COMPARATIVE POLITICS 95/96

Thirteenth Edition

Editor

Christian Søe
California State University, Long Beach

Christian Søe was born in Denmark, studied in Canada and the United States, and received his doctoral degree in political science from the Free University in Berlin. He is a political science professor at California State University, Long Beach. Dr. Søe teaches a wide range of courses in comparative politics and contemporary political theory, and actively participates in professional symposiums in the United States and abroad. His research deals primarily with developments in contemporary German politics, and he has been a regular observer of party politics in that country, most recently during the campaign leading up to the 1994 election of a new Bundestag. At present Dr. Søe is observing the shifts in the balance of power within the German party system, with particular attention to its implications for the formation of new government coalitions and changes in policy directions. Three of his most recent publications are a biographical essay on Hans-Dietrich Genscher, Germany's foreign minister from 1974 to 1992, in *Political Leaders of Contemporary Western Europe;* a chapter on the Free Democratic Party in *Germany's New Politics;* and another chapter on the Danish-German relationship in *The Germans and Their Neighbors.* Dr. Søe is also coeditor of the latter two books. He has been editor of *Annual Editions Comparative Politics* since its beginning in 1983.

Cover illustration by Mike Eagle

Annual Editions
A Library of Information from the Public Press

Dushkin Publishing Group/
Brown & Benchmark Publishers
Sluice Dock, Guilford, Connecticut 06437

This map has been developed to give you a graphic picture of where the countries of the world are located, the relationship they have with their region and neighbors, and their positions relative to the superpowers and power blocs. We have focused on certain areas to more clearly illustrate these crowded regions.

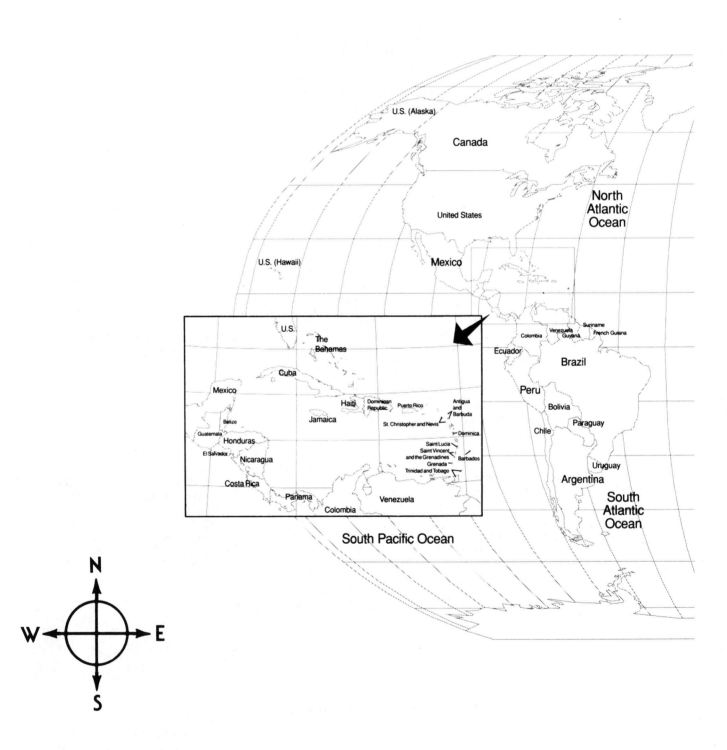

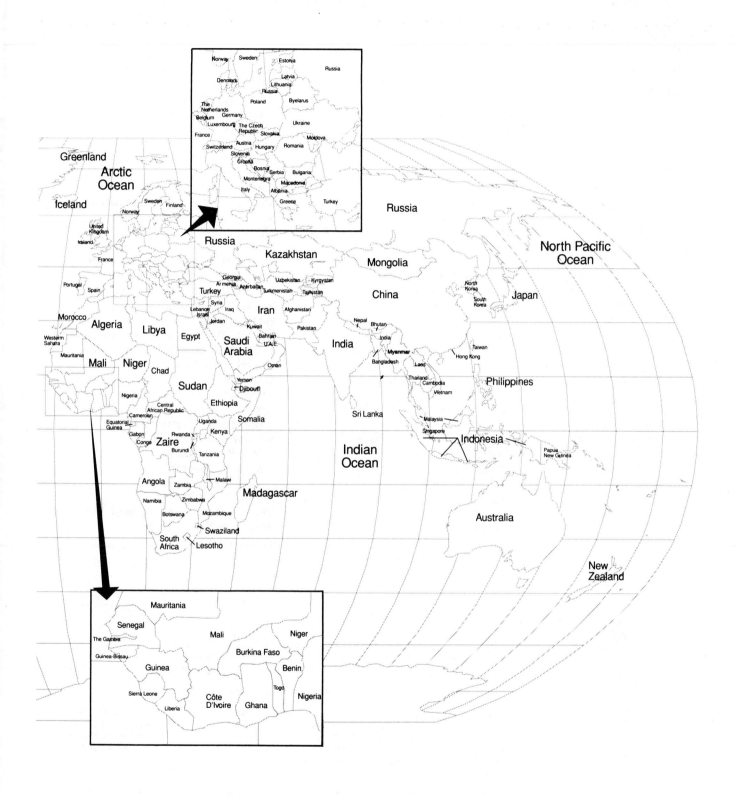

The Annual Editions Series

Annual Editions is a series of over 65 volumes designed to provide the reader with convenient, low-cost access to a wide range of current, carefully selected articles from some of the most important magazines, newspapers, and journals published today. Annual Editions are updated on an annual basis through a continuous monitoring of over 300 periodical sources. All Annual Editions have a number of features designed to make them particularly useful, including topic guides, annotated tables of contents, unit overviews, and indexes. For the teacher using Annual Editions in the classroom, an Instructor's Resource Guide with test questions is available for each volume.

Printed on Recycled Paper

VOLUMES AVAILABLE

Africa
Aging
American Foreign Policy
American Government
American History, Pre-Civil War
American History, Post-Civil War
Anthropology
Archaeology
Biology
Biopsychology
Business Ethics
Canadian Politics
Child Growth and Development
China
Comparative Politics
Computers in Education
Computers in Business
Computers in Society
Criminal Justice
Developing World
Drugs, Society, and Behavior
Dying, Death, and Bereavement
Early Childhood Education
Economics
Educating Exceptional Children
Education
Educational Psychology
Environment
Geography
Global Issues
Health
Human Development
Human Resources
Human Sexuality
India and South Asia

International Business
Japan and the Pacific Rim
Latin America
Life Management
Macroeconomics
Management
Marketing
Marriage and Family
Mass Media
Microeconomics
Middle East and the Islamic World
Money and Banking
Multicultural Education
Nutrition
Personal Growth and Behavior
Physical Anthropology
Psychology
Public Administration
Race and Ethnic Relations
Russia, the Eurasian Republics, and
   Central/Eastern Europe
Social Problems
Sociology
State and Local Government
Urban Society
Violence and Terrorism
Western Civilization,
   Pre-Reformation
Western Civilization,
   Post-Reformation
Western Europe
World History, Pre-Modern
World History, Modern
World Politics

Cataloging in Publication Data

© 1995 by Dushkin Publishing Group/Brown & Benchmark Publishers, Guilford, CT 06437
Main entry under title: Annual Editions: Comparative Politics. 1995/96.
      1. World politics—Periodicals. 2. Politics, Practical—Periodicals. I. Søe, Christian, comp.
II. Title: Comparative Politics.
ISBN 1-56134-348-X   909′.05   83-647654

Thirteenth Edition

Printed in the United States of America

Editors/ Advisory Board

EDITOR

Christian Søe
California State University
Long Beach

ADVISORY BOARD

Members of the Advisory Board are instrumental in the final selection of articles for each edition of Annual Editions. Their review of articles for content, level, currentness, and appropriateness provides critical direction to the editor and staff. We think you'll find their careful consideration well reflected in this volume.

STAFF

To the Reader

In publishing ANNUAL EDITIONS we recognize the enormous role played by the magazines, newspapers, and journals of the *public press* in providing current, first-rate educational information in a broad spectrum of interest areas. Within the articles, the best scientists, practitioners, researchers, and commentators draw issues into new perspective as accepted theories and viewpoints are called into account by new events, recent discoveries change old facts, and fresh debate breaks out over important controversies.

Many of the articles resulting from this enormous editorial effort are appropriate for students, researchers, and professionals seeking accurate, current material to help bridge the gap between principles and theories and the real world. These articles, however, become more useful for study when those of lasting value are carefully *collected, organized, indexed,* and *reproduced* in a *low-cost format,* which provides easy and permanent access when the material is needed. That is the role played by *Annual Editions.* Under the direction of each volume's *Editor,* who is an expert in the subject area, and with the guidance of an *Advisory Board,* we seek each year to provide in each ANNUAL EDITION a current, well-balanced, carefully selected collection of the best of the public press for your study and enjoyment. We think you'll find this volume useful, and we hope you'll take a moment to let us know what you think.

This collection of readings brings together articles that will help you understand the governments and politics of many foreign countries from a comparative perspective. You will soon discover that such a study not only opens up a fascinating world beyond our borders, but also leads to greater insights into the American political process.

The articles in unit one cover Great Britain, Germany, France, Italy, and Japan in a serial manner. Each of these modern societies has developed its own political framework and agenda, and each has sought to find its own appropriate dynamic balance of continuity and change. Nevertheless, as the readings of unit two show, it is possible to point to some common denominators and make useful cross-national comparisons among these and other representative democracies. Unit three goes one step further by discussing the impact of two major changes that are rapidly transforming the political map of Europe—the irregular but impressive growth of the European Union (EU), which until November 1993 was called the European Community (EC), and the political and economic reconstruction of Central and Eastern Europe after the collapse of the communist regimes in that part of the world. The continuing political importance of Europe has been underscored by these two developments.

Unit four looks at developments in some of the developing countries, with articles on Mexico, sub-Saharan Africa and the Union of South Africa, China, and India. A careful reader will come away with a better understanding of the diversity of social and political conditions in these countries. Additional readings cover the newly industrialized countries of Eastern and Southeastern Asia—the so-called "tigers" or "dragons," which have managed to generate a self-sustaining process of industrial modernization. Here the central question concerns the combination of factors that made such an economic take-off possible or, more specifically, what can be learned about the most promising strategy of development for other developing world countries.

Unit five considers three major trends in contemporary politics from a comparative perspective. The "third wave" of democratization may already have crested, but it is nevertheless important in having changed the politics of many countries. The widespread shifts toward a greater reliance on markets to perform the task of economic allocation, in place of centralized planning and heavy governmental regulation, is also of great significance. The move is frequently toward a "mixed economy," and it should not be misunderstood for a victory of doctrinaire "laissez-faire." Finally, the surge of what has been called "identity politics," with particular emphasis on exclusive cultural or ethnic group assertion, is a development that bears careful watching.

There has rarely been so interesting and important a time for the study of comparative politics as now. We can already see that the political earthquake of 1989–1991 has altered the landscape with consequences that will be felt for many years to come. The aftershocks continue to remind us that we are unlikely to ever experience a condition of political equilibrium.

This is the thirteenth edition of *Annual Editions: Comparative Politics.* It is a sobering reminder that the first edition appeared just as the Brezhnev era had come to a close in what was then the Soviet Union. Over the years, the new editions have tried to reflect the developments that eventually brought about the post–cold war world of today. In a similar way, the present edition tries to present information and analysis that will be useful in understanding today's political world and its role in setting the parameters for tomorrow's developments.

A special word of thanks goes to my own past and present students at Long Beach State. Susan B. Mason, who received her master's degree in political science at my university several years ago, continues to add to her long record as a superb research assistant. Another graduate of our M.A. program, Deborah Lancaster, has for a second year provided me with some very useful suggestions and articles for the reader. My current graduate assistant, Linda Wohlman, has continued to be resourceful, energetic, and cheerful in helping me survive the paper battles.

I am very grateful to members of the advisory board and the Dushkin Publishing Group/Brown & Benchmark Publishers as well as to many readers who have made useful comments on past selections and suggested new ones. I ask you all to help me improve future editions by keeping me informed of your reactions and suggestions for change. Please complete and return the postpaid article rating form in the back of the book.

Christian Søe
Editor

Contents

Unit 1

Pluralist Democracies: Country Studies

Twenty-five selections examine the current state of politics in Western Europe, Great Britain, Germany, France, Italy, and Japan.

The concepts in bold italics are developed in the article. For further expansion please refer to the Topic Guide and the Index.

Unit

2

Modern Pluralist Democracies: Factors in the Political Process

Eleven selections examine the functioning of Western European democracies with regard to political ideas and participation, ethnic politics, the role of women in politics, and the institutional framework of representative government.

The concepts in bold italics are developed in the article. For further expansion please refer to the Topic Guide and the Index.

The concepts in bold italics are developed in the article. For further expansion please refer to the Topic Guide and the Index.

Unit 3

Europe — West, Center, and East: The Politics of Integration, Transformation, and Disintegration

Ten selections examine the European continent: the European Union, Western European society, post-communist Central and Eastern Europe, and Russia and the other post-Soviet Republics.

The concepts in bold italics are developed in the article. For further expansion please refer to the Topic Guide and the Index.

Unit 4

Political Diversity in the Developing World

Thirteen selections review the developing world's economic and political development in Latin America, Africa, China, India, and newly industrialized countries.

The concepts in bold italics are developed in the article. For further expansion please refer to the Topic Guide and the Index.

Unit 5

Comparative Politics: Some Major Trends, Issues, and Prospects

Six selections discuss the rise of democracy, how capitalism impacts on political development, and the political assertion of group identity in contemporary politics.

The concepts in bold italics are developed in the article. For further expansion please refer to the Topic Guide and the Index.

Topic Guide

This topic guide suggests how the selections in this book relate to topics of traditional concern to students and professionals involved with the study of comparative politics. It is useful for locating articles that relate to each other for reading and research. The guide is arranged alphabetically according to topic. Articles may, of course, treat topics that do not appear in the topic guide. In turn, entries in the topic guide do not necessarily constitute a comprehensive listing of all the contents of each selection.

Pluralist Democracies: Country Studies

Great Britain, Germany, France, and Italy rank among the most prominent industrial societies in Western Europe. Although their modern political histories vary considerably, they have all become pluralist democracies with diversified and active citizenries, well-developed and competitive party systems, and representative forms of governments. Japan is less pluralist in sociocultural terms, but it occupies a similar position of primacy among the few industrial democracies in Asia. A study of comparative government can usefully begin by examining the politics of these countries more closely through the articles in this and the following two units.

The articles in the first unit cover the political systems of Great Britain, France, Germany, Italy and Japan. Each of these modern societies has developed its own set of governmental institutions, defined its own political agenda, and found its own dynamic balance of continuity and change. Nevertheless, as later readings will show more fully, it is possible to find some common denominators and make useful cross-national comparisons among these and other representative democracies. Moreover, the West European countries all show the impact of three major developments that are transforming the political map of the continent: (1) the growth of the European Union (EU), as the European Community (EC) has been officially known since November 1993, (2) the rise of new or intensified challenges to the established political order after the end of the cold war, often reflected in a weakening of the traditional party system, and (3) the spillover effects from the reconstruction efforts in the countries of Central and Eastern Europe after their recent exit from communist rule.

The continuing political importance of Europe has been underscored by these developments. The integration of the European Community, which led to the European Union, has been a process of several decades, but it accelerated markedly in the last half of the 1980s as a result of the passage and stepwise implementation of the Single European Act, which set as a goal the completion of a free market among the twelve EC-member countries by the end of 1992. The Maastricht Treaty of 1991 outlined a further advance toward supranational integration by setting up the goal of achieving a common European monetary system and foreign policy toward the end of the decade.

The first article reports that the "Europhoria," which a few years ago greeted the end of the cold war and the seemingly inexorable onset of European unification, has given way to a new malaise in much of the continent. The revival of "Europessimism" has been fed by a combination of economic setbacks, sociocultural tensions, political scandals, and a revival of right-wing populist parties and movements. While each country has its own peculiar mix of such problems, the article also points to a common pattern of voter rebellion against incumbents.

Great Britain has long been regarded as a model of parliamentary government and majoritarian party politics. In the 1960s and 1970s, however, the country became better known for its chronic governing problems. Serious observers spoke about the British sickness or "Englanditis," a condition characterized by such problems as economic stagnation, social malaise, political polarization, and a general incapacity of the elected government to deal effectively with such a situation of relative deterioration.

As if to defy such pessimistic analyses, if only temporarily, Britain by the mid-1980s began to pull far ahead of other West European countries in its annual economic growth. This apparent economic turnabout could be linked in part to the policies of Prime Minister Margaret Thatcher, who came to power in May of 1979 and introduced a drastic change in economic and social direction for the country. She portrayed herself as a conviction politician, determined to introduce a strong dose of economic discipline by encouraging private enterprise and reducing the role of government, in marked contrast to what she dismissed as the consensus politics of her Labour and Conservative predecessors. Her radical rhetoric and somewhat less drastic policy changes spawned yet another debate about what came to be called the Thatcher Revolution and its social and political consequences.

For the mass electorate, however, nothing seems to have been so upsetting as the introduction of the community charge, a tax on each adult resident that would replace the local property tax or rates as a means of financing local public services. Although the poll tax was very unpopular, Thatcher resisted all pressure to abandon the project before its full national implementation in early 1990. Not only did such a tax appear inequitable or regressive, as compared to one based on property values, it also turned out to be set much higher by local governments than the national government originally had estimated. The politically disastrous result was that the revenue measure was anything but neutral in its impact. It created an unexpectedly large proportion of immediate losers, that is, people who had to pay considerably more in local taxes than previously, while the immediate winners were people who had previously paid high property taxes. Not surprisingly, the national and local governments disagreed about who was responsible for the high poll tax bills, but the voters seemed to have little difficulty in assigning blame to Margaret Thatcher and the Conservative Party as originators of the unpopular reform. Many voters were up in arms, and some observers correctly anticipated that the tax rebellion would undermine Thatcher's position in her own party and become her political Waterloo.

John Major, who was chosen by his fellow Conservative members of Parliament to be Thatcher's successor as prime minister and leader of the Conservative Party, had long been regarded as one of her closest cabinet supporters. He was thought to support her tough economic strategy, which she often described as "dry," but to prefer a more compassionate or "wet" social policy without indulging in the Tory tradition of welfare paternalism, against which Margaret Thatcher had also railed. Not surprisingly, he abandoned the hated poll tax. His undramatic governing style was far less confrontational than that of his predecessor, and some nostalgic critics were quick to call him dull. In the Persian Gulf War of 1991, Major continued Thatcher's policy of giving strong British support for firm military measures against the government of Iraq, which had invaded and occupied oil-rich Kuwait. Unlike his predecessor after the Falkland

Battle, however, he did not follow up on a quick and popular military victory by calling for general elections.

By the time of Thatcher's 1990 resignation, Labour appeared to be in a relatively good position to capitalize on the growing disenchantment with the Conservative government. The big political question had become whether Prime Minister Major could recapture some of the lost ground. Under its leader, Neil Kinnock, Labour had begun to move back toward its traditional center-left position, presenting itself as a politically moderate and socially caring reform party. Labour had a leading position in some opinion polls, and it won some impressive victories in by-elections to the House of Commons. In the shadow of the Persian Gulf War, Labour was overtaken by the Conservatives in the polls, but its position improved again a few months later.

As the main opposition party, however, Labour was now troubled by a new version of the Social Democratic and Liberal alternatives that had fragmented the non-Conservative camp in the elections of 1983 and 1987. The two smaller parties, which had operated as an electoral coalition or "Alliance" in those years, had drawn the conclusion that their organizational separation was a hindrance to the political breakthrough they hoped for. After the defeat of 1987, they joined together as the Social and Liberal Democrats (SLD) but soon became known simply as Liberal Democrats. Under the leadership of Paddy Ashdown, they have attempted to overcome the electoral system's bias against third parties by promoting themselves as a reasonable centrist alternative to the Conservatives on the Right and the Labour Party on the Left. Their strategic goal was to win the balance of power in a tightly fought election and then, as parliamentary majority makers, enter a government coalition with one of the two big parties. One of their main demands would then be that the existing winner-takes-all or plurality electoral system, based on single-member districts, be replaced by some form of proportional representation (PR) in multimember districts. Such a system, which is used widely in Western Europe, would almost surely guarantee the Liberal Democrats not only a relatively solid base in the House of Commons, but also a pivotal role in a future process of coalition politics in Britain. Given their considerable electoral support, the Liberal Democrats would then enjoy a position comparable to or even better than that of their counterparts in Germany, the Free Democrats (FDP), which has been a junior member of governments in Bonn for decades.

The rise of this centrist "third force" in British electoral politics during the 1980s had been made possible by a temporary leftward trend of Labour and the rightward movement of the Conservatives. The challenge from the middle had the predictable result of the two main parties seeking to "recenter" themselves, as became evident in the general election called by Prime Minister Major for April 9, 1992. The timing seemed highly unattractive for the governing party, for Britain was still suffering from its worst recession in years. Normally, a British government chooses not to stay in office for a full five-year term. Instead, it prefers to dissolve the House of Commons at an earlier and politically convenient time. It will procrastinate, however, when the electoral outlook appears to be dismal. By the spring of 1992 there was hardly any time left for further delay, since an election had to come before the end of June under Britain's five-year limit. The polls did not look good for the Conservatives, and many observers suggested the likelihood of either a slim Labour victory or, as seemed far more likely, a "hung" Parliament, in which no party would end up with a working majority. The latter result would have led either to a minority government, which could be expected to solve the impasse by calling an early new election, or a coalition government including the Liberal Democrats as the majority-making junior partner.

The outcome of the 1992 general election confounded many observers who had expected a change in government. Instead, the Conservatives were enabled to continue into an unprecedented fourth consecutive term of office. Despite the recession, they garnered the same overall percentage of the vote (about 43 percent) as in 1987, while Labour increased its total share only slightly, from 32 to 35 percent. The Liberal Democrats received only 18 percent, about 6 percent less than the share the Alliance had won in its two unsuccessful attempts to "break the mold" of the party system in 1983 and 1987. In the House of Commons, the electoral system's bias in favor of the front-runners showed up once again. The Conservatives lost 36 seats but ended up with 336 of the 651 members—a small but sufficient working majority, unless a major issue should fragment the party. Labour increased its number of seats from 229 to 271—a net gain of 42, but far short of an opportunity to threaten the majority party. The Liberal Democrats ended up with 20 seats, down from 22. A few seats went to representatives of the small regional parties from Northern Ireland, Scotland, and Wales.

In the aftermath of the election, John Major has run into considerable difficulties with a wing of his own party that follows Thatcher in opposing his European policy. It was only by threatening to dissolve Parliament and call a new election that Major brought the dissidents into line during a crucial vote on the Maastricht Treaty in the summer of 1993. The Labour Party, with its newest leader Tony Blair, has made some tremendous advances in the regular opinion polls. The opposition party would probably win a general election today, but it is hampered by its own factional disputes. The major ideological and strategic cleavage runs between traditional socialists and more pragmatic modernizers, who wish to continue the centrist reform policies of Tony Blair. But the issue of Europe would also trouble the Labour Party, if it were to take over the government. Only the Liberal Democrats seem to be united in their commitment to a more fully integrated Europe.

Germany was united in 1990, when the eastern German Democratic Republic or GDR was merged into the western Federal Republic of Germany. The two German states had been established in 1949, four years after the total defeat of the German Reich in World War II. During the next 40 years, their rival elites subscribed to the conflicting ideologies and interests of East and West in the cold war. East Germany comprised the territory of the former Soviet Occupation Zone of Germany, where the communists exercised a power monopoly and established an economy based on central planning. In contrast, West Germany, which emerged from the former American, British, and French zones of postwar occupation, developed a pluralist democracy and a flourishing market economy. When the two states were getting ready to celebrate their fortieth anniversaries in 1989, no leading politician was on record as having foreseen that the German division would come to end during the course of the following year.

Mass demonstrations in several East German cities and the westward flight of thousands of citizens brought the GDR government to make an increasing number of concessions in late 1989 and early 1990. The Berlin Wall ceased to be a hermetical seal after November 9, 1989, when East Germans began to stream over into West Berlin. Collectors and entrepreneurs soon broke pieces from the Wall to keep or sell as souvenirs, before public workers set about to remove the rest of this symbol of the cold war and Germany's division. Under new leadership, the ruling communists of East Germany introduced a form of power sharing with noncommunist groups and parties. It was agreed to seek democratic legitimation through a free election in March 1990, also in the hope of reducing the westward flight of thousands of East Germans with its devastating consequences for the economy.

The East German communists abandoned their claim to an exclusive control of power and position, but by the time of the March 1990 election it was clear even to them that the pressure for national unification could no longer be stemmed. The issue was no longer whether the two German states would be joined together, but how and when. These questions were settled when an alliance of Christian Democrats, largely identified with and supported by Chancellor Kohl's party in West Germany, won a surprisingly decisive victory, with 48 percent of the vote throughout East Germany. It advocated a short, quick route to unification, beginning with an early monetary union in the summer and a political union by the fall of 1990. This also meant that the new noncommunist government in East Germany, headed by Lothar de Maiziere (CDU), followed the short route to merger with the Federal Republic, under Article 23 of the West German Basic Law. The Social Democrats or SPD won only 22 percent of the East German vote in March 1990. That amounted to a defeat for its alternative strategy for unification that would have involved the protracted negotiation of a new German constitution, as envisaged by Article 146 of the Basic Law.

During the summer and fall of 1990, the governments of the two German states and the four former occupying powers completed their so-called two-plus-four negotiations that resulted in mutual agreement on the German unification process. A monetary union in July was followed by a political merger in October 1990. In advance of unification, Bonn was able to negotiate an agreement with Moscow in which the latter accepted the gradual withdrawal of Soviet troops from eastern Germany and the membership of the larger, united Germany in NATO, in return for considerable German economic support for the Soviet Union. The result was a major shift in both the domestic and international balance of power.

The election results of 1990 raised, but did not finally answer, the question of how national unification will eventually reshape the German party system. By the time of the next national election, in October 1994, it became evident that a new east-west division had emerged in German politics. This time, the far-Left PDS was able to attract nearly 20 percent of the vote in the East, where one-fifth of the population lives, but did not quite reach 1 percent in the more populous West. Although the PDS received less than 5 percent of the total German vote, it was able to win proportional representation in the Bundestag by meeting an alternative requirement of winning at least 3 single-member districts. Thus the political descendants of the former ruling communists are now represented in the Bundestag by 30 deputies, where they present themselves as democratic far-Left Socialists.

The articles on Germany include economic and political balance sheets on the challenges and accomplishments of national unification. There are also two analyses of the Bundestag election of 1994 and the implications of its result. The task of postcommunist reconstruction in eastern Germany goes far beyond the transfer of institutions and capital from the West. The transition to pluralist democracy and a market economy in eastern Germany also requires a social and cultural transformation, as several authors suggest. Moreover, there are new problems facing the larger and more powerful Germany on the international scene, as it seeks to deal with a mixture of expectations and anxieties that it arouses abroad. No wonder some

Germans have developed a kind of nostalgia ("Ostalgie," as some call it) for the less complicated and demanding existence before reunification!

France must also cope with major political challenges within a rapidly changing Europe. The bicentennial of the French Revolution was duly celebrated in 1989. It served as an occasion for public ceremonies and a revival of historical-political debates about the costs and benefits of that great exercise in the radical transformation of a society. Ironically, however, for some time before there had been mounting evidence that the sharp ideological cleavages that marked French politics for so much of the past two centuries were losing significance. Instead, there was emerging a more pragmatic, pluralist form of accommodation in French public life.

To be sure, this deradicalization and depolarization of political discourse is by no means complete in France. If the communists have become weakened and ideologically confused, Le Pen's National Front on the extreme Right can arouse populist support with its xenophobic rhetoric directed primarily against the many residents of Arab origin in the country. The apparent electoral appeal of such invective has led some leaders of the establishment parties of the more moderate Right to voice carefully formulated reservations about the presence of so many immigrants. An entirely new and different political phenomenon for France is the appearance of two Green parties, one more conservative and the other more socialist in orientation.

As widely expected, the Socialists suffered a major setback in these parliamentary elections of 1993. After the second round of voting, held a week after the first, it was clear that the conservative alliance of the center-Right Giscardists (the Union pour la Démocratie Française or UDF) and the neo-Gaullists (the Rassemblement pour la République or RPR) had garnered about 40 percent of the popular vote. However, that gave them an overwhelming majority of nearly 80 percent of the seats in the 577-seat National Assembly.

The Socialists and their close allies were among the losers in this largest electoral landslide in French democratic history. Receiving less than 20 percent of the popular vote or about one-half as much as five years earlier, they plummeted from their previous share of 282 seats in 1988 to only 70 seats. The communists, with about half as many votes, were able to win 23 seats, because much of their electoral support is concentrated in a few urban districts. With a similar share of the vote, the National Front won no seats at all. The environmental alliance was doubly disappointed, winning a smaller share of the vote than expected and capturing no seats either.

François Mitterrand's seven-year presidential term did not expire until 1995. After the parliamentary rout of the Socialists in March 1993, he was faced with the question of whether to resign early from the presidency or, as under similar political circumstances in 1986, to enter a period of "cohabitation" with a conservative prime minister. Mitterrand opted for the latter solution, but he made sure to appoint a moderate Gaullist, Edouard Balladur, as the new prime minister. Balladur in turn appointed a new, compact government that included members from all main factions of the conservative alliance. For a time, Balladur enjoyed considerable popularity, and he decided to enter the presidential race in 1995 instead of leaving Jacques Chirac, a former prime minister, to be the only Gaullist candidate. The presidential race tends to become highly individualized, and a few weeks before the first round of the election it appeared as though the tough and outspoken Chirac had pulled ahead of the more consensual and lackluster Balladur. Some observers believe that many French voters are looking for a powerful personality to fill the office. The main socialist candidate was Lionel Jospin, a former education minister and party leader.

The articles in this section provide a perspective on what some observers call "the new France." In fact, contemporary French politics and society combine some traits that reflect continuity with the past and some that suggest considerable innovation. One recurrent theme among observers is the decline of the previously sharp ideological struggle between the Left and the Right. There may well be a sense of loss among some French intellectuals who still prefer the political battle to have apocalyptic implications.

The loss of the great ideological alternatives may help account for the mood of political malaise that many observers claim to observe in contemporary France. But the French search for political direction and identity in a changing Europe has another major origin as well. The sudden emergence of a larger and potentially more powerful Germany next door cannot but have a disquieting effect upon France, even though opinion polls in 1990 showed a strong support for the right of the Germans to choose national unification. French elites now face the troubling question of redefining their country's role in a post–cold war world, in which the Soviet Union has lost its power and influence while Germany has gained in both.

Italy is roughly comparable to France and Great Britain in population and economic output, but it has a different political tradition that includes a long period of fascist rule and a far more persistent element of north-south regionalism. The country became a republic after World War II and, using a system of proportional representation, developed a multiparty system in which the center-Right Christian Democrats played a central role as the major coalition party. The Communists, as second major party, were persistently excluded from government at the national level. They played a considerable role in local politics, however, and embarked relatively early on a nonrevolutionary path of seeking social reforms in a pluralist society. Under their recently adopted new name, Democratic Party of the Left (PDS), the former Communists essentially adopted social democratic reform positions. In 1993 and 1994, they experienced a political revival, as Italian voters abruptly turned away from the Christian Democrats and other corrupt establishment parties.

In late March 1994 Italy finally held what has been regarded as the most important parliamentary elections in over four decades. Once again Italian voters demonstrated their disgust with the old government parties. Using a new electoral system, in which three-quarters of the members of Parliament are elected on a winner-takes-all basis and the rest by proportional representation, they decimated the centrist alliance that included the former Christian Democrats. On the Left, an alliance led by the PDS won 213 of the 630 seats in the Chamber of Deputies, compared to the 46 seats for the main centrist group. But it was the Freedom Alliance of the Right that triumphed by winning 366 seats. It consisted of an incongruous coalition of three main groups, of which the strongest was the *Forza Italia* (Go Italy) movement, led by the media magnate, Silvio Berlusconi. The others were the fascist-descended National Alliance (formerly MSI), led by Gianfranco Fini, and the federalist Northern League, led by Umberto Bossi. Berlusconi, who campaigned against both corruption (the centrists) and communism (the PDS), had catapulted himself and his party to the front by skillful use of the media. He faced the difficult task of creating a government based on a fractious coalition, in which the leader of the federalist Northern League showed contempt for the rhetoric and centralist ideology of the neofascists. Observers, who spoke of a Second Republic in Italy, generally found its start to have been as rocky as that of its predecessor. Berlusconi's coalition had collapsed before the end of the year, the 53rd Italian

government to fall since the end of the fascist control of the country in 1944. A new temporary government of technocrats, headed by the banker Lamberto Dini, took over the reins in January 1995. Observers expect a new election during the second half of the year.

Japan, the fifth country in this study of representative governments of industrial societies, has long fascinated students of comparative politics and society. After World War II, a representative democracy was installed in Japan under U.S. supervision. This political system soon acquired indigenous Japanese characteristics that set it off from the other major democracies examined here.

For almost four decades the Japanese parliamentary system was dominated by the Liberal Democratic Party that, as the saying goes, is "neither liberal, nor democratic, nor a party." It is essentially a conservative political force, comprising several delicately balanced factions. These are often personal followerships identified and headed by political bosses who stake out factional claims to benefits of office. At periodic intervals the LDP's parliamentary hegemony has been threatened, but it was always able to recover and retain power until 1993. In that year, it lost several important politicians who objected to the LDP's reluctance to introduce political reforms. As a result of these defections, the government lost its parliamentary majority. A vote of no confidence was followed by early elections in July 1993, in which the LDP failed to recover its parliamentary majority for the first time in almost four decades. Seven different parties, which span the spectrum from conservative to socialist, thereupon formed what turned out to be a very fragile coalition government. Two prime ministers and several cabinet reshufflements later, the rump LDP had managed by the summer of 1994 to return to the cabinet in coalition with its major former rival, the Socialists. The curious alliance is possible because of the basically pragmatic orientation of the leadership of both parties at this point in Japan's history.

Looking Ahead: Challenge Questions

What are the main issues that seem to divide the Conservatives in the British House of Commons? What are the reasons for the electoral weakening of the Liberal Democrats? How is Tony Blair trying to reform his Labour Party? What are the main institutions that constitutional reformers in Britain wish to change or abolish? How has the situation in Northern Ireland improved during the past year?

How and why did Bonn underestimate the problems of reconstruction in eastern Germany? How did Chancellor Kohl manage to win reelection in 1994, despite a considerable unification malaise in the country? Why were the Free Democrats of crucial importance for the continuation of Kohl's government? What are the sources of strength of the communist-descended PDS? Why did the Social Democrats (SPD) not manage to win?

What are the signs that French politics have become more centrist or middle-of-the-road? How do you explain the conservative landslide in the French elections of March 1993? Who were the main candidates for the French presidency in 1995, and what were their main strengths and weaknesses?

Why has Italy been called the "sick man" of Western Europe? Explain the recent shake-up in the Italian party system.

Explain the political outcome and significance of the 1993 parliamentary elections in Japan. Why do some observers believe that the political changes are more apparent than real?

World Trend:
Voters Reject Incumbents

Ire over 'politics as usual' topples existing governments right and left

Peter Grier

Staff writer of The Christian Science Monitor

WASHINGTON

Some Democrats say President Clinton should focus on foreign policy and overseas tours now that Republicans have captured Capitol Hill. If he does, he may be in for a surprise: The United States has no monopoly on political anger. Election after election shows that a sour throw-the-yobs-out mood pervades rich democracies around the world.

The extent of recent ruling party reversals might actually make Mr. Clinton feel better. In France, President François Mitterrand's Socialists are limping along with only 54 National Assembly seats, down from 270 last year. Canada's Conservatives makes US Democrats look as strong as George Foreman. A year ago they ruled the country with 154 seats. Elections left them two. The Democrats may have suffered its worst electoral setback in some four decades, but at least there are enough of them left in Washington to fill a restaurant booth at lunchtime.

"The common denominator around the world is that people that have been in power for a long time are being tossed out," says Christopher Layne, a former Cato Institute senior analyst and international relations scholar.

In Italian elections last spring, for instance, voters disgusted by widespread corruption utterly repudiated the country's longtime ruling Christian Democrats. In a somewhat pathetic and fruitless bid for votes, Christian Democrat leaders went so far as to rename themselves the "Popular Party."

Similarly, in Japan an electorate tired of money politics last year ended the 38-year continuous rule of the Liberal Democratic Party (LDP).

The LDP has since returned to a measure of power—at the price of entering into a coalition with its longtime archrival, the Socialists.

Germany's Helmut Kohl managed to win reelection last month. But the man who presided over German reunification saw his parliamentary majority slashed from a 66-seat edge to a bare 10-vote advantage.

This trend of battering incumbents does not run along ideological lines. Parties of both the left and right have suffered the slings of voter ire.

Nor are electoral conditions the same in every industrial democracy. Each has its unique, burning issues that bear on the outcome; corruption in Italy and Japan, for instance, puts the US House of Representatives check-kiting scandal to shame.

But there may be enough similarities to lead some analysts to say that in many nations the 1990s is shaping up as the decade of inchoate voter desire for change. The loss of jobs across borders, the press of poor immigrants, the perceived sleaze of those in power—all these factors could be feeding a growing sense of voter discontent.

"There is a feeling that decisions are being made outside of the political territory that one controls," says Charles Maier, a professor of European Studies at Harvard University in Cambridge, Mass.

Hold it a second—isn't this a time when the Western democracies should be feeling good about themselves? They have emerged triumphant from the cold war, after all. Their values of freedom and tradition of market economies seem victorious over all ideological competitors.

In fact, citizens in the rich democracies are backing away from their political leaders in disillusion, according to Professor Maier. He argues that this is evidence of a widespread "moral crisis" of democracy.

One cause of this crisis, says Maier, is a sense that old principles and alignments have disappeared or no longer seem appropriate.

Nothing has yet taken the place of the old cold war certainties. Today's struggles—Bosnia, Rwanda—seem patternless, almost nihilistic.

In this environment of moral crisis, according to Maier, local loyalties—to state, to region, even to race—can begin to seem more important than existing national political structures. Electorates begin to doubt that domestic problems can be solved, particularly by existing big government programs.

Hard-nose responses to social problems are in favor in many nations, notes Maier. In the US, the solution to crime that many voters favor is more prisons.

In Germany and France, a flood of immigrants seeking jobs has launched a political backlash in favor of tighter residence controls.

Overall, voters simply feel alienated from the political process in Bonn and Boston, Milan and Miami, Topeka as well as Tokyo.

"People have the feeling that things are not responding for them," says Maier.

It's not clear where politics proceeds from here: It might descend into further voter alienation, or strong political re-formers could force something of a national "remoralization," says Maier.

Not all analysts think nations today are unhappy in similar ways. Francis Fukuyama of the RAND Corporation says that the conditions causing voter unrest are mostly rooted in each nation's particular problems.

The widespread bribes and political slush funds uncovered in Italy are simply not comparable in scale to anything the US has experienced, for instance. The US, for its part, has immigration and racial problems that are much worse than the backlash against Turkish workers in Germany. Religion plays a far greater role in US politics than it does almost everywhere else in the industrialized world.

"I just don't buy that there's a worldwide phenomenon going on here," says Fukuyama.

Not all ruling parties have suffered equally, points out the RAND analyst. Considering Germany's economic problems, it might count as something of a victory that Helmut Kohl survived at all.

New Paths and Old in British Politics

Hansrudolf Kamer

Just before the summer break, the British political scene was given a facelift. The more or less cosmetic cabinet shuffle in a tired-seeming but tough Tory government, and the selection of the youthful attorney Tony Blair to head a Labour Party still in the throes of renovation, marked a new stage in the struggle for political power in the United Kingdom. The outcome could be of some importance for the future of Europe—because the British, with their cool and distanced attitude toward continental efforts at integration, play the vitally important role of a constructive opposition. While the Germans and French try to pull the strings by means of old-fashioned backroom politicking, it is one of London's tasks to make the game transparent. So the question of who will rule the roost in Whitehall in the years ahead cannot be a matter of indifference to the rest of Europe.

All the prophecies of imminent collapse which Prime Minister John Major has survived and proved false should be enough to discourage similar attempts at prognostication. There are already signs that his government has passed the nadir of its popularity. Britain's economy, which clearly benefited from the pound's abandonment of the European Monetary System, is doing better than was recently expected. Its relatively strong growth could provide the chancellor of the exchequer with a chance to order popular tax cuts next year and thus to prepare the ground for new elections the year after. Provided that the Conservatives avoid new battles over policy toward Europe— a very big "if," however—they could still have a decent chance of once again extending their 15-year time in office.

Much will depend on their opponent. Can Tony Blair, the *Wunderkind* from Islington, succeed where Neil Kinnock, the rose grower from Wales, failed? If one were to believe the opinion polls—a very dubious thing to do in Great Britain—the die is already cast: Labour and Blair enjoy an "unbeatable" lead. The new party leader is benefiting from the reform efforts of his two predecessors, Kinnock and John Smith, as a result of which his mandate is much stronger. In a long and thorough election process, he was elevated to the leadership by a clear majority of the three pillars of his party: the rank-and-file-membership, trade unions and Labour parliamentarians. This could mean that a majority of party supporters are prepared to back the reforms that are necessary if Labour is to return to power.

"The simple justification for democratic socialism," according to the credo of the new Labour leader, "is the belief that individuals thrive best in a strong, active society." The conceptual scaffolding of democratic socialism is now to be reinforced with an emphasis on individual freedom and thus made viable once again. But there is another reason why the credos enunciated by Blair, America's Bill Clinton, and German SPD leader Scharping, sound similar. These men are all professional politicians of a generation which has learned to skillfully handle the hectic pressure of today's political life; they are all extremely image-conscious, smooth, seldom at a loss for the appropriate word, yet cautious about specifics—and they are all in their element in front of the TV camera. In the struggle to succeed his late predecessor, Blair, known as "Bambi" because of his guileless eyes, brought the art of friendly noncommittal to new heights. Whether he, like Clinton and Scharping, will sud-

denly make mistakes when under pressure for a decision, will become evident only when circumstances force him to show his true colors.

In 1974–79 the Conservatives used their "time in the desert" very effectively, laying the foundation for a long period in power. Labour has now had ample opportunity to bathe in the rejuvenating waters of political opposition. The reasons for its election defeats should have been thoroughly examined by now. Vital repairs have been carried out, and the image of the old union-dominated workers' movement, saturated with collectivist ideas, has been overcome. Much has been improved on the tactical level as well. Where formerly self-destructive internecine struggles were carried out in full public view, today the First Commandment of politics—"Thou shalt say nothing ill of a party colleague"—is observed with astonishing discipline. This is in crass contrast to recent wrangles in the Tory ranks.

In gradual stages, much of the old Labour Party's ideological ballast has been heaved overboard, and Labour has moved closer to the gospel of the Post-Thatcher Tories, to a degree clearly illustrated by the new party chief's programmatic statements. In Tony Blair's world view, the market economy has been awarded the label "dynamic." Though a few relics still remain in the party statutes, in Tony Blair's speeches there is no room for old ideas about nationalizing the means of production of goods and services, or the thought that government, in pursuing an active industrial policy, could separate the wheat from the chaff and predict corporate success with the certitude of a sleepwalker. A Labour government headed by Blair would clearly be committed to the understanding that Great Britain cannot be sundered from global competition.

In the realm of public education, according to Tony Blair, it is necessary to once again impose standards and demand performance rather than blame the social environment for failure in school. The purpose of welfare programs, he emphasizes, is not to create dependency but to help people find solutions to problems and to facilitate them. The unemployed have not only rights, but also responsibilities. Criminals should be punished, not only treated therapeutically. The government must be firmly committed to providing the necessary funding for a strong national defense.

If Tony Blair can credibly stand up for such planks in a Labour platform, Labour should be once again able to garner the votes of "Middle England." But if the party's new leadership merely goes through the rhetorical motions, it will not be able to win a national mandate by regaining the confidence of a middle class that is again striving upward after

the end of the recession. More than rhetoric is needed. In the past Labour has all too often found that is efforts at modernization came too late, lagging behind the desires and aspirations of the voters.

Foreign policy, too, deserves more attention. After his successful resistance to the naming of Belgium's Dehaene as president of the EU Commission at the summit meeting on Corfu, John Major was lauded in the House of Commons by shouts of triumph from the formerly deeply divided Tories. The fact that the man selected instead of Dehaene, Luxembourg's Jacques Santer, is apparently no less centralistically inclined than his Belgian colleague, has little significance in British politics. With his opposition to the candidacy "imposed" by France and Germany, Major appealed to more deeply seated feelings shared by far more than just the "Euroskeptics" in the Tory ranks.

The British in general have a difficult time with the Brussels brand of "Europe" and their own membership in that still-alien construction. Germany and

France see European unity as a means of exorcising old specters from their war-filled past. But Britain lacks that connecting link. It has not been subjected to any invasion in its more recent history, and its form of government has continued to evolve over the centuries without interruption. So it should not be surprising that there are fundamental differences over the design of future political and social conditions in an integrated Europe. Each of the three leading powers—Germany, France and Great Britain—represents different and sometimes internally contradictory views.

The new Labour leader is considered decidedly pro-Europe, but he has already announced that fundamental corrections are necessary in the Maastricht integration program. And it has become known that, beneath a surface of tactical unity, the divergence of opinion with Labour is similar to that found on the Conservative side. Those who expect that Britain under a Blair government could be a more comfortable European partner may well be mistaken. Stronger forces are at work here.

Problems of the Conservative Party

The rot within

John Major's rebels have struck again. Can his government survive?

Unlike a fish, which rots from its head, John Major's government is rotting from its tail. The stink pervades the corridors of Westminster as government ministers gloomily calculate the government's chances of survival.

The package of tax increases and public-spending cuts announced by the chancellor, Kenneth Clarke, on December 8th will fill the £1 billion ($1.6 billion) hole ripped, two days earlier, by the eight-vote defeat of the government's plans to increase value-added tax (VAT) on fuel from 8% to 17.5%. A half-point rise in interest rates seemed to restore City confidence. But neither can repair the perception of a government that is "divided, discredited and dying".

That charge was levelled by the Labour leader, Tony Blair, but some Tory MPS mutter much the same in private. The vain, last-minute attempt by the chancellor to buy off the VAT rebellion with a £120m package to ease the burden of the fuel-price increase on pensioners underlined the government's humiliation at the hands of its dissident backbenchers. The strain on Mr Major was clear when he emerged from a late-night meeting with the chancellor after the lost vote. Normally the most courteous of men, the prime minister could not contain himself when he was asked how he felt. "Don't waste my time," he spat as he swept past waiting reporters.

At the heart of the government's loss of authority is Britain's relationship with Europe. Tory backbenchers are deeply divided over a tighter European Union, which between 30 and 50 MPS irreconcilably oppose.

The catalyst for the current crisis was the disciplining of eight backbench MPS who on November 28th, voted against the government in a motion over Britain's increased contributions to the European budget. Kenneth Baker, a former party chairman, called the subsequent withdrawal of the party whip "crass stupidity".

Certainly this disciplinary procedure, which withdraws all party recognition and services from those affected, ensured the government's defeat on Labour's procedural motion on the VAT increase. All but one of the rebels either abstained or voted against it. But, once he had made the European bill a matter of confidence, what else could the prime minister have done? He could hardly have shrugged off a rebellion on a vote upholding an international commitment which, if lost, would have led to the fall of the government.

If the revolt had been ignored, the complaints of weak leadership would have redoubled. Party discipline, already frail, would have collapsed and the job of the whips (party managers) would have become impossible. The simple truth is that the Tory party in its present state is ungovernable. After 15 years in government, it appears to have grown tired of power.

The options now open to Mr Major are limited. Nine of his backbenchers are estranged: eight rebels plus Sir Richard Body, who joined them in disgust. The prime minister heads a minority government vulnerable to every passing controversy and every contentious vote.

Jim fixed it

The crisis does not have to prove terminal. The 1976–79 Labour government led by Jim (now Lord) Callaghan lost a score of votes, including at least three budget resolutions, before finally succumbing to a Tory motion of no-confidence on March 28th 1979. Until that vote, Mr Callaghan had succeeded in shoring up his minority government for two years by striking a deal with the Liberals. In spite of the lost Commons votes, his government was level-pegging with the Tories in the polls by autumn 1978.

Mr Major might like a similar arrangement. But it takes two to tango. The 23 Liberal Democrats are bitterly opposed to the government. The nine Ulster Unionists, headed by James Molyneaux, are not, but their leader has no interest in a formal deal.

The government is not, however, entirely exposed. Its legislative programme for the coming year, set out in the Queen's Speech, was deliberately designed to be uncontroversial. Post Office privatisation has been shelved. A bill to introduce new privacy laws has been dropped. Meanwhile the chancellor holds out hope of tax cuts ahead. The opposition parties will have few opportunities to gang up with Tory dissidents to defeat the government. The bills to end British Gas's distribution monopoly and to equalise the age of male and female retirement at 65 will attract backbench criticism but important defeats are unlikely.

Rows over financial measures, always a potent source of discord, are more likely. Nicholas Winterton, the maverick Tory MP for Macclesfield, is trying to open a new front against the government by criticising the budget's proposal to give home owners who lose their jobs less state help with their mortgage payments.

The prime minister can console himself that his party critics have little in common save alarm about European federalism. They might be soothed if he could bring himself to promise a referendum on Europe. Moreover, the three Eurosceptics in the cabinet, Michael Howard, Peter Lilley and Michael Portillo, have taken care to observe collective responsibility.

The task of restoring unity on the back benches, though difficult, may be eased by the timing of discussions on the next stage of European union. As these are supposed to come to a

head at the European intergovernmental conference of 1996, the government may be able to finesse its final decision on a deal until after a British general election in 1997.

For now Mr Major's last, best hope is to cling to power. A reviving economy might restore his and his government's fortunes. Or Labour blunders might make the opposition seem less attractive. But the usual cure for rot is excision of the affected parts. Mr Major has tried everything on his rebels, from charm to excommunication. The problem, as one minister says, is that they simply do not fear him.

Tory Divide: Bitter, Deep, and a Threat to Major

John Darnton

Special to The New York Times

LONDON, Dec. 7—John Major's authority has been so devastated by Tuesday night's stunning defeat in Parliament that people both inside and outside the Conservative party wondered today if the Prime Minister could survive two-and-a-half more years.

The defeat, which came on the Government's plan to slap a hefty tax increase on home heating fuel and electricity, was being compared to the poll tax, the issue that brought

down Margaret Thatcher, Mr. Major's predecessor.

Except that Mrs. Thatcher managed to push through the poll tax, which raised revenues for localities by head and which was effectively scrapped only after she resigned four years ago. Mr. Major did not get that far. The additional value added tax on fuel was turned back on a procedural amendment, 319 to 311.

What stopped him was a rebellion among the back-benchers in his own Tory party. Divisions and bitterness in the party now run so deep that Mr. Major is hard put to sponsor any bill with even a hint of discord to it.

Already the Government has backed away from what was to have been its showcase legislation this year—privatizing the post office.

The divisions initially cropped up over the issue of closer ties to Europe, a course that the Government is committed to in a lukewarm way but that is vociferously opposed by two dozen or so Conservative Members of Parliament. By now the rent is so big it encompasses everything from personal grudges and recriminations to doubts about Mr. Major's leadership.

The full dimension of his defeat was spelled out in today's headlines and the crowing epitaphs of opposition leaders. The Government, said Tony Blair, the new and popular Labor head, is "in disarray, discredited, no longer in control of events" and "terminally incapable of asserting its authority." Paddy Ashdown, leader of the Liberal Democrats, saw "the drift into decay of what will eventually prove to be a dying government."

What makes these pronouncements different from those of the past is that there is objective evidence to support them. The fuel tax increase, to 17.5 percent from 8 percent, had been agreed upon two years ago and approved by the House of Commons four times already. All in all it was a perfunctory bit of budgetary business, hardly worthy of setting off a rebellion. Not since the Labor Government of the late 1970's have votes on a budget amendment been lost.

The immediate problem for Mr. Major, and for his Chancellor of the Exchequer, Kenneth Clarke, was to fill a $2.3 billion hole in the budget. Mr. Clarke will announce substitute revenue measures Thursday. More pressing is the need to steady the financial markets, which do not take kindly to a political mutiny that unravels the country's fiscal plan.

At 9:30 A.M., today, less than 12 hours after the vote, the Chancellor raised the interest rate by half a point, to 6.25 percent from 5.75 percent. While the raise had been expected at some point, the timing was clearly intended to send the message that the Government was still in charge and aiming to damp down inflation and control economic expansion.

The Premier is hard put to back bills with even a hint of discord.

Over the long run, Mr. Major's challenge will be to restore his credibility and his hold over the party in time for an election, which must be held by mid-1997. In regaining popularity, he is looking to Britain's economic recovery, which is moving ahead, and an emphasis on strong new measures to strengthen the powers of police in questioning criminal suspects.

In dealing with the party, he has tried contradictory tactics, at times threatening the Tory rebels and at other times offering them concessions. Last week he quelled a revolt by "Euroskeptics"—those wary of merging more closely with the rest of Europe as called for by the Treaty on European Unity—by declaring a vote on Britain's contribution to the European Union to be a vote of confidence in his Government.

This meant that when eight Conservatives refused to vote the Government line last week they had to be punished. They were effectively drummed out of the party, at least for the time being. The move backfired. It reversed Mr. Major's slender margin in the House of Commons, giving him control of 322 votes compared to 324 for opposition and Tory rebel votes combined.

When the critical vote on the fuel tax came, the rebels felt free to vote their conscience. All but one either opposed the Government or abstained.

The failed strategy has become another arrow in the critics' quiver. "Crass stupidity" was what Kenneth Baker, former Conservative Party chairman, called the decision to expel the Tory rebels.

To Keep Power, the Tories Must Share It

Vernon Bogdanor

Vernon Bogdanor is Reader in Government, Oxford University, and a Fellow of Brasenose College.

The Government is now formally in a minority in the House of Commons. Whether it also loses its majority on standing committees depends upon the rebel Conservatives. Will they constitute themselves as a separate group in the Commons, or will they support the Government on the procedural motion that determines the composition of standing committees?

Whatever the rebels decide, it is clear that the Government can no longer rely upon their support. For all effective purposes, therefore, there is a hung parliament in which support for government legislation cannot be guaranteed but has to be negotiated anew for each item.

How long can such a parliament last? There have been four hung parliaments in Britain since 1918. The first, the Labour minority government in 1924, lasted for nine uneasy months to be defeated in the general election of October 1924; the second, between 1929 and 1931, was blown out of office by a financial crisis that caused the formation of the National Government.

The third minority government, led by Harold Wilson, survived for just over seven months from March 1974, to gain an overall majority of three in the October 1974 general election. By April 1976, however, this majority had been whittled away, and James Callaghan, who became Prime Minister in that month, inherited the fourth minority government. That government lasted for longer than any of its predecessors, surviving for three

Reprinted from *The Independent*, December 14, 1994, p. 16.

years before being defeated on a vote of confidence and losing the 1979 general election.

How did these minority governments survive? The most common method has been through *ad hoc* majorities on particular issues. But this negative basis prevented such governments from promoting coherent legislative programmes. They survived, but at a price that made it impossible for them to govern.

On two occasions, therefore—in 1930 and in the 1970s—minority governments sought agreements with other parties. The second Labour government secured an informal understanding with the Liberals in 1930, by which Labour would promote electoral reform in return for the Liberals sustaining the government in office for two further years. In 1978–79, the Callaghan government had an informal understanding with the SNP, by which the government would be kept in office until after the devolution referendums; and with the Ulster Unionists, by which the government would be kept in office until extraparliamentary seats had been granted to Northern Ireland.

For all effective purposes there is a hung parliament in which support must always be renegotiated

---

But the main reason for the Callaghan government's survival as a minority administration was the Lib-Lab pact. In 1977, Labour was in a desperate position. Knowing that it faced defeat, it had refused even to contest an adjournment motion on its public expenditure plans which were rejected by 293 votes to 0. Yet, 16 per cent behind in the polls, La-

bour dared not go to the country.

Callaghan, therefore, approached David Steel, the Liberal leader, who declared that he would sustain the government only if a joint committee were established so that the Liberals would enjoy a formal consultative role in legislation. The pact was a novel constitutional experiment, since it was not a coalition and the Liberals did not join the government, but remained on the opposition benches. It lasted, nevertheless, until July 1978. Had Callaghan gone to the country then, rather than hanging on till 1979, he might well have been able to retain office and Thatcherism would never have been heard of again.

Is a similar device open to John Major? He can hardly propose a pact with the Tory rebels, and the only other party that he can depend upon is the Ulster Unionists. But, if he is to avoid presiding over a broken-backed administration, he needs something more than a commitment to support the Government in confidence votes. To make the most of Unionist support, therefore, he needs to negotiate a pact with the party, offering it, as was done in 1977, a consultative role over legislation. That indeed might have avoided the shambles of last week's VAT vote.

A pact with the Ulster Unionists would be perfectly in accordance with Tory traditions

---

A pact with the Unionists would be perfectly in accordance with Tory traditions. Until 1972, after all, the Ulster Unionists took the Tory whip at Westminster. Had they still done so in 1974, the Conservatives rather than Labour would

have been the largest party in the House. Edward Heath sought to recoup his losses by offering the whip to seven of the eleven Unionist MPs returned in March 1974, excluding the Paisleyites, but he was too late and the Unionists rejected him.

Would a pact damage the Irish peace process? There is no reason why it should, since the Conservatives accept that Northern Ireland must remain part of the United Kingdom, while that is the wish of a majority in the province, and the Unionists, by contrast with 1972, will accept a partnership government in Northern Ireland, and non-executive links with the Republic. Moreover, a pact could serve to combat the deep sense of alienation on the part of the majority in Northern Ireland, the most powerful political force in the current politics of the province.

If the Conservatives want to continue to govern, they must learn to share legislative power. That would involve surrendering their unilateral control over the parliamentary timetable, and replacing adversarial politics with the politics of negotiation.

This kind of politics, the politics of sharing power, may become a pointer to the future. The Conservatives were 7.5 per cent ahead of Labour in the 1992 general election, but won an overall majority of only 21. Had they lost another 1 per cent of the vote, there would have been a hung parliament, even though the Conservatives would have been more than 6 per cent ahead.

At the next election, either major party will probably have to gain a lead of at least 4 per cent to secure an overall majority. Such a lead was gained in only two of the nine general elections between 1945 and 1979, when the Conservatives came into office. So, whether or not we like hung parliaments, we may well have to get used to them.

The Resurgence of the Labour Party

Labour's ladder of opportunity

Tony Blair has a chance to redefine Labour as the party of meritocracy

Perhaps the most remarkable thing about Tony Blair's speech as leader to the Labour Party's annual conference on October 4th was that it contained more than one big idea. His pledge to scrap Clause Four—the one about nationalising the means of production, distribution and exchange—rightly made his audience sit up, and dominated the headlines. Nothing so symbolises Labour's attachment to its anti-market past as this bit of socialist rhetoric, and nothing could so demonstrate its commitment to a pro-market future as getting rid of it. Despite his embarrassing defeat in a non-binding conference vote on the issue, Mr Blair is almost certain to get his way.

The other big idea, though it generated fewer headlines, could prove almost as important for Mr Blair's future and far more difficult to achieve: redefining Labour as the party of meritocracy. Running through Mr Blair's speech was the idea that a socialist society must be "built on merit and hard work". Labour, he argued, stands for the silent majority, who are currently being held back by "entrenched interests. The Tories, in contrast, have sold out to a decadent establishment. The Thatcherites may have claimed that they wanted to bust that establishment, but, in fact, all they really wanted to do was to join it. "The new establishment is not a meritocracy," he insisted, "but a power elite of money-shifters, middlemen and speculators."

Mr Blair's speech had a couple of practical ideas for building the meritocracy, too. He pledged his party to getting rid of that standing insult to the meritocracy, "hereditary peers voting on the law of the land". And he insisted that Labour would invest more money in education. This might not sound all that startling—which Labour leader has not promised to invest in education?—but he added an edge to his generosity by promis-ing, in a coded threat to the educational establishment, that his party will no longer tolerate "bad discipline, low standards, mediocre expectation or poor teachers". To drive the point home he added that "if teachers can't teach properly, they shouldn't be teaching at all." These are welcome signs that turning Labour into the "party of opportunity" is more than blather.

Mr Blair has hit on a powerful argument. Meritocracy is a perfect vehicle for a party that claims to be both reforming and responsible, worried about inequality but keen on economic efficiency. The idea advances social justice, by treating people as individuals, rather than just as representatives of social groups, but it also promotes economic efficiency, by allocating jobs to those most capable of doing them.

It could also help Mr Blair to seize the radical baton from the Thatcherites. However much he talks about ditching Clause Four, embracing the global economy and being sensible about taxation, it is desperately hard for Mr Blair to appear more market-friendly than the Conservative Party. But if he mixes meritocracy with markets he may be able to produce a much more radical mixture than the Tories. He may even be able to force John Major to go into the next election defending inherited peerages and unearned wealth.

What is more, Mr Blair can present supporting the mer-itocracy as a return to the party's roots. The meritocratic ideal played a central role in establishing Labour as a serious party—as both a scourge of the old order, with its nepotism, corruption and inefficiency, and a harbinger of the new.

It provided a powerful rebuttal of the laisser-faire claim that the state is inherently inefficient. Certainly, the state was inefficient under Old Corruption, the party argued, but if you throw positions open to free competition and written examinations there is every chance that the public sector will eventually be just as effective as the private one. It also allowed socialists to present themselves as guardians of national efficiency, worried about an educational system which is horribly wasteful of the abilities of the nation's children and disgusted by a snobbish culture which directs such a high proportion of the chosen few into "useless" occupations.

It sounds like a marvellous idea. Unfortunately, reconverting the party to meritocracy could prove almost as difficult as converting it to the market. For the Labour Party includes two powerful groups that are firmly opposed to any sort of meritocracy: the trade unions and the public-sector salariat. And they, too, can summon up an eloquent tradition of left-wing thinking to support their case.

The trade unions, of course, are anti-meritocrats to their fingertips. Their defining philosophy is thoroughly collectivist: their aim is to strike collective deals, regardless of the huge variations in ability, aptitude and industry among their members, and their standard method is to dragoon the workforce into collective action. But many public-sector professionals are just as obsessed by group rights as their trade-union colleagues, though the groups are increasingly women, blacks and other "victims", rather than traditional manual workers. Already, the Labour Party has bowed to this argument by introducing positive discrimination for women in its process for selecting parliamentary candidates.

To these anti-meritocrats, meritocracy is both emotionally repugnant and "sociologically naive". It is emotionally repugnant because it creates an intolerably smug elite, convinced that it deserves all that it gets, and a horribly dispirited underclass, which has no choice but to blame itself for its own misfortunes. It is sociologically naive because it ignores the obvious "fact", demonstrated in a thousand social-science textbooks, that individual differences are the result not of genetic inheritance or personal character but of environmental circumstances: family wealth, parental encouragement and educational advantage. To sort people out according to their "abilities", then, amounts to nothing more than rewarding or punishing them for their family backgrounds.

These anti-meritocrats look to an equally powerful tradition in Labour Party thought, communitarianism. For the communitarians, the greatest good is attachment, the greatest evil alienation; and the principal purpose of political activity is to advance the first at the expense of the second. Communitarians such as William Morris, G. D. H. Cole and R. H. Tawney wanted to do away with social selection, not to improve it; to diminish the division of labour, not to refine it; to abolish social mobility, not to accelerate it; in short, to re-create the organic certainties of the pre-industrial world.

In his conference speech, Mr Blair was careful to flatter communitarians as well as meritocrats. "Community is not some piece of nostalgia," he told his audience. "It means what we share. It means working together." The Tory party's indif-

The ties that bind

THE Labour Party is not alone in showing renewed interest in the word "community". Several right-wing intellectuals, who would not have let the word pass their lips in the 1980s, have recently discovered that they, too, are communitarians. John Gray, who used to be Hayek's stoutest defender in academia, now argues that the market, unconstrained, severs social ties and robs people of the things they hold most dear, such as security and a sense of belonging. He says that the Conservative Party, having thrown in its lot with a clique of free-market purists, now faces electoral oblivion for a generation.

David Willetts, a Conservative MP who used to sit at Mr Gray's feet at Oxford, has criticised this argument. But even Mr Willetts is keen to establish his communitarian credentials. For him, however, it is the market that promotes communities by allowing people to consort with their own kind, and the state that destroys them by crushing voluntary organisations.

David Green, of the free-market Institute of Economic Affairs, laments the

fact that, in the 1980s, the Conservative Party paid so little attention to reinforcing social solidarity. David Selbourne, a former socialist who moved to the right in the 1970s, castigates the government for encouraging egotistical hedonism at the expense of civic responsibility.

Of course, there have long been Conservative intellectuals who waxed lyrical about feudalism, when everybody knew their place. But the new advocates of community would strongly deny that they are neo-feudalists. And there is an old tradition of left and right stealing each other's clothes. One-nation Tories happily quoted Cobbett and William Morris. Leftists such as Raymond Williams and Michael Young heaped praise on T.S. Eliot.

Today the two parties give different twists to the communitarian argument. But for both, the revival of the idea draws its strength from a revulsion against the more chaotic aspects of the modern world and a longing for a steadier society. It is a curious alliance—but one that may have a profound effect on western politics.

ference to community had led to the current epidemic of crime, brutishness and alienation, and one of the Labour government's key tasks will be to repair the ties of community that the Tories have torn asunder.

Mr Blair would no doubt argue that there is no tension between the two positions. Strong communities help their members get ahead, and go-ahead citizens weld their communities together. "We are the party of the individual," Mr Blair declared, "because we are the party of community." But, in fact, meritocrats and communitarians are in conflict over most of the questions that propel people into politics, and that conflict has repeatedly torn the Labour Party asunder.

The party's meritocrats believe, above all, in upward mobility and national efficiency. Asked what is wrong with Britain, they instinctively list titled twits, inherited wealth and lousy education. The communitarians, on the other hand, are worried about social disintegration and personal alienation. Their pet hates are money-grubbing and go-getting, their worst nightmare a world in which we are "all elbows", to quote their favourite thinker, Tawney.

The conflict between the meritocrats and the communitarians came to a head over the grammar schools, as Adrian Wooldridge, our education correspondent, chronicles in a soon-to-be published book*. The meritocrats believed that grammar schools represented Britain's only chance of replacing public-school toffs with carefully-selected meritocrats. Communitarians like Michael (now Lord) Young, Raymond Williams and Richard Hoggart argued that the grammar schools were causing untold harm, reinforcing inequality, tearing the heart and brains out of working-class communities, and churning out dysfunctional, neurotic scholarship winners. This argument was once more divisive than the one about nationalisation, and could be again.

---

*"Measuring the Mind: Education and Psychology in England 1860–1990". To be published on November 10th by Cambridge University Press

So which will it be, community or meritocracy? To answer the question, it will be necessary to look carefully at the way Mr Blair answers three tricky questions, all of which deal, in their different ways, with the application of market principles to the public sector.

THREE TESTS

Should the Labour Party preserve the purchaser-provider split in the National Health Service? Should it encourage market testing and contracting out in the rest of the public sector? And, most controversially of all for a party that invented the comprehensive school, should it allow schools to opt out of local-authority control, fashion their own identities and compete for pupils? If he throws in his lot with meritocracy, he will put himself at odds with powerful sections of his party. If he chooses communitarianism, on the other hand, he will be able to buy short-term political peace, but he will be accused by furious meritocrats of buying it at the cost of inefficiency.

Hard-nosed political commentators would no doubt argue that this is to read too much into a choice of words. After all, talk of "community" is just a way of tickling pressure groups (community values), dressing up hopeless policies (community policing), or sugaring harsh realities (the Toxteth community). But words have consequences, as Mr Blair recognised in his brave decision to scrap Clause Four.

If Mr Blair sides with the communitarians, he will face strong pressure to flunk hard decisions: to give just a little more money to this declining industry, to allow the benefit system to eat more and more of the nation's money, to shirk opportunities and stifle change. If he sides with the meritocrats, on the other hand, he will be seizing—at some risk—a chance of modernising not just his party but his country too.

An instinct for the centre

Tony Blair has ensured that John Major cannot win the next general election by default, says Philip Stephens

You could sense from as far away as Blackpool the ministerial hand-wringing in Whitehall. Mr Tony Blair achieved something rare this week. For the first time since 1979, a Labour leader set the terms for the Tory conference.

As Mr John Major contemplates his week in Bournemouth, he knows his performance will be judged against the powerful debut of his Labour opponent. Mr Blair reached out beyond his party's activists to the disaffected Tory voters who will decide

the next general election. Mr Major must begin to explain why they should return to the Conservative fold.

This should not be a crisis conference for the prime minister. Unusually since the sterling debacle on Black Wednesday, there is no immediate threat to his leadership. The economic recovery is real and well-balanced. For the moment, he has papered over the cracks in his party over Europe.

So, fingers crossed, next week will be, as was always planned, a sedate affair: a mid-term stock-taking exercise with no grand pronouncements, no great visions. Facing an audience still badly bruised by recession and angered by rising crime rates, the message has gone out to ministers to avoid any hint of triumphalism.

After his performance in Blackpool, there will be no real attempt to demolish Mr Blair. The voters are fed up with the politics of knocking; more seriously, ministers have yet to discover a credible line of attack on the Labour leader.

The message Mr Major wants to repaint on his government's peeling shop front is one of quiet, gritty competence. Don't worry, it says to those disillusioned Conservatives, we will arrive before the election.

The prime minister's image-makers are taking a similar tack in rebuilding his reputation with the voters. No, he is not a towering political figure in the mould of his predecessor. But look at how he gets things done.

He has taken hard decisions on the economy; and they are paying off with low inflation and steady growth. He has taken risks in Northern Ireland; and there is the best hope of peace for 25 years. He has stood up for Britain against the hated bureaucrats of Brussels; and he will do again at the 1996 intergovernment conference.

The safety-first approach is understandable. Conservative Central Office has spent the past month quizzing disaffected supporters. The voters are unconvinced by the reality of economic recovery. This is an upturn in which their disposable income is falling, not rising. So are house prices. And there are more tax increases to come.

The electorate shares traditional Tory values on law and order and education. But it judges the government is not delivering safety on the streets or high standards and discipline in the classroom.

Nor are the voters keen on the idea that the new breed of highly-paid bureaucrats in the national health service spend more time furnishing their executive suites than improving patient care. It is no accident that Mr Michael Howard, the home secretary, and Mrs Virginia Bottomley, the health secretary, are among the nation's least popular politicians.

Middle England's malaise

Gillian Tett on the despondency undermining Tory support

Mr Mike Bawden, a long-serving conservative councillor in Swindon, is not a melodramatic man. But as he surveys middle England this autumn, his verdict is that something strange is afoot.

"The government has a big problem," he admits. "All the yardsticks by which we used to measure the economy have changed, and people just don't feel wealthy or good any more."

The failure of the feelgood factor to return with economic growth is troubling the Conservative party as it assembles for its conference next week. An internal inquiry has been launched into the government's low popularity, led by Mr John Maples, one of the party's deputy chairmen. He insists the despondency will lessen in time.

But two years into the recovery, the message from Swindon is not simply that the feelgood factor is elusive but that there is little likelihood of a rapid change in mood.

On paper, Swindon is a manufacturing success story. In the late 1980s, the local economy grew fast as companies such as Honda, the Japanese car maker, opened factories locally. Growth faltered with the recession in the early 1990s, but its economy is expanding again.

Unemployment, which rose from 4 per cent in the late 1980's to 9 per cent in 1992, has fallen back to 6 per cent. The town's retailers detect modest sales growth. And 10,00 homes are being built in what will be Europe's largest private sector housing development.

But, says Mr Geoff Teather, editor of the Swindon Evening Advertiser, "nobody is really thanking the government".

Tax increases such as the imposition of Value Added Tax on domestic power have been introduced gradually, adding to consumer uncertainty. But, says Mr Bawden, the housing market is the real culprit for Middle England's malaise. Flat house prices have not only left the town with myriad tales of negative equity but forced many middle class residents to re-evaluate financial strategies.

David, a 36-year-old project planner, for example, bought a house five years ago for £140,000. He tried, and failed, to sell it for about £120,000 last year. "In the 1980's, people like me thought if we had spare cash we had to get on the housing ladder and keep borrowing and moving up. But now that's ended. We have had to look at our salary again and think a lot harder about saving."

Few people expect an early end to this malaise. Mr Russell Cleverley, of developers Hannick, says that, although the market picked up at the start of the year, it has stalled again. He blames the end of fixed rate mortgages, a crucial marketing tool in a time of low economic confidence. "I was thinking of buying a place for my children, but I won't now they have withdrawn the fixed rate."

There is no shortage of jobs locally. Indeed Mr Andy Cable, of the Response Management mail order group, says he has recruitment problems as he prepares for Christmas demand. But the part-time, flexible jobs he is offering have only limited appeal. "You can get temporary jobs, but there is really not much proper stuff around," says Miss Ann Whitfield, who recently found a job as a receptionist.

Few people in Swindon are yet predicting the three Conservative MPs in the area will be ousted at the next election. But as Mr Teather of the Swindon Evening Advertiser observes: "Labour is re-emerging just as these economic changes are happening. Mr Tony Blair must be hoping that people in Swindon could turn out to be his children of tomorrow."

All of this is perfectly clear to anyone who strays occasionally into the world of real people. But politicians only believe the obvious after they have paid huge sums to discover it from the opinion pollsters.

Mr Major's theme—assuming that he has not ripped up his speech entirely in the wake of Mr Blair's appearance in Blackpool—will be security.

The voters of middle England are troubled by a changing, harsh and competitive world. The middle-class life plan, the bedrock of Tory support in southern England, is threatened by the pace of technological change, by a cash-strapped welfare state and, above all, by an insecure employment market.

The government's answer is the promise of a steady, sustainable recovery instead of a return to boom and bust; a deregulated economy that allows Britain to keep up with world competition; and, when Mr Kenneth Clarke judges they can be afforded, all-important tax cuts.

It is an approach that most in the cabinet have signed up for. Mr Clarke, still hankers for another burst of radicalism, but the consolidators have the ear of No 10 Downing Street. The one controversial announcement scheduled for next week—privatisation of the Royal Mail—has now been delayed until the Tory faithful return home.

There is nothing much now that the Conservatives can do to rewrite the script for Bournemouth, though plenty of ministers will spend the weekend sharpening up their speeches to dispel any hint of complacency. But a strategy tailored to the pressures of the party conference will not be enough to counter the threat from Mr Blair. The opposition now has a leader with the authority and the intellect to take on the Conservatives in the battle of ideas.

Sure, his party still has the capacity to shoot itself in the foot (though in the 1980s it tended to aim the gun at its head). Conference defeats this week on Clause IV public ownership and defence will give ministers much-needed ammunition in Bournemouth.

But Mr Blair knows where he is going: into the political centre ground. Labour is to represent the aspirant classes. For all the talk of modernism, what he is doing is reconnecting it to its traditional roots as the party of opportunity. The voters who elected Mr Clement Attlee in 1945 and Mr Harold Wilson in 1964 were won over not by dewy-eyed socialism but by the promise of a brighter future.

The prime minister's view that the anxieties of middle England will be the most potent force at the next general election is shared by the Labour leader. The difference is that Mr Blair judges that the electorate's instincts have shifted back towards the centre. The individualism of the 1980s has become the insecurity of the 1990s.

It was no accident that in Tuesday's speech Mr Major was not mentioned by name; nor for that matter were Mr Clarke or Mr Douglas Hurd. Mr Blair's targets were the embattled Mr Howard and Mr Michael Portillo, the standard-bearer of the Tory right. Forget Labour's left-wing past, the Tories are the extremists now, he was saying.

There are flaws. It was easy to detect in the speech the tensions between his embrace for the market and the romanticism of Old Labour; easier still in the speeches of shadow cabinet colleagues. He will face serious internal battles over tax before the next general election.

To watch Mr Blair up close though is to understand how determined he is that New Labour will win. He has already in his back pocket a draft of the new statement of aims and values that will replace Clause IV. He is thinking ahead in a way that Mr Neil Kinnock was never allowed to and Mr John Smith never felt inclined to.

Mr Major is not lost. The government might yet recreate itself as the guardian of security in a changing world. Put another dash for integration by Britain's European partners alongside Labour's plans for devolution in Scotland and Wales and you can see the possibility of a campaign built around defence of the (British) Union.

But one thing is clear: 1992 was the last election the Conservatives will win by default.

British Constitutional Reform: Including the Monarchy?

Grim future for UK's ancien régime

Larry Siedentop

The author is fellow in politics at Keble College, Oxford

Britain is in the midst of a constitutional crisis. But it does not yet recognise the fact. One element after another of the old constitution has come under attack or, more dangerously, become the object of ridicule. The monarchy, Parliament and MPs, the electoral system, the role of the courts, local government, the Church and the honours system have become bones of contention.

Thatcherism—with its appeal to market forces, economic rationality, and self-interest—has been fatal to the British *ancien régime*. Alas, those who promoted the Thatcherite revolution did not understand the implications of their own programme. They did not grasp that they were putting the whole assembly of public institutions under the guillotine and that their programme made constitutional change unavoidable.

Which institutions can both sustain and constrain a market economy? How can values of fairness and community be fostered in a capitalist system? Evidently the market alone is not enough. Indeed, the idea of the market alone is a nonsense—for the state and popular habits and attitudes play a crucial role in structuring market relations.

Former Thatcherites have begun to worry about these questions. John Gray, the Oxford philosopher, has so far recanted that he sees the Tories' embracing of free-market ideology as a form of suicide that is likely to remove them from power for a generation. He urges them to return to what he calls their traditional concern for "nurturing communities and the renewal of civic institutions".

Gray's concerns are timely, but his prescription is unconvincing. It relies on a notion of "community" that is pre-individualist and embodies half-mythical solidarities associated with "cosy" relations of superiority and deference.

Like many former Thatcherites, he does not distinguish between free-market ideology and liberalism as a broader creed. The real failure of Thatcherism was its failure to understand that a market model could be safely imposed only if it was joined to a comprehensive social and political liberalism—the creation of a constitutional framework that fosters democratic forms of community to replace the old aristocratic intermediate bodies.

Liberal fairness must be the goal for Britain. Public policy must seek to promote reasonable equality of opportunity. As a test for social institutions, it need not work at the expense of community. But it will ensure that pursuit of the values of community co-operation, loyalty, mutual involvement, participation and consent are founded unambiguously on social equality and free association.

It prevents the appeal to "community" sliding into a yearning for pre-individualist and illiberal forms of social solidarity.

No other western nation has weakened local loyalties in the way the UK has done in recent decades

---

The British have found it difficult to construct a liberal society because of an aristocratic nostalgia that has tended to rely on subtle class roles regulated by accents and manners to encourage people to believe that they fitted into a community. But it is an illusion to suppose that such comforts rested on "fairness" or the "nurturing of community". They rested on social inequality—and they benefited one section of society disproportionately.

The historical consequence was that one section of British society was able to champion free-market ideas without for a moment assuming that it would ever be subject to the insecurities and risks inseparable from a more egalitarian and competitive social order.

The discontents of Middle England receiving so much attention at the moment should not therefore be misunderstood. They are not calls for a retreat from liberal fairness into a fantasy world of cosiness, under-education and, by implication, deference.

Rather, they are evidence that Thatcherism was a monstrously unbalanced programme and that in attending to market inefficiencies, trade union power and feather-bedding it failed to address larger social issues of fairness in anything like an adequate way.

The chief tenet of liberalism has always been that an excessive concentration of power in central government is dangerous—a danger both to individual liberty and to the "communities" that local autonomy and voluntary associations can help to create or strengthen.

No other western nation has weakened local loyalties in the way the UK government has done in recent decades, treating the country as a *tabula rasa* on which an omnipotent central government can impose forms and boundaries at will.

The centralisation of power is the real enemy of community in Britain. We cannot allow a government that has contributed so much to that development, now to hide behind the banner of community.

An idea whose time has passed

"WE MUST not let daylight in upon magic," wrote Walter Bagehot, the finest and most influential writer ever to have been editor of *The Economist*, when in 1865–67 he defined—some would even say created–the constitutional role of the modern British monarchy. Now, with each week of new books, new revelations and new comments from the royal family, there can be no doubt that the magic is thoroughly exposed, though by floodlight more than by daylight. In an institution which might be thought to be above personality, the foibles and weaknesses of the heir to the throne, his wife, his father and even his mother have become a subject of open debate and widespread criticism in a way not seen for decades. Is Prince Charles a suitable future monarch? That is the question on millions of lips, and not only those of republicans or of editors of salacious newspapers.

Yet it is also the wrong question. The right questions, though few dare to pose them in serious company, are the ones Bagehot would have asked: whether a monarchy is any longer a suitable part of Britain's constitutional arrangements, and whether those arrangements remain collectively suitable for this modern democracy. The answers, in *The Economist*'s view, are that the monarchy's time has passed; that the only powerful argument against abolition is that it is not worth the trouble; and that there is an even stronger case for reforming other parts of the constitution, which anyway cannot be done without addressing, and hence altering, the monarchy's role.

The paradox of a royal democracy

The most unpleasant aspect of all the current talk is that it has arisen out of personal revelations. Yet the tittle-tattle has performed a useful service, by prompting the royal family itself to open the debate. Responding to a book by a journalist, Jonathan Dimbleby, about his son, Prince Philip sensibly told the *Daily Telegraph* that a republic was "a perfectly reasonable alternative" to a constitutional monarchy, and that the monarchy should survive only as long as people wanted it.

That is the right starting point, and also the right corrective to any dogmatic republicans. If the British people want a monarchy, they should have a monarchy. That is the contradiction at the heart of a constitutional monarchy: that an unelected institution, redolent of authority and selected by accident of birth, depends for its legitimacy on the popular will. That is why a referendum on the monarchy would be wise, either soon or at the time of the next succession, for it would test the popular will, which is what democracies are all about. It is also, however, why the royal family knows that personal revelations do matter, for they threaten the popular support on which the crown depends.

For the moment, the monarchy remains popular. Opinion polls still show widespread, albeit gradually declining, support: generally 70–75% of people say they favour its retention, though that is down from 85–90% a decade ago. When asked whether Britain will still have a monarchy in 50 years' time, people are more divided: those sure that it will still exist have fallen from 70% in 1990 to a range between 35% and 50% or so in more recent polls. This uncertainty may arise from a view that kings and queens belong to the past, not the future; more likely it also arises from those turbulent royal lives.

Dyed-in-the-wool monarchists hate such polls, and hate even more deeply the idea of a referendum. To them, monarchy is about awe and deference, and to put it to a vote is by definition to destroy its very essence. Yet that is the weakest possible defence of monarchy, to those who value democracy. For the royal family does need popularity. Whereas in the distant past monarchs were remote and invisible, in this age both of television and democracy the royal family has sought to make itself more accessible, and to build an image in which fairy-tale grandeur, a sense of tradition and, perhaps most fatefully, the importance of family life are blended. Some say that it should never have done so. Yet remaining remote was not a real choice: one way or another, modern communications would have made royalty visible; one way or another, an educated populace, eager for information whether profound or prurient, would have wanted to know more. And the more they know, the more they are likely to question.

Not dignified, not a disguise

Like it or not, then, the questions are there. They cannot and, in a democracy, should not be dismissed, as the foreign secretary, Douglas Hurd, tried to this week by attacking "chattering people" who "chip away at our institutions in this country." If Prince Charles is deemed widely to be an unsuitable king, then to allow him to succeed without a referendum would itself harm the institution of the monarchy by removing its own legitimacy. Leave the personal question to one side, however. Does the monarchy deserve support?

On principle, this newspaper is against monarchy. Constitutional or not, it is the antithesis of much of what we stand for: democracy, liberty, reward for achievement rather than inheritance. Surrounded as it is by privilege and patronage, the crown even has a certain, though not inevitable, bias against capitalism. It may be a symbol of unity but it is also a symbol of aristocracy, of feudal honours, of baseless deference.

What might Bagehot think? Our modern Bagehot column . . . summarises what its inspirer wrote about the crown during his mid-Victorian era. Whether he would now have changed his mind depends on what his view would have been of today's democracy. His defence of monarchy, in his book "The English Constitution", depended crucially on a belief in rule by an educated elite and a fear of giving power to the uneducated masses. He saw the "efficient" part of the constitution as the parliament and the cabinet: these took on the complicated and difficult tasks of governing. The monarchy was the "dignified" part, which meant not merely that it was decorative but also that it acted as a "disguise" for the true nature of government. Leadership by a single person was something ordinary people could understand, and accept. Leadership by an assembly, and political parties, could not easily be understood by the ignorant masses. So it was best to use the monarchy as a channel for popular support, deflecting attention from the true centre of power.

Since then, many things have changed. The monarchy no longer disguises the business of government, for the suffrage is universal and the nation far more educated. Bagehot wrote of the monarchy that "among a cultivated population, a population capable of abstract ideas, it would not be required." That is true, and it would be outlandish to argue now that the British people cannot understand democracy. Nevertheless, that it may not be required does not rule out the chance that the monarchy might be wanted.

Questions of value

It might, for example, be felt that in times of transition, of turmoil and division, a monarch could be a steadying, unifying force. Yet Britain does not look like such a country and has not done so for a century or more. In the past five years many other countries, especially ex-communist ones, have endured painful transitions: yet only one, Cambodia, has chosen to restore or create a monarchy.

Another reason for wanting a monarchy might be its neutrality, and the value of using that neutrality in the way Bagehot defined: "the right to be consulted, the right to encourage, the right to warn." The existence of monarchy, in other words, is a useful check on the behaviour of parliament and the prime minister. That it might play such an active role cannot be ruled out altogether. Yet there is also contained within this idea a fiction, a last remnant of Bagehot's notion of the dignified disguise. The modern monarch could not afford to offer any serious opposition to a determined democratic entity. In the monarchy's current state, there are virtually no true checks and balances in the British constitution; but the fiction that one exists is convenient to governments, and therefore dangerous to their subjects.

That leaves three other reasons for wanting a monarchy, one bad but the others perfectly reasonable. The bad reason is one of the most often cited: tourism. Not only is tourism an odd justification for a constitutional arrangement, it is also wrong on its own terms: tourists visit Britain for its history, which would not disappear if the monarchy were to go. The most popular tourist site is the Tower of London, which thankfully has not been in active use by monarchs for some time. Just as the attraction of Versailles has endured for the two centuries since the French revolution, so Britain's historical and monarchical sites would survive the loss of their living inhabitants.

The two good reasons for the monarchy, have, however, far greater force. One is sentiment. People might simply like the monarchy: it is an institution of which some people feel fond, something they would rather have than lose despite the political, symbolic and constitutional arguments. This newspaper would not share that view, but, being based on emotion, it cannot be refuted and should not be ignored. The other good reason is also hard to refute: that even if the monarchy does not deserve support, to abolish it would be more trouble than it is worth. Britain has bigger issues to address than whether to remove the queen's head from postage stamps. Abolition of the monarchy would be a giant distraction.

The interdependent constitution

As long as the monarchy is considered on its own, this view is surely correct. Its symbolism is harmful: the hereditary principle, deference, *folies de grandeur*. But it is hard to prove that doing away with it would bring such powerful benefits as to overcome the costs of doing so. Yet the monarchy should not be considered on its own.

This brings us back, once again, to Walter Bagehot. As he realised, the connections between the parts of Britain's constitution are as important as the parts themselves. Britain's basic constitutional defects arise from the excessive power of the House of Commons, and hence of the cabinet. In Bagehot's view, that power was a marvellous, "efficient secret". Now it is damaging and inefficient, permitting abuses of power, excessive centralisation and a steady erosion in respect for government. Yet it derives from the royal prerogatives that Parliament enjoys; it is reinforced by the weakness, since 1911, of the House of Lords as a scrutineer of legislation; it depends on an electoral system that allows strong majority governments to be chosen by a minority of votes; it is preserved by the lack of a constitutional court and of a bill of rights by which the judiciary could limit over-mighty government; it is protected by the lack of public access to information. Government actions, and the actions of agencies appointed by government, are accountable only to the very Parliament that that government dominates.

To deal with those defects you do not have to change everything entirely and all at once. But if you start to deal with one part of the constitution you will inevitably affect the others. For example, if, as we would argue, the House of Lords should be replaced by an elected second chamber, then to do so would affect the role of the monarchy, and it would alter the case for reforming the Commons's electoral system. The connections continue, from everything to everywhere.

The point is this. The case for constitutional change is, in our view, irresistible; it is one to which this newspaper will return in the coming months. The crucial reforms do not require outright abolition of the monarchy—but they would inevitably alter the monarch's position and open that position to further scrutiny. Those who argue that, for the sake of avoiding a fuss, there should be no examination of the monarchy's future are therefore, deliberately or otherwise, acting to stifle a broader and necessary debate. Constitutional change of any sort is certain to be "troublesome", and is equally certain, one way or another, to raise questions about the crown.

The monarchy is not the most pressing issue facing Britain. In our view, it would be best to abolish it, but the rest of the agenda for constitutional change matters more. In the end, if the people wish, it would be appropriate to preserve the crown. But to protect it from review is indefensible. This would be to preserve its mere dignity, such as it is, at the risk of leaving Britain's constitution unreformed. And that would be plainly and unforgivably wrong.

Tradition, continuity, stability, soap opera

The War of the Windsors is forcing a reluctant Britain to re-examine itself. Is the monarchy a valuable link to the nation's past, or a useful symbol for it in the future?

A TRULY conservative people, with a deep-rooted distaste of "change for change's sake", most Britons would prefer not to tamper with their country's constitutional monarchy. And yet the royal family seems determined to push the question of the monarchy's future underneath everyone's nose.

For the past few years the British media have been full of demeaning royal tittle-tattle, much of it sadly true and much of it leaked by the royals themselves. Every few months someone in the family delivers another bombshell—a confession, a marital separation, a reluctance to pay for a burned castle, an admission that its members ought to pay taxes or a suggestion that the next monarch might not be head of the Church of England.

This week Prince Charles set off the biggest explosion yet when, through an authorised biography whose serialisation began in the *Sunday Times* on October 16th, he complained in excruciating detail not only about his wife's behaviour, but also about the cold treatment meted out to him by his father and mother. The queen, setting out the next day on the first-ever visit by a British monarch to Russia, maintained her usual silence. But Prince Philip delivered an obvious rebuke to his son in an interview with the *Daily Telegraph*, declaring that "I've never discussed private matters and I don't think the queen has either."

This latest episode will force into the open a long-rumbling debate about whether or not Britain should abolish the monarchy. Prince Charles's revelations are different from those of the past on several counts. They come from the heir to the throne and, for the first time, directly involve the queen. They have been almost universally condemned, and prompted direct comparisons with Edward VIII's abdication crisis of 1936. They seemed to herald his divorce from the Princess of Wales, though both his solicitors and hers denied this.

Prince Philip seemed to sense something had changed. In his newspaper interview he pointed out that, because the monarchy had lasted more than 1,000 years, "it can't be all that bad," but added: "There's a perfectly reasonable alternative which is a republic." He then calmly discussed how elected heads of state were chosen elsewhere and declared that monarchy was an alternative only as long as people wanted it. "What it is not," he claimed, "is a desperate attempt by a family to hold on to some sort of situation. Because that isn't the point. I don't think anyone would actively volunteer for this sort of job." He seemed to be saying: "back us or sack us."

Many people would prefer not to make that choice. But further revelations will keep the issue of the monarchy before the public, whether they like it or not. On October 23rd, the *Sunday Times* plans to publish the second instalment of Charles's biography, with his account of his affair with Camilla Parker Bowles. Next month a second book on the Princess of Wales, by Andrew Morton, a journalist, is due to be published, and will again carry her version of events. On December 9th Charles and Diana will have been formally separated for two years, making an easy divorce possible. Even before this flood of confession abates, people already know more about Charles and his family than many know about their neighbours, or their own relatives. As if to underline this, a comic play opened in London on October 19th portraying the queen and her family, having lost the throne, living on a council estate.

The debate about the monarchy's future will be long and complicated. Some will claim that trying to get rid of the monarchy, in scaling it down, is a distraction from "real" issues, though with the country awash with royal stories distraction is already rife. Others, including this newspaper, will argue for, or against, abolition primarily on constitutional grounds. Many will blame media intrusion for the monarchy's loss of status. Many will also blame the royals themselves, especially Diana and Charles, even while arguing that the fate of the institution of monarchy should not be decided by the antics of its current occupants.

However the debate goes, it is likely to reveal much about how Britons view their country, and its future. And the argument for keeping the monarchy with the greatest appeal will be what it has always been: that it is a symbol of continuity and tradition, a cherished link with Britain's past, an embodiment of nationhood.

This view, though still widely held, needs to be re-examined. The monarchy is undeniably a link with Britain's past and it is encrusted with traditions, of a sort. But many of those traditions are recent inventions. And Britain has other national traditions which also link it with its past, but which might serve it far better in the future.

The monarchy may have lasted 1,000 years, but until recently the British have only occasionally treated it with reverence (Charles I lost his head, remember). The current royal family, like the Hanoverians before them, are as much German as British. In fact George V invented the family name Windsor (after his favourite castle) in 1917 at the height of the first world war when the family's real name, Saxe-Coburg & Gotha, had caused grumbling. When the Kaiser heard of this he demanded, in a rare flash of wit, a staging of that famous opera, "The Merry Wives of Saxe-Coburg & Gotha".

As David Cannadine* and other historians have shown, many of the elaborate rituals now associated with the royal family, and widely believed to be the epitome of ancient tradition, are of recent vintage. One of the most important of these, the queen's state opening of Parliament, which takes place this year on November 16th, was not even performed throughout much of the last century. Queen Victoria hated taking part in public ceremonies and opened Parliament only eight times between 1862 and her death in 1901.

In fact, in the early 19th century many Britons themselves not only had little taste for royal ritual, but prided themselves on this very fact, regarding the ostentatious ceremonies of continental monarchs, or the nonsense of Napoleon Bonaparte's self-coronation as Emperor, as symptomatic of despotism. With the country's economy developing faster than any other in the world and confidence soaring after the Napoleonic wars, "free-born Englishmen" seemed to have little use for the monarchy, and often viewed it as an embarrassing anachronism.

....
* see his essay on the British monarchy in "The Invention of Tradition" edited by Eric Hobsbawm and Terence Ranger, Cambridge University Press

When royal ritual was attempted, it was often a dismal failure. In 1817, at the funeral of Princess Charlotte, the daughter of the Prince Regent, the undertakers were drunk. At George IV's coronation in 1821, pugilists had to be employed to keep the peace among guests (not the rabble outside). Victoria's coronation in 1838 was also a shambles according to contemporary accounts.

Journalists and the public also showed little respect for monarchs themselves. On the death of George IV in 1830 *The Times* declared in an editorial that: "There never was an individual less regretted by his fellow creatures." Cartoonists such as Gillray, Rowlandson and Cruickshank attacked the monarch in a manner which would look savage even today.

Victoria was no more popular than her predecessors until her apotheosis near the end of her reign. She was at various times scornfully referred to as "Mrs Melbourne" (for her partiality to her first prime minister) or "Mrs Brown" (for her partiality to her servant John Brown). Her long retirement after the death of Albert was bitterly resented. In 1864 an advertisement was pinned to the railings of Buckingham Palace by some wag: "These premises to be let or sold, in consequence of the late occupant's declining business." She was regularly attacked in newspaper articles. By the mid-1860s republicanism was becoming widely discussed, even fashionable. Republican clubs sprang up throughout the country in the following decade. The monarchy seemed headed for the dustbin of history.

And then something happened. The ruling elite, forced to widen the voting franchise, decided that the country needed the monarchy as a symbol of stability and that they needed it to help them retain control of the government. At the height of the republican agitation, Walter Bagehot wrote his book "The English Constitution", which set out not only to describe the workings of the government, but also to prescribe how a constitutional monarch should behave. In the following decades Victoria was pressed by politicians to participate more actively in public ceremonial. She continued to

resist. But, by the time she was persuaded to take part in her own golden jubilee in 1887, her longevity alone had begun to make her popular.

Royal ceremonial was vastly inflated in the following decades, as it was elsewhere in Europe in a frantic competition for national prestige. Bagehot's "English queen" became "British", even "Imperial", and she came to sit not at the heart of his "English Constitution" but of the "British Constitution". Stirring music was written by the nation's best composers to accompany royal ceremonies, and they were executed with unprecedented precision and care. Long-forgotten medieval rituals were dragged out of the attic, dusted off and performed, such as the investiture of the Prince of Wales in 1911. New ones were invented: the royal Christmas broadcast in 1932. When the public began to grow bored even with this in the 1960s, the cameras were invited in to Buckingham Palace. Two world wars swept Europe's other monarchies away, or cut them down to the size of "first citizens". The Windsors alone remained at the centre of a giant ceremony business (appropriately referring to themselves as "the firm.")

The royal spectacle may, as many monarchists insist, have helped Britain survive the social upheavals of the past century. Whether it will be much help in facing those of the future is doubtful. Many people remain fond of it. But many are also ashamed of the royals for holding themselves, and their nation, up to ridicule.

The British do have other traditions which run through their history as consistently as those of monarchy, and matter far more: of innovation, commercial flair, civility, fairness, tolerance, respect for the individual and a distrust of emotional extremes. In fact, British political thinkers have done more than those of any other nation to help create the modern idea of democracy which is now spreading throughout the world. It is hard to believe that monarchy is vital for the political health of such a nation. How ironic it is that the land of Locke, Hume, Paine, Godwin and Mill should even think it desirable.

Peace in Northern Ireland

Part I
Northern Ireland Takes a Leap On Painstaking Path to Peace

Carole Craig

Special to The Christian Science Monitor

═══════════ **DUBLIN** ═══════════

IN some parts of Ireland, David Ervine, former Protestant paramilitary leader, is a popular man. In the middle-class confines of the mirrored and carpeted Teachers' Club bar in the heart of Dublin, he meets a constant flow of well-wishers wanting to shake his hand.

For many in the Catholic-dominated Irish Republic, Mr. Ervine is the acceptable face of unionism, the political philosophy that for the past 70 years has defended the six majority-Protestant northern counties of Ireland as part of the United Kingdom.

In contrast to members of the establishment-oriented Ulster Unionist Party (UUP) – which threatened to bring down the British government in reaction to controversial peace proposals for Northern Ireland – Ervine asked his supporters to wait and see, and spoke of being "positive" about the future of the north.

The final version of the "framework document" on the future of Northern Ireland is to be unveiled Feb. 22 by British Prime Minister John Major and Irish Prime Minister John Bruton. The UUP preempted the unveiling by setting out its own proposal on Feb. 21, which would go more slowly toward building a new local government in the province.

But it is not certain that all unionists are all behind it, and an apparent division among them could thwart their all-out rejection of the framework document.

Ervine, who served time in prison for transporting a bomb, has a position similar to that of Gerry Adams, president of Sinn Fein, the political wing of the Irish Republican Army.

The IRA's long terrorist campaign to drive the British out of Northern Ireland ended with an IRA cease-fire on Sept. 1 last year. Ervine was among those who reciprocated a few weeks later by announcing a cease-fire of Protestant paramilitary groups.

Although they come from different sides of the struggle for Northern Ireland, both men since last fall have argued for a political process to supersede the 25 years of violence that has cost more than 3,000 lives.

Now that the paramilitary groups have laid down their weapons, the compromises that must be reached through painstaking negotiation – for which the framework document is a stepping stone – are just as critical.

Unionists, representing the majority in Northern Ireland, have to be persuaded that they will not be forced into a united Ireland. Nationalists, representing Catholics who make up about 40 percent of the population in the province, must believe that their desire for links with the Republic of Ireland in the south will become a reality.

Unionists are most upset about the framework document's proposal for "cross-border bodies," which will have authority from both Northern Ireland and the Republic of Ireland to handle areas of mutual economic interest, especially those concerning the European Union—to which both the Republic of Ireland and the United Kingdom belong.

Unionist concern has been hard to allay, especially since some observers see the new cross-border bodies as a push into the Republic of Ireland.

Mitchell McLoughlin, northern chairman of the IRA's political ally, Sinn Fein, says it will look at the framework document "in terms of two aims, the end of partition and the end of British administration."

Enough is enough?

As far as nationalists are concerned, they have already made their fundamental compromise: That Ireland would only be united by the consent of those in the Protestant-dominated North, not by a desire of the island as a whole.

Further compromise may be difficult to draw from the province's Catholics, many of whom feel they were included in Northern Ireland against their will. The old local parliament, which was disbanded in 1972, was infamous for discriminatory policies against Catholics.

But six months of peace under the IRA and Protestant cease-fires may make everyone hungry for more. Ervine, the Protestant paramilitary leader, calls the days of paramilitary violence "hell on earth" and says he will not stand by and watch "hearses roll into the graveyards again."

And unlike many unionists, Ervine and his followers are ready to admit that nationalist

Catholics have a point when they criticize how the unionist Protestants have treated them.

But his bottom line shows that final agreement with the nationalists still is a long way away. He says that speaking with nationalists is "the same old story. You get, 'you know you're not British really, you're Irish. Your future is in a united Ireland and you'll love it when you get there.' Well I ain't going."

Part II
Politicians Place N. Ireland Peace In Public's Hands

Alexander MacLeod

Special to The Christian Science Monitor

═══ LONDON ═══

A YEAR ago, few would have imagined that the prime ministers of the Irish Republic and Britain would come together on the soil of troubled Belfast and introduce a peace deal for Northern Ireland.

Riding on the hopes of nearly six months of peace that followed 25 years of terrorist violence in the British-ruled province, John Major of Britain and John Bruton of the Irish Republic yesterday struck through the blistering attacks of Protestant leaders to appeal directly to the people of Northern Ireland.

The two leaders insisted their plan, a long-awaited formula for negotiations on the province's future, is the best hope for permanent peace among Northern Ireland's Protestants and the Catholic minority.

They will have to keep up their stamina to ride out a storm of criticism by leading Protestant politicians, who are concerned that the document weakens Britain's ties to the province and condemned it even before it was published.

The Rev. Ian Paisley, leader of the hard-line Democratic Unionist Party, called it "a nationalist agenda" and "a declaration of war" on Protestants.

James Molyneaux, leader of the moderate Ulster Unionist Party (UUP), which also favors links with Britain, chose a more subtle tactic. It will likely also be more successful: He preempted London and Dublin by publishing his own alternative plan for Northern Ireland.

Mr. Molyneaux insisted that his proposals were "more realistic and practical" than the joint Anglo-Irish document that appeared the next day.

In what analysts see as a possibly crucial change of tack, Major

KEY POINTS IN ANGLO-IRISH PROPOSAL FOR NORTHERN IRELAND

■ A new Northern Ireland assembly elected by proportional representation will replace the old assembly, scrapped in 1972 by Britain.

■ A new cross-border body will be formed from – and accountable to – the Irish parliament and the new Northern Ireland assembly. The body would have limited powers.

■ The Irish Republic will drop its constitutional claim to Northern Ireland.

■ British law will be changed to recognize the right of self-determination for Northern Ireland, which currently is a province of the United Kingdom.

■ Ireland and Britain will design a new agreement on coodinating their Northern Ireland policies, but neither side will interfere with the new Northern Ireland assembly.

■ Safeguards will be provided for the protection of civil, political, social, and cultural rights of Northern Ireland people.

– **A. M.**

– who met Bruton in Dublin before their peace proposals were published – told the British Parliament on Tuesday that the Molyneaux plan could be used as a basis for discussion, along with the official framework document.

Eleanor Goodman, a leading London-based political analyst, says that by allowing the Molyneaux document to form part of the political agenda, Mr. Major "has made it possible for the unionists to take part in future discussions."

Even so, advisers to Major and Mr. Bruton accept that the two leaders are embarking on a hazardous project that could still go wrong. "They are walking a high wire," one British Cabinet minister said.

"They are pinning their hopes on the war-weariness of the people of Northern Ireland," the minister said. "Those people may not be too impressed if their political leaders adopt rigid positions and destroy the cease-fire that has prevailed since last September."

The Anglo-Irish framework document aims at promoting talks among the London and Dublin governments and Northern Ireland political parties, including Sinn Fein, the political wing of the Irish Republican Army.

The goal is power-sharing between the two communities and creating links in such matters as tourism between Northern Ireland and the Irish Republic.

IRISH premier Bruton called the framework document "balanced and fair" and said it "threatened nobody." The aim was to "facilitate, not preempt dialogue" and not to impose a blueprint over the heads of the people. The people of both parts of Ireland would have the final say, he said.

John Hume, the moderate nationalist politician whose talks in the last two years with Sinn Fein leader Gerry Adams set the peace process going, called for calm appraisal of the framework document. "Dialogue has brought us to where we are, and dialogue is the only way to bring us to agreement," Mr. Hume said. Martin McGuinness, deputy leader of Sinn Fein, said his party would study the document and make its views known after its conference this coming weekend.

Major and Bruton both heavily stressed the "triple lock" element of the framework document, intended to allay unionist fears of a sell-out to the nationalists.

It means that any progress towards a lasting settlement would have to be approved in advance by all the parties, by the London and Dublin parliaments, and by voters in both parts of Ireland through parallel referendums.

The UUP alternative proposals urge the early creation of an interim power-sharing assembly in Northern Ireland but say nothing about links or contacts between Dublin and Belfast.

Initial Unionist reaction to the Anglo-Irish proposals was angry.

Peter Robinson, Mr. Paisley's deputy, said they amounted to an "eviction notice" to leave the United Kingdom.

Ken Maginnis, a leading UUP member of the British Parliament, said it was an attempt to "buy off IRA terrorism."

In Northern Ireland, however, informed commentators say the chances of Major and Bruton being able to ride out the political storm are better today than they would have been in the recent past. They are certain to be encouraged by evidence that the peace process is being strongly supported by the people of Northern Ireland.

According to a poll by Ulster Marketing Services, in 1993 only 6 percent of the population expected a more peaceful year. In 1994 the proportion had risen to 23 percent, and last month it was at 66 percent.

═══ 6. Peace in N. Ireland ═══

Germany:
Urgent Pressures, Quiet Change

"Germany may assert its foreign policy priorities with unaccustomed vigor, and it may express profound disappointment if its initiatives slow or fail, but its commitment to remain part of the Western economic and defense community is firm. Compromise will be the order of the day, not an independent German course."

GARY L. GEIPEL

GARY L. GEIPEL *is a research fellow at the Hudson Institute. He is the editor of* Germany in a New Era *(Indianapolis, Ind.: Hudson Institute, 1993).*

Five years ago, as Germany began the stunning legal and political process that led to reunification, observers argued whether the result would be a "new Germany" or simply an "enlarged Federal Republic." One could play this intellectual game with regard to almost any aspect of Germany's future: its economic strategy, foreign policy, and domestic political landscape all might be dramatically transformed or continue more or less as usual in a postunification, post–cold war world. Underlying the debate was the widespread fear that a new Germany might in fact resemble old Germany and pose grave risks for its neighbors and erstwhile friends. Today the dichotomy of a volatile new Germany versus an old-style stable Federal Republic retains little usefulness. It is time to confront a Germany that is new but not inherently dangerous, stable but not entirely predictable—a Germany that no longer fits the mold from which it sprang.

Dichotomies are insufficient for understanding a nation of paradoxes. Germany is poised to seize the most dramatic economic opportunity in its history—de facto leadership of an expanding European Union (EU)—while agonizing over severe structural problems at home. German foreign policy hovers somewhere between the aggressive hegemony and passive multilateralism of its previous incarnations. German leaders do not avoid or deny their nation's past, but they remain confused about the meaning of old lessons for future policy. Finally, German domestic politics accommodates a variety of extremist agendas and protest parties while sustaining in power what is arguably the most monolithic and enduring political center of any major democracy.

Today's Federal Republic of Germany is fascinating precisely because it is a work in progress. There is no easy recourse to German history or to other international precedents in describing the evolution of the new nation, which is changing for reasons that go well beyond the impact of reunification. Among the large industrialized countries Germany is unique in the pressures it feels to redefine its social contract and its external relationships simultaneously. How it will respond remains to be seen, but recent developments offer important clues.

AN ECONOMY AT RISK?

As late as 1990, when East Germany became part of a unified Germany, the West German "social market economy" enjoyed a degree of reverence bordering on the mystical. The formula of cradle-to-grave social services, consistent economic growth, and close labor-management relations demanded high productivity, technological superiority, and expanding foreign markets. It seemed unstoppable, however, and few Germans questioned its immediate extension to East Germany. Four years later, according to a lead article in Germany's most prominent left-oriented weekly, "*Modell Deutschland*[the German model] is at risk," threatened by "external competition" and "internal tensions."[1] Much as German officials would prefer to attribute their country's economic troubles to the costs of unification, that is only part of the truth. Almost 3 million eastern German workers became unemployed or underemployed after unification, and public transfers from western to eastern Germany are indeed enormous, amounting to 5 percent of GNP. If anything, however, pent-up consumer demand in eastern Germany and the flood of public spending shielded the western German economy from a structural crisis in the years immediately following unification. Today there is no place left to hide.

The German economy suffered the deepest reces-

---

[1] Robert Leicht, "Wenn die Stunde der Politik schlägt," *Die Zeit*, November 12, 1993, p. 1.

sion in its history in 1993, contracting 2.4 percent in western Germany and losing nearly 1 million manufacturing jobs. The unemployment rate in western Germany climbed above 8 percent, where it remains, and topped 18 percent in the formerly Communist eastern Länder (states). Disposable earned income in Germany fell 3.3 percent in 1993, which dampened consumer demand considerably. Modest new growth this year has had virtually no impact on job creation and few economists expect the unemployment rate to drop significantly in the near future. Official estimates suggest that as many as 600,000 additional jobs may be lost to industrial restructuring in Germany. A poll of more than 10,000 German firms by the German Conference of Industry and Trade reports that 30 percent plan to relocate part of their production abroad in the next three years. To fund the rising costs of unemployment and to promote economic development and infrastructure projects in eastern Germany, public sector debt increased from 46 percent of GNP in 1989 to more than 60 percent today.

What went wrong with the vaunted German model? By a variety of important measures, Germany lost ground to international competitors. Labor costs are near the highest in the world, largely because contributions to mandated entitlement and insurance programs now come to more than 85 pfennigs on top of each deutsche mark paid in wages. German labor market regulations remain rigid, discouraging part-time and short-term employment, shift work, and the hiring of pensioners and students. German workers—who enjoy six to eight weeks of paid vacation and more than a dozen annual holidays—put in 15 to 20 percent fewer hours on the job each year than their Asian and North American counterparts. Not surprisingly, the Federal Republic's attractiveness as an investment site is in decline. The productivity increases that resulted from recent industrial restructuring only partially compensate for the high cost of German labor.

Meanwhile, the technological advantages traditionally enjoyed by German manufacturers continue to slip away. Intense regulation, the difficulty of financing risky ventures, a bureaucratized research-and-development culture, and widespread pessimism about the effects of new technology on social life and the environment hold back the development of new technology in Germany. Germany's widely heralded status as a major exporter masks the fact that its global share of the high-technology export market is significantly smaller than its overall market share in manufactured goods. That does not bode well for the future, since it is primarily in the most advanced sectors that German firms will be able to hold off low-wage competitors. German firms also suffer from their minimal presence in the dynamic East Asian economies. Only 7 percent of German exports go to East Asia, about the same share as go to Belgium and Luxembourg.

Germany's structural problems are exacerbated by a major actuarial dilemma: the country stands at what might be called the limits of the welfare state. Taking high unemployment rates into account, Germany soon will approach a situation in which a little more than one-third of the population must finance the education, subsistence, and health-care benefits of the other two-thirds. It is common for university students to reach the age of 30 before entering the workforce, even as the average retirement age in Germany creeps down to 59 and life expectancy increases. Birth rates are low and immigration is discouraged, further reducing the potential infusion of new taxpayers. The way out of this trap is some combination of large-scale job creation, efforts to extend the average working life of Germans, and cutbacks in social welfare spending—a tall political order.

Chancellor Helmut Kohl does not shy away from describing the magnitude of the country's structural and demographic problems. In a blistering speech on the floor of parliament last October, Kohl decried an entitlements mentality and declining work ethic that have made the country resemble "a collective amusement park" rather than an attractive business site. In an effort to keep larger numbers of workers on corporate payrolls, the government this year urged troubled firms to experiment with short-term palliatives such as reduced work weeks and extended vacations in exchange for pay cuts. And by tightening political asylum procedures and encouraging the departure of foreign guest workers, the government succeeded in reducing the number of non-Germans who might compete for jobs, under the popular (but incorrect) assumption that foreigners are a drain on the German economy.[2] Kohl and his government have avoided more drastic corrective measures, however, which is no surprise in an election year.

Thus far it has fallen to German business leaders and to the struggling Free Democratic Party (FDP) to argue the need for more dramatic changes in the German economy, including slashing subsidies to uncompetitive industries, and fostering greater wage differentiation between industries and regions, and trimming social spending. Now that Germany's federal elections are in the past and a fresh four-year legislative period commences, political courage to undertake such measures will probably increase.

Changes of the kind sought by German business **would amount to a redefinition of the country's social**

---

[2]Contrary to popular myth, non-Germans contribute disproportionately to GNP (their 7.8 percent of the population generates 10 percent of Germany's output) and to tax and pension pools (at least $9 billion more per year than they take out). Even in a depressed economy, foreigners often are the only workers in Germany willing to take menial or low-wage jobs.

contract. In exchange for continued growth in real income, citizens would be asked to work a bit more, sacrifice some of the esoteric and excessive benefits of the welfare state, and contend with a more competitive labor market (including, eventually, more immigrants willing to accept low-wage jobs). Germany's economic advantages remain considerable: social peace; a highly educated workforce; an excellent vocational training system; a large market in the EU and central Europe; and a tradition of sound fiscal management and cautious monetary policy. Even with those advantages, however, it is difficult to see how Germany will continue to prosper into the twenty-first century without a more flexible labor market and a more entrepreneurial business climate. The international competition—from Asia, North America, and, increasingly, central Europe—is simply too fierce.

In view of the economic pressures on Germany, it is no wonder the German government acts cautiously in exercising its powerful influence in the European Union. German leaders quite naturally consider the possible evolution of the EU in terms of how it will affect Germany's own economic position. It is not clear, for example, that some visions of a "deeper" Union necessarily would benefit Germany. For example, most Germans recoil at the thought of diluting their sovereignty over monetary policy in the big pool of a European currency. Similarly, the widening of the EU to central Europe, which many German leaders support for sound foreign policy reasons, is not without its economic and political risks at home. Full access to EU markets for countries such as the Czech Republic and Poland, with their low labor costs, would pose an almost insurmountable competitive challenge to older German industries such as chemicals, steel, and shipbuilding. From a long-term and purely economic standpoint, such a shakedown probably would be a good thing. For German politicians, however—like their counterparts elsewhere in the Union—the short-term consequences of widening the EU to central Europe will be difficult to sell.

REPHRASING THE GERMAN QUESTION: GERMANY'S INTERNATIONAL ROLE

If the price of German competitiveness is a new social contract, the price of reunification and the end of the cold war is a more decisive German role in international affairs. Germany's definition of that role has yielded a contentious process at home and a disconcerting spectacle for its neighbors and friends. However, clarity improved this year with the decision of Germany's highest court that the deployment of German troops for peacekeeping and peacemaking purposes under UN auspices does not violate the German constitution. The past year also saw the beginnings of a serious debate in Germany about the country's national interests, heretofore taboo.

For 40 years after the creation of the Federal Republic, its top leaders honed the art of simultaneously pursuing goals that appeared to contradict one another. West Germany proved itself a loyal member of NATO while pioneering *Ostpolitik* to secure stable diplomatic and economic relationships with the Warsaw Pact countries. Bonn kept alive the goal of reunification, which implied the demise of East Germany, while placing its relations with its Communist brethren on an increasingly businesslike footing. West Germany hosted the nuclear weapons of the United States while asserting no right to control their ultimate use and denying any desire for an independent nuclear arsenal. And Bonn unfailingly supported the multinational approaches of the UN to global problems and crises while forbidding the use of its own forces for such contingencies.

Germany was many things to many people during the cold war, but much has changed. Most obviously, the external constraints on German freedom of action no longer exist. The residual rights of the victorious World War II powers in Germany formally ended with reunification. NATO forces remain in the country at the pleasure of the German government, as they did during the cold war, but Germany once again is fully sovereign. More important, the roles of other NATO members in safeguarding the alliance have declined relative to Germany's. This is particularly true in the case of the United States, which has withdrawn all but about 150,000 troops from Europe. Germany continues to be the NATO member that is arguably most exposed to potential instability and aggression originating in central and eastern Europe or in Russia. And while the magnitude of security risks to the North Atlantic alliance obviously declined with the end of the cold war, the diversity and number of smaller risks increased significantly. For example, three major cases this year of plutonium smuggling through Germany from the former Soviet Union elevated the importance of nonproliferation regimes in the minds of many German leaders. Finally, while expectations of Germany in managing European and international crises have increased since reunification, the Federal Republic—like most other members of the Western alliance—devotes fewer resources to its armed forces and lacks the capability to participate in distant, large-scale military actions.

As a result of these changes, Germany is under pressure to make strategic choices for the first time in its existence. Should it focus inward to complete the daunting task of unification or must it take on new global responsibilities? Should it favor the deepening of the EU, the widening of the Union to include new central and eastern European members, or some combination of the two strategies? Should it emphasize the European or the transatlantic dimension of its alliance relationships? Should it remain firmly anchored in "the West," rediscover a historic role in "the East," or become a bridge between the two? Lest anyone thought that the perennial "German question" had been laid to rest, this list demonstrates that the questions have multiplied.

There is a certain unfairness in pressuring Germany to make such choices. Geography did not bless Germany with obvious strategic priorities. Nor is it clear that Germany's neighbors and allies will be entirely happy with any choices that the unified nation might make. No sooner does Germany opt out of military involvement in the Persian Gulf War than it is accused of shirking responsibility. No sooner does it assume a degree of responsibility in the Balkans by recognizing the independence of Croatia and Slovenia than it is called to account for its supposed resurrection of great power politics. It is not surprising, then, that some German leaders still prefer to avoid difficult foreign policy choices with rhetorical finesse. That breed inevitably will be replaced, however, by a new generation never schooled in the art of being all things to all people. The new generation, which came of age after World War II, is far less likely to fear discussions of German interests and will not hesitate to stand up to foreign opposition. The Christian Democratic Union's Volker Rühe and the FDP's Klaus Kinkel are early prototypes. In their respective ministries, defense and foreign affairs, the outlines of a new German role in international relations have begun to emerge in the last two years.

First, the Federal Republic does not look to remain immobile in the West or to defect to the East. Instead, it wants to make the East part of the West, closing the German question forever by surrounding itself with like-oriented countries. This goal entails the incorporation of the central European countries—the Czech Republic, Hungary, Poland, and Slovakia at a minimum—into the key Western institutions: the EU, the Western European Union (WEU), and NATO. If that happens, Germany no longer would sit on the edge of one political universe, peering anxiously into the other. It would be located in the middle of a shared universe, realizing a goal of German leaders—expressed in various ways, some of them reprehensible—for generations.

Second, although it is loathe to make this choice explicit, Germany gives growing priority to the widening of the EU at the expense of its deepening. The strategic rationale for widening flows directly from the first goal of westernizing central Europe. The integrated market is a reality, and German exporters benefit from it tremendously. But in the minds of many Germans, going further—to a common currency, or to pursuing common European policies on everything from the labor market to environmental protection—erodes German flexibility and places German expectations and standards at the mercy of a massive consensus.

Future German leaders will not reject the Maastricht agenda, but they almost certainly will attempt to steer it in the direction of a federal system, leaving maximum power with individual countries and regions rather than creating a new superstate.

German leaders increasingly see it as their mission to "synchronize" the European and transatlantic security institutions, the WEU and NATO. They view Germany's handling of the controversial Eurocorps as the first success in this endeavor. When Chancellor Kohl and French President François Mitterrand agreed in 1991 to form the nucleus of a pan-European army corps under WEU auspices, little thought was given to the formal relationship the Eurocorps would have with NATO. In the wake of considerable American and other allied criticism, Germany obtained French agreement to subordinate the Eurocorps to NATO in the event of a crisis. The German goal is to continue to bind the United States firmly to Europe in security matters, without jeopardizing the formation of a meaningful European security identity.

Moreover, the Federal Republic has become much more active in European security affairs, even as some German leaders continue to argue that the country's troops can never again be deployed to regions occupied by Hitler's armies. In the Balkans, following its controversial recognition of Croatia and Slovenia in early 1992, Germany adopted a more team-oriented approach, alternating with the other transatlantic powers in spearheading negotiations and participating (not without domestic controversy) in the naval blockade of Yugoslavia, airborne relief efforts, and the deployment of NATO AWACS planes to monitor the no-fly zone in Bosnia and Herzegovina. Unlike Britain, France, and the United States, Germany has no troops on the ground in the former Yugoslavia. However, it shoulders a disproportionate share of the refugee burden. In mid-1993, Chancellor Kohl took an outspoken position in favor of lifting the arms embargo against the Bosnian Muslims, but was overruled by his EU allies.

Finally, although it is actively engaged in Europe, Germany's involvement in crisis management elsewhere in the world will remain highly selective. Following the high court decision in July, German troops no longer face legal obstacles to their deployment in any UN operation. German military officials now openly consider crisis-reaction capabilities in their force planning. And German leaders are keen on receiving a permanent UN Security Council seat. In practice, however—since approval by a majority of parliament will be required—German governments will make military deployment decisions on a case-by-case basis, with sober reference to national interests and to the ability of the German armed forces to make a meaningful contribution. The deployment of a German medical unit, other technical specialists, and military police to Somalia in 1993 and 1994 took place without serious casualties, but it is not likely to set a significant precedent. Many observers in Germany questioned the appropriateness of the overall UN mission in Somalia.

This emerging outline of unified Germany's foreign policy will not get rave reviews in every foreign capital. The current administration in Washington, for example, does not favor the rapid expansion of NATO membership to central Europe, fearing the impact of such a move on Russian perceptions of the West's intentions. As an interim substitute for NATO membership, the United States–devised Partnership for Peace initiative met with public support but private disappointment in Germany, particularly in the Defense Ministry. For its part, the French government is not delighted by Germany's fixation on central Europe and its related efforts to widen the EU at the expense of deepening. France's priorities are the reverse of Germany's in this, setting the stage for tension in the bilateral relationship that has driven the EU's evolution. This April, Germany secured France's commitment to use the two countries' back-to-back EU presidencies to develop a "perspective" on central Europe's association with the Union. Little has come of the initiative, and French leaders remain far more preoccupied with an unfolding crisis in Algeria than with the future of central Europe.

Public pronouncements aside, there also is little foreign support for a German seat on the UN Security Council. Britain and France resent Germany's elevation to the status of a strategic player, and the proliferation of European seats on the Security Council would highlight the absence of the common EU foreign and security policy pledged at Maastricht. Finally, German activism in Balkan and eastern European affairs often comes across as one-sided to allied officials, who note that Germany favors decisive action but refuses to deploy its own troops to support such action.

It is at this point that some observers speculate on Germany's reaction if its foreign policy visions meet with hesitation or rejection in the West. Would Germany then go it alone as a central European stabilizer, or revert to some type of condominium with Russia? Would Germany loosen its ties to the EU and NATO? The determined individual can find evidence for these possibilities in today's Germany. A former German EU official, Manfred Brunner, took a constitutional challenge against the Maastricht treaty all the way to Germany's highest court last year and formed an anti-Maastricht political party, the Alliance of Free Citizens. A group of young nationalist intellectuals have begun publishing a weekly newspaper called *Junge Freiheit* (Young Freedom). The paper is a forum for writers who regularly suggest that Germany's *Westbindung* (tie to the West) is not an absolute requirement but rather a marriage of convenience to be maintained only so long as it reflects German interests.

Still, these segments of opinion must be seen in context. Germany's high court rejected Brunner's challenge, and his party won only 1.1 percent of the vote in last June's European Parliament elections in Germany. Intellectual fads, meanwhile, can be easily overemphasized as indicators of impending policy shifts.

Questioning *Westbindung* is a path to oblivion for German politicians. Germany's economic and political stakes in the EU are much greater than its advantages as a central European hegemon. No rational German leader believes that the country could muster the defense investments that would be necessary to replace NATO's security guarantee. As for a special relationship with Moscow, early signs suggest that in the wake of Russia's troop withdrawal, Germany will tend more to bluntness than condominium. This summer, for example, Kohl dispatched a top deputy to give Russian leaders a dressing-down on nuclear safeguards. Germany may assert its foreign policy priorities with unaccustomed vigor, and it may express profound disappointment if its initiatives slow or fail, but its commitment to remain part of the Western economic and defense community is firm.

A FRENZY OF ELECTIONS

In view of the severe economic pressures on Germany and the unsettled nature of the country's international role, it would not seem unusual to find major upheaval in German domestic politics. Such upheaval is not at hand. Germany's Bundestag (federal parliament) elections were to take place on October 16, shortly after this issue went to press. They will culminate an unprecedented streak of 20 German elections this year, including municipal and Länder balloting and elections to the European Parliament. Even without seeing the results of the Bundestag elections, a number of important conclusions can be drawn from this frenzy of political activity.

Germans share the disillusionment with politics that is widespread today in the major democracies, but they are not inclined to stage a revolution at the voting booth. This year the German electorate did not follow the lead of Canadian, Italian, or Japanese voters and precipitate a great shift in the balance of power. Either the Christian Democratic Union/Christian Social Union (CDU/CSU) or the Social Democratic Party (SPD) continues to dominate every state government in Germany. These two large *Volksparteien* (people's parties) lost some ground at the state and local level, and the SPD's performance almost certainly did not live up to its expectations, but combined support for the two parties still accounts for between 70 percent and 80 percent of the vote in almost any election in Germany. In short, the center holds.

Members of Germany's traditional liberal party, the FDP, grumble with considerable justification that they constitute the only non–social democratic party in the country. The CDU/CSU leans to the right and the SPD to the left, but they do not depart from a basic consensus on the inviolability of the welfare state, the importance of collective rather than individual responsibility, and the appropriateness of government intervention in the market. The FDP's struggle this year simply to clear the 5-percent threshold necessary for representation in the Bundestag suggests that there is a small and dwindling constituency in Germany for free-market, civil libertarian ideas. This may complicate the necessary restoration of Germany's international competitiveness.

German voters continue to favor experience over change in their selection of leaders, even (or perhaps especially) in difficult times. The higher the office, the more accurate that observation becomes. In early 1994, polls indicated that SPD Chancellor-Candidate Rudolf Scharping could hire a decorator for his new suite at the Chancellery. By summer, however, lackluster performances on the stump, gaffes, and a failure to control dissent in the SPD had left Scharping with much diminished credibility. He rallied somewhat, but it appears that the best the SPD can hope for is junior status in a Grand Coalition with the CDU, or a continuation of its role as the primary opposition in the Bundestag. It is difficult to overstate the effectiveness of what the newsmagazine *Der Spiegel* called the "power machine" of Helmut Kohl, as well as the grudging respect that most Germans have for the man who appears poised to break Konrad Adenauer's record of 14 years as chancellor of the Federal Republic.

There is much continuity at the top, but German politics is not entirely without surprises. Contrary to all forecasts in the immediate wake of unification, the Party of Democratic Socialism—the successor to the Communist Party that ruled East Germany for 40 years—is a force to be reckoned with. The PDS earned double-digit representation this year in most of the local and state elections held in eastern Germany, and is poised to return to the Bundestag. The PDS retains most of the ingredients necessary for political survival: a natural constituency (former East German Communists and other easterners who feel alienated by the process of unification); a young, charismatic leader (Gregor Gysi, perhaps the most gifted political orator of his generation in Germany); and financial resources (garnered in part from the coffers of the East German Communists).

Another surprise might be called the rise of the mainstream avant garde. Banished from the Bundestag four years ago, the Greens did not so much regroup as ungroup by dumping its Fundi faction—the extremists who tossed pies in the faces of visiting foreign leaders and refused to contemplate coalitions with more established parties. The Greens, who merged with the eastern German civil rights group Alliance '90, now take 10 percent or more of the vote in most German elections and show up in an increasing number of state-government coalitions with the SPD. Despite their continued support for the eventual dissolution of NATO and the German army, it may be only a matter of time before the Greens claim a piece of federal power. One senior Greens leader remarked only half jokingly that his party is now the party of the rich in Germany, since its supporters indeed tend to be well off, young, and well educated; this is an enduring and powerful constituency.

A final, welcome surprise this year is the disarray and electoral failure of the extreme right-wing parties in Germany. They retain seats in some state parliaments but do not seem to be within striking distance of the 5 percent support necessary for Bundestag seats. There is little cooperation between or even within the Republikaner and the German People's Union (DVU), the two most developed far-right parties. Changes in Germany's asylum law defused the immigration issue, which the far-right had used to its advantage. Opinion polls have identified latent sympathy—sometimes on the order of 10 percent or more—for some of the neofascist message in Germany, but even sympathizers pull back from supporting the far-right in the voting booth.

NORMALCY

"There is no German dream. There is only a German nightmare. People talk about returning to normalcy now that the Wall is down. What does 'normalcy' mean in German history? And what does 'return' mean?" asked Norbert Gansel, a senior SPD legislator, in the June 29, 1993 *International Herald Tribune*. With top Geman leaders expressing such anxieties, it is no surprise that foreign observers also worry. Gansel does have a point. Looking back past the Federal Republic, Germans see little worth returning to. But are not the 45 years of the Federal Republic also a part of Gemany's past? And was it not a central goal of the Federal Republic to become "normal" in the sense of being whole, free, stable, self-reliant, and trusted with power? If so, whether or not Germany has returned to normalcy, it does appear to have arrived there.

Everyone a winner

BERLIN

It is a stange week that finds John Major the most secure among the leaders of the big European democracies. In the following article we look at [one of] five leaders in trouble, Helmut Kohl, narrowly re-elected in Germany. [The others are:] Edouard Balladur, scandal-ridden in France, Silvio Berlusconi, ditto in Italy, Viktor Chernomyrdin, ill, allegedly, in Russia and Lech Walesa, criticised in Poland.

NARROW majorities affect German chancellors in different ways. The night Helmut Schmidt won a ten-seat majority in 1976 he chain-smoked his way through a harrowing evening and left for bed after a brief victory speech looking shattered. An ebullient Helmut Kohl, by contrast, declared victory in Germany's general election on October 16th barely an hour after the polls closed and well before his ten-seat majority had been officially confirmed. He could see no reason why his coalition of Christian and Free Democrats would not finish another four-year term.

Together Mr Kohl and his allies won 341 seats in a 672-member Bundestag (enlarged through the working of Germany's mixed proportional and constituency voting). Mr Kohl's Christian Democrats (CDU) and their Bavarian allies (CSU) won 41.5% of the vote, a drop of 2.3 percentage points over 1990, but a good result considering that Mr Kohl has been in office for 12 years. Despite an unbroken string of state election results in which they had won no seats, the liberal Free Democrats (FDP) vaulted over the 5% hurdle to get back into parliament and government.

The opposition Social Democrats (SPD) under Rudolf Scharping won 36.4% of the vote and 252 seats, 13 better than before, but nowhere near a majority, even with the Greens who re-joined their eastern colleagues in parliament as an all-German party with 7.3% of the vote.

As even the remote chance of leading an unstable left-wing coalition vanished, Mr Scharping looked as if a great weight had rolled from him. Germany will be hard to govern in the next four years and Mr Scharping now has the chance to prove himself a national leader for 1998. Leading the opposition is his excellent second best. He has given up as premier of Rhineland-Palatinate and will be at the thick of the action in Bonn as the Social Democrats' new parliamentary leader.

The ex-communist Party of Democratic Socialism (PDS), or Red Socks, which had given tint to a colourless campaign, won four constituencies in Berlin, enough and to spare for the party's 4.4% share of the national vote to count in the overall allocation of seats. The irrepressible Gregor Gysi and Stefan Heym, a writer and parliament's old-

est member, will thus head a 30-member PDS group in the new Bundestag. Though it did not produce a hung parliament, as some had feared, this tiny party attracted much attention. This was an election which had something for everyone.

Mr Kohl would see the silver lining in an asteroid attack. But his confidence in the stability of his fourth government rests on more than animal spirits. To get a German chancellor in or out of the saddle takes half the votes in the Bundestag plus one. Mr Kohl has this; the opposition does not. Germany has no by-elections, so the majority cannot change (dead deputies are replaced from party lists). A ten-seat edge means whips can rise above the odd defection.

Mr Kohl's predecessor, Mr Schmidt, need not have worried that night long ago. He was chancellor for the next six years, until his FDP partners deserted him—for Mr Kohl. The liberals are an unpredictable lot, even to themselves. Later in this parliament they may prove to be a rubber crutch, but not yet. Their priorities are to look like an indispensable part of government and to hang on to the foreign ministry.

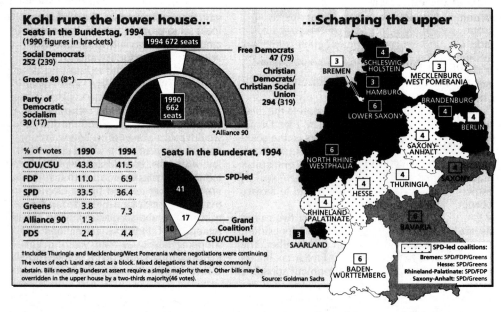

Kohl runs the lower house...

Seats in the Bundestag, 1994
(1990 figures in brackets)

1994 672 seats

Social Democrats 252 (239)

Greens 49 (8*)

Party of Democratic Socialism 30 (17)

1990 662 seats

Free Democrats 47 (79)

Christian Democrats/Christian Social Union 294 (319)

*Alliance 90

% of votes	1990	1994
CDU/CSU	43.8	41.5
FDP	11.0	6.9
SPD	33.5	36.4
Greens	3.8	7.3
Alliance 90	1.3	
PDS	2.4	4.4

Seats in the Bundesrat, 1994

41 — SPD-led

17 — Grand Coalition†

10 — CSU/CDU-led

†includes Thuringia and Mecklenburg/West Pomerania where negotiations were continuing
The votes of each Land are cast as a block. Mixed delegations that disagree commonly abstain. Bills needing Bundesrat assent require a simple majority there . Other bills may be overridden in the upper house by a two-thirds majority(46 votes).

Source: Goldman Sachs

...Scharping the upper

SCHLESWIG-HOLSTEIN 4
BREMEN 3
HAMBURG 3
MECKLENBURG WEST POMERANIA 3
LOWER SAXONY 6
BRANDENBURG 4
BERLIN 4
NORTH RHINE-WESTPHALIA 6
SAXONY-ANHALT 4
SAXONY 4
THURINGIA 4
HESSE 4
RHINELAND-PALATINATE 4
BAVARIA 6
SAARLAND 3
BADEN-WÜRTTEMBERG 6

SPD-led coalitions:
Bremen: SPD/FDP/Greens
Hesse: SPD/Greens
Rhineland-Palatinate: SPD/FDP
Saxony-Anhalt: SPD/Greens

The pressing question is not whether Mr Kohl's government can survive—it can, at least for now—but what it will be able to do. One constraint is that much law-making needs the assent or acquiescence of the Bundesrat, or upper house, where the Social Democrats are strong. There is already, for some purposes, a Grand Coalition in all but name.

The recent big parliamentary decisions—on asylum, state-funded nursing-home insurance and the annual budget—required late-night bargaining between Wolfgang Schäuble, the leader of Mr Kohl's parliamentary group, and his Social Democrat counterparts. Now, the Social Democrats' increased weight in the lower house must also be reckoned with.

The other constraint is Mr Kohl himself. Twilight is long at northern latitudes but his era is unmistakably ending. This is likely to be his last term. He means to use it, he says, to "complete German unity" and to make a leap toward the European kind.

Lame duck already?

"German unity" is code for propping up the eastern economy with welfare and subsidies until it can pay for itself, while lightening the tax-load and further de-regulating the German economy as a whole (see box below). As for European unity, Mr Kohl belongs to the last generation with direct experience of Nazism and world war. He feels a duty to make European integration irreversible to prevent a recurrence. He doubts the next generation of Germans find this as urgent as he does, and he may be right. Mr

Time to shrink

BERLIN

WITH Helmut Kohl safely back in office, businessmen's lobbying for economic change—suspended while the chancellor's re-election was in doubt—can begin again. Almost in unison the associations that represent most employers and industries started demanding lower taxes, less government, reform of social security, more-flexible labour markets, deregulation and a slew of other free-market changes.

Mr Kohl agrees with much, though not all, of this agenda. He will, however, be able to enact only a small part of it during the new four-year parliament. The opposition Social Democrats (SPD), who control the Bundesrat (upper house), are not the only constraint. Mr Kohl has never been one to press visionary reforms that might disturb social tranquillity.

Mr Kohl's tricky task is to shrink government spending while continuing to pay the enormous costs of German unification. The coalition has already vowed to cut government's share of GDP from more than half now to 46% by 2000. To qualify for European monetary union in 1998, Germany must also cut government debt from a projected 64% of GDP next year to 60% or less.

The outgoing government made a start, helped by the ending of recession (after shrinking 1.9% in 1993, western Germany's GDP is expected to grow about 2% this year). In addition, says the OECD, the government's "structural deficit" (the share independent, that is, of the economic cycle) fell from 5.2% of GDP in 1991 to 3.1% last year. A draft 1995 budget, likely to be revived by the new government, would hold nominal federal spending to a scant increase of 1%, in part by restricting now-unlimited unemployment benefits to two years.

Combined government deficits are supposed to fall from a forecast 2.8% of GDP this year to 0.5% by 1998. But debt reduction depends on three things beyond the federal government's control: economic growth, real interest rates and the thrift of *Land* (state) and local governments. Moreover, the SPD-controlled Bundesrat can veto tax measures on which deficit-reduction depends.

Next year's main business will be the wholesale reform of the tax system triggered by a court order to reduce taxes on low incomes; implementing this will cost DM15 billion ($10 billion) or more. Politicians in and out of government will try to

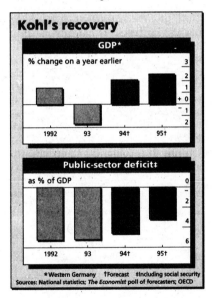

Kohl's recovery

GDP*

% change on a year earlier

1992   93   94†   95†

Public-sector deficit‡

as % of GDP

1992   93   94†   95†

*Western Germany †Forecast ‡Including social security
Sources: National statistics; *The Economist* poll of forecasters; OECD

get their pet programmes on to the inevitable tax bandwagon. The Free Democrats (FDP), junior partners in the coalition, are eager to cut business taxes, particularly two hated levies on capital. The Christian Democrats (CDU) will go along only if money is found to replace the lost revenue.

Tax reform could further two causes dear to both government and opposition: industrial innovation and families. The coalition and the SPD favour tax breaks for research-and-development spending

to promote the high-tech industries they believe Germany lacks. They also want to boost child benefits but quarrel over the method. The CDU would raise the tax deduction for each child but make direct child payments dependent on incomes; the SPD would scrap the tax deduction but raise direct payments.

Prophets of decline dream of more sweeping change. The ageing of Germany's population will drive social-security costs to intolerable levels in the next century, they insist. Zealots like Klaus Murmann, chief of the employers' federation, want sharp cuts in benefits and a change in the way they are financed (away from payroll taxes, as now, to general taxes). The FDP backs these notions; the CDU sees no need for drastic reforms, especially ones that would hurt loyal constituents—older voters, civil servants and the self-employed. Given the FDP's electoral weakening, the government's main social-security initiative is likely to be a continuation of its successful programme for containing health-care costs.

To the extent the coalition can influence employment directly, it is likely to rely on deregulation. Mr Kohl's previous government gave employers more freedom to vary the eight-hour day and let private employment agencies compete with the state monopoly. The current one looks set to promote flexible, lower-wage employment, especially in the under-developed service sector. It wants to encourage part-time work and to boost tax deductions for child care and other domestic services.

The FDP has bolder schemes for tempting the unemployed off the dole. It would replace a range of benefits with one transfer payment and it would subsidise low-wage jobs. Both ideas are probably too radical for its coalition partners. The FDP, its power reduced by the election, may have to settle for a more modest contribution to the service economy: the scrapping of ludicrous restrictions on shopping hours. German voters might then look more kindly on the unloved liberals, at least on Saturday afternoons.

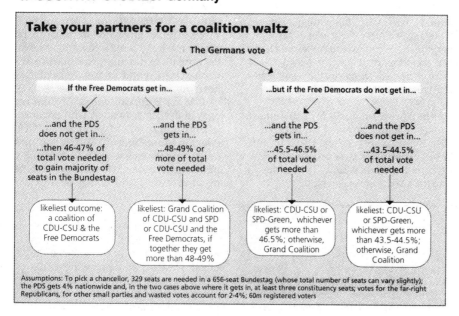

Take your partners for a coalition waltz

The Germans vote

If the Free Democrats get in...

...and the PDS does not get in...

...then 46-47% of total vote needed to gain majority of seats in the Bundestag

likeliest outcome: a coalition of CDU-CSU & the Free Democrats

...and the PDS gets in...

...48-49% or more of total vote needed

likeliest: Grand Coalition of CDU-CSU and SPD or CDU-CSU and the Free Democrats, if together they get more than 48-49%

...but if the Free Democrats do not get in...

...and the PDS gets in...

...45.5-46.5% of total vote needed

likeliest: CDU-CSU or SPD-Green, whichever gets more than 46.5%; otherwise, Grand Coalition

...and the PDS does not get in...

...43.5-44.5% of total vote needed

likeliest: CDU-CSU or SPD-Green, whichever gets more than 43.5-44.5%; otherwise, Grand Coalition

Assumptions: To pick a chancellor, 329 seats are needed in a 656-seat Bundestag (whose total number of seats can vary slightly); the PDS gets 4% nationwide and, in the two cases above where it gets in, at least three constituency seats; votes for the far-right Republicans, for other small parties and wasted votes account for 2-4%; 60m registered voters

Kohl's formidable instinct for what is doable may conflict here with his historical imperatives.

That is a complex equation for a lame-duck chancellor, even one as canny as Mr Kohl. Germany's government will not be in-ert in the next four years. The previous parliament, struggling with unity, distracted by electioneering, was nevertheless not passive. All the same, it would be a mistake to expect from Germany dynamic or consistent leadership.

Those hoping that this election would provide some kind of unequivocal mandate—a clear, renewed conservative vote, or their own turn at last for the Social Democrats—were looking for the wrong thing. This was a year for incumbents in Germany: one premier after another was re-elected at state level, too. But to treat the 1994 elections as showing drift, muddle or plain boredom with politics would also be wrong. The German election has more positive lessons.

One concerned the wrecks and disasters that did not occur. The far-right virtually disappeared. The parties with federal government experience (which excludes the Greens) together still account for four-fifths of the vote. There was no hung parliament.

An intricate voting system reflected well the electorate's rather contradictory wishes. Many more Germans preferred Mr Kohl to Mr Scharping as chancellor. But many of those are fed up with the Christian Democrats and liberals.

An electorate split exactly into left and right, as is Germany's, may look like one that cannot make up its mind or that is at war with itself. But a different explanation applies here: those labels do not mean as much as they did. Voters in both camps seem to be telling politicians, "Together or apart, get on with it."

Kohl's Germany: The Beginning of the End?

Timothy Garton Ash

Taking a break from Germany's rather boring election campaign, I dropped in to the fine new museums that have recently been opened in Bonn. Right at the beginning of the permanent exhibition in the splendid new Museum of the History of the Federal Republic I found a strange black pavilion with, inside, pictures from the Nazi extermination camps. A young German guide was just explaining to a group of visitors that there had been a vigorous debate about whether to show these horrifying pictures. The conclusion, he said, was that "a German museum could not afford not to show these pictures."

At the towering new exhibition hall just down the road there was a fine show of the central and east European avant-garde in the twentieth century. One section was entitled "The Presence of Jewry." Here another young German guide stood before Chagall's 1914 picture *The Feast Day*, showing a rabbi with a miniature rabbi on his head, pointing in the opposite direction. Trying to explain the figure of the miniature rabbi, the guide, a woman in her early twenties, said: "I myself have no direct experience with Jewish people, so I can't really judge, but from what I've read, this spirit of contradiction, this capacity to make fun of yourself, is characteristic of Jewry."

Yes, the past—*that* past—is still here. Whenever you come to Germany you are sure to stumble across it, one way or another. It won't pass away. Yet as the naive comments of the young German guides suggest, it is almost astronomically remote from the life experience of younger Germans today. Painful innocence, not

guilt or even repressed guilt, speaks from those comments.

For me, these flashbacks to a hell made in Germany serve above all as a reminder of the fantastic distance that Germany has traveled over the last half-century: the distance to civility, legality, modernity, democracy. The very fact that, after four years of traumatic change in an only painfully uniting Germany, the election campaign can be boring is itself a measure of that progress. The village pub where I go for lunch with friends turns out also to be a polling station. As we chew our schnitzels, we can watch the civil, genial, utterly matter-of-fact business of voting. In the evening, the "election parties" in the headquarters of the main political parties are even more hot and crowded than at previous elections, with everyone trying to judge everyone else's *Stimmung* as the beer (SPD) and wine (CDU) flow.

An element of drama is given by the closeness of the result, with estimates of the current coalition's new parliamentary majority sinking to as low as a single seat during the evening, before rising again in the small hours to the eventual ten. But the whole nation is hardly biting its nails in suspense. On another television channel there is a comedy show, with a comedian from Paderborn giving a wonderful imitation of the petit-bourgeois *Hauswart* type, obsessed with cleanliness and order. The audience loves it. Who says the Germans can't laugh at themselves? On a third channel, there is a light entertainment program, with viewers invited to contribute by tele-

phone to a charity for cancer victims. Viewers' names are flashed across the screen, with their contributions: 20 DM, 30 DM, 4,000 DM, 40,000 DM. Just before I flick back to the election coverage, the compere announces the latest total. It is 5 million DM ($3.36 million).

Germany—from the banality of evil to the banality of good.

1.

Of course there are still serious matters to be worried about in Germany—even in the results of this election. But the first thing is to keep those matters in proportion.

I have been traveling to Germany for more than twenty years now. For as long as I can remember, I have heard apocalyptic warnings—and none more apocalyptic than those issued by Germans themselves. The *Ölpreisschock*! The terrorists! *Berufsverbot*![1] Franz Josef Strauss! Eurosclerosis! The Greens! The peace movement! Nationalist-neutralism! Rapallo! *Anschluss* (of East Germany)! German-dominated *Mitteleuropa*! Neo-Nazis! For as long as I can remember, the Federal Republic has gone on its quiet, successful, bourgeois way, proving one warning after the other wrong,

---

[1] *Berufsverbot*—roughly "job-ban"—was a term coined by critics of government vetting procedures introduced in the 1970s to combat supposed far-left infiltration, and which resulted in a number of public-sector employees losing their jobs. This was criticized as an infringement of civil liberties.

as it has got steadily richer, stronger, and now bigger.

This election, the thirteenth to a German Bundestag but only the second to an all-German Bundestag, is taken so seriously both because of the pre-1945 past—the ghosts in the museum—and because of the post-1995 future, with Germany as the key power in the center of Europe. And how very seriously it is taken. It is not just the little sermon on television from the Bundestag presidentess (Präsidentin), Frau Professor Dr. Rita Süssmuth, telling people how important it is to turn out to vote, in the dulcet yet pious tones of the "Queen's Speech" broadcast on British television on Christmas Day. It is not just the three or four highly professional polling organizations, producing unbelievably detailed information on every aspect of the voting.

It is also the teams of political scientists and observers from all over the world, flown in to diagnose in minute detail the condition of German Democracy. They (or rather: we) remind me of nothing so much as the huge medical teams assigned to check the health of the President or the Pope. Is there a *slight* irregularity in his pulse?

In the last few years there has been much speculation about a fragmentation of the country's political representation. As a result both of unification and of widespread dissatisfaction with the political elites of the established parties—seen as remote, bureaucratic, and unduly interested in lining their own pockets—local and state elections have seen votes flowing away not just to the Greens in the west and the post-Communist PDS (Party of Democratic Socialism) in the east, but also to new groupings such as the Hamburg-based *Stattpartei*. The name means roughly "the instead party": instead, that is, of the worn-out old established parties.

"Bonn is not Weimar," went the old saying: the Bonn Republic was not going to fall victim to the political fragmentation which helped to doom the Weimar Republic. But perhaps, we all somberly wisecracked, "Berlin could be Weimar." Well, the republic hasn't quite got to Berlin, yet—indeed, the government will probably

still be in Bonn at the next federal election, due in 1998. (Nineteen hundred and ninety-nine is the target date for the move to be completed.) So there is still time for the somber fears to be realized. There are still real concerns about the reputation and future of the political parties.

Yet this election showed a clear swing in the other direction: back to the established parties. With a 79 percent turnout, about 85 percent of the votes cast went to the parties of the old Federal Republic: the wedded Christian Democratic Union and Bavarian Christian Social Union (CDU/CSU), the Social Democrats (SPD), and the Free Democrats (FDP). A further 7.3 percent of the vote went to the combined list of the Greens, who by now must almost count as an "established" party of the Federal Republic, and the Bündnis 90 (Alliance 90), the heirs to the alliance of civil rights and opposition groups formed to fight the elections of 1990.[2]

According to the opinion pollsters, voters were more or less evenly divided about which combination of these parties they wanted to see in power: the present coalition of CDU/CSU and FDP, a "Grand-Coalition" of CDU/CSU and SPD, or "red-green" (SPD-Greens/Alliance 90). (Each of these combinations can already be found in local or state governments.) But that they wanted some combination of these four or, inasmuch as the Bavarian CSU still has a separate identity, five established parties was very clear.

2.

The two main extremist outsiders, the east German post-Communist PDS (Party of Democratic Socialism) and the largely west German, indeed mainly Bavarian, far-right Republikaner, fared differently. Most reassuringly, the Republikaner—or "Reps"—got only 1.9 percent. In Bavaria they have been completely outplayed by the CSU, which has mopped up their votes by a tough line on the issues of law and order and immigration, together with firmly expressed skepticism about further steps of European integration, while, at the same time, avoiding the Reps' extreme nationalist or racist tones. (*Arbeit für Deutsche!* said one of the Reps' election posters.)

At the same time, the Reps have been crippled by internal feuding. A few weeks before the election the leadership (*Parteivorstand*) voted to sack their chairman and founding father, Franz Schönhuber, a former SS man and gifted rabble-rouser, because he had met with the leader of an older-established far-right party, Gerhard Frey of the so-called Deutsche Volksunion. But just three days before the election a Berlin court issued an order suspending Schönhuber's dismissal on the grounds that the proper procedures had not been followed.

Thinking that I would try to attend all the election parties in Bonn, I inad-

---

FEDERAL ELECTION, OCTOBER 16, 1994
Percentage Share of Votes

	CDU/CSU	SPD	FDP	Greens	PDS	Alliance 90	REP
1990:	43.8	33.5	11.0	3.9	2.4	1.2	2.1
1994:	41.5	36.4	6.9	7.3*	4.4	—	1.9

*Represents the percentage of votes for Alliance 90/Greens combined

---

[2]See my "East Germany: The Solution," *The New York Review*, April 26, 1990.

vertently chose the day of the court hearing to telephone the Reps' office in Bonn to ask if they were having a party. "Well," said a slightly confused lady at the end of the line, "we have the food and drink here, but we're waiting for instructions as to whether we have a party." On the election day, I rang again. Yes, I was told, the party was on. At about 8:15 PM, abandoning the packed, excited scrum in the CDU's Konrad-Adenauer-Haus, I took a taxi down to the Reps' headquarters in Bad Godesberg.

We had a little difficulty finding it. No flags or posters hung outside the villa at number 91 Plittersdorfer-strasse. The shutters were down on the windows—but a chink of light shone through them. As I advanced to the front door, automatic security spot-lights flashed on. A muscular character opened the door. Was the party still on? I asked. Yes, he said, but "most of them have gone." Inside, there was a large room with a buffet and drinks. It contained eight people. Two of them turned out to be journalists.

The journalists then interviewed the party's spokesman and deputy chairman, a Herr Hausmann. He spent most of the interview denouncing his temporarily reinstated chairman. However, he said, they would not disappoint the confidence which had been placed in them by their voters, by the *Angestellte* (white-collar workers) and *Beamte* (officials); yes, by the *Polizeibeamte*—the police officers.

His reference to the police was a reminder that the Reps cannot simply be dismissed out of hand. There has been worrying evidence of far-right sympathies among the police. And the Reps still got a total of some 875,000 votes—the population of a medium-size city. The xenophobic, authoritarian, and anti-Maastricht views of these voters will be reflected, not directly but indirectly, especially in the rhetoric of the CSU. Nonetheless, for the time being at least the result puts the Reps themselves right back on the outer margins of German politics.

Not so the post-Communist PDS, which will have thirty members of the new parliament. Indeed, in a curious twist the proceedings of the thirteenth Bundestag will actually be opened by a speech from a PDS member. The foxy old East German writer Stefan Heym, elected on the PDS ticket, is

automatically granted this right as the oldest member of the house.

To understand why the PDS is in parliament one must dwell for a

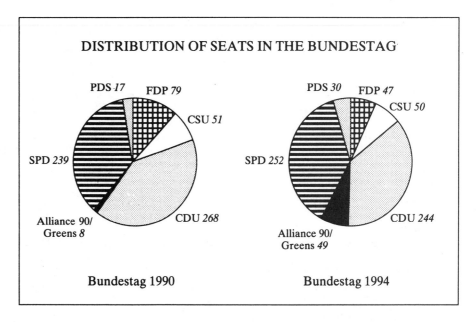

DISTRIBUTION OF SEATS IN THE BUNDESTAG

PDS 17 FDP 79 CSU 51 SPD 239 Alliance 90/ Greens 8 CDU 268

Bundestag 1990

PDS 30 FDP 47 CSU 50 SPD 252 Alliance 90/ Greens 49 CDU 244

Bundestag 1994

moment on the peculiarity of Germany's electoral law. According to this law, each citizen has two votes. The "first vote" goes to an individual candidate, the "second vote" goes to a party. It is the *second* vote that mainly determines the total number of seats each party has in the house. Incidentally, it is not only to foreign readers that this peculiarity needs explaining. Surveys and interviews regularly show that many German voters don't understand it either. They think their "first vote" is as important as or even, as its name suggests, more important than the "second vote."

The so-called "5 percent hurdle" provides that only the parties getting more than 5 percent of the second votes will enter the Bundestag. This provision was introduced to prevent a recurrence of the fragmented party politics of the Weimar Republic— the nightmare of "Bonn becoming Weimar."

So how come the PDS has got into parliament with less than 5 percent of the second votes? Because the law also provides that if the party gets three or more direct candidates elected —by the "first votes," that is—then it should have the full number of seats to which it would be entitled by its percentage of the second votes. And the PDS got not just three but four direct

candidates elected—all of them in what used to be East Berlin.[3]

Through this super-scrupulous loophole in the election law, their Noah's ark sails into parliament, disgorging, besides Stefan Heym, such diverse creatures as the lawyer, wit, and gifted demagogue Gregor Gysi; the former East German economics minister Christa Luft; a great-grandson of Bismarck, Count Heinrich von Einsiedel; a former East German Olympic champion, Ruth Fuchs; and, most repulsively, two people who were almost certainly regular Stasi informers, one Rolf Kutzmutz and the curiously named Kerstin Kaiser-Nicht. What a bunch!

The PDS is, without doubt, the most interesting phenomenon in these elections. It is overwhelmingly an east German party, picking up a little over 300,000 votes in the west, but more than 1.7 million in the east. In what used to be East Berlin, it got a good third of the vote and four of the five constituencies. Since most of the old West Berlin went to the CDU, the capital is now dramatically divided—almost, one is tempted to say, like the di-

---

[3] I say "what used to be East Berlin," because East Berlin actually included the city center—Berlin-Mitte —which is now part of Stefan Heym's constituency.

vision between the white and black parts of Washington, DC.

The vote for the PDS is, in part, a familiar post-Communist phenomenon, as seen in Poland and Hungary: a diverse vote comprising old comrades and functionaries, the losers from the traumatic process of economic transformation, those who yearn for the good old days of social security when "we pretended to work and they pretended to pay us," and some younger protest voters. In the East German case the familiar mix of post-Communist grievances has been ameliorated by the economic transfers from the west, in the order of $100 billion a year; but then it has been exacerbated again by two elements.

First, nowhere in post-Communist Europe has the change in every single aspect of life been so sudden and total as in east Germany. Not just the political, economic, and legal system but the street signs, the banks, the post offices, the health insurance, the cars, the products in the shops, why even the bread has changed. Small wonder there is much dislocation and even nostalgia. Second, nowhere else has one had the strange experience of colonialism in one country. Many west Germans have displayed monstrous condescension, and sheer incomprehension, to their poorer compatriots in the east. At the same time, the east Germans continue to be paid less and bureaucratically discriminated against in countless aspects of everyday life. This is felt most acutely in Berlin, where an easterner working on the next block from his western colleague is paid only 70 or 80 percent of his salary. And the PDS, not the heirs of the opposition in Alliance 90, has become the vehicle of this resentment: the party of eastern protest.

Moreover, the PDS is reveling in the luxury of dissidence, without the risk of persecution (whereas the true dissidents in the GDR were fiercely persecuted by the ruling Communist party—or SED—from which the PDS was born). It is the gamekeeper turned poacher. Its leaders gather all the available arguments against all the established parties, without worrying unduly about internal coherence or a serious program for government. The past master of this kind of left-wing

populism is Gregor Gysi. The diminutive, fast-talking Jewish lawyer, son of a high-ranking official in the old SED, is a Mephistophelean figure. Evidence continues to emerge of how, as a lawyer in Communist East Germany, he cooperated closely with the Stasi. But as a speaker, this miniature Mephisto is terrific—and I would guess almost single-handedly responsible for attracting the party's younger voters. (Almost a quarter of PDS voters are under thirty.)

I saw Gysi in action at the PDS's last election rally in Berlin. As I arrived, a warm-up band was singing "*Komm schlaf mit mir*" (Come, sleep with me), which seemed appropriate. "Once a whore, always a whore," as Orwell remarked in a similar context. A bookstall displayed, among other wares, some of Stalin's works, at 10 DM a volume. I asked the booksellers whether he had many takers. "Oh yes, people buy them out of historical interest. You see, they weren't available in East Germany for a long time."

After speeches by Stefan Heym and two others, it was Gysi's turn. Speaking like a rapid-fire machine gun, Gysi presented the PDS as the only real party of opposition in Germany. He protested against a "one-sided view" of the history of the GDR. Of course "real socialism" had failed because of its own deficiencies, he said, but the alternative was not Herr Kohl but a truly democratic socialism. The east, he said, was being used as a laboratory for the dismantling of the welfare state.

Then there was foreign policy. Of course the Federal Republic had greater responsibilities, but what hypocrisy to call for German participation in peace-making missions when Germany is the third largest arms exporter in the world!

Then there was the growth of right-wing extremism, racism, and anti-Semitism. How about changing the country's *völkisch* electoral law? How absurd that a Turkish citizen living here for years (he was talking in Kreuzberg, where many Turks live) cannot vote, whereas a German from Argentina can come here for three months, vote for Helmut Kohl, and then go back to Argentina, leaving us with Kohl...

Then there was the dismantling of higher education. This must be stopped. Not that he was arguing for endless study. Helmut Kohl had taken sixteen semesters to get his doctorate. In the GDR, he, Gysi, was only allowed eight. "The difference is clearly visible, but I try to make up for it by life experience." At this remark even the policemen standing next to me were laughing.

Then there was the environment. Why didn't they keep up the GDR's system of recycling basic raw materials? Of course the GDR had done it for economic rather than ecological reasons. But it was still sensible. (No mention of the huge environmental damage under the GDR regime.)

Then there was the bureaucracy. "I thought the GDR was the most bureaucratic country in the world. What a mistake!" The west German bureaucracy is much worse. (This is a complaint you hear from east Germans in every walk of life.)

And so on. A catalog of well-made individual points, appealing to the particular experience of particular groups, above all in the east. And the whole spiced with acid wit. It doesn't add up to a policy. But in expressing radical populist opposition it is very effective.

Later I talk with one of the most distinguished of the former east German opposition leaders, the biochemist Jens Reich, about the PDS phenomenon. Like me, he finds it utterly repulsive that these former functionaries, hacks, and Stasi narks are rearing their heads again, even behaving with some of the old arrogance. On the other hand, looking at it coolly, he feels there is an argument that it is better to have these people integrated into the democratic system than to have them working outside and against it. Better to have them inside the tent pissing out rather than outside pissing in, as President Lyndon Baines Johnson once so elegantly observed.

After all, so the argument continues, that's what the Federal Republic did with the old Nazis after 1949: integrate them. Ah yes, comes the answer, but at least the old Nazis were working in newly constituted democratic parties, not in a direct successor to the Nazi party, the NSDAP. Imagine, says a conservative politician, if the NSDAP had just renamed itself the PDSAN—and been voted back into parliament.

In practice, the PDS has so far only affected one major decision in national politics. It was the votes of the PDS members of the Bundestag that, in 1991, gave the narrow majority for the decision to move the capital to Berlin. Whether they can establish themselves as a more permanent feature of the political landscape will clearly depend above all on the progress of reconstruction and "internal unification" in the east in general, and the former East Berlin in particular. But for the period of the thirteenth Bundestag they will be a colorful, raucous, disturbing presence in Bonn, a presence indeed recalling—in a figure like Gysi—the radical left-wing politics of the Weimar Republic, but also seen by many as "the voice of the east."

3.

So much for the small but interesting margins. What of the large but boring center? "He's done it again" is, of course, the first thing to be said of Helmut Kohl, written off by many commentators at the beginning of the year, just as he was being written off by many, even in his own party, in early 1989. Five years ago, it was the way in which he seized the opportunity of unification that brought him back. This year it was three things.

First, it was his personal authority, conviction, and energy. The Christian Democrats fought a presidential election campaign around Helmut Kohl: the colossus of Oggersheim, the "chancellor of unity," the "Bismarck in a cardigan." His face alone stared down from the posters. For the first time ever, polls showed that he was more popular than his party. Indeed, some well-informed sources wonder what exactly will be left of his party when he is gone. By contrast, the Social Democrats had, rather late in the campaign, to bring in two other politicians—their last candidate for chancellor, Oskar Lafontaine, and the man who many think should be their next one, Gerhard Schröder—to stand beside the lackluster Rudolf Scharping in a so-called leadership "troika."

Second, the economic upturn in west Germany and the signs of lasting economic recovery in east Germany came just in time to save Kohl's bacon. Napoleon famously asked about one of his generals the single, all-important question: "Is he lucky?" Helmut Kohl is lucky. In the west, he benefited from the familiar "feel-good factor" at this point in the economic cycle. In the east, it was something more dramatic. Here he had been first adored and then reviled for his famous promise of 1990 to create "flowering landscapes" within a few years. In fact, the transformation has been much slower and more painful than he predicted. Some 14 percent of the east German labor force is still unemployed, and another 4 percent hold artificial, government-subsidized jobs.

Nonetheless, if you travel through east Germany today it is one big building site. In a bold move, Helmut Kohl went back to every place where he had campaigned in the elections of 1990 and said, in effect, "I told you so." And enough people felt their own lives had in fact improved. So in the east, the CDU got the most votes— more than 38 percent to the SPD's 32 percent. Altogether, any claim or perception that the PDS is the "voice of the east" must be qualified by the plain fact that 80 percent of the east German vote went to the established parties and Alliance 90/Greens.

The third reason Helmut Kohl won is that he managed ever so slightly to tar the Social Democrats with the Communist brush. They foolishly gave him the opportunity to do so, by forming a minority government in one of the east German states, Sachsen-Anhalt, in coalition with the Alliance 90/Greens but depending on the votes (or abstention) of the PDS for its continuance in office. Aha, said Kohl, here is a fundamental break with the continuity of the democratic politics of the Federal Republic: a Social Democratic government that is there only on sufferance from the PDS. And adapting a phrase of the early postwar Social Democratic leader Kurt Schumacher, he described the PDS as "red-painted fascists." This, Kohl said to the voters, is what you might get if you vote for the SPD. It was a tactical, some might even say a cynical argument, and it is difficult to judge its pre-

cise effect. Perhaps in east Germany it even won the PDS a few more protest votes. But I think Kohl knew exactly what he was doing.

With this single argument he artfully polarized a contest in which, up to that point, the differences between the Christian Democrats and Social Democrats had been very blurred—so much so, in fact, that wits had combined the two leading candidates for chancellor into an imaginary "Chancellor Kohlping." At the same time, by summoning up the ghost of "red-painted fascists" in a popular front with the SPD, he activated some deep-seated cold war reactions and fears, reinforcing the feeling that it was safer to stick with the devil you know. *Keine Experimente!* (No Experiments!) to quote a famous Christian Democratic slogan from earlier in the history of the Federal Republic.

Yet it was still a close-run thing. In fact, the coalition only got its working majority of ten thanks to another peculiarity of the German electoral system. I said earlier—choosing my words carefully—that the percentage of second votes won by a party "mainly determines" the number of seats it has in parliament. However, if a party gets more direct candidates elected in a particular state (*Land*) than it would be entitled to from its proportion of the "second votes" in that state, then those extra members enter the Bundestag as so-called "overhang mandates." The CDU/CSU got twelve "overhang mandates" against the SPD's four, thus significantly increasing its majority.

Kohl himself immediately pointed out that Helmut Schmidt had governed for four years after 1976 with a majority of ten, and that Willy Brandt had come to power in 1969 with a majority of twelve. Yet Kohl knows as well as anyone that Brandt's majority was then pared down to almost nothing by defections in protest at his Ostpolitik. Narrow majorities sit uneasily with bold policies. And Kohl's position now is significantly weaker than Brandt's or Schmidt's was then. As this article goes to press, there is even speculation that Kohl might not get the absolute majority of votes in the Bundestag needed to elect him chancellor first time round (although the constitution also provides for a second round, in which a chancellor can be elected by a qualified majority). Yet if we assume he is returned, after what are sure to be difficult coalition negotiations, he still faces major new constraints.

For a start, there is the sickness of the Free Democrats. The FDP is a small party that has been in government for all but eight of the forty-five years of the Federal Republic. In the Museum of the History of the Federal Republic you can see one of its earliest election posters, describing it as "the golden center" between red and black, left and right. Over the years, it has become accustomed to being the effective arbiter of German politics. Helmut Kohl originally came to power in 1982 because the FDP switched coalition partners in mid-term, from Helmut Schmidt's embattled SPD to the CDU. A Federal Republic without the FDP would be "a different republic," the party's current leader, Klaus Kinkel, declared in his last pre-election speech: a bold claim for any party leader to make, yet with a grain of truth.

Even under Hans-Dietrich Genscher, foreign minister between 1974 and 1992, the FDP had constantly to struggle to establish its separate identity, and to keep above the 5 percent hurdle in federal and state elections. Genscher quite deliberately organized the switch of coalition partners back in 1982, because in voters' eyes the FDP seemed to be becoming indistinguishable from the SPD, which itself was in trouble. Now the FDP has the opposite problem; but even more so. It has only got back into the Bundestag because more than half a million CDU voters gave their second votes tactically to the FDP, in order to bring back Helmut Kohl as leader of the present center-right coalition. Indeed, by the end of the campaign the FDP was openly pleading for such tactical voting. One poster showed a picture of the retired but still very popular Genscher playing chess. Underneath was the message: "A clever chess-move, second vote for the FDP!"

According to one remarkable poll, 63 percent of those who voted for the FDP named the CDU as their preferred party. According to another poll, just 17 percent of those asked saw the FDP as an independent party, while 72 percent saw it only as a part-

ner of the CDU/CSU. Kinkel has not established himself as a credible successor to Hans-Dietrich Genscher in the role of foreign minister. Their economics minister, Günter Rexrodt, is not the powerful personification of hard-nosed "Manchester liberal" economics that the former party leader Otto Count Lambsdorff was, appealing to the entrepreneurial middle class which has been a vital part of the FDP's traditional constituency. At the same time, the party has failed to strengthen its other wing, identified with more left-liberal positions on law and order, immigration, or education. Most serious of all, this loss of identity, credibility, and leadership has resulted in the party losing its place in most state parliaments. On the day of the Bundestag election it failed to get back into another three state parliaments.

This deep crisis of the FDP does not just mean that the party will be riven with recriminations and worry about its own future. (The internal squabbling started on the very night of the elections.) It also means that some in the FDP will start to think that the party can be saved only by once again changing coalition partners in midterm. The option here would be a so-called "traffic-light coalition," consisting of SPD, FDP, and Alliance 90/Greens (red-yellow-green). Some great "issues of principle" could surely be found for abandoning the FDP's current partner, just as Genscher found them in 1982. Whether this would again save the turncoat party, or finally condemn it to extinction, is a very open question—but the possibility will haunt the coalition Kohl is now trying to reconstitute.

Meanwhile, the Social Democrats have emerged not only strengthened in the Bundestag but also with a clear majority in the federal upper house, the Bundesrat, whose political balance is determined by the composition of state governments. This means that now more than ever the government will need to negotiate its legislative proposals in advance with the SPD, in order to get them through the upper house. Many talk in this connection of a "de facto Grand Coalition"—a reference to the "Grand Coalition" of Christian and Social Democrats, with-

out the FDP, which ruled the Federal Republic between 1966 and 1969. The strengthening of the SPD increases the temptation for the FDP to play its old game of switching sides. On the other hand, the threat of the new constellation also strengthens the temptation for the Christian Democrats to pre-empt the FDP defection by themselves going for a Grand Coalition with the SPD.

To add to the uncertainty, there is the question of the succession to Helmut Kohl. Kohl himself has announced that this will be his last term as chancellor. But if he is to give his "crown prince," Wolfgang Schäuble, or anyone else, a chance to establish their authority before the next Bundestag election, in four years' time, then he will presumably have to step down in 1997, at the latest. So irrespective of the political uncertainties, this is "the beginning of the end of the Kohl era"—because Kohl himself has proclaimed it so.

4.

To describe Kohl as already a "lame duck" would, however, be once again to underestimate a man who has made a habit of being underestimated throughout his extraordinarily successful political career. Helmut Kohl is still the most formidable politician—and statesman—in Europe. He will not lightly be deflected from pursuing the last great task that he has set himself: to bind united Germany into a united Europe. In his view, the Maastricht treaty was a crucial step in that direction. The EU's intergovernmental review conference, scheduled to begin in 1996, and already popularly billed as "Maastricht 2," should be another one. Indeed, I should not be altogether surprised if somewhere at the back of his mind he does not cherish the idea of stepping down after completing "Maastricht 2," having made the integration of Germany into something called the European Union "irreversible"—as he fondly hopes.

Nothing decisive will happen until the French presidential elections next spring, although there will be an intensive half-year of preparation and "policy planning" in the chancellor's office, where German European policy is really made, and in the other chancelleries of Europe. But if he then has the right partner in Paris—and ironically enough the Socialist candidate Jacques Delors must be the favorite for the chancellor who is the scourge of socialism in Germany—then I suspect we will see some very challenging Franco-German initiatives for a further "deepening" of the EU.

These may recall, in substance if not in name, the CDU/CSU parliamentary party's proposals for a "hard core" of the EU, consisting of France, Germany, and the Benelux countries. But the affronted reaction to those proposals, in Britain, in Italy, and elsewhere in Europe, is nothing compared to the furious row that will arise if that really seems to be French and German government policy, in the run-up to the intergovernmental conference. This alone would make it very difficult for Chancellor Kohl to realize his goal in the few years still available to him. Moreover, given the virtual collapse of the European Monetary System and the continued disparities between the economies of even the front-runners for European monetary union, the Maastricht timetable for monetary union looks increasingly unrealistic.

Within Germany itself, the business and banking community is, on the whole, notably unenthusiastic about European monetary union. Altogether, there is much more skepticism in Germany about a further deepening of the existing EU than there was before German unification—a skepticism notably articulated by the Bavarian prime minister Edmund Stoiber. Public opinion is increasingly indignant at Germany's outsize net contribution to the EU's budget, especially at a time when domestic budgets are being cut (although their leaders still try quietly to explain that this contribution is a small price to pay for keeping open Germany's main export market). With Poland just five minutes' flying time from Berlin, and German business already deeply committed to the Czech Republic, enlarging the EU to the east is also widely felt to be a higher priority for Germany.

Nonetheless, on the issue of "Europe" the political leadership of the Social Democrats is by and large on Kohl's side. So while he may ultimately fail to realize his particular vision of "Europe," because other European countries are not ready for it, or have other visions of their own, Germany's politics, as they appear after the election, will probably not stop him trying—and trying very forcefully.

However, the goal most important to Chancellor Kohl personally is not the top priority of most of his compatriots. A poll result published on election night showed "foreign policy" at the very bottom of the list of issues that concerned the respondents. At the very top was job creation, then issues such as the restructuring of the welfare state, health care, and the environment. Despite its strong economic recovery, Germany has daunting domestic problems. It clearly has to cut budgets in order to reduce the public debt, which has soared to 2 trillion DM as a result of the costs of unification. It has to try to restore Germany's competitive edge in world export markets, which probably involves doing some of the things that Britain and America did already in the 1980s—privatization, deregulation, reducing employment costs and the tax disincentives to enterprise. It has to work out what to do about long-term, structural unemployment: a problem common to all of Western Europe, but particularly sensitive because of the disproportionately larger number of long-term unemployed to be found in east Germany. Yet it is not only in east Germany that Gysi's polemic against a "dismantling of the welfare state" will fall on fallow ground. And it is not only in west Germany that the Greens' ecological and feminist concerns will further complicate the process.

With the results of the elections it is clear that, within the present political system, these issues can only be addressed by negotiation between all the established parties. In other words, this is the greatest test so far of what has long been the Federal Republic's greatest strength: its ability to achieve change through consensus. If the attempt fails, then next time round we may yet see a more significant flight of disillusioned voters from the boring center to the interesting margins. Then, indeed, the Berlin republic might after all begin to look like Weimar.

But there we go again: worrying and warning, because of the ghosts in the museum. The Federal Republic has proved the Cassandras wrong so many times before. Let's hope it can do so again. In any case, it's worth remembering that when looking at Germany most people from most of the world, even from quite prosperous countries in the West, will exclaim: "If only we had your problems...."

—*November 3, 1994*

Germany: A Wave of 'Ostalgia'

Those from the east are looking back fondly, even on the hard times under the Communists. They're even taking pride in driving their clunky Trabants.

Mary Williams Walsh

Times *Staff Writer*

BERLIN—"What makes people drive Trabants?"

Albrecht Reither considers the question almost shyly for a moment, sitting in an auto shop decorated with poster-sized photos of the tinny, toylike car, East Germany's contribution to the automative world.

How, indeed, to explain to an outsider why anyone today would still want to suffer the Trabant's noisy two-stroke engine, dollhouse interior, the acrid products of its notion of an exhaust system?

East Germany is long gone, and the Trabant—which, unfortunately for the East Germans, means "satellite"—is no longer in production. There are no Trabbi dealerships. To get a Trabbi today, you have to go well out of your way to find one on the secondhand market and be prepared to withstand the ridicule of your fellow Germans.

But then Reither, a burly spare-parts dealer, turns defiant. "The Trabant is a symbol of protest," he says. "People are saying: 'I drove this car for 30 years, and I'm going to keep driving it. I'm not ashamed to be from the east.' "

Time was, eastern Germans wanted to get clear of anything associated with their Communist past. From bad coffee to the ideological water torture of official discourse, from the baleful Trabbi to the tiresome workplace habit of eating bologna sandwiches every time a colleague had a birthday—in the weeks and months immediately after the Berlin Wall fell, people wanted to discard all of these fixtures of socialist life and anything else that had to do with East Germany.

Of late, however, a wave of nostalgia for *Ostdeutschland*—call it Ostalgia, as many do—has been washing over eastern Germany. Today, people are driving their Trabbis with a vengeance, to the point of joining Trabbi outing clubs and parading through the eastern German countryside.

Shops specializing in made-in-the-East groceries and household products are opening, and it has become socially acceptable to drink eastern Germany's sugar-sweet Little Red Riding Hood sparkling wine and to serve eastern Germany's more chewy dinner rolls.

Ostalgia parties are very much the thing on eastern German campuses. Even the former East German practice of giving all 14-year-olds a sort of secular "first Communion" service—the *Jugendweihe,* or "youth blessing"—has been enthusiastically revived.

"Most people have quickly found out that the dream of the golden West was just an illusion," contends Reither, who had the commercial sense to buy all the Trabbi parts he could find and who now does a thriving trade in them. He has made enough money to buy a Mercedes or a BMW, but his sense of eastern identity keeps him behind the wheel of his 1974 Trabbi.

Eastern Germans have had nearly five years now to plumb the joys of Western capitalism, and, as Reither says, many have found them wanting.

True, they no longer have to live with shootings at the Wall, a censored press, the largest spying network in the Marxist world, or the many other instruments of East German state power.

But some have come to the arresting conclusion that they are worse off today than they were under communism. Many men have lost their jobs. Women have lost child-care centers that cost 20 cents a day; practically all households are paying many times more for rent and sustenance.

And even the eastern Germans who now have "made it"—who have bigger apartments, interesting jobs, telephones, fax machines, plausible newspapers, strawberries year-round—even these easterners talk of a certain *something* that is missing from their lives.

It is, in part, a sense of belonging: They know they aren't East Germans anymore, but five years of unification have convinced them that they don't quite fit into the West either.

So, if they aren't East Germans, and they aren't West Germans, then what are they?

The current conspicuous return to old ways may be, for easterners, a means of finding out. And if nothing else, it serves for many as a heartening reminder that everything about life in the German Democratic Republic wasn't thoroughly evil—that life in the East was in some respects actually better.

"I don't know anyone who says they want the whole German Democratic Republic back," says Hans-Joachim Maaz, a psychiatrist in the eastern German city of Halle who has written on the special psychological problems of his compatriots. "What I hear about is the lack of values. People say, 'We don't want to live in a society where everyone is elbowing their way to the front. We want to have a sense of solidarity. And we want to live in a society where money doesn't influence everything, even relationships between friends.' "

"The tragedy," adds Maaz, "is that there is nobody who really takes these desires seriously."

Well, almost nobody.

On a busy street in what used to be East Berlin, Klaus Eichler has carved out a speciality business centered on Ostalgia: He packages tours for eastern Germans who now miss the very thing they would have spurned in the past—group tours, laced with nonstop ideology, to the old glory spots of the socialist world.

Interested in the space race from the soviet point of view? Eichler has a tour to Baikonur, the Russian Cape Canaveral, where participants undergo mock cosmonaut training and watch a rocket launching. The tour guide is a former East German cosmonaut, Sigmund Jaehn.

Or what about those who like to mix a little sunshine and surf with their politics? For them, Eichler offers two weeks in Cuba, in the capable hands of East Germany's former ambassador to Havana, Hans Langer. Langer takes the Ostalgic tourists to the beaches but also books political discussions with Cuban doctors, farmers and members of the *Asamblea Nacional.*

"Of course, we have to admit that there wasn't enough that was good about East Germany. Otherwise it wouldn't have failed," he says. "But, nevertheless, I think that quite a few people here believe that in East German times we enjoyed a more peaceful way of life, even a more pleasant way of life. It's difficult to explain this, but it has something to do with human feelings and with values—with the feeling that my neighbor was my friend, and not my competitor."

Eichler thinks eastern Germany's fixation with the past may be a sign that a broader quest is under way for a new ideology—some sort of economic arrangement that is neither capitalism nor communism.

To understand why eastern Germans feel the way they do, look with eastern eyes at the way German unification has turned out.

In the early, heady months after the Berlin Wall was breached, people dreamed big dreams of what the future might hold once unification was complete: People would vote in free elections; they would enjoy real representation in an authentic national assembly; inefficient state enterprises would be reorganized and the public would become shareholders; a new, all-German constitution would combine the best elements of the East with those of the West.

But as reunification took hold, it became clear that West Germany had no intention of retaining what may have been "good" about the East.

Free elections were held, true enough, but West German political parties sent in candidates and dominated the political scene. Far from making easterners shareholders in their former country's industrial stock, the unified government sold much of what was salable to outside investors. New, private owners, in many cases, then laid off the easterners by the thousands.

As for a new constitution: It is still being brought up to date, but so far, nothing from East Germany has been kept.

The way things have turned out, the only East German artifact that the unified government has preserved has been the freedom to turn right on some red lights.

Which is why people like Werner Riedel have set about saving bits and pieces all by themselves.

"The practice of celebrating the youth blessing in the German Democratic Republic was not 100% bad," says Riedel, who plucked that East German custom off the endangered list in 1990 and has revived it virtually single-handedly. "It was just sort of exploited by ideology and forced on people."

Indeed. In former times, when East Germans turned 14, they were put through indoctrination courses, then formally initiated into adulthood in a public ceremony. The young people took an oath and were presented with a book about their place in the universe. "The Cosmos, the Earth, and the Human Being." Then, typically, doting relatives took them home, showered them with gifts and fed them a big lunch.

"I can remember my own youth blessing," says Riedel. "It was sort of automatic. I've forgotten the oath, but I still remember all the presents I got, and the big meal."

In the turbulent months after the East German government collapsed, Riedel says he began worrying about young people and thinking maybe they needed proof that somebody cared about them.

In many cases, he says, their parents were thrown out of work and spending all of their time trying to survive. Riedel thought the old youth blessing might put much-needed structure back into their lives—as long as it was stripped of its former ideological content.

He assembled a volunteer staff, organized a curriculum, printed up some brochures and has never looked back. Last year in Berlin, 8,000 14-year-olds received the new, post-Communist youth blessing—10 times as many as those who received their first Communion. Across eastern Germany, about 80,000 adolescents are enrolled in the program this fall.

As it happens, even the young people Riedel is catering to—teenagers who are too young to have arrived at much of an understanding of what it was to be an East German—have joined the Ostalgia kick.

Consider the goings-on at Friedrich-Schiller University in Jena, a city in the southern part of what used to be East Germany. Deep under the city's center, in a campus rathskeller, posters of the late East German dictator Erich Honecker share wall space with portraits of Mikhail S. Gorbachev, the onetime Soviet leader, and the album covers of popular East German musicians.

"Forward to the 300th Anniversary of the German Democratic Republic!" exhorts a banner over the dance floor. Young people swill Vita Cola, an East German soft drink, and an ersatz sangria made only with apples, pears and grapes (it was difficult to find imported fruit in East Germany, so no one ever had oranges or pineapples).

When a young man leaps onto the bar and begins singing, the whole crowd joins in: "Build, build, build! Help us to build a better society! We're going to construct a new homeland, for a better future!" It is an East German classic, and everybody knows the words.

This is an Ostalgia party, a rage on campuses all over the former East. University students show up in polyester clothing that would otherwise never make it out of the darkest corners of their wardrobes.

1. COUNTRY STUDIES: Germany

At the entrance, organizer Steffen Bernhardt sits at a table graced by a pile of transcripts of the late North Korean leader Kim Il Sung's speeches, taking money. He is 27, old enough to remember what it was like in the former times, when the student club was twice shut down by the authorities for minor ideological infractions. But he is prepared to explain why students today are embracing the symbols and impedimenta of the repressive system they used to hate.

"We don't want to deny our own history," he says. "These things are part of our lives, and that's why we keep them."

There is a shriek and a woman runs by, reeking of chemicals; a prankster has just anointed her with a discontinued East German deodorant. A tall man in an army jacket and an enormous red motorcycle helmet comes by, brandishing an old copy of Neues Deutschland, once the official newspaper of the East German Communist Party.

"If I had seen this newspaper five years ago, I'd have said, 'Oh, hell,' " says Dirk Spoerl, a 29-year-old handyman. "But now I can laugh about it."

"We are no nerds," adds Bernhardt. "We can speak like the West Germans. We can write like the West Germans. We are as tall as the West Germans. Yet everything from the German Democratic Republic is being destroyed. That is a mistake. It is history. History will never end."

THE TWO FACES
OF FRANCE

In trade, culture, and outlook, it wonders: Embrace the world, or shut it out?

Howard LaFranchi

Staff writer of The Christian Science Monitor

PARIS

At about the same time last month that France bucked world apathy toward Rwanda's horror by announcing it would mount a "humanitarian intervention" into the central African country, French refugee authorities turned down a Rwandan Tutsi woman's request for asylum, and Paris police ordered her out of the country.

The first event received substantial international attention, while the second was hardly noticed even here. What makes the two events so striking when viewed together is how each one symbolizes the state of France—or, rather, of a particular France. For in the post-Soviet, post–Berlin-Wall, and post-industrial world of 1994, there are two Frances battling to determine where the country heads as it approaches the 21st century.

One France remains open to the world and more prepared than most countries to intervene in international crises.

This is also the France that sees its position as the world's fourth-largest exporter, that takes account of the tremendous economic strides it has made over the past decade—while under Socialist rule—and is determined to face the stiff challenges of a rebalanced international economy.

Another France looks at the world of post–cold-war instability and a changing Europe led by a larger and more consequential Germany, and responds by closing in on itself, by seeking to hold the world at bay and protect what it considers a threatened identity. It sees an emerging global economy where French workers, accustomed to generous health,

vacation, and retirement benefits, face job insecurity. This France pleads for the status quo.

To illustrate how strongly recent changes in Europe and fears of an enlarged Germany have rattled France, Michel Foucher, director of the European Geopolitical Observatory in Lyon, likes to cite a fictitious headline from November 1989: "Berlin Wall falls; one death: France."

"We can see two Frances in every essential aspect of the country's life," says Mr. Foucher, a specialist in Europe's evolution, "from the domestic political scene and the economy to foreign affairs and the geopolitical dimension. In each case there is an open, outward-oriented France and a defensive France responding to mounting fears by turning inward and closing up."

Despite its virtually single-handed intervention in Rwanda, what has stood out most dramatically about France in the '90s is its growing unease with the world. Stupefied foreigners have watched as French farmers—the biggest farm-product exporters in the world after the United States—battled police and dumped foreign produce by the bushel to protest global farm-trade liberations.

YOUTH UPRISING

Following close behind the farmers, students called strikes, filled city boulevards—and sometimes saw their movement degenerate into bloody confrontations with police—until a proposal to lower the minimum wage was scuttled. The move had been intended to create more jobs for youths.

Never mind that France suffers one of the industrialized world's worst youth unemployment rates (25 percent for

those without higher education or qualifications), the reflex even among some youths was to reject change. Before them were striking Air France workers, whose financially troubled, nationalized airline faces extinction even before the government has a chance to privatize it; fishermen, who clashed violently early this year with agents of the same government from which they had sought protection from imported fish; and even the country's elite film industry, which battled to keep out Hollywood.

The French film industry may have won temporary haven from the American steamroller with a "cultural" exception" to audiovisual free trade, but many observers say it will be a Pyrrhic victory once cable and satellite communications make national barriers meaningless.

Signs have grown that the government as well has succumbed to a defensive protection from the outside world. Since conservatives took the reins of power under Prime Minister Edouard Balladur in May 1993, lawmakers have approved a set of laws that in effect targets foreigners as a threat to the country's security and economic well-being.

The tone of the laws, inspired by law-and-order Interior Minister Charles Pasqua, has washed over local authorities and made for an antiforeigner tone: Mixed-nationality marriages are suspect, and many accounts have surfaced of couples forcibly separated when one spouse is ordered to leave the country.

French children of mixed-nationality parentage have been refused access to some public schools. Newspapers have chronicled a new, rougher treatment for foreign youths, mostly African or Arab, at the hands of police.

Even Culture Minister Jacques Toubon's French First (read: anti-English) law, adopted this year, strikes many as reflecting a bunker mentality. The law seeks—with the threat of heavy fines—to weed out such Anglicisms as "cheeseburger" from print, and the airwaves, and advertising, and to curtail the use of English in international conferences here.

"It's a stupid, defensive law," says Alain Costes, director of the internationally renowned LAAS microelectronic and robotics research laboratory in Toulouse, "and whenever you become defensive, you are already the loser." Worried that the law will make France less attractive as a host country for the international conferences that help keep his business in the vanguard of high-tech research, Mr. Costes says, "I simply won't adhere to this law."

NO RESPECT

He's not alone.

A company manager for Car Rental is asked if his company's name will change to respect the new law: "France is finished," he quips. "We now live in Europe—though some people don't seem to know it."

Yet despite the picture of an increasingly protectionist France, rich in what sociologist Michel Crozier calls "considerable advantages in a post-industrial era favoring human resources, conceptual capacities, and a spirit of research and innovation," is flourishing.

This is the France where production per worker outstrips Germany, Japan, and Britain; where foreign investment remains high despite an unsure international economic picture; where products as well-known as the TGV ultrafast railroad and some of the world's best software continue to draw international envy.

Toulouse, a southwestern city targeted in the 1960s to become a high-tech center, is an example of this progressive, future-oriented France.

INTERNATIONAL HUB

At the Toulouse plant of Aérospatiale—the French partner in the European Airbus consortium—new A330 and A340 planes are assembled in a cavernous assembly hangar where the human presence seems curiously sparse. Robots work in a circle around a new plane's fuselage, quietly piercing the metal

frame and attaching thousands of rivets. Aérospatiale has abandoned the traditional assembly line for a "workshop" approach that calls on workers, parts, and machines to move around as needed, and not the aircraft.

"This facilitates the kind of customizing today's clients want," says Dominique Berger, Aérospatiale's deputy technical director.

French aviation had its "cultural revolution" two decades ago, Mr. Berger says, when it embraced the imperatives of the international marketplace. Now Toulouse has also broken free of the traditional image of the French provincial city to embrace the world.

"Here, we are in Europe," Berger says, gesturing beyond the aeronautics plant to the city beyond. "We started building Europe before others were thinking about it." He emphasizes that Airbus is an alliance of aviation companies, not of governments—an innovation for the traditionally state-oriented French, but a key to the consortium's success.

International companies—some as well known as Motorola, others as little known as Storagetek (a Colorado-based world leader in information storage and retrieval systems)—continue to set up R&D units in Toulouse.

"When Storagetek saw what our researchers were coming up with, they forgot their interest in places in Germany or [Britain]," says Alain Ayache, a professor at Toulouse's ENSEEIGHT engineering school. (ENSEEIGHT developed the world's smallest camera, an understandable attraction for a data-storage company.)

HOPES AND FEARS FOR FUTURE

Despite the city's success, Mayor Dominique Baudis—who led the French center-right in recent European Parliament elections—says his city is subject to the same mix of hopes and fears for the future as the rest of France.

The vote on the European Union's Maastricht Treaty in September 1992 "showed us that indeed there are two Frances," Mayor Baudis says, "one made up of those who are confident in the country's future, and those who aren't—who are afraid of the future, afraid of change, afraid of competition."

A certain France, shaken by economic and geopolitical changes in the world,

"tells itself, 'If we circle the wagons we'll be able to save ourselves,' " he says.

But Baudis doesn't see the fearful France growing appreciably. He says France's need—and indeed the key to determining which France ultimately carries the day—is to modernize the democratic process that gives citizens the information they need to understand national challenges, make informed decisions, and develop confidence in the country's advantages.

Among these advantages, Baudis says, are a well-educated population, strong research institutions, and well-developed traditional and organizational infrastructures.

But, he adds, "After decades of talk and projects, France remains too centralized." That centralization stymies citizens' involvement in their own affairs, and encourages the centuries-old tendency to depend on the very central government from which one seeks to break free.

"France is suffering a crisis in its political structures," Foucher says, one that is even deeper than the political crises of such neighbors as Germany.

TRADITIONAL FRANCE

An older, rural, traditional France "that no longer exists" is better represented in many institutions than its younger, working, urban equivalent, he says. "This leaves the country expose to the kind of social turmoil we're already experiencing."

Mr. Crozier agrees. Well-known for his work chronicling the *blocages* (strikes) in France in 1970, Crozier says that while French society today is "tremendously modernized, much more open" than it was 25 years ago, the country's political and administrative structures have not evolved to serve a very different France.

"What is broken in France is the state," he says—a devastating conclusion in a country where the state has been a central element of national identity for centuries.

Crozier cites the case of Air France, the once-proud flagship of national public administration. He notes that an initial rescue plan, presented in traditional French fashion of top-down imposition, led to a catastrophic strike and the plan's withdrawal—along with the firing of Air France's president.

But a second rescue plan, even more severe than the first, was accepted in a referendum earlier this year by 80 percent of the employees. "The difference was the way it was generated and the way it was presented," says Crozier, whose consulting firm, SMG, was contracted by Air France to help develop employee involvement in decisionmaking.

Perhaps most noticeable for lower-echelon employees especially is a drastic reduction in the number of administrative levels in the company: from a staggering 21 to seven.

PRIORITY ON JOBS

Perhaps the best indicator of what will come out of the country's current malaise will be how the French address their staggering problem of nearly 13 percent unemployment.

"The truth is that France has never made the jobs battle its No.-1 priority," Baudis says. The reason is that the vast majority benefits from a nearly un-equaled system of social protection that—along with a marvelous cuisine and varied, temperate natural beauty—has made France synonymous with good living.

The global economy has changed. Will a French majority arguably more coddled and comfortable than any in the world's history make the sacrifices necessary to allow more of their countrymen—especially youths—to work?

Baudis is sanguine about the prospects. "The advantages of the system were developed for those with a job, and they [job-holders] expect it to stay that way," he says. He recalls how he recently tried to adjust municipal pay raises to help create jobs for local youths. City employees refused.

One necessity will be a rebuilding of trust between the French and their leaders, he says, adding that the process probably can't begin until after the country's presidential elections next spring.

Other observers say the French will be ready to make the necessary sacrifices if the reasons are explained—and if those sacrifices are equitably shared.

"People sense that the acquired benefits of our system are threatened, and they're right," says Nicole Belaud, a marketing professor in Toulouse.

Pointing to the country's operation in Rwanda, she says a commitment to what the average French see as "universal values" made intervention a "humanitarian imperative."

The same kind of priority on values like social equality can work to address the unemployment problem, she says, so long as leaders get beyond "managing" a frightened society to explaining, working with people, and acting with courage.

Finessing that expanded sense of values just might indicate that France—despite the global changes that have shaken it up and set its right hand battling its left—is still the France of "The Rights of Man."

France in the Mid-1990s: Gloom but Not Doomed

"As the end of the Mitterrand era nears, there is . . . the risk of yet another crisis of the state. But the French economy is stronger than the British, and the French political system more stable than the Italian."

PATRICK MCCARTHY

PATRICK MCCARTHY *is a professor of European studies at the Johns Hopkins University Bologna Center. He edited* France–Germany 1983–1993: The Struggle to Cooperate *(New York: St. Martin's, 1993).*

France is discontented. Newspaper headlines proclaim that the country is governed by a technocratic elite who have lost touch with the people; conversely, they lament that the government pays too much attention to public opinion polls. Either way, the electorate is turning to populist protest: the parties led by Jean-Marie Le Pen, Philippe de Villiers, and Bernard Tapie won 35 percent of the vote in June elections for the European Parliament. Europe provides ample material for lamentation: France has lost the presidency of the European Commission and the chairmanship of the Socialist group in the European Parliament; it has no European policy and it is becoming a satellite of Germany. When the French worry about their place in the world, American diplomats brace themselves: sure enough, this summer the dollar was too low for Paris's liking and the United States too enthusiastic about the victory in the Rwandan civil war of the guerrilla Rwandan Patriotic Front, the opponents of the regime France formerly supported.

France has genuine problems, but it is worth remembering that each European country has its own way of perceiving its history. The British are ironically complacent, while the French bewail their lot—de Gaulle called it "moaning, groaning, and whining." This is dangerous because a vision of reality becomes part of reality. By depicting themselves as racked by internal divisions, prone to crises, and lagging behind other countries, the French bring on these maladies. There is at present the risk of yet another crisis of the state. But the French economy is stronger than the British, and the French political system more stable than the Italian.

It is tempting to link the mood of discontent with the imminent departure of President François Mitterrand from the office he has held since 1981. But to do

so would be an error, because Mitterrand's rule ended with the defeat of his Socialist Party in the parliamentary elections of March 1993 and because he was unpopular for two years before that. Until his second seven-year term expires next spring Mitterrand is cohabitating with the right-wing government of Prime Minister Édouard Balladur, an enlightened conservative who manages to appear both competent and reasonable. The president retains some power, particularly over foreign policy, and it is thought he pressed hard for the French intervention in Rwanda, whereas Balladur and the military were less enthusiastic. Mitterrand also retains his Machiavellian skill at political infighting, and he has probably succeeded in preventing his old enemy Michel Rocard from becoming the Socialist Party candidate for president. (As party secretary, Rocard was blamed for the Socialists' disastrous 14.5 percent share of the vote in the elections for the European Parliament.)

But Mitterrand, who has prostate cancer, spends much time visiting cemeteries and chatting with visitors about death. It is as if he were trying to disarm and seduce mortality. He expends his political guile in this struggle rather than in running the country. He has also been damaged by financial scandals and by revelations that in his youth he flirted with far-right groups. The France and the Europe Mitterrand helped shape are today revealing their fragility. His era has passed in both his country and the continent, but it contained the seeds of the problems other French leaders are now confronting.

MITTERRAND'S LEGACY: SUCCESS WALKS WITH FAILURE

Mitterrand will go down in French history as a man of consensus. Twentieth-century France has been more stable and more capable of incremental change than many observers had given it credit for, and Mitterrand's role was to make this evident. In 1972 the Socialists, under his leadership, became the junior partners in an alliance with the Communists; 12 years later the Communist Party was reduced to 10 percent of the

 Reprinted with permission from *Current History* magazine, November 1994, pp. 364-368.

electorate and the Socialists were the dominant party of the left. During his first cohabitation (1986–1988) Mitterrand was faced with a fervently neoliberal right; he occupied the center, and in 1988 won both the presidential and parliamentary elections. Now the Balladur government flaunts its centrism.

If the left and the right regularly alternate in power in today's France, and if politics there no longer seems like a war of religion, this is primarily Mitterrand's doing. But since the orthodox left and right do not appear very different, voters often turn to protest parties. Opposition is channeled into Le Pen's National Front, which makes the Arab immigrant the scapegoat for all ills, or it lines up behind right-winger de Villiers and the authority-mocking Tapie, or it disguises itself behind local and single-issue groups such as the Hunters and Fishermen, which received 4 percent of the vote in the European elections. Such movements are present in most European countries, with populism and fragmentation acting as the counterpoint to centrism.

Against the success of dedramatizing mainstream French politics—albeit at the cost of encouraging protest—one must set Mitterrand's role in weakening his own Socialist Party. When he became its head in 1971 the party was divided and languishing. He brought it up to around 35 percent of the vote in the 1980s, but helped precipitate its collapse to 19.7 percent in last year's parliamentary elections. Mitterrand was too much of a loner to be a good party leader. After becoming president in 1981 he used the Socialist Party as a tool to gain support for his policies, over which the party had scant influence.

Since he steered the party toward the economics of rigor, which gives priority to disinflation and a strong franc rather than to social spending, and market forces, he also gradually undermined the socialists' identity. Here again achievement and failure run together. While the Labour Party in Britain and the German Social Democrats were flagging in the 1980s because they were too closely tied to blue-collar workers, the French Socialists attained power by stitching together an alliance of the working class and segments of the middle class, like public-sector employees and junior managers. Mitterrand's ability to reassure was essential. But in 1991 he high-handedly sacked the then popular Rocard as prime minister and imposed the disastrous Edith Cresson, who managed to alienate everyone. By now the Socialists' past success in curbing inflation had been superseded in the electorate's mind by their inability to reduce unemployment. Deprived of influence, the party lapsed into corruption and internal feuds. Mitterrand did nothing to halt the decline, which has created a dangerous vacuum on the center-left.

Yet weaning the Socialists away from statism, nationalization of enterprises, and job-creation by public spending was another of Mitterrand's accomplishments. From 1983 on his government focused on reducing inflation, increasing the percentage of value-added that went to business, and encouraging private investment. By 1990 inflation in France was lower than in Germany and growth topped 3 percent a year. Mitterrand had created a national consensus around disinflation and had spurred acceptance of market values in a country that had long doubted them.

The black spot was unemployment, which remained above the EC average, began to rise in the early 1990s, and now stands at 12.4 percent. How much of this unemployment stems from the policy of rigor, how much is the result of structural factors like an inflexible labor market and poor vocational training, and what part is played by demography in a country where the labor force will not start to shrink until around 2005, is open to discussion. Whatever the explanation for it, high unemployment is part of Mitterrand's legacy.

Reducing inflation meant maintaining a strong franc, which in turn meant binding the franc to the deutsche mark within the European Monetary System. This made possible a partnership with Germany and an expanded role in the EC (now rebaptized the European Union, or EU). Mitterrand was one of the architects of both the 1985 Single Europe Act, which included the creation of a barrier-free EC market by 1992, and the 1991 Maastricht treaty on complete monetary and closer political union for member countries. His alliance with German Chancellor Helmut Kohl was the axis on which the expansion of European unity was founded.

Historians will probably consider this his greatest achievement, yet in today's France it is his most controversial. When the Bundesbank raised interest rates in the aftermath of German reunification, French rates had to keep pace. Indeed, the combination of a risk penalty factor and lower inflation meant that real short-term rates over the last three years have usually been between 3 percent and 4 percent higher in France than in Germany. Moreover, French industry is more dependent on short-term borrowing.

This was merely one strain in Franco-German relations. Differences over what stance the EC should take toward the formerly Communist countries of eastern Europe and over the wars in the Balkans made a mockery of the Maastricht commitment to a common foreign and security policy. The summer of 1993 brought the EC's second monetary crisis, in the course of which the franc was forced out of the European Monetary System's narrow band of allowable values. Underlying these tensions was the fear, which has haunted French elites since the Berlin Wall came down, that a reunited Germany will dominate France and Europe.

This overlaps with the more general fear that France is unable to compete in the European Union's internal market and in the more open world economy being created under the General Agreement on Tariffs and Trade (GATT) Uruguay Round pact. A referendum in 1992 on the Maastricht treaty that Mitterrand held because he thought it offered an easy triumph ended up a near disaster. The yes vote was won by the narrowest of margins, with France's blue-collar workers voting against the treaty because they feared it meant yet more unemployment and its farmers because they considered the EC's agricultural subsidies inadequate.

In the area of security Mitterrand displayed the same mixture of successful adaptation and failure to cope with recent developments. On taking office in 1981 he broke with the left's neutralist tendencies and its distaste for nuclear weapons and endorsed the Gaullist concept that France must be responsible for its own defense. In 1983 he delighted the United States by backing the German government in its decision to accept the basing of NATO cruise missiles in German territory. He supported the United States in the 1991 Persian Gulf War, but he has also during the decade led the campaign to strengthen the Western European Union as an arm of the EC and hence independent of NATO. Simultaneously he maintained—though leaving room for compromise—that France's nuclear deterrent should be used only for its own defense.

Mitterrand seemed unable to grasp that the administration of President Bill Clinton in the United States was not seeking military hegemony and that cooperation with NATO no longer meant subordination. His reluctance to share French nuclear weapons stemmed from the same belief: that France was and must be a world power. Its military was one guarantee, while another was its place at the center of a worldwide francophone community. Mitterrand cultivated economic ties with French Africa, where during his presidency French troops have intervened no fewer than ten times to restore order and defend French interests. The latest such venture is the complex operation in Rwanda.

Although on these points Mitterrand followed the late president, General Charles de Gaulle, the two leaders are very different. De Gaulle was a rebel who dreamed of a France he knew did not exist; he was a man of grand designs and conflicts. Mitterrand's task has been to "banalize": to cure the left of ideology, to emphasize what is economically obvious, and to accept the constraints of a tighter European Union. He prefers complicated maneuvers to grand designs and intricate compromises to solitary defiance.

Mitterrand's legacy is in general positive, and it will last. The best proof is that Prime Minister Balladur has continued the policies of rigor, the strong franc, and cooperation with Germany. It is Mitterrand's misfortune that the bill for his successes has fallen due during his last years as president.

NATIONALISM AND POLITICS

The discontent in France is part of a malaise pervading Europe. Five years ago the European Community was confidently marching toward the completion of the internal market and greater political integration. Today the European Union is plagued with unemployment, does not know what to do about eastern Europe, and lacks the leadership it had with Jacques Delors at the helm of the European Commission and a solid Franco-German partnership.

The political confusion stems from the contrast between the current world economy and an identity that remains national. The discrepancy is especially sharp in France, which has been a leader in the move toward European unity but has historically had a strong state. When they voted against the Maastricht treaty the French blue-collar workers and farmers were telling the government it had not protected them well enough. Similarly, the Gaullists won the 1993 parliamentary elections because they were the party associated with a strong state. The segments of the right that voted in this year's European Parliament contests for Le Pen, and for de Villiers, who had been a leader of the no campaign in the Maastricht referendum, were telling the Balladur government that its policy triad of rigor, a strong franc, and commitment to greater European unity was unacceptable.

The Tapie phenomenon sent the government a different yet similar message. A businessman one step away from bankruptcy and jail, owner of the Marseilles soccer team, Tapie won 12 percent of the vote in the European elections by defying the establishment. When he announced he would introduce a bill in the French parliament making youth unemployment illegal, he was mocking mainstream politicians who had failed to resolve the problem. Tapie's brand of populism resurrected the ancient French habit of voting *against*. It expressed distrust of the state and it weakened the state.

Yet the Tapie phenomenon has a comforting side. Mitterrand's manipulation casts doubt on the notion of the gulf between the elite and the masses. Moreover, Tapie, the standard-bearer of the tiny Left Republicans Party, kept his supporters on the center-left, thus creating a reserve battalion for the Socialists if they produce a leader and a project. This could provide the basis for a strong presidential run that would end the crushing, dangerous superiority of the right.

The most significant split in French politics, however, is no longer between left and right but between supporters of the Mitterrand-Balladur orthodoxy and the heretics who propose more nationalistic policies. This is the context in which the presidential election scheduled for next year should be set. On the left the Communists, who won only 6.9 percent of the vote in the European elections, will put up a candidate to testify that they are still alive. The devastated Socialists would like to run outgoing European Commission President Jacques Delors. His policies differ little from those of Balladur, who would like to run as the candidate of the entire right except for Le Pen's National Front. A Delors-Balladur clash in the second round, in which only the two top candidates participate, would confirm the banalization of French politics.

It would also be preceded in the first round by a strong protest vote for Le Pen and—if he runs—de Villiers, both of whom would denounce the "Brussels technocracy" of the European Union in the name of "the French people." The split in French politics, however, would be more clearly demonstrated by a first-round battle between Balladur and Gaullist Party leader Jacques Chirac, or by a runoff that pitted Chirac against Delors. Chirac has inherited the prickly nationalist strain in Gaullism. He is growing ever more critical of Balladur's rigor, and his supporters wonder aloud whether increased deficit spending and devaluation of the franc are not the only ways to reduce unemployment. Chirac is perceived as a stronger figure than Balladur, better able to defend French interests in forums such as the EU or GATT, or, alternatively, more willing to pull out of international arrangements like the plan for European monetary union.

In the clamor of a presidential campaign Chirac is likely to strike a belligerent pose, but it is hard to see where the nationalistic option would lead. Or rather, it is all too easy to see it leading to inflation, loss of credibility in financial markets, and isolation in Europe. The protagonists of independent action by the French state come up against the fact that modern states exist to bargain with anone other; power flows from the domestic to the international level and back. A government that acquits itself well at GATT talks gains legitimacy at home, and conversely, a united, efficient state can strike better bargains abroad. Intransigent nationalism makes other countries reluctant to bargain and so undermines itself. For this reason centrist politics are likely to continue in France after the presidential election, and if Chirac is elected he will change the style and the details but not the essentials of policy.

OUT OF WORK AND IN DEBT

This leads back to the economic problems that Balladur has been unable to solve. In the year he has been in power unemployment has risen from 11.1 percent to 12.4 percent, where it has now flattened out. Some 140,000 jobs have been lost, while the workforce has grown by 159,000. Moreover, there is no mesh between the few new jobs, in the tertiary sector, and the manufacturing and construction jobs lost. Unemployment is higher among women than men— more than 14 percent to less than 11 percent—and highest among the unskilled young. Among people younger than 30 and without special qualifications, 32

percent are unemployed. Only 1.6 percent to 2 percent growth is predicted for the economy this year, while at least 3 percent is needed to reduce unemployment.

Unemployment is the dominant grievance and is perceived as the cause or the catalyst of most others. Decline in the number of farmers and lack of other jobs in the countryside causes *désertification*: the transformation of rural areas into uninhabited deserts. People move to urban agglomerations like the Ile-de-France, the region around Paris where 20 percent of the population now resides. But there unemployment heightens racial tensions.

Unemployment is threatening the very policy of rigor. Lower tax revenues and increased social spending have sent the government's debt soaring. After increasing by less than 5 percent in 1991, it jumped 13 percent and 17 percent the next two years. Estimates are that it will reach 60 percent of gross domestic product in 1995, which is low compared with Italy, where the debt stands at approximately 120 percent of GDP, but high enough to trigger fears of inflation or of a crowding out of private investment. Balladur's plan to reduce the annual deficit from last year's $70 billion to $55 billion next year separates him from Chirac.

Public anger with unemployment has led to demonstrations and clashes with the police. This March Balladur came up with a plan to reduce the minimum wage for young people by 20 percent where employers provided job training. This provoked a wave of protests from university and high school students. The government offered to amend the proposal and open discussions, but demonstrations persisted and Balladur finally withdrew the proposal.

THE STATE BACKS DOWN

The politics of the unemployment issue were more important than the minimum wage plan's potential impact on joblessness. By backing down the government avoided violent clashes but made itself look weak. Nor was this an isolated incident. The government postponed the restructuring of nationalized Air France after a strike by the airline's employees. Farmers and fishermen have won financial concessions after protests that turned into riots. Balladur is following a strategy based on his reading of French history: clashes between the centralized state and grassroots protesters lead to violence, which undermines the state. But Balladur's current conciliatory strategy cripples his government's ability to take action.

The well-organized French state represents France's advantage in Europe. Giving in to demonstrators encourages other forms of corporatist protest and diminishes the state's ability to arbitrate at home and bargain abroad. Frenchmen's vision of their country as one prone to crises, where an overbearing government clashes with grassroots anarchy, may become a self-fulfilling prophecy. The likelihood of a crisis is strengthened by the tale of a technocratic elite cut off from the people. In this case the political class is acutely aware of the suffering caused by the recession. But genuine solutions like better job training cannot have an immediate impact.

Since the origins of the recession lie partly outside France and one major cause is high German interest rates, the Balladur government has worked hard to revive cooperation with Germany after the conflict provoked by the franc's humiliation in mid-1993. Germany proved helpful in the Uruguay Round, supporting France's campaign to obtain concessions for farmers. Differences continue over eastern Europe, where Germany remains more favorable toward the entry of Poland, Hungary, and the Czech Republic into the EU while France is increasingly worried about the union's southern flank and especially about the disintegration of Algeria. Monetary tensions eased after the franc returned to the narrow band in December and the Bundesbank gradually lowered interest rates. Defense cooperation has become more plausible because the French right distrusts NATO less than Mitterrand, and because of the German Constitutional Court's ruling that German troops may be deployed as peacekeepers anywhere in the world.

Three questions still hang over the future of Franco-German cooperation. The first is whether the two countries can continue to offer leadership to an EU with an enlarged membership and marked by a resurgence of the nation-state. Their failure to impose their candidate, Jean-Luc Dehaene, as head of the European Commission may be symptomatic. One solution, which was adopted with the proposal for a Franco-German army corps, is for France and Germany to push ahead, leaving other countries to follow at their own pace. This raises the second question: whether a reunited Germany still seeks cooperation with France, and in particular, monetary union, or whether it may prefer to go it alone. Many Germans believe their country would benefit from monetary union, which would both stabilize trade with France and prevent the mark from being isolated vis-à-vis the dollar and the yen. Monetary union within a small group—France, Germany, and the Benelux countries—is the most likely scenario, although it has aroused opposition in Britain, Italy, and the other "second-division countries." It, however, is dependent on the third question: Does France want to continue down Mitterrand's road of closer ties with Germany? Under a Delors or Balladur presidency the answer is yes; under Chirac France might drag its feet. Any president will have to take into account the popular mood, which is less anti-German than suspicious of interdependence. It is nurtured by the self-doubts—reawakened in July by Bill Clinton's comment on German leadership in Europe—about France's

ability to keep up with Germany. Both de Gaulle and Mitterrand have tried to cure these doubts, which are exaggerated. France now has a lower inflation rate than Germany, and its military superiority has not, as the Gulf War demonstrated, lost its significance.

The Rwandan expedition stems from the determination to demonstrate that France is a world power, while Germany is not. But it has laid bare the murkier aspects of French policy. France supported the late brutal Hutu president, Juvénal Habyarimana, whose militias massacred ethnic Tutsis. Paris sent troops to the country on a humanitarian mission, but the humanitarian and the political realms are inseparable. They entered Rwanda through Zaire, for which that country's dictator, Mobutu Sese Seko, will exact a price, and they defended the Hutus, deliberately creating a Hutu enclave. Other European nations like Belgium and Italy, which have been reluctant to help, suspect that France was attempting to gain leverage over the Patriotic Front as it set about forming a government. France suspects the Americans are using the front, now ensconced at the head of a new government, to weaken French influence in Africa.

Western power struggles make for a sordid spectacle amid the massacre and the starvation of Africans. Yet the French soldiers saved lives in Rwanda, and the UN actually tried to persuade them to stay before they pulled out July 30. In general it is hard to argue that Africa would be better off without the French presence. Moreover, France's ability to intervene is the sign of an active, resolute state.

A YEAR FOR LIVING DANGEROUSLY

The next year is likely to be perilous for France. The upcoming presidential election will encourage politicians to be irresponsible—especially those of the right, which has a plethora of candidates and believes the left cannot win. Lower German interest rates will not bring about an instant reduction in unemployment. The EU will be more a hindrance than a help, with a weak new commission, a parliament flexing its muscles but unused to power, and flimsy national governments, like John Major's in Britain, that use Europe as a scapegoat. The French and German presidencies of the EU Council of Ministers will be sorely tested. At home there will surely be more racially motivated incidents, while the disintegration of Algeria will have ever greater repercussions in France, which has as many as 3 million residents of Algerian descent.

The critical task is holding state and civil society together during the long recession. France has strengths that French observers underestimate: disinflation has worked and Franco-German cooperation is far from dead. If France can avoid yet another war among the French, it can flourish, and help Europe do so also.

The rise, again, of Jacques Chirac

PARIS

IF THE opinion polls are even half right, Jacques Chirac will be the next president of France. With a month to go before the first round of voting in the presidential election (on April 23rd), the man who seemed to have no chance at all three months ago is now so far ahead that no rival looks able to catch him.

The polls could change again, perhaps. Two months ago they showed the prime minister, Edouard Balladur, as the frontrunner. But spectacular reversals three months before polling day have happened before in France. Even so, no presidential candidate has yet thrown away so large a lead so near an election. Indeed, the opposite often happens: as polling day nears, undecided voters and politicians tend to line up behind the man who looks like winning.

This is already happening to Mr Chirac. His lead in the polls has been stable, or getting bigger, for weeks. President Mitterrand's nephew has backed him. Mr Balladur's most stalwart supporter, Charles Pasqua, the interior minister, is putting out feelers to him. Even Raymond Barre, a former prime minister, and Valéry Giscard d'Estaing, a former president, may follow suit. Mrs Chirac is doubtless measuring the windows of the Elysée for new curtains.

To outsiders, this burst of popularity may seem strange. Mr Chirac lost two presidential campaigns to François Mitterrand, in 1981 and in 1988. He split the Gaullist party in 1974 by throwing his weight behind Mr Giscard d'Estaing in the presidential election of that year. He has twice been prime minister (in 1974-76 and 1986-88)—neither time with notable success. He clashed with both his presidents (Messrs Giscard d'Estaing and Mitterrand). Mr Chirac, it seems, is not easy to work with.

Above all, Mr Chirac has the reputation of an unguided missile. As a youngster, he sold the Communist-party newspaper, *L'Humanité*, on the streets. As prime minister for the second time, he espoused a French version of Thatcherism. Now he presents himself as the true Gaullist, standing above the left-right divide, seeking to reconcile the interests of the whole nation.

On the European Union, he has wobbled just as much. In 1978, he signed a notorious letter called the *appel de Cochin* (after the hospital where he was then laid up). This was a visceral, Europhobic display of French nationalism. Last year he also suggested holding a referendum on economic and monetary union (EMU)—which was taken to be an attempt to prevent it. Yet in 1992, during the referendum on the Maastricht treaty, he campaigned for a Yes vote, though many of his advisers opposed it. He now says he supports EMU.

Why, then, are so many French voters prepared to back so erratic a figure? The answer has nothing to do with his policies: you need a microscope to spot the difference between his manifesto and Mr Balladur's.

It has everything to do with the candidates' personalities. His rivals are weak. The Socialist, Lionel Jospin, a transparently decent man, is a candidate only because Jacques Delors, a former president of the European Commission, chose not to run. Mr Jospin's campaign started well but has faltered recently, as the various factions of the Socialist Party tug him in different directions. Mr Jospin seems undecided about how left-wing to make his appeal. Even traditional Socialist supporters find it hard to imagine him as president.

Mr Balladur's problems are worse. He has failed to overcome his image as a prince of the state, rather than a man of the people. At first, he tried to run an unflamboyant campaign, restricted to a few grand television appearances and public meetings, as if trying to glide in one effortless movement from the Matignon Palace, where the prime minister lives, to the Elysée, the ultimate seat of power. Arguably this was a rational response to electioneering for someone who, unlike Mr Chirac, knows next to nothing about it. Mr Balladur was 56 when he first stood for elected office.

The attempt failed. As his standing in the polls has slumped, Mr Balladur's impeccable suits and silk ties have been hidden under a lumber jacket and woollen scarf. He has tried to coarsen his cool, condescending manner and adopt a more pugnacious style. But the result has simply been to make the patrician prime minister look faintly ridiculous. It is now even possible that he might pull out of the race before the first round, rather than face humiliation.

Yet Mr Chirac is more than not-Jospin and not-Balladur. He has virtues of his own. Experience is one. He has been around in politics a long time. Elected to parliament in 1967, he got his first ministerial post that year at the age of 34. In addition to having been prime minister twice, he has been mayor of Paris for almost two decades. This gives him an important power base—and a record of success. Paris is a city that works.

Resilience in adversity is another. In most democracies, his loss of two presidential elections would count against him. In France it may be regarded as necessary preparation. The French like their leaders tried and tested. Mr Mitterrand also made two failed bids for the presidency before being elected at the age of 64. Many voters feel the 62-year-old Mr Chirac's turn has come.

Above all, Mr Chirac has understood, as Mr Balladur has not, that the French generally want something more from their president than mere competence and continuity. Mr Balladur's message to them is: "You know me. Everything is in safe hands. Go back to sleep." Mr Chirac's is: "France needs a new start. I am the man to give it. There will be something for everyone."

So Mr Chirac offers jobs for the unemployed, wage rises for those in work, cuts in employers' social-security contributions, special grants for the old and infirm, "salaries" for mothers, increases in health spending, more teachers, more money for culture and lower taxes. And, to cap it all, he is promising to reduce the budget deficit to below 3% of GDP, to satisfy the Maastricht criteria. And so what if the figures do not add up? "Politics", says Mr Chirac, "is not the art of the possible, but the art of making possible what is necessary."

The mayor of Paris has sometimes been likened to a dashing cavalry officer—impulsive, colourful, energetic, but lacking in *gravitas* and the capacity for sober judgment. His critics say he has no ideas of his own, only those of the last person he spoke to. His friends reply that the calmer, more reflective figure who seems to have emerged in the present campaign is the "real" Jacques Chirac. Whether that is true is indeed the great question about him. France may well have to live with the answer for the next seven years.

[In the first round of the April 23rd election process, Socialist Lionel Jospin received the most votes with 23.3 percent, a surprise to even his own pollsters. In a very close battle for second place, Paris mayor Jacques Chirac edged out Prime Minister Edouard Balladur, each having 20.8 percent and 19 percent respectively. Right-wing candidates, National Front leader Jean-Marie Le Pen won 15 percent of the vote, and Philippe de Villiers won 4.7 percent. This right-wing showing was the highest for the far-Right in Europe since the end of World War II. On the Left, the Communist Party, the Trotskyites, and environmental candidates won a total of 17.2 percent. The run-off election was held on May 7th, between the top two winners Jospin and Chirac. At this writing, the first polls pick Chirac as the next president of France. *Editor*]

Some Judges in France Battle the Establishment

Business Ties to Politics Are Under Fire

NATHANIEL C. NASH

PARIS, March 17 — For decades in France, it has been an open secret that the nation's business and political elite had intimate and mutually beneficial ties — far more blatant ones than in other countries.

French industrial giants channeled campaign contributions through offshore bank accounts, and in return, their exports were promoted by Government officials. Within France they were given captive markets, and any bribes were considered a necessary cost of doing business. And politicians and chief executives alike were kept mostly beyond the reach of the criminal courts.

But that cozy relationship has been shaken by a series of corruption cases brought against some barons of industry. Corporate chiefs as well known here as Lee Iacocca or Bill Gates is in the United States have been hauled into court and interrogated, on charges including defrauding shareholders, illegal political financing, fraudulent invoicing and using company funds to remodel home bathrooms.

What is happening, political analysts say, is a kind of 20th-century version of the French Revolution — a generational struggle between young, idealistic, rambunctious judges on the lower end of the pay scale and the 60-something members of the establishment who wonder why their power, perks and big salaries are suddenly being questioned. And all this comes as Government-controlled companies are privatized and thrown into a competitive global economy.

Not surprisingly, members of the old guard are indignant, complaining that the scandals will hurt their export markets — and, broadly, that Anglo-Saxon values are being imposed on Gallic corporate governance. Politicians are also presumably indignant, but are mute about the scandals with a presidential election looming in late April.

While some historians and legal experts say the investigators may be going too far, they quickly add that the corporate and political establishment has long exercised political clout with a fierce impunity, and this is the backlash.

"We are going through in France what Italy went through five years ago — the courts beginning to take on the corrupt aspects of the large industrial groups," said Thierry Jean-Pierre, a former judge and now a member of the European Parliament.

The latest and most prominent case involves Alcatel Alsthom S.A., the world's largest maker of telecommunications equipment.

On March 10, its chairman, Pierre Suard, was barred from the executive suite by a French judge investigating him for using corporate funds to remodel his homes and for his reported involvement in a scheme to overcharge France Télécom, Alcatel's largest corporate customer, by more than $100 million.

On Wednesday, on national television, Mr. Suard denied all charges, saying he was the subject of persecution by disgruntled former employees and of a misguided judiciary.

The next day, an association of judges expressed outrage, saying its members were "dumbstruck" by Mr. Suard's "surreal appearance."

And today, a second judge said he had uncovered an Alcatel account in Brussels that had reportedly channeled up to $20 million to accounts operated by French political parties.

Analysts say the Alcatel case has captured the public imagination because it embodies so much of the pent-up frustration with the power elite.

"It is a French tradition that a lot of high managers come from the top ranks of the civil servants," said

A cozy relationship is shaken by corruption cases.

Hervé Joly, a political analyst in Lyon. "Alcatel is one of the best examples of this system."

For the company and Mr. Suard, the trouble began in 1993, when two employees of Alcatel-CIT, a subsidiary, were arrested for setting up a system of false invoicing in which they contracted work to companies they controlled and had Alcatel pay exorbitant fees. To defend themselves, Mr. Suard contends, the two men began implicating top company executives.

On July 4, the police came to Mr. Suard's home and questioned him on renovations done in the apartment he owned in a Paris suburb and in a three-apartment building he had built for himself, his son and his daughter. That same evening, he came face to face with his future nemesis, Judge Jean-Marie d'Huy, who informed him that he had been placed under formal investigation for misuse of corporate funds.

By the end of the year the judge had jailed Pierre Guichet, the head of Alcatel-CIT, for 12 days on charges that he was part of the scheme to overcharge France Télécom.

Mr. Suard has yet to spend any time in jail; he has not been brought before a grand jury or indicted. Under French law, judges have wide latitude to place anyone they consider involved in a crime under investigation and to detain them, almost indefinitely.

For his part, Mr. Suard, an intense man with neatly combed silver hair, a square face and gentle eyes, protests his innocence.

Over a recent lunch, he said he had personally paid for the renovations to his home and had shown the checks to the judge. And he saw no problem with the company's paying for a security system, especially after the Government recommended that companies protect top executives after the 1986 killing of the chairman of Renault.

"I never imagined I could have been a victim of this type of injustice," he said. He said he had paid the $60,000 bill to install the telephone system in his new apartment building. "No one in France could believe that I, head of Alcatel, actually paid for my own telephone installation," he said.

Most of all, he said, he felt helpless against repeated leaks from the courts. "All damages to my honor and to Alcatel have been made by one man, one judge, under the control of nobody," he said. "And I have not been permitted to defend myself."

Judge d'Huy declined requests for interviews.

Some French judges pursuing the corruption cases have become almost folk heroes, although to a lesser extent than in Italy. Mr. Jean-Pierre, for example, who brought some early cases, was elected to the European Parliament on an anticorruption platform.

In the past, judges have often been kept in check by politicians who remove them if they step out of line. But Prime Minister Édouard Balladur, a presidential candidate, has given the court more freedom and interfered less, political analysts say.

This greater liberalism has come back to sting Mr. Balladur, who has seen his once big lead in the polls erode, in part, because of his close ties to Mr. Suard and others caught up in the corporate scandals.

When Mr. Balladur was Finance Minister, from 1986 to 1988, he named Mr. Suard to head Compagnie Générale d'Electricité, which became Alcatel after its privatization a year later.

Before joining the Cabinet, Mr. Balladur had been head of GSI, a software subsidiary of the company, and rejoined the concern as a part-time adviser after leaving office in

Analysts see a struggle between idealism and power.

1988. Over the next five years, he made almost $2 million in capital gains and fees from GSI. He has not been accused of any illegal activities, and he had repeatedly refused to disclose his compensation until last week.

Mr. Suard insisted he would not resign. Yet he is likely to face some pressure from Alcatel shareholders, for reasons quite apart from Judge d'Huy's investigations.

Last year, because of troubles in Germany, Turkey and Brazil, the company's profits plunged 40 percent, sending its stock price reeling. The company's biggest shareholder, the ITT Corporation, which holds 7 percent of Alcatel's shares, appears to be upset. Though it has made no official statement, press reports this week in Paris were filled with thinly veiled warnings from ITT that Alcatel could ill afford a management crisis. Until Mr. Suard's judicial fate is clear, the reports said, Mr. Suard might want to step aside.

France:
Keeping the Demons at Bay

Stanley Hoffmann

1.

Few nations have been so successful at advertising their troubles, at turning their difficulties into dramas and fears into phobias, as the French. In a country where much has changed over the past half-century, the habit of loud self-examination survives intact.

The French have turned the post–World War II years into a myth, that of *les trente glorieuses*, the thirty years when reconstruction, state planning, and the opening of borders transformed the aging and paralyzed nation of peasants and shopkeepers into a major industrial and exporting power, and a predominantly urban country with a growing population. In fact things never were quite so simple —the economic "takeoff" became visible only in the mid-Fifties; the glorious years were also those of intense domestic political warfare, particularly over decolonization in Vietnam and Algeria. But the myth about this period now serves to reinforce French unhappiness with the twenty years of economic difficulty that followed the first world oil shock of 1973.

If French discontent seemed particularly strong during 1993, it is because what might be called the Gaullist afterglow is finally gone. De Gaulle's psychological statecraft flattered the French (even those who disliked or distrusted him) into believing that France had become once again a major player on the world stage. France in this view emerged from the conflicts of the Thirties, from the defeat of 1940, the Nazi occupation, and the loss of empire as an independent, inventive, and ad-

vanced society with a workable set of institutions at last. The new disillusionment results from a series of blows to French pride and hopes, and from the sense that virtually all of the possible political formulas for dealing with the "twenty years crisis" that began in 1973 have been tried in vain.

In the mid-Seventies, many put their hopes on the union of the left —between Communists and Socialists —which finally came to power with Mitterrand's election to the presidency in 1981. Between 1981 and 1993, France went through four phases: (1) Mitterrand's aggressive economic policy of nationalization and public spending, which failed almost instantly, breaking up the union of Socialists and Communists; (2) his subsequent policy of economic austerity emphasizing the need to be competitive in an open world economy; (3) a return of the right to power in 1986 with Jacques Chirac's quasi-Reaganite program of economic deregulation and privatization; (4) a renewal of Socialist rule, after 1988, devoted to preserving a strong franc linked to the deutsche mark. But the most salient fact throughout the period was the rise of unemployment, which none of the six governments—five Socialist and one conservative—had been able to stop between 1983 and 1993.

Unemployment has been the worst of the shocks inflicted on French self-esteem. Each government has tried to cope with it, but the many plans have only succeeded in making the lives of

the unemployed marginally less awful. With more than three million people officially out of work—12 percent of the active population—the situation is unprecedented since World War II. (If unemployed immigrants and others who are not officially registered as looking for jobs are taken into account, the figure may be much higher.)

This is, of course, not an entirely French phenomenon, but why is France worse off than Germany? Nobody has come up with very convincing answers. It seems clear, however, that the policies pursued since the mid-Eighties, which aimed at preparing France for the single European Market of 1992 and for the Monetary Union described in the Maastricht treaty of December 1991, are to a large degree responsible. The end of "indexation"—the linking of price and wage increases—kept inflation down but also depressed domestic demand. Abolishing the regulations protecting workers from being fired has led French private and public enterprises to reduce labor costs by laying off large numbers of manual workers, clerical employees, and low level managers, in order to become more competitive. France never developed the kinds of cooperative links between unions and business that tend to protect employees in bad times—partly because of the weakness and divisions of French unions, partly because of the attitudes of French business. This may account for the difference between unemployment in France and Germany. Too few new jobs have been created,

Reprinted with permission from *The New York Review of Books*, March 3, 1994, pp. 10, 12-16. © 1994 by Nyrev, Inc.

partly because the technical training of workers by business and by the state is far less effective than in Germany.

The rise of unemployment has drawn attention to the weaknesses of France's modern industries, which are competitive mainly in processed foods and luxury consumer goods. Many French exports have been heavily subsidized, especially arms exports. But the subsidies are increasingly being banned by the rules of the European Union and of GATT, and the demand for French weapons has fallen drastically.[1] With unemployment has come another phenomenon, familiar to Americans but new in France: *l'exclusion*—the estrangement of a wide variety of depressed and troubled people from society including the long-term unemployed, unskilled young men and women, illegal immigrants, drug addicts, and criminal gangs, many of them in grim suburbs. Somewhat unexpectedly the new prime minister, the Gaullist Edouard Balladur, called attention to the situation of such people in the last book he published before coming to power.[2]

Political life has also taken a bad turn. In France as in other democratic countries, the prestige of politicians and public trust in politicians seem lower than at any time since 1945. This has happened partly as a result of the politicians' inability to solve pressing economic and social issues, above all unemployment, and partly as a result of the spectacular number of recent cases of proven or suspected corruption—*les affaires* such as the scandals that swirled around the Socialist prime minister Pierre Bérégovoy and may have contributed to his decision to kill himself on May 1, and those around the Marseilles business adventurer and Socialist politician Bernard Tapie, one of whose associates is accused of paying football players to throw games to Tapie's team. In the legislative elections of March 1993, the Socialist share of the votes fell from 34 percent in 1988 to 19 percent, a sign of the voters' disgust with the scandals and feuds that have splintered and demoralized the Socialist Party in recent years. The moderate right coalition of Jacques Chirac and Giscard d'Estaing was able to take power with around 44 percent of the vote—as against 44.5 percent when it won in 1986—but the main beneficiaries of the Socialists'

disgrace were the three "protest" groups: Communists, Ecologists, and Le Pen's National Front, which got more than a third of the votes.

Meanwhile France's position in the world also suffered. Having "overcome Yalta," i.e., the division of Europe—a goal shared by De Gaulle and Mitterrand—the French found themselves far worse off diplomatically than during the cold war. With Germany unified, France faced an unhappy choice between a policy of European integration that could lead to a European Union dominated by Germany, its most economically powerful member, and a policy of "independence" in which France's main asset—its nuclear force—has lost much of its meaning.[3] During the cold war, the French, longing for high international status, could always assert themselves against American "hegemony"; today, the French often complain more about America's withdrawal from Europe than about American imperiousness. They once assumed that as American and Soviet power in Western and Eastern Europe diminished, a Europe led by France would become one of the major forces in the world. But now, in diplomatic and defense matters, Europe remains a congeries of distinctive states without a collective will or adequate military forces. The complete failure of the European Community to act in Yugoslavia has contributed heavily to the post–cold war disillusionment in France.

The intellectuals, for their part, have not been of much help. Between the mid-Seventies and the late Eighties, a strong liberal current swept away most of the Marxist tendencies that had been dominant in French literary and university culture. The main target of liberal intellectuals such as Jean-François Revel and the writers for the quarterly *Commentaire* was French and Soviet communism, and while their analysis of sterile leftist ideas could be refreshing, their anticommunism sometimes sounded like that of the American neoconservatives. A secondary target was French socialism, insofar as it was tactically allied with the Communists and advocated a program of nationalization and state intervention. As the Communists declined and the Socialists reversed their economic policies, some liberal intel-

lectuals, such as the historian François Furet, announced the advent of a "Republic of the Center," in which a kind of Tocquevillian consensus was to overcome the old ideological divisions and bring France closer "to the liberal democratic regimes of America and Britain."[4]

No doubt the liberal thinkers succeeded in discrediting the myth of revolution as the necessary force of social change,[5] but with the collapse of the Soviet Union and the crisis of the French left they have found themselves without a clearly defined cause. The end of the cold war and the persistent economic and social difficulties of France have dissolved many of the old ideological alignments, and writers who once were allies have now split over European integration and over Yugoslavia, as well as over the issues of immigration and nationality. Some ex-Communist intellectuals have been engaging in a bizarre dialogue with extreme right-wing ideologues, expressing mutual sympathy over the "rediscovery" of the Nation, anti-Americanism, and even anti-Semitism.[6] A broad consensus among intellectuals and journalists on the values of liberal democracy has done little to cure the rest of France of its phobias.

2.

Indeed, during much of 1992 and 1993, what was most striking about French political life was its regression into a kind of shrill, defensive, and protectionist nationalism, which recalled previous episodes of chauvinism in French history. In the 1880s, also a period of economic difficulties, the Republic adopted protectionist policies both for agriculture and for industry; the best-selling book of Edouard Drumont, *La France juive*, denounced Jewish cosmopolitanism and corruption as bringing about the decline of traditional France. In the 1930s, when the world recession finally reached France, governments took steps to restrict both competition at home and with foreign countries while tolerating the wave of xenophobia that culminated in the Vichy regime. Despite the extensive changes in French society since the Fifties—far larger than those between 1880 and 1930—many of the old reflexes and prejudices, particularly against poor immigrants, are again evident.

During the last couple of years, it has often seemed as if many of the French were making the outside world responsible for their domestic and external woes. To some, Germany was mainly at fault and, particularly, the Bundesbank, whose policy of high interest rates was aimed at preventing inflation while Germany financed reunification through deficit spending. Some French politicians have denounced the bank's policies as the direct cause of France's recession and unemployment since French leaders have felt they must hold down inflation if the close link between the two currencies in the European Monetary System is to be maintained. Philippe Séguin, the populist Gaullist leader who is now the president of the National Assembly, has been the articulate champion of a radically different economic policy, based on giving priority to employment, a greater measure of state *dirigisme*, and the independence of French monetary policy.[7]

Another target has been *la délocalisation*—an odd term that refers to the transfer of capital from advanced countries with high labor costs to developing countries, mainly in Asia, with very low labor costs—and to the "invasion" of French markets by cheaper products coming from these countries, thus ruining old French industries and depriving French workers of their jobs. A report written by a committee of the French Senate presented a particularly hysterical view of this peril; it concluded that three to five million French jobs were threatened—even though only 8 percent of French imports come from Asia and Eastern Europe. The remedy frequently suggested is tariffs, quotas, and other forms of protection, to be imposed either by the European Union ("*préférence communautaire*") or by France alone if the Union "betrays" its duty.[8]

It is not only the cheap goods produced by overpopulated poor countries that threaten France, it is also their miserable masses attracted by Europe's wealth. As the Gaullist interior minister Charles Pasqua keeps insisting, the door must be closed to them as well. There is a glaring contradiction in his solution for keeping

those masses away: he wants to give more aid to these countries—for example in formerly French-controlled North Africa—while either closing France's borders to their products or refusing to open them any wider. Both the Senate report and the demand for an end to immigration evoke the image of a beleaguered and aging France (and Europe), imperiled by the goods and the peoples of alien cultures.

Large numbers of those foreign invaders are already within the walls; hence the government has shown a new vigor in defending the traditional model of an integrated French nation, and in fostering the already widespread view that multiculturalism *à l'américaine* would balkanize and dismantle the Republic. Foreigners who want to stay in France must be willing to become French by assimilation—by accepting French institutions such as *la laïcité* (i.e., the relegation of religion to the private sphere), by mastering French, and by absorbing French culture. Those who refuse to do so should be punished—expelled from school if they insist on wearing an "Islamic scarf," and from France if they agitate for Muslim fundamentalism. The defense of the traditional ideal of an integrated French society has brought together "Jacobin" left-wingers like the ex-Socialist Jean-Pierre Chevènement, assimilated Jewish intellectuals, and conservative nationalists.

France is not threatened only by the less-developed barbarians. Another threat comes from the overdeveloped barbarian: the United States. In 1992 and 1993 France's complex post-1945 relationship with America and "Americanization" has taken a sour turn with predictable conflicts of interests transformed into a clash of cultures.[9] The three main sticking points in the GATT drama were (1) France's desire to protect a very small part of French agriculture, which is under strong pressure from American competitors demanding greater access to France's market, (2) the American demand that France reduce its subsidies of French farm products competing in foreign markets; and (3) the French insistence that quotas limit the access of American films and TV programs to French screens, and that French films and TV programs be subsidized more than

ever. The French have every right to defend the survival of French (and European) movies. But it seems highly questionable whether imposing quotas will produce better films or TV programs, and, as some French critics have observed, quotas seem a mechanical response to the basic fact that, on the whole, the French public prefers American films, while American demand for French movies, which are often more glossy and arty than exciting, is meager. The government negotiators also insisted that, during the coming years, the concessions on agriculture France would make to the countries outside Europe in the new GATT agreement should not exceed the concessions the French had already painfully agreed to in 1992, for the reform of the ruinous European Common Agricultural Policy. Their obstinacy paid off.

But the public debate went way beyond these technical disputes. During 1993 there was more talk than had been heard in years about France as a rural nation, although only 5 percent of the population is now rural. Many prominent French commentators proclaimed their hostility to an "unregulated," "savage" economic liberalism which cares only for profits and amounts to the crushing of the weak by the strong. They defended French culture against Hollywood's products as if all American films were hopelessly vulgar, and pictured France as a place in which what is good and fair for the country is properly decided by the state, not the market, and by the general interest, not private interests. Such plaintive and often angry convictions combine Catholic and leftist anticapitalist traditions, intellectual dislike for mass culture, and the widespread belief in the universal value of French civilization.

3.

These bitter and often exaggerated protests have led some observers in France and abroad to wonder whether a kind of collective hysteria has been rising in France. And yet, behind the confusion and petulance, one can find many reasons for being, if not optimistic (the French themselves are more pessimistic than ever about their immediate future), at least somewhat reassured. This is not the first time that the French politicians, bureaucrats, journalists, and intellectuals have indulged in a grand psychodrama that leaves what De Gaulle referred to as "the nation in its depths"—most ordinary French people—rather cool.

It may, however, be the first time that in a period of crisis and self-doubt, the scapegoats have been almost exclusively foreign ones. During the 1880s and in the 1930s, not only émigrés from Italy and Eastern Europe but their French accomplices (usually on the left) were accused of being "agents of dissolution." Today the defenders of nationalist rectitude have few targets among French citizens. The Socialists have become the advocates of managerial efficiency while the party is still divided among competing baronies, and communism isn't even a scarecrow anymore. In other words, the feverish condition one finds in France today is not a matter of a war of French against French. This is quite a change.

The main reason for believing that the fever will go down and cool heads prevail is provided by Edouard Balladur's remarkable performance. He presents himself as a Gaullist reformer; so far, in fact, he has introduced few reforms but he has skillfully skirted dangers and corrected mistakes. The electoral law provided the moderate right with the largest majority any party or coalition has enjoyed in the National Assembly: 486 out of 577 seats. But Balladur has been shrewd in giving key positions in the government to members of the majority's second party, the conglomeration of business-minded politicians known as the UDF who are less "statist," less nationalist, and generally more pro-Europe than the Gaullists. In doing so he has weakened the influence in the UDF of such potential rivals to the Gaullists as Raymond Barre and Valéry Giscard d'Estaing. Indeed, two of Balladur's UDF ministers, Simone Veil and François Léotard, have publicly suggested that he should be the right's presidential candidate for 1995. Balladur has also maintained a delicate balance among the different Gaullist tendencies. The two anti-Maastricht leaders, Séguin and Pasqua, have their hands full with domestic affairs, and the pro-Maastricht group, which in-

cludes Balladur and the foreign minister Alain Juppé, control foreign policy. Contrary to what Balladur had promised before coming to power, he also has left members of Parliament with practically no leeway for initiatives of their own.

Without quite saying so Balladur takes the plausible view that economic recovery depends much more on what happens to the American and the German economies than on what France can do alone. He also knows that the National Front's progress, both in percentage of the electorate (12.5 percent in 1993 as against 8.5 in 1988) and in all the traditionally conservative sectors of French society—particularly in rural districts and in the urban lower middle and even upper-middle classes—is a major threat to his own moderate right constituency.[10] With the enthusiastic help of Interior Minister Pasqua, he has proceeded to appease right-wing voters and impatient deputies with tougher laws on immigration and on the requirements for French nationality.[11] In fact the new conditions for becoming French are not very drastic; they preserve the traditional *jus soli*—residence, not blood, is what matters—and merely require that the sons and daughters born in France of foreign parents explicitly request French nationality between the ages of sixteen and twenty-one, instead of receiving it automatically, a change which a distinguished non-partisan commission had already proposed.

The changes in immigration policy have been far more aggressive: they increase the powers of the police and of bureaucrats to control and punish illegal immigration, particularly from North Africa and sub-Saharan Africa. They make it more difficult for foreigners to become residents and to bring their families to France; and they try to prohibit marriages of convenience between French and foreign nationals. When some of these provisions were declared unconstitutional by the Constitutional Council, the government got Parliament to amend the Constitution so as to restrict the right of foreigners to ask for asylum in France, a right the council had said was guaranteed by the preamble of the Constitution of 1946, which was incorporated into the Constitution of 1958. A special new branch of the police has

been established in order to repress illegal immigration.[12]

With very few exceptions (Michel Rocard was one—another was *Le Monde*) the left has reacted tepidly to the new measures, perhaps because, in matters having to do with immigrants, there has been since 1984 a vast discrepancy between the Socialists' rhetoric and their acts. As a clever Machiavellian, Balladur, without making any fundamental changes in French practice, may have pacified the fears of the voters who supported him that French national identity is being eroded. Restrictions on immigration were imposed in 1974 without stopping the flow of immigrants. In a country with open borders, and despite the police's new powers, the new measures may also be ineffectual. There is, however, a change in tone: before Pasqua, nobody except Le Pen had ever proclaimed that France would no longer accept immigrants.

Having satisfied the members of his majority at the expense of immigrants, Balladur proceeded to remove the obstacles his own Gaullist party had used to block both France's European policy and an improvement in France's relations with the US. He rejected both populist and business-inspired protectionism. After all, he argued, France's economy is twice as open as those of Japan and the US. French exports in 1990 were 23 percent of production, and imports 23 percent of consumption.[13] He has preserved the policy of the *franc fort*, arguing that the softer money and low interest rate policies advocated by such critics as George Soros could not guarantee any faster recovery, and would damage French competitiveness through inflation, and, eventually, a devaluation of the franc.[14] After the financial hurricane of July 1993, in which international speculation against the franc obliged the members of the European Monetary System to increase the margin of fluctuation allowed among the European currencies, the franc, in a very short time, recovered the value it had lost.

Balladur had written that France should not lock itself into a purely Franco-German partnership; he nevertheless has given the highest priority to preserving the alliance with Germany that Mitterrand pursued, after some hesitations at the time of German unification. This policy wasn't dictated by any conversion of Balladur to a Federal Europe; he is a Gaullist of the pragmatic Pompidou variety—i.e., someone for whom Europe is not "the ultimate objective of French policy," just "a means at the service of France's interests and permanence."[15] But he also understands that the European Community can be used to accomplish specifically French goals. By repudiating protectionism generally and clinging to the Franco-German scheme for gradual monetary union, he was able to obtain first German and then general European Union support for French demands that French agriculture and movies be protected in the GATT talks; he could claim credit for the US concession allowing France to continue to subsidize agriculture and the US retreat on free entry of movies into France. He could thus appear before Parliament both as the successful defender of French interests and as the man who avoided a crisis between the European Union and the US: no mean accomplishment—even if the defense of French interests often appears crass, as in the case of France's courting of the China market instead of continuing to sell arms to Taiwan, and in the case of two Iranian terrorists who were sent back to Iran instead of being extradited to Switzerland.

Balladur has also tried to keep the temperature low in domestic affairs. Many politicians, especially but not exclusively on the left, have sought a panacea for unemployment in a drastically shorter work week of thirty-two hours. Balladur has quietly resisted this trend, saying that it could easily lead to generalized partial unemployment instead of a "new distribution of work." Many politicians, especially but not exclusively on the right, have called for sharp reductions in social protection (especially against illness, unemployment, and old age); but he has preferred incremental cuts, based on agreements with the representative of the groups concerned. His concern for social peace and quiet led him to scrap the imprudent and authoritarian plan to cut back employees his minister of transport tried to impose on the financially troubled Air France, which resulted in a disruptive strike. Balladur had been Pompidou's chief aide when Pompidou negotiated, at the cost of huge financial concessions to the unions, an end to their nationwide strike of May 1968. He now applied once again the lessons his master had taught him.

Indeed he did so twice. He allowed his minister of education to rush through Parliament a revision of a law of 1850, aimed at allowing local governments to subsidize the investments needed by private (i.e., mainly Catholic) schools—a measure opposed by Mitterrand and the *laïc* left, but designed to appeal to the Catholic and centrist elements of the majority. He decided to drop the matter when the Constitutional Council declared that the bill violated the principle of equality among citizens and after a rally in support of public schools, whose needs are just as great, attracted hundreds of thousands of demonstrators. (Conversely, an attempt by Mitterrand's government in 1984 to tighten state control on subsidized private schools had drawn hundreds of thousands to the streets and forced the Socialists to retreat.) Balladur has now reverted to his favorite means of dealing with social issues that divide the French: consultation with a variety of national leaders.[16]

He still faces a daunting situation. The relatively small economic stimulus plan of the summer (financed largely by a very successful loan) has had little effect; although the recession is not getting any worse, unemployment is expected to keep rising for some time. The efforts to reduce deficits, connected with the *franc fort* policy, have led to cuts in the number of new academic teaching positions planned for a system of higher education that is increasingly, and explosively, overcrowded and understaffed.[17] Yet after nine months in office, Balladur is immensely popular. The esteem in which he is held reminds one of Poincaré, who both stabilized the franc and calmed the public mood after the disastrous financial failure of the left-wing parties in 1924 and 1925.

Poincaré, however, had been France's president during the First World War—whereas Balladur was trained as a civil servant and spent years as a man behind the scenes, first with Pompidou and, after 1980, with Chirac. He was minister of the economy only between 1986 and 1988. But both Poincaré and Balladur have a reputation for personal integrity and devotion to the public good; above all, both are men of few words, who promise little and avoid the jargon —*langue de bois*—of professional politicians, and who deliver more than they promised.

François Mitterrand is therefore being quietly overshadowed as he ends his reign. Balladur has been careful to avoid humiliating him, to respect his prerogatives in foreign policy, to consult with him over most constitutional changes. Mitterrand has tried to capitalize on Balladur's popularity by suggesting he is the prime minister of his own choice. He may be delighted that Balladur's popularity could destroy the presidential prospects, in 1995, of two men he dislikes: Chirac on the right, Rocard on the left. But he can no longer conceal the fact that he now does little more than live at the Elysée Palace. The indiscreet memoirs of his former aide Jacques Attali suggest that since 1983 he has had two preoccupations: appointing his men to key positions and overseeing in minute detail the audio-visual channels of communication, because, as Mitterrand put it, "everything that is *médiatique* is *politique*."[18] Now these two powers have been transferred from the Elysée to the Matignon, the prime minister's office, and Balladur's performance has revived the Gaullist Party, Mitterrand's most overt object of dislike (the less overt one, the Communist Party, he helped to destroy).

None of this means that calm will now descend upon France. Elections for local government and for the European parliament will take place in 1994, and a new president will be elected in 1995. If the economy does not improve, this will give the Socialist Party of Rocard, if he can reorganize it, a better chance to be heard and to emphasize issues on which there are continuing differences between left and right. On many of these issues, however—immigration, privatization, even private schools—the public today clearly leans to the right. Continuing high unemployment will also exacerbate tensions and ambitions within the moderate right: Giscard still wants to give the French a chance to correct the mistake he thinks they made when they threw him out of office in 1981, and Chirac's leadership of the Gaullists is threatened by the superior popularity of Balladur. To date, Chirac is still expected to be the candidate for president, but Balladur is already, if silently, his rival. The drama taking place between the two men, who have been close associates for many years, is intense.

Beyond the struggle among the politicians, France's future remains difficult. The population is aging, which means that the younger people have to pay more for the security of their elders.[19] France shares in the general West European predicament: it has to compete both with advanced and dynamic societies like Japan and (perhaps again) the US, and with the cheap goods of developing countries. The French will try to switch from a long and heady emphasis on independence, which was almost an absolute goal, to a strategy of influence within the groups that France needs to belong to, among them the European Union and NATO. This is a shift that Balladur clearly believes must be made,[20] and a Gaullist may be better able to bring it about than a non-Gaullist; but it remains a delicate gamble.

Today the French are grateful to Balladur for the very modesty of his proposals, for the quiet, if somewhat woolly, elegance of his language. But will lowering the temperature of public debate be enough? Especially in difficult moments, the French like to turn to leaders with a vision—sometimes reactionary and disastrous, like Pétain's, sometimes heroic, like De Gaulle's, sometimes utopian, like Mitterrand's—at least for a few moments in 1981. Balladur's notion of a strong state concentrating on a few essential tasks appeals both to the atavistic French need for a state in firm control of society and to their equally strong instinct of resistance to it. Balladur combines a calm, avuncular, reassuring manner with a vision promising little more than gradual economic recovery and piecemeal bureaucratic reforms. He has only twelve months or so in which to show whether he can provide sufficient inspiration,

and sufficient jobs, to keep the demons at bay.

—February 3, 1994

[1] See *Le Monde*, December 22, 1993, p. 20.

[2] *Dictionnaire de la Réforme* (Paris: Fayard, 1992), pp. 118–120.

[3] For a fuller discussion, see my chapter, "French Dilemmas and Strategies after the Cold War," in Robert Keohane, Joseph Nye, and Stanley Hoffmann, editors, *After the Cold War* (Harvard University Press, 1993).

[4] See Sunil Khilnani's *Arguing Revolution* (Yale University Press, 1993), a stimulating discussion of the rise and fall of the intellectual left's love affair with the idea of revolution in postwar France; but the book suffers from an insufficient understanding of pre-1945 left-wing French thought, which was far richer than he seems to think. And, like Tony Judt in *Past Imperfect* (University of California Press, 1992), he neglects Camus.

[5] Another nail into the myth's coffin is driven—rather obliquely—by Jean-Claude Milner, in his somewhat arcane assault on "*progressisme*," *L'Archéologie d'un échec* (Paris: Editions du Seuil, 1993).

[6] *Le Monde* has been particularly exercised over this; see the issues of July 1, 1993, p. 7, and July 13, 1993, pp. 8–9, which include a "call for vigilance" signed by a group of distinguished intellectuals, such as Pierre Bourdieu, Jacques Derrida, François Jacob, the historian Georges Duby, etc.

[7] He has collected his speeches in two books, *Discours pour la France* (Paris: Grasset, 1992) (this is mainly his onslaught on the Maastricht treaty, seen as destructive of the French nation: "1992 is literally the anti-1979," p. 17) and *Ce que j'ai dit* (Paris: Grasset, 1993) (this is his call for a new economic and social policy, anti-European Union and anti-GATT).

[8] The Senate report—*rapport Arthuis*—is analyzed by Suzanne Berger in "The Coming Protectionism," an unpublished paper for a conference on the new France in the new Europe, Center for German and European Studies, Georgetown University, October 1993; see also Patrick A. Messer-

lin, "La Communauté, la France et l'Uruguay Round," in *Commentaire*, No. 63 (Fall 1993), pp. 497–506. He refers to a working paper by the Commission de réflexion économique of the CNPF—France's top business association—which is trying to rehabilitate the protectionism of the 1930s!

[9] Richard Kuisel, *Seducing the French* (University of California Press, 1993), was attacked in *Esprit* (July 1993, pp. 175–182) as anti-French, and has not yet, I believe, found a publisher in France.

[10] On the National Front's progress, see Pascal Perrineau, "Le Front National, la force solitaire," in Philippe Habert, Pascal Perrineau, and Colette Ysmal, editors, *Le vote sanction* (Paris: Presses de la Fondation National de Sciences Politiques, 1993), pp. 137–160.

[11] See *Dictionnaire de la Réforme*, pp. 155–160.

[12] The constitutional reform incorporates the provisions of the Schengen agreements, signed by nine of the twelve members of the European Union, which allow each state to refuse asylum to a foreigner whose request for asylum has already been turned down by another signatory.

[13] William James Adams, "France and Global Competition," paper for the conference on the new France in the new Europe, Center for German and European Studies, Georgetown University, October 1993.

[14] See George Soros's *Prospect for European Integration*, available from the Soros Foundation, 888 Seventh Avenue, New York, NY 10106.

[15] *Dictionnaire de la Réforme*, p. 112.

[16] In December 1986, he persuaded Prime Minister Chirac to withdraw the university reform plan prepared by University Minister Devaquet, which had provoked a massive student revolt; see Claire Chazal, *Balladur* (Paris: Flammarion, 1993), pp. 128–130.

[17] The *Dictionnaire de la Réforme* has no entry for universities, or higher education.

[18] *Verbatim: Volume I, 1981–1986* (Paris: Fayard, 1993) is marred not only by the notorious "annexation" by Attali of conversations between Mitterrand and Elie Wiesel that were supposed to get published later, but also by the unorthodox and unverifiable publication of endless diplomatic conversations between Mitterrand and other leaders, which are as tedious

as old news reports. As for Mitterrand's *confidences* about himself, they are narcissistic, overblown, and unrevealing.

[19]See *Le Monde*, October 28, 1993, p. 1.

[20]In the *Dictionnaire de la Réforme*, he calls several times for better Franco-American cooperation in a reformed NATO (which the Brussels NATO summit of January 1994 began to achieve), and for a new defense policy, less centered on nuclear weapons and independent means.

This has not prevented a spectacular public rift over Yugoslavia. The French government apparently wants to show two things: first that the Secretary-General of the UN is not willing to use airpower to protect UN forces in Bosnia from the Serbs, and second, that the US is not willing either to put pressure on the Bosnian Muslims to accept a settlement based on the UN and European Union partition plan or to send troops to enforce such a settlement. Having thus demonstrated that they were willing to act but failed to get the necessary support, Mitterrand and the French government would then be free to remove French forces from Bosnia with a good conscience. They could blame the Bosnian government for continuing the war, the Serbs for having thwarted the UN, the Secretary-General of the UN for allowing the Serbs to do so, and the US for being once again both ineffectual and self-righteous. Posturing aimed at putting a good face on one's failure to act appears to be a widely shared tactic in dealing with Bosnia.

The Debate over the Constitutional Council

A Special Court of Law?

*Contrary to What Robert Badinter Claims, the Council Must
Not Be an "Opposition" Institution*

François Terré

Just what is this Constitutional Council that everyone is talking about? A political institution? That is what it was created to be in 1958. But is it a supreme court, bearing witness to the existence of "a government of judges"? Robert Badinter, its presiding judge, has said loud and clear that the members of the Constitutional Council are judges; they constitute a court of law. And the Council is thus establishing itself as an "opposition force."

If it really were such an institution, then the Council would be one of those "special" courts that in the past were so roundly assailed in long drawn-out speeches. And on more than one count it would figure among the least satisfactory of such "special" courts.

1. Special in terms of its very competence, the Council had only a limited role at its inception: overseeing the conformity of laws to the articles of the Constitution. It should have given a strict interpretation to its role. Nothing of the kind occurred: it has involved itself in issues of respect for the preamble and the general principles, dictated their interpretation to the other branches of government, and scrutinized the texts in their minutest detail, all with complete disregard for the sovereignty of the French people.

2. The composition of this pseudo-court of law also makes it special. Given its mission, the Council should have been made up completely of members who were independent and above reproach. Matters did not turn out this way, and it is particularly intolerable for members of the Constitutional Council to simultaneously hold elective office. Either a judge is independent or he is not independent.

3. This special "court," which claims to be supreme, is far from being a model from the standpoint of how it conducts its affairs, employing procedures that shake the foundations of a justice worthy of the name. Before the Council the rights of defendents are not respected and there is no debate; its justice is inquisitorial. The Council likewise does not respect the principle of "pronouncement" according to which a judge must only pronounce upon what has been referred to him. On the contrary, the Constitutional Council has assumed the arbitrary and inordinate power of publishing opinions on all of the articles of a law, or on selected articles even when only others were referred to it. While expeditious, this form of justice lacks the rudiments of wisdom. And the secrecy of its deliberations debases it.

4. The Constitutional Council should remain a truly "exceptional" institution or be restored to that status. Its existence is contrary to our democratic traditions, as well as to those of England. And if the purveyors of constitutional councils have deemed it wise to export such institutions to Eastern Europe and elsewhere, they have often provided cover for apparatchiks. Boris Yeltsin has just had first hand experience with this at home.

5. The presiding judge of a court of law—if this one can be called such—should leave to others the task of defending it when it comes under criticism. Otherwise, he is robbed of the dispassion that properly belongs to him. And he falls victim to the reproach that Voltaire addressed to Montesquieu when the latter defended the venality of public office: "Even the most philosophical among us cannot avoid paying tribute to self-esteem. If a grocer were to discourse on legislative matters, he would want everyone to buy cinnamon and nutmeg."

—François Terré, Le Figaro (Paris),
Thursday, November 25, 1993.
Translated by Thomas W. Casstevens
and David Jaymes, Oakland University.

Update on Italy

THE BIRTH OF THE "SECOND REPUBLIC"

Gianfranco Pasquino

Gianfranco Pasquino is professor of political science at the University of Bologna and adjunct professor of political science at the Bologna Center of the Johns Hopkins University. His most recent books are La nuova politica *(1992) and, with Luciano Bardi,* Euroministri: Il governo dell'Europa *(1994). His essay "Italy: The Twilight of the Parties" appeared in the January 1994 issue of the* Journal of Democracy.

The results of the parliamentary elections that Italy held on 27–28 March 1994 were surprising, if not totally unexpected. To judge from the opinion polls, the victory scored by the Alliance for Freedom—a coalition comprising three conservative groups (the neofascist National Alliance [AN], Forza Italia, and the Northern League [Lega Nord]) plus a few small parties—had been in the making at least since the beginning of March. What was less widely anticipated was the coalition's conquest of a 366-seat majority in the 630-member Chamber of Deputies and a 155-seat near-majority in the 315-member Senate; the two houses together make up the first Parliament chosen under the complex new electoral laws adopted in August 1993. Under the new system, proportional representation

(PR) has been largely abandoned in favor of plurality elections in single-member districts, although a quarter of the seats in each house are allocated according to party-list PR with a 4-percent threshold requirement.[1]

What is more, the respective showings made by each of the three coalition partners were also major surprises. In less than three months, television magnate and soccer-team owner Silvio Berlusconi made a powerful electoral machine out of his brand-new Forza Italia, whose name is borrowed from a sports cheer that means "Go Italy, Go!" Its 20-percent share of the national vote was the largest that any single party received. For a new party in an established democracy, to get one out of every five votes cast is an achievement without parallel.

The National Alliance, which used to be known as the Italian Social Movement and can trace its roots back to Benito Mussolini, ran few "new faces" on its ticket but almost tripled its vote share, polling an unprecedented 13.5 percent. Although appearing as the junior partner in the coalition, the Northern League appealed effectively to its strong regional base and doubled the size of its parliamentary contingent. Thanks to the peculiarities of Italy's revamped electoral system, the strongly anticentralist Lega Nord is

now the largest parliamentary group within the Alliance for Freedom in both the Chamber and the Senate (see Table 1), and one of its Milanese deputies, Irene Pivetti, has been elected speaker of the lower house.

The defeat of the Progressive Alliance, as the loose left-wing coalition was known, appeared as less of a surprise to most observers, though the resounding character of the defeat seems to have stunned many inside the coalition. Having won almost all the important mayoral elections held across the country in November and December 1993, and having achieved a hard-won state of agreement amongst themselves, the Progressives entertained high hopes for a sizeable national victory, to be followed by governmental power at long last. Indeed, their triumph seemed like such a strong possibility that Berlusconi entered the arena precisely to prevent it. Seeking to counter those he called "Communists, former Communists, and post-Communists," he openly exploited what remained of the communist-anticommunist cleavage, once the central divide of Italian politics. The electoral results suggest that what remains of this cleavage is still quite salient, and perhaps even decisive.

Coalescing for the first time in their history (in a move dictated by the logic of the new electoral sys-

Table 1 — Election Results for the Chamber of Deputies

PARTY	% of VOTE on PR BALLOT	TOTAL SEATS
Right-of-Center Groups		
Northern League (Lega Nord)	8.4	122
National Alliance (AN)	13.5	109
Forza Italia	21.0	97
Christian Democratic Center (CCD)	*	32
Lista Pannella	*	6
Centrist Groups		
Italian People's Party (PPI)	11.1	33
Pact for Italy	4.6	13
Left-of-Center Groups		
Democratic Party of the Left (PDS)	20.4	115
Refounded Communists	6.0	40
Democratic Alliance (AD)	*	17
Italian Socialist Party (PSI)	*	15
Greens	*	11
Network (La Rete)	*	9
Social Christians	*	6
Others	*	5
Total Seats		**630**

Sources: *La Repubblica*, 14 April 1994, and International Foundation for Electoral Systems.

*Did not achieve 4-percent threshold.

tem), the left-of-center elements in Italian politics nonetheless found themselves punished with their lowest vote percentage since the critical elections of April 1948. Then, early in the Cold War, the Socialists (PSI) and Communists (PCI)—united as the Popular Front—received only 31 percent of the vote; the Social Democratic Party (PSDI), a recent breakaway from the PSI, obtained 7 percent. In 1946, when they ran separately, the PSI and PCI had posted a combined total of 39 percent. Subsequently, the combined electoral strength of the various left-wing parties fluctuated around 40 percent, reaching a peak of 46 percent in 1976. In 1994, the Progressive Alliance—comprising the Democratic Party of the Left (PDS, as the former PCI is now known), the Refounded Communists, the PSI, the Democratic Alliance, the Greens, the Social Christians, and the anti-Mafia Network party (La Rete)—polled only 34.6 percent. Especially disappointing were the results for the minor left-wing groups. Indeed, only the PDS

(20.4 percent) and the Refounded Communists (6 percent) passed the 4-percent qualifying threshold for participation in the proportional distribution of seats in the Chamber of Deputies. This means that three million leftist votes went to parties that did not earn any of the 157 seats that were awarded on the basis of proportional distribution.

A long and acrimonious discussion has already taken place within the leftist grouping concerning two issues. The first was whether a left-center coalition—one including, or perhaps even led by, the former Christian Democrat and leader of the electoral-reform movement Mario Segni and his newly formed Pact for Italy party and excluding the Refounded Communists—might have defeated or even forestalled Berlusconi's challenge. The second was whether Achille Occhetto, the secretary general of the PDS, was the best leader to take on Berlusconi (or, more pertinently, whether Occhetto should lead next time). From a

purely electoral point of view, Segni's contribution to the Progressive Alliance would have been less than the contribution actually made by the Refounded Communists, especially in some hard-fought, marginal districts: Segni himself lost to a rival from the AN in his own single-member constituency, and his party's 4.6-percent showing barely exceeded the distributional threshold. Thus although Segni might have improved the overall appeal of the Progressive Alliance by helping to shift its image toward the center, such a differently composed coalition would probably still have been unable to stop the Alliance for Freedom.

Berlusconi's Gentle Ruthlessness

Berlusconi's masterful bringing together of the National Alliance and the Northern League was, to use a most apt set of terms from Machiavelli, a balanced blend of *virtù* and *fortuna*. Many politicians had already realized that the new electoral laws would favor those capable of making alliances. Berlusconi's *virtù* lay not only in his ready grasp of the constraints and incentives built into the new rules of the game, but also in his facility at playing the game in a manner at once gentle and ruthless. Patiently and deftly he mollified his reluctant partners; ruthlessly he exploited anticommunism and the power that his television resources gave him. Realizing that, if left to themselves, the Lega's candidates in single-member northern districts and the AN's candidates in single-member southern districts might be no match for rivals backed by the Progressives, Berlusconi showed great skill in acting as a linchpin. His Forza Italia reached electoral agreements in most single-member districts with either the Lega or the AN. As for Forza Italia itself, it was the quasi-miraculous product of Berlusconi's marketing agencies and his television exposure, forces that Italy's confused and inadequate campaign regulations could scarcely contain. Berlusconi also welcomed into his coalition several outgoing parliamentarians belonging to the former Christian Democratic, Liberal, and Republican parties, as well as some ex-Socialists, effectively recycling these members of the old political class and what remained of their electoral appeal.

When it came to setting the agenda for the election campaign, Berlusconi seized the initiative with adventurous proposals for fiscal reform, job creation, and the restructuring of the health and pension systems. The common thread was the idea of reducing the state's role in order to give more space to the market and to private initiatives.

The Progressives reacted with an overcomplicated set of proposals that had little chance of persuading a skeptical electorate. Instead of coining effective slogans of their own, the Progressives zeroed in on some of Berlusconi's personal characteristics: his close friendship with the indicted and discredited former Socialist premier Bettino Craxi, his membership in the secret and illegal P2 Masonic lodge, and his control of television interests. Moreover, the Progressives never realized that they appeared to stand for "business as usual"—for continuity with the old, collapsing political order. In the end, voters faced a choice between a successful entrepreneur telling them to rely on the market and on their own skill and ingenuity, and a group of professional politicians asking for a vote of confidence in its own ability to reform the Italian state.

The private entrepreneur against professional politicians, the market against the state—in essence, this was the nature of the Italian electoral confrontation. A crucial sector of the electorate decided that it wanted less state regulation in the socioeconomic sector and fewer professional politicians in elective offices. These voters were generally people with ample political and socioeconomic resources, confident in their abilities and willing to accept the challenges and opportunities of the market.

They were and are highly dissatisfied with the state, its bureaucracies, and its regulations. In the eyes of these voters, the parties of the left represented both too much political continuity and too much political regulation. Yet there are good reasons to believe that Berlusconi himself will temper change with efforts at restoration. The bloc of socioeconomic forces that shaped Italian public policies during the First Republic is only undergoing a certain realignment. While this bloc is not identical to the one that the Christian Democrats represented and nourished for so long, many of its key members are holdovers, including the association of manufacturers (Confindustria), financial groups such as Mediobanca, and most commercial and professional lobbies. All these groups have already shifted their support to Berlusconi.

Of course it is one thing to win an election, and quite another to create a viable government, much less enact coherent public policies. A preliminary difficulty arose during the electoral campaign, when it was asked whether a major entrepreneur can become prime minister without divesting himself of some or most of his holdings. Although there is nothing in the laws or constitution of Italy to require such personal divestment, and no relevant precedent, Berlusconi himself seems to recognize that even the appearance of a conflict of interests may impair the premier's ability to run the government. Thus even though public pressure in favor of a clear-cut separation of interests has not been overwhelming, Berlusconi has felt obliged to offer the clever idea of appointing three so-called wise men to supervise his activity. Unfortunately, two of them have a history of very close ties to Fininvest, Berlusconi's financial company.

Berlusconi's problems aside, there exist major obstacles to the creation of a viable governmental coalition. Foremost among these impediments are the political and institutional differences separating the AN from the

Lega Nord. The AN's voters, especially in the south, tend to depend on state funds and subsidies—just the sorts of things that the Lega and Forza Italia are avowedly against. While they want not merely to readjust the welfare state, but to cut it back substantially, the AN is wedded to the idea of a strong national state. (It has also voiced irredentist demands for parts of Slovenia where individuals of Italian origin used to live.) The Lega is equally committed to a vision of federalist decentralization. The solution proposed by Berlusconi's advisors is a compromise in which the AN would accept federalism while receiving in exchange a shift in the form of government from parliamentarism to presidentialism. In the end, Italy would become a federal republic with a popularly elected chief executive.

For his part, Berlusconi has already appealed to the remnants of the once all-powerful center: the former Christian Democrats. That Mario Segni has all along been an emperor with no clothes is now clear to everybody. So far he has not been able to redesign his strategy or keep his small band of troops together. But if Berlusconi's appeals have already drawn away some members of Segni's Pact for Italy, most of the Popolari (or PPI, as the former Christian Democrats now call themselves) appear unwilling to collaborate with any coalition that includes the neofascists. Practically, what Berlusconi wants is to drown the neofascist presence in a large and diverse coalition. What the Popolari want is either to form the pivot of a governing coalition or, better yet, to appear as the core around which a viable centrist governing alliance can be rebuilt. For the time being, though, they do not seem to be in any position to mount a credible challenge, and the imperatives of the new electoral system make them very vulnerable.

Elusive Stability

Again, *virtù* and *fortuna* may, at least temporarily, work for Berlusconi. So far, he has been able to mute all the intracoalitional conflicts; he even faced the scathing personal attacks of Lega Nord leader Umberto Bossi with a smile. In trying to reduce tensions, he has had the help of Gianfranco Fini, the AN's cool-headed secretary general, who behaves at all times with Anglo-Saxon phlegm. Although Fini did make the widely quoted remark that Benito Mussolini was "the greatest states-man of the century," this was not a gaffe or a mindless fulmination, but a calculated attempt to reassure the AN's neofascist militants that their past would not be betrayed.

Berlusconi's *fortuna* has both a po-litical and an economic dimension. First, his political opponents are in disarray. The Progressives are cur-rently undertaking an agonizing re-appraisal of their role and strategy, and appear almost paralyzed. There is a crisis of leadership within the PDS; Occhetto may well find himself forced out. Moreover, the left-wing deputies and senators have so far been unable even to organize a caucus, once more projecting the im-age of internal disunity. Finally, the Progressives' analysis of the short-term and long-term causes of their electoral defeat is inadequate. Leftist politicians have put too much em-phasis on Berlusconi's television ex-posure and not enough on their own inability to reach large sectors of the electorate, especially young people and northerners, with a convincing message of concrete and achievable change.

On the economic front, Berlusconi is taking office just as Western Eu-rope seems at long last to be recover-ing from a deep recession. His promises to simplify the fiscal sys-tem and cut taxes (especially on re-turns from investment) seem to have come at the optimal time. Perhaps he will even be blessed with the sponta-neous creation of many new jobs.

Even if all this turns out as well as can be expected, however, serious questions will remain about the fu-ture, the performance, and the qual-ity of Italian democracy. For the first time since the end of the Second World War, neofascist ministers will sit in the cabinet of a European democracy—a worrisome state of af-fairs that several European govern-ments and parties (alarmed by resurgent fascist groups in their own countries) have already begun to de-cry. Clearly, the political and cultural relegitimation of Italian fascism is not good news for the construction of a closer European Union. As for the performance of Italian democ-racy, it will depend on Berlusconi's ability not only to revive the market, but to reform the state. Berlusconi and most of his lieutenants are new to politics. His extensive business holdings are bound to cast a shadow over his premiership, raising the question of conflicts of interest at every turn. There will be frequent quarrels within the majority coali-tion. If political stability is a prereq-uisite for effective decision making, Italian democracy is unlikely to achieve such effectiveness in the wake of the March elections.

Yet more than governability may be at stake. Berlusconi has made it clear that he will not sell his three television networks. Whatever un-certainty lingers about the contribu-tion of Berlusconi's broadcasting empire to his electoral success, it is not at all out of place to worry about the prospect of a prime minister who owns half the mass-media system of a democratic country and whose parliamentary majority has the legal right to appoint the board that over-sees public broadcasting.

With the voting of last March, the collapse of the first Italian republic became an accomplished fact. Unfor-tunately, those who by *virtù* and *for-tuna* have inherited the political system do not as yet appear to be capable of improving either its func-tioning or the quality of its democ-racy. Italy's political transition has not yet come to an end, though it does seem to have entered a phase of socioeconomic and political restora-tion. The Italian democratic frame-work will in all likelihood prove strong enough to withstand the presence in government of some neofascists from the AN, some sep-aratists from the Lega Nord, and some unscrupulous parliamen-tarians from Forza Italia, but test it they will.

NOTE

1. For more details and a precise technical explanation of the whole package of elec-toral laws that Parliament adopted on 4 August 1993, see the chapter by Richard S. Katz in Carol Mershon and Gianfranco Pas-quino, eds., *Italian Politics: Ending the First Republic* (Boulder, Colo.: Westview Press, 1994).

Italy: The Right Break with the Past?

This year's parliamentary elections in Italy saw the dramatic emergence of an entirely new set of parties and politicians. While generally judged a healthy democratic cleansing of a sclerotic political system, the agents of change have worried some observers because of their rightist cast. "Where the lengthy process of reform will lead remains to be seen."

Douglas A. Wertman

Douglas A. Wertman *is a resource analyst at the United States Information Agency in Washington. He has coauthored two books,* Italian Christian Democracy: The Politics of Dominance *(London: Macmillan, 1989) and* U.S.–West European Relations in the Reagan Years: The Perspective of West European Publics *(London: Macmillan, 1992), and has written more than 15 book chapters and articles, mostly on Italian politics. The views expressed herein are those of the author and do not necessarily represent those of the United States Information Agency or the United States Government.*

In the half century since the end of World War II, Italy saw sweeping social, cultural, and economic changes. At the same time, little changed in the Italian political system. The party system set in place in the late 1940s remained largely the same until recently, with Italian voters facing similar choices in parliamentary elections. One party—the Christian Democratic Party—was in every postwar government and held the prime ministership for 42 of the 49 years. Various combinations of the Christian Democrats and their allies—the three small centrist parties (Republicans, Social Democrats, and Liberals) and, beginning in the early 1960s, the Socialists—ruled Italy in every government until this May.

Unlike in other western European democracies, there was never an alternation of power; the second-largest party (the Communists, renamed the Democratic Party of the Left, or PDS, in 1991) has not been in government since 1947. Within the parties there was a limited and gradual turnover of political elites. This was most true of the Christian Democrats, but the party still proved unable to reform itself despite two decades of internal debate. Italy's political institutions also remained unchanged. And there was a final constant: Italian politics over the past few decades was riddled with systematic kickbacks and payoffs, primarily used to finance the party organizations that have dominated the postwar scene.

Much of this has now changed. A number of new parties have been formed in recent years (most important among them the Northern League in the late 1980s and Forza Italia, or Let's Go, Italy, in 1994). The traditional governing parties have collapsed, and in a number of cases, disappeared. Three parties that never before governed Italy, two of which have come into existence only recently, have replaced the traditional governing parties. Substantial turnover of political elites has occurred, with over 80 percent of the members of Parliament newly elected in the 1990s, including 72 percent in 1994 alone. Corruption has been rooted out. Nevertheless, much has not yet changed. Apart from the electoral system, the political institutions remain the same, many of the fractious political practices continue, and the transformation of the party system is far from complete.

WHY CHANGE NOW?

Polls over the past few decades had shown substantial and growing public dissatisfaction with the way Italy was governed. Nevertheless, efforts at reform went nowhere, particularly because of the resistance from established political forces. Given that so little change had taken place for nearly a half century, the fundamental question is why real change in the system has finally begun in the 1990s.

First, the end of the cold war helped shake the foundations of Italy's postwar political structure. The cold war divisions had served as a major defining characteristic of the Italian party system, and anticommunism was a key source of Christian Democratic support. Corruption and inefficiency were long tolerated by many nonleft voters because they believed them a necessary evil in protecting from communism Italy's place in the Western security and economic framework. The end of the cold war did not necessarily mean that the left would gain power, but it did mean that the lock on power of the parties that had governed Italy was no longer secure.

Second, by the early 1990s there was deep and increasing disenchantment with a political system and governing parties unable to bring about institutional reform or to deal effectively with organized crime, poor public services, and longstanding economic problems such as double-digit unemployment, a budget deficit, and a huge national debt.

Then, the ongoing and spreading investigations into the massive public corruption even further discredited the established parties and created deep popular resentment against the ruling elites. More than 6,000 politicians, bureaucrats, and businessmen had either been charged or were under investigation as of the middle of this year. While it had been assumed that political corruption was common, these investigations revealed that it was much greater than expected. The prosecuting magistrates, who staked out their independence from political control from the beginning, have been major protagonists of Italy's political change.

The pressure for reform has accelerated greatly with the growth of movements willing to tap popular discontent directly through the use of the referendum as a tool for institutional change, thereby circumventing Parliament and established parties. Referendums in June 1991 and April 1993 relating to the electoral system, long the central issue in the debate over reform of Italy's political institutions, demonstrated the broad public support for change.

Finally, for the first time in northern Italy in the 1992 elections and throughout the country in the 1994 elections, nonleft voters were given real alternatives to the established parties. These included new parties such as the Northern League and Forza Italia, and an old alternative that has become more acceptable to sizeable numbers of conservative voters—the National Alliance/Italian Social Movement. These alternatives, not coincidentally, developed at the very time that Italy's governing parties were in deep crisis.

THE BEGINNINGS OF CHANGE

The last few years have been marked by one dramatic political development after another in Italy. The first major signal of the greatly increased desire for change was the June 1991 referendum. Nearly 96 percent of those voting supported the reform movement's initiative to switch from multiple-to-single-preference votes in elections for the Chamber of Deputies, Parliament's lower house, despite the opposition of many party leaders. Even though this was a relatively minor aspect of the electoral system, 63 percent of eligible Italians voted in the referendum. The importance of the balloting lay not in the particular modification of the electoral system but in the sweeping popular support for change.

Next, the "clean hands" investigations by Italy's judiciary came before the public's eye in February 1992 with the arrest in Milan of Mario Chiesa, a Socialist involved in a kickback scheme. These investigations had only a limited impact on the April 1992 elections, in part because Antonio Di Pietro, the most prominent magistrate on the team, decided to go slow until after the elections to avoid being charged with

trying to influence them. The investigations have, however, had a major impact on political life since then, with the greatest number of those involved coming from the two largest long-ruling parties, the Christian Democrats and the Socialists. Many former top leaders, including prime ministers, other cabinet ministers, and party secretaries, have been implicated and have left politics. Most still await trial, but some, such as former Prime Minister Bettino Craxi, have already been found guilty.

The 1992 parliamentary elections represented a vote of no confidence in the existing government majority, especially in the north. The balloting witnessed the greatest shift in individual votes since 1948. While dramatic political change did not immediately result, the elections were another key sign that the traditional politics that had so long endured were near an end. The Christian Democratic Party received an all-time low of 29.7 percent of the vote, and the Democratic Party of the Left saw its share fall 10 percent from the last elections, to just over 16 percent. The Northern League—a combination of different northern regional movements—won almost 9 percent, an enormous gain over the 1 percent won by separate leagues in a number of northern regions in 1987.

The Northern League gave northern voters the opportunity to show their discontent with the state of affairs in the country, and also gave them the chance to express their desire for greatly increased regional autonomy (generally within a federal structure, although some of its more extreme advocates and even some top leaders called for splitting Italy apart). At times the league also took on an antisouthern flavor, especially in the attacks on the way government taxation and spending redistributed substantial public resources from the north to the south, and in the claims that the Italian state, often dominated by southern politicians, was a drag on the economically dynamic north. After the league's initial successes in the 1990–1991 regional and local elections, the established parties refused to form any local coalition governments with them; this refusal to ally with them continued through the 1993 local elections.

The Italian Communist Party had been working for years to transform itself into a party considered a legitimate democratic alternative both within and outside Italy. After reaching its high point of 34.4 percent of the vote in the 1976 parliamentary elections yet failing to enter the government as part of either a leftist coalition or a grand coalition, the Communists saw their electoral strength decline to 26.6 percent by 1987. The center-left coalition government continued to remain in power in the 1980s and early 1990s, leaving the Communists largely isolated politically and unable to devise a strategy to emerge from this isolation. After Achille Occhetto became party secretary in 1988, he attempted to transform the group into a moderate, reformist party. At the same time he faced strong opposition from those who considered the link to the party's communist heritage important. When he led the party to change its name to the Democratic Party of the Left in 1991, a sizeable group from the party's leftmost wing formed Communist Renewal. The combination of the lagging transformation of the old party and the siphoning off of votes by Communist Renewal resulted in a serious defeat for the PDS in the 1992 elections.

Between the 1992 and 1994 elections there were two governments, the first from June 1992 to April 1993 and headed by Socialist Giuliano Amato, and the second taking up later that month and headed by Carlo Azegli Ciampi. Both governments marked the beginning of change even though each was based on the traditional coalition formula. The Amato government reduced the number of cabinet positions and undersecretaries, and a few posts, including the key Treasury job, went to nonpoliticians. The Ciampi government—the first government since the 1946 Constituent Assembly elections not headed by a member of Parliament—saw its chief given considerable independence in selecting his cabinet, which included eight nonpoliticians in addition to Ciampi himself.

Both governments were awarded fairly good marks by outside observers for their economic policies, including their efforts to fight Italy's budget deficit, give the Bank of Italy more independent powers in monetary policy, and push privatization of public enterprises. Ciampi also played a key role in prodding Parliament to reform the electoral system for the Chamber of Deputies. However, these two governments were largely a sideshow on the political front, as the old class of politicos lingered on.

In April 1993, 76 percent of Italians turned out to vote on eight referendums, all of which passed and most of which dealt with institutional changes, including abolishing three ministries and ending public financing for political parties. Most important by far, however, was the referendum on the electoral system for choosing the Senate, Parliament's upper house; 82 percent of those voting favored changing it. The precise proportional representation scheme used for selecting members of the Senate and the Chamber of Deputies has long been blamed by many in Italy for the proliferation of small parties and unstable governments.

Polls showed that many Italians were not well informed on the details of the electoral system, but all understood this as a vote for political change. Sponsored by the reformist movement led by Christian Democratic deputy Mario Segni, it was also important because it greatly increased the pressure on the traditional parties to change the Chamber of Deputies electoral system. After long, difficult debate Parliament in August 1993 adopted a system for the Chamber of Deputies that provided for three-quarters of the members to be chosen by plurality in single-member districts and one-quarter to be elected by proportional representation.

The reform movement also pushed for change in the electoral system used in towns and cities, and had in fact collected more than the necessary 500,000 signatures on petitions to have a referendum on the method of electing mayors also voted on in April 1993. Under pressure to avoid the referendum on this issue, Parliament adopted a new system for the direct election of mayors in communities with 15,000 or more people, with a runoff two weeks after the first round between the two candidates who received the most votes if no candidate won an absolute majority. Of key importance in such a system is the ability to form alliances with other parties.

Major local elections in June and then in November and December 1993 saw a number of significant developments. The Christian Democrats fell from the unprecedented 29.7 percent they received in the 1992 parliamentary elections to about 20 percent in the June 1993 local elections, and to only 11 percent in the November elections. In June the party lost primarily in the north, but in the November balloting it also suffered major losses in the south, where it had believed it would continue to garner support. The other traditional government parties also all did poorly in these local elections.

The left won the bulk of the mayoral seats, especially in the larger towns and cities, in both the June and the November elections because it formed broad alliances and the Christian Democrats and other parties failed to do so. While the PDS was seen as a victor in these elections because it won so many mayoral races, this was due more to its alliance strategy than to its image. The Northern League was the single most popular party in all five major northern cities where elections were held in either June or November (Genoa, Milan, Trieste, Turin, Venice), and also did well in most smaller northern cities and towns, winning many mayoral contests. However, among the five large cities it won the mayoralty only in Milan because of its inability to coalesce with other parties. The most stunning result was the success of the neofascist Italian Social Movement (MSI) in the November elections, in particular in the south. The MSI was the single biggest vote-getter in both Naples (31.2 percent) and Rome (30.9 percent), took a sizeable number of votes away from the Christian Democrats, and received many more votes than it had in any local or parliamentary election ever before.

THE RIGHT TURN TO REFORM?

By early 1994 the five traditional governing parties were in serious trouble and likely to suffer large losses in the upcoming parliamentary elections in March. The

Christian Democrats, after failing to bring about real internal reform, dissolved themselves in January and created the Italian Popular Party (PPI), a somewhat changed DC, minus many of the leaders of the past. The left looked clearly in the strongest position, based on its ability to form a coalition and the absence of any opposing coalition, and was likely to win an absolute majority. The two nonleftist parties that then appeared strongest—the Northern League and the MSI—were both expected to do well separately, but were unlikely to enter into alliances with other parties. Among a sizeable bloc of conservative voters, especially in the south, the MSI had overcome its pariah status and had become an acceptable alternative to many who had previously voted for the Christian Democrats and the small centrist parties.

Key to considerations as the balloting approached was the new electoral system. With three-quarters of the seats for each house of Parliament to be chosen by a plurality in single-member districts and only one-quarter by the old proportional representation system, building electoral alliances with other parties was crucial to winning. Silvio Berlusconi and his Forza Italia party's entrance into politics can be explained in the context of the changed electoral method and a situation in which the left appeared likely to win, the traditional governing parties were in disarray, and the two protest parties (Northern League and MSI) were expected to do well but remain isolated.

Silvio Berlusconi is one of Italy's wealthiest citizens; until entering the race this January, he headed a giant media and retail conglomerate, Fininvest. Most important, Berlusconi's group included Italy's three major private television networks as well as sizable magazine and newspaper holdings. Berlusconi was also the owner of the AC Milan professional soccer team. In preparation for a possible foray into politics, Berlusconi had put together hundreds of Forza Italia clubs throughout Italy in the last months of 1993; these were modeled on the fan clubs around the country that supported his soccer team. On January 26, just two months before the elections, Berlusconi announced his candidacy and linked this directly to the possible victory of the left, which he said had not really changed, and the inability of the center and right to come together. He began the scramble to form alliances and assemble his candidate lists and campaign.

The PPI was unwilling to ally with Berlusconi; in fact, the PPI, like its predecessor, the Christian Democratic Party, in the 1993 local elections, failed to organize any broad electoral coalition, ending up in an alliance only with Mario Segni's small centrist grouping. Berlusconi then cleverly put together the victorious alliance. By early 1994, the MSI had changed its name to the National Alliance as part of the effort of its leader, Gianfranco Fini, to modify the image of what he claimed was a new party that was no longer "neofas-

cist" but, rather, "postfascist." Fini had also added some non-MSI conservatives, including a small number of former Christian Democratic deputies, to his party.

Fini, who had fallen just short of winning in his run for mayor of Rome in the November elections, was attempting to overcome the baggage of nearly 50 years during which the MSI had been completely out of power at the national and local levels. He was trying to bring about the democratic legitimation of his party in a short time, something the Communist Party and its successor, the PDS, have not fully accomplished after several decades.

Nevertheless, Umberto Bossi, the leader of the Northern League, remained unwilling to consider teaming up with the National Alliance. Berlusconi then succeeded in forming separate alliances in the north and south—a practical move since all the Northern League's strength was in the north and most of the National Alliance's strength was in Rome and farther south. In the north, in a concession to gain Bossi's assent, Berlusconi agreed that the League would get 70 percent of the seats their alliance won; at that time, of course, Berlusconi's electoral future remained uncertain, while the Northern League had done well in elections over the previous three years. Berlusconi's party joined with the National Alliance in the south, while the National Alliance ran its own separate ticket in the north.

The 1994 elections, even more than the 1992 elections, produced enormous changes in Italy's party system. The new electoral selection method gave Berlusconi's rightist coalition a majority in the Chamber of Deputies and a near majority in the Senate. In the Chamber, the right, which won 42.9 percent of the popular vote, would have had between 280 and 290 seats under the old proportional representation system (short of the 316 needed for a majority) rather than the 372 it ended up with; in the Senate, with 39.9 percent of the vote, it would have had between 130 and 135 seats rather than the 156 it won.

The biggest winners on the right were Forza Italia and the National Alliance. Forza Italia, which did well throughout the country, won the largest share of the vote with 21 percent; its enormous success just months after its formation has no parallel in postwar Italy. The National Alliance surpassed its stunning November 1993 election results and became Italy's third-largest party, winning 13.5 percent. It gained votes in all regions, but the bulk of its strength was in Rome and the south, where it won 21.8 percent, making it the most popular single party there. The third member of the rightist coalition, the Northern League, had mixed results. Contrary to expectations in late 1993, it stayed at the same level as 1992 (8.4 percent of the vote compared to 8.7 percent); however, as a result of the electoral system and the favorable alliance agreement with Berlusconi, it actually doubled its number of seats to win slightly more than the National Alliance.

There were many big losers. As predicted, Italy's five traditional governing parties collapsed. These parties, which together had 51.5 percent of the vote and 57 percent of the seats in Parliament after the 1992 elections, dropped to under 20 percent of the vote and 10 percent of the seats in 1994. Only the PPI, which won 11.1 percent, received more than a handful of votes. The Socialist Party, running as part of the leftist alliance, won only 2.2 percent. Another loser was Mario Segni, the leader of the reformist referendum movement. Segni, heading his own political group, which ran in alliance with the PPI, garnered only 4.6 percent; during 1993 and early 1994, he had squandered his once substantial popularity with his frequent changes in strategy.

The leftist, or progressive, alliance, as it called itself, also was a major loser. The coalition received as a whole only as large a share of the vote in 1994—34.4 percent—as the Italian Communist Party had won by itself at its high point in 1976. In fact, putting together the votes for all the parties that ran as part of the progressive alliance, including the Socialists, the left dropped more than 8 percent from its 42.8 percent in 1992. The presence in the alliance of Communist Renewal, the far-left splinter from the PDS, certainly did not help in attracting former centrist or center-right voters to the progressive alliance. The PDS itself was the second-largest vote-getter, climbing to 20.4 percent from its 1992 showing of 16.1 percent, but this was small consolation for the left's crushing defeat.

Despite the shortest time between elections since the 1940s, the 1994 election produced the greatest changes in Italy's postwar political history. The right's victory can be traced to several factors. First, many Italians voted for a clean break with the past. The three parties of the rightist coalition grabbed the sense of something new. Despite his past ties to Prime Minister Bettino Craxi, Berlusconi was perceived by many voters as something new. His innovative campaign techniques, in particular the massive use of his three television networks during the campaign, furthered this image and played a key role in the success of Forza Italia. Second, while many do not have the same fear of communism they once did, most former Christian Democrat and center/center-right voters found it difficult to break habits after many years of anticommunist voting and were unwilling to vote for the left. Surveys found that most backers of the Christian Democrats and the small centrist parties who did not stick with their old party shifted to one of the parties of the rightist coalition rather than to the left. Finally, after two governments that stressed economic austerity and sacrifice, Berlusconi presented a more upbeat economic message by promising lower taxes and a million new jobs.

CREATING A NEW GOVERNMENT

Forming the coalition government after the election did not prove easy. The results meant that no coalition without all three of the rightist parties was possible. Most of the problems were created by Bossi and the Northern League. Bossi initially said he was unwilling to support Berlusconi as prime minister; he argued that Berlusconi's media and retail empire would create serious conflicts of interest, both as a threat to Italian democracy as well as in economic terms, even though Berlusconi had given up his positions at Fininvest. Bossi also said he was unwilling to serve in a government with the National Alliance, calling into question its democratic credentials.

In addition, there were many disagreements among the coalition partners over policy issues. The most serious of these revolved around the different electoral bases and philosophies of the Northern League, which wanted a federation and attacked the redistribution of resources from north to south, and the National Alliance, which strongly supported a centralized state and the substantial government aid to the south. In the end, Bossi, undoubtedly concerned by the threat of immediate new elections for which he would be held primarily responsible, got the best bargain he could and entered the coalition. Clearly, however, many disagreements were unresolved and continue to haunt the government coalition.

The first reaction both in and outside Italy to the formation of this government was concern over the inclusion in the cabinet of five ministers from the National Alliance. While Alliance leader Fini is clearly different from members of the far right in Germany or France, there continue to be fascist elements within the party. The concerns were also fueled by a number of statements—including some praise for Mussolini—that Fini and some other National Alliance leaders made shortly after the election. The democratic legitimacy of the National Alliance remains a question over which observers disagree. Nevertheless, the government easily won a vote of confidence in the Chamber of Deputies; in the Senate, where it is a few votes short of a majority, it won with the help of a few senators for life and some PPI senators who either abstained or voted for the government.

Berlusconi had an initial honeymoon as prime minister. He was further boosted by Forza Italia's great success in the mid-June European Parliament elections. Berlusconi's image was also helped by United States President Bill Clinton's visit in early June on the fiftieth anniversary of the liberation of Rome and the good publicity he received in Italy as chairman of the Group of Seven summit in Naples in early July. This honeymoon did not, however, last long. Continuing criticism of the conflict between Berlusconi's media and other business holdings and his role as prime minister have forced Berlusconi on the defensive and required him to name experts to draft Italy's first conflict of interest law and to pick a trustee to take over his role in Fininvest. In addition, the investigations into the scandals have created problems for Berlusconi: his brother Paolo, now under house arrest, and other top Fininvest officials have been accused of authorizing bribes to tax officials; however, no charges have been leveled at Berlusconi himself. At about the same time as these revelations, Berlusconi's government, in what it said was an action to prevent abuses of civil liberties, issued a decree abolishing preventive detention for nonviolent crimes. The law was immediately attacked by a number of the leading magistrates in the "clean hands" investigations, who said it would hamper their work and then threatened to resign; these threats, a strong public reaction, and a quick backing away from the law by Bossi and Fini, led to the decree being withdrawn after only six days.

The government is holding together thus far, but it is no more united than were previous governments. It faces major economic and other decisions likely to divide the government parties further. It will not have an easy job getting its program approved by Parliament, especially since it lacks a stable majority in the Senate.

The opposition parties, however, have at least as many, if not more, problems. The PPI, now only one-third the size of its Christian Democratic predecessor, has just gone through a divisive fight over the party secretaryship that may be difficult to heal. Achille Occhetto resigned as PDS secretary immediately after his party's mediocre results in the European Parliament elections. His replacement, Massimo D'Alema, must deal with the same problems the PDS and the left more generally have long faced, and find a political strategy that will lead to electoral victory. Gaining government power appears as difficult for the PDS today as it has over the past few decades.

Italy's political transition has begun, but it has a long way to go. Where the lengthy process of reform will lead remains to be seen. Making progress on institutional reforms, such as further changing the electoral system to eliminate the use of proportional representation, granting greater regional autonomy, strengthening the executive, or weakening the role of the Senate so that the two houses no longer have identical powers (a feature of the Italian system unique among western democracies), will be difficult. Further transformation of the party system will undoubtedly occur over the next several parliamentary elections. The investigations into Italy's past political corruption will continue to have an impact for some time. The roots of democracy, however, will remain firmly planted in Italy as the process of change, with all its fits and starts, continues.

The Fall of Berlusconi's Government

Italian Premier's Fall: Perils of Overreaching

Alan Cowell

Special to The New York Times

ROME, Dec. 23—When they come to sum up his career, the line they might reserve for Silvio Berlusconi is: He wanted it all.

Not content to follow his father into banking, he built a business empire that now stands among Italy's biggest. Unwilling to remain on the political sidelines, he became Prime Minister. And, not satisfied with high office, he moved to stamp his mark on a swath of institutions, from broadcasting to the judiciary.

Searching for reasons why Italy's grand new experiment in renewal collapsed, as it did Thursday when Mr. Berlusconi resigned, some might say its failure was inevitable because the disparate forces that formed the cumbersome coalition bore the seeds of its own, rapid destruction.

But others might argue that Mr. Berlusconi himself gave his enemies the ammunition they needed to ambush him.

The Prime Minister drew no clear line between his business and political domains, hesitating to sell companies or place his holdings in some kind of trust, thereby laying himself open to charges of conflict of interest.

Because a large part of his Fininvest business empire is rooted in three successful commercial television stations, he was vulnerable to the charge of seeking unfair advantage in the electronic stadium of modern politics, not only by using his networks to project his message, but by trying to control state television, too.

And because Fininvest is under investigation for corruption, his moves to curb the judiciary smacked too much, for

his adversaries, of an attempt to use his office to protect his investments.

"In a democracy, the phase of conquering power ends when the ballot-boxes are opened and the winner is anointed," said Ezio Mauro, a columnist for the newspaper La Stampa. "In Italy's democracy of 1994, by contrast, the conquest of power obsessed Berlusconi and his men right up to yesterday, far more than the problems of government."

Umberto Bossi, the leader of the Northern League, a nominal coalition partner, who ended up siding with the opposition against the Government, said: "Berlusconi behaves as if he has been robbed of something. But he cannot behave as if the state were his own corporation."

Mr. Berlusconi resigned after it became clear the opposition had enough votes to pass any of three no-confidence motions. President Oscar Luigi Scalfaro must now decide whether to call new elections or name someone else to try to form a government or even ask Mr. Berlusconi to patch together a new coalition.

The task of forming a new government out of this Parliament is difficult because the Northern League itself has split under the weight of its rebellion, so it is now hard to see where a new line-up might be found to command a parliamentary majority.

Mr. Scalfaro, by all accounts wants to delay elections until new electoral and antitrust laws are framed. Mr. Berlusconi wants a quick vote while he still commands the levers of power as caretaker Prime Minister.

The question, said Mino Fuccillo, a commentator in the opposition newspaper La Repubblica today, is whether the interim period is run as a "government of vendetta" by Mr. Berlusconi and

his allies, or as a "cease-fire government" by someone else.

Mr. Mauro, the columnist for La Stampa, said: "This is more than just the end of a government. This is the end of an adventure that was born to implant a new epoch, not just a ministry."

In elections in March, Mr. Berlusconi was hoisted to power on the dreams of Italians who, after the collapse of their political old guard in a miasma of corruption, seemed ready to grasp at his promises of political renewal and economic revival.

No matter that in the freewheeling 1980's, he had been closely associated with former Prime Minister Bettino Craxi, the Socialist Party leader who now lives in exile in Tunis and is regarded by many Italians as the arch-villain of the corruption scandals.

For Berlusconi, business and politics mixed.

No matter that his own brother, Paolo Berlusconi—given a five-month suspended sentence Thursday on corruption charges—was already under investigation by the anti-graft magistrates in Milan.

No matter that he aligned his Forza Italia Movement with the neo-Fascist National Alliance, which had for years remained on the fringes of Italian politics.

At that time, many Italians seemed willing to see only what they needed to see: a promise of change after the years of scandal, a home in the political center after the old political center provided by the defunct Christian Democrats collapsed.

Mr. Berlusconi stood square for the free market and liberty, and just as squarely against the former Communists who, only a year ago, seemed poised to take power.

As he addressed his invited audiences during the campaign, microphone in hand like a talk-show host or a television evangelist, oozing reassurance, he seemed the Italian dream come true. Indeed, one of his most vociferous critics called him "the great seducer, the vendor of dreams."

The initial enthusiasm carried through to European elections in June in which his Forza Italia movement won more than 30 percent of the vote, assuming the central position once occupied by the Christian Democrats.

Then things began to unravel.

With a decree in July, Mr. Berlusconi tried to curb the powers of pretrial arrest used freely by the anticorruption magistrates as they closed in on companies, including his own, accused of paying bribes and kickbacks to political parties in exchange for government contracts.

Such was the outcry from Italians that the Prime Minister backed down.

"From then on he was on the defensive," a European official said, "July was the turning-point."

But if he had already lost, he did not show it, behaving more like a corporate executive frustrated by uppity directors than a politician in trouble. He fought a bruising battle with the magistrates that sapped his authority as he sought to deny their suspicions that he had known about money paid to the tax investigators in return for favorable audits.

The fighting within the coalition between himself and Mr. Bossi grew ever more rancorous, leaving many Italians to ponder what had happened to their "revolution."

The conflict with the Milan magistrates reached such proportions that the most popular of the investigators, Antonio Di Pietro, resigned on Dec. 6, saying political maneuvering was making his work impossible. The move that further damaged Mr. Berlusconi's standing.

And when, one week later, Mr. Berlusconi himself was called before the magistrates for seven hours of interrogation, he seemed irreparably harmed, even though he insisted that the investigators had produced nothing to substantiate their suspicions that he knew about his company's payments to the tax auditors.

For all that, Mr. Berlusconi seems still to want it all. As a political campaigner, he has far greater skills of slick projection than his adversaries. Indeed, his mercurial rise and fall since he entered politics last January suggests that he is much better at winning power than holding on to it. And already, he is shaping a re-election bid around the image of himself as the hero brought low by the callow treachery of his supposed ally.

"Rightly or wrongly, he feels he could have done better, and if he didn't do better it's not really so much his fault as the fault of the situation he found and the alliances he had to make," said his spokesman, Jas Gawronski. "But he doesn't feel humiliated at all. He rather feels like running again."

Ah, Sweet Mystery,
Thy Name Is Italy

Alan Cowell

ROME

Yet another Italian government has fallen on its face, giving outsiders yet another chance to reinforce their stereotype of Italy as Europe's court jester. But that's not entirely how the Italians see it.

Since the Second World War, 52 governments have come and gone, like players on a gaudy stage, but the real business of being Italian—skirting the rules, securing advantage, making way in an untrustworthy world—has continued despite them.

While the politicians have fumbled and fallen, Italy has undergone an industrializing revolution and rebuilt itself from the ruins of war. It has molded a reputation for finely made things from Gucci shoes and Ferragamo clothes to Ferraris and spectacle frames and dental drills. It is at the forefront of style and life style.

TRUTH AND STEREOTYPE

That is why the outsiders' stereotype is only partly true. Politically, Italy is indeed slapstick. But the daily battle of getting by is deadly earnest, a fight for survival-in-comfort shot through with a melancholy perception that Italy will always do things in its own idiosyncratic way that outsiders will never accept as normal. Only the outsiders see Italy as nonstop pantomime or gaiety.

While people in other countries respect the state, the Italians construct shields around self and family, or build cartels and clubs among their associates, venturing forth to plunder the state. If that seems improbable, consider why the Mafia was born in Italy, or why all Italian big business is centered on the patriarchs of private enterprise, be it Agnelli's Fiat cars, or Pirelli's tires, Benetton's sweaters or De Benedetti's Olivetti computers, not to mention the family-run media empire of acting Prime Minister Silvio Berlusconi.

Successive governments, including Mr. Berlusconi's seven-month, just-departed administration, simply do not disrupt the nation's core, made up 57 million people with arguably the keenest sense of self-interest in the world. It has suited Italians to weaken their state by circumventing its laws: Why pay taxes when the state has been made so feeble? Why stop at stoplights when the sense of self achieves far greater satisfaction by ignoring irksome rules? Italy has more laws and regulations on its books than any other nation in Europe, but it boasts the least observance of any of them.

But it is not anarchy. Every Italian knows the other sets of rules at play in the process known as "sistemazione" (literally "fixing things up"), that network of personal relationships and favors given or received, of marriages and jobs and patronage.

Indeed, such was the effort to undermine state functions that, in the past, Italy's now-discredited political parties actually supplanted the state and took over its role as provider. Need a new street lamp? Ask the local political party boss.

That has changed, leaving Italians questing for reference points in the confused landscape of their new political order. But the basics still exist: an uncle at City Hall is worth far more than a string of qualifications. And wherever power finishes up in Italy's oft-vaunted Second Republic, is custodians can expect the same stream of supplicants. Old habits die hard.

Indeed, that creates the real crunch facing the country, even as it struggles to find its 53d government: new, international rules are coming in to play that not only threaten la dolce vita, but also introduce a new rigor that is beyond "sistemazione."

The Maastricht Treaty on European integration, for instance, tells governments how austerely they must run their economies to maintain their membership in the European Club. Italy's challenge is to find a government that recognizes this new reality and can pass on the message to its people—and make them heed it.

No one wants that to mean the end of the essential well-being that Italians have built on their carefully structured revolt against authority—what Luigi Barzini in his classic study "The Italians" 30 years ago called "the ancient ruses to defeat boredom and discipline, to forget disgrace and misfortune, to lull man's angst to sleep and comfort him in his solitude." No one, that is, wants Frankfurt-on-the-Tiber.

But, equally, many people are aware that some kind of new start is overdue. For much of this century, the Italians' curious relationship with their state had led them to the brink of—and beyond—disaster. Benito Mussolini's Fascism drew them to defeat and destruction in the Second World War. Decades of postwar rule by the Christian Democrats and their allies left them saddled with debt. And it is the source of the Italians' deepest, secret melancholy that they were co-conspirators in it all.

When Mussolini was strung up by his heels in Milan's Piazzale Loreto on April 29, 1945, wrote historian Christopher Hibbert, a man in the crowd recalled later that the mob fell silent. "It was as if we had all in those few seconds shared the realization that Il Duce was really dead at last, that he had been slaughtered without trial and that there had been a time when we would have given his dead body not insults and degradation but the honors due to a hero and prayers worthy of a saint." That is the side of the Italians that lives with defeat and deceit and compromise, with the sense that it is Italy's very pursuit of individual interests and comforts that precludes the collective grandeur they yearn for.

BEMOANING THEIR DESTINY

Mussolini quested in vain for military glory. Today's Italians desperately want to be acknowledged by their European peers as equal players in the great new European marketplace. But then the government falls, the public debt worsens, and the court jester replaces the svelte entrepreneur. It is not surprising that, for all their skills in making themselves comfortable, Italians bemoan their destiny so often and so openly.

No conversation can get far beyond the opening formalities without national self-deprecation on a huge scale. Thirty years ago, Barzini wrote that the Italian way of life "solves no problems." He continued: "It makes them worse. It would be a success of sorts if it made Italians happy. But it does not." The same is true today.

Italy Names Banker with No Party Ties New Prime Minister

Celestine Bohlen

Special to The New York Times

ROME, Jan. 13—Italy's search for a new Prime Minister ended today with the appointment of the current Treasury Minister, a nonpolitical banker with international financial credentials, to replace Silvio Berlusconi and form a government of technocrats to guide a program of fiscal and election reform through Parliament.

After three weeks of fretful negotiations, President Oscar Luigi Scalfaro named Lamberto Dini, a 63-year-old veteran of the Italian Central Bank, as his choice to try to lead Italy out of its political stalemate and to reassure jittery financial markets.

Mr. Dini, who has no political affiliation, served as Treasury Minister in the coalition led by Mr. Berlusconi, who resigned Dec. 22 after seven turbulent months in office. In his first statement, Mr. Dini said he would form a government of "technicians," who would be "free of political ties," to tackle Italy's unfinished agenda of fiscal and political reforms.

But within hours of his nomination, it was clear that a Dini Government, which must win a vote of confidence from Parliament once it is formed, will come up against the same political pressures and contradictions that were at the heart of Italy's latest crisis.

Mr. Berlusconi, who clearly intends to stay in politics, said the new government should be transitional only, put in place to pave the way for new national elections.

"Only a rapid return to the ballot box will create a coalition government that is capable of insuring full stability and political authority," the media magnate said at a news conference tonight. "Arrivederci. I am reasonably sure that mine is a brief goodbye."

Mr. Berlusconi has argued throughout the crisis that any new government should reflect the center-right forces that won Italy's last elections, in March, with his Forza Italia movement at the head. Though Mr. Dini is not a member of any political party, his presence in the outgoing government made him widely regarded as a Berlusconi man.

While Mr. Berlusconi was saying he would support Mr. Dini only as a transitional figure, Umberto Bossi of the Northern League, whose defection from Mr. Berlusconi's coalition last month precipitated the fall of his Government, was still arguing against any early elections.

"The government cannot be a limited-term government which brings the country to elections," Mr. Bossi said shortly after Mr. Dini's nomination was made public. "It would be impossible to hold national elections in June. This would lead to devastating tensions."

Gianfranco Fini, leader of the neo-Fascist National Alliance, which has remained a loyal partner in the Berlusconi coalition, said that a Dini government offered a way out of the stalemate, but that it lacked a mandate to govern for long.

"It is a reasonable solution, and it will certainly lighten the political climate," he said. "But it does not resolve the problem of the majority. The technical ministers will be but a parenthesis. Once their four-point program is enacted, they will have no further reason to exist."

Mr. Dini's appointment came one year after the resignation of another nonpolitical Prime Minister, Carlo Azeglio Ciampi, a former Central Bank Governor who led a Government for nine months at the height of the corruption scandals and pushed the first election reforms through Parliament.

Mr. Dini today committed himself to an ambitious program of reform, including a review of Italy's bloated pension system—an issue dropped by Mr. Berlusconi last fall under pressure from labor unions—and further budget cuts to tackle the country's deficit.

The Prime Minister-designate also promised a new electoral law that would complete Italy's change-over from a proportional representation system to one in which voters elect their representative directly. And, he said, legislation is needed to "discipline" the distribution of telecommunications—an issue that Mr. Berlusconi, whose Fininvest company owns three national channels, had avoided during his turn in office.

Some political observers attribute the causes of this latest political crisis to the tensions endemic to a hybrid system, which combines the old party system, which dominated Italian politics since World War II and led to a wave of corruption scandals, and the more populist politics personified by Mr. Berlusconi.

The question now is whether Mr. Dini will have the support in Parliament he needs to push through the unfinished business of political reform, and to weather protests against further cuts in social programs.

There was an immediate positive reaction to his appointment on financial and currency markets, as the value of the Italian lira stabilized after weeks of steady decline. Part of this, according to financial analysts, was a result of Mr. Dini's reputation in financial circles: he served for more than 10 years as the director general of the Bank of Italy, and before that, as an executive in the International Monetary Fund. He also earned high praise in financial circles for his handling of the budget presented this year by the Berlusconi Government.

But given the volatility of Italian politics, financial analysts were cautious in predicting his success at tackling Italy's fiscal deficits, one of the highest in Europe.

"It is essentially a caretaker government," said Peter Sullivan, an investment strategist at Merrill Lynch in London. "But it is a safe pair of hands until the next elections."

Massimiliano Casini, an Italian specialist at Robert Fleming Securities, said; "It is not going to be easy. But at least in this tricky bargaining period, which will be like a great horse-trading bazaar, there will be someone who is going to keep his eye on the deficit."

Neo-Fascists Remodel Their Party in Italy

Celestine Bohlen

Special to The New York Times

FIUGGI, Italy, Jan. 29—In the final hour of Italy's neo-Fascist party, which died here this weekend to make way for a more moderate successor, a wave of emotion swept through the delegates to a party congress. Some wept openly, others sang the old party anthem, and a few leapt on their chairs to throw out their right arms in one last demonstration of the Fascist salute.

By Saturday morning, the Italian Social Movement—a party formed in 1946 by Benito Mussolini's last followers—was gone, replaced by the National Alliance. As an embryonic umbrella organization, the Alliance passed its first test in Italy's elections last spring, with 13.5 percent of the vote.

A right-wing party joins the mainstream

"It was our family," explained Antonio Pezzella, a 46-year-old deputy from Naples, as he emerged from the congress hall Friday night with tears in his eyes. "Today, we are abandoning our fathers' house and moving into our own. Tonight, I thought of my father, and all these emotions came rushing out."

Various events conspired to give birth this weekend to the National Alliance as a full-fledged party, the first mainstream right-wing party to emerge in Italy since World War II, and one that many now consider a formidable contender in its ever-shifting political sweepstakes.

It took the political upheaval of the last few years, which began with a wave of corruption scandals and ended with the collapse of the old party system. It took Gianfranco Fini, a suave 43-year-old leader who had the diplomatic skills to build a modern party without alienating an old guard still openly nostalgic for Mussolini. Most of all, it took time— five decades, to be exact, from the time that Italy's last true Fascists were flushed from the Italian political system, leaving behind a troubled legacy that their heirs have only now been able to shake off.

"This congress was historic because after 50 years, it was able to resolve the whole Fascist question, which had been open until now," said Gennaro Malgieri, editor of Secolo d'Italia, the party newspaper.

The charter of the new party makes a commitment to democratic values, which, it says explicitly, Fascism had "trampled underfoot." It condemns racial hatred as a "form of totalitarianism," and "all forms of anti-Semitism even when they are hidden under the sheen of anti-Zionism and anti-Israeli polemic." The old anthem, "Hymn to Rome," was replaced by a new one, "Liberty."

In his closing speech to the National Alliance congress today, Mr. Fini again drew the line against any echoes of Fascism. "Nobody ever again will be able to say that the right is synonymous with nostalgia," he said. "There are no nostalgics here. The nostalgics are those who want to deny the evidence."

Not all the old "missini"—as members of the Italian Social Movement were called for the party's initials in Italian, M.S.I.—could stomach these changes. Pino Rauti, a 68-year-old "missino" stalwart, walked out of the congress Friday in protest against the changes and met today with other disaffected members to discuss the formation of a new party.

But for most of the approximately 1,600 delegates who gathered this weekend in this spa town, known for its healing waters and gentle hills, the transformation of the old party was a welcome transition that at long last would release them from the uncomfortable associations of the past.

"This will eliminate a confusion that had been forced upon us with the purpose of discrediting us," said Luigi Natali, an 80-year-old member of the Italian Senate. "We were falsely called undemocratic."

Yet the definition of the Italian right still remains nebulous for many of its members. When asked to define their beliefs, many revert to formulas that would warm the heart of the Christian right in the United States; "God, Country and Family" is the most common.

But for most delegates, the appeal of the right remains its opposition to the left. "We are the social right, and we have greater respect for the individual," said Stefano Di Magni, a 29-year-old architect from Rome. "They want a type of Communism, to make all people equal."

The biggest opportunity for the National Alliance—and its allies in the coalition that governed Italy for most of last year—comes from the widespread disgust with the political system that governed Italy since World War II. Under that system, the governing centrist party, the Christian Democrats, held onto political power through a series of compromises with the old Communist Party. The result was not only corruption, but also a state administration that became bloated, costly, inefficient and unpopular.

"The Italian system after World War II was a system that began with the center and moved to the left," said Lucio Colletti, a noted Marxist philosopher at the University of Rome. "The crisis of the public deficit, of high taxes and bad services has freed up a public opinion that is favorable to the right, as long as it is liberal and constitutional."

A more moderate stance for Mussolini's heirs.

As a member of Silvio Berlusconi's Freedom Alliance, which won Italy's elections last spring and governed the country for seven months, the National Alliance, which includes some other small parties on the right, has already succeeded on a national scale. On the eve of the congress, some polls indicated that as many as 17.5 percent of voters supported it—more than triple the roughly 5 percent the Italian Social Movement used to win in pre-1994 elections.

The National Alliance continues to have its troublesome elements. Most of the "missini" who were giving the Fascist salute on Friday were members of the new party by Saturday. But many observers are convinced that the lure of future political victories will prove stronger than any tugs to the past.

"Sentiments have little to do with politics," Mr. Malgieri said. "The Italian right wants to work in an environment with values that are shared by everybody."

Mirko Tremaglia, a former hardliner who has embraced the new party, said: "We are not dying. We are alive and we want to win."

Italy's Spaghetti Politics Untangle Strand at a Time

Richard L. Wentworth
Special to The Christian Science Monitor

ROME

IN his office in the heart of Rome, Mario Segni keeps a huge photograph of téns of thousands of the politician's supporters in a Roman sports arena.

People came from all over Italy to hear the message of Mr. Segni, a deputy of Parliament, that it was time for Italy to create a bipolar electoral system to give Italy more stable governments.

When Segni's proposal was put to the nation as a referendum question in 1993, 4 out of 5 Italians approved it.

"The referendum has deeply changed the culture of the Italians, their behavior, their conception of politics," Segni says. "The Italians are more bipolar than the law that we made."

Italians used to vote for a dozen or so political parties, which then argued over who would be prime minister, which parties would go into the ruling coalition, and what their government program would be.

In the next elections, however, voters will likely be choosing between two leaders: ex-Prime Minister Silvio Berlusconi on the center-right and economist Romano Prodi on the center-left.

"It's the first time that there are two candidates, one on the right, one on the left," says Segni, a political moderate who supports Mr. Prodi.

The electoral law that Parliament approved following the referendum throws a bone to those people nostalgic for the frag-

DAVE HERRING – STAFF

The Parties of Italy

Each of the 18 parties has representatives in the Chamber of Deputies. In the next election, these often fractious parties may coalesce into left-right blocs, effectively creating a two-party system.

Christian Democratic Center

Cristiano-Sociali

Communist Refoundation

Democratic Alliance

Democratic Party Of the Left

Forza Italia

Greens

Italian Popular Party

Italian Socialists

La Rete

Lista Cito

Lista Pannella

National Alliance

Northern League

Patto Segni

Unione Di Centro

Unione Valdotaine

Sudtiroler Volkspartei

mented political spectrum by leaving one-fourth of the parliamentary seats under the old Italian system.

But the rest are elected under a British-style system, which strongly encourages the parties "to be either here or there," as Italians like to put it.

"Anything that's under 50 percent loses, by definition. Therefore, it forces the others to group together," says Giuliano Urbani, the former public administration minister in the Berlusconi government. "This is really something absolutely new in Italian political life."

The next electoral test will be soon, if Mr. Berlusconi has his way. The former prime minister and his allies are daily hammering away at a single theme: that the Italians did not elect the technocratic government of Prime Minister Lamberto Dini and that early elections must therefore be held as soon as possible, preferably in June. This appears increasingly likely to happen.

One of the four points in the Dini government's program is to create equal political access to television, a key question since Berlusconi owns three TV networks that compete directly with the three state-owned networks.

"This is really an unfair situation," says political analyst Paolo Flores D'Arcais, and it goes beyond news broadcasts. For example, he says, "the idea that you can't use an entertainment pro-

Sinking Lira Putting Italians in the Soup

ROME

SEEKING to rescue the sinking lira, Prime Minister Lamberto Dini warned lawmakers this week that opposition to his deficit-cutting plans could plunge Italy onto "an irreversible and devastating financial crisis."

"When the house is burning, you can't wait for months to put out the fire," Mr. Dini told the Senate Budget Commission.

The Italian currency has plummeted to record lows against the German mark because of fears that lawmakers may try to water down or block Dini's plans, which rely heavily on tax increases.

The lira rebounded slightly Tuesday after Dini's address. He also got a boost when the leader of the right-wing National Alliance, Gianfranco Fini, promised not to try to bring down the government over the package.

THE lira was at 1,135 to one deutsche mark in late European trading, compared with 1,143.09 to the mark on Monday.

A Senate vote on Dini's economic measures may come later this week. If it passes, the bill then moves to the lower house of parliament.

Shrinking Italy's $100 billion deficit is the main goal of Dini's month-old government, Italy's 54th since 1945. But former Premier Silvio Berlusconi has demanded elections this spring and has suggested his Forza Italia party could raise obstacles to the economic proposals.

– Associated Press

---

gram to make political propaganda is considered obvious in the States. It's not considered obvious in Italy."

The only real solution, in Mr. Flores D'Arcais's view, is for Berlusconi to sell at least two networks, which Berlusconi seems strenuously opposed to doing.

Meanwhile, with the possibility of elections around the corner, political parties are siding with Berlusconi or Prodi.

The Italian Popular Party is a key example. The successor to the Christian Democrats at first maintained that it was the true center in Italy and that other parties must move toward it.

But recently, under public pressure to choose the left or the right, party leader Rocco Buttiglione said he wanted to ally his party with Berlusconi.

The left wing of the party rebelled because Berlusconi is allied with the National Alliance, which opponents say is neofascist. The Popular Party appears on the verge of breaking up.

"The fact that this is happening means that there's a push in Italian politics at this point toward clarity, toward two alternative blocs," Segni says.

But Segni adds that these two poles are at the same time themselves becoming more moderate, so they can attract more support.

The problem is that moderation is not happening fast enough to make either side completely attractive to Italian voters.

On the extreme left, there's the Communist Refoundation, a party that gets between 5 and 10 percent of the vote.

"It's a big problem, really a big problem, because they have 5 percent, but this 5 percent is strictly necessary for the center-left to win," says Flores D'Arcais, editor of the left-wing journal MicroMega. "But this reference to this utopian communism is sufficient to frighten a crucial percentage of the Italians."

On the extreme right, there's the National Alliance, whose leader has identified himself as a "post-fascist." His party has become more moderate but . . . not enough to satisfy all of its critics.

"They don't really openly condemn fascism, the ideology, the history, the mentality and the habits, the culture of fascism," says Flores D'Arcais. "So I think it's a little dangerous to trust them so completely as Berlusconi demands the Italians do."

Former administration minister Urbani, whose family fought in the antifascist resistance during World War II, confesses that [he] was at first uneasy about being in a government with the National Alliance, but says he no longer feels uncomfortable.

"I've discovered something, that courage is needed, the courage to bet on the future and consider the past closed. And why?," he asks. "For the simple reason that to relive the past is a luxury that we can no longer afford.

"This doesn't mean, naturally, that we don't have to remain alert to the danger of radicalization of every kind," he adds. "We have to be very alert."

Japan's long march

Opaque politics has stifled the views of ordinary Japanese and produced governments incapable of tackling vested interests. Thanks to this year's electoral reform, however, a stronger democracy may be emerging

TOKYO

When Japan held its first parliamentary election in 1890, Kazuo Hatoyama was among the candidates elected. Armed with a doctorate in law from an American university, he laid down the rules for Japan's new democracy; he became speaker of the lower house, and wrote the standard manual on its procedure. Later Hatoyama's son fought to entrench Japanese democracy as well, and became prime minister in the 1950s. But the elder Hatoyama's pluralist ideals have had to wait until now, the era of his great-grandsons, to begin to be realised.

Recently Kunio Hatoyama held a party in the family home, a mansion built (fittingly) in the western style during the 1920s. Half Japan's political world was there—the half that is in opposition. For the great-grandson is part of a great scheme, to unite a dozen or so splinter groups into a single party. This would give Japan a challenger to the formidable Liberal Democratic Party (LDP), which dominates the current coalition government. It might just create the kind of stable two-party democracy that the elder Hatoyama wanted.

This would make quite a change. Until the second world war, parliamentary democracy was undermined by Japan's constitution, which laid down that the cabinet would stand above the Diet (as the parliament is known) and could ignore it on most issues. Since the war the LDP has held power almost continuously. Then, in July 1993, its fall prompted a period of flux: in the past year there have been three prime ministers, each wobbling atop squabbling multi-party coalitions. A middle way, with strong governments changing every decade or so, has so far proved elusive.

As a result, Japan's democracy has suffered. Continuous rule by a big party and chaotic rule by many small ones share one characteristic: they deprive the electorate of the chance to choose between clear sets of policies. In the absence of a policy choice, voters are swayed by white envelopes full of money. Politicians, in turn, become captive to the lobbies that supply the cash that buys the votes.

Electoral corruption has a further consequence: it lowers the standing of politicians, with the result that real power is wielded by bureaucrats. Japan's prime ministers can seldom claim a popular mandate for change, so they float passively upon the stream of briefs that gushes from the ministries. Indeed, the politicians are beholden to the bureaucrats, who grant the favours that keep the dirty money coming.

In short, Japan's political system stifles popular participation. It favours insiders (notably big firms and the well-organised farm lobby) who get government preference, often to the detriment of less-well-connected outsiders (small firms, foreign firms, consumers). Often this has absurd results: Tokyo's international airport has only one runway, because local farmers refuse to give up the paddy fields that block that airport's extension. Finally, Japan's political system makes it bad at changing direction.

For more than a decade Japan's trading partners have urged the country to deregulate the economy and let in more imports; the trade talks with America that came to a head this week were the latest chapter in this episode. Most Japanese accept that deregulation is needed, both to assuage foreigners and to boost economic efficiency. But Japan's political confusion prevents a leader from gaining the mandate needed to tackle the vested interests that obstruct market opening.

Equally, many Japanese see that a pacifist constitution adopted in the aftermath of war makes little sense now that Japan has a strong army. But muddled politics frustrates the politicians who might otherwise seek to change this. This lends an awkward tone to Japan's foreign policy. When, on September 27th, Japan formally launched its campaign to sit permanently on the United Nations Security Council, this gesture of confidence was mixed with a meek plea: Japan wants to be excused the nasty work of international peacekeeping.

1955 AND ALL THAT

A two-party system, with elections that expressed the popular will and so conferred a popular mandate, would go some way to curing this paralysis. But the politicians who gathered at Mr Hatoyama's family home know that more is needed. For, in the 1950s, the same house hosted an earlier effort to overcome Japan's political malaise by forging a new party. And though at first that effort seemed to work, it turned out to compound the problem.

The chief schemer of the time was Ichiro Hatoyama, son of the dynasty's American-educated founder. In 1955 he united Japan's two conservative parties under him, creating the LDP. This prompted two leftist parties to unite later that year, forming the Socialist Party (in 1991 the party changed its official English name to Social Democratic Party). Politics seemed to have divided neatly into two blocks, with clearly distinct visions: a pro-rearmament, pro-business group squared off against pacifists with roots in the trade unions. But the two-party system born in 1955 soon decayed into continuous LDP rule, because it was unsupported by other important measures.

One missing ingredient was electoral reform. Japan's earliest parliamentary elections resembled those of Britain today, with each electoral district choosing a single candidate. But the modernisers of the 19th century were soon alarmed by the emergence of political parties, intent on using parliament's say over the budget to control the supposedly independent cabinet.

So in 1899 a new electoral system was imposed: each constituency would henceforth return several candidates to the Diet, so that a tiny share of the vote would be enough to be elected. This encouraged splinter parties that could not have survived under the first-past-the-post system. Strong, policy-based parties suffered, just as the rulers had intended.

But now, electoral reform has been enacted. A series of corruption scandals shamed politicians into voting four reform bills through the Diet in March; a further bill, laying down the boundaries of the new electoral districts, is due to be passed in the Diet session starting on September 30th. The prime mover in this has been Ichiro Ozawa, the chief strategist of the opposition groups that met in the Hatoyama home. This is apt: in the 1950s Mr Ozawa's father supported an unsuccessful campaign for electoral reform led by Hatoyama.

The electoral-reform laws replace the multi-member constituencies with a mixture of single-member districts (there will be 300 of these) and proportional representation (which will send another 200 people to the Diet). Only the LDP, which has 200 members in the lower house, can hope to put up a candidate in all 300 single-member districts; the next biggest party, the Social Democrats, has a mere 68 lower-house members. If the LDP's opponents field multiple candidates against the LDP, they are sure to be demolished. So, although they are riven by personality splits, the guests at Mr Hatoyama's house have formed an alliance, even though this falls short of being a proper party. On September 28th they launched a parliamentary group called Renovation, which boasts 187 lower-house members.

THE SHADOW OF MEIJI

Whereas the old electoral system tended towards splintered politics, weak party leadership, and thus bureaucratic power, Japan's new system tends towards the opposite. But electoral reform on its own may not be enough to make Japan's democracy work. It is possible, instead, that the 1955 set-up went sour for lack of other preservatives. If so, Japan's current attempt to entrench democracy may fail as surely as the previous one did.

What, apart from multi-member constituencies, might have doomed the 1955 system? The most popular answer lies in Japan's political culture. The country often seems to avoid vigorous and open argument in order to preserve the appearance of consensus. Vague public debate frustrates the process by which politicians might seek and win clear popular mandates. Decisions seem to be made secretively, by people whose power to decide is not advertised in their job descriptions. Japan's cabinet ministers seem to be puppets, manipulated by unseen masters.

One school of thought traces this dissemblance far back into Japan's history. In the seven centuries to 1868, the myth of imperial rule masked the power of shoguns; and Confucian ethics stressed harmony over discussion. Then came the Meiji restoration, which launched Japan on the road to modernity. In other countries such revolutions

Japan meets the world	
1639	Japan cuts links with the outside world
1853	America demands that Japan open itself to trade
1868	Meiji restoration
1877	Takamora Saigo's rebellion against modernisation
1890	First parliamentary election
1894-95	Sino-Japanese war
1904-5	Russo-Japanese war
1910	Annexation of Korea
1923	Great Tokyo earthquake
1925	Male suffrage
1931	Japanese invasion of Manchuria
1933	Japan leaves League of Nations
1940	Tripartite pact between Japan, Germany and Italy
1941-45	Pacific war
1945	Atom bombs dropped on Hiroshima and Nagasaki
1945-52	Occupation of Japan by allied forces
1946	New, American-designed constitution promulgated
1951	US-Japan security treaty signed
1955	Formation of Liberal Democratic Party and Socialist Party
1993	Fall of LDP
1994	LDP regains power in coalition

have been conducted in the name of political ideas: republicanism, democracy, socialism. But in Japan the revolutionaries masked their scheme to westernise Japan by claiming that they wished to "expel the barbarians". And, although they were bent on destroying feudal hierarchy, their other slogan was "honour the emperor".

The Meiji leaders' traditionalist slogans place them in a different era: in feudal Europe rebels called for the restoration of a bygone age, rather than philosophising about the ideal society of the future. This is no coincidence: until 1868 Japan, too, was feudal. Status derived from land and caste, both of which were inherited; there was little in the way of an educated meritocracy to feed a democratic culture.

From the Meiji restoration Japan started to catch up. New ideas were imported from America and Europe. Realising the importance of education to his pluralist ideals, the elder Hatoyama helped to found Waseda, a school for politicians that is now one of Japan's most prestigious universities. But the Meiji clique was more interested in industrial might than pluralism. As a result, schools taught pupils what to think, not how to think; universities mostly trained people to serve industrialisation as scientists and civil servants. When it came to drafting a constitution, the reformers chose authoritarian Germany as the model.

According to the historical explanation for Japan's weak democracy, then, pluralism has never taken root because of modern Japan's anti-democratic origins. The Americans tried to impose liberalism on Japan after the second world war, but within a decade Japan's antidemocratic tendencies had reasserted themselves.

Even today, the shadow of the Meiji past is visible. Like the Meiji clique before them, today's senior civil servants regard fiscal or foreign policy as technical matters for experts to decide, not as the stuff of democratic discussion. The bureaucrats that head each ministry are called "vice-ministers", a term coined in Meiji times to underscore their importance relative to politicians.

Meanwhile, politicians justify corrupt behaviour in terms designed to recall the old Japan: *giri ninjo*—the loyalty and sympathy that bind faction members to their boss—is presented as a virtue higher than loyalty to policy. Bureaucrats who resist deregulation, even though they know it would serve the interests of Japan, invoke the name of Takamori Saigo—a revealing choice of hero. Saigo helped to instigate the Meiji Restoration's modernising reforms, but later felt obliged to side with fellow samurai from his region who revolted against the loss of feudal privilege. Saigo represents the triumph of loyalty over political ideas. Since its appearance in 1975, a series of books about him has sold 8.4m copies.

CULTURE, PART TWO

History naturally shapes a country's ideas; but it is extreme to argue that modern Japan is captive to the events of the past century. Germany's past authoritarianism, after all, has given way to exemplary democracy. Yet the historical explanation for Japan's weak pluralism does not stop here. A second school of thought sees its roots in America's post-war occupation policies.

The central charge against America is that, by taking the big post-war decisions itself, it prevented the Japanese from debating how their country should be rebuilt. It was this kind of post-war debate, after all, that launched western Germany on the democratic road; the country's Basic Law, which entrenches freedom and guards against concentrated power, was conceived and written by German jurists. Because this had not been imposed from outside, the country embraced it with a passion.

The Japanese were not allowed to do the same. The Americans occupied Japan from 1945 to 1952, and for these seven years Japanese politicians were their puppets. In 1945 Prince Fumimaro Konoe, a former prime minister (and grandfather of one of today's reformists, Morihiro Hosokawa), tried to revise Japan's constitution in a way that would appease America's liberal ideas; he committed suicide after his efforts were rejected.

As to foreign policy, the Americans ensured that Japan would remain only half-sovereign even after the occupation was over. This was achieved partly by means of the new constitution that the Americans drafted. Its ninth article laid down that Japan renounce the use of force abroad; it therefore made Japan dependent on America's armed forces.

In 1951 Japan's dependency was formalised in the two countries' security treaty, which gave America near sovereign rights over its military bases on Japanese territory. The treaty empowered America to veto a third power's military presence in Japan, and even to intervene in Japanese affairs to stem domestic disorder. Again, the Japanese had no say in this. The treaty's contents were secret until after it was signed, making public debate impossible.

In the post-occupation years, Ichiro Hatoyama resented the slight to Japan's sovereignty imposed by the constitution's pacifist clause, and tried to revise it. As with electoral reform, he lacked the parliamentary strength to achieve this. Half a century later Japan has potentially one of the strongest armies in the world, and small bits of it have done non-combatant jobs for UN peacekeeping missions. But the constitution has still not been revised; the military build-up has been made possible by its tortuous reinterpretation.

As with the Meiji legacy, the effects of the American occupation can still be seen. Sophistry over the pacifist clause in Japan's constitution adds to the vagueness of Japan's political discussion. Foreign policy is still affected, too: if war broke out in the Korean peninsula, for example, Japan could not help to control the mess, since the constitution forbids it to use force beyond its own borders. Whereas foreign crises sometimes strengthen the leaders of other democratic states, Japan's politicians are nearly always humbled by them.

A QUICK CHANGE?

But, as with the Meiji legacy again, the American occupation's influence does not seem insurmountable. Defence dependency discourages the emergence of strong political leadership, just as the books about Takamori Saigo discourage principle in politics. But strong leadership is not impossible: in the mid 1980s, for example, the succession of fleeting prime ministerships was interrupted by the five-year rule of Yasuhiro Nakasone. Given a sufficiently hard shove, Japan's political culture could change rather quickly.

Japan has already had a taste of this, when last year's election toppled the LDP from government. Television discussions on politics had suddenly been worth watching: for a change, the outcome of the election had been uncertain. The LDP's opponents used the media to woo voters in a manner shocking to the old guard, for whom politics meant deals in backrooms. Very soon, however, the LDP had caught on, wheeling out its younger and more telegenic men to face the television cameras.

The prime minister who emerged from that campaign, Morihiro Hosokawa, enjoyed the closest thing Japan had seen to a popular mandate. His opinion poll ratings rose to around 70%, three times higher than those of his LDP predecessor. He appeared on television to explain his policies to ordinary Japanese, so distancing himself from the old guard whose power had been bought with dirty money. And Mr Hosokawa's popularity yielded a lasting result: he and his allies used it to push electoral reform through parliament.

This achievement guarantees that Japan's old political culture will suffer more knocks. Electoral reform is driving the opposition parties together, making it likely that Japan will have two big political camps, each capable of winning power. This promises more televised debate, and a new chance for a leader to emerge with popular backing. The next election, or perhaps the one after that, may be won by the opposition men who met at Mr Hatoyama's house. If so, yet more change may follow.

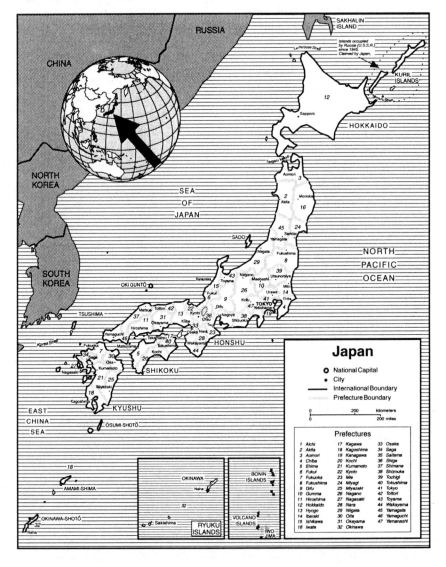

Uncertainty Shuffles the Deck in Japanese Politics

Predictability has dissolved along with the domination of a single party.

Sam Jameson

Times *Staff Writer*

TOKYO—The rule of thumb that once applied to Japanese prospects—political control by a single party that would preside over an ever-prospering economy—has disappeared. And no new guidepost has appeared.

Politics has been turned on its head. Total uncertainty has replaced virtual predictability.

The turmoil, combined with burgeoning growth in Asia and the end of the Cold War, also has contributed to snarled trade negotiations with the United States and a reduced importance placed both on ties with Washington and on the U.S.–Japan Security Treaty that permits U.S. bases in Japan. Yet no new geopolitical visions are emerging.

Suddenly, an economy in which setbacks had always been cyclical, and eventual return to long-range growth a foregone conclusion, now appears unpredictable.

What economist Isamu Miyazaki called "the biggest, longest and broadest" recession in post–World War II history—a reaction to Japan's rocketing "bubble economy" of the late 1980s—has sent corporate profits, stocks and land prices plummeting, staggered banks with bad loans, raised the specter of growing unemployment, reversed investment from boom to bust and resisted $300 billion worth of government pump-priming.

Only one familiar element remains: Japan's trade surpluses and growing exports, spurred on by the recession at home even as Japan's stronger yen cuts into trade profits.

Yesterday's unthinkable—a Socialist prime minister—has become today's reality.

"It was as if an east German had been named chancellor of Germany," an astonished former Prime Minister Morihiro Hosokawa said when Tomiichi Murayama was elected June 29. The August, 1993, election of Hosokawa, head of a fledgling, 15-month-old political party, had itself been only slightly less astonishing.

Within the last 13 months, a country that had not ousted the Liberal Democratic Party as its single ruling party for 38 years has seen two changes of government, the ouster of three prime ministers and the sharing of power by 11 political parties. Former archrivals—the Socialists, who suffered their worst defeat in the last election and may not survive the next, and the Liberal Democrats—now rule the country together.

Reforms unattainable under stability were carried out amid instability.

The most sweeping overhaul of the political system since the postwar U.S. occupation, to be completed this fall, will

JAPAN: Politics and Economics

Seats

In the lower house of Parliament, which elects the prime minister:

Party	1/21/93	Current
Liberal Democrats	274	200
Socialists	140	73
Komei Party	46	52
Communists	16	15
Democratic Socialists	13	19
Japan New Party	-	33
Renewal Party	-	62
New Party Harbinger	-	21
Freedom Party	-	7
New Future Party	-	5
Reform Assn.	-	4
Koshi Assn.	-	6
Unaffiliated	8	12
Vacant	15	2
TOTAL	512	511

Note: The number of seats in the lower house was reduced by one in a July, 1993, election. Parties listed as holding no seats in 1993 all came into existence shortly before or after the July, 1993, election.

Gross national product

For calendar years:

Trillions of yen

Real growth

Source: Official Japanese reports

A Fallen Premier Reflects Upon Japan's Year of Tumult

Sam Jameson
Times *Staff Writer*

In an interview with The Times, Kiichi Miyazawa, the first of three prime ministers to be ousted in the past year of political tumult in Japan, gave his views on developments in his country:

On a diminishing sense of urgency in Japan about economic frictions with the United States:

"We've made all sorts of efforts for countless years, but our surplus with America hasn't gone down at all. We've come to a kind of resignation, a feeling of giving up hope. . . . There also has been a reaction in Japan to [the Clinton Administration's] harsh approach. And . . . leadership in taking up this problem directly at the top level has disappeared in Japan. . . . Concern has fallen."

On Japan's trade surplus with the United States:

"During the last 20 years, exports from Japan have been 'built into' American society—not just consumer goods but capital goods—even into [defense] sectors. A part of the two nations' economies has been integrated."

On security policy:

"[Japan] doesn't have any inclination to become a military power or to change the constitution. Therefore, the framework for Japan's security into the 21st Century is the U.S.–Japan Security Treaty structure as a stabilizer for all of Asia. . . . What Asian countries, including Japan, are most worried about in the 21st Century is the direction China will take. The American presence is very important."

On sending noncombat troops on U.N. peacekeeping missions:

For decades Japan paid no attention to "whatever happened overseas, and we got fat doing that. The Gulf War forced us to go through great soul-searching. We gave money—$13 billion. But we didn't even shed perspiration." Condemnation of that hurt. Japanese concluded they "probably should have perspired" to give something beyond money but aren't prepared "to shed blood, whatever the cause."

On why $300 billion in government pump-priming has not yet resuscitated the economy:

"The economy was swallowed up . . . in a black hole [of deflation]. . . . Everyone misread the depth of the black hole. I too misread it."

On bad debts that have crippled banks:

"The fact that banks couldn't fulfill their normal function really hurt the economy. . . . Money, which is the blood of the economy, didn't flow smoothly. . . . I offered a government rescue to the banks." But they rejected it. They feared if they accepted taxpayers' money, the government inevitably would "start meddling in their business."

On the future of the economy:

"Downsizing has come to Japan. But while Japan too must do restructuring, its labor customs—lifetime employment, seniority—have many merits. Managers won't easily mimic the United States. . . . This has been a terrible recession, but Japan's potential has not been uprooted."

On economic reform:

"What Japan has learned through this recession is cost-consciousness. . . . Reforms will emerge from what recently has been called the 'destruction of price structures.' But deregulation can only occur slowly. . . . Japan is a safe society because government protection has been broadly extended. It's a regulated society."

On political and economic turmoil:

"It's appealing to try to see change in the economy in parallel with politics, and then conclude that both are in a terrible mess—a shambles. . . . [But] what has happened [in the last year] is proof that changing cabinets ceaselessly is not a change. We must wait until an election is carried out under the single-seat districts to see what will happen."

On efforts by the opposition to form a new conservative party to oppose Miyazawa's Liberal Democratic Party (LDP):

"I don't think the Renewal party [of former Prime Minister Tsutomu Hata] and that bunch . . . will be able to build a substantial, consistent platform that is different from ours. I am very skeptical that politics will develop into a confrontation between two big conservative parties. If it does, it would develop into a battle over revising the constitution. That would be a misfortune."

On Prime Minister Tomiichi Murayama abandoning 40 years of Socialist ideological policies:

"I don't think the Socialists have lost their function. We conservatives will support a market economy, smaller government, deregulation. But a market economy has its faults. There is a need for a party that speaks out for weaker people who lose out in competition . . . and other problems, like environmental issues, social welfare."

On voters' attitudes:

"The LDP was viewed as tainted, rotten. [Former Prime Minister Morihiro] Hosokawa didn't have that image at the beginning, and people saw him as a change after more than 30 years of LDP rule. . . . [Now] most voters are apathetic about politics. There's no crisis facing Japan from the outside. Despite the recession, no layoffs have occurred. People don't face a bad situation in their daily lives. So they have little interest in politics."

slash the disproportionate electoral clout of farmers by about a third. It also will plunge the country into the unknown when the next ballot for the lower house of Parliament is held. The possible post-election scenarios for change are many.

In an ideal development envisioned by former Defense Minister Kazuo Aichi, politics would revolve around two large parties. Representatives would vote on bills as they do in the United States—largely by individual decision, not mandatory party dictates. Yet voters in new single-seat districts would cast ballots with the aim of making their candidate's party leader the next prime minister, like the British parliamentary system, he said.

Policies, and not the pork barrel, would highlight campaigns, said Aichi, a policymaker in the opposition Renewal Party, which staged a mass defection in June, 1993, to deprive the Liberal Democrats of their historic majority in the powerful lower house.

But another scenario, though remote, would see conservatives regrouping, making the LDP a bigger monolith than before, Aichi acknowledged. Already, one band of LDP defectors, the splinter New Party Harbinger, has rejoined the Liberal Democrats as a junior partner in the coalition.

"Right now, the LDP is halfway back into power," said former Prime Minister Kiichi Miyazawa.

An old confrontation that perennially dogged Japanese defense policy disappeared as Murayama scrapped his Socialist Party's bedrock insistence on dismantling the nation's 240,000-strong armed forces and abolishing its security treaty with the United States.

Yet military experts like Seiki Nishihiro, a former vice defense minister, worry about a "hollowing out" of support for the U.S.-Japan Security Treaty on both sides of the Pacific.

He said that with the Soviet threat gone, some Americans are asking, "Why do we need Japan?" Similarly, some Japanese are asking, "Why do we need the U.S. bases in Japan?"

LDP politicians in Okinawa, where 75% of the U.S. bases are located, in July started advocating abolition of all American military facilities there in a bid to curry favor with voters on the southern island. But party headquarters in Tokyo, led by Foreign Minister Yohei Kono, has said nothing opposing U.S. bases in Japan.

Although President Clinton and Murayama affirmed the importance of the U.S.-Japan Security Treaty in July—as leaders of the two countries always have done—neither they nor any other top official has bothered to explain why the treaty is still important, Nishihiro complained.

To Japanese defense experts, the importance is to ensure that the United States retains a military presence in Asia as a "balancer," Nishihiro said. "Japan abandoned its World War II goal of seeking hegemony in Asia. But that does not mean it wants China or Russia to assume hegemony."

Murayama's turnabout included acceptance of dispatching troops overseas to participate in humanitarian and noncombat U.N. pacekeeping missions—a move his party opposed vociferously only two years ago. But other than pledging to work for disarmament, the prime minister has offered no vision for a new security policy.

And now that America's relative economic importance to Japan is dwindling in proportion to growth in Asia, where Japan's trade surplus now exceeds its black ink with the United States, U.S.-Japan trade disputes that once caused alarm in Tokyo draw far less attention from both prime ministers and the press.

"The 21st Century will be China's century—and Japan's foreign policy will revolve on the dual axis of Japan–U.S. relations and Japan–China relations," said Kosuke Ito, a member of the Liberal Democrats' policy board.

Previously, the United States was cited as the only axis of Japan's diplomacy.

The choice of Murayama as prime minister and his policy flip-flop, which proved that even the wildest of presumably inconceivable events was possible, wiped out the credibility of political forecasting in Tokyo. "So much has changed that we don't know which precedents mean anything for the future," said an American political analyst, who asked not to be named.

Policy differences that remain—such as whether to do as much, or as little, as possible, to help solve international disputes—now divide individual politicians more than party lines. Doves and hawks roost across the spectrum.

"Can't Find an Axle for Political Confrontation," an Asahi headline said of the new political structure.

New political jokes have emerged. An example: "To a Japanese politician, policy is like a subway station. You only stand on the platform until the train comes in."

Koichi Kato, a rising star in the Liberal Democrat ranks, predicted that Japan would be ruled by coalition governments for at least five, and possibly 10, years.

Minoru Morita, a respected political commentator, said an expected Socialist debacle in an upper house election next July could mark the end of the present government.

The Socialists' alliance with the Liberal Democrats will deprive the party of the large number of anti-LDP protest votes it once received, said Katsumi Samata, who served 35 years as a Socialist staff member.

And now that Murayama has wiped out the old doctrine, Socialists are likely to lose the party's ideologues as well, he pointed out.

"Murayama is being called the 'chairman of the Socialists' funeral committee'—in charge of burying the party," Samata said.

Political analysts, however, are making few other predictions. They confess they are not even sure what groups will run in the next lower house election. Already defections, feuds and shifting alliances have created a new political map splotched with 17 political parties and "associations." The Liberal Democrats, for

Japan's Defense Budget
For fiscal years:

	Yen amount (in trillions)	Dollar amount (in billions)
1983	2.8	$11.7
1984	2.9	12.0
1985	3.1	14.2
1986	3.3	20.9
1987	3.5	25.4
1988	3.7	28.8
1989	3.9	27.4
1990	4.2	29.4
1991	4.4	32.9
1992	4.6	36.5
1993	4.6	43.0
1994	4.7	46.8
1995*	4.7	47.3

*Projected Source: Japan Defense Agency

example, have lost nearly a third of the seats they held in 1993 through defections alone.

In 1989, Takeo Tanaka, who runs a children's clothing store in the Kameari section of Tokyo, was enraged by LDP politicians pocketing windfall profits from capital gains in a stock-for-favors scandal even as they imposed a consumption tax on daily necessities of the Japanese people. And his opinion of politicians hasn't changed today as politicians debate increasing the consumption-tax rate.

"Before raising the tax, why don't politicians reform government to cut expenses and set a model themselves?" he complained. "In Japan, as soon as you become a politician, you become rich."

Polls show once again that the political party favored by the biggest plurality is "none of the above."

Average Japanese, nonetheless, consistently express high levels of satisfaction with their living standards. Nearly 90% of families consider themselves middle class. And despite astronomical costs of housing, nearly two-thirds of Japanese are satisfied with their present living conditions, a poll by the prime minister's office showed in August.

Indeed, 60% of families own their own living unit.

Despite the political turmoil and the economic recession, "most people don't have a sense of crisis. They aren't worried about their livelihoods," said Ryoko Yamaguchi, a therapist.

"In our family, our biggest concern is whether our son [who is 22 and will graduate from college next March] will get a job or not. He's not worried. If he doesn't find a job, he says he'll support himself for a year doing part-time work, and try again next year. And he is telling us: 'Don't worry. I won't impose on you,' " she said.

The recession, nonetheless, is making consumers more cautious.

"People who used to think that using things and throwing them away after a while was fine are now trying to conserve goods. The feeling that money will keep flowing in is gone," Yamaguchi said.

Shopkeeper Tanaka has felt the impact directly.

"Fifteen or 16 [neighboring] shops have closed, and it's the same in every neighborhood," he said. But the villain is only partially the recession, which he said "has tightened the purse strings of consumers."

The bigger blow, he said, has come from revisions of the Large Retail Store Law that were carried out at the insistence of the George Bush Administration on the theory that large stores handle more imports than mom-and-pop shops.

Government restrictions on the hours and the number of days that department stores and supermarkets can operate have been eased, squeezing the shop sector, Tanaka complained. "It's now useless to oppose the opening of new large stores," he added. "The law may as well have been repealed."

Hosokawa succeeded in putting deregulation—the easing and removal of government restrictions on business—near the top of the political agenda, said economist Miyazaki, a former vice minister of the government's Economic Planning Agency who now heads the Daiwa Research Institute. "Nowadays, *kisei kanwa* [easing of restrictions] appears everywhere in government reports," he said.

Hideo Ishihara, chairman of Goldman Sachs Japan, added, "For the first time in history, we are re-examining and reappraising our system on our own, without being forced to do so by Americans." But he also said he was "not optimistic about deregulation because so many people have their vested interests and livelihood at stake."

Despite the political upheaval of the last year, very little change has occurred in daily life, he noted.

The common denominator today is uncertainty. Although the Economic Planning Agency declared last week that the economy has taken a turn toward "moderate recovery," pessimism remains widespread.

"Capital markets play the role of a heart which pumps blood to the economy. Just as a politician with a weak heart cannot become a top-class statesman, an economy with a weak heart cannot become top class in the world. Right now, [capital markets] are not functioning. the surgeon is trying to make up his mind whether to prescribe medication or conduct a major surgery," said Hideo Sakamaki, president of Nomura Securities.

Kenneth S. Courtis, strategist and senior economist for Deutsche Bank Capital Markets Asia, said bad debts held by banks "represent a massive negative for the entire economy" that make it "problematic for the economy to expand anytime soon." And without domestic growth to pull in imports, Japan's trade surpluses for the decade of the 1990s could reach $1 trillion, he warned.

Corporate income has plunged by more than 50%, driving volume on the stagnant Tokyo Stock Market down to a quarter of its peak and sending prices plummeting to barely half their previous level, said Sakamaki, the Nomura Securities president.

"Six times the central discount rate has been lowered. Three overall economic [pump-priming] packages have been announced. But the economy still hasn't taken off," he said.

Miyazaki also said he was confounded by the failure of the pump-priming packages to make an impact on the economy.

"Where has all that money gone?" he asked. "It's not clear."

"The economy that emerges from the recession will be—and must be—completely different from the one that existed before the recession," Miyazaki said.

Already, even with no increase in domestic demand, labor-intensive manufactured imports from neighboring Asian nations are increasing, he noted. Yen appreciation, in effect, is forcing Japan to "import labor" indirectly to cut costs, and that trend will be a feature of the "new economy," he insisted.

As a result, Japan will face, for the first time, "jobless growth," or an economy in which the GNP rises by an annual 3.5% or more without producing new jobs. Unemployment, he said, is likely to become a new issue for the country.

Japanese Politics Meander Nowhere

New opposition party hopes to steer a country unsure of its future but happy with status quo

Cameron W. Barr

Staff writer of The Christian Science Monitor

TOKYO

More than at any time since the end of post-war US occupation, Japan is adrift.

The Japanese have achieved their goal of prosperity, but now their economy has problems they seem unable to fix. The political system that guided them for the past four decades has been in gradual collapse for more than a year, giving way to confusion and an effluence of rhetoric that inspires little enthusiasm.

Left standing is Japan's mighty bureaucracy, the officials who have shepherded the growth of the economy and the evolution of a stable society.

Many here are convinced that these bureaucrats stand between Japan and its future, but acting on that conviction is another matter.

Tatsuya Miyamoto, a student at Tokyo's prestigious Keio University, puts it plainly: "In Japan today there is a lack of destiny. . . . We have to wait for new people with new ideas to come out. We need a new system."

A group of politicians is trying to meet that challenge. Tomorrow, 216 opposition members of Japan's national legislature, the Diet, will launch the New Frontier Party.

The New Frontier Party (NFP)—known in Japanese as Shin Shinto—is being inaugurated with a glitz and media flair that is new to Japanese politics. Organizers have styled the event as the third great opening of Japan (the arrival

of Commodore Matthew Perry in 1853 and the period of United States control following World War II are said to be the others) and the first the Japanese have undertaken themselves. To emphasize the point, the event is being held in the port city of Yokohama, near Tokyo, and a nautical motif is planned. The party's logo is supposed to represent a ship's steering wheel.

NEW PROMISES

These politicians have so far been divided among nine fractious parties, but they promise that the new group will not be rent by internal division and vow to press for national elections. Analysts here believe they could force a vote as early as next spring.

The NFP will then try to defeat the unlikely coalition that has ruled the country since the end of June. The current government is led by a Socialist, Prime Minister Tomiichi Murayama, but the real power lies with the Liberal Democratic Party (LDP), whose members hold 201 of the 294 seats in the coalition. (The Diet's powerful lower house, which elects the prime minister, has 511 seats.)

The LDP alone ran the country from 1955 until an election held in July 1993, when they lost their parliamentary majority. That led to two non-LDP coalition governments that were unified only in their opposition to the conservative, collusive, pro-business politics that LDP rule symbolized.

The LDP again became a governing party this summer by uniting with the

Social Democratic Party of Japan (SDPJ), which opposed them so stridently during the post-war years. The association has caused the Socialists to abandon many longheld SDPJ policies, such as its insistence that Japan's military was not constitutional.

Realizing that voters have not been impressed by their rapid ideological backtracking, some SDPJ members want to remake the party, which could result in a large defection possibly to a third party. That could bring down the government and lead the way to national elections even without any agitation from the opposition.

Amid all of this political gamesmanship, there is growing consensus on the key question that Japan faces. Many people recognize the sense of rootlessness—"We have to find a new energy and a new elan, otherwise we will gradually decline," says Yuriko Koike, a Diet member and NFP spokeswoman—and argue for drastic change.

Political analyst Minoru Morita frames the issue this way: Is Japan to remain a closed society with a big government, or become an open society with a small government? The task at hand is what is known here as "administrative reform"—decentralizing power, loosening regulations on business, and giving politicians greater control over policy.

"Japan is full of this kind of rhetoric," notes Tokyo University political scientist Takeshi Sasaki. The issue is, he continues, who can make it happen.

One problem, Mr. Morita observes, is that neither the NFP or the LDP—the two main parliamentary forces come tomorrow—are unified in their answers to Morita's question.

LDP leaders have claimed the mantle of reform, but the party also includes many politicians loyal to the status quo.

THE MORE THINGS CHANGE. . . .

Some NFP leaders have openly pressed for the open society/small government formula, but the opposition alliance remains a divisive bunch.

It took weeks of wrangling just to decide how to choose a leader, which they finally did yesterday, electing a former LDP member and Prime Minister Toshiki Kaifu to head the party. Running the NFP political machinery as general secretary will be Ichiro Ozawa, also former LDP member.

The past lives of these two men raise another problem. Many Japanese wonder just where exactly the "new frontier" is, when the key figures in the NFP were such prominent members of the system they now purport to oppose. Polls show only tepid enthusiasm for the NFP.

The mix and match nature of the two main parties does not bode well of the cohesiveness of the NFP. "I firmly believe that another major realignment is required," Morita says.

WHAT COMFORTS JAPANESE

There is also no clear indication that the nation wants a radical remake of the way Japan is governed, one reason why a national election seems inevitable at this stage. A strong central government dates back to the reign of the shoguns, and it can at times be a source of comfort, as a recent instance of official intervention illustrates.

Recently a spate of shootings, including some murders, has worried many Japanese and caused commentators to wonder aloud about the erosion of the country's much-beloved "public order."

Three weeks ago the nation's top law-enforcement bureaucrat—Takaji Kunimatsu, head of the National Policy Agency—spoke up. He told police chiefs gathered for a meeting. "I would like you to plan to eradicate armed offenses completely."

In most other countries, such an order would be seen as grandiose and improbable, but in Japan it's possible to believe that concerted government action could accomplish the goal. More importantly, people here felt relieved that their government responded.

This reaction suggests why administrative reform may be difficult. "Many people in this country are still satisfied with the status quo," says Professor Sasaki. "That's the reality."

Intellectual Warfare

The reviews of James Fallows's latest book are emblematic of our complacency
about the nature and implications of Japan's economic strength

Chalmers Johnson

Chalmers Johnson is the president of the Japan Policy Research Institute, in Los Angeles, California. He is the author of many books on East Asian politics, including Japan: Who Governs?

LOOKING AT THE SUN:
The Rise of the
New East Asian Economic
and Political System

by James Fallows.
Pantheon, 517 pages,
$25.00.

THE Cold War has now been over for five years, but there's been no real change in America's military pretensions. Less than three years remains before Hong Kong, the world's third largest financial center (after New York and London), is turned over to China. The English-language business press proclaims that the U.S. economy is strong and the Japanese economy weak, even though the Japanese save just under a fifth of their national income and the Americans save next to nothing. Japan's 1993 per capita income was $36,615, as compared with the United States' $24,075; Japan's 1993 current-account surplus was $131.1 billion, while the current account deficit of the United States was $105.7 billion; and Japan's economy is starting to revive as the headquarters for the East Asian manufacturing megalopolis, while the U.S. economy still depends primarily on domestic overconsumption. It will not be long before Americans will have to start paying premium interest rates to attract foreign sav-

ings to finance their self-indulgence. And there seems not to be a single American leader devoting one iota of attention to this situation.

Kenneth Courtis, the chief strategist for the Deutsche Bank in East Asia, in a recent essay called "Before the Storm," warned that this inattention to the trend of events is highly dangerous. I believe that it is caused by the grip of vested interests perpetuating the Cold War system—a resistance to reality rivaling that of Brezhnev's Russia in its complacency and hostility to new information. There are many indications that we are artificially becalmed, trapped in the horse latitudes, and waiting for some incident to make the intrinsic situation extrinsic. Such an incident would reveal how the global balance of power has changed and how hollow our claims of being the unipolar superpower actually are.

The current drift of events suggests an extended version of France's *drôle de guerre*, which lasted from the declaration of war in September of 1939 until the actual arrival of the German armies in May of 1940. As was the case then, we are today in an eerie time, stranded in the inertia of Cold War relationships while we wait for the real contours of the new world order to emerge from the fog. Some people are preparing for the approaching storm; others do not want to think about it; a great many are trying to kill the meteorologists who are predicting it.

ONE example of the current intellectual warfare being waged is the reception given to James Fallows's *Looking at the Sun*, which was published last year. According to strict publishing standards, I

should not be discussing Fallows's book and *The Atlantic* should not be publishing my remarks. Fallows is the Washington editor of this magazine, which published several excerpts from his book, the manuscript of which I read and vetted. I am indelibly linked with Fallows because we are both what the Japan lobby calls "revisionists"—that is, people who have had the temerity to "revise" orthodox theoretical pronouncements: either that since Japan is rich, it must have learned how to operate its economy from the Econ 101 courses taught in American universities, or that since Japanese economics do not fit the gospel according to Saint Adam Smith, Japan's economy is doomed to collapse any day now.

But the issue here is not the conventions of the publishing world but the biggest and most misunderstood event of the end of the twentieth century: the shift of the global economic center of gravity to the Western Pacific. The end of the Cold War has finally exposed to view something that the Cold War itself both fostered and camouflaged: the enrichment of Asia. How that happened and what it means for the future are the keys to the new world order.

JIM Fallows, a journalist with an Oxford degree in economics, is the author of *National Defense*, which won the National Book Award in 1981. Having heard about the enrichment of Asia, and being curious about the people who produced it, he took himself and his family to live there for four years. Fallows divided his time between Japan, the superpower of the region, and Malaysia, the richest

First published in *The Atlantic Monthly*, January 1995, pp. 99-104. © 1995 by Chalmers Johnson. Reprinted by permission of the author.

of the platforms for Japanese manufacturing in Southeast Asia. His book does not deal with China or take Korea or Indonesia as seriously as it might have. But Fallows studied and wrote unerringly on the likely next entries into the category of miracle economies—Vietnam and perhaps Burma—and every American should read his chapter on the Philippines, since that country is the only part of Asia whose legacy is unambiguously ours. I know of no better contemporary guide than Fallows to the role of the ethnic Chinese in Southeast Asia, the historical underpinnings of Japan's state-guided capitalism, or the differences between the Thai and Malay outlooks on the world. But none of these aspects of his book has surfaced in any of the savage attention it has received.

Instead Fallows has been excoriated for a "visceral hostility" to Japan (the *Los Angeles Times*), for being a "MITI lover" (*The Wall Street Journal*; the reference is to Japan's Ministry of International Trade and Industry, an economic-strategy agency that has guided Japan's postwar growth and is similar to the American Joint Chiefs of Staff), and for writing "a defective guide to what economics teaches about national development strategies and the functioning of modern industries" (*The New York Times*). The last reviewer acknowledges that he is "an infrequent Asian traveler" and that "laissez-faire theories fit the Asian experience badly," but he nevertheless cites an American economist from the 1880s—a time when the United States was one of the most heavily protected economies on earth—to the effect that Asia has nothing to teach us about economic growth. Writing in *The New Republic*, Ian Buruma declares Fallows to be a "neo-Orientalist," of the never-the-twain-shall-meet persuasion (Buruma actually quotes Kipling's bromide), and faults him for failing to understand that the Japanese machine politician Ichiro Ozawa really admires "British parliamentary democracy."

Buruma is an interesting case. A British-accented author of books about Japanese sexual fantasies, travel in Asia, cricket, and how the Germans have wept enough for their wartime deeds but the Japanese have not, Buruma really is innocent of the structure and properties of

the Japanese economy. Nonetheless, *de haut en bas*, Buruma takes Fallows up on the subject of economics.

> Even if we assume, for the sake of argument, that Fallows is absolutely right, that there is such a thing as a specifically Asian system, combining mercantilism with authoritarian politics, does this disprove the main case for classical economics? Ricardo and Smith said that nations benefit from keeping their markets open for trade, even if other nations keep their markets closed. Consumers benefit from cheaper products, and competition keeps producers efficient and quality-conscious. Fallows does not believe this. He thinks it is a dogma that blinds the Anglo-Saxon world to the reality of the East. This is why he thinks the United States should devise an industrial strategy if it is not to follow Britain's giggling slide into the sea.

With the statement "Fallows does not believe this," Buruma begins to reveal that reviews of Fallows's book are not really book reviews at all but acts of faith —what the Inquisition called *autos-da-fé*—and are intended to warn the unsuspecting of possible heresy. This kind of warning disguised as criticism is becoming a regular, if subliminal, feature of discussions about Asian capitalism. Fallows is certainly not the first writer about the challenge of Asia to be savaged by reviewers and yet still be widely read. Michael Crichton was called politically incorrect, a Japan-basher, and a racist for writing his novel *Rising Sun*, about how a Japanese company seeking a share of the American microelectronics market bribed and blackmailed a U.S. senator—a fictional treatment of the daily occurrences Pat Choate detailed in *Agents of Influence*. It now looks as if Jeff Shear's excellent and revealing *The Keys to the Kingdom: The FS-X Deal and the Selling of America's Future to Japan* is to be accorded similar treatment. *The Wall Street Journal* has recently declared Shear to be a "New Mercantilist" who favors supporting high-tech industries in the United States. Shear's reviewer says this viewpoint is silly, because "countries don't compete in most business, businesses do" and "no trade [in the Pacific] is going to occur except win-win transactions."

The issue raised by Fallows is the possibility that the Japanese have put together the institutions of capitalism in a more effective way than is taught in English and American academies. He has also remembered what Adam Smith had to say about the functions of the state in market economies. Even the functions that Smith considered basic—appropriate education of the labor force, construction of the infrastructure on which manufacturing depends, the "night watchman" functions of guaranteeing public safety—our state fails to fulfill in a competitive manner. And Smith was interested in the minimalist state. The Japanese have shown the world that there are many things the state can do in a market economy in order to make it work well—things that never crossed Smith's mind or that would not have mattered in his eighteenth-century setting. These include the management of technology (the great variable that cancels "comparative advantage"), the management of the change of industrial structure (for example, from capital-intensive to knowledge-intensive industries), and the management of competition to ensure the availability of high-value-added jobs (for example, the making of computer chips instead of potato chips) for one's own citizens. When Fallows's critics intone that he fails "to recognize that the enemy was really us" (*New York Times*) and that "the Japanese people aren't so different from us after all" (*Wall Street Journal*), they are deliberately deflecting scrutiny from what Fallows actually says. His book is the most straightforward kind of call to action: the challenge of Asia, like the Cold War itself, requires acknowledgment of the challenge and policies to match it, not just incessant knocking on wood by vested interests fearful of change.

ECONOMICS has become the Marxism-Leninism of our society—the official ideological expression of how the United States works and why it "won" the Cold War. Its adepts, the professional economists of our society, have the same interest in preserving their usually tenured (in violation of market forces) positions as did the masters of ML at Moscow State University until August of 1991. The greatest single threat to their continued dominance is the prowess of the Japanese economy and the emulation of that economy by everybody else in Asia, from China to Kazakhstan. It is not the wealth of Asia that is threatening but how the Asians obtained it. Conventional U.S. economic theory says that the state cannot be effective in the economy. We believe this because of our own history of struggles against the state and because the ideology of the Cold War maintains that laissez-faire vanquished socialism. We also have practical evidence that our nonmilitary bureaucrats are often more expensive than they are effective. But the evidence from East Asia is overwhelming. Nonadversarial relations between the public and private sectors can produce safe, sane societies with astonishingly high levels of evenly distributed income. Our theorists must either dismiss this evidence or start thinking about the only choices left to them—retooling in the Japanese language (very hard to do after age thirty-five) or early retirement.

Fallows knows this, and should not be too surprised by the treatment he has received. It is a good sign that he scored. But readers should ignore the reviews and read the book, because it is also an excellent guide to the struggles that will almost certainly dominate our politics within a very short period of time. China and Japan are the only two foreign countries today that could threaten the national security of the United States if we had relations of conflict with them. One is the world's biggest society, the other among the world's richest in terms of per capita income. Just as the century changes, the world is witnessing a basic change in Asia from enrichment to empowerment. The nineteenth century was the time of the victimization of Asia. In China it took the form of imperialist enclaves, of which Hong Kong is one of the last remaining. In the rest of Asia (except for the buffer state of Thailand) it took the form of European, American, and Japanese colonialism. The twentieth century has been the time of revolt against this imperialism, including the Chinese Revolution (the biggest revolution among all the cases), revolts by subject peoples during interimperialist wars, and wars of national liberation in Indonesia, Indochina, and Malaya.

These wars are now over, and only a few embers from them still smolder. Rich Americans are starting to take luxury cruises to Vietnam, disembarking at Danang for a quickie bus tour to Hue. Vestiges of the old victimization and its consequences still linger in the soon-to-change status of Hong Kong, the not-soon-to-change status of Taiwan, the partition of Korea, and the influence of the U.S. Seventh Fleet. The enrichment of Asia occurred during the Cold War and depended to one degree or another on the opportunities made available by the conditions that prevailed. Today enrichment is a self-sustaining process, still benefiting from the openness of the American market but no longer dependent upon it. During 1993, using Japan's definitions and accounting methods, Japan had a trade surplus of $53.6 billion with the rest of Asia, as against a surplus of $50.2 billion with the United States. The shift from mere enrichment to empowerment is clearly on the agenda. It has started to show up in Asians' growing irritation with the American tendency to deliver sermons on human rights, free trade, multilateral diplomacy, democracy, and virtually anything else, regardless of the United States' own rather tacky record in many of these areas. (Singaporeans, when we lectured them on the evils of flogging, commented on how we dealt with some of our dissidents at Waco, Texas.)

THE empowerment of Asia is going to come as a shock to a lot of Americans. They have not been "looking at the sun," as Jim Fallows puts it, but have been following the advice of the *Los Angeles Times*: "America, take off your sunglasses." Nor are our universities doing a good job of preparing people for the Pacific century. Professors these days are totally devoted to what they call theory—nineteenth-century English economic theory, rational-choice theory, French literary theory, and gender theory—to the exclusion of all forms of empiricism, language study, and awareness of differences in national character. In contrast to the days when universities provided expertise on Russia and China, today people seeking such knowledge must turn to think tanks.

This is one of the reasons I retired early from the University of California and am involved in creating a research institute devoted to policy issues in the Asia-Pacific region. The government itself has access to less genuine expertise on Asia—that is, the expertise of people who have studied and lived in Asia and who read and speak an Asian language—than it has had at any other time since the 1940s.

When Americans wake up to the shift in the balance of power to Asia, they are likely to feel betrayed and angry. They will wonder why they were not warned. Jim Fallows is one of the few issuing a warning. He is also responding seriously to Japan's emergence as a major economic power—one whose economy is three fifths the size of the United States, the first economy in history to produce a $100 billion trade surplus, and the economic equivalent of two Germanys in the Pacific. History teaches us that inattention, drift, and appeasement are not the proper ways to deal with such a nation. In the past comparable policies have led to war. Copying Japan is also not the way to go, and Fallows explicitly warns against it. We must use our own national heritage and resources to match Japan, not copy it, just as we matched but did not copy the former USSR. We would be crazy to imitate, for example, Japan's persistent waste of female talent because of the influence of its rigid gender-based division of labor. We are decades ahead of Japan in terms of integrating women and minorities into all levels of our labor force. This is not a time for complacency, however. Shortly the widespread American belief that Japan is finished will be exposed as an idiotic conceit. We will then have the choice of either matching Japan or adjusting to its ascendancy.

Fallows and the few others like him are not anti-Japanese. They may well be the only true friends Japan has in the West. The issue for the next century, as it has been for the one now ending, is how, short of war, to adjust to the rise of new sources of power and the decline of old ones. Complex factual knowledge of the sort contained in *Looking at the Sun* is the first requirement.

Modern Pluralist Democracies: Factors in the Political Process

- **Political Ideas, Movements, Parties (Articles 26–28)**
- **The Ethnic Factor in Western European Politics (Article 29)**
- **Women and Politics (Articles 30–32)**
- **The Institutional Framework of Representative Government (Articles 33–36)**

Observers of Western industrial societies frequently refer to the emergence of a new politics in these countries. They are not always very clear or in agreement about what is supposedly novel within the political process or why it is significant. Although few would doubt that some major changes have taken place in these societies during the past couple of decades, affecting both political attitudes and behavior, it is very difficult to establish clear and comparable patterns of transformation or gauge their endurance and impact. Yet making sense of continuities and changes in political values and behavior must be one of the central tasks of a comparative study of government.

Since the early 1970s, political scientists have followed Ronald Inglehart and other careful observers who first noted a marked increase in what they called postmaterial values, especially among younger and more highly educated people outside the nonindustrial occupations in Western Europe. Such voters showed less concern for the traditional material values of economic well-being and security, and instead stressed participatory and environmental concerns in politics as a way of improving democracy and the general "quality of life." Studies of postmaterialism form a very important addition to our ongoing attempt to interpret and explain not only the so-called "youth revolt" but also some more lasting shifts in lifestyles and political priorities. It makes intuitive sense that such changes appear to be especially marked among those who grew up in the relative prosperity of Western Europe, after the austere period of reconstruction that followed World War II. In more recent years, however, there appears to have been a revival of material concerns among younger people. There are also some indications that political reform activities evoke less interest and commitment than earlier.

None of this should be mistaken for a return to the political patterns of the past. Instead, we may be witnessing the emergence of a still somewhat incongruent new mix of material and postmaterial orientations, along with old and new forms of political self-expression by the citizenry. Established political parties appear to be in somewhat of a quandary in redefining their positions, at a time when the traditional bonding of many voters to one or another party seems to have become weaker. Many observers speak about a widespread condition of political malaise in advanced industrial countries, suggesting that it shows up not only in opinion polls but also in a marked decline in voter participation and, on occasion, a propensity for voter revolt against the establishment parties and candidates. Without suggesting a simple cause-effect relationship, Martin Jacques points to parallels between electoral malaise or dealignment and the vague rhetoric offered by many political activists and opinion leaders. He believes that the end of the cold war and the collapse of communism in Europe have created a situation that demands a reformulation of political and ideological alternatives. In that sense, he finds some paradigmatic significance in the great political shakeup of the Italian party system.

At this point it seems unlikely that Italy will set an example for many other democracies. Most established parties seem to have developed an ability to adjust to change, even as the balance of power within each party system shifts over time and occasional newcomers are admitted to the club. Each country's party system remains uniquely shaped by its political history, but there do seem to be some very general patterns of development. One frequently observed trend is toward a narrowing of the ideological distance between the moderate Left and Right in many European countries. It now often makes more sense to speak of the center-Left and center-Right respectively.

Despite such convergence, there are still some important ideological and practical differences between the two orientations. Thus the Right is usually far more ready to accept as "inevitable" the existence of social or economic inequalities. It normally favors lower taxes and the promotion of market forces, with some very important exceptions, intended to protect certain favorite groups and values. And it sees the state primarily as an instrument that should provide security, order and protection of an established way of life. The Left, by contrast, emphasizes that government has an important task in promoting opportunities, delivering services, and reducing social inequities. On issues such as higher and more progressive taxation or the relative concern for rates of unemployment and inflation, there will still be considerable differences between moderates of the Left and Right.

Even as the ideological distance between Left and Right narrows but remains important, there are also signs of some political differentiation within each camp. On the center-Right side of the party spectrum in European politics, economic neoliberals (who speak for business and industry) can be distinguished from the social conservatives (who advocate traditional values and authorities). European liberalism has its roots in a tradition that favors civil liberties and tolerance but that also values individual achievement and laissez-faire economics. For such European neoliberals, the state has an important but very limited role to play in providing an institutional framework within which individuals and social groups pursue their interests. Traditional conservatives, by contrast, emphasize the importance of social stability and continuity, and point to the social danger of disruptive change. They often value the strong state as an instrument of order, but many of them also show a paternalistic appreciation for welfare state programs that will keep "the social net" from tearing apart.

In British politics, Margaret Thatcher promoted elements from each of these traditions in what could be called her own mix of "business conservatism." The result is the peculiar tension between "drys" and "wets" within her own Conservative Party, even after she has ceased to be its leader. In France, on the other hand, the division between neoliberals and conservatives runs more clearly between the two major center-Right parties, the Giscardist UDF and the neo-Gaullist RPR. In Germany, the

Free Democrats would most clearly represent the traditional liberal position, while some conservative elements can be found among the Christian Democrats.

There is something of a split identity also among the Christian Democrats, who until recently were one of the most successful political movements in Europe after World War II. Here idealists, who subscribe to the socially compassionate teachings of the Church, have found themselves losing influence to more efficiency-oriented technocrats or success-oriented political managers. The latter seem to reflect little of the original ideals of personalism, solidarity, and subsidiarity that originally set the Christian Democrats off from both neoliberals and conservatives in postwar Europe. It remains to be seen whether political setbacks for the Christian Democrats in Italy will lead to more than a face-lift. Their new name of Popular Party seems unintentionally self-ironic and has done little if anything to stem their recent electoral losses. In Germany, however, the Christian Democrats have managed to remain chancellor party despite some slippage in their electoral appeal.

On the Left, democratic Socialists and ecologists stress that the sorry political, economic, and environmental record of communist-ruled states in no way diminishes the validity of their own commitment to social justice and environmental protection in modern industrial society. For them, capitalism will continue to produce its own social problems and dissatisfactions. No matter how efficient capitalism may be, they argue, it will continue to result in inequities that require politically directed reforms. Many on the Left, however, show a pragmatic acceptance of the modified market economy as an arena within which to promote their reformist goals. Social Democrats have long been known for taking such positions, but parties further to the Left have also moved in that direction in recent years. Two striking examples of this shift can be found among the Greens in Germany and in what used to be the Communist Party of Italy. The Greens are by no means an establishment party, but they have served as a pragmatic coalition partner with the Social Democrats in several state governments and have gained respect for their mixture of practical competence and idealism. Their so-called realist faction (Realos) has clearly outmaneuvered its more radical rivals in the party's so-called fundamentalist or Fundi wing. The Italian Communists have come even further toward a center-Left position. Years before they adopted the new name of Democratic Party of the Left (PDS), they had abandoned the Leninist revolutionary tradition and adopted reformist politics similar to those of social democratic parties elsewhere in Western Europe.

Both center-Left and center-Right moderates face a dual challenge from populists on the Right, who often seek lower taxes, drastic cuts in the social budget, and a curtailment of immigration, and neofascists on the ultra-Right. The two orientations should be distinguished, as in Italy where the populist Northern League and the partly neofascist National Alliance represent positions that are polar opposites on such key issues as government decentralization (favored by the former, opposed by the latter). In part, the electoral revival of the right-wing parties can be linked to anxieties and tensions that affect some socially and economically insecure groups in the lower middle class and some sectors of the working class. Ultra-Right nationalist politicians and their parties typically eschew a complex explanation of the structural and cyclical problems that beset the European economies. Instead, their simple answer blames external scapegoats, namely the many immigrants and refugees from eastern Europe as well as developing world countries in northern Africa and elsewhere. The presence of the far-Right parties inevitably has an effect on both the balance of power and the political agendas that occupy the more centrist parties. Almost everywhere, for example, some of the established parties and politicians have been making symbolic concessions on the refugee issue, in order to prevent it from becoming monopolized by extremists.

Women in politics is the concern of the third section in this unit. There continues to be a strong pattern of underrepresentation of women in positions of political and economic leadership practically everywhere. Yet there are some notable differences from country to country as well as from party to party. Generally speaking, the parties of the Left have been readier to place women in positions of authority, although there are some remarkable exceptions, as the center-Right cases of Margaret Thatcher in Britain and Simone Weil in France illustrate.

On the whole, the system of proportional representation gives parties both a tool and an added incentive to place female candidates in positions where they will be elected. But here too, there can be exceptions, as in the case of France in 1986 when women did not benefit from the one-time use of proportional representation in the parliamentary elections. Clearly it is not enough to have a relatively simple means, such as proportional representation, for promoting women in politics: There must also be a will among decision makers to use the available tool for such a purpose.

This is where a policy of affirmative action may be chosen as a strategy. The Scandinavian countries illustrate better than any other example how the breakthrough may occur. There is a markedly higher representation of women in the Parliaments of Denmark, Finland, Iceland, Norway, and Sweden, where the political center of gravity is somewhat to the Left and where proportional representation makes it possible to set up party lists that are more representative of the population as a whole. It is of some interest that Iceland has a special women's party with parliamentary representation, but it is more important that women are found in leading positions within most of the parties of this and the other Scandinavian countries. It usually does not take long for the more centrist or moderately conservative parties to adopt the new concern of gender equality, and they may even move to the forefront. Thus women now lead three of the main parties in Norway (the Social Democrats, the Center

Party, and the Conservatives), which together normally receive more than two-thirds of the total popular vote. It is worth pointing out that in contrast to Margaret Thatcher, who included no women in her cabinet between 1979 and 1990, Norway's first female prime minister, Gro Harlem Brundtland, used that position to advance the number of women in ministerial positions (8 of 18 cabinet posts).

In another widely reported sign of change, the relatively conservative Republic of Ireland has chosen Mary Robinson as its first female president. It is a largely ceremonial post, but it has a symbolic potential that Mary Robinson, an outspoken advocate of liberal reform in her country, is willing to use on behalf of social change. Perhaps most remarkable of all, the advancement of women into high political ranks has now touched Switzerland, where they did not get the right to vote until 1971.

Altogether, there is undoubtedly a growing awareness of the pattern of gender discrimination in most Western countries. It seems likely that there will be a significant improvement in this situation over the course of the next decade if the pressure for reform is maintained. Such changes have already occurred in other areas, where there used to be significant political differences between men and women. At one time, for example, there used to be a considerably lower voter turnout among women, but this gender gap has been practically eliminated in recent decades. Similarly the tendency for women to be somewhat more conservative in party and candidate preferences has given way to a more liberal disposition among younger women in foreign and social policy preferences than among men. These are aggregate differences, of course, and it is important to remember that women, like men, do not represent a monolithic bloc in political attitudes and behavior but are similarly divided by other interests and priorities. One generalization seems to hold, namely that there is much less inclination among women to support parties or candidates that have a decidedly "radical" image. Thus the vote for extreme left- or right-wing parties in contemporary Europe tends to be considerably higher among male voters.

In any case, there are some very important policy questions that affect women more directly than men. Any statistical study of women in the paid labor force of Europe could supply conclusive evidence to support three widely shared impressions: (1) there has been a considerable increase in the number and relative proportion of women who take paid jobs; (2) these jobs are more often unskilled and/or part-time than in the case of men's employment; and (3) women generally receive less pay and less social protection than men in similar positions. Such a study would also show that there are considerable differences among Western European countries in the relative position of their female workers, thereby offering support for the argument that political intervention in the form of appropriate legislation can do something to improve the employment status of women—not only by training them better for advancement in the labor market but also, and importantly, by changing the conditions of the workplace to eliminate some obvious or hidden disadvantages for women.

The framework of government is the subject of the fourth section of this unit. Here the authors examine and compare a number of institutional arrangements: (1) essential characteristics and elements of a pluralist democracy; (2) two major systems of representative government; (3) different electoral systems; and (4) the presidential and prime ministerial forms of executive.

The topic of pluralist democracy is a complex one, but Philipe Schmitter and Terry Lynn Karl manage to present a very comprehensive discussion of the subject in a short space in their article. Gregory Mahler focuses on the legislative-executive relationship of parliamentary and congressional systems, drawing mainly upon the British, Canadian, and American examples. He avoids the trap of idealizing one or the other way of organizing the functions of representative government. The article "Electoral Reform: Good Government? Fairness? Or Vice Versa. Or Both" examines the supposed advantages and disadvantages of different electoral systems, showing that proportional representation need not result in political instability or paralysis. Richard Rose compares the political executive in the United States, Britain, and France. He finds that each system has its own constraints upon arbitrary rule, which can easily become obstacles to prompt and decisive action.

Looking Ahead: Challenge Questions

How do you explain the apparent shifts toward the political center made by parties of the moderate Left and moderate Right in recent years? How do Social Democrats present themselves as reformers of capitalism? What are the main sources of electoral support for the far-Right political parties?

Why are women so poorly represented in Parliament and other positions of political leadership? How do institutional arrangements, such as elections systems, sometimes help or hinder an improvement in this situation? Which parties and countries tend to have a better record of female representation?

Would you agree with the inventory of democratic essentials as discussed by Philippe Schmitter and Terry Karl ("What Democracy Is . . . And Is Not")? What do you regard as most and least important in their inventory? What are some major traits of a good constitution?

What are some of the major arguments made in favor of the parliamentary system of government? What are the main arguments against and in favor of proportional representation? How do you explain that regionalism and federalism have gained new attention and respect in recent years?

A victim of outdated ideologies and lackluster leaders

The End of Politics

MARTIN JACQUES

Martin Jacques is a journalist and broadcaster. He currently writes for the Sunday Times. *He is also an occasional contributor to various international publications, including* Volkskrant, New York Times, New Republic, *and* Le Monde Diplomatique. *He is chairman of the independent think-tank Demos. For many years he was editor of* Marxism Today *and has co-edited three books on contemporary politics. He was educated at Manchester and Cambridge Universities, where he received his doctorate, and was an academic before becoming a journalist. He now lectures to senior management at Templeton College, Oxford. He is a keen sportsman and writes for the* Financial Times *about motor racing, which has been a lifelong passion.*

THE SUNDAY TIMES

Britons all know that their government is extraordinarily weak. They know that John Major has been the most unpopular prime minister since records began. At any other time this century, the beneficiary would have been the opposition. Yet nobody believes that the Labor Party would make a better fist of things, either. The nation has lost confidence in politicians. We don't believe in them anymore. And the same applies elsewhere. It is difficult to think of a single political leader in the democratic world who is riding high. Governments everywhere are confronted with a crisis of credibility. The French elections saw the biggest defeat for the sitting government this century. German Chancellor Helmut Kohl is but a pale shadow of the figure that strutted the German scene in the heady days of reunification. In

Italy, the political class is discredited, the political system is disintegrating, and all the old governing parties are facing oblivion. Even in the United States, where, unlike in Europe, the people voted for a new kind of leader from a different generation, the president already finds himself an embattled figure.

What the hell is happening, you might ask. If this spectacle were confined to one country, it would be easier to explain, but that is not the case: It is almost a universal condition of the Western world. Two explanations are generally served up. First, recession makes governments unpopular, espe-

cially when they haven't got a clue what to do about it. We have had recessions before, though, and they have not led to this kind of political crisis. Second, the present generation of political leaders is, by historical standards, mediocre. But we have had mediocre leaders before, and it did not produce a universal collapse of confidence in the political class.

Shouldn't we be asking a rather more fundamental question altogether? Are we not witnessing a much more general crisis of politics as an activity, a clutter of institutions, and a body of people? There is plenty of circumstantial evidence. Membership of political parties, not only in Britain but across the developed world, has long been in decline. The British Labor Party now has about 200,000 members, compared with 1 million in the early 1950s. The Conservative Party has more, but it, too, is shrinking. The days of the mass-membership party, with high levels of participation, are over. Fewer and fewer people believe in the party as a vehicle for change and as an object of their activities and affections. The vast and mushrooming range of alternatives—Greenpeace, the Royal Society for the Protection of Birds, the local health and fitness group, and Amnesty International—generally seem more attractive and a lot more useful.

Or consider this fact: The present generation of political leaders—Clinton, Major, Kohl, and Co.—may be the most unpopular bunch since the war. But political leaders have been suffering a steadily declining popularity rating ever since 1945, the most popular leaders being the immediate postwar generation—the Churchills, Attlees, Trumans, and Adenauers. Political leaders, in other words, command declining respect. When we watch the antics in the House of Commons, we are more likely to be appalled or alienated than impressed. Politics and politicians are now judged by more worldly standards. They stand before us like the emperor with no clothes, stripped of the aura that once protected them.

Politics is like a declining sector of the economy: defensive, conservative, nostalgic, incapable of generating new ideas and practices, attracting fewer and fewer able people. Of all areas of society, the political world displays the least ability to learn. It remains male-dominated, resistant to new technology, and rooted in tradition. Society has changed, and politics has failed to keep pace. As a result, it is of declining importance in people's lives. People are less likely to take their identities from either parties or the state.

In the postwar decades, society was characterized by hierarchy and deference. People knew their place. Society consisted of large homogeneous blocs, with class as the foundation stone. Change was marked by certainty and predictability for individuals and institutions alike. But that world has slowly given way to something very different. Hierarchy and deference have been replaced by market-driven egalitarianism, where rank and title matter increasingly little. Certainty has been replaced by uncertainty. Previously, a company lived in the relative calm and safety of a national market; now there is no hiding place. Public-sector institutions such as hospitals and schools are similarly faced with growing uncertainty. And the same applies to people's lives: multiple careers, holidays in different places, and several partners are now *de rigueur*.

Homogeneity and class have been supplanted by diversity and multi-identity. We are confronted with a profusion of styles, ethnicities, identities. Society has become gloriously different. Order has given way to confusion. This is the pick-and-choose society. From food to holidays, from sport to fabrics, from sexual identity to clothes, we can choose as never before.

Society was once dominated by vertical structures that oozed hierarchy. Now society has gone lateral and horizontal. The old lines of connection and loyalty have been replaced. Crucial to this change has been the role of the media. Of course, television and the press are characterized by a certain hierarchy of their own, of editors and owners, controllers and producers. But that misses the point. The modern media have become the mirror, the interlocutor, the enabler of this new society. They are the source of information and opinion, symbol and humor. They have made people worldly rather than parochial. They have made society porous where once it was segmented. The media are now the template of society, defining success and failure in everything from sport to politics, from entertainment to ideas.

Politicians feel deeply uneasy about the change. The true object of their scorn is not this columnist or that program but what the media represent and symbolize in this new society. The media are the means by which political discussion and opinion, fact and revelation, are made universal. Governments and politicians can no longer control as they once did. As a result, they view the media with a mixture of fear and respect, resentment and anxiety. The politicians are fallen idols, and the media have played no small role in their downfall.

For politics, the most dramatic single aspect of the new culture is the decline of the state. In the postwar period, the state stood at the apogee of society, a source of respect and authority. The state was indubitably a commanding height, and those who presided over it enjoyed commensurate prestige. Now the state has turned full circle and come to symbolize the past, inefficiency, and special interests. The implications for politicians have been profound. The state—national and local government—is where politicians do their business. It is their theater. Of course, as the left has always been rather more attached to the idea of the state as an instrument of change than has the right, so its decline has hurt the left more than the right. Taking the broad picture, though, this is nit-picking. The process has undermined the power and importance of all politicians.

But power has not only drained away from the state into, quite literally, thousands of groups within civil society. It has also seeped through the boundaries of the nation-state into the international ether. Things that the British government could do 30 years ago are no longer within its power. In some cases, no one or no body can exercise such control. In others, an institution such as the European Community has acquired some of the power. The decline of the nation-state and national sovereignty has eroded the importance of national politics.

There is another, rather different reason for the crisis of politics. European politics has been predominantly structured around the right-left polarity since the establishment of modern suffrage. There is ample evidence to suggest that the ability of this ideological system to explain the problems of society and offer solutions is in decline. Over the past 20 years or so, we have seen the rise of new issues such as gender, sexuality, and the environment, all of which transcend the traditional lines between left and right.

More recently, we have witnessed a growing crisis of the traditional bases of leftist politics. There are several ingredients: the demise of the Keynesian welfare model, the decline of the modern state and therefore the efficacy of state intervention, the rise of a more flexible and heterogeneous society, and the decline of the working class. Of these, the most important, arguably, is the latter. The industrial working class and its organizations furnished social-democratic parties, including Labor, with their culture, support, organizations, members, and voters. The decline of the working class has, unsurprisingly, thrown all socialist parties into crisis. But the consequences are far wider. If class was the central dynamic of the political system, then its decline disorganizes not only the left but also the right—and politics as a whole. When one pole is undermined, the other does not, by definition, remain unaffected.

The most obvious bipolar analogy is the cold war. The collapse of communism did not leave the West unscathed and unchallenged, as most expected in 1989. On the contrary, the demise of bipolarity has thrown the West into crisis. An overriding enemy provides a sense of purpose, helps to subordinate and discipline other potential conflicts, gives a clear moral framework, and furnishes a sense of identity. Without it, these questions rise to the surface in a new way, begging answers that are novel and profound.

The other dimension of the exhaustion of the left-right system is the decline of ideology. The 20th century has been dominated by grand ideologies: communism, socialism, fascism, neo-liberalism. In all cases, the hope kindled by them has been disappointed. As we approach the end of the millennium, there is, throughout the democratic world, a turn away from ideology toward pragmatism. Great transformative ideologies seem less and less appropriate in an environment of flux and uncertainty. The new era demands organizations able to engage in permanent innovation and experiment, whose natural habitat is a steep learning curve: exactly the opposite of the political party, which we once loved but now find increasingly uninteresting.

Historical crises are never the product of a single factor. They are a combination of long-term trends and short-term causes. The sheer tenaciousness of this recession, and the impotence of governments in the face of it, has created a general disillusionment in politicians and governments. More important, the end of the cold war has created a sense of malaise in the West, which has worsened as the Bosnia crisis has replaced the triumphalism of the Persian Gulf war.

So where is this crisis of politics leading? As always, it is easier to analyze a crisis than to predict its outcome. The added difficulty in this case is that this is a crisis of the old paradigm with no new paradigm yet in view. It would be wrong to assume that it will inevitably lead to some kind of apocalyptic change. That may happen; it is certainly what is occurring in Italy. More probable is a slow process of change and adjustment. This is likely to have two basic components. First, politics will come to occupy a less exalted position in society. This has already begun.

The second component is more intriguing. Politics must go through a process of reform that brings it more into line with how society has changed and is changing. That process, too, is already under way. A more open and pluralistic society suggests political parties that are more socially diverse in terms of membership, votes, and funding; that are not beholden in the same way to specific vested and material interests. Parties themselves are culturally anachronistic. Their decline is imposing powerful strains on the political system. The basis for the selection of candidates, policy, and, ultimately, governments is becoming increasingly narrow and unhealthy. Politics has effectively become the preserve of a small professional political class.

Yet it is difficult to imagine a political system without parties. Perhaps in time they will be looser and more porous, drawing people outside their ranks into decision-making, along the lines of the American model, and spawning leaders who have more diverse backgrounds, a wider range of cultural experience, and who, as a consequence, are able to speak to a broader constituency. But the decline of the political party and the shrinking importance of the formal political world suggest that there is a need for this to be complemented by forms of direct democracy as a means of enabling wider participation in the democratic process. The widespread use of referendums, for example, would allow more people to have a direct say in policy decisions while reducing the power of the parties. New television-based technology will soon revolutionize possibilities at local and national levels. Referendums would allow a little fresh air into a political system that now smells distinctly musty.

The left's new start

A future for socialism

IN MUCH of Europe, left-wing politics is enjoying a revival. Scandinavian voters, who not long ago seemed to have abandoned their tradition of social democratic government, are putting left-of-centre parties into office again. Last month Hungary ditched its reformist pro-business government in favour of a "socialist" party made up of former communists; Social Democrats will do well in Germany's elections in October, opinion polls say; in Britain, the Labour Party trounced the Tories in recent local elections and stands a good chance of forming the next government; across the European Union, socialists expect to do well in elections to the European Parliament on June 9th and 12th. The revival is by no means universal—socialist parties are in trouble in Spain, France and Italy, to name just three—but it is nonetheless striking.

Just as striking is the fact that traditional ideas cannot claim the credit for the left's popularity. Today's socialist parties have all but abandoned many of their old policies. By the end of the 1980s most of Europe's left-of-centre parties already advocated (albeit grudgingly) slimmer government, lower taxes and privatisation—measures to which they were once bitterly opposed. Where parties called "socialist" are doing better, it is partly because they no longer espouse socialism.

This is a good thing. The left's traditional policies of widespread public ownership and punitive taxation only ever promised equality of disappointment. However, the realignment of the left is not as good a thing as it could be. Traditional socialists who ask why the left should seek power at all, if it is only to implement a soft-focus version of conservatism, ask a good question. For the sake of intelligent debate about public policy (ie, for the sake of good government) the left needs to do more than ditch the discredited policies of its past. It needs to develop a new programme that is not just economically literate, welcome though that would be, but distinctive as well.

Same means, different ends

In a variety of countries, attempts to do this are under way (see pages 17-19). Few of these efforts are promising, for a reason that is both revealing and dispiriting: most socialist modernisers remain instinctively hostile to market economics.

Some "market socialists" say, for instance, that capitalism would be all right as long as firms worked in a different way. They propose batteries of regulation to increase worker participation in management, to oblige firms to take a longer-term view, to make them more sensitive to the needs of their "stakeholders" (as opposed to the people who merely own them), and what not. Other modernisers see environmental questions as the niche for a new socialism. Still others emphasise the role of trade and industrial policies in maintaining some supposedly desirable mix of activities. The list goes on—each such policy justified by an elaborate appeal to the concept of "market failure". This idea remains the hallmark even of modernised socialism, central both to its substance and its presentation. The market alone cannot do this, cannot do that. State intervention—cleverer than before, but broadly based and, in its way, hardly less ambitious—remains the offered remedy.

Such thinking is profoundly misguided. In a sense market failure is pervasive. Competition is "imperfect", production and exchange involve externalities, the future is uncertain; for all these reasons, markets fail to allocate resources precisely as they would in the textbook world of basic economics. By the same test, there is much to be said for central planning. But this century's most important economic lesson is that, except in textbooks, government failure is broader, more damaging in economic terms and much more threatening to individual liberty than market failure.

The question is whether socialists can accept that truth whole-heartedly; rather than, as at present, half-heartedly, with

From *The Economist*, June 11, 1994, pp. 11-12. © 1994 by the Economist, Ltd. Distributed by the New York Times Special Features. Reprinted by permission.

10,000 qualifications, or not at all. The answer may well be No. For many, "socialism" by definition cannot accept the market as the right framework for organising society. After all, socialism has a history. Its roots lie in an analysis of society that denies not merely the efficiency but also the moral content of free interaction among economic agents. If that analysis is bankrupt (and it is), what is there left for "socialism" to say?

Plenty, as it happens—with or without that label. The aims of socialism as a programme of social and economic reform, as opposed to the analysis of socialism as an intellectual discipline, have always been the source of its popular support. Goals such as reducing poverty, promoting equality of opportunity, and improving the quality of public services for all remain enormously appealing. In these aims, not in the arcane theories of economic planning, lies the reason why so many people for years invested in socialism their hopes for a happier and healthier society.

If those goals, as opposed to the ideological apparatus in which they were once couched, matter most to today's socialists, there is no reason why the left cannot be as vigorous in its enthusiasm for market economics as the right. If leftist parties could bring themselves to believe that the market is wonderful (not merely useful if kept in its place), that it has delivered the vast majority (not a privileged minority) of people in the West to material well-being which they would never have attained otherwise, that it must be trusted to co-ordinate the great bulk of society's activities, then they could be far more effective in pursuing their aims as social reformers.

These aims constitute an agenda that is not only distinctive but which also attacks the right at its weakest spot. In many countries (notably Britain), conservative governments have failed to reform welfare systems in such a way as to prevent, let alone reverse, increasing poverty. They have failed to invest adequately in the forms of education (notably nursery education, and basic training in literacy and numeracy) that do most to interrupt the transmission of failure from one generation to the next. They have failed to maintain the supply of some public services (such as public transport) to those who have no choice but to rely on them.

Left-of-centre parties account for this partly by saying that conservative governments, unlike them, are not chiefly concerned about the people who suffer as a result. By and large, this is true. But the policies that are needed in response do not call for a searching critique of the market economy. In the aggregate, the market provides the resources for effective action; case by case, moreover, it is often the only effective way to deliver help to the people who need it. The goals of defeating poverty, expanding economic opportunities for the less well-off, and improving the quality of public services will only in fact be achieved by people who can say the words "market" and "capitalism" without sneering.

Exploiting the market

In framing market-friendly policies with aims such as these in view, left-of-centre parties actually have two decisive advantages over their conservative counterparts. First, they can more readily attack certain sorts of privilege. In many countries in Europe and elsewhere, the fiercest opponents of change are those who have traditionally benefited from the restrictive practices established over the years by the middle-class professions: doctors, accountants, lawyers and so forth. The left may be—and certainly ought to be—less willing than the right to defer to such interests. Second, the left's motives in reform are less in doubt. As a result, as "socialist" governments in Australia and New Zealand have shown, leftist reformers can often be more radical than right-of-centre governments in pursuit of efficiency, as well as in pursuit of equity.

This is especially true in management of the public sector. By getting better value for taxpayers' money, and by pruning subsidies to the better off, socialists can deliver more and better services to the people who need them.

Consider Britain's reforms of the National Health Service. By the end of the 1970s, the NHS had become a startlingly wasteful bureaucracy. The best that could be said for it was that it was comparatively cheap: Britain spent massively on health care, but less so than most other rich industrial countries. The service worked badly. Access to medicine and treatment was controlled by rationing; the system was slow and growing slower; standards of treatment and hospital accommodation compared poorly with those abroad.

The reforms undertaken by successive Conservative administrations—the attempt to introduce an "internal market", to ensure that resources were allocated according to the needs of users rather than the convenience of producers—made good sense. In principle, the changes were entirely consistent with the preservation of taxpayer-financed health care for all. In principle, they were capable of putting whatever resources the government devoted to the NHS to better use—meaning faster, better care, including for the least well-off. Voters remained intensely suspicious, however, not least because the government presented its plans as though saving money counted for more than improving the quality of the service. And the Labour Party vilified the reforms from the start, arguing that market economics has no place in the provision of health care.

If Labour wins power, it should think again. However much it plans to spend on health care, the intelligent use of market forces within the system would be its greatest ally in helping those who rely upon it. And because Labour would be trusted by the electorate to keep the NHS intact and free at the point of use, it could actually go further and faster than the Tories in improving the system.

The same goes for socialist parties in other countries, and for other forms of public investment. Adopt road-use pricing, for instance, and use the proceeds from that market-friendly policy to increase investment in railways and other forms of public transport. Introduce competition and market forces into education, by extending the freedom of parents to choose their children's schools, thus encouraging popular schools to grow and unpopular ones to shrink. In these and other areas, left-of-centre governments might still choose to spend more on public investment than conservative ones. That could make sense—but only if a framework (the market) was in place to ensure that the resources were well used.

Respect for market forces and incentives, together with a determination to help the unfortunate, can be expensive. A policy to equip the unemployed for work costs a lot: more, often, than it costs to keep failing industries afloat. However, measures that improve training opportunities for the unemployed make better sense than measures to defend a dying firm. They speed the creation of jobs in the right industries, promoting growth across the economy as a whole. Welfare reform is even more difficult than labour-market reform. It is costly and complicated to help the poor without worsening the poverty trap that is caused by the interaction of benefits and taxation. The remedy involves benefits that are better-targeted, but withdrawn more gradually as income rises, and minimal taxation at the bottom of the income scale. This costs money.

A left-of-centre party should nonetheless be ambitious in both these areas—making it all the more important to pare public spending of the kind that helps people who do not need to be helped. Here too, a left-of-centre government could be more daring than a conservative one. Acting as always in the name of equity and efficiency, it could make benefits to the elderly poor more generous, but reduce or eliminate benefits to the elderly not-poor; it could recover more of the costs of university education from the beneficiaries; it could narrow tax breaks and subsidies for the well-off; it could launch a vigorous assault on support (in the form of inflated prices and other subsidies) for farmers, thereby raising revenue for other purposes while cutting the cost of food.

A question of priorities

Much of this may seem unthinkable for Europe's socialists—like support for privatisation ten years ago. If so, it is because the character of the left, though altered and improved, needs to change further. Socialism must continue to define itself less in terms of means (we will manage the economy and civilise the market) and more in terms of priorities (we will help society's losers). The left should do this not merely to strengthen its electability further, though that would be one result. It should do it mainly because, once in power, it would then be far more likely to change society, as it wants to, for the better.

Western Europe's nationalists

The rise of the outside right

BERLIN, ROME AND PARIS

Pessimists fear that the spectre of fascism is stalking Europe. But how strong—and how fascist—is the new phenomenon?

AT FIRST blench, it has been a disturbingly good few weeks for Europe's far right. An Austrian with a taste for populist nationalism won nearly a quarter of the vote at a general election on October 9th. On the same day in Antwerp, Belgium's second city, more than a quarter of voters in local elections plumped for an anti-immigrant party. In Italy, the leader of the most right-wing big party is, according to the latest opinion polls, the country's most popular politician. In France, the tally of seats won in the summer's Euro-election by two parties to the right of the mainstream conservatives suggests that nearly a quarter of French voters might now support the "extreme right".

What to make of this? The usually stolid *Le Monde* shuddered: "It is as if, in one day, the mythic gateways of the Ancient Continent—its North Sea port and the capital of Central Europe—had been swept away by a wave of extremism moving across Europe." Western European democracies, the newspaper argued, must now accept that one-fifth of their voters oppose tolerance and openness.

To define the problem as one of a worryingly large minority seems justified.

The far right is more powerful, in more countries, than it has been in the recent past. Reasons for its appeal exist other than a thuggish liking for intolerance and violence: fear of crime, inflation and immigration; fear of the erosion of "family values", fear (perhaps) of losing national identity to the European Union.

But what does not seem justified, for now at least, is the idea that parties of the far right might have a chance of running a government in Europe, except perhaps as a junior coalition partner (as in Italy). It is not justified to say that the far right is growing across the continent. Counter-examples come from Germany, where the far right is collapsing, and from Britain, where the far right party lost the only munipical seat it previously held at recent local elections.

Still less is it justified to think that this means the horrors of the 1930s may be repeated. True, some symptoms and causes of the old disease have reappeared. The most consistent is a feverish assertion of nation-statehood, accompanied by a hatred of immigrants. Anti-semitism still permeates virtually all the parties of the far-right.

Yet the new far right is not technically fascist—or neo-fascist, semi-fascist, even palaeo-fascist. Hitler and Mussolini are no longer models. Most leaders eschew the symbols of the 1930s (though their brutal admirers are less bashful about parading in swastikas). In economics, the new far right is not corporatist, but liberal. Most important, the leaders say they accept pluralist democracy as the best form of government. Many mean it. There is nothing to suggest that the rise of some kind of fascism is inexorable.

The good Germans

In the country which has historical reasons for being most nervous of fascism, the far-right is self-destructing. Some people worried that in the long run of elections in **Germany** this year, the two main grouplets of the far-right, the Republicans and the German People's Union, would win enough seats to affect the outcome of the general election.

This fear has not proved justified. The Republicans, the more feared of the two, with 14 seats in the Baden-Württemberg state parliament, have sidelined their eccentric, former Waffen-ss leader, Franz Schönhuber, and will be lucky to win 2% in the election on October 16th.

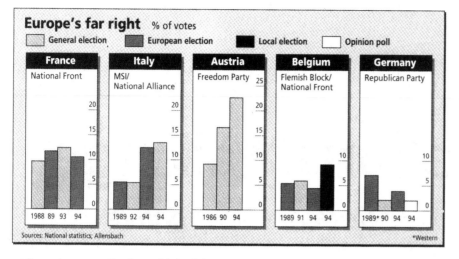

Europe's far right % of votes

☐ General election   ▨ European election   ■ Local election   ☐ Opinion poll

France	Italy	Austria	Belgium	Germany
National Front	MSI/ National Alliance	Freedom Party	Flemish Block/ National Front	Republican Party
1988 89 93 94	1989 92 94 94	1986 90 94	1989 91 94 94	1989* 90 94 94

Sources: National statistics; Allensbach

*Western

The main reason for the curbing of the far right is that Germany's big conservative party, the Christian Democratic Union, together with its Bavarian ally, the Christian Social Union, are broad churches. They heed the advice of the late Franz Josef Strauss, the CSU's former leader, to leave no "enemies to the right". The mainstream of conservatism in Germany is pro-European and internationalist; German nationalists exist only among its furthest fringes. When the parties' leaders sense that anti-immigrant sentiment is rising, they take note. Hence the curbing, two years ago, of Germany's generous asylum law. If a right-of-centre government continues in office, there is no reason to believe that Germany's far right will revive.

In most other countries in Western Europe, the far right has grown slightly during the recession (see chart), but not alarmingly so. Unusually high votes are confined to cities such as Antwerp, where a large immigrant population rubs against a working-class indigenous population. In **Belgium**, **Holland** and **Denmark**, extreme right-wingers, even during the recession, have not captured more than 6% of the vote in general elections. True, Belgium's assorted far right-wingers have doubled their vote over the past five years, but the 9% that they captured in last week's local elections was slightly less than their score in the European elections this summer: they may have peaked.

In **Britain**, where the voting system penalises small parties, the anti-immigrant parties have never won a seat in parliament; they have gained the barest handful in local elections. As in Germany, the broad church of the Conservative Party prevents supporters drifting to the far right. In **Spain** and **Portugal**, run for decades by authoritarian right-wing regimes, the anti-democratic right enjoys minimal support. Neo-Nazis in the **Nordic countries** remain powerless.

The **French** case is more complex. Over the past decade, support for Jean-Marie Le Pen and his National Front has hovered at 10-14%. It won 12.4% in the parliamentary elections last year and 10.5% in this summer's Euro-vote. Though its support has remained consistently at this (relatively) high level, it has never broken through the 15% barrier. But do Philippe de Villiers and his new Struggle for Values movement also qualify as "far right"?

Mr de Villiers shares some of the views of the far right: he is opposed to European integration, to open borders within the European Union and to free trade. He trumpets "traditional values": the family, the nation, the Catholic church. On the other hand, he is not racist or anti-Semitic and has not put hostility to immigration at the heart of his programme. The platform his movement supported won 12% of this summer's vote for the European Parliament. If it is deemed part of the far right, then nearly a quarter of French voters back this wing.

But that is too simple. At least some—perhaps many—of his supporters voted for him not because they share his Catholic fundamentalist, ultra-nationalist views, but merely because they share his hostility to the Maastricht treaty.

Nibbling at the centre

As in Germany and Britain, France's mainstream right has fended off the far right partly by stealing its thunder. In the late 1980s, Charles Pasqua, a Gaullist who is France's tough interior minister, said that the National Front and the mainstream right "shared many of the same values". The ruling conservatives have tightened French citizenship laws and introduced spot identity checks, deportation of illegal immigrants and restrictions on families joining immigrants living in France. Mr Pasqua now says he wants "zero immigration". So long as such figures have clout, anti-immigrant voters need not rush to the embrace of Mr Le Pen.

While, in almost all big western European countries, the far right is contained, there are two places where it might break out to wield greater influence: **Austria** and **Italy**. Austria's Freedom Party, which won 22.6% of the vote on October 9th, now has a small chance (which may grow) of joining a coalition government, should the long-standing ruling combination of centre-left and centre-right parties wither. The far-right Italian Social Movement (MSI), the key component of the National Alliance which won 13.5% in a general election in March, is already part of Silvio Berlusconi's ruling coalition; opinion polls say the MSI's leader, Gianfranco Fini, is more popular than the prime minister.

The question is not whether these far-right parties are gaining in strength—clearly they are—but how great is their potential for mischief in the future. At the moment, the answer is unclear. On the one hand, both Jörg Haider, leader of the Freedom Party, and Mr Fini, leader of the post-fascist (as he likes to term it) MSI, are well spoken men in their early 40s, who wear neat suits and sound reasonable. They are not corporatist. They have no feverish messianic vision. They do not rant.

On the other hand, Mr Haider is fiercely xenophobic, and has been goaded more than once into praising Hitler's employment policies. As for Mr Fini, while he says he wishes to bury his party's past (its parentage goes back to Mussolini), *Il Duce*'s granddaughter Alessandra, an MSI member of parliament for Naples, says that "grandfather would have done what he [Mr Fini] is doing". Respect for democracy does not seem instinctive to either man.

What both men have in common is that they have have benefited from popular disdain for the corrupt or decayed establishments that have run their countries for the past few decades. During the cold war, much of Europe's anti-establishment vote went to Marxists. That option, for most, has shrunk. Instead, people like Mr Fini and Mr Haider, posing as outsiders against systems of cosy patronage, are sweeping up the protest vote. Significantly, they are both hostile to the supranational bureaucracy of Brussels: Mr Haider campaigned against Austria's entry into the European Union. Mr Fini is more ambivalent.

Thus the success of Austria's and Italy's far right does not mean that fascism is creeping up on Europe. But it may mean that parties of the mainstream right will have to pay more attention to the mood of sourness and suspicion that is helping the far right. It may mean that mainstream parties will pander more to xenophobia and other ugly emotions. And that, in turn, may mean that the post-war consensus of Social Democratic and Christian Democratic Europeanism could give way to a narrower, less tolerant, less open kind of Europe of prickly nation-states.

The Migration Challenge

Europe's Crisis in Historical Perspective

James F. Hollifield

James F. Hollifield is Assistant Professor of Political Science at Auburn University.

Few issues have had a greater impact on the politics and society of contemporary Western Europe than immigration. The variety of national responses to the migration crisis would seem to indicate that each state is designing its own policy, and that there is little to link one national experience with another. Moreover, a majority of West European governments and elites have rejected any comparisons with the American experience, arguing that the United States is a nation of immigrants, with much greater territory and a political culture that is more tolerant of ethnic and cultural differences. In recent years, the American "model" of a multicultural and immigrant society has been deemed by many political and intellectual elites in Western Europe a bad model, which can only lead to greater social and political conflict—such critics point to the 1992 riots in Los Angeles. Yet the problems of immigration control (and ultimately the assimilation of foreign populations) in Europe are much the same as in the United States, for two reasons.

First, the global economic dynamic which underlies the migration crisis is similar in the two regions. The great postwar migrations to Western Europe and the United States began, for the most part, in response to the demand for cheap labor and the pull of high-growth economies, which in the 1950s and 1960s literally sucked labor from poorer countries of the periphery, especially Mexico, the Caribbean, southern Europe, North Africa and Turkey. These labor migrations (and *demand-pull* forces) were subsequently legitimized by the receiving states through what came to be known as guestworker and bracero policies. This economically beneficial movement of labor was consistent with the liberal spirit of the emerging global economy.

But what started as an efficient transfer of labor from poor countries of the South to the North, rapidly became a social and political liability in the 1970s, when growth rates in the OECD countries slowed in the aftermath of the first big postwar recession of 1973-74. The recession led to major policy shifts in Western Europe to stop immigration or, at least, to stop the recruitment of foreign workers. At the same time, however, demand-pull forces were rapidly giving way to *supply-push* forces, as the populations of poorer, peripheral countries began to grow at a rapid pace and their economies weakened. Informational and kinship networks had been established between immigrants and their home countries (via families and villages). These networks helped to spur immigration, despite the increasingly desperate attempts by receiving states in Western Europe to stop all forms of immigration.

Global economic (push-pull) forces provide the necessary conditions for international migration, especially the continuation of immigration in Western Europe after the implementation of restrictionist policies in the 1970s. But to understand fully the crisis of immigration control in the 1980s and 1990s, we must look beyond economics to liberal political developments in the major receiving states. The struggle to win civil and social *rights* for marginal groups, including ethnic minorities and foreigners, and the institutionalization of these rights in the jurisprudence of liberal states provide the sufficient conditions for continued immigration. Therefore, to get a complete picture of the migration crisis we must look at the degree of institutionalization of rights-based politics in the countries of Western Europe and at the struggle to redefine citizenship and nationhood in states such as France, Britain and Germany.

The migration tides of the 1950s and 1960s created new and reluctant lands of immigration in Western Europe

Reprinted with permission from *Harvard International Review*, Summer 1994, pp. 26-29, 67-69.

and brought to the fore questions of citizenship, the rights of minorities and multiculturalism. The migration crisis also led to the rise of anti-immigrant, right-wing parties opposed to the extension of rights to non-citizens, ethnic minorities and asylum seekers. These right-wing political and social movements amounted to a populist/nativist backlash tinged with neofascism and opposed to rights-based, liberal politics. But the migration crisis also demonstrated the extent to which new civil and social rights for foreign and ethnic minorities had become embedded in the jurisprudence, institutions and political processes of the West European states since 1945. A new sensitivity to the rights of minorities and refugees grew out of the experiences of the Second World War and the Cold War, making it difficult for states simply to expel or deport unwanted migrants, as was done in earlier periods.

Origins of the Migration Crisis

The origins of the migration crisis in Western Europe can be traced to three historical developments, each of which contributed to the political-economic dynamic described above. First is the crisis of *decolonization* which led to an unsettled period of mass migrations from roughly 1945 to 1962-63. The political and economic significance of these movements of populations early in the postwar period should not be underestimated, for it was the aftermath of war and decolonization that created new ethnic cleavages and a new ethnic consciousness in these societies and, thereby, laid the groundwork for the rise of extremist, populist and nativist movements such as the *Front National* in France and the *Republikaner* in Germany.

The second and perhaps most important wellspring of the migration crisis in Western Europe is the set of public policies known as guestworker (*Gastarbeiter*) or rotation policies. These policies for recruiting ostensibly temporary foreign workers began as early as 1945 in Switzerland, whose policy came to be viewed as the model for guestworker programs in other West European countries. The central feature of these policies was the concept of rotation, whereby foreign unmarried male workers could be brought into the labor market for a specified, contractual period and sent back at the end of this period. They could be replaced by new workers as needed. This was a rather neat macroeconomic formula for solving what was shaping up to be one of the principal obstacles to continued high rates of non-inflationary growth in the 1950s and 1960s. In fact, it seemed to be working so well in the Swiss case that the newly reorganized Organization for Economic Cooperation and Development (OECD) recommended the policy to European states that were experiencing manpower shortages. The Bonn government forged a consensus in 1959-60 among business and labor groups to opt for a policy of importing labor rather than taking industry, capital and jobs offshore in search of lower labor costs, as was being done in the United States. This was the beginning of the largest guestworker program in Western Europe, which would eventually bring millions of Turks, Yugoslavs and Greeks to work in German industry.

Two fateful turning points in the history of the German guestworker program are of interest. The first came in 1967-68, following the shallow recession of 1966. It was at this point that the Grand Coalition government (1966-69) successfully stopped Turks and other guestworkers from entering the labor market, and sent many of them home. This operation was so successful that there was little resistance to bringing the guestworkers back in 1969-70, when the West European economies were heating up again. The second fateful turning point in the history of the *Gastarbeiter* program in Germany came in 1973 when the attempt was made to stop all recruitment of foreign workers, to repatriate them and to prevent family reunification. It was at this point that the relatively new liberal features of the German state came fully to the fore to prevent the government and administrative authorities from stopping immigration (especially family reunification) and deporting unwanted migrants.

France is often mentioned as a European country that pursued guestworker-type policies, a somewhat misleading conception. The Provisional or Tripartite Government under General Charles de Gaulle (1945-46), as well as the first governments of the Fourth Republic, did put in place policies for recruiting foreign labor. But the new workers were defined from the outset as *travailleurs immigrés* (immigrant workers). Policies of Fourth Republic governments encouraged foreign workers to settle permanently because immigration was part and parcel of population policy, which was itself a reflection of pronatalist sentiments among the political elites.

As the French economy boomed in the 1960s, authorities rapidly lost all control over immigration. But instead of sucking more labor from culturally compatible neighboring countries, such as Italy and Spain (which were beginning to develop in their own right), the French economy was supplied principally by the newly independent states of North Africa (Algeria, Morocco and Tunisia). By the end of the 1960s, Algerians were rapidly becoming the most numerous immigrant group. Their special post-colonial status gave them virtual freedom of movement into and out of the former *metropole* of France. The principal "mode of immigration" during this period was immigration "from within," whereby foreigners would enter the country (often having been recruited by business), take a job and then have a request be made on their behalf by the firm for an adjustment of status.

By the early 1970s, the rapid increase in North African immigration convinced the Pompidou government that something had to be done to regain control of immigration. The deep recession of 1973-74, which brought an abrupt end to the postwar boom, simply confirmed this judgment. The new government under Valery Giscard d'Estaing took fairly dramatic steps to close the immigration valve, using heavy-handed statist and administrative measures to try to stop immigration, repatriate immigrants and deny "rights" of family reunification. Thus, the French followed much the same logic as the Germans in attempting to use foreign workers, on one hand, as a kind of industrial reserve army and, on the other, as shock absorbers to solve social and economic problems associated with recession—especially unemployment. Other labor-importing states in Western Europe followed the same guestworker logic in changing from policies of recruitment to suspension.

2. FACTORS IN THE POLITICAL PROCESS: Ethnic Factor

The migration crisis in Western Europe in the 1980s and 1990s cannot be fully understood apart from the history of the guestworker programs. These programs created the illusion of temporary migration, leading some states (especially Germany) to avoid or postpone a national debate over immigration and assimilation policy. This problem was compounded by the statist attempts in 1973-74 to stop immigration and repatriate foreigners, which furthered the "myth of return" and heightened public expectations that governments could simply reverse the migratory process. Also, taking such a strong, statist stance against further immigration made it virtually impossible for French and German governments in the 1980s and 1990s even to discuss an "American-style," legal immigration policy. Instead, immigration became a highly charged partisan issue, leading to soul-searching debates about national identity and citizenship. The more practical questions—which an American policymaker or politician might ask—of "how many, from where, and in what status," simply could not be asked. The result of trying to slam shut the "front door" of legal immigration led to the opening of side doors and windows (for family members and seasonal workers). Most importantly, the "back door" was left wide open (especially in Germany) for refugees and asylum-seekers. Not surprisingly, many would-be legal and illegal immigrants (as well as legitimate asylum-seekers and others) flooded through the back door in the 1980s and 1990s.

At present, it would appear that the politics of xenophobia, nativism and restrictionism prevail and that each state is defining immigration and refugee policies in idiosyncratic and nationalistic terms.

The third historical development in the migration crisis is the influx of *refugees* and *asylum-seekers*, which is causally related to colonialism and to the failed guestworker policies. Large-scale refugee migrations began in Europe in the aftermath of the Second World War and with the advent of the Cold War. In practice, flight from a communist regime was sufficient grounds for the extension of political asylum in most of the countries of Western Europe. The famous Article 16 of the West German Basic Law, which granted an almost unconditional right to asylum for any individual fleeing persecution, was written with refugees from the East in mind, especially ethnic German refugees.

Refugee and asylum policies in Western Europe functioned rather well for almost three decades from roughly 1950 to 1980 (during most of the Cold War), but with the closing of front-door immigration policies in the 1970s, political asylum became an increasingly attractive mode of entry for unwanted migrants who would come to be labeled "economic refugees." As governments across Western Europe struggled to redefine their immigration and refugee policies in the wake of severe economic recessions and rising unemployment, the pace of refugee migrations increased. The first efforts to address this new movement of populations came at the level of the European Community, where it was thought that national governments could simultaneously reassert control over refugee movements and avoid the painful moral and political dilemmas involved in limiting the right to asylum. The Single European Act of 1985 set in motion a new round of European economic integration, which included the goal of "free movement of goods, persons, services and capital"—in effect, the establishment of a border-free Europe. It quickly became clear, however, that achieving this goal would require European states to agree upon common visa and asylum policies.

Toward this end, five states (France, Germany, and the Benelux countries) met in the Dutch town of Schengen, and in 1985 unveiled the Schengen Agreement as a prototype for a border-free Europe. The Agreement called for the elimination of internal borders, the harmonization of visa and asylum policies and the coordinated policing of external borders, leading to the construction of a symbolic "ring fence" around the common territory. Schengen, which was enlarged to include Italy, Spain and Portugal, was followed in 1990 by the Dublin Agreement, which established the principle that refugees must apply for asylum in the first EC member state in which they arrive. But no sooner had the states of Western Europe begun to focus on a common policy for dealing with the refugee and asylum issue, than had the entire international system in Europe changed with the collapse of communist regimes in East-Central Europe and, finally, the collapse of the Soviet Union itself.

The euphoria associated with the "triumph of liberalism" over communism did contribute, at least briefly, to a surge of refugee migration. That surge lasted for about four years, from 1989 to 1993. Governments were forced to reconsider and rewrite sweeping constitutional provisions, which guaranteed the right to asylum, at the same time that new irredentist movements swept the Balkans, Transcaucasia, and other formerly communist territories, leading to civil wars and new refugee migrations.

How have the states of Western Europe and the EC responded to the migration crisis? The responses can be identified at three levels. The first is political, in the sense that politicians, especially on the right, have exploited the migration crisis for political gain. The second is a policy-level response, which has lurched from one extreme to another. Liberal and assimilationist policies of amnesty (for illegals) have been followed by harsh crackdowns on asylum-seekers and attempts to make naturalization more difficult. Finally, emerging from this cauldron of political and policy debates is a search for national "models" of immigration, which range from tempered pluralism in Britain to stringent assimilation in France.

The Search for a National Model

France was the first state in Western Europe to feel the full political force of the migration crisis, in part because of the stunning victory of the left in the presidential and parliamentary elections of 1981. The socialists won the elections partly on a liberal platform, which promised to improve civil rights for immigrants by giving them a more firm legal standing. To carry out these promises, the first socialist government of Pierre Mauroy enacted a conditional amnesty, which led to the legalization of well over 100,000 undocumented immigrants. Other measures also were taken to limit the arbitrary powers of the police to carry out identity checks, to grant long-term (10-year) resident permits to foreigners and to guarantee the rights of association for immigrant groups. These liberal policies, carried out in the wake of the left's electoral breakthrough and with the right in a state of temporary disarray, provided an opening for a little-known populist and neo-fascist candidate, Jean-Marie Le Pen, and the *Front National* (FN). The early 1980s was also a period of recession, rising unemployment and general insecurity, especially among workers. Le Pen and his group seized the moment and won what seemed to be a small victory (16.7 percent of the vote) in the town of Dreux, near Paris. But this was the beginning of an intense period of immigration politics, as the right struggled to regain power and Le Pen, under the banner of *La France aux français*, garnered more support from an extremely volatile electorate.

The traditional parties of the right, *Rassemblement pour la République* (RPR) and *Union pour la Démocratie Française* (UDF), under the leadership of Jacques Chirac, Mayor of Paris, began to attack the socialists' handling of the immigration issue. The socialists responded by defending liberal and republican principles of naturalization and assimilation, holding out the prospect of voting rights for resident aliens in local elections, while promising to enforce labor laws (employer sanctions) in order to crack down on illegal immigration. In the parliamentary elections of 1985, which were fought under new rules of proportional representation, the right won a narrow victory. The FN won over 30 seats in the new parliament, giving Le Pen a forum in which to pursue his anti-immigrant, populist, nativist agenda. The Minister of the Interior in the government of *cohabitation* (headed by Chirac), Charles Pasqua, launched a series of initiatives and bills, which came to be known as *la loi Pasqua*. They intended to give greater power to the police to arrest and deport undocumented migrants, and to deny entry to asylum-seekers, who would not be allowed to appeal their cases to the office for protection of refugees (OFPRA).

Immigrant rights groups, such as *SOS-racisme, France Plus,* MRAP and the GISTI, organized protests and legal appeals to stop the reform. Thousands marched in the streets under banners that read *ne touche pas mon pote* (don't touch my buddy) and the French Council of State was called upon to review the legality (and constitutionality) of the government's immigration policy. In the end, the government made a decision to appoint a special commission composed of leading intellectual and political figures. The commission held public hearings and wrote a long report, concluding that French republican principles of universalism and the right of foreigners born in France to naturalize (*jus soli*) should be upheld. At the same time, the commission stressed the importance of maintaining the assimilationist, republican principles, inherent in French immigration law and practice. The right lost the presidential

and parliamentary elections of 1988, essentially failing to capitalize on the immigration issue, while Jean-Marie Le Pen succeeded in gaining 14.5 percent of the vote on the first ballot of the presidential elections. But the FN received only one seat in the new parliament, which was elected according to the old two-round, single member district rules used throughout the history of the Fifth Republic until 1985. Le Pen cried foul, arguing that the voices of a significant proportion of the French electorate were not being heard, and opinion polls, which showed that over a third of the voters supported the positions of the FN, seemed to bear him out.

The socialist government of François Mitterrand and Michel Rocard continued to defend rights of foreigners, but also launched a campaign for tougher enforcement of labor laws and set up a new council for integration (*Haut Conseil à l'Intégration*) to study ways of bringing immigrants into the mainstream of French social, economic and political life.

French Immigration Policy in the 1990s

Immigration in France continued during this period of the 1980s at a rate of about 100,000 annually, and refugee migrations picked up to about 25,000 annually. As the country slipped slowly into recession in 1991-92, the left began to lose its nearly decade-long grip on power. The parliamentary elections of 1993 were fought in part over the issue of immigration control, with the right feeling little compulsion to restrain anti-immigrant, populist and nativist sentiments among the public. In fact, the decision was made to try to steal the thunder of Le Pen and the FN by proposing harsh measures for dealing with illegal immigration and asylum seekers. The badly divided socialist party suffered a crushing defeat in March 1993, and the reinvigorated right (RPR-UDF), under the new leadership of Edouard Balladur, wasted little time in implementing draconian measures (by French standards) to stop immigration. Once again, Pasqua was named to head the Interior Ministry, and with the right controlling nearly 80 percent of the seats in the National Assembly, he proposed a series of bills to reform immigration, naturalization and refugee law (*la loi Pasqua II*). These measures amounted to a broadside attack on the civil and social rights of foreigners. They sought to undermine key aspects of the republican model, as spelled out in the *Ordonnances* of 1945, especially residency requirements for naturalization, the principle of *jus soli* and the guarantee of due process for asylum-seekers.

La loi Pasqua II also included a bill designed to prevent illegal immigrants from benefiting from French social security, particularly health care. This legislation immediately opened a rift in the new French cabinet between the hardline Minister of Interior and Regional Development, Pasqua, and the more liberal-republican Minister of Social, Health and Urban Affairs, Simone Veil, who argued successfully that emergency medical care should not be denied to foreigners. *Pasqua II* also sought to limit the civil rights of immigrants and asylum-seekers, by increasing the powers of the police and the administration to detain and deport unwanted migrants. Under the new policy, the police are given sweeping powers to check the identity of "suspicious persons." Race is not supposed to be sufficient grounds for stopping an individual, but any immigrant (legal or otherwise) who threatens "public order" can be arrested and deported.

Immigrant workers and students are obliged to wait two years, rather than one, before being allowed to bring their families to join them in France, and illegal immigrants cannot be legalized simply by marrying a French citizen. Finally, *Pasqua II* resurrected the Chirac government's proposal to reform French nationality law (1986), which requires the children of foreigners born in France to file a formal request for naturalization between the ages of 16 and 21, rather than automatically attributing French citizenship to them at age 18.

These repressive measures, which were designed specifically to roll back the rights of foreigners, immigrants and asylum seekers, immediately drew fire from those institutions of the liberal and republican state that were created to protect the rights of individuals. The Council of State, as it had done several times before, warned the government that it was on shaky legal ground, especially with respect to the "rights" of family reunification and political asylum. But the rulings of the Council of State are advisory; no matter how much moral, political and legal weight they may carry, the government can choose to ignore them. The rulings, however, can presage binding decisions of the Constitutional Council, which has limited powers of judicial review. This is precisely what happened in August 1993, as the Constitutional Council found several provisions of the new policy (*Pasqua II*) to be unconstitutional.

All this political and legal maneuvering in 1993 has led inexorably to a full constitutional debate over immigration and refugee policy in France. French President François Mitterrand, who has considerable constitutional responsibilities and political and moral authority, has stayed for the most part on the sidelines. The Minister of the Interior, Pasqua, has continued doggedly to pursue more restrictionist immigration and naturalization policies, at the levels of both symbolic and electoral politics. Any political victories on this front would seem to come at the expense of the principal rivals of the RPR-UDF, namely the FN on the right and the Socialist Party on the left.

These policy and political responses to the migration crisis in France constitute a tacit recognition that there is only so much any state can do to alter push-pull forces, and that a "roll back" of civil and social rights is the most effective way to control or stop immigration. But in France, as in the US and Germany, administrative and executive authorities are confronted with a range of constitutional obstacles associated with the liberal and republican state. The republican model, with its universalistic and egalitarian principles, remains essentially intact, despite repeated assaults from the French right. France still has the most expansive naturalization policies of any state in Western Europe and it has preserved the principles of *jus soli*, as well as due process, equality before the law and the right to asylum. Whether the republican model will survive the current assault and whether it can serve as a broader European model remains to be seen.

The German Response

Until recently, debates over immigration and refugee policy in Germany were confined to policy and administrative elites or academic and intellectual circles. But in the late 1980s, and especially since unification, politicians have seized on the immigration and refugee issue. A full-blown national debate has erupted, with politicians vying for mass support and various social movements on the left and the right seeking to influence policymaking. Unlike France, Germany does not have an established "national model" around which to organize this debate. Debates over immigration, naturalization and refugee law are not, however, devoid of ethno-nationalist or ethno-cultural arguments. The current German nationality law dates from 1913; there are clear historical and national overtones in the debate. But the experience of the Holocaust and the defeat suffered in World War II make it difficult for German authorities to appeal to the past as a way of coping with immigration. Until 1989, a consensus existed among political and policy elites simply to avoid debates over immigration, naturalization and citizenship issues. Foreigners were granted social and civil rights, but barriers to naturalization remained high and the politically explosive issue of reforming the nationality code was avoided.

This ostrich-like approach to immigration policy and the elite's consensus not to raise the issue simply fell apart under the pressure of events in the 1980s. Decades of repressed nationalism have come bubbling to the surface in contemporary party politics. Polls, which showed rising opposition to immigration, encouraged politicians to take up the issue. When Helmut Kohl was chosen to head the new government of the right in 1982, he introduced a new *Ausländerpolitik*, but in the election campaign of 1982-83, the issue simply disappeared from the national agenda. In effect, policy and political elites decided to return to the earlier consensus of silence. Also strong was an appeal to the founding (economic) myth of the Federal Republic, or *Wirtschaftswunder*, that seemingly intractable social, economic and even political problems could be solved by another German economic miracle. But this economic solution proved insufficient to solve the problems of immigration control and assimilation, especially with rising unemployment rates and severe housing shortages. By the mid- to late-1980s, foreigners were increasingly being blamed for taking jobs, housing and public services away from German citizens.

In the Bavarian *Landtag* elections of 1986, the CSU raised the issue of immigration control, in part to counter the break-away of a small faction of the party, under the leadership of a former talk show host, Franz Schonhuber. This faction became the *Republikaner* party and gained 3 percent of the vote. In the following years the *Republikaner* continued to make inroads at the level of state and local politics. With the collapse of the German Democratic Republic and the unification of Germany in 1989-90, it appeared that the *Republikaner* had lost its appeal. It received only 2.1 percent of the vote in the first all-German, federal election in 1990. But its fortunes were to improve in the early 1990s. Clearly, with the collapse of Communism and the end of the Cold War, some of the restraints on overt expressions of German nationalism were removed and the immigration issue was no longer taboo. A new anti-foreigner slogan, *Ausländer raus*, became the rallying cry of far-right, skinhead and neo-Nazi groups. The massive influx of asylum seekers from 1989-93 contributed to the atmosphere of crisis, placing more pressure on the government to act, and making it easier for politicians (of the right) to use the immigration and asylum issue to get votes.

In 1990, the newly reelected government of Kohl faced two problems: how to facilitate the integration and naturalization of the large foreign population, without alienating more of the right-wing electorate, and how to build a consensus for changing Article 16 of the German Constitution to stem the rising tide of asylum seekers, while keeping the front door open to ethnic German refugees from the East. The first task was at least partially accomplished by rushing a bill through parliament to facilitate naturalization of second-generation immigrants, thereby solidifying the rights of resident aliens, and removing some of the legal ambiguities concerning residency, work permits and family reunification. This was done quietly in the midst of the social and political euphoria following unification.

The sufficient conditions for immigration...are likely to persist, even if they are weakened by attacks from the extreme right and lack of popular support.

Reform of immigration and refugee policy was given a new urgency in 1992 and 1993 by a series of much-publicized racist attacks against foreigners, including a fire-bombing by skinheads in the town of Solingen resulting in the death of five Turks who were permanent residents of the Federal Republic. More racist attacks occurred, however, just weeks after the Christian-Liberal government and the Social Democrats agreed in May 1993 to amend Article 16 of the Constitution. Although the language of the new asylum law, which states that "those politically persecuted enjoy the right to asylum," is consistent with the Geneva Convention, in practice the new law allows the German government to turn back asylum-seekers who arrive through a safe country. Since about 80 percent of refugees enter through Poland and the Czech Republic, an agreement had to be reached with these states to allow for the *refoulement* of asylum-seekers. Since the new policy was instituted, the number of migrants apprehended trying to enter the country illegally has skyrocketed.

Despite a great deal of rhetoric following racial violence and fatal attacks on foreigners in 1993 and 1994, the Kohl government was unable to change German nationality law, which dates from 1913 and rests on the principle of *jus sanguinis* (blood, rather than soil or place of birth). The German law also does not allow dual citizenship. Hence, millions of foreign residents have been granted some civil and social rights, but without naturalization. They remain outsiders without full political rights, even though in many cases they have been born, reared and educated in Germany.

The Immigration Issue in Southern Europe

The countries of southern Europe—Italy, Spain, Greece and Portugal—are still far from developing national models for immigration control and assimilation. As the traditional receiving states in northern Europe tried to close their borders to new immigration in the 1970s and 1980s, more unwanted migrants (especially from Africa) began to enter the EC via the soft underbelly of Italy, Spain and Greece. Political change (democratization in Greece, Spain and Portugal) together with high levels of economic growth contributed to the influx of unwanted migrants. Policy responses have lurched from one extreme to another, in the face of a growing political backlash against foreigners, especially in northern Italy where the anti-immigrant Northern League has been capturing about one fifth of the vote in recent elections. Amnesty was extended to illegal immigrants in Spain (1985) and Italy (1987) in the hopes of bringing marginal groups and ethnic minorities into the mainstream of society by offering protections under the rubric of social welfare. But the push to establish a border-free Europe, as a result of the Single European Act, the Schengen Agreement and, finally, the Maastricht Treaty (which holds out the prospect of a kind of European citizenship in the next century), has forced the states of southern Europe to reformulate their immigration and refugee policies. To be a part of a border-free Europe, they must demonstrate a capacity for controlling their borders and stopping illegal immigration.

The perceived failure of national policies and the lack of a dominant national model for dealing with the migration crisis have led many governments in Western Europe to look for a Europe-wide solution to the problem of immigration control. The hope here is that the states of the European Union will be able to accomplish together what they have been unable to accomplish alone: stop immigration.

A European Solution to a Global Problem?

From the Treaty of Rome (1957) to the Maastricht Treaty, the logic of European integration has driven the states of Western Europe to cooperate on border control issues. The logic is one of both inclusion (free movement of goods, services, capital and *people*) and exclusion (a common tariff policy, an economic and monetary union and common visa and asylum policies). But common visa and asylum policies have proved illusive. The prospect of a truly border-free Europe places enormous pressure on member states to cooperate in the policing of external borders.

Control over population and territory are key aspects of national sovereignty that strike at the heart of notions of citizenship and national identity. Since ceding this aspect of sovereignty to a supranational organization such as the EU is a potentially explosive political issue, member states, as well as the European Council and the Commission, have proceeded with great caution. In Dublin in 1990, the European Council established the principle that refugees can apply for political asylum in only one member state. Shortly thereafter, the Schengen Group, which had been enlarged from the original five (France, Germany and Benelux) to include Italy, Spain and Portugal, met to sign the Convention that set in motion a process for lifting all border controls among these states. Britain, as an island-nation, steadfastly refused to get involved in the Schengen process for fear of losing its natural advantage in border control. Still, the inclusionary and exclusionary logic of Schengen seems to be taking hold in post-cold war Europe, as other states and regions have scrambled to join the border-free club. Only Switzerland and Denmark have been reluctant to jump on this bandwagon.

How will "Europe" respond to the global migration crisis? We can learn some things by looking at the recent past, especially the liberal dynamic of *markets* (demand-pull and supply-push) and *rights* (civil, social and political) described above. We must also compare the European and American experiences, because the EU and the United States will be the pacesetters in searching for an international solution to the global migration crisis. Will there be separate American and European models for coping with migration, or will the two models converge? The liberal dynamic and the recent past point to convergence. With the end of the Cold War, all OECD states have experienced an upsurge in migration because (happily) people are freer to move, and because (sadly) ethnic and nationalist forces have been unleashed, causing a wave of refugee migration. The liberal logic of interdependence and economic integration has reinforced the propensity of people to move, in search of higher wages and a better way of life. Supply-push remains strong, but demand-pull is weak. Most of the OECD states are in (or just emerging from) recession. Nevertheless, with slower population growth (especially in Western Europe and Japan) and higher levels of economic growth, demand for immigrant labor is likely to increase as we move closer to the turn of the century. The necessary economic conditions for immigration are present and likely to strengthen, hence all OECD states will be forced to deal with this reality. But what will political conditions, which are the sufficient conditions for immigration, be like in the receiving states?

At present, it would appear that the politics of xenophobia, nativism and restrictionism prevail and that each state is defining immigration and refugee policies in idiosyncratic and nationalistic terms. The rights of immigrants and refugees have been restricted and infringed in Europe and the United States, as governments (freed from the bipolar constraints of the Cold War) have sought to roll back some of the liberal political developments (especially in the area of civil rights) of the past forty years. But liberal-republican institutions and laws are quite resilient. It seems unlikely that what have come to be defined as basic human or civil rights will simply be suspended for non-citizens. Therefore, the sufficient conditions for immigration, which are closely linked to the institutions and laws of the liberal-republican state, are likely to persist, even if they are weakened by attacks from the extreme right and lack of popular support. It is also unlikely that liberal-republicanism will be abandoned or overridden by supranational institutions, such as the EU. The same institutional and legal checks found at the level of the nation-state are evident at the European level.

Since immigration is likely to continue, pressure will mount for states to cooperate in controlling and managing the flow. The states of Western Europe already have taken several steps in this direction at the level of the European Union. But no national or regional model for integration of the large and growing foreign populations has emerged. Policies for controlling the doors of entry (front, side and back) will emerge, barring some unforeseen international catastrophe. Redefining citizenship and nationhood in the older states of Western Europe, however, will be a much longer and more painful process. It remains to be seen which states are best equipped, politically and culturally, to face this challenge.

Women, Power and Politics:

The Norwegian Experience

Irene Garland

Irene Garland, a Norwegian social scientist, lives in London.

Three Scandinavian countries all have more than one third of women representatives in their national assemblies. In Norway the Prime Minister is a woman as are 9 out of 19 cabinet ministers as well as the leaders of 2 of the other political parties.

Commentators trying to explain this phenomenon have looked back through history and pointed to the independence of Norwegian women as far back as the Viking era, when they kept the homefires burning while their menfolk were away plundering. Others have referred to more recent times. Outstanding women, however, are to be found in most countries at some time or another. The reason for Norwegian women being so successful in gaining political power must therefore be found somewhere else. My belief is that the explanation is of a practical nature and is to be found in the post-war era.

Common to the three Scandinavian countries is a structure of progressive social democracy and election systems based on proportional representation. If one compares the number of women in parliaments across the world, one finds that proportional representation is the single most important element for women to gain entry into politics. However, it was the ability to use this system to their advantage, and the fact that a group of women managed to agree on a common course across party lines, that made it possible to break the mold of the male dominated political scene in Norway.

A SPECTACULAR BEGINNING

The year was 1967 and Brigit Wiik—editor, author, mother and leader of the Oslo Feminist Movement—recalls in her book a chance meeting between herself and Einar Gerhardsen on the street in Oslo. Einar Gerhardsen was a leader of the Labor Party and had been Prime Minister almost continuously since the war. He was, at the time, in opposition, having lost the previous election. With the local elections coming up he agreed to a quota for women on the Labor party lists. In doing so he saw an opportunity to activate a new group of voters for his party, and when his agreement was presented to the party in power, they felt compelled to do the same. With the two largest parties both agreeing to give a quota to women, representatives from The National Advisory Council for Women, The Working Women's Association and the Oslo Feminist Movement, formed a group to lead the campaign to get women into politics by harnessing the female vote. They used a professional PR firm to lead the campaign—a first in Norway. The result surprised everyone; there was a national increase in women representatives of 50%, and whereas there had been 179 local communities without women's representation prior to the election, afterwards the number was reduced to 79. Subsequent campaigns further increased the number of women in local government by 50%—except for 1975.

From *Scandinavian Review*, Vol. 79, No. 3, Winter 1991, pp. 18-25. Reprinted courtesy of the American-Scandinavian Foundation.

WOMEN IN THE NATIONAL ASSEMBLY—
THE STORTING

Though there was no campaign to elect women to the national assembly, there seems to have been a spill-over effect. Political parties were quick to recognize the advantage in gaining the female vote and soon extended the quota system to parliamentary elections.

Women's representation in parliament increased steadily from the 1969 election in parallel with what happened in the local elections.

WOMEN START WINNING THE ARGUMENTS

After the 1967 election the Central Bureau of Statistics started to separate voters by gender for the first time, and the 1970s saw an upsurge in research into the history of women's lives and living conditions. Young female researchers were for the first time given the opportunity and the funding to look into their own past, a hitherto ignored area of academic research, and much empirical data was collated during this decade. The history of women's lives ran to 18 volumes and a history of women writers to 3 volumes.

Once they gained entry into the corridors of power, women were increasingly taking up issues of importance to themselves and to the family. Such issues gained in importance by producing results at the ballot box. They could, therefore, not be ignored in party politics and as a result, became part of the overall political agenda.

Enabling policies such as the right to maternity leave and the ability to return to work after giving birth were important for women who wanted to have the choice between having a career and becoming a full-time housewife. With the increased number of women investing in higher education, going back to work was not only seen as a means of personal fulfillment, but became an economic necessity for those who needed to pay back their student loans. The availability of choice was also seen as central to the equality debate— why should men be able to have both a family and a career while women were forced to make a choice? The idea that there was such a thing as a "natural" place for a woman in the home despite qualifications or inclinations was rejected. If women were designed for domesticity by nature itself, then how could one explain the fact that women, given a chance, did very well in the outside world? The patriarchs were at a loss for an answer.

LAWS ARE CHANGED

The 1970s saw a number of typical feminist arguments being brought forward and legislation or common practices changed as a result. One such issue was the one over Miss and Mrs. Throughout the 1960s feminists had opposed the use of these titles and the alternative Ms. had not won approval. During the 1960s ardent feminists would reply to anyone asking if

THE INCREASE IN WOMEN'S REPRESENTATION

Local government elections	pre-1967	1967	1971	1975	1979
Women as a % of total	6.3	9.5	15	15	22.8
Parliamentary elections	1945–53	1969	1973	1977	1981
Women as a % of total	4.7	9.3	15	23.9	25.8

Maternity leave	2 weeks prior to confinement 30 weeks after confinement with full pay
Leave from work & the right to return	mothers have the right to a further year off work without pay
Paternity leave	fathers have the right to 2 weeks off work with pay, dependent on trade union agreement (applies to all civil servants)
Breast-feeding	mothers have their hours of work cut to accommodate breast-feeding
Children's illness	both parents have a right to 10 days off work with pay when a child under 12 is ill

	Born	Married	Children	Education
Gro H. Brundtland Prime Minister (Labor)	1939	1960	4	Degree in medicine; MA (Harvard)
Ase Kleveland Minister of Cultural Affairs (Labor)	1949	Co-habits	None	Part law degree; Studied music
Anne E. Lahnstein Leader, Centre Party	1949	1975	3	Social worker
Kaci K. Five Leader, Conservative Party	1951	1972	2	Political Science degree

they were Miss or Mrs. that it was none of their business whether they were married or not. These days no one would ask and such titles are not in general use.

Another issue was that of surnames upon marriage. Women regarded giving up their own names as losing their identities. The law on surnames has now changed so that couples can choose which name to use. Some prefer to keep their maiden name. Some couples take on her name after marriage instead of his, but many women prefer to attach their husbands' name to their own. The latter is the case with the three female party leaders. Children are no longer automatically given their fathers' surname—again it is subject to parental choice.

The debate on surnames formed part of a wider debate about the right to a separate identity for women after marriage. The argument was for women to be able to carry on with their own careers and not to take on the role of supporting player to that of their husbands. Marriage should not become synonymous with taking on the cooking, cleaning and entertaining in addition to their own jobs. Entertaining could equally well be done in a restaurant anyway. Men would have to grow up and stop relying on their wives taking over where their mothers had left off. Cooking and darning became part of every boy's curriculum at school—the emphasis was on enabling men to become self-sufficient.

This also extended to quotas being set for men in certain professions, such as nursing, which until then had been dominated by women.

WOMEN IN POWER TODAY

The quota system helped the Prime Minister, **Gro Harlem Brundtland,** on her way to power. When she became Prime Minister in 1981 for the first time, it was she who introduced the idea of 50/50 gender representation in the cabinet. Having formed her third government at the most recent election, she has taken with her a team of young and capable women. Mrs. Brundtland followed in her father's footsteps—he was a doctor and a cabinet minister—and has been involved in politics from an early age. She is known for her enormous capacity for work, and certainly her record of achievements bears witness to just this. In addition to working full time she has managed to raise a family of four children. Her first job was as a medical officer on the Oslo Board of Public Health. The first ministerial position came in 1974 when she was appointed Minister for the Environment. She was appointed leader of the Labor Party in 1981, the same year that she became Prime Minister at the age of 42, the youngest ever to hold this office.

Internationally she has served on The Palme Commission which published its report on "Common Security" in 1982. This was followed by her chairing the World Commission on Environment and Development whose report, "Our Common Future," was published in 1987. She has published many scientific papers and received numerous prizes in acknowledgement of her work in different fields.

The new leader of the Conservative Party, **Kaci Kullman Five,** also started in politics quite young. Her mother, an elegant looking lady in her 60s, is still active in the local conservative party in Baerum where Mrs. Five first started out. After serving as deputy leader locally, she joined the national party, and was elected

to parliament in 1981. Her first major office was as Deputy Secretary of State for commercial affairs in the Foreign Office in 1989. Having a degree in political science, she has served on the standing committees for foreign policy and constitutional affairs and on the finance committee. She has also published a book.

The third female party leader is **Anne Enger Lahnstein** of the rural Centre Party, who comes from a farming background. She headed the national action against free abortion in 1978–79, and was a member of the Nordic Council from 1979 on, but she did not enter parliament until 1985. She was head of the Oslo Centre Party from 1980–83. From 1983 on, she served as the deputy leader of the national party until she took over as its leader this year.

Ase Kleveland, the new Minister of Culture, differs from the others in that she has not gone through the rank and file of a party. She studied classical guitar and music theory for a number of years and during the '60s and '70s was one of Norway's best known popular singers. Ms. Kleveland won the Norwegian finals of the Eurovision Song Contest and later hosted the TV program for this contest the year it was held in Norway. She headed the Norwegian Musician's Union for a period and her most recent job was as a manager of the first amusement park in Norway. She was due to take over as Cultural Director for the Olympics to be held in Lillehammer in 1994 on the very day she was offered her cabinet post.

COMBINING CAREER AND FAMILY

Combining career with family commitments is no easy task, though office hours in Norway are short—9 to 4—giving more time for both parents to spend with their children. The smaller towns and communities constitute less danger to children which also makes it easier on working parents. Often though, it would seem that having a husband with flexible working arrangements such as a researcher or a journalist helps, and there is no doubt that joint efforts are necessary when both parents work. Fathers do take a much greater part in the up-bringing of their children and in the running of homes, than previously. This "new" role for fathers has now become the norm.

The Prime Minister's children are all grown up now and she is in fact a grandmother, but her husband's job as a researcher and writer no doubt being able to work from home when the need arose, must have been a help. Anne Lahnstein's children are in their teens, only Kaci Five has a young child (8 years old), and she said in an interview that she had to work very hard in order to make time for the family—something she viewed as important. Her husband is an editor and doubtless has to take his turn in looking after the children.

SOUR GRAPES?

It is perhaps inevitable that dissenting voices be heard when so many women reach such high positions in society. Recently a study has been published suggesting that men are leaving politics in Norway because, since it has become dominated by women, it is also becoming a low-paid occupation. Men, it is claimed, are opting for the better paid, higher status jobs in the private sector.

With increased internationalization, they argue, there are many constraints on national assemblies, and important decisions are being made elsewhere; Parliament is no longer the power house it used to be.

Research by Ms. Hege Skjeie from the Institute for Social Studies, disagrees with these conclusions. It is quite true that politicians whose wages are part of the civil service wage scale are lower than those received for the top jobs in the private sector and also that many professions dominated by women are badly paid. However, wages in the state sector have always been considered low relative to private industry, and this was the case before women started to take an interest in a career in politics. Ms. Skjeie's studies found that the men leaving politics did so because of age—they had all served for quite some time. Others had in fact lost their seats or been ousted from positions of leadership within their parties—some by women. There was certainly no difficulty in recruiting young men into

politics, and as regards the power and status associated with politics one could point to Ase Kleveland, Minister of Culture, who had the choice between politics and the Olympic Committee, and chose politics in spite of its uncertainties.

"I'M ON QUOTA—AND I LOVE IT!"

There can be no doubt that it was the quota system that made it possible for Norwegian women to enter politics in such a big way. The power that comes from parliament cannot be underestimated—it has given weight to arguments that had been previously ignored and as such has changed social attitudes of both sexes to the roles and rights of men and women alike. This change could not have taken place without political backing and without such backing, it would not have received such broad social acceptance. However, it is clear that when women work together across party lines, as was the case in Norway during the early days, that is when they achieve the most. Campaigning is also necessary as the experience of 1975 showed—no campaign, no increase in women's representation. The clock cannot be turned back, but even in Norway many women feel that there is no ground for complacency.

Political power is only half the battle

Norwegian women still lag in the workplace

Norway is the only country where children ask their parents if a boy can grow up to be prime minister and get told that at present, the answer is "no way."

Nowhere else in the world do women have more political clout. In last fall's national election, Prime Minister Gro Harlem Brundtland and the leaders of the nation's two main opposition political parties were women. Helped by a quota system that recommends women make up at least 40 percent of every political party's list of candidates for Parliament, women hold almost half the seats in the cabinet and in Parliament. Norway has even changed its Constitution to allow the first-born daughter—rather than just the eldest son—to succeed to the throne upon the death of the monarch. "Norway is a leading country in the field of equal rights," says Brundtland, a physician, a mother of four and the daughter of a doctor and former cabinet minister.

---

*One of a continuing series on the
status of women around the world*

She is only half right. Despite their political gains, Norwegian women remain second-class citizens in the job market. They are hired last, fired first, denied equal pay for the same work as men and held back from promotions to top executive jobs. New laws pushed through by women politicians were supposed to end all that. But Norway's experience suggests that reforming the law is not enough to guarantee women a fair shake.

Anne Soyland, spokesperson for the Norwegian Women's Front, a feminist lobby, blames the women politicians for the disparity between women's political gains and their lowly status in the workplace. "They are not real women," she says. "Once they get elected, they join the elite and stop working as hard as they should for feminist causes."

Where men still rule. Others think the real reason is that legislation can only do so much. New laws have not changed the realities of private industry, where men still rule—and do the hiring and promoting. "Put crudely," says sociologist Oystein Holter, "that means men inject male values into personnel decisions. Perhaps a man gets the job because his military service is regarded as a better qualification than a woman rival's child-care experience. No sexual discrimination is involved, just a value judgment, and you cannot legislate against that. Instead, you have to change attitudes."

A Norwegian woman's place has traditionally been in the home, as in Henrik Ibsen's classic play *A Doll's House*. Wives stayed away from business; husbands never put the teakettle on. Inflation and economic necessity have now pushed wives into the work force but largely in lower-paying positions, such as nurses or secretaries.

Catching up. That is changing, but slowly. Women now outnumber men in Norway's law and medical schools but trail significantly in business schools. Meanwhile, Norway's legislative reforms have produced some surprising results. Women now get 52 weeks of paid maternity leave, but only if the husband takes off the first month, too. If he doesn't, the wife's paid leave is cut in half. The idea is to encourage fathers to help with a baby from the beginning, in the belief that once they start, they will stay engaged in child rearing. But the policy has led to unexpected results: In many divorce cases, Norwegian fathers are now fighting for child custody.

Women politicians wind up in some seemingly no-win situations. Greta Berget, then a very pregnant minister of family affairs, announced last year that she would take only a two-month maternity leave, rather than the full year, because she was too busy in her government job. Feminists denounced her as a traitor for not taking the full entitlement. Male chauvinists said a government minister had no business getting pregnant and taking any time off.

For all the advances in women's rights, Norwegians are not sure that they ultimately will be more successful than other nations in creating a society in which women can be equally fulfilled as wives, mothers and professionals. For now, they are counting on improvements in child care and job rights to allow women to put families first at some stages of their lives, and to focus on their careers at others.

For all that has changed in Norway, much remains the same. "There is nothing more feminine than being pregnant," insists government minister Berget. Nor do men consider themselves emasculated by the rising political power of women. "Sexual attraction is alive and well in Norway," confirms sociologist Holter.

BY FRED COLEMAN IN NORWAY

Kohl's Party Sets Quotas for Women

Germany: Christian Democrats will set aside one-third of candidacies, posts. Polls have shown a loss of female voters.

Marjorie Miller

Times Staff Writer

BONN—Chancellor Helmut Kohl's Christian Democratic Union, seeking to broaden its appeal after a bare-bones election victory, decided Monday to adopt a quota system to boost the power and profile of women in the party.

The measure, narrowly approved at the Christian Democrats' annual congress, ensures that a third of all party posts will go to women and that women will make up a third of CDU candidates in elections at all levels beginning next year.

Kohl, who was reelected as chancellor for a fourth term this month by a one-vote margin in Parliament, spoke out for the quota system as a way to begin strengthening the party for 1998 elections.

"If we want to get a start into the future, we have to do it now," Kohl said. "The image of the CDU is colored by how it deals with change in society."

The CDU and its Bavarian sister party, the Christian Social Union, are seen as socially conservative and dominated by graying men like Kohl, elected to his 11th term as party chief at the daylong congress.

Women have been campaigning for more power within the party for years, yet less than 14% of the CDU's new parliamentary delegation is female—contrasted with an average of 26% for the entire German legislature and 59% for the leftist Greens party.

The Social Democrats, Germany's leading opposition party, and the Greens adopted quotas in the 1980s, but the Christian Democrats had resisted.

That was clear at the party congress, a predominantly suit-and-tie gathering where women delegates gathered in groups to discuss strategy for prodding stodgy men.

"We have tried for 10 years to change the situation and we have had no luck," delegate Ingeborg Mittelstaedt said. "I think this quota system is necessary. There is a generation of men [in charge] that believes a man is more intelligent, stronger and not disturbed by family affairs."

The measure was controversial even among women, however, with some objecting that it reduced them to tokens and second-class citizens.

"I am decidedly against this quota, because we should judge people for their qualifications, not their gender," said delegate Tonia Meyer. "For my part, I don't want to get elected to a post and afterward have all men look at me with a patronizing air and thinking, 'Our quota women.' "

The party's most prominent woman and parliamentary leader, Rita Suessmuth, answered critics, saying that "if it went by ability and the qualification of women, we wouldn't be fighting about a third today but rather about an equal participation of women and men."

The quota system was approved by a 416-361 vote. It goes into effect next year for a five-year trial period.

CDU polls showing that the party has lost women and younger voters clearly prompted Kohl to make one of the more surprising moves of his 12 years as chancellor—naming a 28-year-old woman from the former East Germany to his new Cabinet as minister for women, family, youth and pensioners.

But the minister, Claudia Nolte, is a crusading Roman Catholic anti-abortionist whose far-right positions are so extreme that some people in the party fear she could scare off as many women as she might attract.

Nolte once suggested that women who have had abortions should be required to work in a hospital for year to make amends. Since her appointment, she has said she strongly favors the idea of the state's paying women a cash bonus of 1,000 German marks (about $640) for each newborn baby.

Many women from the former East Germany feel that they have lost rights since the fall of communism and the 1990 reunification with the former West Germany. Unemployment is high among eastern women, who under communism had guaranteed jobs and child care centers.

Even westerners have their doubts about the new minister, noted for having curtsied before Kohl at a party meeting in Dresden in her efforts to draw his attention.

"Perhaps she is not the figure to integrate the women in Germany, especially the ones in the east," said Karin Gedaschko, a lawyer and CDU delegate. "Her problem seems to be that she is not typical of the women in the CDU and eastern Germany too, for her age. I'm five years older, and I don't feel that she represents me too well."

Kohl's attention to women's issues is groundwork for the 1998 election, when the chancellor has vowed to step down. It is generally acknowledged that Kohl carried his governing coalition to its narrow, 10-seat majority in Parliament. The party needs to broaden its base if it hopes to continue its reign.

WHAT DEMOCRACY IS . . . AND IS NOT

Philippe C. Schmitter & Terry Lynn Karl

Philippe C. Schmitter *is professor of political science and director of the Center for European Studies at Stanford University.* **Terry Lynn Karl** *is associate professor of political science and director of the Center for Latin American Studies at the same institution. The original, longer version of this essay was written at the request of the United States Agency for International Development, which is not responsible for its content.*

For some time, the word democracy has been circulating as a debased currency in the political marketplace. Politicians with a wide range of convictions and practices strove to appropriate the label and attach it to their actions. Scholars, conversely, hesitated to use it—without adding qualifying adjectives—because of the ambiguity that surrounds it. The distinguished American political theorist Robert Dahl even tried to introduce a new term, "polyarchy," in its stead in the (vain) hope of gaining a greater measure of conceptual precision. But for better or worse, we are "stuck" with democracy as the catchword of contemporary political discourse. It is the word that resonates in people's minds and springs from their lips as they struggle for freedom and a better way of life; it is the word whose meaning we must discern if it is to be of any use in guiding political analysis and practice.

The wave of transitions away from autocratic rule that began with Portugal's "Revolution of the Carnations" in 1974 and seems to have crested with the collapse of communist regimes across Eastern Europe in 1989 has produced a welcome convergence toward [a] common definition of democracy.[1] Everywhere there has been a silent abandonment of dubious adjectives like "popular," "guided," "bourgeois," and "formal" to modify "democracy." At the same time, a remarkable consensus has emerged concerning the minimal conditions that polities must meet in order to merit the prestigious appellation of "democratic." Moreover, a number of international organizations now monitor how well these standards are met; indeed, some countries even consider them when formulating foreign policy.[2]

WHAT DEMOCRACY IS

Let us begin by broadly defining democracy and the generic *concepts* that distinguish it as a unique system for organizing relations between rulers and the ruled. We will then briefly review *procedures*, the rules and arrangements that are needed if democracy is to endure. Finally, we will discuss two operative *principles* that make democracy work. They are not expressly included among the generic concepts or formal procedures, but the prospect for democracy is grim if their underlying conditioning effects are not present.

One of the major themes of this essay is that democracy does not consist of a single unique set of institutions. There are many types of democracy, and their diverse practices produce a similarly varied set of effects. The specific form democracy takes is contingent upon a country's socioeconomic conditions as well as its entrenched state structures and policy practices.

Modern political democracy is a system of governance in which rulers are held accountable for their actions in the public realm by citizens, acting indirectly through the competition and cooperation of their elected representatives.[3]

A *regime or system of governance* is an ensemble of patterns that determines the methods of access to the principal public offices; the characteristics of the actors admitted to or excluded from such access; the strategies that actors may use to gain access; and the rules that are followed in the making of publicly binding decisions. To work properly, the ensemble must be institutionalized—that is to say, the various patterns must be habitually known, practiced, and accepted by most, if not all, actors. Increasingly, the preferred mechanism of institutionalization is a written body of laws undergirded by a written constitution, though many enduring political norms can have an informal, prudential, or traditional basis.[4]

For the sake of economy and comparison, these forms, characteristics, and rules are usually bundled together and given a generic label. Democratic is one; others are autocratic, authoritarian, despotic, dictatorial, tyrannical, totalitarian, absolutist, traditional, monarchic, oligarchic, plutocratic, aristocratic, and sultanistic.[5] Each of these regime forms may in turn be broken down into subtypes.

2. FACTORS IN THE POLITICAL PROCESS: Representative Government

Like all regimes, democracies depend upon the presence of *rulers*, persons who occupy specialized authority roles and can give legitimate commands to others. What distinguishes democratic rulers from nondemocratic ones are the norms that condition how the former come to power and the practices that hold them accountable for their actions. The *public realm* encompasses the making of collective norms and choices that are binding on the society and backed by state coercion. Its content can vary a great deal across democracies, depending upon preexisting distinctions between the public and the private, state and society, legitimate coercion and voluntary exchange, and collective needs and individual preferences. The liberal conception of democracy advocates circumscribing the public realm as narrowly as possible, while the socialist or social-democratic approach would extend that realm through regulation, subsidization, and, in some cases, collective ownership of property. Neither is intrinsically more democratic than the other—just *differently* democratic. This implies that measures aimed at "developing the private sector" are no more democratic than those aimed at "developing the public sector." Both, if carried to extremes, could undermine the practice of democracy, the former by destroying the basis for satisfying collective needs and exercising legitimate authority; the latter by destroying the basis for satisfying individual preferences and controlling illegitimate government actions. Differences of opinion over the optimal mix of the two provide much of the substantive content of political conflict within established democracies.

> *"However central to democracy, elections occur intermittently and only allow citizens to choose between the highly aggregated alternatives offered by political parties . . ."*

Citizens are the most distinctive element in democracies. All regimes have rulers and a public realm, but only to the extent that they are democratic do they have citizens. Historically, severe restrictions on citizenship were imposed in most emerging or partial democracies according to criteria of age, gender, class, race, literacy, property ownership, tax-paying status, and so on. Only a small part of the total population was eligible to vote or run for office. Only restricted social categories were allowed to form, join, or support political associations. After protracted struggle—in some cases involving violent domestic upheaval or international war—most of these restrictions were lifted. Today, the criteria for inclusion are fairly standard. All native-born adults are eligible, although somewhat higher age limits may still be imposed upon candidates for certain offices. Unlike the early American and European democracies of the nineteenth century, none of the recent democracies in southern Europe, Latin America, Asia, or Eastern Europe has even attempted to impose formal restrictions on the franchise or eligibility to office. When it comes to informal restrictions on the effective exercise of citizenship rights, however, the story can be quite different. This explains the central importance (discussed below) of procedures.

Competition has not always been considered an essential defining condition of democracy. "Classic" democracies presumed decision making based on direct participation leading to consensus. The assembled citizenry was expected to agree on a common course of action after listening to the alternatives and weighing their respective merits and demerits. A tradition of hostility to "faction," and "particular interests" persists in democratic thought, but at least since *The Federalist Papers* it has become widely accepted that competition among factions is a necessary evil in democracies that operate on a more-than-local scale. Since, as James Madison argued, "the latent causes of faction are sown into the nature of man," and the possible remedies for "the mischief of faction" are worse than the disease, the best course is to recognize them and to attempt to control their effects.[6] Yet while democrats may agree on the inevitability of factions, they tend to disagree about the best forms and rules for governing factional competition. Indeed, differences over the preferred modes and boundaries of competition contribute most to distinguishing one subtype of democracy from another.

The most popular definition of democracy equates it with regular *elections*, fairly conducted and honestly counted. Some even consider the mere fact of elections—even ones from which specific parties or candidates are excluded, or in which substantial portions of the population cannot freely participate—as a sufficient condition for the existence of democracy. This fallacy has been called "electoralism" or "the faith that merely holding elections will channel political action into peaceful contests among elites and accord public legitimacy to the winners"—no matter how they are conducted or what else constrains those who win them.[7] However central to democracy, elections occur intermittently and only allow citizens to choose between the highly aggregated alternatives offered by political parties, which can, especially in the early stages of a democratic transition, proliferate in a bewildering variety. During the intervals between elections, citizens can seek to influence public policy through a wide variety of other intermediaries: interest associations, social movements, locality groupings, clientelistic arrangements, and so forth. *Modern democracy, in other words, offers a variety of competitive processes and channels for the expression of interests and values—associational as well as partisan, functional as well as territorial, collective as well as individual. All are integral to its practice.*

Another commonly accepted image of democracy identifies it with *majority rule*. Any governing body that makes decisions by combining the votes of more than half of those eligible and present is said to be democratic, whether that majority emerges within an electorate, a parliament, a committee, a city council, or a party caucus. For exceptional purposes (e.g., amending the constitution or expelling a member), "qualified majorities" of more than 50 percent may be required, but few would deny that democracy must involve some means of aggregating the equal preferences of individuals.

A problem arises, however, when _numbers_ meet _intensities._ What happens when a properly assembled majority (especially a stable, self-perpetuating one) regularly makes decisions that harm some minority (especially a threatened cultural or ethnic group)? In these circumstances, successful democracies tend to qualify the central principle of majority rule in order to protect minority rights. Such qualifications can take the form of constitutional provisions that place certain matters beyond the reach of majorities (bills of rights); requirements for concurrent majorities in several different constituencies (confederalism); guarantees securing the autonomy of local or regional governments against the demands of the central authority (federalism); grand coalition governments that incorporate all parties (consociationalism); or the negotiation of social pacts between major social groups like business and labor (neocorporatism). The most common and effective way of protecting minorities, however, lies in the everyday operation of interest associations and social movements. These reflect (some would say, amplify) the different intensities of preference that exist in the population and bring them to bear on democratically elected decision makers. Another way of putting this intrinsic tension between numbers and intensities would be to say that "in modern democracies, votes may be counted, but influences alone are weighted."

Cooperation has always been a central feature of democracy. Actors must voluntarily make collective decisions binding on the polity as a whole. They must cooperate in order to compete. They must be capable of acting collectively through parties, associations, and movements in order to select candidates, articulate preferences, petition authorities, and influence policies.

But democracy's freedoms should also encourage citizens to deliberate among themselves, to discover their common needs, and to resolve their differences without relying on some supreme central authority. Classical democracy emphasized these qualities, and they are by no means extinct, despite repeated efforts by contemporary theorists to stress the analogy with behavior in the economic marketplace and to reduce all of democracy's operations to competitive interest maximization. Alexis de Tocqueville best described the importance of independent groups for democracy in his _Democracy in America,_ a work which remains a major source of inspiration for all those who persist in viewing democracy as something more than a struggle for election and re-election among competing candidates.[8]

In contemporary political discourse, this phenomenon of cooperation and deliberation via autonomous group activity goes under the rubric of "civil society." The diverse units of social identity and interest, by remaining independent of the state (and perhaps even of parties), not only can restrain the arbitrary actions of rulers, but can also contribute to forming better citizens who are more aware of the preferences of others, more self-confident in their actions, and more civic-minded in their willingness to sacrifice for the common good. At its best, civil society provides an intermediate layer of governance between the individual and the state that is capable of resolving conflicts and controlling the behavior of members without public coercion. Rather than overloading decision makers with increased demands and making the system ungovernable,[9] a viable civil society can mitigate conflicts and improve the quality of citizenship—without relying exclusively on the privatism of the marketplace.

Representatives—whether directly or indirectly elected—do most of the real work in modern democracies. Most are professional politicians who orient their careers around the desire to fill key offices. It is doubtful that any democracy could survive without such people. The central question, therefore, is not whether or not there will be a political elite or even a professional political class, but how these representatives are chosen and then held accountable for their actions.

As noted above, there are many channels of representation in modern democracy. The electoral one, based on territorial constituencies, is the most visible and public. It culminates in a parliament or a presidency that is periodically accountable to the citizenry as a whole. Yet the sheer growth of government (in large part as a byproduct of popular demand) has increased the number, variety, and power of agencies charged with making public decisions and not subject to elections. Around these agencies there has developed a vast apparatus of specialized representation based largely on functional interests, not territorial constituencies. These interest associations, and not political parties, have become the primary expression of civil society in most stable democracies, supplemented by the more sporadic interventions of social movements.

The new and fragile democracies that have sprung up since 1974 must live in "compressed time." They will not resemble the European democracies of the nineteenth and early twentieth centuries, and they cannot expect to acquire the multiple channels of representation in gradual historical progression as did most of their predecessors. A bewildering array of parties, interests, and movements will all simultaneously seek political influence in them, creating challenges to the polity that did not exist in earlier processes of democratization.

PROCEDURES THAT MAKE DEMOCRACY POSSIBLE

The defining components of democracy are necessarily abstract, and may give rise to a considerable variety of institutions and subtypes of democracy. For democracy to thrive, however, specific procedural norms must be followed and civic rights must be respected. Any polity that fails to impose such restrictions upon itself, that fails to follow the "rule of law" with regard to its own procedures, should not be considered democratic. These procedures alone do not define democracy, but their presence is indispensable to its persistence. In essence, they are necessary but not sufficient conditions for its existence.

Robert Dahl has offered the most generally accepted listing of what he terms the "procedural minimal" conditions that must be present for modern political democracy (or as he puts it, "polyarchy") to exist:

1. Control over government decisions about policy is constitutionally vested in elected officials.
2. Elected officials are chosen in frequent and fairly conducted elections in which coercion is comparatively uncommon.
3. Practically all adults have the right to vote in the election of officials.
4. Practically all adults have the right to run for elective offices in the government. . . .
5. Citizens have a right to express themselves without the danger of severe punishment on political matters broadly defined. . . .
6. Citizens have a right to seek out alternative sources of information. Moreover, alternative sources of information exist and are protected by law.
7. . . . Citizens also have the right to form relatively independent associations or organizations, including independent political parties and interest groups.[10]

These seven conditions seem to capture the essence of procedural democracy for many theorists, but we propose to add two others. The first might be thought of as a further refinement of item (1), while the second might be called an implicit prior condition to all seven of the above.

8. Popularly elected officials must be able to exercise their constitutional powers without being subjected to overriding (albeit informal) opposition from unelected officials. Democracy is in jeopardy if military officers, entrenched civil servants, or state managers retain the capacity to act independently of elected civilians or even veto decisions made by the people's representatives. Without this additional caveat, the militarized polities of contemporary Central America, where civilian control over the military does not exist, might be classified by many scholars as democracies, just as they have been (with the exception of Sandinista Nicaragua) by U.S. policy makers. The caveat thus guards against what we earlier called "electoralism"—the tendency to focus on the holding of elections while ignoring other political realities.
9. The polity must be self-governing; it must be able to act independently of constraints imposed by some other overarching political system. Dahl and other contemporary democratic theorists probably took

this condition for granted since they referred to formally sovereign nation-states. However, with the development of blocs, alliances, spheres of influence, and a variety of "neocolonial" arrangements, the question of autonomy has been a salient one. Is a system really democratic if its elected officials are unable to make binding decisions without the approval of actors outside their territorial domain? This is significant even if the outsiders are relatively free to alter or even end the encompassing arrangement (as in Puerto Rico), but it becomes especially critical if neither condition obtains (as in the Baltic states).

PRINCIPLES THAT MAKE DEMOCRACY FEASIBLE

Lists of component processes and procedural norms help us to specify what democracy is, but they do not tell us much about how it actually functions. The simplest answer is "by the consent of the people"; the more complex one is "by the contingent consent of politicians acting under conditions of bounded uncertainty."

In a democracy, representatives must at least informally agree that those who win greater electoral support or influence over policy will not use their temporary superiority to bar the losers from taking office or exerting influence in the future, and that in exchange for this opportunity to keep competing for power and place, momentary losers will respect the winners' right to make binding decisions. Citizens are expected to obey the decisions ensuing from such a process of competition, provided its outcome remains contingent upon their collective preferences as expressed through fair and regular elections or open and repeated negotiations.

The challenge is not so much to find a set of goals that command widespread consensus as to find a set of rules that embody contingent consent. The precise shape of this "democratic bargain," to use Dahl's expression,[11] can vary a good deal from society to society. It depends on social cleavages and such subjective factors as mutual trust, the standard of fairness, and the willingness to compromise. It may even be compatible with a great deal of dissensus on substantive policy issues.

All democracies involve a degree of uncertainty about who will be elected and what policies they will pursue. Even in those polities where one party persists in winning elections or one policy is consistently implemented, the possibility of change through independent collective action still exists, as in Italy, Japan, and the Scandinavian social democracies. If it does not, the system is not democratic, as in Mexico, Senegal, or Indonesia.

But the uncertainty embedded in the core of all democracies is bounded. Not just any actor can get into the competition and raise any issue he or she pleases—there are previously established rules that must be respected. Not just any policy can be adopted—there are conditions that must be met. Democracy institutionalizes "normal," limited political uncertainty. These boundaries vary from country to country. Constitutional guarantees of property, privacy, expression, and other rights are a part of this, but the most effective boundaries are generated by competition among interest groups and cooperation within civil society. Whatever the rhetoric (and some polities appear to offer their citizens more dramatic alternatives than others), once the rules of contingent consent have been agreed upon, the actual variation is likely to stay within a predictable and generally accepted range.

This emphasis on operative guidelines contrasts with a highly persistent, but misleading theme in recent literature on democracy—namely, the emphasis upon "civic culture." The principles we have suggested here rest on rules of prudence, not on deeply ingrained habits of tolerance, moderation, mutual respect, fair play, readiness to compromise, or trust in public authorities. Waiting for such habits to sink deep and lasting roots implies a very slow process of regime consolidation—one that takes generations—and it would probably condemn most contemporary experiences *ex hypothesi* to failure. Our assertion is that contingent consent and bounded uncertainty can emerge from the interaction between antagonistic and mutually suspicious actors and that the far more benevolent and ingrained norms of a civic culture are better thought of as a *product* and not a producer of democracy.

HOW DEMOCRACIES DIFFER

Several concepts have been deliberately excluded from our generic definition of democracy, despite the fact that they have been frequently associated with it in both everyday practice and scholarly work. They are, nevertheless, especially important when it comes to distinguishing subtypes of democracy. Since no single set of actual institutions, practices, or values embodies democracy, polities moving away from authoritarian rule can mix different components to produce different democracies. It is important to recognize that these do not define points along a single continuum of improving performance, but a matrix of potential combinations that are *differently* democratic.

1. *Consensus:* All citizens may not agree on the substantive goals of political action or on the role of the state (although if they did, it would certainly make governing democracies much easier).
2. *Participation:* All citizens may not take an active and equal part in politics, although it must be legally possible for them to do so.
3. *Access:* Rulers may not weigh equally the preferences of all who come before them, although citizenship implies that individuals and groups should have an equal opportunity to express their preferences if they choose to do so.
4. *Responsiveness:* Rulers may not always follow the course of action preferred by the citizenry. But when

they deviate from such a policy, say on grounds of "reason of state" or "overriding national interest," they must ultimately be held accountable for their actions through regular and fair processes.

5. *Majority rule:* Positions may not be allocated or rules may not be decided solely on the basis of assembling the most votes, although deviations from this principle usually must be explicitly defended and previously approved.
6. *Parliamentary sovereignty:* The legislature may not be the only body that can make rules or even the one with final authority in deciding which laws are binding, although where executive, judicial, or other public bodies make that ultimate choice, they too must be accountable for their actions.
7. *Party government:* Rulers may not be nominated, promoted, and disciplined in their activities by well-organized and programmatically coherent political parties, although where they are not, it may prove more difficult to form an effective government.
8. *Pluralism:* The political process may not be based on a multiplicity of overlapping, voluntaristic, and autonomous private groups. However, where there are monopolies of representation, hierarchies of association, and obligatory memberships, it is likely that the interests involved will be more closely linked to the state and the separation between the public and private spheres of action will be much less distinct.
9. *Federalism:* The territorial division of authority may not involve multiple levels and local autonomies, least of all ones enshrined in a constitutional document, although some dispersal of power across territorial and/or functional units is characteristic of all democracies.
10. *Presidentialism:* The chief executive officer may not be a single person and he or she may not be directly elected by the citizenry as a whole, although some concentration of authority is present in all democracies, even if it is exercised collectively and only held indirectly accountable to the electorate.
11. *Checks and Balances:* It is not necessary that the different branches of government be systematically pitted against one another, although governments by assembly, by executive concentrations, by judicial command, or even by dictatorial fiat (as in time of war) must be ultimately accountable to the citizenry as a whole.

While each of the above has been named as an essential component of democracy, they should instead be seen either as indicators of this or that type of democracy, or else as useful standards for evaluating the performance of particular regimes. To include them as part of the generic definition of democracy itself would be to mistake the American polity for the universal model of democratic governance. Indeed, the parliamentary, consociational, unitary, corporatist, and concentrated arrangements of continental Europe may have some unique virtues for guiding polities through the uncertain transition from autocratic to democratic rule.[12]

WHAT DEMOCRACY IS NOT

We have attempted to convey the general meaning of modern democracy without identifying it with some particular set of rules and institutions or restricting it to some specific culture or level of development. We have also argued that it cannot be reduced to the regular holding of elections or equated with a particular notion of the role of the state, but we have not said much more about what democracy is not or about what democracy may not be capable of producing.

There is an understandable temptation to load too many expectations on this concept and to imagine that by attaining democracy, a society will have resolved all of its political, social, economic, administrative, and cultural problems. Unfortunately, "all good things do not necessarily go together."

First, democracies are not necessarily more efficient economically than other forms of government. Their rates of aggregate growth, savings, and investment may be no better than those of nondemocracies. This is especially likely during the transition, when propertied groups and administrative elites may respond to real or imagined threats to the "rights" they enjoyed under authoritarian rule by initiating capital flight, disinvestment, or sabotage. In time, depending upon the type of democracy, benevolent long-term effects upon income distribution, aggregate demand, education, productivity, and creativity may eventually combine to improve economic and social performance, but it is certainly too much to expect that these improvements will occur immediately—much less that they will be defining characteristics of democratization.

Second, democracies are not necessarily more efficient administratively. Their capacity to make decisions may even be slower than that of the regimes they replace, if only because more actors must be consulted. The costs of getting things done may be higher, if only because "payoffs" have to be made to a wider and more resourceful set of clients (although one should never underestimate the degree of corruption to be found within autocracies). Popular satisfaction with the new democratic government's performance may not even seem greater, if only because necessary compromises often please no one completely, and because the losers are free to complain.

Third, democracies are not likely to appear more orderly, consensual, stable, or governable than the autocracies they replace. This is partly a byproduct of democratic freedom of expression, but it is also a reflection of the likelihood of continuing disagreement over new rules and institutions. These products of imposition or compromise are often initially quite ambiguous in nature and uncertain in effect until actors have learned how to use them. What is more, they come in the aftermath of serious struggles motivated by high ideals. Groups and individuals with recently acquired autonomy will test certain rules, protest against the actions of certain institutions, and insist on renegotiating their part of the bargain. Thus the presence of antisystem parties should be neither surprising nor seen as a failure of democratic consolidation. What counts is whether such parties are willing, however reluctantly, to play by the general rules of bounded uncertainty and contingent consent.

Governability is a challenge for all regimes, not just democratic ones. Given the political exhaustion and loss of legitimacy that have befallen autocracies from sultanistic Paraguay to totalitarian Albania, it may seem that only democracies can now be expected to govern effectively and legitimately. Experience has shown, however, that democracies too can lose the ability to govern. Mass publics can become disenchanted with their performance. Even more threatening is the temptation for leaders to fiddle with procedures and ultimately undermine the principles of contingent consent and bounded uncertainty. Perhaps the most critical moment comes once the politicians begin to settle into the more predictable roles and relations of a consolidated democracy. Many will find their expectations frustrated; some will discover that the new rules of competition put them at a disadvantage; a few may even feel that their vital interests are threatened by popular majorities.

> " . . . democracies will have more open societies and polities than the autocracies they replace, but not necessarily more open economies."

Finally, democracies will have more open societies and polities than the autocracies they replace, but not necessarily more open economies. Many of today's most successful and well-established democracies have historically resorted to protectionism and closed borders, and have relied extensively upon public institutions to promote economic development. While the long-term compatibility between democracy and capitalism does not seem to be in doubt, despite their continuous tension, it is not clear whether the promotion of such liberal economic goals as the right of individuals to own property and retain profits, the clearing function of markets, the private settlement of disputes, the freedom to produce without government regulation, or the privatization of state-owned enterprises necessarily furthers the consolidation of democracy. After all, democracies do need to levy taxes and regulate certain transactions, especially where private monopolies and oligopolies exist. Citizens or their representatives may decide that it is desirable to protect the rights of collectivities from encroachment by individuals, especially propertied ones, and they may choose to set aside certain forms of property for public or cooperative ownership. In short, notions of economic liberty that are currently put forward in neoliberal economic models are not synonymous with political freedom—and may even impede it.

Democratization will not necessarily bring in its wake economic growth, social peace, administrative efficiency, political harmony, free markets, or "the end of ideology." Least of all will it bring about "the end of history." No doubt some of these qualities could make the consolidation of democracy easier, but they are neither prerequisites for it nor immediate products of it. Instead, what we should be hoping for is the emergence of political institutions that can peacefully compete to form governments and influence public policy, that can channel social and economic conflicts through regular procedures, and that have sufficient linkages to civil society to represent their constituencies and commit them to collective courses of action. Some types of democracies, especially in developing countries, have been unable to fulfill this promise, perhaps due to the circumstances of their transition from authoritarian rule.[13] The democratic wager is that such a regime, once established, will not only persist by reproducing itself within its initial confining conditions, but will eventually expand beyond them.[14] Unlike authoritarian regimes, democracies have the capacity to modify their rules and institutions consensually in response to changing circumstances. They may not immediately produce all the goods mentioned above, but they stand a better chance of eventually doing so than do autocracies.

NOTES

1. For a comparative analysis of the recent regime changes in southern Europe and Latin America, see Guillermo O'Donnell, Philippe C. Schmitter, and Laurence Whitehead, eds., *Transitions from Authoritarian Rule*, 4 vols. (Baltimore: Johns Hopkins University Press, 1986). For another compilation that adopts a more structural approach see Larry Diamond, Juan Linz, and Seymour Martin Lipset, eds., *Democracy in Developing Countries*, vols. 2, 3, and 4 (Boulder, Colo.: Lynne Rienner, 1989).

2. Numerous attempts have been made to codify and quantify the existence of democracy across political systems. The best known is probably Freedom House's *Freedom in the World: Political Rights and Civil Liberties*, published since 1973 by Greenwood Press and since 1988 by University Press of America. Also see Charles Humana, *World Human Rights Guide* (New York: Facts on File, 1986).

3. The definition most commonly used by American social scientists is that of Joseph Schumpeter: "that institutional arrangement for arriving at political decisions in which individuals acquire the power to decide by means of a competitive struggle for the people's vote." *Capitalism, Socialism, and Democracy* (London: George Allen and Unwin, 1943), 269. We accept certain aspects of the classical procedural approach to modern democracy, but differ primarily in our emphasis on the accountability of rulers to citizens and the relevance of mechanisms of competition other than elections.

4. Not only do some countries practice a stable form of democracy without a formal constitution (e.g., Great Britain and Israel), but even more countries have constitutions and legal codes that offer no guarantee of reliable practice. On paper, Stalin's 1936 constitution for the USSR was a virtual model of democratic rights and entitlements.

5. For the most valiant attempt to make some sense out of this thicket of distinctions, see Juan Linz, "Totalitarian and Authoritarian Regimes" in *Handbook of Political Science*, eds. Fred I. Greenstein and Nelson W. Polsby (Reading Mass.: Addison Wesley, 1975), 175–411.

6. "Publius" (Alexander Hamilton, John Jay, and James Madison), *The Federalist Papers* (New York: Anchor Books, 1961). The quote is from Number 10.

7. See Terry Karl, "Imposing Consent? Electoralism versus Democratization in El Salvador," in *Elections and Democratization in Latin America, 1980–1985*, eds. Paul Drake and Eduardo Silva (San Diego: Center for Iberian and Latin American Studies, Center for US/Mexican Studies, University of California, San Diego, 1986), 9–36.

8. Alexis de Tocqueville, *Democracy in America*, 2 vols. (New York: Vintage Books, 1945).

9. This fear of overloaded government and the imminent collapse of democracy is well reflected in the work of Samuel P. Huntington during the 1970s. See especially Michel Crozier, Samuel P. Huntington, and Joji Watanuki, *The Crisis of Democracy* (New York: New York University Press, 1975). For Huntington's (revised) thoughts about the prospects for democracy, see his "Will More Countries Become Democratic?," *Political Science Quarterly* 99 (Summer 1984): 193–218.

10. Robert Dahl, *Dilemmas of Pluralist Democracy* (New Haven: Yale University Press, 1982), 11.

11. Robert Dahl, *After the Revolution: Authority in a Good Society* (New Haven: Yale University Press, 1970).

12. See Juan Linz, "The Perils of Presidentialism," *Journal of Democracy* 1 (Winter 1990): 51–69, and the ensuing discussion by Donald Horowitz, Seymour Martin Lipset, and Juan Linz in *Journal of Democracy* 1 (Fall 1990): 73–91.

13. Terry Lynn Karl, "Dilemmas of Democratization in Latin America," *Comparative Politics* 23 (October 1990): 1–23.

14. Otto Kirchheimer, "Confining Conditions and Revolutionary Breakthroughs," *American Political Science Review* 59 (1965): 964–974.

Parliament and Congress:

Is the Grass Greener on the other side?

Gregory S. Mahler

Gregory Mahler is chair of the Political Science Department at the University of Mississippi.

*A*ristotle long ago observed that man is a "political animal." He could have added that man, by his very nature, notes the political status of his neighbours and, very often, perceives their lot as being superior to his own. The old saying "the grass is greener on the other side of the fence" can be applied to politics and political structures as well as to other, more material, dimensions of the contemporary world.

Legislators are not immune from the very human tendency to see how others of their lot exist in their respective settings, and, sometimes, to look longingly at these other settings. When legislators do look around to see the conditions under which their peers operate in other countries, they occasionally decide they prefer the alternative legislative settings to their own.

Features which legislators admire or envy in the settings of their colleagues include such things as: the characteristics of political parties (their numbers, or degrees of party discipline), legislative committee systems, staff and services available to help legislators in their tasks, office facilities, libraries, and salaries. This essay will develop the "grass is greener" theme in relation to a dimension of the legislative world which is regularly a topic of conversation when legislators from a number of different jurisdictions meet: the ability or inability of legislatures to check and control the executive.

The Decline of Parliament

The theme of the "decline of parliament" has a long and well-studied history.[1] It generally refers to the gradual flow of true legislative power away from the legislative body in the direction of the executive. The executive does the real law-making — by actually drafting most legislation — and the legislature takes a more "passive" role by simply approving executive proposals.

Legislators are very concerned about their duties and powers and over the years have jealously guarded them when they have appeared to be threatened. In Canada (and indeed most parliamentary democracies in the world today), the majority of challenges to legislative power which develop no longer come from the ceremonial executive (the Crown), but from the political executive, the government of the day.

It can be argued that the ability to direct and influence public policy, is a "zero sum game" (i.e. there is only room for a

limited amount of power and influence to be exercised in the political world and a growth in the relative power of the political executive must be at the expense of the power of the legislature). It follows, then, that if the legislature is concerned about maintaining its powers, concerned about protecting its powers from being diminished, it must be concerned about every attempt by the political executive to expand its powers.

Others contend that real "legislative power" cannot, and probably never did reside in the legislature. There was no "Golden Age" of Parliament. The true legislative role of parliament today is not (and in the past was not) to create legislation, but to scrutinize and ratify legislation introduced by the Government of the day. Although an occasional exception to this pattern of behavior may exist (with private members' bills, for example), the general rule is clear: the legislature today does not actively initiate legislation as its primary *raison d'être*.

Although parliamentarians may not be major initiators of legislation, studies have indicated a wide range of other functions.[2] Certainly one major role of the legislature is the "oversight" role, criticizing and checking the powers of the executive. The ultimate extension of this power is the ability of the legislature to terminate the term of office of the executive through a "no confidence" vote. Another role of the legislature involves communication and representation of constituency concerns. Yet another function involves the debating function, articulating the concerns of the public of the day.

Professor James Mallory has indicated the need to "be realistic about the role of Parliament in the Westminster system."[3] He cites Bernard Crick's classic work, *The Reform of Parliament:* "...the phrase 'Parliamentary control,' and talk about the 'decline of parliamentary control,' should not mislead anyone into asking for a situation in which governments can have their legislation changed or defeated, or their life terminated... Control means influence, not direct power; advice, not command; criticism, not obstruction; scrutiny, not initiation; and publicity, not secrecy."[4]

The fact that parliament may not be paramount in the creation and processing of legislation is no reason to condemn all aspects of parliamentary institutions. Nor should parliamentarians be convinced that legislative life is perfect in the presidential-congressional system. In fact, some American legislators look to their parliamentary brethren and sigh with envy at the attractiveness of certain aspects of parliamentary institutions.

Reprinted courtesy of *Canadian Parliamentary Review*, Winter 1985–86, pp. 19–21.

Desirability of a Congressional Model for Canada?

Many Canadian parliamentarians and students of parliament look upon presidential-congressional institutions of the United States as possessing the answers to most of their problems. The grass is sometimes seen as being greener on the other side of the border. The concepts of fixed legislative terms, less party discipline, and a greater general emphasis on the role and importance of individual legislators (which implies more office space and staff for individual legislators, among other things) are seen as standards to which Canadian legislators should aspire.

A perceived strength of the American congressional system is that legislators do not automatically "rubber stamp" approve executive proposals. They consider the president's suggestions, but feel free to make substitutions or modifications to the proposal, or even to reject it completely. Party discipline is relatively weak; there are regularly Republican legislators opposing a Republican president (and Democratic legislators supporting him), and vice versa. Against the need for discipline congressmen argue that their first duty is to either (a) their constituency, or (b) what is "right", rather than simply to party leaders telling them how to behave in the legislature. For example, in 1976 Jimmy Carter was elected President with large majorities of Democrats in both houses of Congress. One of Carter's major concerns was energy policy. He introduced legislative proposals (that is, he had congressional supporters introduce legislation, since the American president cannot introduce legislation on his own) dealing with energy policy, calling his proposals "the moral equivalent of war." In his speeches and public appearances he did everything he could to muster support for "his" legislation. Two years later when "his" legislation finally emerged from the legislative process, it could hardly be recognized as the proposals submitted in such emotional terms two years earlier.

The experience of President Carter was certainly not unique. Any number of examples of such incidents of legislative-executive non-cooperation can be cited in recent American political history, ranging from President Wilson's unsuccessful efforts to get the United States to join the League of Nations, through Ronald Reagan's contemporary battles with Congress over the size of the federal budget. The Carter experience was somewhat unusual by virtue of the fact that the same political party controlled both the executive and legislative branches of government, and cooperation still was not forthcoming. There have been many more examples of non-cooperation when one party has controlled the White House and another party has controlled one or both houses of Congress.

This lack of party discipline ostensibly enables the individual legislators to be concerned about the special concerns of their constituencies. This, they say, is more important than simply having to follow the orders of the party whip in the legislature. It is not any more unusual to find a Republican legislator from a farm state voting against a specific agricultural proposal of President Reagan on the grounds that the legislation in question is not good for his/her constituency, than to find Democratic legislators from the southwestern states who voted against President Carter's water policy proposals on the grounds that the proposals were not good for their constituencies.

Congressional legislators know that they have fixed terms in office — the President is simply not able to bring about early

elections — and they know that as long as they can keep their constituencies happy there is no need to be terribly concerned about opposing the President, even if he is the leader of their party. It may be nice to have the President on your side, but if you have a strong base of support "back home" you can survive without his help.

Are there any benefits to the public interest in the absence of party discipline? The major argument is that the legislature will independently consider the executive's proposals, rather than simply accepting the executive's ideas passively. This, it is claimed, allows for a multiplicity of interests, concerns, and perspectives to be represented in the legislature, and ostensibly results in "better" legislation.

In summary, American legislative institutions promote the role of the individual legislator. The fixed term gives legislators the security necessary for the performance of the functions they feel are important. The (relative) lack of party discipline enables legislators to act on the issues about which they are concerned. In terms of the various legislative functions mentioned above, congressmen appear to spend a great deal of their time in what has been termed the legislative aspect of the job: drafting legislation, debating, proposing amendments, and voting (on a more or less independent basis).

While many parliamentarians are impressed by the ability of individual American legislator to act on their own volition it is ironic that many congressional legislators look longingly at the legislative power relationships of their parliamentary bretheren. The grass, apparently, is greener on the *other* side of the border, too.

Desirability of a Parliamentary Model

The "decline of congressional power" is as popular a topic of conversation in Washington as "the decline of parliamentary power" in Ottawa or London. Over the last several decades American legislators have sensed that a great deal of legislative power has slipped from their collective grasp.[5] Many have decried this tendency and tried to stop, or reverse this flow of power away from the legislative branch and toward the executive.

One of the major themes in the writings of these congressional activists is an admiration for the parliamentary model's (perceived) power over the executive. Many American legislators see the president's veto power, combined with his fixed term in office, as a real flaw in the "balance of powers" of the system, leading to an inexorable increase in executive power at the expense of the legislature. They look at a number of parliamentary structures which they see as promoting democratic political behavior and increased executive responsibility to the legislature, including the ability to force the resignation of the executive through a non-confidence vote. The regular "question period" format which insures some degree of public executive accountability is also perceived as being very attractive .

Critics of the congressional system do not confine their criticism only to the growth of executive power. There are many who feel there is too much freedom in the congressional arena. To paraphrase the words of Bernard Crick cited earlier, advising has sometimes turned into issuing commands; and criticism has sometimes turned into obstruction. This is not to suggest that congressional legislators would support giving up their ability to initiate legislation, to amend executive proposals, or to vote in a manner which they (individually) deem proper. This does suggest, however, that even congressional legislators see that independence is a two-sided coin: one side involves individual legislative autonomy and input into the legislative process; the other side involves the incompatibility of complete independence with a British style of "Responsible Government".

In 1948 Hubert Humphrey, then mayor of Minneapolis, delivered an address at the nomination convention of the Democratic Party. In his comments he appealed for a "more responsible" two party system in the United States, a system with sufficient party discipline to have *meaningful* party labels, and to allow party platforms to become public policy.[6] Little progress has been made over the last thirty-seven years in this regard. In the abstract the concept of a *meaningful* two party system may be attractive; American legislators have not been as attracted to the necessary corollary of the concept: decreased legislative independence and increased party discipline.

While American Senators and Representatives are very jealous of executive encroachments upon their powers, there is some recognition that on occasion — usually depending upon individual legislators' views about the desirability of specific pieces of legislation — executive leadership, and perhaps party discipline, can serve a valuable function. Congressional legislators are, at times which correspond to their policy preferences, envious of parliamentary governnments' abilities to carry their programs into law because MPs elected under their party labels will act consistent with party whips' directions. They would be loath to give up their perceived high degrees of legislative freedom but many of them realize the cost of this freedom in this era of pressing social problems and complex legislation. Parliamentary style government is simply not possible without party discipline.

A Democratic Congressman supporting President Carter's energy policy proposals might have longed for an effective three-line whip to help to pass the energy policies in question. An opponent of those policy proposals would have argued, to the contrary, that the frustration of the president's proposals was a good illustration of the wisdom of the legislature tempering the error-ridden policy proposals of the president. Similarly, many conservative Republican supporters of President Reagan have condemned the ability of the Democratic House of Representatives to frustrate his economic policies. Opponents of those policies have argued, again, that the House of Representatives is doing an important job of representing public opinion and is exercising a valuable and important check on the misguided policies of the executive.

Some Concluding Observations

The parliamentary model has its strengths as well as its weaknesses. The individual legislator in a parliamentary system does not have as active a role in the actual legislative process as does his American counterparts, but it is not at all hard to imagine instances in which the emphasis on individual autonomy in the congressional system can be counterproductive because it delays much-needed legislative programs.

The problem, ultimately, is one of balance. Is it possible to have a responsible party system in the context of parliamentary democracy which can deliver on its promises to the public, and also to have a high degree of individual legislative autonomy in the legislative arena?

It is hard to imagine how those two concepts could coexist. The congressional and parliamentary models of legislative behavior have placed their respective emphases on two different priorities. The parliamentary model, with its responsible party system and its corresponding party discipline in the legislature, emphasizes efficient policy delivery, and the ability of an elected government to deliver on its promises. The congressional model, with its lack of party discipline and its emphasis on individual legislative autonomy, placed more emphasis on what can be called "consensual politics": it may take much more time for executive proposals to find their way into law, but (the argument goes) there is greater likelihood that what does, ultimately, emerge as law will be acceptable to a greater number of people than if government proposals were "automatically" approved by a pre-existing majority in the legislature acting "under the whip".

We cannot say that one type of legislature is "more effective" than the other. Each maximizes effectiveness in different aspects of the legislative function. Legislators in the congressional system, because of their greater legislative autonomy and weaker party discipline, are more effective at actually legislating than they are at exercising ultimate control over the executive. Legislators in the parliamentary system, although they may play more of a "ratifying" role in regard to legislation, do get legislation passed promptly; they also have an ultimate power over the life of the government of the day.

The appropriateness of both models must also be evaluated in light of the different history, political culture and objectives of the societies in which they operate. Perhaps the grass is just as green on both sides of the fence.

Notes

[1] There is substantial literature devoted to the general topic of "the decline of legislatures." Among the many sources which could be referred to in this area would be included the work of Gerhard Loewenberg. *Modern Parliaments: Change or Decline?* Chicago: Atherton. 1971; Gerhard Loewenberg and Samuel Patterson, *Comparing Legislatures*, Boston: Little, Brown, 1979; or Samuel Patterson and John Wahlke, eds., *Comparative Legislative Behavior: Frontiers of Research*, New York: John Wiley, 1972.

[2] A very common topic in studies of legislative behavior has to do with the various functions legislatures may be said to perform for the societies of which they are a part. For a discussion of the many functions attributed to legislatures in political science literature, see Gregory Mahler, *Comparative Politics: An Institutional and Cross-National Approach* (Cambridge, Ma.: Schenkman, 1983, pp. 56-61.

[3] J. R. Mallory, "Can Parliament Control the Regulatory Process?" *Canadian Parliamentary Review* Vol. 6 (no. 3, 1983) p. 6.

[4] Bernard Crick, *The Reform of Parliament*, London, 1968, p. 80.

[5] One very well written discussion of the decline of American congressional power in relation to the power of the president can be found in Ronald Moe, ed., *Congress and the President*, Pacific Palisades, Calif.: Goodyear Publishing Co., 1971.

[6] Subsequently a special report was published by the Committee on Political Parties of the American Political Science Association dealing with this problem. See "Toward a More Responsible Two-Party System," *American Political Science Review* Vol. 44 (no. 3, 1950), special supplement.

ELECTORAL REFORM

Good government? Fairness?
Or vice versa. Or both

Italians want to junk proportional representation. Others could usefully adopt it. Which electoral system is best? The arguments are many. So are the answers

BRITAIN elects its House of Commons by the simplest possible system: single-member constituencies in which the front-runner wins, even if he has under 50% of the votes. In 1983, 7.8m votes, a quarter of the total, went to the "third party", the Alliance. It got 23 seats. The Labour Party got 8.5m votes—and 209 seats. No wonder half of all Britons say they would like a fairer system.

Italy uses systems of proportional representation (PR) that are elaborately fair. It has also had 52 governments, mostly coalitions, since 1945, all dominated by the Christian Democrats. Italian government is famously inept, its parties—not only the Christian Democrats—infamously corrupt. No wonder Italians have just voted massively to adopt the British system for three-quarters of their Senate seats; the Chamber of Deputies will probably go much the same way.

These two countries exemplify—in parody—the arguments about electoral reform. Britain's "first past the post" system (FPTP) nearly always produces a single-party government with an overall, and solid, Commons majority. Unless that party itself is split—as now, over the Maastricht treaty—the government can override all opposition. The result, given a decisive prime minister, should always be decisive government.

In contrast, look at Italy, Israel or Poland. Their PR is as fair as it comes. Umpteen parties, even tiny ones with 1-2% of the national vote, can win seats. With 3% or 4%,

they can make or break policies and governments, as Israel's religious parties notoriously have done. It sounds like a recipe for feeble government, with the tail—as the enemies of PR put it—wagging the dog.

The choice looks clear: good government or fair representation? In fact, not so. British governments have often been feeble; Israel's often decisive, even fierce. Italy's governments are unstable and inept; not so Germany's, although the Bundestag they rest on is shaped by PR. True, it keeps out small parties. Yet most post-1949 German governments have had a "tail", the Free Democrats (FDP).

As for the corruption now disgusting Italy's voters, its cause, arguably, is too long tenure of office, not the electoral system. Japan has no formal PR, but its ever-ruling Liberal Democrats are hardly clean. True, PR at times prevents complete clear-outs of government; but the parties that stay in office, despite swings among voters, are usually small, as in Germany (Italy is a special case; its large Communist party was not acceptable as an alternative in government to the Christian Democrats).

Corruption anyway springs more from the climate of society—and state control of the economy—than from any parliamentary arrangements. Most government in India (an FPTP country) is corrupt within weeks of taking office. The African minister

who is not, by British standards, corrupt, is acting very oddly indeed by African ones (or indeed by British ones of the 18th century: not to help one's friends—and oneself—is, like elective democracy, a recent, North European curiosity of human behaviour).

So FPTP offers no monopoly, or even guarantee, of good government. But neither does PR of fairness. Americans fret about many aspects of their political system, but not its fairness between parties; and—given that no third party exists—its results are decently proportional. Still not fair, maybe. All Americans have one vote, but of wildly different values: Alaska's 400,000 voters elect two senators, as do California's 23m. Yet why is that so? Because the founding fathers chose so. And few Americans are bothered by this either.

That is a reminder that fairness has many faces. As much as a party, the voter may want a given person to speak for him. FPTP allows for this. He may want one kind of person. Women hold few seats: in the late 1980s, about 30% in the Nordic PR countries, 5-20% in many others whose parties, in filling the party lists used in PR, take little, if any, note of this; and 5-15% in FPTP countries. Even fewer members come from poor, ethnic minorities. A few constitutions (India's, eg) reserve seats for them. Some American electoral boundaries are drawn to help them. Mostly, they must rely on accidents of geography, notably inner-city concentration.

Nor is the voter picking only his representative. He votes for certain policies, and—save in presidential systems—for a government; a serious one, not a bunch of clowns. A PR system could be as fair as Snow White in reflecting party support, and yet, at times, frustrate all these hopes. Would the result fairly represent the electorate?

It depends who, where and for what

America offers another reminder: that neither fairness nor effectiveness exists *in vacuo*. They depend on their context.

An elected body may spring from long democratic tradition or little, from a multi-cultural society or a homogeneous one. It may be national or local. It may be part of a two-house set-up (America gets territorial fairness in its Senate, demographic from the House). It may provide a government, as do European parliaments, or just legislate and oversee one, as in America. It may be mainly a sounding-board, like the 12-nation parliament of the European Community. And what is "right" here, or for one function, may be wrong there, or for another.

Britain offers an example. Its local government cries out for PR, since the national demography to which parties adapt is not reproduced locally. Voting in 1991 left 15 of 36 English "metropolitan" districts with councils that were 80%-plus Labour (nine of them 90%-plus). Of 296 "non-met"—less urban—councils, 31 had no Labour members, 35 no Liberal Democrats. Point made? Yet it proves nothing about the Commons.

With so many ifs and buts, it is easy to say if it ain't broke don't even think of fixing it. Who would today invent Britain's House of Lords, a jumble of hereditary peers, bishops and judges, plus assorted notables (or party hacks) picked by successive prime ministers? Yet, in its way, it works. If it can survive—and reforming it is a barely an issue in Britain—maybe anything can, even should.

Should? A wise country leaves well, or even only moderately well, alone. After Holland's PR elections, it can take months even to form a government. Yet few Dutchmen worry, any more than Americans do about Alaska. But when a majority (Italy) or a large minority (Britain) feels grossly ill-served or ill-treated, it is time to think again.

Beside Italy, Poland has recently opted for change. Its infant post-Communist democracy chose extreme PR, and in its late-1991 elections paid the price. In all, 67 "parties" fought; the best-placed won only 13% of the vote, and the legislature now includes 29—often shifting—groups. A new electoral law, though it too is PR-based, will limit such follies.

New Zealand, now using FPTP, may go the other way. A referendum last September backed a switch to PR (mainly, as in Italy, to punish politicians). Even Britain's Labour Party is looking at PR, if less because of Liberal complaints than of its own fears that FPTP—which in the past served it well—may leave its Tory rivals for ever running solid one-party governments on 40% of the vote.

Britain's love of FPTP is criticised beyond its borders, because, except in Northern Ireland, it elects members to the European Parliament by this system. So the Tory-Labour balance swings wildly, while large Euro-constituencies crush other national parties. In 1984, the Alliance won 18.5% of the Euro-vote, but no seats; ditto the Greens in 1989, with 14.5%. The result distorts not just British representation but the make-up of the whole parliament.

France's recent elections aroused worries about its two-round voting. This was de Gaulle's substitute for the instabilities of PR, only briefly replaced by PR again in the mid-1980s. Its results can be fair enough. Not this year. Right-wing parties, with 39% of the vote, took 80% of the seats. The National Front, with 12$\frac{1}{2}$%, got none. Nasty as the Front is, many Frenchmen doubt that democracy should leave so many voters voiceless.

Pros and cons

Italians' dislike of PR far outruns French or British anxieties the other way. That is natural: they identify it with lousy government. And bad government both hits the whole nation and impinges visibly and constantly on daily life; the disfranchisement felt by third-party voters does neither. Yet worries about FPTP and related systems go deeper. It is representative democracy, not good government, that is the essence of "western" politics. *The Economist*, discussing these issues two years ago, wrote flatly that

> And since the perception of fairness is the acid test for democracy—the very basis of its legitimacy—the unfairness argument overrules all others.

There is a more pragmatic reason. Politicians can, and in Europe mostly do, provide decent government with PR. Unless, as in America, history has dumped third parties, FPTP cannot, except by chance, and normally does not provide fair representation. Human wit can get round the faults of PR; it cannot—except in drawing electoral boundaries—act on the crude mechanics of FPTP.

Yet any shift toward PR must, if possible, avoid its faults in advance. Its critics list many, not all as solid as they sound:

• **Too complicated.** Nonsense. What some think the best system, the single transferable vote, is indeed complex. But the Irish can work it, so why not others?

• **Too many small parties.** That depends how far fairness is pushed. A threshold can hold numbers down: Germany's fierce 5% one has usually kept the Bundestag to just four parties, rarely five. Is it acceptable to exclude 4.9% of opinion—or, as recently in Eastern Europe, several times 4.9%? FPTP too can let in many small parties, if (but only if) each has a regional base.

• **Too many weak coalitions.** Coalitions, yes. Weak, maybe. PR produces both.

• **Too much power for small "pivotal" parties.** Germany's FDP is often cited. In 1982 it quit a coalition with the SDP and joined the CDU. Undemocratic? Six months later the policy shift that the FDP had sought was endorsed by the voters. The "tail-and-dog" case too is weak. On minor issues dear to them, small parties may get their way (as in Israel). On big issues, in politics as in physics, small bodies can only influence large ones, not rule them. West German unification-seeking softness toward Russia in 1989 is cited. That began with the FDP foreign minister; but it was backed by Chancellor Kohl.

• **Policy decided in inter-party haggling after an election, not by voters during it.** Often true, shamefully so in Italy, though its smoke-shrouded deals were more about posts than policy. But the idea that it is "unfair" for those who backed the biggest party in a coalition to see its policy then diluted is bogus: in politics as in marriage, if you cannot win outright, you must compromise.

• **Too much power for party bosses.** In party-list systems, that is nearly always true. But STV lets voters choose among a party's candidates; so does Japan's simple system. Any coalition adds to the power of party machines in government—and (notoriously in Italy, notedly in Germany) in patronage and appointment to public bodies, not least state television. One can argue whether or not one-party patronage, as in Britain, is even worse. A better answer is open under any system: less patronage.

• **Weak links between a member and his constituents.** This is true of PR using large electoral districts, not in the ones of 3-5 members used in Ireland (and Japan). Members of the Irish Dail feel pressure, they say, to look after constituents, because their support may slip away not only to rival parties but to other members of their own. British critics fear such a member may care only for a section of his constituents. That may happen; PR supporters, in reply, praise the voter's freedom to choose which member he turns to. Districts of 5-7 members, as in most of Belgium, Spain or France in its PR days, allow both PR and acceptable member/voter links.

Many answers

For countries seeking less PR, the considerations, curiously, are much the same, since not even the angry Italians want the pure milk of FPTP. For them too the trick is to find a balance between proportionality and the faults voters feel in their form of PR. They too must remember the many faces of fairness, and ask, in each case, what function the elected body serves, what they want to achieve (punishing politicians, however deservedly, is an inappropriate answer) and is it worth the upheaval? Only zealots think one solution fits every case.

Presidents and Prime Ministers

Richard Rose

Richard Rose is professor of public policy at the University of Strathclyde in Glasgow, Scotland. An American, he has lived in Great Britain for many years and has been studying problems of political leadership in America and Europe for three decades. His books include Presidents and Prime Ministers; Managing Presidential Objectives; Understanding Big Government; *and* The Post-Modern Presidency: The World Closes in on the White House.

The need to give direction to government is universal and persisting. Every country, from Egypt of the pharoahs to contemporary democracies, must maintain political institutions that enable a small group of politicians to make authoritative decisions that are binding on the whole of society. Within every system, one office is of first importance, whether it is called president, prime minister, führer, or dux.

There are diverse ways of organizing the direction of government, not only between democracies and authoritarian regimes, but also among democracies. Switzerland stands at one extreme, with collective direction provided by a federal council whose president rotates from year to year. At the other extreme are countries that claim to centralize authority, under a British-style parliamentary system or in an American or French presidential system, in which one person is directly elected to the supreme office of state.

To what extent are the differences in the formal attributes of office a reflection of substantive differences in how authority is exercised? To what extent do the imperatives of office—the need for electoral support, dependence upon civil servants for advice, and vulnerability to events—impose common responses in practice? Comparing the different methods of giving direction to government in the United States (presidential), Great Britain (prime ministerial and Cabinet), and France (presidential and prime ministerial) can help us understand whether other countries do it—that is, choose a national leader—in a way that is better.

To make comparisons requires concepts that can identify the common elements in different offices. Three concepts organize the comparisons I make: the career that leads to the top; the institutions and powers of government; and the scope for variation within a country, whether arising from events or personalities.

Career Leading to the Top

By definition, a president or prime minister is unrepresentative by being the occupant of a unique office. The diversity of outlooks and skills that can be attributed to white, university-educated males is inadequate to predict how people with the same social characteristics—a Carter or an Eisenhower; a Wilson or a Heath—will perform in office. Nor is it helpful to consider the recruitment of national leaders deductively, as a management consultant or personnel officer would, first identifying the skills required for the job and then evaluating candidates on the basis of a priori requirements. National leaders are not recruited by examination; they are self-selected, individuals whose driving ambitions, personal attributes, and, not least, good fortune, combine to win the highest public office.

To understand what leaders can do in office we need to compare the skills acquired in getting to the top with the skills required once there. The tasks that a president or prime minister must undertake are few but central: sustaining popular support through responsiveness to the electorate, and being effective in government. Success in office encourages electoral popularity, and electoral popularity is an asset in wielding influence within government.

The previous careers of presidents and prime ministers are significant, insofar as experience affects what they do in office—and what they do well. A politician who had spent many years concentrating upon campaigning to win popularity may continue to cultivate popularity in office. By contrast, a politician experienced in dealing with the problems of government from within may be better at dealing effectively with international and domestic problems.

Two relevant criteria for comparing the careers of national leaders are: previous experience of government, and previous experience of party and mass electoral politics. American presidents are outstanding in their experience of campaigning for mass support, whereas French presidents are outstanding for their prior knowledge of government from the inside. British prime ministers usually combine experience in both fields.

Thirteen of the fourteen Americans who have been nominated for president of the United States by the Democratic or Republican parties since 1945 had prior experience in running for major office, whether at the congressional, gubernatorial or presidential level. Campaigning for office makes a politician conscious of his or her need for popular approval. It also cultivates skill in dealing with the mass media. No American will be elected president who has not learned how to campaign across the continent, effectively and incessantly. Since selection as a presidential candidate is dependent upon winning primaries, a president must run twice: first to win the party nomination and then to win the White House. The effort required is shown by the fact that in 1985, three years before the presidential election, one Republican hopeful campaigned in twenty-four states, and a Democratic hopeful in thirty. Immediately after the 1986 congressional elections ended, the media started featuring stories about the 1988 campaign.

Campaigning is different from governing. Forcing ambitious politicians to concentrate upon crossing and recrossing America reduces the time available for learning about problems in Washington and the rest of the world. The typical postwar president has had no experience working within the executive branch. The way in which the federal government deals with foreign policy, or with problems of the economy is known, if at all, from the vantage point of a spectator. A president is likely to have had relatively brief experience in Congress. As John F. Kennedy's career illustrates, Congress is not treated as a

---

Looking presidential is not the same as acting like a president.

---

means of preparing to govern; it is a launching pad for a presidential campaign. The last three presidential elections have been won by individuals who could boast of having no experience in Washington. Jimmy Carter and Ronald Reagan were state governors, experienced at a job that gives no experience in foreign affairs or economic management.

A president who is experienced in campaigning can be expected to continue cultivating the media and seeking a high standing in the opinion polls. Ronald Reagan illustrates this approach. A president may even use campaigning as a substitute for coming to grips with government; Jimmy Carter abandoned Washington for the campaign trail when confronted with mid-term difficulties in 1978. But public relations expertise is only half the job; looking presidential is not the same as acting like a president.

A British prime minister, by contrast, enters office after decades in the House of Commons and years as a Cabinet minister. The average postwar prime minister had spent thirty-two years in Parliament before entering 10 Downing Street. Of that period, thirteen years had been spent as a Cabinet minister. Moreover, the prime minister has normally held the important policy posts of foreign secretary, chancellor of the exchequer or both. The average prime

minister has spent eight years in ministerial office, learning to handle foreign and/or economic problems. By contrast with the United States, no prime minister has had postwar experience in state or local government, and by contrast with France, none has been a civil servant since World War II.

The campaign experience of a British prime minister is very much affected by the centrality that politicians give Parliament. A politician seeks to make a mark in debate there. Even in an era of mass media, the elitist doctrine holds that success in the House of Commons produces positive evaluation by journalists and invitations to appear on television, where a politician can establish an image with the national electorate. Whereas an American presidential hopeful has a bottom-up strategy, concentrating upon winning votes in early primaries in Iowa and New Hampshire as a means of securing media attention, a British politician has a top-down approach, starting to campaign in Parliament.

Party is the surrogate for public opinion among British politicians, and with good reason. Success in the Commons is evaluated by a politician's party colleagues. Election to the party leadership is also determined by party colleagues. To become prime minister a politician does not need to win an election; he or she only needs to be elected party leader when the party has a parliamentary majority. Jim Callaghan and Sir Alec Douglas-Home each entered Downing Street this way and lost office in the first general election fought as prime minister.

The lesser importance of the mass electorate to British party leaders is illustrated by the fact that the average popularity rating of a prime minister is usually less than that of an American president. The monthly Gallup poll rating often shows the prime minister approved by less than half the electorate and trailing behind one or more leaders of the opposition.

In the Fifth French Republic, presidents and prime ministers have differed from American presidents, being very experienced in government, and relatively inexperienced in campaigning with the mass electorate. Only one president, François Mitterrand, has followed the British practice of making a political career based on Parliament. Since he was on the opposition side for the first two decades of the Fifth Republic, his experience of the problems of office was like that of a British opposition member of Parliament, and different from that of a minister. Giscard d'Estaing began as a high-flying civil servant and Charles de Gaulle, like Dwight Eisenhower, was schooled in bureaucratic infighting as a career soldier.

When nine different French prime ministers are examined, the significance of a civil service background becomes clear. Every prime minister except for Pierre Mauroy has been a civil servant first. It has been exceptional for a French prime minister to spend decades in Parliament before attaining that office. An Englishman would be surprised that a Raymond Barre or a Couve de Murville had not sat there before becoming prime minister. An American would be even more surprised by the experience that French leaders have had in the ministries as high civil servants, and particularly in dealing with foreign and economic affairs.

The traditional style of French campaigning is plebiscitary. One feature of this is that campaigning need not be incessant. Louis Napoleon is said to have compared elections with baptism: something it is necessary to do—but to do only once. The seven-year fixed term of the French president, about double the statutory life of many national leaders, is in the tradition of infrequent consultation with the electorate.

The French tradition of leadership is also ambivalent; a plebiscite is, after all, a mass mobilization. The weakness of parties, most notably on the Right, which has provided three of the four presidents of the Fifth Republic, encourages a personalistic style of campaigning. The use of the two-ballot method for the popular election of a president further encourages candidates to compete against each other as individuals, just as candidates for the presidential nomination compete against fellow-partisans in a primary. The persistence of divisions between Left and Right ensures any candidate successful in entering the second ballot a substantial bloc of votes, with or without a party endorsement.

On the two central criteria of political leadership, the relationship with the mass electorate, and knowledge of government, there are cross-national contrasts in the typical career. A British or French leader is likely to know far more about government than an American president, but an American politician is likely to be far more experienced in campaigning to win popular approval and elections.

Less for the President to Govern

Journalistic and historical accounts of government often focus on the person and office of the national leader. The American president is deemed to be very powerful because of the immense military force that he can command by comparison to a national leader in Great Britain or France. The power to drop a hydrogen bomb is frequently cited as a measure of the awesome power of an American president; but it is misleading, for no president has ever dropped a hydrogen bomb, and no president has used atomic weapons in more than forty years. Therefore, we must ask: What does an American president (and his European counterparts) do when not dropping a hydrogen bomb?

In an era of big government, a national leader is more a chief than an executive, for no individual can superintend, let alone carry out, the manifold tasks of government. A national leader does not need to make major choices about what government ought to do; he inherits a set of institutions that are committed—by law, by organization, by the professionalism of public employees, and by the expectations of voters—to appropriate a large amount of the country's resources in order to produce the program outputs of big government.

Whereas political leadership is readily personalized,

government is intrinsically impersonal. It consists of collective actions by organizations that operate according to impersonal laws. Even when providing benefits to individuals, such as education, health care, or pensions, the scale of a ministry or a large regional or local government is such as to make the institution appear impersonal.

Contemporary Western political systems are first of all governed by the rule of law rather than personal will. When government did few things and actions could be derived from prerogative powers, such as a declaration of war, there was more scope for the initiative of leaders. Today, the characteristic activities of government, accounting for most public expenditure and personnel, are statutory entitlements to benefits of the welfare state. They cannot be overturned by wish or will, as their tacit acceptance by such "antigovernment" politicians as Margaret Thatcher and Ronald Reagan demonstrates. Instead of the leader dominating government, government determines much that is done in the leader's name.

In a very real sense, the co-called power of a national leader depends upon actions that his government takes, whether or not this is desired by the leader. Instead of comparing the constitutional powers of leaders, we should compare the resources that are mobilized by the government for which a national leader is nominally responsible. The conventional measure of the size of government is public expenditure as a proportion of the gross national product. By this criterion, French or British government is more powerful than American government. Organization for Economic Cooperation and Development (OECD) statistics show that in 1984 French public expenditure accounted for 49 percent of the national product, British for 45 percent, and American for 37 percent. When attention is directed at central government, as distinct from all levels of government, the contrast is further emphasized. British and French central government collect almost two-fifths of the national product in tax revenue, whereas the American federal government collects only one-fifth.

When a national leader leads, others are meant to follow. The legitimacy of authority means that public employees should do what elected officials direct. In an era of big government, there are far more public employees at hand than in an era when the glory of the state was symbolized by a small number of people clustering around a royal court. Statistics of public employment again show British and French government as much more powerful than American government. Public employment in France accounts for 33 percent of all persons who work, more than Britain, with 31 percent. In the United States, public employment is much less, 18 percent.

The capacity of a national leader to direct public employees is much affected by whether or not such officials are actually employed by central government. France is most centralized, having three times as many public employees working in ministries as in regional or local government. If public enterprises are also reckoned as part of central government, France is even more centralized. In the United States and Great Britain, by contrast, the actual delivery of public services such as education and health is usually shipped out to lower tiers of a federal government, or to a complex of local and functional authorities. Delivering the everyday services of government is deemed beneath the dignity of national leaders in Great Britain. In the United States, central government is deemed too remote to be trusted with such programs as education or police powers.

When size of government is the measure, an American president appears weaker than a French or British leader. By international standards, the United States has a not so big government, for its claim on the national product and the national labor force is below the OECD average. Ronald Reagan is an extreme example of a president who is "antigovernment," but he is not the only example. In the past two decades, the United States has not lagged behind Europe in developing and expanding welfare state institutions that make government big. It has chosen to follow a different route, diverging from the European model of a mixed economy welfare state. Today, the president has very few large-scale program responsibilities, albeit they remain significant: defense and diplomacy, social security, and funding the federal deficit.

By contrast, even an "antigovernment" prime minister such as Margaret Thatcher finds herself presiding over a government that claims more than two-fifths of the national product in public expenditure. Ministers must answer, collectively and individually in the House of Commons, for all that is done under the authority of an Act of Parliament. In France, the division between president and prime minister makes it easier for the president of the republic to avoid direct entanglement in low status issues of service delivery, but the centralization of government necessarily involves the prime minister and his colleagues.

When attention is turned to the politics of government as distinct from public policies, all leaders have one thing in common, they are engaged in political management, balancing the interplay of forces within government, major economic interests, and public opinion generally. It is no derogation of a national leader's position to say that it has an important symbolic dimension, imposing a unifying and persuasive theme upon what government does. The theme may be relatively clear-cut, as in much of Margaret Thatcher's rhetoric. Or it may be vague and symbolic, as in much of the rhetoric of Charles de Gaulle. The comparative success of Ronald Reagan, an expert in manipulating vague symbols, as against Jimmy Carter, whose technocratic biases were far stronger than his presentational skills, is a reminder of the importance of a national political leader being able to communicate successfully to the nation.

In the United States and France, the president is both head of government and head of state. The latter role makes him president of all the people, just as the former role limits his representative character to governing in the name of a majority (but normally, less than 60 percent) of the voters. A British prime minister does not have the symbolic obligation to represent the country as a whole; the queen does that.

The institutions of government affect how political management is undertaken. The separate election of the president and the legislature in the United States and France create a situation of nominal independence, and bargaining from separate electoral bases. By contrast, the British prime minister is chosen by virtue of being leader of the largest party in the House of Commons. Management of Parliament is thus made much easier by the fact that the British prime minister can normally be assured of a majority of votes there.

An American president has a far more difficult task in managing government than do British and French counterparts. Congress really does determine whether bills become laws, by contrast to the executive domination of law and decree-making in Europe. Congressional powers of appropriation provide a basis for a roving scrutiny of what the executive branch does. There is hardly any bureau that is free from congressional scrutiny, and in many congressional influence may be as strong as presidential influence. By contrast, a French president has significant decree powers and most of the budget can be promulgated. A British prime minister can also invoke the Official Secrets Act and the doctrine of collective responsibility to insulate the effective (that is, the executive) side of government from the representative (that is, Parliament).

Party politics and electoral outcomes, which cannot be prescribed in a democratic constitution, affect the extent to which political management must be invested in persuasion. If management is defined as making an organization serve one's purpose, then Harry Truman gave the classic definition of management as persuasion: "I sit here all day trying to persuade people to do the things they ought to have sense enough to do without my persuading them. That's all the powers of the President amount to." Because both Democratic and Republican parties are loose coalitions, any president will have to invest much effort in persuading fellow partisans, rather than whipping them into line. Given different electoral bases, congressmen may vote their district, rather than their party label. When president and Congress are of opposite parties, then strong party ties weaken the president.

In Great Britain, party competition and election outcomes are expected to produce an absolute majority in the House of Commons for a single party. Given that the prime minister, as party leader, stands and falls with members of Parliament in votes in Parliament and at a general election, a high degree of party discipline is attainable. Given that the Conservative and Labor parties are themselves coalitions of differing factions and tendencies, party management is no easy task. But it is far easier than interparty management, a necessary condition of coalition government, including Continental European governments.

The Fifth Republic demonstrates that important constitutional features are contingent upon election outcomes. Inherent in the constitution of the Fifth Republic is a certain ambiguity about the relationship between president and prime minister. Each president has desired to make his office preeminent. The first three presidents had no difficulty in doing that, for they could rely upon the support of a majority of members of the National Assembly. Cooperation could not be coerced, but it could be relied upon to keep the prime minister subordinate.

Since the election of François Mitterrand in 1981, party has become an independent variable. Because the president's election in 1981 was paralleled by the election of a Left majority in the assembly, Mitterrand could adopt what J.E.S. Hayward describes in *Governing France* as a "Gaulist conception of his office." But after the victory of the Right in the 1986 Assembly election resulted in a non-Socialist being imposed as premier, Jacques Chirac, the president has had to accept a change of position, symbolized by the ambivalent term *cohabitation*.

Whether the criterion is government's size or the authority of the national leader vis-à-vis other politicians, the conclusion is the same: the political leaders of Great Britain and France can exercise more power than the president of the United States. The American presidency is a relatively weak office. America's population, economy, and military are not good measures of the power of the White House. Imagine what one would say if American institutions were transplanted, more or less wholesale, to some small European democracy. We would not think that such a country had a strong leader.

While differing notably in the separate election of a French president as against a parliamentary election of a British prime minister, both offices centralize authority within a state that is itself a major institution of society. As long as a French president has a majority in the National Assembly, then this office can have most influence within government, for ministers are unambiguously subordinate to the president. The linkage of a British prime minister's position with a parliamentary majority means that as long as a single party has a majority, a British politician is protected against the risks of cohabitation à la française or à la americaine.

Variations within Nations

An office sets parameters within which politicians can act, but the more or less formal stipulation of the rules and resources of an office cannot determine exactly what is done. Within these limits, the individual performance of a president or prime minister can be important. Events too are significant; everyday crises tend to frustrate any attempt to plan ahead, and major crises—a war or domestic disaster—can shift the parameters, reducing a politician's scope for action (for example, Watergate) or expanding it (for example, the mass mobilization that Churchill could lead after Dunkirk).

In the abstract language of social science, we can say that the actions of a national leader reflect the interaction of the powers of office, of events, and of personality. But in concrete situations, there is always an inclination to emphasize one or another of these terms. For purposes of exposition, I treat the significance of events and personality separately: each is but one variable in a multivariate outcome.

Social scientists and constitutional lawyers are inherently generalizers, whereas critical events are unique. For example, a study of the British prime ministership that ignored what could be done in wartime would omit an example of powers temporarily stretched to new limits. Similarly, a study of Winston Churchill's capacities must recognize that his personality prevented him from achieving the nation's highest office—until the debacle of 1940 thrust office upon him.

In the postwar era, the American presidency has been especially prone to shock events. Unpredictable and nonrecurring events of importance include the outbreak of the Korean War in 1950, the assassination of President Kennedy in 1963, American involvement in the Vietnam War in the late 1960s, and the Watergate scandal, which led to President Nixon's resignation in 1974. One of the reasons for the positive popularity of Ronald Reagan has been that no disastrous event occurred in his presidency—at least until Irangate broke in November 1986.

The creation of the Fifth French Republic followed after events in Vietnam and in Algeria that undermined the authority and legitimacy of the government of the Fourth Republic. The events of May 1968 had a far greater impact in Paris than in any other European country. Whereas in 1958 events helped to create a republic with a president given substantial powers, in 1968 events were intended to reduce the authority of the state.

Great Britain has had relatively uneventful postwar government. Many causes of momentary excitement, such as the 1963 Profumo scandal that embarrassed

The French tradition of leadership is ambivalent.

Harold Macmillan, were trivial. The 1956 Suez war, which forced the resignation of Anthony Eden, did not lead to subsequent changes in the practice of the prime ministership, even though it was arguably a gross abuse of power vis-à-vis Cabinet colleagues and Parliament. The 1982 Falklands war called forth a mood of self-congratulation rather than a cry for institutional reform. The electoral boost it gave the prime minister was significant, but not eventful for the office.

The miner's strike, leading to a national three-day working week in the last days of the administration of Edward Heath in 1974, was perceived as a challenge to the authority of government. The prime minister called a general election seeking a popular mandate for his conduct of industrial relations. The mandate was withheld; so too was an endorsement of strikers. Characteristically, the events produced a reaction in favor of conciliation, for which Harold Wilson was particularly well suited at that stage of his career. Since 1979 the Thatcher administration has demonstrated that trade unions are not invincible. Hence, the 1974 crisis now appears as an aberration, rather than a critical conjuncture.

While personal factors are often extraneous to government, each individual incumbent has some scope for choice. Within a set of constraints imposed by office and events, a politician can choose what kind of a leader he or she would like to be. Such choices have political consequences. "Do what you can" is a prudential rule that is often overlooked in discussing what a president or prime minister does. The winnowing process by which one individual reaches the highest political office not only allows

---

Campaigning for office makes a politician conscious of a need for popular approval.

---

vidual reaches the highest political office not only allows for variety, but sometimes invites it, for a challenger for office may win votes by being different from an incumbent.

A president has a multiplicity of roles and a multiplicity of obligations. Many—as commander in chief of the armed forces, delivering a State of the Union message to Congress, and presenting a budget—are requirements of the office; but the capacity to do well in particular roles varies with the individual. For example, Lyndon Johnson was a superb manager of congressional relations, but had little or no feel for foreign affairs. By contrast, John F. Kennedy was interested in foreign affairs and defense and initially had little interest in domestic problems. Ronald Reagan is good at talking to people, whereas Jimmy Carter and Richard Nixon preferred to deal with problems on paper. Dwight D. Eisenhower brought to the office a national reputation as a hero that he protected by making unclear public statements. By contrast, Gerald Ford's public relations skills, while acceptable in a congressman, were inadequate to the demands of the contemporary presidency.

In Great Britain, Margaret Thatcher is atypical in her desire to govern, as well as preside over government. She applies her energy and intelligence to problems of government—and to telling her colleagues what to do about them. The fact that she wants to be *the* decision-maker for British government excites resentment among civil servants and Cabinet colleagues. This is not only a reaction

to her forceful personality, but also an expression of surprise: other prime ministers did not want to be the chief decision-maker in government. In the case of an aging Winston Churchill from 1951-55, this could be explained on grounds of ill health. In the case of Anthony Eden, it could be explained by an ignorance of domestic politics.

The interesting prime ministers are those who chose not to be interventionists across a range of government activities. Both Harold Macmillan and Clement Attlee brought to Downing Street great experience of British government. But Attlee was ready to be simply a chairman of a Cabinet in which other ministers were capable and decisive. Macmillan chose to intervene very selectively on issues that he thought important and to leave others to get on with most matters. Labor leader Neil Kinnock, if he became prime minister, would adopt a noninterventionist role. This would be welcomed in reaction to Thatcher's dominating approach. It would be necessary because Kinnock knows very little about the problems and practice of British government. Unique among party leaders of the past half-century, he has never held office in government.

In France, the role of a president varies with personality. De Gaulle approached the presidency with a distinctive concept of the state as well as of politics. By contrast, Mitterrand draws upon his experience of many decades of being a parliamentarian and a republican. Pompidou was distinctive in playing two roles, first prime minister under de Gaulle, and subsequently president.

Differences between French prime ministers may in part reflect contrasting relationships with a president. As a member of a party different from the president, Chirac has partisan and personal incentives to be more assertive than does a prime minister of the same party. Premiers who enter office via the Assembly or local politics, like Chaban-Delmas and Mauroy, are likely to have different priorities than a premier who was first a technocrat, such as Raymond Barre.

Fluctuations in Leaders

The fluctuating effect upon leaders of multiple influences is shown by the monthly ratings of the popularity of presidents and prime ministers. If formal powers of office were all, then the popularity rating of each incumbent should be much the same. This is not the case. If the personal characteristics of a politician were all-important, then differences would occur between leaders, but each leader would receive a consistent rating during his or her term of office. In fact, the popularity of a national leader tends to go up and down during a term of office. Since personality is held constant, these fluctuations cannot be explained as a function of personal qualities. Since there is no consistent decline in popularity, the movement cannot be explained as a consequence of impossible expectations causing the public to turn against whoever initially wins its votes.

The most reasonable explanation of these fluctuations in popularity is that they are caused by events. They may be shock events, such as the threat of military action, or scandal in the leader's office. Alternatively, changes may reflect the accumulation of seemingly small events, most notably those that are reflected in the state of the economy, such as growth, unemployment, and inflation rates. A politician may not be responsible for such trends, but he or she expects to lose popularity when things appear to be going badly and to regain popularity when things are going well.

Through the decades, cyclical fluctuations can reflect an underlying long-term secular trend. In Europe a major secular trend is the declining national importance of international affairs. In the United States events in Iran or Central America remain of as much (or more) significance than events within the United States. In a multipolar world a president is involved in and more vulnerable to events in many places. By contrast, leaders of France and Great Britain have an influence limited to a continental scale, in a world in which international relations has become intercontinental. This shift is not necessarily a loss for heads of government in the European Community. In a world summit meeting, only one nation, the United States, has been first. Japan may seek to exercise political influence matching its growing economic power. The smaller scale of the European Community nations with narrower economic interests create conditions for frequent contact and useful meetings in the European arena which may bring them marginal advantages in world summit meetings too.

If the power of a national leader is measured, as Robert A. Dahl suggests in *Who Governs?*, by the capacity that such an individual has to influence events in the desired direction, then all national leaders are subject to seeing their power eroded as each nation becomes more dependent upon the joint product of the open international economy. This is as true of debtor nations such as the United States has become, as of nations with a positive trade balance. It is true of economies with a record of persisting growth, such as Germany, and of slow growth economies such as Great Britain.

A powerful national leader is very desirable only if one believes that the *Führerprinzip* is the most important principle in politics. The constitutions and politics of Western industrial nations reject this assumption. Each political system is full of constraints upon arbitrary rule, and sometimes of checks and balances that are obstacles to prompt, clear-cut decisions.

The balance between effective leadership and responsiveness varies among the United States, Great Britain, and France. A portion of that variation is organic, being prescribed in a national constitution. This is most evident in a comparison of the United States and Great Britain, but constitutions are variables, as the history of postwar France demonstrates. Many of the most important determinants of what a national leader does are a reflection of changing political circumstances, of trends and shock events, and of the aspirations and shortcomings of the individual in office.

Europe—West, Center, and East: The Politics of Integration, Transformation, and Disintegration

- The European Union: From EC to EU (Articles 37–39)
- Revamping the Welfare State (Articles 40 and 41)
- Post-Communist Central and Eastern Europe (Articles 42 and 43)
- Russia and the Other Post-Soviet Republics (Articles 44–46)

Most of the articles in this unit are in some way linked to one or the other of two major developments that have fundamentally altered the political map of Europe in recent years. The first of these major changes is the long-term movement toward supranational integration of many Western European states within the institutional framework of the European Community or EC, which officially became the European Union or EU on November 1, 1993. Here the development has primarily been one by which sovereign states give up piecemeal some of their traditional independence, especially in matters dealing with economic and (to a lesser degree) monetary policy. Some important decisions that used to be made by national governments in Paris, Rome, Bonn, and Copenhagen have become the province of the EU representatives in Brussels. To be sure, the trend toward integration is neither automatic nor irreversible, as recent events have underlined. Nevertheless, the process continues to be very important in shaping the politics of Western Europe.

It is an important indication of the EU's continuing attractiveness that other countries seek to join. Austria and two more Scandinavian countries (Sweden and Finland)) became the newest EU members in 1995, after their entry had been approved in national referendums in each country. In the case of another Scandinavian country, Norway, the voters decided against membership for the second time in recent history. In Norway, there is a deep split between supporters and opponents, with an overwhelming resistance to membership coming from farmers and fishers as well as many women. A similar but weaker gender split is noticeable in the other Scandinavian countries, including Denmark, which has been a member since 1973. It appears that many Scandinavian women fear losing some of their social rights inside a European Union in which gender equality has not yet reached the level of their own countries.

The second major challenge to the established European state system is far more abrupt and goes in another, far more dislocating direction. It consists of the recent and rapid disintegration brought about by the sudden collapse of communist rule in Central and Eastern Europe. Here states, nations, and nationalities have broken away from an imposed system of central control, and now assert their independence from the previous ruling group and its communist ideology. In their attempts to construct a new order for themselves, the postcommunist countries are encountering enormous difficulties. Their transition from one-party rule to pluralist democracy and from centrally planned state socialism to a market-based economy has turned out to be much rougher than had been anticipated. The resulting destabilization has had an enormous impact in the western part of the continent as well. There is already considerable evidence that many people have a nostalgia for the basic

material security provided by the communist welfare states of the past. Communist-descended parties have responded by abandoning much of their Leninist baggage and engaging in the competitive bidding for votes with promises of social fairness and security.

A closer look at the countries of Western Europe reveals that they have their own internal problems, even if in a far less acute form than their counterparts to the East. Their relative prosperity rests on a base built up during the prolonged postwar economic boom of the 1950s and 1960s. By political choice, a considerable portion of their affluence was channeled toward the public sector and used to develop generous systems of social services and social insurance. Between the early 1970s and the mid-1980s, however, Western industrial societies were beset by economic disruptions that brought an end to the long period of rapidly growing prosperity. The last half of the 1980s marked some improvement in the economic situation throughout most of Western Europe, partly as a result of some favorably timed positive trade balances with the United States. In the early 1990s, however, economic recession took these countries in its grip once again. It is becoming clear that there are more fundamental reasons why they no longer can take increasing affluence for granted in a more competitive global economy. Almost every one of them is today beset by economic problems that economists deem to be structural in origin, rather than just cyclical and therefore passing. In other words, it will take more than an upturn in the business cycle to energize these economies.

The earlier economic shock that first interrupted the prolonged postwar boom had come in the wake of sharp rises in the cost of energy, linked to successive hikes in the price of oil imposed by the Organization of Petroleum Exporting Countries (OPEC) after 1973. In the 1980s, OPEC lost its organizational bite, as its members began to compete against each other by raising production and lowering prices rather than abiding by the opposite practices in the manner of a well-functioning cartel agreement. The resulting improvement for the consumers of oil helped the West European economies recover, but as a whole they did not rebound to their earlier high growth rates. The short Persian Gulf War did not seriously hamper the flow of Middle East oil in 1991, but it once again underscored the vulnerability of Europe to external interruptions in its energy supply.

Because of their heavy dependence on international trade, West European economies are especially vulnerable to the kind of global recessionary tendencies we have encountered during the past few years. Another important challenge to these affluent countries is found in the stiff competition they face from the newly industrialized countries (NICs) of East and South Asia, where productivity is higher and labor costs remain much lower.

The emergent Asian factor probably contributed to the increased tempo of the European drive for economic integration in the late 1980s. Some observers have warned of the possibility that major trading blocs in Europe, North America, and Eastern Asia could replace the relatively free system of international trade established in the post-1945 period.

A related issue is how the increase in international trade within and outside the European Community will affect the established "social market economies" of continental Europe. The economic gains derived from international competition could have a positive consequence, by providing a better base for consolidating and invigorating the social welfare systems, as described by Joel Havemann in his article "Diagnosis: Healthier in Europe." However, a different scenario seems to be starting, in which there will be a drastic pruning and reduction in social services, carried out in the name of efficiency and international competitiveness. The social problems that have resulted in Europe's growing "underclass" are presented in the essay "Europe and the Underclass: The Slippery Slope." There are other demographic and economic challenges to the corporatist and welfare state arrangements that appear to have served these countries so well for so long. The debate about the best policy response to such problems will probably continue to agitate West Europeans for years to come.

In the mid-1980s, there was widespread talk of a malaise or "Europessimism" that had beset these countries. Thereafter the mood appeared to become more upbeat, and for a while some observers even detected a swing toward what they labeled "Europhoria." It is advisable to add some salt to such easy generalizations about swings in the public mood, but by now there seems once again to be a more sober or even pessimistic spirit abroad in Western Europe. Observers plausibly link this latest shift in mood to the economic and social problems associated with recessionary developments as well as the impact of the dislocations that have accompanied the end of the cold war.

The demise of the Soviet bloc removed one major external challenge but replaced it with a set of others. The countries of Western Europe were simply unprepared for the chaotic conditions left behind by the former communist regimes to the East. They are now affected by the fierce competition for scarce capital, as the countries in Eastern Europe seek to attract investments that will build a new and modern economic infrastructure. At the same time, the daily poverty and disorder of life in Eastern Europe have encouraged a migration to the relatively affluent societies of the West.

Those who attempt the big move to the "Golden West" resemble in many ways the immigrants who have been attracted to the United States in the past and present. The major point of difference is that many West Europeans are unwilling to accept what they regard as a flood of unwanted strangers. The newcomers are widely portrayed or perceived as outsiders, whose presence will drain the generous welfare systems and threaten not only economic security but also the established way of life. Such anxieties are the stuff of sociocultural tensions and conflicts. One serious political consequence has been the emergence of anti-immigrant populism on the far Right.

There can be no doubt that the issues of immigration and cultural tensions in Western Europe will occupy a central place on the political agenda in the coming years. Some of the established parties have already made symbolic and substantive accommodations to appease protesting voters, for fear of otherwise losing them to extremist ultra-Right movements. But it is important to remember that there are also groups that resist such compromises and instead oppose the xenophobic elements in their own societies. Some enlightened political leaders and commentators seek to promote the reasonable perspective that migrants could turn out to be an important asset rather than a liability. This argument may concede that the foreign influx also involves some social cost in the short run, at least during a recessionary period, but it emphasizes that the newcomers can be a very important human resource that will contribute to mid- and long-term economic prosperity. Quite apart from any such economic considerations, of course, the migrants and asylum-seekers have become an important test of liberal democratic tolerance on the continent.

Prudent observers had long warned about a premature celebration of "Europe 1992," which really referred to the abolition on restrictions in the flow of goods, capital, services, and labor by January 1, 1993. They suggested that the slogan served to cover up some remaining problems and some newly emerging obstacles to the full integration of the community. The skeptics seemed at least partly vindicated by the setbacks that have followed the supposedly decisive "leap" forward during its meeting at the Dutch town of Maastricht in December of 1991. The Maastricht Treaty foresaw the further supranational integration of the member nations during the 1990s. It envisaged a common monetary system and a federal European Reserve Bank as well as common policies on immigration, environmental protection, external security and foreign affairs. In three of the twelve member countries—Denmark, Ireland, and France—ratification of the treaty was tied to the outcome of national referendums. In the first of these expressions of the popular will, Danish voters in June 1992 decided by a very slim majority of less than two percent to reject the treaty. A huge Irish majority in favor of the treaty was followed by a very slim French approval as well. The negative Danish vote seemed to have the effect of legitimating and releasing many pent up reservations in other member countries. But in May 1993, Danish voters approved a modified version of agreement, and some weeks later British prime minister John Major was able to hammer together a fragile parliamentary majority in the House of Commons. The last formal hurdle to the Maastricht Treaty was passed in Germany, where the Constitutional Court turned down a legal challenge. But the difficult ratification process had revealed widespread political resistance that will continue to hamper the course toward a federal union.

As several of the articles in this section point out, the European Union has effectively reached a crossroads. The European nation-state has turned out to have more holding power than some federalists had expected, especially in a time of economic setbacks and perceived threats to the social order. The absence of a coherent West European response to the violent ethnic conflict in former Yugoslavia has added a further reason for doubt concerning the EU's imminent progression toward an elementary form of political federation. For these and other reasons, the present seems to be a time for new thought and debate about the EU's further goals and its route for reaching them, as Ian Davidson suggests in "Towards 1996: The Making or Breaking of Europe."

While much academic and political ink has been spilled on the problems of a transition from a market economy to state socialism, we have little theory or practice to guide East Europeans who are moving in the opposite direction. A new and major theoretical issue, which has important policy consequences, thus concerns the best strategy for restructuring the economies of the former communist countries. Some academics believe that a quick transition to a market economy is a preferable course, indeed the only responsible one, even though it will be disruptive and painful in the short run. They argue that such a "shock" or "big bang" approach will release human energies and bring economic growth more quickly and efficiently, and warn that halfway measures not only bring stagnation but could end up making the economic plight of these countries even worse than at present.

Others have come out in favor of a more gradual strategy for economic change. They warn that the strategy of the neoclassical economist, who would introduce a market economy by fiat, not only ignore its cultural and historical preconditions but also underestimate the social pain and turmoil that accompany the big transition. In effect, these critics contend that the strategy of shock therapy has brought a lot of shock but very little therapy. Such gradualists, therefore, recommend pragmatic strategies of incremental change, accompanied by a rhetoric of lower expectations, as the politically more prudent course of action. It is likely that a mix of the two approaches will be the practical policy outcome, but after a few years we may have some better insights

into the relative merits of each argument. Decision makers must often learn on the job. They cannot afford to become inflexible and dogmatic in these matters, where the human stakes are so high.

The same debate has been carried out in the former Soviet Union during the past few years. In some ways, it could be argued that Mikhail Gorbachev failed to opt clearly for one or the other approach to economic reform. He seems not only to have been ambivalent about the means but about the ends of his perestroika, or restructuring, of the centrally planned economy. He remained far too socialist for some born-again marketers in his own country, while communist hard-liners never forgave him for dismantling a system in which they had enjoyed at least a modicum of security and privilege.

But the Achilles' heel of the now defunct Soviet Union turned out to be its multiethnic character. Gorbachev was not alone in underestimating the potential centrifugal tendencies of a country that was based on an ideological and political redefinition of the old Russian Empire. Many of the non-Russian minorities were ethnic majorities within their own territory, and this made it possible for them to long for greater autonomy or even national independence in a way that the scattered ethnic groups of the United States do not.

Gorbachev appears to have regarded his own policies of glasnost or openness and democratization as essential accompaniments of perestroika in his modernization program. He seems to have understood (or become convinced) that a highly developed industrial economy needs a freer flow of information along with a more decentralized system of decision making, if its component parts are to be efficient, flexible, and capable of self-correction. In that sense, a market economy has some integral feedback traits that make it incompatible with the traditional Soviet model of a centrally directed, authoritarian command economy.

But glasnost and democratization were clearly incompatible with a repressive political system of one-party rule as well. They served Gorbachev as instruments that weakened the grip of the communist hard-liners and at the same time rallied behind him some reform groups, including many intellectuals and journalists. Within a remarkably short time after he came to power in 1985, a vigorous new press emerged in the Soviet Union headed by journalists who were eager to ferret out misdeeds and report on political reality as they observed it. A similar development took place in the history profession, where scholars used the new spirit of openness to report in grim detail about past atrocities of the Soviet system that had previously been covered up or dismissed as bourgeois lies. There was an inevitable irony to the new truthfulness. Even as it served to discredit much of the past along with any reactionary attempts to restore "the good old days," it also brought into question the foundations of the Soviet system and the leading role of the Communist Party. Yet Gorbachev had clearly sought to modernize and reform the system, not to bring it down.

Most important of all, glasnost and democratization gave those ethnic minorities in the Soviet Union, which had a territorial identity, an opportunity to demand autonomy or independence. The first national assertions came from the Baltic peoples in Estonia, Latvia, and Lithuania, who had been forced back under Russian rule in 1940, after some two decades of national independence. Very soon other nationalities, including the Georgians and Armenians, expressed similar demands through the political channels that had been opened to them. The death knell for the Soviet Union sounded in 1991, when the Ukrainians, who constituted the second largest national group in the Soviet Union after the Russians, made similar demands for independence.

In a very real sense, then, Gorbachev's political reforms ended up as a threat not only to the continued leadership role by the Communist Party but also to the continued existence of the Soviet Union itself. Gorbachev seems to have understood neither of these ultimately fatal consequences of his reform attempts until quite late. This explains why he could set in motion forces that would ultimately destroy what he had hoped to make more attractive and productive. The attempted hard-liner coup against the reformer and his reforms, in August 1991, came far too late and was too poorly organized to have succeeded. In fact, the would-be coup d'état became instead a coup de grace for the Soviet Communists and, in the end, the Soviet Union as well. Somewhat reluctantly, Gorbachev declared the party illegal soon after he returned to office. The coup was defeated by a popular resistance, led by Russian president Boris Yeltsin, who had broken with communism earlier and far more decisively.

There is an undeniable gloom or hangover atmosphere in many of the accounts of postcommunist and post-Soviet Europe. It seems clear that much will get worse before it gets better in the economic and social life of these countries. The political consequences could be very important, for social frustrations can now be freely articulated and represented in the political process. The transition from one-party rule to pluralist democratic forms has turned out to be neither easy nor automatic. A turn to some form of authoritarian nationalist populism cannot be ruled out in several countries, including Russia. Former communists with leadership skills are likely to play a major role in the process in countries like Poland and the Ukraine.

Specialists on the former Soviet Union disagree considerably in their assessments of the current situation or what brought it about. One of the hotly debated issues concerns President Yeltsin's decision in September 1993 to use a preemptive strike to break a deadlock between his government and a majority in the Russian Parliament. When a majority of the legislators, who had been elected over two years earlier, persisted in blocking some of his major economic reforms, Yeltsin dissolved Parliament and called new elections to be held in December 1993.

The electoral result was a political boomerang for Yeltsin. It resulted in a major setback for the forces that backed rapid and thoroughgoing market reforms. The new Parliament, based on a two-ballot system of elections, is highly fragmented, but Nationalists and former communists occupy pivotal positions in the Duma. President Yeltsin now plays a more subdued role than previously and the new government pursues far more cautious reform policies than previously. The military invasion of Chechnya, a break-away Caucasian republic located within the Russian federation, has not given Yeltsin the quick and easy victory that might have reversed his slide into political unpopularity among Russians. Nor has it stemmed the surge of Russian nationalist politics, which seems based on a demand for cracking down on crime and social disorder. But neither the ultra-Right nor the former communists, who reject drastic market reforms, seem eager to return to a centrally planned economy. In that limited sense, at least, the long Soviet chapter of Russian history appears to have been closed, even though the experience will continue to disturb the pattern of the country's future development.

Looking Ahead: Challenge Questions

What are the major obstacles to the emergence of a more unified Europe? What differentiates the optimists and the skeptics as they assess the outlook for greater integration? What are the major institutional characteristics of the European Union, and why is there a widespread call for reform?

What is the evidence that the economic problems of Western Europe are not just cyclical but also structural in origin? What has been the impact of economic stagnation on the social services provided by the welfare state?

What are the main problems facing the newly elected governments in Eastern and Central Europe? How well are they doing in coping with the transition to political pluralism and a market economy?

Was Gorbachev mistaken in believing that the Soviet Union could be reformed without being dissolved? How did he and Yeltsin differ in their views about reform before the abortive coup in August 1991?

Why did Boris Yeltsin call an early parliamentary election in December 1993, and how did its outcome represent a setback for the market reformers?

TOWARDS 1996

The making or breaking of Europe

The European Union is moving erratically but inexorably towards a new showdown over its future. The catalyst for this showdown will be the expansion of the union to include most or all of the countries of Eastern Europe, which will top the agenda at the Inter-Governmental Conference of 1996. That conference cannot fail to be a turning point in the history of Europe; and the upshot will either be a radical transformation of the union, and the beginning of a new era in its development, or the biggest crisis in its history.

History has overtaken the European Union, and presented it with problems on a scale beyond all expectation and precedent

---

It is obvious that Europe is not ready for such a showdown because it has not fully recovered from the trauma of the Maastricht treaty of 1991. It is even more obvious that the British Conservative Party has become increasingly, almost suicidally, divided in its feelings about Europe.

Nevertheless, we shall probably find that Maastricht was just a modest hors d'ouevre in comparison with the much more traumatic Inter-Governmental Con-

ference looming ahead. If you thought Maastricht was a nightmare, but you're glad it's over, just wait for 1996: it will be much worse.

The reason for this is that history has overtaken the European Union, and presented it with problems on a scale beyond all expectation and precedent. When the Maastricht negotiation was being planned, the governments were moving painstakingly towards a precisely defined programme for Economic and Monetary Union for the 12 member states.

By the time the Maastricht conference was in session, in 1991, the map of Europe had changed. The Berlin Wall had fallen, and the member governments were confronted with the seismic event of the resurgence of a unified Germany at the heart of the European Union.

But it is only now, three years after the Maastricht treaty was signed, that the member states have gradually realised that the real issue they must deal with is not in fact the unification of Germany but the unification of the whole of Europe.

This will have two consequences. The first is that building this larger Europe almost certainly means abandoning the EU's traditional, incrementalist approach to integration, the accumulation of layer upon layer of limited economic bargains for political purposes which never had to be made explicit.

The new Europe will be too large and diverse for that approach to be feasible,

so it will be necessary to bring fundamental constitutional issues out into the open.

The second consequence, as a result, is that the debate about the larger Europe is bound to turn into a confrontation between the majority of member states (eg, Germany), which want a more tightly integrated Union, and the minority (eg, Britain), which want a looser Europe. It goes without saying that the outcome of that confrontation will not be decided by the minority.

Ever since their liberation from the Soviet empire, all the countries of Central and Eastern Europe have been claiming a place in the European Union, and two of them (Poland and Hungary) have already put in formal membership applications.

Some of the existing member states (such as France) at first resisted the idea of early admission of East European states. But over time reluctance has succumbed to German insistence; the European Union has effectively committed itself to offer membership to all the East European countries; and most member governments now accept that this expansion is unavoidable, and may have to come sooner rather than later.

The reason the Germans feel so strongly is that they see themselves at the precarious frontier between the stability of the European Union in the west and the potential instability of the rest of Europe to the east. So they believe it is vital to the national interests of Germany,

Reprinted from *The Independent*, December 9, 1994, p. 19.

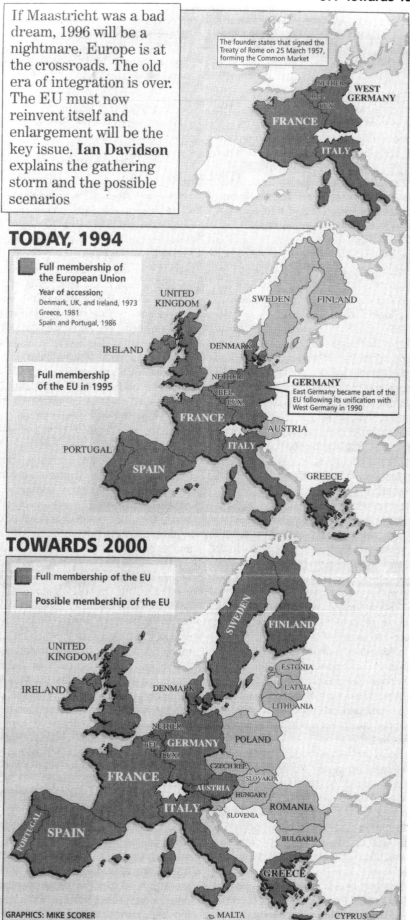

and of Europe, that the whole of Europe should be stabilised, by bringing all the countries of Eastern Europe into an enlarged union.

To be precise, this would mean the admission of six countries from Central Europe, three Baltic states and Slovenia, plus Cyprus and Malta, or an extra 12 member states. This would come on top of the existing 12 member states, plus the three new countries from the European Free Trade Area: Austria, Finland and Sweden.

In other words, the 12 are talking about a truly colossal expansion, an enlarged union of 27 states, and an increase in the population from 345 million to around 480 million.

Such a union would encompass an extraordinary diversity of geography, history, politics and culture, extremes of riches and poverty, and possibly serious conflicts of economic and political interests.

Naturally, no one expects all 12 of these candidates to join on the same day: the Czechs and Hungarians will be ready for membership long before the Bulgarians. But the point is that the union is treating the expansion into Eastern Europe as a question of general principle: all these European countries will join. As a result, the 12 are looking towards an expansion *programme* whose scale must entail far-reaching system changes in the union.

First, it will require the union to make fundamental reforms in some of its existing spending policies, notably the Common Agricultural Policy, the Regional Fund and the Social Fund.

Most East European countries are poor and dependent on agriculture, so they would stand to benefit enormously from the CAP and from the regional and other structural funds. Unfortunately, their entry might nearly double the costs of these policies, which already take 85 per cent of the EU budget (around 66bn Ecus, or £53bn) and high CAP prices in Eastern Europe would provoke an explosion of farm production.

But the rich member states will not pay for such a budget explosion and world trade rules would ban any explosion of subsidised farm exports. In essence, the union will have three options: to exclude the new members from the social, regional and agricultural policies; to reform the policies so as to spread the benefits differently; or even to abandon these social and redistributive policies entirely.

It is easy to foresee a bitter conflict of interest between the poor and/or agri-

If Maastricht was a bad dream, 1996 will be a nightmare. Europe is at the crossroads. The old era of integration is over. The EU must now reinvent itself and enlargement will be the key issue. **Ian Davidson** explains the gathering storm and the possible scenarios

The founder states that signed the Treaty of Rome on 25 March 1957, forming the Common Market

TODAY, 1994

Full membership of the European Union

Year of accession;
Denmark, UK, and Ireland, 1973
Greece, 1981
Spain and Portugal, 1986

Full membership of the EU in 1995

GERMANY
East Germany became part of the EU following its unification with West Germany in 1990

TOWARDS 2000

Full membership of the EU

Possible membership of the EU

GRAPHICS: MIKE SCORER

cultural countries of the existing member states, and the even poorer countries of Eastern Europe. But the deeper problem is that each of these options means abandoning what has hitherto been an inviolate principle, known in French as the "*acquis communautaire*", meaning something like "the accumulated inheritance".

Previously, all candidates for membership have had to accept the whole of the community and all its accumulated policies lock, stock and barrel. The reason was that the "*acquis communautaire*" represented bargains and trade-offs between the existing member states.

The recent increase in the size of the regional and other structural funds, for example, was an explicit concession by the rich member states, to persuade the poor to accept the extra competition of the Single Market.

The implication of expansion to the east is that some of those earlier bargains might be reopened. Which would imply a fundamental rewriting of the EU's ledger and of its rule book. The second problem is that such a mega-Europe will need a radical revision of the Union's decision-making rules: more and easier majority voting, and bigger voting weights for the big countries. This would mean a big step down the road towards political integration.

It is easy to foresee a furious conflict of principle between those countries (such as Germany and the Benelux) that want a more federal Europe and those (such as Britain) that do not; but the combined logic of these two issues (majority voting and national voting weights) will be lethal for Britain. Voting weights will be the key. The small countries have always had much bigger voting weights in the Council of Ministers than the large countries, in relation to their population. In the original European Community this was manageable, because the community was small and homogeneous and only half the member states were small (the Benelux countries).

But in the future mega-Europe, with a possible 27 member states, only six will be large and 21 will be small. This means that a handful of large countries could be outvoted by a swarm of small countries with only a fraction of their population. The big countries will therefore demand a reweighting of voting strengths in their favour.

The problem is that this reweighting will not come free. All the small countries will want something in exchange; and the three Benelux countries, which have learned from experience that their only protection lies in strong community institutions, will only be willing to sell their voting premiums in exchange for much more majority voting and more powers for the European Parliament.

That is a bargain the Germans would be more than happy with, and the French would probably settle for it, if less happily; but for the British government it is a no-win situation.

If we take stock of the argument so far we are driven to some mutually incompatible propositions.

■ Proposition One: the wholesale expansion of the European Union, to include at least 10 new member states from Eastern Europe, is now a strategic imperative of the post–Cold War world and a political commitment on the part of the Twelve.

■ Proposition Two: an expansion on this scale is without precedent; it is almost certainly not attainable without radical changes in the present policies and institutions of the European Union; but such changes will meet fierce resistance from different groups of member states.

■ Proposition Three: it is therefore not clear that wholesale enlargement to the east can be negotiated on terms that will be acceptable to all the present member states. In strategic terms, it may be an overriding imperative; but in practical terms, it may be irreconcilable with existing bargains between the 12; and without unanimous agreement, it will not happen.

It is obvious that something has to give. The contradiction between mega-enlargement and the *acquis communautaire* points to three layers of conclusions:

First, there is a question of the balance of power inside the existing union. Germany is unequivocally and passionately committed to the principle of enlargement, and it will have allies; but they may be heavily outnumbered by others with serious reservations, either economic or political. A balance-of-power struggle might therefore result in the exclusion of the East Europeans; but only at the cost of a serious political crisis, in the EU and in Europe at large.

The second conclusion is rather different. The EU has over 40 years accumulated experience of increasing integration; and it seems unlikely that a contradiction in which such vast political and strategic issues are at stake can be settled in a crude power struggle between winners and losers. The confrontation between the old community and of the *acquis communautaire* and the new union of the larger Europe will create enormous incentives to enlarge the parameters of the debate, and to engage, almost for the first time, in a fundamental showdown over political first principles.

If the union can no longer expand and grow through the accretion of new layers and partial bargains, and if expansion to the east has a genuine claim to be a strategic necessity, then the union may have to rethink its basic principles. If it is forced, by the claims of eastern expansion, partially to deconstruct the policies and the institutions it has acquired from the past, it may need to go one step further, and reconstruct the union more radically from the ground up. It is unlikely that we shall see the convening of a constituent assembly for the writing of a new European constitution. But the questions implied by a constitution will hover permanently in the background.

If the 1996 Inter-Governmental Conference fails, it is not absolutely improbable that the European Union could break up

---

The third conclusion follows from the second. It may prove too difficult to secure unanimous agreement on the terms for enlarging to the east; and it may prove too difficult to secure unanimous agreement on a new phase of political integration between all of the 12 (or 15, as they will be). But we can be sure that the Germans, who are raising the stakes on the agenda for 1996, both on enlargement to the east and on constitutional reform, will not settle for nothing.

If the Inter-Governmental Conference fails, it is not absolutely improbable that the European Union could break up. What is much more likely is that it will disintegrate into different layers of membership in which Germany, together with France and the Benelux (and perhaps others) would press ahead to create an inner political and economic core. That is the kind of power struggle—in which different member states vote with their feet—that may lie at the end of the Inter-Governmental Conference of 1996.

1996 and all that

Europe should agree to disagree

John Andrews

VARIABLE geometry, multi-track, multi-speed, two-tier, hard core, concentric circles, à la carte, deepening, widening ... More than ever, Europe's politicians are mixing their metaphors.

The confusion stems from the part of the Maastricht treaty that calls for a conference of member states in 1996 "to examine those provisions of this Treaty for which revision is provided, in accordance with the objectives set out in Articles A and B." Those objectives are economic and monetary union, "ultimately including a single currency"; a common foreign and security policy, "which might in time lead to a common defence"; and "close cooperation on justice and home affairs".

These are big ambitions. The job of the 1996 intergovernmental conference is to correct any mistakes the Maastricht drafters may have made in the "process of creating an ever closer union among the peoples of Europe". Since there are some profound disagreements over what this union should mean, the 1996 debate could be extremely lively.

Why then has it started prematurely? The best explanation is that Germany, which now holds the six-month rotating presidency of the union, has a vision of an expanding, federalist Europe for which it feels that national electorates, and fellow governments, need to be prepared. After all, one lesson of the Maastricht process—shown by the wafer-thin referendum majority in France in 1992 and the need for Denmark to hold a second referendum in 1993—is that Europe's leaders can easily misread the public mood. Even those who do not share Germany's vision will concede that some kind of EU reform is inevitable.

Age limits

As presently constituted, the EU can barely cope with the present, let alone the future. Bear in mind that this is a club of unequals. Member states range from unified Germany, with 80m people, to tiny Luxembourg with a mere 395,000. They range in wealth from Denmark, with a GDP per head of over 21,000 ecus, to Greece, with about 7,500 ecus. Now look at three main institutions.

The commission is a body of permanent civil servants and government appointees which administers EU business and proposes and drafts legislation. The Council of Ministers, attended by appropriate government ministers from the member

countries, is the EU's legislature, the only one in the democratic world which normally deliberates in secret. The European Parliament, which holds its committee meetings in Brussels but its plenary sessions in Strasbourg, is the one EU body directly elected by the union's citizens and yet has few of the powers of any national parliament and counts for less than either the council or the commission.

This structure was designed for a club of six, and it has just about coped with the doubling to 12. But how can it deal, the rule-book unchanged, with a club that in the next two decades could expand to a membership of a score or more?

The bigger the club, the tougher it will be to maintain an acceptable balance between large countries and small. Of the six founding members, France, West Germany and Italy had big populations; Holland, Belgium and Luxembourg small ones. Today the big members have been joined by

From *The Economist*, October 22, 1994, pp. Survey 19-21. © 1994 by the Economist, Ltd. Distributed by the New York Times Special Features. Reprinted by permission.

Britain, with Spain close behind, and the small countries have been bolstered by Ireland, Denmark, Greece and Portugal. Harmony of sorts is maintained by a system of checks and balances: big countries have more votes in the Council of Ministers so that they cannot be out-voted by a gaggle of small ones. In turn, small countries are protected by a system of weighted voting. Of the council's 76 votes, 54 are currently needed to form a "qualified", or decisive, majority—and only 23 are therefore needed to form a blocking minority.

So far, so good. The present arithmetic means that the big five, with 48 votes between them and representing four-fifths of the union's population, can muster a qualified majority only if they gain the support of at least two small states. Similarly, to get their way the small states need the backing of three big states. Conversely, two big countries can form a blocking minority if they can get the support of any small country other than Luxembourg. Roughly speaking, a qualified majority normally represents 70% of the EU's people, a blocking minority 30%.

The problem is the future. From January 1st the EU is supposed to grow, by four more countries, to 16 members. Extend the arithmetic and the qualified majority will go up to 64 votes out of 90 (see table 1); and the blocking minority to 27. By John Major's pocket calculator that means that Britain, Germany and Holland, a liberal economic group, would be unable to form a blocking minority against illiberal nonsense even though they would represent over 40% of the union's population. By contrast, eight small countries could gang together and get 27 votes even though they represent only 12% of the European Union's people.

Viewing this as an unacceptable shift in the union's balance, Britain threatened until last March to hold up the accession treaties with the applicant countries. Then a compromise was reached: if two big countries wanting to block a decision could not gather the 27 votes needed, fellow members would try for a "reasonable" period to reach a compromise acceptable to them.

The British have a point—it is already bizarre that Germany should have only one council vote

for every 8m people while Luxembourg has one for every 198,000—and the point will grow more obvious if tiddlers such as Malta and Cyprus join the union. But, in practice, council meetings tend to be bazaar-like bargaining sessions in which calculators are seldom needed. Of some 233 single-market decisions taken in the five years to last December only 91 actually went to a vote. The implicit message of Britain's obduracy was that it is more important to be able to block legislation than to pass it.

Is such an attitude sustainable in an expanding union? True followers of Monnet would say that no minority should be allowed to paralyse the European process. The concept of majority voting was in the original Treaty of Rome and was put into effect for all legislation affecting the single market. The aim must surely be to increase the scope for majority voting, not to go backwards towards more of the unanimity still needed for such areas as taxation and foreign policy—and for the revision of the treaties and the acceptance of new members.

On the other hand, no club can be happy if some members are constantly overruled, especially if it is a club of conflicting interests and rival cultures. And that it surely is. Some members, such as Germany, Holland, Denmark and Britain, instinctively believe in free trade and open markets; others, such as France and Spain, mistrust market forces that they cannot influence. Some, notably Germany and Britain, put into the communal budget far more than they get out, while others, especially Greece, Ireland, Spain and Portugal, do the reverse (see chart 2 on next page). There are plenty of what John Major once called "fault lines" to threaten the union's solidity.

Speed limits

Up to now the union has tried to finesse such differences. That is why the Maastricht treaty deals with the single market, economic affairs and trade relations as communal matters to be supervised by the commission, but decrees that a common foreign and security policy, along with justice and home affairs, are matters to be settled between governments. This enables France and Britain, the two countries with lingering imperial responsibilities and also the will, tradition and—just about—the means to project military force around the world, to keep control of their foreign interests. Similarly, Germany, which is particularly sensitive about immigration, can more easily ignore the liberal attitudes of the commission and the parliament.

Yet it is unlikely that intergovernmentalism, the practice of leaving tricky decisions for agreement among individual member governments, can provide a perfect solution. René Foch, secretary-general of a lobbying group, the Comité d'Action pour l'Europe, argues that there are at least three weaknesses. One is inefficiency: since 1985 nine EU states—all except Britain, Ireland and Denmark— have signed the Schengen agreement to abolish all passport checks and other obstacles to the free movement within the EU of its citizens. And yet they have still not fully implemented the agreement. By contrast, the single market, achieved on a

Little and large 1		
1994	Population est. m	Votes in Council
Germany	81.6	10
Britain	58.2	10
Italy	58.1	10
France	58.0	10
Spain	39.2	8
Holland	15.4	5
Greece	10.5	5
Belgium	10.1	5
Portugal	9.4	5
Sweden	8.8	4
Austria	8.0	4
Denmark	5.2	3
Finland	5.1	3
Norway	4.3	3
Ireland	3.6	3
Luxembourg	0.4	2
Sources: European Commission; OECD		

community basis and by qualified-majority voting, is up and (mainly) running.

The second failing is that intergovernmentalism can increase the "democratic deficit"—the extent to which EU affairs are decided outside the direct control of elected representatives. Mr Foch cites the example of Europol, the body set up this year to foster co-operation among the union's police forces: it is specifically excluded by the Maastricht treaty from supervision by the parliament and the European Court, but in reality is also beyond the supervision of national parliaments.

Lastly, intergovernmentalism does not fill in any fault lines, it merely papers them over. The theory is that all participants in intergovernmental organisations are equal—but the practice, from the United Nations down, is that some are more equal than others and a few may be dominant. As the EU expands, so the inequities will tend to worsen. "However democratic the new Germany may be", says Mr Foch, "its sheer size and position in the

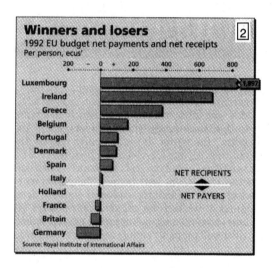

Winners and losers
1992 EU budget net payments and net receipts
Per person, ecus'

Source: Royal Institute of International Affairs

heart of Europe would inexorably lead it—without seeking any such role and even against its will—to dominate a merely intergovernmental Europe."

Mrs Thatcher's answer to that problem was to declare that only the military and political engagement of the United States in Europe, and close relations between the other two strongest sovereign states in the region—Britain and France—could balance German power. She went on to argue that no such balancing arrangements could be achieved within a European super-state. That, however, depends on how you design your super-state.

Pick the metaphor

There are two kinds of design problem here. The first concerns the structure of the institutions. There are now 17 commissioners (two each for the five big countries, one each for the small ones), whose pronouncements have to be translated into nine official languages. If the union grows to 16 members on January 1st there will be 21 commissioners and 12 official languages (the Austrians speak German, which is already an official EU tongue); parliament will increase from 567 to 641 members; the European Court of Justice from 13 judges to 17.

And so it goes on . . . but not indefinitely. Before the union gets bigger still there will have to be a decision at the 1996 conference to have either a smaller commission, or one in which some commissioners are junior to others. Big countries, for example, could have one commissioner each; small countries could take turns to have a commissioner.

That will cause quarrels enough. So will the question of voting arrangements within an expanding Council of Ministers. In August 1993 Karl Lamers, the CDU's parliamentary spokesman on foreign affairs, suggested that successful votes should require a "double majority": a majority of member states representing also a majority of the EU's population. Votes that now need to be unanimous could in future be made by a "super-qualified" majority: say four-fifths, or three-quarters, of the member states representing four-fifths or three-quarters of the union's people.

But the worst quarrels could concern the parliament, not least because—at the urging of Chancellor Kohl—parliament's representatives are to help prepare the 1996 conference. Having won extra powers from the Maastricht treaty (it can, for example veto much legislation and its approval is needed for the appointment of the commission and its president), the parliament will want still more. But only Germany and the Benelux countries are keen to transfer any more power to the parliament; France and Britain are firmly against.

Europe's institutions, however, are simply the means to an end. The real problem is the end itself, that "ever closer union among the peoples of Europe". Can the union become "ever closer" while it is also getting bigger—can "deepening" coincide with "broadening"? Germany and the Benelux countries, true followers of Monnet, believe so almost as an act of principle. Pragmatic Britain, as ever, is sceptical.

Since Chancellor Kohl says that the EU convoy must not be forced to travel at the pace of the slowest ship, the solution will inevitably be some kind of agreement to disagree. There are good precedents: the Maastricht treaty allows Britain to "opt out" both from the goal of a single currency and from the EU's commitment to enhance its "social policy"; Denmark has excused itself likewise from the single currency and, in an agreement after the treaty, from provisions on defence, foreign and judicial policies and European citizenship.

The question is how far there precedents can be taken before the club loses its sense of identity. That is what others object to in the British desire for an "à la carte approach": member states would sign up only to the policies they like—in other words, there could be lots of broadening but no need to deepen. Better, say France and Germany, to take the same path but let some proceed faster than others.

In May, in an article coinciding with a Franco-German summit in Mulhouse, Alain Lamassoure, the French minister for European affairs, called for a "new founding contract" by which a core group of EU members—including France and Germany—would commit themselves to some basics: economic and monetary union, a common defence policy (including Eurocorps), immigration control and co-operation on police matters. Any country not wishing to sign up to these areas would lose the right to vote on them.

Now add Mr Lamassoure's article to the CDU's "reflections" and to remarks by his prime minister, Edouard Balladur, made just before the CDU paper. Mr Balladur talked of an inner circle building a monetary and military union for themselves; other EU members, including new ones, could co-operate on foreign policy, security and trade; a third circle, embracing all of Europe, would co-operate still more loosely on diplomacy and trade. You do not have to be a conspiracy theorist—nor even John Major—to see a Europe which Antonio Martino, Italy's foreign minister, fears will be a Europe of "two speeds" and divisively "variable geometry".

But is there a better alternative? It is true that the inner core might grow increasingly distant from the outer—and poorer—circles. Over time, the inner core might also be less prepared to foot the bill for the development funds that help the others. But the French and the Germans make one thing clear: any country—even Britain—is very welcome to join the inner core. Provided, that is, it believes in an "ever closer" Europe.

THE FUTURE OF EUROPE

Beyond the Year 2000

Daniel Bell

DANIEL BELL is Scholar-in-Residence at the American Academy of Arts and Sciences.

For five hundred years, Europe has been the center of world civilization. In that time, it initiated—one can even say invented—the idea and the fact of sustained economic growth. Since Galileo, it has been the cradle of modern technology, particularly with navigation and scientific instruments. In philosophy, music, painting, and literature, it transformed our conceptions of perspective and perception, of tonality and the diatonic scale, and of the relation of fiction to reality. All this, in a sense, was the application of an idea of rationality unknown to the non-Western world.

And yet, in that same period of time, the plains of Europe saw some of the most devastating wars in the history of human civilization: from Napoleon's revolutionary army crossing to and retreating from Russia to the two world wars, involving all the major and minor powers, in which more than fifty million people were killed. The latter part of the nineteenth century saw the rapid spread of imperialism to almost all of Africa and Asia (with the exception of Japan), so that before World War II, 80 percent of the land mass of the world, and 80 percent of the world's peoples, were under Western domination. And the twentieth century saw the rise of the two most deadly ideologies in history, communism and fascism, which ended in the Gulag and the Holocausts of Stalin and Hitler.

Since the end of World War II, Western imperialism has almost completely disappeared, with a rapidity that future historians will find astonishing (though the legacies of tribalism, colonialism, and ill-fitting national boundaries remain, especially in Africa). Both communism and fascism have collapsed, their ideologies transformed into new nationalisms, especially in the old Soviet-dominated areas. War between the Great Powers—Great Britain, Germany, France, Italy—is entirely unlikely.

In the last decade and a half, Europe—and here I concentrate specifically on Western Europe—has begun an experiment that, from a historical perspective, is unparalleled—at least on such a scale. This is the effort of the twelve countries, now all democratic, to create a single harmonious community that would coordinate their economic and political institutions and by the year 2000—at least according to the original plan—create a unified currency and an integral political federation. The only parallel is Switzerland, which, after the Congress of Vienna in 1815, became a Federal Republic, half Catholic, half Protestant, with three different languages (German, French, and Italian), and twenty-six cantons, or local districts, with their own system of courts.

But beyond all this is the larger, more fateful, historical question—the role of Europe in a new and enlarged world society, with a global economy, and a great shift of power to the Pacific-rim nations in the twenty-first century. Even if there were a unified Europe, could it still play a major role in the economics, politics, and culture of world society in the next century?

The effort to create a "new Europe" can be identified in four steps, as follows.

This article is part of a larger study of the future of Europe, dealing with political, monetary, and cultural issues, and concentrates here largely on Europe's economy and welfare systems.

From *Dissent*, Fall 1994, pp. 445-452. © 1994 by Daniel Bell. Reprinted by permission of the author.

3. EUROPE: European Union

1. **The Common Market**, which is basically a customs union among the members, an area of free trade, and an external common tariff. This is now legally in effect.

2. **The Single Market** (a situation similar to that in the United States except for the currency), in which there would be complete free movement of capital and labor, the harmonization of welfare and labor policies, and the free establishment of services (financial, insurance, and legal) throughout the community. Here, in principle, the new freedoms are established, though there are many practical barriers.

3. **An Economic and Monetary Union**. This would mean a harmonization of economic policies, ceilings for public deficits, and, eventually, a single currency used by all members. But the first-step agreement to keep exchange-rate parities among members has broken down, because of actions last year by the German Bundesbank. (See my "Behind the European Currency Crisis," *Dissent*, Winter 1993.)

4. **A Political Federation**. A European Parliament now exists, with members elected from all nations. And there is a large administrative bureaucracy in Brussels. But the key to political federation was the Maastricht Treaty signed in December 1991, which adopted "convergence criteria" that would give the European Parliament veto power in several areas. Consumer protection, health, and education would come under community scrutiny, and steps would be taken to encourage a common foreign and defense policy. But Maastricht, and the fear of a central bureaucracy, has proven to be a stumbling block toward a united Europe.

The European Economic Arena, consisting of the twelve European Community countries (plus Scandinavia, Switzerland, and Austria, if they join), is now the largest trading bloc on earth, with more than 40 percent of the world's Gross Domestic Product (GDP) within its fold. Germany was considered to be the major powerhouse. The fall of the Berlin Wall and the reunification of Germany were going to create a two trillion dollar dream economy whose skilled workers and world-class manufacturers would make it the envy of the world.

Yet little has turned out that way. For the past three years, Europe has been in the midst of an agonizing economic recession. In 1992, real GDP growth in Europe was 0.5 percent. And in 1993, *every* country in Europe experienced *negative* growth. The German economy was hit the worst, experiencing a 2

percent drop in GDP, and industrial production in 1993 was 7 percent below that of 1992, reflecting the worst postwar recession. No one expects more than 1 percent growth in 1994.

Some of this is cyclical, reflecting the usual ups and downs of the business cycle, and the effects of the worldwide recession. But the more important question is how much is structural, likely to persist even in a recovery. One way to answer this question is to measure the budget deficits in each country as they widen or narrow. An OECD (Organization for Economic Cooperation and Development) study last year showed that in Europe the causes of the recession were largely structural. In Germany, the budget deficit as a percentage of GDP was 4.1 percent, of which 3 percent was structural. In Italy it was 9.5 percent, of which 7.4 was structural. And in France it was 5.7 percent, of which 3.1 was structural. The economies will probably turn up for cyclical reasons, but the deeper problems remain.

The structural question is central for understanding the long-term prospects of the economy. In Europe, the major structural problems are social welfare costs and aging, inefficient industries propped up by subsidies. These eat away at government revenues and reduce productive investment. A corollary factor is rigid labor markets (the costs of reducing a work force by benefit payments, and the unwillingness or inability of workers to move, for family reasons or because of cultural differences).

The most surprising issue is social welfare. Forty or so years ago, Marxist theory said that the capitalist state would spend for warfare, but not for welfare. But it is welfare that now may be strangling the capitalist state.

The modern welfare state was proposed fifty years ago in Great Britain by the famous "Beveridge Report" (though Germany had initiated some social insurance fifty years before, to "buy off" the growing socialist movement). Written during the war, the report proposed the end of hunger and poverty, and the use of the resources of the state to provide not only a "safety net" against the hazards of unemployment, but a framework of benefits that would guarantee an individual and a family the basis of self-respect. Beveridge proposed a comprehensive system of national insurance, financed by employer contributions, that would provide unemployment benefits, health services, and old-age pensions. In addition, there were family allowances for children, services for the disabled, and social-service counseling for family and mental health problems. The plan vastly increased the power of the state, which for the first time assumed responsibility for the relief of poverty and the welfare of the society. The Attlee Labour government in Great Britain initiated the program. And every country in Europe followed suit.

In Europe, public spending as a whole (government administrative expenses, subsidies to industry and farmers, and social welfare) amounts to about 49 percent of Gross Domestic Product (as against 37 percent twenty years ago). That compares with 37 percent in the United States and 32 percent in Japan. But social-security expenditures accounted for 25 percent of the total GDP in Europe, compared to 15 percent in the United States and 10 percent in Japan.

The welfare state has been most costly in Germany, with Italy second. One-third of German GDP goes for social spending, and social-insurance contributions (split 50-50 between employers and workers) amount to about 40 percent of gross pay. The average German manufacturing worker, the highest-paid in Europe, receives about $27 an hour in wages and benefits, of which $12.50 comes in the form of social benefits. Italian workers receive more in benefits than wages in their $21-an-hour compensation. (In contrast, in the U.S. a worker's $16 an hour has only $4.50 in benefits.) Hourly manufacturing labor costs in Germany are about 35 percent higher than in the United States, Japan, or even Great Britain.

Looking ahead, there are the rising costs of pensions. By the year 2015, the number of Germans over age sixty-five will rise by 50 percent, from twelve million to nearly eighteen million. By the year 2030, the number of Germans over age sixty will be double that under age twenty. According to the OECD, the present value of future pensions in Germany is 1.6 times current GDP.* In Italy, deficits in social programs accounted for half of the 1992 budget deficit, or a huge 10 percent of GDP. Italian old-age pensions are the most generous in Europe (and a person can retire, in many instances, at age 55, then seek another job) and about 40 percent of the members of the CGIL, the largest trade-union movement in Italy, are

today on retirement pensions. According to Luigi Spaventa, one of the most talented economists in Europe, and the minister of the budget in the caretaker "technocratic" government, pensions are the largest "fiscal drag" in the Italian budget.

Social spending has reached a limit in Europe for political, economic, and even moral reasons. Under the Maastricht agreement, setting up convergence criteria on public-sector debt and deficits, only Luxembourg, of the twelve European Community members, is in compliance. Economic costs have reduced industrial competitiveness, while the large social-insurance benefits reduce labor mobility, since workers often prefer to draw on unemployment compensation rather than move elsewhere. Assar Lindbeck, the Swedish economist, has argued that incentives to work and to produce are destroyed when the state takes away too much from those who are working and gives too much to those who are idle.

The other major structural problem is industrial. Europe led the way in the first two industrial revolutions. The first one was in England, where the invention of steam power by James Watt, and the application of energy to machines, began the transformation of the world. Steam power gave us locomotives and steamships. By applying steam power to machines, we began factory production. But there were other ways, equally important, unremarked in the textbooks. The most crucial was the creation of steam pumps, so that one could pump the water out of coal mines and dig deep down. England is an island that was bedded on coal, especially in the Midlands. By digging up the coal, one could create a steel industry. And with steel, the associated products in metals engineering, shipyards, and automobiles. Textiles and steel were the foundations of England's early wealth.

The second industrial revolution began in Germany around the 1880s. This was the creation of the large chemical and electrical industries. With chemicals, for the first time, humans could make things that were not found in nature, such as plastics, and with oil, the petrochemicals. With electricity we had both the new sources of amplified power and the transformation of night and day by light, as well as the ability to send coded messages and then voice on electrical lines, creating the telegraph and the telephone.

All this is why Europe was able to lead the world in its industrial transformations. England

---

* Both Germany and Italy are increasing the retirement age to restrain expenditures. Germany's pension-law reform, which went into effect last January, provides that by 2001, the normal retirement age for men and women would be raised to 65.

and Germany were the sources of these transformations. One forgets that before World War II, France and Italy were not industrial societies. Theirs were small workshop industries run by family firms. After World War II, both were transformed. France opened a large new steel industry in Alsace-Lorraine and began the development of chemicals and electricity. Italy expanded its textile and chemical industries, as well as rubber. And all the major countries of Europe went in heavily for the manufacture of automobiles.

The major problem is that Europe has not made the transition, as have the United States and Japan, largely to the postindustrial sectors of information and knowledge (computers and telecommunications). There are some large individual firms in these sectors, such as NV Philips in the Netherlands, Erickson in Sweden, Siemens in Germany, Cable and Wireless in the United Kingdom, and Nokia in Finland. Yet in the crucial areas of microchip technology and software, there are no major players in Europe.

Europe is still struggling with the industrial society, particularly steel and automobiles. (The shipyard industry is gone almost completely.) The European Coal and Steel Commission (the forerunner of the European Community itself) was formed in 1951 to "rationalize" the industry. In the past twenty years it helped close down many mills and eliminate 500,000 jobs. But gluts and surplus capacity remain. The industry last year lost $4.5 billion, and it has sought to "dump" steel abroad to cover costs, prompting retaliation by the United States (which itself had lost 500,000 jobs). The European Commission wants to reduce capacity to about 80 percent of the current 190 million tons and cut 50,000 more jobs. But state-owned and subsidized steelmakers in Italy, Spain, and Germany have resisted. The European Commission, for example, wanted to reduce the tonnage of Ilva, a government-owned steel plant in Taranto, in southern Italy. But the government, which wanted to privatize part of the company, refused. And in Germany and other regions, local communities have bought the steel mills and continue to subsidize them to save jobs.

The same problem, only writ larger, exists in automobiles. There are now six major automobile companies in Europe—Fiat, Renault, Peugeot, Volkswagen, and the subsidiaries of Ford and General Motors. But the markets are now "mature," with little growth, and the intra-European competition will pit the major producers against each other. Fiat, which has been the major (if not the only) Italian firm, has concentrated its hopes on a new small car, the Punto. But European demand is estimated to grow by less than 400,000 cars a year, which is about half the decline in Fiat sales last year alone. BMW, the large luxury-car maker in Germany, has just taken over the English Rover (leaving England with no British-owned car manufacturer) and thus will increase the competition for mass sales. And Japanese factories in England are moving toward the production of a million cars a year by the year 2000, when all limits on Japanese imports into Europe are due to end.

Germany finds itself in increasing difficulty. Four big industries—autos, machinery and machine tools, electrical engineering, and chemicals—account for about 60 percent of Germany's $425 billion export trade. But increased competition has hurt Germany badly, especially in autos, which account for nearly 20 percent of German exports. Volkswagen, the highest-cost big-volume car producer in Europe, which last year made 3.5 million cars, did not earn a pfennig. The result is that it cut its work force by 15 percent. And all over Europe, manufacturing jobs are shrinking rapidly.

Europe can succeed only if it can make the transition to postindustrial sectors. Just as "motors" were the engines of industrial production, "microprocessors" are the engines of the postindustrial, information-based economies. Yet in the area of microchips, the United States produces 47 percent and Japan 41 percent of all micro-electronic units. Germany spends more on subsidies for its older "smokestack" industries, such as coalmining and shipbuilding ($6.4 billion), than for basic research ($5.6 billion).

Germany is today in the midst of a *techno-Angst*, and for good reason. It is losing out in computers, communication electronics, office technology, lasers, and energy technology. In the field of biotechnology and genetic engineering, which is predicted to be a $100 billion industry by the year 2000, German companies now spend an estimated 75 percent of their research-and-development budgets abroad, principally in the United States. Even more important, the revolution in materials technology, which is only now getting seriously under way, means that the older resource-based production becomes less important than technological substitutions (for example, fiber optics for copper). And it is the growth of "technology complexes" and "networking" that cross borders and favor regional developments that is now the source of economic growth. And that poses a challenge to the national state.

Can the transitions be made? All this, theoretically, is manageable in the cycle of industrial restructuring. Japan, from 1960 to 1990, was the world's shining example. It began with textiles and light industry, but when these were taken over by Hong Kong and cheaper producers, Japan moved into optics and instruments, and then to steel, shipbuilding, and automobiles. But after the oil shock of the 1970s, and the increasing costs of energy, it moved quickly into knowledge-based, and electronic and computer-based, industries. But where is Europe to go? The strong rigidities in the major industrial sectors have inhibited structural changes.

There are "rays of hope"—the growth of small-scale, cottage-type manufacturing areas, based on network-linked companies that share market information and allow workers to move about—as in the Prato and Veneto in northern Italy (making textiles and furniture, for example), or in southern Germany, with small machine-tools and parts, or in the Jutland area of Denmark. But these are not sizable enough to affect the major problems.

The single largest economic and social problem in Europe today is unemployment: about thirty-five million persons are without work. In France, Italy, Germany, Denmark, and Great Britain, more than 10 percent of the labor force is unemployed, and this figure may rise to 12 percent, as an average, by the end of 1994. (Spain is a special case, where 23 percent of the population is listed as unemployed, due largely to the delayed transition out of agriculture and the failure of industry to take up the slack.) All of this is politically explosive, especially since few political parties or the trade unions want to take the strong medicine necessary to reduce wage costs, increase labor mobility, or limit pensions and social spending.

In a remarkable report issued in December 1993, the European Commission proposed lowering the minimum wage and cutting social security payments in the hope of creating fifteen million jobs by the year 2000. In a statement presenting the report, Jacques Delors, the president of the commission and a French socialist, declared: "If we want to safeguard the current model of European society and its welfare state, we must adopt this program. *We are no longer in a world where everything is guaranteed.*" (Emphasis added.)

Western Europe, in the fifty years after World War II, was re-created on the model of social democracy. Eastern Europe was shaped on the model of communism or state socialism. The Eastern European model has collapsed. And now the model of social democracy faces an impasse. This is the basis for the coming political crisis of the left in Europe.

DIAGNOSIS: HEALTHIER IN EUROPE

By most standards, Western Europeans are in better medical shape than Americans. And costs are sharply lower. But bureaucracies and under-the-table payments mar the system.

Joel Havemann

Times Staff Writer

BRUSSELS—For someone with a potentially fatal disease, Regine Delvaux is exceptionally healthy. A diabetic for 26 of her 37 years, Delvaux holds down a part-time office job in Brussels and, in the past four years, has been able to adopt two young children.

She owes her active life to the Belgian national health system, which, like those of other Western European governments, guarantees that virtually all Belgians are insured and pays the lion's share of the costs. That means Delvaux receives virtually free care, including the regular insulin she needs to fend off kidney failure, blindness and the other scourges that diabetes can bring.

The contrast with the United States is striking. Europeans have better access to health care than Americans, an estimated 35 million of whom are uninsured. By most objective measures, they are healthier.

And what is most extraordinary, Europe actually spends less for health care—about one-third to one-half less in most countries—than the United States. The U.S. health bill, growing far faster than overall inflation, will reach something like $800 billion this year, or about 13.5% of the nation's entire economic output.

No wonder President-elect Bill Clinton is looking at Europe as he seeks to redeem his campaign promise to overhaul the U.S. health care system. Clinton has promised to require employers to provide insurance to all workers, to guarantee public insurance for those who do not work and to set a national limit on overall health-care spending.

Most Western European countries already do all this.

Clinton and his health-care planners will not want to copy everything they find across the Atlantic. European-style health care is hardly trouble-free.

Inflexible bureaucracies sometimes interfere with the delivery of care. Some doctors, unwilling to settle for government-prescribed fee schedules, take part of their payments under the table. For a minor operation to correct nearsighted-ness, a Brussels clinic charges not only the official rate of about $300 but also another $900 in unreported cash.

Medical services are rationed, especially in countries that spend relatively little on health care. In Britain, which spends less than all but the poorest Western European nations, the elderly frequently wait two years for hip replacements and cataract operations.

Even in the Netherlands, which spends 30% more per person than Britain for health care, a recent survey found that one-third of all hospital admissions came only after excessive waits. At the same

---

Who Pays the Freight?

Here is the share of health care spending paid by governments and by private individuals and insurers, 1989:

	Governments	Private
France	75%	25%
Germany	72	28
Britain	87	13
Italy	79	21
Netherlands	73	27
Sweden	90	10
United States	**42**	**58**

HOW DOCTORS ARE DOING

The average after-tax income of general practitioners in 1985, the latest year with available data:

France	$24,700
Germany	48,200
Britain	27,900
Netherlands	32,400
Sweden	22,200
United States	**77,900**

Reliable figures for salaries of Italian doctors were not available.
Sources: American Medical Assn., Organization for Economic Cooperation and Development

---

 From *Los Angeles Times*, December 30, 1992, pp. A1, A9. © 1992 by The Los Angeles Times. Reprinted by permission.

time, under pressure from health care providers and patients, the Dutch government pays for such dubious treatments as herbal medicine and psychic healing.

In a range of European countries, rising costs have triggered reform movements that have a distinctly American flavor. The Netherlands, for example, is edging toward competition between insurance companies in an effort to introduce incentives to control costs.

Yet for all the flaws, analysts on both sides of the Atlantic rank European health care miles ahead of America's. "What can Europeans learn from Americans about the financing and organization of medical care?" asked Alain C. Enthoven, a health-care financing specialist at Stanford University. "The obvious answer is, 'Not much.'"

The reasons that America spends more and gets less are legion: uncontrolled use of sophisticated medical technology, massive administrative costs, expensive malpractice insurance and higher-paid doctors, to name a few.

All this is rooted in the uniquely American pioneer experience and distrust of big government. The legacy is an every-man-for-himself approach to health care. Except for the elderly and the very poor who are enrolled in Medicare and Medicaid, those on the receiving end of the health care system get what they—or their employers—can pay for.

"In America, part of your population is accustomed to getting every available medical technology," said Henk ten Have, a professor of medical ethics at Catholic University in Nijmegen, the Netherlands. "But another large part gets no care at all."

COLLECTIVE CARE

Health care in Europe, by contrast, is grounded in collective responsibility. European governments either directly provide most health care, as in Britain, or require that everyone be insured, while paying for most of their citizens' insurance, as in Germany.

Either way, European countries operate on the same principle that governs public education in the United States: All of society benefits from a healthy citizenry, and all of society should shoulder the costs.

It is an attitude that Abram de Swaan, a University of Amsterdam sociologist,

---

Health Care: America vs. Europe

For all the flaws, analysts on both sides of the Atlantic rank European health care far ahead of what the U.S. offers.

Americans Spend More . . .

(health expenditures per capita, 1990)

United States	**$2,566**
France	1,543
Germany	1,487
Sweden	1,479
Netherlands	1,266
Italy	1,234
Britain	974

. . . but Are Less Satisfied . . .

(share of persons who believe the health care system works pretty well and only minor changes are needed)

United States	**10%**
Netherlands	47
France	41
Germany	41
Sweden	32
Britain	27
Italy	12

. . . and Achieve Poorer Results

(infant mortality rates per 1,000 births, 1990)

United States	**9.2%**
Italy	8.5
Britain	7.9
Germany	7.5
France	7.2
Netherlands	6.9
Sweden	5.9

Sources: Organization for Economic Cooperation and Development; Robert J. Blendon, Harvard School of Public Health

---

traces back 150 years to cholera epidemics that broke out in urban slums throughout Europe and claimed the lives of the rich as well as the poor. Out of self-protection more than charity, Europe developed modern sewage systems. Now cholera is largely under control, but the principle of collective responsibility remains intact.

"The social welfare systems in West European countries promote the dignity and well-being of all persons and the welfare of society as a whole," said

---

Reinhard Priester of the Center for Biomedical Ethics at the University of Minnesota. "In contrast, the United States embraces individualism, sees provider autonomy as the preeminent value and neglects community-oriented values."

In only two of the 24 industrial nations that make up the Organization for Economic Cooperation and Development does the government pay for less than half of the health care. Those two are the United States and Turkey.

In Western Europe, by contrast, all governments pick up at least two-thirds of health care costs. Each country has its own approach.

In Britain and Sweden, the government owns and operates most of the health care system, with the money coming largely from income tax revenue. Most other countries offer a mix of public insurance and compulsory, government-subsidized private insurance, with the government's contribution coming from a Social Security-like tax on employers and workers.

The Netherlands relies relatively heavily on private insurance. But even there, the 70% of the population at the bottom of the income scale is covered mostly by public insurance; for the rest, a combination of public and private insurers pays most of the bills.

No matter what the system, patients may generally choose their doctors, and they can buy supplementary insurance to cover what their government-financed insurance does not. Most governments dictate what doctors may charge, and some play a role in determining what procedures are appropriate to diagnose and treat particular conditions.

PATIENT SATISFACTION

To Americans, the European approach might seem heavily centralized, bureaucratic and rigid. But Europeans are happier with their approach than Americans are with theirs.

A 1990 study by the Harvard School of Public Health found that only 10% of Americans said their "health care system works pretty well." That put the U.S. system squarely at the bottom of the 10 nations included in the survey.

Of the six European countries surveyed, satisfaction levels ranged from 47% in the Netherlands to 12% in Italy. Canadians, whose national health insurance system is much more European than

American, were the most satisfied of all, with a 56% rating.

These ratings square with the few objective ways of measuring national health. Although America's diverse population, with its many minority groups, makes comparisons with more homogeneous Europe somewhat uncertain, it is nevertheless true that the United States falls consistently below Western European nations in infant mortality rates and life expectancy.

Europe achieves these results even though it spends substantially less for health care than the United States—typically 7% to 9% of national economic output, compared with America's 13.5%. Central to Europe's approach is a technique that seems unthinkable in the United States: Governments set strict health-care budgets, and local health authorities must live within their allowances.

"The strict planning systems for hospital care in Switzerland and the Netherlands, the two European systems most similar to those of the United States, are the major reason why expenditures are constrained in these countries," said Bengt Jonsson, a health specialist at the Stockholm School of Economics.

With strict health-care budgets, Europe has escaped America's uncontrolled growth in the purchase of medical technology. Two nearby European hospitals may not both buy the same piece of sophisticated machinery unless they can show a clear need; instead, one gets the equipment, and the patients at both hospitals use it.

Dr. Niek Klazinga, an official with the Dutch National Organization for Quality Assurance in Hospitals, said a single hospital in Houston three years ago had 13 sophisticated and expensive magnetic resonance imaging machines, more than all of the Netherlands.

American hospitals, armed with the latest medical gadgetry, are compelled to use it to recoup the cost. "When a patient with a headache is told that he needs a brain scan to make sure he doesn't have a tumor, his natural reaction is, 'Where do I lie down?'" said Arthur L. Caplan, director of biomedical ethics at the University of Minnesota.

In most of Europe, by contrast, the expensive brain scan may be used as a last resort—or not at all. In the Netherlands, every neighborhood has a general practitioner who serves as the gatekeeper to medical technology.

"General practitioners know that 70% of all headaches are emotional," Klazinga said. Before they permit brain scans to check for tumors, he said, they test all other possible causes.

Joseph Newhouse, a professor of health policy at Harvard, estimates that "technological change, or what might loosely be called the march of science and the increased capabilities of medicine," accounts for at least half the explosive growth of U.S. medical costs in the last half-century.

Robert Brook, senior health services researcher at the RAND Corp. in Santa Monica, said the use of costly technology often does not help and sometimes is downright dangerous to patients' health.

"Perhaps one-third of the financial resources devoted to health care today are being spent on ineffective or unproductive care," Brook and Kathleen Lohr of RAND's Washington office wrote recently.

FOOTING THE BILL

Technology aside, Europe is more willing to pay for preventive care than is the United States, where the uninsured generally benefit from no such care at all and even those with insurance sometimes find reimbursement unavailable.

Americans, and especially the poor, must typically get sicker than Europeans before they can get the care they need, said Jean-Pierre Poullier, a health policy analyst with the Paris-based Organization for Economic Cooperation and Development. That has the perverse effect, he said, of jacking up the cost of their treatment when they finally get it.

Diabetes provides a stark example. Dr. Ann Owen, an American who was born and trained as a physician in the United States but has specialized in treating diabetics in Belgium since 1983, said uninsured or underinsured diabetics in the United States often have no access to the insulin they need to control their blood sugar. Nor can they afford to care for the non-life-threatening complications of their disease.

"That means many people have to go into a coma before they can get treatment," Owen said. "By then, they need intensive care at a hospital, and in a few days you're up to $50,000."

"In Belgium," she added, "insulin is considered so essential to life that it's available for free."

Delvaux, the long-term diabetic, is glad it is. Since 1989, when the Belgian government set up a special program for diabetics, Delvaux has also been reimbursed for most of the costs of her regular doctor visits and blood sugar tests. "I have hardly had to pay more than a couple of hundred francs [about $7] a month," she said.

Thanks to her regular treatment, which includes a steady supply of insulin that is administered by a pump permanently implanted in an underarm, she has not been hospitalized for about 20 years.

In Los Angeles, Felipe Perez shows what might have happened to Delvaux. Perez, 39, has a less serious form of diabetes. Although he does not require regular insulin, he would benefit from other forms of routine treatment.

But as one of America's 35 million uninsured persons, he does not receive it. Two years ago, Perez lost his paid health insurance when he was laid off from his city job. Once last year he went to a community health clinic in Lincoln Heights and was prescribed medication for his diabetes. But he couldn't afford to buy it.

Earlier this year, he landed a part-time job with Los Angeles County as a home health-care worker for the elderly, but he gets no health benefits himself.

As a consequence, he found himself at L.A. County-USC Medical Center for the better part of a week recently so that doctors could treat an infection in his underarm that, because of his diabetes, had grown to the size of a walnut. The cost, most of which will be absorbed by the hospital: about $5,500.

DOCTORS' PAY

Medical salaries are another part of the cost-quality equation. General practitioners in the United States earned an average income of $77,900 in 1985 after covering their expenses but before paying taxes, according to the American Medical Assn.'s most recent data. That compares with $48,200 in Germany, $32,400 in the Netherlands, $24,700 in France and $19,700 in Belgium.

The United States has fewer doctors for its population than most European countries, with the notable exception of

Britain, and its supply of registered nurses falls at about the European average.

Yet its health care system employs more people than Europe's—especially those who sell health insurance and administer claims. "Behind every hospital bed in the United States is a clerk filling out forms," said Poullier of the OECD.

Jack A. Meyer, an analyst with New Directions for Policy, a Washington research group, said administrative costs soak up 22% of U.S. health-care spending. The American urban landscape, said Caplan of the University of Minnesota, is dotted with insurance company towers (Prudential, John Hancock) and even an entire city (Hartford, Conn.).

"We have a huge administrative bureaucracy to keep the rich from having to share costs with the poor, the healthy from having to share costs with the sick and the able-bodied from having to share costs with the disabled," Caplan said.

European nations avoid a substantial share of these administrative costs because they do not make such distinctions. At least in this respect, their decision to make health a collective rather than an individual responsibility actually saves money. **Times staff writer Somini Sengupta in Los Angeles contributed to this story.**

EUROPE AND THE UNDERCLASS

The slippery slope

ROTTERDAM

As yet, Western Europe does not have an urban underclass to compare with that of the United States. But the growth of long-term unemployment seems to be dragging it inexorably in that direction

IN ROTTERDAM'S vast harbour, a million containers a year are loaded and unloaded. Giant cranes poke towards the sky. Dry docks and oil refineries stretch to the horizon. But for all the gigantism of the harbour—the big ships, big machines, big statistics—there is something missing. People. The modernisation that began in the 1970s has meant that the burly types who used to do the heavy work have been mechanised out of their jobs. It is possible to cruise around Europe's busiest port on an average day and see only a handful of workers.

The decline of port employment, combined with a collapse of the Dutch textile industry, means that Rotterdam, a hardworking city where, it is said, shirts are sold with the sleeves already rolled up, has an unemployment rate of more than 20%. Of the 50,000 jobless, 32,000 have been unemployed for more than a year, and many for more than three years. Even this has come against a background of economic recovery. The finance and retail industries expanded in Rotterdam in the 1980s, yet unemployment still tripled. Few longshoremen were ready to become financial analysts.

In poor parts of the city where unemployment has become almost the norm, crime, drug abuse and one-parent families are increasingly common. The uneven concentration of unemployment—35% of Turks and 42% of Moroccans in Holland are unemployed, compared with 7% of ethnic Dutch—has provided fertile ground for political extremism. "People feel rejected. They don't participate in the social process. It's kind of a time bomb," says Jaap Timmer, a Dutch social scientist.

Lumped together

Such conditions are far from unique to Rotterdam. In cities across Western Europe—such as Frankfurt and Berlin, Lyons and Paris, Amsterdam and Utrecht, Naples and Dublin, Liverpool and Manchester—the shadowed lives of the urban poor are getting darker. Does Europe have an underclass to compare with that of America? Not yet. But the situation is deteriorating in ways that cause the question to be posed more often and more plausibly. And there are no ready solutions in view.

In America, the term "underclass" entered common usage in the 1970s and was a cliché, albeit a controversial one, by the end of the 1980s. It came to connote ghetto populations that were overwhelmingly black, isolated, unemployed, welfare-dependent, poorly educated and with disrupted family patterns. The origins of the underclass lay somewhere in a mix of racial inequality, middle-class black flight from the cities, public-housing policy and the loss of industrial jobs. As the underclass grew more entrenched, so too did a perception that those who peopled it were fundamentally different from other Americans—a universe of teenage moms, crack addicts, drop-outs and criminals.

When America was discerning the early outlines of its underclass in the 1970s, Europe had no poverty debate to speak of. There were some poor people in Europe's cities, certainly, but it was assumed they would not stay that way for very long; the welfare state, that most generous of European inventions, would help them to help themselves. Two decades on, that confidence seems tragically misplaced. Even the richest European countries are seeing new, intractable and growing problems among troubled urban populations. Hamburg, Europe's richest city measured by income per head, had by 1990 Germany's highest proportion of millionaires—and its highest proportion of people on social welfare. Unemployment was 40% higher than the national average. A third of industrial jobs had disappeared in the past 15 years.

"You could use the old Marxist concept of a *lumpenproletariat*", says Pierre Bourdieu, a professor at the Collège de France in Paris. "That describes more exactly the kind of people below the level they need to be at in order to behave rationally, to be able to master the future. The main thing is, there are many, many poor people. When you have many, you have a sort of destruction of solidarity. Nobody can help the others."

Unlike in America, where the fundamental urban tension is that of race, the fundamental tension pulling at the social fabric of Europe's cities is that caused by long-term unemployment. But the effect, in both cases, is one of polarisation and marginalisation. The question is whether Europe's cities are now in the process of producing their distinctive brand of "underclass", different in its origins from that of America but equally damning to those that it claims.

For every new job of aerobics instructor or government clerk created in Europe in the past few decades, at least one older job, probably an industrial one, has disappeared. Blue-collar workers have suffered the most. People who are unskilled, uneducated or merely thick have little chance of finding even a toehold in the workforce. Job shifts are a natural part of economic progress: no surprise that there are far fewer blacksmiths and chimney sweeps, for example, than a century ago. The disappearance of some kinds of jobs would not be an issue if new jobs were springing up to absorb those affected. The problem is they are not. More than 40% of the 17m unemployed in the European Union have been out of work for at least a year; a third have never worked at all. In the United States, which creates and destroys jobs with a verve Europe gawps at, only 11% of the unemployed have been looking for work for more than a year.

But if Europe's unemployment is not fundamentally a racial issue—the majority of poor or unemployed people in any European country are indigenous whites—minorities and first- and second-generation migrants often have a particularly tough time. Large numbers of North Africans came to France, Turks to Germany, Surinamese to Holland, Cape Verdeans to Portugal and West Indians to Britain 20 or 30 years ago to do dirty work that Europeans spurned. When those jobs disappeared in the 1980s and 1990s, they and their children were often ill-equipped to adapt.

Coming to no good

Historically, immigration has been a positive economic force around the world. America absorbed large immigrant surges in the late 19th century and in the 1980s; its wide-open economy put to good use the commitment and hard work of those who made the effort to get in. But Europe does not have the same tradition of openness and individual enterprise, and new arrivals can find these more structured societies tough to crack. Generous social benefits may also blunt the sense of urgency that drives many immigrants in America.

Over time, these later immigrants to Europe, or their children, or their children's children, will probably make themselves at home as other immigrants have done before them. But the shorter-term outlook is so troubling because economic conditions are so straitened. In the former West Berlin, the number of unemployed foreigners nearly doubled between 1989 and 1993, while the unemployment rate for ethnic Germans rose by less than a third.

Unemployment exacerbates geographical divides as easily as it does racial ones. Mr Bourdieu evokes a street in the town of St Marcellin, central France: on one side are nice little single-family dwellings where working families live, on the other are big ugly buildings into which the poorest are stuffed. He speaks of a "translation of economic division into spatial division." People on the wrong side of the line start to cut themselves off from society, sometimes in minor but telling ways. In Holland, disproportionate numbers of the long-term unemployed opt for unlisted telephone numbers; in Ireland they attend church less often.

In Europe as in America, when middle-class people start deserting a district and leaving it to the poor, the process feeds on its own momentum. The only people willing to move in become those with nowhere else to go. Private commerce shrinks or retreats. Long-term unemployment and economic segregation become mutually aggravating. Theft and violence rise as frustrated youths turn to crime and drugs. Because non-working men are less marriageable, illegitimacy rates rise (see chart, next page); the proliferation of one-parent families creates a new hard core of dependency. Public order can easily become fragile. Examples of such places can be found across Europe. Many Frankfurters will name Gallusviertel and Gutleutviertel as areas to avoid; residents of Griesheim, says Michael Wegener of the University of Dortmund in a report to the European Commission, "view their neighbourhood as a ghetto—the Bronx in Frankfurt." Some taxi drivers in Manchester refuse to take fares to Moss Side, an area of high unemployment notorious nationally for its incidence of violent crime.

Overlapping concentrations of urban decay and immigrant communities also provide an easy target for racists and political extremists. In Dreux, near Paris, five youths recently fired shots at a group of North Africans. Racist political parties have struck a chord in distressed neighbourhoods in France, Belgium, Germany, Holland, Italy and Britain. The technique is simple: blame foreigners (preferably non-white ones) for economic problems, call for them to be kicked out, and collect the votes. In Sossenheim in western Frankfurt, ex-

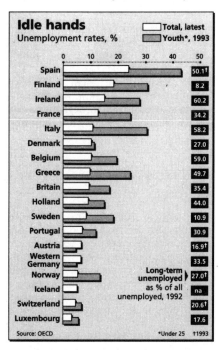

Idle hands
Unemployment rates, %

Total, latest — Youth*, 1993

	Total, latest	Youth*, 1993
Spain		50.1†
Finland		8.2
Ireland		60.2
France		34.2
Italy		58.2
Denmark		27.0
Belgium		59.0
Greece		49.7
Britain		35.4
Holland		44.0
Sweden		10.9
Portugal		30.9
Austria		16.9†
Western Germany		33.5
Norway		27.0†
Iceland		na
Switzerland		20.6†
Luxembourg		17.6

Long-term unemployed as % of all unemployed, 1992

Source: OECD   *Under 25 †1993

tremist parties won 20% of the vote, the highest in the city. They have made similar breakthroughs in Rotterdam's Nieuwe Westen and in the East End of London.

A theory of relativity

Still, in important ways, Europe's poor are better off than America's. In the American perception, the underclass is threatening because those who compose it are believed to be different—a perception often reinforced by racial prejudice. Europe has managed to avoid this extreme degree of marginalisation, although there are hints of it in some British political attitudes and in the way some of France's wilder *banlieusards* are regarded. The continuing willingness of the mainstream of society to go on identifying with its poorest members (and vice-versa), and the preservation of a generally superior physical environment, is still sufficient to deny Europe anything classifiable as a full-blown underclass.

Europe's poor are less segregated than America's; their streets are cleaner and safer; and they are more likely to have access to medical care. Schools do not have gun detectors. In Wilhelmsburg, one of the poorest parts of Hamburg, there are boutiques, banks and grocery shops, even a travel agency and a Mormon church—the sort of institutions that have trouble keeping a foothold in America's ghettos. Public telephones work, and the modest three-storey brick council flats are in good shape. Even the dodgier bits of Manchester, London or Brussels look positively serene compared with America's urban war zones.

In another contrast with America, the living standards of Europe's poor have risen in absolute terms over the past couple of decades, even if differentials with those of Europe's rich have widened. The Policy Studies Institute, an independent British think-tank, found that infant mortality rates declined throughout Britain between 1977 and 1990 because people were generally better off, better fed and better cared-for*. Older Germans can remember being rationed to 700 calories a day after the war. Today, 96% of German households dependent on social-welfare benefits have a colour television, 89% have a washing machine and 52% have a car.

The reassurance communicated by such statistics may be misleading, however. Colour televisions cannot make people feel useful, or feel that they matter to the community in which they live; and these are the fault-lines along which Europe's social foundation is cracking. "I now hear constantly the question: Are we going to become like Los Angeles?" says Michael Parkinson of the European Institute for Urban Affairs at John Moores University in Liver-

* "Urban Trends 1". Edited by Peter Wilmott and Robert Hutchison. Policy Studies Institute, London, 1992

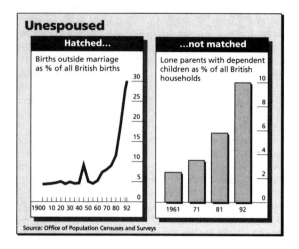

Unespoused

Hatched...

Births outside marriage as % of all British births

1900 10 20 30 40 50 60 70 80 92

...not matched

Lone parents with dependent children as % of all British households

1961 71 81 92

Source: Office of Population Censuses and Surveys

pool. "Crime, drugs, poverty, unemployment, social exclusion, segregation ... People are beginning to raise the spectre of the ghetto in the [American] sense."

Many of Europe's young adults may never work, or work only occasionally, and are going to pass their frustration and isolation on to their children. Even when Europe's economies are doing as well as most were in the late 1980s, they have ceased to create the kinds of jobs needed to absorb the long-term unemployed. "Roughly, until the 1970s, the expansion of the economy translated into improvements at the bottom of the class structure," says Loïc Wacquant, a scholar at the Russell Sage Foundation, a New York think-tank, who has compared urban poverty in the United States and Europe. "Now when the economy goes into a downward spiral, neighbourhoods of exclusion get worse. But when it goes into an upward progression, they don't join in."

A system stalled

An absence of work promotes a growth in dependency among those who lose the energy to keep plugging away for an opening or for a chance to upgrade their skills. But there is, too, a kind of considered, calculated dependency practised by those who devote their energies to "working the system" as an end in itself. When four Dutch sociologists interviewed hundreds of people in three Dutch cities, they found that about 55% of the long-term unemployed in their sample had stopped looking for work[†]. More than half of this group had quit because they had found "other activities to give meaning to their lives: hobbies, volun-

....

[†] "Cultures of Unemployment: A Comparative Look at Long-Term Unemployment and Urban Poverty". By Godfried Engbersen, Kees Schuyt, Jaap Timmer and Frans Van Waarden, foreword by William Julius Wilson. Westview Press, Boulder, Colorado, and Oxford, England, 1993

tary work, studying, or working in the informal economy." Such findings seem to bear out the contention of an American sociologist, Charles Murray, that some people will, given the chance, make a rational economic choice to live on social welfare. The Dutch researchers concluded that Holland, with its generous, multifarious benefits, had produced "a group of enterprising and calculating unemployed people . . . the strategically operating welfare client." Across Europe, this kind of willful semi-poverty can be seen evolving into something entrenched, even socially acceptable. The mayor of Roubaix in northern France, for example, has complained publicly that too many residents prefer to collect their basic welfare payments rather than to seek work.

Such is the perverse destiny of a European model of a welfare state, devised in the expectation of universal full-time employment for men. The idea was that lots of people would pay into the system and far fewer would take money out of it. Most benefits would be administered through the payroll. But the balance has swung far away from those early expectations. The number of people receiving benefits has kept growing, while the proportion of people in work in European Union countries has been falling since 1960. The European Commission, in a report published last year, estimated Europe's needy at 52m poor, 17m unemployed, 3m homeless. Holland has only four full-time workers for every three people on full-time benefits. In western Germany, the number of recipients of social benefits doubled in the 1980s. "The worst scenario is people not feeling responsible for each other," says Radboud Engbersen, a social worker who lives in one of Rotterdam's poorer areas. "And yes, this is happening."

Yet, for all the evidence accumulating around them, many of Europe's academics

and politicians have still to drop the presumption that poverty and unemployment can best be addressed by, in effect, subsidising the poor and unemployed. The French prime minister, Edouard Balladur, gave a warning earlier this year of the risks of "social explosion" if France's 1.4m hard-core poor stayed that way. But the French poverty debate centres on purported solutions such as work-sharing, guaranteed incomes, liberation from employment and enhanced social benefits: ideas that are at best illusory, at worst dangerous. Europe cannot afford to spend any more than it does on welfare and other social programmes. In many instances, it cannot afford what it is spending already. In headier days Frankfurt spent 11% of its budget on culture; now it is DM8.5 billion ($5.4 billion) in debt and fighting off bankruptcy.

If Europe is to reverse the drift towards an underclass of American finality, the answer must lie in creating more jobs rather than in helping people to get by without them. Unfortunately, job-creation is something for which Europe seems to have lost the knack. The public sector, provider of millions of jobs over the past 30 years, is stretched to the limit; and the private sector seems incapable of filling the gap. As the European Commission's 1994 white paper on employment acknowledged, European industrial policy has concentrated "too much on the rents and positions established in traditional industries."

In effect, Europe has priced much of its labour force out of employment, compensating it with welfare payments. Only a thoroughgoing reversal of that strategy can do much to get Europe's unemployed off the park bench and back into work. Encouraging the kind of dynamic economy in which lots of jobs are created will mean hacking away at policies that have long operated in favour of rigid work rules, high social costs, subsidies and protectionism; and that may mean things getting worse for the poor before they can get better.

For years, Europeans sniffed at America's frisky but cruel economy. The New World opted for high risk and high reward, and left its losers to be pushed far from the economic and social mainstream. The Old World favoured a stabler, more secure economic order in which the losers would be looked after. Seen in those terms, the trade-off was a defensible one. But the terms were not what they seemed. As even prosperous cities like Hamburg, Rotterdam and Paris can testify, the European model has proved insecure and unsustainable. In Europe, too, there are millions in danger of slipping beyond the point of no return.

A consumer report

Freedom in Post-Communist Societies

Richard Rose

Measures of freedom often emphasize the absence of freedom—and this was very appropriate in assessing Communist regimes that stretched from East Berlin and Prague to the vastness of Siberia. In *Freedom in the World,* the annual Freedom House review of political rights and civil liberties, then-Communist regimes in Bulgaria,

---

Since the fall of the Berlin Wall in 1989, how much freedom do people in post-Communist societies really enjoy? A straightforward way to find out is to ask the people who live there.

Romania and the Soviet Union ranked along with Angola, Iran and Saudi Arabia as countries where freedom was conspicuously absent. In such circumstances, public opinion does not exist; the only public opinions are official opinions.

In Eastern Europe* today, we can welcome the absence of repression. There are monuments to freedom in every post-Communist country; they are the empty plinths on which formerly stood statues of Lenin, Marx, and the local dictator. Their statues are now consigned to the dust bin of history to which they had promised to send their enemies. So too is the

---

* Eastern Europe is here used as a political rather than geographical term to describe all those societies in Central and Eastern Europe that were formerly under the control of Communist parties.

apparatus of repression, such as border guards ready to shoot to kill fellow citizens who want to travel abroad, informers who report on what is said within the family, and Party officials who assess people as qualified or not for education or jobs based on loyalty to the Party.

However, news from post-Communist countries also highlights problems. The difficulties of transforming a corrupt command economy into some kind of market system leads people who are not Marxists to jump to the conclusion that if living standards do not rise rapidly East Europeans will abandon freedom in favor of traditional or new forms of authoritarian rule. Some historians may point to the past as evidence that some cultures in Eastern Europe are collectivist by tradition, and do not value individual autonomy. The election of governments led by ex-Communists in Hungary and Poland and the results of ballots in the former Soviet Union cause alarm, too.

A consumer index of freedom

Since the fall of the Berlin Wall in 1989, how much freedom do people in post-Communist societies really enjoy? A straightforward way to find out is to ask the people who live there.

A consumer index of freedom is based on what people believe they can do in their everyday lives; it should not be based on the reports of those—legislators, civil servants, judges—who in the recent past served an authoritarian regime. Social scientists are accustomed to measuring public opinion by interviewing a representative sample of the national population. In Eastern Europe it makes a lot more sense to ask people about personal freedom than about things that are remote, such as their opinion of the United States or the European Union. The New Democracies Barometer of the Paul Lazarsfeld

From *Freedom Review,* September/October 1994, pp. 19-22. *Freedom Review,* published by Freedom House, New York, NY 10005.

Society, Vienna (named after the Viennese-born academic who conducted the first voting study in America in 1940) annually surveys public opinion across ten countries of Central and Eastern Europe and the former Soviet Union. After a half century of silence, the great majority of people are happy to give public voice to their views about changes in their lives.

Freedom can be measured in many different ways. First is the existence of civil liberties, freedom from state controls; second comes political rights, such as the right to vote in free elections. Communist party-states had a totalitarian vocation: the party-state not only ruled out free elections but also sought to dictate what people said and did in many spheres of social life. Communist doctrine did not tolerate the existence of civil society, that is, institutions independent of the state. Nor could it tolerate civil liberties, that is, individuals thinking and acting independent of the party-state. In the inverted language of Marxist distinctions between "false" and "real" consciousness, the principle was: "If you want to know what people think, don't ask the people; ask the party."

In Eastern Europe today, freedom thus means what Isaiah Berlin has described as *freedom from* the state. "Destatization," the reduction in the role of the state in everyday life, is now manifest in the "deconstruction" of institutions of repression. Even if East European regimes have yet to become established democracies, they can promote freedom through weakness, letting citizens say and do what they like free of state control.

Since every East European has experienced a Communist regime as well as their new regime, asking people to compare what they can do today with what they could do five years ago gives a consumer assessment. Even though the situation over the past five years is not ideal, it can still be an improvement over what it was in the previous fifty years. Hence, each of the 1,000 persons interviewed in each of the ten New Democracies surveyed was asked:

> Please think of the difference between the old system of government under the Communists and our present system. I will read out a series of statements on this card. Please tell me for each whether you think our present political system, by comparison with the Communist, is much better, somewhat better, equal, worse, much worse.

There followed a list of six different everyday activities that are taken for granted in free societies, but which former Communist regimes had sought to control.

All kinds of freedom greater now

On each measure of freedom, a majority of people surveyed in New Democracies Barometer feel freer today than before. The only difference is in the size of the majority who feel their daily lives have been made freer by the fall of Communist regimes (*Table 1*).

Religion: 86 percent. Communist regimes were not just secular, they were militantly atheist. The big boost in freedom

Table 1
Increased Freedoms in
East European New Democracies

(percentage feeling more free now than under Communist regime)

	Speech	Join Organization	Travel	No fear of arrest	Interest in Politics	Religion
Bulgaria	90	95	95	88	97	98
Czech Republic	84	90	96	73	84	94
Slovakia	82	88	88	62	80	96
Hungary	73	81	76	59	na	83
Poland	83	78	75	71	69	70
Romania	94	94	90	81	92	95
Croatia	66	78	42	53	66	72
Slovenia	74	82	62	54	59	77
Belarus	73	74	48	37	57	87
Ukraine	79	76	49	42	60	84
	--	--	--	--	--	--
Mean	80	84	72	62	74	86

Source. Paul Lazarsfeld Society, Vienna, *New Democracies Barometer III*. A multi-national survey with 11,087 interviews conducted between late November, 1993 and early April, 1994, sponsored by the Austrian Federal Ministry for Science and Research and the Austrian National Bank. For full details, see R. Rose and Christain Haerpfer, *New Democracies Barometer III* (Glasgow: Strathclyde Studies in Public Policy No. 232).

gained by turning off propaganda for dialectical materialism does not, however, mean that people are flocking back to churches. In every country except Poland, a large majority are infrequent churchgoers or free-thinkers.

Joining any organization: 84 percent. The suppression of organizations independent of the state was a mark of the totalitarian aspirations of communism. Individuals must have the right to start their own business or join a union or voluntary association of their own choice if a civil society is to come into being—and this is happening.

The right to say what you think: 80 percent. If people cannot say what they think, then public opinion must be kept private. This is no longer the case in post-Communist societies.

Whether or not to take an interest in politics: 74 percent. Political participation is considered a civic virtue in democracies, but not in one-party states that compelled people to participate in party activities. Given such experience, freedom from the party and compulsory political mobilization is the freedom that counts, and this has expanded everywhere due to the collapse of Communist parties.

Traveling and living where you want: 72 percent. In Communist societies the right to travel abroad was severely restricted by the need for a passport and exit visas, and controls were also imposed upon moving from one city to another. This system has disappeared except in the former Soviet Union. A shortage of cash and housing is now the big restriction on movement.

No fear of unlawful arrest: 62 percent. Terror was important for securing compliance in Stalinist regimes. De-Stalinization prior to the collapse of communism reduced the significance of terror; the collapse of communism has reduced fear of unlawful arrest even further.

The past five years have made a big difference to people across Central and Eastern Europe. More than 70 percent now feel freer to decide for themselves about religion, join any organization, say what they think, take no interest in politics if they prefer, and travel wherever they might want to go. These

---

Dostoyevsky was only half right. Russians do place a high value upon the collective symbol of "one and indivisible Russia" and upon Christianity in its Orthodox form. But they also place a high value on freedom.

---

are *sine qua non* characteristics of any democratic political system—and they are rights that affect what a person can or cannot do each day, Only 6 percent of East Europeans on average see themselves as less free today than before. For the minority who see no improvement, the alternative is to see things staying the same.

The gains in freedom are greatest where regimes were previously very repressive, such as Ceausescu's Romania, and Bulgaria. They are also very high in the Czech and Slovak republics, where Soviet troops remained in place to prevent the recurrence of another Prague Spring. The gains are less in Hungary, where the former regime had been cynical about enforcing Communist orthodoxies. Its laissez faire doctrine was expressed by former Communist leader Janos Kadar as: "He who is not against us is with us." Gains are also less in Croatia, where the war with Serbia imposes many restrictions, and in Belarus and the Ukraine, where it has yet to be established what kind of regimes will rule there.

Dostoyevsky is dead—Hitler and Honneker, too

Because Communist regimes in Central and Eastern Europe were imposed by the Soviet Union, today's sense of freedom may be a national sense of relief from foreign domination rather than a feeling of individual liberation. If this were true, Russians would not regard the demise of the Soviet Empire as increasing their freedoms but as diminishing their capacities. Such an argument is also consistent with Dostoyevsky's view, as argued in *The House of the Dead*, that Russians can adjust to anything, including tyranny. Some Soviet experts interpreted the apparent durability of the Communist regime as evidence that the silent majority of Russians preferred things that way.

Survey research shows that Dostoyevsky was only half right. Russians do place a high value upon the collective symbol of "one and indivisible Russia" and upon Christianity in its Orthodox form. But they also place a high value on

freedom. Notwithstanding the economic chaos following the collapse of the command economy and a large increase in crime, the great majority of Russians see their freedoms as having increased *(Figure 1)*. At least seven in ten Russians see themselves as freer today than under communism to say what they think, join any organization and treat religion as a matter of personal choice, and a large number also feel free to adopt a take-it-or-leave it attitude toward politics. The Russian sense of freedom is very similar to that found in other post-Communist societies.

Yet Russians do not feel that they yet have thrown off all forms of control by the state. A majority do not see any improvement in their ability to travel, because of the mainte-nance of a bureaucratic system of visas and permits and a lack of money. A majority see the threat of unlawful arrest unchanged from the early 1980s, a period when arrests were far fewer than before. Some institutions of surveillance also remain in opera-tion.

East Germany presents a different yet equally tough test for popular recognition of freedom. During Hitler's Third Reich, it was sometimes argued that German culture was inimical to freedom, and the concept of the authoritarian personality was developed by German social scientists. The so-called German Democratic Republic in East Germany demonstrated that

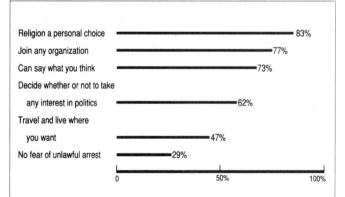

Figure 1   Improvement in Freedom Since Fall of Communist Regimes

(percentage of Russians saying freedom greater now than in Communist times)

Religion a personal choice	83%
Join any organization	77%
Can say what you think	73%
Decide whether or not to take any interest in politics	62%
Travel and live where you want	47%
No fear of unlawful arrest	29%

Source: Paul Lazarsfeld Society, Vienna, and Centre for the Study of Public Policy, University of Strathclyde, Glasgow, *New Russia Barometer III,* a nationwide representative sample survey of 3,535 Russians interviewed in March-April 1994.

18,000,000 Germans could shift from Nazi to Communist rule. The region is populated by families who did not choose freedom by fleeing West in the sixteen years before the Berlin Wall was built. Instead, they knuckled under to a very repressive regime led by Erich Honneker.

The idea of the authoritarian personality is awakened by every new outburst of neo-Nazi violence in East Germany. East Germans have shown a greater readiness than most East Europeans to vote for their revamped Communist organiza-tion, now called the Party for Democratic Socialism. Reunification has brought a hard currency and tastes of West German prosperity, but the dislocation arising from the collapse of the command economy has created new problems of adaptation.

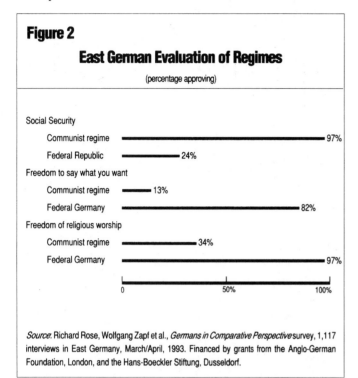

Figure 2

East German Evaluation of Regimes

(percentage approving)

Social Security
Communist regime — 97%
Federal Republic — 24%
Freedom to say what you want
Communist regime — 13%
Federal Germany — 82%
Freedom of religious worship
Communist regime — 34%
Federal Germany — 97%

0   50%   100%

Source: Richard Rose, Wolfgang Zapf et al., *Germans in Comparative Perspective* survey, 1,117 interviews in East Germany, March/April, 1993. Financed by grants from the Anglo-German Foundation, London, and the Hans-Boeckler Stiftung, Dusseldorf.

When East Germans are asked to rate their old and new regimes in terms of social security, the Communist regime comes off best by a margin of four to one *(Figure 2)*. Notwithstanding the recognition of greater social welfare benefits under the Honneker regime, East Germans do not ignore the big gains in freedom achieved by becoming part of a *Rechtsstaat* (rule of law) state, the Federal Republic of Germany. More than four-fifths of East Germans now feel free to say what they think compared to one in eight in the Communist era. Similarly large gains have been made in religious freedom.

When evaluating the old East German regime and the Federal Republic, East Germans give a much higher rating to the regime that increases their freedoms than to the regime that was better for social security. When asked to rate the old and new regimes as a whole, only 32 percent of East Germans approve the old Communist regime, compared to 60 percent endorsing the Federal Republic of which they are now a part.

What freedom is not

The classic liberal belief that people everywhere will appreciate freedom if it is offered to them is an assumption. The New Democracies Barometer offers empirical evidence supporting that faith. Half a century or more of repression by Communist (and sometimes Nazi) forces have not destroyed the ability of people to distinguish between the presence and absence of

> **Half a century or more of repression by Communist (and sometimes Nazi) forces have not destroyed the ability of people to distinguish between the presence and absence of freedom.**

freedom. Even though the transition has imposed costs upon many people, it has also granted a great boon: an increase in freedoms in everyday life. This has been felt in places as far apart as Kiev and Prague, Bucharest and Gdansk.

Freedom from the state is not the only political goal in post-Communist societies. Whereas freedom has been achieved through the "deconstruction" of the state, other goals require positive state action. This is even true of creating a market economy for, as Friedrich von Hayek emphasized, the market requires laws and order that only the state can supply. The example of Russia shows that getting state enterprises away from the control of bureaucrats and Party officials is not easy. Nor is it easy to ensure that the new owners have a rightful claim to their new property. Maintaining law and order in the face of new criminal organizations also requires an effective as well as a civil police force.

Finally, freedom is different from democracy. When the New Democracies Barometer asks people how much influence they have on government today compared with the past, a third say they have more, but half say that things are much the same. A low sense of political efficacy should not be ignored, even though it is often found in established democracies too.

But East Europeans know that being unable to influence government is not the worst thing that can happen to them. The worst has already happened: decades of repressive, sometimes Stalinist regimes. Weak and imperfect as the new regimes may be, those who have lived with both old and new see one great advantage: the new regimes of Eastern Europe grant people much more freedom to say and do what they like.

In the Dark Shadow of History

Success stories obscure the facts: Most Eastern Europeans now alive will not reach Western standards of living. Ever.

WALTER MEAD

Walter Mead is the senior policy advisor at the World Policy Institute at the New School. Research assistance: Matthew Crozat.

History is back in Eastern Europe—and it's hungry. When you walk the streets of Warsaw, as I did recently, Western goods beam from the stores; crowds of shoppers share the streets with Western cars. Beguiled by the spectacle, I found that for hours at a time I could convince myself that Poland and the rest of Eastern Europe would one day soon join the economically developed West.

But then, sadly, a bit of history would remind me that this vision of the future is not inevitable; in fact, it's extremely unlikely. It's hard to forget history for long in Warsaw: The city still bears the scars of its past. The Nazis bombed Warsaw in 1939 and razed it five years later. Rebuilt by a poor and struggling communist regime not noted for its architectural taste or its deft touch in city planning, Warsaw today sits uneasily in the shadow of past wars.

For a while, the excitement of the transition from communism let Poles ignore that shadow. But people here and across much of the rest of Eastern Europe have by now settled into a new routine of democracy and market economics, and life for most Poles is hard. Unlike Prague, a city that already seems to be part of the West, or Berlin, where the clash of Eastern and Western ideas and cultures is creating a new and dynamic urban culture, Warsaw, like Sofia, Kiev, and Bratislava, seems relegated to the second or third tier of European cities: a backwater—again.

The past and the questions of the past haunted the dozen political and security analysts who gathered this summer in a restored castle just north of Warsaw. The question that preoccupied us was an old one: Why is Eastern Europe so different from the West? Baron Sigismund von Herberstein, ambassador from the Emperor Frederick III to the Russian court from 1517 through 1526, asked the same question more than 400 years ago as he pondered the differences between Russian and the West. "I do not know if it is the character of the Russian people that has created such dictators, or if the dictators themselves have given this character to the nation," mused the Baron.

In the 20th century both the communists and Western economists have said, change the regime, and national character will change. Bad economic conditions created bad social and political conditions. Fix the Russian and East European economies, and the East would become a utopia.

Of course, the economies that the communists wanted to fix were the primitive pseudocapitalist ones that characterized Russia and the rest of Eastern Europe in 1917. The Western experts, in contrast, felt at the end of the Cold War that what needed to be fixed were the command economies created by Lenin and Stalin. Fix Eastern Europe's communist economies according to free-market principles, and Russia and all of Eastern Europe would quickly turn into normal—that is to say Western–European societies. Lenin's mistake hadn't been to think that he could remake his society with an economic blueprint; he had just picked the wrong blueprint.

This belief—I would call it a delusion—helped to shape the foreign policies of both the Bush and the hapless Clinton administrations. It's easy to understand the attraction of this vision. Western economics would turn Eastern Europe into an extension of Western Europe and expand the group of affluent European democracies into the Eurasian heartland. That in turn would tilt the global balance of power irreversibly in favor of Western values and policies. Peaceable and prosperous democracies stretching from Vancouver to Vladivostok would encircle the northern hemisphere and guarantee global stability. Both administrations expected a new world order to emerge from the collapse of European communism.

If everything went right and the Russian economy grew as fast as Thailand's, Russia would reach parity with the U.S. in 2132.

Now that some of the dust created by the fall of the Berlin Wall has settled, however, it seems that the best indicator of current and future economic performance in Eastern Europe remains past political and economic performance. It's now clear that the future will be more like the past than almost anyone thought in the heady rush of the downfall of communism.

Take, for example, what was once Czechoslovakia. That country, and especially the territory of the Czechs, was widely considered the most modern and democratic of these countries before the World Wars—and so it is today. In the new Czech Republic, Czechs, freed of the burden of the more backward Slovaks, speak confidently of a future in which they see no military threats to their security and only temporary obstacles to their prosperity. As long as Germany remains democratic and Western Europe is prosperous, say the Czechs, they have nothing to worry about. They are right.

Their Eastern neighbors, however, look into the future and see—with alarm—their past. Poland desperately wants to join the two clubs of Western Europe—the European Economic Union and NATO. It will, however, be years before Poland is ready for either one, and meanwhile the Russian bear is stirring. Belarus, a Slavic country that occupies the territory between Poland and Russia, is on the verge of reintegrating with Russia. That event would put Russian troops once more on Poland's borders.

The Polish economy is also a prisoner of its past. Poland's small farmers were the hard core of resistance to communism; their unity and their Catholic faith enabled them to resist collectivization. An unfettered free market would doom these politically influential farmers: Their "two hectares and a mule" farms can never compete with agribusiness in Western Europe. A program of agricultural investment would probably produce prosperity for some farmers, but others would be forced off the land—a process familiar from our own history. But unless Poland improves the efficiency of its agricultural sector, productivity and incomes will remain low. Although the Polish economy is, at long last, beginning to grow once again, wages—approx-

imately $300 a month including earnings in the underground economy—are extremely low. Most of the population now living cannot expect to reach Western standards of living. Ever. The politics of the past and the economics of the future pull in opposite directions. Care to bet which will be stronger?

Farther south, the Balkan countries, where the Ottoman Empire persisted into the 19th century, are even more heavily weighted down by their past. The consequences are most tragically evident in the wars now raging in the former Yugoslav republics, but in countries like Bulgaria and Romania, tense interethnic relations between aggrieved minorities and traditional ruling groups promise generations of violence. In this region most governments have been simultaneously authoritarian, incompetent, and corrupt.

Within the former Soviet Union, conditions are even worse. Ukraine and Moldova lack the ethnic cohesion and economic base for national independence. The trans-Caucasian former Soviet Republics—Armenia, Georgia, and Azerbaijan—have reverted to the clan feuding that dominated their history until the imposition of Russian rule in the 19th century. As Russia's experiment with democracy dissolves into a morass of anarchy and crime, it seems inevitable that sooner or later the Russian people will demand the strong leadership of—at best—a modern Peter the Great or—at worst—a new Ivan the Terrible.

This shouldn't have surprised anybody in the West, least of all the conservatives who claim to understand the role of tradition in modern society. Unfortunately, we fell victim to our own cold-war propaganda. We compared France with Bulgaria and simple-mindedly attributed the differences to the nature of communism and capitalism.

This was a mistake. Bulgaria was much poorer than France long before the Red Army reached it; Russia was backward and primitive before Lenin was born; the Balkans were considered Europe's most backward region when Karl Marx was eating teething biscuits. More than the Iron Curtain divided Eastern and Western Europe.

Let's look at some numbers. Currency fluctuations and the unreliability of old statistics make it difficult to compare the gross domestic products of European economies before the Second World War, but some indicators can give us an idea of the relative levels of development in prewar, precommunist Europe. By 1938, the United States was producing 1,156.2 kilowatt hours of electricity per person per year and had 0.24 motor vehicles per person on the roads. Britain and France, respectively, were producing 0.85 and 0.51 kilowatt hours of electricity per person, and Britain had 0.06 motor vehicles per person on the road. Infant mortality in the United States was 47 per 1,000 live births for whites and 79 for blacks; it was 53 in Britain and 70 in France.

Now look at the East. In 1938, Russia produced 0.27 kilowatt hours of electricity per person. Infant mortality was 155 per 1,000 in 1928. Romania, still at that time a capitalist country, produced 0.06 kilowatt hours of electricity per person and had 0.002 motor vehicles per person on the road. Infant mortality was 183 per 1,000.

If anything, many Eastern European countries gained on the West during much of the period of communist rule. According to the 1992 National Economic Report of the President, Eastern Europe's centrally planned economies grew 2.0 percent faster than Western Europe's from 1971 to 1975. Even as late as 1985, the Soviet Union was outperforming the European Community. From 1950 to 1975, electricity generation grew 309 percent in France and 282 percent in the United States, compared with 703 percent in the USSR, 690 percent in Poland and 2,015 percent in Romania.

This doesn't mean communism was working or that these countries would have ever passed the West under communist rule, but it should help us focus on the real issue. Eastern Europe's real problem isn't that it was communist but that it is and was underdeveloped. Some Eastern Europeans may have nuclear weapons, but much of Eastern Europe is in the Third World and is likely to stay there for decades to come.

Again, the numbers are sobering. In 1992, the per capita gross domestic product in Poland was $1,882.39, in France $22,150.76, and in the United States $23,678.54. Take the best-case assumption: that Poland can grow as fast as Thailand—one of the world's fastest-growing capitalist economies—while the West will continue to see the slow growth of the past ten years. This would mean that Poland's per capita gross domestic product would grow at 5.8 percent per year, while the U.S. would grow at 2.5 percent and France would grow at 2.2 percent. Under these assumptions, Poland would achieve parity with France in 2064 and with the United States in 2072. In 2050, Poland would still have a per capita gross domestic product that was only 50 percent of the U.S. level.

Russia is even worse off. Assuming the Russian economy bottoms this year and starts to grow like Thailand's, Russia can expect parity with the United States in 2132.

Remember, this is a best-case scenario. Most of these countries will grow more slowly than Thailand, and some of them may not grow at all. Political instability in parts of the East could slow economic growth and establish a vicious cycle: no political stability without economic prosperity, no economic prosperity without foreign investment, but no foreign investment without political stability. These cycles are depressingly common in international life.

The lesson of Eastern Europe is sad but important: The future is rooted in the past. No economic reforms and no paper constitutions can cancel out the effects of centuries of conflict, culture, and tradition. This is the lesson that conservatives ought to be teaching and that liberals ought to be learning. It is a sad commentary on the intellectual and political life of the West that at this critical moment in world history we seem to have forgotten it—just like the Bolsheviks.

Six Reasons for Optimism About Russia

Crime headlines belie steady political and economic progress

Harley Balzer

Harley Balzer is director of the Russian area studies program at Georgetown University in Washington.

Three years after the August 1991 putsch, one could almost believe that Russia is becoming a normal country. This is not the impression that one gets from reading accounts by journalists who focus on Vladimir Zhirinovsky or the mafia. It does not come through in the wails of pain from Russians obsessed with unsafe streets. But despite the danger of using the word "normal" to refer to the land of Gogol and Bulgakov, some important developments are evident:

1. Russia is not yet a democracy, but it is more democratic. Political interests and groupings are being defined. People are exerting a genuine effort to make an awkward system function. Potential candidates are establishing organizations and beginning to "test the waters" for future elections. The political noise level has undergone a major reduction in decibel count.

This may well change when everyone returns from summer vacations and is likely to cycle at varying levels for a long time. Though political battles over fundamental principles will continue, it is unlikely that any of the players will find it in their interest to kick over the game board.

Most important, there is vastly more political discussion, information is more widely available, and there are far more points of access to the political system than in the Soviet era. If money becomes as important as political control in allocating TV time, the next presidential election, whenever it is held, will be a genuine contest. President Boris Yeltsin has failed to make the transition from

political hero to political leader. Like many Russian liberals before 1917 (and like George Washington), he abhors political parties, seeing in them the basis for divisive partisanship. A product of a system that put a high premium on the appearance of unanimity, he fails to comprehend the positive aspects of political conflict. But others are aware of the need for real parties, and they will eventually assert themselves.

Few understand that Russia has real financiers and that this summer's pyramid scandals are a circus of transitory significance.

---

2. It would be almost impossible to reintroduce a dictatorship. The perpetrators of the August 1991 coup mistakenly thought all they had to do was grab the levers of power, as Leonid Brezhnev did in 1964. They did not understand that the levers were no longer connected to anything.

Mr. Yeltsin could proclaim himself emperor and his decrees would have about as much impact as they do now. In the unlikely event that someone like Mr. Zhirinovsky were elected president, his promised draconian measures would be implemented about as effectively. The society has become too complex, too open, too wealthy, and too decentralized. Everyone talks about the need for an "iron hand," but when people are questioned about specific policies that a strict regime might implement (censorship, concentration camps, abolition of political parties), the only one that elicits

majority support is a vague "crackdown on crime."

One of the most pernicious myths about Russia is that the hideous regime imposed by Joseph Stalin was something "normal" in Russian political life, that it responded to the popular desire for order and an iron hand, and that the people did little or nothing to resist. In the countryside, resistance was fierce and sometimes bloody. At the Potsdam, when Winston Churchill sought to ingratiate himself with the Soviet leader by commiserating about wartime losses, Stalin replied, "Collectivization, that was a war." It took a decade to impose Stalinism, costing tens of millions of lives. No one wants a repetition.

3. A new middle class is emerging, a real middle class that receives far less attention than the mafia. But it is not a European middle class, and the "rules of the game" for doing business in Russia are likely to be idiosyncratic for a long time.

Few journalists understand that Russia has real financiers and that this summer's MMM pyramid scandals are a circus of transitory significance. Many more Americans know the names Ivan Boesky and Michael Milkin than could name the CEOs of five Fortune 500 corporations. Most real Russian financiers do not want publicity, especially under current conditions. The "current conditions" bring us to the issue of crime. Yes, it is bad. The question is whether Russia is becoming a totally criminalized state or is a state with a serious criminal problem that requires a major political effort. The latter is more likely. With luck, it may do as well—or as badly—as Italy.

The USSR was a regime that practically forced its people to violate laws to survive. The political class was thoroughly corrupt, and even the "honest" officials adhered to norms much closer to those prevailing in the Middle East or Latin America than the West. No one should belittle the pain of Russians who have been robbed and seen friends and relatives murdered. Everyone is afraid. And fear is likely to produce a political response.

Recent public opinion surveys indicate that crime has replaced inflation as the No. 1 Russian concern. This suggests that political demands for safer streets will be a major issue—and not only for the demagogues. Despite the rise in crime, there has been no corresponding increase in Zhirinovsky's popularity. Polish merchants in Warsaw recently staged a strike to protest the lack of police protection in their city. Throughout the former Soviet bloc, criminals will be stopped when communities take direct measures and demand better conditions from their leaders.

There is support for law and order among a growing financial, economic, business, and specialist class who are not dishonest (except when it is unavoidable) and who still retain norms and values of the intelligentsia. Their coverage in the press is rare compared with that of the mafia because they seek no publicity and make less-exciting reading. We need to know much more about them.

4. A corollary to the new middle class is a recent and critically important shift toward investment in newly privatized Russian industries. There are no accurate statistics and the entire climate of Russian business encourages camouflaging rather than disclosing the real financial condition of companies. But reports from towns as diverse as Angarsk, Novosibirsk, Yakutsk, and Novgorod indicate that businesspeople have begun to put money into their enterprises.

5. New investment is accelerating an already rapid process of regional differentiation. Few Russians can imagine a time when Moscow and St. Petersburg merchants competed to influence tariff policy, with huge stakes involved. Most are shocked at the image of local stock-exchange committees seeking to influence the location of railroad lines or the building of universities, much less building the universities themselves. This heritage is now being reclaimed. Will some of the localities opt to build stadiums rather than decent hospitals? Almost inevitably. That, too, is part of the heritage.

Local development is driving a major redistribution of regional power and wealth. Under the imperial regime, and especially under the Soviet regime, the importance of urban areas and regions was artificial. It depended on administrative fiat, political and military needs, and the whim of individuals in power. Communities were created at enormous cost that are no longer sustainable without special subsidies and supply systems, such as in the far north, the science cities, and special military facilities. We are already seeing shifts in regional status and wealth, based on the natural resources available and the quality of local leadership.

6. Overall living standards appear to have improved. This is a crucial question, and even Yeltsin's top advisers lack solid data. The "visual" evidence suggests that people are better off. Not only are the stores well-stocked, but people are buying. Yet everyone also talks about the growing gap between haves and have-nots, something that was not so visible in Soviet society. It will take some getting used to, but many societies have adapted to sharp income differentials.

Perhaps my optimism is a result of limited expectations. If Russia can avoid another dictatorial regime, if its economy gradually improves, and if the number of those living below the poverty line is more in the range of 20 percent than 50 percent, it will not have a bad outcome. And it will not be likely to create conditions encouraging another coup.

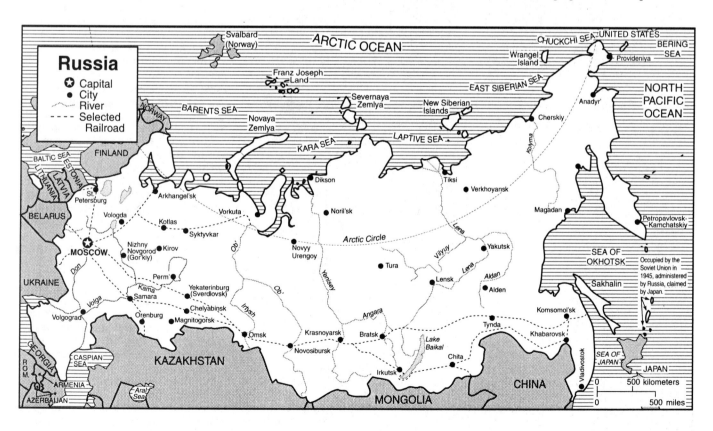

RUSSIA AFTER CHECHNYA

The rise of the new right

MOSCOW

A look at the neo-nationalist reactionaries who may shape Russia's future

BORIS YELTSIN had to take a hard decision after the parliamentary election of December 1993, when Russia's reformers did so badly and wild Vladimir Zhirinovsky strode on to the political stage. Either President Yeltsin could see the election as proof that "he had to use his powers to push more energetically towards a free market, democracy and respect for the rule of law and human rights; or he could go along with those who had concluded that Russia needs a bigger state, more state controls [and] more aggressive foreign . . . policies."

Those are the words of Yegor Gaidar, who was prime minister for much of 1992 (when he launched a radical economic reform), leads the largest party in the Duma, the lower house of parliament, and was until a few weeks ago one of Mr Yeltsin's most loyal supporters. But the president's decision to solve the three-year-old dispute with Chechnya by invading the place is proof, says a regretful Mr Gaidar, that Mr Yeltsin has chosen the wrong, second course.

Mr Yeltsin is a consummate politician, whose instinct for survival has in the past enabled him to escape from some desperate corners—for example, after Mikhail Gorbachev had kicked him out of the Politburo in 1988. But now four things are reshaping Russian politics. Between them, they could be too much even for Mr Yeltsin.

The first of the four is the sense of near-despair that grips many Russians. People are tired of feeling that "we're living in a madhouse and those in charge don't care," says Dmitri Vasiliev. Few Russians share the other opinions of Mr Vasiliev, who is a monarchist and an ultra-nationalist. But most of them would agree that they want to lead a "normal life", meaning that they yearn for calm and order, and do not much care if normality is achieved in a democracy or under a dictatorship.

The second phenomenon is the battle for power between generations. The three men who have done most to reform Russia's economy, Yegor Gaidar, Anatoly Chubais and Boris Fedorov, have an average age of 38. The six men who form the core of what Russians call the "party of war", the group of advisers who lured Mr Yeltsin into the Chechen mess, are on average a decade older. It is people between 45 and 55 who find the changes Russia has undergone since 1990 particularly hard to bear. Too set in their ways to change, but too young to accept that their working lives are over, they resent watching younger men take charge of reform and mere striplings make millions in the new private sector. They want another chance to run things.

These older people are driven by something else, too. They grew up believing that the Soviet Union was the equal of America. So they suffer most from the third hard fact of today's Russian politics, the bitter sense of humiliation caused not only by Russia's loss of empire but by its steady slide down the world's economic league table.

For centuries Russians have talked of their country as a Eurasian power. How can these people explain to themselves not only that the economic gap between Russia and the West is wider than ever but that some Asian nations have now leapfrogged past Russia? The sense of national humiliation is reinforced by the fact that life expectancy for a Russian male—a perhaps over-rosy 64 in 1985—is now only 59.

The fourth politics-shaping fact is the warning finger that history wags at Russia. Every period of radical reform in that country has been followed by a period of reaction. It happened after Peter the Great, who turned Russia towards the West, and after Alexander II, who freed the serfs. Catherine the Great flirted with Voltaire's ideas in the early part of her reign but turned to despotism after the French revolution.

The last tsars confronted a dilemma: how to retain absolute power while at the same time modernising Russia. Mr Yeltsin is not facing exactly that problem. He is supposed to be building a democracy. Yet by launching the war in Chechnya, and bungling it, Mr Yeltsin has made democracy-building vastly harder. Russia's past military humiliations in the Crimea, against the Japanese in 1905, in the first world war and in Afghanistan all led to great changes in Russian politics. The Chechen war is not on the scale of those defeats, to be sure. But it too has caused a crisis big enough to bring, quite possibly, a radical change of direction.

It's everybody else's fault

Which way will things move now? The answer to that question starts from a major consequence of the collapse of the Soviet Union. The Russians, no longer the dominant group in a multi-ethnic empire, have

to find a new identity. Emil Pain, a sociologist who advises Mr Yeltsin, has spent much of the past two years studying what form this new identity might take. His polls have come up with some worrying conclusions.

Over half the people polled believe that Russians are "offended people, lied to and exploited", writes Mr Pain. Exploited by whom? Popular suspects include Russia's own leaders, the mafia, Communists, democrats and, not least, the West, which is widely believed to have a plan for plundering Russia's natural resources. A substantial minority of those questioned say that non-Russians living in Russia have too many rights. Hostility is especially strong against Chechens, Azeris, people from Central Asia and Jews (in Russian internal passports the nationality of Jews is set down as "Jewish", not "Russian").

Mr Pain argues that this xenophobia is "nothing more than the death throes of Soviet consciousness". It is true that Soviet imperialism was obsessed with external enemies: the West, NATO, "international Zionism". Such thinking is still the norm in the party of war, the people who pulled Mr Yeltsin into the Chechen business.

Alexander Korzhakov, Mr Yeltsin's chief bodyguard and a leader of the war party, reckons that Russia must be "protected" from foreign investment. The Counter-Intelligence Service (part of the body that succeeded the KGB) released a report in January accusing George Soros, Harvard University, the Peace Corps and most other westerners currently working in Russia of being in cahoots with the CIA. Andrei Kozlov, a senior official at the Central Bank, honestly believes that American banks have a "thought-out strategy to take over Russia's financial system".

Yet Mr Pain may be too blithe in saying that such things are merely the death throes of the communist period. It may be that the roots of irrational xenophobia go deeper into Russia's past.

For two centuries the "westernisers" and the "Slavophiles" of Russia have been at loggerheads with each other. The Russia the Slavophiles wanted was a theocracy administered by a tsar. Russians had freely given all political power to the tsar, ran the argument, in exchange for the enjoyment of spiritual freedom. Secular, liberal forms of government copied from the West were not suitable for Russia because they would create a "spiritual bondage".

After Napoleon's defeat, Slavophilia went through a messianic stage. Its proponents were convinced that Russia had been entrusted with a divine mission to revive the world by sharing with it the revelation which had been granted to Russia. As the 19th century progressed the movement degenerated into Russian chauvinism, which found its ugliest expression at the turn of the century in the Black Hundreds, a motley collection of gangs that operated under the umbrella of the Union of Russian People.

Sergei Witte, one of the ablest men in the government of the last tsar, said of the Black Hundreds: "This party can instigate the most frightening pogroms and convulsions, but it is incapable of anything positive. It embodies a wild, nihilistic patriotism that thrives on lies, slander and deceit; it is a party of wild, cowardly despair but has no room for courageous, far-sighted, creative thinking. The bulk of the membership comes from the wild, ignorant masses; its leaders are political villains."

The three horsemen of the reaction

The Black Hundreds are back. It is reckoned that about 80 ultra-nationalist groups are now active in Russia. Many of them are the offspring of Mr Vasiliev, the man who calls Mr Yeltsin's Russia a "madhouse". In 1986, Mr Vasiliev was allowed to found Pamyat ("Memory", in Russian). Pamyat today is the leading exponent of the first of three sorts of reaction. It stands for a return to tsarism and submission to the authority of the Russian Orthodox church.

Mr Vasiliev receives visitors seated on a small throne beneath a portrait of Nicholas II. During the audience young men dressed in tsarist uniforms line the wall, listening intently as their leader explains that "monarchy is the only acceptable system of government for Russia," and that the proper role of a monarch is to serve as a "dictator who tells the people how to live properly". Mr Vasiliev has made one theoretical breakthrough: "It is not necessary to be Jewish to be a Jew. Anyone who helps Jews encroach on others' traditions is a Jew. Everybody in power is a Jew, or their wives are." What would Mr Vasiliev do about this? "Jews have inflicted humiliation after humiliation on Russians. You must kill them, it's the only solution. It's a filthy business."

The second lot of reactionaries are the neo-communists, who refuse to co-operate with the main Communist Party (which has 45 seats in the Duma) because they regard it as a bunch of compromisers. They are not monarchists, though they too are fiercely anti-Semitic. They call for the overthrow of the present government and the restoration of the Soviet Union, by violence if necessary. They are split into several groups, such as the Russian Communist Workers' Party

and the All-Union Communist Party of the Bolsheviks. Since their supporters are mostly old and poor, they will probably fade from the scene before long.

Would that this were true of the third force of reaction—the nationalists who are neither ex-Communists nor religio-tsarist enthusiasts. This third group has been more successful than anybody else in modern Russia at bringing young people into politics. Vladimir Zhirinovsky, the best-known member of the school, has always been careful to court young men; his party headquarters has a shop that sells heavy metal music by bands with names like "Vomit".

But Mr Zhirinovsky, though a familiar name outside Russia, is a waning star in his own country. He pulled in large numbers of votes in 1993 because he was then an outsider, an unknown with a stinging tongue. By the time the next parliamentary election is held, in December, he will have been in the heart of Russian politics for two years; and, as with the cavalry officer who was so stupid that even the other cavalry officers noticed, familiarity has not helped him.

The far right's real hard core views Mr Zhirinovsky with contempt. "We would never work with him, not because he's a Jew, but because he's crazy," says Alexander Barkashov, the leader of Russian National Unity. Mr Barkashov himself would be less worrying if he showed more signs of being crazy. He is building a neo-fascist movement with grim coolness.

Parts of 41-year-old Mr Barkashov's life sound eerily familiar. He came from a modest family, and received no higher education. He trained as an electrician and served in the army, where he rose to the rank of lance-corporal and qualified as a karate instructor. In 1987 he joined Pamyat, but was expelled three years later. Pamyat's Mr Vasiliev says of him that "he's a very limited person. We kicked him out for his Nazi ideas. And he's a KGB agent." Mr Barkashov hurls that last insult back at Mr Vasiliev.

His Russian National Unity, founded in 1991, has a rigid hierarchy. At the bottom are sympathisers who include, Mr Barkashov claims, many officers of the army and the former KGB. Some sympathisers are invited to become *soratniki*, a cheery sort of word best translated as "companions", who have to take an oath of loyalty. This binds them, among other things, "to be always ready, by order of the Chief Companion, to . . . fight to the last breath against the internal and external enemies of Russia and the Russian nation", to "remember that Russia has no friends", and to "cleanse [themselves] of disgrace only by blood". By the end of 1994 Mr Barkashov claimed to have 20,000 *soratniki*, 4,500 of them in Moscow.

Mr Barkashov, while denying that he is a fascist, is an admirer of Hitler. How can a nationalist from a country invaded by Nazi Germany in 1941 admire the Nazis' leader?

Attack, a magazine published by Russian National Unity, offers an answer.

The second world war was the result of a plot by Jews, Freemasons and the Vatican to drive a wedge between the two great Aryan races, the Russians and the Germans. The Holocaust was a diversion, claims Mr Barkashov: "The Holocaust against Jews was created artificially to conceal a Jewish-inspired genocide which killed 100m Russians." For good measure, the Bolshevik revolution of 1917 was a plot financed by Jewish bankers in New York in order to gain control of Russia's wealth. This bit of paranoia is shared by nearly all national patriots, who never tire of drawing attention to the original names of three of the leading Bolsheviks: Bronstein (Trotsky), Apfelbaum (Zinoviev) and Rosenfeld (Kamenev).

Flavour of the year

A return to religion and tsarism, the restoration of the Soviet Union, and something alarmingly like Hitlerism: the three components of Russia's reaction are an ill-assorted lot, and even in the near-desperation of today's Russia seem unlikely election-winners. What chance is there that these people might come to power?

On the surface, not much. A candidate fielded by Russian National Unity in a Moscow by-election last November came sixth in a field of 12, winning 5.9% of the votes. The far-rightists might pose more of a threat if they were capable of uniting, but their leaders' egos are too rampant for that.

Could they seize power by force? In the Moscow uprising of October 1993, a poorly organised rabble nearly took control of Russia's capital. The army's recent performance in Chechnya shows how hard it might be to regain control of the capital once it had been lost. Yet this may be too melodramatic a view. The main reason why the October uprising almost succeeded was the vacuum of power created by the quarrel between the executive and legislative arms of government. Mr Yeltsin may not be exactly popular at the moment but there is no equivalent institutional crisis at the heart of Russian politics. Mr Barkashov's *soratniki* and their friends cannot assume they would bring off a March on Moscow.

The real danger posed by the ultra-nationalists is subtler. To an alarming extent, they are setting the tone of political debate. Mr Zhirinovsky's Liberal Democrats were the only large party in the Duma to support Mr Yeltsin throughout the Chechen war. That leads Ernest Ametistov, a member of the Constitutional Court (Russia's highest court), to conclude that "our present 'democratic' government follows the policies of the most reactionary forces." The tsar-restoring Mr Vasiliev says that "they used to blame me for ideas which now underlie the main policy of the Russian state."

3. EUROPE: Russia and Post-Soviet Republics

A century ago, some of the tsar's entourage gambled that the Black Hundreds would be an effective weapon against radicals and revolutionaries. The Okhrana, the tsarist secret police, supported some extremist groups (and may have had a hand in producing the "Protocols of the Elders of Zion", a particularly vicious example of anti-Semitism). Now, some members of Mr Yeltsin's entourage are donning the nationalist cloak with a different end in mind.

The unelected men who run Russia's state machinery and control its regions are for the most part relics of the Soviet era. Their main aim is to hang on to their jobs. They see nationalism as "a way of shifting blame for their own mistakes on to the policies of Gaidar, whom they condemn for sacrificing Russia's interests to please the West," argues Mr Pain. These nomenklatura nationalists are supported by people in the unreformed parts of the economy—agriculture, coal and defence—who know they cannot survive unless they go on getting huge state hand-outs.

The good news is that Russia's neo-nationalists face some considerable obstacles. The old apparatchiks are aware that the parts of the economy they still control have no money, whereas the thriving parts of the new private sector are dominated by younger men who played no part in the old regime. The Chechen war has proved that the Russian press can say what it likes. It has done a good job in exposing the incompetence of the party of war and its supporters. Today's neo-nationalists may in the end be no more successful at staving off the inevitable than were the attempts to prop up tsarism by using the Black Hundreds.

The bad news is that the death throes of the old system could set back, for years, Russia's attempt to establish some form of liberal democracy. The war in Chechnya has broken the alliance between Mr Yeltsin and the leaders of Russia's democratic movement. This is bad for both sides. Until recently, Mr Yeltsin had been the only top politician around whom the democrats could rally; the democrats, in turn, pulled in votes for Mr Yeltsin. The democrats may perform better in this year's parliamentary election if they do not have to support an increasingly unpopular president. But, for the time being at least, they have no convincing alternative to Mr Yeltsin to back in the presidential election due to be held in June next year.

This opens the door to a dismal possibility. The sort of person most likely to push himself to the top of Russian politics may be neither a committed democrat nor a neo-fascist nationalist, but someone who offers the prospect of "normality", meaning the imposition of order, without too much fuss about doing it lawfully. The likeliest place to look for such a man is the armed forces, now seething with anger about their ill-usage by the politicians. Russia's crisis still seems unlikely to place the country in the hands of a Russian Hitler. But the botched war in Chechnya and the continued unwillingness to take the tough measures needed to save the economy have made a Russian Bonaparte or Pinochet a more likely prospect.

Russian Politics:
The Calm Before the Storm?

"Compared to the tumultuous previous three years, 1994 has proved a relatively stable period for post-Communist politics in Russia. . . [But] Russia is still midway into one of the greatest social, economic, and political transformations ever undertaken. . . Calm in the Kremlin does not necessarily signal the end of turmoil in society."

MICHAEL MCFAUL

MICHAEL MCFAUL *is a senior associate at the Carnegie Endowment for International Peace, currently in residence at Carnegie's Moscow office. He is the author of* Post-Communist Politics: Democratic Prospects in Russia and Eastern Europe *(Washington: Center for Strategic and International Studies, 1993); with Sergei Markov,* The Troubled Birth of Russian Democracy: Parties, Personalities and Programs *(Stanford: Hoover Institution Press, 1993); and editor with Tova Perlmutter of* Privatization, Conversion and Enterprise Reform in Russia *(Boulder, Colo.: Westview Press, 1994). The author would like to thank James Chavin for his comments on this essay.*

Presidential Decree No. 1400, issued September 23, 1993, fundamentally altered the course of Russia's political transition. Debilitating polarization during the two years before between President Boris Yeltsin's government and parliament had resulted in the virtual collapse of the Russian state. As Yeltsin explained when he announced the decree: "All political institutions and politicians have been involved in a futile and senseless struggle aimed at destruction. A direct effect of this is the loss of authority of state power as a whole. . ."

In an attempt to resolve this impasse, Yeltsin's decree disbanded the 1,000-plus–member Congress of People's Deputies and the Supreme Soviet, and simultaneously called for a referendum on a new constitution and elections for a new bicameral legislature, both to be held in December. But Decree No. 1400 could not be realized without bloodshed. Most members of the Congress of People's Deputies regretted but accepted Yeltsin's decree. However, a small, resolute group of deputies led by Congress Speaker Ruslan Khasbulatov and Russian Vice President Aleksandr Rutskoi combined forces with militant fascist and Communist groups to defy the presidential initiative by occupying the "White House," the building that housed the Congress. The standoff ended on October 3 and 4 as military forces loyal to Yeltsin first thwarted an attack by parliamentary forces on the national televi-sion station and the Moscow mayor's office, and then counterattacked by shelling the White House itself. Russia's peaceful revolution had ceased to be peaceful.

THE DECEMBER SURPRISE

The so-called "October events" created an inauspicious context for Russia's first post-Communist election. Voters were asked to go to the polls just two and a half months after one branch of the government had forcefully liquidated the other. More generally, the two-year interval between the fall of communism in August 1991 and the first national election had further tainted Russia's democratic beginning. Denied the opportunity to compete in elections during the euphoric moment after communism's collapse, almost all Russia's reformist political parties founded in 1990 and 1991 had decayed or disappeared by fall 1993. Without elections or parliamentary seats, Russian political parties had no *raison d'être*. During polarizing crises, including most notably the challenges to Yeltsin's presidency and the subsequent referendum on it in April 1993, Democratic Russia—the umbrella organization for dozens of anti-Communist movements and parties that had spearheaded the struggle against communism in 1990 and 1991—remobilized to play a crucial role in helping the forces of reform coalesce. When not engaged in these struggles, however, Democratic Russia took few constructive steps toward becoming a post-Communist political party. Thus no parties championing reform existed when Yeltsin announced the elections for the new parliament.

More important, much had happened, most of it bad, between the attempted coup of August 1991 that precipitated the end of the Soviet era and December 1993. Acute economic hardship in 1992 and 1993, including double-digit monthly inflation rates and catastrophic declines in production, helped sustain Soviet political groups such as the Communist and Agrarian Parties. Additionally, the collapse of the Soviet empire combined with these economic woes to stimulate the development of extreme nationalist parties and movements. Under these circumstances (and also considering that the election was held in the winter and not, as has been traditional, in the spring) it is difficult to think of a worse time for a first election after communism.

Despite all this, most polls and political analysts predicted that Russia's proreform forces would win the largest share of the vote. After all, only several months earlier Russian voters had firmly supported Yeltsin and his economic reform policies in the April referendum. Russia's Choice, the liberal reformist electoral bloc headed by Yegor Gaidar, anticipated that it would win between 30 percent and 40 percent of the popular vote.[1] Polls conducted in October and early November suggested that Grigori Yavlinsky's Yabloko electoral bloc would garner as much as 20 percent of the popular vote. Even in the worst-case scenario, reformist electoral blocs were certain they would constitute a solid majority in the Duma, the new lower house.

They were wrong. To everyone's surprise, Vladimir Zhirinovsky's ultranationalist Liberal Democratic Party won 23 percent of the popular vote, and Russia's Choice only 16 percent. With totals for its parties counted together, the antireformist bloc received 43 percent of the vote compared with 34 percent for proreformist forces.

INVITATION TO DEFEAT

Without question, the explanation for this electoral outcome must begin with the economy and the "October events." Two years of radical economic reform had produced dislocation, discontent, and uncertainty about the future—a recipe for a vote for the opposition. Judging by recent elections results in Poland, Lithuania, and even Russia's own referendum that April, it should have shocked no one that a significant part of the electorate voted against those associated with market reforms.

Moreover, the use of military force by one branch of government against another must have fueled apathy about and antipathy toward the "democrats" and the "democratic process." Apathy was reflected in the low voter turnout: despite being the first true multiparty election in more than 70 years, barely 50 percent of the electorate voted.[2] Polls indicate that the majority of those who did not vote would have supported reformist parties. Antipathy resulting from October, though more difficult to measure, surely contributed to the success of political groups not affiliated with either side in the tragic events, as disenchanted reformers cast their ballot for Yavlinsky and newly mobilized antireformers threw their support behind Zhirinovsky.

These two factors, however, are not sufficient for explaining the election results. Opinion polls, while always suspect in Russia, had shown support for Russia's Choice at nearly 30 percent, while only 2

December 1993 Election Results	
Electoral Bloc	Percentage of Popular Vote
Agrarian Party of Russia	8.0
Yabloko (Yavlinsky-Boldyrev-Lukin)	7.9
*Future of Russia-New Names	1.3
Russia's Choice (Gaidar)	15.5
*Civic Union	1.9
Democratic Party of Russia	5.5
*Dignity and Charity	0.7
Communist Party of the Russian Federation	12.4
*Constructive Ecological Movement	0.8
Liberal Democratic Party of Russia	22.9
Party for Russian Unity and Accord	6.7
Women of Russia	8.1
*Russian Movement for Democratic Reforms	4.1

*These blocs did not receive the necessary 5 percent in order to gain seats through the system of proportional representation.

Source: Byulleten', no. 1(12) (Moscow: Tsentral'noi Izbiraltel'noi Kommissii Rossiiskoi Federatsiya, 1994), p. 67.

percent of those surveyed planned to vote for Zhirinovsky's Liberal Democratic Party. More proximate factors—factors that had little to do with shock therapy or the October events—also shaped this very different outcome.

First, the mixed electoral system for parliamentary races benefited the LDP. The system of proportional representation for parties used to apportion half the Duma seats allowed the party to ride on the coattails of its charismatic leader, Vladimir Zhirinovsky. Capturing 23 percent of the popular vote on the party-preference list, the LDP won 57 seats in the Duma by this means. In single-constituency races, however, the party's candidates won only 5 seats in the Duma and none in the upper house, the Federal Council. In a pure majoritarian system, the Liberal Democratic Party would have won fewer than 10 seats.

Second, the LDP ran the most effective campaign. Given the short electoral season, television was the only effective means of campaigning. After Russia's Choice the well-funded LDP had more television time than any other party or bloc, and as an individual candidate Zhirinovsky had more television exposure than any of the others. Equally important, Zhirinovsky used his time very effectively. In his snappy, professionally produced commercials, he spoke in short sentences using simple language and addressed issues that concerned voters: housing for military officers, "unfair" prices in farmers markets, and the need for more police officers for crime-ridden cities. He lambasted the government, saying it was composed of theoreticians who cared little about the people. He identified scapegoats—gangsters from the Caucasus, Jews, the West—for Russia's woes. In short, Zhirinovsky explained everything and promised everything to everyone.

In turning from the success of Zhirinovsky to the failures of the reformist forces, a significant factor was the split among "democrats." Proreform forces ran as four separate electoral blocs—Russia's Choice, Yabloko, Party for Russian Unity and Accord (PRES), and Russian Movement for Democratic Reform (RDDR)—rather than one. While there were nuanced ideological differences between the four, the real source of division was personal ambition. These divisions had several deleterious consequences. Because the vote for democratic parties in the party-preference balloting was split, the democratic defeat looked worse than it really was. (An electoral outcome in which a democratic coalition received 34 percent of the popular vote—the combined total for Russia's Choice, Yabloko, PRES, and the RDDR—would have looked quite different from the December outcome, in which the leading democratic party won just 15 percent.)

In terms of parliamentary seats, the democrats could have acquired an additional 10 or 11 seats had the RDDR and its 4 percent of the popular vote been part of one of the proreform parties that exceeded the 5 percent threshold. Even more important, however, was the effect of these splits on how the proreform parties conducted their campaigns. Gaidar and Yavlinsky spent most of their campaign time quarreling with each other rather than criticizing opponents such as Zhirinovsky.

Perhaps the most significant factor in the electoral results was that Yeltsin did not participate in the elections. With members of his government divided among several blocs, the president not only did not side with any electoral bloc, but refrained from speaking about the elections at all. His only public statement about the elections during the campaign was a 10-minute national television address in which he urged voters to approve his draft constitution. Yeltsin's nonparticipation left Russia's Choice without a strong, charismatic figure to rally support. In previous elections Yeltsin's backers had been of two distinct varieties: Western-oriented liberal reformers from major metropolitan areas such as Moscow, St. Petersburg, and Ykaterinburg (formerly Sverdlovsk), and anticorruption, anti-elite, anti-Moscow voters in medium-sized cities in Siberia and the Far East. While Russia's Choice could win the support of the former group, it

had no chance with the latter without Yeltsin as their leader. It was captured instead by Zhirinovsky.

Finally, the dreadful performance of the leading democratic bloc, Russia's Choice, must be fully appreciated within the context of the democrats' poor showing. Foremost among its weaknesses, Russia's Choice lacked organization. Formally, the bloc had united seven different political movements and organizations when it convened its founding congress last October, less than two months before the election. In reality, the bloc was an incomplete fusion of new government elites, both federal and regional, from the Russia's Choice movement with old grassroots activists from the Democratic Russia movement. The divisions between these two allies plagued the campaign effort in November and December. In many regions they were never resolved, resulting in several candidates from the same bloc running for one seat, handing Communists or nationalists the victory for as little as 15 percent of the vote.

These splits were especially costly, since they kept Russia's Choice from establishing any regional organization. Thousands of posters were sent but not displayed. Leaflets collected dust in regional offices. No coherent party message was developed that linked regional candidates to the Russia's Choice party-preference list. Many local elites from Russia's Choice who stood as candidates for single-constituency seats ran and won without identifying themselves as supporters of Russia's Choice.

Complementing this lack of organization was the absence of an effective campaign strategy. The bloc's chief strategist, Gennadi Burbulis, planned to create an image of a party already in power and destined to win in December. Russia's Choice leaders thus promised nothing to voters, and instead insolently asserted there was no alternative to their course of reform but a return to the Communist system. To the extent that they did explain the government's plan of action, Gaidar and others delivered long, monotonous, academic monologues on the macroeconomics of financial stabilization that were in stark contrast to the pithy, pointed ads aired by Zhirinovsky.

This arrogant philosophy engendered a passive campaign. Little attempt was made to mobilize social organizations to campaign for Russia's Choice. But perhaps the greatest strategic error was the bloc's failure to respond to Zhirinovsky. Instead of spelling out the implications of the LDP leader's campaign promises—wars with most neighboring countries and possibly even with the United States—Russia's Choice decided not to challenge him directly. When it finally did in the last week of the campaign, the bloc paid for television time to run old Zhirinovsky speeches. Hoping to scare people into voting against him, the free exposure instead helped establish Zhirinovsky as the leading opposition candidate.

FROM CHAOS, ORDER?

Immediately after the election, most predicted continued instability if not civil war in Russia. Radical voices in Russia's Choice called on Yeltsin to liquidate the new parliament immediately and establish an authoritarian regime, saying this was the only way to avoid a fascist takeover. Resigning from the government after their electoral defeat, deputy prime ministers Yegor Gaidar and Boris Fyodorov predicted hyperinflation, price controls, and the end of privatization. Western commentators warned that a new imperial Russia would soon be haunting the West.[3]

In the long run these predictions may come true. But in the short run the exact opposite has been the case. Paradoxically, Russian politics has been more stable and "normal" during the first nine months of 1994 than in the first two years after communism. This political stability has in turn served to sustain economic reform, not derail it. So far this year, the monthly inflation rates have not once exceeded 10 percent, the voucher program for privatization was completed and the second stage of privatization and postprivatization restructuring announced, and price controls, while hinted at by Prime Minister Viktor Chernomyrdin immediately after the election, have not been reinstated. After Russia's Choice's defeat, Chernomyrdin boldly announced the "end of market romanticism." To date, however, the end of the romantic period has meant further consolidation of practical economic reform.

The More Powerful Government

Progress on the economic front has resulted, in part, from a stabilization of Russia's new political institutions and a formalizing of relations between them. While supporting Zhirinovsky's LDP and other antireformist groups such as the Agrarian and Communist parties in the parliamentary elections, Russian voters also ratified Yeltsin's constitution. Compared to Western constitutions, Russia's new basic law grants inordinate power to the executive branch of government. By laying out the political rules of the game, however, this document—the first post-Communist Russian constitution—has so far helped smooth and regulate relations between the president, the government, and the legislature.

The new constitution has also aided in preventing political intervention on economic issues. Under the Soviet constitution, the economy was hostage to the whims of the Congress of People's Deputies and the entire system of soviets subordinate to this "highest state organ." The new constitutional configuration of the Russian state gives the Russian parliament a consultative role rather than primary responsibility for reforming and managing the economy. An antireform or fascist president could use these new rules for far different ends, but for now this political reform has furthered economic reform.

This new institutional setting has allowed the prime minister to sustain most of the basic tenets of Gaidar's reform program. Chernomyrdin has been emboldened to maintain a tight fiscal budget by establishing real interest rates for government credits from the Russian Central Bank and curtailing government subsidies to state enterprises. Rather than responding to requests for spending from the Duma, Chernomyrdin's government submitted a federal budget to parliament this spring. With the (surprising) support of the Liberal Democratic Party, the budget was approved with only minor amendment.

Approval of a new privatization law proved more difficult, but again demonstrated the preeminence of the executive in the formulation of strategic economic policy. After heated debate the Duma failed to approve the government's draft law on privatization before its summer recess this July. The day after the chamber adjourned, Yeltsin signed Presidential Decree No. 1535, implementing by fiat what the Duma had rejected. But signaling his desire to cooperate with the Duma, Yeltsin included in his decree several amendments that had been suggested during parliamentary discussions. Likewise, the decree explicitly stated that it is a temporary stand-in for a new law on privatization. With the decree in place, however, it will be difficult for the Duma to adopt a fundamentally different privatization law without risking major confrontation with Yeltsin.

Informally, Chernomyrdin also has established his authority as sole leader of the government. It must be remembered that Chernomyrdin has been prime minister since December 1992. Nonetheless, the government was still split and Chernomyrdin's personal authority questioned so long as radical reformers such as Gaidar and Fyodorov retained portfolios. After the election only one senior member of Gaidar's original reform team—the deputy prime minister in charge of privatization, Anatoli Chubais—remained in Chernomyrdin's government.

The government, in fact, in no way represents the balance of forces elected in December. Civic Union, the bloc claiming to represent Chernomyrdin's "centrist," "industrialist" orientation, won only 2 percent of the popular vote, but Chernomyrdin's government is dominated by like-minded people. At the same time the LDP, which captured 23 percent of the vote, has no representative in the government, while Russia's Choice (having received 16 percent of the vote) and the Communist and the Agrarian parties (20 percent) have only one representative each in the government.

In addition to this consolidation within his government, Chernomyrdin's political stature has also risen because of Yeltsin's decline. Since last October, Yelt-

The Duma's Makeup

Party Fraction	Leader	Number of Deputies
Liberal Democratic Party	Vladimir Zhirinovsky	57
Russia's Choice	Yegor Gaidar	71
*New Regional Politics	Vladimir Medvedev	64
Agrarian Party	Mikhail Lapshin	55
Communist Party	Gennadi Zyuganov	45
Yabloko	Grigori Yavlinsky	27
Party for Russian Unity and Accord	Sergei Shakrai	33
Women of Russia	Yekatarina Lakhova	23
Democratic Party of Russia	Nikolai Travkin	15
**"Union 12th of December"	Boris Fyodorov	28
**Russian Path	Sergei Baburin	14
**Derzhava (Power)	none	5

*Fraction formed after the elections.
**Factions formed after the elections that do not have the requisite 35 members to be formally registered as a fraction. (Blocs with fewer than 35 members that were formed before the elections are still registered as fractions.)

Source: Federalnoe Sobranie, no. 4 (Moscow: "Panorama," July 14, 1994). Derzhava, the faction of five members at the end of this table, is made up of former members of the Liberal Democratic Party.

sin's popular support has fallen gradually, reaching its nadir this summer. Yeltsin's infrequent public appearances, in contrast with Chernomyrdin's daily exposure, have created the impression that the prime minister is running the country. With questions about Yeltsin's health a continual topic of gossip, many observers and political leaders have begun to discuss Chernomyrdin as Russia's next president.

The Less Fractious Parliament

Few predicted that any good would come from the newly elected parliament, especially the Duma. A body that includes ultranationalists, neo-Communists, and neoliberals was, by definition, not destined to govern. After one of the chamber's first acts—a grant of amnesty to those who had participated in the August 1991 aborted putsch and the October 1993 "events"—many Yeltsin supporters reiterated their plea for him to dissolve the lower house before polarization between the executive and legislative branches of government crystallized.

Since the amnesty vote, however, both the Duma and Federal Council have avoided direct confrontation with the president and the government. Possibly because of these threats of disbandment, as well as the chastening effect of what had happened to the previous parliament, Duma deputies focused on constructing an effective organization; institutional survival was the imperative. Their first and perhaps most important act

was to create real incentives for deputies to organize as "fractions"—Russia's equivalent of a parliamentary party. For example, chairmanships of committees were allocated proportionally according to fraction size. Deputies elected in single-constituency districts could only chair committees if they joined a fraction. Similarly, deputies voted to create a Duma Council comprised of representatives from each fraction and committee, and this council was accorded the power to set the legislative calendar. To date the organizational decisions have stimulated the consolidation of the multiparty parliament. Whereas the vast majority of deputies in the old congress were "independents," only 11 representatives in the current legislature have not joined a political party or fraction.

The reputation and effectiveness of the Duma have also been enhanced by the conduct of its officers. The speaker, Ivan Rybkin, from the Agrarian Party, has proved extremely adept at reaching compromise with all fractions in the Duma as well as working cooperatively with other branches of government. From Gaidar to Zhirinovsky, almost all deputies have praised Rybkin for his outstanding leadership during a difficult time. Without detracting from Rybkin's personal accomplishment, the new organization of parliament has also served to lessen tensions between members and their leaders. Unlike in the Supreme Soviet and the Congress of People's Deputies, Rybkin's office does not maintain monopoly control over committee chair appointments, staff assignments, or internal financial questions (including perks for individual deputies) in the Duma. These and other organizational changes have helped the Duma function more like a legislative body than its predecessor.

Parliament's upper house, the Federal Council, is deliberately not organized along party lines. Instead, members of this chamber have stronger regional affiliations; 42 of them are "heads of administration," equivalent to the governor of an American state. The new constitution has relegated the Federal Council to a role closer to a consultative body concerning federal issues than a lawmaking legislative organ. As political decentralization continues, the real power and interest of the council's regional leaders remains at the provincial and republic level.

The Inchoate Political Forces

The relative stability in government and parliament has not been reflected in a commensurate consolidation of political parties or civic organizations. While electoral blocs coalesced quickly to participate in the December elections, it remains uncertain whether they will be around for the next parliamentary elections, scheduled for the end of 1995. The creation of new parties, a reshuffling of allies, and a reorientation of many existing political organizations are under way across the political spectrum.

Among liberal reformist parties, disaggregation— not consolidation—continues. Immediately after the December elections, leaders from several reformist groups called for the formation of one prodemocratic, antifascist coalition. Though a congress to create such an organization is scheduled for this October, little progress has been made in constructing a workable coalition. On the contrary, the electoral blocs of December have begun to split rather than unite with other parties and movements. Four separate groups have emerged from the remnants of the Russia's Choice bloc: Democratic Russia, which is planning to become a party this fall; the political party Democratic Russia's Choice, headed by Gaidar, which held its founding congress in June; Russia's Choice Movement; and the 12th of December faction in the Duma.

Yabloko is also showing signs of disintegration. Yuri Boldyrev, one of the three bloc's original leaders, has effectively quit because of sharp disagreements with Yavlinsky. Likewise, two electoral partners in the December elections—the Social Democratic Party of Russia and the Republican Party of Russia—are also considering leaving. After much hesitation Yavlinsky has begun to organize a national Yabloko movement in major regions throughout Russia, but it remains to be seen how successful this new association will be in an already crowded field. The Party for Russian Unity and Accord has taken few steps toward further organiza-

tion, but has resisted invitations to join forces with other movements and parties. The Russian Movement for Democratic Reform, after failing to cross the 5 percent threshold in the December elections, has all but disappeared.

Centrists may run the government, but centrist parties and organizations are also in disarray. Civic Union, once considered the most powerful political group in Russia, has all but disappeared after its dismal showing in December. Nikolai Travkin's Democratic Party of Russia, the one former Civic Union coalition member to break the 5 percent barrier, has also begun to decay with Travkin's neglect of party activities since his appointment as deputy prime minister. The New Regional Politics fraction has pretensions to form a new centrist party focused on regional and industrial issues; however, voting records for this fraction indicate that its deputies have few common issues beyond being from regions outside Moscow and St. Petersburg. Finally, Yuri Skokov, the former head of the Security Council, who is closely associated with the military-industrial complex, has begun courting allies to create yet another new party. The "center" thus remains amorphous.

Since December the most active political groups outside parliament have been those affiliated with the so-called "red-brown" coalition—nationalist and Communist organizations such as the Liberal Democratic Party, the Communist Party of the Russian Federation, and new Communist patriotic groups such as Aleksandr Rutskoi's Derzhava (Power) and Soglasie vo imya Rossii (Accord in the Name of Russia). The term "red-brown coalition" has always been a misnomer since ultranationalist and neo-Communist groups have never succeeded in forming a durable united front.[4] Extremist nationalists such as Zhirinovsky have been shunned by Communists, while many patriotic groups reject Communist ideology as being just as Western, and thus as alien to the Russian soul, as capitalism. However, figures like Rutskoi and Gennadi Zyuganov have managed to close the gap between patriots and Communists by concentrating on themes important to both camps, such as distress over the dissolution of the Soviet Union and contempt for the mafia-dominated market. With polls indicating that more than two-thirds of the Russian people have similar views regarding the collapse of the Soviet Union and crime, this political orientation could attract new support in the near future.

Winning an election, of course, is only one way to power for authoritarian leaders. The heads of several militant groups—including Zhirinovsky and Rutskoi—have again hinted they will assume power by any means necessary. If they try, the Russian military will ultimately play the decisive role. The political loyalties and ideological orientation of this institution remain ambiguous, however. Officers have publicly expressed their disappointment with the government's handling of demobilization and the conversion of defense industries to civilian production. Less publicly, they have also criticized Defense Minister Pavel Grachev for not defending the military's interests inside the government. Renegade regional commanders such as General Aleksandr Lebed in Moldova expose the weakness of the Defense Ministry's control over the army by defying Moscow and winning. Nonetheless, translation of this discontent and disarray into support for a putsch seems unlikely since the military's most recent involvement in domestic politics, in October 1993, proved tragic for all concerned.

MIDSTREAM IN RUSSIA

Compared to the tumultuous previous three years, 1994 has proved a relatively stable period for post-Communist politics in Russia. The adoption of a new constitution has helped formalize the division of power between the different branches of government. Similarly, despite—or perhaps as a result of—its limited mandate, the new Russian parliament has been more effective than originally expected. Under Chernomyrdin's direction, Russia's post-December government has been more successful at implementing Gaidar's reform program than Gaidar himself was.

But focusing exclusively on these short-term stabilizing tendencies serves to obfuscate many structural problems in society that remain unresolved. Russia is still midway into one of the greatest social, economic, and political transformations ever undertaken. As these revolutionary changes continue, the discontent that accompanies the reorganization of any society will continue for years if not decades. Under these circumstances common-denominator ideologies such as nationalism and imperialism can quickly mobilize forces outside the state that are disenchanted with both the Communist past and the democratic present. Calm in the Kremlin does not necessarily signal the end of turmoil in society.

---

[1]The "popular vote" in the December 1993 elections actually represents only one of three ballots that voters cast in electing members of parliament. The 450 seats in the lower house were allocated according to a mixed system. Half went to candidates winning the most votes in single-constituency districts while the remaining 225 were allocated to parties according to a system of proportional representation for parties receiving at least 5 percent of the vote. The "popular" vote thus refers to how parties performed on the latter ballot. Balloting for the upper house employed a first-past-the-post system that awarded seats to the two candidates who received the highest number of votes in each district.

[2]Of those who did vote, more than 15 percent cast their ballot for "none of the above."

[3]See, for example, Zbigniew Brzezinski, "The Premature Partnership," *Foreign Affairs,* vol. 73, no. 2 (March/April 1994).

[4]The National Salvation Front, created during fall 1992 and banned after the "October events," was the closest approximation to a united front of Communist and nationalist organizations. Significantly, Zhirinovsky was not a member of this coalition.

Political Diversity in the Developing World

- Politics of Development (Articles 47 and 48)
- Latin America: Mexico (Articles 49 and 50)
- Africa (Articles 51–53)
- China (Articles 54–56)
- India (Article 57)
- Newly Industrialized Countries (Articles 58 and 59)

Until recently, the Third World was a widely used umbrella term for a disparate group of states that are now more frequently called the developing world countries. Their most important shared characteristic may well be what these countries have *not* become—namely relatively modern industrial societies. Otherwise they differ considerably from each other, in terms of their past and present situations as well as their future prospects. The designation Third World has been used so variously that it is dismissed by some critical observers as a category that produces more confusion than analytical precision or political insight. Their objections should at least make us cautious when speaking about the Third World. Perhaps the time has come to let go of the slippery concept, as the first article suggests. But as this essay acknowledges, there are some commonalities among these countries that need conceptual recognition of some kind. Moreover, as Barbara Crossette next explains, the "spirit" or "vision" of a Third World still retains some of its power.

Originally the term third world referred to countries—many of them recently freed former colonies—that chose to remain nonaligned in the cold war confrontation between the First World (or Western bloc) and the Second World (or communist bloc). It was common to speak of "three worlds," but the categories of First World and Second World themselves never gained wide usage. They make very little sense today in view of the collapse of communist rule in central and eastern Europe, including Russia and the other former Soviet republics.

The derivative category Third World continues to be a handy, if imprecise and sometimes misleading, term of reference. It sometimes still carries the residual connotation of non-Western and noncommunist. Increasingly, however, the term is used to cover all largely nonindustrial countries that are predominantly nonmodern in their economic and social infrastructures. In that sense, the remaining communist-ruled countries would belong to the Third World category, with China and a few of its Asian neighbors as prime examples. In the same sense, Cuba is one of many Third World countries in Latin America, although it differs from the others in being communist-ruled.

Most of the Third World nations also share the problems of poverty and, though now less frequently, rapid population growth. However, their present economic situation and potential for development vary considerably, as a simple alphabetical juxtaposition of countries such as Angola and the Argentines, Bangladesh and Brazil, or Chad and China illustrates. An additional term, Fourth World, has therefore been proposed to designate countries that are so desperately short of resources that they appear to have little or no prospect for self-sustained economic improvement. Adding to the terminological inflation and confusion, the Third World countries are now often referred to collectively as the "South" and contrasted with the largely industrialized "North." Most of them in fact are located in the southern latitudes of the planet—in Latin America, Africa, Asia, and the Middle East. But Greenland would also qualify for Third World status along with much of Russia and Siberia, while Australia or New Zealand clearly would not. South Africa would

be a case of "uneven" or "combined" development, as would some Latin American countries where significant enclaves of advanced modernity are located within a larger context of premodern social and economic conditions.

It is very important to remember that the countries of the Third World vary tremendously in their sociocultural and political characteristics. Some of them have representative systems of government, and a few of these even have an impressive record of stability, like India. Many more are governed by authoritarian, often military-based regimes that advocate an ideologically adorned strategy of rapid economic development. Closer examination will sometimes reveal that the avowed determination of leaders to improve their societies may carry less substance than their determination to maintain and expand their own power and privilege. In any case, the strategies and politics of development or modernization in these countries vary enormously.

In recent years, market-oriented development has gained in favor in many countries that previously subscribed to some version of heavy state regulation or socialist planning of the economy. The renewed interest in markets resembles a strategic policy shift that has also occurred in former communist-ruled nations or the more advanced industrial countries. It usually represents a pragmatic acceptance of a "mixed economy" rather than a doctrinaire espousal of laissez-faire capitalism. In other words, state intervention continues to play a role in economic development, but it is no longer so pervasive or heavy-handed as often in the past, and the belief in some form of centralized state planning has long since withered away.

In studying the attempts by Third World countries to create institutions and policies that will promote their socioeconomic development, it is important not to leave out the international context. The political and intellectual leaders of these countries have often drawn upon some version of what is called *dependency theory* to explain their plight, often combining it with demands for special treatment or compensation from the industrial world. Dependency theory is itself an outgrowth of the Marxist theory of imperialism, according to which advanced capitalist countries have established exploitative relationships with the weaker economic systems of the Third World. The focus of such theories has been on finding external reasons for a country's failure to generate self-sustained growth. They differ strikingly from explanations that give greater emphasis to a country's internal obstacles to development (whether sociocultural, political, environmental, or a combination of these). Such theoretical disagreements are not only of academic interest. The theories themselves are likely to provide the framework for strikingly different policy conclusions and strategies for development. In other words, theory has consequences.

The debate has had some tangible consequences in recent years. It now appears that dependency theory in its simplest form has lost intellectual and political support. Instead of serving as an explanatory paradigm, it is now more frequently encountered as a part of more pluralist explanations of lagging development that recognize the diversity of internal and external factors that are likely to affect economic development. There is much to be said for paying greater attention to the contextual or situational aspects of each case of development. On the whole, multivariable explanations seem preferable to monocausal ones. Strategies of development that may work in one setting may come to naught in a different environment.

Sometimes called the Group of 77, but eventually consisting of some 120 countries, the Third World states used to link themselves together in the United Nations to promote whatever interests that they may have had in common. In their demand for a New International Economic Order, they focused on promoting changes designed to improve their relative commercial position vis-à-vis the affluent industrialized nations of the North. This common front, however, has turned out to be more rhetorical than real. It would be a mistake to assume that there is a necessary identity of national interest among these countries or that they pursue complementary foreign policies.

Outside the United Nations, some of these same countries have tried to increase and control the price of industrially important primary exports through the building of cartel agreements among themselves. The result has sometimes been detrimental to other Third World nations. The most successful of these cartels, the Organization of Petroleum Exporting Countries (OPEC), was established in 1973 and held sway for almost a decade. Its cohesion has since eroded, resulting in drastic reductions in oil prices. While this development has been welcomed in the oil-importing industrial world as well as in many developing countries, it left some oil-producing nations such as Mexico in economic disarray for a while. Moreover, the need to find outlets for the huge amounts of petrodollars, which had been deposited by some oil producers in Western banks during the period of cartel-induced high prices, led financial institutions to make huge and often ill-considered loans to many Third World nations. The frantic and often unsuccessful efforts to repay on schedule created new economic, social, and political dislocations, which hit particularly hard in Latin America during the 1980s. The memory of these recent misadventures is likely to have some prudential influence on policymakers in the future.

The problems of poverty, hunger, and malnutrition in much of the developing world are socially and politically explosive. In their fear of revolution and their opposition to meaningful reform, the privileged classes often resort to brutal repression as a means to preserve a status quo favorable to themselves. In Latin America, this led to a politicalization of many lay persons and clergy of the Roman Catholic Church, who demanded social reform in the name of what was called liberation theology. For them, some variant of dependency theory filled a very practical ideological function by providing a relatively simple analytical and moral explanation of a complex reality. It also gave some strategic guidance for political activists who were determined to change this state of affairs. Their views on the inevitability of class struggle, and the need to take an active part in it, often clashed with the Vatican's outlook.

The collapse of communist rule in Europe has had a profound impact on the ideological explanation of the developing world's poverty and on the resulting strategies to overcome it. The Soviet model of modernization, which until recently fascinated many Third World leaders, now appears to have very little of practical value to offer these countries. The fact that even the communists who remain in power in China have been willing to experiment with market reforms, including the private profit motive, has added to the general discredit of the centrally planned economy. Perhaps even more important is the positive demonstration effect of some countries in Africa and Latin America that have pursued more market-oriented strategies of development. On the whole, they appear to have performed much better than some of their more statist neighbors. That may help explain the intellectual journey of someone like Michael Manley, the former prime minister of Jamaica, who broke away from the combination of dependency theory and socialist strategies that he had once defended vigorously. During the 1980s, Manley made an intellectual U-turn as he gained a new respect for market-oriented economic strategies, without abandoning his interest in using reform politics to promote the interests of the poor. More recently, Jorge Castañeda has called upon the Left in Latin America to abandon utopian goals and seek social reforms within "mixed" market economies.

Latin America: Mexico illustrates the difficulty of establishing stable pluralist democracies in many parts of the developing world. Some authors have argued that its dominant political tradition is basically authoritarian corporatist rather than competitively pluralist. They see the region's long tradition of centralized authoritarian governments, whether of the Left or the Right, as the result of an authoritarian "unitary" bias in the political culture. From this perspective, there is little hope for a lasting pluralist development, and the current trend toward democratization in much of Latin America is unlikely to last. Today, however, the cultural explanation for the prevalence of authoritarian governments in Latin America appears to meet with more skepticism than it did a few years ago. One simple reason is the fact that one after the other dictatorships in the region have been replaced by an elected government. The demonstration effect of democratic governments in Spain and Portugal may also have been important for the Latin American countries. Finally, the negative social, economic, and political experience with authoritarian rulers may well be one of the strongest cards held by their democratic successors. But unless they also meet the pragmatic test ("Does it work?"), by providing evidence of social and economic progress, the new democracies in Latin America could also be in trouble shortly. They may yet turn out to have been short interludes between authoritarian regimes that achieve a modicum of political and social order through repression.

In much of Latin America there has been a turn toward a greater emphasis on market economics, replacing the traditional commitment to strategies that favored statist interventions. An important example is the attempt by former president Carlos Salinas of Mexico to move his country toward a more competi-

(PRI) and given new outlets for protest. But critics of Salinas argued that his approach was too technocratic in its assumption that economic modernization can be accomplished without a basic change of the political system. During his last year in office, Salinas was confronted by an armed peasant rebellion in the southern province of Chiapas, which gave voice to the demand for land reform and economic redistribution. Mexican criticism of Salinas intensified after he left office in December 1994 and three months later sought political exile in the United States. Since then, some top Mexican officials and their associates have been accused of having links to major drug traffickers with a sordid record of corruption and political assassination.

The successor to Salinas was elected in August 1994, in a competitive contest that was reported as not seriously distorted by fraud. The ruling party won with 51 percent of the vote. The PRI's first presidential candidate, Luis Donaldo Colosio, had been assassinated earlier in March. His place was taken by Ernesto Zedillo, an economist and former banker who fits the technocratic mold of recent Mexican leaders. He was expected to continue the basic economic policies of Salinas, but he appeared ready to listen to demands for meaningful political reform. He had hardly taken office at the beginning of December 1994, however, before the Mexican peso collapsed and brought the economy to ruins. A major factor was the country's huge trade deficit and the resultant loss of confidence in the peso, as Lucy Conger explains in her article. It remains to be seen whether Mexico's political institutions will be more resilient than its economic ones have proven to be.

Africa: South Africa faces the monumental task of introducing democracy in a multiracial society where the ruling white minority has never shared political or economic power with black Africans or Asian immigrants. A new transitional constitution was adopted in late 1993, followed by the first multiracial national elections in April 1994. Former president Frederik de Klerk will go into history as an important reformer, but his political work cannot possibly please a broad cross section of South African society. His reforms have simply gone much too far and too fast for a privileged white minority, and they have not gone nearly far or quickly enough for many more who demand policies that would promote much more than formal racial equality.

Nelson Mandela, who succeeded de Klerk, has an even more difficult historical task. He has some strong political cards, in addition to his undisputed leadership qualities. He clearly represents the aspirations of a long-repressed majority, but he has managed to retain the respect of a sizable number of the white minority. It will be important that he continues to bridge the racial cleavages that otherwise threaten to ravage South African society. The reformers have sought political accommodation through an institutional form of power-sharing. The task of keeping such a coalition government together will be only one of Mandela's many problems. In order for the democratic changes to have much meaning for the long suppressed majority, it will be necessary to find policies that reduce the social and economic chasm separating the races. The politics of redistribution will be no simple or short-term task, and one may expect many conflicts

tive form of market enterprise. His modernization strategy included Mexico's entry into the North American Free Trade Agreement (NAFTA) with the United States and Canada. In a time of enormous socioeconomic dislocations, however, Salinas showed considerable reluctance to move from an economic to a thorough political reform. Such a shift would have undermined the long-time hegemony of his own Institutional Ruling Party in the future. Nevertheless, for the first time since the beginning of colonization, South Africa now offers some hope for a major improvement in interracial relations.

China is the homeland of over a billion people, or more than one-fifth of the world's population. Here the reform communists, who took power after Mao Zedong's death in 1976, began much earlier than their Soviet counterparts to steer the country toward a relatively decontrolled market economy. They also introduced some political relaxation, by ending Mao's recurrent ideological campaigns to mobilize the masses. In their place came a domestic tranquillity such as China had not known for over half a century. But the regime encountered a basic dilemma: it wished to maintain tight controls over politics and society while reforming the economy. When a new openness developed in Chinese society, comparable in some ways to the pluralism encouraged more actively by Gorbachev's glasnost policy of openness in the Soviet Union, it ran into determined opposition among hard-line communist leaders. The aging reform leader Deng Xiaoping presided over a bloody crackdown on student demonstrations in Beijing's Tiananmen Square in May 1989. The regime refuses to let up on its tight political controls of society, but it has continued to loosen the economic controls. In recent years, China has experienced a remarkable economic surge with growth rates that appear unmatched elsewhere in the world. A still-unanswered question is whether the emerging industrial society can long coexist with a repressive political system. It would be surprising, if the succession in political leadership does not produce tensions and conflicts at the elite level.

India is often referred to as a subcontinent. With its almost 900 million people, this country ranks second only to China in population and ahead of the continents of Latin America and Africa combined. India is deeply divided by ethnic, religious, and regional differences. In recent years, Hindu extremists have become politicized and now constitute a threat to the Muslim minority as well as the secular foundation of the state. For the vast majority of the huge population, a life of material deprivation seems inescapable. However, some policy critics point to the possibility of relief if the country's struggling economy were freed from a long tradition of heavy-handed state interference. There have been some promising steps in that direction. The potential for political crisis nevertheless looms over the country. In 1992 the national elections were marred by the assassination of Rajiv Gandhi, the former prime minister and leader of the Congress party. Prime Minister P. V. Narasimha Rao, the political veteran who took charge of a tenuous minority government after the election, has followed in the steps of other reform governments in the Third World by adopting more market-oriented policies. This attempt to bring India, with its long tradition of heavy state regulation and protectionism, into the world economy bears careful watching.

The Newly Industrialized Countries (NICs) are the subject of the two final articles in this unit. They have received much attention as former Third World nations that have succeeded in breaking out of the cycle of chronic poverty and low productivity. It is not fully clear what lessons we can draw from the impressive records of the four or five "tigers" or "dragons"—Singapore, Hong Kong, South Korea, Taiwan, and possibly Thailand or Malaysia. Some observers have suggested that their combination of authoritarian politics and market economics have provided a successful mix of discipline and incentives that have made the economic take-off possible. Others point to the presence of special cultural factors in these countries (such as strong family units and values that emphasize hard work, postponement of gratification, and respect for education), which supposedly encourage rational forms of economic behavior. It would also be possible to cite some geopolitical and historical advantages that helped the NICs accumulate investment capital at a critical phase. The subject is of great importance and it seems bound to become one of the main topics in the field of study we call the politics of development. These countries are clearly of interest as possible role models for economic development. They can also serve as examples of how authoritarian political and social traditions can be reformed in tandem with the development of a more affluent consumer society. The authors give a perspective on the newly industrialized countries by carefully reviewing the debate concerning the relative contributions made to their remarkable economic development by market forces, state intervention, and cultural and social factors.

Looking Ahead: Challenge Questions

Why is the term Third World of little analytical value? What have these countries in common, and how are they diverse? Is there any value in keeping the concept, or should we scrap it? What is meant by the term Fourth World?

How do explanations of Third World poverty and slow development differ in assigning responsibility for these conditions to external (foreign) and internal (domestic) factors? Why can theories of development be important factors in shaping strategies of modernization?

What is dependency theory, and why has it had so much appeal especially in Latin America? How do you explain the current wave of market-oriented reforms? How did the widespread optimism about Mexico's economic development arise, and why did it come to such an abrupt end?

Why do economic development and representative government run into such difficulties in most of Latin America and much of Africa? What are some of the major political, economic, and social problems that South Africa still has to face in overcoming the legacy of apartheid?

How do you explain China's relative success in turning toward market reforms for the economy, as compared to the Soviet Union? Why can we expect future political tension at the elite and mass levels of Chinese society?

How has India managed to maintain itself as a parliamentary democracy, given the many cleavages that divide this multi-ethnic society?

What can the newly industrialized countries of Asia teach us about the possibility of economic modernization and democratic reform?

LET'S ABOLISH THE THIRD WORLD

It never made much sense, and it doesn't exist in practice.
So why not get rid of it in theory?

Sometimes language lags history. Take the Third World. Did we ever have another name for the poor, unstable nations of the south? In fact, the Third World is a 1950s coinage, invented in Paris by French intellectuals looking for a way to lump together the newly independent former European colonies in Asia and Africa. They defined *le tiers monde* by what it wasn't: neither the First World (the West) nor the Second (the Soviet bloc). But now the cold war is over, and we are learning a new political lexicon, free of old standbys like "Soviet Union" that no longer refer to anything. It's a good time to get rid of the Third World, too.

The Third World should have been abolished long ago. From the very beginning, the concept swept vast differences of culture, religion and ethnicity under the rug. How much did El Salvador and Senegal really have in common? And what did either share with Bangladesh? One of the bloodiest wars since Vietnam took place between two Third World brothers, Iran and Iraq. Many former colonies remained closer to erstwhile European metropoles than to their fellow "new nations."

Nevertheless, the Third World grew. Intellectuals and politicians added a socioeconomic connotation to its original geopolitical meaning. It came to include all those exploited countries that could meet the unhappy standard set by Prime Minister Lee Kuan Yew of Singapore in 1969: "poor, strife-ridden, chaotic." (That was how Latin America got into the club.) There's a tendency now to repackage the Third World as the "South" in a global North-South, rich-poor division. To be

sure, in this sense the Third World does refer to something real: vast social problems—disease, hunger, bad housing—matched by a chronic inability to solve them. And relative deprivation does give poor nations some common interests: freer access to Western markets, for example.

But there are moral hazards in defining people by what they cannot do or what they do not have. If being Third World meant being poor, and if being poor meant being a perennial victim of the First and Second Worlds, why take responsibility for your own fate? From Cuba to Burma, Third Worldism became the refuge of scoundrels, the "progressive" finery in which despots draped their repression and economic mismanagement. Remember "African socialism" in Julius Nyerere's Tanzania? It left the country's economy a shambles. A good many Western intellectuals hailed it as a "homegrown" Third World ideology.

Paternalism is one characteristic Western response to a "victimized" Third World. Racism is another. To nativists such as France's Jean-Marie Le Pen or Patrick Buchanan, "Third World" is a code phrase for what they see as the inherent inferiority of tropical societies made up of dark-skinned people. Either way, the phrase Third World, so suggestive of some alien plant, abets stereotyping. "The Third World is a form of bloodless universality that robs individuals and societies of their particularity," wrote the late Trinidad-born novelist Shiva Naipaul. "To blandly subsume, say, Ethiopia, India, and Brazil under the one banner of Third Worldhood is as

absurd and as denigrating as the old assertion that all Chinese look alike."

Today, two new forces are finishing off the tattered Third World idea. The first is the West's victory in the cold war. There are no longer two competing "worlds" with which to contrast a "third." Leaders can't play one superpower off the other, or advertise their misguided policies as alternative to "equally inappropriate" communism and capitalism. The second is rapid growth in many once poor countries. The World Bank says developing countries will grow twice as fast in the '90s as the industrialized G-7. So much for the alleged immutability of "Third World" poverty—and for the notion that development must await a massive transfer of resources from north to south. No one would call the Singapore of Lee Kuan Yew poor, strife-ridden or chaotic: per capita GNP is more than $10,000, and its 1990 growth rate was 8 percent. South Korea, Taiwan and Hong Kong also have robust economies, and Thailand and Malaysia are moving up fast.

American steelmakers have recently lodged "dumping" complaints against half a dozen Asian and Latin American countries. Cheap wages explains much of these foreign steelmakers' success, but the U.S. industry's cry is still a backhanded compliment. "A nation without a manufacturing base is a nation heading toward Third World status," wrote presidential candidate Paul Tsongas. But Tsongas was using obsolete imagery to make his point: soon, bustling basic industries may be the *hallmark* of a "Third World" nation.

Patina of modernity: Nor can the Third World idea withstand revelations about what life was really like in the former "Second World." It was assumed that, whatever the U.S.S.R.'s political deformities, that country was at least modern enough to give the West a run for its money in science and technology. In fact, below a patina of modernity lay gross industrial inefficiency, environmental decay and ethnic strife. Nowadays, it's more common to hear conditions in the former Soviet Union itself described as "Third World," and Russia seeks aid from South Korea. Elsewhere in Europe, Yugoslavia's inter-ethnic war is as bad as anything in Asia or Africa. The United States itself is pocked with "Third World" enclaves: groups with Bangladeshi life expectancies and Latin American infant-mortality rates.

A concept invoked to explain so many things probably can't explain very much at all. The ills that have come to be associated with the Third World are not confined to the southern half of this planet. Nor are democracy and prosperity the exclusive prerogatives of the North. Unfair as international relations may be, over time, economic development and political stability come to countries that work, save and organize to achieve them. Decline and political disorder come to those who neglect education, public health—and freedom. The rules apply regardless of race, ethnicity, religion or climate. There's only one world.   CHARLES LANE

The 'Third World' Is Dead, but Spirits Linger

Indonesia saw a movement born, and now hosts its wake.

Barbara Crossette

Not more than 60 miles down the highway from the Indonesian hill town of Bogor, where President Clinton will take part this week in an economic summit of Asian-Pacific nations, is a genteel city that once symbolized everything the third world believed in and hoped for when it was young. The city is Bandung. There, another generation of world leaders—Nehru, Nasser, Nkrumah, Sukarno, Zhou Enlai—met at another summit, the 1955 Afro-Asian Conference, a gathering full of post-colonial promise, with dreams of self-sufficiency, solidarity among newly independent nations and commitment to an anti-superpower international policy that became known as nonalignment.

"Sisters and brothers!" President Sukarno of Indonesia told the delegates. "How terrifically dynamic is our time!"

The fraternal third world these founders envisioned is dead. The agenda for Bogor, where the heirs of the Bandung generation plan to talk mostly about economic liberalization, competition for foreign investment and free trade, is its obituary. The hollowness of the dream of Afro-Asian commonality is never so starkly evident as when Pacific Rim countries get together, a number of them boasting higher living standards than some European nations.

Nehru's India is barely on the horizon of this world; Nkrumah's Africa isn't even in the picture.

The "third world," a phrase first used by French journalists in the 1950's, was meant to describe those who were not part of the industrial world or the Communist bloc. The distinction has no more relevance now than the idea that developing nations automatically have much in common with each other. People speak of the "tigers" who form a class of their own, or a "fourth world" of the poorest countries. A "fifth world" might be found among proliferating populations of rootless refugees. And so on.

"We no longer have a coherent image of the third world," says Jean-Bernard Mérimée, France's chief delegate to the United Nations and a former Ambassador to India. "It is now composed of totally different elements. What do nations like Burkina Faso and Singapore have in common? Nothing, except a sort of lingering perception that they belong to something that had the tradition of opposing the West and the developed world." All that is left, the envoy said, are "remnants of the Bandung attitude" and memories of the fight against colonialism that once bonded emerging nations.

Bandung's oratory lives on, however, resurfacing regularly in the frustration of poor countries looking for easy explanations for develop-ment shortcomings. The new "imperialists" now tend to be lending organizations like the World Bank and International Monetary Fund, which have tried to impose stringent fiscal regimes. The "neocolonial" tag has also been attached to donor nations asking questions about rights abuses, child labor, religious or sex discrimination and population policy. At the recent United Nations population conference in Cairo, some of the hottest buttons and bumper stickers proclaimed angrily, "No to Contraceptive Imperialism."

The days of Bandung were heady days of shared underdevelopment, before yawning material gaps between the richest and poorest of these nations began to widen. In Asia, Pakistani business leaders say ruefully that a few decades ago their nation was roughly on a par with South Korea and both had military governments. Both are now democracies, at least on paper, but South Koreans live a decade longer, earn 10 times as much and send 10 times as many children to college with less than half Pakistan's population. In Egypt, intellectuals recall how their country once exported skilled labor to other Arabic-speaking nations that now import a more educated work force, even for menial jobs, from Southeast Asia. In decades of building organizations—the Nonaligned Movement, the Group of 77—third world nations never devised effective mechanisms to help one another.

Ideologies, economic policies, cultural differences and the creation of superpower clienteles all played a part in widening fissures among developing countries. Different growth rates were not always predictable. Singapore's lack of natural resources did not prevent it from growing into an economic powerhouse. A sea of oil has not turned Nigeria into Texas or Mexico. Authoritarian policies contributed to the boom in some nations. Repression and corruption drained the life of others, or drove the dispossessed into violence.

Dirt Poor, With Tanks

What happened to the shared dreams of the third world is documented in the United Nations' Human Development Index. Looking at daily lives rather than macroeconomic figures, the index has for the last five years ranked more than 100 developing nations in education, access to basic services and conditions of women, among other topics. "What emerges is an arresting picture of unprece-dented human progress and unspeak-able human misery, of humanity's advances on several fronts mixed with humanity's retreat on several others, of a breath-taking globaliza-tion of prosperity side by side with a depressing globalization of poverty," the 1994 report says.

This year, the index focuses on big military spenders. "Many nations have sacrificed human security in the search for more sophisticated arms," it says. "For example, India ordered 20 advanced MIG-29 fighters that could have provided basic edu-cation to all the 15 million girls now out of school. Nigeria bought 80 bat-tle tanks from the United Kingdom at a cost that would have immunized all two million unimmunized chil-dren in that country while also pro-viding family-planning services to nearly 17 million couples."

While the third world had divided itself into unequal streams of devel-opment well before the end of the cold war, developing nations hoped there would be peace dividends for them after the collapse of commu-nism. They have been disappointed. Not only have sources of aid from the former Soviet bloc withered, as Cuba has discovered most painfully, but also the European nations reborn as democracies—now labeled "econ-omies in transition"—have moved in to claim a lot of attention and scarce development funds.

What to do? Development experts say doing nothing about the Global South—the new term—will lead only to more ethnic wars, migrations from overpopulated regions and rapid de-pletion of natural resources. On the other hand, those "remnants of the Bandung attitude" that the French envoy identified do not want the industrialized world to get an oppor-tunity to intervene in national policies as a condition of granting more aid.

"You get a certain feeling that on many issues—social policies, environ-mental policies, human rights—the de-veloping countries get a feeling of interference," said Austria's United Nations delegate, Ernst Sucharipa. "We would not say this is true, though I can see why some countries would feel that way. We have to have an open discussion on issues of global consequence." The need for universal sisterhood and brother-hood is now no longer confined to the world of Bandung.

Mexico: The Failed Fiesta

"With the devaluation of the peso in December, the structures of rationalism were fractured and the conflict over who the Mexicans are and what type of nationhood best suits their unique amalgam has resurfaced... For the reformist option to survive, not to mention flourish, Mexicans must once again believe in the future."

LUCY CONGER

LUCY CONGER, *Mexico correspondent for* Institutional Investor *magazine and the newspaper* Jornal do Brasil, *has reported on Mexican politics and economics for the past 11 years.*

In the early evening of election night, August 21, 1994, a small group of reporters crossed the windy, empty esplanade encircling the two office buildings that are headquarters to the world's oldest state party, the Institutional Revolutionary Party (PRI). Only a few party hacks loitered about the stairwells and narrow corridors; the usual gaggles of congenial Mexican politicians whispering excitedly or slapping each other on the back were nowhere to be seen.

Inside the Hall of Presidents, the secluded meeting room where the PRI national executive committee makes its decisions, a number of young men wearing suits—the foreign-trained economists and political scientists who designed the election campaign of Ernesto Zedillo—chatted amiably and masked their excitement at being on the winning team.

At 7:25 P.M., only minutes after the polls had closed in western Baja California state, Zedillo stepped up to the microphones and declared victory. "We have a quick count and it makes us very satisfied about the results," the bespectacled bureaucrat remarked. "This election says Mexico believes in democracy, a united country, loves social peace, and is a very solid country."

Ernesto Zedillo had just won the presidency in the most openly contested race in modern Mexican history, running against two strong challengers and fighting uphill against a stagnating economy. By all accounts this election night marked a resounding triumph for Zedillo and the divided PRI. The government could boast the cleanest elections ever held. Mexicans, who at the beginning of the year had expressed greater anger with the government than at any other time in recent memory, turned out in record numbers (an astonishing 80 percent) to give the PRI and Zedillo a solid mandate.

But, in this land of fiestas, there was no fiesta. Inside PRI headquarters the mood was flat. Outside the voters who had swept Zedillo to victory never took to the streets to celebrate their candidate's triumph. "The election was won in sadness, in melancholy but not in resignation," says Roger Bartra, a social critic and author. The mood that night reflected a broad and deep sadness that permeated Mexican society throughout the year. Zedillo, after all, was an accidental candidate, the man who became the PRI's presidential nominee only because of the tragic assassination of President Carlos Salinas's first choice, Luis Donaldo Colosio. In death Colosio had become the great reformer who would have led Mexico to democracy, the charismatic politician who was now the favorite candidate of the man and woman on the street. And even before Colosio's murder, from New Year's Day when the Zapatista National Liberation Army burst onto the scene in January, the nasty specter of political violence and civil war cast a long shadow over the land.

On that August night there was no joy at the PRI, no electric aura around Zedillo. It was not clear what this means, but the fact that the mood at PRI headquarters was indecipherable is important. The strange air surrounding Zedillo's victory signaled Mexico's entrance into a new realm of unclarity, a time of indefinition. Some observers described this new uncertainty in strictly political terms. "The country is divided between a system—which has guaranteed stability but today has fewer resources for sustaining it—and a part of the society and politics that seeks to make changes although it has not yet managed to convince the rest of society that those changes will lead to a new stability," wrote Manuel Camacho Solís, former Chiapas peace commissioner and former Mexico City mayor, in his pointedly titled manifesto, *Change without Rupture*. But the indistinct reality that enshrouds Mexican life today appears to be part of a broader cultural malaise. "There are ideological commotions, political problems, disturbances to the mind. Also, there is a sickness of the heart which is sunken in darkness as we [Mexicans] are moving from one cultural era to another," said Roger Bartra in an interview.

OF PHANTOMS AND PROVIDENTIAL MEN

Why Zedillo and the PRI won the election with a resounding mandate of 51 percent of the vote remains a subject of wonderment and debate in Mexico. A lackluster candidate and unexciting campaigner, Zedillo's victory was nonetheless unquestionable. In a count not seriously distorted by fraud, he received 24 percent more of the vote than National Action Party candidate Diego Fernández de Cevallos, the closest challenger. But why this paradox of a glittering victory for a lackluster candidate? Some say voters stayed with the ruling party out of loyalty, robotism, or fear of change. Independent civic leaders charged that the overwhelming pro-PRI bias of television coverage poisoned the election and tilted opinion toward the PRI. And, as social commentator Carlos Monsiváis rightly quipped, people who had ranted and raged against Zedillo five minutes before still stepped up to the ballot box and cast a vote for him.

Despite stagnation in the economy, opinion polls showed that people did not think conditions had deteriorated under President Carlos Salinas de Gortari. "Strangely enough, there was not a perception that the economic situation was adverse because inflation was low and there was the sense that a process was going on that would allow you to get on board," Adolfo Aguilar Zínser, a congressman, said in an interview. Although Zedillo embodied continuity in the strict economic reforms of the past decade and signified an extension of the PRI regime into its seventh decade, exit polls showed that 65 percent of those who voted for Zedillo favored a change in social and economic policy.

The most compelling explanation for the PRI-Zedillo victory is fear. In 1994 phantoms hovered over Mexico. Political turbulence shattered Mexicans' most fondly held illusions and stirred up their deepest fears. The Zapatista National Liberation Army guerrilla uprising in January had reawakened long-standing dread of violence and a civil war fueled by an endless stream of recruits drawn from the millions of impoverished peasants. The photographs of army troop movements and the five Zapatistas with their hands tied behind their backs who had been executed by soldiers evoked the horror of the 1968 Tlatelolco massacre, when the army mowed down student protesters in Mexico City. The killing of Colosio, less than one year after the machine-gun slaying of Cardinal Juan Jesús Posadas Ocampo during a shootout between two drug gangs at Guadalajara's airport, unleashed the specter of drug wars driving politics. A popular, persistent rumor about Colosio's unexplained assassination blamed the crime on druglords enraged over their failure to cut a deal with the heir apparent. The horrifying instant in which part of Colosio's head was blown sideways was replayed on television hundreds of times, drilling terror into the consciousness of even the dullest viewer. The widespread belief that opposing factions in the PRI engineered Colosio's assassination touched people's deepest fear: that a bitter, internecine struggle would tear the political fabric to shreds, ending the vaunted 65 years of social peace that was the PRI's strongest claim to legitimacy.

Throughout the year, frequent reports of sightings of other guerrilla groups scattered around the country constantly churned anxieties about violence. Alleged national security reports leaked to the press painted grim scenarios of postelection strife in strategic states ringing Mexico City and dotted across the country from the Texas border down to the Pacific and Gulf coasts.

Other phantoms lurked in the dark corners of the Mexican mind in 1994. The highly publicized kidnappings of Alfredo Harp Helú and Angel Lozada, top executives of the Banamex bank and Gigante supermarket chain, were bitter reminders of mounting problems with crime and a lack of security. The threat of economic disorder often reared its head as the guerrilla war and the Colosio assassination triggered sharp stock market drops, and NAFTA-induced investment stayed away from a Mexico that was now home to a guerrilla threat. "Only the PRI guarantees economic stability and certainty," said Mexican Bankers' Association president Roberto Hernández at the height of the Zedillo campaign; he evoked businesspeople's worst fears of a populist-inspired spending spree, loss of confidence, and devaluation should left-wing candidate Cuauhtémoc Cárdenas become president.

Against this backdrop Zedillo won power, but the economist and former central banker failed to arouse hopes or inspire confidence. He would not make Mexicans tremble, as have his predecessors in the all-powerful presidency. "The election resolved the problem of Zedillo but not the problem of governability of the country," said Luis Hernández, adviser to the national coordinator of Coffee Producer Organizations and an independent social activist.

The election left a desolate landscape in which no other leader was standing on the political horizon. Colosio's rival within the PRI, Manuel Camacho, was squeezed out of politics because his role as Chiapas peace commissioner had eclipsed the PRI's presidential campaign. Cárdenas, the caudillo who nearly won the presidency in 1988 running against Carlos Salinas and demonstrated, for the first time ever, that the PRI was not invincible, was sidelined by the meager 16 percent of the vote he received. The blustery conservative National Action Party candidate, Diego Fernández de Cevallos, who led his party to its best-ever vote, simply abandoned the political arena, reigniting rumors that he was ill or had cut a deal with the PRI. Finally, the election shattered the myth of the "hombre providencial," the strong man who gives direction and leadership to a country in crisis. "The Mexican political class has no providential figures," said social critic Bartra.

DECONSTRUCTING CHIAPAS

The Chiapas conflict irrevocably changed political life in Mexico by creating a permanent threat of war. That threat, along with the steady stream of poetic texts from the Zapatista leader, SubComandante Marcos, kept the issues of poverty, democratization, and indigenous autonomy on the national agenda and added pressure for clean elections. Why the world's newest guerrilla force should explicitly back the demands of civil society for political reform and social justice remains a mystery, as does the identity of its charismatic masked leader. Remarkably, the government's unilateral cease-fire and peace talks with the Zapatistas achieved a truce that has held for more than a year. Given Mexicans' deep concerns about violence, the Zapatista army "awakens a force that is not bellicose but rather is pacifist," says Carlos Monsiváis, referring to the powerful antiwar civic mobilizations stirred by the Chiapas conflict that succeeded in bringing about the cease-fire.

But new rumblings in December, when the Zapatistas broke out of the military encirclement that had apparently confined them to the Las Margaritas area of the Lacandon jungle, shook Mexicans' confidence. Small bands of young guerrillas erected roadblocks and occupied the plazas of 38 towns in northern Chiapas, thrusting the conflict back onto the national stage and creating new tensions in the state. The army bolstered defenses in the region and intensified surveillance, but ultimately both the army and the Zapatistas made strategic retreats. Zapatista operations were initially blamed for the devaluation debacle that shattered confidence in the 19-day-old Zedillo administration and cost Finance Minister Jaime Serra his job.

The troubles in Chiapas precipitated a deep reconsideration of the political and social order, as activists and intellectuals groped to explain the causes of the conflict and envision solutions. In the past year, the way the uprising is viewed has become more complex. It "never was a conflict between two armies, it is a civil conflict between landholders and peasant peons," said Luis Hernández. And the age-old dispute over land is now complicated by a political dispute initiated by the leftist Democratic Revolution Party (PRD), which demands the PRI state governor be deposed because of alleged election fraud. Six people were killed in a shootout between PRD protesters and local police in the Chiapas town of Chicomuselo on January 10, adding political violence to the ongoing social violence of land evictions and the threat of war. Chiapas remains a cauldron of conflict, an impoverished and polarized state in which Indians are pitted against Ladinos; ranchers against peasants; and Protestants against Catholics.

But even when the Zapatistas remained on alert, a number of influential intellectuals seemed to have assimilated the guerrillas as a civil force, a call to social sensitivity, a democratic imperative, and a new cultural phenomenon. According to this interpretation, the Chiapas conflict had been contained. "The psychological impact [of Chiapas] is that it brings back the indigenous problem, the problems of poverty and inequality, problems which Mexico has always faced and always refused to deal with," opposition intellectual Jorge Castañeda said in an interview. The Zapatistas and SubComandante Marcos "removed the persuasiveness of the neoliberal dream [and showed that] history that is not for justice is nothing," says Monsiváis. Ultimately the explanation for these sanguine assessments may lie in the curious nature of the Zapatista guerrillas; they are "armed reformers," in the words of political writer Joel Ortega.

Former Chiapas Peace Commissioner Manuel Camacho sees the conflict as a call to nationwide reform. "The reestablishment of the political unity of the country will demand a peace accord in Chiapas and a commitment to combat violence on the part of all political forces and social organizations of the country. A profound political change would ease negotiations and reinforce the peace process in Chiapas," he has written. Although during the peace talks Camacho avowed that the problem could be resolved mainly inside the borders of the impoverished state, he now takes a larger view. "If it [the conflict] is part of a broader program for political reforms, then there is space for finishing the negotiations. But if it's just seen in terms of Chiapas, then there's no more hope for a peaceful agreement," Camacho told me in November.

In mid-January, the threat of guerrilla war suddenly evaporated as the Zapatistas declared a cease-fire for an "indefinite time" after an extraordinary meeting with Zedillo's interior minister, Esteban Moctezuma, and troop withdrawals from two towns.

BACK TO THE THIRD WORLD

In 20 quick days in December, the great myth of Carlos Salinas's presidency collapsed. The illusion that Mexico's entry into the North American Free Trade Agreement would bring Mexico into the promised land of the first world vanished. In two days in December, the government lost $11 billion in a vain attempt to sustain that illusion by preserving a strong, stable currency. On January 4, when Zedillo announced the government's emergency economic program, he boldly smashed the Salinas myth and proclaimed the harsh new reality of Mexico: "The development of Mexico demands that we recognize, with full realism, that we are not a rich country, but a nation of grave needs and lacks." His stark language represented a breakthrough in Mexico's traditionally convoluted political rhetoric; and called a halt to the Salinas administration's rosy portrayal of Mexico's fragile economy.

The economic ruin spread by the devaluation signaled the end of another Salinas myth, that of the infallible technocrat. The irony that some of the world's best-trained and most highly praised economists could lead the country to the brink of economic disaster was not lost on Mexicans, even as they licked their wounds. The public repeatedly asked how the Harvard and Yale doctorates in the cabinet could have overlooked the gaping trade deficit that, in the last four years of the Salinas administration, averaged almost $255 million annually. As popular discontent with the economic emergency spread, opposition politicians and businesspeople alike attacked the former Salinas administration for the huge deficit that had caused the devaluation. The PRD filed a brief with the attorney general's office demanding that Salinas, former Finance Minister Pedro Aspe, central bank chief Miguel Mancera, and Zedillo's first finance minister, Jaime Serra, stand trial for conspiring to conceal the truth about the nation's financial situation. "We want those who plunder the people to be judged by history, but also by the people, and to be sanctioned by law," said PRD congressional leader Jesús Ortega. The scramble to lay blame for the economic crisis marked the culmination of the devastation left by the turmoil of 1994; it trained Mexicans' discontent on the all-powerful presidency, the arrogance and unaccountability of technocrats, and the new fragility of Mexican institutions.

FROM TRANSPARENCY TO OPACITY

Under the Salinas administration, official rhetoric touted "transparency" as a catchword to signal the modernization process that opened the economy to imports and foreign investment, and to suggest a new, straightforward style of doing business. "Transparency" was first used to refer to new foreign investment rules, and was bandied about by Trade Minister Jaime Serra to appeal to investors' universal demand for clear rules of the game. When the Salinas privatization drive got under way, "transparency" became the buzzword to portray the bidding process as clean and forthright. The transparency propaganda was supposed to convince vital foreign investment that Mexico was a safe haven for foreign capital, and it had the desired effect. But, clearly, the numbing repetition of the term was meant to rub off on the administration at large, creating an image of a crystalline business environment in a country known for corruption, backroom deals, intrigue, and betrayal.

The last year of the Salinas administration clouded the image of transparency. The assassinations, fraud, kidnappings, narco-Catholic confabs, and economic debacles of 1994 would even boggle the mind of a Mexican. Nationally publicized high crimes, seared into the national consciousness, showed the pervasiveness and power of dark forces in Mexican public life: the assassinations of Luis Donaldo Colosio and PRI secretary general José Francisco Ruiz Massieu; a $700-million bank loan scam engineered by Carlos Cabal Peniche, the suddenly wealthy businessman-banker whose empire allegedly flourished thanks to high-level contacts in government; revelations that Papal Nuncio Gerónimo Prigione had twice received in his offices two of Mexico's most wanted drug traffickers, Benjamín Arellano Félix and his brother Javier, who have been linked to Cardinal Posadas's murder; and the 106-day-long kidnapping of Banamex executive Alfredo Harp Helú, which ended when his family paid the kidnappers a record $30 million. None of these crimes have been solved. Until the government prosecutes the crimes, business continues as usual in Mexico—where disclosure remains a dream and impunity prevails.

The Colosio investigation is the prime example of opacity in the era of "transparency." The first special prosecutor, Miguel Montes, abandoned his theory that the crime was a conspiracy that involved several members of the Colosio security team and adopted a lone-assassin theory that was instantly debunked in Congress and by the public. Salinas was forced to name a new prosecutor, Olga Islas, who did not generate any new findings. Mario Aburto, the man who fired the pistol into Colosio's head, is behind bars, but a mastermind has not been named or prosecuted, and doubts remain about a second gunman and the motives for the murder, which are widely believed to be political.

The investigation into the Ruiz Massieu murder nearly caused a state crisis just days before Zedillo was to take power. Deputy Attorney General and Special Prosecutor Mario Ruiz Massieu, the victim's brother, charged that Salinas lacked the political will to pursue the inquest, accused the two top leaders of the PRI of blocking the investigation, and resigned from it. "The demons are loose, and they have won," the aggrieved Ruiz Massieu said, apparently referring to the ascendancy of the PRI old guard over the reformist faction led by his slain brother. Before his resignation, Ruiz Massieu managed to put 14 suspects behind bars, but the PRI congressman accused of being the mastermind, Deputy Manuel Muñoz Rocha, remains on the lam.

Reports about the Cabal Peniche scandal point to Cabal's close links with senior PRI political figures, including a former cabinet official and three state governors. Cabal has published advertisements in national newspapers pledging to continue to run Banco Unión Cremi, but his whereabouts are unknown. Suspicions about the Salinas-era privatizations intensified in 1994, especially after *Forbes* magazine released its list of billionaires, including 24 Mexicans, in July. According to the magazine, 23 of the super rich became billionaires during Salinas's term, and many of their fortunes ballooned after they bought state enterprises. As questions swirled around these sudden, fabulous fortunes, a hypersensitive government issued a 600-page white paper on the privatization process in an effort to prove its "transparency."

In the last year of Salinas's term, persistent rumors linked politicians to drug trafficking and drug money to the privatizations. The political assassinations and the killing of Tijuana police chief José Federico Benítez López were blamed on a power struggle between druglords and authorities in popular versions of the crimes; these will continue to shape opinion until the authorities release satisfactory findings.

MAGIC AND MYSTERY

While the magic and joy of Mexico may seem to have taken leave, the country has not lost its capacity to surprise. Mexico remains a mystery to political and economic observers alike. Before the vote, distinguished historians and political analysts on the left and the right proclaimed the 1994 election the "end of the regime," the deathknell of the PRI's hegemony. Yet Zedillo and the PRI emerged with an uncontested victory and a strong popular mandate. Some of the finest minds in Mexico City and Wall Street, who predicted economic growth of 3.5 to 4 percent for 1994 and continuing improved growth thereafter, were baffled by the December devaluation.

Reflecting on the significance of Mexico's annus horribilis became a vocation for citizens and spawned a cottage industry in publishing. As tensions increased in Chiapas and Mexicans were jolted by the devaluation and financial crisis, making sense of the jumbled events of the year became a matter of urgency. During one of our periodic rumination sessions in January, a friend said to me brightly, "I can sum it all up in three words: Back to normality." The democratic reform is unrealized, the value of the peso has returned to its proper level, wealthy industrialists retain tax benefits and trade protectionism while the national debt is passed on to the poor, impunity reigns, nobody trusts the government, and the mafias of oligarchs, politicians, and drug traffickers are in control as always in Mexico and throughout Latin America, he said.

If there is an upside to the traumas and torments Mexico weathered last year, it is that the national agenda is now clear and a wide range of structures and organizations are in place that could nurture and lead a transition to democracy. In recent years, opposition parties and social groups alike have demanded reforms that would separate the PRI from government and government financing; limit presidential powers; provide greater independence for the legislative and judicial branches; end corruption; allow free and fair elections; break up the private television monopoly; and create rules of open competition in banking.

President Zedillo endorsed many of these reforms and surprised most observers with his unexpected political adroitness in mid-January when he brought the three leading opposition parties together with the

PRI to sign a pact to forge sweeping political reforms to achieve a peaceful transition to democracy. The administration capitalized on the economic crisis to bring the country back from the brink of ungovernability and build bridges with even the PRD which had been relentlessly persecuted under Salinas.

The pact reflects the new political reality of Mexico in which the PRI can no longer govern without allies from across the political spectrum. The long-awaited political reform is a trade-off aimed at quelling political protest and maintaining consensus around the emergency economic program.

The situation has evolved since 1988, when change and reform were seen to be the function of a single man—Cuauhtémoc Cárdenas—who was vested with the mission of democratizing Mexico. Though wracked by bitter divisions, the PRD today is a party, not just a caudillo. Moreover, the diverse watchdog organizations of civil society have channeled discontent and galvanized demonstrations against violence and war.

Ultimately, for the democratization reforms to succeed, Zedillo and the PRI must reach beyond political parties to draw in peasant and urban popular groups, human rights, and other special interest groups as well as individual thinkers and activities. Proposals abound for establishing the new social, political, and economic order that could offer the promise of democracy, peace, plurality, and growth to Mexico in the twenty-first century. As political writer Joel Ortega points out, "a reformist option" is coming into view, most notably through the recent writings of PRIista Manuel Camacho, centrist novelist Carlos Fuentes, and opposition intellectual Jorge Castañeda. In his pointedly titled *Change without Rupture*, Camacho calls for formation of a "democratic center" made up of civic organizations, institutions, and individuals from across the political spectrum; this center would bring about a phased-in transition to democracy that would end the PRI's political hegemony. Fuentes rails against the false and dysfunctional compartmentalization of Mexico's modern state. In his reflection on 1994, *Nuevo Tiempo Mexicano*, Fuentes sounds a compelling call for "inclusive modernization"—a process of political modernization to complete the country's economic modernization and recapture the noble attempt of the 1910 social revolution "to recognize the cultural totality of Mexico." Castañeda's *Sopresas te da la Vida* calls for building a broad current of opinion "situated between the PRD and the PRI" to advance democratic reform.

The impulse for a new synthesis is not idle. The PRI successfully ruled Mexico for decades as a sui generis alliance that incorporated most of society's disparate elements and channeled contradictory tensions within Mexico. Culturally and historically, Mexicans feel more comfortable with a consensus-building inclusionary dynamic, rather than the adversarial politics of other latitudes.

Analysts and scholars have long noted the tension between rationality and magic in Mexico. When Mexicans wax sentimental about their country—as they often do—a favored way of summing up their feelings is to talk of "Mexico mágico." Nobody who knows Mexico would deny that magical people and events tend to appear here just when needed. Little more than a year ago, who would have imagined a witty masked poet leading an indigenous guerrilla force that would remind a rapidly yuppifying Mexico of its Indian origins and neglected peasant masses—and willingly negotiate with the government just six weeks after launching attacks on the army? "The genius of Mexicans consists of preserving the values of progress without giving up affirmation of the right to mystery, the right to amazement and endless self-discovery," writes Carlos Fuentes, obviously warming to his subject.

During the past decade of intense reforms, Mexico's economic and political metamorphosis was grounded in pragmatism and rationalism, as the foreign-trained technocrats shifted into overdrive to apply conventional modern economic theory to Mexico. With the devaluation of the peso in December, the structures of rationalism were fractured and the conflict over who the Mexicans are and what type of nationhood best suits their unique amalgam has resurfaced. The financial crisis even pulled the rug out from under the businesspeople and bankers, the privileged few who had clearly benefited from the economic reform. The devaluation spread discontent into every corner of society, crushed confidence, and demolished faith in the country's institutions. "With each passing day, one believes less in the possibility that there can be a change," remarked artist Gabriela Ortiz Monasterio. For the reformist option to survive, not to mention flourish, Mexicans must once again believe in the future. In the meantime, they are placing their trust in powerful, ethereal forces that have long graced and shaped their history. "Magic is the source of my stability regarding my country," said Rogelio Fuentes, an industrial designer.

The Larger Lessons of the Mexican Crisis

Mexico must reform a political system that allows presidents to manipulate public policy for their own ends

Richard Seid

Richard Seid, an American who has lived in Mexico for 23 years, writes on Mexican politics and society.

The government crackdown on the Zapatista rebels over the weekend, spurring demonstrations in Mexico City and leading many observers there to question the judgment of President Ernesto Zedillo Ponce de León, may have pushed the peso crisis off the front pages.

But the astute observation Sen. Phil Gramm (R) of Texas made before the Clinton administration's loan guarantee was announced still should be heeded.

He said that Mexico started 1994 with its bucket full but ended the year with it empty. He wondered whether or not the administration had considered where the holes were before committing more funds to an obviously leaky bucket.

I am not saying that short-term assistance to Mexico isn't necessary right now; it is. But the United States must be careful not to prop up an outmoded political system that contributes to Mexico's continual economic crises. The main "hole" is the inflexible, almost-dictatorial powers wielded by Mexican presidents.

The blame for Mexico's financial crisis has centered on former President Carlos Salinas de Gortari. What the finger-pointing shows is frustration with presidentialism gone wrong. The accusations, including the threat of a trial, charge that Mr. Salinas used his extraordinary powers as chief executive for personal gain and against the best interests of the Mexican people. Specifically, Salinas is said to have improperly depleted Mexico's dollar reserves in 1994 from approximately $30 billion to less than $7 billion in a futile attempt to defend an overvalued peso. Why? So that his image as author of the "Salinas economic miracle" would remain untarnished at the end of his presidential term last Dec. 1 and he could be elected head of the new World Trade Organization.

Unfortunately, for a Mexican president to manipulate public policy for his own private ends and ego is nothing new. Almost 20 years ago, in November 1975, as President Luís Echeverría was nearing his last year in office, he thought it might be a nice career move to become secretary-general of the United Nations. To gain votes, he decided to join the Arabs, Communists, and many other third-world countries in backing the infamous UN resolution defining Zionism as "a form of racism." Mr. Echeverría had to have been aware that Mexico was quite dependent on tourism dollars and that a large proportion of those dollars came from Jewish tourists. Some apologists still insist that it did not occur to Echeverría that the US Jewish community might be so upset that they would boycott Mexican resorts. The consequent damage to Mexico was horrendous. We were in Acapulco the following month and the usually bustling resort was practically dead at what should have been the height of the season. The embarrassment, from hotel managers to shopkeepers, was impressive. Never have we seen more gold Stars of David displayed on the shelves.

The tragedy is that nobody will tell a Mexican president that he is hurting the country until after the fact. Even when a president isn't acting for personal gain, the system of unilateral decisionmaking often leads to wrong, foolish, policy.

President José López Portillo followed Echeverría. The first years of his administration were euphoric, given the news that untold reserves of petroleum had been recently discovered. The mood was so giddy that Mr. López Portillo crowed about how Mexico would spend its riches—and borrowed from first-world institutions all too eager to lend.

Then, oil prices started to fall. The head of Mexico's petroleum monopoly, Pemex, prepared to lower Mexico's rates accordingly. "No," López Portillo cried, "Mexico will not reduce its prices!" Of course, Mexico eventually had to give in, but the delay cost it billions of dollars, and perhaps caused the innumerable devaluations that followed.

Unfortunately, there are still no checks on the authoritarian rule of Mexican presidents. President Zedillo, in partnership with the legislature, should make the necessary changes so that the hole in the bucket will be permanently repaired.

Ignorant of the real situation in Latin America, the Clinton administration and American investors stumbled

William Ratliff

William Ratliff is a senior research fellow at the Hoover Institution at Stanford University in Stanford, Calif.

Mexico's peso crisis is a warning to the Clinton administration and Americans in

Reprinted from *The Christian Science Monitor*, February 13, 1995, 0. 18. © 1994 Richard Seid and William Ratliff.

general to take Latin America more seriously.

The danger is that we may use this crisis as an excuse to write off much of Latin America altogether. If we do, we will pay a high price for our provincialism.

The United States today has an enormous and growing economic, political, and human stake in Latin America. However, our knowledge of this region, which is undergoing its most profound change in five centuries, is superficial.

This superficiality is evident in the White House and Congress, in most investment firms, and among Americans generally. It contributed to the current crisis and will bring even more trouble in the future.

In recent years, frustration with lack of development in Latin America was replaced by a mindless euphoria and a propaganda snow-job about the future. For example, the North American Free Trade Agreement (NAFTA), an essential instrument of change, was shamelessly oversold by supporters. Early reforms led naive and overzealous investors to believe that Latin economies were suddenly good for safe, easy, and endless profits.

Thus, US ties increased exponentially through direct investments by millions of Americans in Mexican telephones, Argentine petroleum, and Chilean wines, and by investments in Latin stock markets, especially through mutual funds.

But the Chiapas rebellion in Mexico in January 1994 reminded us that change must benefit everyone. Now the peso crisis has shown that leaders generally on the right path can still make serious mistakes—through inexperience or playing politics—that hurt their own people and investors while casting a shadow over their country's free-market revolution.

Many Americans have looked on South America as simply other southern provinces of Mexico. When the peso crisis hit, and their investment portfolios were flattened, they panicked. The Mexican crisis became a warning about what they thought would happen in all of latin America.

The responsibility for this US attitude falls partly on a Clinton administration that has allowed itself and Americans to get distracted by side issues, such as Haiti. If the president had devoted as much time to conscientiously developing former President Bush's hemispheric free-trade plan as he has to Haiti, every country in the hemisphere would have been better off today. The current crisis might have been averted, or at least softened.

Ironically, the Summit of the Americas in Miami last December demonstrated the Clinton administration's lack of interest in Latin America. During the year between when it offered invitations and the summit, the White House largely ignored the event and the region. In the end, frantic to find something concrete to accomplish in Miami, Clinton decided to invite Chile to Join NAFTA. But if he had really been interested in the region, he would have issued that invitation a year ago—Chile has long had the strongest economy in Latin America.

From Argentina to Mexico, reform-minded officials complain of a lack of US support for the basic reforms that are central to successful political and economic change. They note that increasingly petty US protectionism reflects true US policy better than speeches lauding free trade. Legitimate US objectives, such as securing intellectual property rights, are often pursued with much subtlety.

Finally, some policies the US does push, like dragging Latin military forces into the drug war, alienate Latin leaders and breed corruption while leaving untouched the basic and more politically volatile problem of demand for drugs in the US.

The Clinton administration has offered help in stabilizing the peso. But it must continue with a more informed and constructive role in the region. Investors who invest knowledgeably and for the long term in Latin America can make profits for themselves and help create more vibrant economies that in turn become markets for US exports.

"As a result of its economic marginalization and relatively feeble attempted [economic] reform, Africa is in many respects lost between state and market. It wanders between ineffective states and weak markets, both domestic and international, and the latter are increasingly indifferent."

Africa: Falling Off the Map?

THOMAS M. CALLAGHY

THOMAS M. CALLAGHY *is an associate professor of political science at the University of Pennsylvania; he is coeditor, with John Ravenhill, of* Hemmed In: Responses to Africa's Economic Decline *(New York: Columbia University Press, 1993). This article is a revised and updated version of a chapter in* Africa in World Politics, *2d edition, edited by John Harbeson and Donald Rothchild (Boulder, Colo.: Westview Press, paperback, 1994; cloth, 1995), and appears by permission.*

In the mid-nineteenth century, after the end of the slave trade and before the imposition of direct colonial domination, Africa found itself both marginalized from the world economy and highly dependent on it. A leading historian of Africa has pointed out this paradox, and noted that it operated in the opposite direction as well: the world's "increasing involvement in the African economy. . .[was] at odds with the decreasing economic importance of Africa" for the world economy.[1] At the end of the twentieth century, this paradox still holds; in fact, it is truer now than it was in the pre-colonial period.

Africa's increased marginalization has been both economic and political-strategic, but the former is most significant. Africa is no longer very important to the international division of labor or to the major actors in the world economy—multinational corporations, international banks, the economies of the major Western countries or those of the newly industrializing countries such as South Korea, Taiwan, Brazil, and Mexico. Africa generates a declining share of world output. The main commodities it produces are becoming less sought after or are more effectively produced by other ʰⁱʳd world countries. Trade is declining, nobody

wants to lend, and few want to invest except in selected parts of the mineral sector.

Africa's per capita income levels and growth rates have declined since the first oil crisis in 1973, while its percentage of worldwide official development assistance rose from 17 percent in 1970 to about 38 percent in 1991. Since 1970, nominal gross domestic product has risen more slowly than in other developing countries, while real GDP growth rates have dropped dramatically since 1965.

Other developing countries performed better in spite of the poor world economic climate, especially in the 1980s. For the period 1982–1992, average annual GDP growth for Africa was 2 percent; for South Asia, the most comparable region, it was a little over 5 percent, while the East Asian rate was 8 percent. The rate for all developing countries was 2.7 percent. The per capita GDP rates are even more revealing: Africa, 1 percent; South Asia, 3 percent; and East Asia, 6.4 percent. The World Bank's baseline projections for the decade beginning in 1992 are more optimistic, projecting annual GDP growth of 3.7 percent for Africa, but the bank's estimates for Africa have often proved overly hopeful, and the assumptions of the current forecast are startling. They assume less unfavorable external conditions, including a break in falling commodity prices; more liberalized world trade regimes; and no real decline in the growth of industrial countries; less civil strife; improvement in economic policies and implementation; a higher percentage of foreign investment; the continuation of current foreign aid; and no major adverse weather! The forecast does, however, anticipate a 50 percent rise in the number of poor people, from 200 million to 300 million, making Africa the only region in the world with an overall increase in poverty.

In addition, African export levels have stayed relatively flat or have actually declined since 1970, while

---

[1]Ralph Austen, *African Economic History* (London: James Currey, 1987), pp. 102, 109. In this article, Africa means sub-Saharan Africa minus South Africa.

From *Current History* magazine, 80th Anniversary Issue, January 1994, pp. 31-36. From *Africa in World Politics,* 2d edition, edited by John Harbeson and Donald Rothchild, 1995. © 1995 by Westview Press, Boulder, Colorado. Reprinted by permission.

those of other developing countries have risen significantly. For example, the continent's share of developing-country agricultural exports slumped from 17 percent to 8 percent between 1970 and 1990, with South and East Asian exports expanding rapidly. Africa's marginalization becomes more startling when its performance is compared with that of other low income regions, particularly South Asia. The difference between the two is striking for per capita GDP growth; Africa's has slipped markedly while that of South Asia has climbed slowly but steadily as the African population growth rate continues to rise while that of South Asia has begun to decline.

The most important differences, however, relate to the level and quality of investment. Africa's investment as a percentage of GDP declined in the 1980s, while that of South Asia continued to increase despite the difficult economic conditions of the decade. South Asia followed better economic policies, and above all provided a much more propitious socioeconomic and political environment for investment. This is most vividly manifested in the rate of return on investment: in Africa, the rate fell from almost 31 percent in the 1960s to just 2.5 percent in the 1980s, while in South Asia it inched steadily upward, from 21.3 percent to 22.4 percent.

Given this dismal economic performance, both substantively and comparatively, it is not surprising that world business leaders take an increasingly jaundiced view of Africa. As one business executive said to this author, "Who cares about Africa; it is not important to us; leave it to the IMF [International Monetary Fund] and the World Bank." Some observers have referred to this phenomenon as "postneocolonialism." For the most dynamic actors in a rapidly changing world economy, even a neocolonial Africa is not of much interest anymore, especially after the amazing changes wrought in Eastern Europe and elsewhere beginning in 1989. According to this viewpoint, the African crisis really should be left to the international financial institutions, and if their salvage effort works, fine; if not, so be it, the world economy will hardly notice.

Thus, whatever one thinks about the role of foreign business and capital, it is important to remember that Africa increasingly imposes enormous difficulties for them, such as political arbitrariness and administrative, infrastructural, and economic inefficiency. Because foreign capital has the considerable ability to select the type of state with which it cooperates, it is very doubtful that Africa will play any significant role in current shifts in the patterns of production in the international division of labor. For most businesspeople from abroad Africa has become a sinkhole that swallows their money with little or no return. Two arresting facts further underscore Africa's marginalization: the amount of external financing through bonds for East

Asia in 1991 was $2.4 billion, and for South Asia $1.9 billion, while it was zero for Africa; and flight capital as a percentage of GDP at the end of 1990 was 15 for South Asia, 19 for East Asia, and 28 for developing Europe and for Central Asia, while it was 80 for Africa.

Disinvestment, in fact, has emerged as a trend. During the 1980s, for example, 43 of 139 British firms with industrial investments in Africa withdrew. Ironically, the retrenchment has in part been due to economic reforms that have done away with overvalued exchange rates and import tariff protection. The British firms were unwilling to inject new capital to make their investments efficient by world standards of competitiveness. While Japan is now the major donor, it is not likely to be a major investor in Africa; in the 1980s, for example, the number of Japanese commercial companies operating in Kenya dwindled from 15 to 2.

The second aspect of Africa's marginalization is at the strategic level, which has also had negative economic consequences. Africa has become of much less interest to the major world powers with the dramatic changes in the international arena, especially the end of the cold war. As one senior African diplomat put it, "Eastern Europe is the most sexy beautiful girl, and we are an old tattered lady. People are tired of Africa. So many countries, so many wars." The rise of warlords in regional and civil wars similar to those in nineteenth-century Africa has challenged the very notion of the nation-state borrowed at independence in the 1960s. Eritrea's independence from Ethiopia, made official last year, and the potential breakup of countries such as Zaire, raise the potentially inflammatory issue of redrawing old colonial boundaries sacrosanct for 30 years. External intervention on the scale seen in Somalia recently is not likely to be repeated; the malign neglect applied to the greater Liberian, Angolan, and Sudanese civil wars is likely to be the more common reaction to such conflicts.

THE NEW NEOCOLONIALISM

Yet in other ways Africa has become more tightly linked to the world economy. This increased involvement has two aspects: an extreme dependence on public actors from outside Africa, particularly the IMF and the World Bank, in the determination of African economic policy; and the liberal or neoclassical thrust of the policy so developed, which pushes the continent toward more intense reliance on and integration with the world economy. Both these aspects are directly linked to Africa's debt crisis.

In 1974 total African debt was about $14.8 billion; by 1992 it had reached an estimated $183.4 billion, or about 109 percent of Africa's total GNP. (In comparison, in South Asia it was 36 percent, and in East Asia 28 percent.) Much of the recent rise has come through borrowing from international financial institutions, especially the IMF and the World Bank, that has been associated with economic reform programs sponsored from outside, usually referred to as structural adjustment. In 1980 debt through international financial institutions constituted 19 percent of the total, whereas by 1992 it accounted for 28 percent. This cannot be rescheduled and significant arrears are accumulating, with the result that IMF and World Bank assistance to some countries has been cut off. Much of the rest of Africa's debt is bilateral or government-guaranteed private medium- and long-term debt and thus is rescheduled by leading Western governments through the Paris Club, and not by the private banks as in Latin America. Countries cannot obtain Paris Club rescheduling relief without being in the good graces of the IMF and the World Bank.

Despite its relative smallness by world standards, the enormous buildup of African debt puts terrible strains on fragile economies. By the end of the 1980s the debt was the equivalent of 350 percent of exports. Africa's debt service ratio (debt service owed as a percentage of export earnings) averaged a little less than 30 percent by the mid-1980s. By 1992 it still averaged more than 25 percent, with some African countries showing much higher rates; Uganda's, for example, was 80 percent. The debt service ratios would be significantly lower, however, if African export growth had kept pace with the performance of other less developed countries. Only about half of debt service owed is paid in any given year, which tends to dampen foreign direct investment.

Given such debt, African countries have benefited from rescheduling concessions such as longer terms and grace periods, lower interest rates, and the rescheduling of previously rescheduled debt. Between 1989 and 1991, about $10 billion in concessional debt, especially that incurred by the continent's low-income nations, was written off by Western countries, including the initially unwilling United States. Despite strong pressure from the IMF, the World Bank, various UN agencies, and private organizations such as Oxfam, most of the major donor countries are still resisting significant debt cancellation.

As in other areas of the third world, this external debt burden and the consequent desperate need for foreign exchange have left African countries highly dependent on a variety of actors from outside the continent, all of which have used their leverage to "encourage" economic liberalization. This process, which some have referred to as "the new neocolonialism," means intense dependence on international financial institutions and major Western countries for the design of economic reform packages and for the resources needed to implement them. Specific economic policy changes are requested in return for the lending of resources. The primary intent of these economic reform efforts is to more fully integrate African economies into the world economy by resurrecting the primary-product export economies that existed at independence and making them work better this time by creating a more "liberal" political economy.

The track record of IMF and World Bank economic reform in Africa since the early 1980s has been quite modest. Ghana under the authoritarian military government of Jerry Rawlings has been about the only case of sustained economic transformation, and it is still fragile. Even African countries that traditionally did relatively well economically in the postcolonial period are now in considerable trouble—Nigeria, Kenya, Ivory Coast, Cameroon, and Senegal have grave economic problems and weak or failed economic reform efforts.

As a result of its economic marginalization and relatively feeble reform efforts, Africa is in many respects lost between state and market. It wanders between ineffective states and weak markets, both domestic and international, and the latter are increasingly indifferent. Many African officials fail to realize just how unimportant Africa is becoming to the world economy. Many are still looking for a quick fix, while the last decade of world history shows that one does not exist. If African countries are to survive, changes must be made. If not, changes in the world political economy will continue to pass Africa by, with very serious long-term consequences for the people of the continent.

DEBATING WHAT TO DO

By the end of the 1980s, with obstacles to reform on all sides, the key question remained: what should Africa do to cope with its devastating economic crisis? The answer from outside, led by the World Bank, was to persevere with the thrust of reforms while making modifications to make them work more effectively. Many Africans remained unconvinced. This fundamental disagreement had simmered quietly throughout the decade behind what appeared to many as a growing consensus around a modified neo-orthodox position.

This disagreement erupted with surprising vigor in what could be called "the bloody spring of 1989." A major battle ensued between the World Bank and the UN's Economic Commission for Africa (ECA) as the former tried to defend structural adjustment and the latter attack it and present its own alternative strategy. Both sides made inappropriate claims. The record of structural adjustment was not nearly as strong as the World Bank tried to make it appear. On the African side, the ECA's "alternative framework" was a warmed-over version of earlier statist and "self-reliant" policies that were vague, often contradictory, and could not be implemented under the best of conditions—all linked to staggering demands for money and other resources. Many Africans were still running from the world economy while looking for a shortcut to development.

By late 1989 the visceral emotions of the bloody spring had been substantially tamed, though without resolution of many of the underlying disagreements. One of the main pacifying factors was the World Bank's release of its long-awaited "long-term perspective study," *Sub-Saharan Africa: From Crisis to Sustainable Growth,* which had been drafted following extensive consultation with Africans—from government officials and entrepreneurs in both the formal and informal economies to the heads of African private volunteer organizations. The report demonstrated that the World Bank had learned many lessons from the attempts at structural adjustment in the 1980s, especially the desperate need for institutional change and for a slower, more sequenced transition that recognized the sociopolitical obstacles to change. Its major themes were that Africa requires an enabling environment—above all, technical and administrative capacity (both state and private) and better political governance.

The report sought a second-generation development strategy in which the state listens carefully to the market even if it does not precisely follow it. Although not put in these terms, this strategy would attempt a move away from the predatory and inefficient mercantilism of the first 30 years of independence and back toward a more productive and efficient, though limited, version of what some have called "benign mercantilism"—that is, toward a more productive tension between state and market.

From the African point of view, this second-generation strategy is clearly a second-best one. But critics of structural adjustment, both inside and outside Africa, do not have a viable alternative to this modified version of neo-orthodoxy. The current African state does not have the capabilities for the more interventionist versions of benign mercantilism represented by South Korea and Taiwan. Governments can, and should, work in that direction, but the transition will be slow and uneven.

Creative tinkering with the neo-orthodox strategy by both African governments and the IMF and World Bank could begin to move the continent in useful directions. The long-term perspective study seemed to represent a step down that road. Ultimately it is not just a question of finding the "precarious balance" between state and market or state and society, but rather of searching for the balance between state, market, and the international arena.

This author would argue that the debate was reignited because many of the nice-sounding "lessons" of *From Crisis to Sustainable Growth,* which were meant to placate a variety of critics, have either been very difficult to implement or the IMF and the World Bank have simply not tried to do so seriously. Largely this is because structural adjustment requires difficult tradeoffs that most opponents refuse to face squarely. Structural adjustment cannot be all things to all people; if it could, there would be no crisis.

DEMOCRACY AND ECONOMY

The three-way balance between state, market, and the international arena has proved hard to achieve. In part this is because the international arena has a habit of presenting new and unexpected challenges for African rulers. While *From Crisis to Sustainable Growth* was initially well received by many Africans, it contained a time bomb called governance—the issue of how African states are ruled—which has brought considerable new tension and uncertainty to relations between Africans and influential groups from outside, and to economic policy.

With the shifts in the world since 1989, especially in Eastern Europe but also in Central America and South Africa, and the search for a new direction in foreign policy to replace containment—what the Clinton administration has recently called "enlargement" of the world's free community of market democracies—governance has been transformed by the major Western industrial democracies into a strategy for the promotion of democracy. The convergence of these two policy thrusts—one largely technocratic from the World Bank, the other distinctly political from the major powers—has posed a real dilemma for Africa.

Political conditionality, or making bilateral assistance and loans from international financial institutions conditional on domestic political changes, greatly increases African dependence on outside actors. Many African leaders fear this, including a few who are committed to economic reform. Guinea's finance minister, Soriba Kaba, for example, recently complained about the proliferation of conditions that African regimes have to face, "especially relating to governance and performance," saying that "application of these criteria, without agreed parameters and precise definitions, may be used as a pretext to reduce the volume of resource flows to our continent."[2] Some leaders resist energetically, such as Zaire's Mobutu Sese Seko; others, such as Kenya's Daniel arap Moi and Cameroon's Paul Biya, stall while playing charades with critics both inside and outside their countries.

However, a major contradiction may indeed exist between economic and political conditionality, one that Western governments either do not see or ignore. The primary assumptions appear to be that economic structural adjustment and political liberalization are mutually reinforcing processes, and that since authoritarian politics in large part caused the economic malaise, democratic politics can help lift it. Yet evidence from the second and third worlds over the last decade does not support such optimism. This is not to

---

[2]Cited in "The IMF and the World Bank: Arguing about Africa," *Africa Confidential,* vol. 34, no. 20 (October 8, 1993), p. 3.

say that authoritarian regimes can guarantee economic reform or even produce it very often. Nor is it to say that economic reform under democratic conditions is impossible; it is just very difficult.

Presumptions about the mutually reinforcing nature of political and economic reform in Africa rely on an extension of neoclassical economic logic: economic liberalization creates sustained growth, growth produces winners as well as losers, winners will organize to defend their newfound welfare and create sociopolitical coalitions to support continued economic reform. This logic, however, does not appear to hold for Africa, even under authoritarian conditions, much less under democratic ones.

The winners of economic reform in Africa are few, appear only slowly over time, and are hard to organize politically. The neoclassical political logic of reform is too mechanistic for Africa; there are real "transaction costs" to organizing winners, and not just infrastructural ones. Other organizational bases of political solidarity exist—ethnic, regional, religious, linguistic, and patron-client—that make mobilization around policy-specific economic interests difficult in much of Africa.

Some have argued that Africa does not have a democratic tradition, but in fact it has a vivid one, although its day was brief and ended in failure, and the reasons for its demise have not disappeared. The periodic reemergence of democratic regimes in Ghana and Nigeria over the last two decades indicates that old patterns of politics reappear with amazing vigor; political liberalization is not likely to guarantee the appearance of new political alignments that favor sustained economic reform.

The progress of democratization in Africa has been very uneven. Outside actors tried political conditionality in Kenya only to have it undermined by the maneuvering of the Moi government and the inability of the opposition to come up with a single presidential candidate and slate of legislators. In Zambia, where a full transition did take place in late 1992, the new government of Frederick Chiluba has been confronted with political factionalism, renewed corruption, ethnic and regional tension, and uneven economic performance, despite good intentions and help from abroad.

Is this version of the "thesis of the perverse effect"— that political liberalization might have a negative impact on the chances for sustained economic reform— likely to hold across the board for Africa? No, it is not. It is important to assess particular countries. But if not handled properly, political conditionality might well impede rather than facilitate Africa's relinking to the world economy in more productive ways. The widespread emergence of what UCLA professor Richard Sklar has called "developmental democracies" is not likely in Africa any time soon.

Finally, the actions of Western governments in other areas of the world will be important. Many Africans, for example, are likely to see recent support for Russian President Boris Yeltsin's accumulation of executive power and manipulation of constitutional and electoral practices, largely in the hope of getting more coherent economic reform, as highly hypocritical: one standard for strategically important Russia and another for marginal and dependent Africa.

ENDING AS THEY BEGAN

With or without political conditionality, what are the prospects that African countries will engage successfully in economic reform and establish more a productive relationship with the world economy? The answer appears to be that simultaneous marginalization and dependence are likely to continue, and probably increase, for most countries. A few, with hard work, propitious circumstances, and luck, may begin to improve their situation. Differentiation among African states, long evident, may well increase; a few countries will stay in the third world and do relatively better economically, while most will continue to descend. The countries likely to do better are those that are already more advantaged, partly because of better performance over the last 30 years: Kenya, Ivory Coast, Cameroon, Nigeria, Zimbabwe, and possibly Senegal. As noted above, however, even these cases are now fragile, largely for political reasons. A handful of countries in serious decline, such as Ghana, may be able to reverse course, but chances for this are even more tenuous.

A quiet debate is under way among Western officials and business executives about what to do with Africa. Should they provide some resources to all countries to create a sort of international social safety net for declining countries, which then become de facto wards of the world community, or should they "pick a few and work with them," as one Western official has put it? With the first option, it is not at all clear how effective such an international safety net would be, as the recent intervention in Somalia has shown. With the second option, resources would be concentrated in countries that have some good prospects for sustained economic performance, and possibly some strategic importance—Nigeria and Zimbabwe, for example. This is a delicate political task, however, and the recent performance of both of these countries might give one considerable pause.

The trajectory of individual countries will be affected by both internal and external factors. On the internal side, the degree of effective "stateness"—the technical and administrative capabilities to formulate and implement rational economic policies—will be crucial. On average, Africa has the lowest level of state capabilities of any region in the world. As the IMF and the World Bank have begun to realize, it takes a relatively capable state to implement their neo-orthodox economic reform consistently over time. To sustain a solid base in the international political economy, a country needs a high degree of "stateness," including the crucial ability to bargain with all types—private business groups, states, and the international financial institutions. Whether "stateness" will emerge or increase in many places, however, is questionable; certainly political dynamics will play a vital role in arriving at a productive balanced tension between state and market and between state and society. Some African leaders, such as Jerry Rawlings in Ghana, have begun to understand this.

Although it is largely a self-help world, external factors are also very important. They revolve around two central issues. First is the degree of openness of the world political economy. Second is the degree to which both sides fulfill their part of the "implicit bargain" between international financial institutions and the major Western countries and Africans: if African countries successfully reform their economies with the help and direction of the IMF and the World Bank, then new international private bank lending and direct foreign investment will be made available.

John Ruggie has characterized the current international political economy as one of "embedded liberalism," in which the major Western countries intervene in their domestic economies to buffer the costs of adjusting to shifts in the world economy. A precarious openness, based on liberal economic norms, is maintained, despite increasing tensions. Others, such as Robert Gilpin, see the world moving toward an increasingly conflictual and closed international political economy, which might be characterized as "malign mercantilism." Africa's prospects would not be very bright under a shift from embedded liberalism to malign mercantilism by the major Western powers. Despite its marginalization and dependence, Africa desperately needs openness in the world economy; in fact, the neo-orthodox adjustment strategy is predicated on it. Whether some form of benign mercantilism would benefit Africa is also open to question.

Chances for fulfillment of the "implicit bargain" may not be much better, however. Because private actors in the world economy increasingly pass Africa by, Western countries and the international financial institutions will continue to play central roles. If African countries are to have any hope of making economic progress, these actors must help to fulfill this bargain, primarily through increased aid levels and substantial debt relief. Given the domestic politics of Western industrial democracies, debt relief might be the easier route to take, since it is more politically malleable. But major debt relief has not occurred, and there are signs that aid levels may decline as these Western countries become increasingly preoccupied with domestic problems and those of more important regions.

Because resources are scarce, aid and debt relief should be given only to those actually undertaking difficult economic reforms and without being tied automatically to political change. The Jerry Rawlingses of Africa should be supported; nonreforming leaders should not. It is not clear, however, how many leaders like Rawlings actors outside Africa can actually support at the level required for sustained economic change. Since such reform is difficult, stop-and-go cycles are a fact of life, and external actors need to learn to adjust to them more effectively. The primary obstacle is how to cope with a huge debt and substantial arrears to the IMF and the World Bank without setting precedents with worldwide implications.

Finally, given the enormous obstacles confronting African countries, undue optimism and inflated expectations about what is possible in Africa can be dangerous. Slow, steady, consistent progress is preferable. Neither international nor African policymakers can unduly hasten, control, or speed up social processes such as institution and capacity building. Change is incremental, uneven, often contradictory, and dependent on the outcome of unpredictable socioeconomic and political struggles. Policymakers must try to bring about important changes, but they need to retain a sense of the historical complexity involved. Today's policy fads can easily become tomorrow's failed initiatives.

Africa really is caught between a rock and a hard place when it comes to the world economy and the international state system, and all will have to work extremely hard to alter this fact. Although pessimism about Africa is appropriate analytically, try they must, for not trying to keep Africa from falling off the map could have even worse consequences for its long-suffering peoples.

Why Is Africa Eating Asia's Dust?

While one scrambles toward development, the other slips into despair

Keith B. Richburg

Washington Post Foreign Service

NAIROBI—Ugandan President Yoweri Museveni is a thoughtful, analytical man who often takes on a professorial tone when discussing Africa's myriad problems. So he seemed uncharacteristically at a loss when asked at a recent news conference: Why has African development lagged so far behind that of East Asia, a region that suffered from a somewhat similar set of obstacles?

After offering several well-explored explanations, he paused and admitted some hesitancy to go further. Finally, he said what seemed most on his mind: "The discipline of Asians compared to Africans." People from East Asian countries with scarce resources and large populations "may tend to be more disciplined than people who take life for granted," he said. Some Africans, he intoned, "have so much land that they don't know what to do with it."

It is an explanation heard time and again to a question that fascinates and perplexes anyone who has spent time in both Africa and East Asia. Why has East Asia over the past two decades become a model of economic success, while Africa, since independence, has seen largely failure—increasing poverty, hunger and economies propped up by foreign aid? Is it largely a matter of discipline, as Museveni suggests, or are other factors at work?

There was nothing innate in the peoples of East Asia and Africa that made this outcome inevitable. In 1957, Ghana—one of the bright hopes of black Africa—had a higher gross national product than South Korea, then emerging from a devastating war. Now South Korea is a newly industrialized country—one of the "four dragons" of Southeast Asia. Ghana, meanwhile, has actually slid backwards; its gross national product is lower than it was at independence. It is fair to ask, what happened?

For four years, from 1986 until late 1990, I traveled throughout Southeast Asia as a Washington Post correspondent, seeing firsthand the economic dynamism of a region that has been largely defined by its successful growth and development. Some countries—Singapore, Malaysia and Indonesia—emerged just as Africa did from under colonial tutelage. Singapore became independent as a tiny city-state, with no natural resources. Indonesia and Malaysia at independence were as divided, along ethnic, religious and linguistic lines, as many African countries are today. Thailand, which was never colonized, was a front-line state for the Indochina wars of the late 1960s and was beset by its own Communist insurgency.

Yet from these uncertain beginnings, Southeast Asian nations have prospered. Their average growth rates for the 1980s measured between 8 percent and 10 percent. They avoided the pitfall of heavy external debt through deft management of their economies. And they have successfully diversified away from reliance on single commodity exports, making them less vulnerable to world market price shocks.

There are, of course, examples in East Asia of nonprospering countries, such as Cambodia, Vietnam and Laos—all of which opted for a Communist path and were wracked by lengthy wars. And the Philippines—once the most prosperous country in East Asia—was ravaged by 20 years of authoritarian rule by Ferdinand Marcos.

Moving last year to sub-Saharan Africa, I found a continent in a dismal state of disrepair. From the statistics and the background briefings, one expects to find Africa underdeveloped; the surprise is discovering just how underdeveloped it is. Africa has most of the world's poorest nations. Its children are most likely to die before the age of 5. Its adults are least likely to live beyond the age 50. Africans are, on the whole, more malnourished, less educated and more likely to be afflicted by fatal diseases than any other people on earth.

Any Asia-Africa comparison must allow for many important differences. Although the two continents became independent at roughly the same time, they didn't begin the economic race at the same starting point. East Asian

ECONOMIC DISPARITY

A generation ago, Nigeria's gross national product and exports topped those of South Korea, Malaysia and Thailand. Today, however, Nigeria lags behind its Asian counterparts.

Nigeria is not atypical. In Ghana, Kenya, Tanzania and Zaire as well, per capita gross national product has declined over the past decade even as it has increased steadily in Asia's Little Dragons.

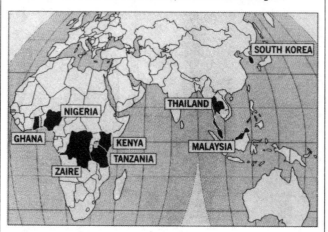

PER CAPITA GROSS NATIONAL PRODUCT
IN THOUSANDS OF U.S. DOLLARS

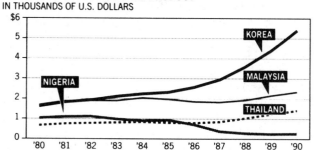

GROSS NATIONAL PRODUCT
IN BILLIONS OF U.S. DOLLARS

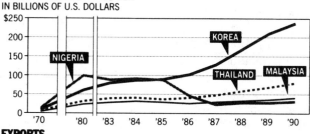

EXPORTS
IN BILLIONS OF U.S. DOLLARS

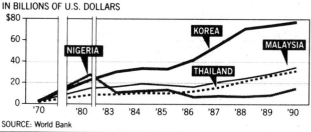

SOURCE: World Bank

push from the West. In the years since independence, they have received far more Western and Japanese investment. And East Asia, unlike Africa, did not have to spend its early post-colonial years recovering from the physical and psychological trauma associated with three centuries of slavery.

What follows is not a detailed statistical comparison; it is rather a set of interviews and impressions gathered by a reporter who has lived in both places. For the past seven months, I have lived in Kenya and traveled to seven other countries of this troubled continent. One, Somalia, has in fact ceased to be a functioning country, divided as it is between armed warring clans and now in a state of anarchy. Zaire and Malawi are reeling under repressive dictatorships—and in Zaire, years of corruption and neglect have brought the official economy to collapse. Ethiopia and Uganda are struggling to emerge from the shadow of decades of ethnic conflict and dictatorial repression that have driven the economies of both those countries into the ground.

Tanzania in many ways is the saddest, because it has enjoyed 30 years of peace and considerable foreign assistance, but its economy has been ravaged by years of socialist mismanagement. Dar es Salaam, its capital, is in a worse state of disrepair than Hanoi; the road system has collapsed, telephones do not work, electricity is sporadic, its store shelves are bare. Tanzania remains, by many estimates, the third-poorest place on earth.

Kenya and Nigeria, along with Ghana, represented hope in sub-Saharan Africa. But neither has realized its potential. Both have seen their economic advances canceled out by debilitating corruption. Nigeria has often been compared to Indonesia—big, diverse and oil-rich. But where Indonesia managed the oil boom of the 1970s successfully, and has begun to diversify away from its dependence on oil, Nigeria used the boom years to borrow heavily, creating a debt burden that today constrains government action. And Nigeria, unlike Indonesia, remains dependent on oil for 95 percent of its export earnings and 80 percent of its budget receipts.

These resource-rich African countries need not have emerged as basket cases. And Tanzania and Malawi have had ample opportunities to develop through foreign assistance.

Foreign reporters often are criticized for not reporting more "good news" from Africa. There seems a simple reason for that: So much of what happens here is so bad. In East Asia, the stories are largely about economic growth. But in Africa, the issues are more basic. Thirty years after independence, Africans are still trying to learn how to live together in civil societies and how to forge a sense of national identity inside the artificial boundaries of their nation-states.

The continent today is on the economic sidelines. It accounts for a mere pittance of the world's trade. Its share of world markets has fallen by half since the 1970s.

economies had a substantial head start; they had developed elaborate patterns of trade and development long before the European colonists arrived. The East Asians, in addition to starting out ahead, also have had a stronger

African trade accounts for less than 0.1 percent of North American imports.

How did Africa reach this current predicament? And what lessons, if any, does the East Asian success hold for this troubled region?

Africans themselves, when asked the questions, often point to a familiar list of reasons: the legacy of colonialism; the problem of having diverse ethnic groups within national boundaries; the long-running East–West conflict that constrained Africa's independent decision-making; small countries with fragmented markets; widespread corruption of Africa's ruling elite; and now, more recently, the lack of popular participation in governance. "There is absolutely no way you can achieve economic development without democracy," said Museveni.

Yet many of the East Asian nations also have had to contend with these problems. East Asia, more than Africa, became a playing field for the East–West rivalry. Some of East Asia's most economically successful countries—Thailand, Malaysia and Indonesia, for example—are notoriously corrupt. And precious few East Asian countries can be called democratic, as evidenced by the recent protests in Thailand against the military's continued domination of politics.

An answer, then, would seem to lie deeper. It may be found in the respective patterns of colonialism, in the economic choices pursued and in the differences in the post-independence leadership that emerged in East Asia and Africa. And, as Museveni suggests, it may also be a question of differing cultural traditions.

At a restaurant in Washington last year, a diplomat from the Embassy of Cameroon was explaining to a reporter the problem of Africa's black elite. Go to the cafes and the bistros, he said. See them in their European suits, reading the latest editions of European newspapers. The problem of African development, he said, is that the educated elite have never developed indigenous models, but instead have tried to transplant Europe to Africa.

It doesn't take long in Africa to see what the diplomat was talking about. Basil Davidson, a renowned British scholar on Africa, writes in his new book "The Black Man's Burden" how European colonialism in Africa set out to deny and eventually eliminate the continent's precolonial history. And in that, the Europeans found willing accomplices among Africa's European-oriented elite, the "modernizers," who were in constant conflict with Africa's "traditionalists," including the acknowledged tribal chiefs.

These modernizing Africans clung to the notion that anything traditional was by definition primitive. And it was this elite that came to the forefront of the independence movements and proceeded to impose European models on their new African states. Rather than seek to build on tradition, as the Confucianist societies of East Asia tried to do even in their revolutionary phases, the new Africans often sought to purge what was deepest and most authentic in their cultures.

That influence can still be seen today. Judges in Kenyan courts wear white wigs and speak in a flowery, archaic English that might be considered "quaint." Governmental institutions in the former British colonies—from parliaments to the "special branch" internal security forces—are near-duplicates of their counterparts at Westminster and Whitehall. Colonial governments in Africa were dictatorships backed up by a top-heavy bureaucracy. Independence seems to have substituted black autocrats for the old white colonial governors, with little thought of Africa's traditions.

The suppression of indigenous culture has been especially pronounced in the former French colonies of West Africa, which were treated as an overseas department of France, notes Pauline Baker, an Africa specialist with the Aspen Institute. "The French tried to have black Frenchmen," she says.

After traveling through East Africa, the late Shiva Naipaul concluded in his book "North of South" that the black man's contact with the European had only succeeded in destroying African culture. "Black Africa, with its gimcrack tyrannies, its field marshals and emperors, its false philosophies, its fabricated statehoods, returns to Europe its own features," he wrote, "but grotesquely caricatured—as they might be seen in one of those distorting funhouse mirrors."

Black African leaders also point to the deleterious effects on their continent's development, heritage and traditions caused by slavery. They note that slavery robbed the continent of its brightest and most ablebodied men and women for more than 300 years, and some leaders today are going so far as to demand "reparations" from the West.

Contrast that to East Asia. A common feature of Western colonialism was that it never managed to supplant historic traditions—be it the emphasis on education, the hierarchical respect for elders, or the religious traditions of Confucianism, Buddhism and, in Indonesia and Malaysia, Islam, which had come later. Only in the Philippines did the Spanish friars succeed in converting most of the population to Roman Catholicism.

Today, a common theme of East Asian leaders is how to modernize without Westernizing, how to pick and choose the most relevant of Western technology without losing sight of their traditions. A fear commonly voiced around Asia is that encroaching Westernization threatens to erode East Asian culture. Four years ago, Singapore's deputy prime minister, Lee Hsien Loong, summed up the challenge in an interview. "If we reach the point where we all become Americanized," he said, "then that's the end of Singapore."

After independence, many of the African countries became swayed by socialism, the ideology in vogue throughout Europe at the time. Theirs became an African variety, whether dubbed "humanism" as in Zambia, or *ujamaa* in Tanzania. But even in avowedly capitalist countries such as Kenya, the result became the same: government ownership of most enterprises, and a distrust of private-sector initiative and foreign investment.

Asia found another way. Theirs was a brand of state-centered capitalism that was neither completely free enterprise nor dogmatically Marxist. The state intervened in the economy, but in a positive way, supporting "winning" corporations and settling wage disputes. East Asia also had three wars fought on its soil—World War II, Korea and Vietnam—leading the United States to offer benign trading relations to secure stable partners in its fight against Communist expansion.

In a paper examining East Asian and African responses to the global debt crisis, World Bank economist Ishrat Husain detailed how from the mid-1970s, East Asian countries adopted "outward" development policies—meaning liberal trade with low tariff barriers to imports, and realistic exchange rates that enhanced exports. This outward orientation allowed the East Asians to diversify their imports while the international competition improved the efficiency of its producers.

Africa, on the other hand, pursued "inward" economic policies, throwing up trade restrictions and maintaining overvalued currencies.

Herman Cohen, the U.S. assistant secretary for African affairs, sees another reason East Asia has largely prospered. "They did all the right things—plus land reform," he says. By privatizing land holdings, East Asian countries saw agricultural production increase, Cohen says. In Africa, land was communally owned in traditional society and expropriated by the state after independence; prices for farm products typically have been set by state marketing boards.

In comparing East Asia and Africa, it has become fashionable among those who know both regions to say the key difference is that Africa has not produced a Lee Kuan Yew. As long-time prime minister of tiny Singapore, Lee has come to personify the idea of benevolent authoritarianism, a paternalistic ruler who brooked no dissent but nonetheless guided his city-state into the ranks of East Asia's "little dragons."

Africa has had its share of towering figures. But by contrast, some of the best known—such as Tanzania's Julius Nyerere and Zambia's Kenneth Kaunda—ran their countries' economies into the ground. Africa also has produced more than its share of dictators, tyrants and buffoons—such as Uganda's Idi Amin and Jean Bedel Bokassa, who declared himself emperor and his impoverished country the Central African Empire. Zaire's Mobutu Sese Seko and Malawi's H. Kamuzu Banda cling to power through repression. In between are a host of corrupt dictators and military men who seem more intent on padding their European bank accounts than improving the lot of their impoverished peoples.

To be sure, Asia is not without its corruption. In Thailand, corrupt military officers and unscrupulous politicians are involved in a host of illegal activities. But there is a difference between corruption Asian-style and its African equivalent. In Asia, the corruption has not been as debilitating to economic growth. In fact, corruption and growth seem to run parallel.

A Western economist in Nigeria, who lived previously in Indonesia, puts it this way: "In Indonesia, the president's daughter might get the contract to build the toll roads, but the roads do get built and they do facilitate traffic flow. . . . That sort of corruption is productive corruption as opposed to malignant corruption."

In Addis Ababa, an official of the Organization of African Unity, Mamadon Bah, was explaining to a visiting reporter the problem of bringing more democracy to the continent. "What we need in Africa these days is mainly discipline," he said, "but discipline from the top."

Any discussion of cultural differences between Asians and Africans by definition treads on explosive ground, since it feeds on past racist stereotypes of Asians as hard-working and Africans as lazy.

"People work like dogs in Kenya," says Makau wa Mutua, a Kenyan exile at the Harvard University law school's human rights program. "Nobody sits around waiting for mangos to drop from trees." Referring to Museveni's comments about discipline, Mutua recalls how Kenyan President Daniel arap Moi once visited Asia and similarly came back urging Kenyans to emulate the Asian example. "As a leader, one has to talk about discipline to get people to work harder," Mutua says. "That is the stereotype of the Asian machine, that people work so hard. But I think that's pure garbage."

Still, many other Africans agree with Museveni and the OAU official that cultural factors do play a role in development. They argue that lack of discipline among African leaders is a particular problem. For even the hardest-working African has difficulty building a solid life if his country's political leadership is corrupt and undisciplined.

Pauline Baker speaks of the "five bads" that she says help explain Africa's poor record of economic development: "bad luck, bad environment, bad policy, bad government and bad faith [by Western governments that failed to deliver on expected aid and investment]." Baker says that although cultural analysis has gone out of fashion among academics, it may be appropriate to add a sixth factor—"bad outlook."

As examples of the cultural factors that enrich African life but may limit economic development, Baker cites "the role of the extended family" and "the role of tradition." In Africa, she notes, "the real obligations are blood ties to the family or tribe, rather than national ties." The extended family provides a private welfare system that helps take care of people, but it also limits the development of a middle class. The lucky entrepreneur who makes a little money finds he is expected to house, feed and educate his cousins, nieces and nephews. He is pulled back, toward family and village. It is typical, says Baker, that the first thing a newly wealthy city dweller will do with his money is build a big house back in his village.

In most of the Southeast Asian countries, discipline has been imposed from the top. Singapore's People's Action Party under Lee Kuan Yew has been highly authoritarian, micro-managing people's lives to the point of prohibiting chewing gum, using financial incentives to encourage better-educated couples to have more children and launching nationwide campaigns to encourage people to smile more. Governments in Malaysia and Indonesia, trying to forge cohesion out of diverse populations, have force-fed their people a common language policy. In all the Southeast Asian countries except the Philippines, civil liberties are sacrificed as a necessary price of stability—something Asians call the "social contract" between rulers and the ruled.

These Asian regimes draw support from cultural traditions that foster order, hierarchy and stability. The Confucian tradition, for example, is widespread throughout East Asia. It encourages a disciplined work ethic and a stable, stratified political system; it also reinforces the Asian emphasis on education, which is prized in disciplined, authoritarian societies such as Korea and China almost as a secular religion.

Africa has had its share of authoritarian regimes. But far from fostering discipline, most of them have led to chaos. Dictators who tried to enforce unity and discipline—Ethiopia's Mengistu Haile Mariam and Somalia's Mohamed Siad Barre are just two examples—were overthrown last year in bloody revolutions; other African autocrats are teetering. The single feature of African autocracies seems to be their inability to impose their will on their populations.

Even when the military tries to impose political discipline from the top down, as in Nigeria, moral discipline remains lax among the top leaders—and corruption is widespread.

On the individual level, the question of discipline is more difficult to address. No one, for example, would say that the average farmer in Tanzania or Malawi works less than his Asian counterpart. People in hard-pressed Kinshasa, Zaire, survive only by their endurance—working several jobs, selling goods on the streets. In Uganda, government offices are largely empty during the daytime, because low-paid bureaucrats are out running private businesses. In Kenya, even when no milk was available on store shelves because of government price controls, farmers with cows were busy building their own networks of urban buyers. Together, this private sector activity accounts for a disciplined economic sector often overlooked in official statistics.

Lawrence Harrison, a retired Foreign Service officer who has written two books exploring cultural values in the developing world, says he has found Confucianism to be the key ingredient in East Asian development.

"Confucius imparts to his followers a strong sense of future, the importance of education, the importance of merit, the importance of saving for future generations," he says. "All of those things in an economic sense are things that you don't associate with the African culture."

But some African leaders are beginning to express similar themes in their own terms. As Museveni put it recently in Kampala, Uganda, this is the time "for the people of Africa to take their destiny in their own hands."

South Africa's Change, Mandela's Challenge

Thomas R. Lansner

Thomas R. Lansner was an international election observer in South Africa and is an advisor on election and human rights issues to the democratic opposition in Gabon.

Optimists must take South Africa's April election as a toweringly good omen for that country's future. Despite considerable confusion, intermittent ineptitude, instances of sabotage and a spate of terror attacks, the electoral process worked well enough to sanction the democratic transfer of power to Nelson Mandela's African National Congress from the long-dominant National Party.

Election success

On 27-30 April, people lined up patiently, sometimes for many hours and usually in good humor, to cast their ballots. Overall, throughout the country, the bloody violence that has so wounded South Africa's transition from apartheid took a

> **As a political exercise measuring the spirit of consensus and compromise, then, these elections bode well for South Africa's ability to negotiate a difficult future.**

holiday. And when white extremists launched a terror campaign that killed over twenty people in several bombings, the security forces demonstrated a welcome loyalty to black majority rule by quickly rounding up the plotters.

The turnout of nearly 20 million voters—most of them black Africans voting for the first time—was immensely encouraging. Serpentine queues at voting stations spoke not only of hitches in administration, but of the huge and highly successful voter education campaign that saturated the country's media for months before the election and helped bring people to the polls. Even the South African Police sought to establish a newly neutral role, promising a quick response in flyers that asked, "Are You Being Threatened or Intimidated in Any Way?"

Perhaps most significant was the large-scale participation through every phase of the electoral process by South Africans of every race. From voter education to political party work to voting stations and counting center officials, hundreds of thousands of people contributed long hours and untold effort and energy to make the election happen. South Africa's ability to conduct proper elections, and the civil society needed to underpin democratic institutions, were immeasurably strengthened by the exercise.

The presence of international observers during the voting—some 2,500 from the United Nations and smaller contingents from the Organization of African Unity, European Union,

Commonwealth and a slew of nongovernmental and church groups—calmed some tense and potentially very ugly situations in which people were losing faith or patience with local officials. In this alone, the international observer presence probably averted violence and saved lives.

Even as voting continued, representatives of the United Nations and other observer missions offered reassurance that the elections were "substantially free and fair"—using the semantically and politically elastic phraseology that was the official guideline for assessing the election's conduct. Officials of South Africa's Independent Election Commission unsurprisingly soon followed suit. These statements in no way claimed the voting was smooth or totally free of fraud. They did reflect the broad political consensus, inside and outside South Africa, that the country's first all-race vote would be a "legitimating election," providing an institutional and democratic context for the transfer to majority rule, rather than a test of adherence to the letter of electoral law.

As a political exercise measuring the spirit of consensus and compromise these elections bode well for South Africa's ability to negotiate a difficult future. The results also fragment power in a manner that may moderate radicals in several camps. The African National Congress's 63 percent showing gives President Nelson Mandela a comfortable ruling margin but not the "super-majority" needed to make constitutional changes. On the strength of their national performances, the National Party and the Inkhata Freedom Party are represented in the new government of national unity. And in Western Cape Province and Natal, respectively, the two parties won regional races that will place them in public view as ruling parties, and should assure their engagement in the democratic process.

Mandela's challenge

Yet this division of power also presents Nelson Mandela with his first great presidential challenge. National Party (NP) support came mostly from white and mixed-race voters fearful of their future under black African majority rule. The Inkhata Freedom Party (IFP) garnered nearly all its backing among Zulu people in Natal, where feelings run high against what is deemed to be domination of the African National Congress (ANC) by people of Xhosa ethnicity. Zulus are the most numerous of the country's ethnic groups, and the Xhosa are second.

The new government of national unity will need to address issues that touch these highly charged questions of racial and ethnic identity with caution and sensitivity. Minority fears of "affirmative action" and expropriation are not merely paranoia. The culture of compromise developed over the last half-decade in South Africa offers some hope for a peaceful evolution to a multi-racial and multi-ethnic society. The composition of the new cabinet gives this vision a tangible face in the presence of

From *Freedom Review,* July/August 1994, pp. 22, 24-26. *Freedom Review,* published by Freedom House, New York, NY 10005.

NP chief F.W. de Klerk and IFP leader Mangosuthu Buthulezi. Their cooperation, in tandem with moderation of the ANC's more radical tendencies, could douse the embers of racial and ethnic antagonism that still threaten to flare into the kind of violence that cost over 13,000 lives over the last four years.

But Nelson Mandela must move quickly to answer other needs, and other constituencies, as well. Whatever the potential for a genuine "rainbow coalition" in South Africa, the most important long-term goal is seeking the pot of gold at its end. Demonstrable material gains from the transition to majority rule are awaited, sometimes with impatience. Bringing basic services to the underclass long deprived under apartheid is an initial goal. The ANC's "Reconstruction and Development Programme" served as the party's 1994 election platform. It pledges a $55 billion five-year effort to build a million low-cost homes and electrify a total of 2.5 million residences. Free and compulsory primary school education is to be instituted nationwide, and over two million people put to work in a massive public works program. There is a pledge to give land to the poor, but only vague inklings of how and when it will be done.

While the ANC's 1955 "Freedom Charter" was a rousing call to socialist revolution with massive redistribution of the country's wealth and land, the 1994 Reconstruction and Development Programme is clothed in pragmatic cautions. "Making promises is easy, but carrying them out as a government is much more difficult," the document warns, adding, "Each and every expectation will not be realized and each and every need will not be realized immediately."

There is certainly no guarantee of South Africa's economic resurgence. The country's foreign debt is low and its well-developed infrastructure and wealth of mineral resources make it a potentially rich land, but poor management could sink that promise. It is important to remember that, a half century ago,

---

The Mandela government must tackle the issue of crime. South Africa's murder rate is eight times that of the U.S.

---

one of the prime goals of apartheid was to bring the largely rural and poor Boer [Afrikaner] population a much larger share of the country's wealth. Now, a rapidly burgeoning population of about forty million-plus—there are no reliable census figures—is swelling the ranks of millions of unemployed faster than jobs are created. Export commodity values, on which South Africa relies heavily for hard currency, remain flat.

Retention of several key economic advisors from the previous government will go some way to allay the fears of foreign capital, but much job-creating investment will simply not be attracted—the country's unionized industrial labor costs do not compete with those of the huge low-wage, little-regulated labor pools available in several Asian countries. And the "peace dividend" of funds freed from the administration of apartheid and its repressive security apparatus may prove illusory, disappearing into the bureaucracies of the nine new provinces and higher salaries for the revamped South African National Defense Force and the South African Police. Much of the national budget will still go for salaries and pensions of (mainly white) civil servants, whose status is guaranteed by the interim constitution.

Crimes and rights

An immediate issue the Mandela government must tackle is crime. South Africa's murder rate is eight times that of the United States. Many of the country's townships are simply unpoliced, run by assortments of criminal gangs and local militia sometimes affiliated with the ANC or other parties, while security forces mostly remain bunkered in sandbagged police stations. The phenomenon of "jack-knifing"—random gang-rapes—is now common in townships. Few doubt the difficulties of bringing many of the "lost generation" of youths—who made schools boycotts ("Liberation before Education!") a primary instrument of the anti-apartheid struggle and adopted an anti-authority outlaw lifestyle—into the economically productive mainstream.

Mounting a massive anti-crime drive without widespread human rights violations will also be a daunting task. The ANC faces the task of truly instituting and properly respecting the rule of law in a country with a 300-year record of repression and resistance. Chapter III of the transitional constitution provides over thirty sections guaranteeing an array of human rights, and then qualifies them all by introducing a clause that allows them to be restricted by law when "reasonable" and "necessary." The temptation in troubled times for any government to find reasons and necessities to abridge fundamental freedoms will be an ongoing measure of the ANC's commitment to respect human rights.

While the Afrikaners' long belief in themselves as a "chosen people" helped reinforce their ferocious excesses, South African courts have maintained some degree of integrity. It is unclear whether the ANC will improve on this tradition. Its record in exile inspires little confidence; executions, torture and detention without trial were common currency at its training bases in Tanzania, Uganda and elsewhere. The appointment as a deputy minister of Winnie Mandela, convicted of responsibility in the murder of a township youth and tarred by association with other thuggery, is equally troubling.

The continuing use of Section 29 of the Internal Security Act to hold detainees without trial, despite the ANC's pledge to quickly repeal the law, is early warning that the new government might hold its current security needs to be more important than promised protections of civil liberties. The existence of strong constitutional guarantees, a relatively independent judiciary and a flourishing free media could be significant checks on the government's powers, as will its need to face the electorate once again, in a starkly different atmosphere, five years from now.

Whither the ANC?

As a grand coalition of varied interests coalesced to fight for single cause of ending apartheid, the ANC has reached its primary goal. But with that momentous achievement behind it, the ANC will no longer be all things to most of the people. To maintain a popular base, it will have to transform itself into a party with a solid platform of identifiable, realistic policies—and, crucially, solid accomplishments in governance—to sustain its appeal to a broad electorate. The slow pace of reform and economic pragmatism many observers believe necessary to reassure whites and entice foreign investment may alienate the black African working class. The Congress of South African Trade Unions (Cosatu), one of the country's best-

South Africa

Nelson Mandela, who served 27 years in prison during the era of apartheid, was chosen by the National Assembly as president of the Republic of South Africa, following the decisive victory of his African National Congress in the country's first nonracial parliamentary elections on April 26–28. President Mandela's inaugural address, delivered on May 10, is reprinted in its entirety below:

Your Majesties, your Highnesses, distinguished guests, comrades and friends.

Today, all of us do, by our presence here, and by our celebrations in other parts of our country and the world, confer glory and hope to newborn liberty. Out of the experience of an extraordinary human disaster that lasted too long must be born a society of which all humanity will be proud.

Our daily deeds as ordinary South Africans must produce an actual South African reality that will reinforce humanity's belief in justice, strengthen its confidence in the nobility of the human soul and sustain all our hopes for a glorious life for all. All this we owe both to ourselves and to the peoples of the world who are so well represented here today.

To my compatriots, I have no hesitation in saying that each one of us is as intimately attached to the soil of this beautiful country as are the famous jacaranda trees of Pretoria and the mimosa trees of the bushveld.

Each time one of us touches the soil of this land, we feel a sense of personal renewal. The national mood changes as the seasons change.

We are moved by a sense of joy and exhilaration when the grass turns green and the flowers bloom.

That spiritual and physical oneness we all share with this common homeland explains the depth of the pain we all carried in our hearts as we saw our country tear itself apart in a terrible conflict, and as we saw it spurned, outlawed and isolated by the peoples of the world, precisely because it had become the universal base of the pernicious ideology and practice of racism and racial oppression.

We, the people of South Africa, feel fulfilled that humanity has taken us back into its bosom, that we, who were outlaws not so long ago, have today been given the rare privilege to be host to the nations of the world on our own soil.

We thank all our distinguished international guests for having come to take possession with the people of our country of what is, after all, a common victory for justice, for peace, for human dignity. We trust that you will continue to stand by us as we tackle the challenges of building peace, prosperity, non-sexism, non-racialism, and democracy.

We deeply appreciate the role that the masses of our people and their political mass democratic, religious, women, youth, business, traditional and other leaders have played to bring about this conclusion. Not least among them is my Second Deputy President, the Honourable F. W. de Klerk.

We would also like to pay tribute to our security forces, in all their ranks, for the distinguished role they have played in securing our first democratic elections and the transition to democracy from bloodthirsty forces which still refuse to see the light.

The time for the healing of the wounds has come.

The moment to bridge the chasms that divide us has come.

The time to build is upon us.

We have, at last, achieved our political emancipation. We pledge ourselves to liberate all our people from the continuing bondage of poverty, deprivation, suffering, gender and other discrimination.

We succeeded to take our last steps to freedom in conditions of relative peace. We commit ourselves to the construction of a complete, just, and lasting peace.

We have triumphed in the effort to implant hope in the breasts of the millions of our people. We enter into a covenant that we shall build a society in which all South Africans, both black and white, will be able to walk tall, without any fear in their hearts, assured of their inalienable right to human dignity—a rainbow nation at peace with itself and the world.

As a token of its commitment to the renewal of our country, the new Interim Government of National Unity will, as a matter of urgency, address the issue of amnesty for various categories of our people who are currently serving terms of imprisonment. We dedicate this day to all the heroes and heroines in this country and the rest of the world who sacrificed in many ways and surrendered their lives so that we could be free. Their dreams have become reality. Freedom is their reward.

We are both humbled and elevated by the honour and privilege that you, the people of South Africa, have bestowed on us, as the first President of a united, democratic, non-racial and non-sexist South Africa, to lead our country out of the valley of darkness.

We understand that there is no easy road to freedom. We know well that none of us acting alone can achieve success. We must therefore act together as a united people for national reconciliation, for nation building, for the birth of a new world.

Let there be justice for all.

Let there be peace for all.

Let there be work, bread, water, and salt for all.

Let each know that for each the body, the mind, and the soul have been freed to fulfill themselves.

Never, never, and never again shall it be that this beautiful land will again experience the oppression of one by another and suffer the indignity of being the skunk of the world.

The sun shall never set on so glorious a human achievement.

Let freedom reign.

God bless Africa.

---

organized political forces, will be loathe to accept a watered-down reform program and even less tolerant of any deterioration in living standards.

However, an expanding South African economy would stimulate growth throughout Southern Africa and perhaps further afield. The frontline states suffered various degrees of economic loss, political destabilization and direct military aggression during the apartheid years. Revitalized rail and road links far north into Central Africa could stimulate trade and help revive a number of nearly moribund economies. Demands for raw materials by a growing South African industrial base could bolster declining commodity prices and supply hard currency to other African countries. Technical cooperation would offer the benefit of *African* experience in crucial areas of mining and farming.

South Africa's political example will also be keenly assessed. Like South Africa, colonial mapmaking left most African countries a bewildering mélange of racial, religious and ethnic groups. If a culture of consensus and compromise truly takes root

in a multi-racial and multi-ethnic South Africa, it will be held as a model for other nations seeking a stable transition to democratic rule. And the lesson will not be lost to outside powers that pushed for an end to apartheid but offer only lukewarm support for democratization elsewhere on the continent.

At seventy-five years of age, Nelson Mandela has succeeded in leading the overthrow of white minority rule in South Africa. But the end of apartheid is only the "beginning of the beginning" of a long and arduous period of change. President Mandela's new challenge is far more complex: persuading the skilled white minority to preserve and expand the formidable economic base built largely on the backs of black labor; assuring by example to South Africa's diverse ethnic and racial groups that the rule of law applies equally to all; and, perhaps most difficult, convincing his own supporters that the material fruits of apartheid's demise will not arrive suddenly, as manna, but can accrue slowly but surely only as the entire country's economy grows.

TARNISHED REVOLUTION

After 45 Years, Beijing Tries to Polish Ideology

Sheila Tefft

Staff writer of The Christian Science Monitor

Beijing

Forty-five years ago, Sidney Shapiro was swept up in China's communist movement and has stuck with it.

But today, Mr. Shapiro, an expatriate lawyer from the United States and one of a handful of Western Marxists to have lived through a turbulent half-century of Chinese communism, sees few remnants of the idealism that helped lift the Communists to victory in 1949. In its place, he says, is a disturbing passion for money rooted in the capitalist-style reforms instituted 15 years ago by paramount leader Deng Xiaoping.

"No one wants to talk [about communist idealism] these days. Then, what Mao [Zedong] used to say was construed as the 'Sermon on the Mount,' " says Shapiro, an author and translator of Chinese classics and fiction, speaking at his home here. "Now, they say it's all right to make money. The whole ethical and moral structure seems to be going. I'm not sure whether they can build a new moral structure."

As China's socialism flags amid the race to make money, the country's leaders are struggling to shore up their party in the face of communism's collapse elsewhere in the world and mounting economic and social disarray at home.

On the eve of the 45th anniversary of the founding of communist China on Oct. 1, the Chinese leadership has issued a new clarion to rejuvenate the party and has planned for tomorrow an old-style propaganda extravaganza to rally the Chinese public.

This week, the Communist Party's senior officials met in a four-day plenum and called for renewed efforts to halt corruption, bolster sagging local party support, and develop a new generation of young party leaders to take charge after the death of the ailing Mr. Deng.

In recent years, the disintegration of the Soviet Union and communist Eastern Europe, Beijing's loosening control over the provinces, a deluge of official bribery, embezzlement and nepotism, and party divisions over China's growing economic woes have thrown Chinese Communists into turmoil.

Capitalist-style reforms have undermined socialist ideology and central planning and have fueled graft, despite repeated anticorruption campaigns. Recently, the government reported that corruption cases rose more than 16 percent in the first half of 1994 and that Beijing authorities face obstruction from local officials in ending abuses.

Many Chinese eschew politics to get rich quick and acquiesce to Communist rule out of fear of the chaos presently gripping Russia. But rapid economic change has also marginalized and embittered many farmers, the core of traditional party support, who struggle to make a living on the land or flood the cities looking for jobs.

"It is necessary to continue to improve the Party's work style and deepen the struggle against corruption in a sustained way," said the party communiqué, which did not deal with the problems of inflation and economic overheating now splitting the party leadership. "It is also necessary to further carry forward the fine tradition of hard work and link the Party closely with the masses."

To mount a brave front, the government tomorrow will stage a Chinese-style pep rally of dancing, singing, speeches, and fireworks for 100,000 Chinese officials and foreign guests in Tiananmen Square. For the festivities, which will be broadcast nationally to ordinary Chinese who are not allowed to attend, a giant dragon mascot has been built in the square, and even Mao's portrait overlooking Tiananmen Square has been exchanged for a larger version.

The spectacular has excited many Beijing residents, who receive a four-day holiday and, in many cases, a hefty increase in their usual monthly pay, to participate in the preparations. "People are getting extra work and know this will be a big event because it only happens every five years," says one city worker.

But the festivities have been overshadowed by a security crackdown to ensure that no dissidence or violence disrupts the holiday. In an onslaught against official corruption and the country's worsening crime wave, large numbers of executions have taken place in many Chinese cities, according to press reports here.

The New China News Agency reported that more than 60,000 people "who posed dangers on the city's security" have been arrested in the runup to the National Day observance in Beijing.

For old Marxists like Shapiro, such extravaganzas cannot mask the cynicism that has accompanied rapid change in China and stands in marked contrast to the idealism of 45 years ago when people "hoped for a society in which they could have a chance to earn their livelihood."

"They wanted the anarchy of crime and corruption in the [pre-1949] society to be stopped," he says, referring to conditions under the Nationalist government of Chiang Kai-shek.

But many Western and Chinese analysts are comparing today's conditions to those preceding the Communists' victory. Shapiro maintains that China is groping to redefine itself amid changing world conditions, although he questions if the communist ideology he believes in can survive.

"Each person is protecting his own turf," he observes. "When money comes in the door, ideology goes out the window."

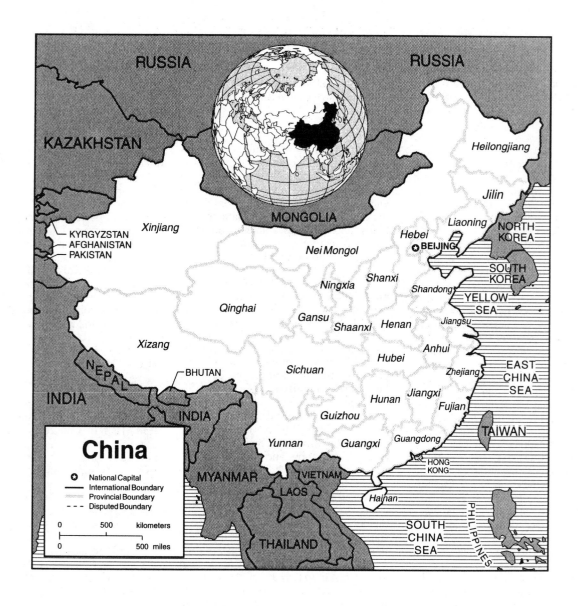

CHINA'S COMMUNISTS

The road from Tiananmen

BEIJING AND HONG KONG

With the Tiananmen Square massacre five years ago, China's Communist Party saw off the latest serious challenge to its rule. The next challenge is coming from within, as the party's get-rich-quick policies breed corruption and regional rivalries that are tearing at its own fabric

FOR a political organisation born supposedly of mass mobilisation and peasant revolution, the Chinese Communist Party has always set a lot of store by exclusivity. On the eve of China's "liberation" from the Nationalist government in 1949, only one person in a thousand in China was a Communist Party member, according to the late Lazlo Ladany, a Jesuit priest and China-watcher. Marshal Nie Rongzhen, who commanded Mao Zedong's forces in northern China, wrote in a memoir that there were just 3,000 party members and 5,000 collaborators in Beijing when the communist armies swept into the city. In Shanghai, a city of 9m people even in 1949, there were just 8,000 party members to orchestrate "the people's will". Hardly surprising that photographs of the PLA's triumphant entry into both cities show that the crowds lining the streets were wearing expressions of suspicion as often as of jubilation.

Once in government, the party has never allowed its membership to rise above 5% of China's population. The figure today is 4.3%, or 52m people, of whom 30m are cadres (full-time party officials or managers of state-owned firms). A monopoly of political power over all China resides formally with this relative handful of people.

The formative years of organising illegally through underground cells and guerrilla units shaped the Communist Party into a force that was disciplined, motivated, loyal and obsessively secretive. It came to power convinced of the need to create socialism, determined to bend China to its will, and prepared to root out not merely those who were known to be its enemies but also anyone who it thought disposed to be-

come an enemy in the future. Institutions that might have checked the party's power—the courts, for example—were devalued or destroyed. The state continued in name, but without any authority distinct from that of the Communist Party. Organisations of all kinds, including government ministries and large corporations, were run by the party committees planted within them.

Individuals were allowed no private life exempt from the scrutiny of officialdom, no freedom to choose where they lived or worked. Neighbourhood committees kept watch on local streets. Travel was impossible without a myriad of papers and permissions. The media were controlled by the party and used primarily for propaganda. Businesses were seized. In the towns, the party controlled all jobs. In the countryside, it bought all produce and owned all land. A person "belonged" in every sense of the word to his work-unit, which allocated housing, education and health care. By these means, and by the often savage punishment of resisters, the communist elite controlled a billion people.

As the years passed, however, so the memory of China's pre-revolutionary hardships began to fade. They were supplanted by memories of more recent hardships engineered by the Communist Party itself—such as the Great Leap Forward of 1958-61, an attempt at cottage-industrialisation which produced a famine that killed 30m-40m people; and the Cultural Revolution, which plunged the country into anarchy from 1966-69 with after-shocks well into the mid-1970s. After the death of Mao in 1976 and the chaotic interlude of the Gang of Four, a powerful section of the party leadership saw that China had been taken as far as it would

go down the road of autarkic stagnation and political strife. If Mao Zedong had found little to inspire him in the notions of social calm and rising living standards, these were the things for which those who had been his subjects now hungered. Deng Xiaoping, who rose to power in 1977-78, decided that economic growth had to take precedence over class-struggle politics. This crucial reversal, once it had been accepted as party doctrine in late 1978, made possible the opening wide of China's economy to foreign trade and investment (see chart), and with it an era of fabulous growth.

Heirs of the dogma

Today, 16 years after Deng Xiaoping's ascent, it is far from clear that even Mr Deng himself saw how far his programme of economic reform would eventually lead. Half of China's industrial output, and perhaps 75% of its total output, is now accounted for by private or "collective" firms: something drastic will have to be done with the half of industry that remains in state hands, for it is an all but insupportable drain on the national budget. And, while it is not quite true to claim—as even some of China's own communists now do—that economic reform has led the Communist Party to abandon ideology altogether, its policies and rhetoric are deeply confused.

Not even the most hard-line of Chinese communists now dares challenge the principles of Deng Xiaoping's reforms, even if some might secretly like to. But the party still numbers "Marxism-Leninism-Mao-Zedong-Thought" among its "four cardinal principles"; and even for the more progressive communists, decades of knee-jerk obedience to Marxist slogans have created habits of mind that are hard to shake off. The upshot is that, even while money-madness sweeps China, slogans which pay lip-service to socialist values are still popular.

In 1987, when Zhao Ziyang was at his zenith as Communist Party general secretary (he fell in disgrace during Tiananmen), the party settled on the notion that China was in a "primary stage of socialism". This was shorthand for the argument that socialism had to be built on a strong economy, and that non-socialist methods might be needed to achieve that strength. The reformers could thus get on with liberalising the economy while pretending that their long-term plan was still to build socialism.

Mr Zhao's slogan disappeared with him. Deng Xiaoping's own ingenious coinage, "socialism with Chinese characteristics", has proved more durable—perhaps because it is as much nationalist as it is socialist. Its precise meaning changes with each new policy: these days party members add "market" to the beginning of the phrase. Crustier communists prefer to stay close to the "four cardinal principles", which are (in addition to Marxism-Leninism-Mao-Zedong-Thought) the socialist road; the dictatorship of the proletariat; and the leadership of the Communist Party. With Mr Deng now 89 years old and failing, the interplay of slogans may reveal something of what one American China-watcher, Andrew Nathan of Columbia University, calls the "pre-post-Deng manoeuvrings". Supporters of Mr Deng's camp are now championing him as China's "Great Theorist"—elevating him, in effect, above Mao. Opponents are appealing even more than usual to the "four cardinal principles", a way to celebrate Mao but not Mr Deng. Jiang Zemin, whose positions as China's president and Communist Party general secretary give him a claim to be seen as Mr Deng's successor, is busy recommending the assiduous study of his patron's writings.

These internal and doctrinal arguments pale, however, beside the question of whether the party as a whole can preserve its grip on political power in the face of the economic liberalisations it has unleashed. The

party survived the 1989 challenge to that power by ordering the massacre of people demonstrating in Beijing against its dictatorship. To judge from its internal panic, the leadership saw that event as a close-run thing. Now, five years later and despite a brief austerity drive in 1990-91, economic reform is running faster and further still, shrinking the party's power to plan the economy from the centre, strengthening the position of cities and provinces, and giving many more people previously unheard-of freedoms including the choice of where to live, work and spend money.

In 1979 there were—officially at least—no Chinese recorded as working in privately-owned businesses. Now, the official figure is 30m, and that is doubtless a substantial underestimate. "Township and village enterprises" (TVEs)—light industrial groups with shared and often informal ownership—employ another 90m, and account for over a third of China's industrial output. The new mobility of labour has undermined the household registration system. Farmers, too, have been largely freed from the constraints of the state. To see how this hurts the party, start at ground level.

More equal than others

Its big cities aside, China is a vast country of 4m rural villages and 700m farm-workers. One of the Communist Party's strengths is, still, to be the nearest thing China has to a universal organisation; but its rural presence is decaying fast.

In the 1950s and 1960s, the hey-day of collectivisation, village cadres would transmit the orders from on high about how collectivisation should be carried out or carried further, what was to be grown, and what prices the government would pay for crops to feed the cities. But Mr Deng's "family responsibility system" abolished Mao's collective farms, restored households as the unit of production, and allowed part of the crop to be sold on the free market. As the countryside grew richer, prosperity lured some cadres back to the family farm or into private enterprise, leaving empty desks behind them. Others hung on to their authority simply in order to extort money from the villagers under their control. In the main,

according to John Burns of the University of Hong Kong, who has studied village organisation in China, villages have returned to the kinship politics that prevailed before the communist revolution.

This loss of authority in the countryside might be less worrying for the Communist Party were it not that the countryside has at the same time been growing more restless. Rural incomes, which rose fast during the 1980s, are now stagnating. Farm prices are being capped again by the central government as an anti-inflation measure. Peasants who have remained on the land are growing envious of the much-flaunted new wealth of China's cities. Worse, some local governments have been paying for crops with IOUs that they cannot redeem; and remittances sent back to the farms by peasants who have migrated to work in the booming coastal provinces of Guangdong and Fujian appear to be drying up, or vanishing along the way. *Contemporary*, a Hong Kong China-watching journal, reports that 44 rural post offices have been ransacked in the past year by angry farmers.

The effect of stagnant incomes and increases in farm productivity is to drive people off the land at a growing pace. The World Bank estimates that there are 100m-150m displaced rural workers on the move in China, a huge and potentially volatile population. The great past challenges to authority in China—the Taiping rebellion of 1850-64, the communist revolution itself—came from the countryside. To judge from the urgency with which the Communist Party has been calling for rural "stability" this past year, it appears to be seriously worried that rural dissatisfaction might once again boil over into insurrection.

The problem would undoubtedly be more acute still, had the TVEs not been so successful in soaking up labour. Their proliferation was encouraged by the party as a buffer between countryside and city that might absorb the shock of population movements. They have done that job well, but they have also proved so profitable that they have drifted almost entirely out of the party's control. In its place have come other groups including clans, syndicates of local businessmen and—particularly along the so-called "Gold Coast" of the maritime provinces—diverse extortionists, smugglers and criminal gangs, whose interest in paying taxes to or otherwise co-operating with the central government is minimal.

Breaking with Beijing

Relations between the central government on the one hand, and China's 22 provinces, three metropolitan areas and five "autonomous regions", on the other, are even more troubling for the party. The extreme case is Guangdong, which leads China in trade and inward investment and is largely self-financing. It pays little of its tax revenues to

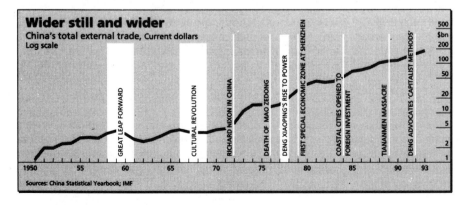

Wider still and wider
China's total external trade, Current dollars
Log scale

GREAT LEAP FORWARD
CULTURAL REVOLUTION
RICHARD NIXON IN CHINA
DEATH OF MAO ZEDONG
DENG XIAOPING'S RISE TO POWER
FIRST SPECIAL ECONOMIC ZONE AT SHENZHEN
COASTAL CITIES OPENED TO FOREIGN INVESTMENT
TIANANMEN MASSACRE
DENG ADVOCATES 'CAPITALIST METHODS'

500
$bn
200
100
50
20
10
5
2
1

1950   55   60   65   70   75   80   85   90   93
Sources: China Statistical Yearbook; IMF

the central government and receives little central-government investment in return. This year, the central government is trying to bring China's growth rate down to 9% from 13% last year. Guangdong's response has been to thumb its nose at instructions and carry on profiting from its inflows of foreign investment and its synergies with Hong Kong. Shenzhen, the "special economic zone" next to Hong Kong, grew by 30% in real terms last year and has no plans to grow by a piffling 9% anytime soon. With Guangdong setting, to all intents and purposes, its own economic policy, the reality is a schism between at least one big provincial Communist Party and the central authorities in Beijing.

The central government is desperate to ensure that China's other economic powerhouses do not follow Guangdong towards de facto autonomy. Shanghai is only now being granted, slowly, the autonomy that Guangdong was given a decade ago. But the process of devolution, and the regional rivalries it has created, may already be too far advanced for the centre to regain its grip. Even poor and inaccessible provinces are setting up economic zones to mimic those of coastal provinces. Beggar-my-neighbour policies—tariffs and import controls at provincial borders, tax breaks for local businesses—are becoming a way of life. Provincial governments hungry for new revenues are neglecting investment in infrastructure while they speculate in property and invest in light industries and service businesses that they hope will bring quick returns. Taxes are handed over grudgingly, if at all; the ratio of central government revenue to GNP has dropped from more than 30% at the end of the 1970s to 19% today. It remains to be seen whether the national tax reforms enacted at the beginning of this year will succeed in giving more control over China's purse-strings back to the central authorities.

As dreams of wealth have gone to the heads of local governments, so they have gone to the heads of many individual Communist Party members. Corruption is widespread and flagrant at the township, county and even provincial level. An anti-corruption drive, reputedly the biggest in a decade,

is now under way, with mass public trials and summary executions; a clutch of cadres was shot last month in Shenzhen. But while this may be enough to strike fear briefly into local cadres, the higher ranks of the party are still being left untouched. Official newspapers are sometimes directed to rail against the "big monkeys"; but China's senior officials have neither the will nor perhaps the means to go about purging their own.

The depth of corruption within the party is impossible to gauge but easy to guess at—just count the stolen limousines with smoked-glass windows that cruise the boulevards of China's cities. So completely has the culture of money saturated the party that anything done in the name of wealth-creation, save for the crudest bribe-taking, seems permissible. How, for example, to judge the minister who, ordered to hive off a state-owned conglomerate, simply quits his government job after naming himself head of the company?

Few of the party's most senior members need to stoop to enriching themselves; they have families to do it. Entrepreneurs and bankers in China and Hong Kong will flock to bring foolproof deals to the son or daughter of a leader, hoping for favours in return. These "princelings" may be the children of provincial grandees, or central committee members, or even of Deng Xiaoping himself: the interests of one of Mr Deng's sons, Zhifang, include a private property company in Hong Kong that does business with mainland companies listed on the colony's stock exchange.

Big money from China, some of it hot and some of it not, is conspicuous in Hong Kong's property and share markets. Probably more than $20 billion of Chinese capital has flowed over the border into Hong Kong shell companies in recent years. Often, the money is channelled back into China as the "foreign investment" component of a joint-venture project; this wins the tax and foreign-exchange privileges granted to such projects. In theory, this money may still belong to such-and-such a Chinese organisation; but in practice much of it has passed into the control of individuals who cannot be held to account.

When the party's over

Officially, the Communist Party professes itself aware of the need for vigilance and reform. It sees that economic liberalisation has raised people's expectations and it is trying hard to co-opt interests that might otherwise coalesce into rival centres of power. It is starting to champion consumer rights, workers' rights against foreign employers, even environmental concerns. It is wondering, too, how to streamline a central government that boasts 400 different ministries and bureaus, and it is circling again around an idea—once advocated by Mr Zhao—of developing a more professional civil service to give more backbone to the state. But these are all, essentially, refinements. It is still heresy to question the party's basic claim to control every lever of political power.

If it does worry privately about its future, the party may take comfort from its relatively steady relations with the army, despite a purge of fractious officers in 1992. Mao held that the "the party rules the gun"; in practice, the relationship has proved rather more ambivalent, the two hierarchies being scarcely separable. Every officer of the PLA is a party member; the army's interests are championed by a retired general, Liu Huaqing, who holds a seat on the Standing Committee of the Politburo, the apex of the party's command structure. The PLA's budget has been raised by a quarter this year. Many of its units are profiting from economic reform: they run private businesses on the side. By one estimate, the PLA now owns about 20,000 commercial companies, half of them in Guangdong.

There is little to suggest, therefore, that the army would not do again today what it did at Tiananmen Square in 1989, if the party were faced with another challenge to its monopoly of power. And that might be enough to secure the party's place, were history simply to repeat itself. But in the years since Tiananmen, the new dangers that face the party may have grown into more of a threat to it than idealistic students could ever hope to be. Its enemies now are corruption, fragmentation and loss of purpose. Against those, tanks can offer no defence.

What next for China?

BEIJING AND HONG KONG

POLITICAL chat in Beijing is a little ghoulish these days: the latest gossip is that Deng Xiaoping has a cotton wad stuffed in his cheek lest signs of drooling send Shanghai's stockmarket plunging further. Since its summer peak, the market has fallen by nearly half, largely because of fears that China's paramount leader, who is 90, has entered a swift decline. Mr Deng's family denies this, claiming that his health is stable and that he merely suffers from an unspecified "old man's disease"—reckoned to be Parkinson's disease, from which Mao Zedong also suffered.

With Mr Deng (attended by two score western-trained doctors) neither dead nor politically alive, the leadership in Beijing seems to be paralysed. No big decisions are being made, and nobody has clearly grabbed the reins of power. Yet the small signs from which China-watchers have to infer big shifts in Beijing suggest that power is shifting towards a hereditary elite of technocrats with a bias towards state control.

A year ago, the picture looked quite different. A troika from the Politburo's Standing Committee was to lead the country: Jiang Zemin, state president, party general secretary and Mr Deng's chosen successor; Li Pen, the premier; and Zhu Rongji, the vice-premier in charge of the economy. In November 1993, the party published its blueprint for economic liberalisation, in effect renouncing one of the Communists' "four cardinal principles"— state ownership.

Three crucial changes were meant to follow: a central-banking law was to allow the People's Bank to run something like a monetary policy; the rest of the banking sector was to be reformed; state-owned industry was to be reconstructed. To show the world it was serious, Beijing celebrated the new year by revamping the country's creaky tax system and unifying a dual exchange-rate system that punished foreign investors.

Since then the government has done little in the way of reform. Instead, it has fuelled inflation. The target for inflation this year was 10%. On October 18th it was admitted that, year-on-year, September's inflation hit 27.4%, up from 25.8% in August.

While proclaiming austerity, the government has been pumping money into the economy in a bid to keep the state-sector afloat. State-sector enterprises currently absorb 70% of all China's investment funds, mostly to keep the two-thirds that lose money afloat. The government would rather court high inflation than risk the unemployment that reforming the state-owned enterprises would entail.

Recently there have been further signs that the reforms are in jeopardy. The government has announced that all further liberalisation has been put on hold until the end of the year. Price controls have been reimposed on food and cotton. The State Planning Commission, which should have died long ago, has begun publicly to define a central role for itself in industrial policy. State-owned enterprises will not now be reformed until 1996, and then only on an "experimental" basis. And in a move that reverses Mr Deng's attempts to get the Communist Party out of the day-to-day running of enterprises, the People's Daily announced this month that party units would be the "beachhead and vanguard" for the socialist modernisation of business.

Since Mr Jiang, the heir apparent, is a reformist, why is this happening? Probably because he does not have the clout to command. China-watchers are therefore speculating on who really will hold power.

Some argue that China's economic problems open the way for the rise of a kind of neo-Maoism. They see as this movement's ring-leader an ideologist, Deng Liqun, who has been in the political wings since being passed over as party general-secretary in 1982. Though this Mr Deng once wrote the first party tract repudiating the Cultural Revolution (which Mao's wife, Jiang Qing, called "the political manifesto for the restoration of capitalism"), he rails these days against the "bourgeois liberalisa-

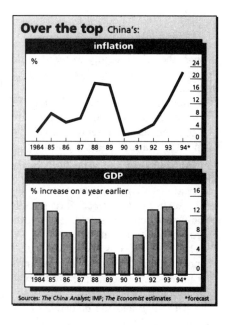

Over the top China's:

inflation

%

1984 85 86 87 88 89 90 91 92 93 94*

GDP

% increase on a year earlier

1984 85 86 87 88 89 90 91 92 93 94*

Sources: *The China Analyst*; IMF; *The Economist* estimates   *forecast

tion" spawned by his namesake's reforms. On October 17th it was announced that the mouthpiece of Mr Deng and his cohorts, *In Search of Truth*, had been ordered to close down by the end of the year.

But closer to the party's core is a group of what are being called "neo-conservatives". They are mostly western-educated technocrats, whose power springs from their pedigree. The most powerful of the princelings is probably Chen Yuan, the vice-governor of the central bank and the son of Chen Yun, the country's second-most eminent revolutionary. It was he, this summer, who ordered the monetary taps to be turned on to keep the state-owned enterprises afloat. Others include Li Peng's son, Li Xiaoyong, whose clout in the power sector may explain his father's enthusiasm for the vast Three Gorges Dam power-generation project: another is Pan Yue, vice-chief of the state land bureau and son of Liu Huaqing, an army general and member of the Politburo's Standing Committee.

Willy Wo-Lap Lam, a Hong Kong-based China-watcher, calls the neo-conservatives' agenda "high-tech feudalism with Chinese characteristics". Their creed is a recent best-seller in China, "Viewing China Through a Third Eye", purportedly written by a German academic. It argues that reforms are threatening China's social stability.

The neo-conservatives seem to believe that the market is fine so long as it does not undermine the apparatus of state and party control. They are, for instance, against letting people move around, even though China's geographically uneven growth demands labour mobility. And they argue that, in the interests of stability, the party should get more involved in business—rather than, as western observers still cheerily expect, pulling out. Their model here is Taiwan, and the vast corporate holdings of its ruling party, the Kuomintang.

When Mr Deng dies, this elite is likely to try to grab more power; Mr Zhu may claim to be their patron. Others will vie for influence, notably those of Mr Deng's generation who are still living. The elder Mr Chen has promised to give up work only when he dies. Bo Yibo, Wan Li (who is now close to Mr Deng) and Yang Shangkun (who was revered) are gerontocrats. They are not yet putting on their slippers.

With its abundance of king-makers and princelings, the Communist Party is almost as faction-riven as the one that Mr Deng inherited in 1978. It may take a man as forceful as Mr Deng to push China into the next stage of reform; but none is available.

INDIA

Pride and Prejudice

India's lower castes are demanding a greater share of political power and government patronage—and getting it. But the politics of caste could endanger economic reform.

Hamish McDonald in New Delhi

Foreign consular officials here are used to hearing all kinds of claims about political persecution to back up applications by Indians for immigrant visas—many of them quite far-fetched.

But in recent months, their jaws have dropped at the line a new class of would-be refugee is pushing. Brahmins and other members of the top castes in the Hindu hierarchy—those whose social and economic pre-eminence reflects millennia of privilege—are telling American and Australian consular officials that they and their children have no future in India.

Just as statistics are beginning to show that three years of economic liberalisation are about to deliver higher growth rates, many of the very people who would seem best positioned to take advantage of the new economic order say their country is going to the dogs. They contend that the standards of virtually all Indian institutions are being diluted because the lower castes are taking over.

As such attitudes indicate, India's economic and political cultures seem headed in opposite directions. On the one hand, the newly assertive lower castes are using their numerical advantage to steadily wrest control of political power. With it, they believe, will come favourable government-job and college-admission quotas and myriad other forms of official patronage. Yet, even as the lower castes grasp for a greater share of state largesse, the government is leaving an increasing number of investment and consumption decisions to the markets.

Indeed, the state's ability to redistribute the economic pie is being reduced drastically.

In the short term, the aspirations of the lower castes will boost the pressure on government to reserve—hence the term reservation—more government jobs, college places and so on for them. The state even may be forced to apply reservation to currently exempt institutions, such as the armed forces. And equal-opportunity laws could see quotas encroach on the private sector.

What does all this mean for India's economic future? Clearly, the country's new lower-caste rulers will have to tread a tightrope between pressure for more state patronage and the demands of the free market. But in a classic Catch 22, such a balancing act won't be successful without sustained economic growth—which won't come easy if the state is squeezed too hard for patronage.

Finance Minister Manmohan Singh alluded to the issue in September, when he warned of "tensions in our democracy" if wealth was not expanded rapidly. "Politics can end up being a zero-sum game if the economy is not growing fast enough," he said.

Foreign investors could be scared off if caste-based violence runs out of control. Indeed, even as Singh was speaking in Delhi, upper-caste protesters in the hill regions of Uttar Pradesh state were continuing to clash with police over their demand for a separate state.

Reform could also be hampered by the anger of lower castes who feel betrayed by the reduction in state control of the economy. Indeed, some of them already see the whole reform process as a high-

caste trick to deny them the fruits of advancement. "The traditional elite can see their power being reduced as real democracy is extended," says a lower-caste government official. "Now that the patronage is slipping from their hands, they are all for liberalisation."

Some lower-caste leaders see it differently, however. Leading sociologist Rajni Kothari says these leaders believed that when the elites opposed the West—or multinationals—they were merely protecting the existing social order. According to Kothari, "when the elite warns about the multinationals coming, the lower castes say: What's wrong with that? It can only create opportunities for us."

India's caste upheaval will also have an effect on the composition of its middle class, now estimated at some 200 million people and the target of worldwide business. Market experts S. L. Rao and I. Natarajan of the National Council of Applied Economic Research in New Delhi predict that as most of the lower castes are predominantly rural, a pro-rural bias could arise in government policies on prices, taxes and subsidies.

The fulfilment of lower-caste aspirations need not necessarily be antithetical to free-market liberalisation, however. Many Indians believe that a nondiscriminatory social order would provide a better climate for business in the long run, while a discriminatory one would always contain within it the seeds of strife and upheaval. However, Kothari says the lower-caste push could lead to a reduction in the strength of familiar national parties such as the Congress. Al-

The System

Indians use two words to describe it. One is *varna,* which can be translated literally as colour. This refers to the four main categories in the Hindu social order based on descending levels of ritual purity.

On top are the Brahmins, the priests and interpreters of ancient Sanskrit texts. Then come the Kshatriyas, the rulers and warriors—who often are the big land-holders. Third are the Vaishyas, the merchants and bankers. On the bottom are the Shudras, the artisans.

As the term varna suggests, there is a racial element to the classification, originating from the ancient conquest of the indigenous peoples of the subcontinent by light-skinned Aryans from Central Asia. The three top varnas are the "twice-born," entitled to wear a sacred

thread, a loop of string over one shoulder. The Shudras, sometimes not considered "caste Hindus," are descended perhaps from the original darker-skinned inhabitants of India, the Dravidians.

As the Aryans elaborated their system of ritual purity, yet another underclass emerged from those engaged in the most polluting tasks such as cleaning latrines, washing laundry, disposing of the dead and working leather. They became the untouchables—those beyond the pale of caste.

However, varna is less spoken of than *jati*—the thousands of occupation-based groups within the broad varna groups. These are akin in some ways to clans or occupational guilds—but observe far stricter rules against social contact and intermarriage. His or her jati is a more

conscious term of identity than varna for most Indians. At the narrow apex of the social pyramid that is presided over by the Brahmin, however, jati and varna are virtually merged.

Within the varnas, the jatis also have a vertical hierarchy of status. Even among the ex-untouchables, for example, the Chamars (leather workers) have a higher status than the Bhangis (sweepers). And the status of a particular jati can vary from region to region.

A final complication is that India stopped collecting statistics on caste in the 1931 census. So all figures of the caste breakup are extrapolations from more than 60 years ago.

Hamish McDonald

ready, lower-caste alliances have taken power in the states of Bihar and Uttar Pradesh. The latter is India's most populous state and has provided most of its prime ministers.

The political awakening of India's lower castes has been a long time coming. In the 1930s, the Congress Party leadership conceded that places should be reserved in parliament, the civil service (excluding the military) and state colleges for untouchables, tribals and "other backward classes." Initially, only untouchable and tribal groups were listed in the Ninth Schedule of the Constitution (hence the term "scheduled" castes or tribes). National parties balked at extending reservation to the Shudra (artisan) castes in the "other backward classes."

The green revolution of the 1960s and 1970s spread wealth into the landowners among the lower castes in the north, such as the dairy-herding Yadavs in the Ganges plains. To satisfy these groups, Uttar Pradesh state introduced 15% reservation for other "backward" castes—in addition to the long-standing reservations for scheduled castes and tribes.

In 1989–90, then-Prime Minister V. P. Singh's Janata Dal government was forced by its lower-caste allies to dust off a report by the late Bihar state politician B. P. Mandal, who had recommended 27% res-

ervation for the "other backward classes." This was Singh's downfall, prompting the Hindu-revivalist Bharatiya Janata Party (BJP), a party dominated by upper-caste Hindus, to end its support for his minority government. The BJP then stepped up its anti-Muslim campaign, culminating in the destruction of the Babri mosque in Ayodhya in December 1992.

This polarising trend in north Indian politics squeezed out the Congress, the traditional party of the middle, although its strong showing in southern and western states brought it back to power at the federal level in mid-1991. Congress tried to play both sides, taking a "me too" line on the Mandal recommendations and making vague pledges that a temple to Ram as well as a new mosque would be built in Ayodhya.

The result was disastrous. The fearful upper castes deserted to the BJP. The lower castes and Muslims turned to Uttar Pradesh Chief Minister Mulayam Singh Yadav's Samajwadi (Socialist) Party, and the allied Bahujan Samaj Party led by Kanshi Ram, who comes from a former untouchable caste.

"I don't see the Muslims and scheduled castes coming back to Congress in large numbers," says Bhupendra Kumar Joshi, director of the city's Giri Institute of Development Studies. Congress will probably work out some modus vivendi

with Yadav's coalition, just as it has for two decades with the anti-Brahmin Dravidian parties in southern Tamil Nadu state.

Tellingly, even reformist Prime Minister P. V. Narasimha Rao is playing caste politics with gusto, both in his home state of Andhra Pradesh and in the neighbouring southern state of Karnataka. With assembly elections due in both states in November–December, the local Congress machines are putting up backward-caste politicians as chief ministers. They are also pushing for considerable increases in reservation.

What new social order—or disorder—will result from India's caste turmoil is hard to sketch. But many Indians regret that, almost 50 years after their country achieved independence as a secular democracy, they see caste becoming more, not less, important in political life. The irony, as Kothari sees it, is that "the very sufferers from the [caste] system . . . are invoking caste identity and claims."

For now, reservation seems to be a tide no-one can stop, and it is only part of the tectonic changes in caste relations reverberating across India. The key question is: Could Finance Minister Manmohan Singh's market-led growth provide a solution to the problem of caste, when other gods such as Nehruvian socialism, Marxism and nationalism have failed?

Miracles beyond the free market

Michael Prowse

The biggest challenge for economists today is understanding the extraordinary success of east Asia. The region has nearly quadrupled per capita incomes in the past quarter of a century—a record unparalleled in economic history. On present trends it may begin to overtake much of the industrialised west early in the 21st century.

If its startling success could be replicated elsewhere, billions of people in developing and formerly communist countries could look forward to improved living standards. And the hope, eventually, of eliminating the scourge of grinding poverty would seem less quixotic.

Yet the region is as puzzling as three-dimensional chess. It has done far better than conventional theories predict, even allowing for such quantifiable pluses as macroeconomic stability, high rates of investment and a focus on exports. There is just no generally accepted explanation for its main distinguishing feature—supercharged rates of productivity growth.

The puzzle is deepened by the region's lack of homogeneity. The high-fliers are far from being carbon copies. At one extreme, Hong Kong has pursued a broadly free market approach; at the other, South Korea has intervened in just about every way conceivable. And the magic formula for growth has entirely eluded some countries in the region, such as the Philippines.

At the World Bank in Washington, an exhaustive analysis of the "Asia miracle" is nearing completion. Bank staff are distilling lessons from Japan, the four "tigers"—South Korea, Taiwan, Hong Kong and Singapore—and the so-called "cubs"—Malaysia, Thailand and Indonesia. They have also taken a look at the recent explosive growth in parts of southern China.

The study was undertaken partly at the instigation of Japan, the bank's second-largest shareholder, which has long wanted to play a bigger role in policy design. Japan has been critical of aspects of conventional World Bank/International Monetary Fund prescriptions and, justifiably, believes more attention should be paid to its own outstandingly successful development strategies—which formed a model for much of east Asia.

In 1991, Japan's Overseas Economic Co-operation Fund told the bank it was putting too much emphasis on deregulation and privatisation and made a case for selective import protection in developing countries and for the use of subsidised credits as a tool in industrial policy.

Mr John Page, a senior member of the bank's Asia miracle team, says the Japanese criticism struck a chord because the results of market-oriented reforms had often proved disappointing in developing economies. By cutting budget deficits, eliminating market distortions and shrinking government, client countries had stabilised their economies. But too often they had not achieved a virtuous cycle of rapid growth; they still lay "at the bottom of the league table relative to east Asia". The question became: "What now?"

The bank's benchmark for judging Asian policies is not an extreme free market philosophy, which would have the public sector shun responsibility for just about everything bar national defence. It is rather the less controversial "market friendly" strategy set out at length in the bank's 1991 World Development Report.

This clearly delineates the role of markets and the state. Development would be fastest, it claimed, when government concentrated on two jobs: maintaining macroeconomic stability through conservative fiscal and monetary policies; and investing in people through public education, training and healthcare programmes.

Beyond this, developing countries should rely on market forces. They should create as competitive as possible a regime in industry, commerce and the financial sector. And they should eliminate all barriers to trade and foreign investment. The core idea is that governments should focus on the things only they can do and leave everything else to markets.

It turns out that most of the Asian high-fliers have adopted a more permissive attitude to the role of government. Indeed, Mr Page argues that the success of the region can best be understood in terms of a "strategic growth" model that focuses more on what has to be done to achieve rapid growth than on who should do what.

On the strategic theory, development will be rapid provided countries find a way of: accumulating capital rapidly; allocating resources efficiently; and catching up technologically.

But there is no presumption that any of these functions should be reserved exclusively for the private sector. The miracle economies appear to have used a mixture of market incentives and state intervention in each of these areas:

• Accumulation. Gross domestic investment averages a startling 37 per cent of GDP in east Asia against an average of 26 per cent in developing countries as a whole. Yet this advantage was not won purely by adhering to the market-friendly approach.

The region has admittedly created a positive climate for business investment by pursuing conservative fiscal and monetary policies—inflation has averaged 9 per cent over the past 30 years, less than half the rate in other developing countries. The public sector has also invested effectively in people (enrollment in primary education far exceeds levels elsewhere, as does attention to vocational education), although it has not spent an atypical proportion of national income on social services.

But most of the Asian high-fliers have also interfered with market mechanisms.

They have limited the personal sector's ability to consume and heavily regulated the financial sector so as to ensure a predictable supply of low-cost capital for industry. Mechanisms for forcibly shifting resources from consumption to investment vary—Japan, South Korea and Taiwan, for example have maintained stringent controls on consumption and housing. The net effect, however, is the same everywhere: an abnormally high rate of savings.

• Efficient allocation of resources. Governments have striven to ensure that the most important market of all—that for labour—is flexible, if not fully competitive. Wages have largely reflected market supply and demand, partly because trade unions have been suppressed. Focusing hard on success in export markets has also imposed crucial competitive discipline and prevented domestic prices for industrial inputs moving far out of line with world markets.

Yet bank research indicates governments have also intervened vigorously. While less protectionist than the third world as a whole, few accepted western free-trade principles. Many have used import controls to protect strategic sectors (for example, quotas in South Korea, high tariffs in Thailand) and showered offsetting subsidies on export industries. At one time or another state-owned industries have played an important role in many of the economies, including South Korea, Taiwan, Indonesia, Singapore and Thailand. Many have not hesitated to direct the supply of credit to particular sectors. Both South Korea and Taiwan provided automatic credit for exporters in the early stages of development.

• Technological catch-up. The lesson again is that remarkable productivity growth only partly reflects market-oriented policies. Singapore, Malaysia, Thailand and, to some degree, Taiwan, have welcomed foreign investment. Early developers such as Japan and South Korea used other devices, such as licences letting them copy foreign technology. But unlike many other developing countries none tried to rely on home-grown technology.

However, all high-fliers intervened selectively to promote particular industries, with varying intensity and success. The process of trying to shift industrial output towards high-valued-added sectors is described by enthusiasts as "getting prices wrong in order to create dynamic comparative advantage".

South Korea provides a wealth of examples of aggressive and successful intervention. The government's most audacious move was perhaps to create from scratch a domestic steel industry despite foreign donor opposition and lack of private-sector enthusiasm. The state-run business went on to become the world's most efficient steel producer.

An internal bank memo sums up South Korea's record: "From the early 1960s, the government carefully planned and orchestrated the country's development. . . . [It] used the financial sector to steer credits to preferred sectors and promoted individual firms to achieve national objectives. . . . [It] socialised risk, created large conglomerates (*chaebols*), created state enterprises when necessary, and moulded a public-private partnership that rivalled Japan's."

Singapore provides another classic example of directed growth. When private sector companies failed to respond to opportunities identified by bureaucrats, state-owned or controlled groups were often pushed to the fore, the memo says. The bank has documented selective interventions throughout the region, even in supposedly free market Hong Kong.

The Asian example poses a dilemma for bodies such as the IMF and the World Bank, especially in former communist countries. Does it still make sense to advocate a form of "shock therapy"—the doctrine that deregulating and privatising everything as fast as possible is the optimum policy? Or should they recommend east Asia's slower, more interventionist path to economic maturity? It all depends on whether east Asia's deviations from orthodoxy can be replicated.

There are some grounds for caution. Mr Vinod Thomas, the bank's chief economist for east Asia and an architect of the market-friendly strategy, points out that government activism outside east Asia has produced dismal results. A distinction should also be drawn between the earlier "northern tier" of Asian highfliers—Japan, South Korea and Taiwan—and the later "southern tier" of Malaysia, Thailand and Indonesia.

Until the 1980s, countries such as South Korea were able to promote exports and protect imports without provoking much criticism. But pressure for a more level playing field has since grown intense. Broadly speaking, the southern tier of later developers has pursued more market-oriented policies than the first wave of Asian stars. Indus-

trial interventions have also tended to be less successful. A bank memo describes Malaysia's efforts as "by and large a costly failure" and Thailand's as "largely ineffective".

Less tangible political and cultural factors may also be crucial. Most Asian highfliers benefited from long periods of stable (if authoritarian) political rule. This encouraged long-term horizons. Public-sector bureaucracies have also tended to be more able and less corrupt than in most other third world countries. Governments were thus unusually well placed to implement development strategies.

Policymakers were also remarkably pragmatic; if a policy did not work it was rapidly dropped. South Korea, for example, went through several phases. It was relatively market-oriented in the early 1960s, became highly interventionist during the "heavy and chemical industries" drive of the 1970s, and then reverted to greater reliance on market forces in the mid-1980s. No region, it seems, has been less weighed down by ideology or more willing to seek advice from abroad.

The bank has only just begun the politically charged process of drawing conclusions from mountains of research papers. But senior officials believe the study may lead to a new paradigm for development in the 1990s. The evidence confirms that the miracle economies did indeed "do things differently". In many instances, "government played a big role, trade was not open and financial markets were repressed", concedes Mr Thomas.

"If we're right," says Mr Page, "the economic policy arsenal has many more weapons than we suspected." Mr Thomas agrees: the lesson from east Asia is that "you need a government guiding hand; you cannot just abdicate development to the private sector". He predicts that the bank will pay more attention to the role of institutions and to the potential for partnerships between the public and private sectors.

The most encouraging aspect of the Asian story, officials say, is that habits and institutions crucial for economic success were created rather than inherited. To raise the social standing of entrepreneurs, for example, South Korea had to overcome its Confucian traditions, which had glorified the scholar-bureaucrat. Singapore raised its savings rate from 1 per cent in 1965 to more than 40 per cent today. The implication is that sufficiently determined governments can work similar miracles in other places.

The "New Authoritarianism" in East Asia

"Authoritarianism in East Asia is an integral part of development strategy, useful not just for steadying societies in developmental flux but for creating the class that carried all before the modern world—the entrepreneurial class—and in the shifting of resources to that class. Authoritarian politics is not something genetically encoded in Confucian civilization, but a tried-and-true political arrangement in East Asia in its rush to industrialize."

MEREDITH WOO-CUMINGS

MEREDITH WOO-CUMINGS *is an associate professor of political science at Northwestern University. She is the author, under the name Jung-en Woo, of* Race to the Swift: State and Finance in Korean Industrialization *(New York: Columbia University Press, 1991). She has also edited a number of books, of which the most recent is* The Developmental State in Comparative Perspective *(forthcoming).*

In April I was in Tokyo for a conference on regional institutions. At a public forum afterward I gave a brief talk on the Asian Development Bank, but the audience seemed less interested in this low-profile bank based in Manila than they were in the scandal of the month—namely, the imminent caning of Michael Fay in Singapore. Most of the questions I fielded concerned the incident, and like most callers to American radio talk shows, the audience in Tokyo cheerfully supported the Singaporean resolve to cane the American teenager for his alleged vandalism. It seemed the world had suddenly discovered draconian politics in the Shining City in the Pacific, and liked it.

Political discipline and economic performance have always gone hand in hand in East Asia. For most of the past three decades Japan and the "Four Tigers" (South Korea, Taiwan, Hong Kong, and Singapore) experienced rapid economic growth under either one-man or one-party rule, with colonial Hong Kong not even permitted to exercise the right of self-determination.

In the last few years much has changed: the military has turned over the government to civilians in South Korea, and the dominant parties are allowing for greater electoral competition in Taiwan and Singapore— even the redoubtable Liberal Democratic Party in Japan briefly suffered the humiliation of being the opposition. Yet the East Asian nations remain profoundly conservative, distrustful of changes that purport to do away with the political formula that has served them well in the race to get rich. Moreover, the increasingly confident elites of the region do not appreciate hectoring by the United States about the shortcomings of

their political system, not to mention chastisement of their venerable culture.

Hence the authorities in Singapore proceeded to give the American youth the promised whipping. Meanwhile the leadership in Beijing, with the connivance of the American business establishment, mocked the China policy of President Bill Clinton's administration, taking the steam out of Secretary of State Warren Christopher's human rights crusade this spring.

TAILORING THE AUTHORITARIANS' NEW CLOTHES

In the heyday of Pax Americana, when American parochialism worked as well as universalism and the reigning social science idea was modernization theory, scholars and policymakers believed in the redemption and ultimate democratization of the heathens. Authoritarianism in East Asia was seen as an aberration, soon to be eclipsed by liberalism. Not so today. In the summer 1993 issue of *Foreign Affairs,* Harvard professor Samuel P. Huntington presented a stylized version of the global divide after the cold war that emphasized the remarkable persistence of cultural and civilizational boundaries. He singled out "Confucian civilization," along with Islamic civilization, as the most resistant to the Western perspective and hence a threat in the next phase of global politics. (He threw China and North Korea into the Confucian camp, but not Japan—an interesting departure that would not occur to any East Asian specialist.) Leaders in Beijing could not have been pleased that America's premier strategic thinker portrayed China as the next evil empire. But the argument on civilizational autonomy would be to their liking, if only to justify their human rights record.

The Chinese have not shrunk from proclaiming that Singapore-style authoritarianism as their formula for political and ideological stability while carrying out paramount leader Deng Xiaoping's economic reform program, since Communism would not serve the purpose. Their preferred term is "New Authoritarianism," connoting both continuity and change, the former occurring in the political and the latter in the economic realm—a political means of holding all other things "equal" while pursuing economic growth.

The new authoritarianism presupposes an older version. Latin Americanists equate the old authoritarianism with the caudillo or oligarchic politics characteristic of economies that relied on the export of primary commodities, or with the populist regimes that wanted to foster a self-reliant, indigenous industrial base—the Peronistas being the classic example. The new authoritarianism, according to the Argentine political scientist Guillermo O'Donnell, developed to provide stability in the transition from self-reliance to an export-led system, holding together the rapidly developing, outward-looking, capitalist economy, with transnational actors and technocrats as administrative linchpins.

Deng presumably had in mind a similiar combination of continuity and change. Old authoritarianism in China would refer to the inward-looking, state-centric economic development Mao Zedong pursued. New authoritarianism, Chinese style, would correspond to the state-centrism of an outward-looking and coastal-oriented economy, with emphasis on light industrial exports, market reforms, and reliance on the private sector.

Tracing this political trajectory in the newly industrialized economies of East Asia is perhaps problematic, but if the Chinese emulated anything it was not the bureaucratic authoritarianism of the militarists in Latin America but the strong states of South Korea and Taiwan, and the industrial might of Japan. Openly emulating Japan is difficult for anyone to do in postwar Asia, however, which is why the Beijing leadership has made Singapore the shining example of "New Authoritarianism" and its presumed economic payoffs.

If the political economy of the People's Republic before 1978 was based on the predictability of political and economic outcomes (repression combined with state planning), and if Western liberal democracy rests on the predictability of procedures (rule of law, a formal constitution, regular elections, and so on) but not the outcomes of politics and markets, then the new authoritarianism seems to offer a way to have one's cake and eat it too. Political predictability reins in the anarchic behavior of both the market and the polity, through state intervention in the market and political behavior, but it does not become a Stalinist smothering of market and polity. This approach is said to be workable because it appears to have worked already in the "mirror of the future" for China: Japan, Taiwan, Singapore, and South Korea.

The attractiveness of the newly industrializing country model also comes from a sense that East Asian countries have essentially the same political culture. On this score, a whole phalanx of Western political scientists is available to help Deng out, pulling the concept of "culture" from the dustbin of history and

informing the world that the success of East Asian capitalist economies is based on the region's traditional culture. But they introduce a new twist: instead of Weber's notion in *The Religion of China* that Confucian society squashed capitalist activity and possessed no "ethic" conducive to commerce, Confucius is suddenly active, promoting aggressive Confucianism, samurai Confucianism, post-Confucianism, and maybe one day even appearing in an Adam Smith tie.[1]

EXPLANATIONS FOR A MIRACLE

So what is this East Asian political economy? For all the sound and fury about the East Asian miracle, there is no comprehensive thesis. At the more coherent end is Chalmers Johnson's 1982 work, MITI *and the Japanese Miracle,* which employs an institutional analysis, including a genealogy of prominent bureaucrats' careers, to unlock the secret of Japanese neomercantilism. Johnson vigorously eschews any cultural argument in this book, since a better one already exists in the political economy of "late" development. The developmental state that emerges from his study, however, is an ideal-type of Japan; the book does not provide a structural understanding of how things came to be the way they are.

Other writers merely assert that the East Asian state guides industrialization, or—in the neoclassical attempt to account for the state—that it pursues "hand-waving" and other such gesticulations to influence market mechanisms. Still less impressive are the cultural determinists mentioned earlier, who find causality emanating from residual categories labeled aggressive Confucianism, or historical evolution in a region assumed to have a common "tradition," or the diffuse concept of "emergence," which harks back to the modernization literature.

It is probably Johnson's ideal-type, however, that comes closest to Beijing's notion of an authoritarian valhalla at the end of the developmental path. MITI *and the Japanese Miracle* does not just explicitly include capitalist nations in East Asia other than Japan, but goes on to assert that what is unique about the East Asian political economy is its combination of "soft authoritarianism" and high-growth economies. This can be termed "plan-rational authoritarianism"—a deeply seductive notion for former Stalinists accustomed to plan-irrational outcomes (as Johnson puts it). In other words, Johnson takes us perilously close to the Dengist notion of new authoritarianism.

---

[1]See Kent Calder and Roy Hofheinz, Jr., *The Eastasia Edge* (New York: Basic Books, 1982); Lucian Pye, *Asian Power and Politics* (Cambridge: Harvard University Press, 1982); and Michio Morishima, *Why Has Japan Succeeded?* (New York: Cambridge University Press, 1982).

4. DEVELOPING WORLD: Newly Industrialized Countries

The developmental juggernaut in East Asia exhibits the following characteristics, according to analyses by Johnson and others, including my own work:

- autonomy of the state

- state-exercised financial control over the economy

- coordinated or corporatized labor relations (which are or had better be tranquil, even if this is achieved by terrorizing labor)

- bureaucratic autonomy (especially for key economic bureaucracies)

- "administrative guidance," which pushes some industries over others

- the existence of special private-sector organizations, especially general trading companies and industrial conglomerates favored by government (whether zaibatsu, keiretsu, chaebol, or caifa)

- a limited role for foreign capital[2]

This is an ideal-type of a statist utopia that would make Adam Smith turn over in his grave: the state wields power over society and the market at home, and holds foreign interests at bay by means of its formidable gate-keeping power. Whether this describes the reality of the East Asian industrial countries is another question entirely, but it is no wonder the Chinese leadership likes a formula that combines political stability, control of the gates against the imperialists, and rapid growth. It is a "Great Leap Forward" without the costs.

There is one problem with this picture, of course: it is a portrait of a capitalist developmental state. It does not matter whether the cat is black or white, Deng once said, so long as it catches mice. But as he himself must have learned during the 1989 Tiananmen revolt, the color of the cat does matter. The aforementioned characteristics of East Asian political economy may not be goods that can be chosen as if off a supermarket shelf. They are closely linked, and together form the gestalt of late capitalist development.

Development in East Asia is a temporal phenomenon, which makes it hard to emulate in different times and other countries. It took place in the context of a kind of benign neglect by a hegemonic power—the United States—which has tolerated neomercantilist

---

[2]Chalmers Johnson, "Political Institutions and Economic Performance: The Government-Business Relationship in Japan, South Korea, and Taiwan," in Frederic Dexo, ed., *The Political Economy of the New Asian Industrialism* (Ithaca, N.Y.: Cornell University Press, 1987).

practices so long as they occur in the interstices of the world market or when America dominates a broad range of industrial markets. Japan enjoyed such benign neglect from about the turn of the century to the 1930s, and then again from the 1950s to about the mid-1980s. South Korea and Taiwan have had their chance from the 1960s to the 1990s, relying above all else on the vast American market. Seizing the opportunity created by United States sponsorship—in particular the decision to keep the American market open to East Asia's industrial commodities, in spite of increasing protectionist pressures—the capitalist states in East Asia built export powerhouses, while insulating their own markets and prevailing over their own societies. In the prophylactic realm they created, these states produced mechanisms that would serve as substitutes for—in economic historian Alexander Gerschenkron's formulation—"missing" prerequisites for an economic takeoff, the most important of these being entrepreneurial segments and domestic capital for industrialization.

THE CONSEQUENCES OF CAPITALISM

The example of China immediately makes clear the hazards of pursuing this model in a different time and place. As several analysts have recently pointed out, if the textile sector were not so heavily protected —especially with the quotas and other barriers in the American market—China would quickly become the world's premier textile exporter. In the protectionist 1990s, as opposed to the open 1960s, textiles probably cannot be a "leading sector" for China as they were for South Korea and Taiwan. China cannot rely overwhelmingly on exports, as have other newly industrialized East Asian countries that have—Japan excepted—paltry domestic markets. China's huge domestic market must be able to absorb not only its own manufactures but vast quantities of foreign imports as well, in part to assure continuing access to markets for its exports.

The 1960s and 1970s were also indulgent toward "soft authoritarianism," with much hortatory literature penned by political scientists touting the virtues of putting the military in the saddle of "political development." Paradoxically, China went from "hard" to "soft" authoritarianism just in time to get bashed for bashing Chinese students—a reprehensible and terrible action, but arguably not worse than what happened in South Korea in 1980 or Mexico City in 1968.

The East Asian newly industrialized countries, however, during the earlier periods erected a huge bureaucratic apparatus to incubate a nascent capitalist class. From this logic flowed a set of repressive policies that characterized prewar Japan and postwar South Korea and Taiwan: financial repression by the state, in the form of a non-market-determined, exceedingly low price for capital, so that large sums were transferred from savers to corporate borrowers; labor repression, so that a class could be broken and a new one created; discrimination against foreign commodities to protect domestic capital; and finally, repression of the popular sector, which is to say, democracy.

Thus in South Korea the historical task of the authoritarian state was the creation (not re-creation, as in more advanced capitalist countries) of a capitalist class. This was particularly urgent because Korea inherited a tiny capitalist class on liberation in 1945—Japanese colonialism having been less interested in incubation than infanticide when faced with independent Korean capitalist development.

If the authoritarian state in South Korea is thus viewed as an entity that has jump-started not just a stagnant economy but an entire capitalist constellation—with the Korean conglomerates, the chaebol groups, the first major fruit—the implications of China's emulation of the South Korean political economy are highly interesting. They imply a transition from communism to capitalism, with the octogenarian Communists who cling to power in Beijing playing midwife to the birth not just of export-led growth but the capitalist classes their dictatorship of the proletariat was designed to quash.

What all this means is that authoritarianism in East Asia is an integral part of development strategy, useful not just for steadying societies in developmental flux but for creating the class that carried all before the modern world—the entreprenuerial class—and in the shifting of resources to that class. Authoritarian politics is not something genetically encoded in Confucian civilization, but a tried-and-true political arrangement in East Asia in its rush to industrialize.

Comparative Politics:
Some Major Trends, Issues, and Prospects

- **The Democratic Trend: How Strong, Thorough, and Lasting? (Articles 60 and 61)**
- **The Turn toward the Market: What Role for the State? (Articles 62 and 63)**
- **Ethnic and Cultural Conflict: The Political Assertion of Group Identities (Articles 64 and 65)**

The articles in this unit deal with three major political trends or patterns of development that can be observed in much of the contemporary world. It is important at the outset to stress that, with the possible exception of Benjamin Barber, none of the authors predict some form of global convergence in which all political systems would become alike in major respects. On closer examination, even Professor Barber turns out to argue that a strong tendency toward global homogenization is offset by a concurrent tendency toward intensified group differentiation and fragmentation.

Thus the trends or patterns discussed here are neither unidirectional nor universal. They are situationally defined, and therefore come in a great variety of forms and "mixes." They may well turn out to be temporary and at least partly reversible. Moreover, they do not always reinforce one another, but show considerable mutual tension. Indeed, their different forms of development are "the very stuff" of comparative politics, which seeks an informed understanding of the political dimension of social life by making careful comparisons across time and space.

After such cautionary preliminaries, we can proceed to identify three recent developments that singly and together have had a very important role in changing the political world in which we live. One is the *democratic revolution*, which has been sweeping much of the world. This refers to a widespread trend toward some form of popular government that often, but not always, takes the form of a search for representative, pluralist democracy in countries that were previously ruled by some form of authoritarian oligarchy or dictatorship.

Another trend, sometimes labeled the *capitalist revolution*, is the even more widespread shift toward some form of *market economy*. It includes a greater reliance on private enterprise and the profit motive, and it involves a concurrent move away from heavy regulation, central planning, and state ownership. But this need not mean laissez-faire capitalism. The "social market economy," found in much of Western Europe, allows a considerable role for the state in providing services, redistributing income, and setting overall societal goals. In some of the Asian communist-ruled countries, above all China, we have become used to seeing self-proclaimed revolutionary socialists introduce a considerable degree of capitalist practices into their formerly planned economies. Some wits have suggested that it is time to speak of "Market-Leninists."

The third major trend could be called the *revival of ethnic or cultural politics*. This refers to a growing emphasis on some form of an *exclusive group identity* as the primary basis for political expression. In modern times, it has been common for a group to identify itself by its special ethnic, religious, linguistic, or other cultural traits and to make this identity the basis for a claim to

rule by and for itself. The principle of national self-determination received the blessing of U.S. president Woodrow Wilson, and it continues to have a democratic appeal, even though some critics warn against the potential dangers that may stem from a fractious politics of ethnocracy. They detect a collectivist or antipluralist potential in this form of political expression, and point out that it can contribute to intolerance and conflicts among groups as well as between the group and the individual.

The articles in the first section cover democratization as the first of these trends, that is, the startling growth in the number of representative governments in recent years. Even if this development is likely to be reversed in some countries, we need to remember how remarkable it has been in the first place. Using very different criteria and data, skeptics on both the Right and the Left for a long time doubted whether representative government was sufficiently stable, efficient, accountable, attractive, or, ultimately, legitimate to survive or spread in the modern world. It would be instructive to review their more recent discussion of the 1970s and early 1980s, not in order to refute the pessimists but to learn from their insights as well as their oversights.

Samuel Huntington is one of the best known observers of democratization, who in the past emphasized the cultural, social, economic, and political obstacles to representative government in most of the world. In the aftermath of the collapse of communist regimes in Eastern and Central Europe, he has identified a broad pattern of democratization that began already in the mid-1970s, when three dictatorships in southern Europe came to an end (in Greece, Portugal, and Spain). In the following decade, democratization spread to most of Latin America. Central and Eastern Europe followed, and the trend has also reached some states in East and South Asia as well as some parts of Africa, above all South Africa.

In a widely adopted phrase, Huntington identifies this trend as the "third wave" of democratization in modern history. The "first wave" was both slow and long in its reach. It began in the 1820s and lasted about one century, until 1926, a period during which first the United States and subsequently 28 other countries established governments based on a wide and eventually universal suffrage. In 1922, however, Benito Mussolini's capture of power in Italy began a period of reversal, which lasted until the early 1940s. During these two decades, the number of democracies fell from 29 to 12, as many became victims of dictatorial takeovers or military conquests.

A "second wave" of democratization started with the Allied victory in World War II and continued during the early postwar years of decolonization. This wave lasted until about 1962 and resulted in the conversion of about two dozen previous authoritarian systems into democracies or quasi democracies, sometimes of very short duration. There followed a second reverse wave, lasting from 1962 to 1973. During this period, the number of democracies fell from 36 to 30 and the number of non-democracies increased from 75 to 95 as various former colonies or fresh democracies fell under authoritarian or dictatorial rule. In the mid-1970s, then, the "third wave" of democratization got its start.

At the beginning of the 1990s, Huntington counted about 60 democracies in the world, which amounts to a doubling of their number in less than two decades. It is an impressive change, but he points out that the process is likely to be reversed once again in a number of the new democracies. His discussion supports the conclusion that democracy's advance has always been a "two steps forward, one step back" kind of process. The expectations associated with the coming of democracy are in some countries so high that disappointments are bound to follow. Already, the "third wave" of democratic advances in countries like the Sudan, Nigeria, Algeria, and Peru have been followed by authoritarian reversals. Haiti has gone through its own double wave. The prospects for democracy on that poverty-stricken Caribbean island do not seem bright, despite the 1994 return to office of President Jean-Bertrand Aristide (elected in 1991 and overthrown by a military coup in the same year). There are ominous signs of an authoritarian revival in some parts of the former Soviet Union.

What are the general conditions that inhibit or encourage the spread and stabilization of democracy? Huntington and other scholars have identified some specific historical factors that appear to have contributed to the "third wave." One important factor is the loss of legitimacy by both right- and left-wing authoritarian regimes, as they have become discredited by failures. Another factor is the expansion in some developing world countries of an urban middle class, with a strong interest in representative government and constitutional rule. In Latin America, especially, the influence of a more liberal Catholic Church has been important. There have also been various forms of external influence by the United States and the European Union, as they have tried to promote a human rights agenda. A different but crucial instance of external influence took the form of Mikhail Gorbachev's shift toward nonintervention by the Soviet Union in the late 1980s, when he abandoned the Brezhnev Doctrine's commitment to defend established communist rulers in Eastern Europe and elsewhere against "counter-revolution." Finally, there is the "snowballing" or demonstration effect of a successful early transition to democracy in countries like Spain or Poland, which served as models for other countries in similar circumstances. This has also been very important in Latin America.

Huntington's rule of thumb is that a democratic form of government can be considered to have become stable when a country has had at least two successive peaceful turnovers of power. Such a development may take a generation or longer to complete, even under fortunate circumstances. Many of the new democracies have little historical experience with a democratic way of life. Where there has been such an experience, it may have been spotty and not very positive. There may be important cultural or socioeconomic obstacles to democratization, according to Huntington. Like most other observers, he sees extreme poverty as a principal obstacle to successful democratization.

Both old and new democracies face dangers, as Philipe Schmitter points out in his article. Schmitter gives a very systematic analysis of the many internal standards against which democracies are measured by their citizenry. Popular dissatisfaction normally focuses on the government in the established political systems, but where representative government itself is a new development there is a danger that democracy itself may become the target of criticism.

Germany provides a valuable case study for testing some of these interpretations of democracy. After World War I, anti-democratic critics identified the Weimar Republic with international disaster, socioeconomic ruin, and political weakness and instability. After World War II, by contrast, the Federal Republic became increasingly credited with stability and prosperity. At first accepted passively, the fledgling West German state soon generated an increasing measure of pragmatic support from its citizenry, based on its widely perceived effectiveness. In time, the new republic also appeared to gain a deeper, more effective support from much of the population. A major question is how national reunification, with its accompanying wrenching changes and inevitable disappointments, will influence German attitudes toward representative government. In the new eastern states, in particular, reunification was linked to unrealistic expectations of almost immediate socioeconomic alignment with the prosperous West. How will East Germans react, as the new polity fails to deliver promptly and bountifully? Unfortunately, many of the new democracies face dislocations that make them more comparable to the conditions of either the Weimar Republic or Eastern Germany rather than the successful West German state after World War II.

The second section of this unit covers the trend toward capitalism or, better, market economics. Here Gabriel Almond explores the connections between capitalism and democracy in an article that draws upon both theory and empirical studies. His systematic discussion shows that there are ways in which capitalism and democracy support each other, and ways in which they tend to undermine each other. Is it possible to have the best of both? Almond answers at length that there is a nonutopian manner in which capitalism and democracy can be reconciled, namely in democratic welfare capitalism.

Almond's discussion can be linked to a theme emphasized by some contemporary political economists. They point out that the economic competition between capitalism and socialism, in its communist form of state ownership and centralized planning, has become a largely closed chapter in history. The central question now is which form of capitalism or market economy will be more successful. A similar argument is made by the French theorist, Michel Albert, who also distinguishes between the British-American and the continental "Rhineland" models of capitalism. The former is more individualistic, antigovernmental, and characterized by such traits as high employee turnover and short-term profit maximizing. It differs considerably from what the Germans themselves like to call their "social market economy." The latter is more team-oriented, emphasizes cooperation between management and organized labor, and leaves a considerable role for government in the setting of general economic strategy, the training of an educated labor force, and the provision of social welfare services.

These different conceptions of capitalism can be linked to different histories. Both Britain and the United States experienced a head start in their industrial revolutions and felt no need for deliberate government efforts to encourage growth. By contrast, Germany and Japan both played the role of latecomers, who looked to government protection in their attempts to catch up. To be sure, governments were also swayed by military considerations to promote German and Japanese industrialization. But the emergence of a kind of "social capitalism" in other continental countries of Europe suggests that cultural rather than military factors played a major role in this development.

The third section deals with the revival of the ethnic and cultural dimension in politics. Until recently, relatively few observers foresaw that this element would play such a fractious role in the contemporary world. There were forewarnings, such as the ethnonationalist stirrings in the late 1960s and early 1970s in peripheral areas of such countries as Britain, Canada, or Spain. It also lay behind many of the conflicts in the newly independent countries of the developing world. But most Western observers seem to have been poorly prepared for the task of anticipating or understanding the resurgence of politicized religious, ethnic, or other cultural forces. Many non-Westerners were taken by surprise as well. Mikhail Gorbachev, for example, grossly underestimated the centrifugal force of the nationality question in his own country.

The politicization of religion in many parts of the world falls into this development of a "politics of identity." In recent years, religious groups in parts of Latin America, Asia, the Middle East, sub-Saharan Africa, Asia and southern Europe have variously set out on the political road in the name of their faith. As Max Weber warned in a classic lecture shortly before his death, it can be dangerous to seek "the salvation of souls" along the path of politics. The coexistence of people of divergent faiths is possible only because religious conviction need not fully determine or direct a person's or group's politics. When it does, it can add an element of fervor and an unwillingness to compromise that makes it difficult to live harmoniously with people who believe differently. Pluralist democracy requires an element of tolerance, which for many takes the form of a casual "live and let live" attitude, rather than a well-intentioned determination to make others conform to one's central beliefs.

There is an important debate among political scientists concerning the sources and scope of politics based on ethnic, religious and cultural differences. Samuel Huntington argues forcefully that our most important and dangerous future conflicts will be based on clashes of civilizations. In his view, they will be far more difficult to resolve than those rooted in socioeconomic or even ideological differences. His critics, including the German Josef Joffe, argue that Huntington distorts the differences among civilizations and trivializes the differences within civilizations as sources of political conflict. Chandra Muzaffar, a Malaysian commentator, goes much further by contending that Huntington's thesis provides a rationalization for a Western policy goal of dominating the Third World.

In the final article, Benjamin Barber brings a broad perspective to the discussion of identity politics in the contemporary world. He sees two major tendencies that threaten democracy. One is the force of globalism, brought about by modern technology, communications, and commerce. Its logical end station is what he calls a "McWorld," in which human diversity, individuality, and meaningful identity are erased. The second tendency works in the opposite direction. It is the force of tribalism, which drives human beings to exacerbate their group differences, become intolerant and engage in holy wars or "jihads" against each other. Barber argues that globalism is at best indifferent to democracy, while militant tribalism is deeply antithetical. He argues in favor of seeking a confederal solution, based on democratic civil societies, which could provide human beings with a nonmilitant, parochial communitarianism as well as a framework that suits the global market economy fairly well.

Looking Ahead: Challenge Questions

What is meant by the first, second, and third waves of democratization? Describe the reversals that followed the first two.

Where are most of the countries affected by the third wave located? What factors appear to have contributed to their democratization?

What are some main problems and dilemmas of old and new democracies, according to Philippe Schmitter ("Dangers and Dilemmas of Democracy")?

In what ways can market capitalism and liberal democracy be said to be mutually supportive? How can they undermine each other?

Why is it so difficult to resolve political conflicts that arise from the political assertion of an exclusive religious or ethnic identity?

What does Benjamin Barber mean when he warns that democracy is threatened by globalism and tribalism?

A NEW ERA IN DEMOCRACY
DEMOCRACY'S THIRD WAVE

SAMUEL P. HUNTINGTON

*Mr. Huntington is
professor of
government at
Harvard
University.*

Between 1974 and 1990, at least 30 countries made transitions to democracy, just about doubling the number of democratic governments in the world. Were these democratizations part of a continuing and ever-expanding "global democratic revolution" that will reach virtually every country in the world? Or did they represent a limited expansion of democracy, involving for the most part its reintroduction into countries that had experienced it in the past?

The current era of democratic transitions constitutes the third wave of democratization in the history of the modern world. The first "long" wave of democratization began in the 1820s, with the widening of the suffrage to a large proportion of the male population in the United States, and continued for almost a century until 1926, bringing into being some 29 democracies. In 1922, however, the coming to power of Mussolini in Italy marked the beginning of a first "reverse wave" that by 1942 had reduced the number of democratic states in the world to 12. The triumph of the Allies in World War II initiated a second wave of democratization that reached its zenith in 1962 with 36 countries governed democratically, only to be followed by a second reverse wave (1960-1975) that brought the number of democracies back down to 30.

At what stage are we within the third wave? Early in a long wave, or at or near the end of a short one? And if the third wave comes to a halt, will it be followed by a significant third reverse wave eliminating many of democracy's gains in the 1970s and 1980s? Social science cannot provide reliable answers to these questions, nor can any social scientist. It may be possible, however, to identify some of the factors that will affect the future expansion or contraction of democracy in the world and to pose the questions that seem most relevant for the future of democratization.

One way to begin is to inquire whether the causes that gave rise to the third wave are likely to continue operating, to gain in strength, to weaken, or to be supplemented or replaced by new forces promoting democratization. Five major factors have contributed significantly to the occurrence and the timing of the third-wave transitions to democracy:

1. The deepening legitimacy problems of authoritarian regimes in a world where democratic values were widely accepted, the consequent dependence of these regimes on successful performance, and their inability to maintain "performance legitimacy" due to economic (and sometimes military) failure.

2. The unprecedented global economic growth of the 1960s, which raised living standards, increased education, and greatly expanded the urban middle class in many countries.

3. A striking shift in the doctrine and activities of the Catholic Church, manifested in the Second Vatican Council of 1963-65 and the transformation of national Catholic churches from defenders of the status quo to opponents of authoritarianism.

4. Changes in the policies of external actors, most notably the European Community, the United States, and the Soviet Union.

5. "Snowballing," or the demonstration effect of transitions earlier in the third wave in stimulating and providing models for subsequent efforts at democratization.

I will begin by addressing the latter three factors, returning to the first two later in this article.

Historically, there has been a strong correlation between Western Christianity and democracy. By the early 1970s, most of the Protestant countries in the world had already become democratic. The third wave of the 1970s and 1980s was overwhelmingly a Catholic wave. Beginning in Portugal and Spain, it swept through six South American and three

From *Current,* September 1991, pp. 27-39. From "Democracy's Third Wave," as it appeared in *Journal of Democracy,* Spring 1991, pp. 12-34.

Central American countries, moved on to the Philippines, doubled back to Mexico and Chile, and then burst through in the two Catholic countries of Eastern Europe, Poland and Hungary. Roughly three-quarters of the countries that transited to democracy between 1974 and 1989 were predominantly Catholic.

By 1990, however, the Catholic impetus to democratization had largely exhausted itself. Most Catholic countries had already democratized or, as in the case of Mexico, liberalized. The ability of Catholicism to promote further expansion of democracy (without expanding its own ranks) is limited to Paraguay, Cuba, and a few Francophone African countries. By 1990, sub-Saharan Africa was the only region of the world where substantial numbers of Catholics and Protestants lived under authoritarian regimes in a large number of countries.

THE ROLE OF EXTERNAL FORCES

During the third wave, the European Community (EC) played a key role in consolidating democracy in southern Europe. In Greece, Spain, and Portugal, the establishment of democracy was seen as necessary to secure the economic benefits of EC membership, while Community membership was in turn seen as a guarantee of the stability of democracy. In 1981, Greece became a full member of the Community, and five years later Spain and Portugal did as well.

In April 1987, Turkey applied for full EC membership. One incentive was the desire of Turkish leaders to reinforce modernizing and democratic tendencies in Turkey and to contain and isolate the forces in Turkey supporting Islamic fundamentalism. Within the Community, however, the prospect of Turkish membership met with little enthusiasm and even some hostility (mostly from Greece). In 1990, the liberation of Eastern Europe also raised the possibility of membership for Hungary, Czechoslovakia, and Poland. The Community thus faced two issues. First, should it give priority to broadening its membership or to "deepening" the existing Community by moving toward further economic and political union? Second, if it did decide to expand its membership, should priority go to European Free Trade Association members like Austria, Norway, and Sweden, to the East Europeans, or to Turkey? Presumably the Community can only absorb a limited number of countries in a given period of time. The answers to these questions will have significant implications for the stability of democracy in Turkey and in the East European countries.

The withdrawal of Soviet power made possible democratization in Eastern Europe. If the Soviet Union were to end or drastically curtail its support for Castro's regime, movement toward democracy might occur in Cuba. Apart from that, there seems little more the Soviet Union can do or is likely to do to promote democracy outside its borders. The key issue is what will happen within the Soviet Union itself. If Soviet control loosens, it seems likely that democracy could be reestablished in the Baltic states. Movements toward democracy also exist in other republics. Most important, of course, is Russia itself. The inauguration and consolidation of democracy in the Russian republic, if it occurs, would be the single most dramatic gain for democracy since the immediate post-World War II years. Democratic development in most of the Soviet republics, however, is greatly complicated by their ethnic heterogeneity and the unwillingness of the dominant nationality to allow equal rights to ethnic minorities. As Sir Ivor Jennings remarked years ago, "the people cannot decide until somebody decides who are the people." It may take years if not decades to resolve the latter issue in much of the Soviet Union.

During the 1970s and 1980s the United States was a major promoter of democratization. Whether the United States continues to play this role depends on its will, its capability, and its attractiveness as a model to other countries. Before the mid-1970s the promotion of democracy had not always been a high priority of American foreign policy. It could again subside in importance. The end of the Cold War and of the ideological competition with the Soviet Union could remove one rationale for propping up anti-communist dictators, but it could also reduce the incentives for any substantial American involvement in the Third World.

PROMOTION OF DEMOCRACY

American will to promote democracy may or may not be sustained. American ability to do so, on the other hand, is limited. The trade and budget deficits impose new limits on the resources that the United States can use to influence events in foreign countries. More important, the ability of the United States to promote democracy has in some measure run its course. The countries in Latin America, the Caribbean, Europe, and East Asia that were most susceptible to American influence have, with a few exceptions, already become democratic. The one major country where the United States can still exercise significant influence on behalf of democratization is Mexico. The undemocratic countries in Africa, the Middle East, and mainland Asia are less susceptible to American influence.

Apart from Central America and the Caribbean, the major area of the Third World where the United States has continued to have vitally important interests is the Persian Gulf. The Gulf War and the dispatch of 500,000 American troops to the region have stimulated demands for movement toward democracy in

Kuwait and Saudi Arabia and delegitimized Saddam Hussein's regime in Iraq. A large American military deployment in the Gulf, if sustained over time, would provide an external impetus toward liberalization if not democratization, and a large American military deployment probably could not be sustained over time unless some movement toward democracy occurred.

The U.S. contribution to democratization in the 1980s involved more than the conscious and direct exercise of American power and influence. Democratic movements around the world have been inspired by and have borrowed from the American example. What might happen, however, if the American model ceases to embody strength and success, no longer seems to be the winning model? At the end of the 1980s, many were arguing that "American decline" was the true reality. If people around the world come to see the United States as a fading power beset by political stagnation, economic inefficiency, and social chaos, its perceived failures will inevitably be seen as the failures of democracy, and the worldwide appeal of democracy will diminish.

SNOWBALLING

The impact of snowballing on democratization was clearly evident in 1990 in Bulgaria, Romania, Yugoslavia, Mongolia, Nepal, and Albania. It also affected movements toward liberalization in some Arab and African countries. In 1990, for instance, it was reported that the "upheaval in Eastern Europe" had "fueled demands for change in the Arab world" and prompted leaders in Egypt, Jordan, Tunisia, and Algeria to open up more political space for the expression of discontent.

The East European example had its principal effect on the leaders of authoritarian regimes, not on the people they ruled. President Mobutu Sese Seko of Zaire, for instance reacted with shocked horror to televised pictures of the execution by firing squad of his friend Romanian dictator Nicolae Ceauşescu. A few months later, commenting that "You know what's happening across the world," he announced that he would allow two parties besides his own to compete in elections in 1993. In Tanzania, Julius Nyerere observed that "If changes take place in Eastern Europe then other countries with one-party systems and which profess socialism will also be affected." His country, he added, could learn a "lesson or two" from Eastern Europe. In Nepal in April 1990, the government announced that King Birendra was lifting the ban on political parties as a result of "the international situation" and "the rising expectations of the people."

If a country lacks favorable internal conditions, however, snowballing alone is unlikely to bring about democratization. The democratization of countries A and B is not a reason for democratization in country C, unless the conditions that favored it in the former also exist in the latter. Although the legitimacy of democratic government came to be accepted throughout the world in the 1980s, economic and social conditions favorable to democracy were not everywhere present. The "worldwide democratic revolution" may create an external environment conducive to democratization, but it cannot produce the conditions necessary for democratization within a particular country.

WORLDWIDE DEMOCRATIC REVOLUTION

In Eastern Europe the major obstacle to democratization was Soviet control; once it was removed, the movement to democracy spread rapidly. There is no comparable external obstacle to democratization in the Middle East, Africa, and Asia. If rulers in these areas chose authoritarianism before December 1989, why can they not continue to choose it thereafter? The snowballing effect would be real only to the extent that it led them to believe in the desirability or necessity of democratization. The events of 1989 in Eastern Europe undoubtedly encouraged democratic opposition groups and frightened authoritarian leaders elsewhere. Yet given the previous weakness of the former and the long-term repression imposed by the latter, it seems doubtful that the East European example will actually produce significant progress toward democracy in most other authoritarian countries.

By 1990, many of the original causes of the third wave had become significantly weaker, even exhausted. Neither the White House, the Kremlin, the European Community, nor the Vatican was in a strong position to promote democracy in places where it did not already exist (primarily in Asia, Africa, and the Middle East). It remains possible, however, for new forces favoring democratization to emerge. After all, who in 1985 could have foreseen that Mikhail Gorbachev would facilitate democratization in Eastern Europe?

In the 1990s the International Monetary Fund (IMF) and the World Bank could conceivably become much more forceful than they have heretofore been in making political democratization as well as economic liberalization a precondition for economic assistance. France might become more active in promoting democracy among its former African colonies, where its influence remains substantial. The Orthodox churches could emerge as a powerful influence for democracy in southeastern Europe and the Soviet Union. A Chinese proponent of *glasnost* could come to power in Beijing, or a new Jeffersonian-style Nasser could spread a democratic version of Pan-Arabism in the Middle East. Japan could use its growing economic clout to encourage human rights and democracy in the poor countries to which it makes loans and grants. In 1990, none of these possibilities seemed very likely, but after the surprises of 1989 it would be rash to rule anything out.

A THIRD REVERSE WAVE?

By 1990 at least two third-wave democracies, Sudan and Nigeria, had reverted to authoritarian rule; the difficulties of consolidation could lead to further reversions in countries with unfavorable conditions for sustaining democracy. The first and second democratic waves, however, were followed not merely by some backsliding but by major reverse waves during which most regime changes throughout the world were from democracy to authoritarianism. If the third wave of democratization slows down or comes to a halt, what factors might produce a third reverse wave?

Among the factors contributing to transitions away from democracy during the first and second reverse waves were:

1. the weakness of democratic values among key elite groups and the general public;

2. severe economic setbacks, which intensified social conflict and enhanced the popularity of remedies that could be imposed only by authoritarian governments;

3. social and political polarization, often produced by leftist governments seeking the rapid introduction of major social and economic reforms;

4. the determination of conservative middle-class and upper-class groups to exclude populist and leftist movements and lower-class groups from political power;

5. the breakdown of law and order resulting from terrorism or insurgency;

6. intervention or conquest by a nondemocratic foreign power;

7. "reverse snowballing" triggered by the collapse or overthrow of democratic systems in other countries.

Transitions from democracy to authoritarianism, apart from those produced by foreign actors, have almost always been produced by those in power or close to power in the democratic system. With only one or two possible exceptions, democratic systems have not been ended by popular vote or popular revolt. In Germany and Italy in the first reverse wave, antidemocratic movements with considerable popular backing came to power and established fascist dictatorships. In Spain in the first reverse wave and in Lebanon in the second, democracy ended in civil war.

The overwhelming majority of transitions from democracy, however, took the form either of military coups that ousted democratically elected leaders, or executive coups in which democratically chosen chief executives effectively ended democracy by concentrating power in their own hands, usually by declaring a state of emergency or martial law. In the first reverse wave, military coups ended democratic systems in the new countries of Eastern Europe and in Greece, Portugal, Argentina, and Japan. In the second reverse wave, military coups occurred in Indonesia, Pakistan, Greece, Nigeria, Turkey, and many Latin American countries. Executive coups occurred in the second reverse wave in Korea, India, and the Philippines. In Uruguay, the civilian and military leadership cooperated to end democracy through a mixed executive-military coup.

In both the first and second reverse waves, democratic systems were replaced in many cases by historically new forms of authoritarian rule. Fascism was distinguished from earlier forms of authoritarianism by its mass base, ideology, party organization, and efforts to penetrate and control most of society. Bureaucratic authoritarianism differed from earlier forms of military rule in Latin America with respect to its institutional character, its presumption of indefinite duration, and its economic policies. Italy and Germany in the 1920s and 1930s and Brazil and Argentina in the 1960s and 1970s were the lead countries in introducing these new forms of nondemocratic rule and furnished the examples that antidemocratic groups in other countries sought to emulate. Both these new forms of authoritarianism were, in effect, responses to social and economic development: the expansion of social mobilization and political participation in Europe, and the exhaustion of the import-substitution phase of economic development in Latin America.

Although the causes and forms of the first two reverse waves cannot generate reliable predictions concerning the causes and forms of a possible third reverse wave, prior experiences do suggest some potential causes of a new reverse wave.

First, systemic failures of democratic regimes to operate effectively could undermine their legitimacy. In the late twentieth century, the major nondemocratic ideological sources of legitimacy, most notably Marxism-Leninism, were discredited. The general acceptance of democratic norms meant that democratic governments were even less dependent on performance legitimacy than they had been in the past. Yet sustained inability to provide welfare, prosperity, equity, justice, domestic order, or external security could over time undermine the legitimacy even of democratic governments. As the memories of authoritarian failures fade, irritation with democratic failures is likely to increase. More specifically, a general international economic collapse on the 1929–30 model could undermine the legitimacy of democracy in many countries. Most democracies did survive the Great Depression

POTENTIAL CAUSES

of the 1930s; yet some succumbed, and presumably some would be likely to succumb in response to a comparable economic disaster in the future.

SHIFT TO AUTHORITAR-IANISM

Second, a shift to authoritarianism by any democratic or democratizing great power could trigger reverse snowballing. The reinvigoration of authoritarianism in Russia or the Soviet Union would have unsettling effects on democratization in other Soviet republics, Bulgaria, Romania, Yugoslavia, and Mongolia and possibly in Poland, Hungary, and Czechoslovakia as well. It could send the message to would-be despots elsewhere: "You too can go back into business." Similarly, the establishment of an authoritarian regime in India could have a significant demonstration effect on other Third World countries. Moreover, even if a major country does not revert to authoritarianism, a shift to dictatorship by several smaller newly democratic countries that lack many of the usual preconditions for democracy could have ramifying effects even on other countries where those preconditions are strong.

If a nondemocratic state greatly increased its power and began to expand beyond its borders, this too could stimulate authoritarian movements in other countries. This stimulus would be particularly strong if the expanding authoritarian state militarily defeated one or more democratic countries. In the past, all major powers that have developed economically have also tended to expand territorially. If China develops economically under authoritarian rule in the coming decades and expands its influence and control in East Asia, democratic regimes in the region will be significantly weakened.

Finally, as in the 1920s and the 1960s, various old and new forms of authoritarianism that seem appropriate to the needs of the times could emerge. Authoritarian nationalism could take hold in some Third World countries and also in Eastern Europe. Religious fundamentalism, which has been most dramatically prevalent in Iran, could come to power in other countries, especially in the Islamic world. Oligarchic authoritarianism could develop in both wealthy and poorer countries as a reaction to the leveling tendencies of democracy. Populist dictatorships could emerge in the future, as they have in the past, in response to democracy's protection of various forms of economic privilege, particularly in those countries where land tenancy is still an issue. Finally, communal dictatorships could be imposed in democracies with two or more distinct ethnic, racial, or religious groups, with one group trying to establish control over the entire society.

All of these forms of authoritarianism have existed in the past. It is not beyond the wit of humans to devise new ones in the future. One possibility might be a technocratic "electronic dictatorship," in which authoritarian rule is made possible and legitimated by the regime's ability to manipulate information, the media, and sophisticated means of communication. None of these old or new forms of authoritarianism is highly probable, but it is also hard to say that any one of them is totally impossible.

OBSTACLES TO DEMOCRATIZATION

Another approach to assessing democracy's prospects is to examine the obstacles to and opportunities for democratization where it has not yet taken hold. As of 1990, more than one hundred countries lacked democratic regimes. Most of these countries fell into four sometimes overlapping geocultural categories:

1. Home-grown Marxist-Leninist regimes, including the Soviet Union, where major liberalization occurred in the 1980s and democratic movements existed in many republics;

2. Sub-Saharan African countries, which, with a few exceptions, remained personal dictatorships, military regimes, one-party systems, or some combination of these three;

3. Islamic countries stretching from Morocco to Indonesia, which except for Turkey and perhaps Pakistan had nondemocratic regimes;

4. East Asian countries, from Burma through Southeast Asia to China and North Korea, which included communist systems, military regimes, personal dictatorships, and two semi-democracies (Thailand and Malaysia).

The obstacles to democratization in these groups of countries are political, cultural, and economic. One potentially significant political obstacle to future democratization is the virtual absence of experience with democracy in most countries that remained authoritarian in 1990. Twenty-three of 30 countries that democratized between 1974 and 1990 had had some history of democracy, while only a few countries that were nondemocratic in 1990 could claim such experience. These included a few third-wave backsliders (Sudan, Nigeria, Suriname, and possibly Pakistan), four second-wave backsliders that had not redemocratized in the third wave (Lebanon, Sri Lanka, Burma, Fiji), and three first-wave democratizers that had been prevented by Soviet occupation from redemocratizing at the end of World War II (Estonia, Latvia, and Lithuania). Virtually all the 90 or more other nondemocratic countries in 1990 lacked significant past experience with democratic rule. This obviously is not a decisive impediment to democratization—if it were, no countries would now be democratic—but it does make it more difficult.

Another obstacle to democratization is likely to disappear in a number of countries in the 1990s. Leaders who found authoritarian regimes or rule them for a long period tend to be-

LEADERSHIP CHANGE

come particularly staunch opponents of democratization. Hence some form of leadership change within the authoritarian system usually precedes movement toward democracy. Human mortality is likely to ensure such changes in the 1990s in some authoritarian regimes. In 1990, the long-term rulers in China, Côte d'Ivoire, and Malawi were in their eighties; those in Burma, Indonesia, North Korea, Lesotho, and Vietnam were in their seventies; and the leaders of Cuba, Morocco, Singapore, Somalia, Syria, Tanzania, Zaire, and Zambia were sixty or older. The death or departure from office of these leaders would remove one obstacle to democratization in their countries, but would not make it inevitable.

Between 1974 and 1990, democratization occurred in personal dictatorships, military regimes, and one-party systems. Full-scale democratization has not yet occurred, however, in communist one-party states that were the products of domestic revolution. Liberalization has taken place in the Soviet Union, which may or may not lead to full-scale democratization in Russia. In Yugoslavia, movements toward democracy are underway in Slovenia and Croatia. The Yugoslav communist revolution, however, was largely a Serbian revolution, and the prospects for democracy in Serbia appear dubious. In Cambodia, an extraordinarily brutal revolutionary communist regime was replaced by a less brutal communist regime imposed by outside force. In 1990, Albania appeared to be opening up, but in China, Vietnam, Laos, Cuba and Ethiopia, Marxist-Leninist regimes produced by home-grown revolutions seemed determined to remain in power. The revolutions in these countries had been nationalist as well as communist, and hence nationalism reinforced communism in a way that obviously was not true of Soviet-occupied Eastern Europe.

One serious impediment of democratization is the absence or weakness of real commitment to democratic values among political leaders in Asia, Africa, and the Middle East. When they are out of power, political leaders have good reason to advocate democracy. The test of their democratic commitment comes once they are in office. In Latin America, democratic regimes have generally been overthrown by military coups d'état. This has happened in Asia and the Middle East as well, but in these regions elected leaders themselves have also been responsible for ending democracy: Syngman Rhee and Park Chung Hee in Korea, Adnan Menderes in Turkey, Ferdinand Marcos in the Philippines, Lee Kwan Yew in Singapore, Indira Gandhi in India, and Sukarno in Indonesia. Having won power through the electoral system, these leaders then proceeded to undermine that system. They had little commitment to democratic values and practices.

Even when Asian, African, and Middle Eastern leaders have more or less abided by the rules of democracy, they often seemed to do so grudgingly. Many European, North American, and Latin American political leaders in the last half of the twentieth century were ardent and articulate advocates of democracy. Asian and African countries, in contrast, did not produce many heads of government who were also apostles of democracy. Who were the Asian, Arab, or African equivalents of Rómulo Betancourt, Alberto Llera Camargo, José Figueres, Eduardo Frei, Fernando Belaúnde Terry, Juan Bosch, José Napoleón Duarte, and Raúl Alfonsin? Jawaharlal Nehru and Corazon Aquino were, and there may have been others, but they were few in number. No Arab leader comes to mind, and it is hard to identify any Islamic leader who made a reputation as an advocate and supporter of democracy while in office. Why is this? This question inevitably leads to the issue of culture.

CULTURE

It has been argued that the world's great historic cultural traditions vary significantly in the extent to which their attitudes, values, beliefs, and related behavior patterns are conducive to the development of democracy. A profoundly antidemocratic culture would impede the spread of democratic norms in the society, deny legitimacy to democratic institutions, and thus greatly complicate if not prevent the emergence and effective functioning of those institutions. The cultural thesis comes in two forms. The more restrictive version states that only Western culture provides a suitable base for the development of democratic institutions and, consequently, that democracy is largely inappropriate for non-Western societies. In the early years of the third wave, this argument was explicitly set forth by George Kennan. Democracy, he said, was a form of government "which evolved in the eighteenth and nineteenth centuries in northwestern Europe, primarily among those countries that border on the English Channel and the North Sea (but with a certain extension into Central Europe), and which was then carried into other parts of the world, including North America, where peoples from that northwestern European area appeared as original settlers, or as colonialists, and laid down the prevailing patterns of civil government." Hence democracy has "a relatively narrow base both in time and in space; and the evidence has yet to be produced that it is the natural form of rule for peoples outside those narrow perimeters." The achievements of Mao, Salazar, and Castro demonstrated, according to Kennan, that authoritarian regimes "have been able to introduce reforms and to improve the lot of masses of people, where more diffuse forms of political authority had failed."

Democracy, in short, is appropriate only for northwestern and perhaps central European countries and their settler-colony offshoots.

The Western-culture thesis has immediate implications for democratization in the Balkans and the Soviet Union. Historically these areas were part of the Czarist and Ottoman empires; their prevailing religions were Orthodoxy and Islam, not Western Christianity. These areas did not have the same experiences as Western Europe with feudalism, the Renaissance, the Reformation, the Enlightenment, the French Revolution, and liberalism. *WESTERN CULTURE THESIS* As William Wallace has suggested, the end of the Cold War and the disappearance of the Iron Curtain may have shifted the critical political dividing line eastward to the centuries-old boundary between Eastern and Western Christendom. Beginning in the north, this line runs south roughly along the borders dividing Finland and the Baltic republics from Russia; through Byelorussia and the Ukraine, separating western Catholic Ukraine from eastern Orthodox Ukraine; south and then west in Romania, cutting off Transylvania from the rest of the country; and then through Yugoslavia roughly along the line separating Slovenia and Croatia from the other republics. This line may now separate those areas where democracy will take root from those where it will not.

A less restrictive version of the cultural obstacle argument holds that certain non-Western cultures are peculiarly hostile to democracy. The two cultures most often cited in this regard are Confucianism and Islam. Three questions are relevant to determining whether these cultures now pose serious obstacles to democratization. First, to what extent are traditional Confucian and Islamic values and beliefs hostile to democracy? Second, if they are, to what extent have these cultures in fact hampered progress toward democracy? Third, if they have significantly retarded democratic progress in the past, to what extent are they likely to continue to do so in the future?

CONFUCIANISM

Almost no scholarly disagreement exists regarding the proposition that traditional Confucianism was either undemocratic or antidemocratic. The only mitigating factor was the extent to which the examination system in the classic Chinese polity opened careers to the talented without regard to social background. Even if this were the case, however, a merit system of promotion does not make a democracy. No one would describe a modern army as democratic because officers are promoted on the basis of their abilities. Classic Chinese Confucianism and its derivatives in Korea, Vietnam, Singapore, Taiwan, and (in diluted fashion) Japan emphasized the group over the individual, authority over liberty, and responsibilities over rights. Confucian societies lacked a tradition of rights against the state; to the extent that individual rights did exist, they were created by the state. Harmony and cooperation were preferred over disagreement and competition. The maintenance of order and respect for hierarchy were central values. The conflict of ideas, groups, and parties was viewed as dangerous and illegitimate. Most important, Confucianism merged society and the state and provided no legitimacy for autonomous social institutions at the national level.

In practice Confucian or Confucian-influenced societies have been inhospitable to democracy. In East Asia only two countries, Japan and the Philippines, had sustained experience with democratic government prior to 1990. In both cases, democracy was the product of an American presence. The Philippines, moreover, is overwhelmingly a Catholic country. In Japan, Confucian values were reinterpreted and merged with autochthonous cultural traditions.

Mainland China has had no experience with democratic government, and democracy of the Western variety has been supported over the years only by relatively small groups of radical dissidents. "Mainstream" democratic critics have not broken with the key elements of the Confucian tradition. The modernizers of China have been (in Lucian Pye's phrase) the "Confucian Leninists" of the Nationalist and Communist parties. In the late 1980s, when rapid economic growth in China produced a new series of demands for political reform and democracy on the part of students, intellectuals, and urban middle-class groups, the Communist leadership responded in two ways. First, it articulated a theory of "new authoritarianism," based on the experience of Taiwan, Singapore, and Korea, which claimed that a country at China's stage of economic development needed authoritarian rule to achieve balanced economic growth and contain the unsettling consequences of development. Second, the leadership violently suppressed the democratic movement in Beijing and elsewhere in June of 1989.

In China, economics reinforced culture in holding back democracy. In Singapore, Taiwan, and Korea, on the other hand, spectacular growth created the economic basis for democracy by the late 1980s. In these countries, economics clashed with culture in shaping political development. In 1990, Singapore was the only non-oil-exporting "high-income" country (as defined by the World Bank) that did not have a democratic political system, and Singapore's leader was an articulate exponent of Confucian values as opposed to those of Western democracy. In the 1980s, Premier Lee Kwan Yew made the teaching and promulgation of Confucian values a high priority for his city-state and took vigorous measures to limit and suppress dissent and to prevent media criticism of the government and its policies. Singapore was thus an authoritarian Confucian anomaly among the wealthy countries of the world. The interesting question is whether it will remain so now that Lee, who created the state, appears to be partially withdrawing from the political scene.

TAIWAN AND KOREA In the late 1980s, both Taiwan and Korea moved in a democratic direction. Historically, Taiwan had always been a peripheral part of China. It was occupied by the Japanese for 50 years, and its inhabitants rebelled in 1947 against the imposition of Chinese control. The Nationalist government arrived in 1949 humiliated by its defeat by the Communists, a defeat that made it impossible "for most Nationalist leaders to uphold the posture of arrogance associated with traditional Confucian notions of authority." Rapid economic and social development further weakened the influence of traditional Confucianism. The emergence of a substantial entrepreneurial class, composed largely of native Taiwanese, created (in very un-Confucian fashion) a source of power and wealth independent of the mainlander-dominated state. This produced in Taiwan a "fundamental change in Chinese political culture, which has not occurred in China itself or in Korea or Vietnam—and never really existed in Japan." Taiwan's spectacular economic development thus overwhelmed a relatively weak Confucian legacy, and in the late 1980s Chiang Ching-kuo and Lee Teng-hui responded to the pressures produced by economic and social change and gradually moved to open up politics in their society.

In Korea, the classical culture included elements of mobility and egalitarianism along with Confucian components uncongenial to democracy, including a tradition of authoritarianism and strongman rule. As one Korean scholar put it, "people did not think of themselves as citizens with rights to exercise and responsibilities to perform, but they tended to look up to the top for direction and for favors in order to survive." In the late 1980s, urbanization, education, the development of a substantial middle class, and the impressive spread of Christianity all weakened Confucianism as an obstacle to democracy in Korea. Yet it remained unclear whether the struggle between the old culture and the new prosperity had been definitively resolved in favor of the latter.

THE EAST ASIAN MODEL

The interaction of economic progress and Asian culture appears to have generated a distinctly East Asian variety of democratic institutions. As of 1990, no East Asian country except the Philippines (which is, in many respects, more Latin American than East Asian in culture) had experienced a turnover from a popularly elected government of one party to a popularly elected government of a different party. The prototype was Japan, unquestionably a democracy, but one in which the ruling party has never been voted out of power. The Japanese model of dominant-party democracy, as Pye has pointed out, has spread elsewhere in East Asia. In 1990, two of the three opposition parties in Korea merged with the government party to form a political bloc that would effectively exclude the remaining opposition party, led by Kim Dae Jung and based on the Cholla region, from ever gaining power. In the late 1980s, democratic development in Taiwan seemed to be moving toward an electoral system in which the Kuomintang (KMT) was likely to remain the dominant party, with the Democratic Progressive Party confined to a permanent opposition role. In Malaysia, the coalition of the three leading parties from the Malay, Chinese, and Indian communities (first in the Alliance Party and then in the National Front) has controlled power in unbroken fashion against all competitors from the 1950s through the 1980s. In the mid-1980s, Lee Kwan Yew's deputy and successor Goh Chok Tong endorsed a similar type of party system for Singapore:

> I think a stable system is one where there is a mainstream political party representing a broad range of the population. Then you can have a few other parties on the periphery, very serious-minded parties. They are unable to have wider views but they nevertheless represent sectional interests. And the mainstream is returned all the time. I think that's good. And I would not apologize if we ended up in that situation in Singapore.

A primary criterion for democracy is equitable and open competition for votes between political parties without government harassment or restriction of opposition groups. Japan has clearly met this test for decades with its freedoms of speech, press, and assembly, and reasonably equitable conditions of electoral competition. In the other Asian dominant-party systems, the playing field has been tilted in favor of the government for many years. By the late 1980s, however, conditions were becoming more equal in some countries. In Korea, the government party was unable to win control of the legislature in 1989, and this failure presumably was a major factor in its subsequent merger with two of its opponents. In Taiwan, restrictions on the opposition were gradually lifted. It is thus conceivable that other East Asian countries could join Japan in providing a level playing field for a game that the government party always wins. In 1990 the East Asian dominant-party systems thus spanned a continuum between democracy and authoritarianism, with Japan at one extreme, Indonesia at the other, and Korea, Taiwan, Malaysia, and Singapore (more or less in that order) in between.

Such a system may meet the formal requisites of democracy, but it differs significantly from the democratic systems prevalent in the West, where it is assumed not only that political parties and coalitions will freely and equally compete for power but also that they are likely to *alternate* in power. By contrast, the East Asian dominant-party systems seem to involve competition for power but not alternation in power, and participation in elections for all, but participation in office only for those in the "mainstream" party. This type of political system offers democracy without turnover. It represents an adaptation of Western democratic practices to serve not Western values of competition and change, but Asian values of consensus and stability.

Western democratic systems are less dependent on performance legitimacy than authoritarian systems because failure is blamed on the incumbents instead of the system, and the ouster and replacement of the incumbents help to renew the system. The East Asian societies that have adopted or appear to be adopting the dominant-party model had unequalled records of economic success from the 1960s to the 1980s. What happens, however, if and when their 8-percent growth rates plummet; unemployment, inflation, and other forms of economic distress escalate; or social and economic conflicts intensify? In a Western democracy the response would be to turn the incumbents out. In a dominant-party democracy, however, that would represent a revolutionary change. If the structure of political competition does not allow that to happen, unhappiness with the government could well lead to demonstrations, protests, riots, and efforts to mobilize popular support to overthrow the government. The government then would be tempted to respond by suppressing dissent and imposing authoritarian controls. The key question, then, is to what extent the East Asian dominant-party system presupposes uninterrupted and substantial economic growth. Can this system survive prolonged economic downturn or stagnation?

ISLAM

"Confucian democracy" is clearly a contradiction in terms. It is unclear whether "Islamic democracy" also is. Egalitarianism and voluntarism are central themes in Islam. The "high culture form of Islam," Ernest Gellner has argued, is "endowed with a number of features—unitarianism, a rule-ethic, individualism, scripturalism, puritanism, an egalitarian aversion to mediation and hierarchy, a fairly small load of magic—that are congruent, presumably, with requirements of modernity or modernization." They are also generally congruent with the requirements of democracy. Islam, however, also rejects any distinction between the religious community and the political community. Hence there is no equipoise between Caesar and God, and political participation is linked to religious affiliation. Fundamentalist Islam demands that in a Muslim country the political rulers should be practicing Muslims, *shari'a* should be the basic law, and *ulema* should have a "decisive vote in articulating, or at least reviewing and ratifying, all governmental policy." To the extent that governmental legitimacy and policy flow from religious doctrine and religious expertise, Islamic concepts of politics differ from and contradict the premises of democratic politics.

Islamic doctrine thus contains elements that may be both congenial and uncongenial to democracy. In practice, however, the only Islamic country that has sustained a fully democratic political system for any length of time is Turkey, where Mustafa Kemal Ataturk explicitly rejected Islamic concepts of society and politics and vigorously attempted to create a secular, modern, Western nation-state. And Turkey's experience with democracy has not been an unmitigated success. Elsewhere in the Islamic world, Pakistan has made three attempts at democracy, none of which lasted long. While Turkey has had democracy interrupted by occasional military interventions, Pakistan has had bureaucratic and military rule interrupted by occasional elections.

The only Arab country to sustain a form of democracy (albeit of the consociational variety) for a significant period of time was Lebanon. Its democracy, however, really amounted to consociational oligarchy, and 40 to 50 percent of its population was Christian. Once Muslims became a majority in Lebanon and began to assert themselves, Lebanese democracy collapsed. Between 1981 and 1990, only two of 37 countries in the world with Muslim majorities were ever rated "Free" by Freedom House in its annual surveys: the Gambia for two years and the Turkish Republic of Northern Cyprus for four. Whatever the compatibility of Islam and democracy in theory, in practice they have rarely gone together.

Opposition movements to authoritarian regimes in southern and eastern Europe, in Latin America, and in East Asia almost universally have espoused Western democratic values and proclaimed their desire to establish democracy. This does not mean that they invariably would introduce democratic institutions if they had the opportunity to do so, but at least they articulated the rhetoric of democracy. In authoritarian Islamic societies, by contrast, movements explicitly campaigning for democratic politics have been relatively weak, and the most powerful opposition has come from Islamic fundamentalists.

ECONOMIC
PROBLEMS
In the late 1980s, domestic economic problems combined with the snowballing effects of democratization elsewhere led the governments of several Islamic countries to relax their controls on the opposition and to attempt to renew their legitimacy through elections. The principal initial beneficiaries of these openings were Islamic fundamentalist groups. In Algeria, the Islamic Salvation Front swept the June 1990 local elections, the first free elections since the country became independent in 1962. In the 1989 Jordanian elections, Islamic fundamentalists won 36 of 80 seats in parliament. In Egypt, many candidates associated with the Muslim Brotherhood were elected to parliament in 1987. In several countries, Islamic fundamentalist groups were reportedly plotting insurrections. The strong electoral showings of the Islamic groups partly reflected the absence of other opposition parties, some because they were under government proscription, others because they were boycotting the elections. Nonetheless, fundamentalism seemed to be gaining strength in Middle Eastern countries, particularly among younger people. The strength of this tendency induced secular heads of government in Tunisia, Turkey, and elsewhere to adopt policies advocated by the fundamentalists and to make political gestures demonstrating their own commitment to Islam.

Liberalization in Islamic countries thus enhanced the power of important social and political movements whose commitment to democracy was uncertain. In some respects, the position of fundamentalist parties in Islamic societies in the early 1990s raised questions analogous to those posed by communist parties in Western Europe in the 1940s and again in the 1970s. Would the existing governments continue to open up their politics and hold elections in which Islamic groups could compete freely and equally? Would the Islamic groups gain majority support in those elections? If they did win the elections, would the military, which in many Islamic societies (e.g., Algeria, Turkey, Pakistan, and Indonesia) is strongly secular, allow them to form a government? If they did form a government, would it pursue radical Islamic policies that would undermine democracy and alienate the modern and Western-oriented elements in society?

THE LIMITS OF CULTURAL OBSTACLES

Strong cultural obstacles to democratization thus appear to exist in Confucian and Islamic societies. There are, nonetheless, reasons to doubt whether these must necessarily prevent democratic development. First, similar cultural arguments have not held up in the past. At one

point many scholars argued that Catholicism was an obstacle to democracy. Others, in the Weberian tradition, contended that Catholic countries were unlikely to develop economically in the same manner as Protestant countries. Yet in the 1960s, 1970s, and 1980s Catholic countries became democratic and, on average, had higher rates of economic growth than Protestant countries. Similarly, at one point Weber and others argued that countries with Confucian cultures would not achieve successful capitalist development. By the 1980s, however, a new generation of scholars saw Confucianism as a major cause of the spectacular economic growth of East Asian societies. In the longer run, will the thesis that Confucianism prevents democratic development be any more viable than the thesis that Confucianism prevents economic development? Arguments that particular cultures are permanent obstacles to change should be viewed with a certain skepticism.

Second, great cultural traditions like Islam and Confucianism are highly complex bodies of ideas, beliefs, doctrines, assumptions, and behavior patterns. Any major culture, including Confucianism, has some elements that are compatible with democracy, just as both Protestantism and Catholicism have elements that are clearly undemocratic. Confucian democracy may be a contradiction in terms, but democracy in a Confucian society need not be. The real question is which elements in Islam and Confucianism are favorable to democracy, and how and under what circumstances these can supersede the undemocratic aspects of those cultural traditions.

Third, cultures historically are dynamic, not stagnant. The dominant beliefs and attitudes in a society change. While maintaining elements of continuity, the prevailing culture of a society in one generation may differ significantly from what it was one or two generations earlier. In the 1950s, Spanish culture was typically described as traditional, authoritarian, hierarchical, deeply religious, and honor-and-status oriented. By the 1970s and 1980s, these words had little place in a description of Spanish attitudes and values. Cultures evolve and, as in Spain, the most important force bringing about cultural changes is often economic development itself.

ECONOMICS

Few relationships between social, economic, and political phenomena are stronger than that between the level of economic development and the existence of democratic politics. Most wealthy countries are democratic, and most democratic countries—India is the most dramatic exception—are wealthy. The correlation between wealth and democracy implies that transitions to democracy should occur primarily in countries at the mid-level of economic development. In poor countries democratization is unlikely; in rich countries it usually has already occurred. In between there is a "political transition zone": countries in this middle economic stratum are those most likely to transit to democracy, and most countries that transit to democracy will be in this stratum. As countries develop economically and move into the transition zone, they become good prospects for democratization.

In fact, shifts from authoritarianism to democracy during the third wave were heavily concentrated in this transition zone, especially at its upper reaches. The conclusion seems clear. Poverty is a principal—probably *the* principal—obstacle to democratic development. The future of democracy depends on the future of economic development. Obstacles to economic development are obstacles to the expansion of democracy.

The third wave of democratization was propelled forward by the extraordinary global economic growth of the 1950s and 1960s. That era of growth came to an end with the oil price increases of 1973–74. Between 1974 and 1990, democratization accelerated around the world, but global economic growth slowed down. There were, however, substantial differences in growth rates among regions. East Asian rates remained high throughout the 1970s and 1980s, and overall rates of growth in South Asia increased. On the other hand, growth rates in the Middle East, North Africa, Latin America, and the Caribbean declined sharply from the 1970s to the 1980s. Those in sub-Saharan Africa plummeted. Per capita GNP in Africa was stagnant during the late 1970s and declined at an annual rate of 2.2 percent during the 1980s. The economic obstacles to democratization in Africa thus clearly grew during the 1980s. The prospects for the 1990s are not encouraging. Even if economic reforms, debt relief, and economic assistance materialize, the World Bank has predicted an average annual rate of growth in per capita GDP for Africa of only 0.5 percent for the remainder of the century. If this prediction is accurate, the economic obstacles to democratization in sub-Saharan Africa will remain overwhelming well into the twenty-first century.

The World Bank was more optimistic in its predictions of economic growth for China and the nondemocratic countries of South Asia. The current low levels of wealth in those countries, however, generally mean that even with annual per capita growth rates of 3 to 5 percent, the economic conditions favorable to democratization would still be long in coming.

In the 1990s, the majority of countries where the economic conditions for democratization are already present or rapidly emerging are in the Middle East and North Africa (see Table 1). The economies of many of these countries (United Arab Emirates, Kuwait, Saudi Arabia, Iraq, Iran, Libya, Oman) depend heavily on oil exports, which enhances the control of the state bureaucracy. This does not, however, make democratization impossible. The state bureaucracies of Eastern Europe had far more power than do those of the oil exporters. Thus at some point that power could collapse among the latter as dramatically as it did among the former.

In 1988 among the other states of the Middle East and North Africa, Algeria had already reached a level conducive to democratization; Syria was approaching it; and Jordan, Tunisia, Morocco, Egypt, and North Yemen were well below the transition zone, but had grown rapidly during the 1980s. Middle Eastern economies and societies are approaching the point where they will become too wealthy and too complex for their various traditional, military, and one-party systems of authoritarian rule to sustain themselves. The wave of democratization that swept the world in the 1970s and 1980s could become a dominant feature of Middle Eastern and North African politics in the 1990s. The issue of economics versus culture would then be joined: What forms of politics might emerge in these countries when economic prosperity begins to interact with Islamic values and traditions?

In China, the obstacles to democratization are political, economic, and cultural; in Africa they are overwhelmingly economic; and in the rapidly developing countries of East Asia and in many Islamic countries, they are primarily cultural.

ECONOMICS VERSUS CULTURE

ECONOMIC DEVELOPMENT AND POLITICAL LEADERSHIP

History has proved both optimists and pessimists wrong about democracy. Future events will probably do the same. Formidable obstacles to the expansion of democracy exist in many societies. The third wave, the "global democratic revolution" of the late twentieth century, will not last forever. It may be followed by a new surge of authoritarianism sustained enough to constitute a third reverse wave. That, however, would not preclude a fourth wave of democratization developing some time in the twenty-first century. Judging by the record of the past, the two most decisive factors affecting the future consolidation and expansion of democracy will be economic development and political leadership.

Most poor societies will remain undemocratic so long as they remain poor. Poverty, however, is not inevitable. In the past, nations such as South Korea, which were assumed to be mired in economic backwardness, have as-

TABLE 1. Upper and Middle Income Nondemocratic Countries—GNP Per Capita (1988)

Income level	Arab-Middle East	Southeast Asia	Africa	Other
Upper income (>$6,000)	UAE[a] Kuwait[a] Saudi Arabia[a]	Singapore		
Upper middle income ($2,000–5,500)	Iraq[a] Iran[a] Libya[a] Oman[a,b] Algeria[b]		(Gabon)	Yugoslavia
Lower middle income ($500–2,200)	Syria Jordan[b] Tunisia[b]	Malaysia[b] Thailand[b]	Cameroon[b]	Paraguay
$1,000	Morocco[b] Egypt[b] Yemen[b] Lebanon[b]		Congo[b] Côte d'Ivoire Zimbabwe Senegal[b] Angola	

Source: World Bank, *World Bank Development Report 1990* (New York: Oxford University Press, 1990), 178–181.

[a]Major oil exporter.
[b]Average annual GDP growth rate 1980–1988 > 3.0%.

tonished the world by rapidly attaining prosperity. In the 1980s, a new consensus emerged among developmental economists on the ways to promote economic growth. The consensus of the 1980s may or may not prove more lasting and productive than the very different consensus among economists that prevailed in the 1950s and 1960s. The new orthodoxy of neoorthodoxy, however, already seems to have produced significant results in many countries.

Yet there are two reasons to temper our hopes with caution. First, economic development for the late, late, late developing countries—meaning largely Africa—may well be more difficult than it was for earlier developers because the advantages of backwardness come to be outweighed by the widening and historically unprecedented gap between rich and poor countries. Second, new forms of authoritarianism could emerge in wealthy, information-dominated, technology-based societies. If unhappy possibilities such as these do not materialize, economic development should create the conditions for the progressive replacement of authoritarian political systems by democratic ones. Time is on the side of democracy.

Economic development makes democracy possible; political leadership makes it real. For democracies to come into being, future political elites will have to believe, at a minimum, that democracy is the least bad form of government for their societies and for themselves. They will also need the skills to bring about the transition to democracy while facing both radical oppositionists and authoritarian hard-liners who inevitably will attempt to undermine their efforts. Democracy will spread to the extent that those who exercise power in the world and in individual countries want it to spread. For a century and a half after Tocqueville observed the emergence of modern democracy in America, successive waves of democratization have washed over the shore of dictatorship. Buoyed by a rising tide of economic progress, each wave advanced further—and receded less—than its predecessor. History, to shift the metaphor, does not sail ahead in a straight line, but when skilled and determined leaders are at the helm, it does move forward.

Dangers and Dilemmas
of Democracy

Philippe C. Schmitter

Philippe C. Schmitter is professor of political science at Stanford University. He has previously taught at the University of Chicago and the European University Institute in Florence. This is an abbreviated version of a longer essay written at the request and with the financial support of UNESCO. It is published here with the permission of UNESCO's Division on Human Rights and Peace.

The celebrations that have accompanied shifts from autocracy to democracy since 1974 have tended to obscure some serious dangers and dilemmas. Together, these presage a political future that, instead of embodying "the end of history," promises to be tumultuous, uncertain, and very eventful. Far from being secure in its foundations and practices, modern democracy will have to face unprecedented challenges in the 1990s and beyond.

For the world's established liberal democracies, the very absence in the present context of a credible "systemic" alternative is bound to generate new strains. Defenders of these regimes have long argued—and their citizens have generally agreed—that whatever its faults, this mode of political rule was clearly preferable to any of several forms of autocracy. Now, these external models for comparison have (mostly) disappeared, or in any case are no longer supported by the propaganda and military might of a great power. All that remains are internal standards for evaluation enshrined in a vast body of normative democratic theory and in the expectations of millions of ordinary citizens. What will happen when well-entrenched elite practices in such countries are measured against these long-subordinated ideals of equality, participation, accountability, responsiveness, and self-realization?

Second, the widespread desire of fledgling neo-democracies to imitate the basic norms and institutions of established liberal democracies is by no means a guarantee of success. There is no proof that democracy is inevitable, irrevocable, or a historical necessity. It neither fills some indispensable functional requisite of capitalism, nor corresponds to some ineluctable ethical imperative in

social evolution. There is every reason to believe that its consolidation demands an extraordinary and continuous effort—one that many countries are unlikely to be able to make.

My focus here will be limited to the dangers and dilemmas inherent in the difficult and uncertain task of consolidating democracy in the aftermath of the recent collapse, overthrow, or self-transformation of autocracy. I will set aside the many problems involved in reforming and religitimating "real existing" liberal democracies, although I know that the two challenges are linked in the longer run. To the extent that citizens in established democracies, who have long been accustomed to limited participation and accountability, begin to question these practices and to express their disenchantment openly, they are bound to have some impact on their counterparts in new democracies, who are just aspiring to acquire these same practices. Conversely, the failure of many of these young regimes to consolidate themselves will certainly shake the confidence of liberal democrats in the West and increase pressures for more substantial institutional and policy reforms.

AN EXPLORATION OF DANGERS

"Democracy," in some form or another, may well be the only legitimate and stable form of government in the contemporary world—if one sets aside those entrenched autocracies where monarchs, dictators, technocrats, fundamentalists, or nativists have thus far been able to sell the notion that competitive elections, freedom of association, civil liberties, and executive accountability are merely instruments of Western imperialism or manifestations of cultural alienation. It is striking how few contemporary parties or movements openly advocate a nondemocratic mode of rule. Even the above-mentioned *régimes d'exception* sometimes hold (rigged) elections, tolerate (limited) contestation, and usually claim that their (authoritarian) tutelage will eventually lead to some culturally appropriate kind of democracy.

If democracy has become "the only game in town" in so many polities, why bother to explore its dangers? Is

 From *Journal of Democracy*, April 1994, pp. 57-74. © 1994 Johns Hopkins University Press. Reprinted by permission.

not the absence of a plausible alternative enough to ensure the success of its consolidation in most if not all neodemocracies? The answer is no, for two reasons:

1) Democracy's current ideological hegemony could well fade as disillusionment with the actual performance of neodemocracies mounts and as disaffected actors revive old authoritarian themes or invent new ones.

2) Even if autocracy fails to experience a revival, democracies may stumble on without satisfying the aspirations of their citizens and without consolidating an acceptable and predictable set of rules for political competition and cooperation.[1]

The first scenario implies a "sudden death," usually by coup d'état; the second involves a "lingering demise," whereby democracy gradually gives way to a different form of rule.[2]

So far, the first scenario has occurred with astonishing rarity. One of the most striking things about the more than 40 transitions that have transpired since the demise of the Salazar-Caetano regime in Portugal on 25 April 1974 is how few of these experiments have failed outright. Soon after each of the previous periods of widespread democratization (in 1848–52, 1914–20, and 1945–56, respectively), many, if not most, of the affected polities regressed to the *status quo ante* or worse. Recent neodemocracies, however, have so far avoided this most serious danger. Moreover, even the few apparent exceptions—Burma, Burundi, Haiti, Togo, Gabon, the Congo, Algeria, Suriname—suggest that the most vulnerable moment usually comes with the attempt to hold a "founding election." If the autocrats tolerate such a vote and allow the rise of a government accountable to parliament, then the odds against outright regression improve dramatically. Thailand and Nigeria seem to be rather special cases of persistent oscillation in regime type. The former has shown signs recently of swinging back toward greater democracy, whereas the latter has yet to break the cycle. Haiti is a particularly telling example. Its initial experiment with free and contested elections of uncertain outcome resulted in a reassertion of military power. The democratic trajectory resumed after a short interlude, but again met with a violent overthrow by the armed forces. The outcome has long hung in the balance. In mid-1993, it seemed to be moving toward an internationally mediated solution with President Jean-Bertrand Aristide resuming office, but this subsequently met with the intransigence of the Haitian military. As the recent case of Guatemala demonstrates, massive external intervention, when combined with internal fragmentation, can quickly turn back an authoritarian challenge and even leave the polity more dramatic than before.

Which is not to say that, having survived the founding experience, these polities are surely on the road to consolidation. There is no simple choice between *regression* to autocracy and *progression* to democracy, for at least two other alternatives are available: 1) a hybrid regime that combines elements of autocracy and democracy; and 2) persistent but unconsolidated democracy.

Especially when the transition is initiated and imposed from above, the previous rulers attempt to protect their interests by "embedding" authoritarian practices within the emergent regime. Where they liberalize without democratizing (i.e., where they concede certain individual rights but do not render themselves accountable to the citizenry), the hybrid has been labeled *dictablanda*. For those cases where they appear to democratize but do not liberalize (i.e., where elections are held, but under conditions that guarantee the victory of the governing party, that exclude specific sociopolitical groups from participating, or that deprive those elected of the effective capacity to govern), the neologism *democradura* has been proposed. Neither outcome in itself deserves to be called democratic, although both could lead eventually to competitive and accountable rule. *Dictablandas* may not last long, since liberalization can lead to a resurgent civil society that winds up gaining more rights than the autocrats ever meant to concede. Elections in *democraduras* have a habit of producing unexpected winners who, in turn, may use the authority of civilian government to reduce the prerogatives of authoritarian enclaves like the military. But let us not exaggerate. These hybrid arrangements can also serve as facades for enduring autocracy. Once external pressures diminish or internal foes lose resolve, the rulers may quickly revert to the *status quo ante* or worse.

Dictablandas and *democraduras* have become increasingly common, especially in Central America and Africa, as authoritarian rulers seek to introduce democratic mechanisms into their polities in order to placate international forces demanding democratization. Guatemala was one such *democradura* in which elections have been held regularly since 1984–85, but where civilian officials have found their actions restricted by the military. El Salvador, where elections since 1982 have been accompanied by the systematic violation of political and human rights, is another such case, although it may cross the threshold to democracy if UN-negotiated peace accords manage to guarantee a different context for the 1994 elections. Kenya, Togo, Gabon, Zaire, Côte d'Ivoire, and many other African cases seem more like *dictablandas*—increased contestation and even multiparty activities are tolerated, but elections (if held at all) are manipulated to favor the governing clique. In neither region do hybrid regimes seem capable of providing a stable solution to the problems of transition. In central America, one can hope that their likely demise will give rise to genuine experiments with democracy. In Africa, they may be more usefully viewed as improvisations by rulers who are buying time, waiting for the international climate to change so they can engineer a regression to autocracy.[3]

In South America, Eastern Europe, and Asia the specter haunting the transition is not hybridization but nonconsolidation. Many polities in these regions may fail to establish a form of stable self-governance that is appropriate to their respective social structures or accepted by their respective citizenries. Democracy in its most generic sense persists after the demise of autocracy, but never gels into a specific, reliable, and generally accepted set of rules. These countries are "doomed" to remain democratic almost by default. No serious alternative to democracy seems available. Elections are held; associations are tolerated; rights may be respected; arbitrary treatment by authorities may decline—in other words, the procedural minima are met with some degree of regularity—but regular, acceptable, and predictable democratic patterns never quite crystallize. "Democracy" is not replaced, it just persists by acting in *ad hoc* and *ad hominem* ways as successive problems arise. Under these circumstances, there is no underlying consensus defining relations among parties, organized interests, and ethnic or religious groups.

Argentina is often cited as an exemplar of persistently unconsolidated democracy punctuated by periodic returns to dictatorship. Virtually no two successive elections proceed by the same rules; each party fears the hegemonic pretensions of its opponents; voter preferences swing dramatically from one party to another; constitutional rules are no guarantee against intervention by the central government; executive power is concentrated and exercised in a personalistic fashion; and segments of the military remain involved in a permanent conspiracy against elected officials. Brazil, Peru, and the Philippines also seem more or less to fit this description.[4] It is a bit too early to tell, but "Argentinization" may be the most likely prospect for several new democracies in Eastern Europe and the successor republics of the former Soviet Union.

A TAXONOMY OF DILEMMAS

One way in which analysts have tried to introduce greater precision into this discussion of the dangers of democratization is through the notion of "dilemmas."[5] All new democracies, if they are to consolidate a viable set of institutions, must make difficult choices. Unlike the decisions of the transition, which are usually made in a hurry and under the influence of an overriding agreement on the need to get rid of autocracy, the choices involved in consolidation usually require protracted and explicit negotiations among actors who not only have much greater information about one another's intentions and resources, but are fully aware that the outcome will have a lasting impact on how they cooperate and compete in the future. There are no illusions that everyone or nearly everyone can benefit equally, but only the unavoidable realization that preferences with regard to rules and institutions are incompatible and that any alternatives chosen will hurt some and help others. It is by resolving these dilemmas, by making disagreeable procedural choices, that a given polity chooses "its" type of democracy. If these choices somehow do not get made, then the danger of regression, hybridization, or nonconsolidation increases greatly.

Given the high initial expectations of the people at large, it may come as a shock to realize that the fall of tyrants fails to spell the rise of endless harmony and good feelings: that the popular uprising or the resurrection of civil society is powerless to produce an actionable "general will"; that "honest democrats" can bicker incessantly over seemingly minor details; that the mere advent of democracy does not also bring freedom and equality, growth and equity, security and opportunity, efficiency and responsiveness, autonomy and accountability, *la pluie et le beau temps*. Is it any wonder, then, that disenchantment sets in and that more and more people begin to question whether democracy is really worth so much anxiety and uncertainty?

What is needed is some generic idea of what these dilemmas are. Obviously, each new democracy will have perplexing and painful choices to make that are peculiar to its own history, geostrategic situation, and natural and human resources, but there will surely be common threads. If we could specify these shared dilemmas, we would be better able to assess the probable dangers—although to predict the outcome in any given case, we would still have to incorporate an understanding of all the relevant particulars.

Let us begin by distinguishing two overall categories of dilemmas: 1) those that are *intrinsic* to modern democracy, no matter where it exists or when it came into existence; and 2) those that are *extrinsic*, in the sense that they call into question the compatibility of emerging democratic rules and practices with existing social, cultural, and economic circumstances.

INTRINSIC DILEMMAS

It may come as another shock to discover that democracy, even if stable and well-entrenched, does not always work well. These intrinsic difficulties will occupy us only briefly in this essay, partly because scholars have already extensively treated them, and also because it is the extrinsic class of dilemmas that most preoccupies new democracies. Still, it seems likely that the intrinsic dilemmas that I am about to list will interact with the difficulties of coming up with rules and practices compatible with prevailing social, cultural, or economic institutions.

1) *Oligarchy:* Roberto Michels was the first to observe that even in the most democratic institutions, professional leaders and staff tend to possess certain advantages of incumbency that insulate them from the threat of being deposed by challengers. His "Iron Law" implies that parties, associations, and movements—to say nothing of legislatures—all become increasingly oligarchic and therefore less accountable to their members or the public at large.[6]

2) *"Free-riding"*: Mancur Olson may not have been the first, but he has been the most systematic in demonstrating that much of what sustains and is produced by democracy consists of public goods to which individuals have no rational incentive to contribute voluntarily. In the absence of private selective payoffs, citizens in a democracy should "learn" that it is not worth their while to vote, to join associations or movements, or even to participate in public affairs since their various discrete contributions will normally have little or no impact upon the outcome. Increasingly, they will leave most of this activity to professional "political entrepreneurs" acting more or less independently of their followers, constituents, or clients.[7]

3) *"Policy-cycling"*: All modern democracies have to make decisions involving the uneven distribution of costs and benefits among groups and individuals. Whenever this is done by majority vote, rather than by unanimity, the possibility arises of "cycling," i.e., of unstable majorities formed by shifting coalitions composed of groups with incompatible preferences on other issues. If choices are presented pairwise, no stable majority emerges, and there may ensue a vacillating series of policy measures that pass in sequence, but have the net effect of alienating everyone.[8]

4) *Functional autonomy:* All democracies must depend for their survival on specialized institutions that cannot themselves be democratic—the armed forces and the central bank are the most obvious examples. For these to perform their respective functions efficiently, they must be insulated from popular pressures and partisan competition. To the extent that the role of such institutions increases in a more turbulent, competitive, and (as we shall see below) internationally interdependent environment, the power of the experts who run these institutions will increase at the expense of congressional and executive leaders accountable to the citizenry.

5) *Interdependence:* All contemporary democracies, even the largest and most powerful of them, are entangled in complex webs of interdependence with other democracies and some autocracies. In principle, elected national leaders are sovereign (i.e., accountable to no authority higher than their own countries' constitutions). In practice, however, they are quite limited in their ability to control the decisions of transnational firms, the movement of ideas and persons across their borders, and the impact of their neighbors' policies. Their authority confined to nation-states, these leaders find themselves decreasingly capable of ensuring the welfare and security of their own citizens.

EXTRINSIC DILEMMAS

Such are the major generic dilemmas that are plaguing established democracies. They will have to be faced eventually by fledgling democracies. But before the institu-

tions of the latter can become oligarchic, before the diminishing enthusiasm of their citizens teaches them to free-ride, before policy-cycling can settle in, maybe even before their armed forces and central banks can establish their functional autonomy, and before they can come to terms with their de facto restricted national sovereignty, politicians in new democracies are going to have to settle on rules and practices for resolving even more pressing extrinsic dilemmas.

The core of the problem with regard to these extrinsic dilemmas is well-captured by the Spanish verb *adecuar*, which means to come up with solutions that are at least adequate, if less than optimal. The trick is to make binding and collective choices (or, as we shall see, nonchoices) between alternative institutional arrangements that are compatible with existing socioeconomic structures and cultural identities. In the longer run, it may become possible for consolidated democracies to change these "confining conditions."[9] In the shorter run, those polities that have democratized and *simultaneously* sought to produce rapid changes in the rights of property owners, the distribution of wealth, the balance of public-private power, and so forth have usually failed and, in so doing, rendered the consolidation of democracy much more difficult. The Portuguese learned this the hard way in 1974–75. The Spaniards next door took the lesson to heart and resolved their major extrinsic dilemmas one after another. The Chileans, faced with more deliberately placed "confining conditions" than any other recently democratizing nation, have moved very carefully and gradually to remove them. Alas, in Eastern Europe and the successor republics of the old Soviet Union, the gradualist option is unavailable. These countries face a knotty tangle of dilemmas that simultaneously demand urgent attention and force crucial decisions affecting virtually all realms of political, social, economic, and cultural life.[10]

The response to these extrinsic dilemmas may involve varying degrees of "reflection and choice." The "classic" model (best exemplified by the Philadelphia Convention of 1787) is that of a constituent assembly, composed of delegates deliberating (perhaps secretly) about the country's rules and institutions. Spain is the best recent example of how that founding moment can be seized to great effect.[11] In some countries, by contrast, the key players have agreed on a "nonchoice" by simply reviving some previously employed institutional format, either because the ensuing authoritarian period was short and relatively inconsequential (as in Greece in the late 1970s), or because some ancient founding document was thought still to be adequate (as in Argentina and Lithuania more recently). In the Philippines, the metaprocedural choices were made not by deliberation among elected representatives or by resuscitation of the past, but by a committee of experts. Chile continues to operate under a document imposed on it by onetime dictator Augusto Pinochet. Brazil and some East European countries have taken a long time before formally attempting to "adequate" their institutions. Russia stands out as an extreme case of incapacity to choose any set of self-limiting institutions.

Few democratizing countries face their extrinsic dilemmas in a purely reflective and logical manner. Most have historical experience to draw upon, even if they may be compelled to modify their choices in the light of subsequent economic, demographic, generational, and cultural changes. Sentiment and habit also play a role. This does not always ensure an adequate institutional fit, much less an optimal one, but at least the comforts of familiarity are secured.

The last 20 years of democratization have included an unusual number of polities that either have had virtually no previous experience with democracy (Paraguay, Mongolia, Albania, Bulgaria, Ethiopia, Angola, all the Central Asian republics, Taiwan, and Russia), or whose previous experiences with it have been notoriously short and unsuccessful (Hungary, Poland, Romania, Estonia, Latvia, Lithuania, Mali, the Congo, Benin, Togo, Thailand, and South Korea). In principle, this should place them in a more favorable position to select adequate institutions; in practice, one suspects that most will end up relying extensively (if clandestinely) upon outside advisors and foreign models. As we shall see below, political science may have little to say about what are the most adequate institutions for resolving specific dilemmas.

It should also be kept in mind that those who make the metachoices governing long-term democratic consolidation must also pay attention to banal near-term considerations like staying in office. This is especially significant today, when most democratizers are career politicians. They may have no other vocation and source of income than politics and, therefore, are even less likely to put general interests ahead of their own immediate interests in pursuing their political careers.

The single most important influence on these choices—beyond that of habit and precedent—is the mode of transition.[12] Differences in the level of mass mobilization (as opposed to elite domination) and in the extent of violence (as opposed to negotiation) produce variations in constraints and opportunities. The most favorable context for an eventual consolidation is a "pacted transition" in which elites from the previous autocracy and its opposition reach a stalemate and find themselves compelled to respect each other's interests. The least favorable is a revolution, with mobilized masses using force to topple the *ancien régime*. Falling somewhere in between are: imposed transitions, in which elements of the autocracy dictate the conditions and pace of the changeover; and reform transitions, in which mass mobilization plays a vital role but incumbents are not violently removed from power.

As we briefly describe the major extrinsic dilemmas, let us remember that only by knowing the habits instilled by a given country's experience with democracy, and only by situating the actors within their respective modes of

transition, does it become possible to estimate the most adequate institutional response.

1) *Boundaries and identities:* If there is one overriding political requisite for democracy, it is the prior existence of a legitimate political unit. Before actors can expect to settle into a routine of competition and cooperation, they must have some reliable idea of who the other players are and what will be the physical limits of their playing field. The predominant principle in establishing these boundaries and identities is that of "nationality." Unfortunately, it is not always clear what constitutes a nation—before, during, or even after democratization. Common ancestry, language, symbols, and historical memories may all play a role, but there always remain residual elements of opportunistic choice and collective enthusiasm. All one can say for sure is that the sentiment of national identity and boundaries is the outcome of arcane and complex historical processes that are, nevertheless, subject to manipulation. Democratization itself may encourage actors to attempt such manipulations in order to create constituencies favorable to their respective purposes, but it does not and cannot resolve the issue. *There is simply no democratic way of deciding what a nation and its corresponding political unit should be.* Slogans such as the self-determination of peoples and devices such as plebiscites or referenda simply beg the question of who is eligible to vote within which constituencies, and whether the winning majority can legitimately impose its will on eventual minorities.

2) *Capitalist production, accumulation, and distribution:* All of the established democracies are located in countries in which economic production and accumulation are largely in the hands of privately owned firms and in which distribution is mainly effected through market mechanisms. In all of these polities, however, the outcome of these processes is affected—admittedly in different ways and to different degrees—by public intervention that has been decided by democratic governments and generally supported by most of the citizenry. The paradoxical conclusion is inescapable that 1) capitalism must be a necessary (though not sufficient) condition for democracy; and 2) that capitalism must be modified significantly to make it compatible with democracy.

The dilemma is not merely the static one of deciding on what mix of public-private ownership, income redistribution, monetary intervention, welfare expenditure, health-and-safety regulation, consumer protection, credit subsidization, industrial promotion, tariff protection, and so on will best satisfy citizens' expectations of justice or fairness without stifling economic growth (and impeding the incumbents' chances for reelection). It also involves a dynamic set of choices concerning the development of capitalism at different stages and in different locations within the world system. Playing "catch-up" seems to require greater reliance on state intervention by peripheral economies; overcoming critical thresholds in capital accumulation may even require recourse to authoritarian methods, if not to outright bureaucratic-authoritarian rule.[13]

In the best of circumstances, the preceding autocracy may have already concentrated profits, encouraged private accumulation, increased the state's fiscal capacity, developed the country's physical infrastructure, and improved its international competitiveness, thereby doing much to resolve this dilemma. New democracies that have inherited this sort of legacy—Spain, Chile, and to a much lesser extent Turkey, Greece, Uruguay, and Brazil—have found the task of consolidation easier.

In the worst of circumstances, the *ancien régime* leaves a legacy of corruption, protectionism, price distortions, foreign indebtedness, inefficient public enterprises, trade imbalances, and fiscal instability. The Argentinean and Peruvian cases demonstrate how costly it is to put off dealing with these issues. The experience of Bolivia and, in a different way, Portugal suggest that it may be possible to tackle such problems and still make progress toward consolidation. The countries of Eastern Europe and the former Soviet Union find themselves in a dramatically more difficult situation. Not only must many of the institutions of pricing, credit, monetary policy, collective bargaining, consumer protection, and the like, be created *ex nihilo*, but this must be done at the same time that key political arrangements are being chosen. The first project often implies an exaggerated dependence on foreign models and advice; the latter will likely involve serious unexpected coincidences and unforeseen interaction effects.

It is important to stress that the problematic relationship between capitalism and democracy—"necessary, but necessarily modified"—is structural. It stems from the root difference between a polity that distributes power and status relatively equally and an economy that distributes property and income relatively unequally. This poses a dilemma no matter how well the economic system is performing at a given moment.[14]

Not surprisingly, however, most observers assume that crises in growth, employment, foreign-exchange earnings, and debt repayment bode ill for the consolidation of democratic rule, and few would question the long-run value of growth for political stability. But austerity may have some perverse advantages, at least for initial survivability. In the context of the difficult economic conditions of the late 1980s and early 1990s, the exhaustion of utopian ideologies and even of rival policy prescriptions has become painfully evident. Neither the extreme right nor the extreme left has a plausible alternative to offer. Populism, driven by the disappointment of rising expectations and disenchantment with the travails of democracy, is always a possibility, but unlike in the past, it can deliver no immediate rewards to the masses.

To the extent that this situation diminishes the rewards expected from engaging in antisystem activity, the likelihood is enhanced that some form of democracy will persist. This suggests that the conditions for bargaining over rules and institutions may be as favorable in times of austerity as in time of plenty. Such conditions are likely to worsen, however, when the economy is fitful, going through stop-and-go cycles or experiencing sudden gluts or shortages.

3) *Overload and ungovernability:* Democracies are not anarchies. They must be capable of governing, of using public authority to modify the behavior of individual citizens, and of regulating the performance of firms and markets. One of the enduring mysteries of established democracies is their source of political obligation. Why do citizens generally obey the law and pursue their demands through regular institutional channels, even when there might seem to be a greater payoff and little fear of punishment from doing otherwise? The usual answers of political scientists rest on such abstract notions as "tradition," "trust in institutions," "socialization" and, of course, "legitimacy." Unfortunately, they are rarely very explicit about where these things come from in the first place—often noting only the gradual accumulation of custom and the explicit inculcation of norms through the educational system. These lessons are not likely to give much comfort to those concerned with the consolidation of democracy in a relatively short period of time.

Moreover, there is growing evidence from the older democracies that traditional partisan identifications, habits of self-restraint, trust in institutions, and belief in the legitimacy of rulers have all been persistently and markedly declining, whether measured by attitudes in surveys or behavior in polling booths or in the streets. The reasons for such declines have been extensively (if inconclusively) discussed: greater physical mobility, higher levels of education, more leisure time, decline in the quality of public education, increasing intellectual disaffection, and so forth.[15]

The problem for so many new democracies is that their own respective populations are often subject to the same trends and are therefore more mobile, educated, disaffected and, certainly, skeptical than were the citizens of older democracies when those countries went through their early phases of political development. Most importantly, modern mass communications have made citizens vastly more aware of events taking place elsewhere in the world and of alternative means for pursuing their interests and passions. Hence the shift away from political parties as the exclusive intermediaries for citizens and the primary source of legitimacy for rulers. Interest associations (and more recently, various kinds of social movements) have moved into this space. They are particularly important in expressing the demands of classes, professions, generations, religions, ethnic groups, and other segments of the population whose numbers preclude them from creating or dominating parties, but whose interests and passions motivate them to participate with special intensity.[16]

New democracies thus need legitimacy in order to build institutions, and institutions in order to establish legitimacy. Success will depend on many factors, especially the mode of transition and prior experience with democracy. Even though most new democracies today contain relatively sophisticated, well-informed groups whose interests are diverse and whose organizational skills are formidable, political parties will probably still provide the principal linkage between citizens and government, and it is likely that the choice of rules and institutions will involve bargaining between party leaders. Hence the nature of the emerging party system will be a major determinant of governability. But it will not be the only one. Today's fledgling democracies will not repeat the trajectory of their older cousins. They will have to cope with (and govern with) the full range of associations and movements that have accumulated in the meantime—all the exotic flora and fauna of a media-saturated, urbanized, postindustrial society.

4) Corruption and decay: At first glance, especially given recent headlines in Western Europe and the United States, this would seem an intrinsic dilemma. All democracies, old as well as new, are subject to the abuse of power and the appropriation of public goods for private benefit—evils ultimately held in check by the periodic opportunity citizens have to go to the polls and "throw the rascals out." The criteria of malfeasance may shift a bit from one culture to another; the magnitude seems to vary inversely with the extent to which capitalism offers alternative sources of self-enrichment. Democracies as a group are still far behind autocracies when it comes to either corruption or decay.

The element which makes the dilemma extrinsic is the professionalization of politics. When democratic politicians were usually well-to-do male amateurs, positions of representation were usually unremunerated. Upon losing them, officeholders would return to private life, often at a profit to their fortunes. This began to change with the rise of socialist parties in the early twentieth century, and has continued unabated. Today, not only do those who hold elected office expect to be well-paid for their services, but many have no other source of income. Add to this the spiralling costs of getting elected and servicing one's constituents, and the problem of extracting sufficient revenues to pay for democratic politics becomes even more acute.

How do the citizens pay for democracy? At what point does its peculiar "political economy" become a serious impediment to its legitimacy, even its perpetuation? Some more senior democracies—Japan, France, Italy, and Spain—are currently facing this issue; others have had to deal with recurrent scandals in the past. New democracies are usually born in a burst of civic enthusiasm and moral outrage against the corrupt decadence of the *ancien régime*, so that the dilemma only emerges later. When it does, the effect can be particularly devastating, for politicians have less secure alternative sources of income, while citizens are less convinced of the need to pay their representatives generously.

What tends to compound the problem in fledgling democracies is that regime transition is often accompanied by the simultaneous need to make major transformations in other socioeconomic domains: property rights, industrial subsidies, price controls, privatization, deregulation, licensing of services and media, and the like. Even where the thrust of change is toward "unleashing market forces," the process of accomplishing this offers very attractive opportunities for illicit enrichment on the part of the politicians who set the norms, sell off the enterprises, and award the contracts. Ironically, while the long-term intent is precisely to reduce the rent seeking intrinsic to public ownership and regulation, the short-term effect is to increase the potential payoffs to be had from the exploitation of public authority.

The crux of the matter is that modern democratic practice, especially given its professionalization and the expansion of its policy tasks, has never come to terms with its own political economy. Understandably, democratic citizens find the financing of parties, the remunerating of deputies, the extracting of fees-for-service, and the profiting from government contracts to be murky and often repugnant. It should therefore come as no surprise to discover that they are reluctant to pay—even for the type of regime that they manifestly prefer.

5) External security and internal insecurity: The advent of democracy does not guarantee national security. Depending on a country's size, resources, strategic location, and neighbors, it may even make the problem worse. Fledgling democracies can present an attractive "target of opportunity" to aggressors as the case of Bosnia tragically testifies. They may also, however be able to count upon greater regional and global solidarity—consider Macedonia, where 1,100 foreign troops are now stationed to guard its territorial integrity.

Furthermore, almost every country undergoing the changeover to democracy has suffered from greater domestic insecurity: higher crime rates, increases in political violence, and more frequent disruptions of basic services. In a few cases, dissidents have even resorted to terrorism in their efforts to redefine the identity of the political unit (e.g., the Basque-based ETA in Spain); to bring about a rupture with capitalism (e.g., Sendero Luminoso in Peru); or simply to return the country to autocracy (e.g., the *carapintada* officer clique in Argentina).

At the center of the security dilemma lies the very delicate issue of civil-military and civil-police relations—a dilemma made all the more acute if the previous regime was a military dictatorship. Not only will the transition have to face the issues of extricating the armed forces from power and meting out justice for crimes committed during their tenure, but the consolidation will have to give the soldiers a satisfactory and credible role under democratic auspices. In the past, this was not too difficult since the communist threat could provide reason (or rationale) enough for retaining an autonomous national defense capability. Communism's collapse, plus that of most domestic armed insurrections, has left a "functional vacuum" in several areas of the world. membership in NATO was sufficient in the 1970s to provide a *raison d'être* (and substantial military assistance) to the armed forces of Southern Europe's neodemocracies. Two of these Greece and Turkey, even had plausible enemies in each other! Elsewhere, especially in Latin America, it will take more imagination to find the armies a plausible role.

Moreover, civilian governments in new democracies that lack border conflicts or internal insurrections find themselves assailed with competing demands from myriad newly enfranchised groups. To the extent that these governments are simultaneously following neoliberal strictures to cut budget imbalances, implement austerity measures, and privatize public (and often military-run) enterprises, the military must seem like the most likely place for cuts. One can hardly blame citizens for thinking that military expenditures were swollen under the preceding dictatorship and should be slashed drastically—just when the shift to a new mission might temporarily require additional expenditures. And these potential new missions—such as combatting drug traffic, policing common crime, repressing social unrest, building infrastructure, providing health and relief services to stricken areas, and participating in UN and regional peacekeeping forces—all have their risks. Some virtually invite officers to intervene in policy making outside their traditional domain; others are profoundly repugnant to their usual sense of mission; none of them would provide a sufficient excuse for maintaining existing levels of expenditure and personnel for very long.

Establishing control over the police can also pose some delicate choices—especially where it has previously been under the control of the military or the intelligence services. On the one hand, there is the enhanced need for policing due to the likely increase in crime. On the other, there is the enhanced expectation that the police will respect due process of law and basic human rights. Few things can be more subversive of trust in institutions and the legitimacy of the government than the popular perception that "nothing has changed" at the level of face-to-face contacts between police authorities and the population. Here is an area where a modest but firm investment in civilian control can yield high symbolic benefits (as happened in Spain), and where its absence can undermine not only the regime's legitimacy but the authority of the state itself.

As with all of these extrinsic dilemmas, the long-run prospects are favorable—provided that the neodemocracies cope with the nearer-term consequences of the choices that they have made (or not made) during the transition. Eventually, civil-police relations will become institutionalized, and guarantees for human rights will be made to stick. Internal security should stabilize, if not increase, once consolidation is accomplished. The proliferation of popularly accountable governments within a given region or across the entire globe should be good for

external security. One of the few "invariant laws" of international relations is that democracies do not go to war with other democracies. Autocracies have frequently fought each other as well as democracies, but a world or a region populated by democracies is definitely likely to be less insecure and less violent. Its member states will still have their quarrels but are much more likely to resort to negotiation, mediation, or adjudication to settle them. Barring the regression of any of its members to autocracy, such a democratized region should be able to organize itself into a "security community" wherein the resort to arms would be unimaginable.[17] This, in turn, should facilitate a firm assertion of civilian supremacy and perhaps even a gradual reduction in military expenditures and personnel.

FORBEARANCE AND DISENCHANTMENT

This essay has suggested that there are some good reasons to be less than triumphal about the longer-term prospects for contemporary democratization. Historically, very few countries have ever consolidated democracy on their first try. All previous waves of regime change eventually receded—and it may be too early to tell how many polities will be swept back to autocracy this time. Certainly, those that have not yet resolved the dilemma of defining their national identity and territorial boundaries are unlikely to make much progress in other domains. Moreover, with most neodemocracies facing declining economic performance, accelerating inflation, heavy loads of foreign debt, severe budgetary and fiscal imbalances, and the pressure of international competition and capital flight in the new global economy, resolving the fundamental structural dilemmas concerning capitalist institutions is not getting any easier.

What is most striking so far is that citizens have responded to these dilemmas of choice and strains of adjustment by focusing their discontent on governments rather than on democracy as such. They have frequently voted transitional leaders and parties out of office, but they have rarely demanded or supported a return to authoritarianism in any guise. Despite this rather remarkable display of forbearance, there are growing signs of what the Spaniards have called *desencanto* (disenchantment) with democracy itself. The perception is widespread that corruption has increased and that decay has set in even *before* consolidation has been assured. With astonishing regularity, one hears complaints that professional politicians have arranged disproportionate salaries and perquisites for themselves; that political parties are clandestinely enriching themselves; that privileged groups are evading the law; that entrenched powers such as the military have protected and even increased their share of the budget; that crime has increased; that violations of human rights by police forces persist; that taxes are unfairly distributed or collected; and that unsavory nationals or even foreigners are reaping too many of the benefits from privatization and deregulation. Complaints like these suggest that one or more extrinsic dilemmas are not being addressed.

But these problems of economic suffering and political disappointment pale when compared to those generated by cultural conflict. Autocracies commonly suppress or manipulate ethnolinguistic minorities; nascent democracies then inherit the resulting resentments while providing an environment in which they can be freely aired. In Southern Europe and Latin America, where national borders and identities have long been secure, the demands of subnational groups proved to be relatively easy to accommodate through policies of territorial devolution, although in the case of the Spanish Basques this was accomplished only after a lengthy and bloody armed struggle. In Eastern Europe and Africa, where historical resentments run much deeper and existing political frontiers often run through rather than around nations, ethnolinguistic divisions can become explosive and easily overwhelm the usual social cleavages—of class, status, profession, generation, and the like—that underlie stable party and interest-group systems.

The suggestion that the current wave of regime changes is likely to be followed by fewer regressions to autocracy than in the past may prove of scant comfort to those presently attempting to consolidate new democracies. They still must face some formidable dilemmas and make some arduous choices before settling into the routinized patterns of political cooperation and competition that will ensure the perpetuation of democratic rule.

NOTES

1. See Juan Linz, *The Breakdown of Democratic Regimes: Crisis, Breakdown and Reequilibration* (Baltimore: Johns Hopkins University Press, 1978). Linz observed that, on many occasions in the interwar period, the worst enemies of democracy were themselves genuine democrats who believed that by taking certain extraordinary measures they were protecting democracy. The breakdown came, not because the alternative was so popular or overwhelming, but because the existing regime had transformed itself into a quasiautocracy.

2. Cf. Guillermo Ó'Donnell, "Transitions, Continuities and Paradoxes," in Scott Mainwaring et al., eds., *Issues in Democratic Consolidation: The New South American Democracies in Comparative Perspective* (Notre Dame: University of Notre Dame Press, 1992), 17–56.

3. For a detailed account of this tendency in Africa, with some references to Latin America, see Max Liniger-Goumax, *La démocrature: Dictature camouflée; démocratie truquée* (Paris: Editions L'Harmattan, 1992).

4. Guillermo O'Donnell has drawn attention to other aspects of this subset of countries, which he calls "delegative democracies." See his "Delegative Democracy," *Journal of Democracy* 5 (January 1994): 55–69.

5. The first to have done so (to my knowledge) was Terry Karl in her "Dilemmas of Democratization in Latin America," *Comparative Politics* 23 (October 1990): 1–23. Much of my thinking on this subject has been influenced by this article and subsequent conversations with her.

6. Roberto Michels, *Political Parties: A Sociological Study of the Oligarchic Tendencies of Modern Europe* (New York and London: The Free Press, 1962).

7. Mancur Olson, *The Logic of Collective Action: Public Goals and the Theory of Groups* (Cambridge: Harvard University Press, 1965).

8. The classic statement of this problem is Kenneth J. Arrow, *Social Choice and Individual Values* (New York: John Wiley, 1951). For a more recent restatement, along with other logical dilemmas of collective choice, see Dennis C. Mueller, *Public Choice II* (Cambridge: Cambridge University Press, 1989), 63ff.

9. Cf. Otto Kirchheimer, "Confining Conditions and Revolutionary Breakthroughs," *American Political Science Review* 59 (1965): 964–74.

10. Several authors have stressed this issue of simultaneity: Claus Offe, "Capitalism by Democratic Design? Democratic Theory Facing the Triple Transition in East Central Europe," *Social Research* 58 (Winter 1991): 865–92; Jon Elster, "Constitution-Making in Eastern Europe," *Public Administration* (forthcoming, 1994); Philippe C. Schmitter and Terry Karl. "The Types of Democracy Emerging in Southern and Eastern Europe and South and Central America." in Peter Volten, ed., *Bound to Change: Consolidating Democracy in Central Europe* (New York: IEWSS, 1992), 42–68.

11. A. Bonimé-Blanc, *Spain's Transition to Democracy: The Politics of Constitution-Making* (Boulder and London: Westview Press, 1987). For general remarks on the desirability of seizing this moment early, see Bruce Ackerman, *The Future of Liberal Revolution* (New Haven: Yale University Press, 1992).

12. Terry Lynn Karl and Philippe C. Schmitter, "Modes of Transition in Latin America, Southern and Eastern Europe." *International Social Science Journal* 128 (1991)l 269–84; also Donald Share, "Transitions to Democracy and Transition through Transaction," *Comparative Political Studies* 19 (1987): 545.

13. See Alexander Gerschenkron, *Economic Backwardness in Historical perspective* (Cambridge: Harvard University Press, 1962); and Guillermo O'Donnell, *Modernization and Bureaucratic Authoritarianism: Studies in South American Politics* (Berkeley: University of California, Institute of International Studies, 1973).

14. No one has pursued this theme more exhaustively than Adam Przeworski. For his latest exploration, see *Democracy and the Market* (New York: Cambridge University Press, 1992).

15. The *locus classicus* of this discussion is Michel Crozier, Samuel P. Huntington, and Joji Watanuki, *The Crisis of Democracy* (New York: New York University Press, 1975). For Huntington's revised thoughts on the prospects for democracy, see his "Will More Countries Become Democratic?" *Political Science Quarterly* 99 (Spring 1984): 193–218.

16. This theme is further developed in Philippe C. Schmitter, "The Consolidation of Democracy and Representation of Social Groups," *American Behavioral Scientist* 35 (March–June 1992): 422–49.

17. See Michael W. Doyle, "Liberalism and World Politics," *American Political Science Review* 80 (December 1986): 1151–70; and Bruce Russett, "Political and Alternative Security: Towards a More Democratic and Therefore More Peaceful World," in Burns H. Weston, ed., *Alternative Security: Living Without Nuclear Deterrence* (Boulder, Colo.: Westview Press, 1990). For a case study of the impact of democratization upon foreign relations in the Southern Cone of Latin America, see Philippe C. Schmitter, "Change in Regime Type and Progress in International Relations," in Emanuel Adler and Beverly Crawford, eds., *Progress in Postwar International Relations* (New York: Columbia University Press, 1991), 89–127.

DEMOCRACY AND GROWTH

Why voting is good for you

Believers in the "Asian Way" argue that democracy undermines economic development. They are wrong. Democracy entrenches economic freedoms, and in doing so underpins growth

IN 1992 Lee Kuan Yew, Singapore's leader for many years and one of the world's most successful economic policy-makers, told an audience in the Philippines: "I do not believe that democracy necessarily leads to development. I believe that what a country needs to develop is discipline more than democracy. The exuberance of democracy leads to indiscipline and disorderly conduct which are inimical to development."

Several other Asian leaders have echoed those thoughts. The unelected ones may reasonably be suspected of bias. More telling, in a way, is that some elected leaders have said the same for much longer, without meaning to commend authoritarian rule. For years Indian politicians excused their country's slow growth as the price of democracy, albeit one worth paying. Having to justify policies to an electorate, they said, made it harder to get things done. (In 1991, nonetheless, India launched bold economic reforms; let that pass.) Lately, the theme has been taken up by many in the West who recognise the success of the East Asian tigers—South Korea, Taiwan, Singapore and Hong Kong—as one of the great human achievements of modern times. What did these places have in common? One answer: in varying degree, undemocratic government.

There are plausible economic reasons why "strong government" should be associated with economic success. A much-cited study of Taiwan, by Robert Wade of Sussex University's Institute of Development Studies, argues that Taiwan's government was able to intervene intelligently in economic management partly because it was spared popular pressure to intervene unintelligently* (for footnotes, see final page). Instead of saving jobs in doomed industries it could concentrate on policies likely to create new jobs and new wealth.

Then, compare East Asia with Eastern Europe and the former Soviet Union, where democracy arrived before economic reform—making it much more difficult, you might argue, for governments to introduce the policies that were needed to promote rapid economic growth. It has become a cliché to hold that the Soviet Union got its political and economic reforms the wrong way round—unlike China, with its repressive politics and booming economy.

The grip that these ideas and examples have taken on many shades of western opinion is in one way unsurprising. Authoritarianism has a strong populist appeal. No free speech, perhaps, but the trains run on time. The more politically sophisticated find subtler arguments for agreeing that democracy and economic efficiency are at odds. The left, loosely speaking, thinks markets are unjust; democracy is a good thing precisely because it can subordinate efficiency to fairness. The right, again loosely speaking, sees the same trade-off in a different way: democracy sometimes entails things, such as levying punitive taxes, which cause economic harm and which infringe freedoms more basic than the right to vote. But there is broad agreement on the proposition that democracy and economic growth are in conflict: a consensus which ought to be surprising indeed, since, according to the most obvious evidence, the proposition is false.

A map on the next page shows a three-way classification of the world's political systems. It counts countries as free, partly free, or not free, according to whether they have free and fair elections, protection of civil liberties, multi-party legislatures, an uncontrolled press and so forth. The distribution has changed a lot in recent years. Democracy has spread across much of Latin America and the former Soviet block; sev-

eral of the tigers have become less authoritarian; many other countries have become less free. But it remains true that nearly all of the world's richest countries are free (meaning, among other things, democratic) and nearly all of the poorest countries are not. A map that classified the world into rich, middle-income and poor, according to income per head, would not look very different from this political map. Across the world, in other words, the correlation between political freedom and prosperity is a close one.

The democratic rich

This correlation may not, on further examination, mean much—but on one point the map brooks no argument. It is absurd to conclude from East Asia's success, and from that fact alone, that non-democratic government is best for development. To account for East Asia's growth, factors common to that region but not to others need to be identified. East Asia's governments were not unusual in being non-democratic. This was, and is, something common to much of the third world. If dictators made countries rich, Africa would be an economic colossus.

The correlation between wealth and democracy must not be pressed too far. It does not prove that democracy promotes growth, for instance. Arguably, as people grow richer, democracy is one of the things they want, and it becomes ever more difficult for governments to deny them. So it may be that growth promotes democracy, rather than the other way round. Despite the correlation, therefore, non-democratic government may still be conducive to (though plainly not sufficient for) radical change, such as a successful shift from agriculture to industry, say, or from communist central planning to market economics. And, more

5. COMPARATIVE POLITICS: Turn toward the Market

generally, it could still be true that democracy, once in place, inhibits growth.

But other evidence suggests that these ideas are wrong, too. First, consider the demands of radical economic change. Such change usually makes some groups—and often, for a time, the population at large—worse off. It poses a great challenge to democratic governments. But it poses just as great a challenge to authoritarian governments. These, too, need to retain the support of certain constituencies (trade unions, say, or the army) in order to hang on to power. It is unclear in principle, therefore, which form of government should cope best with the pressures of economic change. A strong authoritarian government may be more secure, and thus a more effective reformer, than a weak democratic government—just as a strong democracy may be more secure than a weak dictator. But one-off comparisons are unhelpful. It is better to consider a range of cases, and look for some general lessons.

Studies that do this have given democratic governments high marks for effectiveness in economic reform. A recent one edited by John Williamson, of the Institute for International Economics, looked at 13 cases of bold reform (typically, radical trade liberalisation and/or drastic changes in taxes and public spending)**. The sample included rich and poor countries, democratic and non-democratic regimes.

In four cases, the governments "would generally be classified as authoritarian" when the reforms began: Chile in 1983, Indonesia in 1982, Mexico in 1987 and South Korea in 1979. The study judged all these programmes to have worked—the changes were successfully introduced and consolidated. The case of Turkey (1980), is more complicated: a democratic government began the reforms but was overthrown by the army, which gave way to another democratic government that continued them. This programme was a success too.

Six of the governments were "unambiguously democratic": Australia in 1983, Colombia in 1989, New Zealand in 1984, Poland in 1990, Portugal in 1985 and Spain in 1982. The reforms in Poland and Spain were exceptionally far-reaching. All these programmes succeeded. In two cases, Brazil (1987) and Peru (1980), democratic governments failed to stay the course of reform, but in both countries democracy had been newly restored in difficult circumstances.

A crunchy result

There is little in that to support the view that democratic governments are worse than non-democratic ones at carrying out re-

form. It is worth noting, too, that in every case bar that of Chile, successful authoritarian reformers were dealing with problems that they or their authoritarian predecessors had helped to create; and that the most radical of the successful democratic reformers, Poland and Spain, were coping with problems inherited from non-democratic days.

So much for the view that democracy and radical economic change do not mix. What of the idea that democracy, once in place, inhibits growth? This question has been much analysed by political scientists, less so (surprisingly) by economists. On the whole, their research has been inconclusive. In some studies democracy appears to promote growth, in others to retard it; and as a rule the results are statistically insecure.

However, a recent paper by Surjit Bhalla, formerly of the World Bank, improves on the methodology of earlier work[†]. It uses an econometric technique to test the direction of causation—ie, it asks explicitly whether democracy affects growth or vice versa. It examines 90 countries for the period 1973-90, looking not just at growth, which it measures in three different ways, but also at two other measures of economic progress: falls in infant mortality, and increases in secondary-school enrolment. And it is careful

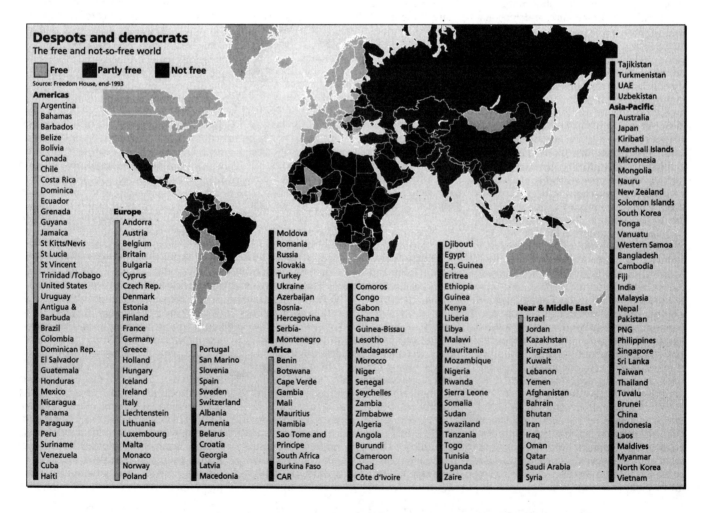

Despots and democrats
The free and not-so-free world

☐ Free   ■ Partly free   ■ Not free

Source: Freedom House, end-1993

Americas
Argentina
Bahamas
Barbados
Belize
Bolivia
Canada
Chile
Costa Rica
Dominica
Ecuador
Grenada
Guyana
Jamaica
St Kitts/Nevis
St Lucia
St Vincent
Trinidad /Tobago
United States
Uruguay
Antigua &
Barbuda
Brazil
Colombia
Dominican Rep.
El Salvador
Guatemala
Honduras
Mexico
Nicaragua
Panama
Paraguay
Peru
Suriname
Venezuela
Cuba
Haiti

Europe
Andorra
Austria
Belgium
Britain
Bulgaria
Cyprus
Czech Rep.
Denmark
Estonia
Finland
France
Germany
Greece
Holland
Hungary
Iceland
Ireland
Italy
Liechtenstein
Lithuania
Luxembourg
Malta
Monaco
Norway
Poland

Portugal
San Marino
Slovenia
Spain
Sweden
Switzerland
Albania
Armenia
Belarus
Croatia
Georgia
Latvia
Macedonia

Moldova
Romania
Russia
Slovakia
Turkey
Ukraine
Azerbaijan
Bosnia-
Hercegovina
Serbia-
Montenegro

Africa
Benin
Botswana
Cape Verde
Gambia
Mali
Mauritius
Namibia
Sao Tome and
Principe
South Africa
Burkina Faso
CAR

Comoros
Congo
Gabon
Ghana
Guinea-Bissau
Lesotho
Madagascar
Morocco
Niger
Senegal
Seychelles
Zambia
Zimbabwe
Algeria
Angola
Burundi
Cameroon
Chad
Côte d'Ivoire

Djibouti
Egypt
Eq. Guinea
Eritrea
Ethiopia
Guinea
Kenya
Liberia
Libya
Malawi
Mauritania
Mozambique
Nigeria
Rwanda
Sierra Leone
Somalia
Sudan
Swaziland
Tanzania
Togo
Tunisia
Uganda
Zaire

Near & Middle East
Israel
Jordan
Kazakhstan
Kirgizstan
Kuwait
Lebanon
Yemen
Afghanistan
Bahrain
Bhutan
Iran
Iraq
Oman
Qatar
Saudi Arabia
Syria

Tajikistan
Turkmenistan
UAE
Uzbekistan

Asia-Pacific
Australia
Japan
Kiribati
Marshall Islands
Micronesia
Mongolia
Nauru
New Zealand
Solomon Islands
South Korea
Tonga
Vanuatu
Western Samoa
Bangladesh
Cambodia
Fiji
India
Malaysia
Nepal
Pakistan
PNG
Philippines
Singapore
Sri Lanka
Taiwan
Thailand
Tuvalu
Brunei
China
Indonesia
Laos
Maldives
Myanmar
North Korea
Vietnam

to distinguish between different sorts of freedom—an especially important point.

India, for example, has real democracy, which is one sort of political freedom. But it is much less impressive on civil rights; and, at least until recently, it imposed repressive controls on economic activity. Most firms needed government licences to start up, close down, change prices or products, sell to new customers or shift suppliers. Previous research tended to see in India an association between slow growth and freedom—even though, in important ways, India was not free. Similarly, successful East Asian economies which scored high on economic freedom but low on political freedom tended to be pigeon-holed as places where fast growth was associated with authoritarian rule. Mr Bhalla separates economic freedoms from civil and political freedoms, and measures the effect of each in turn.

First comes a finding that is no surprise: economic freedom, as measured by the extent of various price distortions, promotes growth. The next is more interesting: civil and political freedoms do the same. Ranking countries on a seven-mark scale ranging from free (America is 1) to not free (Iraq is 7), the implication is this: other things being equal, an improvement of one mark in civil and political freedom raises annual growth per head by roughly a full percentage point. On this scale, admittedly, one mark is quite a big change. Still, the effect on growth is extremely strong. It persists in many different versions of the model used by Mr Bhalla, and survives batteries of statistical tests.

How is this result to be explained? Democracies are notoriously susceptible to interest-group pressure: they favour policies, such as trade protection, that benefit the few at the expense of the many and that reduce incomes in the aggregate. Democracies also arouse, and try to meet, demands for relief from poverty and for other forms of social insurance—policies that call for taxes on the non-poor. Such arrangements, however desirable, blunt incentives for rich and poor alike to work. Democracy might thus be expected to curb output. Evidently, however, it does the opposite.

It is easy to see why economic freedom encourages growth. The clearest lesson from the collapse of communism is that, to prosper, an economy must be allowed to order itself spontaneously in the main, according to the principles of competition and voluntary exchange. The invisible hand, in other words, works better than the visible boot. The question is why political freedom adds to the economic benefits already secured by economic freedom. The answer may be that it encourages firms and people to behave as if those freedoms will endure.

For centuries it has been argued that security of property (protection from theft, legal or otherwise) is the foundation for material progress. In effect, the concept of economic freedom looks at security of property in the present, by asking whether taxes are non-confiscatory, contracts are enforced, trade is free and so on. But people also need to know that these freedoms, where they exist, will not soon disappear. Here lies the decisive advantage conferred by political freedom—meaning democracy, and the dispersion of political power that goes with it.

A benevolent dictator may do everything right in economic policy; and if he does, his economy will grow faster. But he cannot promise credibly that freedoms created by these policies will last: partly because he can suspend them at a moment's notice, and partly because when he dies or steps down he may be replaced by a non-benevolent dictator. Not, of course, that democracy offers cast-iron guarantees. Democratic governments can be overthrown, constitutions torn up. But it is plausible to believe that, over time, democracy entrenches economic freedoms, making them more stable and more credible. In this way, political freedom makes a contribution in its own right to economic growth.

Rulers and ranchers

Mancur Olson, of the University of Maryland, is a leading analyst of the economic weaknesses of democratic government. His is the definitive account of the economics of rent-seeking, free-riding, lobbying and the destructiveness of interest-group politics. Yet he also argues forcefully that democracy is far more conducive to long-term economic growth than dictatorship, even of an apparently benevolent kind[††].

Mr Olson agrees that security of property is more firmly anchored under democracy than under autocratic rule. He argues that regard for individual rights is necessary for lasting democracy, and that regard for exactly the same rights is also needed if there is to be any lasting commitment to security of property and enforcement of contracts. That is why countries tend to have democracy and security of property together, or not at all. Mr Olson then takes the argument further. Throughout history, despots have tended to take the most income possible from their subjects. Note, that did not mean taking everything, for the subjects would then have had no reason to work, leaving the ruler with nothing. A revenue-maximising autocrat taxes at a rate that is punitive rather than self-defeating. He even invests in some public goods, such as protection from outlaws, in order to encourage production and thereby improve his own income.

Such a government, therefore, is not really a "predatory state" (a term often used to describe some modern third-world dictatorships). A predator kills and moves on.

Rather, a despot is a rancher. The sensible autocrat takes care of his cattle in order to maximise his yield. That is why, for all his faults, he is a lot better than no government at all.

Taking an equally unsentimental view of democracy, Mr Olson asks how far a vote-buying democratic leader would raise taxes on the whole economy in order to reward the constituencies that put him in power. The answer is: maybe a lot, but most likely less than the revenue-maximising despot would do. The reason is simple. The despot does not care about the income left over for his subjects, only about his own slice. The democratic majority cares about both—the slice taken in taxes from everybody and redistributed in its direction, and its own post-tax income. On this account, democracy is superior economically in two ways: tax proceeds are shared with at least some of the citizenry, and the incentive to grab as much as possible is muted.

Accordingly, Mr Olson and others see the centuries-long pattern of economic growth in Europe and its former colonies as intimately linked to the earlier development of democracy. After the Glorious Revolution of 1688, rights to property were more secure in Britain, with a limited monarchy and an independent judiciary, than anywhere else. Britain, not long after, was where the industrial revolution began. In the same spirit, other work has discovered a strong correlation between absolutist rule and economic stagnation in Europe's cities over the seven centuries to 1800.

All this may seem remote from the issues of political and economic reform that now confront developing countries. It is not. The claim that authoritarian government works best for development is a claim about history—but it draws mainly on evidence from one region, East Asia, over a comparatively short period. This evidence is anyway unpersuasive: East Asia may well be special, but not because it has had authoritarian rulers. Broaden the evidence, chronologically and geographically, and the claim looks weaker still. Dictatorships with wise economic policies can achieve rapid economic growth; but they are rare, and, being dictatorships, will lack the economic strengths of stable democracy. Far from inhibiting growth, democracy promotes it.

....

* "Governing the Market: Economic Theory and the Role of Government in East Asian Industrialisation". Princeton University Press, 1990
** "The Political Economy of Policy Reform". Institute for International Economics, Washington, DC, 1994
† "Free Societies, Free Markets and Social Welfare". Unpublished paper to be presented at this month's Nobel symposium on democracy, Uppsala University
†† See, eg, "Dictatorship, Democracy and Development". *American Political Science Review*, September 1993

Capitalism and Democracy*

Gabriel A. Almond

Gabriel A. Almond, professor of political science emeritus at Stanford University, is a former president of the American Political Science Association.

J oseph Schumpeter, a great economist and social scientist of the last generation, whose career was almost equally divided between Central European and American universities, and who lived close to the crises of the 1930s and '40s, published a book in 1942 under the title, *Capitalism, Socialism, and Democracy.* The book has had great influence, and can be read today with profit. It was written in the aftergloom of the great depression, during the early triumphs of Fascism and Nazism in 1940 and 1941, when the future of capitalism, socialism, and democracy all were in doubt. Schumpeter projected a future of declining capitalism, and rising socialism. He thought that democracy under socialism might be no more impaired and problematic than it was under capitalism.

He wrote a concluding chapter in

*Lecture presented at Seminar on the Market, sponsored by The Ford Foundation and the Research Institute on International Change of Columbia University, Moscow, October 29–November 2.

the second edition which appeared in 1946, and which took into account the political-economic situation at the end of the war, with the Soviet Union then astride a devastated Europe. In this last chapter he argues that we should not identify the future of socialism with that of the Soviet Union, that what we had observed and were observing in the first three decades of Soviet existence was not a necessary expression of socialism. There was a lot of Czarist Russia in the mix. If Schumpeter were writing today, I don't believe he would argue that socialism has a brighter future than capitalism. The relationship between the two has turned out to be a good deal more complex and intertwined than Schumpeter anticipated. But I am sure that he would still urge us to separate the future of socialism from that of Soviet and Eastern European Communism.

Unlike Schumpeter I do not include Socialism in my title, since its future as a distinct ideology and program of action is unclear at best. Western Marxism and the moderate socialist movements seem to have settled for social democratic solutions, for adaptations of both capitalism and democracy producing acceptable mixes of market competition, political pluralism, participation, and welfare. I deal with these modifications

of capitalism, as a consequence of the impact of democracy on capitalism in the last half century.

At the time that Adam Smith wrote *The Wealth of Nations,* the world of government, politics and the state that he knew—pre-Reform Act England, the French government of Louis XV and XVI—was riddled with special privileges, monopolies, interferences with trade. With my tongue only half way in my cheek I believe the discipline of economics may have been traumatized by this condition of political life at its birth. Typically, economists speak of the state and government instrumentally, as a kind of secondary service mechanism.

I do not believe that politics can be treated in this purely instrumental and reductive way without losing our analytic grip on the social and historical process. The economy and the polity are the main problem solving mechanisms of human society. They each have their distinctive means, and they each have their "goods" or ends. They necessarily interact with each other, and transform each other in the process. Democracy in particular generates goals and programs. You cannot give people the suffrage, and let them form organizations, run for office, and the like, without their developing all kinds of ideas as to

From *PS: Political Science and Politics,* September 1991, pp. 467-474. © 1991 by The American Political Science Association. Reprinted by permission.

how to improve things. And sometimes some of these ideas are adopted, implemented and are productive, and improve our lives, although many economists are reluctant to concede this much to the state.

My lecture deals with this interaction of politics and economics in the Western World in the course of the last couple of centuries, in the era during which capitalism and democracy emerged as the dominant problem solving institutions of modern civilization. I am going to discuss some of the theoretical and empirical literature dealing with the themes of the positive and negative interaction between capitalism and democracy. There are those who say that capitalism supports democracy, and those who say that capitalism subverts democracy. And there are those who say that democracy subverts capitalism, and those who say that it supports it.

The relation between capitalism and democracy dominates the political theory of the last two centuries. All the logically possible points of view are represented in a rich literature. It is this ambivalence and dialectic, this tension between the two major problem solving sectors of modern society—the political and the economic—that is the topic of my lecture.

Capitalism Supports Democracy

Let me begin with the argument that capitalism is positively linked with democracy, shares its values and culture, and facilitates its development. This case has been made in historical, logical, and statistical terms.

Albert Hirschman in his *Rival Views of Market Society* (1986) examines the values, manners and morals of capitalism, and their effects on the larger society and culture as these have been described by the philosophers of the 17th, 18th, and 19th centuries. He shows how the interpretation of the impact of capitalism has changed from the enlightenment view of Montesquieu, Condorcet, Adam Smith and others, who stressed the *douceur* of commerce, its "gentling," civilizing effect

on behavior and interpersonal relations, to that of the 19th and 20th century conservative and radical writers who described the culture of capitalism as crassly materialistic, destructively competitive, corrosive of morality, and hence self-destructive. This sharp almost 180-degree shift in point of view among political theorists is partly explained by the transformation from the commerce and small-scale industry of early capitalism, to the smoke blackened industrial districts, the demonic and exploitive entrepreneurs, and exploited laboring classes of the second half of the nineteenth century. Unfortunately for our purposes, Hirschman doesn't deal explicitly with the capitalism–democracy connection, but rather with culture and with manners. His argument, however, implies an early positive connection and a later negative one.

Joseph Schumpeter in *Capitalism, Socialism, and Democracy* (1942) states flatly, "History clearly confirms . . . [that] . . . modern democracy rose along with capitalism, and in causal connection with it . . . modern democracy is a product of the capitalist process." He has a whole chapter entitled "The Civilization of Capitalism," democracy being a part of that civilization. Schumpeter also makes the point that democracy was historically supportive of capitalism. He states, ". . . the bourgeoisie reshaped, and from its own point of view rationalized, the social and political structure that preceded its ascendancy. . ." (that is to say, feudalism). "The democratic method was the political tool of that reconstruction." According to Schumpeter capitalism and democracy were mutually causal historically, mutually supportive parts of a rising modern civilization, although as we shall show below, he also recognized their antagonisms.

Barrington Moore's historical investigation (1966) with its long title, *The Social Origins of Dictatorship and Democracy; Lord and Peasant in the Making of the Modern World,* argues that there have been three historical routes to industrial modernization. The first of these followed by Britain, France, and the United States, involved the subordination and transformation of the

agricultural sector by the rising commercial bourgeoisie, producing the democratic capitalism of the 19th and 20th centuries. The second route followed by Germany and Japan, where the landed aristocracy was able

---

The relation between capitalism and democracy dominates the political theory of the last two centuries.

---

to contain and dominate the rising commercial classes, produced an authoritarian and fascist version of industrial modernization, a system of capitalism encased in a feudal authoritarian framework, dominated by a military aristocracy, and an authoritarian monarchy. The third route, followed in Russia where the commercial bourgeoisie was too weak to give content and direction to the modernizing process, took the form of a revolutionary process drawing on the frustration and resources of the peasantry, and created a mobilized authoritarian Communist regime along with a state-controlled industrialized economy. Successful capitalism dominating and transforming the rural agricultural sector, according to Barrington Moore, is the creator and sustainer of the emerging democracies of the nineteenth century.

Robert A. Dahl, the leading American democratic theorist, in the new edition of his book (1990) *After the Revolution? Authority in a Good Society,* has included a new chapter entitled "Democracy and Markets." In the opening paragraph of that chapter, he says:

It is an historical fact that modern democratic institutions . . . have existed only in countries with predominantly privately owned, market-oriented economies, or capitalism if you prefer that name. It is also a fact that all "socialist" countries with predominantly state-owned centrally directed economic orders—command economies—have not enjoyed democratic governments, but have in fact been ruled by authoritarian dictatorships. It is also an historical fact that some "capitalist" countries have also been, and are, ruled by authoritarian dictatorships.

To put it more formally, it looks to be the case that market-oriented economies are necessary (in the logical sense) to democratic institutions, though they are certainly not sufficient. And it looks to be the case that state-owned centrally directed economic orders are strictly associated with authoritarian regimes, though authoritarianism definitely does not require them. We have something very much like an historical experiment, so it would appear, that leaves these conclusions in no great doubt. (Dahl 1990)

Peter Berger in his book *The Capitalist Revolution* (1986) presents four propositions on the relations between capitalism and democracy:

Capitalism is a necessary but not sufficient condition of democracy under modern conditions.

If a capitalist economy is subjected to increasing degrees of state control, a point (not precisely specifiable at this time) will be reached at which democratic governance becomes impossible.

If a socialist economy is opened up to increasing degrees of market forces, a point (not precisely specifiable at this time) will be reached at which democratic governance becomes a possibility.

If capitalist development is successful in generating economic growth from which a sizable proportion of the population benefits, pressures toward democracy are likely to appear.

This positive relationship between capitalism and democracy has also been sustained by statistical studies. The "Social Mobilization" theorists of the 1950s and 1960s which included Daniel Lerner (1958), Karl Deutsch (1961), S. M. Lipset (1959) among others, demonstrated a strong statistical association between GNP per capita and democratic political institutions. This is more than simple statistical association. There is a logic in the relation between level of economic development and democratic institutions. Level of economic development has been shown to be associated with education and literacy, exposure to mass media, and democratic psychological propensities such as subjective efficacy, participatory

aspirations and skills. In a major investigation of the social psychology of industrialization and modernization, a research team led by the sociologist Alex Inkeles (1974) interviewed several thousand workers in the modern industrial and the traditional economic sectors of six countries of differing culture. Inkeles found empathetic, efficacious, participatory and activist propensities much more frequently among the modern industrial workers, and to a much lesser extent in the traditional sector in each one of these countries regardless of cultural differences.

The historical, the logical, and the statistical evidence for this positive relation between capitalism and democracy is quite persuasive.

Capitalism Subverts Democracy

But the opposite case is also made, that capitalism subverts or undermines democracy. Already in John Stuart Mill (1848) we encounter a view of existing systems of private property as unjust, and of the free market as destructively competitive—aesthetically and morally repugnant. The case he was making was a normative rather than a political one. He wanted a less competitive society, ultimately socialist, which would still respect individuality. He advocated limitations on the inheritance of property and the improvement of the property system so that everyone shared in its benefits, the limitation of population growth, and the improvement of the quality of the labor force through the provision of high quality education for all by the state. On the eve of the emergence of the modern democratic capitalist order John Stuart Mill wanted to control the excesses of both the market economy and the majoritarian polity, by the education of consumers and producers, citizens and politicians, in the interest of producing morally improved free market and democratic orders. But in contrast to Marx, he did not thoroughly discount the possibilities of improving the capitalist and democratic order.

Marx argued that as long as capitalism and private property existed there could be no genuine democracy, that democracy under capitalism was bourgeois democracy,

which is to say not democracy at all. While it would be in the interest of the working classes to enter a coalition with the bourgeoisie in supporting this form of democracy in order

There is a logic in the relation between level of economic development and democratic institutions.

to eliminate feudalism, this would be a tactical maneuver. Capitalist democracy could only result in the increasing exploitation of the working classes. Only the elimination of capitalism and private property could result in the emancipation of the working classes and the attainment of true democracy. Once socialism was attained the basic political problems of humanity would have been solved through the elimination of classes. Under socialism there would be no distinctive democratic organization, no need for institutions to resolve conflicts, since there would be no conflicts. There is not much democratic or political theory to be found in Marx's writings. The basic reality is the mode of economic production and the consequent class structure from which other institutions follow.

For the followers of Marx up to the present day there continues to be a negative tension between capitalism, however reformed, and democracy. But the integral Marxist and Leninist rejection of the possibility of an autonomous, bourgeois democratic state has been left behind for most Western Marxists. In the thinking of Poulantzas, Offe, Bobbio, Habermas and others, the bourgeois democratic state is now viewed as a class struggle state, rather than an unambiguously bourgeois state. The working class has access to it; it can struggle for its interests, and can attain partial benefits from it. The state is now viewed as autonomous, or as relatively autonomous, and it can be reformed in a progressive direction by working class and other popular movements. The bourgeois democratic state can be moved in the direction of a socialist state by political action short of violence and institutional destruction.

Schumpeter (1942) appreciated the tension between capitalism and democracy. While he saw a causal connection between competition in the economic and the political order, he points out ". . . that there are some deviations from the principle of democracy which link up with the presence of organized capitalist interests. . . . [T]he statement is true both from the standpoint of the classical and from the standpoint of our own theory of democracy. From the first standpoint, the result reads that the means at the disposal of private interests are often used in order to thwart the will of the people. From the second standpoint, the result reads that those private means are often used in order to interfere with the working of the mechanism of competitive leadership." He refers to some countries and situations in which ". . . political life all but resolved itself into a struggle of pressure groups and in many cases practices that failed to conform to the spirit of the democratic method." But he rejects the notion that there cannot be political democracy in a capitalist society. For Schumpeter full democracy in the sense of the informed participation of all adults in the selection of political leaders and consequently the making of public policy, was an impossibility because of the number and complexity of the issues confronting modern electorates. The democracy which was realistically possible was one in which people could choose among competing leaders, and consequently exercise some direction over political decisions. This kind of democracy was possible in a capitalist society, though some of its propensities impaired its performance. Writing in the early years of World War II, when the future of democracy and of capitalism were uncertain, he leaves unresolved the questions of ". . . Whether or not democracy is one of those products of capitalism which are to die out with it. . ." or ". . . how well or ill capitalist society qualifies for the task of working the democratic method it evolved."

Non-Marxist political theorists have contributed to this questioning of the reconcilability of capitalism and democracy. Robert A. Dahl, who makes the point that capitalism historically has been a necessary precondition of democracy, views contemporary democracy in the United States as seriously compromised, impaired by the inequality in resources among the citizens. But Dahl stresses the variety in distributive patterns, and in politico-economic relations among contemporary democracies. "The category of capitalist democracies" he writes, "includes an extraordinary variety . . . from nineteenth century, laissez faire, early industrial systems to twentieth century, highly regulated, social welfare, late or postindustrial systems. Even late twentieth century 'welfare state' orders vary all the way from the Scandinavian systems, which are redistributive, heavily taxed, comprehensive in their social security, and neocorporatist in their collective bargaining arrangements to the faintly redistributive, moderately taxed, limited social security, weak collective bargaining systems of the United States and Japan" (1989).

In *Democracy and Its Critics* (1989) Dahl argues that the normative growth of democracy to what he calls its "third transformation" (the first being the direct city-state democracy of classic times, and the second, the indirect, representative inegalitarian democracy of the contemporary world) will require democratization of the economic order. In other words, modern corporate capitalism needs to be transformed. Since government control and/or ownership of the economy would be destructive of the pluralism which is an essential requirement of democracy, his preferred solution to the problem of the mega-corporation is employee control of corporate industry. An economy so organized, according to Dahl, would improve the distribution of political resources without at the same time destroying the pluralism which democratic competition requires. To those who question the realism of Dahl's solution to the problem of inequality, he replies that history is full of surprises.

Charles E. Lindblom in his book, *Politics and Markets* (1977), concludes his comparative analysis of the political economy of modern capitalism and socialism, with an essentially pessimistic conclusion about contemporary market-oriented democracy. He says

> We therefore come back to the corporation. It is possible that the rise of the corporation has offset or more than offset the decline of class as an instrument of indoctrination. . . . That it creates a new core of wealth and power for a newly constructed upper class, as well as an overpowering loud voice, is also reasonably clear. The executive of the large corporation is, on many counts, the contemporary counterpart to the landed gentry of an earlier era, his voice amplified by the technology of mass communication. . . . [T]he major institutional barrier to fuller democracy may therefore be the autonomy of the private corporation.

Lindblom concludes, "The large private corporation fits oddly into democratic theory and vision. Indeed it does not fit."

There is then a widely shared agreement, from the Marxists and neo-Marxists, to Schumpeter, Dahl, Lindblom, and other liberal political theorists, that modern capitalism with the dominance of the large corporation, produces a defective or an impaired form of democracy.

Democracy Subverts Capitalism

If we change our perspective now and look at the way democracy is said to affect capitalism, one of the dominant traditions of economics from Adam Smith until the present day stresses the importance for productivity and welfare of an economy that is relatively free of intervention by the state. In this doctrine of minimal government there is still a place for a framework of rules and services essential to the productive and efficient performance of the economy. In part the government has to protect the market from itself. Left to their own devices, according to Smith, businessmen were prone to corner the market in order to exact the highest possible price. And according to Smith businessmen were prone to bribe public officials in order to gain special privileges, and legal monopolies. For Smith good capitalism was competitive capitalism, and good government provided just those goods and services which the market needed to flourish, could not itself provide, or would not provide. A good government according to Adam Smith was a minimal government, providing for the national defense, and domestic order. Particularly important for the economy were the rules pertaining to commercial life such as the regulation of weights and measures, setting and enforcing building standards, providing for the protection of persons and property, and the like.

For Milton Friedman (1961, 1981), the leading contemporary advocate of the free market and free government, and of the interdependence of the two, the principal threat to the survival of capitalism and democracy is the assumption of the responsibility for welfare on the part of the modern democratic state. He lays down a set of functions appropriate to government in the positive inter-

---

. . . one of the dominant traditions of economics from Adam Smith until the present day stresses the importance for productivity and welfare of an economy that is relatively free of intervention by the state.

---

play between economy and polity, and then enumerates many of the ways in which the modern welfare, regulatory state has deviated from these criteria.

A good Friedmanesque, democratic government would be one ". . . which maintained law and order, defended property rights, served as a means whereby we could modify property rights and other rules of the economic game, adjudicated disputes about the interpretation of the rules, enforced contracts, promoted competition, provided a monetary framework, engaged in activities to counter technical monopolies and to overcome neighborhood

effects widely regarded as sufficiently important to justify government intervention, and which supplemented private charity and the private family in protecting the irresponsible, whether madman or child. . . ." Against this list of proper activities for a free government, Friedman pinpointed more than a dozen activities of contemporary democratic governments which might better be performed through the private sector, or not at all. These included setting and maintaining price supports, tariffs, import and export quotas and controls, rents, interest rates, wage rates, and the like, regulating industries and banking, radio and television, licensing professions and occupations, providing social security and medical care programs, providing public housing, national parks, guaranteeing mortgages, and much else.

Friedman concludes that this steady encroachment on the private sector has been slowly but surely converting our free government and market system into a collective monster, compromising both freedom and productivity in the outcome. The tax and expenditure revolts and regulatory rebellions of the 1980s have temporarily stemmed this trend, but the threat continues. "It is the internal threat coming from men of good intentions and good will who wish to reform us. Impatient with the slowness of persuasion and example to achieve the great social changes they envision, they are anxious to use the power of the state to achieve their ends, and confident of their own ability to do so." The threat to political and economic freedom, according to Milton Friedman and others who argue the same position, arises out of democratic politics. It may only be defeated by political action.

In the last decades a school, or rather several schools, of economists and political scientists have turned the theoretical models of economics to use in analyzing political processes. Variously called public choice theorists, rational choice theorists, or positive political theorists, and employing such models as market exchange and bargaining, rational self interest, game theory, and the like, these theorists have produced a substantial literature throwing new and often controversial light on dem-

ocratic political phenomena such as elections, decisions of political party leaders, interest group behavior, legislative and committee decisions, bureaucratic, and judicial behavior, lobbying activity, and substantive public policy areas such as constitutional arrangements, health and environment policy, regulatory policy, national security and foreign policy, and the like. Hardly a field of politics and public policy has been left untouched by this inventive and productive group of scholars.

The institutions and names with which this movement is associated in the United States include Virginia State University, the University of Virginia, the George Mason University, the University of Rochester, the University of Chicago, the California Institute of Technology, the Carnegie Mellon University, among others. And the most prominent names are those of the leaders of the two principal schools: James Buchanan, the Nobel Laureate leader of the Virginia "Public Choice" school, and William Riker, the leader of the Rochester "Positive Theory" school. Other prominent scholars associated with this work are Gary Becker of the University of Chicago, Kenneth Shepsle and Morris Fiorina of Harvard, John Ferejohn of Stanford, Charles Plott of the California Institute of Technology, and many others.

One writer summarizing the ideological bent of much of this work, but by no means all of it (William Mitchell of the University of Washington), describes it as fiscally conservative, sharing a conviction that the ". . . private economy is far more robust, efficient, and perhaps, equitable than other economies, and much more successful than political processes in efficiently allocating resources. . . ." Much of what has been produced ". . . by James Buchanan and the leaders of this school can best be described as contributions to a theory of the failure of political processes." These failures of political performance are said to be inherent properties of the democratic political process. "Inequity, inefficiency, and coercion are the most general results of democratic policy formation." In a democracy the demand for publicly provided services seems to be insatiable. It ultimately turns into a special interest, "rent seeking" society. Their remedies take the form of proposed constitutional limits on spending power and checks and balances to limit legislative majorities.

One of the most visible products of this pessimistic economic analysis of democratic politics is the book by Mancur Olson, *The Rise and Decline of Nations* (1982). He makes a strong argument for the negative democracy–capitalism connection. His thesis is that the behavior of individuals and firms in stable societies inevitably leads to the formation of dense networks of collusive, cartelistic, and lobbying organizations that make economies less efficient and dynamic and polities less governable. "The longer a society goes without an upheaval, the more powerful such organizations become and the more they slow down economic expansion. Societies in which these narrow interest groups have been destroyed, by war or revolution, for example, enjoy the greatest gains in growth." His prize cases are Britain on the one hand and Germany and Japan on the other.

> The logic of the argument implies that countries that have had democratic freedom of organization without upheaval or invasion the longest will suffer the most from growth-repressing organizations and combinations. This helps explain why Great Britain, the major nation with the longest immunity from dictatorship, invasion, and revolution, has had in this century a lower rate of growth than other large, developed democracies. Britain has precisely the powerful network of special interest organization that the argument developed here would lead us to expect in a country with its record of military security and democratic stability. The number and power of its trade unions need no description. The venerability and power of its professional associations is also striking. . . . In short, with age British society has acquired so many strong organizations and collusions that it suffers from an institutional sclerosis that slows its adaptation to changing circumstances and technologies. (Olson 1982)

By contrast, post-World War II Germany and Japan started organizationally from scratch. The organizations that led them to defeat were all

dissolved, and under the occupation inclusive organizations like the general trade union movement and general organizations of the industrial and commercial community were first formed. These inclusive organizations had more regard for the general national interest and exercised some discipline on the narrower interest organizations. And both countries in the post-war decades experienced "miracles" of economic growth under democratic conditions.

The Olson theory of the subversion of capitalism through the propensities of democratic societies to foster special interest groups has not gone without challenge. There can be little question that there is logic in his argument. But empirical research testing this pressure group hypothesis thus far has produced mixed findings. Olson has hopes that a public educated to the harmful consequences of special interests to economic growth, full employment, coherent government, equal opportunity, and social mobility will resist special interest behavior, and enact legislation imposing anti-trust, and anti-monopoly controls to mitigate and contain these threats. It is somewhat of an irony that the solution to this special interest disease of democracy, according to Olson, is a democratic state with sufficient regulatory authority to control the growth of special interest organizations.

Democracy Fosters Capitalism

My fourth theme, democracy as fostering and sustaining capitalism, is not as straightforward as the first three. Historically there can be little doubt that as the suffrage was extended in the last century, and as mass political parties developed, democratic development impinged significantly on capitalist institutions and practices. Since successful capitalism requires risk-taking entrepreneurs with access to investment capital, the democratic propensity for redistributive and regulative policy tends to reduce the incentives and the resources available for risk-taking and creativity. Thus it can be argued that propensities inevitably resulting from democratic politics, as Friedman, Olson and many others argue, tend to reduce productivity, and hence welfare.

But precisely the opposite argument can be made on the basis of the historical experience of literally all of the advanced capitalist democracies in existence. All of them without exception are now welfare states with some form and degree of social insurance, health and welfare nets, and regulatory frameworks designed to mitigate the harmful impacts and shortfalls of capitalism. Indeed, the welfare state is accepted all across the political spectrum. Controversy takes place around the edges. One might make the argument that had capitalism not been modified in this welfare direction, it is doubtful that it would have survived.

This history of the interplay between democracy and capitalism is clearly laid out in a major study involving European and American scholars, entitled *The Development of Welfare States in Western Europe and America* (Flora and Heidenheimer 1981). The book lays out the relationship between the development and spread of capitalist industry, democratization in the sense of an expanding suffrage and the emergence of trade unions and left-wing political parties, and the gradual introduction of the institutions and practices of the welfare state. The early adoption of the institutions of the welfare state in Bismarck Germany, Sweden, and Great Britain were all associated with the rise of trade unions and socialist parties in those countries. The decisions made by the upper and middle class leaders and political movements to introduce welfare measures such as accident, old age, and unemployment insurance, were strategic decisions. They were increasingly confronted by trade union movements with the capacity of bringing industrial production to a halt, and by political parties with growing parliamentary representation favoring fundamental modifications in, or the abolition of capitalism. As the calculations of the upper and middle class leaders led them to conclude that the costs of suppression exceeded the costs of concession, the various parts of the welfare state began to be put in place—accident, sickness, unemployment insurance, old age insurance, and the like. The problem of maintaining the loyalty of the working classes through two world wars resulted in additional concessions to working class demands: the filling out of the social security system, free public education to higher levels, family allowances, housing benefits, and the like.

Social conditions, historical factors, political processes and decisions produced different versions of the welfare state. In the United States, manhood suffrage came quite early, the later bargaining process emphasized free land and free education to the secondary level, an equality of opportunity version of the welfare state. The Disraeli bargain in Britain resulted in relatively early manhood suffrage and the full attainment of parliamentary government, while the Lloyd George bargain on the eve of World War I brought the beginnings of a welfare system to Britain. The Bismarck bargain in Germany produced an early welfare state, a postponement of electoral equality and parliamentary government. While there were all of these differences in historical encounters with democratization and "welfarization," the important outcome was that little more than a century after the process began all of the advanced capitalist democracies had similar versions of the welfare state, smaller in scale in the case of the United States and Japan, more substantial in Britain and the continental European countries.

We can consequently make out a strong case for the argument that democracy has been supportive of capitalism in this strategic sense. Without this welfare adaptation it is doubtful that capitalism would have survived, or rather, its survival, "unwelfarized," would have required a substantial repressive apparatus. The choice then would seem to have been between democratic welfare capitalism, and repressive undemocratic capitalism. I am inclined to believe that capitalism as such thrives more with the democratic welfare adaptation than with the repressive one. It is in that sense that we can argue that there is a clear positive impact of democracy on capitalism.

* * *

We have to recognize, in conclusion, that democracy and capitalism are both positively and negatively related, that they both support and subvert each other. My colleague, Moses Abramovitz, described this dialectic more surely than most in his presidential address to the American Economic Association in 1980, on the eve of the "Reagan Revolution." Noting the decline in productivity in the American economy during the latter 1960s and '70s, and recognizing that this decline might in part be attributable to the "tax, transfer, and regulatory" tendencies of the welfare state, he observes,

> The rationale supporting the development of our mixed economy sees it as a pragmatic compromise between the competing virtues and defects of decentralized market capitalism and encompassing socialism. Its goal is to obtain a measure of distributive justice, security, and social guidance of economic life without losing too much of the allocative efficiency and dynamism of private enterprise and market organization. And it is a pragmatic compromise in another sense. It seeks to retain for most people that measure of personal protection from the state which private property and a private job market confer, while obtaining for the disadvantaged minority of people through the state that measure of support without which their lack of property or personal endowment would amount to a denial of individual freedom and capacity to function as full members of the community. (Abramovitz, 1981)

Democratic welfare capitalism produces that reconciliation of opposing and complementary elements which makes possible the survival, even enhancement of both of these sets of institutions. It is not a static accommodation, but rather one which fluctuates over time, with capitalism being compromised by the tax-transfer-regulatory action of the state at one point, and then correcting in the direction of the reduction of the intervention of the state at another point, and with a learning process over time that may reduce the amplitude of the curves.

The case for this resolution of the capitalism-democracy quandary is made quite movingly by Jacob Viner who is quoted in the concluding paragraph of Abramovitz's paper, ". . . If . . . I nevertheless conclude that I believe that the welfare state, like old Siwash, is really worth fighting for and even dying for as compared to any rival system, it is because, despite its imperfection in theory and practice, in the aggregate it provides more promise of preserving and enlarging human freedoms, temporal prosperity, the extinction of mass misery, and the dignity of man and his moral improvement than any other social system which has previously prevailed, which prevails elsewhere today or which outside Utopia, the mind of man has been able to provide a blueprint for" (Abramovitz, 1981).

References

Abramovitz, Moses. 1981. "Welfare Quandaries and Productivity Concerns." *American Economic Review,* March.

Berger, Peter. 1986. *The Capitalist Revolution.* New York: Basic Books.

Dahl, Robert A. 1989. *Democracy and Its Critics.* New Haven: Yale University Press.

_____. 1990. *After the Revolution: Authority in a Good Society.* New Haven: Yale University Press.

Deutsch, Karl. 1961. "Social Mobilization and Political Development." *American Political Science Review,* 55 (Sept.).

Flora, Peter, and Arnold Heidenheimer. 1981. *The Development of Welfare States in Western Europe and America.* New Brunswick, NJ: Transaction Press.

Friedman, Milton. 1981. *Capitalism and Freedom.* Chicago: University of Chicago Press.

Hirschman, Albert. 1986. *Rival Views of Market Society.* New York: Viking.

Inkeles, Alex, and David Smith. 1974. *Becoming Modern: Individual Change in Six Developing Countries.* Cambridge, MA: Harvard University Press.

Lerner, Daniel. *The Passing of Traditional Society.* New York: Free Press.

Lindblom, Charles E. 1977. *Politics and Markets.* New York: Basic Books.

Lipset, Seymour M. 1959. "Some Social Requisites of Democracy." *American Political Science Review,* 53 (September).

Mill, John Stuart. 1848, 1965. *Principles of Political Economy,* 2 vols. Toronto: University of Toronto Press.

Mitchell, William. 1988. "Virginia, Rochester, and Bloomington: Twenty-Five Years of Public Choice and Political Science." *Public Choice,* 56: 101-119.

Moore, Barrington. 1966. *The Social Origins of Dictatorship and Democracy.* New York: Beacon Press.

Olson, Mancur. 1982. *The Rise and Decline of Nations.* New Haven: Yale University Press.

Schumpeter, Joseph. 1946. *Capitalism, Socialism, and Democracy.* New York: Harper.

A Debate on Cultural Conflicts

The Coming Clash of Civilizations—Or, the West Against the Rest

Samuel P. Huntington

Samuel P. Huntington is professor of government and director of the Olin Institute for Strategic Studies at Harvard. This article is adapted from the lead essay in the summer issue of Foreign Affairs.

World politics is entering a new phase in which the fundamental source of conflict will be neither ideological or economic. The great divisions among mankind and the dominating source of conflict will be cultural. The principal conflicts of global politics will occur between nations and groups of different civilizations. The clash of civilizations will dominate global politics.

During the cold war, the world was divided into the first, second and third worlds. Those divisions are no longer relevant. It is far more meaningful to group countries not in terms of their political or economic systems or their level of economic development but in terms of their culture and civilization.

A civilization is the highest cultural grouping of people and the broadest level of cultural identity people have short of that which distinguishes humans from other species.

Civilizations obviously blend and overlap and may include sub-civilizations. Western civilization has two major variants, European and North American, and Islam has its Arab, Turkic and Malay subdivisions. But while the lines between them are seldom sharp, civilizations are real. They rise and fall; they divide and merge. And as any student of history knows, civilizations disappear.

Westerners tend to think of nation-states as the principal actors in global affairs. They have been that for only a few centuries. The broader reaches of history have been the history of civilizations. It is to this pattern that the world returns.

Global conflict will be cultural.

Civilization identity will be increasingly important and the world will be shaped in large measure by the interactions among seven or eight major civilizations. These include the Western, Confucian, Japanese, Islamic, Hindu, Slavic-Orthodox, Latin American and possibly African civilizations.

The most important and bloody conflicts will occur along the borders separating these cultures. The fault lines between civilizations will be the battle lines of the future.

Why? First, differences among civilizations are basic, involving history, language, culture, tradition and, most importantly, religion. Different civilizations have different views on the relations between God and man, the citizen and the state, parents and children, liberty and authority, equality and hierarchy. These differences are the product of centuries. They will not soon disappear.

Second, the world is becoming smaller. The interactions between peoples of different civilizations are increasing. These interactions intensify civilization consciousness: awareness of differences between civilizations and commonalities within civilizations. For example, Americans react far more negatively to Japanese investment than to larger investments from Canada and European countries.

Third, economic and social changes are separating people from longstanding local identities. In much of the world, religion has moved in to fill this gap, often in the form of movements labeled fundamentalist.

Such movements are found in Western Christianity, Judaism, Buddhism, Hinduism and Islam. The "unsecularization of the world," . . . George Weigel has remarked, "is one of the dominant social facts of life in the late 20th century."

Fourth, the growth of civilization consciousness is enhanced by the fact that at the moment that the West is at the peak of its power a return-to-the-roots phenomenon is occurring among non-Western civilizations—the "Asianization" in Japan, the end of the Nehru legacy and the "Hinduization" of India, the failure of Western ideas of socialism and nationalism and, hence, the "re-Islamization" of the Middle East, and now a debate over Westernization versus Russianization in Boris Yeltsin's country.

More importantly, the efforts of the West to promote its values of democracy and liberalism as universal values, to maintain its military predominance and to advance its economic interests engender countering responses from other civilizations.

The central axis of world politics is likely to be the conflict between "the West and the rest" and the responses of non-Western civilizations to Western power and values. The most prominent example of anti-Western cooperation is the connection between Confucian and Islamic states that are challenging Western values and power.

Fifth, cultural characteristics and differences are less mutable and hence less easily compromised and resolved than political and economic ones. In the former Soviet Union, Communists can become democrats, the rich can become poor and the poor rich, but Russians cannot become Estonians. A person can be half-French and half-Arab and even a citizen of two countries. It is more difficult to be half Catholic and half Muslim.

Finally, economic regionalism is increasing. Successful economic regionalism will reinforce civilization consciousness. On the other hand, economic regionalism may succeed only when it is rooted in common civilization. The European Community rests on the shared foundation of European culture and Western Christianity. Japan, in contrast, faces difficulties in creating a comparable economic entity in East Asia because it is a society and civilization unique to itself.

As the ideological division of Europe has disappeared, the cultural division of Europe between Western Christianity and Orthodox Christianity and Islam has re-emerged. Conflict along the fault line between Western and Islamic civilizations has been going on for 1,300 years. This centuries-old military interaction is unlikely to decline. Historically, the other great antagonistic interaction of Arab Islamic civilization has been with the pagan, animist and now, increasingly, Christian black peoples to the south. On the northern border of Islam, conflict has increasingly erupted between Orthodox and Muslim peoples, including the carnage of Bosnia and Sarajevo, the simmering violence between Serbs and Albanians, the tenuous relations between Bulgarians and their Turkish minority, the violence between Ossetians and Ingush, the unremitting slaughter of each other by Armenians and Azeris and the tense relations between Russians and Muslims in Central Asia.

The historic clash between Muslims and Hindus in the Subcontinent manifests itself not only in the rivalry between Pakistan and India but also in intensifying religious strife in India between increasingly militant Hindu groups and the substantial Muslim minority.

Groups or states belonging to one civilization that become involved in war with people from a different civilization naturally try to rally support from other members of their own civilization. Decreasingly able to mobilize support and form coalitions on the basis of ideology, governments and groups will increasingly attempt to mobilize support by appealing to common religion and civilization identity. As the conflicts in the Persian Gulf, the Caucasus and Bosnia continued, the positions of nations and the cleavages between them increasingly were along civilizational lines. Populist politicians, religious leaders and the media have found it a potent means of arousing mass support and of pressuring hesitant governments. In the coming years, the local conflicts most likely to escalate into major wars will be those, as in Bosnia and the Caucasus, along the fault lines between civilizations. The next world war, if there is one, will be a war between civilizations.

Only Japan is non-Western and modern.

If these hypotheses are plausible, it is necessary to consider their implications for Western policy. These implications should be divided between short-term advantage and long-term accommodation. In the short term, it is clearly in the interest of the West to promote greater cooperation and unity in its own civilization, particularly between its European and North American components; to incorporate into the West those societies in Eastern Europe and Latin America whose cultures are close to those of the West; to maintain close relations with Russia and Japan; to support in other civilizations groups sympathetic to Western values and interests; and to strengthen international institutions that reflect and legitimate Western interests and values. The West must also limit the expansion of the military strength of potentially hostile civilizations, principally Confucian and Islamic civilizations, and exploit differences and conflicts among Confucian and Islamic states. This will require a moderation in the reduction of Western military capabilities, and, in particular, the maintenance of American military superiority in East and Southwest Asia.

In the longer term, other measures would be called for. Western civilization is modern. Non-Western civilizations have attempted to become modern without becoming Western. To date, only Japan has fully succeeded in this quest. Non-Western civilizations will continue to attempt to acquire the wealth, technology, skills, machines and weapons that are part of being modern. They will attempt to reconcile this modernity with their traditional culture and values. Their economic and military strength relative to the West will increase.

Hence, the West will increasingly have to accommodate to these non-Western modern civilizations, whose power approaches that of the West but whose values and interests differ significantly from those of the West. This will require the West to develop a much more profound understanding of the basic religious and philosophical assumptions underlying other civilizations and the ways in which people in those civilizations see their interests. It will require an effort to identify elements of commonality among Western and other civilizations. For the relevant future, there will be no universal civilization but instead a world of different civilizations, each of which will have to learn to co-exist with others.

Global debate on a controversial thesis

A Clash Between Civilizations —or Within Them?

SüddeutscheZeitung

■ *A recent essay by Harvard professor Samuel P. Huntington in "Foreign Affairs" magazine—"The Clash of Civilizations?"—has attracted a good deal of attention not only in the U.S. but abroad, as well. Huntington is attempting to establish a new model for examining the post-cold-war world, a central theme around which events will turn, as the ideological clash of the cold war governed the past 40 years. He finds it in cultures. "Faith and family, blood and belief," he has written, "are what people identify with and what they will fight and die for." But in the following article, Josef Joffe, foreign-affairs specialist at the independent "Süddeutsche Zeitung" of Munich, argues that "kulturkampf"—cultural warfare—is not a primary threat to world security. And in a more radical view, Malaysian political scientist Chandra Muzaffar writes for the Third World Network Features agency of Penang, Malaysia, that Western dominance—economic and otherwise—continues to be the overriding factor in world politics.*

A ghost is walking in the West: cultural warfare, total and international. Scarcely had we banished the 40-year-long cold war to history's shelves, scarcely had we begun to deal with the seductive phrase "the end of history," when violence broke out on all sides. But this time it was not nations that were behind the savagery but peoples and ethnic groups, religions and races—from the Serbs and Bosnians in the Balkans to the Tiv and Jukun in Nigeria.

Working from such observations, one of the best brains in America, Harvard professor Samuel Huntington, produced a prophecy, perhaps even a philosophy of history. His essay "The Clash of Civilizations?" has caused a furor. For centuries, it was the nations that made history; then, in the 20th century, it was the totalitarian ideologies. Today, at the threshold of the 21st century, "the clash of civilizations will dominate global politics." No longer will "Which side are you on?" be the fateful question but "What are you?" Identity will no longer be defined by passport or party membership card but by faith and history, language and customs—culture, in short. Huntington argues that "conflicts between cultures" will push the old disputes between nations and

Reprinted with permission from *World Press Review*, February 1994, pp. 24-26. Originally from *SüddeutscheZeitung*.

265

ideologies off center stage. Or put more apocalyptically: "The next world war, if there is one, will be a war between civilizations."

Between which? Huntington has made a list of more than half a dozen civilizations, including the West (the U.S. plus Europe), the Slavic-Orthodox, the Islamic, the Confucian (China), the Japanese, and the Hindu. At first glance, he seems to be right. Are not Catholic Croats fighting Orthodox Serbs—and both of them opposing Muslim Bosnians? And recently, the ruthless struggle between the Hindus and Muslims of India has re-erupted. Even such a darling of the West as King Hussein of Jordan announced during the Persian Gulf war: "This is a war against all Arabs and all Muslims and not against Iraq alone." The long trade conflict pitting Japan against the United States (and against Europe) has been called a "war"—and not only by the chauvinists. Russian Orthodox nationalists see themselves in a two-front struggle: against the Islamic Turkic peoples in the south and the soulless modernists of the West. And even worse: The future could mean "the West against the rest."

But this first look is deceptive; after a closer look, the apocalypse dissolves, to be replaced by a more complex tableau. This second look shows us a world that is neither new nor simple. First of all, conflicts between civilizations are as old as history itself. Look at the struggle of the Jews against Rome in the first century, or the revolt of the Greeks against the Turks in the 19th century. The Occident and Orient have been in conflict, off and on, for the last 1,300 years. Second, the disputes with China, Japan, or North Korea are not really nourished by conflicts among civilizations. They are the results of palpable national interests at work. Third, if we look only at the conflicts between cultures, we will miss the more important truth: Within each camp, divisions and rivalries are far more significant than unifying forces.

The idea of cultural war seems to work best when we examine Islam. The demonization of the West is a part of the standard rhetoric of Islamic fundamentalists. The Arab-Islamic world is one of the major sources of terrorism, and most armed conflicts since World War II have involved Western states against Muslim countries. But if we look more closely, the Islamic monolith fractures into many pieces that cannot be reassembled. There is the history of internecine conflicts, coups, and rebellions: a 15-year-long civil war of each against all in Lebanon (not simply Muslims against Maronite Christians), the Palestine Liberation Organization against Jordan, and Syria against the PLO. Then consider the wars among states in the Arab world: Egypt versus Yemen, Syria against Jordan, Egypt versus Libya, and finally Iraq versus Kuwait. Then the wars of ideologies and finally, the religiously tinted struggles for dominance within the faith—between Sunnis and Shiites, Iraq and Iran.

But most important: What does the term "Islam" really mean? What does a Malay Muslim have in common with a Bosnian? Or an Indonesian with a Saudi? And what are we to understand by "fundamentalism"? The Saudi variety is passive and inward-looking, while the expansive Iranian variety arouses fear. It is true that, from Gaza to Giza, fundamentalists are shedding innocent blood. But most of the Arab world sided with the West during the Gulf war. And, beyond this, only 10 percent of the trade of the Middle East takes place within the region; most of it flows westward. Economic interdependence, a good index of a common civilization, is virtually nonexistent in the Islamic world.

The real issue is not a cultural war but actually another twofold problem. Several Islamic nations are importing too many weapons, and some are exporting too many people. The first demands containment and denial, calling for continued military strength and readiness in the West. And what of the "human exports"? They are not just a product of the Islamic world but of the entire poor and overpopulated world—no matter what culture they are part of. Along with the spread of nuclear weapons and missiles, this is the major challenge of the coming century, because massive migrations of people will inevitably bring cultural, territorial, and political struggles in their wake. No one has an answer to this. But a narrow vision produced by the "West-against-the-rest" notion is surely the worst way to look for answers.

—*Josef Joffe*

The West's Hidden Agenda

Third World Network
FEATURES

Like Francis Fukuyama's essay "The End of History?" published in 1989, Samuel Huntington's "The Clash of Civilizations?" has received a lot of publicity in the mainstream Western media. The reason is not difficult to fathom. Both articles serve U.S. and Western foreign-policy goals. Huntington's thesis is simple enough: "The clash of civil-izations will dominate global politics. The fault lines between civilizations will be the battle lines of the future."

The truth, however, is that cultural, religious, or other civilizational differences are only some of the many factors responsible for conflict. Territory and resources, wealth and property, power and status, and individual personalities and group interests are others. Indeed, religion, culture, and other elements and symbols of what Huntington would regard as "civilization identity" are sometimes manipulated to camouflage the naked pursuit of wealth or power—the real source of many conflicts.

 Reprinted with permission from *World Press Review*, February 1994, pp. 25-26. Originally from *Third World Network Features*.

But the problem is even more serious. By overplaying the "clash of civilizations" dimension, Huntington has ignored the creative, constructive interaction and engagement between civilizations. This is a much more constant feature of civilization than conflict per se. Islam, for instance, through centuries of exchange with the West, laid the foundation for the growth of mathematics, science, medicine, agriculture, industry, and architecture in medieval Europe. Today, some of the leading ideas and institutions that have gained currency within the Muslim world, whether in politics or in economics, are imports from the West.

That different civilizations are not inherently prone to conflict is borne out by another salient feature that Huntington fails to highlight. Civilizations embody many similar values and ideals. At the philosophical level at least, Buddhism, Christianity, Hinduism, Islam, Judaism, Sikhism, and Taoism, among other world religions, share certain common perspectives on the relationship between the human being and his environment, the integrity of the community, the importance of the family, the significance of moral leadership, and, indeed, the meaning and purpose of life. Civilizations, however different in certain respects, are quite capable of forging common interests and aspirations. For example, the Association of Southeast Asian Nations encompasses at least four "civilization identities," to use Huntington's term—Buddhist (Thailand), Confucian (Singapore), Christian (the Philippines), and Muslim (Brunei, Indonesia, and Malaysia). Yet it has been able to evolve an identity of its own through 25 years of trials.

It is U.S. and Western dominance, not the clash of civilizations, that is at the root of global conflict. By magnifying the so-called clash of civilizations, Huntington tries to divert attention from Western dominance and control even as he strives to preserve, protect, and perpetuate that dominance. He sees a compelling reason for embarking on this mission. Western dominance is under threat from a "Confucian-Islamic connection that has emerged to challenge Western interests, values, and power," he writes. This is the most mischievous—and most dangerous—implication of his "clash of civilizations."

By evoking this fear of a Confucian-Islamic connection, he hopes to persuade the Western public, buffeted by unemployment and recession, to acquiesce to huge military budgets in the post-cold-war era. He argues that China and some Islamic nations are acquiring weapons on a massive scale. Generally, it is the Islamic states that are buying weapons from China, which in turn "is rapidly increasing its military spending." Huntington observes that "a Confucian-Islamic military connection has thus come into being, designed to promote acquisition by its members of the weapons and weapons technologies needed to counter the military power of the West." This is why the West, and the U.S. in particular, should not, in Huntington's view, be "reducing its own military capabilities."

There are serious flaws in this argument. One, it is not true that the U.S. has reduced its military capability; in fact, it has enhanced its range of sophisticated weaponry. Two, though China is an important producer and exporter of arms, it is the only major power whose military expenditures consistently declined throughout the 1980s. Three, most Muslim countries buy their weapons not from China but from the U.S. Four, China has failed to endorse the Muslim position on many global issues. Therefore, the Confucian-Islamic connection is a myth propagated to justify increased U.S. military spending.

It is conceivable that Huntington has chosen to target the Confucian and Islamic civilizations for reasons that are not explicitly stated in his article. Like many other Western academics, commentators, and policy analysts, Huntington, it appears, is also concerned about the economic ascendancy of so-called Confucian communities such as China, Hong Kong, Taiwan, Singapore, and overseas Chinese communities in other Asian countries. He is of the view that "if cultural commonality is a prerequisite for economic integration, the principal East Asian economic bloc of the future is likely to be centered on China." The dynamism and future potential of these "Confucian" economies have already set alarm bells ringing in various Western capitals. Huntington's warning to the West about the threat that China poses should be seen in that context—as yet another attempt to curb the rise of yet another non-Western economic competitor.

> **"U.S. and Western dominance is at the root of global conflict."**

As far as the "Islamic threat" is concerned, it is something that Huntington and his kind have no difficulty selling in the West. Antagonism toward Islam and Muslims is deeply embedded in the psyche of mainstream Western society. The rise of Islamic movements has provoked a new, powerful wave of negative emotions against the religion and its practitioners. Most Western academics and journalists, in concert with Western policy makers, grant no legitimacy to the Muslim resistance to Western domination and control. When Huntington says, "Islam has bloody borders," the implication is that Islam and Muslims are responsible for the spilling of blood. Yet anyone who has an elementary knowledge of many current conflicts will readily admit that, more often than not, it is the Muslims who have been bullied, bludgeoned, and butchered.

The truth, however, means very little to Huntington. The title of his article "The Clash of Civilizations?" is quoted from [British educator] Bernard Lewis's "The Roots of Muslim Rage," an essay that depicts the Islamic resurgence as an irrational threat to Western heritage. Both Huntington and Lewis are "Islam baiters" whose role is to camouflage the suffering of and the injustice done to the victims of U.S. and Western domination by concocting theories about the conflict of cultures and the clash of civilizations. Huntington's "The Clash of Civilizations?" will not conceal the real nature of the conflict: The victims—or at least some of them—know the truth.

—Chandra Muzaffar

Jihad vs. McWorld

The two axial principles of our age—tribalism and globalism—clash at every point except one: they may both be threatening to democracy

Benjamin R. Barber

Benjamin R. Barber is the Whitman Professor of Political Science at Rutgers University. Barber's most recent books are Strong Democracy *(1984),* The Conquest of Politics *(1988), and* An Aristocracy of Everyone.

Just beyond the horizon of current events lie two possible political figures—both bleak, neither democratic. The first is a retribalization of large swaths of humankind by war and bloodshed: a threatened Lebanonization of national states in which culture is pitted against culture, people against people, tribe against tribe—a Jihad in the name of a hundred narrowly conceived faiths against every kind of interdependence, every kind of artificial social cooperation and civic mutuality. The second is being borne in on us by the onrush of economic and ecological forces that demand integration and uniformity and that mesmerize the world with fast music, fast computers, and fast food—with MTV, Macintosh, and McDonald's, pressing nations into one commercially homogenous global network: one McWorld tied together by technology, ecology, communications, and commerce. The planet is falling precipitantly apart and coming reluctantly together at the very same moment.

These two tendencies are sometimes visible in the same countries at the same instant: thus Yugoslavia, clamoring just recently to join the New Europe, is exploding into fragments; India is trying to live up to its reputation as the world's largest integral democracy while powerful new fundamentalist parties like the Hindu nationalist Bharatiya Janata Party, along with nationalist assassins, are im-

periling its hard-won unity. States are breaking up or joining up: the Soviet Union has disappeared almost overnight, its parts forming new unions with one another or with like-minded nationalities in neighboring states. The old interwar national state based on territory and political sovereignty looks to be a mere transitional development.

The tendencies of what I am here calling the forces of Jihad and the forces of McWorld operate with equal strength in opposite directions, the one driven by parochial hatreds, the other by universalizing markets, the one re-creating ancient subnational and ethnic borders from within, the other making national borders porous from without. They have one thing in common: neither offers much hope to citizens looking for practical ways to govern themselves democratically. If the global future is to put Jihad's centrifugal whirlwind against McWorld's centripetal black hole, the outcome is unlikely to be democratic—or so I will argue.

MCWORLD, OR THE GLOBALIZATION OF POLITICS

Four imperatives make up the dynamic of McWorld: a market imperative, a resource imperative, an information-technology imperative, and an ecological imperative. By shrinking the world and diminishing the salience of national borders, these imperatives have in combination achieved a considerable victory over factiousness and particularism, and not least of all over their most virulent traditional form—nationalism. It is the realists who are now Europeans, the utopians who dream nostalgically of a resurgent England or Germany, perhaps even a resurgent Wales or Saxony. Yesterday's

wishful cry for one world has yielded to the reality of McWorld.

The market imperative. Marxist and Leninist theories of imperialism assumed that the quest for ever-expanding markets would in time compel nation-based capitalist economies to push against national boundaries in search of an international economic imperium. Whatever else has happened to the scientistic predictions of Marxism, in this domain they have proved farsighted. All national economies are now vulnerable to the inroads of larger, transnational markets within which trade is free, currencies are convertible, access to banking is open, and contracts are enforceable under law. In Europe, Asia, Africa, the South Pacific, and the Americas such markets are eroding national sovereignty and giving rise to entities—international banks, trade associations, transnational lobbies like OPEC and Greenpeace, world news services like CNN and the BBC, and multinational corporations that increasingly lack a meaningful national identity—that neither reflect nor respect nationhood as an organizing or regulative principle.

The market imperative has also reinforced the quest for international peace and stability, requisites of an efficient international economy. Markets are enemies of parochialism, isolation, fractiousness, war. Market psychology attenuates the psychology of ideological and religious cleavages and assumes a concord among producers and consumers—categories that ill fit narrowly conceived national or religious cultures. Shopping has little tolerance for blue laws, whether dictated by pub-closing British paternalism, Sabbath-observing Jewish Orthodox fundamentalism, or no-Sunday-liquor-sales Massachusetts puritanism. In the context of common markets, international law ceases to be a vision of justice and becomes a workaday framework for getting things done—enforcing contracts, ensuring that governments abide by deals, regulating trade and currency relations, and so forth.

Common markets demand a common language, as well as a common currency, and they produce common behaviors of the kind bred by cosmopolitan city life everywhere. Commercial pilots, computer programmers, international bankers, media specialists, oil riggers, entertainment celebrities, ecology experts, demographers, accountants, professors, athletes—these compose a new breed of men and women for whom religion, culture, and nationality can seem only marginal elements in a working identity. Although sociologists of everyday life will no doubt continue to distinguish a Japanese from an American mode, shopping has a common signature throughout the world. Cynics might even say that some of the recent revolutions in Eastern Europe have had as their true goal not liberty and the right to vote but well-paying jobs and the right to shop (although the vote is proving easier to acquire than consumer goods). The market imperative is, then, plenty powerful; but, notwithstanding some of the claims made for "democratic capitalism," it is not identical with the democratic imperative.

The resource imperative. Democrats once dreamed of societies whose political autonomy rested firmly on economic independence. The Athenians idealized what they called autarky, and tried for a while to create a way of life simple and austere enough to make the polis genuinely self-sufficient. To be free meant to be independent of any other community or polis. Not even the Athenians were able to achieve autarky, however: human nature, it turns out, is dependency. By the time of Pericles, Athenian politics was inextricably bound up with a flowering empire held together by naval power and commerce—an empire that, even as it appeared to enhance Athenian might, ate away at Athenian independence and autarky. Master and slave, it turned out, were bound together by mutual insufficiency.

The dream of autarky briefly engrossed nineteenth-century America as well, for the underpopulated, endlessly bountiful land, the cornucopia of natural resources, and the natural barriers of a continent walled in by two great seas led many to believe that America could be a world unto itself. Given this past, it has been harder for Americans than for most to accept the inevitability of interdependence. But the rapid depletion of resources even in a country like ours, where they once seemed inexhaustible, and the maldistribution of arable soil and mineral resources on the planet, leave even the wealthiest societies ever more resource-dependent and many other nations in permanently desperate straits.

Every nation, it turns out, needs something another nation has; some nations have almost nothing they need.

The information-technology imperative. Enlightenment science and the technologies derived from it are inherently universalizing. They entail a quest for descriptive principles of general application, a search for universal solutions to particular problems, and an unswerving embrace of objectivity and impartiality.

Scientific progress embodies and depends on open communication, a common discourse rooted in rationality, collaboration, and an easy and regular flow and exchange of information. Such ideals can be hypocritical covers for power-mongering by elites, and they may be shown to be wanting in many other ways, but they are entailed by the very idea of science and they make science and globalization practical allies.

Business, banking, and commerce all depend on information flow and are facilitated by new communication technologies. The hardware of these technologies tends to be systemic and integrated—computer, television, cable, satellite, laser, fiber-optic, and microchip technologies combining to create a vast interactive communications and information network that can potentially give every person on earth access to every other person, and make every datum, every byte, available to every set of eyes. If the automobile was, as George Ball once said (when he gave his blessing to a Fiat factory in the Soviet Union during the Cold War), "an ideology on four wheels," then electronic telecommunication and information systems are an ideology at 186,000 miles per second—which makes for a very small planet in a very big hurry. Individual cultures speak particular languages; commerce and science increasingly speak English; the whole world speaks logarithms and binary mathematics.

Moreover, the pursuit of science and technology asks for, even compels, open societies. Satellite footprints do not respect national borders; telephone wires penetrate the most closed societies. With photocopying and then fax machines having infiltrated Soviet universities and *samizdat* literary circles in the eighties, and computer modems having multiplied like rabbits in communism's bureaucratic warrens thereafter, *glasnost* could not be far behind. In their social requisites, secrecy and science are enemies.

The new technology's software is perhaps even more globalizing than its hardware. The information arm of international commerce's sprawling body reaches out and touches distinct nations and parochial cultures, and gives them a common face chiseled in Hollywood, on Madison Avenue, and in Silicon Valley. Throughout the 1980s one of the most-watched television programs in South Africa was *The Cosby Show.* The demise of apartheid was already in production. Exhibitors at the 1991 Cannes film festival expressed growing anxiety over the "homogenization" and "Americanization" of the global film industry when, for the third year running, American films dominated the awards ceremonies. America has dominated the world's popular culture for much longer, and much more decisively. In November of 1991 Switzerland's once insular culture boasted best-seller lists featuring *Terminator 2* as the No. 1 movie, *Scarlett* as the No. 1 book, and Prince's *Diamonds and Pearls* as the No. 1 record album. No wonder the Japanese are buying Hollywood film studios even faster than Americans are buying Japanese television sets. This kind of software supremacy may in the long term be far more important than hardware superiority, because culture has become more potent than armaments. What is the power of the Pentagon compared with Disneyland? Can the Sixth Fleet keep up with CNN? McDonald's in Moscow and Coke in China will do more to create a global culture than military colonization ever could. It is less the goods than the brand names that do the work, for they convey life-style images that alter perception and challenge behavior. They make up the seductive software of McWorld's common (at times much too common) soul.

Yet in all this high-tech commercial world there is nothing that looks particularly democratic. It lends itself to surveillance as well as liberty, to new forms of manipulation and covert control as well as new kinds of participation, to skewed, unjust market outcomes as well as greater productivity. The consumer society and the open society are not quite synonymous. Capitalism and democracy have a relationship, but it is something less than a marriage. An efficient free market after all requires that consumers be free to vote their dollars on competing goods, not that citizens be free to vote their values and beliefs on competing political candidates and programs. The free market flourished in junta-run Chile, in military-governed Taiwan and Korea, and, earlier, in a variety of autocratic European empires as well as their colonial possessions.

The ecological imperative. The impact of globalization on ecology is a cliché even to world leaders who ignore it. We know well enough that the German forests can be destroyed by Swiss and Italians driving gas-guzzlers fueled by leaded gas. We also know that the planet can be asphyxiated by greenhouse gases because Brazilian farmers want to be part of the twentieth century and are burning down tropical rain forests to clear a little land to plough, and because Indonesians make a living out of converting their lush jungle into toothpicks for fastidious Japanese diners, upsetting the delicate oxygen balance and in effect puncturing our global lungs. Yet this ecological consciousness has meant not only greater awareness but also greater inequality, as modernized nations try to slam the door behind them, saying to developing nations, "The world cannot afford *your* modernization; ours has wrung it dry!"

Each of the four imperatives just cited is transnational, transideological, and transcultural. Each applies impartially to Catholics, Jews, Muslims, Hindus, and Buddhists; to democrats and totalitarians; to capitalists and socialists. The Enlightenment dream of a universal rational society has to a remarkable degree been realized—but in a form that is commercialized, homogenized, depoliticized, bureaucratized, and, of course, radically incomplete, for the movement toward McWorld is in competition with forces of global breakdown, national dissolution, and centrifugal corruption. These forces, working in the opposite direction, are the essence of what I call Jihad.

JIHAD, OR THE LEBANONIZATION OF THE WORLD

OPEC, the World Bank, the United Nations, the International Red Cross, the multinational corporation . . . there are scores of institutions that reflect globalization. But they often appear as ineffective reactors to the world's real actors: national states and, to an ever greater degree, subnational factions in permanent rebellion against uniformity and integration—even the kind represented by universal law and justice. The headlines feature these players regularly: they are cultures, not countries; parts, not wholes; sects, not religions; rebellious factions and dissenting minorities at war not just with globalism but with the traditional nation-state. Kurds, Basques, Puerto Ricans, Ossetians, East Timoreans, Quebecois, the Catholics of Northern Ireland, Abkhasians, Kurile Islander Japanese, the Zulus of Inkatha, Catalonians, Tamils, and, of course, Palestinians—people without countries, inhabiting nations not their own, seeking smaller worlds within borders that will seal them off from modernity.

A powerful irony is at work here. Nationalism was once a force of integration and unification, a movement aimed at bringing together disparate clans, tribes, and cultural fragments under new, assimilationist flags. But as Ortega y Gasset noted more than sixty years ago, having won its victories, nationalism changed its strategy. In the 1920s, and again today, it is more often a reactionary and divisive force, pulverizing the very nations it once helped cement together. The force that creates nations is "inclusive," Ortega wrote in *The Revolt of the Masses.* "In periods of consolidation, nationalism has a positive value, and is a lofty standard. But in Europe everything is more than consolidated, and nationalism is nothing but a mania. . . ."

This mania has left the post-Cold War world smoldering with hot wars; the international scene is little more unified than it was at the end of the Great War, in Ortega's own time. There were more than thirty wars in progress last year, most of them ethnic, racial, tribal, or religious in character, and the list of unsafe regions doesn't seem to be getting any shorter. Some new world order!

The aim of many of these small-scale wars is to redraw boundaries, to implode states and resecure parochial identities: to escape McWorld's dully insistent imperatives. The mood is that of Jihad: war not as an instrument of policy but as an emblem of identity, an expression of community, an end in itself. Even where there is no shooting war, there is fractiousness, secession, and the quest for ever smaller communities. Add to the list of dangerous countries those at risk: In Switzerland and Spain, Jurassian and Basque separatists still argue the virtues of ancient identities, sometimes in the language of bombs. Hyperdisintegration in the former Soviet Union may well continue unabated—not just a Ukraine independent from the Soviet Union but a Bessarabian Ukraine independent from the Ukrainian republic; not just Russia severed from the defunct union but Tatarstan severed from Russia. Yugoslavia makes even the disunited, ex-Soviet, nonsocialist republics that were once the Soviet Union look integrated, its sectarian fatherlands springing up within factional motherlands like weeds within weeds within weeds. Kurdish independence would threaten the territorial integrity of four Middle Eastern nations. Well before the current cataclysm Soviet Georgia made a claim for autonomy from the Soviet Union, only to be faced with its Ossetians (164,000 in a republic of 5.5 million) demanding their own self-determination within Georgia. The Abkhasian minority in Georgia has followed suit. Even the good will established by Canada's once promising Meech Lake protocols is in danger, with Francophone Quebec again threatening the dissolution of the federation. In South Africa the emergence from apartheid was hardly achieved when friction between Inkatha's Zulus and the African National Congress's tribally identified members threatened to replace Europeans' racism with an indigenous tribal war after thirty years of attempted integration using the colonial language (English) as a unifier, Nigeria is now playing with the idea of linguistic multiculturalism—which could mean the cultural breakup of the nation into hundreds of tribal fragments. Even Saddam Hussein has benefited from the threat of internal Jihad, having used renewed tribal and religious warfare to turn last season's mortal enemies into reluctant allies of an Iraqi nationhood that he nearly destroyed.

The passing of communism has torn away the thin veneer of internationalism (workers of the world unite!) to reveal ethnic prejudices that are not only ugly and deep-seated but increasingly murderous. Europe's old scourge, anti-Semitism, is back with a vengeance, but it is only one of many antagonisms. It appears all too easy to throw the historical gears into reverse and pass from a Communist dictatorship back into a tribal state.

Among the tribes, religion is also a battlefield. ("Jihad" is a rich word whose generic meaning is "struggle"—usually the struggle of the soul to avert evil. Strictly applied to religious war, it is used only in reference to battles where the faith is under assault, or battles against a government that denies the practice of Islam. My use here is rhetorical, but does follow both journalistic practice and history.) Remember the Thirty Years War? Whatever forms of Enlightenment universalism might once have come to grace such historically related forms of monotheism as Judaism, Christianity, and Islam, in many of their modern incarnations they are parochial rather than cosmopolitan, angry rather than loving, proselytizing rather than ecumenical, zealous rather than rationalist, sectarian rather than deistic, ethnocentric rather than universalizing. As a result, like the new forms of hypernationalism, the new expressions of religious fundamentalism are fractious and pulverizing, never integrating. This is religion as the Crusaders knew it: a battle to the death for souls that if not saved will be forever lost.

The atmospherics of Jihad have resulted in a breakdown of civility in the name of identity, of comity in the name of community. International relations have sometimes taken on the aspect of gang war—cultural turf battles featuring tribal factions that were supposed to be sublimated as integral parts of large national, economic, postcolonial, and constitutional entities.

THE DARKENING FUTURE OF DEMOCRACY

These rather melodramatic tableaux vivants do not tell the whole story, however. For all their defects, Jihad and McWorld have their attractions. Yet, to repeat and insist, the attractions are unrelated to democracy. Neither McWorld nor Jihad is remotely democratic in impulse. Neither needs democracy; neither promotes democracy.

McWorld does manage to look pretty seductive in a world obsessed with Jihad. It delivers peace, prosperity, and relative unity—if at the cost of independence, community, and identity (which is generally based on difference). The primary political values required by the global market are order and tranquillity, and freedom—as in the phrases "free trade," "free press," and "free love." Human rights are needed to a degree, but not citizenship or participation—and no more social justice and equality than are necessary to promote efficient economic production and consumption. Multinational corporations sometimes seem to prefer doing business with local oligarchs, inasmuch as they can take confidence from dealing with the boss on all crucial matters. Despots who slaughter their own populations are no problem, so long as they leave markets in place and refrain from making war on their neighbors (Saddam Hussein's fatal mistake). In trading partners, predictability is of more value than justice.

The Eastern European revolutions that seemed to arise out of concern for global democratic values quickly deteriorated into a stampede in the general direction of free markets and their ubiquitous, television-promoted shopping malls. East Germany's Neues Forum, that courageous gathering of intellectuals, students, and workers which overturned the Stalinist regime in Berlin in 1989, lasted only six months in Germany's mini-version of McWorld. Then it gave way to money and markets and monopolies from the West. By the time of the first all-German elections, it could scarcely manage to secure three percent of the vote. Elsewhere there is growing evidence that *glasnost* will go and *perestroika*—defined as privatization and an opening of markets to Western bidders—will stay. So understandably anxious are the new rulers of Eastern Europe and whatever entities are forged from the residues of the Soviet Union to gain access to credit and markets and technology—McWorld's flourishing new currencies—that they have shown themselves willing to trade away democratic prospects in pursuit of them: not just old totalitarian ideologies and command-economy production models but some possible indigenous experiments with a third way between capitalism and socialism, such as economic cooperatives and employee stock-ownership plans, both of which have their ardent supporters in the East.

Jihad delivers a different set of virtues: a vibrant local identity, a sense of community, solidarity among kinsmen, neighbors, and countrymen, narrowly conceived. But it also guarantees parochialism and is grounded in exclusion. Solidarity is secured through war against outsiders. And solidarity often means obedience to a hierarchy in governance, fanaticism in beliefs, and the obliteration of individual selves in the name of the group. Deference to leaders and intolerance toward outsiders (and toward "enemies within") are hallmarks of tribalism—hardly the attitudes required for the cultivation of new democratic women and men capable of governing themselves. Where new democratic experiments have been conducted in retribalizing societies, in both Europe and the Third World, the result has often been anarchy, repression, persecution, and the coming of new, noncommunist forms of very old kinds of despotism. During the past year, Havel's velvet revolution in Czechoslovakia was imperiled by partisans of "Czechland" and of Slovakia as independent entities. India seemed little less rent by Sikh, Hindu, Muslim, and Tamil infighting than it was immediately after the British pulled out, more than forty years ago.

To the extent that either McWorld or Jihad has a *natural* politics, it has turned out to be more of an antipolitics. For McWorld, it is the antipolitics of globalism: bureaucratic, technocratic, and meritocratic, focused (as Marx predicted it would be) on the administration of things—with people, however, among the chief things to be administered. In its politico-economic imperatives McWorld has been guided by laissez-faire market principles that privilege efficiency, productivity, and beneficence at the expense of civic liberty and self-government.

For Jihad, the antipolitics of tribalization has been explicitly antidemocratic: one-party dictatorship, government by military junta, theocratic fundamentalism—often associated with a version of the *Führerprinzip* that empowers an individual to rule on behalf of a people. Even the government of India, struggling for decades to model democracy for a people who will soon number a billion, longs for great leaders; and for every Mahatma Gandhi, Indira Gandhi, or Rajiv Gandhi taken from them by zealous assassins, the Indians appear to seek a replacement who will deliver them from the lengthy travail of their freedom.

THE CONFEDERAL OPTION

How can democracy be secured and spread in a world whose primary tendencies are at best indifferent to it (McWorld) and at worst deeply antithetical to it (Jihad)? My guess is that globalization will eventually vanquish retribalization.

The ethos of material "civilization" has not yet encountered an obstacle it has been unable to thrust aside. Ortega may have grasped in the 1920s a clue to our own future in the coming millennium.

Everyone sees the need of a new principle of life. But as always happens in similar crises—some people attempt to save the situation by an artificial intensification of the very principle which has led to decay. This is the meaning of the "nationalist" outburst of recent years. . . . things have always gone that way. The last flare, the longest; the last sigh, the deepest. On the very eve of their disappearance there is an intensification of frontiers—military and economic.

Jihad may be a last deep sigh before the eternal yawn of McWorld. On the other hand, Ortega was not exactly prescient; his prophecy of peace and internationalism came just before blitzkrieg, world war, and the Holocaust tore the old order to bits. Yet democracy is how we remonstrate with reality, the rebuke our aspirations offer to history. And if retribalization is inhospitable to democracy, there is nonetheless a form of democratic government that can accommodate parochialism and communitarianism, one that can even save them from their defects and make them more tolerant and participatory: decentralized participatory democracy. And if McWorld is indifferent to democracy, there is nonetheless a form of democratic government that suits global markets passably well—representative government in its federal or, better still, confederal variation.

With its concern for accountability, the protection of minorities, and the universal rule of law, a confederalized representative system would serve the political needs of McWorld as well as oligarchic bureaucratism or meritocratic elitism is currently doing. As we are already beginning to see, many nations may survive in the long term only as confederations that afford local regions smaller than "nations" extensive jurisdiction. Recommended reading for democrats of the twenty-first century is not the U.S. Constitution or the French Declaration of Rights of Man and Citizen but the Articles of Confederation, that suddenly pertinent document that stitched together the thirteen American colonies into what then seemed a too loose confederation of independent states but now appears a new form of political realism, as veterans of Yeltsin's new Russia and the new Europe created at Maastricht will attest.

By the same token, the participatory and direct form of democracy that engages citizens in civic activity and civic judgment and goes well beyond just voting and accountability—the system I have called "strong democracy"—suits the political needs of decentralized communities as well as theocratic and nationalist party dictatorships have done. Local neighborhoods need not be democratic, but they can be. Real democracy has flourished in diminutive settings: the spirit of liberty, Tocqueville said, is local. Participatory democracy, if not naturally apposite to tribalism, has an undeniable attractiveness under conditions of parochialism.

Democracy in any of these variations will, however, continue to be obstructed by the undemocratic and antidemocratic trends toward uniformitarian globalism and intolerant retribalization which I have portrayed here. For democracy to persist in our brave new McWorld, we will have to commit acts of conscious political will—a possibility, but hardly a probability, under these conditions. Political will requires much more than the quick fix of the transfer of institutions. Like technology transfer, institution transfer rests on foolish assumptions about a uniform world of the kind that once fired the imagination of colonial administrators. Spread English justice to the colonies by exporting wigs. Let an East Indian trading company act as the vanguard to Britain's free parliamentary institutions. Today's well-intentioned quick-fixers in the National Endowment for Democracy and the Kennedy School of Government, in the unions and foundations and universities zealously nurturing contacts in Eastern Europe and the Third World, are hoping to democratize by long distance. Post Bulgaria a parliament by first-class mail. Fed Ex the Bill of Rights to Sri Lanka. Cable Cambodia some common law.

Yet Eastern Europe has already demonstrated that importing free political parties, parliaments, and presses cannot establish a democratic civil society; imposing a free market may even have the opposite effect. Democracy grows from the bottom up and cannot be imposed from the top down. Civil society has to be built from the inside out. The institutional superstructure comes last. Poland may become democratic, but then again it may heed the Pope, and prefer to found its politics on its Catholicism, with uncertain consequences for democracy. Bulgaria may become democratic, but it may prefer tribal war. The former Soviet Union may become a democratic confederation, or it may just grow into an anarchic and weak conglomeration of markets for other nations' goods and services.

Democrats need to seek out indigenous democratic impulses. There is always a desire for self-government, always some expression of participation, accountability, consent, and representation, even in traditional hierarchical societies. These need to be identified, tapped, modified, and incorporated into new democratic practices with an indigenous flavor. The tortoises among the democratizers may ultimately outlive or outpace the hares, for they will have the time and patience to explore conditions along the way, and to adapt their gait to changing circumstances. Tragically, democracy in a hurry often looks something like France in 1794 or China in 1989.

It certainly seems possible that the most attractive democratic ideal in the face of the brutal realities of Jihad and the dull realities of McWorld will be a confederal union of semi-autonomous communities smaller than nation-states, tied together into regional economic associations and markets larger than nation-states—participatory and self-determining in local matters at the bottom, representative and accountable at the top. The nation-state would play a diminished role, and sovereignty would lose some of its political potency. The Green movement adage "Think globally, act locally" would actually come to describe the conduct of politics.

This vision reflects only an ideal, however—one that is not terribly likely to be realized. Freedom, Jean-Jacques Rousseau once wrote, is a food easy to eat but hard to digest. Still, democracy has always played itself out against the odds. And democracy remains both a form of coherence as binding as McWorld and a secular faith potentially as inspiriting as Jihad.

Credits/ Acknowledgments

Cover design by Charles Vitelli

1. Country Studies
Facing overview—British Information Service. 38—Chart from *The Economist,* October 8, 1994.

2. Factors in the Political Process
Facing overview—United Nations photo by Milton Grant.

3. Europe—West, Center, and East
Facing overview—Novosti photo/Soviet Mission of the United Nations.

4. Developing World
Facing overview—United Nations photo. 213—Box from *Journal of Democracy.*

5. Comparative Politics
Facing overview—United Nations photo by J. Isaac.

PHOTOCOPY THIS PAGE!!!*

ANNUAL EDITIONS ARTICLE REVIEW FORM

NAME: _____ DATE: _____

TITLE AND NUMBER OF ARTICLE: _____

BRIEFLY STATE THE MAIN IDEA OF THIS ARTICLE: _____

_____

_____

_____

_____

LIST THREE IMPORTANT FACTS THAT THE AUTHOR USES TO SUPPORT THE MAIN IDEA:

_____

_____

_____

_____

_____

WHAT INFORMATION OR IDEAS DISCUSSED IN THIS ARTICLE ARE ALSO DISCUSSED IN YOUR TEXTBOOK OR OTHER READING YOU HAVE DONE? LIST THE TEXTBOOK CHAPTERS AND PAGE NUMBERS:

_____

_____

_____

_____

_____

_____

LIST ANY EXAMPLES OF BIAS OR FAULTY REASONING THAT YOU FOUND IN THE ARTICLE:

_____

_____

_____

_____

LIST ANY NEW TERMS/CONCEPTS THAT WERE DISCUSSED IN THE ARTICLE AND WRITE A SHORT DEFINITION:

_____

_____

_____

_____

_____

*Your instructor may require you to use this Annual Editions Article Review Form in any number of ways: for articles that are assigned, for extra credit, as a tool to assist in developing assigned papers, or simply for your own reference. Even if it is not required, we encourage you to photocopy and use this page; you'll find that reflecting on the articles will greatly enhance the information from your text.

ANNUAL EDITIONS:
COMPARATIVE POLITICS 95/96
Article Rating Form

Here is an opportunity for you to have direct input into the next revision of this volume. We would like you to rate each of the 65 articles listed below, using the following scale:

1. **Excellent: should definitely be retained**
2. **Above average: should probably be retained**
3. **Below average: should probably be deleted**
4. **Poor: should definitely be deleted**

Your ratings will play a vital part in the next revision. So please mail this prepaid form to us just as soon as you complete it.
Thanks for your help!

Rating	Article	Rating	Article
	1. World Trend: Voters Reject Incumbents		34. Parliament and Congress: Is the Grass Greener on the Other Side?
	2. New Paths and Old in British Politics		35. Electoral Reform: Good Government? Fairness? Or Vice Versa. Or Both
	3. Problems of the Conservative Party		
	4. The Resurgence of the Labour Party		36. Presidents and Prime Ministers
	5. British Constitutional Reform: Including the Monarchy?		37. Towards 1996: The Making or Breaking of Europe
	6. Peace in Northern Ireland		38. 1996 and All That
	7. Germany: Urgent Pressures, Quiet Change		39. The Future of Europe
	8. Everyone a Winner		40. Diagnosis: Healthier in Europe
	9. Kohl's Germany: The Beginning of the End?		41. Europe and the Underclass: The Slippery Slope
	10. Germany: A Wave of 'Ostalgia'		42. Freedom in Post-Communist Societies
	11. The Two Faces of France		43. In the Dark Shadow of History
	12. France in the Mid-1990s: Gloom but Not Doomed		44. Six Reasons for Optimism about Russia
	13. The Rise, Again, of Jacques Chirac		45. Russia after Chechnya: The Rise of the New Right
	14. Some Judges in France Battle the Establishment		46. Russian Politics: The Calm before the Storm?
	15. France: Keeping the Demons at Bay		47. Let's Abolish the Third World
	16. The Debate Over the Constitutional Council: A Special Court of Law?		48. The "Third World" Is Dead, but Spirits Linger
	17. Update on Italy: The Birth of the "Second Republic"		49. Mexico: The Failed Fiesta
			50. The Larger Lessons of the Mexican Crisis
	18. Italy: The Right Break with the Past?		51. Africa: Falling Off the Map?
	19. The Fall of Berlusconi's Goverment		52. Why Is Africa Eating Asia's Dust?
	20. Neo-Fascists Remodel Their Party in Italy		53. South Africa's Change, Mandela's Challenge
	21. Italy's Spaghetti Politics Untangle Strand at a Time		54. After 45 Years, Beijing Tries to Polish Ideology
	22. Japan's Long March		55. China's Communists: The Road from Tiananmen
	23. Uncertainty Shuffles the Deck in Japanese Politics		56. What Next for China?
	24. Japanese Politics Meander Nowhere		57. India: Pride and Prejudice
	25. Intellectual Warfare		58. Miracles beyond the Free Market
	26. The End of Politics		59. The "New Authoritarianism" in East Asia
	27. The Left's New Start		60. A New Era in Democracy: Democracy's Third Wave
	28. Western Europe's Nationalists: The Rise of the Outside Right		
	29. The Migration Challenge: Europe's Crisis in Historical Perspective		61. Dangers and Dilemmas of Democracy
			62. Democracy and Growth: Why Voting Is Good for You
	30. Women, Power, and Politics: The Norwegian Experience		63. Capitalism and Democracy
	31. Political Power Is Only Half the Battle		64. A Debate on Cultural Conflicts
	32. Kohl's Party Sets Quotas for Women		65. Jihad vs. McWorld
	33. What Democracy Is . . . and Is Not		

(Continued on next page)

ABOUT YOU

Name_____ Date_____

Are you a teacher? ☐ Or student? ☐

Your School Name _____

Department _____

Address _____

City _____ State _____ Zip _____

School Telephone #_____

YOUR COMMENTS ARE IMPORTANT TO US!

Please fill in the following information:

For which course did you use this book? _____

Did you use a text with this Annual Edition?   ☐ yes   ☐ no

The title of the text? _____

What are your general reactions to the Annual Editions concept?

Have you read any particular articles recently that you think should be included in the next edition?

Are there any articles you feel should be replaced in the next edition? Why?

Are there other areas that you feel would utilize an Annual Edition?

May we contact you for editorial input?

May we quote you from above?

ANNUAL EDITIONS: COMPARATIVE POLITICS 95/96

BUSINESS REPLY MAIL

First Class   Permit No. 84   Guilford, CT

Postage will be paid by addressee

Dushkin Publishing Group/
Brown & Benchmark Publishers
DPG **Sluice Dock**
Guilford, Connecticut 06437

No Postage
Necessary
if Mailed
in the
United States

Autodesk 3ds Max 2017 Fundamentals

ASCENT – Center for Technical Knowledge®

Publications

SDC Publications
P.O. Box 1334
Mission KS 66222
913-262-2664
www.SDCpublications.com
Publisher: Stephen Schroff

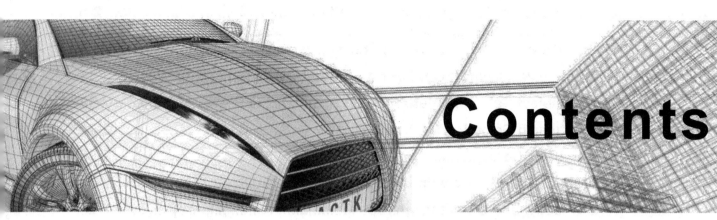

Contents

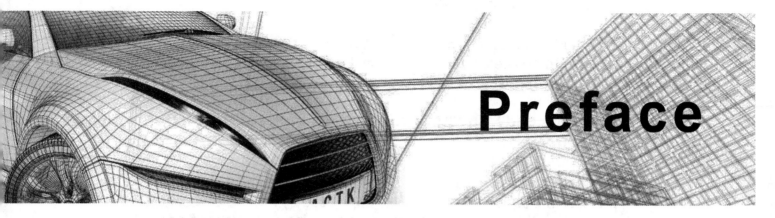

Preface

The Autodesk 3ds Max 2017: Fundamentals student guide provides a thorough introduction to the Autodesk 3ds Max 2017 (R1) software that will help new users make the most of this sophisticated application, as well as broaden the horizons of existing, self-taught users.

The practices in this student guide are primarily geared towards real-world tasks encountered by users of the Autodesk 3ds Max software in the Architecture, Interior Design, and Civil Engineering industries.

Advanced topics, such as character animation and rigging, are not covered in this student guide.

Topics Covered

- Introduction to Autodesk 3ds Max 2017 (R1)

- Autodesk 3ds Max Interface and Workflow

- Assembling Files by importing, linking, or merging

- 3D Modeling with Primitives and 2D Objects

- Using Modifiers to create and modify 3D objects

- Materials and Maps

- Autodesk 3ds Max Lighting

- Lighting and Rendering with mental ray

- Rendering and Cameras

- Animation for Visualization

Note on Software Setup

This student guide assumes a standard installation of the software using the default preferences during installation. Lectures and practices use the standard software templates and default options for the Content Libraries.

Students and Educators can Access Free Autodesk Software and Resources

Autodesk challenges you to get started with free educational licenses for professional software and creativity apps used by millions of architects, engineers, designers, and hobbyists today. Bring Autodesk software into your classroom, studio, or workshop to learn, teach, and explore real-world design challenges the way professionals do.

Get started today - register at the Autodesk Education Community and download one of the many Autodesk software applications available.

Visit www.autodesk.com/joinedu/

Note: Free products are subject to the terms and conditions of the end-user license and services agreement that accompanies the software. The software is for personal use for education purposes and is not intended for classroom or lab use.

Lead Contributor: Renu Muthoo

Renu uses her instructional design training to develop courseware for AutoCAD and AutoCAD vertical products, Autodesk 3ds Max, Autodesk Showcase and various other Autodesk software products. She has worked with Autodesk products for the past 20 years with a main focus on design visualization software.

Renu holds a bachelor's degree in Computer Engineering and started her career as a Instructional Designer/Author where she co-authored a number of Autodesk 3ds Max and AutoCAD books, some of which were translated into other languages for a wide audience reach. In her next role as a Technical Specialist at a 3D visualization company, Renu used 3ds Max in real-world scenarios on a daily basis. There, she developed customized 3D web planner solutions to create specialized 3D models with photorealistic texturing and lighting to produce high quality renderings.

Renu Muthoo has been the Lead Contributor for *Autodesk 3ds Max: Fundamentals* since 2010.

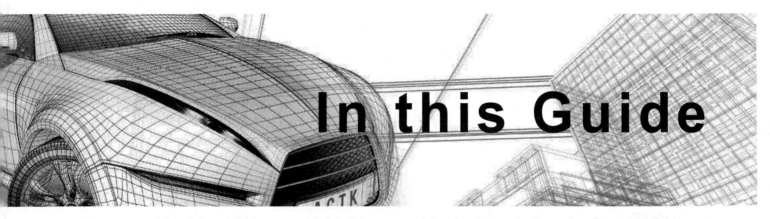
In this Guide

The following images highlight some of the features that can be found in this Student Guide.

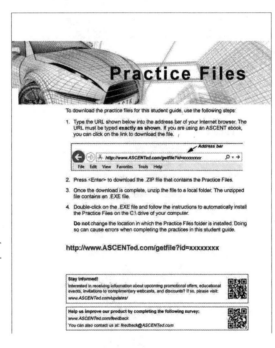

FTP link for practice files

Practice Files

The Practice Files page tells you how to download and install the practice files that are provided with this student guide.

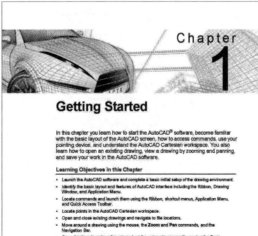

Learning Objectives for the chapter

Chapters

Each chapter begins with a brief introduction and a list of the chapter's Learning Objectives.

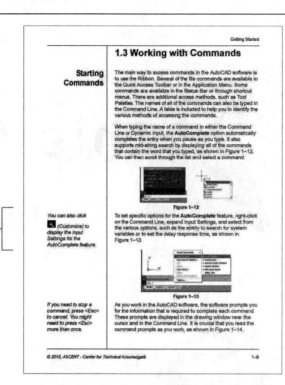

Side notes

Side notes are hints or additional information for the current topic.

Instructional Content

Each chapter is split into a series of sections of instructional content on specific topics. These lectures include the descriptions, step-by-step procedures, figures, hints, and information you need to achieve the chapter's Learning Objectives.

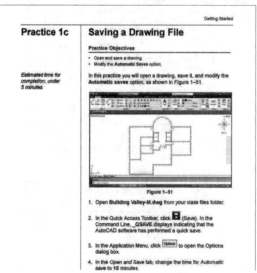

Practice Objectives

Practices

Practices enable you to use the software to perform a hands-on review of a topic.

Some practices require you to use prepared practice files, which can be downloaded from the link found on the Practice Files page.

Chapter Review Questions

Chapter review questions, located at the end of each chapter, enable you to review the key concepts and learning objectives of the chapter.

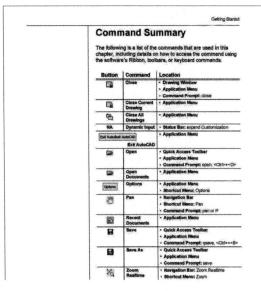

Command Summary

The Command Summary is located at the end of each chapter. It contains a list of the software commands that are used throughout the chapter, and provides information on where the command is found in the software.

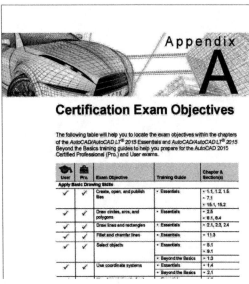

Autodesk Certification Exam Appendix

This appendix includes a list of the topics and objectives for the Autodesk Certification exams, and the chapter and section in which the relevant content can be found.

Icons in this Student Guide

The following icons are used to help you quickly and easily find helpful information.

New in **2017**	Indicates items that are new in the Autodesk 3ds Max 2017 (R1) software.
 **Enhanced** in **2017**	Indicates items that have been enhanced in the Autodesk 3ds Max 2017 (R1) software.

Practice Files

To download the practice files that are required for this training guide, type the following in the address bar of your web browser:

SDCpublications.com/downloads/978-1-63057-031-6

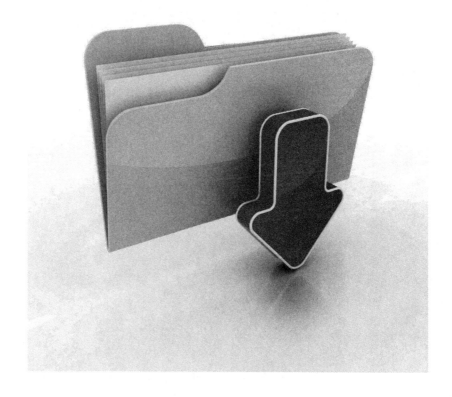

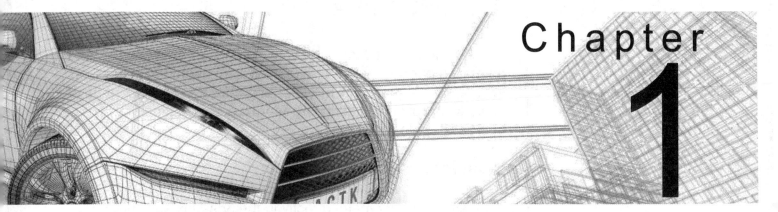

Chapter 1

Introduction to Autodesk 3ds Max

The Autodesk® 3ds Max® software is a modeling, rendering, and animation package used for the visualization and presentation of scenes. Projects can be created and modeled in the software or files from other software packages can be linked/imported for use in the software. A solid understanding of the interface, configuration settings, and the workflow used to create, render, and animate models enable you to visualize your models prior to building the final design.

Learning Objectives in this Chapter

- Identify the various data sources that can be imported into and then output from the Autodesk 3ds Max software.
- Understand the common workflow process to plan your visualization projects.
- Understand the various components of the interface.
- Set the preferences for the scene.
- Set the project folder to organize all of the files in the project.
- Set the path locations of reusable data files and reconfigurable items.
- Identify the display drivers available with the software.
- Identify the viewport display labels and the various options available in them.

1.1 Overview

The Autodesk® 3ds Max® software is a modeling, rendering, and animation package used for design visualization. It can be used to create high-quality 3D models, single-frame still renderings of virtually any size (including large-format presentation graphics), and desktop animations.

Input Into Autodesk 3ds Max

You can create geometry directly in the 3ds Max software or import it from multiple data sources, including the following:

- **AutoCAD® drawing files (.DWG, .DXF):** Including objects created in AutoCAD vertical applications, such as the AutoCAD® Architecture and AutoCAD® Civil 3D® software.

- **Autodesk® Revit® Architecture designs:** Linked into the Autodesk 3ds Max software using .RVT files or the exported .FBX or .DWG files. The Autodesk® Revit® Structure and Autodesk® Revit® MEP software can also be imported using .DWG.

- **AutoCAD® Civil 3D® (VSP3D):** Using **Autodesk Civil View**, you can import files from various civil design programs.

- **Autodesk® Inventor® files (.IPT, .IAM):** The Autodesk Inventor software must be installed on the same machine as the Autodesk 3ds Max software to import these files.

- **3D Studio Mesh format (.3DS):** A common data format used when transferring between 3D applications.

- Autodesk® Alias® .Wire files and the Autodesk® Showcase® .APF (Autodesk Packet File).

- LandXML and DEM data files.

- **Adobe Illustrator (.AI):** The Autodesk 3ds Max software only supports the Adobe Illustrator 88 software.

Vector Data

The input data formats are considered to be vector data. Graphics displayed from vector data formats are defined by point locations and mathematical formulas. Since their data is defined mathematically, vector graphics can be redrawn or regenerated at different scales or from different 3D viewpoints. The Autodesk 3ds Max software file format (.MAX file) is also a vector data file.

Output from Autodesk 3ds Max

Autodesk 3ds Max software stores its data in vector-based .MAX files, used to generate raster images as final products. These images, called *renderings*, can be configured as simple illustrations or fully realized photorealistic images. The most common Autodesk 3ds Max animations are created by combining a series of individually-rendered raster images into a desktop animation file (e.g., Windows .AVI or QuickTime .MOV).

Raster Data

Raster graphics consist of a grid of colored points called pixels Pixels are viewed at a resolution at which they cannot be identified individually, and instead are permitted to present a unified image, as shown in Figure 1–1.

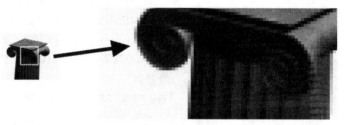

Figure 1–1

The Autodesk 3ds Max software is also used to create raster images or raster based animations (Autodesk 3ds Max renderings). Raster image renderings must be recreated (re-rendered) if the point-of-view is animated or otherwise changed. Common raster file formats include .JPEG, Windows bitmap (.BMP), and .TIFF files. They can also be used as input into the Autodesk 3ds Max software to supplement the vector geometry as follows:

- Scanned or digital photographs of a proposed construction site can be used as a background image.

- Images that illustrate material texture, such as wall coverings, wood grain, or a scratched metal surface.

- Image files created in other computer graphic applications can be used as signs, posters, or company logos.

1.2 Visualization Workflow

Each visualization project can be very different from the next, but most follow a common general workflow. A suggested approach to plan your visualization project is as follows.

1. Setting Goals and Expectations

Every project should start with a clear understanding of the deliverables and expectations.

- Determine viewpoints, animation paths, lighting conditions, etc. before modeling.
- Sketch a mock-up storyboard to agree on the content and scope of an animation.
- Incorporate resolution time in your time estimates. Simple oversights and design problems are often found during the visualization process.

2. Scene Creation and Modeling

The next step is to gather data together into scenes (.MAX files).

- Create a project folder to store all of your data and source material, such as site photos, textures, drawings, scans, in the appropriate locations.
- Import or link 2D or 3D data into one or more scene files, when it is available from other design applications.
- Merge together or externally reference scene files when a project requires multiple scene files.
- Add modeled geometry at this stage. The **Graphite Modeling** tools have many new features for creating new geometry on the surfaces of imported files.

3. Material Design

Materials define how surfaces display and how light interacts with them. Often the next step is to configure the surface characteristics using the Material Editor. It is recommended that you consider the lighting and rendering as materials might need to be coordinated with renderers and lights.

- Detail materials to help simplify the geometry. For example, you do not need to model the grout along a brick wall. Material definitions, such as bump mapping, can add the appearance of depth.

- Fine-tune the material properties, as required, to make them realistic.
- Lighting and materials are often adjusted together, but it can be useful to have a first draft of your materials completed before adding lights.

4. Lighting Design

For realistic results, the 3D models need light sources to illuminate the objects.

- There are different approaches to lighting scenes in the Autodesk 3ds Max software, some are more straightforward and some are more technical.
- Most scenes might require lighting adjustments.

5. Configuring Rendered Views and Animations

Once your model, materials, and lights have been initially configured, you can focus on the final output.

- The length of any animations, their frame rate, and the required time display should be assigned first.
- Camera objects can then be positioned to set up both single-frame still renderings and animations.
- Objects are animated and animated details such as clouds blowing through the sky, pedestrians on the sidewalks, etc. can then be added.
- The rendering options should be configured at this stage.

6. Testing and Final Adjustments

Test the rendering and adjust the model, materials, and lights to achieve the required results. Note that computer processing of the renderings can be very time-consuming, especially for long animations or large still renderings.

7. Post Production

You can add details to your final renderings outside the Autodesk 3ds Max software using third-party image editing programs (Adobe Photoshop or Adobe AfterEffects) and other video post-production software (Autodesk Combustion). Usually, the finished animation segments are mixed with actual video footage, voice-over narration, background sound effects, and music in a different software (such as Apple's Final Cut Pro, or another video editing and assembly tool).

1.3 The Autodesk 3ds Max Interface

To launch the Autodesk 3ds Max software, use one of the following methods:

- Double-click on ▨ (3ds Max) on your desktop.

- Click **Start** in the Windows Task Bar and select **All Programs>Autodesk>Autodesk 3ds Max 2017> 3ds Max 2017**.

Welcome Screen

If you are opening the software for the first time, a Welcome screen displays, as shown in Figure 1–2. It contains three separate panels: Learn, Start, and Extend. This is a starting point for users as it provides access to help, information for learning the software and new and enhanced features, options for starting a new scene or opening a file. You can do the following:

- Clear the **Show this Welcome Screen at startup** option to prevent the Welcome Screen from displaying when you launch the Autodesk 3ds Max software.

- Close the dialog box by clicking ▨.

- Open the Welcome Screen any time during the current session by selecting **Welcome Screen** in the Help menu.

Learn

The Learn Panel (shown in Figure 1–2) contains:

- Startup videos, sample scenes, and online resources that help you to learn about the new features in the current release of the software.

- Learning movies on the Autodesk 3ds Max YouTube Channel, and additional resources on the web.

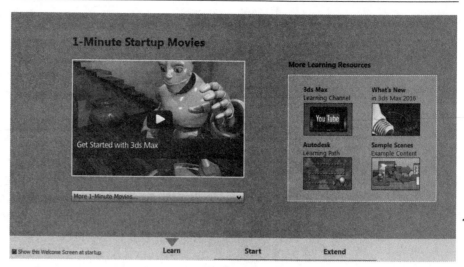

Figure 1–2

Start

The Start Panel contains:

- Options for opening an already saved .MAX file (**Browse**) or opening a file from the list of recently opened files.

- Five standard start-up templates (shown in Figure 1–3) are available for creating a new empty scene. These templates contain built-in settings (rendering, environment, lighting, units, etc.) optimum for that particular type of scene enabling you to quickly and easily create a new scene. Select a template and click **New Using Selected Template** to open a scene from a template.

- The **Open Template Manager** options enable you to create new templates or modify the existing ones.

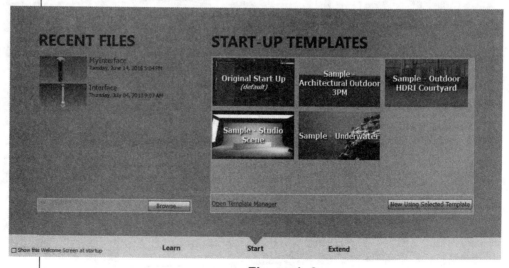

Figure 1–3

Extend

This page provides links to the Autodesk Exchange Apps center and Autodesk 360 to access online services. It enables you to connect to the online community of artists and forums such as Scriptspot and Area.

Interface

The Autodesk 3ds Max software consists of a main modeling window, called the *viewport*, which is surrounded by interface tools and panels. Figure 1–4 shows an example of a model created using various modifiers in the Command Panel, to display the different interface features.

*For printing purposes, the UI color scheme used in the figures is **ame-light** (Menu bar: Customize>Custom UI and Defaults Switcher> UI schemes), and the Theme has been set to **Light** in the Customize User Interface dialog box>Colors tab.*

- By default, the scene is set as one viewport/four equal viewports that display the model at different viewing angles.

- You can toggle between the four viewport displays or one maximized viewport (as shown in Figure 1–4), by clicking

  (Maximize Viewport) or pressing <Alt>+<W>.

- The active viewport displays a yellow border. Clicking in empty space in a viewport makes it active.

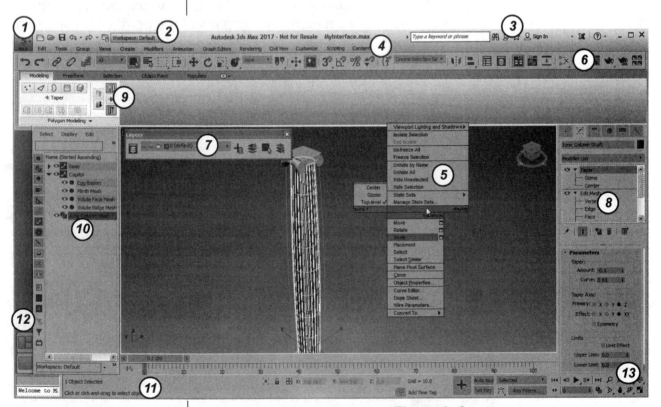

Figure 1–4

1. Application Menu

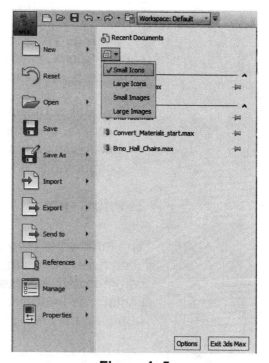 (Application Menu) provides access to the file commands, settings, and recently opened files, as shown in Figure 1–5. The Recent Documents can be sorted by date and pinned in the stack to prevent them from scrolling. Using [image], the display can be customized to display them as icons or viewport thumbnails as shown in Figure 1–5.

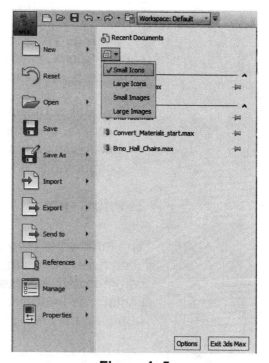

Figure 1–5

2. Quick Access Toolbar

The Quick Access Toolbar (shown in Figure 1–6) contains:

- One-click tools for saving, opening, or creating new scenes, using undo/redo, and setting the project folder.

- The Undo and Redo stack: Can be accessed using the drop-down arrows.

- [image]: Opens a drop-down list where you can select tools to create a custom quick access toolkit.

- The workspaces list (shown in Figure 1–6): Enables you to manage and switch between different interface setups. You can create a custom interface setup, containing commonly used toolbars, menus, quad menus, viewport layout settings, ribbon tools, and hotkeys for commands.

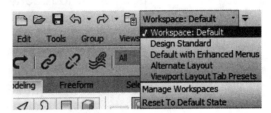

Figure 1–6

- **Manage Workspaces**: Opens the Manage Workspaces dialog box, in which you can add new workspaces, edit workspaces, and delete workspaces.

- **Default with Enhanced Menus:** Displays an enhanced interface containing additional menus in the menu bar, tooltips linking to relevant help topics, a display that is highly configurable, and a keyboard search for menu commands.

3. InfoCenter

The InfoCenter (shown in Figure 1–7) enables you to quickly search for help on the web, access the subscription services and communication center, open the Autodesk Exchange Apps center, save and access topics as favorites, sign into Autodesk A360, and access the Autodesk 3ds Max help.

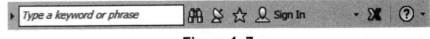

Figure 1–7

4. Menu Bar

The display of the menu bar can be controlled using the Quick Access Toolbar by clicking ☰ and selecting ***Hide/Show Menu Bar*** *in the drop-down list.*

The Menu Bar contains working commands that are grouped together in the menu titles. There are two different menu bars: Standard and Enhanced. The menus in the Standard Menu Bar are described as follows:

Edit	Contains undo and redo functions, object selection options, copying (cloning), and delete functions.
Tools	Contains the **Mirror**, **Array**, **Align**, and **Measure Distance** options.
Group	Contains tools to create and edit Autodesk 3ds Max group objects. Groups function similar to AutoCAD groups.

Views	Contains features, such as preset viewport views, viewport display options, and ViewCube and SteeringWheel options.
Create	Contains options that enable you to create objects, such as 3D geometry, 2D shapes, cameras, and lights.
Modifiers	Contains sub-menus categorized by the available modifiers.
Animation	Contains common features used when creating animations.
Graph Editors	Contains several Track View features. Track View offers advanced controls for animations.
Rendering	Contains functions for rendering, such as setting up the scene environment, advanced lighting controls, and output image resolution.
Civil View	Contains features that can be used for displaying the contents of a scene created in a civil design program and to create visualizations of civil engineering projects. It offers support for various civil design programs, including the AutoCAD® Civil 3D® software. If you are opening Civil View for the first time, you need to initialize it and set the system units, country resource kit, and start mode.
Customize	Contains features for customizing the user interface, setting up the drawing units, and setting the overall Autodesk 3ds Max default options.
Scripting	Contains tools for working with the MAXScript programming language used by the Autodesk 3ds Max software.
Content	Links you to the Creative Market Store, which lists 3D and 2D assets . These assets can be licensed for use in your project. You can also launch the Autodesk Exchange App Store, where the Autodesk 3dx Max Asset Library is available for download along with various other apps.
Help	The **Help** menu connects you directly to the Autodesk 3ds Max Help documentation on the autodesk.com website. It contains features, such as Online Reference manuals, Tutorials, and Network-version license borrowing and return options.

Enhanced Menu Bar

The Enhanced Menu Bar can be displayed by selecting **Default with Enhanced Menus** in the Workspaces drop-down list in the Quick Access Toolbar. The Enhanced Menu Bar contains various menus: **Objects, Edit, Modifiers, Animation, Simulate, Materials, Lighting/Cameras, Rendering, Scene, Civil View, Lighting Analysis, Customize, Script, Content**, and **Help**.

- The commands and functions are organized as menu items, with submenus containing the relevant commands.

- Hovering the cursor over an item displays an information tooltip (as shown in Figure 1–8), and provides a link to the relevant help topic.

Figure 1–8

Hint: Global Menu Search

You can search for any menu command or action using the global menu search method. Press <X> to open the Search actions edit box at the cursor location and enter the name of the command or action that you want to use. As you enter the first letter of the command, a list of matching actions displays, as shown in Figure 1–9. Select an option in the list or enter another letter to display a more specific list of actions. To clear the search action, click the red **X** icon in the upper right corner of the *Search* edit box. Click in empty space or press <Esc> to exit the search feature.

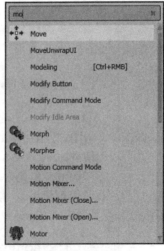

Figure 1–9

5. Quad Menu

The Quad Menus (shown in Figure 1–10) are a series of context-sensitive menus that open when selecting and right-clicking on one or more objects in the viewport. The commands are displayed in different quadrant areas and each quad menu can have a maximum of four quadrant areas, as shown in Figure 1–11.

- Quad menus also display when nothing is selected.

- Different quad menus display when <Ctrl>, <Alt>, or <Shift> are combined with right-clicking.

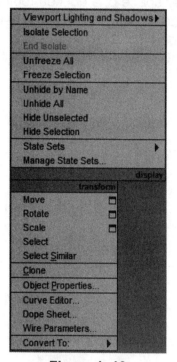

Figure 1–10

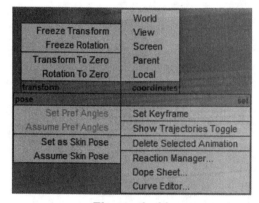

Figure 1–11

6. Main Toolbar

The Main Toolbar (shown in Figure 1–12), is visible by default and contains tools for some of the most commonly used options. These include the **Selection**, **Transforms**, **Snap**, and **Rendering** tools.

Figure 1–12

- The Main Toolbar can extend beyond the interface and some of the tools are not visible on the screen. To slide the buttons left or right, hover the cursor over the gray empty area until the cursor changes into a Pan cursor (hand icon), hold the left mouse button and drag.

- If the Main Toolbar is not visible, you can display it by selecting **Customize>Show UI>Show Main Toolbar**.

7. Toolbars

By default, the toolbars (except the Main Toolbar) are not displayed. Right-click on the title bar of an open toolbar or on the gray empty space of a docked toolbar to open the **Customize Display** menu (shown in Figure 1–13) where you can select the required toolbar name to display it. As with other interface components, you can float or dock the toolbars.

Figure 1–13

8. Command Panel

*The options in the lower portion of each panel are grouped into rollouts. You can expand and collapse the rollouts by clicking on the title bar of the rollout, or the **+/-** signs (or upward/downward facing double arrows).*

The Command Panel enables you to efficiently create, edit, and manage the settings of 3D objects. It contains six different panels or tabs, each with a different appearance and function. Figure 1–14 shows the Object Type rollout in the Create panel ().

Figure 1–14

- If the list of rollouts are extensive and extend beyond the bottom of the interface, pan the list up and down by holding and dragging the mouse button in the Command Panel.

- By default, the Command Panel is docked along the right side of the viewport window. You can minimize the Command Panel by hovering the cursor over the top right edge of the Command Panel until the cursor displays as , then right-clicking and selecting **Minimize**. Once minimized, hover the cursor over the Command Panel title bar, (displayed vertically) to display it. To maximize it, right-click along the right edge of the Command Panel and select either **Dock>Right** or **Dock>Left**.

Create Panel

The Create panel enables you to interactively create objects in the Autodesk 3ds Max software and contains the following categories of object types:

	Geometry is 3D objects.
	Shapes are 2D objects.
	Lights are used to illuminate the scene.
	Cameras are objects that provide scene views.
	Helpers are non-rendering tools that help with layout or work with other objects, such as a distance measuring tape object.
	Space warps are non-renderable objects that deform or otherwise influence the geometry of other objects. They are used to create ripples and waves, using forces such as wind and gravity.
	Systems contains the Sunlight and Daylight Systems, Biped, and the controls for some 3rd party plug-ins.

Modify Panel

The Modify panel shows the selected object's parameter values, a list of modifiers added to an object, and the parameters that apply to them.

- Modifiers are geometric modifications and additional property controls that can be added to objects, as required.

- Object and modifier parameters can be changed at any time after the object's creation, if the Modifier Stack remains intact.

- The **Modifier List** drop-down menu contains all of the modifiers that can be applied to the current selection.

- The Modifier Stack lists the modifiers that have been applied to an object. Figure 1–15 shows the Modifier Stack of a circle that was edited, extruded, and tapered into a 3D column shaft.

- The Modify panel is blank if no object is selected or if more than one object is selected.

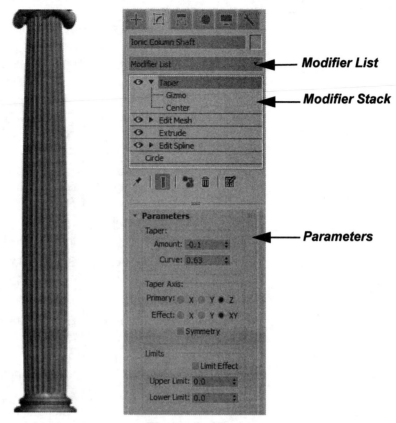

Figure 1–15

Hierarchy Panel

The Hierarchy panel contains controls for objects that are linked together into hierarchies, such as for mechanical equipment with interconnected parts.

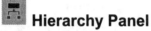 Motion Panel

The Motion Panel contains sophisticated motion controls for animating.

Display Panel

The Display panel contains object-level visibility controls, enabling you to hide or unhide objects individually or by category, independent of the layer settings.

Utilities Panel

The Utilities panel contains a number of miscellaneous utilities as follows:

Asset Browser	Enables you to review and select content such as 3D objects or 2D bitmaps from your local drive or across the web.
Perspective Match Utility	Helps match the position and field of view of the camera in your 3D scene to the perspective photographic background image.
Collapse Utility	Removes the modifiers from an object's stack, turning the object into an editable mesh or poly.
Color Clipboard Utility	Stores color swatches for copying from one map or material to another.
Measure Utility	Lists the surface area and volume of objects.
Motion Capture Utility	Enables you to animate virtual objects with the real-time movement of the mouse or they input device.
Reset XForm Utility	Removes rotation and scale values of an object, applying them to the XForm modifier gizmo.
MAXScript	Accesses a scripting language that can be used to automate repetitive functions or build new tools and interfaces.
Flight Studio Utility	Enables you to open and manage the open Flight models.
More...	Provides access to a complete list of Utilities, including the controls for many 3rd party plug-in applications.

9. Modeling Ribbon

The Modeling ribbon (shown in Figure 1–16) provides easy access to polygon modeling tools, including the editing and modification tools used at sub-object level. The ribbon contains most of the commonly used tools that are also found in the Command Panel's Modify panel (at the Edit Poly sub-object level).

*If the ribbon is not displayed, in the menu bar, select **Customize> Show UI>Show Ribbon**. You can also click ⊞ (Toggle Ribbon) in the Main Toolbar or select **Ribbon** in the Customize Display right-click menu.*

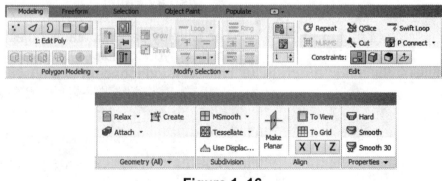

Figure 1–16

The ribbon contains five tabs: *Modeling*, *Freeform*, *Selection*, *Object Paint*, and *Populate* that are further subdivided into various panels that are context dependent. All of the tools are grouped based on context and are placed in separate panels.

- For example, the *Modeling* tab contains the tools used for modeling and are grouped in the Polygon Modeling panel, Modify Selection panel, Edit panel, etc. Each of the panels has a set of related tools and commands present for easy access. For example, the Polygon Modeling panel contains tools used for **Edit Poly** modifier, as shown in Figure 1–17.

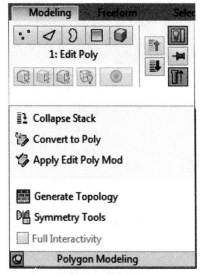

Figure 1–17

- The ribbon might be minimized to the panel tiles, and is docked under the Main Toolbar. Click ▣ to maximize the ribbon.

- The display of the tabs and panels can be controlled by right-clicking on the ribbon and select the options in the menu, as shown in Figure 1–18.

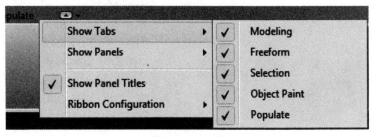

Figure 1–18

- If you are continuously using the options from a panel, you can click 🔲 in the expanded panel to lock it.

Hint: Caddy Display for Edit Poly Modifier

The caddy display (shown in Figure 1–19) enables you to enter values on the screen for various modifiers at the Edit Poly sub-object level. The modifications are dynamically updated and reflected in the model.

- The values can be typed in the edit boxes or you can hold and drag the spinner arrows for dynamical viewing and updating of the changes.

- Click ⊘ to accept the change ⊕ to accept the change and continue in the same modifier.

Figure 1–19

- The caddy interface can be accessed through:

  - **Modeling ribbon**: Hold <Shift> and select the sub-object level modifier tool or click the down arrow next to the modifier and select the setting, as shown for the Bevel modifier in Figure 1–20.

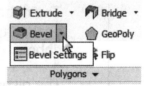

Figure 1–20

  - **Command Panel**: Click ■ (Settings) next to the sub-object level modifier option. This enables you to enter the values while performing the operation.

  - The display of the caddy interface is controlled by the **Enable Caddy Controls** option in the Preference Settings dialog box>*General* tab>*UI Display* area. By default, the option is selected.

Hint: Design Workspace

The Design Workspace Ribbon contains the commonly used 3ds Max commands and features grouped together in tabs, as shown in Figure 1–21. It can be started by selecting **Design Standard** in the Workspaces drop-down list in the Quick Access Toolbar, or by opening a template, which uses a Design Standard workspace from the Welcome screen>Start panel.

Figure 1–21

The various tabs included are:

- **Get Started**: Commands for starting a new scene, opening an already saved scene, and linking geometry and files from other 3D data software. It also contains commands for customizing the software and accessing to learning resources.

- **Object Inspection**: Commands used to control the display of objects in viewports and also explore the geometry in the scene.

- **Basic Modeling**: Tools for creating new geometry in the scene.

- **Materials**: Tools for creating, managing, and editing the materials.

- **Object Placement**: Tools for moving, placing and editing geometry. You can also open Civil View from this tab.

- **Populate**: Tools for adding animated or idle people to a scene.

- **View**: Commands to add cameras and control the viewport display.

- **Lighting and Rendering**: Tools for adding lights and creating renderings of the scene.

10. Scene Explorer

The Scene Explorer (shown in Figure 1–22) lists all of the objects that are present in a scene in the form of a tree structure, along with each object's properties displayed in a tabular form.

- By default, the Scene Explorer is docked along the left side of the viewport. You can float it or dock it to left/right by hovering the cursor over on the top or top left edge till the cursor displays as ⬓, then right-clicking and selecting the required option.

- It is a modeless dialog box that can remains open while you are working in the scene.

- You can open and manage the Scene Explorer from the Tools menu bar.

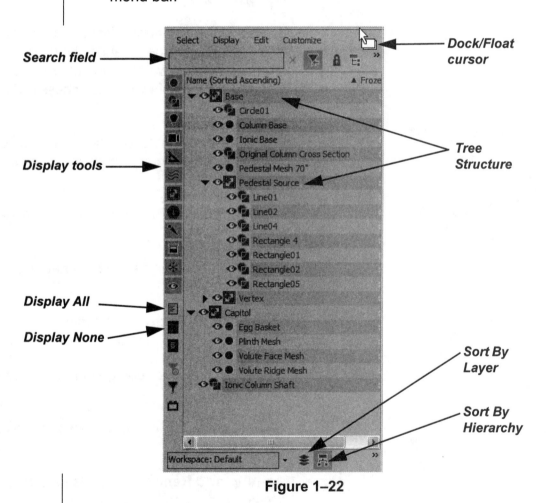

Figure 1–22

- A default Scene Explorer is included for each workspace and can be saved with a specific name with that workspace.

- The objects can be toggled to be displayed either as hierarchies (![icon]) or as layers (![icon]).

- Objects and layers can be nested to any depth. Use the arrow next to the name to expand or collapse the group.

- You can perform actions and modifications such as sorting, filtering, selecting, renaming, hiding, and freezing objects, directly in the Scene Explorer.

- You can drag and drop objects and layers to reorganize the groups.

- A toolbar is provided along the left edge of the Scene Explorer that enables you to list only those objects that belong to a particular category. There are tools for various categories such as ![icon] (Display Geometry), ![icon] (Display Cameras), ![icon] (Display Lights), etc. When the tool for a category is active (i.e., displays with a yellow background), the objects belonging to that category are listed. The ![icon] (Display All) tool lists all of the different categories of objects. To only list the objects belonging to the category that you need, use ![icon] (Display None) to clear any existing selections, and then select the required display category.

- To easily find and select an item, use the *Search* field.

11. Status Bar

The Status Bar (shown in Figure 1–23) found along the bottom left and center of the interface contains the following elements:

Figure 1–23

MAXScript Mini-Listener	Enables you to enter commands and receive feedback (MaxScript commands)
Status Line	Identifies the number of objects selected
Prompt Line	Prompts for the next action or input that is required.
(Isolate Selection Toggle)	Zooms the current selection in the active viewport while temporarily hiding unselected objects in all viewports (except the **Camera** viewport). This enables you to work on the required object without the other objects getting in your way. You can also access this command by selecting Tools>Isolate Selection or pressing <Alt>+<Q>.
(Selection Lock Toggle)	Toggles a lock to prevent you from changing your current selection between options. Pressing the space bar toggles this on or off.
or (Absolute/Offset Transform Mode Toggle)	Enables you to toggle between Absolute mode (which sets the coordinates in the world space) and the Offset transform mode (which transforms the objects relative to its coordinates).
Transform Type In	Enables you to review and adjust transform values for the X, Y, and Z coordinates.
Grid Setting Display	Controls the distance between grid lines. Select Tools>Grids and Snaps>Grid and Snap Settings to open the dialog box. Use the *Home Grid* tab to adjust the spacing. To toggle the Grid on or off, press <G>.
(Adaptive Degradation Toggle)	Enables you to toggle adaptive degradation on or off. Right-click to open the Viewport Configuration dialog box in the *Display Performance* tab (the Adaptive Degradation tab is for legacy drivers). You can improve the viewport quality progressively and set the resolution for the texture display (for nitrous drivers). It also contains options for controlling adaptive degradation.
Time Tag	Enables you to add or edit time tags, which are labels describing specific points of an animation.

12. Viewport Layouts tab bar

The Viewport Layouts tab bar is a vertically, expandable bar containing a list of viewport layouts that can be selected to quickly change the layout of the viewports, as shown in Figure 1–24.

- For a new scene, a single layout tab is available. Once you have saved additional viewport layouts, they are listed along with the default one. The Viewport Layouts tab bar displays the default layout and three additional viewport layouts that were saved.

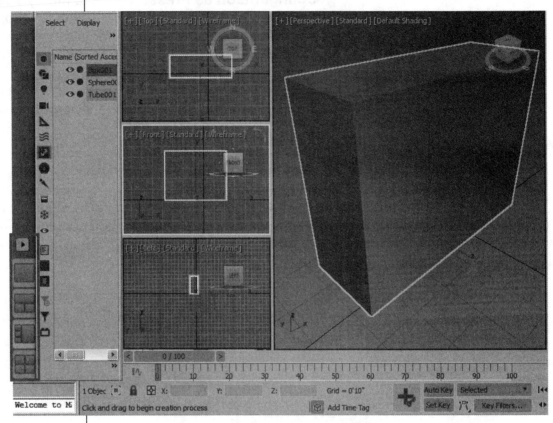

Figure 1–24

- Click 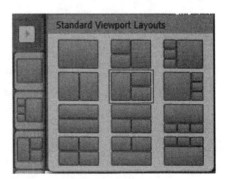 (as shown in Figure 1–25), to open the available standard viewport layouts for selection and customization. Once you have selected a layout, it is listed in the tab bar with any previously saved layouts. The viewports are displayed as the new layout.

Figure 1–25

- To customize a preset layout, select it from the preset layouts, move the boundaries by clicking and dragging them to new positions, set the required Point of View and Shading modes, and then save the custom viewport layout. Save it by right-clicking on the newly custom tab and selecting **Save Configuration as Preset**. Set its name by entering a new name in the edit box. The newly saved viewport configuration is saved along with the scene for easy retrieval in a later session.

- To display or hide the tab bar, right-click in an empty area of the Main Toolbar, and toggle the **Viewport Layout Tabs** option.

13. Viewport Navigation Tools

The navigation tools are discussed in detail later in the student guide.

The navigation tools (shown in Figure 1–26), are located in the lower right corner of the interface and contain tools for navigating and displaying objects in the viewports. The tools are dependent on the active viewport.

Figure 1–26

1.4 Preferences

The Preference Settings dialog box (shown in Figure 1–27) contains tabs that control the display and operational settings at the program level. The dialog box is available through the **Application Menu>Options** or in the menu bar **Customize> Preferences**.

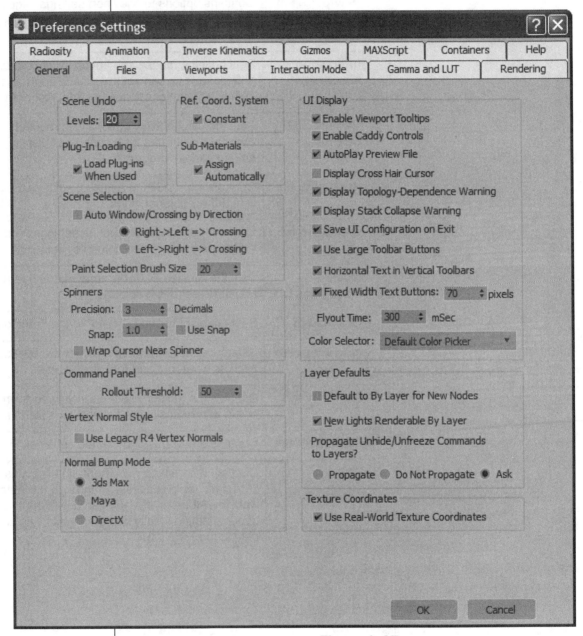

Figure 1–27

The various tabs are described as follows:

General tab	Controls the interface settings, such as Number of Scene Undo steps (levels) that are saved, settings for the transform center, user interface display options, etc.
Files tab	Contains options for file handling, such as Automatic backup save settings.
Viewports tab	Contains options for viewport settings, highlighting options for selection and preview, and setting the display drivers.
Interaction Mode tab	Sets how the mouse and keyboard shortcuts are going to behave. You can set the mouse shortcut behavior to match with earlier releases of 3ds Max or Maya.
Gamma and LUT tab	Sets the compatibility options with respect to other Autodesk programs for a consistent display of colors among various programs
Rendering tab	Controls the rendering settings, such as the ambient light default color settings.
Animation tab	Controls the various animation settings. You can assign the sound plug-ins and controller defaults.
Inverse kinematics tab	Sets the Applied IK (for accuracy) and Interactive IK (for real-time response) settings.
Gizmos tab	Sets the display and behavior of the Transform gizmos.
MAXScript tab	Sets the various features used for the MAXScript editor, such as what font and font size to use.
Radiosity tab	Controls the radiosity settings in viewports and if the light levels with radiosity are saved with a file or not.
Containers tab	Controls the Status and Update settings in viewports.
Help tab	Controls where help documentation is accessed from. By default, help is accessed through the Autodesk.com website. Alternatively, you can download the documentation locally and then specify its installation path in the *Help* tab.

Hint: Gamma and LUT Settings Mismatch

Gamma and LUT Settings are saved with the defaults for the current file based on the current UI. Opening or merging a scene, whose file gamma or LUT settings are different from the gamma and LUT settings of the system in which it is being opened, causes the Mismatch dialog box to open, as shown in Figure 1–28. It provides you with options to use the current settings or adopt the file settings.

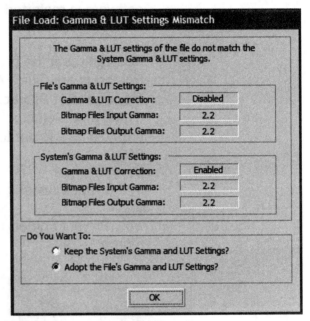

Figure 1–28

1.5 Setting the Project Folder

Setting a project folder enables you to better organize all of the files for a project.

- By default, the project folder is set to your local */3dsmax* folder. Once the project folder is created, a series of subfolders (e.g., scenes, render output) are generated. The project folder is maintained when the Autodesk 3ds Max software is restarted.

- You can reset the project folder by clicking 🗎 (Project Folder) in the Quick Access Toolbar or **Application Menu> Manage>Set Project Folder** to open the Browse For Folder dialog box. Select a folder to be set as your project folder or create a new folder to be used as your project folder and click **OK**.

- In the Quick Access Toolbar, hover the cursor over

  🗎 (Project Folder) to display its name, as shown in Figure 1–29.

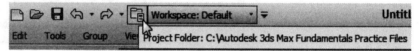

Figure 1–29

1.6 Configure Paths

Projects can use external files such as fonts, image maps for materials, IES (Illuminating Engineering Society) data files for lights, etc. The locations of these and other required data files are identified in the Configure System Paths and Configure User Paths dialog boxes. These dialog boxes can be opened by selecting **Customize>Configure System Paths/Configure User Paths**.

Configure System Paths

The Configure System Paths dialog box (shown in Figure 1–30) stores paths to data files and contains the following tabs:

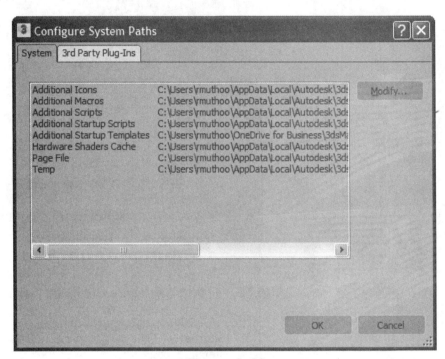

Figure 1–30

System	Paths used for additional buttons, macros, scripts and startup scripts, and temp files.
3rd Party Plug-Ins	Default paths to search for add-on application data (some standard functions and 3rd party products).

Configure User Paths

The Configure User Paths dialog box (shown in Figure 1–31) stores items that might be reconfigured for different users or for different projects. The User path settings can be saved as a path configuration (.MXP) file and later re-loaded as required. The dialog box has the following tabs:

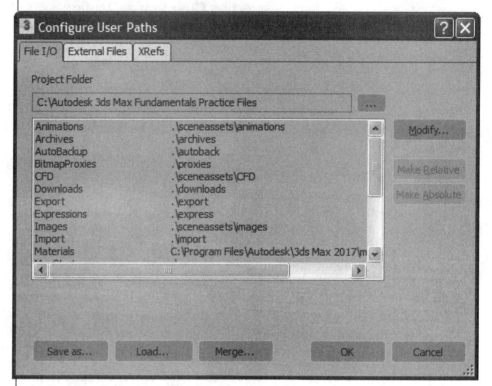

Figure 1–31

File I/O	Paths used to locate files for options such as open, save, export, etc.
External Files	Paths to external data files such as image maps, IES files, etc.
XRefs	Paths that are searched to find externally referenced objects and scene files.

- Since multiple workstations often make use of the same data files, it is often helpful to create shared network locations for these files (especially when network rendering).

- Relative paths are used to help prevent *missing external files* problems when sharing or moving files from one location to another. In the Configure User Paths, all of the paths are preceded with a dot and backslash (.\) indicating a relative path.

- You can use the Configure User Paths dialog box to change hard-coded absolute paths from earlier versions to Relative paths. Select the path and click Make Relative.

> **Hint: Asset Tracking**
>
> In the **Application Menu>References**, select **Asset Tracking** to change hard-coded absolute paths from earlier versions to relative paths. In the Asset Tracking dialog box, select *Paths* tab>**Make Path Relative to Project Folder**, as shown in Figure 1–32.
>
>
>
> **Figure 1–32**

1.7 Display Drivers

The Nitrous Direct3D 11 driver is the default and recommended display driver, but you can change to the other Nitrous drivers or legacy drivers. Nitrous Direct3D 9 is set as the default driver if the graphics card or operating system on your system does not support Nitrous Direct3D 11.

To open the Preference Settings dialog box, select **Customize> Preferences** or **Application Menu>Options**. In the *Viewports* tab, and in the *Display Drivers* area, click **Choose Driver**. Then, select the required driver in the Display Driver Selection dialog box, as shown in Figure 1–33. If you change the display driver, you need to close and reopen the software for the changes to take effect.

You can also change the graphics driver outside the software using the Windows Start menu. Select Windows Start>All Programs> Autodesk>Autodesk 3ds Max 2017> Change Graphics Mode. This launches the software and provides the option of selecting the display driver.

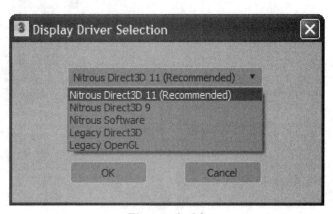

Figure 1–33

The following display drivers are available:

*   **Nitrous Direct3D 11:** The Nitrous Direct 3D 11 driver requires Direct 3D 11.0. This driver takes advantage of video card features (when available), and provides high quality realistic viewport display options and faster rendering times. The visual display is render quality and supports unlimited lights, shadows, tone mapping, etc. The Nitrous driver also enables you to display your scenes in stylized images (pencil, acrylic, ink, etc.) in the viewports.

*   **Nitrous Direct3D 9:** The Nitrous Direct 3D 9 driver requires Direct3D 9.0. It works in the same way as the Direct3D 11 driver.

*The **OpenGL** and **Direct3D** options are useful if your system supports those forms of hardware acceleration. Experiment with these options to determine the best option for your workstation.*

- **Nitrous Software:** The Nitrous Software driver has similar capabilities to the other nitrous drivers, but the hardware support is not required and it might be slower during rendering.

- **Legacy Direct3D:** The Direct3D driver supports data culling and works well for the high-color displays.

- **Legacy OpenGL:** The OpenGL driver works well for hardware acceleration, including geometry acceleration and rasterization acceleration. You cannot display shadows or ambient occlusion in viewports while using this driver.

1.8 Viewport Display and Labels

Geometry opens in the software through one or more viewports, which can be configured to show objects from different viewing angles and with different viewport shading modes.

Three Viewport label menus (shown in Figure 1–34) display in the upper left corner of each viewport. Note that the four labels are only available for the Nitrous displays, while the legacy driver display shows only three labels.

Figure 1–34

General Viewport

Click on **[+]** to open the **General Viewport** label menu, as shown in Figure 1–35. It includes the ability to display grids, the ViewCube, and the SteeringWheels. It also contains tools for the **xView** functionality, which enables you to show statistics and diagnose problems in polygonal geometry such as overlapping faces, unwelded vertices, or face normal orientation issues.

Figure 1–35

Point Of View

The **Point of View** label displays the name of the view projection (i.e., Perspective, Orthographic) that is being shown in the viewport. Clicking on this Viewport label opens the **Point of View** label menu (shown in Figure 1–36), which enables you to change the view type.

The three most common view types are:

*You can also change the view using the shortcut keys that are listed next to the type in the label menu (e.g., <T> for **Top**, <B> for **Bottom**, etc.).*

- **Perspective View:** This view displays what is seen with human vision and uses vanishing points to make distant objects appear to recede from view. The most realistic output is shown through perspective views or the camera view, as shown in Figure 1–37.

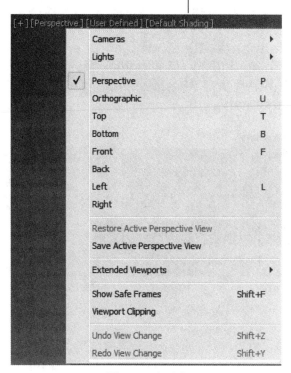

Figure 1–36

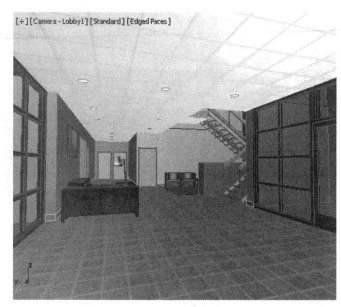

Figure 1–37

- **Orthographic (Axonometric Rotated) View:** Orthographic views (shown in Figure 1–38) do not use vanishing points or convergence; therefore objects do not seem to recede over distance. You can think of Orthographic views as being similar to Isometric views (Isometric views are special cases of Axonometric views where the axes are equally inclined to the screen).

You might find Orthographic views easier to navigate (especially when zooming with a mouse wheel), but the rendered output often does not display as realistic as from a perspective view.

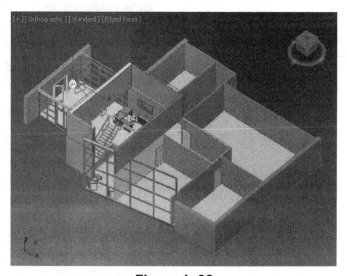

Figure 1–38

- **Other Views:** The **Left**, **Right**, **Top**, **Bottom**, **Front**, and **Back** views are all types of predefined views, which show a 2D projection of the model.

Shading Viewport

The Shading Viewport label provides options to change the shading display methods used in the viewport, such as **High Quality**, **Standard**, **Performance**, **DX Mode**, and **User Defined** (as shown in Figure 1–39). In addition to shading, this menu contains tools for the **Lighting and Shadows**, and display of materials with textures and maps.

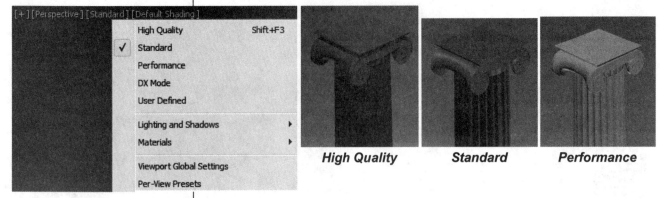

High Quality   *Standard*   *Performance*

Figure 1–39

Per-View Preference

The Per-View Preference label menu (shown in Figure 1–40) displays the visual style methods for a view, such as **Default Shading**, **Facets**, **Bounding Box**, **Clay**, etc. You can select different edge modes and with the selected shading method. This menu also contains tools for various **Stylized** options, **Lighting and Shadows**, and **Viewport Background**. You can use the **Display Selected** options to control the display of selected geometry in shaded viewports.

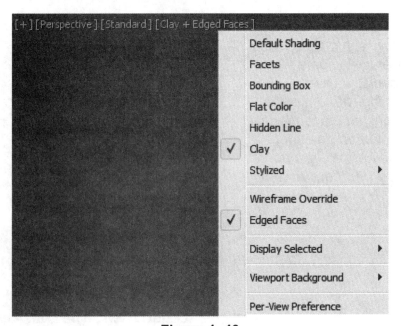

Figure 1–40

Some of the visual style modes (using the Standard shading viewport display) are shown in Figure 1–41.

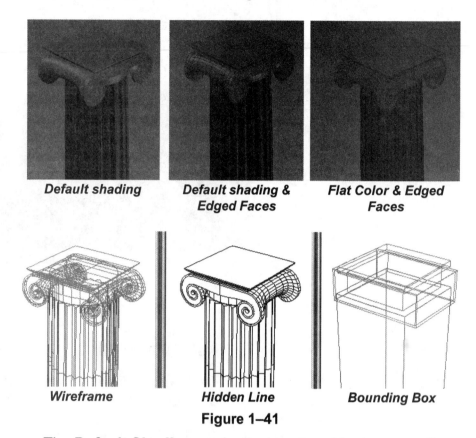

Default shading

Default shading & Edged Faces

Flat Color & Edged Faces

Wireframe

Hidden Line

Bounding Box

Figure 1–41

- The **Default Shading** mode displays the object as smooth with Phong shading being applied to it.

- In the **Flat Color** mode, lighting effects are disabled and the object is displayed with just the color.

- The **Edged Faces** option overlays a wireframe over any other visual style, such as Default shading, Facets, Clay, and others.

- The **Facets** option always displays the geometry as faceted even if the Smooth modifier or Smoothing have been applied to the object. This enables you to precisely locate the edges in the model and makes it easier to work with the geometry.

- The **Hidden Line** option improves the Wireframe display by hiding the lines that are on the backside of the objects.

- The **Bounding Box** option is useful when scenes are extremely complex and software performance is an issue. Alternatively, in this situation, individual objects can be set to view as bounding boxes through Object Properties.

- The **Clay** option displays the geometry in a terracotta color without any material or texture color.

- The **Stylized** menu options enables you to display objects with a variety of effects that are non-photorealistic, as shown in Figure 1–42.

| *Graphite* | *Color Pencil* | *Pastel* |

Figure 1–42

Hint: Legacy Driver Display Labels

The legacy driver display shows only three labels:

- The **General Viewport** label and the **Point of View** label contains the same menu options as for the nitrous drivers.

- The **Shading Viewport** label has menu options pertaining to the legacy drivers, as shown in Figure 1–43.

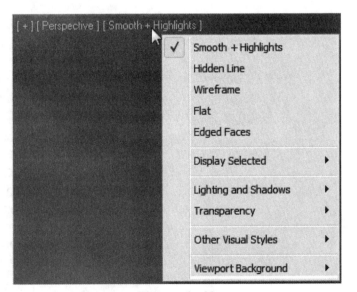

Figure 1–43

Practice 1a

Organizing Folders and Working with the Interface

Practice Objectives

- Set the project folder and configure User Paths.
- Create Viewport Layouts and navigate the graphic user interface
- Modify an object using the Command Panel and using the Scene Explorer.

Estimated time for completion: 20 minutes

In this practice you will work with the Autodesk 3ds Max software by setting the project folder to organize the files in the project. You will also configure the user paths to set the folders. You will then create different Viewport layouts by changing the viewing angles and different shading modes. You will also navigate the graphic user interface. To complete the practice you will open a file and modify the objects using different interface components.

For printing purposes, the UI color scheme used for this practice is **ame-light** (Menu bar: Customize>Custom UI and Defaults Switcher>ame-light in UI schemes list), and the *Theme* has been set to **Light** in the Customize User Interface dialog box.

Task 1 - Set the Project Folder.

1. Install the practice files by launching the self-extracting .EXE file. Ensure that the files are located in the *C:\Autodesk 3ds Max Fundamentals Practice Files* folder.

2. Launch the Autodesk 3ds Max 2017 (R1) software.

   - If a Welcome Screen is displayed, clear **Show this Welcome Screen at startup** and close the Welcome Screen.

   - If it is already running, reset the program by selecting **Reset** in the **Application Menu**. This closes the current file and opens a new blank file. If an unsaved scene is open, you might be required to save or discard the changes to the scene. Click **Don't Save**. Click **Yes** to reset the file.

3. In the Quick Access Toolbar, click (Project Folder).

4. In the Browse For Folder dialog box, navigate to C:\ and select the *Autodesk 3ds Max Fundamentals Practice Files* folder.

If an Invalid Path dialog box opens, click OK.

5. Click **OK**. You only have to set the project folder once.

6. In the Quick Access Toolbar, hover the cursor over

   (Project Folder) to display the set project folder. Ensure that it displays as C:*Autodesk 3ds Max Fundamentals Practice Files*, as shown in Figure 1–44.

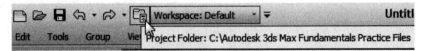

Figure 1–44

Task 2 - Setting Preferences.

*Alternatively, you can also select **Application Menu> Options**.*

1. In the menu bar, select **Customize>Preferences**. The Preference Settings dialog box opens.

2. In the *General* tab, in the *Ref. Coord. System* area, select **Constant**, as shown in Figure 1–45. This enables the Transform types to use the same Reference Coordinate System.

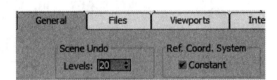

Figure 1–45

3. In the *Layer Defaults* area, clear **Default to By Layer for New Nodes**, if not already cleared, as shown in Figure 1–46. Click **OK**.

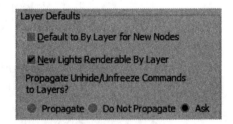

Figure 1–46

Task 3 - Configure the User Paths.

1. Select **Customize>Configure User Paths** to open the Configure User Paths dialog box.

2. Verify that the *File I/O* tab is selected. In the list, select **Materials** and click **Modify**. In the Choose Directory for Materials dialog box, browse to *C:\Program Files\Autodesk\ 3ds Max 2017\materiallibraries*. Click **Use Paths**. The path is displayed as shown in Figure 1–47.

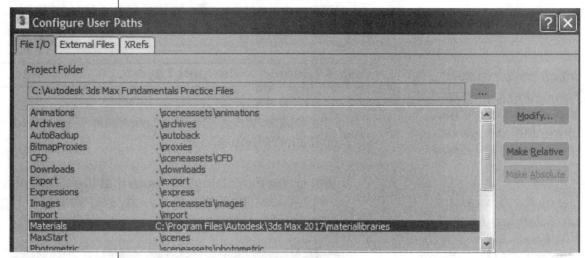

Figure 1–47

3. In the Configure User Paths dialog box, select the *External Files* tab and click **Add**.

*If you double-click on a folder, you are not required to click **Use Path**.*

4. In the Choose New External Files Path dialog box, navigate to *C:\Autodesk 3ds Max Fundamentals Practice Files* (select it but do not double-click). Click **Use Path**. Double-click on the *Maps* folder and click **Use Path**. Verify that you have returned to the Configure User Paths dialog box. This enables all of the folders under the main folder to be searched for missing external files.

The paths are searched in order from top to bottom, so moving a custom path to the top saves time when searching for files.

5. In the Configure User Paths dialog box, verify that the Maps new path is still selected and continue clicking **Move Up** until the new path is at the top of the list, as shown in Figure 1–48.

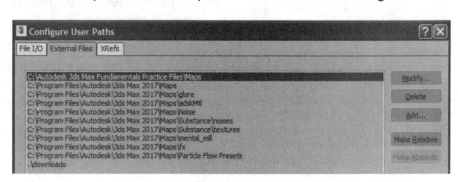

Figure 1–48

6. Select the *XRefs* tab and click **Add...**. In the Choose New XRef Path dialog box, navigate to your practice files folder (C:*Autodesk 3ds Max Fundamentals Practice Files)*, double-click on the *scenes* folder and click **Use Path**.

7. Click **OK** to exit the Configure User Paths dialog box. These settings are not specific to the scene file, so there is no need to save the file at this point.

Task 4 - Setting a Viewport Layout.

1. In the Quick Access Toolbar, click  (Open File) or use Application Menu>**Open**.

2. In the Open File dialog box note that the *...\scenes* folder in your practice files folder is already set, shown in Figure 1–49. Select the file **Interface.max** and click **Open**.

Figure 1–49

3. The model should display similar to that shown in Figure 1–50. Note that it opens in one maximized viewport layout, which was previously saved with the scene.

4. Verify that the Viewport Layout tab bar and the Scene Explorer are displayed and docked along the left side of the viewport.

5. In the Scene Explorer toolbar, click ■ (Display None) to clear all the categories. Note that the object list is empty.

6. Click 📄 (Display All) to activate all the different categories of objects. All of the selected tools have a blue background, indicating that they are active. Note the three main objects that make up the model are listed, as shown in Figure 1–50.

If you have created something in the current scene, you might be prompted to save or discard any changes.

*If a dialog box opens prompting you about a File Load: Mismatch for Gamma & LUT settings, click **OK** to accept the default values.*

If the ribbon is covering the top portion of your model, minimize it by clicking ▣.

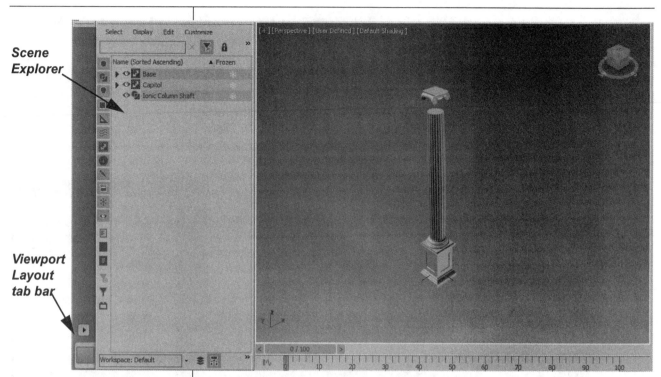

Scene Explorer

Viewport Layout tab bar

Figure 1–50

- The file can be zoomed out by rolling the middle mouse button to display the complete model in the viewport.

7. In the Viewport Layouts tab bar, click  to expand the Standard Viewport Layouts panel. Select the layout, as shown in Figure 1–51 (second row, second column).

   - Note that the model displays in three viewport layouts and the newly selected layout is added to the tabs list, as shown in Figure 1–52.

Figure 1–51   Figure 1–52

8. Note that a yellow border displays around the **Top** viewport, indicating that it is the active viewport. In this viewport, click on **[Wireframe]** (Per-View Preference label) to display the menu.

9. Select **Stylized>Graphite**, as shown in Figure 1–53. Note the change in the display of objects in this view only.

10. Click on **[Top]** (Point of View label) and select **Right**, as shown in Figure 1–54. Alternatively, you can press <R> to display the **Right** view of the object.

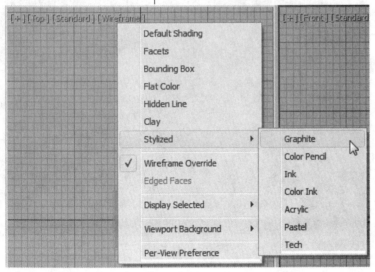

Figure 1–53

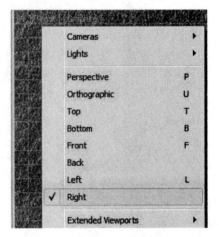

Figure 1–54

11. Use the mouse wheel to zoom out so that the complete model is displayed in this viewport. While holding the middle mouse button, drag the cursor to pan the objects so that they are centrally located in the viewport.

*Click on **[Left]** (Point of View label) will be referred to set the Left Point of View label.*

12. Click in empty space in the lower right viewport (**Left** view). Note that the yellow border now displays around this viewport, indicating that it is the active viewport. Set the following:

  • *Left* Point of View label: **Perspective**
  • *Wireframe* Per-View Preference: **Default Shading**

13. Press <Z> to zoom in to the objects in this viewport.

14. In the top right viewport, ensure that the *Point of View* is set to **Front** and change the *Wireframe* Visual Style to **Clay**.

15. Use the middle mouse button to pan and zoom to display the objects in this view.

  • The objects and the viewport layout should look similar to those in Figure 1–55.

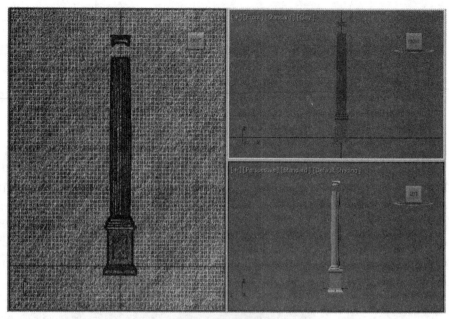

Figure 1–55

Task 5 - Modifying the objects using the Command Panel.

1. In the Viewport Layout tab bar, select the initial layout that existed with the scene, as shown in Figure 1–56. The objects display in a single viewport in the **Perspective** view with the **Default Shading** Visual Style.

2. In the Command Panel, select the Create panel ($+$), if required (active by default), as shown in Figure 1–57.

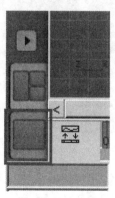

Figure 1–56   **Figure 1–57**

3. Select the *Geometry* category by clicking ● (Geometry), if required (active by default). The different types of geometry that you can create are listed here.

4. In the Command Panel, select the Modify panel (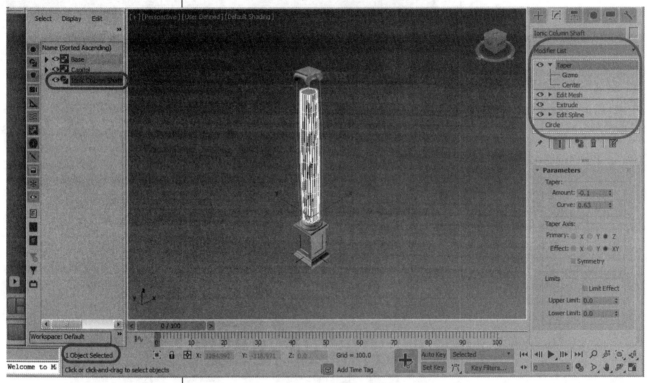). The panel is empty as no objects are currently selected.

5. In the Main Toolbar, click ▨ (Select Object), if required (active by default).

Names only display when the cursor is hovered over an unselected object. Once the object has been selected, its name is displayed in the Modifier Stack.

6. In the viewport, hover the cursor over the cyan (blue) object to display its name, **Ionic Column Shaft**. Click the object to select it. The **Ionic Column Shaft** is also highlighted in the Scene Explorer, indicating that it is selected. The name and modifiers that have been applied are displayed in the Command Panel. The Status Line at the bottom of the viewport, displays **1 Object Selected**, as shown in Figure 1–58.

Figure 1–58

7. In the Command Panel, next to the object name **Ionic Column Shaft**, select the color swatch. Select a different color and click **OK** to change the color of the column shaft.

8. In the Modifier Stack, the list of modifiers that have been used on the column shaft are displayed, as shown in Figure 1–59.

   Click 👁 (eye) next to the **Taper** modifier to toggle the taper off and then on again and note the effect on the object. Leave it on.

You can adjust parameters at any level of the Modifier Stack. To change the parameter, enter the value in the Amount edit box or use the spinners 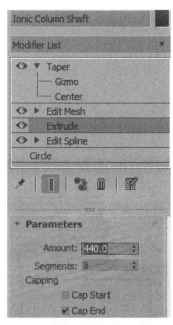.

9. In the Modifier Stack, select the **Extrude** modifier. In the Warning dialog box, click **Hold/Yes** to continue.

10. The **Extrude** parameters are displayed in the rollouts. Note that the *Amount* displays the height of the shaft. Change it to **440.0** (as shown in Figure 1–60) and press <Enter>. The column shaft is extended and touches the top. The modifiers above the extrude are automatically reapplied to the object with its new height.

Figure 1–59

Figure 1–60

Task 6 - Using the Scene Explorer.

---

1. In the Scene Explorer, note an arrow besides the objects **Capitol** and **Base,** indicating that each have a group of objects inside it. Click on the arrow besides **Capitol** to expand the group and note the different objects sorted in a hierarchical fashion, as shown in Figure 1–61.

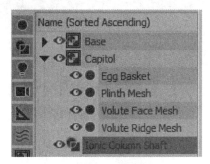

Figure 1–61

2. Click in empty space in the viewport to clear the selection. Note that the Command Panel is empty as there are no objects currently selected. Also note that nothing is highlighted in the Scene Explorer.

3. In the viewport, hover the cursor over the top gray square portion of the object. It displays the name as **[Capitol] Plinth Mesh**, as shown in Figure 1–62.

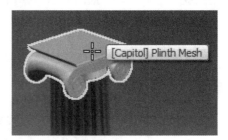

Figure 1–62

4. As the  (Select Object) is already active, click on **[Capitol] Plinth Mesh** in the viewport to select it. The complete object is selected although, the Plinth Mesh is just the top square portion.

5. Click in empty space in the viewport to clear the selection.

6. In the Scene Explorer, click on 👁 for **Plinth Mesh** and note that only the top most square object of the Capitol is hidden in the viewport, as shown in Figure 1–63.

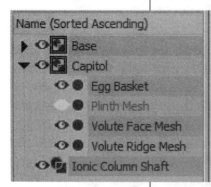

Figure 1–63

7. Similarly, in the Scene Explorer, click on  for **Volute Face Mesh** and **Volute Ridge Mesh** and note that only the inner cylindrical object remains visible, as shown in Figure 1–64.

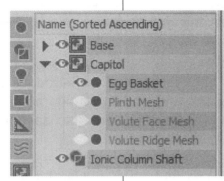

Figure 1–64

8. In the Scene Explorer, click on (grayed out eye) for the three hidden sub objects to make them visible again.

9. Select **Application Menu>Save As** and save your work as **MyInterface.max**.
   - When you save a file, verify that it is being saved to the ...\scenes folder.

*Clicking (Save File) in the Quick Access Toolbar or selecting **Save** in the **Application Menu**, overwrites the existing file. If you are saving an unnamed file for the first time, these options work as **Save As**.*

Practice 1b | Autodesk 3ds Max Quickstart

Practice Objective

- Create primitive objects and apply basic animation to a primitive object.

Estimated time for completion: 15 minutes

In this practice, you will model and animate a teapot driving through a city of pyramids. This practice will introduce you to the Autodesk 3ds Max interface and workflow fundamentals. Many of the commands used in this practice are discussed later in the student guide.

Many of you will probably never need to animate a teapot driving through a city of pyramids. This practice is designed to introduce you to interactive 3D modeling and animation, and working with the interface.

Task 1 - Create Primitive Objects.

If an unsaved scene is open, you might be required to save or discard any changes to the scene.

1. Select **Application Menu>Reset** to start a new file. Click **Yes** in the confirmation dialog box.

2. In the Command Panel, verify that the Create panel (➕) and ● (Geometry) are selected (active by default). Also, ensure that the *Standard Primitives* sub-category is displayed.

3. In the Object Type rollout, click **Pyramid** to activate it, as shown in Figure 1–65.

Figure 1–65

*If the Scene Explorer is not displayed, select **Tools>Scene Explorer** and then dock it.*

4. In the **Perspective** viewport (which is maximized), near the center of the grid, click and drag to create the base for a pyramid, as shown in Figure 1–66. Release the mouse button and continue to move the cursor up to set the height of the pyramid. When your pyramid displays correctly (similar to that shown in Figure 1–67), click to end the creation process. In the Scene Explorer, note that a highlighted geometry is listed with the name **Pyramid001,** indicating that it is selected.

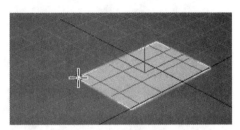

Figure 1–66   **Figure 1–67**

To make any changes, the object should be selected.

5. In the Command Panel, click the **Color** swatch to the right of the pyramid name (**Pyramid001**), select a different color in the Object Color dialog box and verify that **Assign Random Colors** is selected. This enables you to create objects with different colors automatically. Click **OK**. Note that the color of the pyramid and the swatch change in the viewport.

6. In the Navigation toolbar, found in the lower right corner of

   the interface, click ◼ (Maximize Viewport) or use <Alt>+<W>. Note that the pyramid is displayed in four equal viewports with different viewing angles.

The transform tools are discussed in detail, later in the student guide.

7. You might need to move the pyramid to the upper left quadrant of the home grid. In the Main Toolbar, click

   ◼ (Select and Move). In the **Top** view (upper left viewport), right-click to make it active with the object still selected.

   • Clicking in a viewport makes it active, but loses the selection of objects. To maintain the selection of objects, right-click to activate the viewport.

8. Click and hold the yellow square (anywhere along the two outer edges when the cursor displays as a move cursor) of the Transform gizmo, as shown in Figure 1–68. While holding the object, drag it to the new location. Leave the gizmo once the object is at the correct location.

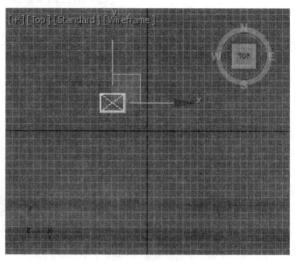

Figure 1–68

9. In the Object Type rollout, click **Pyramid** again. In the **Top** viewport, click and drag to create the base for another pyramid on the lower side of the main grid line, opposite to the first one. Release the mouse button and continue to move the cursor up to set the height of the pyramid. Because you are in the **Top** viewport, the height of the pyramid is not displayed. You can visually note the height in other three viewports in which the height is displayed. Once the pyramid displays as required, click to complete the command.

You can create objects in any viewport, but the orientation of the objects depends on the viewport created. Note that their creation is also displayed interactively in other viewports.

10. Similarly, create a number of pyramids on the home grid. Create a row of pyramids in one direction and a few others to create a street corner in the pyramid city, as shown in Figure 1–69. Try to keep all of the pyramids in the grid visible in the **Perspective** viewport.

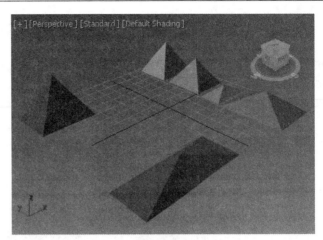

Figure 1–69

To display all of the pyramids in a viewport, use the middle mouse wheel to zoom in and out and press, hold, and drag it to pan.

11. Once the required number of pyramids have been created, right-click in empty space or press <Esc> to exit the **Pyramid** command.

12. Make the **Perspective** viewport active and maximize the viewport by clicking (Maximize Viewport) or use <Alt>+<W>. You can click anywhere in empty space to clear a selected object and activate the viewport.

13. In the Create panel (+)> (Geometry), in the Object Type rollout, click **Teapot** to activate it.

14. In the lower left area of the **Perspective** viewport, click and drag to create a teapot, as shown in Figure 1–70.

Figure 1–70

Animation controls are discussed in detail later in the student guide.

Task 2 - Add Basic Animation.

1. The Animation controls are next to the Status Bar at the bottom of the screen. Click **Auto Key**, as shown in Figure 1–71. Once you click it, the time slider bar and border around the active viewport (**Perspective** viewport) are highlighted in red.

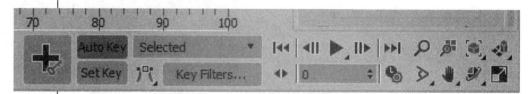

Figure 1–71

2. Drag the time slider in the red slider bar until the frame indicator displays **30/100** ( 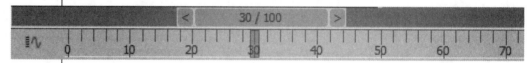), as shown in Figure 1–72.

Figure 1–72

3. Click on the teapot, if not already selected, right-click and select **Move** in the **transform** quad menu, as shown in Figure 1–73. Alternatively, in the Main Toolbar, click

     (Select and Move) after selecting your teapot.

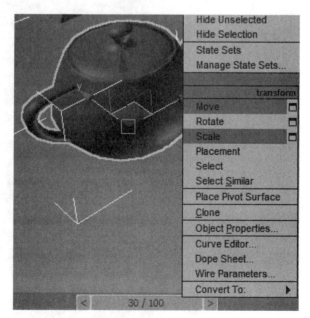

Figure 1–73

4. Move the cursor over the X axis (red arrow) of the teapot Move gizmo so that it displays in yellow. Hold and drag to move the teapot in the X direction, as shown in Figure 1–74. Move it to midway between the original position and the intersection of the home grid.

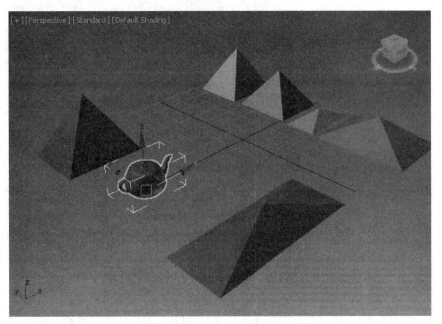

Figure 1–74

5. Move and drag the time slider again to read **60/100**.

6. Move the teapot in the X direction till it reaches the intersection of the horizontal street, as shown in Figure 1–75.

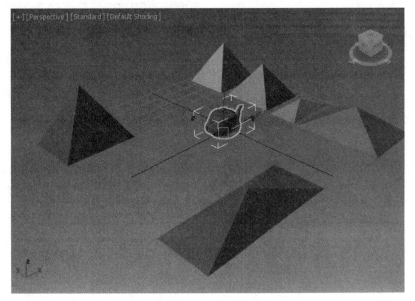

Figure 1–75

7. Move and drag the time slider to read **90/100**. Move the teapot in the Y direction (left, green arrow) till it reaches the end of the horizontal street, as shown in Figure 1–76.

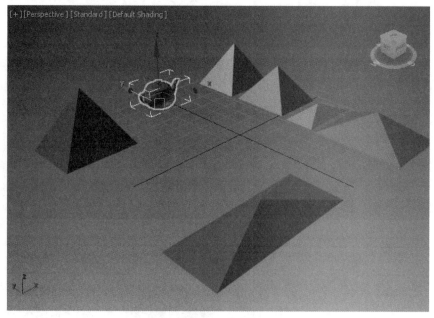

[+] [Perspective] [Standard] [Default Shading]

Figure 1–76

- The track bar below the time slider now has four red boxes indicating that the keyframes have been set at frames 0, 30, 60, and 90.

8. In the Animation Controls (⏮ ◀‖ ▶ ‖▶ ⏭) located near the bottom right of the screen, click ▶ (Play). The teapot is now animated in the viewport, moving through the pyramid city. Click ⏸ (Stop Animation) to stop the animation.

9. You can add a rotation to the teapot. Drag the time slider to frame **60**.

10. Click ⬈ (Maximize Viewport) to change to four equal viewports. In all of the viewports, note that the teapot has moved to the grid intersection position. Right-click on the teapot and select **Rotate**. You can also click ↻ (Select and Rotate) in the Main Toolbar.

11. The Rotation Transform gizmo is displayed on the teapot. Move the cursor over the horizontal axis (yellow circle). Rotate the teapot counter-clockwise so that the spout is pointing to the left. The rotation angle is displayed in the viewport, as shown in Figure 1–77. The rotation angle is also displayed in the *Transform Type-in* fields in the Status Bar.

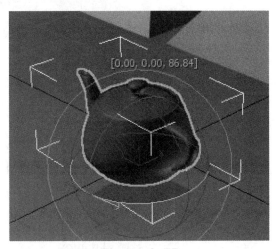

Figure 1–77

- At frame 60, the time slider now displays a red and green box indicating both rotation and position keys

12. Play the animation using ▶ (Play). Click ▮▮ (Stop) to stop the animation. You can also view the animation by dragging the time slider back and forth. This is called *scrubbing* the time slider.

13. To only rotate the teapot after frame 45, add a keyframe rotation of **0** at frame 45. Play the animation to view the changes.

14. Toggle off **Auto Key** mode by clicking the red **Auto Key**.

15. Click in empty space to clear the object selection.

16. Select **Application Menu>Save As** and save your work as **MyPyramidCity.max**. Verify that it is being saved in the ...*scenes* folder.

- You can also open **Pyramidcity.max** from your practices files folder to compare with a similar type file.

Chapter Review Questions

1. Which of the Autodesk 3ds Max interface components contains ▣ (Selection Lock)?

   a. Modeling Ribbon

   b. Status Bar

   c. InfoCenter

   d. Quick Access Toolbar

2. Which of the following tabs are part of the Modeling ribbon? (Select all that apply.)

   a. Freeform

   b. Display

   c. Utilities

   d. Modeling

3. In the Configure User Paths dialog box, which tab stores the location of the files for open, save, export, etc.?

   a. *XRefs* tab

   b. *System* tab

   c. *External Files* tab

   d. *File I/O* tab

4. Which display driver does not require hardware support?

   a. Nitrous Direct3D 11

   b. Nitrous Direct3D 9

   c. Nitrous Software

5. Which of the following is not a **Stylized** menu option?

   a. **Color Pencil**

   b. **Graphite**

   c. **Shaded**

   d. **Pastel**

Command Summary

Button	Command	Location
+	**Create panel**	• **Command Panel**
	Open	• **Quick Access Toolbar** • **Application Menu:** Open>Open
	Project Folder	• **Quick Access Toolbar** • **Application Menu:** Manage
	Ribbon	• **Main Toolbar** • **Customize:** Show UI>Show Ribbon
N/A	**Save As**	• **Application Menu:** Save As
	Save File	• **Quick Access Toolbar** • **Application Menu:** Save
N/A	**Scene Explorer**	• **Tools:** Saved Scene Explorers>Workspace:Default

Autodesk 3ds Max Configuration

The Autodesk® 3ds Max® software layout and unique to other Autodesk products. Becoming familiar with its navigation tools, viewing the model in the viewport, and how to work with the model in the interface is an important step to efficiently create a visualization project.

Learning Objectives in this Chapter

- Move around in a scene using the various navigation tools.
- Set the layout and viewport configuration settings.
- Select objects using the object selection tools.
- Assign and change units in a scene.
- Group similar objects together in a layer and adjust layer properties.
- Modify the display settings of layers and objects.

2.1 Viewport Navigation

Navigation tools are used to change the point of view in viewports. Perspective, User, and Orthographic views (non-camera views such as Top, Front, etc.) share common viewport controls. The navigation tools are different in the non-camera and camera views.

Viewport Navigation Toolbar

The navigation tools (shown in Figure 2–1) are available in the lower right corner of the interface.

Figure 2–1

- When selected, the tool button is highlighted. Press <Esc> or select another tool to toggle a selected tool off.

- Several buttons contain an arrow symbol in the lower right corner, which you can hold to expand a flyout.

Zooming with the mouse wheel in a perspective view might not work in all scenes due to roundoff issues. If you are unable to zoom, click (Zoom Extents) and use (Zoom) instead of the mouse wheel.

	Zoom: When this tool is active, click, hold, and drag the cursor to zoom in or out of the active viewport.
	Zoom All: Activate and then click and drag to zoom in or out simultaneously in all viewports.
/	**Zoom Extents/Zoom Extents Selected:** Zooms to the extents of all visible objects/selected objects only in the active viewport.
/	**Zoom Extents All/Zoom Extents All Selected:** Zoom to the extents of all visible objects/selected objects only in all viewports.
	Zoom Region (zoom window) in the active viewport.
	Field of View: This is a flyout option in Zoom Region, available only in **Perspective** or **Camera** view. It adjusts the perspective of the view, similar to changing the focal length of a camera. Even small changes to the Field of View setting can cause large distortions. To reset, enter a default field of view value of **45 degrees** in the Viewport Configuration dialog box.
	Pan View: Hold in a viewport and drag to pan your objects. You can also hold and drag the middle mouse wheel to pan.

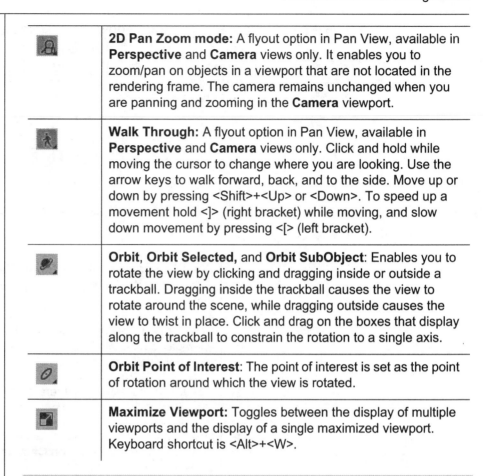	**2D Pan Zoom mode:** A flyout option in Pan View, available in **Perspective** and **Camera** views only. It enables you to zoom/pan on objects in a viewport that are not located in the rendering frame. The camera remains unchanged when you are panning and zooming in the **Camera** viewport.
	Walk Through: A flyout option in Pan View, available in **Perspective** and **Camera** views only. Click and hold while moving the cursor to change where you are looking. Use the arrow keys to walk forward, back, and to the side. Move up or down by pressing <Shift>+<Up> or <Down>. To speed up a movement hold <]> (right bracket) while moving, and slow down movement by pressing <[> (left bracket).
	Orbit, **Orbit Selected**, and **Orbit SubObject**: Enables you to rotate the view by clicking and dragging inside or outside a trackball. Dragging inside the trackball causes the view to rotate around the scene, while dragging outside causes the view to twist in place. Click and drag on the boxes that display along the trackball to constrain the rotation to a single axis.
	Orbit Point of Interest: The point of interest is set as the point of rotation around which the view is rotated.
	Maximize Viewport: Toggles between the display of multiple viewports and the display of a single maximized viewport. Keyboard shortcut is <Alt>+<W>.

New in 2017

Hint: Switching Maximized Viewports

When you maximize a single viewport from a multi-viewport layout, you can switch to other viewports while in the current maximized viewport display. In the maximized viewport display, hold <Win> (the Windows logo key, which might also be <Start>) and then press <Shift> (do not hold <Shift>). An overlay opens displaying all of the available viewports and the currently maximized viewport highlighted with a yellow border, as shown in Figure 2–2. While holding <Win>, press <Shift> repeatedly to highlight the next viewport option and release <Win> to maximize the highlighted viewport.

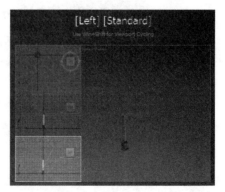

Figure 2–2

Viewport Navigation Toolbar (Camera Viewport)

Camera viewports show what is visible to the camera object based on its Field of View. Similar to other viewports, camera viewports can be directly navigated, but some of the controls are slightly different, as shown in Figure 2–3.

Figure 2–3

- Note that most of these controls actually move the camera or target object.

	**Dolly Camera** is similar to **Zoom**. The flyout contains options to dolly (move) the camera, the target, or both along the camera's directional axis.
	**Perspective** is a combination of **Field of View** and **Dolly** that attempts to maintain the same scene composition while changing the camera's Field of View.
	**Roll Camera** rotates a camera along the axis of its view.
	**Orbit Camera** rotates a camera around the target position similar to **Orbit**. The flyout option (**Pan Camera**) rotates the target around the camera instead.
	Truck Camera is similar to Pan when used in a **Camera** view.

Viewport Navigation using the ViewCube

The ViewCube (shown in Figure 2–4) is a navigation tool and by default, it displays in the top right corner of each viewport indicating the orientation of the scene. The ViewCube is activated by hovering the cursor over it in the active viewport.

- Selecting any of the ViewCube faces or edges, causes the viewport to immediately swing around to that view. You can also select the ViewCube and drag the mouse to quickly rotate the Viewport.

- When the ViewCube is active, the **Home** icon becomes visible near the top left corner. Clicking the **Home** icon resets the viewport.

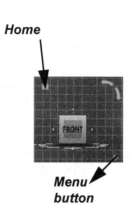

Home

Menu
button

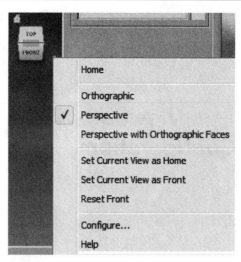

Home

Orthographic

✓ Perspective

Perspective with Orthographic Faces

Set Current View as Home

Set Current View as Front

Reset Front

Configure...

Help

Figure 2–4

*The ViewCube tool options can also be accessed in the **Views** menu.*

- Clicking on the menu button or right-clicking on the ViewCube provides you with additional options (shown in Figure 2–4) that enable you to set the current view as Home, Orthographic, Configure etc.

- Selecting the **Configure** option, opens the Viewport Configuration dialog box in the *ViewCube* tab containing options to show or hide the ViewCube, control its size and display, control what happens when dragging on the ViewCube, and displaying the compass below the ViewCube.

Viewport Navigation using the SteeringWheel

The SteeringWheel (shown in Figure 2–5) is another navigation tool and it can be toggled on by pressing <Shift>+<W> where it gets attached to the cursor.

- It provides instant access to zoom/pan, orbit, etc. The **Rewind** feature is unique to this tool and provides a thumbnail of all of your previous views. It also enables you to visually select any of them to return to that view. Press <Shift>+<W> to toggle the SteeringWheel on and off. You can also press <Esc> to hide its display.

*The Steering wheel tool options can also be accessed in the **Views** menu.*

Figure 2–5

2.2 Viewport Configuration and Settings

Viewport Configuration

The layout and display settings of your viewports can be set through the Viewport Configuration dialog box. In the Viewport label, click [+] (General label) to display the label menu and select **Configure Viewports**, as shown in Figure 2–6. Alternatively, select the **Shading Viewport** label>**Viewport Global Settings**.

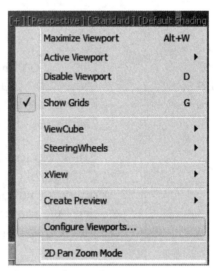

Figure 2–6

If you have selected one of the legacy display drivers (Direct 3D or OpenGL), the Rendering Method tab displays.

The Viewport Configuration dialog box opens and contains tabs which differ based on the selected display driver. By default, the Viewport Configuration dialog box opens with the *Display Performance* tab active. Some of the tabs that are available in the Viewport Configuration dialog box are described in the following section. The remaining tabs are discussed throughout the student guide, as required.

Layout tab

You can also set up multiple viewport layouts and switch between them by selecting the saved tabs in the Viewport Layouts tab bar.

The *Layout* tab in the Viewport Configuration dialog box (shown in Figure 2–7) enables you to set the size and shape of viewports and its view type. Select one of the preset viewport layouts to select a view type.

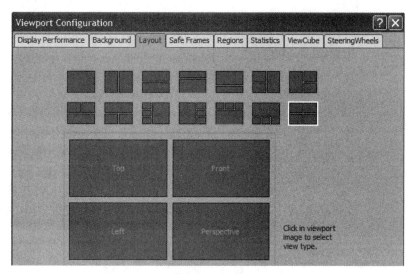

Figure 2–7

SteeringWheels tab

The *SteeringWheels* tab (shown in Figure 2–8) enables you control the properties of the Steering Wheel such as displaying them as Big or Mini Wheels and setting their respective sizes and opacity. You can also set the options for tools, such as the **Zoom** tool and the **Orbit** tool.

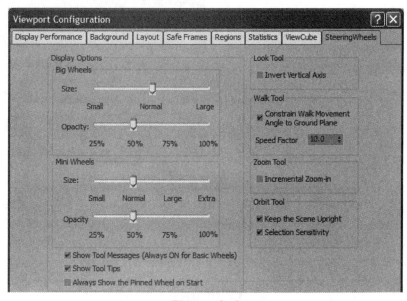

Figure 2–8

ViewCube tab

Similar to the *SteeringWheels* tab, the *ViewCube* tab has options for controlling the display of the ViewCube. You can control the size of the ViewCube, what the ViewCube displays when selected, and the position of the compass.

Statistics tab

The *Statistics* tab enables you to customize the display of various statistics for the selected geometry or the complete scene. In the viewports, you can display the number of polygons in a scene, number of triangular faces, number of edges, number of vertices, etc. The statistics can be displayed on the screen, near the left hand corner of the active viewport by selecting **Show Statistics in Active View** in the dialog box. You can also display statistics by selecting **Show Statistics** in the **General Viewport label menu>xView** or by pressing <7>.

Background tab

The *Background* tab (shown in Figure 2–9) enables you to set an image, environment map, or animation as the background of your active viewport or all viewports.

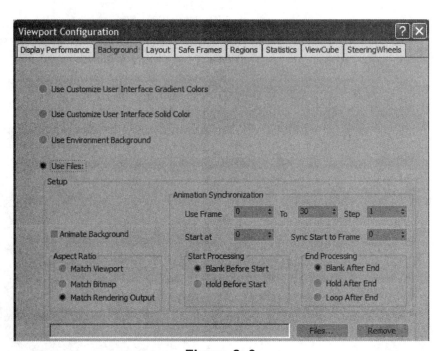

Figure 2–9

Viewport Setting and Preferences

New in 2017

You can control the viewport display of the models in the Viewport Setting and Preference dialog box, as shown in Figure 2–10. To open the dialog box, in the viewport, click the **Shading Viewport** label and in the label menu select **Per-View Presets**, as shown in Figure 2–10. Alternatively, select **Per-View Preference>Per-View Preference**.

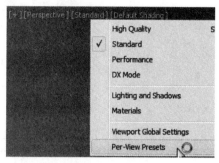

Figure 2–10

The Viewport Setting and Preference dialog box contains two tabs: *Per-View Presets* and *Per-View Preferences*. The *Per-View Presets* tab (shown in Figure 2–11), has the following options:

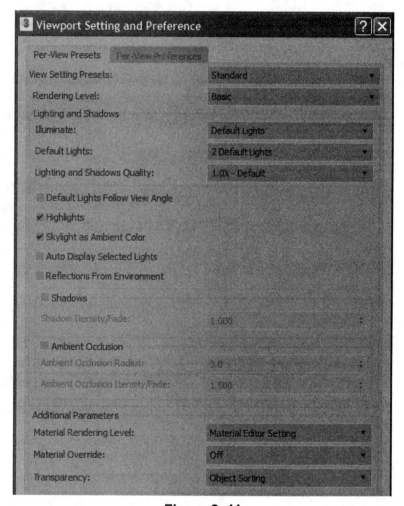

Figure 2–11

- You can create and add a user-defined view setting preset to the list of choices. Note, however, that you can have only one user-defined view setting, and you cannot change the four existing presets (i.e., High Quality, Standard, Performance or DX mode).

- The **Default Lights** are used to illuminate the viewports, providing even illumination. You can select **1 Default Light** or **2 Default Lights**.

- The **Default Lights Follow View Angle** option tracks changes to the position of the viewport using two default lights.

- The **Skylights as Ambient Color** option causes the skylights to emit ambient color and not cast shadows.

- The **Shadows** options renders the scene with shadows and the **Ambient Occlusion** helps improve the display of shadows.

- The *Additional Parameters* area contains settings for various material-related options, such as Material override and Transparency.

The *Per-View Preferences* tab (shown in Figure 2–12) enables you to control the display of selected objects in a specific viewport. You can set a selection to display using a selection bracket, or shade the selected faces/objects with or without edges.

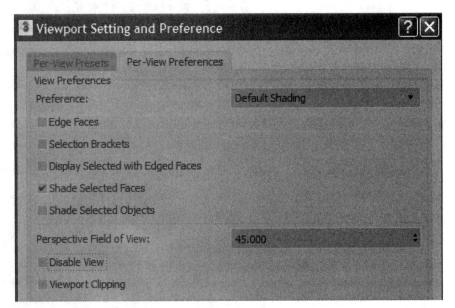

Figure 2–12

Practice 2a

Viewport Configuration and Navigation

Estimated time for completion: 5 minutes

Practice Objectives

- Set the configuration of the viewport.
- Move around a scene using different navigation tools.

In this practice, you will set various configuration option for an exiting viewport layout. You will then move around a scene and experiment with changing the camera position by using navigations tools such as **Zoom**, **Orbit**, **Pan View** and other **SE Camera** options.

1. In the Quick Access Toolbar, click ☞ (Open File) or click **Application Menu>Open>Open**, to open the Open File dialog box. If you were working in the software, you might be prompted to save or discard any changes to the scene.
   - In the Open file dialog box, note that the *C:\Autodesk 3ds Max Fundamentals Practice Files\scenes* folder is set, because you have already set the Project Folder. If you did not set the path to your practice files folder, return to **Chapter 1: Introduction to Autodesk 3ds Max** and complete Task 1 to Task 3 in **Practice 1a: Organizing Folders and Working with the Interface**. You are required to set the project folder only once.

*If a dialog box opens prompting you about a Mismatch, click **OK** to accept the default values.*

2. In the Open File dialog box, select **Navigation.max** and click **Open**.
   - If the Viewport Layout tab bar is not displayed, right-click in an empty space of the Main Toolbar, clear and select the **Viewport Layout Tabs** option, and then dock it. If the Scene Explorer is not displayed, select **Tools>Scene Explorer** and then dock it.
   - The file opens the objects in four equal sized viewports. Along the left edge of the interface, in the Viewport Layouts tab bar, note that the file has been saved with two viewport layouts.

Alternatively, select the required viewport layout in the Viewport Configuration dialog box>Layout tab.

3. To create another layout, in the Viewport Layouts tab bar,

   click ▶ to expand the Standard Viewport Layouts panel. Select the layout shown in Figure 2–13.

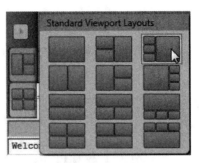

Figure 2–13

- The pillar objects display in the **3 X 1** viewport layout and another layout tab is added to the Layouts tab bar.

4. Note that the **Top** viewport is the active viewport (it displays a yellow border). In the Navigation toolbar, note the available navigation tools are for the **Orthographic** view, as shown in Figure 2–14.

Figure 2–14

5. The complete objects are not displayed in the viewports. In the Zoom Extents flyout, click 🔲 (Zoom Extents All) to zoom to the extents of all of the objects in all of the viewports.

6. Click on empty space in the **Front** viewport to activate it.

*If the Scene Explorer is not displayed, select **Tools>Scene Explorer** and then dock it.*

7. In the Scene Explorer, select **Base** to select the base objects in all the viewports, as shown in Figure 2–15.

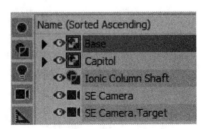

Figure 2–15

8. In the Zoom Extents All flyout, click 🔲 (Zoom Extents All Selected). Note that you are zoomed to the extents of the selected objects (Base) in all of the viewports.

9. With the Base still selected, click 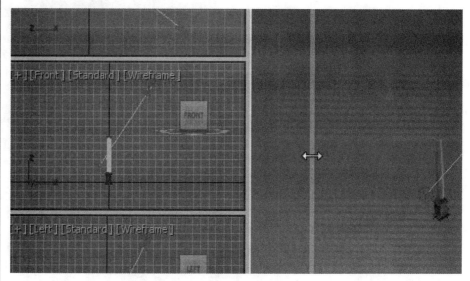 (Zoom Extents All). The camera zooms to the extents of all of the objects in all of the viewports.

10. Right-click in empty space in the **Left** viewport. Note that the **Left** viewport becomes active and the base object remains selected.

11. Click in empty space in the **Top** viewport to make it active. Note that this also clears the selection.

12. Hover the cursor over the left edge of the **Perspective** viewport. The cursor displays as a two-sided arrow. Click and drag the arrow horizontally to resize the viewports, as shown in Figure 2–16.

Figure 2–16

13. Click in the **Perspective** view to make it active. In the

Viewport navigation tools, click (Maximize Viewport Toggle) to maximize the active viewport. Select the toggle again to return to the four viewport arrangement. Alternatively, press <Alt>+<W> to toggle between the maximized single viewport and multiple viewports. Leave the **Perspective** viewport maximized.

You must hold <Win> continuously for the overlay to display.

14. Hold <Win> (windows logo or the <Start> key) continuously and press <Shift> once. An overlay displays all of the available viewports in the layout, as shown in Figure 2–17. With <Win> still pressed, press <Shift> repeatedly to cycle through all of the viewports. When [Left] [Wireframe] is highlighted (as shown in Figure 2–17), release <Win> to maximize the viewport.

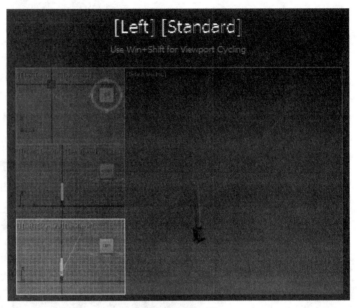

Figure 2–17

15. Select the **[Left]** Point of View label. In the label menu, select **Cameras>SE Camera**, as shown in Figure 2–18, to display the **Camera** view.

Figure 2–18

- Note that the navigation tools are different in a camera viewport, as shown in Figure 2–19.

Figure 2–19

16. Click ![icon](Maximize Viewport Toggle) to toggle to the four viewport display.

17. Click ![icon] (Zoom Extents All). Note that the **SE Camera** (lower left viewport) does not change because the non-camera navigation tools do not affect the camera views.

18. Click in the **Perspective** view to make it active and note how the navigation tools change.

19. Click in the **SE Camera** viewport to make it active.

20. Click ![icon] (Orbit Camera) and use it in the **SE Camera** viewport to orbit the camera. In the other viewports, note that the camera object is moving simultaneously as the pillar object moves in the camera viewport.

21. Experiment with changing the camera position using ![icon] (Roll Camera) and ![icon] (Dolly Camera).

You can use the mouse wheel to zoom in and out in a viewport and hold and drag the middle mouse button to pan.

22. In the **Perspective** viewport, practice navigating with the **Zoom**, **Zoom All**, **Orbit**, and **Pan View** options.

23. Close the file without saving.

2.3 Object Selection Methods

Working with modifiers and other functions requires you to select objects accurately, using various methods. The recommended method is to click on the required geometry in one of the viewports to select it. It uses the (Select Object) tool in the Main Toolbar which is active by default.

Selection Preview

In the Nitrous viewports, hovering the cursor over an object displays a yellow outline for that object. This enables you to easily determine the object that is going to be selected. Once you click on an object a blue outline displays indicating the selection, as shown in Figure 2–20.

Preview (yellow outline)

Selected (blue outline)

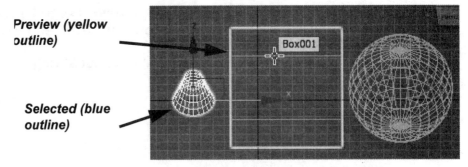

Figure 2–20

The highlighting can be controlled in the Preference Settings dialog box>*Viewports* tab, as shown in Figure 2–21.

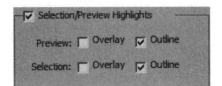

Figure 2–21

Scene Explorer

If the Scene Explorer is not displayed, click

(Scene Explorer) *in the Min toolbar or select **Tools>Scene Explorer**. Dock the Scene Explorer.*

Being a modeless interface component, you can have the Scene Explorer open while working in the viewports.

- The Scene Explorer can be used to easily select objects. If you know the name of the object, locate it in the tree list and select it, as shown in Figure 2–22. It gets selected in the viewports interactively. Use <Ctrl> to click on multiple objects in the list to select them together.

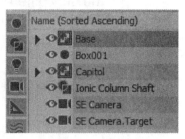

Figure 2–22

- You can use the Scene Explorer toolbar to list only those objects that belong to the particular type and then select it.

    Use (Display None) first to clear all the selected categories, and then select the tools for the required categories to list only the objects belonging to that category.

- To easily find and select an item you can use the *Find* field in the Scene Explorer. Enter the initial letters to select only the objects that begin with the entered letters

- In the **Display** menu, verify that the **Display Children**, **Display Influences**, and **Display Dependants** are cleared for all the objects to be displayed in the list.

Main Toolbar

A variety of selection tools are provided in the Main Toolbar, as shown in Figure 2–23.

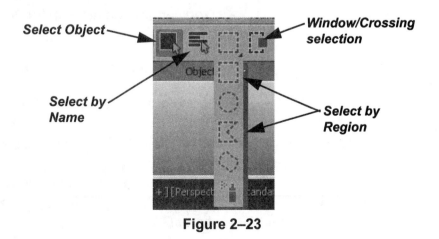

Figure 2–23

Select by Name tool

(Select by Name) opens the Select From Scene dialog box (shown in Figure 2–24), which enables you to select one or more objects. It is a modal version of the Scene Explorer, and therefore works the same way as the Scene Explorer. However, the only difference is that after selecting objects in the list of the dialog box, you must click **OK** to close the dialog box in order to continue working with the selection.

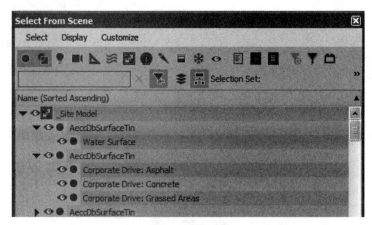

Figure 2–24

Select Object tool

(Select Object) enables you to select objects and to drag selection regions inside your viewports depending on the selected Region selection type.

- You can add to your current selection if you select or drag a region while holding <Ctrl>. You can remove items from the selection with <Alt>.

- You can also select with the **Move**, **Rotate**, **Scale**, and **Place** tools.

- You can access **Select** in the quad menu.

- If one of the **Transform** tools is active, you can click

  (Select Object) or press <Q> to activate select objects.

  If (Select Object) is already active, press <Q> repeatedly to cycle through the various Region selection types.

Rectangular Selection Region

(Rectangular Selection Region) in the Main Toolbar enables you to draw the shape of your selection region. The default is a rectangular region. There are also flyout options for **Lasso**, **Paint**, **Circular**, and **Fence** selections, as shown in Figure 2–23. Paint selection is particularly useful when you have thousands of objects or vertices that need selecting.

Window/Crossing

/ (Window/Crossing) enables you to define the *Window Selection Region* (only objects completely within the region are selected), or the *Crossing Region* (objects within or crossing the boundary are selected) as the selection toggle.

Edit Menu

The **Edit** menu also has a number of important selection options including **Select All**, **Select None**, **Select Invert**, **Select Similar**, **Select Instances**, and **Select By** (e.g., **Color**). These options also work in Sub-object mode.

Layer Explorer

(Layer Explorer) (in the Main Toolbar) lists and select objects directly from the Layer Explorer.

Edit Named Selection Sets

(Edit Named Selection Sets) (in the Main Toolbar) enables you to create and edit named selection sets. Named Selection Sets are different than layers, in that an object can be in many different named selections. An object can only be on one layer, making Named Selection Sets more flexible.

Practice 2b

Estimated time for completion: 5 minutes

*If prompted that there is a File Load: Mismatch, click **OK** to accept the default values.*

*Depending on how you rotate the viewing angle, it might be difficult to select a specific object. Setting the viewport shading to **Wireframe Override** can make it easier to select.*

Selection Methods

Practice Objective

- Select objects using **various** selection tools.

You must set the paths to locate the External files and Xrefs used in the practice. If you have not done this already, return to **Chapter 1: Introduction to Autodesk 3ds Max** and complete Task 1 to Task 3 in **Practice 1a: Organizing Folders and Working with the Interface**. You only have to set the user paths once.

In this practice you will select objects in a scene using the Window and Crossing selection tools. You will also use the Scene Explorer and Select from Scene dialog box to select objects.

1. In the Quick Access Toolbar, click ▱ (Open File) to open the Open File dialog box. If you were working in the software, you might be prompted to save or discard any changes to the scene. Open **Selection Methods.max**.

2. Click in the **Perspective** viewport to make it active.

3. Maximize the **Perspective** viewport to fill your screen by clicking ▱ (Maximize Viewport Toggle) or by pressing <Alt>+<W>.

4. In the viewport, click on one of the parking lot light poles. Note that it is selected as a blue outline that encloses the object and all the face edges of the geometry are highlighted as white, with white bounding brackets enclosing the geometry.

5. Hover the cursor on the other parking lot light poles and note that it is highlighted with a yellow outline indicating the selection preview as shown in Figure 2–25.

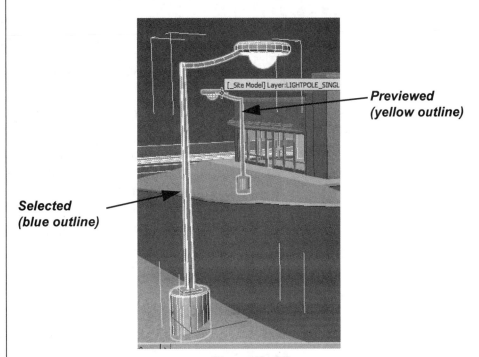

Previewed
(yellow outline)

Selected
(blue outline)

Figure 2–25

6. Click on the **[Edged Faces]** Per-View Preference viewport label and select **Per-View Preference** in the label menu. The Viewport Setting and Preferences dialog box>*Per-View Preferences* tab opens. Select the **Display Selected with Edged Faces** option, and then clear all of the other options, as shown in Figure 2–26. Ensure that **Apply to All Views** (near the bottom of the dialog box) is cleared. Click **OK**.

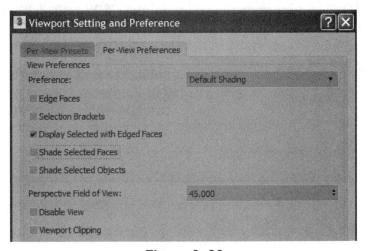

Figure 2–26

• In the viewport, note how the white bounding brackets are no longer displayed.

7. Open the Viewport Setting and Preferences dialog box. In the *Per-View Preferences* tab, select **Selection Brackets** and then click **OK**. The selection brackets are displayed.

8. Expand the **Edit** menu, and click **Select None** or click in empty space to clear your selection.

9. In the Main Toolbar, verify that the Window/Crossing toggle is set to [icon] (Crossing) and the Selection Region is set to [icon] (Rectangular). Starting in a blank area, near the top left corner of the parking lot light, click and drag the cursor diagonally down to create a rectangular crossing region around the light pole. The scene is complex and the crossing window will select several other objects in the background, in addition to the light pole.

    - In the Status Line, near the bottom left of the screen, note the number of objects selected.

10. Click in empty space to clear the selection.

11. Toggle the **Selection/Crossing** toggle from [icon] (Crossing) to [icon] (Window). Drag the selection region around the light pole completely.

    - In the Status Line, note that you selected fewer objects than before, but some additional objects are also selected.

If the Scene Explorer is not displayed, click

[icon] *(Scene Explorer) in the Main toolbar or select Tools>Scene Explorer.*

12. In the Scene Explorer toolbar, click [icon] (Display None). Note that the list is empty.

13. In the Scene Explorer toolbar, click [icon] (Display All). Note that the list of objects is very long as all the different categories of objects are listed.

14. In the Scene Explorer toolbar, click ■ (Display None) and then click ● (Display Geometry) to display all of the geometry objects in the scene. Note that some objects are highlighted (as shown in Figure 2–27), indicating that they are selected in the viewport.

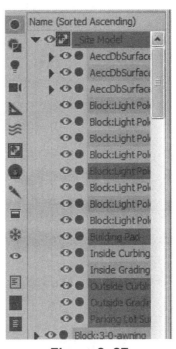

Figure 2–27

15. Click in empty space in the viewport to clear the selection.

16. In the Main Toolbar, click ▦ (Select by Name) to open the Select From Scene dialog box.

The Select From Scene dialog box is similar to the Scene Explorer.

17. The objects listed depend on the selection tools that are toggled on in the toolbar in the dialog box. In the toolbar, click ■ (Display None) to clear any selection group. Verify that ▦ (Sort by Hierarchy) is selected, as shown in Figure 2–28.

Figure 2–28

18. In the Select From Scene dialog box, click  (Display Shapes), as shown in Figure 2–29. This enables you to filter the number of items listed in the dialog box so that you can easily select the required items.

Figure 2–29

19. Select all of the **Block:Light Pole- Single** shapes. Click **OK** to close the dialog box. Note that all of the Single light poles are selected.

20. Click in empty space in the viewport to clear the selection.

21. In the Scene Explorer toolbar, click ■ (Display None) and click (Display Shapes) as shown in Figure 2–30. Expand the tree list, if required.

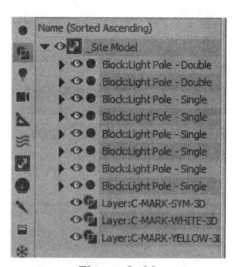

Figure 2–30

22. Select the first **Block:Light Pole - Single**. Note that it is not the light pole in the viewport because it is not selected.

23. Select the second **Block:Light Pole - Single** and keep on selecting the next ones. The third **Block:Light Pole - Single** selects the light pole in the view as shown in Figure 2–31.

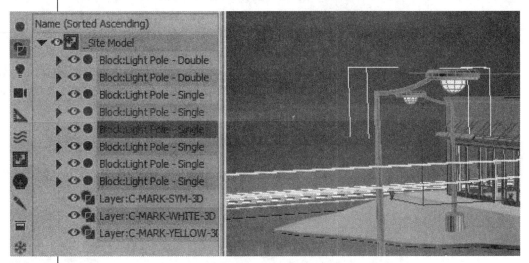

Figure 2–31

24. In the list, click again on the highlighted entry to convert it into an edit box and rename it to **Block:Light Pole - Front Left** and then click anywhere. Note that the newly-named entry moves above **Block:Light Pole - Single,** as shown in Figure 2–32, as the list is sorted in ascending order.

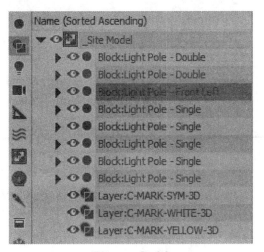

Figure 2–32

25. Select **Application Menu>Reset**. Click **Don't Save** and click **Yes** to close the current file without saving it.

2.4 Units Setup

Each scene file is based on a unit of measurement called the System Unit Scale. You can change and assign the units settings using the Units Setup dialog box. Select **Customize> Units Setup** to open the Units Setup dialog box, as shown in Figure 2–33. In the dialog box, click **System Unit Setup** to open the System Unit Setup dialog box, as shown in Figure 2–34.

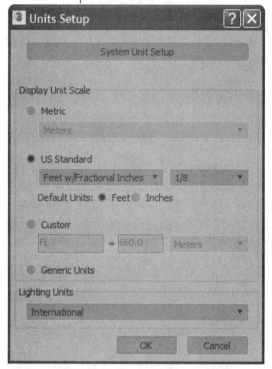

Figure 2–33   Figure 2–34

- For efficient viewport rendering, the Autodesk 3ds Max software might incur round off errors to very large and very small numerical values, as displayed by the slider bar in the System Unit Setup dialog box. These round off errors become problematic when the geometry is located further away from the center of the virtual universe.

- The Autodesk 3ds Max Help recommends that you center scene geometry close to the origin and not have any significant details smaller than one system unit. (For example, a unit scale of meters might not be appropriate for architectural work. Instead, you might consider using a **System Unit Scale** of inches, millimeters, or centimeters.) It is recommended not to make changes to the System Unit Scale unless there is a viewport problem due to very small or large models.

The Display Unit Scale does not need to match the System Unit Scale.

- Assign the unit scale before adding any geometry to the scene. Changing the System Unit Scale later does not rescale the existing objects. (To rescale objects, use the **Rescale World Units** utility in the Command Panel's Utilities panel (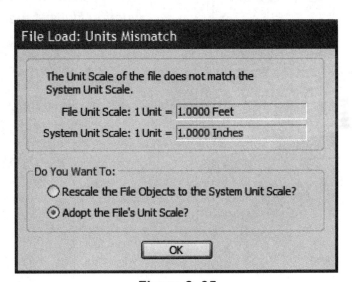).

- Selecting **Respect System Units in Files** enables individual scene files that have different Unit Scales assigned to them to be scaled when merging them together.

- The *Display Unit Scale* area defines the units to be displayed by the interface when measuring coordinates and distances.

- When the Display Unit Scale is set to **Feet w/Fractional Inches** or **Feet w/Decimal Inches,** the **Default Units** option identifies how a distance is read if a value is entered without a unit designation (' or ").

- If the current System Unit Scale does not match that of a file that is opened, you are warned with the Units Mismatch dialog box, as shown in Figure 2–35. It is recommended to select **Adopt the File's Unit Scale**, unless you specifically want to change the Unit Scale of the file being opened.

File Load: Units Mismatch

The Unit Scale of the file does not match the System Unit Scale.

File Unit Scale: 1 Unit = 1.0000 Feet

System Unit Scale: 1 Unit = 1.0000 Inches

Do You Want To:

○ Rescale the File Objects to the System Unit Scale?

⊙ Adopt the File's Unit Scale?

OK

Figure 2–35

Practice 2c

Estimated time for completion: 5 minutes

If an unsaved scene is open, you might be required to save or discard the changes to the scene.

Working with Units Setup

Practice Objective

- Assign and set up units in a scene.

In this practice you will setup units for the projects.

1. Select **Application Menu>Reset** and click **Yes** in the confirmation dialog box.

2. Select **Customize>Units Setup** to open the Units Setup dialog box. Click **System Unit Setup**.

3. In the System Unit Setup dialog box, in the *System Unit Scale* area, verify that *1 Unit =* is set to **1.0** and to **Inches**. Click **OK**.

4. You are returned to Units Setup dialog box. Select **US Standard**, and then select **Feet w/Fractional Inches** and **1/8** in the respective drop-down lists, as shown in Figure 2–36.

5. Set the following, as shown in Figure 2–36:
   - *Default Units:* **Inches**
   - *Lighting Units:* **American**

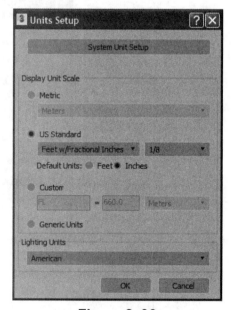

Figure 2–36

6. Click **OK** to close the Units Setup dialog box.

7. Select **Application Menu>Save As** to save your work as **MyUnits Setup.max**. Verify that it is being saved in the ...*scenes* folder.

2.5 Layer and Object Properties

It is convenient to group similar objects into layers to modify these objects' properties and control their visibility together.

Layers Toolbar

By default, the Layers toolbar is not displayed. To display it, right-click anywhere on the blank space in the Main Toolbar and select **Layers**, as shown in Figure 2–37. The toolbar enables you to set an active layer by selecting it from the drop-down list. Additionally, it contains various tools.

Figure 2–37

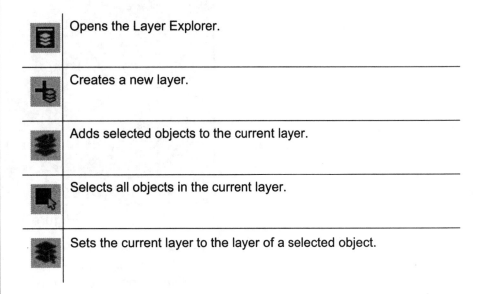	Opens the Layer Explorer.
	Creates a new layer.
	Adds selected objects to the current layer.
	Selects all objects in the current layer.
	Sets the current layer to the layer of a selected object.

Layer Explorer

Enhanced in **2017**

To open the Scene Explorer - Layer Explorer with (Sort by Layer) selected, click (Layer Explorer) either in the Main Toolbar or in the Layers toolbar, or select **Tools>Layer Explorer**. This version of Scene Explorer has tools and functions that are specific to layers, as shown in Figure 2–38.

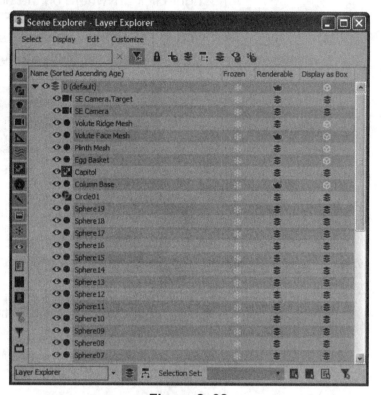

Figure 2–38

- View all of the objects on a layer by expanding the layer and clicking the arrow beside it, as shown in Figure 2–38. Right-clicking on an object in the list enables you to select and/or change its **Object Properties**.

- Click (gray layer icon) next to a layer to make the layer active. Active layers display the (blue layer icon).

Tools in the Layer Explorer

You can create and adjust layers using the tools in the Layer Explorer toolbar.

	Creates a new layer and makes it the active layer. Using this button in the Layer Explorer automatically moves selected objects to a new layer. If no objects are selected, an empty layer is created.

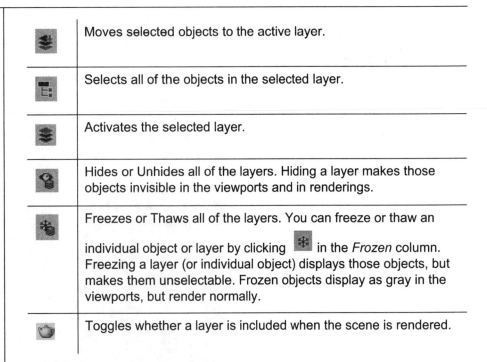	Moves selected objects to the active layer.
	Selects all of the objects in the selected layer.
	Activates the selected layer.
	Hides or Unhides all of the layers. Hiding a layer makes those objects invisible in the viewports and in renderings.
	Freezes or Thaws all of the layers. You can freeze or thaw an individual object or layer by clicking ✳ in the *Frozen* column. Freezing a layer (or individual object) displays those objects, but makes them unselectable. Frozen objects display as gray in the viewports, but render normally.
	Toggles whether a layer is included when the scene is rendered.

- The **Layers** quad menu (shown in Figure 2–39) opens by right-clicking on the name of the layer in the Layer Explorer and enables you to view and adjust other layer properties.

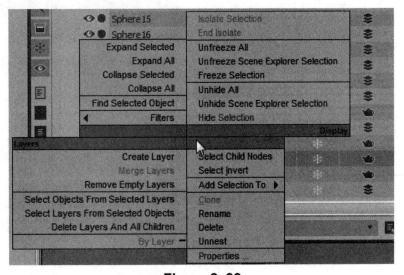

Figure 2–39

- You can also modify the display settings of one or more layers using the Layer Properties dialog box, that can be opened by selecting **Properties** in the **Layers** quad menu. Layer properties apply to all objects on that layer that do not have overrides set in their Object Properties.

Layer Properties

The Layer Properties dialog box (shown in Figure 2–40) contains two tabs:

- *General* tab: Used to set the display properties, hide and freeze options, or the rendering options of the layer.

- *Adv. Lighting* tab: Used to set the radiosity properties such as whether the layer objects can cast shadows and receive illumination.

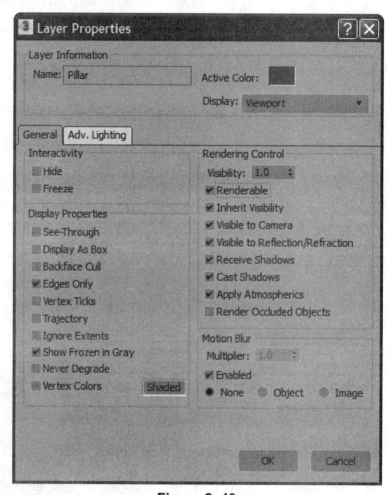

Figure 2–40

Object Properties

Right-clicking on an object in the Scene Explorer or Layer Explorer opens the quad menu for the object, as shown in Figure 2–41. In this menu, you can quickly edit or modify the properties of an object. Using the menu to edit the Display Properties is shown in Figure 2–41.

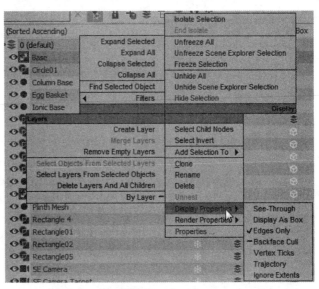

Figure 2–41

You can modify the detailed properties of an object in the Object Properties dialog box, as shown in Figure 2–42. The Object Properties dialog box is opened by selecting **Properties** in the quad menu. Alternatively, you can right-click on an object in a viewport and select **Object Properties**.

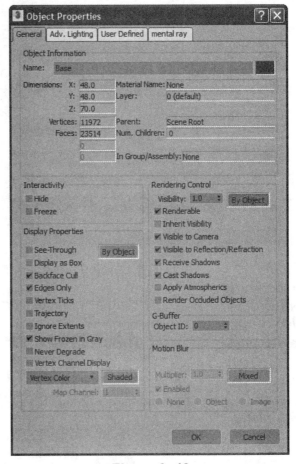

Figure 2–42

- It lists important information about an object, such as the name of the object, how many faces it consists of, the material assigned to it, whether its properties are controlled by layer or by object, etc.

- Changes made in the Object Properties dialog box override any layer settings for that object. The *Rendering Control* area in the Object Properties dialog box enables you to change setting for casting shadows on individual objects in a layer. This is useful when you do not want an object to cast shadows, while keeping the display of the other objects.

- To override the layer properties for an object, click the appropriate **By Layer** so that it changes to **By Object**.

Display Panel

The Command Panel's Display panel (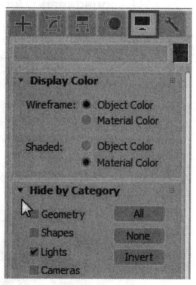) also contains controls for hiding and freezing objects, as shown in Figure 2–43.

Figure 2–43

The Display panel enables you to:

- Hide all objects by category (all lights, all geometry, etc.).

- Hide or Freeze objects individually or by selecting them first.

- Unhide or Unfreeze all objects, or do so by object name. You can also freeze or hide by hit.

*A Display Floater is available in the **Tools** menu, where you can **Hide**, **Unhide**, **Freeze**, and **Unfreeze** objects.*

*You can also use the right-click on the **Display** quad menu.*

Practice 2d

Estimated time for completion: 10 minutes

*Use 📂 (Open File) in the Quick Access Toolbar or click **Application Menu > Open>Open**.*

*If a dialog box opens prompting you about a File Load: Mismatch, click **OK** to accept the default values.*

Layer and Object Properties

Practice Objectives

- Create a new layer and move objects into a layer.
- Adjust properties of the layer and objects in the layer.

In this practice you will create a new layer and move several objects into it. You will also set and modify the properties of the layer and of an individual object using Layer Properties and Object Properties respectively.

You must set the paths to locate the External files and Xrefs used in the practice. If you have not done this already, return to **Chapter 1: Introduction to Autodesk 3ds Max** and complete Task 1 to Task 3 in **Practice 1a: Organizing Folders and Working with the Interface**. You only have to set the user paths once.

Task 1 - Practice Layer Management.

1. Open **Layers.max** from the ...*scenes* folder.

2. In the Main Toolbar, right-click anywhere on the blank space and select **Layers** to display the Layers toolbar. Click

   🗂 (Layer Explorer) in the Main Toolbar or in the Layers toolbar to open the Layer Explorer (Scene Explorer in the Layer mode).

3. In the Layer Explorer, next to layer **0 (default)** note the

   🗂 (blue layer icon) indicating that it is the active layer. Verify that the **Name (Sorted Ascending)** is displayed as the title heading to display the **0 (default)** at the top of the list. If it does not display as mentioned, keep on clicking on the title to cycle through different options.

4. Select the arrow beside **0 (default)** to expand it and list all of the objects on this layer.

5. Scroll down in the object list and locate the objects **Parking Lot Surface**, **Outside Grading**, **Outside Curbing**, **Inside Grading**, **Inside Curbing**, and **Building Pad**.

6. These objects are ground surfaces and part of a group called **Site XREF**. You can verify it by selecting one of these objects such as the **Building Pad** (shown in Figure 2–44) in the

Layer Explorer. Then, click  (Sort by Hierarchy) to shift to the hierarchy mode. Note that **Site XREF** is expanded and all of the objects in the group are highlighted, as shown in Figure 2–45. Scroll down and note that **Building Pad** is also listed and highlighted.

Figure 2–44

Figure 2–45

7. Zoom out in the viewport so that all the objects are visible.

8. In the Layer Explorer click ⧨ (Sort by Layers).

9. In layer **0 (default)**, select **Site XREF**. Note that a number of objects are selected in the viewport and that **1 Group Selected** displays in the Status Bar.

10. With **Site XREF** selected, select **Group>Open** in the menu bar. The Site XREF group is now open. Note that nothing is selected now.

- To verify this, select **Building Pad** in layer **0 (default)** and

  click ▦ (Sort by Hierarchy). Note that only the single object is highlighted and the complete group is not highlighted.

If you already have objects selected, click in empty space in the viewport to clear selection.

11. In the Layer Explorer, click 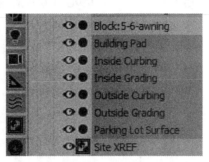 (Sort by Layers). Select the six ground surfaces by using <Shift> **or** <Ctrl> as shown in Figure 2–46.

Figure 2–46

12. In the menu bar, select **Group>Detach**.

You can also use

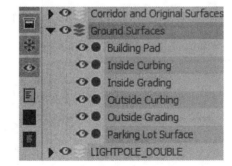 *(Create New Layer) in the Layer toolbar, which opens a dialog box. Verify that **Move Selection to New Layer** is selected and then click **OK**.*

13. In the Layer Explorer with the six ground surfaces selected, click (Create New Layer). A new layer called **Layer001** is automatically created with the six building surfaces placed in it, as shown in Figure 2–47. Note that the software automatically sets this layer to be the current layer, which is indicated by ⬚ (blue icon).

14. Right-click on the layer **Layer001** and select **Rename**. Rename the layer as **Ground Surfaces**, as shown in Figure 2–48.

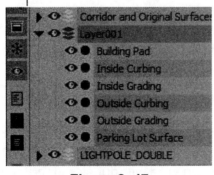

Figure 2–47

Figure 2–48

15. Expand layer **Corridor and Original Surfaces|Surfaces** and note that there are eight ground surfaces in it. Right-click on this layer to open the menu and note that **Delete** is unavailable (grayed out), because the layer contains objects.

*You can also select **Select Child Nodes** in the right-click quad menu.*

16. With the **Corridor and Original Surfaces|Surfaces** layer selected, in the Layer Explorer toolbar, click ⬚ (Select Children). This selects all of the objects in this layer.

You can also select Add Selection To>New Parent (pick) and then select the required layer to move.

17. In the Layer Explorer toolbar, click 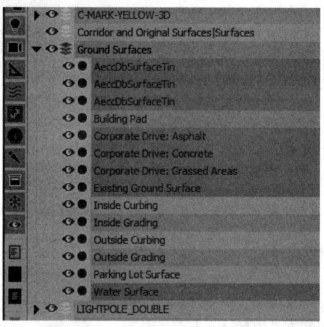 (Add to Active Layer). The eight objects from the **Corridor and Original Surfaces|Surface** layer are moved to the **Ground Surfaces** layer (which is the active layer), as shown in Figure 2–49.

Figure 2–49

18. Right-click **Corridor and Original Surfaces|Surfaces** and note that **Delete** is now available. Select **Delete** to remove **Corridor and Original Surfaces|Surfaces**.

19. Select (gray layer icon) next to layer **0 (default)** to make the layer active which toggles the icon to (blue layer icon).

Task 2 - Set Layer and Object Properties.

Set the ground surfaces so that it does not cast shadows although they will still receive shadows. This simplification can save rendering time without significantly affecting the final output when using relatively flat ground surfaces.

1. In the Layer Explorer, select and right-click on the layer **Ground Surfaces**, and then select **Properties**.

2. In the Layer Properties dialog box, in the *Rendering Control* area, toggle off **Cast Shadows** (as shown in Figure 2–50) and click **OK**

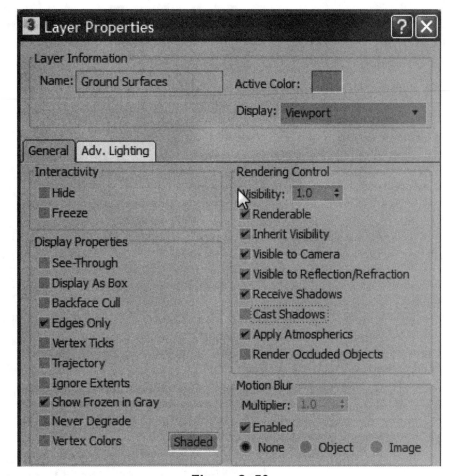

Figure 2–50

3. You can override this setting for one of the ground surfaces. In the Layer Explorer, in the layer **Ground Surfaces**, select and right-click on **Outside Grading**. Select **Properties** to open the Object Properties dialog box.

4. In the Object Properties dialog box, in the *Rendering Control* area, click **By Layer** so that it changes to **By Object**. Verify that **Cast Shadows** for this object is enabled and click **OK**.

5. Close the Layer Explorer.

6. Select **Application menu>Save As**, and save your work as **MyLayers.max**.

Chapter Review Questions

1. Which tool can be used to zoom to the extents of all visible objects in all viewports?

   a. (Zoom Extents)

   b. (Zoom All)

   c. (Zoom Extents All)

   d. (Zoom Region)

2. After selecting a number of objects, which key do you press to remove items from the selection?

   a. <Shift>

   b. <Ctrl>

   c. <Alt>

   d. <Esc>

3. In the maximized viewport display, along with holding <Win>, which key do you need to press to open the viewport overlay where you can switch to a different viewport?

   a. <Shift>

   b. <Ctrl>

   c. <Alt>

   d. <Tab>

4. You should assign the unit scale before adding any geometry to the scene. Changing the **System Unit Scale** later does not rescale objects that are already present.

   a. True

   b. False

5. In the Layer Explorer, which option makes objects unselectable, but leaves them visible in the viewport and renders them normally?

a. **Hide**

b. **Freeze**

c. **Render**

d. **Radiosity**

6. In the Layer Explorer toolbar, selecting a few objects and then clicking (Create New Layer) creates:

a. A new inactive layer that is empty.

b. A new active layer that is empty.

c. A new inactive layer that contains the selected objects.

d. A new active layer that contains the selected objects.

Command Summary

Button	Command	Location
Layers		
	Add Selection to Current Layer	• **Layers Toolbar**
	Add to Active Layer	• **Scene Explorer Toolbar**
	Create New Layers	• **Layers Toolbar** • **Scene Explorer Toolbar**
	Manage Layers	• **Main Toolbar** • **Layers Toolbar**
	Select Objects in Current Layer	• **Layers Toolbar**
	Set Current Layer to Selection's Layer	• **Layers Toolbar**
Object Selection		
	Crossing	• **Main Toolbar:** Window/Crossing Toggle
	Rectangular Selection Region	• **Main Toolbar**
	Select Object	• **Main Toolbar**
	Select by Name	• **Main Toolbar**
	Window	• **Main Toolbar:** Window/Crossing Toggle
Viewport Navigation		
	Dolly Camera	• **Viewport Navigation Toolbar (Camera Views):** Dolly Camera flyout
	Field-of-View	• **Viewport Navigation Toolbar:** Zoom Region flyout in Perspective and Camera views
	Maximize Viewport Toggle	• **Viewport Navigation Toolbar**
	Orbit Camera	• **Viewport Navigation Toolbar (Camera Views)**
	Orbit	• **Viewport Navigation Toolbar (Non-Camera Views):** Orbit flyout

	Orbit Point of View	• **Viewport Navigation Toolbar (Non-Camera Views):** Orbit flyout
	Pan View	• **Viewport Navigation Toolbar**
	Perspective	• **Viewport Navigation Toolbar (Camera Views)**
	Roll Camera	• **Viewport Navigation Toolbar (Camera Views)**
	Truck Camera	• **Viewport Navigation Toolbar (Camera Views)**
	Walk Through	• **Viewport Navigation Toolbar:** Pan View flyout in Perspective and Camera views
	Zoom	• **Viewport Navigation Toolbar (Non-Camera Views)**
	Zoom All	• **Viewport Navigation Toolbar (Non-Camera Views)**
	Zoom Extents	• **Viewport Navigation Toolbar (Non-Camera Views):** Zoom Extents flyout
	Zoom Extents Selected	• **Viewport Navigation Toolbar (Non-Camera Views):** Zoom Extents flyout
	Zoom Extents All	• **Viewport Navigation Toolbar:** Zoom Extents All flyout
	Zoom Extents All Selected	• **Viewport Navigation Toolbar:** Zoom Extents All flyout
	Zoom Region	• **Viewport Navigation Toolbar (Non-Camera Views)**

Assembling Project Files

The files used in the Autodesk® 3ds Max® software can be modeled directly in the software, referenced by linking, or directly imported from another source. Linking files enables you to incorporate objects or other scene files into the current scene by externally referencing them. Once referenced, the connection between the two files can be maintained. If files are imported, they are merged with the project and no link is established. Understanding the benefits and drawbacks of using external data helps you decide how to best reference it in a project.

Learning Objectives in this Chapter

- Understand the difference between File Linking and File Importing, and edit the linked data files.
- Combine entities from .DWG, .DXF, .FBX, and .RVT files into an active Autodesk 3ds Max scene.
- Understand how to link AutoCAD® DWG, DXF, generic FBX files, and Autodesk® Revit® RVT/FBX files.
- Create and modify presets.
- Incorporate objects or other scene files into the current scene by externally referencing them.
- Manage data using the asset tracking systems.

3.1 Data Linking and Importing

Although the Autodesk 3ds Max software has a robust 2D and 3D modeling system, it might be efficient to link or import some or all of the design data from other Autodesk software, such as AutoCAD®, Autodesk® Revit® Architecture, AutoCAD® Architecture, or Autodesk® Inventor®.

Linking vs. Importing

You can link or import files using the **File Link** and **Import** tools. You can link files such as .DWG, .DXF, .FBX, and .RVT, and import files such as Autodesk® Inventor® (.IPT, .IAM), Autodesk® Alias® .Wire, Autodesk® Showcase® .APF (Autodesk Packet File), LandXML and DEM data files, and Adobe Illustrator (.AI).

- Linked geometry differs from imported geometry in that it remains connected to the source file. If the source file is edited, the Autodesk 3ds Max Scene can be updated to show those changes. Imported geometry maintains no connection to the source file.

- If a source .DWG, .DXF, .FBX, or .RVT file is likely to change (or you would prefer to make changes in the .DWG, .DXF, .FBX, or .RVT directly), then using **File Linking** might be the best way to incorporate this data into the Autodesk 3ds Max software.

- **Importing** can be used as a faster alternative to linking to bring large amounts of data into the software. Complex geometry might be faster to reimport than to update through a file link.

- File links and imports are launched from the Application Menu (as shown in Figure 3–1):

    - Expand (Application Menu), expand **Import**, and select **Link Revit/Link FBX/Link AutoCAD**, or

    - Expand (Application Menu), expand **Import**, and select **Import**.

Figure 3–1

Editing Linked Data

- Linked geometry can be edited but not directly deleted from a scene file. Alternatively, the layer on which the objects are placed might be ignored during a reload, or set to **Hide** in the Layer dialog box.

- Edits applied to linked geometry (such as through modifiers) are reapplied after a link is updated. Some complex modifications might not apply as expected, so you should always review your geometry carefully after a link is updated.

- Links to drawing files are not bi-directional, so that changes you make to the data in the Autodesk 3ds Max software do not update the original .DWG, .FBX, .DXF, or .RVT file.

- In linked files that are bound, the geometry stays in the scene file as-is, but the connection to the source file is dropped.

Importing

You can export an .FBX file from the Autodesk Revit software and import it in Autodesk 3ds Max software. The FBX importer is an independent plug-in that is frequently updated. In the FBX Import dialog box, use **Web Update** to check for web updates, download the latest updates, and install them. Close 3ds Max when you do the install.

Merging Autodesk 3ds Max Scene Files

Objects already saved in Autodesk 3ds Max scenes (.MAX files) are imported into the current scene using the **Merge** option (**Application Menu>Import>Merge**). Merging files is a one-directional transfer that does not maintain any connection between the two files. Using the **Merge** option, you can either load a few objects from a scene or you can load a complete scene into the current one.

Practice 3a

Ground Surfaces using Civil View

Practice Objective

Estimated time for completion: 20 minutes

- Open a Civil 3D data file in a scene file.

In this practice you will open a .VSP3D file for importing ground surfaces using Civil View. You will then modify the material assignment for various ground surfaces using the Civil View Explorer.

You must set the paths to locate the External files and Xrefs used in the practice. If you have not done this already, return to **Chapter 1: Introduction to Autodesk 3ds Max** and complete Task 1 to Task 3 in **Practice 1a: Organizing Folders and Working with the Interface**. You only have to set the user paths once.

Task 1 - Initialize Civil View.

It is recommended that you import 3D ground surfaces from Civil/Survey products, such as AutoCAD Civil 3D or Land Desktop using the vsp3d data format.

You have to initialize Civil View once.

1. In the menu bar, select **Civil View>Initialize Civil View**. If you have already initialized Civil View, go to Step 5.

2. In the Initialize Autodesk Civil View dialog box, set the *System Units* to **Feet** because the civil project that you will be opening uses Feet as its unit of measurement. Verify that **Don't warn me about System Units again** is selected.

3. In the *Select a Country Resource Kit* area, select **US IMPERIAL** and verify that *Start Mode for Civil View* is set to **Manual**. Click **OK**. In the Information dialog box, click **OK**.

4. Exit and then restart the Autodesk 3ds Max software.

5. Start Civil View by selecting **Civil View>Start Civil View**.

Hint: Starting Civil View

Although Civil View is initialized next time you launch the Autodesk 3ds Max software, you are still required to start Civil View if the *Start Mode for Civil View* is set as **Manual**. You can change this setting in the Civil View Preferences dialog box, in the *General* tab, by select **Automatically start Civil View?**, as shown in Figure 3–2.

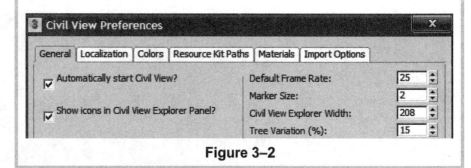

Figure 3–2

Task 2 - Opening a Civil 3D File.

1. Open **Civil Base XRef.max** from the *...\scenes* folder. If a Mismatch dialog box opens, click **OK** to accept the default values. If prompted again, click **OK**. This is an empty scene in which the System Unit Scale has been set to **1 Unit=1.0 Feet**.

2. In the menu bar, select **Civil View>Geometry Import>Civil 3D (VSP 3D) File**, as shown in Figure 3–3.

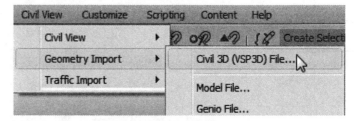

Figure 3–3

3. In the Civil 3D Import Panel dialog box, click **Open**. In the Select a VSP3D File dialog box, browse to the *...\import* folder in the practice files folder and open **Civil surfaces.vsp3d**.

The objects listed include surfaces, site/ grading featurelines, corridor (surfaces, baselines, featurelines etc.),and point groups, etc.

4. In the Civil 3D Import Panel dialog box, a list of objects that are in the AutoCAD Civil 3D file are listed. In the left pane, select **Surfaces [9]** to display all of the surfaces in the right pane. Select **Building Pad**, hold <Shift>, and select **Parking Lot Surface** to highlight the first seven surfaces. Select the checkbox for **Building Pad** to select all seven highlighted surfaces, as shown in Figure 3–4. You can select them individually as well.

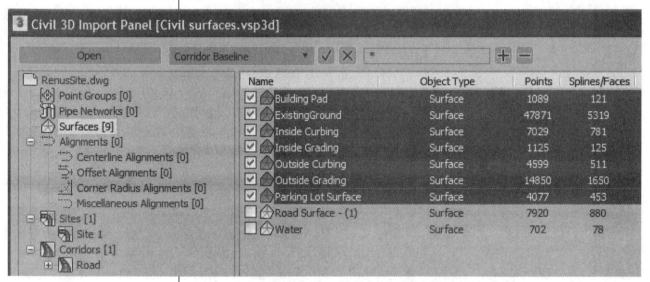

Figure 3–4

5. You will select the corridor surfaces and the baseline. In the left pane, select **Corridors [1]** and in the right pane, click in the checkboxes for **PrimaryAccess**, **Region(1)**, **Region(2)**, and **Region(3)**, as shown in Figure 3–5.

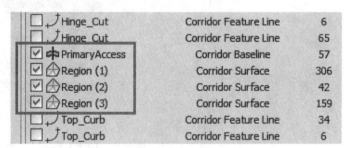

Figure 3–5

6. Click **OK**. In the Civil View Information, click **Yes** to accept the global shift values.

7. Click **Yes** to proceed without a feature interpretation style.

8. In the Warning dialog box, click **OK**. In the Error dialog box, click **OK**.

It takes a few minutes to load the file.

9. The ground surfaces, building pad, corridor, and parking lot are displayed in all of the viewports. If they are not, click

   (Zoom Extents All). In the Perspective viewport, note that only the corridor displays the right surface material but the rest of the surfaces display a checkerboard material.

Right-click on the title bar and select Dock>Left.

10. In the menu bar, select **Civil View>Civil View>Civil View Explorer** to open the Civil & View Explorer. Dock it along the left side of the screen.

Task 3 - Modify Material Assignment.

1. Verify that the *Civil Explorer* tab is selected. Expand **Civil View Objects>Imported Objects**, if not already expanded. Select **Surfaces** and note that the corridor is selected in the viewports. The Object List rollout opens with all of the surfaces listed, as shown in Figure 3–6.

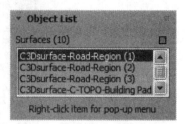

Figure 3–6

A material is not required for the first three corridor regions.

2. In the Object List rollout, select **C3Dsurface-C-TOPO-Building Pad**. In the Surface Parameters rollout, select the *Statistics* tab and note that in the *Face Selection Sets*, in *By Material ID*, **[31] Ground Type 4** has been assigned, as shown in Figure 3–7.

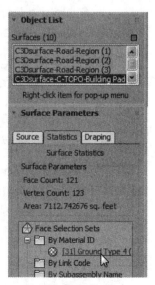

Figure 3–7

The complete list might not be visible in the Explorer. Hover the cursor in empty space in the information area until it displays as a Pan (hand) cursor. Slide up or down, using the hand cursor or the scroll button to display all of the information.

3. Right-click on **[31] Ground Type 4** and select **Modify Material ID Assignment**, as shown in Figure 3–8.

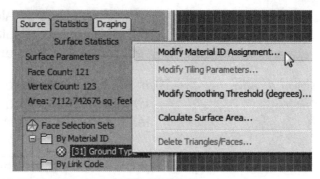

Figure 3–8

4. Click **Yes** in the Warning dialog box.

5. In the Modify material channel dialog box, select **[22] Concrete Type 1** as shown in Figure 3–9. Click **OK**.

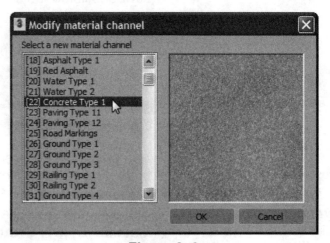

Figure 3–9

6. In the **Perspective** viewport, use **Zoom** and **Pan** to zoom into the building pad. Note how the new material is applied.

7. Select **Surfaces** again and in the Object List rollout, select **C3Dsurface-C-TOPO-Existing Ground**. In the Surface Parameters rollout, in the *Statistics* tab, right-click on **[31] Ground Type 4**, and select **Modify Material ID Assignment**. In the Warning dialog box, click **Yes**.

8. In the Modify material channel dialog box, select **[28] Ground Type 3** and click **OK**. In the **Perspective** viewport, note that the new ground type material is applied to the ground surface.

A material is not required for the first three corridor regions.

9. Similarly, for the other surfaces, apply the material types as follows:

- C3Dsurface-C-TOPO-Inside Curbing:
  [38] Concrete Type 3
- C3Dsurface-C-TOPO-Inside Grading:
  [28] Ground Type 3
- C3Dsurface-C-TOPO-Outside Curbing:
  [38] Concrete Type 3
- C3Dsurface-C-TOPO-Outside Grading:
  [28] Ground Type 3
- C3Dsurface-C-TOPO-Parking Lot Surface:
  [39] Asphalt Type 4

10. Close the Civil View Explorer.

You might need to undock the explorer first to close it.

11. Click 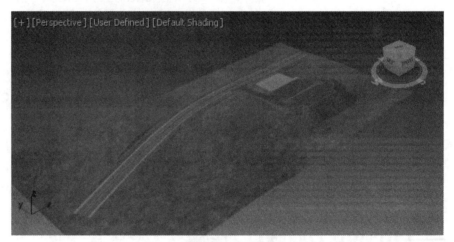 (Zoom Extents All). In the **Perspective** view, the scene displays as shown in Figure 3–10.

Figure 3–10

12. Save your work as **MyCivil Base XRef.max**.

3.2 Linking Files

File Linking is used to incorporate data from other Autodesk software such as Autodesk Revit and AutoCAD into the Autodesk 3ds Max scene. If the incorporated data is changed in the originating software, the file link enables you to update those changes in the 3ds Max scene. File linking is useful when you are working on a visualization project and know that all design decisions have not yet been made. You can link files using the Manage Links dialog box that can be opened as follows:

- (Application Menu)>Import>Link Revit: Links the .RVT files from the Autodesk Revit Architecture software.

- (Application Menu)>Import>Link FBX: Links the .FBX files that can be created in the Autodesk Revit, Autodesk MotionBuilder, Autodesk Maya, and Autodesk Mudbox software.

- (Application Menu)>Import>Link AutoCAD: Links the .DWG and .DXF files from the AutoCAD software.

- You can also open the Manage Links dialog box outside of the Link commands (**Application Menu>References> Manage Links**) and modify the Link settings.

Linking DWG Files

In CAD data files it is common to have large numbers of objects. When linking or importing AutoCAD .DWG or .DXF files, it is efficient to combine multiple, related objects together into a single Autodesk 3ds Max object to control their display and visibility.

- When multiple entities are combined into compound Autodesk 3ds Max shapes (2D objects) and meshes (3D objects), you can still access and adjust the original geometry using the Sub-object level modifiers, such as **Edit Spline**, **Edit Mesh**, and **Edit Poly**.

- Once multiple entities are combined, you can detach objects or portions of an objects to form new ones for individual editing control.

Linking FBX and RVT Files

The Autodesk Revit and Autodesk 3ds Max software share a mental ray renderer. Both products use the Autodesk Material Library materials.

- The .RVT and .FBX file format supports the import of photometric lights, both interior artificial lights and exterior daylight systems.

- Detailed .RVT and .FBX file formats can become very large in size and importing them as single files cannot be accomplished. In such cases, use a section box in the **3D View** in the Autodesk Revit software to limit the amount of the scene you are exporting.

Manage Links Options

The Manage Links dialog box (shown in Figure 3–11) contains the following tabs:

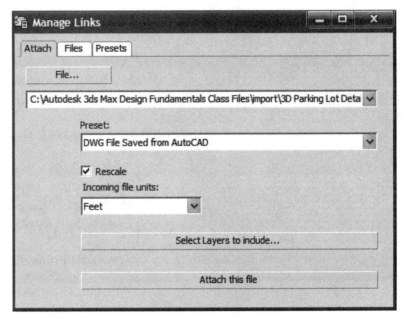

Figure 3–11

Attach Tab

The options available in the *Attach* tab are described as follows:

- **File...** enables you to open a file (.DWG, .DXF, .FBX, or .RVT) for linking. The selected filename and its path display in the File drop-down list. If the file that you selected is a .RVT file with more than one camera view, you are prompted to select a camera view.

- The Preset drop-down list enables you to select the preset settings. The Presets listed here can be created or modified using the *Presets* tab. You can set the units by selecting them in the Incoming file units drop-down list.

- **Select Layers to include** is only available with .DWG and .DXF file formats and enables you to select the layers that you want included with the drawing file.

- **Attach this file** links the selected file with the specified preset settings to the current Autodesk 3ds Max scene.

Files Tab

The *Files* tab displays a list of files that are linked to the current scene with a specific status icon.

- If the linked file has been modified, ▣ displays with the linked filename.

- ▣ indicates that the linked file is unchanged and does not have any errors.

- When a file is highlighted, the following options are available:

Reload...	When the original file has been changed, it displays the changes in the current scene.
Detach...	Use when you want to remove the link with the original file. This option removes all geometry associated with the linked file.
Bind...	Removes the link with the original file, but the geometry stays in the current scene, although the link between the original file is broken. Changes made to the original linked file cannot be reloaded.

Presets Tab

Many options are available before files are linked to your current scene. These options are configured and saved as **Presets** and can be used when linking files at a later stage. Many of these options require trial and error to find the most appropriate settings. You can link a file and then reload (or detach and relink) with different settings until you achieve the required results.

If you are linking a file for the first time, it is recommended that you create a new preset.

The *Presets* tab lists all existing presets and contains options for creating new presets, modifying existing presets, copying existing ones, renaming and deleting them. You need to select a preset for the **Modify**, **Copy**, **Rename**, and **Delete** options to be available, as shown in Figure 3–12. If no preset is selected, **Copy** is replaced by **New** and is the only available option.

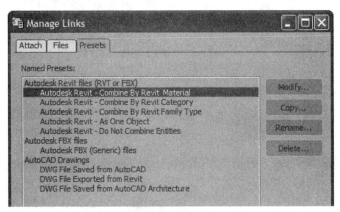

Figure 3–12

Depending on the type of preset selected (.RVT, .FBX, or .DWG), clicking **Modify...** opens a specific File Link Settings dialog box, which enables you to define the way you want the geometry to be linked, what portions of the file are to be modified on **Reload**, and how the geometry is combined.

File Link Settings: DWG Files

In the Manage Links dialog box, in the *Presets* tab, selecting an AutoCAD DWG file preset and clicking **Modify...** opens the File Link Settings: DWG Files dialog box, as shown in Figure 3–13.

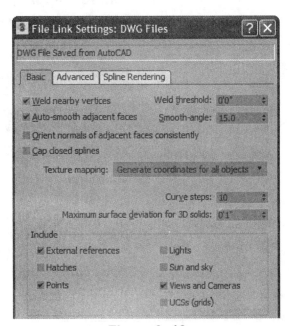

Figure 3–13

Basic Tab

The options available in the *Basic* tab are described as follows:

- **Weld nearby vertices** and **Weld threshold:** Welding joins together vertices of the same object that fall in the weld threshold. If the objects are joined by layer, this option removes duplicate vertices so that the adjacent 2D objects on the same layer are automatically combined into splines. Adjacent 3D objects that are welded become faces in a single mesh that share common vertices.

- **Auto-smooth adjacent face** and **Smooth-angle:** Auto-smooth enables adjacent faces in the same 3D mesh to display smooth if the angles of separation between their face normals (a directional vector perpendicular to the face) is equal to or less than the Smooth-angle. Otherwise, the adjacent faces have a faceted edge between them. This is the same smoothing process used in the Edit Mesh and Edit Poly modifiers.

- **Orient normals of adjacent faces consistently:** This option coordinates the face normals of linked objects. This option should be left off by default unless some faces of your 3D objects are missing after the link.

- **Cap closed splines:** It assigns an Extrude modifier to all closed 2D geometry (e.g., circles and closed polylines).

- **Texture mapping:** Texture mapping is used to locate texture maps on objects. Two options are available:

Generate coordinates on-demand	• Links objects without adding any texture mapping. • Adds the mapping when it is first called for by the software. • Enables a faster link but might cause some discrepancies.
Generate coordinates for all objects	• Adds texture mapping to all objects at the time of the link, matching any that might have existed in the original drawing file.

- **Curve steps:** This setting defines the number of segments to subdivide each 2D curve segment into if they are later extruded in the Autodesk 3ds Max software. This setting applies to circles, arcs, polyline curves, spines, and similar curved objects.

You can adjust smoothing later if you still encounter smoothing issues after import.

- **Maximum surface deviation for 3D solids:** This setting defines the allowed deviation distance from a parametric AutoCAD 3D curve (such as a curved AutoCAD extrusion) and the resulting Autodesk 3ds Max mesh. The lower the value, the more a 3D curve is subdivided. In the Autodesk 3ds Max software, all 3D curves must be segmented.

This value can be set as low, (0.01).

- **Include area options:** These options enable you to select the type of objects to be brought into the scene. Note that the **Lights** option only brings in Lights from AutoCAD drawings pre-2007. If you have Sun and Sky checked, a daylight system is created based on the information in the incoming DWG file from the Autodesk Revit 2009 software.

Advanced Tab

The *Advanced* tab (shown in Figure 3–14) controls the import of AutoCAD primitives and the effect of scene materials while importing.

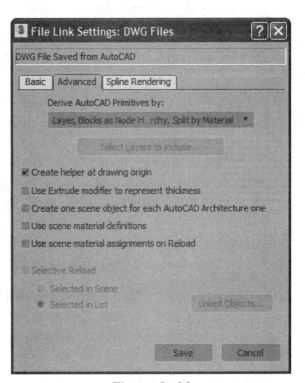

Figure 3–14

The options available in the *Advanced* tab are described as follows:

- **Derive AutoCAD Primitives by:** Controls how AutoCAD objects are combined when linked.

Layer	Creates one object for each AutoCAD layer. Each AutoCAD block links as a single object called a VIZBlock.
Layer, Blocks as Node Hierarchy	This option preserves material assignments in linked AutoCAD blocks. It structures each as a hierarchy of objects rather than single objects.
Layer, Blocks as Node Hierarchy, Split by Material	This option works similarly to the one above but takes into account drawings that have more than one material applied to objects on the same layer. Separate hierarchies are created for each material type on each layer.
Entity, Blocks as Node Hierarchy	This option includes all non-blocks as separate, individual objects. Blocks are preserved as hierarchies, however, organized by layer.
Color	Combines AutoCAD objects by color. All objects of one color are joined in as a single object, regardless of layer.
Entity	Does not combine AutoCAD objects at all. Instead, each AutoCAD object becomes an individual object.
One Object	This option combines all AutoCAD objects into a single object.

- **Create helper at drawing origin:** Adds an origin point helper at the origin of the current coordinate system. All of the linked geometry is part of a hierarchy parented by this helper, so all of the linked objects can be repositioned as one by transforming the helper.

- **Use Extrude modifier to represent thickness:** When disabled, linking 2D AutoCAD objects with a non-zero thickness value translates the objects into the Autodesk 3ds Max software as a 3D mesh. When enabled, objects translate as 2D objects with a parametric extrude modifier. The resulting geometry is the same but when this option is enabled, the extrusion properties (such as height) can be modified after the link or imported using the modifier stack.

- **Create one scene object for each AutoCAD Architecture one:** When unchecked, AutoCAD Architecture and AutoCAD MEP objects are subdivided into separate objects by material.

- **Use scene material definitions:** When unchecked, the Autodesk 3ds Max software includes the current state of any material applied to the linked objects in the AutoCAD software. If selected and the current scene has a material with the same exact name as the AutoCAD material, the scene material is used instead.

- **Use scene material assignments on Reload:** When unchecked, the Autodesk 3ds Max software re-loads the current state of any AutoCAD materials present in the drawing file when the link is updated. When enabled, the Autodesk 3ds Max software maintains the current state of any materials in the scene file after a link is updated. Select this option if you intend to adjust linked materials in the Autodesk 3ds Max software or leave it unchecked if you intend to adjust them the AutoCAD software.

- **Selective Reload:** Enables you to reload a subset of the original file. You can select objects to reload by selecting them in the scene or by selecting them from a list. If you select **Selected in List**, and click **Linked Objects** a list opens.

Hint: Hierarchies and File Linking

Autodesk 3ds Max Hierarchies are collections of objects linked together into parent/child relationships where transform applied to a parent are automatically passed on to its children. Connecting multiple objects in a hierarchical chain can enable sophisticated animations in the Autodesk 3ds Max software, such as the motion of jointed robotic arms.

In the case of the **hierarchy** file link options, incoming AutoCAD blocks are brought into the Autodesk 3ds Max software as multiple objects so that they can maintain multiple material assignments from the AutoCAD software. The parent object itself does not have any geometry and does not render. Most modifiers (such as **Substitute**) must be applied to the objects in the hierarchy rather than the parent.

Spline Rendering Tab

The options available in the *Spline Rendering* tab (shown in Figure 3–15) enable linear objects (2D and 3D lines, polylines, etc.) to display as extruded 3D objects in the viewports or rendering. Normally, splines cannot be rendered because they do not have surface area to interact with scene lighting. These options enable splines to link into the Autodesk 3ds Max software as 3D linear objects with a cross-sectional radius or a rectangular length and width. This provides the surface area for rendering.

Figure 3–15

- If splines are to be rendered with materials then options such as smoothing, mapping coordinates, and/or real-world map size are often important.

- When enabled, all of the splines linked with this setting are renderable, and all have the same cross-section geometry.

- To make only certain 2D objects renderable (or want some to render differently than others) you could apply a Renderable Spline modifier directly to those objects after linking.

File Link Settings: Revit Files (RVT or FBX)

In the Manage Links dialog box, in the *Presets* tab, selecting an Autodesk Revit file and clicking **Modify...** opens the File Link Settings: Revit Files (RVT or FBX) dialog box, as shown in Figure 3–16. Additionally, you can also select the Autodesk FBX (Generic) file preset and click **Modify...**.This opens the File Link Settings: FBX Files dialog box, as shown in Figure 3–17. This dialog box is similar to the Autodesk Revit Files (.RVT and .FBX) but without a *Geometry* area for controlling the segments and smoothing the linked geometry.

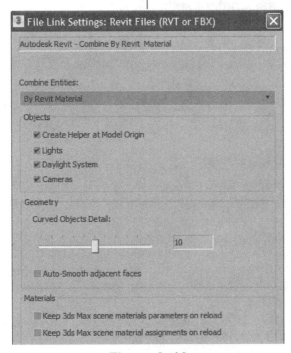

Figure 3–16

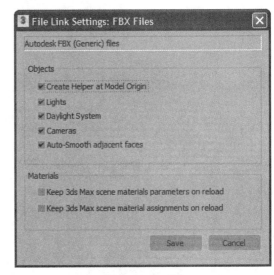

Figure 3–17

The options available in the File Link Settings: Revit Files (RVT or FBX) dialog box are described as follows:

It is recommended that you combine entities to reduce the number of objects.

- **Combine Entities** list: Enables you to select the Autodesk Revit entities that you want to combine, as shown in Figure 3–18. For example, if you select **By Revit Material**, all of the entities that have the same material are linked in the current Autodesk 3ds Max scene as a single object.

Figure 3–18

- ***Objects*** area: The selected options in this area are linked from the .RVT file to your current scene. If the .RVT file or .FBX file contains photometric lights, interior artificial lights, cameras, and exterior daylight systems, you can select the associated options in the File Link Settings dialog box.

- ***Geometry*** **area:** Enables you to set the number of segments for your curved entities and apply auto-smoothing to them.

- ***Materials*** **area:** Enables you to control the material definitions and assignment settings.

Practice 3b

Linking an AutoCAD DWG

Practice Objectives

- Create a preset to link an AutoCAD .DWG file and reposition it.
- Revise the link settings and reload the linked file.

Estimated time for completion: 20 minutes

In this practice you will link AutoCAD geometry to represent the parking lot details, such as pavement markings and other details. You will reposition this file using the Helper object, and will create 3D markings by projecting 2D lines to the elevation of a terrain model.

You must set the paths to locate the External files and Xrefs used in the practice. If you have not done this already, return to **Chapter 1: Introduction to Autodesk 3ds Max** and complete Task 1 to Task 3 in **Practice 1a: Organizing Folders and Working with the Interface**. You only have to set the user paths once.

Task 1 - Link an AutoCAD .DWG File.

*If a dialog box opens prompting you about a File Load: Mismatch, click **OK** to accept the default values.*

1. Open **Civil Base.max** from the *...\scenes* folder.

2. Select **Application Menu>Import>Link AutoCAD**. In the Open dialog box, browse and open the *...\import* folder in the Practice Files folder. Select **3D Parking Lot Detail.dwg** and click **Open**. The Manage Links dialog box opens with the path and the filename displayed, as shown Figure 3–19.

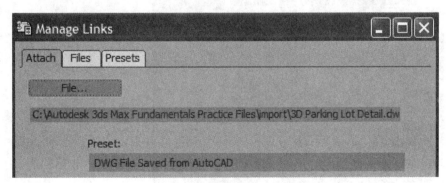

Figure 3–19

*If no preset is selected, only **New...** is available.*

3. Select the *Presets* tab and click **New...** to create a new link preset.

4. In the New Settings Preset dialog box, set *New Name* as **AutoCAD – Derive by Layer**. Note that the *Format* is selected as **AutoCAD Drawings**. Click **OK**.

5. In the Manage Links dialog box, select the new **AutoCAD – Derive by Layer** preset, as shown in Figure 3–20. Click **Modify...**.

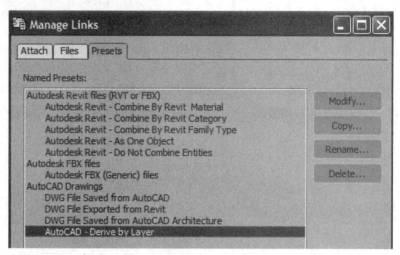

Figure 3–20

*The **Create Helper at drawing origin** option adds a helper object at the origin of the linked file.*

6. In the File Link Settings: DWG Files dialog box, in the *Basic* tab, set the link options, as shown in Figure 3–21. Select the *Advanced* tab and select **Create helper at drawing origin**, as shown in Figure 3–22. Leave all other options as defaults (clear).

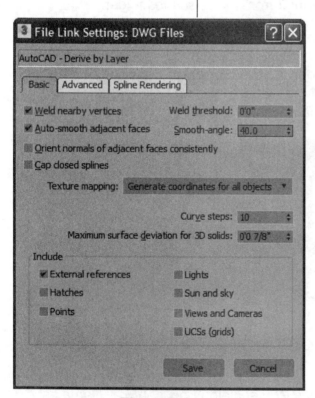

Figure 3–21

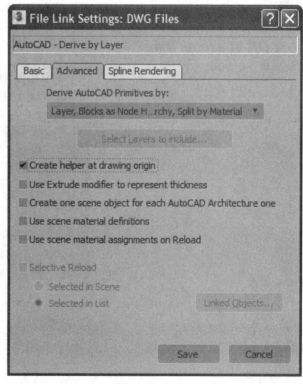

Figure 3–22

7. Select the *Spline Rendering* tab and verify that the link options are set to the defaults, as shown in Figure 3–23.

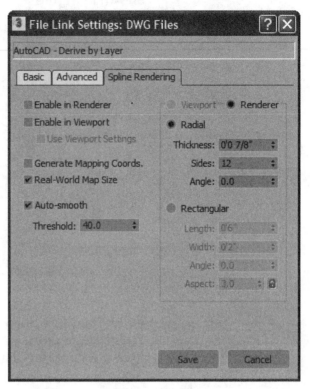

Figure 3–23

8. Click **Save**.

9. In the Manage Links dialog box, select the *Attach* tab. Set *Preset* to **AutoCAD – Derive by Layer**, as shown in Figure 3–24. Click **Select Layers to include....**

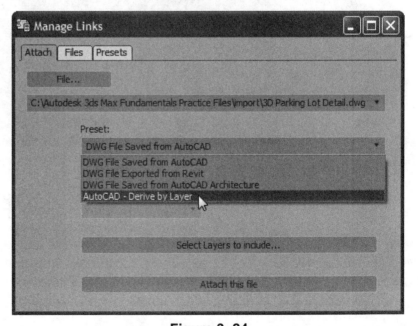

Figure 3–24

10. In the Select Layers dialog box, select **Select from list**. Clear **0** and **DEFPOINTS** and leave all other layers as selected, as shown in Figure 3–25. Click **OK**.

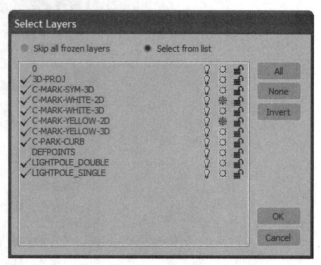

Figure 3–25

11. In the Manage Links dialog box, click **Attach this file**. Close the Manage Links dialog box. Note that the parking lot details have been added to the scene, but are located far away from the origin, as shown in the **Top** viewport in Figure 3–26.

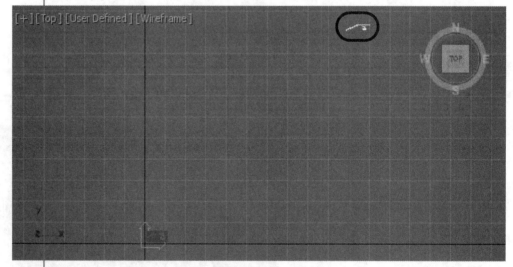

Figure 3–26

Task 2 - Relocate the Linked Geometry.

You might need to start Civil View, if it is not set to start automatically.

1. You need to move the parking lot details by the global shift values in Civil View. In the menu bar, select **Civil View>Civil View>Civil View Explorer**.

2. In the Civil View Explorer, select **Scene Settings**, as shown in Figure 3–27. In the Scene Settings rollout, note the *Global Import Shift* values for *X Shift* and *Y Shift (-9901)*, as shown in Figure 3–28. Close the Civil View Explorer.

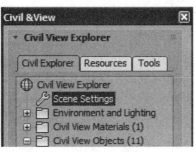

Figure 3–27

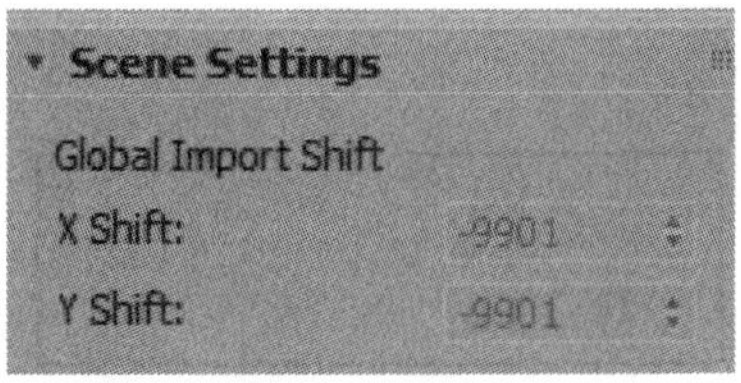

Scene Settings

Global Import Shift

X Shift: -9901

Y Shift: -9901

Figure 3–28

3. In the Main Toolbar, click 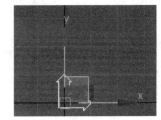 (Select and Move).

If the Scene Explorer is not displayed, select ***Tools>Scene Explorer*** *and then dock it.*

4. In the Scene Explorer, click ((Display None) and

(Display Helpers)), and then select the helper object **3D Parking Lot Detail.dwg**, as shown in Figure 3–29. Note that the **User Coordinate System** icon located at the origin is selected, as shown in Figure 3–30.

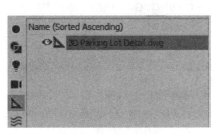

Figure 3–29

Figure 3–30

5. In the Status Bar, ensure that (Absolute Mode Transform) is displayed. Set the following, as shown in Figure 3–31:

- *X* edit box: **-9901'0"**
- *Y* edit box: **-9901'0"**

X: -9901'0"   Y: -9901'0"   Z: 0'0"

Figure 3–31

6. Press <Enter>.

7. Click (Zoom Extents All). Note how the parking lot details are placed exactly on the parking lot surface.

8. In the **Perspective** viewport, use 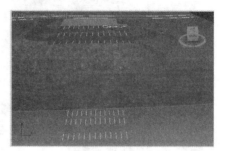 (Zoom) and (Orbit) to zoom into the Parking lot area and tilt the view to display the area below the surfaces, similar to that shown in Figure 3–32. Note that in addition to the 3D pavement markings, 2D line markings are imported through the link.

Figure 3–32

Task 3 - Revise the Link Settings.

In the Files tab, if the linked file has been modified, displays.

1. Click **Application Menu>References>Manage Links** to open the Manage Links dialog box.

2. In the Manage Links dialog box, select the *Files* tab and note that the linked file displays , indicating that the file has not changed. (*Although the linked file has not changed, use Reload... to revise the link settings.*) Verify that **Show Reload options** is selected, and click **Reload....**

You can use:
***Reload...** to update the file in the scene.*
***Detach...** to remove a linked drawing from the scene.*
***Bind...** to insert the drawing as is and removes the connection.*

3. The File Link Settings: DWG Files dialog box opens. In the *Advanced* tab, click **Select Layers to include....** Clear the 2D layers (**C-MARK-WHITE-2D**and **C-MARK-YELLOW-2D)**, and the two **LIGHTPOLE** layers, as shown in Figure 3–33.

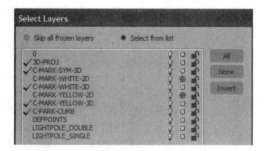

Figure 3–33

The 2D linework should no longer display, keeping the scene smaller.

4. Click **OK** twice to close both dialog boxes. Click to close the Manage Links dialog box. In the **Perspective** viewport, note that the 2D line markings are not displayed.

5. Save your work as **MyCivil Base.max**.

Practice 3c

Linking and Reloading Autodesk Revit File

Practice Objectives

- Link and reposition an Autodesk Revit file to the current scene.
- Reload a modified .RVT file.

In this practice you will link a .RVT file into a 3ds Max scene. You will reposition the Revit file using the Helper object. You will then reload a modified version of the .RVT linked file to incorporate the changes made to the original Autodesk Revit file using **Reload**.

You must set the paths to locate the External files and Xrefs used in the practice. If you have not done this already, return to **Chapter 1: Introduction to Autodesk 3ds Max** and complete Task 1 to Task 3 in **Practice 1a: Organizing Folders and Working with the Interface**. You only have to set the user paths once.

Estimated time for completion: 20 minutes

Task 1 - Link an Autodesk Revit (.RVT) file.

1. Open **Civil Base Link.max** from the *...\scenes* folder.

2. Select **Application Menu>Import>Link Revit**.

3. In the Open dialog box, in the *...\import* folder, select **Revit Building-1.rvt** and click **Open**.

*If a dialog box opens prompting you about a File Load: Mismatch, click **OK** to accept the default values.*

It might take a few minutes to load the file.

4. The Status Bar is replaced by the Loading file bar, indicating the progress of the file as it loads. Once loaded, the Select Revit View dialog box opens, as shown in Figure 3–34.

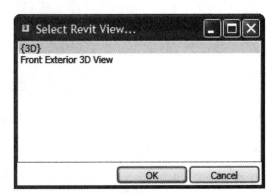

Figure 3–34

5. Select **Front Exterior 3D View** and click **OK**.

6. In the Manage Links dialog box, select the *Presets* tab. Click **New...** to create a new preset. In the New Settings Preset dialog box, set the following:
    - *New Name*: **Revit Preset**
    - *Format*: **Autodesk Revit (*.rvt,*.fbx)**.

7. Click **OK**.

8. In the Manage Links dialog box, select **Revit Preset** and click **Modify**.

*The **Create Helper at Model Origin** option adds a helper object at the origin of the linked file. Selecting and applying transforms (move, rotate, or scale) to the helper object applies the transform to the linked geometry together.*

9. In the File Link Settings dialog box, do the following, as shown in Figure 3–35:
    - In the Combine Entities drop-down list, select **By Revit Category**.
    - In the *Objects* area, clear **Lights** and **Daylight System**.
    - In the *Objects* area, select **Create Helper at Model Origin** and **Cameras**.
    - In the *Geometry* area, set *Curved Objects Detail* to **6**.
    - In the *Materials* area, verify that **Keep 3ds Max scene materials parameters on reload** and **Keep 3ds Max scene material assignments on reload** are cleared.

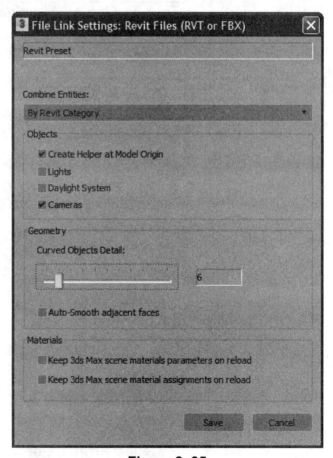

Figure 3–35

10. Click **Save**.

11. Select the *Attach* tab. Expand the Preset drop-down list and select **Revit Preset**.

12. Click **Attach this file**. Note that the Autodesk Revit building and camera are loaded at the 0,0,0 location in the viewports.

13. Click ❌ to close the Manage Links dialog box.

14. In the Scene Explorer, click ⬛ (Display None) and ◣ (Display Helpers) and then select the helper object **Revit Building-1.rvt**, as shown in Figure 3–36.

(It might take a few minutes to load the file).

*If the Scene Explorer is not displayed, select **Tools>Scene Explorer** and then dock it.*

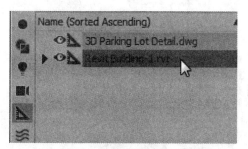

Figure 3–36

15. Right-click on the **Top** viewport to make it active and to maintain the selection. In the Main Toolbar, click ✛ (Select and Move). The Transform gizmo is displayed at the helper location, which is the origin of the linked Autodesk Revit file.

16. In the Status Bar, verify that ▦ (Absolute Mode Transform) is displayed. Set the following, as shown in Figure 3–37:
    - *X* edit box: **800'0"**
    - *Y* edit box: **382'0"**
    - *Z* edit box: **154'6"**

The position of the building pad from the origin has been calculated.

Figure 3–37

17. Press <Enter>.

18. Click 🔲 (Zoom Extents All). Note how the building is placed on the building pad.

Grid has been hidden for clarity. Press <G>.

19. In the **Front** viewport, use  (Zoom Region) and create a rectangular window around the building to zoom into the building. Select the **User Defined** Visual Style label and select **High Quality.** Select the **Wireframe** Visual Style label and select **Default Shading**. Select the **Default Shading** Visual Style label again and select **Edged Faces** to define the windows and doors. The building should display similar to that shown in Figure 3–38.

[+] [Front] [High Quality] [Edged Faces]

Figure 3–38

20. In the **Left** viewport, select the **Wireframe** Visual Style label and select **Default Shading** and then **Edged Faces**.

21. Select the **Left** Point of View label, and select **Cameras>Views: Front Exterior 3D View**, as shown in Figure 3–39.

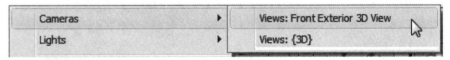

| Cameras | ▶ | Views: Front Exterior 3D View |
| Lights | ▶ | Views: {3D} |

Figure 3–39

22. Use  (Pan Camera) and (Field-of-View) to display the complete building in the **Left** viewport, similar to that as shown in Figure 3–40.

23. In the **Perspective** viewport, use (Zoom) and (Orbit) to zoom into the building and parking lot area so that the display is similar to that shown in Figure 3–40.

Figure 3–40

Task 2 - Reload the variation of the .RVT file.

A variation to the .RVT linked file (windows have been added) has been included in the ...\import folder.

1. In Windows Explorer, open the ...\import folder.

2. Right-click on **Revit Building-1.rvt** and select **Rename**. Rename the file as **Revit Building-1_ORIGINAL.rvt**.

3. Right-click on **Revit Building-2.rvt**, and select **Copy**. Paste a copy of this file into the same directory. Right-click on the copied file, select **Rename**, and rename the file as **Revit Building-1.rvt**. This must be the same name as the original file that was linked to indicate that the original linked file has changed.

4. Return to the Autodesk 3ds Max software. Select **Application Menu>References>Manage Links** to open the Manage Links dialog box.

5. In the Manage Links dialog box, select the *Files* tab. Note that 🗒 displays in front of the .RVT filename (as shown in Figure 3–41), indicating that changes have been made to the original linked file.

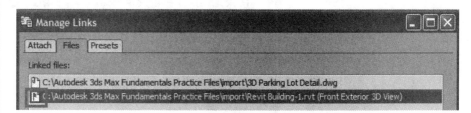

Figure 3–41

6. Select the complete path of **Revit Building -1.rvt** (if not already selected) and click **Reload...**. The Loading file bar displays the progress.

7. In the File Link Settings dialog box that opens, in the *Materials* area, select **Keep 3ds Max scene material assignments on reload**. Click **OK**. The scene is refreshed with the new changes.

8. In the Manage Links dialog box, in the *Files* tab, the icon has changed to , as shown in Figure 3–42. This indicates that there are no differences between the original file and the linked file.

Figure 3–42

9. Close the Manage Links dialog box.

10. In the viewports, the modified building is displayed. More windows are added to the building, as shown in Figure 3–43.

Figure 3–43

11. Save the file as **MyCivil Base Link.max**.

3.3 References

External References (XRef)

Autodesk 3ds Max Scene files can reference data from other .MAX scene files by expanding **Application Menu> References>XRef Objects or XRef Scene**. The XREF data remains linked to the source (.MAX) scene file so that changes in the source file can be reflected in any scene that contains the XREF.

- External References are useful to break up large projects into more manageable pieces, permit more than one person to work on the same project at the same time in separate files, and to enable the same core scene geometry to be used in multiple files.

- **XRef Scenes** bring in the entire scene. All of the XREF objects are non-selectable and cannot be modified.

- **XRef Objects** enable you to select individual objects (or all) from an XREF scene. These objects remain selectable and modifiable in the XREF scene file.

- You can snap to XREF and use XREF objects with AutoGrid. You can also use XREF objects as alignment targets and you can select an XREF object's coordinate system for object transformation. XREF support parameter wiring and you can XREF the controllers.

- Objects in scenes (.MAX) are imported into other . MAX scenes using the **Merge** option.

Data Management and Asset Tracking

The Autodesk 3ds Max software enables you to manage your data through Data Management (DM) solutions, referred to as Asset Tracking Systems (ATSs).

- DM solutions such as the Autodesk® Vault software enables you to store scene files and any supporting data (such as material maps) in a single database repository.

- These systems can be accessed simultaneously by multiple users with different rights assigned based on their project responsibilities. Data can be checked out for editing by one individual at a time while still being referenced by other users. Users can see who is editing which portion of the project at any time.

- By centralizing the files in a DM system it is much easier to adjust paths for external files such as image maps.

- Data files can be versioned through DM solutions, so that the older versions can be readily accessed, if required.

- For more information see *Asset Tracking* in the Autodesk 3ds Max Help files. Asset Tracking is available through the **Application Menu>References> Asset Tracking**.

Practice 3d

XRef and Merge Objects

Practice Objective

- Link an AutoCAD .DWG file and incorporate objects from another scene file into the current scene.

Estimated time for completion: 15 minutes

In this practice create a new scene file that will contain linked AutoCAD objects and XRef objects from the Civil Base scene. You will then merge objects into the current scene file.

You must set the paths to locate the External files and Xrefs used in the practice. If you have not done this already, return to **Chapter 1: Introduction to Autodesk 3ds Max** and complete Task 1 to Task 3 in **Practice 1a: Organizing Folders and Working with the Interface**. You only have to set the user paths once.

Task 1 - Assemble the Data.

If an unsaved scene is open, you need to save or discard the changes to the scene.

1. Click **Application Menu>Reset** and click **Yes** to reset the scene.

2. For this scene, set the *System Unit Scale* to **Inches**. Select **Customize>Units Setup**. In the dialog box, verify that the following is set:
   - *Display Unit Scale:* **US Standard**, **Feet w/ Fractional Inches**
   - *Default Units*: **Inches**
   - *Lighting Units*: **American**

3. Click **System Unit Setup**. In the System Unit Setup dialog box, set *System Unit Scale* to **Inches**. Click **OK** in both the dialog boxes.

4. Expand **Application Menu>References** and select **Manage Links**.

5. In the Manage Links dialog box, in the *Attach* tab, click **File....** In the ...*import* folder, select **Exterior AutoCAD Architectural Model.dwg**. Click **Open**.

*The **AutoCAD – Derive by Layer** preset was created in the **Practice: Linking an AutoCAD DWG**. Complete the above mentioned practice to create the preset if not already done so.*

6. In the *Preset* drop-down list, select **AutoCAD – Derive by Layer** and click **Attach this file**. Once the file has been loaded, close the Manage Links dialog box.

   - The AutoCAD Architectural objects were not joined together by layer. Each was subdivided by material type into different objects. Materials previously assigned in AutoCAD Architecture were preserved on these separate objects.

7. Click ![icon](Maximize Viewport Toggle) or use <Alt>+<W> to display the four viewport view.

8. Click ![icon](Zoom Extents All) to display all of the objects in all of the viewports.

9. In the **Front** viewport, select all of the objects by creating a window around the objects. In the Main Toolbar, in the *Named Selection Sets* field, enter **exterior AutoCAD Architectural building**, as shown in Figure 3–44. Press <Enter>.

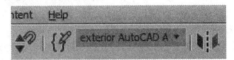

Figure 3–44

You select objects to XREF rather than the entire scene because XREF scene objects cannot be individually selected or modified.

10. Click **Application Menu>References>XRef Objects**. In the XRef Objects dialog box, click ![icon](Create XRef Record from File) as shown in Figure 3–45.

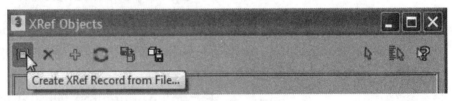

Figure 3–45

11. In the Open File dialog box, select **Parking Lot Detail.max** (from the ...\import folder) and click **Open**.

12. If the Units Mismatch dialog box opens, click **OK**. This rescales the XRef objects to the system units.

13. The Duplicate Material Name dialog box opens prompting you that there is an incoming material with the same name as an existing scene material. Select **Apply to All Duplicates** to keep both materials, as shown in Figure 3–46. Click **Auto-Rename Merged Material**.

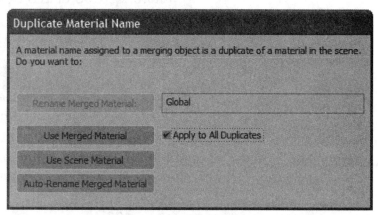

Figure 3–46

14. In the XRef Objects dialog box, note that the .MAX filename is displayed. Click ☒ to close the dialog box.

15. Click ![zoom] (Zoom Extents All). Note that the Civil Base objects are located far from the origin. This is a coordinate system discrepancy and not a scale issue. It is common for Architectural drawings to be based in a different coordinate system and scale than the accompanying Civil/Survey drawings.

Task 2 - Coordinate the Data.

In this task you will relocate the Civil Base in the Architectural Data. To line up the data accurately you will need the exact coordinate translation and rotation. You can measure ahead of time in programs, such as AutoCAD by comparing the coordinates of points common to both files.

Alternatively, you can use the Scene Explorer to select all the XRef objects.

1. In the Scene Explorer (![icon] (Display None) and ![icon] (Display Object XRefs)), select all of the XRef objects in the list (use <Shift> and then select the first and last).

2. With these XRef objects selected, select **Group>Group** from the menu bar.

3. In the Group dialog box, set the *Group name* to **Site XRef** and click **OK**.

4. In the Main Toolbar, click  (Select and Move). In the Reference Coordinate System, select **World**, as shown in Figure 3–47. Click (Use Transform Coordinate Center).

Figure 3–47

The translation coordinates have already been measured in AutoCAD.

5. In the Status Bar, verify that (Absolute Mode) is displayed. In the *Transform Type-in* area, set the following, as shown in Figure 3–48:

- *X:* **-197'4"**
- *Y:* **-30'0"**
- *Z:* **-4'11"**

Figure 3–48

6. Press <Enter>.

7. In the Main Toolbar, click (Select Object) to exit the **Move** transform operation.

8. Click (Zoom Extents All).

9. In the **Perspective** viewport, change the Standard visual display to **High Quality** to display the materials.

10. In the **Perspective** viewport, use 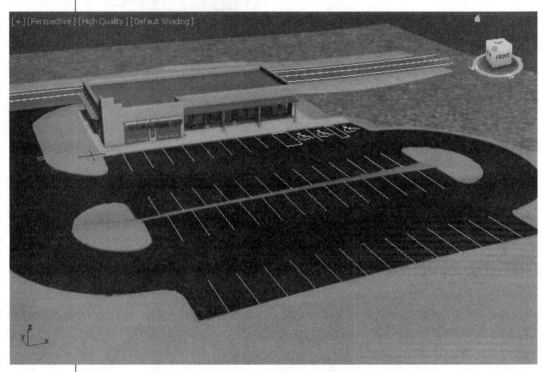 (Orbit Point of Interest) and click to place a point on the building and then orbit around that point. Using **Pan** and **Zoom**, zoom into the parking lot and building area (as shown in Figure 3–49), and verify that the building is located on the building pad. Although the XREF had a different Unit Scale (feet), it scaled correctly to the active scene (in inches).

Figure 3–49

11. Save your work as **MyArchitectural Scene.max**.

Task 3 - Merging Objects.

---

1. Expand **Application Menu>Import>Merge**. In the Merge File dialog box, select **Light Poles for Project1.max** from the *...\scenes* folder. Click **Open**.

2. In the Merge dialog box, click **All**, as shown in Figure 3–50. Click **OK**.

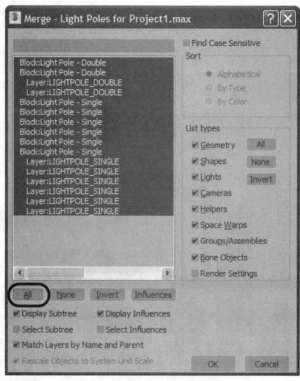

Figure 3–50

Merge enables both objects to have the same name, Skip ignores the incoming object, and Delete Old removes the original object.

3. The Duplicate Name dialog box opens, prompting you that an object with the same name already exists in the scene. Select **Apply to all Duplicates** and click **Auto-Rename**.

4. The light poles are displayed in the scene, as shown in Figure 3–51.

Figure 3–51

5. Save your work.

Chapter Review Questions

1. The following file types can be linked to the current Autodesk 3ds Max scene:

   a. .DWG, .OBJ, .APF, .FBX

   b. .DWG, .DXF, .FBX, .RVT

   c. .DWG, .DXF, .MAX, .RVT

   d. .DWG, .OBJ, .FBX, .RVT

2. In the Manage Links dialog box, in the *Files* tab, which of the following options do you use to remove the link with the original linked file but maintain its geometry in the current scene?

   a. **Reload...**

   b. **Detach...**

   c. **Bind...**

3. Which command do you use to combine objects from a saved Autodesk 3ds Max scene (.MAX file) into your current .MAX scene?

   a. **Import**

   b. **Link**

   c. **Open**

   d. **Merge**

4. While linking Autodesk Revit files in the current Autodesk 3ds Max scene, which of the following options are provided in the Combine Entities List? (Select all that apply.)

   a. By Revit Material

   b. By Revit Layer

   c. As One Object

   d. By Revit Camera

5. When an entire .MAX scene is brought into the current scene using **XREF Scenes**, the XREF objects are selectable but cannot be modified.

   a. True

   b. False

Command Summary

Button	Command	Location
	Absolute Mode	• **Status Bar**
N/A	Asset Tracking	• **Application Menu:** References
N/A	Import	• **Application Menu:** Import
N/A	Link AutoCAD	• **Application Menu:** Import
N/A	Link FBX	• **Application Menu:** Import
N/A	Link Revit	• **Application Menu:** Import
N/A	Manage Links	• **Application Menu:** References
N/A	Merge	• **Application Menu:** Import
	Select by Name	• **Main Toolbar**
	Select Object	• **Main Toolbar**
	Use Transform Coordinate Center	• **Main Toolbar**
N/A	XRef Objects	• **Application Menu:** References
N/A	XRef Scene	• **Application Menu:** References

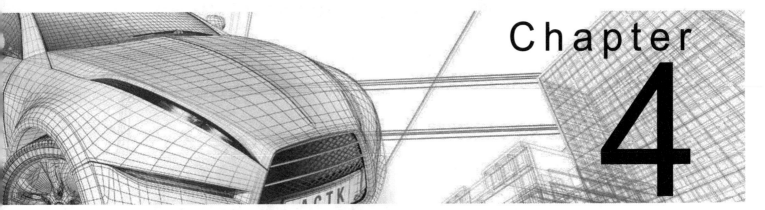

Basic Modeling Techniques

Autodesk® 3ds Max® is a rendering and animation software that allows for objects to be directly modeled in the software. Modeling can be accomplished using Primitive Objects or Polygon Modeling tools that are further manipulated using Modifiers and Transforms to move, rotate, and scale them. Additionally, sub-object modes can be used to further modify and control the resulting objects.

Learning Objectives in this Chapter

- Identify the various primitive objects provided with the software.
- Apply changes to the model geometry using modifiers.
- Move, rotate, scale, and place objects, and constrain the movement of the Transform tools.
- Modify objects at a sub-object level.
- Work with various coordinate systems and transform systems.
- Create copies of the same object using various Clone options and create a single unit by grouping multiple objects together.
- Create and modify objects using the Polygon modeling tools.
- Review the status of the overall model and display information about the scene, such as polygon count, number of vertices, etc.

4.1 Model with Primitives

The Autodesk 3ds Max software enables you to create and adjust 3D geometry by creating a complex model from simple 3D objects called primitives, as shown in Figure 4–1.

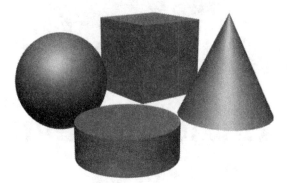

Figure 4–1

- All various types of already built objects (i.e., Standard Primitives, Extended Primitives, Compound Objects, etc.) are listed in the **Create>Geometry** Command Panel, as shown in Figure 4–2. Each of these categories consists of a group of objects that can be modeled and modified to create simple or complex objects.

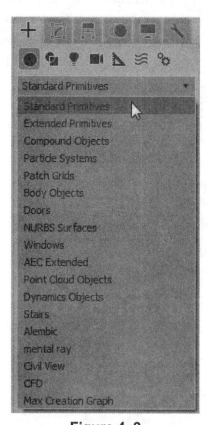

Figure 4–2

- You can model the selected 3D object directly in the viewport by using the mouse to locate and specify the starting point and then dragging the mouse to pick the locations (length, height, etc.).

- You can also enter the precise values in the edit boxes of the Keyboard Entry rollout in the Command Panel (as shown in Figure 4–3), and then click **Create**. You can either enter the values or use the spinner arrows to increase or decrease the values. After entering a value in a field, click in another field or press <Enter> to assign the values to the object.

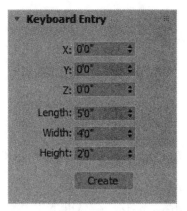

Figure 4–3

- You can also create geometry by modeling with modifiers, creating loft compound objects, or creating a 3D terrain from 2D contour objects.

Practice 4a

Modeling with Primitives

Practice Objective

- Create primitive objects by using standard primitives and the modify the object.

Estimated time for completion: 10 minutes

In this practice you will model the base for the parking lot light fixtures by modeling the object using a standard primitive and then modifying its parameters using the Modify panel in the Command Panel.

You must set the paths to locate the External files and Xrefs used in the practice. If you have not done this already, return to **Chapter 1: Introduction to Autodesk 3ds Max** and complete Task 1 to Task 3 in **Practice 1a: Organizing Folders and Working with the Interface**. You only have to set the user paths once.

*If a dialog box opens prompting you about a File Load: Mismatch, click **OK** to accept the default values.*

1. Open **Modeling with Primitives.max**. It is an empty base scene file.

2. Click in the **Top** viewport to make it active. The orientation of the object being created depends on the active viewport. For this practice, you will create the cylinder with its height in the Z-axis direction.

3. In the Command Panel, verify that the Create panel (![+]) >

    ![•] (Geometry) is selected with **Standard Primitives** displayed in the drop-down list, as shown in Figure 4–4. In the Object Type rollout, click **Cylinder**.

Figure 4–4

The 0,0,0 location corresponds to the default axes (center of the active grid) of the construction plane. Any value entered for X,Y, and Z, offsets the object by that number in the specified direction.

You can enter the values in their respective fields or use the spinner arrows to increase or decrease the values. After entering a value in a field, click in another edit field or press <Enter> to assign the values to the object.

4. Click on the Keyboard Entry title bar to expand the rollout. Leave the X, Y, Z coordinates at **0'0"**. The software places the base center of the cylinder at 0,0,0, location. Set the following, as shown in Figure 4–5:

   - *Radius*: **1'0"**

   - *Height*: **3'0"**

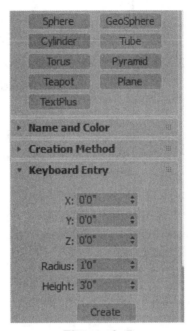

Figure 4–5

5. Click **Create**. Note that a cylinder is created and is displayed in all viewports.

Hint: Creating Objects

After creating an object, you cannot change the parameters in the Keyboard Entry rollout. Changing the parameters in the Keyboard Entry rollout and clicking **Create** adds a second object. If you created another object, in the Quick Access Toolbar, click ⤶ ▾ once to undo the creation of the second object. Use the Modify panel ( ) to change the parameters.

---

6. Click (Zoom Extents All) display the base more clearly. Note that it zooms into the cylinder in all of the viewports.

7. With the cylinder still selected, in the Command Panel, select the Modify panel (![]). At the top of the modifier list, in the *Name* field, rename the object from *Cylinder001* to **LP Base**.

8. In the Parameters rollout, set the following, as shown Figure 4–6. Note the effect on the geometry:
   - *Radius*: **1'6"**
   - *Height Segments*: **1**
   - *Cap Segments:* **1**
   - *Sides*: **20**

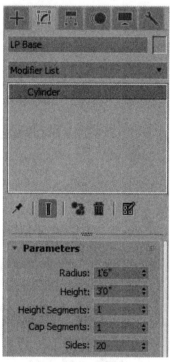

Figure 4–6

9. Select the Create panel (![+]) and in the Object Type rollout, click **Box** to create the anchor base plate. In the Keyboard Entry rollout set the following, as shown in Figure 4–7:
   - *X* coordinates: **0'0"**
   - *Y* coordinates: **0'0"**
   - *Z* coordinates: **3'0"**

   This will create the center of the base of the box at the 0,0,3 location, which is the top of the cylinder (the height of the cylinder is 3'-0").

   - *Length*: **1'4"**
   - *Width:* **1'4"**
   - *Height*: **0'2"**

10. Click **Create**. A box is created on top of the **LP Base** cylinder, as shown in Figure 4–7.

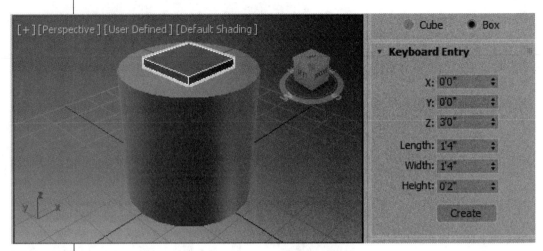

Figure 4–7

11. With the box still selected, select the Modify panel ( ) and rename the *Box001* as **LP Anchor Base**.

12. Save your work as **MyLight Pole.max**.

4.2 Modifiers and Transforms

The Autodesk 3ds Max software includes various modifiers and transforms that enable you to modify your geometry. They are described as follows:

Modifiers	• Adds geometric and property alterations to objects such as Extrude, Taper etc. • Listed in the Modifier Stack and their parameter values are available for adjustment afterwards.
Transforms	• Transforms are used to translate and scale objects in the scene. • Initiated by selecting the required buttons in the Main Toolbar or by using the Transform modes in the right-click quad menu. • Conducted by accessing a transform mode and entering new values, or graphically transforming objects on the screen. • Applied to objects after basic parameters and modifiers have been taken into account (except world-space modifiers). For example, if you scale a box, the **Length** parameter shown in the Modifier Stack does not take into account the effects of the scale transform.

- An object can have any number of modifiers, but only has a single set of transform values at any time.

- Transforms and almost all object and modifier parameters can be animated. For example, a walkthrough animation can be created using Move Transform to move the camera, its target, or both.

Modifiers

Any object that you create can be modified using the modifiers in the Modifier List, as shown in Figure 4–8. This list is located in

the Command Panel's Modify panel ( ) on top of the Modifier Stack. Click the down arrow to display the list and use the scroll bar to navigate through the complete list of modifiers. If you know the name of the modifier, you can enter the first letter to jump to that part of the selection list.

Modifiers are placed in groups and then listed alphabetically.

Figure 4–8

Transform Tools

The Transform tools are available in the Main Toolbar, as shown in Figure 4–9.

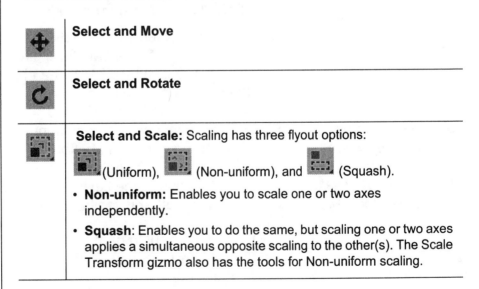

Figure 4–9

The available Transform tools are described as follows:

⊕	**Select and Move**
↻	**Select and Rotate**
▣	**Select and Scale:** Scaling has three flyout options: (Uniform), (Non-uniform), and (Squash). • **Non-uniform:** Enables you to scale one or two axes independently. • **Squash:** Enables you to do the same, but scaling one or two axes applies a simultaneous opposite scaling to the other(s). The Scale Transform gizmo also has the tools for Non-uniform scaling.

Select and Place / Select and Rotate: Enables you to locate and position/locate and rotate an object with respect to the surface of another object.

Right-click on **Select and Place** and use the Placement Settings dialog box (as shown in the image below) to customize how the objects are aligned. Right-clicking on **Select and Rotate** opens the same dialog box with the Rotate option selected.

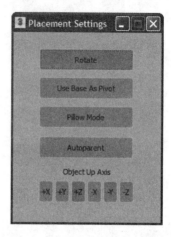

- **Rotate:** Enables you to click and drag an object to rotate around the local axis that is specified with the object Up Axis.
- **Use Base As Pivot:** Constrains the base of the object as the contact point with the surface of another object. By default, the pivot point of the object is used as the contact point.
- **Pillow Mode:** Enables you to move the objects around each other, but restricts them from intersecting. Useful when moving the object over uneven surfaces.
- **Autoparent:** Automatically links the object that is being placed as a child of the object it is being placed on, creating a hierarchical relationship.
- **Object Up Axis:** The selected up axis is used as the local axis on the object that is being moved.

Hint: XForm Modifier with Scale

To avoid problems in animation, it is recommended that you do not to use the Scale transform directly on objects. Instead, apply an XForm modifier to the objects and then **Scale** the XForm gizmo.

To display a toolbar, right-click anywhere on an empty space in the Main Toolbar and select the required toolbar.

- Transforms can be constrained to one or two axes by selecting one of the buttons in the Axis Constraints toolbar, as shown in Figure 4–10. However, it is more common to use the gizmos or the keyboard shortcuts to constrain the transforms. This toolbar is hidden by default.

- When a transform mode is active, a Transform gizmo displays (as shown in Figure 4–11) on the selected object on the screen.

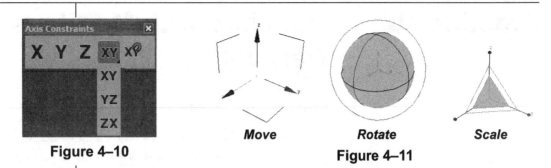

Figure 4–10

Move   **Rotate**   **Scale**

Figure 4–11

- Clicking and dragging over the gizmo enables you to perform the transform interactively on the screen. You can also constrain the transform by highlighting an axis handle on the gizmo before clicking and dragging.

- You can change the display size of the transform gizmo interactively in the viewport. Pressing <-> decreases its display size while as pressing <=> increases its display size.

- You can apply a transform accurately by entering (or using spinners) the required transform values in the *Transform Type-In* area, in the Status Bar, as shown in Figure 4–12.

X: 50.0   Y: -32.0   Z: 11.0

Figure 4–12

- In the Main Toolbar, right-click on **Transform** to open its Transform Type-In dialog box, as shown in Figure 4–13 for the Move transform. The Transform Type-In dialog box can be also be accessed by clicking ▣ (Settings) in the right-click quad menu, as shown in Figure 4–14.

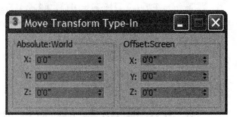

Figure 4–13

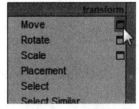

Figure 4–14

- Transform modes remain active until they are canceled by either clicking ◳ (Select Object) in the Main Toolbar or by pressing <Q>.

- Click ◳ (Select Object) after you have finished a transform to avoid accidentally moving, rotating, or scaling objects while making selections.

Practice 4b

Modeling with Modifiers and Transforms

Practice Objectives

- Create a 2D shape and then extrude it into a 3D object.
- Create primitive solids dynamically and modify objects.
- Transform objects to place them at the right location.

Estimated time for completion: fS30 minutes

In this practice you will refine the parking lot lighting fixture by creating a 2D shape and then extruding it to create a 3D object. You will create primitive objects dynamically in the viewport and then modify the objects using various modifiers in the Command Panel. You will also use Transforms (**Move**, **Rotate**, and **Place**) to place the created objects in the correct scene positions.

You must set the paths to locate the External files and Xrefs used in the practice. If you have not done this already, return to **Chapter 1: Introduction to Autodesk 3ds Max** and complete Task 1 to Task 3 in **Practice 1a: Organizing Folders and Working with the Interface**. You only have to set the user paths once.

Task 1 - Extrude and Adjust the Light Pole.

Modeling 3D geometry from 2D shapes is discussed in detail later in the Student Guide.

To create the rectangular light pole, create a 2D cross-section shape and then extrude it into a 3D object. This approach is another way to create 3D geometry.

1. Open **Modeling with Modifiers and Transforms.max**.

2. Verify that the **Top** viewport is active. In the Create panel (+), click (Shapes) to create 2D objects. Verify that *Splines* is displayed in the drop-down list and click **Rectangle**, as shown in Figure 4–15.

Figure 4–15

The corner radius fillets the corners of the rectangle.

3. In the Command Panel, expand the Keyboard Entry rollout and set the following:

   - *X:* **0'0"**
   - *Y:* **0'0"**
   - *Z:* **3'2"**
   - *Length:* **0'6"**
   - *Width:* **0'6"**
   - *Corner Radius:* **0'1"**

4. Click **Create**. A 2D rectangle is created on top of the base plate.

The modifiers in the Modifier drop-down list are placed in groups and then listed alphabetically. Use the scroll bar to navigate through the list.

5. With the rectangle still selected, select the Modify panel (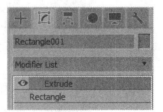). Expand the Modifier List (click down arrow) and select **Extrude** in the *OBJECT SPACE MODIFIERS* category. Note that Extrude is listed in the Modifier Stack above the Rectangle entry, as shown in Figure 4–16.

Figure 4–16

6. Rename the object *Rectangle001* as **LP Pole**.

7. In the Parameters rollout, set *Amount* to **15'0"** and leave the other parameters as the defaults. Note that the rectangle is extruded and becomes a rectangular-shaped pole.

8. In the **Perspective** viewport, use 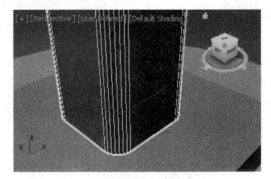 (Zoom) and **Pan** to get a closer look at the light pole, as shown in Figure 4–17. Note how much detail the light pole's fillet adds to the model.

Figure 4–17

Hint: Simple Models

If the object is to be used only as a background item, you should remove any unnecessary detail. Keeping models simple reduces the file size and speeds up software performance and rendering times.

Although the Extrude modifier is listed directly above the Rectangle object in the Modifier Stack, the rectangle's parameters are still accessible and can be changed anytime.

9. In the Modify panel (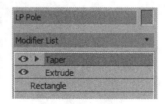), in the Modifier Stack, select **Rectangle**. It is highlighted as dark gray. In the Interpolation rollout, change *Steps* to **2** and press <Enter>, as shown in Figure 4–18. The fillet divisions are reduced, as shown in Figure 4–19.

Figure 4–18	Figure 4–19

10. Save your work as **MyLightPole01.max**.

Task 2 - Taper the Light Pole.

Use the scroll bar to navigate to Taper near the bottom of the list.

1. In the Modifier Stack, select **Extrude** (so that the next modifier *Taper* is applied after it). In the Modifier List, select **Taper**. Note that the *Taper* displays above the *Extrude* in the Modifier Stack, as shown in Figure 4–20. The Modifier Stack lists modifiers in reverse historical order.

Figure 4–20

2. With Taper selected, in the Parameters rollout, set *Amount* to **-0.5** and press <Enter>. You can still adjust the original **Rectangle** and **Extrude** parameters by selecting them in the Modifier Stack.

3. Click 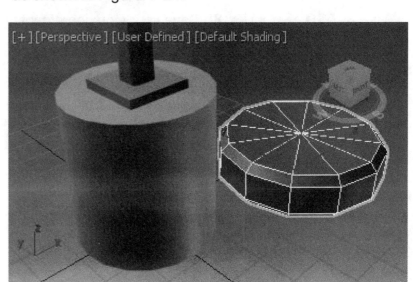 (Zoom Extents All) to see all of the objects in the viewports. Note the taper on the pole towards the top.

4. Save your work incrementally as **MyLightPole02.max**.

Task 3 - Create the Fixture Housing and Globe.

1. In the **Perspective** viewport, zoom in so that the LP Base object is displayed.

2. In the Create panel ( )> (Geometry), in the Standard Primitives drop-down list, select **Extended Primitives** as a sub-category. In the Object Type rollout, click **ChamferCyl**.

3. In the **Perspective** viewport, next to the base (LP Base), click and drag the left mouse button to size the radius to roughly **2'0"** (Note the Parameters rollout in the Command Panel where the Radius changes interactively as you move the cursor). After releasing the mouse button, move the cursor up the screen slightly to give the cylinder a height of approximately **1'0"**. Click a second time to set the cylinder height. Then move the cursor up and down the screen until you can roughly define a **0'2"** fillet. Complete the object creation process with a third click. The object should display as shown in Figure 4–21.

You do not have to be accurate because you will modify the dimensions later.

[+][Perspective][User Defined][Default Shading]

Figure 4–21

4. With the **ChamferCyl** object still selected, in the Command Panel, select the Modify panel ( ). Name the object **LP Fixture Housing** and modify the parameters, as shown in Figure 4–22.

5. In the Create panel ( ), verify that ● (Geometry) is selected. In the drop-down list, select **Standard Primitives.** In the Object Type rollout, click **Sphere** to create the fixture's globe. Click and drag anywhere on the screen to size a sphere of approximately **1'0"** in radius. Select the Modify panel ( ) and assign the parameters, as shown in Figure 4–23.

*A value of **0.5** for the hemisphere creates half a sphere.*

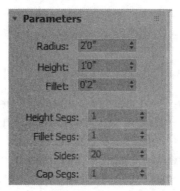

Figure 4–22

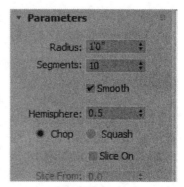

Figure 4–23

6. Select **Squash**. This option generates more faces and creates a smoother appearance.

7. Rename the hemisphere **LP Fixture Globe**.

8. Save your work incrementally as **MyLightPole03.max**.

Task 4 - Use Transforms to Position Objects.

---

1. Select the **LP Fixture Housing** (the chamfered cylinder) and in the Main Toolbar, click ✛ (Select and Move).

2. In the Main Toolbar, set the *Reference Coordinate System* to **World** and click  (Use Pivot Point Center), as shown in Figure 4–24.

Figure 4–24

3. The Move gizmo displays over the object, as shown in Figure 4–25. Move the fixture housing by clicking and dragging the gizmo's axis handles and plane handles. By default, the gizmo displays at the object's pivot point, located at the bottom center for this object.

Figure 4–25

*The ▣ (Absolute Mode) toggles with ▤ (Offset Mode). If the values are entered in **Offset Mode**, they are added to the current coordinates. This option is useful if you want to move an object a certain distance from the current position.*

4. To position the object correctly, verify that ▣ (Absolute Mode Transform Type-In) is displayed in the Status Bar. Set the following in the type in edit boxes, as shown in Figure 4–26:
   * *X*: **0'0"**
   * *Y*: **-6'0"**
   * *Z*: **19'0"**

Figure 4–26

5. Click ⏣ (Zoom Extents All) to display all of the objects in the viewports. In the **Left** viewport, note that the **LP Fixture Housing** (the chamfered cylinder) has now moved to the top right side of the light pole assembly.

6. As the **Move** transform and **Absolute Mode** are already active, select **LP Fixture Globe** (hemisphere) and enter the same X, Y, Z coordinates as you did for LP Fixture Housing (*X: 0'0"*, *Y: -6'0"*, *Z: 19'0"*). The half globe moves inside the fixture housing.

7. With the half globe still selected, in the Main Toolbar, click

   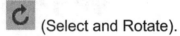 (Select and Rotate).

8. In the Status Bar, the *X, Y, Z Transform Type-In* fields display the current rotations of **0**. Set *X* to **180** and note the position of the globe is inverted. The object should display as shown in Figure 4–27 in the **Left** viewport.

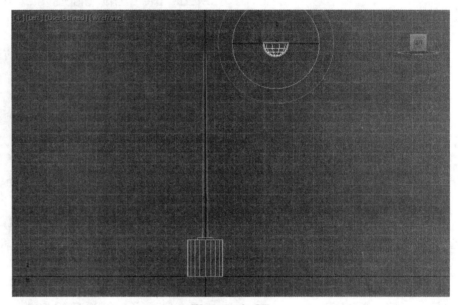

Figure 4–27

9. Click (Select Object) or press <Q> to end the **Rotate** transform to avoid rotating objects accidentally.

10. Save your work incrementally as **MyLightPole04.max**.

Task 5 - Use Additional Transforms to Place Objects.

You will create a nut and bolt group and place it on the top surface of the anchor plate.

1. In the **Perspective** viewport, zoom into LP Base (base cylinder).

2. In the Create panel (**+**), ensure that ● (Geometry) and **Standard Primitives** as a sub-category is selected. In the Object Type rollout, click **Cylinder**.

3. In the **Perspective** viewport, using the mouse, create a cylinder that is smaller than the base object.

4. With the new cylinder selected, select the Modify panel (⟨⌐⟩). Rename the new cylinder as **LP Nut** and assign the parameters shown in Figure 4–28.

Figure 4–28

5. With **LP Nut** still selected, click ⟨⟩ (Zoom Extents All Selected) so that it is zoomed in on all the viewports.

6. Click in the **Top** viewport to activate it and clear the selection.

7. In the Command Panel>Create (**+**)> ● (Geometry), verify that **Standard Primitives** is selected. In the Object Type rollout, click **Cylinder**, and in the **Top** viewport create a small cylinder next to LP Nut (6 sided cylinder).

8. With the new cylinder selected, select the Modify panel

( 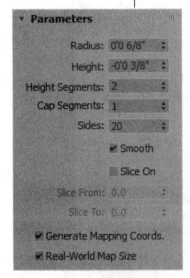). Rename the new cylinder as **LP Bolt** and assign the parameters, as shown in Figure 4–29. The bolt displays as shown in Figure 4–30.

Figure 4–29

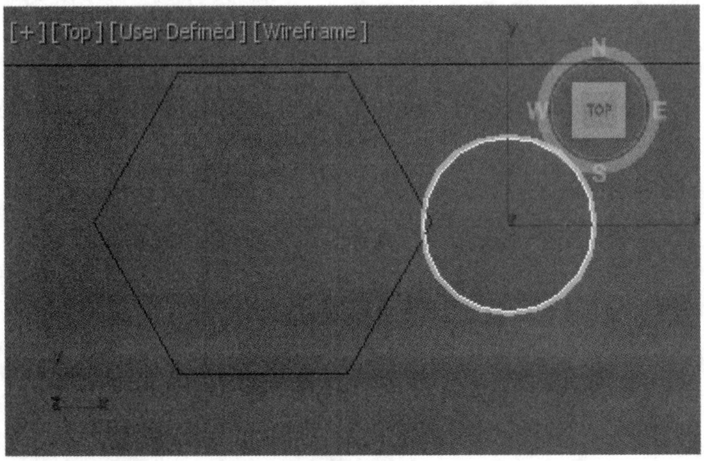

Figure 4–30

9. With **LP Bolt** selected, in the Main Toolbar, click ⬤ (Select and Place).

10. In the **Perspective** viewport, click and hold ✥ over the selected **LP Bolt** object. While holding, drag it over the **LP Nut** object. Note that when you move the **LP Bolt** object along the sides of the **LP Nut** object, it automatically flips on its side, as shown in Figure 4–31. Drag the selected **LP Bolt** object along the top surface of the **LP Nut** object and note how it flips so that its base touches the top surface. Place the **LP Bolt** object at the approximate center of the **LP Nut** object, as shown in Figure 4–32.

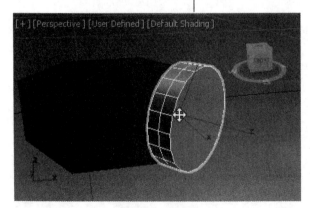

Figure 4–31

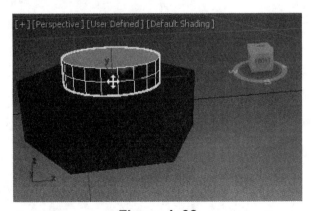

Figure 4–32

11. Click (Select Object) in the Main Toolbar to exit the Placement command.

12. Select both the **LP Nut** and the **LP Bolt** objects (<Ctrl>) and select **Group>Group**. In the Group dialog box, name the grouped object as **LP Anchor**.

13. Activate the **Perspective** viewport (if not already active) and click (Maximize Viewport Toggle), or use <Alt>+<W> to maximize the viewport.

14. Zoom and pan so that you can clearly see the **LP Anchor** group and the **LP Anchor Base**, as shown in Figure 4–33.

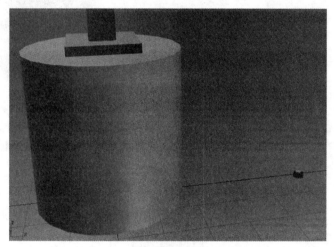

Figure 4–33

15. In the Main Toolbar, click (Select and Place). Click and hold on the **LP Anchor** group and then drag it on top of the LP Anchor Base plate object. Place the **LP Anchor** group near one of the corners of the plate, as shown in Figure 4–34.

- Note that the group object is placed halfway inside the LP Anchor Base object.as shown in Figure 4–35.

Figure 4–34

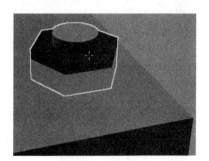

Figure 4–35

16. Right-click on 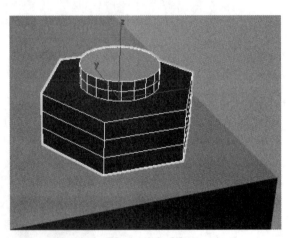 (Select and Place). In the Placement Settings dialog box, select **Pillow Mode** to activate it.

17. Click on the **LP Anchor** group object and slightly move it. Note how its base now touches the top surface of the anchor plate. Place it in one of the corners, as shown in Figure 4–36.

Figure 4–36

*It might be easier to copy the object in the **Top** viewport.*

18. Hold <Shift> and then click and drag a copy of the **LP Anchor** group object to place it near the next corner of the plate. Click **OK** in the Clone Options dialog box.

19. While still holding <Shift>, place two more copies of the objects at the other corners of the plate. A total of four **LP Anchor** group objects should now be placed at the four corners of the anchor plate, as shown in Figure 4–37.

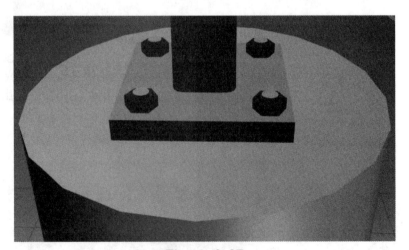

Figure 4–37

20. Save your work incrementally as **MyLightPole05.max**.

4.3 Sub-Object Mode

Many of the objects and modifiers available in the Autodesk 3ds Max software contain sub-objects that can be independently adjusted through transforms and special modifier controls. These sub-objects are adjusted through a special Autodesk 3ds Max state called Sub-object mode. For example, the **Taper** modifier in the column has Gizmo and Center sub-objects (as shown in Figure 4–38) that can be adjusted to position the Taper.

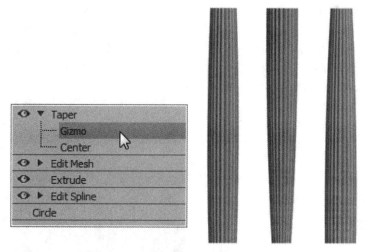

Figure 4–38

Working in Sub-Object Mode

Sub-object mode is activated through the Modifier Stack. You can expand the modifier by clicking ▶ (arrow) next to the object or modifier that has sub-objects, then clicking the sub-object level to be adjusted.

- You can only have one object selected to enter the Sub-object mode. When Sub-object mode is active, the sub-object level (or the modifier name if the sub-object list has not been expanded) is highlighted in blue (with the default user interface settings).

- You cannot clear the currently selected object while in Sub-object mode. Therefore, to edit another object you must first exit Sub-object mode. To do so, click the level of the Modifier Stack presently highlighted in yellow to toggle it off.

Geometric Edits through Sub-objects

*You can also use the **Polygon Modeling** tools in the ribbon to perform modeling and use modifiers with the **Edit Poly** technique.*

A whole range of explicit geometric changes can be made through Sub-object mode.

- Objects imported into the Autodesk 3ds Max software often take the shape of **Editable Splines** or **Editable Meshes**. These have sub-object controls that can be edited directly. For example, a group of vertices in an Editable Mesh can be selected, moved, or deleted separate to the rest of the geometry.

- Many Autodesk 3ds Max objects can also have the controls applied to them through an **Edit Spline** modifier (for 2D objects) or an **Edit Mesh** or **Edit Poly** modifier (for 3D objects). This includes geometry linked to AutoCAD drawings that list only as *Linked Geometry* in the Modify panel.

- Figure 4–39 shows an example of a Box that is being edited geometrically by lowering two of its vertices with the **Move** transform.

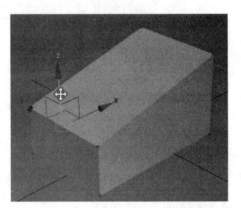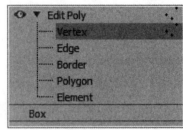

Figure 4–39

- The **Edit Mesh** modifier is best for objects based on a triangular mesh, such as triangulated terrain models.

- The **Edit Poly** modifier is best for objects with faces of more than three vertices, such as rectangular objects.

- To easily review and make changes, it is recommended to adjust objects through their core parameters (such as the length, width, and height of a primitive) and standard modifiers. When required, you can use Spline, Mesh, and Poly for editing.

New in 2017

- A single hotkey can be used to easily and quickly toggle between the various sub-object levels. This speeds up your overall modeling workflow. To use this, to hover your cursor over the required sub-object level and press the hotkey.

Geometric Sub-Objects

The Editable Spline, Editable Mesh, and Editable Poly objects (and any other object with an Edit Spline, Edit Mesh, or Edit Poly Modifier applied to it) share a number of common Sub-object modes. These are described as follows:

	Vertex: The individual 3D points that define an object (Edit Spline, Edit Mesh, or Edit Poly).
	Segment: A single line or curve segment of an Editable Spline.
	Spline: A series of one or more connected Editable Spline segments. Segments are considered connected if they share a common vertex.
	Edge: The linear segments connecting vertices with Edit Mesh or Edit Poly. Three edges are shown in the button.
	Face: The triangular surface area defined by three edges (Edit Mesh only).
	Border: A series of edges that define an opening in an Editable Poly (only).
	Polygon: Enables you to work with coplanar faces (Edit Mesh) or a defined polygon (Edit Poly).
	Element: Enables you to work with all of the faces or polygons that form a contiguous whole (Edit Mesh or Edit Poly).

Smoothing

One of the most important properties controlled at the face or polygon sub-object level is smoothing. Figure 4–40 shows the same geometry without and with smoothing applied.

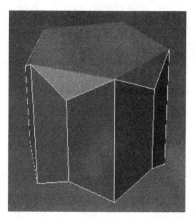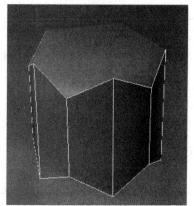

Figure 4–40

- The Autodesk 3ds Max software can have two adjacent faces appear to be smooth or faceted. When smoothed, faces display smooth but the software does not adjust the actual geometry.

- Smoothing is controlled by smoothing groups. Each face or polygon can be a member of up to 32 smoothing groups. If two adjacent faces share a common smoothing group, the software attempts to blend the surfaces together to disguise the edge that separates them.

- Figure 4–41 show an example of the smoothing groups for the selected faces that controls polygon smoothing groups (in Edit Mesh and Edit Poly). When some but not all selected faces fall into a particular smoothing group, that group's box is shown without a number.

Figure 4–41

- Alternatively, the **Auto Smooth** feature automatically places adjacent selected faces into smoothing groups if their normal vectors have an angle of separation equal to or less than the Auto Smooth angle.

Practice 4c

Modeling with Edit Poly in Sub-Object Mode

Practice Objective

Estimated time for completion: 15 minutes

- Modify objects at a sub-object level.

In this practice you will add some detail to the concrete base of the light pole by chamfering (beveling) the outside top of the cylinder and then add smoothing to it.

You must set the paths to locate the External files and Xrefs used in the practice. If you have not done this already, return to **Chapter 1: Introduction to Autodesk 3ds Max** and complete Task 1 to Task 3 in **Practice 1a: Organizing Folders and Working with the Interface**. You only have to set the user paths once.

1. Open **Edit Poly in Sub-Object Mode.max**.

2. In the **Perspective** viewport, select **LP Base** and click (Zoom Extents Selected). Use (Zoom) and (Orbit) to display a base similar to that shown in Figure 4–42.

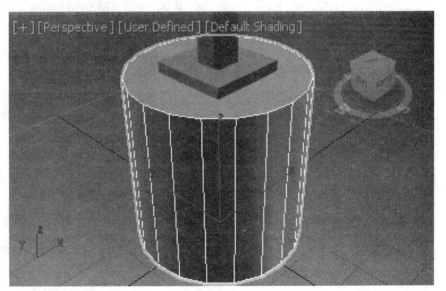

Figure 4–42

3. In the Modify panel ( ), select **Edit Poly** from the Modifier List. Click ▶ (arrow sign) for Edit Poly to display its Sub-object modes. Select **Polygon** to activate the Sub-object mode at the Polygon level. The highlighting in the Modifier Stack indicates that you are in the Polygon Sub-object mode, as shown in Figure 4–43.

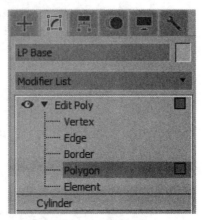

Figure 4–43

Hint: Using Modeling Tools in the Ribbon

You can also perform all of the commands using the **Polygon Modeling** tools in the Modeling ribbon. With the object selected, select the *Polygon Modeling* tab in the *Modeling* tab, in the ribbon. In the drop-down list, select **Apply Edit Poly**

Mod, as shown in Figure 4–44. Click ☐ for **Polygon** sub-object level. Note that the selections that you make in the ribbon are reflected in the Command Panel and vice-versa.

Figure 4–44

---

4. Select the polygon at the top of the cylinder, as shown in Figure 4–45. The selected polygon tuns red.

Figure 4–45

5. Creating a 1" bevel will raise the cylinder top by 1". In preparation, you will first lower the top of the cylinder by that same 1". In the Main Toolbar, click ✛ (Select and Move). Note that the Move gizmo only displays for the selected polygon.

6. In the Status Bar, click ⊞ (Absolute Mode Transform) to toggle it to ⟰ (Offset Mode Transform) and set Z to **-0'1"**. Press <Enter>. The cylinder geometry is adjusted by moving the polygon down.

7. Right-click to activate the **Left** viewport (keeping the polygon selected) and zoom into the base area. Note that the base is not touching the base plate anymore.

*The rollouts in the Command Panel might extend below the display window. To scroll, hover the cursor over an empty gray area until it displays as a **Hand** icon, then hold and drag the cursor up or down to locate the required rollout.*

8. In the Command Panel, scroll down and locate the Edit Polygons rollout. Expand the Edit Polygons rollout, and next to **Bevel** click ▣ (Settings), as shown in Figure 4–46.

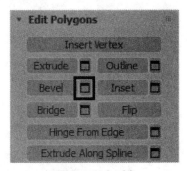

Figure 4–46

In the caddy display, when you select the edit box, its icon displays as a spinner and the edit name (Height or Outline) is displayed in addition to the modifier name (Bevel) at the top. You can enter new values in the edit box or use the spinner to change the values.

9. The caddy display opens on the screen, in the **Left** viewport. Hover the cursor over the 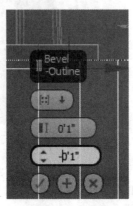 *Height* edit box and set its value to **0'1"** and an *Outline* of **-0'1"**, as shown in Figure 4–47. Click . Verify that the caddy display closes and the base is beveled, as shown in Figure 4–48.

Figure 4–47   **Figure 4–48**

10. To make the newly created faces smooth you will adjust the smoothing groups. While still in Polygon Sub-object mode, in the menu bar, expand **Edit** and select **Select All** to select all of the polygons in the base object.

11. In the Command Panel, scroll down and locate the Polygon: Smoothing Groups rollout. Click **Clear All** to remove the existing smoothing. Set the *AutoSmooth angle* to **30**, as shown in Figure 4–49. Click **Auto Smooth**.

Figure 4–49

12. To end Sub-object mode, in the Command Panel>Modifier Stack, click the **Polygon** that is highlighted in blue to clear the selection.

*To display the smoothing effect, toggle off **Edged Faces** in the Viewport Shading label, if it is enabled.*

13. To display the effect of the smoothing change, in the **Perspective** viewport, clear the object selection by clicking anywhere in empty space. The 30 degrees angle enabled the newly created faces to smooth across each other, but the faces are not smoothed with the top of the cylinder, as shown in Figure 4–50. This is the chamfered appearance that was originally intended. A larger smoothing angle enables the chamfered faces between the top and sides to smooth out.

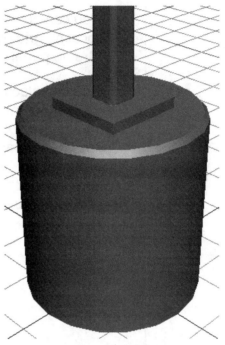

Figure 4–50

14. In the Main Toolbar, click (Select Object) to end the Move Transform mode as a precaution to avoid moving objects accidentally while making further selections.

15. Save your work as **MyLightPole06.max**.

4.4 Reference Coordinate Systems and Transform Centers

All geometry in the Autodesk 3ds Max software is referenced to a base coordinate system called the Home Grid.

- You can create your own coordinate systems by creating and locating grid objects, available in the Helpers Category in the Create panel.

- You can also create objects in the Auto-grid mode, which creates a temporary 3D Grid aligned to the object directly under the crosshairs. The **AutoGrid** option can be found in the Create panel, in the Object Type rollout, as shown Figure 4–51. If you hold <Alt>, the AutoGrid remains available for future use. If you use AutoGrid without any key pressed, the grid disappears after object creation.

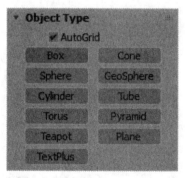

Figure 4–51

Reference Coordinate Systems

Enhanced
in 2017

The current Reference Coordinate System might differ depending on which view you are in and which transform is active. It is recommended that new users stay in the **World** system to avoid confusion from changing axis labels. By default, the Reference Coordinate system is set to **View**.

- In the Main Toolbar, the options listed in the Reference Coordinate System drop-down list (shown Figure 4–52) control how transform values are read. Note that A single grid is active at any one time.

Figure 4–52

- In the **World** coordinate system the X, Y, and Z axes are interpreted based on the Home Grid, even if a user-defined grid is active. To use the coordinates of the active user-defined grid instead, select the **Grid** option.

- In the **Screen** coordinate system the X-axis is always measured along the bottom of the viewport, the Y-axis is always measured along the side, and the Z-axis is measured perpendicularly out of the screen.

- The **View** system is a combination of **World** and **Screen**. In an orthographic view, the **Screen** system is used, while in other views the **World** system is used.

- The **Local** system considers the coordinate system of the selected object. Note that only the Z axis of the object is considered, which can cause unpredictable changes along the X and Y axis.

- The **Grid** system is based on the currently active grid and uses its coordinate system.

- The **Working** option enables you to use the Working Pivot. It is a temporary modeling pivot tool you create from the Hierarchy panel's *Pivot* tab. Generally you need to assign a hotkey to **Use Working Pivot** and **Edit Working Pivot** to make them functional tools.

- The **Local Aligned** option is used with sub-objects in an editable mesh or poly. It calculates all three (X,Y,Z) axes by using the coordinate system of the selected object. It can be used when multiple sub-objects need to be adjusted at the same time.

- The **Pick** option enables you to pick any object in the viewport or from a list and use the reference coordinate system of that object as the reference for transforms. You can use XRef objects with the **Pick** option.

Transform Centers

Transforms are applied through a Transform Center point indicated by the Transform gizmo. The Transform Center options are available in the Main Toolbar, in the Transform Center flyout, as shown Figure 4–53.

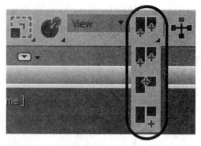

Figure 4–53

 Pivot Point Center: Transforms are applied through each selected object's pivot point. Pivots often default to the bottom center or geometric center of objects. Pivot points can be adjusted through controls in the Hierarchy panel. Select this option if you want to rotate many objects, each around its own center.

 Selection Center: Transforms are applied through the geometric center of all selected objects.

 Transform Coordinate Center: Transforms are applied through the origin point of the current Reference Coordinate System. For example, if you wanted to rotate objects around their individual pivot points about the World Z-axis, you would select the World Coordinate System and Pivot Point Transform Center. Alternatively, to rotate all of the objects around the origin, you would do the same with the Transform Coordinate Center.

- The Transform Center might automatically change depending on whether one or multiple objects are selected, and on the active transform.

- The Reference Coordinate System and Transform Center can be held using **Constant** in the Preference Settings dialog box, in the *General* tab, as shown in Figure 4–54.

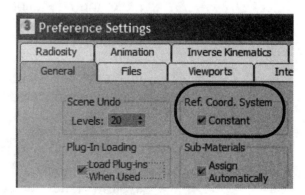

Figure 4–54

4.5 Cloning and Grouping

Cloning

In Autodesk 3ds Max, objects can be duplicated using the **Clone** option (**Edit>Clone**), which opens the Clone Options dialog box, as shown in Figure 4–55. To access the **Clone** command, an object should be selected first, otherwise it remains grayed out.

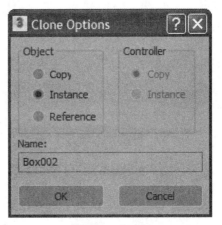

Figure 4–55

Copy	Makes an independent copy without a dynamic link to the source object.
Instance	Makes the duplicate and original Instances of each other. Changes made to any Instance automatically update all Instances, including changes to Modifiers, property changes, and material assignments (except for Transforms).
Reference	A one-directional link where changes made to the original object affect the duplicate. You can apply Modifiers to the Reference without affecting the Source object.

- You can also clone an object by holding <Shift> while transforming through a click and drag on the Transform gizmo. In this procedure, you have an additional option for specifying the number of copies you want to make, which are arrayed at the same Transform value.

- The *Controller* area in the Clone Options dialog box applies to objects in a group or hierarchy.

- Objects that are instanced or referenced display with the Modifier Stack text in bold type. Instancing or referencing can be disabled by right-clicking on the item in the Modifier Stack and selecting **Make Unique**.

Grouping

Enhanced in 2017

Grouping enables multiple objects to be treated as a single unit, for selection and transforms. The various grouping options are available in the **Group** menu, as shown in Figure 4–56.

Figure 4–56

Group	Creates a group out of all of the currently selected objects. Groups can have other groups inside them (nested groups).
Ungroup	Dissolves any selected groups back into their constituent objects.
Open/Close	Enables you to select, modify, and transform individual group members as if they were not in a group. The group is still defined; however, it can be Closed to treat the objects as a single unit again.
Open Recursively	Enables you to select, modify, and transform individual members at any level in a group. The group is still defined. Use the **Close** command to restore the original group.
Attach	Enables you to add another object to a group. First select the objects to be attached, then select the **Attach** option in the **Group** menu. When prompted, select a closed group to which to add the objects.
Detach	Enables you to remove selected objects from a group. You must first open the group to select the objects to be detached.
Explode	Dissolves the selected groups and any groups nested inside them.
Assembly	Special case object grouping that are intended for creation of lighting assemblies called luminaires, and for character assemblies.

- Groups are located in the Command Panel's Modify panel, with group name in bold type, and a blank Modifier Stack. The Modifier Stack of individual group members is displayed if it is opened.

- Groups can be copied, instanced, and referenced.

- It is recommended not to use grouping on objects that are linked into a hierarchy and then animated.

Practice 4d

Modeling with Coordinate Systems

Practice Objective

- Create an object and modify the parameters.

Estimated time for completion: 10 minutes

In this practice you will add the Light Pole Mounting Arm to the Light Pole model by creating the model and modifying the parameters.

You must set the paths to locate the External files and Xrefs used in the practice. If you have not done this already, return to **Chapter 1: Introduction to Autodesk 3ds Max** and complete Task 1 to Task 3 in **Practice 1a: Organizing Folders and Working with the Interface**. You only have to set the user paths once.

*If a dialog box opens prompting you about a File Load: Mismatch, click **OK** to accept the default values.*

1. Open **Modeling with Coordinate Systems.max**.

2. Activate the **Front** viewport, if required.

3. Use a combination of **Zoom** and **Pan** to zoom into the top portion, as shown in Figure 4–57. If the Grid is showing in the **Front** view, in the Viewport label, click [+] and select **Show Grids** to clear it. Alternatively, you can press <G> to toggle the grid on or off.

4. In the Create panel (➕)> ⬤ (Geometry), click **Box**. Use the cursor to create a small box near the top of the light pole with approximate dimensions for *Length*, *Width*, and *Height*, as shown in Figure 4–58.

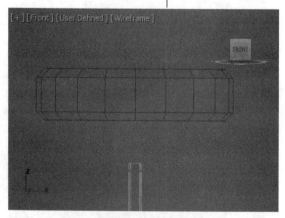

Figure 4–57

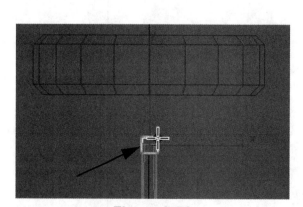

Figure 4–58

The object creation orientation depends on the viewport in which it is being created.

5. With this box still selected, in the Modify panel ( ), in the Parameters rollout, set the following, as shown in Figure 4–59:

- *Name:* **LP Mounting Arm**
- *Length*: **0'3"**
- *Width:* **0'3"**
- *Height*: **4'6"**
- *Height Segs*: **6**

6. In the **Perspective** view, use a combination of **Zoom**, **Pan**, and **Orbit** to zoom into the **LP Mounting Arm**, as shown in Figure 4–59. Since you created the box in the **Front** viewport, the height of the box is measured perpendicular to the view, in this case along the world Y-axis.

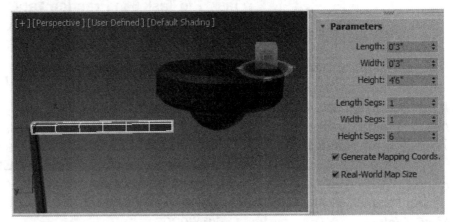

Figure 4–59

7. With the LP Mounting arm selected, click (Select and Move). In the Status Bar, set the transform mode to

 (Absolute mode) and set the location of the mounting arm with the Z value at **18'0"**, as shown in Figure 4–60.

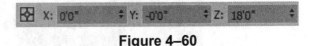

Figure 4–60

8. In the Modifier List, select **Bend** to curve the arm to the housing. In the Parameters, set the following:

- *Bend Angle*: **30** degrees
- *Direction:* **-90** degrees

Note that the arm is bent and extended.

9. Save your work as **MyLightPole07.max**.

Practice 4e

Cloning and Grouping

Practice Objectives

- Create a single unit of multiple objects.
- Clone an instance of the group and modify it.

Estimated time for completion: 10 minutes

In this practice you will complete the model of the light pole using Cloning and Groups. You will first create a single unit by grouping multiple objects. You will then clone an instance of a group and modify the instance so that the original object is modified as well.

You must set the paths to locate the External files and Xrefs used in the practice. If you have not done this already, return to **Chapter 1: Introduction to Autodesk 3ds Max** and complete Task 1 to Task 3 in **Practice 1a: Organizing Folders and Working with the Interface**. You only have to set the user paths once.

1. Open **Cloning and Grouping.max**.

*If the Scene Explorer is not displayed, select **Tools>Scene Explorer** or click* ▦ *(Toggle Scene Explorer) in the Main Toolbar.*

2. In the Scene Explorer, (■ (Display None) and ● (Display Geometry) to display the scene geometry only. Select **LP Fixture Housing**, **LP Fixture Globe**, and **LP Mounting Arm** (use <Ctrl> to select multiple items), as shown in Figure 4–61. Note that the three items are selected in the viewports.

3. In the menu bar, select **Group>Group** to combine the three objects together into a single, selectable unit. In the Group dialog box, name the group **LP Fixture**, as shown in Figure 4–61. Click **OK**.

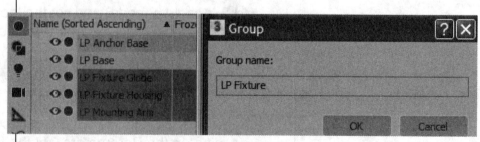

Figure 4–61

4. In the Scene Explorer, note that the group name is identified with the 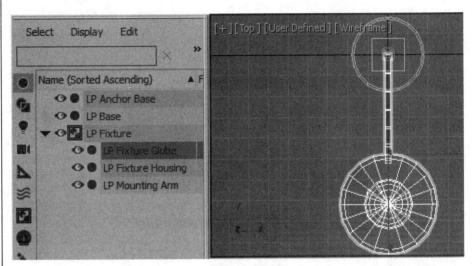 symbol and the geometry objects displayed under it, as shown in Figure 4–62. In the Scene Explorer, select the group (**LP Fixture**) and note that all the three objects are selected in the viewport. Similarly, select **LP Fixture Globe** in the Scene Explorer and note that the three objects are still selected in the viewports, as shown in Figure 4–62.

Figure 4–62

5. In the Scene Explorer, select the group (**LP Fixture**) and then in the menu bar, select **Group>Open**. The group remains intact but a pink bounding box encloses the group objects indicating that it is an open group. Here, you can select, manipulate, and transform the three component objects individually.

6. With one or more of the group components selected, in the menu bar, select **Group>Close**. The pink bounding box is cleared with all of the group objects selected, indicating that it is treated as a single object and that the components cannot be modified separately.

7. With the **LP Fixture** group selected, in the menu bar, select **Edit>Clone**.

8. In the Clone Options dialog box, in the *Object* area, select **Instance** (if not already selected) leaving all other options at their default values, as shown in Figure 4–63. Click **OK**.

   • The original and the copy now directly overlay each other. Note that in the Scene Explorer, another group with the name **LP Fixture001** is created.

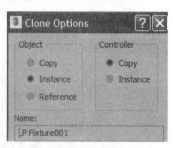

Figure 4–63

9. In the Scene Explorer, select **LP Fixture001**.

10. In the **Left** viewport, zoom and pan to the selected group.

11. Right-click in the **Front** viewport to activate it and keep the selection intact.

12. In the Main Toolbar, click ⟳ (Select and Rotate).

13. The position of the Transform gizmo is dependent on the active **Use Transform**. In the Main Toolbar, in the Use Transform flyout, click (Use Pivot Point Center). Note in the **Left** viewport that the Rotate transform gizmo is in the center of the group, as shown in Figure 4–64. This rotation will not place **LP Fixture001** in the correct position.

14. Verify that the **Front** viewport is still active. In the Use Transform flyout, click (Use Transform Coordinate Center). In the **Left** viewport, note that the Rotation gizmo moves to the base of the left side, as shown in Figure 4–65.

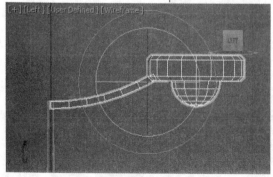

Figure 4–64

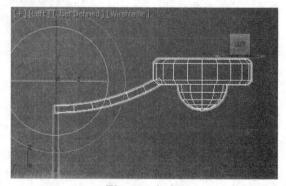

Figure 4–65

15. In the Status Bar, in the *Transform Type-In* area, set *Z* to **180.0** (as shown in Figure 4–66) to rotate **LP Fixture001** by **180°** about the Z axis. Press <Enter>. The round off error might result in a -180° value. This is a common occurrence and is not indicative of a problem.

Figure 4–66

- The cloned group is moved opposite to the original group, as shown in Figure 4–67.

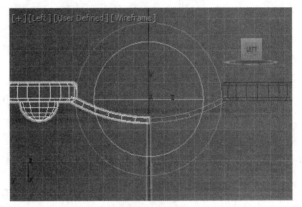

Figure 4–67

16. Click  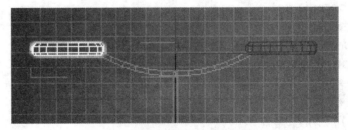 (Select Object) to end the Rotate transform mode.

17. To verify that the groups are instanced, with **LP Fixture001** selected, select **Group>Open**. A pink bounding box displays around the group.

18. In the Scene Explorer, select **LP Fixture Housing001**.

19. In the Modify panel (), in the Parameters rollout, reduce the *Height* from **1'0"** to **0' 8"**. Both Fixture Housings update and have reduced height as shown in Figure 4–68.

Figure 4–68

20. Select **Group>Close** to close **LP Fixture001**.

21. Save your work as **MyLightPole08.max**

4.6 Polygon Modeling Tools in the Ribbon

The Autodesk 3ds Max software is a powerful environment for creating a variety of 3D models. The box modeling technique, also called polygon modeling or mesh modeling, is an interactive method for creating vertices, edges, faces, and surfaces in a free form way.

- Box modeling can be performed using either the **Edit Mesh** or **Edit Poly** modifiers, or be converted to an **Editable Mesh** or **Editable Poly** object. Any of these methods give you the access to the sub-object levels required to do this type of modeling.

- The **Edit Poly** modifier is a commonly used modeling technique, although you can convert the object to an editable mesh or editable poly object and discard the modifier. You can also use the **Edit Mesh** modifier which is the most stable.

- The Modeling ribbon (*Modeling* tab) provides easy access to polygon modeling tools, including the editing and modification tools used at sub-object level. The ribbon contains many of the commonly used tools that are present in the Command Panel's Modify panel, at the Edit Poly sub-object level. In the *Modeling* tab, the polygon modeling and modifying tools are organized into panels.

- By default, the ribbon can be minimized to the panel tiles by clicking ▣ and can be docked under the Main Toolbar. By default, **Minimize to Panel Titles** is set in the drop-down list, as shown in Figure 4–69. Click ▣ to maximize the ribbon. You can also set the ribbon to be minimized to tabs or Panel Buttons by selecting the respective option in the drop-down list.

If the ribbon is not displayed, in the menu Bar, select Customize UI>Show Ribbon or

click ▦ *(Toggle Ribbon) in the Main Toolbar.*

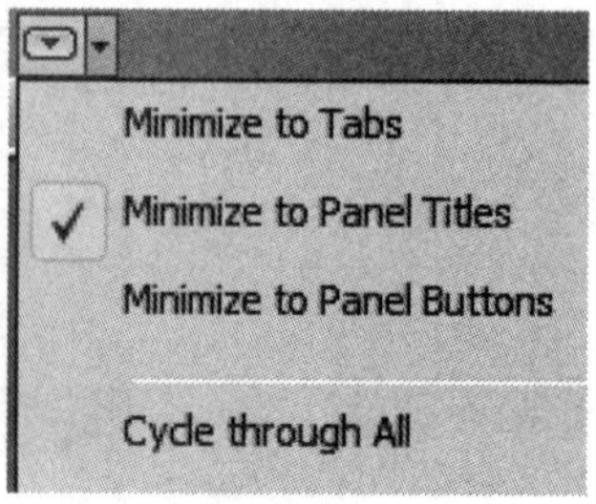

Figure 4–69

Practice 4f

Poly Modeling Using the Ribbon (Optional)

Practice Objective

- Create and modify a model using the box modeling technique.

In this practice you will learn to create a model using some of the tools and techniques of box modeling. You will also use the **Edit Poly** modifier and the modifier tools available in the ribbon.

Task 1 - Model the Armchair.

Estimated time for completion: 40 minutes

*If required, reset the scene by selecting **Application Menu>Reset**.*

The model is created in any color.

1. In the Create panel (+)> ● (Geometry), click **Box** in the Object Type rollout to activate the **Box** tool.

2. In the **Perspective** viewport, create a box of any size by clicking and dragging to define the length and width of the rectangle. Click and continue moving the mouse upwards to define the height.

3. Initially you can use the Parameters rollout in the Create panel to enter the values. After completing a command, you will use the Modify panel ( ) to edit the values. Set the following:
   - *Length*: **4'2"**
   - *Width*: **2'9"**
   - *Height*: **0'10"**

   Press <Enter>. In the **Perspective** viewport, the box should look similar to that shown in Figure 4–70.

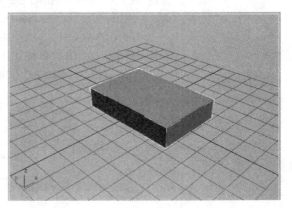

Figure 4–70

4. Name the object **armchair**.

5. To display the edges more clearly, change the display mode to wireframe by selecting the **Visual Style** label and selecting **Wireframe Override**.

6. Press <G> to hide the grid.

7. If the Modeling ribbon is only displaying Panel titles, click ⊡ (Show Full Ribbon).

8. Verify that the *Modeling* tab is active. Ensure that the armchair model is selected. Expand the Polygon Modeling panel and select **Apply Edit Poly Mod**, as shown in Figure 4–71. This adds an Edit Poly modifier to the armchair model. This is also displayed in the Command Panel. Note that the Modify panel (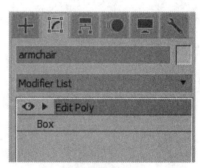) is already open and that the Modifier Stack displays the **Edit Poly** modifier, as shown in Figure 4–72.

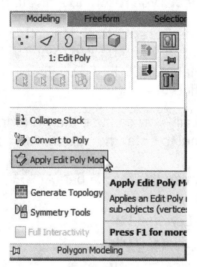

Figure 4–71

Figure 4–72

9. In the Modeling panel of the ribbon, click ◁ (Edge) to activate Edge Selection, as shown in Figure 4–73. Alternatively, you can press <2> to select it. Expand the **Edit Poly** modifier in the Modifier Stack and note that **Edge** is already selected (highlighted in blue).

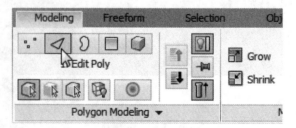

Figure 4–73

10. In the Navigation toolbar, click ![icon] (Zoom Extents All Selected) and using **Pan** and **Zoom** fill the viewport with the box.

11. Hold <Ctrl> and select the upper two long edges, as shown in Figure 4–74. The selected edges display in red.

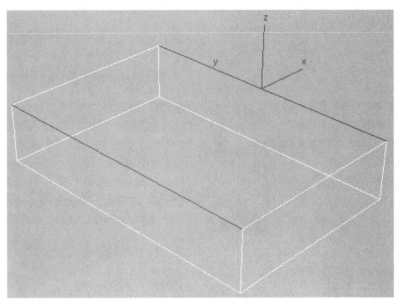

Figure 4–74

12. Hold <Shift>, and in the ribbon, in the Loops panel, click ![icon] (Connect) to open the **Connect Edges** caddy display.

In the Caddy display, hover the cursor on the edit box to display the option in its title.

13. In the Connect Edges caddy display, set *Segments* to **2** and *Pinch* to **70**. Press <Enter> (leaving *Slide* as **0**). Note that two edges are placed along the two short edges, as shown in Figure 4–75.

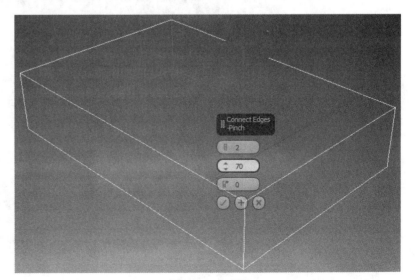

Figure 4–75

Use 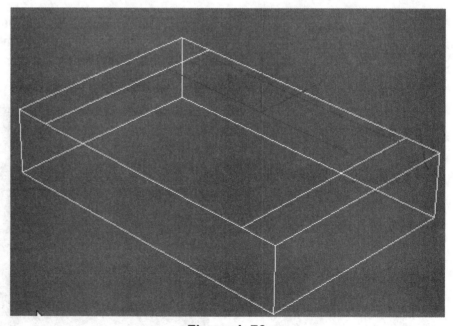 (Apply and continue) when you need to continue in the same tool. If you want to use another tool, use (OK) to exit the caddy display.

Pinch moves the lines in opposite directions, while Slide moves both of them in the X-direction

14. If your *Pinch* edit box is still highlighted (white) with the cursor in the edit box, you are required to exit it first. You can also verify this by hovering the cursor over ⊕.

   • If it highlights, then you need to click ⊕ once to apply and continue.

   • If it does not highlight, then you need to click ⊕ twice, first to exit the *Pinch* edit box and then to place a new set of segments along the long edge of the box.

15. Leave the *Segments* at **2**. Using the spinner arrows to change the *Pinch* and *Slide* values to create a rectangle towards the back of the armchair, as shown in Figure 4–76. You can drag their slider arrows in either direction viewing the changes dynamically. The values of *Pinch* and *Slide* are approximately **-30** and **-180** respectively. Press <Enter> each time if you enter a new value in the edit box, to see how it affects the lines. Click ⊘ (OK) to accept the changes and exit the caddy display. (Hover the cursor over ⊘ and if it highlights, click ⊘ once. If it does not highlight click ⊘ twice).

Figure 4–76

16. In the Modeling panel, click (Polygon), or press <4> to change the sub-object selection level from *Edge* to **Polygon**. Alternatively, select **Polygon** in the **Edit Poly** modifier in the Modifier Stack. In the viewport, right-click and select **Select**. Hold <Ctrl> and select the two polygons along the shorter side of the box, as shown in Figure 4–77.

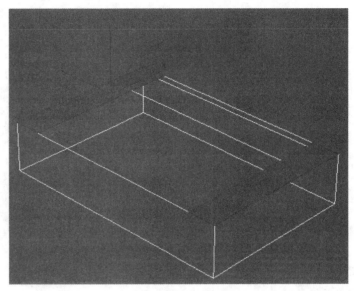

Figure 4–77

Hover the cursor over and if it highlights, click once. If it does not highlight click twice). The first time it accepts the values and the second time it exits the caddy display.

17. In the Modeling ribbon, in the Polygons panel, hold <Shift> and click (Extrude) to open the **Extrude Polygons** caddy display. Set *Height* to **0'2"** and click , as shown in Figure 4–78. Click again to exit the caddy display.

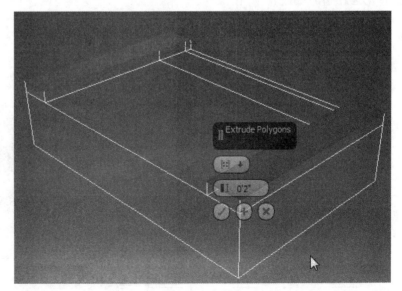

Figure 4–78

18. In the Polygons panel, hold <Shift> and click 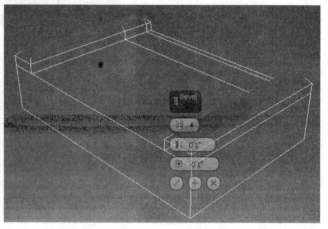 (Bevel) to open the **Bevel** caddy display. Set the following, as shown in Figure 4–79:

- *Height*: **0'1"**
- *Outline*: **-0'1"**

19. Click ⊘ to accept the changes and click ⊘ again to exit the caddy display.

Figure 4–79

The shortcut for Orbit is <Alt> + middle mouse button.

*You might need to right-click in empty space to exit the **Orbit** command first and then select the polygon.*

20. In the Navigation toolbar, click (Orbit) to orbit in the **Perspective** viewport so that you can see the back of the armchair.

21. Select the long, thin rectangle at the top (along the longer end) for the back of the chair. In the Polygons panel, hold <Shift> and click (Extrude). In the **Extrude Polygons** caddy display, set extrude to **0'5"** (as shown in Figure 4–80) and press <Enter>. Click ⊘ to exit the caddy display.

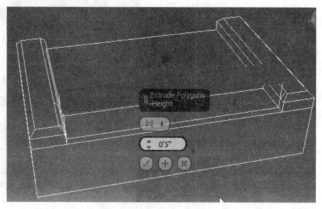

Figure 4–80

22. With the polygon still selected, in the Polygons panel, hold

<Shift> and click 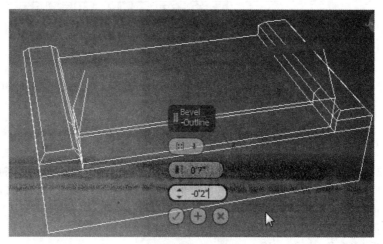 (Bevel) to access the Bevel caddy display. Bevel up the back of the chair, as shown in Figure 4–81. Do not to bevel too much or the edges will overlap. The values are approximately **0'7"** for *Height* and

-0'2" for *Outline*. Press <Enter> and click ⊘ either once or twice to exit the caddy display.

Figure 4–81

*Use 🪐 (Orbit) or hold <Alt> and use the middle mouse button to orbit in the **Perspective** viewport for a better view around the object.*

23. In the Main Toolbar, click ✛ (Select and Move) and move the selected polygon backwards along the X-axis, as shown in Figure 4–82. Orbit the viewport to view the design.

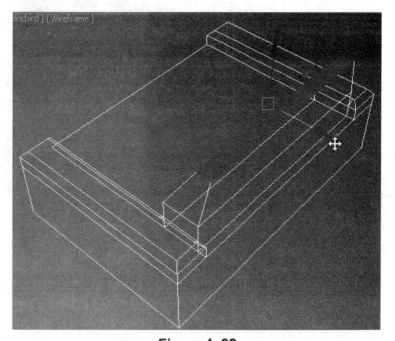

Figure 4–82

Alternatively, click

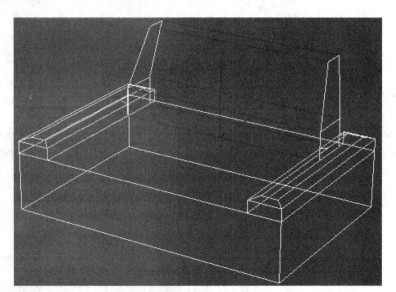 *(Edge) in the Modeling panel or select* **Edge** *in the Modifier Stack.*

Use (Orbit) *or hold <Alt> and use the middle mouse button to orbit in the* **Perspective** *viewport for easy access for clicking the edges at the back side.*

24. Press <2> to change to the **Edge** selection level. If some edge(s) have already been selected, click in an empty area in the viewport to clear the selection.

25. In the Modify Selection panel, click (Ring Mode) at the bottom of the panel (Ensure that you select **Ring Mode** and not **Ring**). This enables to select a ring of edges when a single edge is selected.

26. Select one of the long edges at the top of the chair back. Because the **Ring Mode** is toggled on, all of the other edges along the first edge are selected and display in red.

27. In the Modify Selection panel, click (Ring Mode) again to toggle it off.

28. In the Modify Selection panel, click (Shrink Ring) to clear one edge on either side of the ring. Alternatively, you can hold <Alt> and select one edge in front and one edge in the back to remove them from the selection. Only six edges should be selected, as shown in Figure 4–83.

Figure 4–83

29. In the Loops panel, hold <Shift> and click ▦ (Connect). In the **Connect Edges** caddy display, reset the Pinch and Slide to 0, set the segments to **21** and press <Enter>. This adds 21 vertical segments, as shown in Figure 4–84. Click ✅ (OK) either once or twice to exit the caddy display.

Sometimes clicking ⊕ does not work correctly when you need to continue in the same modifier. You can use ✅ and then reopen the modifier.

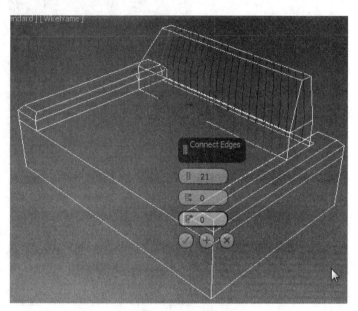

Figure 4–84

30. Hold <Shift> and click ▦ (Connect) to open the **Connect Edges** caddy display. Change the *Segments* to **3** and press <Enter>. This adds three rows of horizontal segments between two horizontal edges along the armchair back. Click ✅ either once or twice to exit the caddy display.

31. Clear the selection by clicking in empty space.

32. Maximize the **Left** viewport (Use <Win> + <Shift> to open the overlay). Use the **Zoom** and **Pan** tools to fill the viewport with the model.

33. In the Modeling ribbon, in the Polygon Modeling panel, click ▦ (Vertex) or press <1>.

Click ⟲ (Undo) if you selected the wrong vertices.

34. Click ✥ (Select and Move) and using a selection rectangle, select only the middle vertices in the top row leaving four vertices on each side unselected, as shown in Figure 4–85.

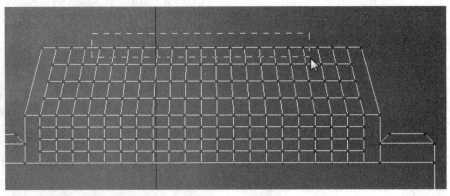

Figure 4–85

- The row of vertices selected display in red.

35. Maximize to display all of the four viewports. In the **Perspective** view, orbit around and verify that you have selected the correct row (only the top most row) of vertices.

36. In the Command Panel, note that you are in the Modify panel with the Modifier Stack indicating that you are at the **Edit Poly>Vertex** level. Expand the Soft Selection rollout and select **Use Soft Selection**. A rainbow color is displayed. The Red/Yellow/Orange/Green vertices will be affected by the selected transform (e.g., **Move**), while the Dark Blue vertices remain unaffected. You can change the Falloff values to add or remove vertices from the affected/unaffected group. Using the spinners in *Falloff,* note that decreasing the falloff changes the cyan colored vertices to a dark blue. Set the *Falloff* similar to that shown in Figure 4–86. Note that the resulting model might differ from that shown.

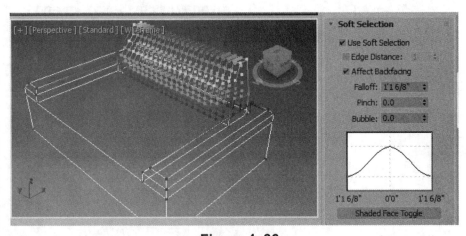

Figure 4–86

You can change the size of the Transform gizmo using the <->(hyphen) and <=> (equal sign).

37. Use 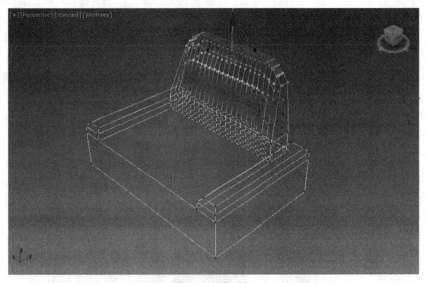 (Select and Move) and move the vertices up by moving the gizmo along the Z-axis, to create the curved chair back, similar to that shown in Figure 4–87. Note that while moving the vertices, the dark blue vertices remain unaffected.

Figure 4–87

Hint: Assign Hotkey

You can assign a hotkey to interactively adjust the Soft selection falloff and pinch in the viewport. To do this, assign a hotkey to **Edit Soft Selection Mode**. Refer to **To edit a soft selection** in the Autodesk 3ds Max Help.

---

38. In the Modifier Stack, select **Edit Poly** to toggle off the sub-object selection

*Alternatively, you can click the **Viewport Shading** menu and select **Realistic** and **Edged Faces**.*

39. Click anywhere in empty space in the **Perspective** viewport to clear the selection. Press <F3> to toggle from *Wireframe* to **Default Shading** mode and press <F4> to toggle on **Edged Faces** mode. The model displays similar to that shown in Figure 4–88.

40. Press <F4> to end the **Edged Faces** mode and display the model using the **Default Shading** mode. In the Display Method label menu, select **High Quality**, as shown in Figure 4–89. Note that there are some problems with smoothing and that the chair looks faceted.

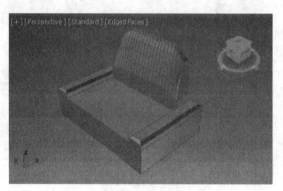

Figure 4–88

Figure 4–89

41. Select the chair and in the Modifier Stack or ribbon, select **Polygon** or press <4> to access the **Polygon** sub-object level.

42. In the Command Panel, scroll down and expand the Polygon: Smoothing Groups rollout. Press <Ctrl>+<A> to select all of the polygons, and click **Auto Smooth** in the rollout, as shown in Figure 4–90.

Figure 4–90

43. Click in empty space in the viewport to clear all of the selections. Note that the faceted problem has been fixed, as shown in Figure 4–91.

Figure 4–91

Task 2 - Apply Geometric Smoothing.

In this task you will add Geometry Smoothing using the **MSmooth** operation.

*You can add divisions to the seat portion of the chair for the **MSmooth** modifier to have a smoother effect. Use the **Slice** modifier to add divisions.*

1. In the **Perspective** view, select the chair, if not already selected. In the Modeling ribbon, in the Polygon Modeling panel, click ▢ (Polygon), or press <4>.

2. Press <Ctrl>+<A> to select all of the polygons. If they are completely displayed in red, press <F2> to only display the faces in a red outline (edges).

3. In the Modeling ribbon, in the Subdivision panel, hold <Shift> and click ▦ (MSmooth). **Msmooth** changes the geometry by adding density to the mesh, as shown in Figure 4–92.

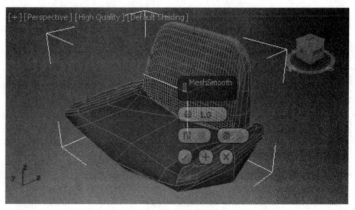

Figure 4–92

4. Click ✓ to exit the caddy display.

5. Save the file as **My Armchair.max**.

Task 3 - Using Freeform tools. - Optional

If you have time, you can soften the model using the **Freeform** tools.

1. In the *Polygon Modeling* tab, click 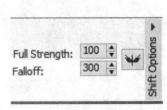 (Polygon), if it is not selected. Press <Ctrl>+<A> to select all of the polygons.

2. Select the *Freeform* tab, as shown in Figure 4–93.

Figure 4–93

3. In the Paint Deform panel, click (Shift).

4. When you start this command, a Shift Options panel displays on the screen. Also note that the cursor displays as two circles in the active viewport, specifying the brush size. Set the values shown in Figure 4–94.

In the Quick Access Toolbar, click

(Undo) if you moved the wrong vertices.

5. Right-click to activate the **Left** viewport (with the selection on) and hover the cursor, which displays as two circles over the top of the back. Stretch the back upward, as shown in Figure 4–95.

Full Strength: 100
Falloff: 300

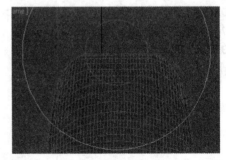

Figure 4–94   **Figure 4–95**

Task 4 - Optimize the Mesh.

The shape of the chair has been softened. Now you need to reduce the polycount so the file can be used efficiently. The ProOptimizer modifier will achieve this.

1. Select the **Edit Poly** modifier in the stack to disable Sub-object mode. In the Modifier drop-down list, select **ProOptimizer**, as shown in Figure 4–96.

2. In the Command Panel, in the Optimization Levels rollout, click **Calculate**. Change the *Vertex %* to **22**. Use the spinner to move it up or down as shown in Figure 4–97. Keep watching the viewport and also the statistics are displayed in the rollout.

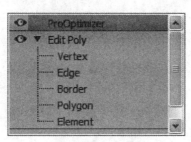

Figure 4–96

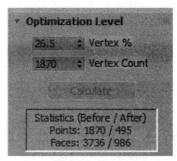

Figure 4–97

3. Save your work as **Myarmchair_softened.max**.

Hint: Using Optimize and MultiRes Modifiers

The **Optimize** and **MultiRes** modifiers are both accessed from the Modifier List. They can be used to reduce the number of vertices and polygons.

- **Optimize:** Reduces the model geometry, but does not critically change the appearance of the model.

- **MultiRes**: Reduces the model geometry and enables you to specify the exact vertex count to be used for reduction. This modifier should be used if you have to export the models to other 3D applications because it maintains the map channels.

4.7 Statistics in Viewport

While Box modeling it is recommended to frequently review the status of your model. You can expand **Application Menu> Properties >Summary Info** to get details about the file. You can also **Show Statistics** directly in the viewport by, clicking **[+]>xView>Show Statistics**. The total number of polygons, vertices, and Frames Per Second are displayed in the viewport (as shown in Figure 4–98), and are dependent on the options selected in the Viewport Configuration dialog box. Alternatively, press <7> to toggle the statistics display in the viewport on and off, in the active viewport.

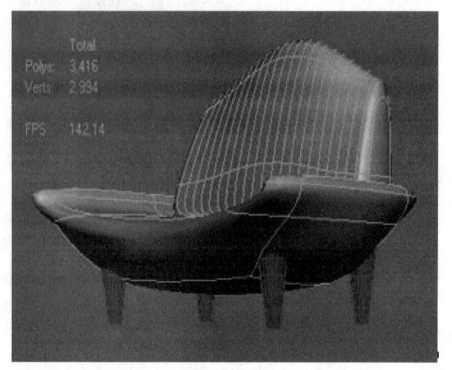

Figure 4–98

The statistics options can be controlled by selecting **Views> Viewport Configuration** and in the *Statistics* tab of the Viewport Configuration dialog box, as shown in Figure 4–99. Here, you can customize the display (e.g., **Polygon Count**, **Triangle Count**, **Edge Count**, **Vertex Count**, etc.).

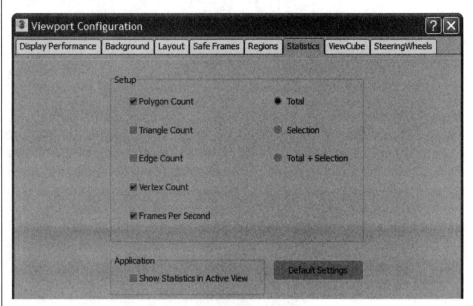

Figure 4–99

Hint: Low Polygon Count

When designing, it is recommended to keep the **Polygon Count** or **Triangle Count** as low as possible to speed up rendering and viewport performance. If you are creating real time models, this impacts the interactive viewport navigation and playback speed.

Performance might be improved if you keep this off when not in use.

• You can toggle the view of the statistics on and off, as required.

Hint: Use Summary Info

Sometimes **Show Statistics** does not give correct results. To check the information, expand **Application Menu> Properties>Summary Info** and then compare the Vertex/Face/Poly count displayed there.

Chapter Review Questions

1. Which of the following are the **Transform** tools in the Autodesk 3ds Max software? (Select all that apply.)

   a. **Move**

   b. **Stretch**

   c. **Trim**

   d. **Scale**

2. Which of the following do you press to change the size (shrink and enlarge) of the Transform gizmo?

   a. <-> and <+>

   b. <+> and <=>

   c. <-> and <=>

   d. </> and <+>

3. Which **Transform center** option do you select if you want to rotate many objects, each around its own center?

   a. (Pivot Point Center)

   b. (Selection Center)

   c. (Transform Coordinate Center)

4. Which clone option creates a one-directional link in which changes made to the original object affect the duplicate, but the modifiers applied to the duplicate do not affect the source object?

   a. **Copy**

   b. **Instance**

   c. **Reference**

5. In addition to the **Polygon Modeling** tools, the *Modeling* tab in the Ribbon contains the commonly used tools from which panel of the Command Panel?

    a. Modify panel ( )

    b. Hierarchy panel ( )

    c. Display panel ( )

    d. Utilities panel ( )

6. Which key on the keyboard can be used as a shortcut to toggle the statistics display in the viewport on and off?

    a. <1>

    b. <3>

    c. <5>

    d. <7>

Command Summary

Button	Command	Location
	Ribbon (Graphite Modeling Tools)	• **Main Toolbar** • **Customize**>Show UI>Show Ribbon
	Select and Move	• **Main Toolbar** • **Edit**>Move
	Select and Place	• **Main Toolbar** • **Edit**>Placement
	Select and Rotate	• **Main Toolbar** • **Edit:**>Rotate
	Select and Uniform Scale	• **Main Toolbar:** Scale flyout • **Edit**>Scale
	Select and Non-uniform Scale	• **Main Toolbar:** Scale flyout
	Select and Squash	• **Main Toolbar:** Scale flyout
	Use Pivot Point Center	• **Main Toolbar:** Transform Center flyout
	Use Selection Center	• **Main Toolbar:** Transform Center flyout
	Use Transform Coordinate Center	• **Main Toolbar:** Transform Center flyout

Modeling From 2D Objects

In addition to Primitive Objects or Polygon Modeling tools, models in the Autodesk® 3ds Max® software can also be created using 2D shapes that are subsequently used to generate 3D geometry. Tools such as Lathe, Extrude, and Sweep Modifiers enable you to create 3D geometry from a 2D shape.

Learning Objectives in this Chapter

- Create 2D shapes, such as lines and closed shape objects.
- Revolve a profile around an axis using the Lathe modifier.
- Add and subtract shapes using the 2D Boolean operations.
- Add depth to a 2D shape to create 3D geometry using the Extrude modifier.
- Combine two or more 3D objects to generate a third 3D object by performing Boolean operations on their geometry.
- Modify shapes and geometry with precision using various snap modes.
- Create 3D geometry based on a 2D section that follows a series of spline segment paths using the Sweep modifier.

5.1 3D Modeling from 2D Objects

The Autodesk 3ds Max software enables you to create 2D shapes in the form of splines and NURBS, and using various modifiers, to create organic smooth curved surfaces from the shapes. Shapes can be created using 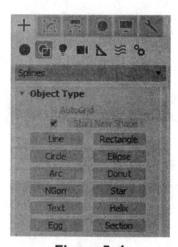 (Shapes) in the Command Panel's Create panel ( ), as shown in Figure 5–1. The splines consist of:

Although the software includes 2D tools, it is not a drafting application.

- Basic shapes: **Line**, **Rectangle**, **Ellipse**, etc.

- Extended shapes: **WRectangle**, **Channel**, **Angle**, etc.

Figure 5–1

The software enables you to draw lines and curves in a freeform interactive manner by clicking points in the viewport. Lines can be drawn to create three kinds of shapes: open, closed, and self-intersecting.

You cannot draw a 2D line that forks or branches.

- Closed shapes can also be created using other shape object types, such as Rectangle, Ellipse, Ngon, or Text.

- Open shapes and self-intersecting shapes can be extruded to create 3D objects, but these objects have mixed face normals. Some faces do not render and might not be visible in the viewport.

- The **Edit Spline** modifier: Enables you to apply edits such as trim, extend, fillet, and chamfer to 2D objects.

- The **Extrude** modifier: Enables you to create 3D objects by extruding closed shapes. The outside of these objects is visible and renderable from all sides. All face normals point away from the center of the object.

- The **Lathe** modifier: Enables you to create 3D objects by using on open shapes where a profile is revolved.

- The Transform Type-In functionality: Enables you to achieve precision using snaps and vertices, which can be shifted after placement.

The **Line** tool has two basic drawing techniques:

Method 1

You can draw straight line segments by clicking and moving the cursor repeatedly. This method does not create any curves at first. All of the vertices created are Corner type. After clicking to set the vertices, you select the line vertices individually or in sets and then change their type from Corner to **Bezier** or **Smooth** to create curves.

> ### Hint: Preventing Self-intersecting Shapes
>
> If you draw too quickly when drawing using Method 1, the program might translate your motions into press and drag, and self-intersecting shapes can be inadvertently drawn. To prevent this, in the Create panel's Creation Method rollout, change the drag type to **Corner**. In doing so, you are not able to drag curves interactively.

Method 2

*You cannot create **Bezier** vertices by clicking, holding, and dragging if both the Initial Type and Drag Type have been set to **Corner** in the Creation Method rollout, in the **Line** tool.*

Draw curves directly by clicking, holding, and dragging to create **Bezier** vertices rather than **Corner** vertices. This is a faster method but harder to control, since you are defining the curve on both sides of the vertex in a single move. Holding <Alt> while dragging enables you to define the curve on the leading side of the vertex, introducing an angle between the vertex handles.

- Using either method, these curved segments are created out of smaller straight line segments. Increasing the segments makes the curve smoother. The *Steps* value in the Interpolation rollout sets the number of segments.

- Drawing while holding <Shift> also draws straight lines and perpendicular lines.

- Press <Backspace> to undo the last drawn vertex in a line.

Practice 5a

Drawing Lines

Practice Objectives

- Create an open and closed 2D shape.
- Move the location of a vertex and change the shape of a curve.

Estimated time for completion: 20 minutes

In this practice you will create, open, and close 2D shapes using the **Line** command. You will then move the location of a vertex and change the shape of a curve using the Bezier handles. Finally, you will create a candlestick model using the 2D shapes drawn.

You must set the paths to locate the External files and Xrefs used in the practice. If you have not done this already, return to **Chapter 1: Introduction to Autodesk 3ds Max** and complete Task 1 to Task 3 in **Practice 1a: Organizing Folders and Working with the Interface**. You only have to set the user paths once.

Task 1 - Drawing 2D lines.

1. Reset the scene.

2. Maximize the **Front** viewport from the layout overlay using <Shift> and <Win>. Alternatively use ⬈ (Maximize Viewport) or press <Alt>+<W>.

*If a dialog box opens prompting you about a File Load: Mismatch, click **OK** to accept the default values.*

3. Press <G> to hide the grid.

4. In the Command Panel>Create panel (+), click ⬚ (Shapes), as shown in Figure 5–2.

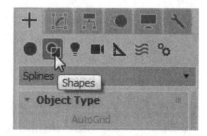

Figure 5–2

5. In the Object Type rollout, click **Line**.

6. In the **Front** viewport, draw a saw-tooth pattern line, as shown in Figure 5–3. Click to set the first point, move the cursor to the next location of the point and click to place the second point. The first line displays. Continue the pattern. Right-click to end, once you have placed the last line. An open shape is created.

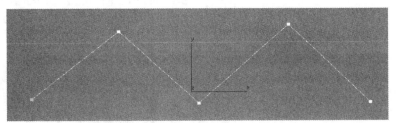

Figure 5–3

7. With the line still selected, delete the lines by pressing <Delete>.

*Closed shapes and open shapes are both used in creating 3D objects. Modifiers, such as **Extrude**, **Lathe**, and **Surface**, can be used to build 3D surfaces based on 2D shapes.*

8. Still in the **Line** command, repeat the drawing process to create a closed shape, as shown in Figure 5–4. Click to set each point and select the starting point (yellow vertex) to complete the shape. In the Spline dialog box, click **Yes** to close the shape. Right-click in the empty space to exit the command. Do not delete this shape.

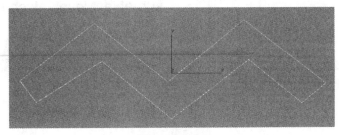

Figure 5–4

9. To draw curved lines, in the Object Type rollout, click **Line**. Then, in the Creation Method rollout, change the *Drag Type* to **Bezier**, as shown in Figure 5–5.

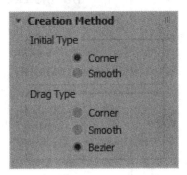

Figure 5–5

10. Click to set the first point, move the cursor, then click and drag to create a Bezier curve running through the second point. Each time you click and drag, the curve extends through the new point. This draws a curve, but it is difficult to control, since dragging affects the curve on both sides of the point at the same time. Draw a curved line similar to the one shown in Figure 5–6. Right-click to exit the command and press <Delete> to delete to this curved line.

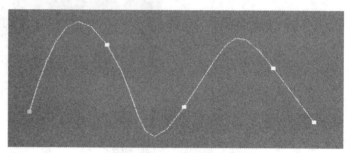

Figure 5–6

11. Right-click in empty space to exit the **Line** command.

12. Select the closed shape that was previously created. In the Command Panel, select the Modify panel ( ). Click ► in the Modifier Stack to expand **Line**. Select **Vertex** at the sub-object level, as shown in Figure 5–7.

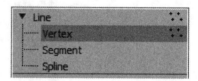

Figure 5–7

13. In the viewport, select one vertex at the top left of the saw tooth pattern. The selected vertex displays in red. Right-click and select **Bezier** in the tools 1 quadrant of the quad menu. Note that the vertex corner is replaced by a Bezier curve and that the Bezier handles are displayed.

14. In the Main Toolbar, click (Select and Move). The Transform gizmo is displayed with the bezier handles. Click the yellow plane at the interior of the gizmo and move the location of the vertex from its initial position. Click and drag either handle end (green square) to modify the curve shape, as shown in Figure 5–8. The handle movement is constrained by the Transform gizmo usage. Note that dragging one handle moves the other handle simultaneously.

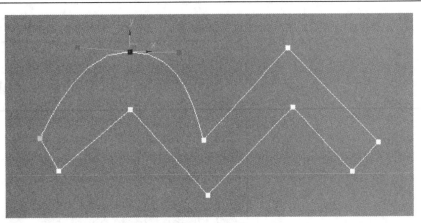

Figure 5–8

Hint: Transform Gizmo Size

<-> (hyphen) and <=> (equal sign) can be used to decrease or increase the size of the Transform gizmo. If the Transform gizmo handles extend beyond the vertex handles, you might have trouble moving the vertex handles.

If you move the Transform gizmo in one axis, the movement of the bezier handles is constrained to that axis. To have the handles move freely, select the yellow square of the gizmo to have movement in the XY-axes. This can also be controlled using the Axis Constraints toolbar.

15. Hold <Shift> and move one of the handles. This changes the command to **Bezier Corner** and enables you to break the continuity of the curve to manipulate the handles on one side of the curve separately from the other, as shown in Figure 5–9. Right-click on the vertex and select **Reset Tangents** to return the original curve shape. To return to **Bezier**, right-click and select it again in the quad menu.

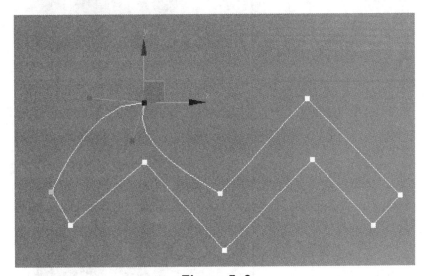

Figure 5–9

Task 2 - Using 2D Shapes to draw a candlestick model.

In this task you will draw a model of a candlestick. A reference photo (**Candlestick_pewter.jpg**) of an actual candlestick as shown in Figure 5–10, is located in the *...\Maps* folder.

1. In the Modifier Stack, select **Line** to exit sub-object selection mode. If required, select the shape and any other lines that you might have drawn and delete them using <Delete>.

2. In the Create panel, click (Shapes) and click **Line**. In the Creation Method rollout, in the *Drag Type* area, select **Corner**, if required.

Holding <Shift> creates straight lines at a 90 degree angle (vertical direction) and 180 degree angle (horizontal direction).

3. Start at the bottom right (the yellow vertex indicates the start point) and click to place the first line vertex, as shown-in Figure 5–11. Hold <Shift>, move the cursor left, and click to draw the base of the candlestick. Still holding <Shift>, move the cursor up to draw the long straight vertical line segment, and then click to place the vertex. Release <Shift> and continue clicking and drawing in a clockwise direction.

• Press <Backspace> to undo the points if you make a mistake.

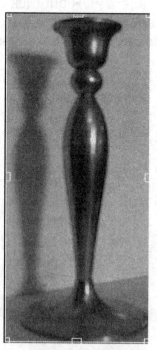

Figure 5–10

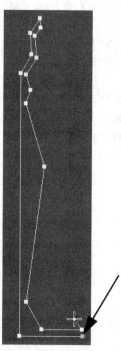

Figure 5–11

4. Continue to place approximately 16 points and close the shape by clicking over the first point. Click **Yes** and then right-click to exit the **Line** command.

5. In the Modify panel (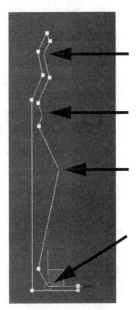), in the Modifier Stack, expand **Line** and select the **Vertex** sub-object level. Hold <Ctrl> and select the four red vertices, as shown in Figure 5–12. Right-click and select **Bezier** in the quad menu. This changes the vertices to **Bezier** vertices with handles

Figure 5–12

6. Adjust the handles of each vertex using 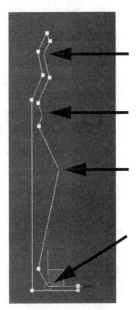 (Select and Move) to obtain a shape similar to that shown in Figure 5–13. Move the vertices and handles to get a shape similar to that shown in Figure 5–14.

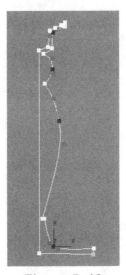

Figure 5–13

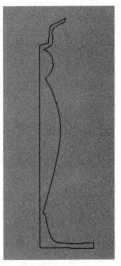

Figure 5–14

7. Save your work as **MyCandlestickProfile.max**. For comparison, you can open the file **Candlestick_Profile.max**.

5.2 The Lathe Modifier

The **Lathe** modifier enables you to create a 3D object by revolving a profile (2D shape) around an axis. It can be accessed in the Modifier List, in the Modify panel (image) in the Command Panel.

How To: Create a 3D Object Using the Lathe Modifier

1. Select a profile (usually a line object).
2. Apply a **Lathe** Modifier.
3. Adjust the axis of revolution.
4. Adjust the alignment of the axis with the profile.

Practice 5b

Creating a Candlestick

5–11

Practice Objective

- Revolve a 2D shape around its axis.

Estimated time for completion: 5 minutes

In this practice you will resolve a 2D shape around its axis, using the **Lathe** modifier to create the solid geometry for the candlestick.

You must set the paths to locate the External files and Xrefs used in the practice. If you have not done this already, return to **Chapter 1: Introduction to Autodesk 3ds Max** and complete Task 1 to Task 3 in **Practice 1a: Organizing Folders and Working with the Interface**. You only have to set the user paths once.

*If a dialog box opens prompting you about a File Load: Mismatch, click **OK** to accept the default values.*

1. Open **Candlestick_Profile.max**.

2. Maximize the **Front** viewport.

3. Select the profile. In the Modify panel ( ), in the Modifier Stack, verify that the **Line** is highlighted and that no sub-object level is highlighted.

4. In the Modifier List, select **Lathe**. The profile revolves around a center point, but the alignment is off, as shown in Figure 5–15.

*Sometimes, lathed objects display inside-out. If something looks wrong with your candlestick, use the **Flip Normals** option in the Parameters rollout.*

5. In the Parameters rollout, in the *Align* area, click **Min**. The candlestick should now display as shown in Figure 5–16.

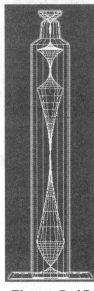

Figure 5–15

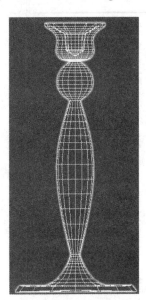

Figure 5–16

6. In the Modifier Stack, expand **Lathe** and select **Axis**. Using 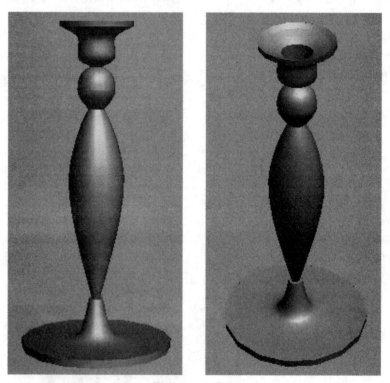 (Select and Move), move the X-axis to display the candlestick in various positions.

7. In the Quick Access Toolbar, click (Undo) or press <Ctrl>+<Z> to undo the axis moves.

8. Select **Lathe** (highlighted) to exit the Sub-object mode. Maximize the viewport to display the four viewports.

9. Assign a color to the geometry by selecting the candlestick first, selecting the color swatch next to the **Line** name, and selecting a color in the Object Color dialog box.

10. In the Viewport Navigation toolbar, click (Orbit) and examine the geometry as shown in Figure 5–17.

Figure 5–17

11. Save your work as **MyCandlestick.max**.

5.3 2D Booleans

- 2D Boolean operations enable you to create shapes by combining drawn lines and shapes. Using the **Edit Spline** modifier, you can add or subtract shapes at the sub-object level.

- 2D Boolean operations are available in the Spline sub-object level, in the **Geometry** parameters, as shown in Figure 5–18.

- All shapes that are to be combined must be part of a single shape. The **Edit Spline** modifier enables you to convert a shape to an editable spline while the **Attach** command enables you to combine multiple shapes into a single shape.

- When drawing shapes, if you clear the **Start New Shape** option in the Object Type rollout (as shown in Figure 5–19), all of the subsequent shapes that you create are joined into one single shape. If you already have a shape selected, anything you draw becomes part of that shape. By default, the **Start New Shape** option is selected before you start drawing any shapes.

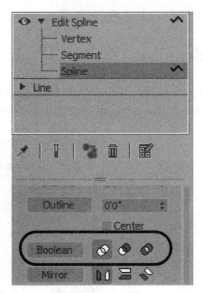

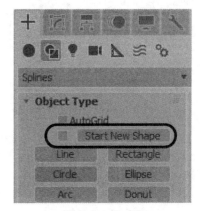

| Figure 5–18 | Figure 5–19 |

- No history is associated with 2D Boolean operations that are saved with the file and you are not able to retrieve the various Boolean components after saving.

Practice 5c

2D Booleans

Estimated time for completion: 5 minutes

*If a dialog box opens prompting you about a File Load: Mismatch, click **OK** to accept the default values.*

Practice Objective

- Modify a shape using 2D Booleans.

In this practice you will add and subtract rectangles using 2D Booleans to change the shape of the profile for the candlestick.

You must set the paths to locate the External files and Xrefs used in the practice. If you have not done this already, return to **Chapter 1: Introduction to Autodesk 3ds Max** and complete Task 1 to Task 3 in **Practice 1a: Organizing Folders and Working with the Interface**. You only have to set the user paths once.

1. Open **Candlestick.max**.

2. Maximize the **Front** viewport and zoom to the extents of all objects.

3. Select the candlestick. In the Modify panel (   ), in the Modifier Stack, click   (eye) next to the **Lathe** to toggle the **Lathe** modifier off. The line profile and the **Lathe** axis displays in the viewport.

4. In the Create panel (+   ), click   (Shapes).

5. Click **Rectangle**. Draw four rectangles intersecting the right edge of the profile, similar to that shown in Figure 5–20.

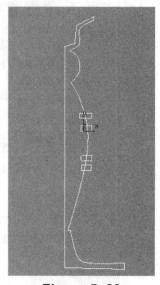

Figure 5–20

6. Right-click to cancel the command.

7. Select the candlestick profile. Open the Modify panel ( ), and in the Modifier Stack, select **Line**.

8. Scroll down and in the Geometry rollout, click **Attach Mult**.

9. In the Attach Multiple dialog box, click (Display Shapes) to activate it, if not already active. Select all of the four rectangles and click **Attach**. All of the rectangles become part of the candlestick profile spline object.

10. In the Modifier Stack, select the **Spline** sub-object in the **Line** object and select the candlestick profile in the viewport. The selected profile displays in red and the rectangles remain white (unselected).

11. In the Geometry rollout, scroll down and click **Boolean** to activate it. Verify that (Union) is already active.

12. In the viewport, hover the cursor over the topmost rectangle, and note that the cursor displays as a Union cursor ( ). Select the topmost rectangle and then select the second rectangle. Note that in each case, the profile is extended to the right to include part of the rectangle, and the inner part of the rectangle is discarded.

13. In the Command Panel, click (Subtraction) to activate it. Hover the cursor over the third rectangle to display the cursor as a Subtraction cursor ( ).

14. Select the third rectangle and then select the last rectangle. For these shapes, the rectangle is subtracted from the candlestick. The first two rectangles create a rim, and the last two create an inscribed groove, as shown in Figure 5–21.

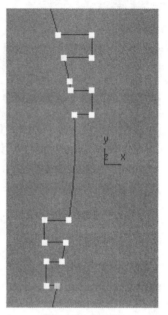

Figure 5–21

15. In the Modifier Stack, select **Lathe**, and then click (grayed out eye) next to **Lathe** to toggle it on.

16. Press <Alt>+<W> to return to four viewports. Activate the **Perspective** viewport and review the results in **Default Shading** display mode. The two rims and two grooves are created in the candle stick, as shown in Figure 5–22.

Figure 5–22

17. Save your work as **MyCandlestick01.max**.

18. (Optional) Modify some of the vertices. Select the candlestick, if required. In the Modify panel (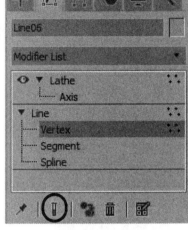), select **Line** and **Vertex** sub-objects. Select one of the vertices in the first rim that you created, as shown in Figure 5–23.

19. (Optional) In the Modifier Stack, click 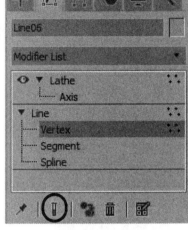 (Show end result on/off toggle), as shown in Figure 5–24. This tool enables you to see the object as an end product.

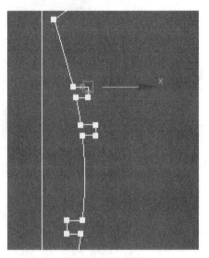

Figure 5–23

Figure 5–24

20. (Optional) Move the selected vertex in the viewport. You are now sculpting the candlestick in real time, as shown in Figure 5–25.

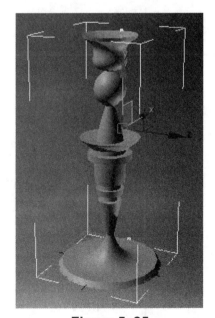

Figure 5–25

21. Save your work as **MyCandlestick01.max**.

5.4 The Extrude Modifier

The **Extrude** modifier enables you to add depth to a 2D shape to create 3D geometry. As with other modifiers, the Extrude modifier is available in the Modifier List, in the Command Panel's Modify panel ( ), as shown in Figure 5–26.

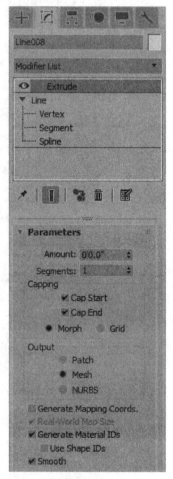

Figure 5–26

Capping area

The capping options are located in the Parameters rollout, in the *Capping* area, as shown in Figure 5–26.

- Capping only applies to closed extruded shapes. Open shapes can be extruded but they cannot be capped.

- Closed shapes often do not cap if they cross themselves or if they have more than one vertex at the same location.

- You can also extrude with a height of **0** to create a flat surface. In this situation, only the start or end cap is required.

- Figure 5–27 shows **various** capping options.

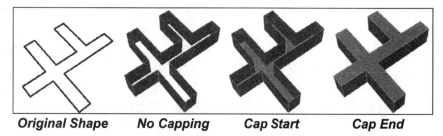

Original Shape   **No Capping**   **Cap Start**   **Cap End**

Figure 5–27

- **Morph** capping type linearly interpolates across the vertices to create the cap, as shown in Figure 5–28. This option creates less geometry and is the default setting.

- **Grid** capping type breaks down the cap into a repeating grid of vertices, in square shapes, as shown in Figure 5–29. The grid method enables more complex modeling on the surface of the cap, but adds a great deal of geometry.

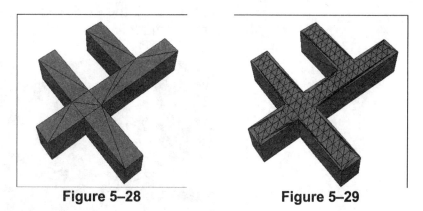

Figure 5–28   **Figure 5–29**

Output area

The *Output* area options controls the kind of object that is derived if you simplify (collapse) the object. It is recommended to select the default **Mesh** option. **Patch** and **NURBS** options are used to create complex curved geometry.

Mapping Coordinates

The options for mapping coordinates and real-world map sizing are described with materials.

- For surfaces that have tiled, repeating textures of a specific size (e.g., carpeting, wall surfaces, metal, etc.) select **Generate Mapping Coords** and **Real-World Map Size**.

- For surfaces meant to show textures that are scaled explicitly (e.g., signs, labels, company logos, paintings, computer screens, etc.) you might use **Generate Mapping Coords option,** but the **Real-World Map Size** option can be cleared.

- Select **Generate Material IDs** to apply a different material to the sides, start, and end cap through a Multi/Sub-object material.

- Selecting **Use Shape IDs** assigns material IDs that have been applied to the segments of the spline that you extruded.

Extruding Nested Splines

When linked or imported geometry is merged together (such as by layer with the weld option) or, when 2D objects become attached to form complex splines, these objects are called **nested splines**. When extruding a nested spline (as shown in Figure 5–30), the enclosed areas form solid masses and can be used for modeling wall systems and similar geometry.

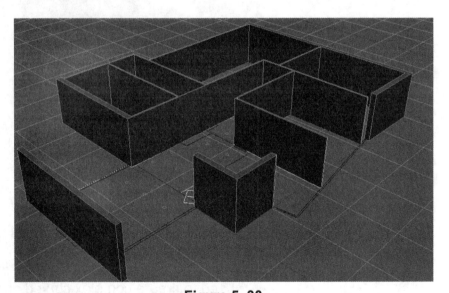

Figure 5–30

5.5 Boolean Operations

Boolean operations enable you to graphically bring together two 3D objects to generate a third 3D object. This is an intuitive way to create complex geometry from simple 3D primitives and extruded 2D shapes.

The Boolean objects are available in the Create panel (![plus icon]), by clicking ![geometry icon] (Geometry) and selecting **Compound Objects** in the drop-down list. You can select the required Boolean object in the Object Type rollout, as shown in Figure 5–31.

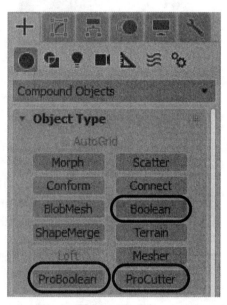

Figure 5–31

The three types of Boolean objects that can be created, are described as follows:

Enhanced in **2017**

Boolean compound object	Combines two 3D objects to generate a third 3D object by applying a logical operation. The Boolean compound object offers improved stability.
ProBoolean compound object	Similar to the Boolean compound object, this option has more advanced functionality and alternate workflow.
ProCutter compound object	Enables you to separate objects into pieces so that you can use them in dynamic simulations.

Boolean Operations

The original objects are referred to as **Operands** and the final result is a **Boolean** object. The operands can be combined in three ways, as shown in Figure 5–32:

- By subtraction of one from the other.

- By finding the intersection where their geometries overlap.

- By the union of the two together.

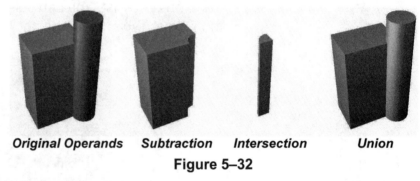

Original Operands   *Subtraction*   *Intersection*   *Union*

Figure 5–32

- Boolean operations can be nested where the results of one operation can be used as input to the next. **ProBooleans** offer superior methodology when creating objects with multiple operands. It enables you to reorder and change the operations interactively.

- Boolean operations can be animated, this is often a technique used to reveal or hide geometry in a presentation.

New
in 2017

Boolean Explorer

The Boolean Explorer can help you to keep track of the various operands that are being used, as shown in Figure 5–33. The Boolean Explorer is only available with the Boolean compound object.

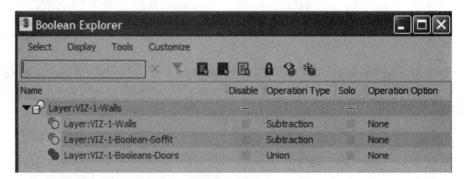

Figure 5–33

- To open the Boolean Explorer, in the Boolean Parameters rollout, click **Open Boolean Explorer**.

- Whenever you add an operand, it is displayed in the Boolean Explorer.

- If you change the order of the operands, the change is reflected in the Boolean Explorer.

Adjusting Boolean Results

The results of a Boolean operation can be adjusted dynamically by making changes to the operands' parameters or modifier stack. This dynamic update requires that operands be identified as a reference or instance on creation (or an extracted operand is selected to be an instance).

- The original operands can be maintained for editing after the fact or they can be reconstituted (extracted) from the Boolean result later on.

- The practical application of adjusting Boolean results is best left for Intermediate course material.

Best Practices

Boolean operations are known to produce unexpected results if the operand geometries had certain issues such as: gaps, irregular face normals, did not overlap each other, etc. It is recommended to avoid the following issues whenever possible:

- Avoid coplanar operands, whenever possible, to minimize Boolean complexity.

- Boolean operations expect water-tight geometry. If the geometry does not cleanly define a volume, the Boolean might not work, as shown in Figure 5–34.

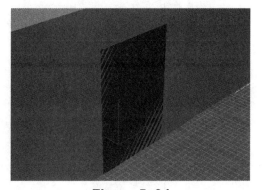

Figure 5–34

Collapsing Booleans

When an object has been sufficiently modeled with Boolean operations you can leave the result as a Boolean object or simplify (collapse) it to a mesh.

- To collapse a Boolean object to an editable mesh, in the Modifier Stack, right-click on the Boolean and select **Convert to: Editable Mesh** or **Convert to: Editable Poly**.

- If you are using a Boolean result as an operand for another Boolean operation and are not getting the expected results, it might help to convert the original Boolean object to an editable mesh before the second operation. It is recommended to use ProBooleans if you have multiple operands.

If you select a selective reload and avoided the layers used to create your Booleans, any connected Boolean objects would be removed from the scene.

- Boolean objects that originate from linked AutoCAD geometry might react unpredictably after an updated DWG link.

- Many other kinds of 3D objects besides Booleans can be collapsed to a mesh to simplify them.

- Once an object is converted to a mesh, it loses all of its parametric controls. Therefore, converted Boolean objects cannot be updated by editing instanced operands or a file link update.

Practice 5d

Extrude Walls and Create Wall Openings

Practice Objective

- Add depth to a 2D spline to create 3D walls and openings in 3D walls.

In this practice you will extrude walls from a spline to create 3D walls. You will then refine the walls by creating openings for a corridor and doors, using the **Extrude** modifier. Additionally, you will use **ProBoolean** objects to graphically subtract two objects from the walls.

You must set the paths to locate the External files and Xrefs used in the practice. If you have not done this already, return to **Chapter 1: Introduction to Autodesk 3ds Max** and complete Task 1 to Task 3 in **Practice 1a: Organizing Folders and Working with the Interface**. You only have to set the user paths once.

Estimated time for completion: 20 minutes

Task 1 - Extrude the Walls.

1. Open **Spline Walls Bound.max**.

2. In the Scene Explorer toolbar, click ▉ (Display None) and click 🔲 (Display Shapes). Select **Layer:VIZ-1-Walls** and note that the 2D lines for the walls (cyan colored shapes) are selected in the viewport. .

*If a dialog box opens prompting you about a File Load: Mismatch, click **OK** to accept the default values.*

*If the Scene Explorer is not displayed, select **Tools>Scene Explorer** or click ▦ (Toggle Scene Explorer) in the Main Toolbar.*

3. In the Command Panel, select the Modify panel (🔲). The name **Layer:VIZ-1-Walls** displays in the Command Panel and it is an **Editable Spline**.

4. In the Modifier List, select **Extrude**. In the Parameters rollout, set *Amount* to **11'0"** (the height of the first floor walls), as shown in Figure 5–35. Press <Enter>.

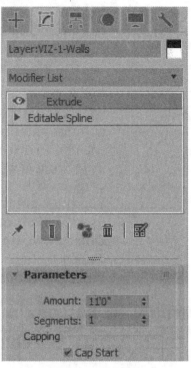

Figure 5–35

The missing wall sections eventually contain curtain walls.

5. Click 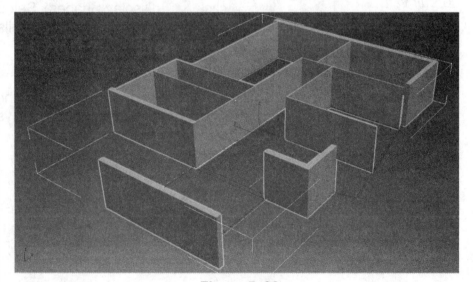 (Zoom Extents All). Only the areas enclosed by the wall linework are extruded, as shown in Figure 5–36.

Figure 5–36

Task 2 - Creating the Subtraction Operands.

The Layer Explorer is a modeless dialog box and can remain open while you are working in the viewport.

1. In the Main Toolbar, click 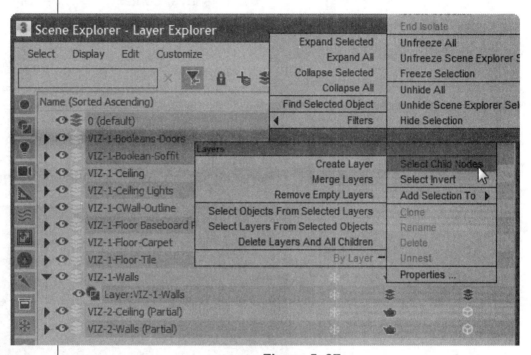 (Layer Explorer). In the Layer Explorer, select the two layers **VIZ-1-Booleans-Doors** and **VIZ-1-Boolean-Soffit**. Right-click on any of the selected layer and click **Select Child Nodes**, as shown in Figure 5–37. These layers contain closed polylines that define the openings to be created. Note that these layers are selected as well.

Figure 5–37

2. To avoid a coplanar face along the floor, first move these objects below the floor level. In the Main Toolbar, click

   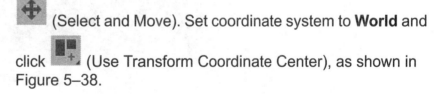 (Select and Move). Set coordinate system to **World** and

   click  (Use Transform Coordinate Center), as shown in Figure 5–38.

Figure 5–38

3. In the Status Bar, in the *Transform Type-In* area, activate

   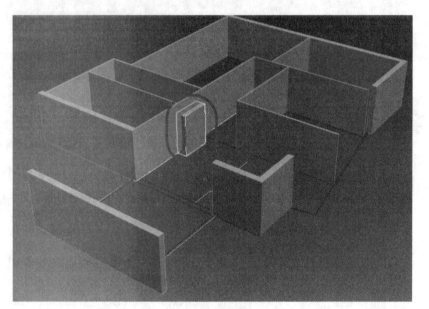 (Offset Mode Transform), enter **-1'0"** in the *Z* field, and press <Enter>.

4. In the Main Toolbar, click (Select object).

5. Click anywhere in empty space to clear the selection. In the Layer Explorer, highlight only the layer **VIZ-1-Boolean-Soffit**. Right-click on the selected layer and click **Select Child Nodes**. This layer contains a single polyline defining an opening in one of the walls.

6. In the Command Panel>Modify panel ( ), verify that the name **Layer:VIZ-1-Boolean-Soffit** displays in the panel.

7. In the Modifier List, select **Extrude**. In the Parameters rollout, set *Amount* to **9'0"** and press <Enter> (this is **8'** + the **1'** that was just used to lower the object). The first subtraction operand (8'0") is created, as shown in Figure 5–39.

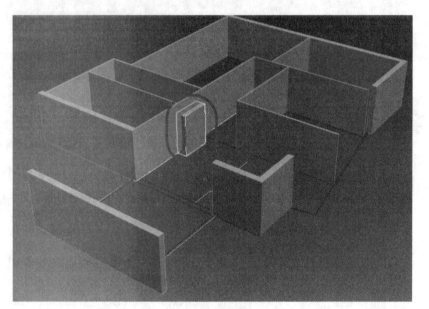

Figure 5–39

8. Repeat Steps 5 to 7 for **VIZ-1-Booleans-Doors**. Select the child layer of **VIZ-1-Booleans-Doors** and extrude it with an *Amount* of **8'0"**. The 7'0" subtraction operands are created, as shown in Figure 5–40.

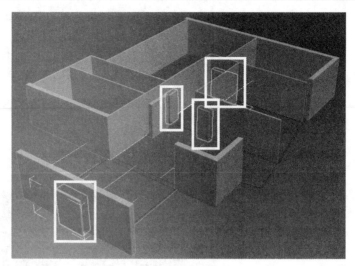

Figure 5–40

Task 3 - Creating the Wall Openings.

1. In the Layer Explorer, select **VIZ-1-Walls.** Right-click on the selected layer and click **Select Child Nodes**.

2. In the Create panel (+)> ● (Geometry), select **Compound Objects** in the drop-down list, as shown in Figure 5–41. Click **ProBoolean** to convert the wall system into a Boolean object. The selected walls **(VIZ-1-Walls)** are now your Operand A.

3. In the Pick Boolean rollout, verify that **Move** is selected and click **Start Picking**.

4. In the Parameters rollout, in the *Operation* area, verify that **Subtraction** is selected, as shown in Figure 5–42. This subtracts **Operand B** (the soffit opening) from **Operand A** (the walls).

Figure 5–41

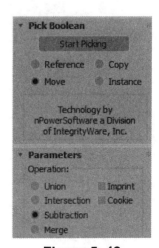

Figure 5–42

5. In the viewport, select the Boolean Soffit extrusion (**VIZ -1-Boolean Soffit**, the 9'0" operand that was created first). The volume contained by the Soffit object is removed from the walls, as shown in Figure 5–43.

6. Click any of the **VIZ-1-Boolean-Doors** objects to complete the second ProBoolean subtraction operation. The volume contained by the Doors object is also removed from the walls, as shown in Figure 5–43.

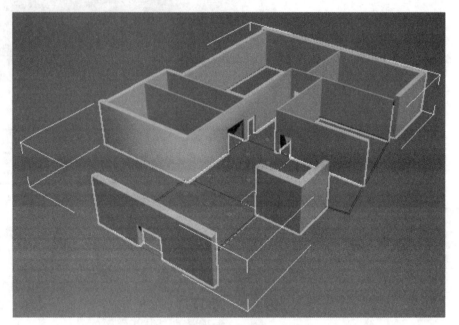

Figure 5–43

7. Click **Start Picking** to end the ProBoolean operation.

8. The ProBoolean operation has the ability to change the way the faces are built in the object using the Quadrilateral Tessellation function. In the Layer Explorer, with the **VIZ-1-Walls** highlighted, right-click on **VIZ-1-Walls** and select **Properties**. In the Object Properties dialog box, verify that the *Name* displays as **Layer:VIZ-1-Walls**. In the *Display Properties* area, click **By Layer** to toggle it to **By Object**. Clear **Edges Only** and click **OK**.

9. Press <F4> to display the edges of the newly created faces, as shown in Figure 5–44. Note the way long triangular faces are created on some of the walls.

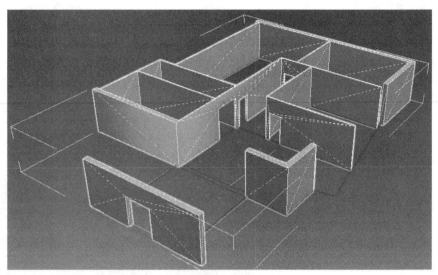

Figure 5–44

10. In the Command Panel>Modify panel ( ), note that the **ProBoolean** is displayed in the Modifier Stack. Expand the Advanced Options rollout (collapse Pick Boolean and Parameters rollouts). In the *Quadrilateral Tessellation* area, select **Make Quadrilaterals**, as shown in Figure 5–45. Note how the geometry has changed. There are no long triangular faces, as shown on the right in Figure 5–46.

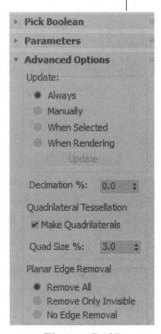

Figure 5–45

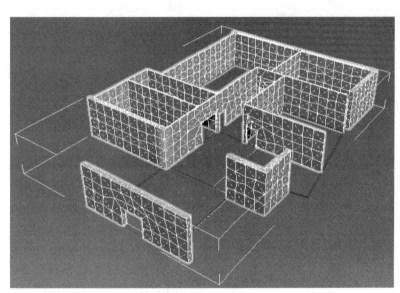

Figure 5–46

11. Increase the *Quad Size %* to **10.0**. This modifies the geometry so that the polygons are bigger, as shown in Figure 5–47.

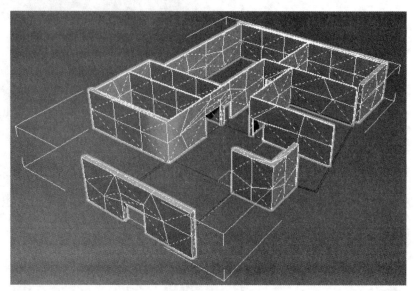

Figure 5–47

12. You can collapse the **ProBoolean** to a simple mesh. In the Modifier Stack, right-click on **ProBoolean** and select **Editable Poly**.

13. Save your work as **MySpline Walls Bound.max**.

Hint: Controlling Edge Line Visibility

After a Boolean or other complex operation, there might be missing or unnecessary edge lines in a wireframe or default shading viewport rendering mode. To easily read the geometry on the screen, only certain edges across your 3D object are visible.

To display the edges, right-click on the object and select **Object Properties**. In the *Display Properties* area, clear **Edges Only**. The **Edges Only** is available in **By Object**. Click **By Layer** to change it to **By Object**.

Alternatively, in the Modify panel, add an **Edit Mesh** modifier to your object and select **Edge** Sub-object mode. In the **Edit** menu, select **Select All**. In the Surface Properties rollout, click **Invisible** to make all edges invisible. Click **Auto Edge** to show only the edges with 24°+ separation. To get required results on curved objects (including curved walls), you might have to enter different separation angles.

5.6 Using Snaps for Precision

Snaps enable you to create, move, rotate, and scale objects with precision and are activated using the buttons in the Main Toolbar, as shown in Figure 5–48. Press <S> to toggle Snaps on and off while drawing lines, creating primitives, or transforming objects.

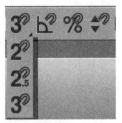

Figure 5–48

The available Toggle options are described as follows:

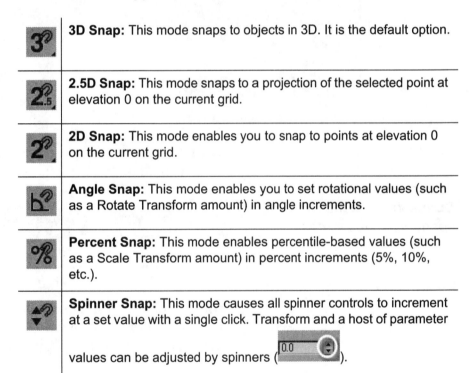	**3D Snap:** This mode snaps to objects in 3D. It is the default option.
	2.5D Snap: This mode snaps to a projection of the selected point at elevation 0 on the current grid.
	2D Snap: This mode enables you to snap to points at elevation 0 on the current grid.
	Angle Snap: This mode enables you to set rotational values (such as a Rotate Transform amount) in angle increments.
	Percent Snap: This mode enables percentile-based values (such as a Scale Transform amount) in percent increments (5%, 10%, etc.).
	Spinner Snap: This mode causes all spinner controls to increment at a set value with a single click. Transform and a host of parameter values can be adjusted by spinners ( ).

- Snap settings, such as the increment values for angle and percent snap, can be set in the *Options* tab of the Grid and Snap Settings dialog box, as shown in Figure 5–49. The dialog box can be accessed by right-clicking on **2D**, **2.5D**, **3D**, **Angle**, or **Percent Snap**, from **Tools>Grids and Snaps>Grid and Snap Settings**, or by holding <Shift> and right-clicking anywhere in the viewport.

- The active snaps are selected in the *Snaps* tab of the Grid and Snap Settings dialog box, as shown in Figure 5–50.

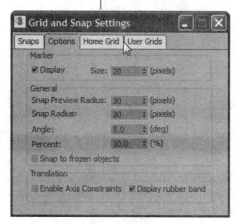

Figure 5–49

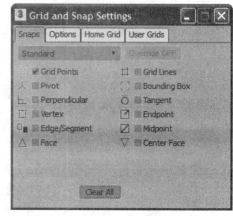

Figure 5–50

*Right-click on empty space in the Main Toolbar and select **Snaps** in the menu to open the Snaps toolbar.*

- You can activate snaps by selecting buttons in the Snaps toolbar (hidden by default), as shown in Figure 5–51.

Figure 5–51

- You can also activate snaps in the **Snaps** quad menu (hold <Shift>, right-click anywhere in the viewport, and select **Standard**, as shown in Figure 5–52.

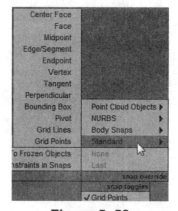

Figure 5–52

- The toolbar contains buttons for the most common snap settings. These are described as follows:

 Grid Points: Snaps to grid intersections.

 Pivot: Snaps to the pivot point of an object.

 Vertex: Snaps to vertices on splines, meshes, or similar geometry.

 Endpoint: Snaps to the vertices at the end of a spline segment, mesh edge, or similar geometry. Similar to Vertex except that not all vertices are at the endpoints of spline segments and mesh edges.

 Midpoint: Snaps to the middle of spline segments, mesh edges, or similar geometry.

 Edge/Segment: Snaps to anywhere along spline segments, mesh edges, or similar geometry.

 Face: Snaps anywhere on the surface of a face.

 Snap to Frozen Objects: Enables other snaps to reference frozen objects.

 Snaps Use Axis Constraints: Forces result along the selected axis constraints set in the Axis Constraints toolbar.

- The following additional snaps are available in the Snap and Grid Settings dialog box and the **Snaps** quad menu.

Grid Lines	Snaps to anywhere along a grid line.
Bounding Box	Snaps to the corners of an object's bounding box.
Perpendicular	Snaps perpendicularly to a spline segment.
Tangent:	Snaps tangent to a curved spline segment.
Center Face	Snaps to the center of triangular faces.

By default, these snapping methods are not directly available in the software interface and are required to be added to the toolbar.

- The two additional snap functions available in the Autodesk 3ds Max software are described as follows:

 Ortho Snapping: Forces a transform in the horizontal or vertical directions based on the active grid.

 Polar Snapping: Forces results to the angle increment set in the Grid and Snap Settings dialog box.

Hint: Adding Snapping modes to toolbar

1. Extend the Snaps toolbar by dragging either edge.
2. Open the Customize User Interface dialog box>*Toolbars* tab (**Customize>Customize User Interface**).
3. Select **Ortho Snapping Mode/ Polar Snapping Mode in** the Action list.
4. Drag the snap mode into the Snaps toolbar.

Hint: Snap to XRef Objects

You can snap to XRef objects just like any other object. In earlier versions, XRef objects were displayed in the scene, but were not recognized by the snap functions.

Practice 5e

Creating a Door with Snaps

Learning Objective

- Create doors at precise locations using snaps.

Estimated time for completion: 10 minutes

In this practice you will add a door to an opening, using snaps to position it precisely.

You must set the paths to locate the External files and Xrefs used in the practice. If you have not done this already, return to **Chapter 1: Introduction to Autodesk 3ds Max** and complete Task 1 to Task 3 in **Practice 1a: Organizing Folders and Working with the Interface**. You only have to set the user paths once.

*If a dialog box opens prompting you about a Mismatch, click **OK** to accept the default values.*

1. Reset the scene and open **Creating a Door.max**.
   - The scene contains extruded walls with openings and extruded carpet and tile areas. A camera has also been added.

2. Maximize the **Perspective** viewport.

3. In a **Perspective** viewport, use 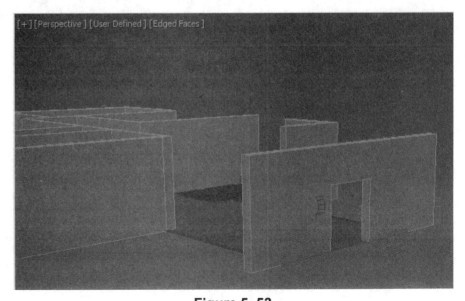 (Zoom) and (Orbit) to display the west side of the model (where the space for the outer door is located), as shown in Figure 5–53. Verify that the **Perspective** viewport displays as Default **Shading with Edged Faces**.

[+] [Perspective] [User Defined] [Edged Faces]

Figure 5–53

4. Using  (Zoom) and (Pan), zoom into the doorway opening (as shown in Figure 5–54) to display the points for snapping.

Figure 5–54

5. In the Main Toolbar, click (3D Snaps) to activate it. In the Command Panel, verify that Create panel> (Geometry) is open. In the Standard Primitives drop-down list, select **Doors**.

Hint: Create Window and Door Objects

By default, Autodesk 3ds Max Doors and Windows are created by:

- **Clicking and dragging:** To define the width of the door/window.

- **Releasing and picking:** A point to define the depth of the wall opening.

- **Releasing and picking:** A point to define the height of the opening.

---

6. In the Object Type rollout, click **Pivot** to start the door creation process, as shown in Figure 5–55.

*You can also press <Shift> and right-click to open the **Snaps** quad menu and select **Standard>Endpoint**.*

7. Open the Snaps toolbar, and click (Snap to Endpoint Toggle), as shown in Figure 5–56.

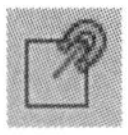

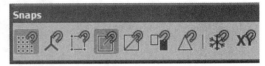

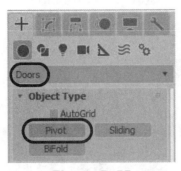

Figure 5–55

Figure 5–56

8. Hover the cursor at the bottom left corner of the door opening. Note that when the cursor hovers over the endpoint (corner), it snaps to that point and a small yellow square (endpoint marker) displays, as shown in Figure 5–57.

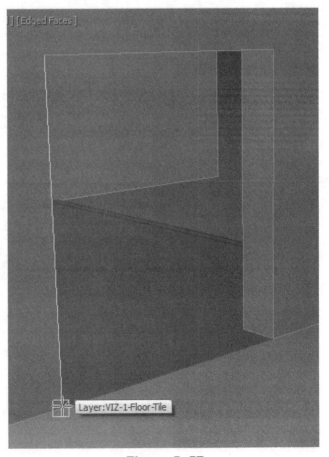

Figure 5–57

9. Click and hold at this point and then while still holding, drag the cursor over to the lower right corner. Once it snaps to the lower right corner (as shown in Figure 5–58), release the mouse button to define the width of the door.

- If you have difficulty with this, change the orientation of the **Perspective** viewport, as shown below. You might also want to change to Wireframe display.

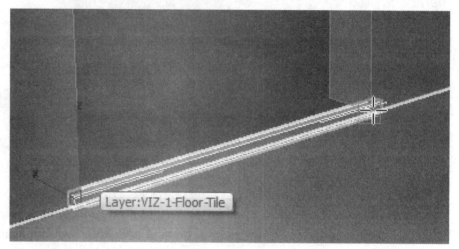

Figure 5–58

10. Move the cursor to the back corner of the door opening and click (not click and drag) to define the depth of the opening, as shown in Figure 5–59.

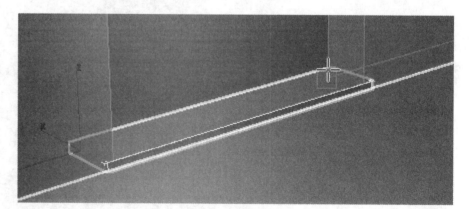

Figure 5–59

11. Move the cursor to the upper right corner of the door opening and click (not click and drag) to define the height, as shown in Figure 5–60. Sometimes this is difficult to do, depending on the angle of your view. You can toggle off the Snap by pressing <S>, then adjust the height using the Parameters rollout.

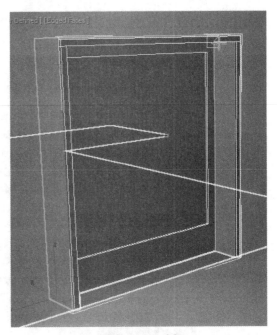

Figure 5–60

12. With the door still selected, in the Command Panel, select the

    Modify panel ( ). In the Parameters rollout, select **Double Doors**. Set the *Open* angle to **45°**. In the Leaf Parameters rollout, in the *Panels* area, select **Beveled**. Note that in the viewport, the door will change to double doors with beveled panels and will be open at a **45°** angle, as shown in Figure 5–61.

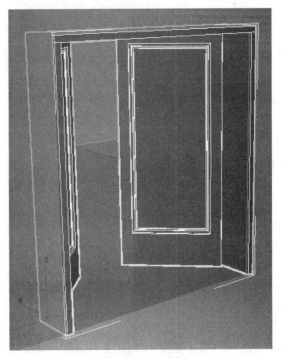

Figure 5–61

13. Set the *Open* angle to **0°** to display the panels as closed.

14. Save your work as **MyCreating a Door.max**.

Hint: Holes in Walls using Window and Door Objects

When you use Autodesk 3ds Max Wall objects combined with Window or Door objects, you can automatically create holes for the doors and windows using snaps to align them in place. If you create the door or window away from the wall, you can move it so it intersects with the wall. Use **Select and Link** to link the door or window to the wall to automatically create the hole. You can use Edge snap to align the doors with the walls.

The advantage is that if you move the door or window, the hole moves with it. However, this functionality only works when you create Autodesk 3ds Max wall objects and it is not available when you are extruding linked geometry.

5.7 The Sweep Modifier

The Sweep modifier is a simple and effective option to create 3D geometry based on a 2D section that follows a series of spline segment paths.

- This modifier can create 3D pipe networks, curbing, moldings, and similar types of geometry, very quickly.

- Sweeps are created by adding the Sweep modifier to the path, followed by adjusting cross-section settings and other parameters in the Modify panel.

- You can select a predefined cross-section shape such as, boxes, pipes, tees, and angles, or you can use a custom shape.

- Although this functionality is also available through the Loft compound object, the Sweep modifier is easier to configure.

To use the Sweep modifier, select a spline and then in the Modify panel (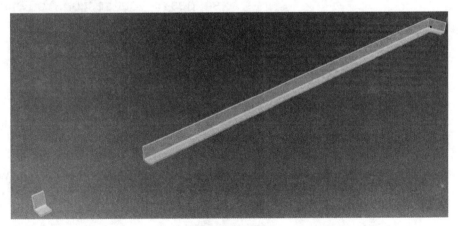), select **Sweep** from the Modifier List. Figure 5–62 shows an example of a wall baseboard created using the Sweep modifier.

Figure 5–62

Sweep Parameters

Section Type

In the Section Type rollout, you can select the type of profile that you want to sweep along the spline segments.

- If you selected **Use Built-In Section**, a list of precreated cross-sections is available as your profile, as shown in Figure 5–63. The **Angle** is the default cross-section.

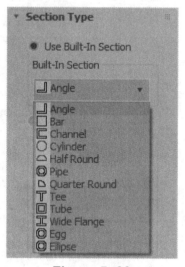

Figure 5–63

- You can select **Use Custom Section** to use a custom shapes as your section. You can either create your section in the current scene or obtain it from another .MAX file.

Interpolation

In the Interpolation rollout, you can control the smoothness of the cross-section by adding or removing vertices.

- Steps can be set to **0** for cross-section shapes that have sharp edges (no curves). Otherwise this value should be kept low to reduce complexity. The two options available are described as follows:

Optimize	Groups the supplemented vertices closer to the corners rather than evenly along the shape.
Adaptive	Tessellates (break into segments) curves in the section shape. Select Adaptive results in a wireframe rendering mode to reduce complexity

Parameters

In the Parameters rollout, you can control the size and shape of the predefined cross-sections.

Sweep Parameters

In the Sweep Parameters rollout, you can control the placement and orientation of the cross-section shape along the path object.

- If a sweep result is backwards or upside down, use the two mirroring options to correct it. The options available are described as follows:

Offset	This option enables you to shift the horizontal and vertical position of the sweep geometry away from the spline path
Angle	This options rotates the section relative to the plane. The spline path is drawn as defined by its pivot point.
Smooth Section/ Smooth Path	Selecting these options enables you to make the object smooth, even if the path object or shape are not smooth. In the case of the swept wall baseboard, the section is smoothed to make the cross-section display as filleted, not because the baseboard follows the angled corners of the wall.
Pivot Alignment	This options enables you to anchor the cross-section shape to the path based on the shape's pivot point.
Banking	This options rotates a cross-section shape assigned to a 3D path, similar to an airplane rolling during a turn

Practice 5f

Sweeping the Wall Baseboard

Practice Objective

- Create a wall baseboard by extruding a pre-created cross-section along a selected spline.

Estimated time for completion:15 minutes

In this practice you will create a vinyl baseboard object around the walls using the **Sweep** modifier.

You must set the paths to locate the External files and Xrefs used in the practice. If you have not done this already, return to **Chapter 1: Introduction to Autodesk 3ds Max** and complete Task 1 to Task 3 in **Practice 1a: Organizing Folders and Working with the Interface**. You only have to set the user paths once.

Task 1 - Sweep the path.

*If a dialog box opens prompting you about a Mismatch, click **OK** to accept the default values.*

1. Open **Sweep Modifier.max**.
   - The scene contains the extruded walls and main door in the closed position. A camera has also been added.

2. Open the Layer Explorer (Main Toolbar> ▤ (Layer Explorer). Select and right-click on **VIZ-1-Floor Baseboard Path**. In the menu, select **Select Child Nodes**. This layer contains a series of lines and polylines that define the base of the wall with gaps at the openings. Close the Layer Explorer.

*You can also right-click in the viewport and select **Isolate Selection** or press <Alt>+<Q> to activate the Isolate Selection.*

3. In the Status Bar, click ⬚ (Isolate Selection Toggle) to only display the selected sweep path (2D line). Click anywhere in the **Perspective** viewport to clear the selection. Zoom in so that the path (lines) are displayed as shown in Figure 5–64.

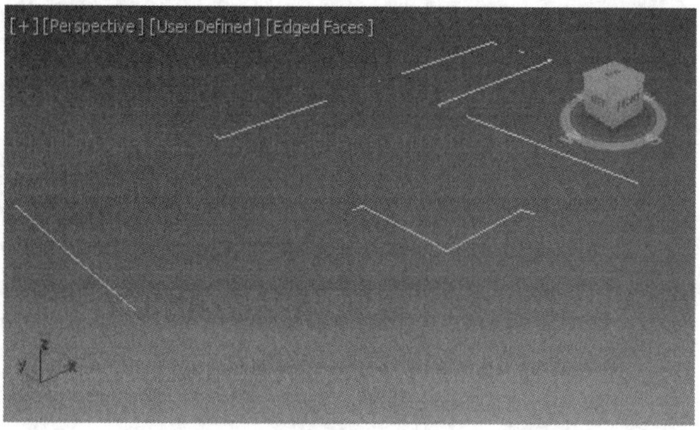

Figure 5–64

4. In the **Perspective** viewport, click on the 2D line to select it.

You can also create a custom profile to be swept along the sweep spline.

5. In the Command Panel, select the Modify panel (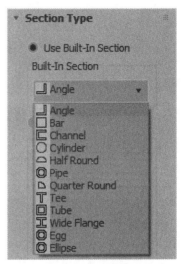). The name **VIZ-1-Floor Baseboard Path** is displayed. In the Modifier List, select **Sweep**. The **Sweep** modifier displays in the Modifier Stack. In the **Perspective** viewport, zoom in on the left side baseboard. Note that the lines have extruded along an angled cross-section, as shown in Figure 5–65. The shape of the extrusion depends on the selected *Built In Selection* in the Section Type rollout. The **Angle** type is the default selection, as shown in Figure 5–66.

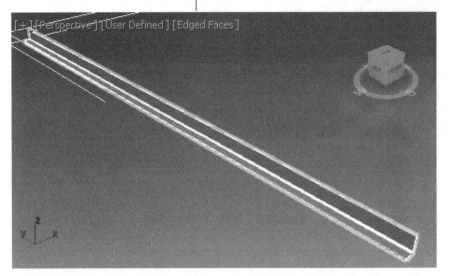

Figure 5–65

Figure 5–66

6. In the Interpolation rollout, set *Steps* to **0**. (Since all of the wall corners are square, there are no curves required to interpolate along the path.)

7. In the Parameters rollout, set the values shown in Figure 5–67. This shape is meant to create a baseboard with minimal detail. In the viewport, note how the baseboard detail changes.

8. The angle is still facing outward (in the wrong direction). In the Sweep Parameters rollout, select **Mirror on XZ Plane** to reverse the angle face. Clear **Smooth Path** (all of the corners are square and should not display as rounded). Anchor the

   Pivot Alignment option by clicking ⬚ in the lower right corner. This option creates the 3D geometry object by sweeping the lower left corner of the baseboard cross-section along the baseboard path. Select **Gen. Mapping Coords.** and **Real-World Map Size**, as shown in Figure 5–68.

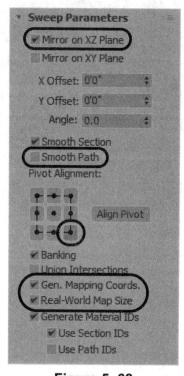

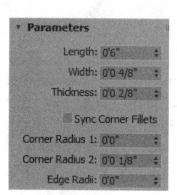

Figure 5–67   Figure 5–68

9. In the Status Bar, click ⬚ (Isolate Selection Toggle) again to clear it. The walls and other geometry are now displayed.

10. In the **Front** viewport, select the **Front** Point of View label and select **Cameras>Camera002-Door**. This displays the door from the inside. Select the **Visual Style** label and select **Default Shading** and **Edged Faces**. Note that the baseboard runs along the entire wall, including the door, as shown in Figure 5–69.

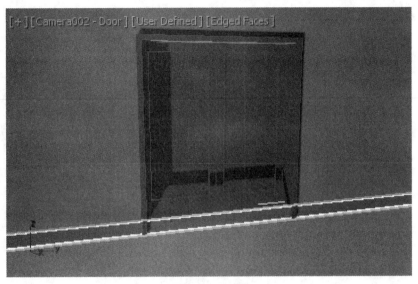

Figure 5–69

Task 2 - Modify the path.

1. Maximize the **Camera002-Door** viewport.

2. Click anywhere on the baseboard to select it. In the Modify

    panel (), verify that *Name* displays **Layer:VIZ-1-Floor Baseboard Path**.

3. In the Modifier Stack, in Editable Spline, select **Vertex**. In the viewport, note that the baseboard is not displayed because you have selected an option before the **Sweep** modifier.

4. In the Geometry rollout, click **Refine**.

5. Verify that snap is cleared. In the viewport, click on the spline to place a vertex on either side and outside of the door frame, as shown in Figure 5–70. Once the two vertices have been placed, click **Refine** again to clear it.

Figure 5–70

6. In Editable Spline, select **Segment**. In the viewport, click on the segment between the two vertices, in front of the door. It displays as a red line, as shown in Figure 5–71.

Figure 5–71

7. With the segment selected, press <Delete> to remove the segment.

8. In the Modifier Stack, select **Sweep**. In the viewport, note that the baseboard has been modified and does not pass in front of the door, as shown in Figure 5–72.

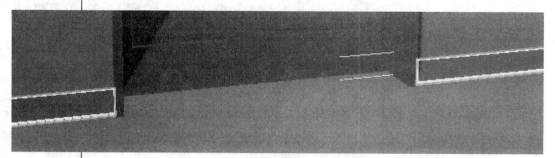

Figure 5–72

9. Maximize to open the four viewports display.

10. In the Application Menu, expand **Import**, and select **Merge**. In the Merge File dialog box, select **Interior Furnishings and Detail.max**. Click **Open**. In the Merge dialog box, click **All** at the bottom left to select all of the objects and click **OK**.

11. In the **Perspective** viewport, select the **Perspective** Point of View Viewport label and select **Cameras>Camera001 – Lobby1**. This changes the display to look through the newly merged **Camera – Lobby1**, as shown in Figure 5–73.

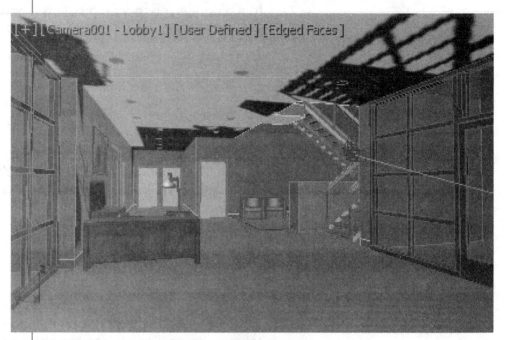

Figure 5–73

12. Select **Edit>Select None** to clear the object selection.

- Note that the desk, chairs, and other furnishings are AutoCAD Architecture 3D blocks. The curtain walls, stairs, and doors are examples of architectural objects that can be created. Save your work as **MySweep Modifier.max**.

Hint: Precreated Objects

Instead of modeling all of your scene content from scratch, look for royalty-free or low-cost objects posted on the Internet. Consider 3D blocks from other software, such as AutoCAD Architecture, Autodesk Revit, AutoCAD Civil 3D, or directly from manufacturer's web sites.

Chapter Review Questions

1. While editing a spline at the vertex sub-object level, which tool enables you to manipulate the handles on one side of the curve separately from the other handle?

    a. **Bezier**

    b. **Bezier Corner**

    c. **Smooth**

    d. **Smooth Corner**

2. To combine shapes using the 2D Boolean operations, which sub-object level in the **Edit Spline** modifier should be selected?

    a. Vertex

    b. Segment

    c. Spline

3. Which **Sweep** modifier option in the Sweep Parameters rollout rotates a cross-section shape assigned to a 3D path?

    a. **Offset**

    b. **Angle**

    c. **Banking**

    d. **Pivot Alignment**

4. Which of the following Snap mode enables you to snap to points at elevation **0** on the current grid?

    a. (Angle Snap)

    b. (3D Snap)

    c. (2.5D Snap)

    d. (2D Snap)

5. You cannot snap to XRef objects as with any other object because the XRef objects are not recognized by the snap functions.

   a. True

   b. False

Command Summary

Button	Command	Location
3	3D Snap	• **Main Toolbar:** Snaps flyout
2.5	2.5D Snap	• **Main Toolbar:** Snaps flyout
2	2D Snap	• **Main Toolbar:** Snaps flyout
	Angle Snap	• **Main Toolbar**
	Isolate Selection	• **Status Bar** • **Keyboard:** <Alt>+<Q>
	Manage Layers	• **Main Toolbar** • **Layers Toolbar**
N/A	Merge	• **Application Menu:** Import
	Offset Mode	• **Status Bar**
	Percent Snap	• **Main Toolbar**
	Shapes	• **Command Panel:** *Create* panel • **Create:** Shapes
	Snap to Edge/ Segment	• **Snaps Toolbar**
	Snap to Endpoint	• **Snaps Toolbar**
	Snap to Frozen Objects	• **Snaps Toolbar**
	Snap to Grid Point	• **Snaps Toolbar**
	Snap to Midpoint	• **Snaps Toolbar**
	Snap to Pivot	• **Snaps Toolbar**
	Snap to Vertex	• **Snaps Toolbar**
XY	Snaps use Axis Constraints	• **Snaps Toolbar**

Materials

To create a realistic visualization, materials are used to more accurately represent the model as a realistic real-world design. The Autodesk® 3ds Max® software provides material libraries that can be used to assign materials to objects in a scene or to create and customize materials. Materials control such attributes as color, texture, transparency, and a host of other physical properties that you can adjust to create a realistic representation of the model.

Learning Objectives in this Chapter

- Understand the role of materials and maps in visualization.
- Control the various attributes of a material using various shaders, components, and maps.
- Display and manage all of the materials used in a scene using the Material Explorer.
- Use various types of Standard materials and control the parameters of the material shaders.
- Assign bitmaps or procedural maps to replace the shader parameters in materials.
- Control transparency, embossed or pitted appearance, glass or mirror effect on objects using various mapping techniques.
- Understand the various types of mental ray materials and control their various attributes.

6.1 Understanding Materials and Maps

Introduction to Materials

Materials can be used to create believable visualizations and to dress up geometry so that it resembles objects in the real world. Materials control how light interacts with surfaces in 3D models. If an object is shiny it reflects the light, however, if transparency is applied, the light passes through the object.

- Materials use Maps to paint the surfaces with all types of textures to resemble the actual construction materials for your design.

- Different material types use different material shaders to generate their work. Shaders are algorithms that create the image. Each shader has its own set of parameters.

In the 3D visualization process, to create an image in the viewport or in a image file, a *renderer* is employed. The viewport display uses an interactive viewport renderer however the image is created using an *image* (production) renderer. The renderer determines what the pixel's RGB (red, green, blue) values are in the image based on the material assignments.

Materials and Renderers in the Autodesk 3ds Max software

In the Autodesk 3ds Max software, you can use the scanline, quicksilver, iray renderer, or mental ray renderers as image renderers.

- The viewport renderer can use Nitrous Direct 3D 11 (default), Nitrous Direct3D 9, Nitrous Software, Legacy Direct3D, or Legacy OpenGL graphics drivers to create the real-time interactive display.

- The standard material type is associated with the Autodesk 3ds Max scanline renderer.

- mental ray materials (*Autodesk Material Library/Arch & Design* materials) work with the mental ray renderer.

Materials are deeply interconnected with the renderers. The rendering process is similar for any material type using any renderer. The viewport provides a frame around the image and the output resolution determines the number of pixels to be created in that frame. The renderer then examines the geometry in the scene, first looking at the face normals, removing the faces whose normals face away from the camera (face normals are directional vectors perpendicular to the surface of the face). The remaining faces are z-sorted, the faces in front covering up the ones further away.

- Once the faces are determined, the color, transparency, shininess, texture, reflection, bumpiness, and other values are defined based on the material type, shaders, and map channels.

- The visible faces are calculated using the UVW mapping coordinates and the scene illumination. This determines RGB values, which are applied to the pixels in the image.

Material Components

Materials have several fundamental components. Standard materials have channels that determine the color applied in the calculation based on the lighting interaction. The components available are described as follows:

- The *Diffuse* channel represents those faces that are receiving illumination.

- The *Ambient* channel paints the faces that are in darkness, and it contributes color to all faces in the scene.

- The *Specular* channel determines color based on shininess and lighting information.

- The Shininess is controlled by various parameters, such as **Specularity** and **Glossiness**. Shininess also plays a part in reflection and refraction.

- A Transparency quality is determined by *opacity* values, which can have advanced features such as *falloff* and *additive* or subtractive behavior.

- Materials are defined by maps and other physical properties (diffuse, ambient, shininess, etc.).

Maps

Maps are the key components when working with materials. Maps are based on either 2D image files (bitmaps) or are formula-based, computer-generated images called procedural maps. Some maps can be configured as composites or adjustments to other maps.

- Materials can include multiple maps to serve different purposes.

- Map also serve in other roles, such as an environment background or a lighting projection (a gobo).

When a material containing a map is applied to an object, mapping coordinates are required for the software to render correctly.

- Maps cannot be applied directly to objects in a scene; instead, they are assigned to materials. These materials are then directly applied to objects, as shown in Figure 6–1.

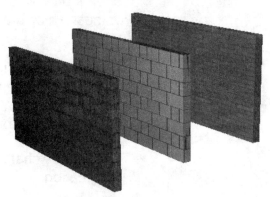

Figure 6–1

- Two of the most commonly used maps types are **diffuse color** and **bump**.

Diffuse Color	Defines the color of objects under normal lighting.
	• Digital or scanned photographs can be used as Diffuse Color maps.
	• The figure below is a brick image map (left) and a rendering of an object with a brick material that uses it (right).

Bump maps	Make objects appear to have texture without modifying object geometry.
	• Bump maps are used to describe indentations, relief, and roughness.
	• In bump maps the lighter-colored areas display projected away from the surface while the darker areas display recessed.
	• The figure below displays a brick bump map (left) and a rendering of an object with a brick material that uses it (right).
	• You can apply both the diffuse and bump map to a single object.
	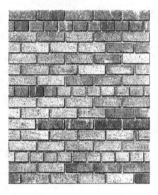 

• In addition to these two map types, the Autodesk 3ds Max software can use maps to control many different material parameters that might vary across a surface, including shininess, transparency, and more.

6.2 Managing Materials

Materials are managed through the Material Editor (Slate or Compact). The Slate Material Editor has the Material/Map Browser included with it whereas the Compact Material Editor has an option for accessing the Material/Map Browser.

- Use the Slate Material Editor to design and build materials.

- Use the Compact Material Editor to apply existing materials.

Slate Material Editor Interface

The Slate Material Editor is a graphical interface for listing, creating, modifying, and assigning different kinds of materials. It enables you to graphically create and modify complex materials by wiring the maps and materials to different channels of the parent material. It also enables you to edit and modify the parameters of already created materials. In the Main Toolbar, in the Material flyout, use 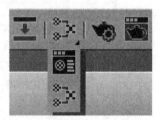 (Slate Material Editor) to open the Slate Material Editor, as shown in Figure 6–2.

Figure 6–2

The interface of the Slate Material Editor has the following main areas:

Material/Map Browser

The Material/Map Browser area (shown in Figure 6–3) contains an extensive list of predefined materials and maps. You can use the predefined materials directly or as a base for modifying them to get the required material effect.

*You can also select **Rendering>Material Editor>Slate Material Editor**. Pressing <M> opens the last material editor that was used.*

Figure 6–3

*You can also open the Material/Map Browser independent of the Material Editor by selecting **Rendering> Material/Map Browser** in the menu bar.*

- The Browser displays by default, but you can temporarily close it by clicking **X** in the title bar. You can open it by selecting **Tools>Material/Map Browser** in the Slate Material Editor's menu bar (as shown in Figure 6–4) or by pressing <O> when the Slate Material Editor is the active window.

- At the top of the Material/Map Browser, click ▼ to open the drop-down list (options menu), as shown in Figure 6–5. It contains options that enable you to control the display of the libraries, materials, maps, and other groups of materials. It also enables you to create and manage new custom libraries and groups.

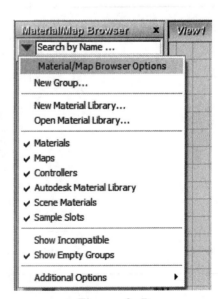

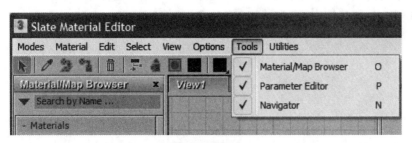

Figure 6–4

Figure 6–5

The materials and maps listed in the Material/ Map Browser are dependent on the active renderer.

- The *Search by Name* box enables you to enter the first few characters of the material/map name to display the list of materials/maps that you want to use.

- The materials in the Browser are organized in the form of libraries and groups. The groups are organized on the basis of their attributes such as Maps, Materials, etc and are further divided into subgroups (For example, **Materials>Standard**). Each library or group has a +/- sign, to expand or contract, along with its heading.

- The *Materials* and *Maps* groups contain the type of materials and maps that can be used as templates for creating custom materials and maps.

- The *Controller* group contains the animation controllers that can be used for material animation.

- The Autodesk Material Library contains the mental ray Arch and Design materials and only displays when the active production renderer is set to **NVIDIA iray**, **NVIDIA mental ray**, or **Quicksilver Hardware Renderer**.

- All of the materials used in the scene are listed in the *Scene Materials* group. A solid wedge shaped red band displayed with a scene material name indicates that the **Show Shaded Material In Viewport** option has been selected.

- The materials listed in the Browser are dependent on the type of renderer currently in use. To see all of the materials independent of the renderer, select **Show Incompatible** option in the Material/Map Browser drop-down list (click ▼ to open the options menu).

Active View

The Active View is an area in the Slate Material Editor that displays the expanded view of materials with all its elements shown as nodes, as shown in Figure 6–6. You can graphically create and modify complex materials by wiring their nodes together, and further edit their parameters through this view.

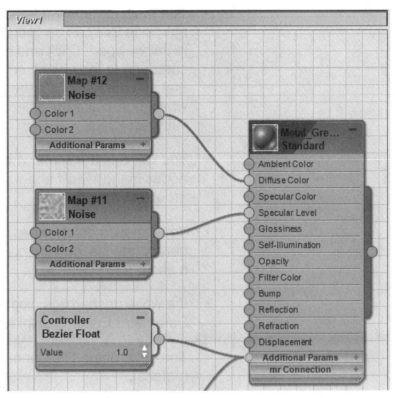

Figure 6–6

You can also double-click on the material in the Map/Material Browser to automatically place it on the View1 sheet.

- To display a material in the active view (*View1*, by default), drag the material from the Map/Material Browser and then drop it on the *View1* sheet. These are called nodes.

- Once the material node is loaded on the active view, the title bar with a preview icon is displayed and the list of various channel slots are listed, as shown in Figure 6–6. You can wire each of these slots to another map or material. On the left side, each node has a number of input sockets (small circles) for each slot. On the right side of each node is a single output socket. These can be wired to the sockets of other material. If a map or material is wired to a channel, the slot displays in green. This material, with its input sockets wired, becomes the parent material and the materials and maps that are wired to the slots become the children. You can further wire the children to other materials to create complex material trees.

- You can also right-click in an empty area of the active view to open a menu containing options for selecting any material/map/controller listed in the Material/Map Browser.

- The main material node has a blank output socket on the right side that can be used to assign this material to geometry in the viewport. Click and hold the output socket and drag the cursor on to the object. A temporary wire displays indicating that you are assigning the material. Assigning material in this way ignores already selected objects or geometry in the viewport.

- You can use the scroll wheel to zoom in or zoom out on the nodes in the *View1* sheet. Hold the scroll wheel to pan around in the sheet.

- You can also delete wires to cut the connection between the parent material and the child material. To delete a wire, select it and press <Delete>.

- If a white dashed line displays as a border around a node, its Parameter Editor is displayed in the active view.

- The color of the title bar of the node indicates the type of material.

Blue node	Indicates that it is a material.
Green node	Indicates that it is a Map.
Yellow node	Indicates that it is a Controller

- A diagonal line dividing the title bar into two colors (red and blue) indicates that the **Show Shaded Material In Viewport** option is selected for that material.

- Right-clicking on a title bar of a node displays a specific right-click menu containing the options for managing that material or map. The options enable you to control the display and how you want the preview to be displayed on the active sheet. It also enables you to organize the material nodes and their children more efficiently.

- You can select multiple material/map nodes together, then right-click to open the combined menu and use the options for all of the nodes at the same time.

- You can toggle between a large and small material preview icon by double-clicking on the icon in the node title bar.

- The outline of a preview icon indicates whether the material is assigned or not (hot or cold) to objects in the viewport.

	No white boundary around the icon indicates that the material is not used in the scene and is cold.
	Outlined white triangles at the four corners indicate the material is hot and is being used in the scene. Modifying this material interactively displays the modifications in the scene.
	Solid white triangles at the four corners indicate the material is applied to the currently selected object on the scene.

- Additional sheets can be added to the View area by right-clicking on the default *View1* tab and selecting **Create New View**. Using this menu, you can also rename and delete your views. Once multiple sheets exist, you can select the appropriate tab to active it.

Hint: Active View

To organize your working space, it is recommended that you delete any unused materials from the active view. Deleting a material from the active view does not delete the material from the Scene materials list. You can drag and drop (or double-click) the material back to the active view.

- After you have created and applied materials to a scene, the *View* sheets are saved with the .MAX file. When you open the file again, the sheets display the saved material nodes.

Navigator Window

The Navigator window, which displays by default, provides a quick layout of the nodes in the active sheet, as shown in Figure 6–7. It can be used to pan around in the active view by dragging the outlined red box. The colored nodes indicate the same concepts as that of a sheet. A red and blue node indicates that the **Show Map In Viewport** option is selected for that material.

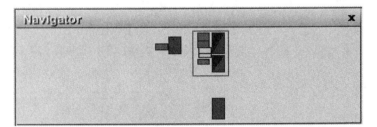

Figure 6–7

Parameter Editor

You can modify a material or a map by adjusting their parameters. Double-click on the material's title bar heading to display the Parameters, as shown in Figure 6–8. A white dashed line border displays around the node indicating that its Parameter Editor is displayed. The parameters are grouped in rollouts and you can click **+** on the rollout name bar to expand the rollout and access its parameters. You can rename the material by entering a new name in the *Name* field of the Parameter Editor.

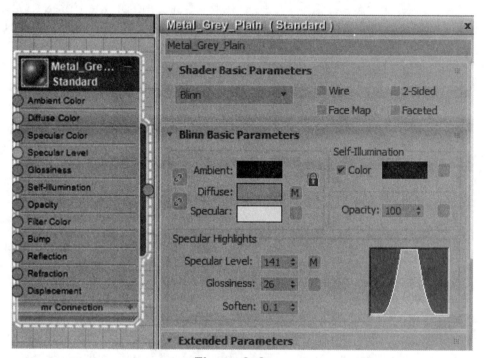

Figure 6–8

Floating the Parameter Editor and hiding the Navigator can help reduce the footprint of the Slate Material Editor on the screen.

- As with any other window, you can move, dock, float, or close the Parameter Editor. To float the Parameter Editor, drag its header outside the Slate Material Editor. To dock it again, double-click on its header.

Toolbar

The Slate Material Editor includes a toolbar (shown in Figure 6–9) at the top left corner of the window and contains the following tools.

Figure 6–9

(Select Tool)	Enables you to select a material node in the Active View. It is the tool that is selected by default.
(Pick Material from Object)	Enables you to pick a material that is assigned to an object in the scene and display it in the active view.
(Put Material to Scene)	Enables you to update objects having an older material whose copy has been edited after it was applied.
(Assign Material to Selection)	Enables you to assign a selected material to selected objects in the viewport.
(Move Children)	Enables you to move the complete material tree when you move the parent material node in the Active View. Clearing this tool, moves the Parent individually and extends the wires as you move the parent
(Show Shaded Material in Viewport)	Enables you to display the maps for the active material. This is helpful when you are modifying the map in the View sheet, you can see the changes interactively in the viewport. You do not have to render to see the map changes.
/ (Lay Out All-Vertical/ Horizontal)	Enables you to organize all of the material nodes and their children in the View sheet either vertically or horizontally.
(Lay Out Children)	Enables you to lay out the children of the currently selected node without changing the position of the parent node.
(Material/Map Browser) (Parameter Editor)	Enable you to control the display of these tools in the Slate Material Editor.
(Select by Material)	Enables you to select objects based on the active material.

Menu Bar

The Slate Material Editor displays a menu bar along the top of the window (shown in Figure 6–10) that contains commands for various actions related to materials.

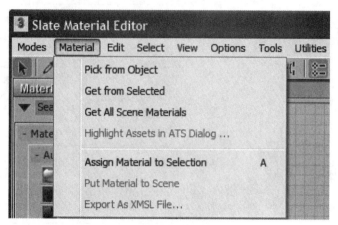

Figure 6–10

Modes	Enables you to toggle between the two editors (Slate and Compact).
Material	Enable you to select a material by picking it from the object in the viewport, by selecting an object in the viewport, or selecting all of the materials used in the scene. You also have the options for assigning materials.
Edit	Enables you to edit the active view and update the preview windows.
Select	Provides different selection options that can be used in the active view.
View	Provides different zoom and pan options and contains options for the layout of the nodes in the active view.
Options	Enables you to further manage the Slate Material Editor.
Tools	Controls the display of the Material/Map Browser, Parameter Editor, and Navigator.
Utilities	Provides the render and object selection options and contains options for managing the materials.

Practice 6a

Introduction to Materials

Practice Objectives

- Load a material library in the Slate Material Editor.
- Create and edit a new material and assign it to objects in the scene.

Estimated time for completion: 20 minutes

In this practice you will assign previously created materials to different objects on the scene. You will then create, edit, and assign new materials to objects in the scene using the Parameter Editor of the Slate Material Editor.

You must set the paths to locate the External files and Xrefs used in the practice. If you have not done this already, return to **Chapter 1: Introduction to Autodesk 3ds Max** and complete Task 1 to Task 3 in **Practice 1a: Organizing Folders and Working with the Interface**. You only have to set the user paths once.

Task 1 - Assigning materials in the Slate Material Editor.

*If a dialog box opens prompting you about a Mismatch, click **OK** to accept the default values.*

1. Open **Intro to Materials and Rendering.max**.
   - The Light pole model is displayed in the viewport.

2. In the Main Toolbar, in the Material flyout, click (Slate Material Editor) to open the Slate Material Editor. Alternatively, you can select **Rendering>Material Editor>Slate Material Editor**.

If you start a new scene file, no materials are listed in the View1 sheet.

3. In the Slate Material Editor, in the *View1* sheet, four materials nodes are displayed, as shown in Figure 6–11. Note that all the materials used in the scene are listed in the *Scene Materials* group (bottom of the list) in the Material/Map Browser.

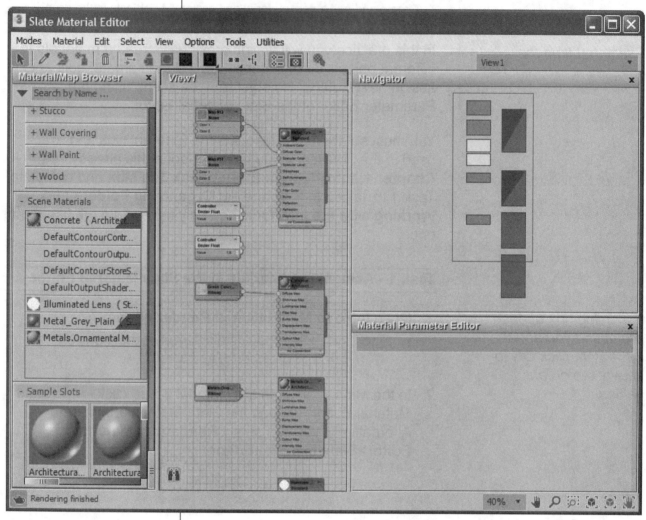

Figure 6–11

A blue node indicates that it is a material, a green node indicates that it is a Map, and a yellow node indicates that it is a Controller.

• A diagonal line dividing the title bar into two colors (red and blue) indicates that the **Show Map In Viewport** option is selected for that material

4. Click in an empty space in the *View1* sheet, and using the scroll wheel on your mouse, zoom into the nodes. Hold the scroll wheel to pan around to see the details of each node. The red bounding box in the *Navigator* area can also be dragged around to quickly access specific areas in the *View1* sheet.

5. Using Zoom and Pan, locate the **Concrete** material (second material node from the top).

You can close the Navigator and Parameter Editor to create more space for displaying the nodes in the active sheet.

6. Move and size the Slate Material Editor in the Drawing window so that you can see both the Material Editor and the model in the viewport window side by side.

7. In the **Concrete** material, click and hold ⬭ (material output socket) on the right side. Drag and drop the **Concrete** material from the *View1* sheet directly to the LP Base object in the viewport window, as shown in Figure 6–12. A temporary wire displays in *View1* indicating that you are assigning the material. (Dragging in this way ignores which objects or geometry are currently selected in the model.) The material is assigned to the object and displays in the viewport.

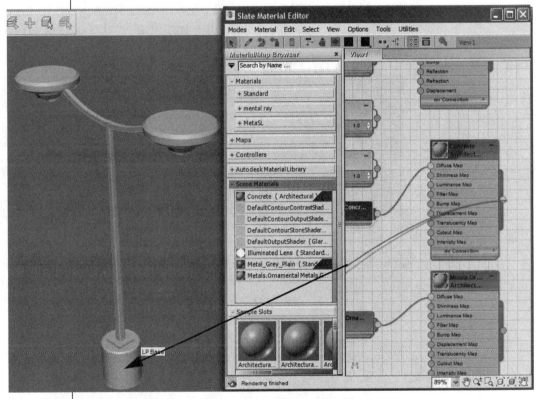

Figure 6–12

Dragging materials in highly complex scenes can be challenging. Instead, you can select objects, select material, and use ⬛ (Assign Material to Selection).

8. Using the Scene Explorer, select the groups **LP Fixture** and **LP Fixture01** (each group contains housing, globe, and mounting arm). You can also select them directly in the viewport.

9. In the Slate Material Editor, in the *View1* sheet, locate **Metal_Grey_Plain** (the first material node). Right-click on the title bar of the material and select **Assign Material to Selection**. The material is applied to all of the objects in the two **LP Fixture** groups.

> **Hint: Group Objects**
>
> To assign a material to individual objects in a group, select the group, select **Group>Open**, and then select the individual object in the group. Then, assign materials to individual parts in the group.

10. Click in the empty space to clear the selection.

11. You can also assign materials directly from the Material/Map Browser. Scroll to the bottom of the Material/Map Browser and expand the *Scene Materials* category, if required, as shown in Figure 6–13. Click and drag **Illuminated Lens** to one of the LP Globe objects in the model. Both globes have **Illuminated Lens** material assigned to them. This method only assigns the material to the object on which you are dropping the material.

Figure 6–13

12. Assign the **Metal_Grey_Plain** material to the LP Base Plate and LP Pole objects using any of the assigning materials method.

A gradient background was added for visual clarity during rendering.

13. Orbit and zoom into all objects in the viewport. In the Main Toolbar, click  (Render Production) to render the scene. The scene is rendered, as shown in Figure 6–14.

Figure 6–14

- The globe material was made to look as if it is illuminated, but it does not actually add any light to the scene.

14. Save the file as **MyLightPoleMaterials.max**.

Task 2 - Working with Materials.

When you are starting a new scene or working in an existing scene you will have to create new materials or edit existing materials. In this task, you will be able to use the Slate Material Editor to create and work with materials.

1. The Material/Map Browser of the Slate Material Editor contains an extensive list of predefined materials that you can use directly or use them as a base for creating your custom materials. You can also import your own material library. Scroll through the list of materials that are available in the list.

2. At the top of the Material/Map Browser, click ▼ to open the **Materials/Map Browser Options** menu.

If the material libraries were not installed, there will be no files in the project folder in the \materiallibraries subdirectory.

3. In the **Materials/Map Browser Options** menu, select **Open Material Library**. The Import Material Library dialog box opens in the *materiallibraries* subdirectory. If required, browse to the path under the root installation (usually *C:\Program Files\ Autodesk\3ds Max 2017*) and open the *\materiallibraries* subdirectory.

4. Select and open **AecTemplates.mat**, as shown in Figure 6–15.

   - In the Material/Map Browser, note that a list of materials is added to the top of with **AecTemplates.mat** listed as the title, as shown in Figure 6–16.

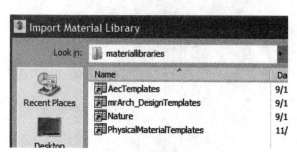

Figure 6–15

Figure 6–16

   - You can remove a library by right-clicking on the category heading and selecting **Close Material Library**. Do not close this library.

Double-clicking on a material in the Material/ Map Browser also displays the material in the View1 sheet, where you can customize the material, as required. Materials do not have to be placed in the View1 sheet unless they are being customized. General materials can be assigned directly from the Material/Map Browser.

5. In the Material/Map Browser, expand the *Materials>General* category. A list of materials is displayed. Right-click on the *General* category and select **Display Group (and Subgroups) As>Medium Icons**. All of the materials in the *General* category now display as thumbnail images. Right-click on the *General* category again and select **Display Group (and Subgroups) As>Icons and Text** to display the materials in the icons and name format.

6. The *View1* sheet already displays the materials used in the scene. To create a new view, right-click on the **View1** label and select **Create New View**, as shown in Figure 6–17.

Figure 6–17

*The Autodesk Material Library is not available in the Material/Map Browser when **Scanline Renderer** or **VUE File Renderer** are set as the active renderers.*

7. Accept the default name, **View2**, and click **OK**. A new empty sheet, *View2*, is added.

8. In the Material/Map Browser, select the *Autodesk Material Library* category.

9. In the list, expand **Metal** and **Steel** to display the materials listed.

10. Double-click on the **Galvanized** material. The material displays as a node on the *View2* sheet, as shown in Figure 6–18.

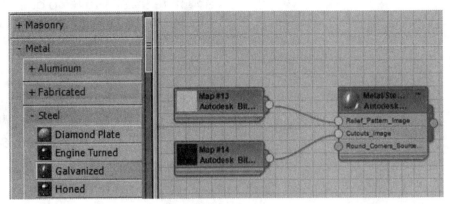

Figure 6–18

Hint: Add Materials to Sheets

Add materials to sheets if they are going to be modified. If they are simply going to be assigned to an object in the scene, select and drag them directly onto the objects.

---

11. In the *View2* sheet, double-click on the title bar of the **Metal/Steel Galvanized** material.

Note that in the active sheet (View2), the material node is surrounded by a dashed white border, indicating that the Parameter Editor for this material is displayed.

12. The Parameter Editor for this material opens in the Slate Material Editor. In the Relief Pattern rollout, note that *Image* displays the map name as **Metals.Metal Fabrications.Metal Stairs. Galvanized.png**. Use the *Amount* slider or enter the value **0.5** directly in the edit box, as shown in Figure 6–19.

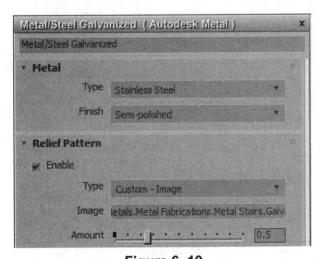

Figure 6–19

> **Hint: Parameter Editor**
>
> You can customize the materials by making changes in the Parameter Editor.

13. In the *View2* sheet, review the preview icon for the material and note that there is no outline around the icon (as shown in Figure 6–20) indicating that it is not assigned to any object and that it is a cold material.

Figure 6–20

14. Using the drag and drop method from the output socket, assign the **Galvanized** material to the **LP Fixture Housings** (the chamfer cylinders) and **LP Mounting Arms** (the arms holding the fixtures to the post).

15. Replace the existing material for the **LP Base Plate** and **LP Pole** with the **Galvanized** material.

16. Review the preview icon for the material. Note that there is now a white outline around the thumbnail, as shown in Figure 6–21. This indicates that the material has been assigned to an object in the scene.

   • Note that this new material is also added to the *Scene Materials* list in the Material Map Browser, as shown in Figure 6–22.

Figure 6–21

Figure 6–22

17. Save the file.

6.3 General Materials

General materials are the most basic materials provided with the Autodesk 3ds Max software. They can be accessed by expanding the *Materials>General* categories in the Material/Map Browser, as shown in Figure 6–23.

Depending on the renderer you are using, the list of the materials might differ from the figure shown.

Figure 6–23

- You can use General materials directly as is or customize them by modifying their parameters to create your own materials, as required.

Physical Materials
New in **2017**

Physical materials are parameters that create reasonable shading effects and are appropriate for scenes with physically-based lighting. Using Physical materials, you can create materials that are based on the physical properties of a material.

- Physical materials are real world materials that are organized in an easy interface that follows a logical layout.

- Materials are comprised of either a base layer that is assigned a diffuse color with dielectric reflections, or a base color with metallic reflections, as shown in Figure 6–23.

- In addition to the diffuse color, the materials have transparency, sub-surface scattering, self-illumination (emission), and a top clear-coat layer, as shown in Figure 6–24.

- These materials contain both standard and advanced parameters that are designed for physically-based material adjustments.

- These materials work well with ART (Autodesk® Raytracer) and the mental ray renderers.

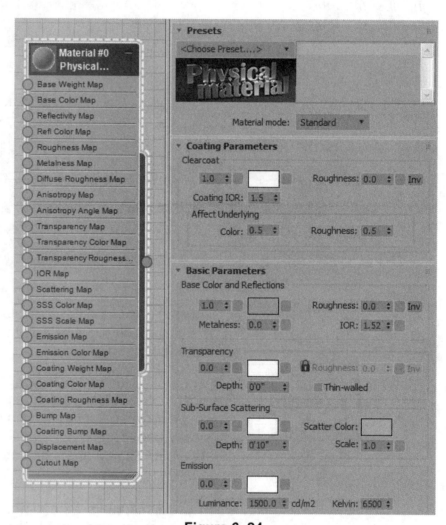

Figure 6–24

Physical Material Parameters

The parameters of the physical materials are easy and follow a simple workflow. The available parameters are:

- The **Coating Parameters** rollout (shown in Figure 6–25) contains options that are used for applying a clear coat onto the finish of the surface.

  - To create a glossy coating on the material, set the *Clearcoat Weight* to **1.0**.

  - *Coating IOR* sets the reflectivity of a clear coat. The higher the value, more reflective the clear coat is.

  - *Roughness* adds a softer sheen and makes a clear coat less glossy.

  - *Affect Underlying* area adds an affect to the base diffuse color.

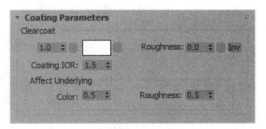

Figure 6–25

- In the **Basic Parameters** rollout (shown in Figure 6–24), the *Base Color and Reflections* area enables you to set the base color of the material surface and add the type and amount of reflectivity.

  - A *Weight* of **0** has no color, and a value of **1** is full color.

  - *Metalness* determines how the surface reflects. A value of **0.0** creates standard reflections (such as for plastics), and a value of **1.0** creates a metal surface (such as for steel or aluminum).

  - *Roughness* and *IOR* work in a similar fashion as the Clearcoat settings, but alter the base surface of the material. A value of **0.0** is a hard surface, and **1.0** is a soft surface.

- In the **Basic Parameters** rollout, the *Transparency* area enables you to create clear materials, like glass.

  - A *Weight* value of **0.0** is completely opaque, and **1.0** is fully transparent.

  - *Thin Walled* creates a glass-like appearance to the surface by making the interior hollow.

- In the **Basic Parameters** rollout, *Sub-Surface Scattering* is a feature that causes light to dissipate through the volume of an object.
  - *Scatter Color* sets the color of the scattered light within the volume of the object.
  - *Depth* sets the distance the light scatters through the object in a real-world distance.

- In the **Basic Parameters** rollout, the *Emission* area enables you to create a material that can emit light and illuminate the scene.
  - An *Emission Weight* of **1** sets the material to full emission and defaults to a *Luminance* of 1500 cd/m² (candelas per meter square).

Multi/Sub-Object Materials

Objects might require different materials on each face. For example, a door or window might need different materials for front and back frames, mullions, and glazing. For this, Multi/Sub-Object materials are used, as shown in Figure 6–26.

- They enable you to stack multiple materials into a single *parent* material, each with a material ID number.

- Faces and polygons of individual objects can have a corresponding ID number assigned through modifiers such as **Edit Mesh** and **Edit Poly**.

- Objects brought into the Autodesk 3ds Max software from vertical applications, such as the AutoCAD Architecture software and the AutoCAD Civil 3D software are divided into multiple objects by material and do not require Multi/Sub-Object materials.

- The Slate Material Editor provides a convenient view that enables you to visually identify all of the materials that make up a Multi/Sub-Object material. Initially, when the material is created, the parent material node opens with 10 default slots. You can wire sub-materials to each slot. Each of the sub-materials can be modified or you can add new materials to the view and rewire into any of the slots. Figure 6–26 shows an example of a Multi/Sub-Object material that is wired to five materials. Slots can be added or deleted using the **Add** or **Delete** options in the Multi/Sub-Object Basic Parameters rollout.

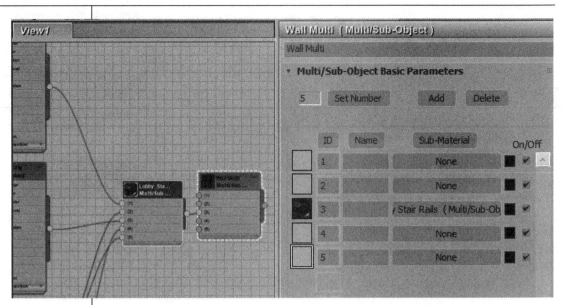

Figure 6–26

Additional Standard Materials

The additional General materials available for use are described as follows:

Blend	Combines two materials to create a third.
Composite	Enables multiple materials to be combined into a single, composite material through additive colors, subtractive colors, or opacity mixing.
DirectX Shader	Enables you to shade objects in the viewport to more accurately display how objects look when exported to real-time viewing.
Double Sided	Enables you to have one material assigned to the outside of objects and another to the inside (the back-facing sides).
Ink 'n' Paint	Creates a flat shaded cartoon rendering with the contours or edges as ink lines.
Shell Material	Used with *texture baking*, which is the process of creating replacement color maps that include the scene illumination (illumination is *baked in*).
Shellac	Superimposes two materials together through additive composition.
Top/Bottom	Assigns different materials to faces with normals pointing *up* and *down*.
XRef Material	Assigns a material applied to an object to another Autodesk 3ds Max scene file. As with Xref scenes and objects, you can only change the material parameters in the original source file.

Enhanced
in 2017

Depending on the current renderer used, the list of the materials might differ.

Architectural materials are applicable to many different kinds of visualization projects, not only Architectural or Civil/Site projects.

6.4 Scanline Materials

Scanline materials are another set of basic materials that are included in the Autodesk 3ds Max software. These materials can be accessed by expanding the *Materials>Scanline* category in the Material/Map Browser, as shown in Figure 6–27.

Figure 6–27

Architectural Materials

Architectural materials are a type of Scanline materials (as shown in Figure 6–27) that are appropriate for scenes with physically-based lighting.

- Architectural materials use a streamlined interface that highlights the parameters and maps that are most likely to change.

- Controls that are not directly available to Standard materials are also available, such as refraction, luminance, and advanced lighting overrides.

Raytrace Material

The Raytrace material is used to create highly configurable, realistic reflections and refractions. These materials support fog, color density, translucency, fluorescence, and other effects. Some Architectural materials (such as ones with the mirror template) automatically generate raytraced results.

Standard Materials

Standard materials are the most basic material and consist of four color components: Ambient color, Diffuse color, Specular color, and Filter color. These materials can be used in most models and can be easily customized.

6.5 Material Shaders

Material Shaders are complex algorithms that describe how light interacts with surfaces. The material color, highlights, self-illumination, and many other features are dependant on the material shaders.

- Standard and mental ray materials enable you to select or use a shader. When using mental ray, a wide range of shaders are available for specific advanced effects. Architectural materials do not provide any shader choice.

- In Standard materials, the shader type is selected through the Shader Basic Parameters rollout, as shown in Figure 6–28.

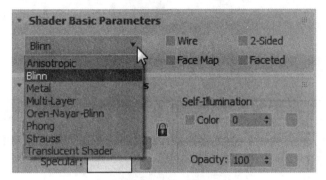

Figure 6–28

- In mental ray materials, shaders can be applied anywhere you might place a map or directly to cameras and lights. They are located using the Material/Map Browser.

- Many shader properties relate to highlights, the bright areas caused by the specular reflection of a light source on the surface of an object.

- The standard shader types are described as follows:

	Anisotropic	Shader for materials with elliptical highlights, such as hair, glass, or brushed metal.
	Blinn	General purpose shader for shiny, smooth objects with soft, circular highlights. Blinn is the default shader for Standard materials.

	Metal	For luminous metallic surfaces.
	Multi-Layer	Enables two sets of anisotropic controls for complex or highly polished surfaces.
	Oren-Nayar-Blinn	A variation of the Blinn shader that provides additional controls for matte surfaces such as fabric or terra cotta.
	Phong	Related to the Blinn shader, also used for shiny, smooth surfaces with circular highlights. The Phong shader generates harder, sharper (often less realistic) highlights than Blinn.
	Strauss	For metallic and similar surfaces, Strauss offers a simpler interface than the Metal shader.
	Translucent Shader	Enables you to control translucency, which is the scattering of light as it passes through the material. Appropriate for Semi-transparent materials, such as frosted glass.

- When using the mental ray renderer, you can apply mental ray shaders to materials, which display with a yellow parallelogram, instead of the green symbol used for maps. The mental ray materials display as yellow spheres.

- The mental ray also enables you to attach shaders directly to lights and cameras for a variety of rendering effects such as contour rendering. If the mental ray render is not selected, the various mental ray shaders are not shown as a possible choice. However, in the Material/Map Browser options, when the **Show Incompatible** option is selected, it displays incompatible materials to that renderer in gray.

Shader (Specific) Basic Parameters

Each material shader has a unique combination of parameters (as shown in Figure 6–29) that can be controlled.

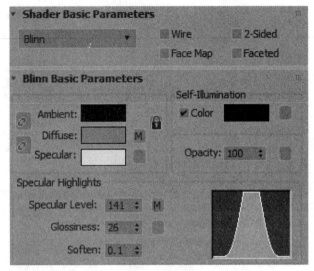

Figure 6–29

- Most of these parameters can be replaced by a map when their values are not constant across the surface. For example, a Diffuse Color Map can be used to replace a single diffuse color for a brick material.

- Colors can be selected by picking on the color swatch next to a color parameter, which opens the interactive Color Selector.

Ambient Color	The color of a material under ambient (background) lighting. It can be assigned globally and through standard lights set to cast ambient light. Ambient and diffuse colors can be locked at the same values, if required.
Diffuse Color	The color of a material under direct lighting. This is the base color of a material (outside of highlights).
Specular Color	The color of material's highlights. It is calculated automatically for the Metal and Multilayer shaders.
Self-Illumination	Values greater than 0 cause materials to appear to be illuminated, but surfaces with this material do not illuminate other objects. This parameter is useful for materials used in light fixtures. Self-illuminated objects do not automatically glow; glows need to be assigned as a special effect (**Rendering>Effects**).
Opacity	This is a percentage measurement of opacity, the opposite of transparency. Materials that have 0% opacity are completely see-through. As an example, a typical clear glass material could have an Opacity between 0-10%.

- Parameters relating to Specular Highlights are listed next to a highlight curve that shows a graphical representation of these settings. Not all of the parameters are available for each shader type. The **Specular Highlights** parameters for Blinn are shown in Figure 6–30.

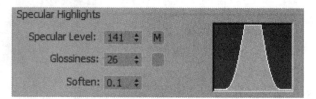

Figure 6–30

- The **Specular Highlights** parameters for Anisotropic shaders are shown in Figure 6–31.

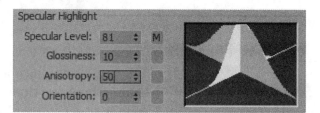

Figure 6–31

Specular Level	A relative measurement of the overall highlight intensity.
Glossiness	A relative measurement of the overall size of highlights. The more glossy an object the smaller and more intense the highlights.
Soften	A relative measurement used to soften the edges of highlights.
Anisotropy	Defines the elliptical shape of Anisotropic highlights, where 0 = round and 100 = a very tight ellipse.
Orientation	Defines the degrees of rotation for an Anisotropic highlight.

6.6 Assigning Maps to Materials

Maps are often assigned to replace the shader parameters, especially Diffuse Color. Maps can be assigned to various materials through the Maps rollout. Figure 6–32 shows the Maps rollout for Standard materials and Figure 6–33 shows the Special Maps and Generic Maps rollout for Physical Materials. Maps include Diffuse Color, Bump maps, Opacity etc.

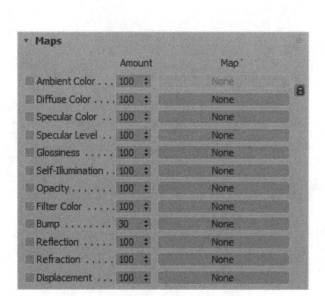

Figure 6–32

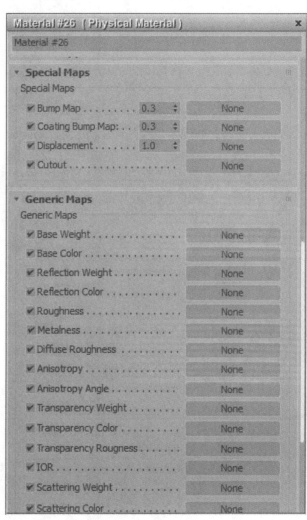

Figure 6–33

Clicking **None** next to a channel opens the Material/Map Browser (shown in Figure 6–34) where you can select a map and assign it or change a map and its settings.

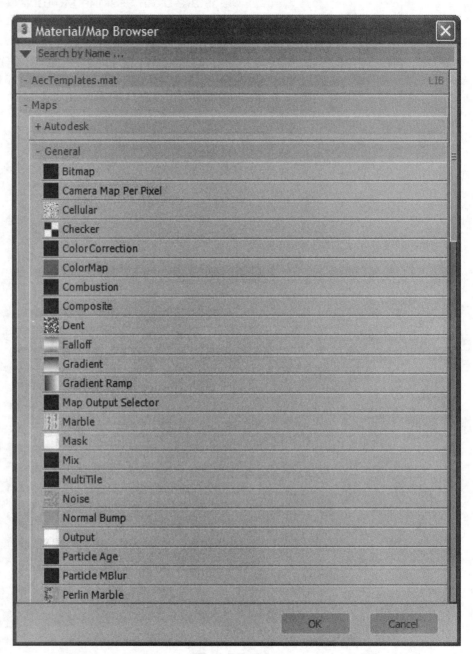

Figure 6–34

- The **Bitmap** map type enables you to assign an external image as a map. Different types of image formats can be used as maps including Windows Bitmaps, JPEGs, PNGs, Targas, TIFFs, and more.

New in **2017**

- **Color Map** enables you to make an instance of a solid color swatch. This helps you be consistent in the solid colors that you use in your models. You can also assign a color bitmap instead of creating a color swatch.

New in **2017**

- **MutiTile** enables you to assign more than one texture maps into a UV editor. The map is designed so that high resolution textures can be opened and displayed. This map type supports patterns created using Mudbox, Zbrush, and Mari.

- The remainder map types are Autodesk 3ds Max **Procedural** maps, which are automatically generated mathematically rather than from image files.

- When you assign (or edit) a map to a material, individual nodes are created and display the maps assigned to the material components. Wires are created automatically between the map and the material component to which the map has been assigned, as shown in Figure 6–35. Maps can also be added individually and wired into a material to establish a link. To edit any of the parameters in the material or maps, double-click on the title bar heading for the item to access its associated Parameter Editor.

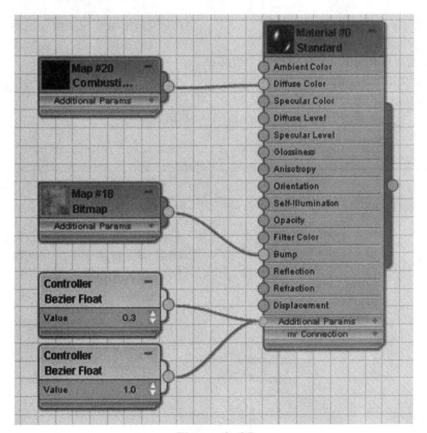

Figure 6–35

Practice 6b

Working with Standard Materials and Maps

Practice Objectives

- Assign a Standard material and modify it.
- Apply an image file and a procedural map to the Diffuse Color of the material.

Estimated time for completion: 20 minutes

In this practice you will assign a Standard material to an object and apply parameter changes to it. You will then apply an image file and a procedural map to an object.

You must set the paths to locate the External files and Xrefs used in the practice. If you have not done this already, return to **Chapter 1: Introduction to Autodesk 3ds Max** and complete Task 1 to Task 3 in **Practice 1a: Organizing Folders and Working with the Interface**. You only have to set the user paths once.

Task 1 - Load Materials into the Material Editor.

*If a dialog box opens prompting you about a Mismatch, click **OK** to accept the default values.*

1. Open **Standard Materials.max**. A model of a guitar displays in the **Perspective** viewport.

2. In the Main Toolbar, click ⬚ to open the Slate Material Editor.

3. In the Slate Material Editor, in the Material/Map Browser, expand the *Scene Materials* category. There are currently nine materials available in this scene, as shown in Figure 6–36.

   - Each material name is listed and is followed by its material type, in parentheses ( ). The square brackets [ ] includes the scene object to which the material has been assigned.

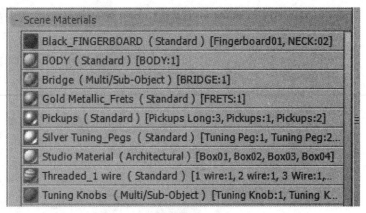

Figure 6–36

4. Note that all of these materials are also displayed in the *View1* sheet and are overlapping each other, as shown in Figure 6–37. In the Slate Material Editor toolbar, click

   (Lay Out All -Vertical) to display the materials vertically in the *View1* sheet.

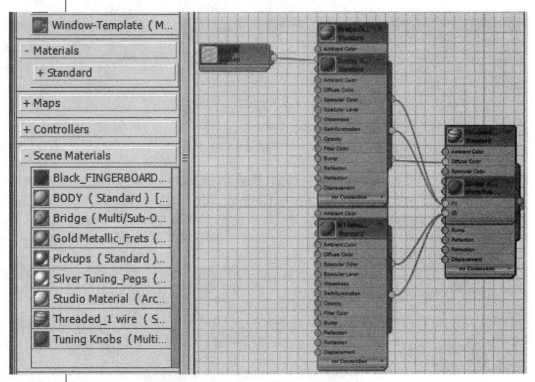

Figure 6–37

Task 2 - Change the material parameters.

1. In the *View1* sheet, using pan and zoom, locate the **BODY Standard** node (name displayed in the title bar), as shown in Figure 6–38. Double-click on the title bar heading to open its Parameter Editor, as shown in Figure 6–39. Note that a white dashed border displays around the node in the *View1* sheet.

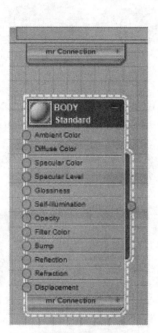

Figure 6–38

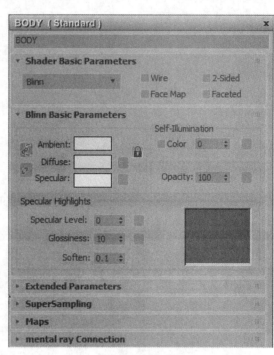

Figure 6–39

2. Note that the **Body** material is a Standard material that uses the Blinn shader. In the Blinn Basic Parameters rollout, select the Diffuse color swatch (currently gray) to open the Color Selector dialog box, as shown in Figure 6–40.

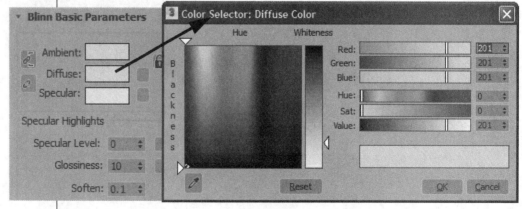

Figure 6–40

3. In the Color Selector dialog box you can select a color from the chart or set RGB (red-green-blue) or HSV (hue-saturation-value) levels. Experiment with different colors for the guitar body and click **OK**.

4. Change the *Shading Viewport* (User Defined) to **High Quality**. The guitar is displayed in the viewport with high quality shading and lighting, as shown in Figure 6–41.

The Slate Material Editor is a modeless dialog box that can remain open when you are working in the viewport or performing other operations that do not pertain to the dialog box. You can minimize it to get more space in the viewport and maximize it when you want to work in it.

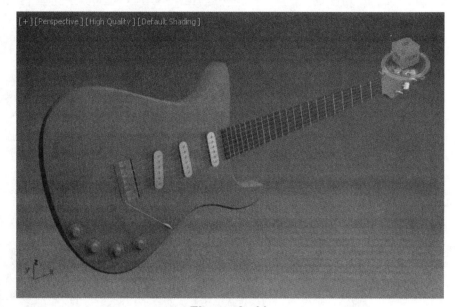

[+] [Perspective] [High Quality] [Default Shading]

Figure 6–41

5. In the *Specular Highlights* area, the material's *Specular Level* is set to **0**, which is appropriate for a material that is not shiny. To simulate a shiny coating, increase the *Specular Level* to **100**, as shown in Figure 6–42. Note the shiny coating on the guitar body.

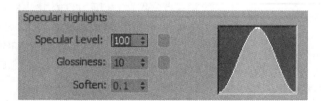

Specular Highlights
Specular Level: 100
Glossiness: 10
Soften: 0.1

Figure 6–42

6. Change the *Glossiness* to **25**. Increasing the glossy value focuses the highlighting in a smaller area.

7. Click (Render Production) in the Main Toolbar to display a more realistic rendered image. Close the Render Window.

Task 3 - Applying a procedural map and image file.

A Procedural Map is generated algorithmically. It is not a digital photo or painting. Procedural Maps are useful for terrains or other objects where the texture should not repeat in a tiled pattern.

1. To replace the Diffuse Color with a procedural map that represents a wood grain, verify that the Body material has a white dashed boundary around it indicating that its parameters are displayed. In the Parameter Editor, expand the Maps rollout, as shown in Figure 6–43. Next to the **Diffuse Color** option, click **None**.

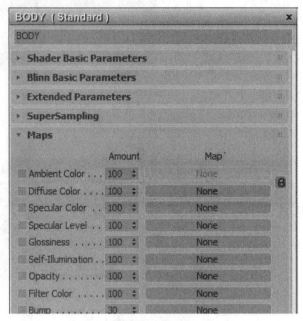

Figure 6–43

*As with all procedural maps, **Wood** is defined by parameters and formulas, not by an image file.*

*The Map number and name **Map #10 (Wood)** replaces **None** for the Diffuse color in the Parameter Editor.*

2. In the separate Material/Map Browser that opens, expand the *Maps>General* categories and select **Wood**. Click **OK** to assign it as a map to the **BODY** Standard material.

3. A new Map node has been added in the *View1* sheet that represents the **Wood** map. The node is wired to the Diffuse Color in the **Body** material, as shown in Figure 6–44. Note that the title bar of this node is green, indicating that the node is a Map node.

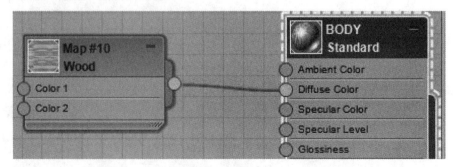

Figure 6–44

4. Double-click on the title bar heading for the **Wood** map. Note that a white dashed border surrounds the Wood Map node, indicating that its parameters are displayed in the Parameter Editor. In the Wood Parameters rollout, set *Grain Thickness* to **8**, as shown in Figure 6–45. This distance is measured in the file's System Unit Scale.

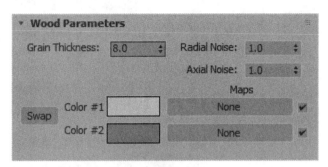

Figure 6–45

5. The wood grain does not display on the guitar body in the viewport. To display the map in the viewport, in the Slate Material Editor toolbar, click ▣ (Show Shaded Material in Viewport). The wood grain displays on the guitar body in the viewport but it is not accurate. Note that the title header of this node has changed to a half diagonal red area and the rest is green.

6. In the Main Toolbar, click ⬛ (Render Production) to render. The wood map is displayed on the body of the guitar, as shown in Figure 6–46. Leave the modeless Render Window dialog box open.

Figure 6–46

- The display in the viewport might not be identical to the rendered display. This is typical of procedural maps. Procedural maps offer some interesting parameter-driven maps, which maintain the wood grain into the third dimension (across the top of the guitar body).

7. To replace the procedural **Wood** map with an image file, in the *View1* sheet, double-click on the title bar heading for the **BODY** material to open its Parameter Editor. Expand the Maps rollout, right-click on **Map #10 (Wood)**, and select **Clear**. Alternatively, you can drag any **None** onto it. Note that in the *View1* sheet, the wiring between the **BODY** material node and the **Wood** map node has been deleted.

8. Click **None** next to the **Diffuse Color** to open its specific Material/Map Browser.

9. In the Material/Map Browser, double-click on **Bitmap** in the *Maps>General* categories, as shown in Figure 6–47.

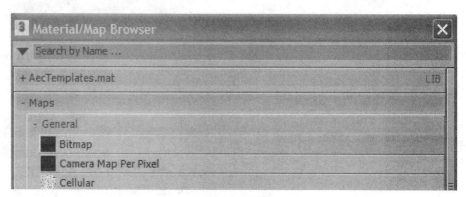

Figure 6–47

You can delete the unused node by clicking its title bar heading and pressing <Delete>. This keeps the active sheet clean. It also removes the material from the active sheet only.

10. The Select Bitmap Image File dialog box opens. Browse to the ...*Maps* folder. Select **GuitarDiffuse.jpg** and click **Open**. A new node for Bitmap is added to the *View1* sheet and its output socket is connected to the Diffuse Color input socket of the **BODY** material node, as shown in Figure 6–48. The new **Bitmap** node and **Wood** Map node might overlap. Select the header of one of the nodes to move them apart.

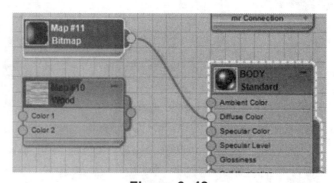

Figure 6–48

11. Double-click on the **Bitmap** node title bar to display its Parameter Editor. In the Coordinates rollout, clear the **Use Real-World Scale** and set the *Tiling* to 1.0 in both **U** and **V**, as shown in Figure 6–49.

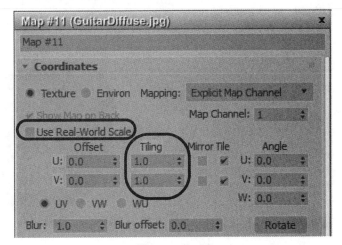

Figure 6–49

12. Click (Show Shaded Material in Viewport) again to display the **BODY** material with the new map in the viewport.

13. If the Render Window is still open, click **Render**, which is located near the top right corner, to display the effect, as shown in Figure 6–50. If you closed the Render Window, open it again from the Main Toolbar by clicking (Render Production). Leave the dialog box open.

Figure 6–50

Hint: Use Mix Map Type

You could also mix the procedural wood grain with the bitmap by selecting a Mix map type. The mix material on the guitar displays as shown in Figure 6–51.

Figure 6–51

14. To use a Color Correction map along with the Bitmap, In the Material/Map Browser, open the *Maps>General* categories. Double-click on the Color Correction map. A new node for Color Correction is added to *View1*, as shown in Figure 6–52. To relocate a node in the active sheet, hold and drag the title bar heading.

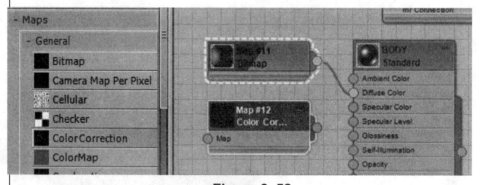

Figure 6–52

15. Select the red wire that connects the Bitmap node to the Diffuse Color of the **BODY** material, press <Delete>.

The input socket of Color correction is used for a Map.

16. For the Bitmap node (**Map # Bitmap**), select the material output socket ⬜ (right socket) and drag/drop the wire to the material input socket (left socket) for the Color Correction node (**Map # Color Correction**), as shown in Figure 6–53. Note that the wired slots display in green.

17. Select 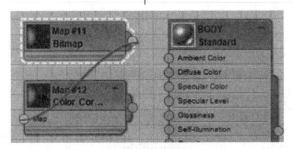 (material output socket) for the Color Correction node and drag the wire to the material input socket for the Diffuse Color entry in the **BODY** material node, as shown in Figure 6–54.

Figure 6–53

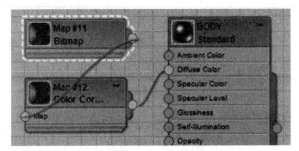

Figure 6–54

18. Select the Color Correction heading and then click (Show Shaded Material in Viewport) to display the map on the guitar in the viewport.

19. Double-click on the Color Correction heading to open its Parameter Editor. In the Color rollout, change the *Hue Shift* slider and note that the guitar changes color interactively in the viewport. Set the slider at any color (such as a green color hue).

20. In the Render dialog box, click **Render** to render the scene, as shown in Figure 6–55.

Figure 6–55

21. Save your work as **MyGuitar.max**.

Practice 6c

Working with Multi/Sub-Object Materials

Practice Objective

- Create a Multi/Sub-Object material and assign different materials to specific faces of a single object.

In this practice you will create a Multi/Sub-Object material with various materials on different material ID's. You will assign an instanced scene material to all the faces of the wall system, an Autodesk material to some of the outside faces, and an accent paint color to other interior faces using material ID numbers of the Multi/Sub-Object material.

You must set the paths to locate the External files and Xrefs used in the practice. If you have not done this already, return to **Chapter 1: Introduction to Autodesk 3ds Max** and complete Task 1 to Task 3 in **Practice 1a: Organizing Folders and Working with the Interface**. You only have to set the user paths once.

Estimated time for completion: 20 minutes

Task 1 - Identify and Apply Multi/Sub-Object Materials.

1. Open **Interior Model.max**.

*If a dialog box opens prompting you about a Mismatch, click **OK** to accept the default values.*

2. In the Main Toolbar, click ![icon] to open the Slate Material Editor.

3. In the Material/Map Browser, expand the *Scene Materials* categories and note that six of the materials in the scene are Multi/Sub-Object materials.

You can leave the modeless Slate Material Editor dialog box open.

4. Click, drag, and drop the **Curtain Wall Doors** material on **PivotDoor07** (door on the left side of the model), as shown in Figure 6–56.

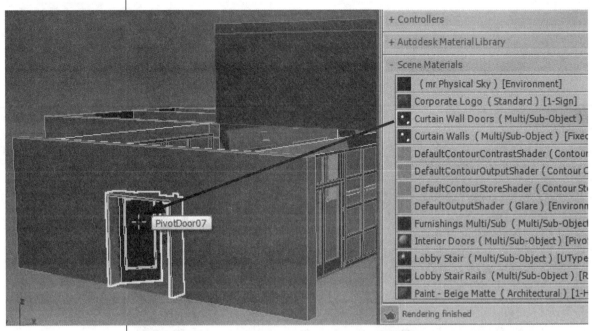

Figure 6–56

5. Select **PivotDoor07** object and click  (Zoom Extents Selected). The doors have glass panels and solid frames, as shown in Figure 6–57.

Figure 6–57

Task 2 - Create a Multi/Sub-Object Material.

1. In the Material/Map Browser, expand the *Materials> General* categories. Double-click on Multi/Sub-Object or drag an instance of it to add it to the *View1* sheet, as shown in Figure 6–58.

2. Right-click on the title bar heading for the new material, and select **Rename**, as shown in Figure 6–59.

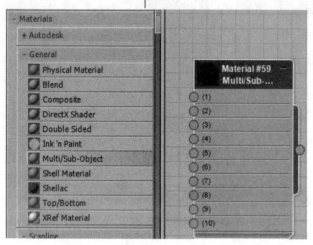

Figure 6–58

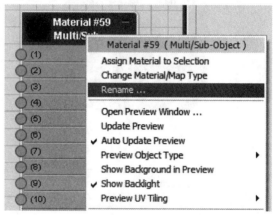

Figure 6–59

3. In the Rename dialog box, enter **Wall Multi** and click **OK**.

4. There are ten default slots in a Multi/Sub-Object material. This material only requires five slots. To set the number of materials, double-click on the Wall Multi material title bar to open its Parameter Editor. Click **Set Number**, enter **5** in the *Number of Materials* edit box and click **OK**. Note that the node has only 5 slots now.

To display all of the materials in the Scene Materials, use its scroll bar.

5. You will use an instanced copy of the **Paint – Beige Matte** material present in the scene for your sub-material 3. (This material displays dark brown in this practice but will look more like beige when lights are added to the scene.) In Material/Map Browser, in *Scene Materials* category, locate **Paint – Beige Matte**, which is an Architectural material.

6. Click and drag the **Paint – Beige Matte** material and place it directly on the input socket 3 in the **Wall Multi** (Multi/Sub-Object material). When you move the cursor on top of the socket, its color changes to green indicating that the socket is selected, as shown in Figure 6–60. Drop the material on this socket.

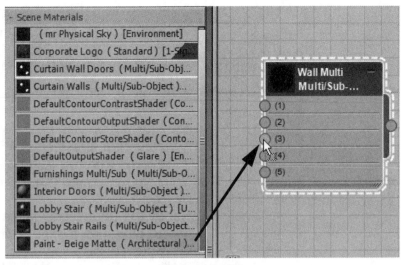

Figure 6–60

7. In the Instance dialog box, verify that **Instance** is selected and click **OK**.

8. The Paint – Beige Matte material node is wired to slot 3 of **Wall Multi** material. Use the pan and zoom (middle mouse button) to display both the material nodes in the *View1* sheet.

9. Verify that the Wall Multi (Multi/Sub-Object material) node has a white dashed boundary indicating that its Parameter Editor is displayed. Note that the **Paint – Beige Matte** material is displayed on the 3 ID slot, as shown in Figure 6–61.

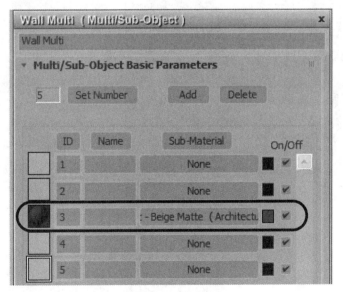

Figure 6–61

10. In the Material/Map Browser, expand the *Autodesk Material Library>Finish* categories and locate **Paint- Varnish** material.

11. Click and drag the **Paint- Varnish** material onto the Wall Multi Parameter Editor and release it over **None** next to *ID* slot 5. Note that the **Paint- Varnish** material is wired to slot 5 of the **Wall Multi** material. Alternatively, you can place the **Paint- Varnish** material on the *View1* sheet and wire it to slot 5.

- You cannot drag and drop Autodesk materials on the input socket for sub-material 5 directly in the *View1* sheet as you did with the **Paint-Beige Matte** scene material. You need to use the Parameter Editor.

12. Not all the nodes are visible and might be overlapping each other in the active sheet (*View1*). In the Slate Material Editor toolbar, click ▓ (Lay Out All - Vertical) to arrange the sub-materials vertically, as shown in Figure 6–62. Note that in the active view, the input socket 5 of Wall Multi material node is wired to the output socket of the Finish (Paint Varnish) material node. Also, note that in the Parameter Editor of the **Wall Multi** material, the ID5 slot now displays **Paint- Varnish (Autodesk Generic)**, as shown in Figure 6–63.

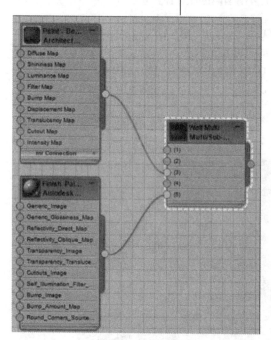

Figure 6–62

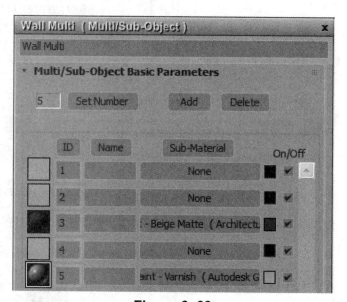

Figure 6–63

13. You will copy and adjust the **Paint – Beige Matte** material into an accent paint material. In Material/Map Browser, in *Scene Materials* category, click and drag the **Paint – Beige Matte** material and place it on the input socket for sub-material 4 in the **Wall Multi** material.

14. In the Instance dialog box, select **Copy** and click **OK**.

Use  *(Lay Out All - Vertical), if required.*

15. Double-click on the title bar heading for the new **Paint – Beige Matte** material (slot 4) to open its Parameter Editor.

16. Change the material name to **Paint – Accent**, as shown in Figure 6–64.

17. In the Physical Qualities rollout, select the Diffuse Color swatch. In the Color Selector set *Value* as **255** and press <Enter>. The color changes, as shown in Figure 6–65. Click **OK**.

Figure 6–64

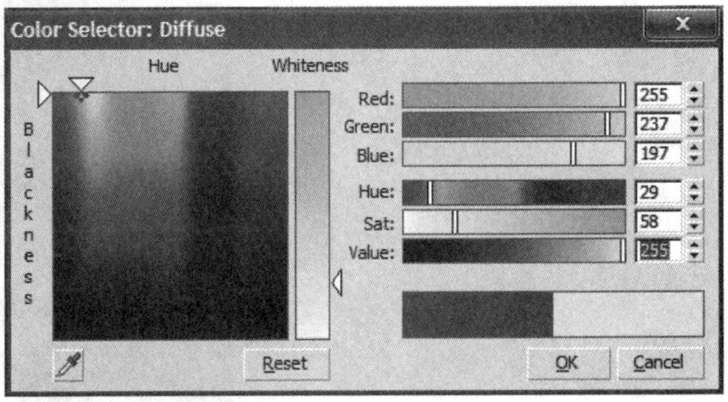

Figure 6–65

18. Close the Slate Material Editor.

Task 3 - Assign Material ID Numbers to the Wall System.

---

1. In the **Perspective** viewport, zoom out and pan so that the entire model is displayed in the viewport.

2. In the Scene Explorer ((Display None) > (Display Geometry)), select **Layer:VIZ-1-Walls**, which selects all of the walls in the lower floor in the viewport.

3. In the Command Panel, in the Modify panel ( ), note that it is an Editable Mesh in the Modifier Stack. Select the **Polygon** Sub-object mode, as shown in Figure 6–66.

Figure 6–66

4. In the viewport, select the **Edged Face** Per-View Preference label and select **Wireframe Override** in the menu. Use

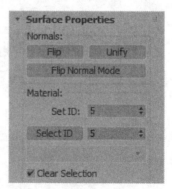 (Orbit) until your model displays as shown in Figure 6–67. Right-click in empty space to exit the command and maintain the selection.

5. Using <Ctrl>, select the two polygons as shown in Figure 6–67.

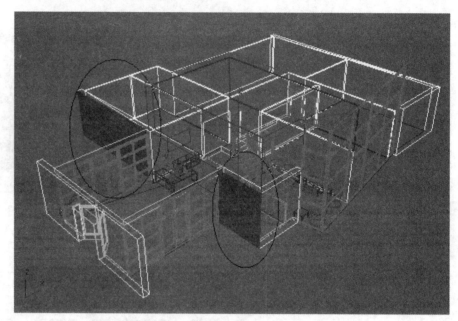

Figure 6–67

6. In the Command Panel, in the Surface Properties rollout, in the *Material* area, set *Set ID* to **5**, and press <Enter>. *Select ID* also changes to **5**, as shown in Figure 6–68. This sets the selected polygons to ID 5 and will associate the Finish (Autodesk Material) with those two walls.

Figure 6–68

7. Clear the selection of the two walls and select the polygon as shown in Figure 6–69. Set *Set ID* to **4** and press <Enter>. This will associate the **Beige - Accent** material with this wall.

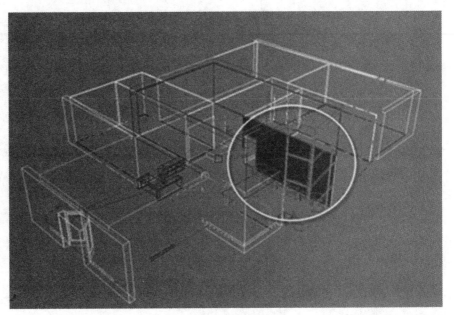

Figure 6–69

8. In the Command Panel, select **Editable Mesh** to exit Sub-object mode.

9. Change the visual display to **Default Shading** and **Edged Faces** by selecting the **Wireframe** (Per-View Preference) label and selecting **Default Shading**. There is no change in the model because the material has not yet been assigned.

10. With the wall object (**Layer:VIZ-1-Walls**) still selected, open the Slate Material Editor, select the Wall Multi material title bar heading in the *View1* sheet. In the Slate Material Editor toolbar, click (Assign material to Selection).

11. Note that the interior wall displays in light beige (**Paint – Accent**) and the two exterior brick walls display in grayish brown (**Paint- Varnish**), as shown in Figure 6–70.

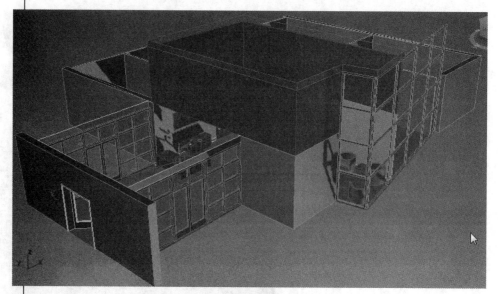

Figure 6–70

12. In the Slate Material Editor, double-click on the **Finish Paint - Varnish** title node to open its Parameter Editor.

13. In the Generic rollout, select the Color bar to open the Color Selector. Change the color to a different one, such as red. In the viewport, note that only the color of the two walls that have ID 5 changes, as shown in Figure 6–71. This indicates that your **Multi-Sub -Object** materials have been applied.

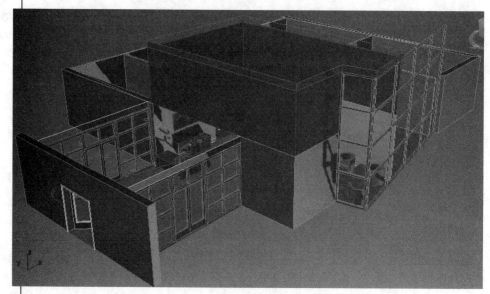

Figure 6–71

14. Save the file as **MyInterior Model MultiMaterials.max**.

6.7 Opacity, Bump, and Reflection Mapping

You can use simple objects with materials and textures applied to them to add detailed effects without adding complex geometry to a scene. For example, leaves on trees or a chain link fence can be generated using a simple model with mapped textures and materials rather that creating it with complex geometry.

Opacity Mapping

Opacity mapping controls the transparency of objects, as shown with the lace curtains in Figure 6–72.

Figure 6–72

To create an Opacity map, add a map to the *Opacity map* channel, under the Maps rollout of the material.

*   The black to white values are mapped to the transparent state, where black creates a hole (completely invisible), white makes a surface (100% opaque), and grays create a semi-transparent effect, good for clouds and fabrics.

*   If a color image is used as an Opacity map, the RGB color is ignored and only the Luminance value is used. Opacity maps are usually created by taking digital photos and manipulating them in other programs.

> **Hint: Two-sided Opacity Mapped Material**
>
> When you create an opacity mapped material, it is recommended to make the material two-sided to see the backsides of faces if looking inside/through an object.

Bump Mapping

The white value raises the surface fully while the black value does not raise it at all.

Bump mapping gives the illusion of an embossed or pitted surface without geometry being present on the model, as shown for a braided carpet in Figure 6–73. As with Opacity mapping, it uses black to white values to generate the appearance of a raised surface.

- When combined with texture mapping, it helps the scene lighting integrate with the textures to place shadows in cracks, and generally add a veneer of three-dimensionality to the surfaces.

Figure 6–73

Reflection Mapping

Reflection mapping gives a surface the ability to mirror the world surrounding the object, as shown on the glass in Figure 6–74.

- Using Standard materials, you can place a bitmap or a reflection map type in the *Reflection map* channel.

- If you add a bitmap to the *Reflection map* channel, the faces reflect the bitmap based on shininess and scene lighting.

- If you add a Reflect/Refract or Raytrace map, the objects in the scene reflect along with the environment.

Figure 6–74

Practice 6d

Opacity and Bump Mapping

Estimated time for completion: 15 minutes

Practice Objective

- Assign a Diffuse Color texture map, Opacity map, and Bump map to an object.

In this practice you will create a chain link fence using opacity and bump mapping to display the cutouts in a solid piece of geometry. You will then add a map to the *Specular Level* channel to add shininess to the object texture.

You must set the paths to locate the External files and Xrefs used in the practice. If you have not done this already, return to **Chapter 1: Introduction to Autodesk 3ds Max** and complete Task 1 to Task 3 in **Practice 1a: Organizing Folders and Working with the Interface**. You only have to set the user paths once.

Task 1 - Assign the texture map.

*If a dialog box opens prompting you about a Mismatch, click **OK** to accept the default values.*

1. Open **start_chainlink.max**.

2. In the *Shading Viewport* (User Defined) label, select **High Quality**.

3. In the viewport, select the object **Line01** (yellow fence object).

4. In the Main Toolbar, click [icon] to open the Slate Material Editor.

5. In the Material/Map Browser, expand the *Materials>General* categories. In the list, double-click on the **Physical Material** material to add it to the *View1* sheet.

6. Assign the **Physical Material** material to the selected fence object by clicking [icon] (Assign Material to Selection) in the Material Editor toolbar. Verify that the fence object now displays in gray in the viewport.

7. In the *View1* sheet, double-click on the **Physical Material** material title bar heading to open its Parameter Editor. To open a separate Material/Map Browser, in the Basic Parameters rollout, next to *Base Color and Reflections* color swatch, click ■ (None), as shown in Figure 6–75.

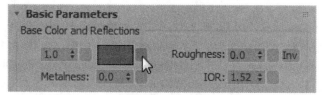

Figure 6–75

8. Expand the *Maps>General* categories and double-click on Bitmap, as shown in Figure 6–76.

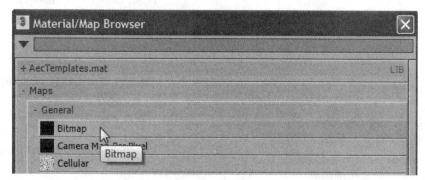

Figure 6–76

The Autodesk Maps are available in your local drive, generally, C:\Program Files\ Autodesk\3ds Max 2017\maps.

9. In the Select Bitmap Image File dialog box, in the Practice Files ...\Maps folder, open **Chain-link.bump.jpg**.

- Note that in the Parameter Editor the icon changes to ⓜ, as shown in Figure 6–77. Also note that in *View1* sheet, the output socket of the Bitmap node is wired to the Base Color Map input socket of the **Physical Material** material, as shown in Figure 6–77.

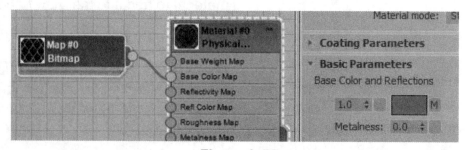

Figure 6–77

10. In the *View 1* sheet, select the **Map # Bitmap** and then click
    ⬚ (Show Shaded Material in Viewport). The **Chainlink**
    texture should display on the **Line01** object in the viewport,
    but does not display correctly because the settings need to
    be changed.

11. In the *View1* sheet, double-click on the **Map # Bitmap** title
    bar heading to open its Parameter Editor.

12. In the Coordinates rollout, clear **Use Real-World Scale** and
    set *Tiling* as **U: 6.0** and **V: 3.0**, as shown in Figure 6–78.
    Press <Enter> for the values to take effect. The **Chainlink**
    texture should display in the viewport.

    • If it does not display, render the scene once (Main

      Toolbar> 🫖 *(Render Production)). Close the Render*

      Window and then click ⬚ (Show Shaded Material in
      Viewport) twice to toggle it off and on again..

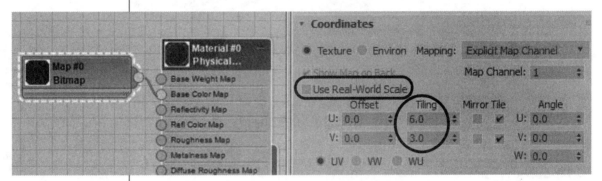

Figure 6–78

13. In the Main Toolbar, click 🫖 (Render Production). The map
    displays in the Render window. Leave the window open.

14. In the menu bar, select **Rendering>Environment**. In the
    Background area, select the color swatch as shown in
    Figure 6–79. In the Color Selector, select a new color (cyan)
    and click **OK**. Close the Environment and Effects dialog box.

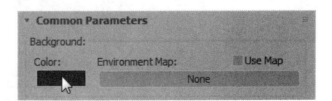

Figure 6–79

15. In the Render window, click **Render**. The Render window should display as shown in Figure 6–80. Leave the window open.

Figure 6–80

Task 2 - Assign the Opacity map.

1. In the Slate Material Editor, in the *View1* sheet, double-click on the **Physical Material** material title bar heading to open its Parameter Editor.

2. Expand the **Generic Maps** rollout and note that chainlink map has already been applied to the *Base* Color channel.

3. Expand the **Special Maps** rollout and click **None** for *Cutout*, as shown in Figure 6–81.

To control the transparency, apply the map to the Opacity channel

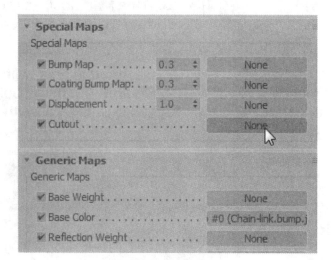

Figure 6–81

The Tiling settings for the Diffuse map and the Opacity map should be the same so that they overlap each other for the cutout to display correctly.

4. In the Material/Map Browser, expand the *Maps>General* categories. Double-click on **Bitmap** to open the Select Bitmap Image File dialog box. Open **Chain-link.cutout.jpg** (from the *...\Maps* folder). Note that this bitmap is wired to **Opacity** in Standard material. It also replaces **None** in the Maps rollout of the Parameter Editor.

5. In the *View1* sheet, double-click on **Map #1 Bitmap** (cutout) title bar heading to open its Parameter Editor. In the Coordinates rollout, clear **Use Real-World Scale** and set the *Tiling* to **U: 6.0** and **V: 3.0**. Press <Enter>.

6. Orbit around in the Perspective view so that the fence is facing you. In the Render window, click **Render** to render the scene. Note that the background is displayed through the fence, as shown in Figure 6–82. This is caused by the map on the *Cutout* channel. The chainlink in your rendering might display a little lighter in color than that shown in Figure 6–82.

Figure 6–82

7. Close the Render window.

Task 3 - Assign the Bump map.

1. In the Slate Material Editor, in the *View1* sheet, double-click on the **Physical Material** material title bar heading to open its Parameter Editor. In the **Special Maps** rollout, for *Bump Map,* click **None** .

*You can also drag and drop the map from the Diffuse channel onto the Opacity channel and select **Copy** in the dialog box.*

2. In the Material/Map Browser, in the *Maps>General* categories, double-click on Bitmap to open the Select Bitmap Image File dialog box. Open **Chain-link.bump.jpg** (from the ...*Maps* folder). Note that this bitmap is displayed on **Bump Map**, as shown in Figure 6–83 (the same map was used on the *Base Color* channel). Note that in the *View1* sheet, it is wired to **Bump Map** in **Physical Material** material, as shown in Figure 6–83.

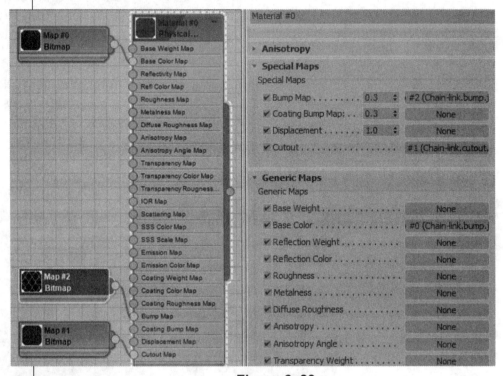

Figure 6–83

If you copied the map, the settings are also copied and you are not required to enter the Tiling values.

3. In the *View1* sheet, double-click on the **Map #2 Bitmap** (*Bump* channel) title bar heading to open its Parameter Editor. In the Coordinates rollout, clear **Use Real-World Scale** and set the *Tiling* to **U: 6.0** and **V: 3.0**.

4. Click ![teapot icon] (Render Production) to render the scene.

5. To make the chain link more realistic (smaller cutouts), set the *Tiling* values for all the three map channels to **U: 18** and **V: 11**. Double-click on each map title bar heading to open its Parameter Editor and change the values.

*To display the various maps correctly in the viewport, in the View1 sheet, select the **Material # Physical Material** heading (parent material node) and then click*

![icon] *(Show Shaded Material) to switch it on.*

6. Render the scene again. The rendered scene is similar to one shown in Figure 6–84.

Figure 6–84

There is no light on this side, so the rendering display might be dark.

7. Click  (Orbit) and navigate in the viewport to the other side of the chain link fence. Render the scene again. Note that the chain link displays. Leave the Render window open.

8. In the viewport, navigate back to the front side of the fence.

9. Save your work as **MyChainLinkFence.max**.

6.8 mental ray Materials

mental ray materials are used with the NVIDIA mental ray renderer to can achieve high-quality images with accurate lighting effects.

*The mental ray material complete list is displayed if the NVIDIA mental ray is assigned to be the current renderer. With ART Renderer, NVIDIA iray, or Quicksilver Hardware Renderer, a limited list of mental ray material is available. The renderer can be made current in the Render Setup dialog box. (**Rendering> Render Setup**).*

- mental ray materials are available in the Material/Map Browser, in the *Materials>mental ray* category, as shown in Figure 6–85.

- **Autodesk** materials are also mental ray materials and are available in a separate *Materials>Autodesk* category, as shown in Figure 6–86.

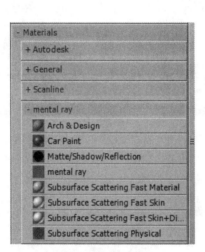

Figure 6–85

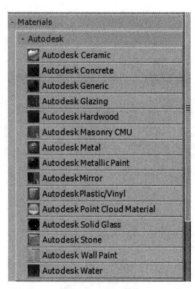

Figure 6–86

Arch & Design Materials

The Arch & Design material type is the most commonly used mental ray material. It provides over 20 different templates for Appearance and Attributes, Finishes, Transparent Materials, and Metals. There are also Advanced Tools for detail enhancement. The Arch & Design templates have default texture bitmaps already assigned when you select them. You can create your own Arch & Design material by modifying its parameters. The templates include the following:

• Matte, Pearl, or Glossy Finish	• Physical Frosted Glass
• Satin or Glossy Varnished Wood	• Translucent Plastic Film with Light Frost
• Rough or Polished Concrete	• Translucent Plastic Film with Opalescent Effect

• Glazed Ceramic/Glazed Ceramic Tiles	• Water, Reflective Surface
• Glossy or Matte Plastic	• Chrome
• Masonry	• Brushed Metal
• Rubber	• Satined Metal
• Leather	• Copper
• Thin or Solid or Physical Glass	• Patterned Copper

Arch & Design materials enable you to do the following:

• Adjust the reflection, refraction, and transparency of the material.

• Control the blurriness of the reflections by using Fast Reflection.

• Control the distance that reflects in a surface.

• Adjust the strength of the reflection based on the angle of viewing (BDRF).

• Add light into the scene using self-Illumination. Unlike standard lights, the self-illumination used with mental ray materials emits illumination in the scene instead of faking the effect.

• Round corners through a post-production pixel shader and an Ambient Occlusion setting that adds subtle detail enhancement to surface corners, cracks, and crevices.

Autodesk Materials

Fifteen **Autodesk** mental ray materials are also available, as shown in Figure 6–86. The materials are:

• Autodesk Ceramic	• Autodesk Mirror
• Autodesk Concrete	• Autodesk Plastic/Vinyl
• Autodesk Generic	• Autodesk Point Cloud Material
• Autodesk Glazing	• Autodesk Solid Glass
• Autodesk Hardwood	• Autodesk Stone
• Autodesk Masonry CMU	• Autodesk Wall Paint
• Autodesk Metal	• Autodesk Water
• Autodesk Metallic Paint	

- In addition to the Autodesk materials in the *Autodesk* category, there are additional categories of Autodesk materials present in the *Autodesk Material Library* category that can be used directly or modified for use in your scenes.

- The Autodesk Material Library materials are simplified versions of the Arch & Design materials. Similar to the Arch & Design materials, Autodesk mental ray materials should also be used with physically accurate (photometric) lights but have a much simpler interface. They contain presets that permit faster selection of specific material parameters and preassigned bitmaps.

- The Autodesk Material Library was designed specifically for architectural visualization and includes material categories for *Ceramic, Concrete, Fabric, Finish, Flooring, Glass, Liquid, Masonry, Metal*, etc.

- These materials are aligned with the latest release of the Autodesk Revit software, so the materials applied in the Autodesk® Revit® Architecture software display as Autodesk Material Library materials inside the Autodesk 3ds Max software.

Car Paint Material

This is a layered material that provides four layers combining to create one surface treatment. Elements such as a base paint layer, an embedded metal flake layer, a clear-coat layer, and a Lambertian dirt layer, each have their own parameters and rollouts. These enables you to create complex highly reflective surfaces. By using your own texture maps with these base materials, and tweaking the various parameters within each, you can achieve an unlimited variety of materials.

Matte/Shadow/ Reflection Material

This is a mental ray version of the Standard Matte/Shadow material. You can create matte objects by using the Matte/Shadow/Reflection (mi) material included in the Production Shaders library. A photographic plate containing real-world objects can be used as the scene background. The material provides various options for combining the photographic background plate with the 3D scene. The options include ambient occlusion, bump mapping, and indirect illumination.

mental ray Material

This is your basic mental ray material. It provides rollouts that enable you to assign component shaders for materials used with the mental ray renderer.

Subsurface Scattering (SSS) Materials

Enables you to create organic materials like skin that do not reflect light at the surface, but scatter or absorb light below in the surface. There are four different types of Subsurface Scattering materials available for use with the mental ray renderer.

> **Hint: Output Rollout**
>
> The Output rollout of the texture bitmap can be used to great advantage when using mental ray materials. Lighten and brighten the output of the texture by enabling the color map or increasing the Output Amount.

Practice 6e

Estimated time for completion: 20 minutes

*If a dialog box opens prompting you about a Mismatch, click **OK** to accept the default values.*

Working with mental ray Materials

Practice Objectives

- Assign a mental ray material template to an object.
- Assign and modify a mental ray material.

In this practice you will explore the mental ray materials, shaders, and templates. You will assign an Arch & Design material to an object and modify the material using a map and a color mapping.

You must set the paths to locate the External files and Xrefs used in the practice. If you have not done this already, return to **Chapter 1: Introduction to Autodesk 3ds Max** and complete Task 1 to Task 3 in **Practice 1a: Organizing Folders and Working with the Interface**. You only have to set the user paths once.

Task 1 - Assign the NVIDIA mental ray renderer.

1. Open **candleholder.max**. The candle holder is displayed in the four viewports layout. A camera view has already been set up.

2. In the Main Toolbar, click to open the Slate Material Editor. In the Material/Map Browser, expand the *Materials* category and note that no mental ray materials or Autodesk materials are available. To work with mental ray materials, you need to set the renderer to mental ray.

3. In the Main Toolbar, click (Render Setup) or select **Rendering>Render Setup**.

4. In the Render Setup dialog box, expand the Renderer drop-down menu and select **NVIDIA mental ray**, as shown in Figure 6–87. Close the Render Setup dialog box.

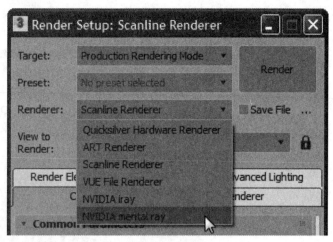

Figure 6–87

Task 2 - Assign the Arch & Design materials.

1. Open the Slate Material Editor, if not already open. In the Material/Map Browser, in the *Materials* category, note that the **mental ray** and **Autodesk** categories are now listed.

2. Expand the *Scene Materials* category at the bottom of the Material/Map Browser. Note that the gray **Standard** materials are being used in the scene.

3. Double-click on each of the gray materials (**CandleHolder**, **Countertop**, **Left Wall**, and **Right Wall**) to place them on the *View1* sheet. They are placed on top of each other. In the

   Material Editor toolbar, click ▪▪ (Lay Out All - Horizontal) to display the four materials horizontally in the *View1* sheet.

4. To change the color on each of these scene materials, double-click on each material node to open the Parameter Editor. In the Blinn Basic Parameters rollout, select the Diffuse swatch, and select a color in the Color Selector. You can use any color (**Countertop** - dark pink, **Right Wall** - blue, **CandleHolder** - dark blue, and **Left Wall** - green).

5. Verify that the **Camera01** viewport is active (yellow border) and in the Main Toolbar, click  (Render Production) or press <F9> to render the scene, as shown in Figure 6–88. Note the shadow cast by the candleholder. There is a shadow casting mental ray spotlight already set up in the scene. Leave the Render window open.

Figure 6–88

6. In the Material/Map Browser in the Slate Material Editor, expand the *Materials>mental ray* categories. Double-click on Arch & Design (as shown in Figure 6–89) to add a new material node to the *View1* sheet.

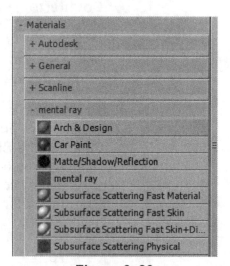

Figure 6–89

7. Double-click on the **Material # Arch & Design** title bar heading to open its Parameter Editor.

8. In the Templates rollout, expand the (Select a template) drop-down list and in the *Metals* sub-category, select **Copper**, as shown in Figure 6–90. The **Copper** material displays as the sample sphere in the material's title bar.

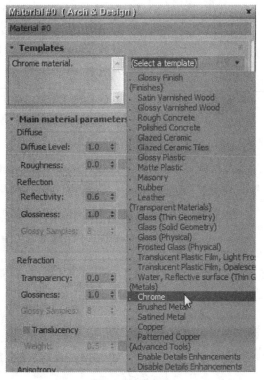

Figure 6–90

*You can select the object in any other viewport but you must activate the **Camera01** viewport before rendering the view.*

9. In the **Camera01** viewport, select the **candleholder** object and in the Slate Material Editor toolbar, click [icon] (Assign Material to Selection).

10. Click **Render** (bottom right of the Render Window), or click

[icon] (Render Production) if the Render window was closed, to render the **Camera01** viewport, as shown in Figure 6–91. The **Copper** material reflects the colors of the walls around it and the lighting in the scene.

*In the Render window, **Render** is located at the bottom right corner of the Settings panel. The rendering time is a little slower due to the calculations for reflections.*

Figure 6–91

11. In the Material/Map Browser, double-click on Arch & Design (*mental ray* category) again to add another material node to the *View1* sheet. Place this new material node to the left of the existing Arch & Design (Copper) node.

12. Double-click on the title bar heading for the new Arch & Design material to access its Parameter Editor.

13. In the Templates rollout, expand the (Select a template) drop-down list and select **Glazed Ceramic Tiles** in the *Finishes* sub-category.

14. In the Camera01 viewport, select the floor object (Box01 which has the countertop material) and in the Slate Material Editor toolbar, click to assign the new ceramic tile to the floor.

15. Click  (Show Shaded Material in Viewport) to see the tiles displayed on the floor in the viewport.

16. Render the **Camera01** viewport, as shown in Figure 6–92. The **Copper** and **Glazed Tile** materials both display in the scene. The rendering is slower (possibly due to the shadow of the candlestick reflecting on the tiles).

17. Double-click on the title bar heading for the Arch & Design material (Copper template). In the Templates rollout, expand the (Select a template) drop-down list and select **Frosted Glass (Physical)** in the *Transparent Materials* category. This material is automatically assigned to the Candlestick. Render the **Camera01** view again, as shown in Figure 6–93. The render time is significantly slower. The **Translucent** material enables the light to pass through it.

The light is casting a ray-traced shadow, rather than a map shadow.

Figure 6–92

Figure 6–93

18. Save your work as **Mycandleholder.max**.

Task 3 - Assign a Car Paint material.

To explore the **Car Paint** material, you will load a different file.

1. Open **MR_guitar.max**. This is the guitar with a plain gray material applied to the body.

2. Open the Slate Material Editor, if required. In the Material/Map Browser, expand the *Materials>mental ray* categories. Double-click on the **Car Paint** mental ray material to add it to the *View1* sheet.

3. Select the **BODY:1** object in the viewport (you can select it in the Scene Explorer as well). In the Slate Material Editor toolbar, click [icon] (Assign Material to Selection) to assign the **Car Paint** material. In the Main Toolbar, click [icon] (Render Production). The **Car Paint** material is applied to the body, as shown in Figure 6–94.

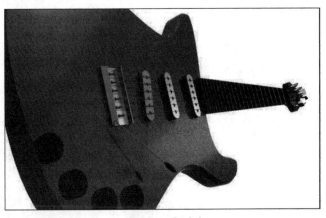

Figure 6–94

4. Note that the pickups and strings reflect in the guitar body, but the body looks a little dull. In the *View1* sheet, double-click on the **Material# Car Paint** title bar heading to open its Parameter Editor. In the Diffuse Coloring rollout, select the *Ambient/Extra Light* color swatch to open the Color Selector. Set the *Value* slider to **100**. Click **OK**.

5. Render the scene and note the change in brightness.

Your rendering might be slightly different than Figure 6–94. It depends on your monitor display and the Gamma and LUT settings.

6. To add a texture map to a mental ray material, in the Diffuse Coloring rollout, click ☐ for **Base Color** as shown in Figure 6–95.

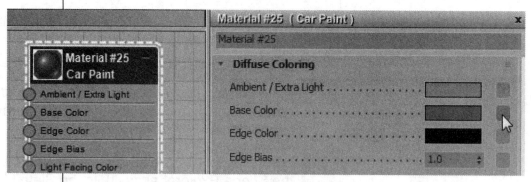

Figure 6–95

7. In the Material/Map Browser, expand the *Maps>Standard* categories and double-click on **Bitmap**. In the Select Bitmap Image File dialog box, browse to the *...\Maps* directory in your Practice Files, open **BURLOAK.JPG**.

8. Render the viewport again. The wood texture is displayed on the guitar body, as shown in Figure 6–96.

Figure 6–96

9. To brighten up the wood texture, in the *View1* sheet, double-click on the **Map # Bitmap** title bar (wired to the Base color of **Car Paint** materials) to open its Parameter Editor.

10. Expand the Output rollout and select **Enable Color Map**. In the Color Map toolbar, click (Add Point) and add a point to the diagonal line at its approximate midpoint, as shown in Figure 6–97.

11. In the Color Map toolbar, click 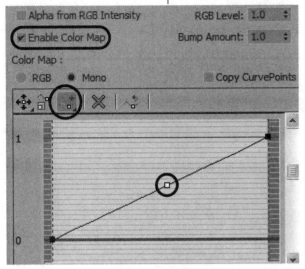 (Move) and drag the right-most point to a *value* of about **2**. You can enter **2** in the right text box at the bottom of graph. Use the **Zoom** tool (located in the lower right corner of the graph window) of the graph to display the point.

12. Move the middle point to **1**, right-click on it and select **Bezier-Smooth**. Move the point and/or handles, as shown in Figure 6–98. The sample sphere for the bitmap updates. Close the Slate Material Editor.

Figure 6–97

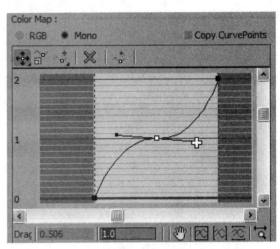

Figure 6–98

13. In the viewport, use  (Field-of-View) to zoom in on the pickups. Render the scene and note the reflections, as shown in Figure 6–99.

Figure 6–99

14. Save your work as **My_MR_guitar.max**.

6.9 The Material Explorer

The Material Explorer enables you to manage all of the materials used in a scene using. It displays the material's *Name*, *Type*, *Show in Viewport* setting, and *Material ID*, as shown in Figure 6–100.

- You can open the Material Explorer dialog box by selecting **Rendering>Material Explorer**, as shown in Figure 6–100.

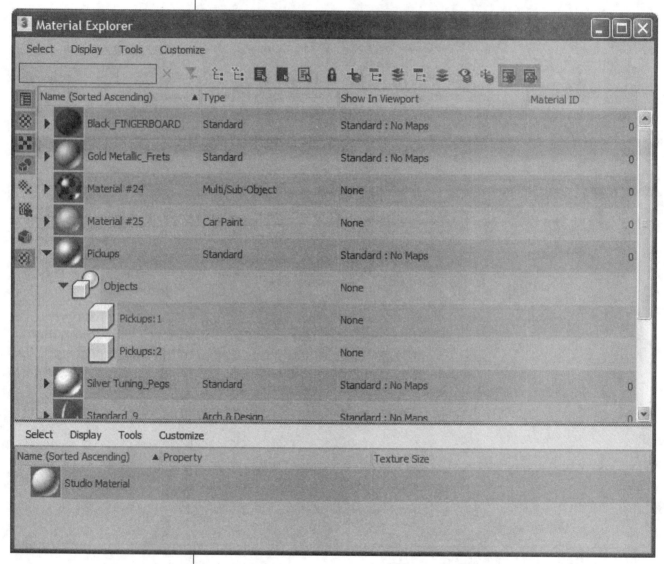

Figure 6–100

- Selecting the various headings sorts the materials in various ways. For example, if you select the *Type* heading, materials of the same type are listed alphabetically according to the material type (such as Architectural, Standard, Arch & Design, etc.).

- The bottom panel of the interface displays information on the maps or other properties of the material. This panel has its own menu that enables you to manipulate each material's properties.

- From the Material Explorer, you can save directly to a new material library (as shown in Figure 6–101) or perform a variety of tasks depending on the type of the material.

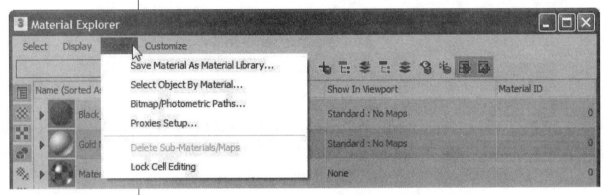

Figure 6–101

Chapter Review Questions

1. What are the three color channels in Standard materials that determine the color applied to an object?

   a. *Ambient, Bump, Specular*

   b. *Bump, Diffuse, Opacity*

   c. *Specular, Opacity, Diffuse*

   d. *Ambient, Diffuse, Specular*

2. The materials and maps listed in the Material/Map Browser are dependent on...

   a. the active scene.

   b. the active renderer.

   c. the active viewport.

   d. the active material editor.

3. In the active view sheet of the Slate Material Editor, the green color (title bar) of a node indicates that it is a...

   a. Material

   b. Map

   c. Controller

   d. Material with the **Show Map In Viewport** option applied.

4. In the active view sheet of the Slate Material Editor, a dashed white border around a material node indicates that the...

   a. Material is being used in the scene.

   b. Map is assigned to one of the channels (socket) of the material.

   c. Parameters of the material are displayed in the Parameter Editor.

   d. Material is a customized material.

5. The Phong shader generates softer, smoother (often more realistic) highlights than the Blinn shader.

   a. True

   b. False

6. Which type of general material enables you to stack multiple materials into a single parent material, each with a material ID number.

    a. Multi/Sub-Object material

    b. Architectural material

    c. Raytrace material

    d. Shell material

7. Which type of mapping gives the illusion of an embossed or pitted surface without actual geometry having to be present on the model?

    a. Opacity mapping

    b. Bump mapping

    c. Reflection mapping

8. Which type of mental ray material is a layered material that provides for four layers (base paint layer, embedded metal flake layer, clear-coat layer, and Lambertian dirt layer) combining to create one surface treatment?

    a. Arch and Design material

    b. Matte/Shadow/Reflection material

    c. Subsurface Scattering (SSS) material

    d. Car Paint material

Command Summary

Button	Command	Location
	Compact Material Editor	• **Main Toolbar** • **Rendering:** Material Editor>Compact Material Editor
N/A	**Material Explorer**	• **Rendering:** Material Explorer
	Render Production	• **Main Toolbar**: Render flyout • **Rendering:** Render
	Render Setup	• **Main Toolbar** • **Rendering:** Render Setup
	Slate Material Editor	• **Main Toolbar** • **Rendering:** Material Editor>Slate Material Editor

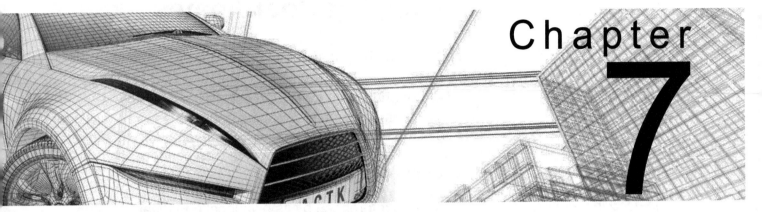

Mapping Coordinates and Scale

When creating a realistic representations of a model, both materials and image texture maps can be used. They can be incorporated in a Material or you can use specific Map Modifiers and Scaling controls to further control how these elements look in a model.

Learning Objectives in this Chapter

- Work with mapping coordinates required for objects with texture maps.
- Assign mapping coordinates using various tools.
- Adjust the size of the image maps using the various map scaling options.
- Assign spline mapping to a curved object.

7.1 Mapping Coordinates

Most of the sample materials provided with the Autodesk® 3ds Max® software are assigned image texture maps, especially the Diffuse Color and Bump maps. Objects that are assigned materials with maps require mapping coordinates to control how the map is projected onto the object. For example, a rectangular sign can use planar or box mapping and a cylindrical can uses cylindrical mapping.

UVW is used instead of XYZ to indicate that the mapping does not need to be aligned with the world XYZ coordinates.

- Mapping is referenced by its own local coordinate system, described by UVW coordinates.

- Many objects (including primitives) are automatically assigned mapping coordinates. This is controlled by **Generate Mapping Coords** in the Command Panel, in the object's Parameters rollout, as shown in Figure 7–1.

- Linked or imported objects with materials assigned in AutoCAD® automatically have mapping coordinates if the **Generate coordinates for all objects** is selected in the import or link preset options, as shown in Figure 7–2.

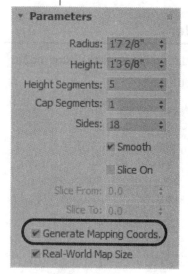

Figure 7–1

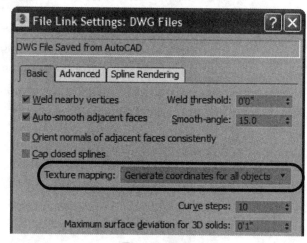

Figure 7–2

- The Autodesk 3ds Max software provides a number of different modifiers (such as **UVW Map**, **Unwrap UVW**, and **MapScaler**) that can be used to reassign mapping manually.

- Mapping is often disturbed by editing (as through an Edit Mesh modifier) and by Boolean operations. The Edit Poly modifier has a Preserve UVW's feature that can be toggled on to prevent the need for remapping.

- If you select to render an object without mapping coordinates, you receive a warning message that the maps might not render correctly.

Mapping Controls in Slate Material Editor

At the map level of the Slate Material Editor, in the Parameter Editor of the map (shown in Figure 7–3), there are controls to manipulate the positioning of a map with mapping coordinates. (Some of these controls are duplicated in the UVW Map modifier, which controls only the object it is applied to.)

Use Real-World Scale On

The **Use Real-World Scale** attempts to simplify the correct scaling of textures by specifying the actual height and width (as shown in Figure 7–3) as represented by the 2D texture map. This option requires that the object use UV texture mapping set to **Real World Map Size** and that the Material also have **Use Real-World Scale** selected. It replaces the *Tiling* fields with a Size value for **Width** and **Height**.

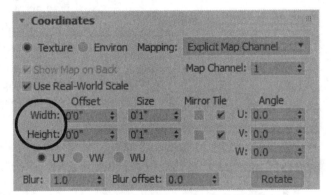

Figure 7–3

Hint: Importing with Use Real-World Scale

Using the **Use Real-World Scale** option when importing from earlier versions of the Autodesk 3ds Max software might cause textures to display incorrectly. It can be due to **Real World Map Size** and **Use Real-World Scale** trying to create an extreme texture. If you leave these on, you need to reset *Tiling* to a different value. You can use **0.01** or a similar small value before you can see the bitmap texture, or go larger and use **10** or **20**. If the texture does not display correctly, it might be easier to toggle off **Use Real-World Scale** and set *Tiling* to **1.0 x 1.0**.

Use Real-World Scale Off

When the **Use Real-World Scale** is toggled off, the map texture is placed with respect to the UV values, as shown in Figure 7–4.

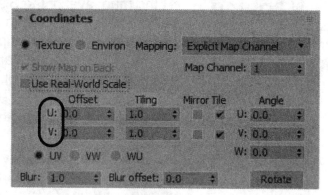

Figure 7–4

Offset	Enable you to move the map on an object relative to the mapping coordinates.
Tiling	Enables you to specify whether the map is repeated or tiled across the surface, in either the U (often width) or V (often height) direction.
Mirror	Causes tiled maps to be mirrored end-to-end as they tile.
Angle (*W-rotation field*)	Controls rotation of the map about the W (local Z) axis. For 2D maps (such as with an image file) this value typically is used to rotate the map on the surface of an object.

MapScaler Modifier

You can use the MapScaler Modifier (Modifier List in the Modify panel ( )) to project a map perpendicular to each face of an object. There are two MapScalers:

• **MapScaler World Space Modifier (WSM)** (shown in Figure 7–5) keeps the map scale constant if the object size changes with the Scale transform.

- **MapScaler Object Space Modifier (OSM)** (shown in Figure 7–6) scales the map proportionally.

Figure 7–5

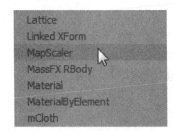

Figure 7–6

MapScalers do not always project well on curved surfaces.

- MapScalers enable automatically generated, continuous tiling across complex geometry that might be difficult with UVW Maps. They tend to work well with geometry imported from the AutoCAD Architecture and the Autodesk Revit software.

- One method of repositioning a map on an object assigned a MapScaler is to adjust the U- and V-offset settings in the Bitmap Parameters rollout in the Material Editor. Otherwise, apply a UVW XForm modifier to the object and apply the offsets there instead.

- MapScaler modifiers are generally used on objects that have tiling material maps but do not have a defined beginning or end point, such as concrete pads, metals, asphalt, grass, and sometimes brick.

UVW Map Modifier

The UVW Map modifier (Modify panel ( )>Modifier List) enables you to apply a map to an object, where you select a specific shape and location to project the map onto.

- The UVW Map modifier has a gizmo for transforming in Sub-object mode.

- UVW Maps might not project as well as MapScalers on geometry that does not lend itself to the standard projection shapes (planar, box, cylinder, etc.).

> **Hint: Unwrap UVW**
>
> The **Unwrap UVW** modifier is another commonly used mapping method. For more information on *Unwrap UVW*, see the Autodesk 3ds Max Help files.

Practice 7a

Applying Mapping Coordinates

Practice Objective

- Adjust the placement of a map on an object.

Estimated time for completion: 10 minutes

In this practice you will adjust the material mapping using the UVW Map and MapScaler (WSM) modifiers.

You must set the paths to locate the External files and Xrefs used in the practice. If you have not done this already, return to **Chapter 1: Introduction to Autodesk 3ds Max** and complete Task 1 to Task 3 in **Practice 1a: Organizing Folders and Working with the Interface**. You only have to set the user paths once.

1. Open **Light Pole Mapping.max**.

*If a dialog box opens prompting you about a File Load: Mismatch, click **OK** to accept the default values.*

2. In the viewport, select the concrete **LP Base** object and then click ![icon](Zoom Extents Selected) to zoom into the base object as shown in Figure 7–7. When this cylinder was created, the mapping coordinates were generated automatically.

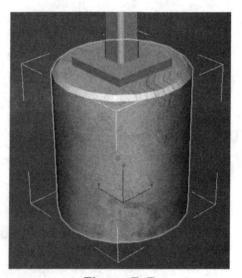

Figure 7–7

*You need to scroll down the list to select the **UVW Map** modifier.*

3. With the **LP Base** object selected, in the Command Panel> Modify panel ( ), expand the Modifier list. In the *OBJECT-SPACE MODIFIERS* group, select **UVW Map**, as shown in Figure 7–8.

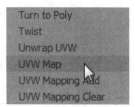

Figure 7–8

4. In the Parameters rollout, in the *Mapping* area, select **Box,** as shown in Figure 7–9. This projects the concrete map onto the object from all six sides of an imaginary box, causing a seam to form in places, as shown in Figure 7–10.

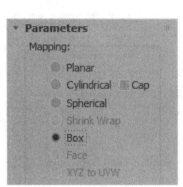

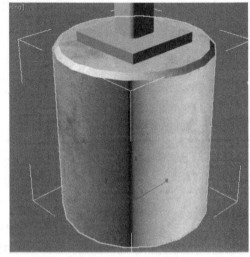

Figure 7–9   **Figure 7–10**

5. Change the projection to *Cylindrical* and then *Planar*, noting the differences.

   • The Cylindrical projection is not handling the beveled top very well, as shown in Figure 7–11.

   • The Planar projection is not displaying the cylindrical base correctly, as shown in Figure 7–12.

   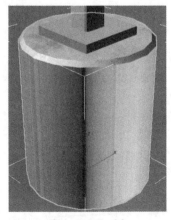

Figure 7–11   **Figure 7–12**

6. Remove the UVW Map modifier from the Modifier Stack by selecting it and clicking 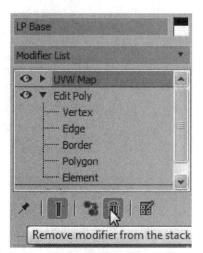 (Remove modifier from the stack), as shown in Figure 7–13.

Figure 7–13

7. In the Modifier drop-down list, in the WORLD-SPACE MODIFIERS, select **MapScaler (WSM)**. The MapScalers are automatically projected perpendicular to each face of an object.

8. Change the Shading Viewport (User Defined) label to **High Quality**.

9. In the Parameters rollout, adjust the *Scale* spinner up or down to visually improve the look of the map, as shown in Figure 7–14.

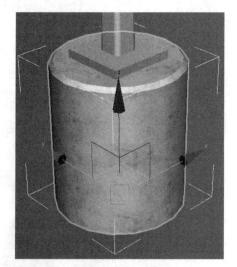

Figure 7–14

10. Save your work as **MyLight Pole Mapping.max**.

Practice 7b

Mapping a Large Scale Image

Practice Objective

- Assign a map to a model and apply mapping coordinates.

In this practice you will apply a scanned image to a terrain model and map it accurately. You will use the Slate Material Editor and the **UVW Map** modifiers to assign a map to a model, apply mapping coordinates, and adjust the map.

You must set the paths to locate the External files and Xrefs used in the practice. If you have not done this already, return to **Chapter 1: Introduction to Autodesk 3ds Max** and complete Task 1 to Task 3 in **Practice 1a: Organizing Folders and Working with the Interface**. You only have to set the user paths once.

Estimated time for completion: 10 minutes

*If a dialog box opens prompting you about a File Load: Mismatch, click **OK** to accept the default values.*

1. Open the file **Mapping a large scale image.max**.

2. If your Units setup is maintained for Imperial, a Units Scale Mismatch dialog box opens. Click **OK** to accept the defaults. The units for this file are set to **Meters** and the *System Unit Scale* is **1 Unit=1 Meter**. This is required because the map that will be used is set for Metric units.

3. In the Main Toolbar, click ![icon] (Material Editor) to open the Slate Material Editor. In the Material/Map Browser, expand the *Materials>Scanline* categories. Double-click on the **Standard** material to add it to the *View1* sheet. Double-click on the title bar heading for this new material to open the Parameter Editor. Change the material name to **Quad Map**.

4. Expand the Maps rollout and for *Diffuse Color*, click **None**, as shown in Figure 7–15. The Material/Map Browser opens.

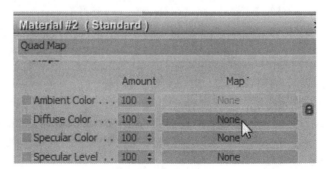

Figure 7–15

5. In the Material/Map Browser, expand the *Maps>General* categories. Double-click on **Bitmap** to open the Select Bitmap Image File dialog box. Open the image **q257938.tif** from the ...*Maps* folder in the Practice Files folder.

6. In the *View1* sheet, note that the **Map # Bitmap** is wired to the Input socket of *Diffuse Color* of the Quad Map material. Double-click on the Bitmap title bar heading to open its Parameter Editor. In the Bitmap Parameters rollout, in the *Cropping/Placement* area, click **View Image** to open the bitmap. Close the Specify Cropping/Placement window.

7. In the Coordinates rollout, clear **Use Real-World Scale**. Clear *Tile* for both **U** and **V** (as shown in Figure 7–16) because you want this map to display only once and in a specific location.

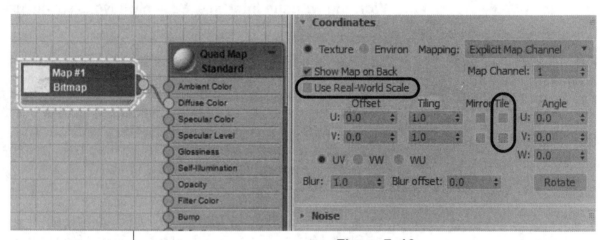

Figure 7–16

8. In the viewport, select the **Terrain01** object. In the *View1* sheet, select the **Quad Map** material and in the Material Editor toolbar, click (Assign Material to Selection). The material does not preview in the viewport.

9. In the viewport, right-click on the **Terrain01** object and select **Object Properties**. In the *Display Properties* area, clear **Vertex Channel Display** and click **OK**. Now the gray color of the material is visible on the terrain, and no texture map indicates a mapping issue.

In the Main Toolbar,

click (Render Production).

10. Render the scene and note the warning message of missing map coordinates. Click **Cancel** in the Missing Map Coordinates dialog box and close the Render window.

11. In the viewport, select the **Terrain01** object, if required. In the Command Panel, select the Modify panel (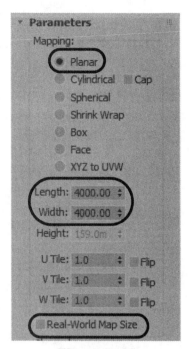), and in the Modifier List, select **UVW Map**. Since the diffuse map is not meant to tile, in the Parameters rollout, verify that **Planar** is selected and clear **Real-World Map Size**, as shown in Figure 7–17.

Figure 7–17

12. Render the scene. The terrain model should now resemble a 3D map, as shown in Figure 7–18.

Figure 7–18

- Without any direct manipulation, it appears that this texture map is being applied correctly. This is because the contours used to create the surface were trimmed very close to the geographic boundary of the image file.

13. Close the Render window. If the map does not display in the viewport, in the Slate Material Editor toolbar, click ■ (Show Shaded Material in Viewport).

14. In the Command Panel, in the Parameters rollout, note that the map was automatically scaled to the correct coordinates displayed in the *Length* and *Width* values.

15. In the Modifier Stack, expand UVW Map and select **Gizmo** to enter Sub-object mode, as shown in Figure 7–19.

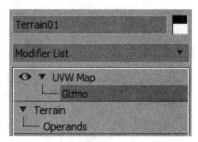

Figure 7–19

16. In the Main Toolbar, click ✛ (Select and Move) and move the image map on the terrain object. You can adjust the map more precisely using the UVW Map gizmo.

17. Save your work as **MyLargeScaleProjectMapped**.

7.2 Mapping Scale

Mapping Scale is directly related to mapping coordinates and both are often addressed at the same time. Objects that use materials with image maps need to have them sized appropriately.

- Procedural maps also need to be scaled, but they are normally controlled by scale parameters at the Map level of the Material Editor.

Explicit Map Scaling

The size parameters of the UVW Map modifier enables you to control the number of times a map is displayed. Examples of this include maps used in materials for 3D models of signs, billboards, computer screens, paintings, etc.

- These kinds of maps are not assigned a real-world scale since they often require to be sized manually for each object. In these situations, clear the **Use Real-World Map Scale** option in the Map Coordinates rollout and clear the **Real-World Map Size** in the **UVW Map** parameters, as shown in Figure 7–20.

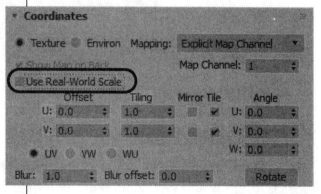
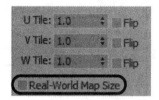

Figure 7–20

- To display the map once, the U and V tile values should be set to **1.0** in both the Map Coordinates rollout of the Material Editor and the **UVW Map** modifier parameters.

- To display the map in the V-direction twice, for example (the map's local Y-direction), set the V tile value to **2** in one of these locations, but not both.

Continuous Map Scaling

When material maps are meant to tile continuously across an object, a continuous approach can be used. The size of these maps can be controlled by a Real World scale that affects all objects using the map, or they can be sized directly using **UVW Map** or **MapScaler** size parameters for each object. Setting a Real World scale makes it easier to affect a global map scale change to multiple objects. You might need to determine the physical size you want to display an image file map in your scene.

Calculating Real World scales

U is the map's local X-axis and V is the local Y.

The **Brick** material uses an image file for a diffuse color map, as shown in Figure 7–21. This image map represents a section of wall that is five bricks wide (measured along the long edges) and 16 courses tall. If you want to use this material to represent bricks that are 11" on center laid in 4" courses, this brick map should be scaled to exactly **4'7" (11" x 5)** in the U direction and **5'4" (4" x 16)** in the V direction.

Figure 7–21

You can set this scale in various ways:

- At a global scale, enable **Use Real-World Scale** and assign appropriate size values in the map's Coordinates rollout, as shown in Figure 7–22.

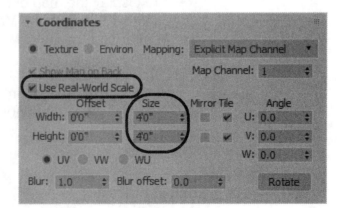

Figure 7–22

- If mapping coordinates are required, apply UVW Maps or Map Scalers to objects displaying this map. UVW Maps should have the **Real World Map Size** option enabled as shown in Figure 7–23. The Map Scalers should be set to a size of one scene unit (such as 1"), as shown in Figure 7–24, in the Parameters rollout of WSM modifier.

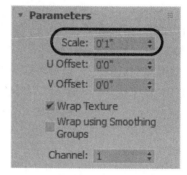

Figure 7–23   **Figure 7–24**

- If you want to control map scaling of individual objects through a UVW Map, clear the **Use Real-World Scale** option in the Coordinates rollout and set the *Tiling* values to **1.0**, as shown in Figure 7–25.

- Objects showing map can be assigned sizes directly through the UVW Map modifier's **Length**, **Width** and **Height** parameter values. Clear **Real-World Map Size** in the **UVW Map** parameters.

- If you want to control map scaling on individual objects with a Map Scaler, clear the **Use Real-World Scale** option, set the *U-Tiling* value to **1.0** and the *V-Tiling* value equal to the ratio of the U-scale divided by the V scale, as shown in Figure 7–26.

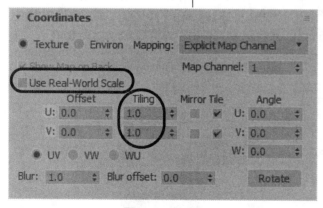

Figure 7–25

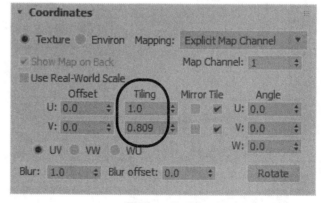

Figure 7–26

- Objects showing this map can be assigned MapScaler modifiers with the **Scale** parameter value set to the U scale.

Practice 7c | Assigning Map Scales

Practice Objectives

- Assign a material that contains an image map.
- Adjust the size of the image maps.

Estimated time for completion: 15 minutes

In this practice you will assign a material containing an image map to an object in a scene. You will then use the **MapScaler (WSM)** modifier to adjust the image map and the scaling options to position it correctly in the scene.

You must set the paths to locate the External files and Xrefs used in the practice. If you have not done this already, return to **Chapter 1: Introduction to Autodesk 3ds Max** and complete Task 1 to Task 3 in **Practice 1a: Organizing Folders and Working with the Interface**. You only have to set the user paths once.

Task 1 - Position and Scale the Brick Maps.

*If a dialog box opens prompting you about a File Load: Mismatch, click **OK** to accept the default values.*

1. Open the file **Interior Mapping.max**. If you completed the Terrain Mapping practice, the *Units* were changed to **Metric**, and a Units Scale Mismatch dialog box now opens. Click **OK** to accept the defaults and adopt the file's units (Imperial).

2. In the Scene Explorer, ■ (Display None) and ● (Display Geometry). Select **Layer:VIZ-1-Walls**, to select all of the walls in the lower floor in the viewport. .

3. In the Modify panel ( ), in the Modifier List, select **MapScaler (WSM)**. In the Parameters rollout, verify that the *Scale* value is set to one system unit **0'1"**, as shown in Figure 7–27.

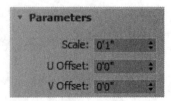

Figure 7–27

4. In the Main Toolbar, click (Material Editor) to open the Slate Material Editor.

5. In the *Scene Materials*, double-click on the **Wall Multi (Multi/Sub-Object)** material to open it on the *View1* sheet. Locate the **Masonry** material, wired to input socket 5 of the **Wall Multi** material, as shown in Figure 7–28. Note that this material has bitmaps wired to the *Diffuse* and *Bump* channels.

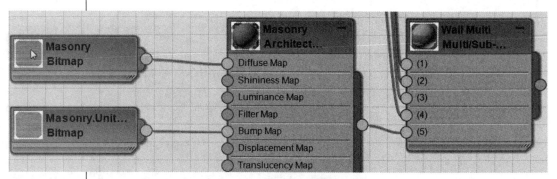

Figure 7–28

6. Double-click on the **Masonry Bitmap** wired to the **Masonry** material's *Diffuse Map* to open its Parameter Editor.

7. In the Coordinates rollout, verify that **Use Real-World Scale** is selected and set the following, as shown in Figure 7–29:

   • *Width, Size*: **4'7"**
   • *Height, Size:* **5'4"**

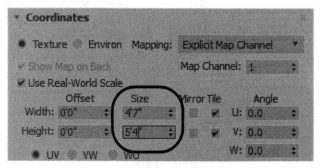

Figure 7–29

8. In *View1* sheet, select the **Masonry Architect** material, click (Assign Material to Selection), and click (Show Shaded Material in Viewport). Note that the **brick** material has been assigned to the walls because **Layer:VIZ-1-Walls** was selected.

The Slate Material Editor is a modeless dialog box and can remain open while you are working in the viewport or other commands. You can minimize or maximize it, as required.

*The brick texture terminates in acceptable positions along the wall edges. If it does not, move the texture along the wall with the **U-** and **V-** offset parameters in the map's Coordinates rollout, or with a UVW XForm modifier.*

9. In the **Perspective** viewport, use the various navigation tools, such as  (Zoom), (Pan), and (Orbit), to zoom into and obtain the required orientation of one of the brick walls. The brick texture displays at the correct scale on the wall objects displaying the brick sub-material, as shown in Figure 7–30.

Figure 7–30

10. For images in a material to be aligned, all of their mapping coordinates' parameters should also match. In the Slate Material Editor, double-click on the title bar heading for the **Masonry.Unit** bitmap, wired to the Bump Map of the **Masonry** material. In the Coordinates rollout, set the *Width* and *Height Size* values that were used for the Diffuse Map. This makes the bitmap texture display more realistic.

Hint: Multiple Sets of Mapping Coordinates

In the example, you scaled a Multi/Sub-Object material map with a single MapScaler Modifier. What if another material's map in Wall Multi required a **UVW Map** or different **MapScaler Scale** parameter?

Material maps can be assigned to separate channels in the Material Editor, so that each can be controlled by separate UVW Maps or MapScaler Modifiers. In such a case, you can apply multiple UVW Maps or MapScaler Modifiers to the same object and assign each the applicable channel identified in the **Map** parameters, as shown in Figure 7–31.

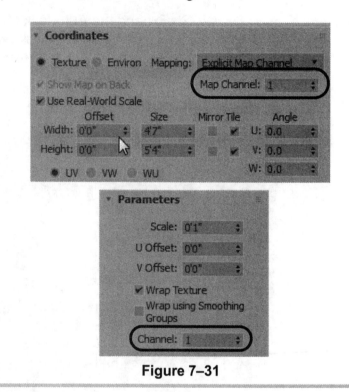

Figure 7–31

Task 2 - Assign the Ceiling Material.

---

1. Change your current view to the **Camera - Lobby1** camera view, by selecting the **Perspective** POV label and selecting **Cameras>Camera - Lobby1**.

2. Change the Shading Viewport (User Defined) to **High Quality**.

The production renderer should be NVIDIA mental ray, NVIDIA iray, ART Renderer, or Quicksilver Hardware Renderer, to display the Autodesk Material Library.

3. In the Material/Map Browser in the Slate Material Editor, locate the Autodesk Material Library.

   • If the Autodesk Material Library is not listed, in the Main

     Toolbar, click 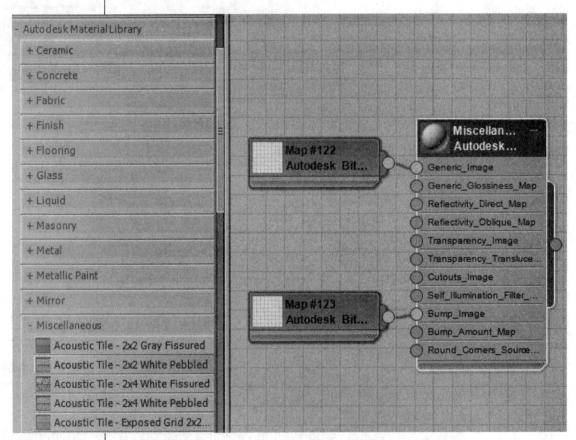 (Render Setup) to open the Render Setup dialog box. In the Renderer drop-down list, select **NVIDIA mental ray** and close the Render Setup dialog box.

4. Right-click on the *View1* label and select **Create New View**. Accept the default view name (*View2*) and click **OK**. The *View2* sheet, which is empty, is the now active sheet.

5. Expand the Autodesk Material Library and the *Miscellaneous* category. Double-click on the **Acoustic Tile - 2x2 White Pebbled** material to display it in *View2* sheet, as shown in Figure 7–32.

Figure 7–32

6. In the viewport, select the ceiling object and note that **Layer:VIZ-1-Ceiling** is displayed in the Command Panel. In the Command Panel, apply a **MapScaler (WSM)** modifier by selecting it from the Modifier List. In the Parameters rollout, verify that *Scale* is set to **0'1"**.

7. In the Slate Material Editor, in the *View2* sheet, select **Miscellaneous** material by clicking on its title bar and click  (Assign Material to Selection).

8. Note that the ceiling displays in white/gray in the viewport. In the Slate Material Editor toolbar, click (Show Shaded Material in Viewport) to preview the diffuse map in the viewport, as shown in Figure 7–33. The ceiling tiles have been sized using the Real-World Map Size that was defined for this material in the Autodesk Material Library (to a 2'x2' grid).

Figure 7–33

9. You can reposition the ceiling texture through the *Offset* fields in the MapScaler modifier. In the Command Panel, in the Parameters rollout, change the *U Offset* and *V Offset* spinner arrows and observe the change in the viewport. Move it so that the left ceiling tile edge coincides with the corner of the ceiling and the left curtain wall window, as shown in Figure 7–34.

Figure 7–34

10. Save your work as **MyInterior Mapping.max**.

7.3 Spline Mapping

Generating mapping coordinates that follow the path of extrusion is useful when a texture needs to follow the curvature of the lofted object. The **Unwrap UVW** modifier enables you to apply spline mapping and to select a spline for the basis of the mapping coordinates. You can use the Mapping gizmo to modify the mapping along the cross-section.

- It is applied at a sub-object level (Polygon or Face), as shown in Figure 7–35.

- It is present in the Wrap rollout of the **Unwrap UVW** parameters, as shown in Figure 7–36.

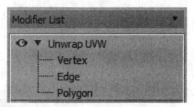

Figure 7–35

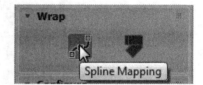

Figure 7–36

Practice 7d

Spline Mapping

Practice Objective

* Apply spline mapping to a curved object.

Estimated time for completion: 15 minutes

In this practice you will apply spline mapping to a curved object using the **Unwrap UVW** modifier and adjust the scale and position to place it appropriately.

You must set the paths to locate the External files and Xrefs used in the practice. If you have not done this already, return to **Chapter 1: Introduction to Autodesk 3ds Max** and complete Task 1 to Task 3 in **Practice 1a: Organizing Folders and Working with the Interface**. You only have to set the user paths once.

Task 1 - Position and Scale the Checker Map.

If a dialog box opens prompting you about a File Load: Mismatch, click OK to accept the default values.

1. Open **Spline Mapping.max**. There are two curved objects. The one on the right has been mapped with spline mapping while the one on the left does not have mapping.

2. Select **Roadshape01** (left object). A spline has already been prepared in this file and it runs (yellow line) through the center of the curved object. You can change the Per-View Preference to **Wireframe Override** to display the spline more clearly and then change it back to **Default Shading**.

3. Expand the Modify panel ( ) and in the Modifier Stack verify that a Line object and an Extrude modifier are listed.

4. In the Main Toolbar, click (Material Editor) to open the Slate Material Editor.

5. In the Material/Map Browser, in the *Scene Materials* category, double-click on **02 - Default** Standard material to place it in the *View1* sheet. This material has already been assigned to the **Roadshape01 o**bject.

6. Double-click on the **02 - Default** title bar to open its Parameter Editor. In the Blinn Basic Parameters rollout, click ▢ (None) for the *Diffuse color* channel, as shown in Figure 7–37.

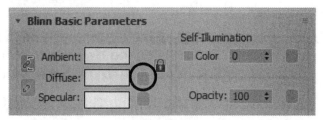

Figure 7–37

7. In the Material/Map Browser that opens, in the *Maps> General* categories, double-click on **Checker**. In the *View1* sheet, note that the Checker node is wired to the input socket of Diffuse Color of the **02- Default** material.

8. In the Slate Material Editor toolbar, click ▣ (Show Shaded Material in Viewport) to display the checker texture on the road shape in the viewport, as shown in Figure 7–38.

Figure 7–38

- Note that the checker map is projected as a single sheet on top of the rectangular object and not generated to follow the curvature of the spline.

9. In the Command Panel>Modify panel (▨), in the Modifier List, select **Unwrap UVW**. Note that the Unwrap UVW is listed above Extrude in the Modifier Stack.

A checker board mapping material is useful for identifying map scaling and orientation issues, which can then be corrected before applying the actual texture map so that it displays correctly.

You can minimize the Slate Material Editor so that it is not in the way while you are working in the Command Panel and the viewport and maximize it when you need it again.

10. In the Modifier Stack, expand Unwrap UVW and select **Polygon**, as shown in Figure 7–39.

Figure 7–39

11. In the viewport, select the top face along the curve of the **Roadshape01** object. Note that the top checker face is displayed in a red hue indicating that the face is selected.

12. In the Command Panel, pan down to the Wrap rollout. Click (Spline Mapping), as shown in Figure 7–40.

Figure 7–40

*Apply **Planar** for roads and planar surfaces with a line cross-section. Use **Circular** Mapping for objects with a circular cross-section.*

13. In the Spline Map Parameters dialog box, set *Mapping* to **Planar** and click **Pick Spline**, as shown in Figure 7–41.

Figure 7–41

14. In the viewport, select the end of the spline (yellow line), which is displayed at either end of the **Roadshape01** object.

15. In the Spline Map Parameters dialog box, click **Commit**.

If the checker map does not display as required, use the spinner for the Size Width to increase or decrease the value and note the interactive changes in the viewport. The checker line should pass through the center, following the curve line.

16. In the Modifier Stack, select **Unwrap UVW** to clear the selection and exit Sub-object mode. The texture is displayed on the shape as a single color indicating that the position and scale need to be corrected.

17. In the Slate Material Editor, in the *View1* sheet, double-click on the **Map # Checker** title bar to display its Parameter Editor. In the Coordinates rollout, set the following, as shown in Figure 7–42:

- *Size Width*: **0'0.8"**
- *Size Height*: **0'0.1"**

Press <Enter> and verify that the *Offset* values are **0'0.0"** for both *Width* and *Height*. It is recommended that you use the spinners to increase and decrease the *Size Width* while checking the interactive display of checker in the viewport.

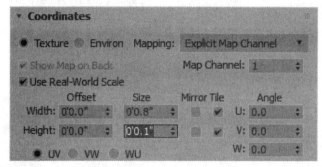

Figure 7–42

The checker map displays as shown in the Figure 7–43. This is the correct position and scale of the **checker** material.

Figure 7–43

Task 2 - Assign the Road Material.

1. In the Material/Map Browser, expand the *Maps>General* categories. Double-click on **Bitmap** to open the Select Bitmap Image File dialog box. Open **TextureForRoad.jpg** (from the ...*Maps* folder).

   - Note that a new node for this bitmap is added in the *View1* sheet.

2. Delete the wire that currently exists between the **Checker** Map and the Diffuse Color of **02 Default** material by selecting the wire and pressing <Delete>.

3. Draw a new wire linking the input socket of the Diffuse Color for **02 Default** material to the output socket of the new Bitmap (**Map #4 Bitmap**), as shown in the Figure 7–44.

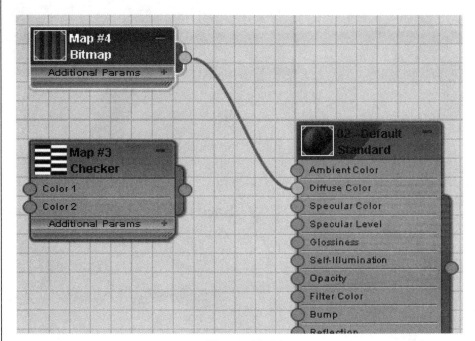

Figure 7–44

4. Select the **02 Default** material title bar and select (Show Shaded Material in Viewport) to display the road texture on the face on **Roadshape01** object.

5. Double-click on the new **Map # Bitmap (TextureForRoad)** material to open its Parameter Editor. In the Coordinates rollout, clear **Use Real-World Scale**.

6. Set *Tiling* for **U: 2** and **V: 8**. Use the **Offset U** and **V** sliders to center the road. Increasing the **Tiling V** brings the dashes closer to the middle of the road while decreasing it makes the dashes longer and farther apart along the center curve. Use the **Offset U** spinner to increase or decrease the value so that the dashed line is placed along the center of the road. The road shape on the left should now look similar to the road shape on the right as shown in Figure 7–45.

Figure 7–45

7. Save your work as **MyStartSplineMapping.max**.

Chapter Review Questions

1. Which option manipulates the positioning of a map with mapping coordinates at the map level of the Slate Material Editor?

   a. Generate coordinates for all objects.

   b. Generate Mapping Coords

   c. Unwrap UVW

   d. Use Real-World Scale

2. The MapScaler in the World Space Modifier keeps the map scale constant if the object size changes with the Scale transform.

   a. True

   b. False

3. The **UVW Map** modifier enables you to.... (Select all that apply.)

   a. Explicitly apply a map to an object by selecting a shape and location.

   b. Use a gizmo for transforming in Sub-object mode.

   c. Perfectly project on geometry with non-standard projection shapes.

   d. All of the above.

4. Which of the following is the correct method for controlling map scaling of individual objects using a UVW Map? These options are accessed in the Parameter Editor of the map in the Slate Material Editor.

   a. Select **Use Real-World Scale** and assign the appropriate size (*Width* and *Height*) values.

   b. Select **Use Real-World Scale** and assign both the *Width* and *Height Size* values to the U-scale value.

   c. Clear **Use Real-World Scale** and set the *Tiling U* and *V* values to **1.0**.

   d. Clear **Use Real-World Scale** and set the *U-Tiling* value to **1.0** and the *V-Tiling* value equal to the ratio of the U-scale divided by the V scale.

5. Which mapping modifier is used to generate a map to follow the curvature of the spline along which the object was extruded (Spline mapping)?

    a. UVW Map

    b. Unwrap UVW

    c. MapScaler (WSM)

    d. MapScaler (OSM)

Chapter 8

Introduction to Lighting

Once materials have been added to an Autodesk® 3ds Max® project, lighting can be used to further enhance and create a realistic representation of the model. Projects automatically include default illumination that can be further enhanced or modified to create local or global illumination. Illumination can be accomplished using either photometric or standard lights.

Learning Objectives in this Chapter

- Work with various lighting strategies such as default lighting, local illumination, and global illumination.
- Work with standard lights and control the various parameter settings.
- Control the specific settings of various types of standard lights.
- Work with different types of shadow casting methods available in the software.
- Control the common parameters and set the specific parameters for each type of shadow casting method.

8.1 Local vs. Global Illumination

The Autodesk 3ds Max software provides several different kinds of scene lighting and enables you to add lighting objects that simulate real lights.Commonly used lighting methods provide either local or global illumination.

Default Illumination

By default, the Autodesk 3ds Max software automatically adds light to unlit scenes with invisible, unselectable light objects referred to as default lighting.

- A key light is located in the front and left of a scene and a fill light behind and to the right. These lights act as omni lights that illuminate in all directions. When user-defined light objects are added to a scene, the default lighting is automatically disabled for rendering.

Local Illumination

With a traditional local illumination approach, light sources only affect those objects that they can directly illuminate. They do not account for the diffuse light that bounces off of one surface to illuminate another nor do the effects of this reflected light become mixed together.

- Using a local illumination strategy, also referred to as Standard Lighting, requires arbitrary fill or ambient lights to simulate indirect lighting.

- Using Ray traced materials in a scene lit by standard lighting permits for the calculation of specular reflections between surfaces, which create mirrored effects and highlights on shiny surfaces.

- When a scene is illuminated with standard lighting (local illumination), without ambient or indirect light, the ceiling and shadows are dark as there are no lights pointed directly at those areas, as shown in Figure 8–1. When the ambient lights are added with standard lighting, the ceiling and shadows become softer, as shown in Figure 8–2.

Figure 8–1

Figure 8–2

Global Illumination

Global Illumination (GI) algorithms describe how light interacts with multiple surfaces. The illumination and rendering methods that take into account GI include mental ray, radiosity, and raytracing.

- Ray tracing is not used as a stand-alone rendering method but rather to compliment the other rendering methods.

- Radiosity and mental ray are two different lighting/rendering strategies that calculate diffuse inter-reflections of light, automatically generating ambient illumination and light mixing, producing realistic results, especially when daylight is involved.

- Radiosity and mental ray are designed to work with physically based (photometric) lights that have parameters derived from real-world lighting properties.

Figure 8–3 was created with global illumination, showing an interior scene with night time lighting. Figure 8–4 was created with global illumination, showing an interior scene with daytime lighting.

Figure 8–3

Figure 8–4

Figure 8–5 shows an example of an indoor scene that uses mental ray lit by physical lighting.

Figure 8–5

Hint: Lighting Analysis

Global Illumination calculations can be rendered as a lighting analysis to reveal illumination levels. Lighting Analysis Assistant generates light meter objects and image overlays based on mental ray physical lighting and materials. This information can be used for green building LEED certification credit 8.1.

Hint: Global Illumination vs Standard Lighting

Although longer to generate, Global Illumination (GI) approaches results are often more realistic. Standard lighting is less time consuming than the GI approaches (although there are exceptions), especially when working with simple scenes that contain a small number of objects or surfaces.

GI approaches are very popular in architecture, interior design, and related fields. However, standard lighting still has a place in these industries for conceptual tasks, projects with short timeframes, or projects that do not require extreme photorealism.

Types of Lights

Two types of lights are provided with the software:

- Standard lights

- Photometric lights

Although both create light objects, there are many different parameters available when you create either type of light. The lights can be created using the Command Panel. In the Create panel (➕), click 💡 (Lights), and select the type of light in the drop-down list, as shown in Figure 8–6. Alternatively, you can select **Create>Lights** and then select the type you want to create.

Figure 8–6

8.2 Standard Lighting

Standard lights (as shown in Figure 8–7) are objects based on computer calculations, which imitate lights used in everyday life. The following specifics apply to working with a standard lighting strategy.

Figure 8–7

- Standard lighting strategies use standard light objects, such as **Spot**, **Directional**, **Omni**, and **Skylights**. They are highly configurable, but are not based on real-world lighting parameters and require arbitrary adjustments to achieve the required effect.

- Objects illuminated with standard lighting can use any material type.

- Scenes lit by standard lighting almost always require additional ambient (fill) lights, either through a global ambient value or ambient light objects.

Exposure control is a method of balancing illumination levels in rendered output. It is essential to working with global illumination, using mental ray or radiosity.

- Lighting results are calculated at render time and are not stored on the objects. Processing standard lights does not increase file size and mesh subdivision is not required (as with radiosity).

- Standard lighting does not require exposure control. In standard lighting, ensure exposure control is not toggled on as it might result in differences between the viewport display and the rendering result

Photometric lights are the preferred lighting technique when working with mental ray.

- Although it also works with mental ray, Standard lighting is designed for use with the Scanline Renderer. The mental ray results are not physically accurate.

- All of the standard lights except for directional lights, are considered Point lights, which cast light from a single point rather than along a line or from an area.

Common Parameters

All standard lights share common General Parameters and Intensity/Color/Attenuation settings. These parameters can be set while creating each type of standard light, as shown in Figure 8–8. Once the lights have been created, you can access these parameters in the Modify panel ( ) in the Command Panel.

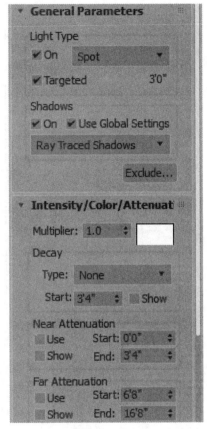

Figure 8–8

General Parameters

The General Parameters rollout enables you to toggle the light on and off in the scene, change the light type (**Spot**, **Directional**, or **Omni**), select to work with a target, and select shadow settings.

Lights cast illumination even if they are on a hidden layer.

> **Hint: Target Lights**
>
> Several types of lights (and some cameras as well) can have a target object. A light always points directly at its target, enabling you to change the direction of the light by moving the target. Target lights are lights with targets and Free lights are lights without targets.

Intensity/Color/Attenuation Parameters

The Intensity/Color/Attenuation rollout provides you with following options:

Multiplier	Controls brightness for standard lights. This is an arbitrary value that needs to be evaluated by trial. Start with a **1.0** value and adjust, as required. Avoid using high Multiplier values, which creates overly bright lighting. The color swatch enables you to select a color to filter the light with.
***Decay* area**	Offers techniques for simulating how light fades over distance.
***Far Attenuation* area**	Provides a similar kind of fading based on explicitly set distances. The *Start* value is where fading begins and the *End* value is the point at which the light fades to zero illumination. Typically you would use either the options in the *Decay* or *Far Attenuation* areas, not both.
Near Attenuation area	Enables you to define a distance from the light where the light starts casting faint illumination and then end with full illumination. Near attenuation does not occur in the real world and is included here as a computer graphics lighting effect
Show (Attenuation option)	Enables a graphical representation of the attenuation distances to remain visible after the object is cleared.

8.3 Types of Standard Lights

The type of standard light objects that can be created are **Spot**, **Directional**, **Omni**, and **Skylights**. They can be selected in the Object Type rollout, as shown in Figure 8–9.

Figure 8–9

Omni Lights

Omni lights (shown in Figure 8–10) are used to represent point lights that cast light equally in all directions, such as an idealized light bulb. Omni lights are also commonly used for ambient fill lights. A single omni light requires six times the computational effort of a single spotlight, so use spotlights in place of omni lights whenever possible.

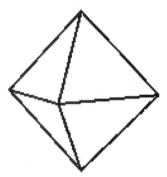

Figure 8–10

Spotlights

Spotlights are used to represent point light sources that cast focused beams of light in a cone with a circular or square base. Figure 8–11 shows an example of a spotlight with a circular base in 2D, and Figure 8–12 shows an example in 3D. Most real world lighting fixtures are more appropriately represented by spotlights rather than omnis or directional lights.

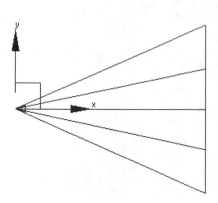

Figure 8–11

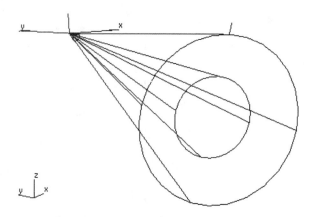

Figure 8–12

Two types of spotlight objects are available:

- **Target Spot:** Light objects cast focused beams of light pointing directly at a target.

- **Free Spot:** Light object casts focused beams of light pointing anywhere without a target object.

In addition to the Common Standard Parameters, spotlights have specific parameters (as shown in Figure 8–13) to control the distribution of the light they cast.

Figure 8–13

- The *Hotspot/Beam* value is the angle over which the full lighting intensity is projected. It is represented as the inner cone, as shown in Figure 8–12.

- The *Falloff/Field* value is the outer angle that illumination projects. It is represented as the outer cone, as shown in Figure 8–12.

- The light fades from full intensity to zero intensity between these two angles. Therefore, when these angles have similar values, the light creates a sharp, defined pool of light. Widely separated angles create a soft, gradual fade.

- The **Overshoot** option enables a spotlight to cast light in all directions (as an omni). However, spotlights only cast shadows within their falloff angle. Overshoot generally looks unnatural and should be used with care.

- The **Aspect** option enables you to define the width and height ratio through a numeric value.

- **Bitmap Fit** enables you to match the rectangular proportions of the lighting area to those of an image bitmap file directly.

Directional Lights

Directional lights are used to represent light sources that cast parallel rays, as shown in Figure 8–14. The best example of parallel light would be the light cast from the sun to an Architectural-scale project or smaller. (The sun could be considered an omni light when dealing with massive visualizations at the continental or global scale.)

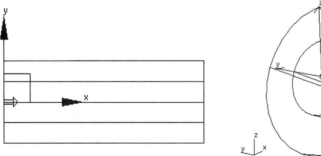
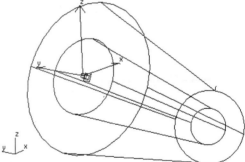

Figure 8–14

Two types of directional light objects are available:

- **Target Direct**

- **Free Direct**

In addition to the Common Standard Parameters, directional lights have specific options available through the Directional Parameters rollout, as shown in Figure 8–15. The Directional Parameters options are nearly identical to those in the Spotlight Parameters rollout options. The only difference is the *Hotspot/Beam* and *Falloff/Field* values. These are measured in terms of a width parameter rather than an angle.

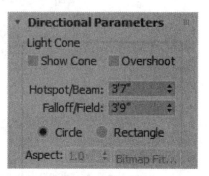

Figure 8–15

Fill Lights

Any light can be used to approximate indirect lighting, which is referred to as a fill light. Fill lights can act as normal lights or they can be specifically set to cast ambient light, by selecting the **Ambient Only** option in the Advanced Effects rollout in the **Standard lights** parameters, as shown in Figure 8–16.

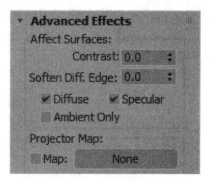

Figure 8–16

- Standard materials have an **Ambient color** parameter that can be used when illuminated using ambient lights. This color can be different from the diffuse color produced by normal (non-ambient) lights. The Ambient color is normally locked to the diffuse or it can be set darker than the diffuse color for emphasis.

- Setting a fill light to cast ambient light automatically disables shadow casting because only real-world light sources (the sun and lighting fixtures) are normally permitted to cast shadows.

- If you want your fill lights to cast normal light (which illuminates a material's diffuse color instead of ambient), do not select the **Ambient Only** option, but rather manually disable shadow casting.

- Architectural materials were designed for radiosity and do not have an **Ambient color** parameter. Otherwise, they function similarly to Standard materials with standard lighting.

- Arch & Design materials were designed for mental ray and also lack an ambient color channel. In mental ray, the concept of ambient lighting is replaced with bounced lighting. It is controlled by the number of diffuse bounces in the Final Gather rollout, as well as reflectivity/transparency, and other material choices.

Skylight and mr Sky

The Standard light category also includes a Skylight object. There is also a mental ray skylight (mr Sky) used with an mental ray sun (mr Sun) to create a sky when rendering with the mental ray renderer. The mr Sky is found in the Photometric category. Both the Skylight and the mr Sky serve as a type of ambient lighting adding global illumination to the scene.

mental ray (mr) Area Omni Light and mental ray (mr) Area Spotlight

Also included in the standard light category are these two area light objects (as opposed to point light objects). They are intended specifically for use with mental ray.

- You can combine the use of mental ray materials and mental ray lighting. This enables for energy-conserving lighting, which is calculated based on the 1st Law of Thermodynamics. mental ray can also use standard lights for rendering.

Practice 8a

Standard Lighting for an Interior Scene

Practice Objectives

- Create standard lights and adjust their parameters.
- Create ambient fill lighting to brighten the dark areas.

In this practice you will model interior lighting conditions by creating a spot light and array it to position it at various locations around the room. You will adjust the parameters to make the scene realistic and add ambient lighting to brighten areas that are not directly illuminated by your standard light objects.

Estimated time for completion: 30 minutes

You must set the paths to locate the External files and Xrefs used in the practice. If you have not done this already, return to **Chapter 1: Introduction to Autodesk 3ds Max** and complete Task 1 to Task 3 in **Practice 1a: Organizing Folders and Working with the Interface**. You only have to set the user paths once.

Task 1 - Create, Array, and Instance Light Objects.

*If a dialog box opens prompting you about a File Load: Mismatch, click **OK** to accept the default values.*

1. Open **Standard Lighting – Interior.max**.

2. You will add lights in the **Top** viewport such that they point toward the floor. Maximize the **Top** viewport, by selecting it from the overlay (Hold <Win> and press <Shift>).

Hold <Win> and press <Shift> repeatedly to cycle through all of the viewports. Release <Win> when the viewport that you want maximized is highlighted.

3. Click ![icon] (Zoom Extents) to refit the model in the **Top** viewport and then zoom into the foyer area (Leftmost area).

4. In the Create panel (![icon]), click ![icon] (Lights). In the drop-down list, select **Standard** and in the Object Type rollout, click **Free Spot**, as shown in Figure 8–17.

Figure 8–17

The small circles represent the opening for recessed lighting.

5. Click near the approximate center of the upper left circle. A free spotlight is added at that location, as shown in Figure 8–18.

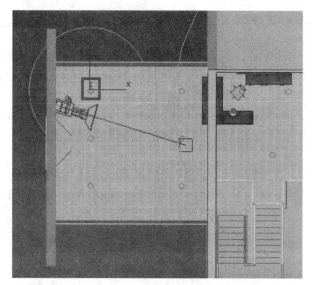

Figure 8–18

6. With the light object still selected, click ⊕ (Select and Move).

7. In the Status Bar, verify that ▦ (Absolute Mode Transform Type-In) is displayed and set the following, as shown in Figure 8–19:

   - X: **84'7"**
   - Y: **126'10"**
   - Z: **9'11"**
   - Press <Enter>

Figure 8–19

In addition to placing the light at the exact center of the recessed fixture, it places the light at a height of 9'11", which is 1" below the ceiling height.

8. In the Command Panel, select the Modify panel ( ) and name the light **Ceiling Downlight 00**.

- To locate your light objects to the center of the circles representing the recessed fixtures, enter the exact coordinates, which were determined using the **Measure** tool in the Autodesk 3ds Max Utilities. The six lights in the foyer area are 12' apart along the world X-direction and 6' apart along the world Y-direction.

*If the Extras toolbar is hidden, in the Main Toolbar area, right-click in empty space, and select **Extras** in the list of toolbars.*

9. With the light selected, in the Extras toolbar, click

 (Array), as shown in Figure 8–20, or in the menu bar select **Tools>Array**.

Figure 8–20

10. In the Array dialog box, click **Preview** to enable the previewed display in the scene.

- For the first dimension of the array, in the *Array Transformation* area, enter *X Incremental* value of **12'0"**.

- In the *Array Dimensions* area, set *1D Count* to **2** to create two columns of lights.

- Select **2D**, set *2D Count* to **3**, and *Incremental Row Y* to **-6'0"** to create three rows of lights.

- In *Type of Object* area, verify that **Instance** is selected so that the parameters of all of the lights can be adjusted at the same time.

- Note that *Total in Array* is automatically set to **6** (two lights in each of the three rows), as shown in Figure 8–21.

Note that the six lights are displayed in the viewport because **Preview** is selected.

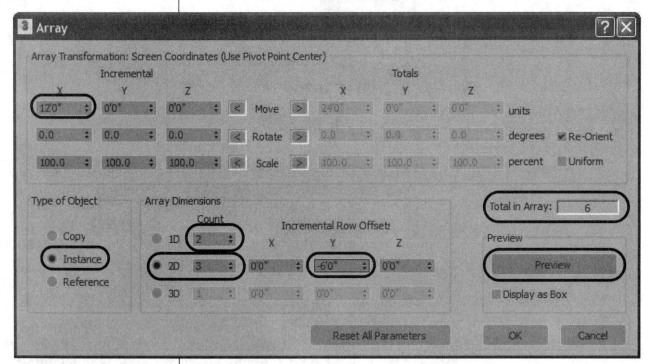

Figure 8–21

11. If the lights preview is in the correct positions (as shown in Figure 8–22) click **OK** in the dialog box.

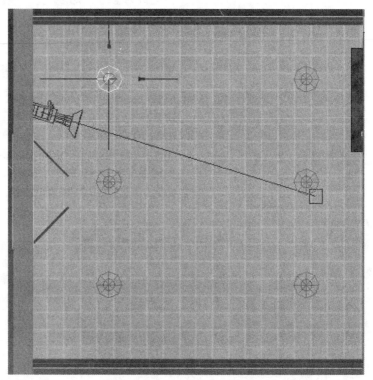

Figure 8–22

When arraying the objects, the software automatically increments the name by 1.

12. Select the light in the upper right corner in foyer (**Ceiling Downlight 001**). Using 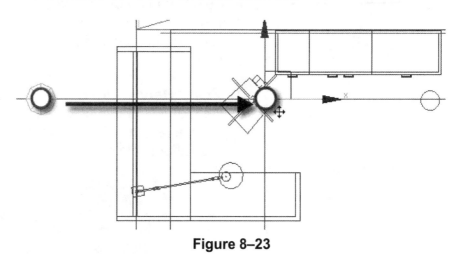 (Select and Move), and holding <Shift>, drag along the Transform gizmo's X-axis to locate the light over the desk area, almost on top of the chair, as shown in Figure 8–23. In the Clone Options dialog box, verify that **Instance** is selected and click **OK**.

Figure 8–23

13. With the light still selected, in the Status Bar, set the *X* value to **104'7"** and ensure that the *Y* value is set to **126'10"** and and the *Z* value is set to **9'11"**, as shown in Figure 8–24:

Figure 8–24

14. Continue to <Shift> + click and drag to instance the remainder of the Ceiling Downlights, to the circles provided for the locations of the recessed lighting, as shown in Figure 8–25. In the interest of time, approximate their positions. You should have 14 lights with the last one named as **Ceiling Downlight 013**.

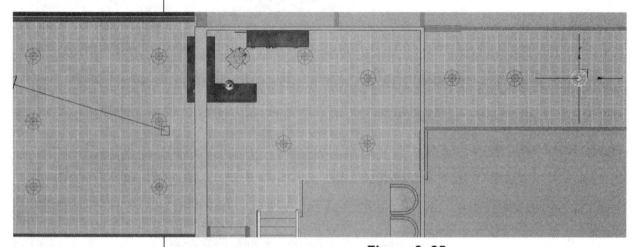

Figure 8–25

Task 2 - Adjust Standard Light Parameters.

In Task 1, you made instances of each of the lights so that their parameters can be adjusted together. You will now adjust lighting levels through light object parameters, avoiding exposure control.

1. Select **Rendering>Exposure Control**. In the Environment and Effects dialog box, in the Exposure Control rollout, clear **Active**, as shown in Figure 8–26. Close the Environments and Effects dialog box.

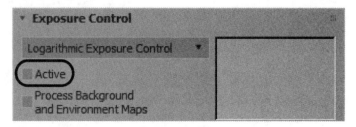

Figure 8–26

2. Select any of the instanced lights. In the Command Panel, verify that the Modify panel () is open and that **Ceiling Downlight** (any number) name is displayed (i.e., selected). In the Spotlight Parameters rollout, set *Hotspot/Beam* to **45**, press <Enter> and verify that **Circle** is selected. Set the *Falloff/Field* to **47.0**, as shown in Figure 8–27.

Figure 8–27

3. Change to the **Camera – Lobby1** view by selecting the **Top** POV label and selecting **Cameras>Camera - Lobby1**. In the Main Toolbar, click  (Render Production). Due to their current hotspot and falloff values, the light objects are only illuminating small pools of light on the floor, as shown in Figure 8–28.

The brightness of your rendering might vary as it is dependent on your computer settings.

Figure 8–28

- The **Layer:VIZ-1-Ceiling Lights** object is formed from extruded circles representing the openings for your recessed lighting. They have been assigned a self-illuminated material to make the openings display brightly lit. The light objects you have just added to the scene do not render.

*If you need to change some of the parameters and render again, you can leave the Rendered Frame Window open because it is a modeless dialog box. After changing a parameter, click **Render** in the Rendered Frame Window to render the viewport again.*

4. In the viewport, select one of the instanced lights, if not already selected. In the Spotlight Parameters rollout, set the *Falloff/Field* value to **170** degrees and press <Enter>.

5. Click 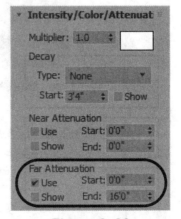 (Render Production) if you closed the Rendered Frame Window or click **Render** if the Rendered Frame Window is open. The illumination now spreads out, but the floor is being lit too brightly and has lost all of its contrast (sometimes referred to as being washed out), as shown in Figure 8–29. Leave the Rendered Frame Window open.

Figure 8–29

6. In the Intensity/Color/Attenuation rollout, in *Far Attenuation* area, select **Use**. Set the following, as shown in Figure 8–30:

- *Start*: **0'0"**
- *End*: **16'0"**

Figure 8–30

7. Click **Render**. The washed out effect is removed but the overall render looks dark, as shown in Figure 8–31.

Figure 8–31

*As with most **Standard Lighting** parameters, attenuation settings are arbitrary and require trial and error to achieve the best result.*

8. Adjust the overall brightness of the lights using the Multiplier. In the Intensity/Color/Attenuation rollout, set *Multiplier* to **2.0**. Click **Render** in the Rendered Frame Window. The surfaces under direct illumination should now become brighter.

Task 3 - Add Ambient Fill Light.

Next use ambient fill lighting to approximate the indirect illumination that would be present in the real world. With a standard lighting approach, fill light is required to brighten areas that are not directly illuminated by your light objects.

1. Add the ambient light globally. Select **Rendering> Environment** to open the Environment and Effects dialog box.

2. In the *Environment* tab, in the Common Parameters rollout, in the *Global Lighting* area, select the **Ambient** color swatch, as shown in Figure 8–32.

Figure 8–32

3. In the Color Selector dialog box, change the *Value* to **25**, and press <Enter>, as shown in Figure 8–33. Leave both the Environment and Effects dialog box and Color Selector dialog box open.

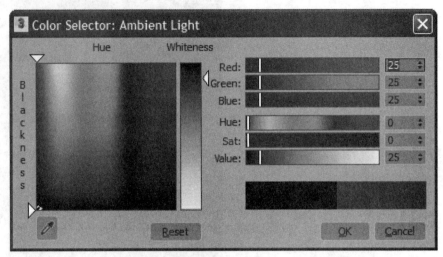

Figure 8–33

4. In the Rendered Frame Window, click **Render** to render the scene. In this rendering many areas have become lighter but the ceiling is still too dark. In the Color Selector dialog box, change the *Value* to **50** and render again. The ceiling is brighter but objects under direct illumination have lost some contrast, as shown in Figure 8–34. The front of the half-wall behind the stairs looks flat because the ambient lighting is so uniform. (This is a pitfall of adding too much global ambient light.)

Figure 8–34

5. This scene might respond better with manually configured ambient light rather than the global settings. In the Color Selector dialog box, set the ambient color *Value* to **0** and press <Enter>. Close all dialog boxes.

6. In the viewport, change to the **Top** viewport by pressing <T> and zoom out to see the floorplan. If (Lights) is not already active, in the Create panel ( ), click (Lights). Verify that **Standard** is displayed, and then click **Omni** to create an omni light.

7. Click once in the center of the six lights in the foyer to add an omni light. In the Name and Color rollout, enter **Lobby Fill Light 00** as the name of the light.

8. Click (Select and Move) and in the Status Bar, change its absolute Z-elevation to **2'0"**.

9. Hold <Shift>, and drag and click to create two instances of the omni light, as shown in Figure 8–35.

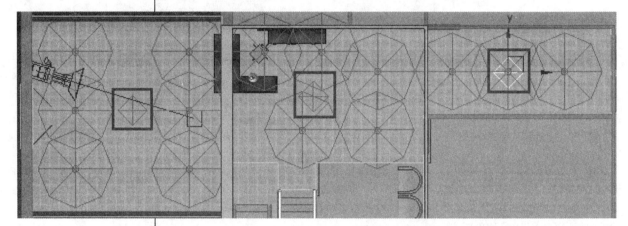

Figure 8–35

10. With one of the omni lights selected, in the Modify panel ( ), in the Advanced Effects rollout, select **Ambient Only**, as shown in Figure 8–36. This setting causes the light to illuminate the ambient color of Standard materials and not to cast shadows.

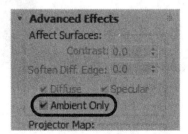

Figure 8–36

11. Change to **Camera – Lobby1** viewport and render the scene. Note that everything is washed out. Ambient lights can wash out a scene with their default settings. Leave the Rendered Frame Window open.

12. With the omni light still selected, in the Intensity/Color/ Attenuation rollout, set *Multiplier* as **0.75** and in the *Far Attenuation* area, select **Use**. Additionally, set the following, as shown in Figure 8–37:

    • *Start*: **0'0"**

    • *End*: **16'0"**

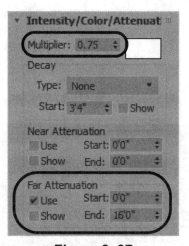

Figure 8–37

Your rendering might not be exactly the same because of your monitor display. You can adjust your Gamma and LUT correction (Preference Settings dialog box> Gamma and LUT tab) to get a similar rendering.

13. Render the scene. The ambient lighting does not look flat, but the floor and desk lamp are illuminated too brightly, as shown in Figure 8–38.

Figure 8–38

14. To resolve the brightness issue, you can exclude these objects from the ambient light. With one of the omni lights (Lobby Fill Light) still selected, in the Modify panel (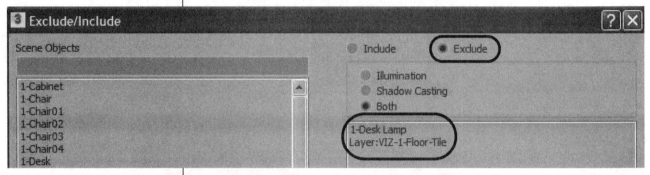), in the General Parameters rollout, click **Exclude**. The Exclude/Include dialog box opens.

15. Verify that **Exclude** is selected. In the list on the left, select **1-Desk Lamp** and **Layer:VIZ-1-Floor-Tile**. Click **>>** to add them to the Exclude list on the right, as shown in Figure 8–39.

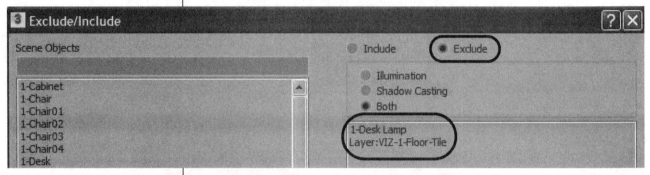

Figure 8–39

16. Click **OK** to close the dialog box.

17. Render the scene. The brightness of the lamp and the floor is removed, as shown in Figure 8–40. Close the Rendered Frame Window.

Figure 8–40

18. Save your work as **MyStandard Lighting – Interior.max**.

8.4 Shadow Types

Autodesk 3ds Max lights are able to cast realistic shadows from opaque objects. There are several shadow-casting methods available, such as Shadow Mapped, Ray Traced, Area, etc. While creating light objects, you can set the type and aspect of shadow by selecting it in the drop-down list (as shown in Figure 8–41), in the *Shadows* area of General Parameters rollout. Alternatively, after creating the light objects, you can

control or change them using the Modify panel () parameters of light objects. Individual lights might cast different kinds of shadows in the same scene and shadow casting can be disabled for specific lights.

Figure 8–41

Figure 8–42 shows the shadow-casting methods available.

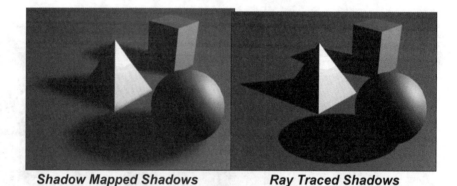

Figure 8–42

Shadow Type	Description, Advantages	Disadvantages
Shadow Map	Traditional approach, shadow mapping is relatively fast and creates soft-edged shadows. **Animation:** Shadows only need to be calculated once when scene geometry is not animated. Most efficient shadow type for omni lights.	Not as accurate as other methods; might not be appropriate for shadow studies. Uses a lot of RAM. Does not support materials with transparency or opacity maps.
Ray Traced Shadows	More accurate than shadow maps, supports transparency and opacity mapping. **Animation:** Shadows only need to be calculated once when scene geometry is not animated. In these cases, RT might be best for animations (including animated shadow studies) in terms of rendering time.	Slower than shadow maps, and shadows have sharp edges. Avoid omni lights with Ray Traced shadows whenever possible, as they require 6x the processing time of spot and directional lights.
Advanced Ray Traced	A good, general-purpose shadow type that is an improvement on RT shadows. It is more accurate than Shadow Maps, supports transparency and opacity mapping. Uses less RAM than standard raytraced shadows, therefore is generally faster for producing still renderings. Offers several parameters that can help soften and smooth shadows.	Slower than shadow maps. **Animation:** Shadows must be calculated at every frame, regardless of whether scene geometry is animated or not. Avoid omni lights with Advanced Ray Traced shadows whenever possible, as they require 6x the processing time of spot and directional lights.
Area Shadows	Enables a simulation of shadows cast from an area light (the other methods assume point light sources). Supports transparency and opacity mapping, uses relatively little RAM.	Generally slower than shadow maps, Ray Traced and Advanced Ray Traced. **Animation:** Shadows must be calculated at every frame, regardless of whether scene geometry is animated or not.

mental ray Shadow Maps	A shadow type optimized for the mental ray renderer. This is not covered in this training course.	Not as accurate as Ray Traced or Advanced Ray Traced shadows.

Common Shadow Parameters

The most commonly used shadow parameters in the Autodesk 3ds Max software are:

General Shadow Parameters

All lights have certain general parameters (*Shadows* area in *General Parameters* area) common to all shadow types, as shown in Figure 8–43.

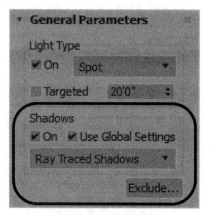

Figure 8–43

On	Enables you to select whether to cast shadows from this light or not and the type of shadows to use.
Use Global Settings	Controls whether the scene's global shadow generator or the light's own individual shadow generator is used.
Drop-down list	Contains all the types of shadows available in the software. Selecting the type provides a shadow specific rollout that can be used to control the advanced settings in the selected shadow type.

Shadow Parameters Rollout

The Shadow Parameters rollout (shown in Figure 8–44) contains settings that are common to all types of shadows.

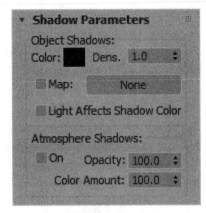

Figure 8–44

Color	Use this swatch to set a shadow to display as a color other than black.
Density	Controls the overall darkness of the created shadows. A density below 1.0 makes shadows lighter, greater than 1.0 makes them darker.
Map	Use this option to have an image map project inside your shadow.
Light Affects Shadow Color	Enables colored light to blend with the assigned shadow color when generating shadows.
Atmosphere Shadows	Enables atmospheric effects to cast shadows.

Shadow Map Parameters

In the General Parameters rollout, in the *Shadows* area, selecting **Shadow Map** in the drop-down list provides a Shadow Map Params rollout, as shown in Figure 8–45. Lights set to cast shadow mapped-shadows have additional controls that are specific to the Shadow Map type of shadow.

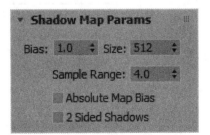

Figure 8–45

Bias	A relative adjustment that can move the shadow closer to or further away from the objects casting them. This value sometimes needs to be adjusted with large scenes.
Size	The height and width (in pixels) of the image map used to create the shadows. Shadow detail and computation time increase as the size increases.
Sample Range	Controls the amount of blending and smoothing. If shadow mapped-shadows appear grainy, increase this value.
Absolute Map Bias	Enables the Bias to be fixed to a value measured absolutely in scene units rather than a relative, normalized value. This option should normally not be used unless shadows flicker and disappear during an animation.
2 Sided Shadows	Enables both sides of a face to cast shadows. Double-sided mode is discussed in the rendering information.

Ray Traced Shadows

In the General Parameters rollout, in the *Shadows* area, selecting **Ray Traced Shadow** in the drop-down list provides a Ray Traced Shadow Params rollout, as shown in Figure 8–46. This rollout contains additional settings for lights set to cast (standard) ray traced shadows.

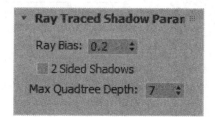

Figure 8–46

Ray Bias	Similar to shadow map bias, ray bias is a relative adjustment to move a shadow closer or further away from an object casting them. This value might need to be adjusted for large scenes.
2 Sided Shadows	Enables both sides of a face to cast shadows.
Max Quadtree Depth	Controls ray-tracing performance. Increasing the quadtree depth can speed up ray-tracing time but requires more RAM. You need to experiment to determine the most efficient quadtree settings for individual scenes (default = 7).

Advanced Ray-Traced Shadows

In the General Parameters rollout, in the *Shadows* area, selecting **Adv. Ray Traced** in the drop-down list provides an Adv. Ray Traced Params rollout, as shown in Figure 8–47 and the Optimizations rollouts, as shown in Figure 8–48. Both rollouts contains additional settings for lights set to cast advanced ray-traced shadows.

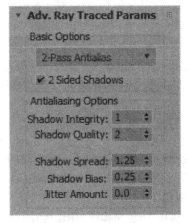

Figure 8–47

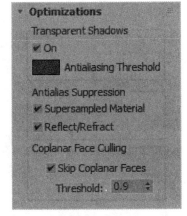

Figure 8–48

Adv. Ray Traced Params Options

Basic Options	The menu assigns either a mode without antialiasing (simple), a single or double-pass antialiasing mode. Antialiasing is an additional calculation made to smooth pixilated edges of shadows.
2 Sided Shadows	Enables both sides of a face to cast shadows.
Shadow Integrity and Quality	Controls the number of rays cast in the calculation. Increasing these values can enhance the final result at the expense of longer calculation time.
Shadow Spread	A parameter to blur or soften shadows, measured in pixels.
Shadow Bias	The minimum distance required to cast a shadow. This parameter should be increased as shadow spread is increased.
Jitter Amount	Blurred shadows sometimes cause artifacts to form. Increasing jitter can help break up the patterns of these artifacts and make them less noticeable.

Optimizations Options

Transparent Shadows	When enabled, transparent objects cast colored shadows based on their transparency and diffuse color.
Antialias Suppression	When using supersampling, reflections or refractions, this option disables the second pass in two-pass antialiased mode. This is a good idea to save time since the second pass often adds little in these situations. (Supersampling is discussed in the rendering and animation material.)
Skip Coplanar Faces	Prevents coplanar faces from shading each other (those that lie overlapped in the same plane).

mental ray Shadow Maps

In the General Parameters rollout, in the *Shadows* area, selecting **mental ray Shadow Map** in the drop-down list displays a mental ray Shadow Map rollout, as shown in Figure 8–49. The options should be used with mental ray lights. You only use these for interior shots that render with mental ray and require physical lighting effects, such as caustics or global illumination.

Figure 8–49

Map Size	Determines the resolution of the shadow bitmap. The size of the map is actually the square of this value. It should be in powers of 2 – 256, 512, 1024, 2048 etc.
Sample Range	Used to create soft-edged shadows when using mental ray lights. You must increase this value AND the Samples values greater than zero to get soft shadow effects.
Samples	Determines the number of samples that are removed from the map to make the shadows soft.
Use Bias	Moves the shadow closer or farther from the object.
Transparent Shadows	Provides controls for finer looking shadows. When enabled, you can add transparency and control shadow color. The *Merge Dist* and *Samp./Pixel* fields enable you to increase shadow quality (this result in additional memory consumption and slower renderings).

Practice 8b

Working with Shadow Parameters

Practice Objective

Estimated time for completion: 10 minutes

* Understand the different types of shadows casting methods.

In this practice you will adjust parameters to refine the shadows in a scene.

You must set the paths to locate the External files and Xrefs used in the practice. If you have not done this already, return to **Chapter 1: Introduction to Autodesk 3ds Max** and complete Task 1 to Task 3 in **Practice 1a: Organizing Folders and Working with the Interface**. You only have to set the user paths once.

*If a dialog box opens prompting you about a File Load: Mismatch, click **OK** to accept the default values.*

1. Open **Shadow Parameters.max**.

2. In the Scene Explorer, ((Display None) and (Display Lights)), select one of the Ceiling Downlight objects, such as **Ceiling Downlight 06**.

3. In the Command Panel, select the Modify panel ( ), and examine its parameters. These lights use the default Advanced Ray Traced shadow type (**Adv. Ray Traced** in General Parameters rollout), as shown in Figure 8–50.

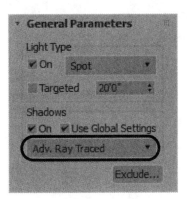

Figure 8–50

4. In the Main Toolbar, click  (Render Production) to render the scene. In the Rendered Frame Window, zoom and pan to the desk area, as shown in Figure 8–51. The edges of the shadow under the desk display jagged. Leave the Rendered Frame Window open.

Figure 8–51

5. In the Modify panel ( ), expand the Adv. Ray Traced Params rollout and in the *Basic Options* area, select **2-Pass Antialias** in the drop-down list. In the *Antialiasing Options* area, set the following, as shown in Figure 8–52:

- *Shadow Integrity*: **2**
- *Shadow Quality*: **3**

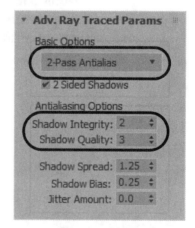

Figure 8–52

6. In the Rendered Frame Window, click **Render**. The shadow edges display more smoothly, but the rendering time has increased.

7. In the General Parameters rollout, in the *Shadows* area, change the type from *Adv. Ray Traced* to **Shadow Map** by selecting **Shadow Map** in the drop-down list.

When soft shadows are required or speed is critical, Shadow maps make a good alternative.

8. Render the scene. These shadows are fuzzier and less accurate (as shown in Figure 8–53) but significantly faster to render.

Figure 8–53

9. To make the shadow-mapped shadows better defined, increase the map size. In the Shadow Map Params rollout, double the *Size* from 512 to **1024**, as shown in Figure 8–54.

10. Render the scene. Zoom into the right side and note that the shadow maps are causing rendering artifacts along the curtain wall, as shown in Figure 8–55.

There might not be a huge difference in shadows under the desk.

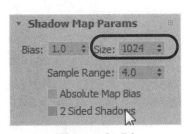

Figure 8–54   **Figure 8–55**

11. Adjust the Shadow map by setting the following:
    - *Size*: **2048**
    - *Bias*: **0.01**

12. Render the scene again. These settings reduce the problem, but can increase rendering time. Also note that the shadows have become slightly more significant under the desk .

13. Save your work as **MyShadow Parameters.max**.

Chapter Review Questions

1. The default lights (key light and fill light) provided by default in the Autodesk 3ds Max scene, act as:

   a. Omni lights

   b. Spotlights

   c. Directional lights

   d. mental ray area omni light

2. Which type of standard lights are used to represent light sources that cast parallel rays?

   a. Omni lights

   b. Spotlights

   c. Directional lights

   d. mental ray area omni light

3. In the Intensity/Color/Attenuation rollout (shown in Figure 8–56), which has common parameters for all of the standard lights, which option does not occur in the real world and is only included as a computer graphics lighting effect?

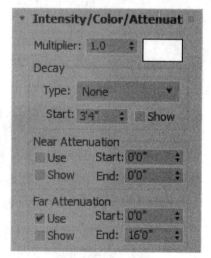

Figure 8–56

   a. Multiplier

   b. Decay options

   c. Near Attenuation options

   d. Far Attenuation options

4. In the Spotlight parameters rollout (shown in Figure 8–57), which option enables a spotlight to cast light in all directions and behave like an omni light? (Hint: Setting this option generally looks unnatural and it should be used with care.)

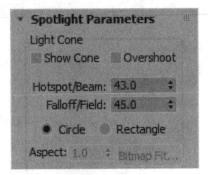

Figure 8–57

a. Show Cone

b. Overshoot

c. Hotspot/Beam

d. Falloff/Field

5. Which one of the following shadow types does not support materials with transparency and opacity maps?

a. Shadow Map

b. Ray Traced Shadows

c. Advanced Ray Traced

d. Area Shadows

6. In the Shadow Map type of shadows, a density value below 1.0 makes the shadow darker and a density value of greater than 1.0 makes the shadow lighter.

a. True

b. False

Command Summary

Button	Command	Location
	Array	• **Extras toolbar** • **Tools:** Array
	Lights	• **Command Panel:** *Create* panel • **Create:** Lights
	Render Production	• **Main Toolbar** • *Rendering:* Render

Lighting and Rendering

Photometric lights are generally used to accurately represent real-world lighting. Once added, their parameters can be further modified to create realism in a design. Additionally, the use of sunlight and skylight in a daytime scene and the use of exposure controls can add additional realism.

Learning Objectives in this Chapter

- Create photometric lights and modify them by changing their parameters.
- Work with different methods of Exposure Control and control the method specific parameters.
- Create Sunlight and Skylight and use their parameters to enhance the lighting in a scene.

9.1 Photometric Light Objects

Photometric light objects are based on quantitative measurements of light levels and distribution. They provide a real-world lighting and accurate scene illumination when used with mental ray and other global illumination solutions. In the Autodesk® 3ds Max® software, photometric lights are the default choice for creating lights.

- Photometric lights take advantage of physically-based color, intensity, and distribution properties. They can be defined with real-world lighting parameters in engineering units.

- Since photometric lights are based on real-world calculations of light energy, they are **scale-specific**. Scenes using photometric lights and mental ray/radiosity should have an appropriate system unit scale.

- All photometric lights automatically decay (attenuate) with an inverse-square relationship. Far attenuation can be controlled manually, to save calculation time and energy.

- Photometric lights work for both the scanline renderer and mental ray renderer.

- Exposure control should be used with Photometric lights objects to adjust the brightness of the scene, the Shadow/Midtones, and Highlight areas of the image. If the Exposure control is not on with the Photometric light type, the software prompts you to use the Logarithmic Exposure Control (for Default Scanline renderer) or the mr Photographic Exposure Control (for the mental ray renderer).

Photometric Light Types

*The **mr Sky Portal** is also included in the Object Type rollout but it is not a standard photometric light type.*

In the Command Panel's Create panel (⊞)> 💡 (Lights), **Photometric** is the default light type, as shown in Figure 9–1. The object types for photometric lights are:

- **Target Light**

- **Free Light**

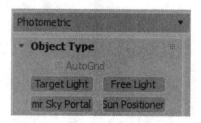

Figure 9–1

While creating a Target Light or a Free Light, you can set different parameters to illuminate the scene accurately and effectively. Once the lights have been created, you can modify the parameters using the Modify panel in the Command Panel.

Templates Rollout

Once you create either a Target or Free light there are Templates to select from, as shown in Figure 9–2. Selecting a template controls the intensity and color temperature of the light.

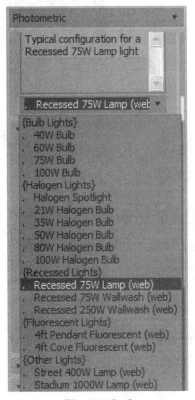

Figure 9–2

General Parameters Rollout

The General Parameters rollout controls some of the basic settings for toggling the light on/off in the scene and the different shadow casting methods (Ray Traced, Adv. Ray Traced, mental ray, Shadow Map, etc.). The options found in the *Light Properties* area and *Shadows* area are similar to the options found in Standard Lights, and can be used in the same manner.

Any Free Light can be changed into a Targeted Light (and vice-versa) by using the **Targeted** option in the *Light Properties* area. When the Targeted option is enabled, a tool tip displays as you move the target indicating the illumination, as shown in Figure 9–3.

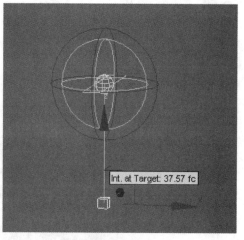

Figure 9–3

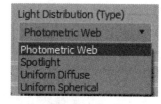

Figure 9–4

*In the General Parameters rollout, many options (Light Properties area options, Shadows area options, and **Spotlight** parameters) are identical or similar to the options used when creating Standard Lights.*

The *Light Distribution* area (shown in Figure 9–4) contains a list of the photometric light distribution types available in the software. These control the way the light illuminates the surrounding space. The options are described as follows:

Uniform Spherical	Casts light in all directions, like a standard Omni light.
Uniform Diffuse	Casts light in one hemisphere only and mimics the way light emits from a surface.
Spotlight	Provides hotspot and falloff parameters identical to standard spotlights.
Photometric Web	Casts light according to a 3D representation of light intensity as determined by a lighting file format, such as IES, LTLI, or CIBSE. These are files provided by lighting manufacturers, usually available via the Internet.

Distribution (Photometric Web) Rollout

If you select Photometric Web in the Light Distribution type list, the Distribution (Photometric Web) rollout displays, as shown in Figure 9–5. Real-world luminaries (lighting fixtures) nearly always cast light in varying amounts in different directions. The Web distribution method enables the Autodesk 3ds Max software to simulate the laboratory-determined light distribution of specific lighting fixtures.

- Photometric lights can make use of web distribution information from IES, LTLI, or CIBSE photometric web data files that can be obtained from lighting manufacturers for specific light fixture models. They are often available directly from manufacturers' web sites.

- Lights with Web distributions are indicated with photometric web icons (as shown in Figure 9–6) that graphically represent the 3D distribution of light cast from the light fixture.

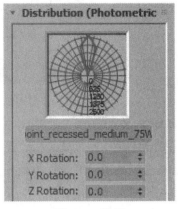

Figure 9–5

Figure 9–6

Web Distribution in Viewports

You can see the web distribution in the viewport. Select the **Shading Viewport** label (such as **High Quality**) and select **Lighting and Shadows>Illuminate with Scene Lights** (as shown in Figure 9–7) to see the lights in the viewport. You can add shadows by selecting **Shadows** and toggle on **Ambient Occlusion** in the viewport to add subtle detail enhancement. These options only take effect in viewport and have no effect on the actual renderings.

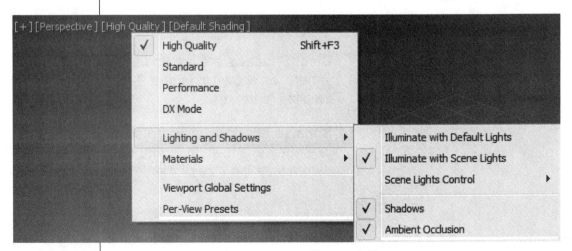

Figure 9–7

Shape/Area Shadows Rollout

The Shape/Area Shadow controls are used to generate a shadow casting shape and to calculate shadows based on a particular shape. The various shapes have different parametric controls and the shapes can be selected in the Shape/Area Shadows rollout, as shown in Figure 9–8.

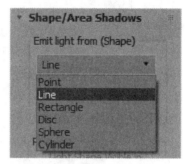

Figure 9–8

- **Point:** Shadows are created as if the light was one single point, as shown in Figure 9–9.

- **Line:** Shadows are created as if the light was one single line, as shown in Figure 9–10. The size of the line is controlled with the **Length** parameter.

Use this for fluorescent tubes or rectangular ceiling lights.

- **Rectangle:** Shadows are created as if the light was a rectangular area (as shown in Figure 9–11) governed by **Length** and **Width** parameters.

Figure 9–9

Figure 9–10

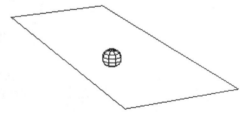

Figure 9–11

- **Disc:** Shadows are created as if the light was a flattened sphere, as shown in Figure 9–12. A radius control determines the size of the disc.

- **Sphere:** Shadows are created as if the light was a round ball or globe, as shown in Figure 9–13. Again a radius control determines the size of the sphere.

- **Cylinder:** Shadows are created as if the light emitter is cylindrical, as shown in Figure 9–14. **Radius** and **Length** are the two parameters to control the cylinder proportions.

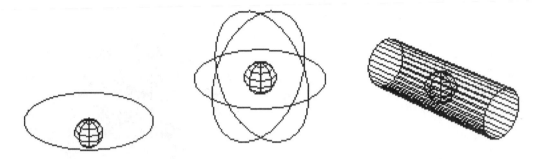

| **Figure 9–12** | **Figure 9–13** | **Figure 9–14** |

In the Shape/Area Shadows rollout, in the *Rendering* area, you can also select the **Light Shape Visible in Rendering** option. This permits the Cylinder, Disc, Sphere, and Rectangle light shapes (as shown on the top in Figure 9–15) to render as objects in the viewport (as shown on the bottom in Figure 9–15). The Point and Line objects do not work with this feature.

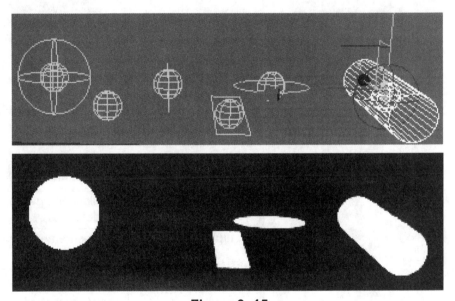

Figure 9–15

Intensity/Color/ Attenuation Rollout

Photometric light color can be assigned through a lamp specification (such as fluorescent, halogen, incandescent, etc.) or through a temperature specified in degrees Kelvin. This color can also be filtered (tinted) through a color swatch. All of these options can be selected in the *Color* area of the Intensity/Color/ Attenuation rollout, as shown in Figure 9–16.

Figure 9–16

The overall brightness of Photometric lights can be specified as one of three intensity values (*Intensity* area):

Luminous flux	The overall output strength of the lamp, measured in lumens (lm).
Luminous intensity	The light energy that is released over time, measured in candelas (cd).
Illuminance	A measurement of how much illumination reaches a surface a set distance away from a lamp with a certain facing. Illuminance is measured in foot-candles (fc, lumens/ft2) or lux (lumens/m2). When using this option, specify both the Luminous flux (lumens) and the distance at which that brightness occurs

---

Hint: Photometric Lights Data

The Autodesk 3ds Max software ships with a host of sample lighting templates that you can use out-of-the-box.

The Autodesk 3ds Max Help lists a number of sample fixtures in the **Common Lamp Values for Photometric Lights** section.

Lights that combine the geometry of a light fixture with the correct photometric light distribution model are referred to as luminaries. These are assemblies with a hierarchy created so that the photometric light is linked to the geometry. You can obtain luminaries from manufacturer websites (such as ERCO). You can also import lighting fixtures from the Autodesk® Revit® software using FBX import.

The *Far Attenuation* area controls the end location of the Photometric light and the area that is graduated as the end of the range is approached, as shown in Figure 9–17.

Figure 9–17

Practice 9a

Working with Photometric Lights

Practice Objectives

- Create photometric lights and modify their parameters.
- Use preset lamps and their provided data.

In this practice you will create and adjust photometric lights. You will use different lamp presets to apply realistic lighting to the lobby model.

You must set the paths to locate the External files and Xrefs used in the practice. If you have not done this already, return to **Chapter 1: Introduction to Autodesk 3ds Max** and complete Task 1 to Task 3 in **Practice 1a: Organizing Folders and Working with the Interface**. You only have to set the user paths once.

Estimated time for completion: 10 minutes

Task 1 - Create free photometric lights.

1. Open **Photometric Lighting start.max**.

*If a dialog box opens prompting you about a File Load: Mismatch, click **OK** to accept the default values.*

2. Using <Win> and <Shift>, display the **Top** viewport as the maximized viewport. Click ![Zoom Extents] (Zoom Extents) to display the floorplan. Change to Wireframe mode by pressing <F3>.

3. In the Create panel (![+]), click ![Lights] (Lights) and verify that **Photometric** is displayed in the drop-down list. In the Object Type rollout, select **Free Light**, as shown in Figure 9–18.

Figure 9–18

You can zoom into the area where the yellow circles are placed, which indicate the slots for lights.

4. Click approximately over the upper left light fixture circle to place a light, as shown in Figure 9–19.

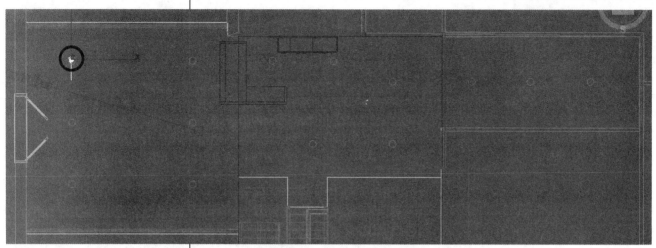

Figure 9–19

Alternatively, right-click

on 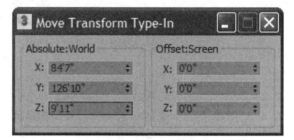 (Select and Move) in the Main Toolbar to open the Transform Type-In dialog box. You can also enter the values in the Status Bar.

5. In the viewport, right-click on the new light and in the quad menu, next to **Move**, select ☐ (Settings). In the Move Transform Type-In dialog box, in the *Absolute:World* area, set the following, as shown in Figure 9–20:
   - *X*: **84'7"**
   - *Y*: **126'10"**
   - *Z*: **9'11"** (elevation)

Figure 9–20

6. Close the dialog box. With the light object selected, in the Modify panel ( ), rename the light object as **Light – Downlight A 00**.

7. In the General Parameters rollout, set *Light Distribution (Type)* to **Spotlight**. Note that the shape of the light object changes in the viewport.

8. In the Intensity/Color/Attenuation rollout, set *Color* to **HID Quartz Metal Halide**, as shown in Figure 9–21.

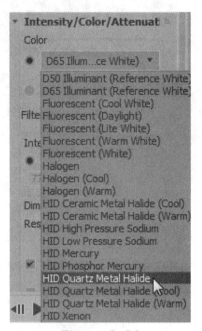

Figure 9–21

Hint: Accessing Photometric Lights Data

When using metal halide lamps, you can find suggestions for their photometric light parameters in the Help system. In the InfoCenter, click in and select **3ds Max Help**. Select the *Search* tab and enter **Common Lamp Values** in the search box. Select **Common Lamp Values for Photometric Lights**. Scroll down to **Par38 Line Voltage Lamps**. The **Medium Beam** has intensities between 1700-4000 candelas, as shown in Figure 9–22. The values for beam and field angles are also displayed.

Par38 Line Voltage Lamps					
Class.	Watts	Type	Intensity	Beam	Field
Narrow Beam	45	Spot	4700	14	28
Narrow Beam	75	Spot	5200	12	25
Narrow Beam	150	Spot	10500	14	28
Medium Beam	45	Spot	1700	28	60
Medium Beam	75	Spot	1860	30	60
Medium Beam	150	Spot	4000	30	60

Figure 9–22

9. With the new light still selected, click 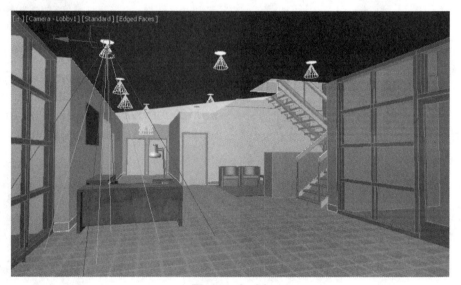 (Select and Move) and then use <Shift> + click and drag to instance the light (the **Instance** option in the Clone Options dialog box). The lights should correspond to the symbols for Ceiling Lights (circles provided for the locations of the recessed lighting). You can approximate their positions and have 14 lights with the last one named **Light - Downlight A 013**.

10. Select Point of View label (Top) and select Cameras> **Camera - Lobby1** to display the **Camera - Lobby1** viewport. Change the *Shading Viewport* to **Standard** and *Per-view Preference* viewport (Wireframe) to **Default Shading + Edged Faces** to display the 14 spotlights, as shown in Figure 9–23.

Figure 9–23

11. Select **Rendering>Exposure Control** to open the Environment and Effects dialog box. Note that this being a legacy file, **Logarithmic Exposure Control** is selected in the Exposure Control rollout.

12. In the Exposure Control rollout, select **Active**. Click **Render Preview** and note the render preview.

13. In the Logarithmic Exposure Control Parameters rollout, increase the *Brightness* to **88**, press <Enter>, and watch the render preview update. Close the dialog box.

14. Click (Render Production) to render the viewport. Note that the scene is quite dark. Leave the Rendered Window open.

Task 2 - Adjust the light parameters.

1. With one of the lights selected, in the Command Panel, in the Distribution (Spotlight) rollout, note that *Hotspot/Beam* and *Falloff/Field* have default values of **30°** and **60°** as stated in the Autodesk 3ds Max Help.

When changing the Light Distribution Type, the shape of the light object (in the viewport) changes accordingly.

2. If you have access to a photometric data file for a light fixture, you can use it for this light. In the General Parameters rollout set *Light Distribution (Type)* to **Photometric Web**, as shown in Figure 9–24.

Figure 9–24

3. In the Distribution (Photometric Web) Parameters rollout, click **< Choose Photometric File >** and in the practice files folder, in the ...*sceneassets\photometric* folder, open **sample_downlight.ies**. The thumbnail diagram of the selected web file is displayed, as shown in Figure 9–25.

The red shape displays the beam.

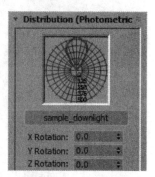

Figure 9–25

4. Note that in the Intensity/Color/Attenuation rollout, in the *Intensity* area, the intensity of the light has been updated to **3298.0 cd**.

5. In the General Parameters rollout, in the *Shadows* area, select **Shadow Map** in the drop-down list, as shown in Figure 9–26.

Figure 9–26

*The **Dimming** parameter should be cleared to control the intensity of light.*

6. Click **Render** in the Rendered Window. Note that the dark areas on the floor have been removed and the floor looks washed out.

7. In the Intensity/Color/Attenuation rollout, in the *Intensity* area, set the intensity to **1100** cd and render the scene again, as shown in Figure 9–27. Close the Render Window.

Figure 9–27

*Selecting **Illuminate with Scene Lights** automatically clears **Illuminate with Default Lights** and vice-versa.*

8. The photometric lights representation is displayed in the viewport and you can control their effects individually. Select the *Shading Viewport* label to display the label menu and select **Lighting and Shadows** and **Illuminate with Scene Lights**. In the menu, also expand Scene Lights Control and select **Auto Display Selected Lights**, as shown in Figure 9–28.

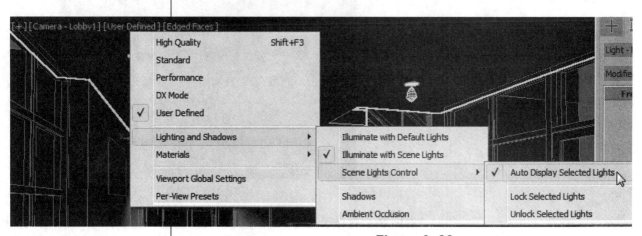

Figure 9–28

If the lights in the viewport are not easily selectable use the Scene Explorer to select the lights.

The display of shadows in the viewport is dependant on the driver you are using. The shadows are previewed in the viewport if you are using Nitrous or the Direct 3D drivers.

9. In the viewport, select one of the lights to enable it. You will see the effect of that light in the viewport. Select another light and see its effect in the viewport. Using <Ctrl>, select a few more lights to activate them together and visually see the effects.

10. In the *Shading Viewport* label menu, verify that **Lighting and Shadows>Shadows** is selected to display the shadows that are cast along with the lighting effect of the light selected.

11. With one of the lights selected, in the Command Panel, in the Templates rollout, select **75 W Bulb**. Note the changes, as shown in Figure 9–29.

Figure 9–29

12. Render the scene. Since the light distribution is spherical, the lighting now illuminates the ceiling and the upper walls, as shown in Figure 9–30.

Figure 9–30

13. In the Templates rollout, select **Recessed 75W Lamp (web)**. This uses a different IES file. Render again. The lighting is dark and moody.

14. Save your work as **MyPhotometricLighting.max**.

Hint: Using Light Lister

The Autodesk 3ds Max software includes a Light Lister utility (as shown in Figure 9–31) (**Tools>Light Lister**) that enables you to view and change light properties without having to select them first. You can change the settings for all lights together or for the selected lights.

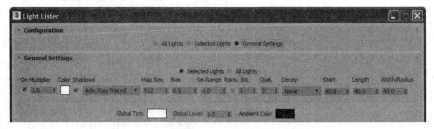

Figure 9–31

Hint: Using mental ray with Standard Lights

The mental ray renderer was designed to be used with photometric light objects. Standard lights can also be used with mental ray, but since they are not physically-based, it cannot achieve accurate results. For better accuracy, it is recommended not to mix standard and photometric lights in the same scene. The following should be considered:

- The luminous intensity of standard lights is equal to the light's multiplier parameter times the Physical Scale value in Logarithmic Exposure Control. (The default Physical Scale value is 1500 candelas in the Logarithmic Exposure Control Parameters rollout in the Environments and Effects dialog box.) You can make drastic changes to the Physical Scale value to compensate for scale problems in lighting a scene. Change this value to 80,000 or 150,000 to brighten a scene.

- To limit the effects of exposure control (i.e., not have the exposure control affect the direct lighting) use the **Affect Indirect Only** option.

- There is an Exposure Control type called **mr Photographic Exposure Control**. In the mr Photographic Exposure Control rollout, in the *Physical scale* area, you can change the scale by selecting **Unitless** and adding a Physical scale value.

Practice 9b

Estimated time for completion: 5 minutes

*If a dialog box opens prompting you about a File Load: Mismatch, click **OK** to accept the default values.*

Materials that Create Lighting

Practice Objective

- Create a self illuminating material.

In this practice you will learn how to toggle on a self-illuminating material and apply it to an object for illuminating the scene.

You must set the paths to locate the External files and Xrefs used in the practice. If you have not done this already, return to **Chapter 1: Introduction to Autodesk 3ds Max** and complete Task 1 to Task 3 in **Practice 1a: Organizing Folders and Working with the Interface**. You only have to set the user paths once.

1. Open **LightPoleSelfIllumination start.max**.

2. Verify that the **Camera01** viewport is active. In the Main Toolbar, click (Render Production) and note the rendered image shown in Figure 9–32. Close the Render Frame Window.

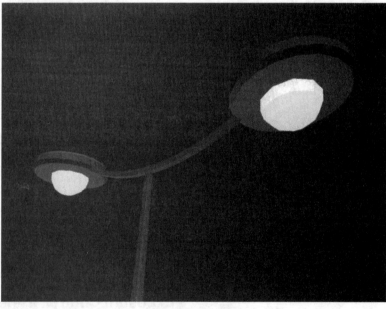

Figure 9–32

3. The globes have a standard material with 100% self-illumination. You will replace the standard material with an Arch & Design Material. In the Main Toolbar, click

   (Material Editor) to open the Slate Material Editor.

4. In the Material/Map Browser, expand the *Materials>mental ray* categories, double-click on Arch & Design to create a new material node in *View1* sheet.

5. Double-click on the title bar heading of the node to open its Parameter Editor. Rename the material **mr Illuminated Lens**, as shown in Figure 9–33.

Figure 9–33

Minimize the Slate Material Editor for use again.

6. Scroll down and in the Self Illumination (Glow) rollout, select **Self-Illumination (Glow)**, as shown in Figure 9–34.

7. In the viewport, select one of the globes and in the menu bar, select **Group>Ungroup** to ungroup the objects. Ungroup the second globe group.

8. In the **Camera01** viewport, select the two globes (inverted hemispheres). In the Slate Material Editor, click (Assign Material to Selection) to apply the material to the globes.

9. Render the **Camera01** viewport. Note that the rendering is identical to the rendering before applying the Arch & Design material.

10. In the Slate Material Editor, in the **mr Illuminated Lens** Parameter Editor, in the Self-Illumination (Glow) rollout, in the *Glow options* area, select **Illuminates the Scene (when using FG)**, as shown in Figure 9–35.

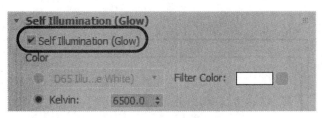

Figure 9–34

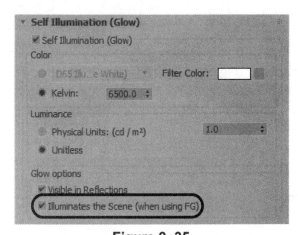

Figure 9–35

11. Render the **Camera01** viewport again. The illumination is still not visible.

12. In the Slate Material Editor, in the Self-Illumination (Glow) rollout, in the *Luminance* area, verify that **Unitless** is selected, and increase its multiplier to **10**, as shown in Figure 9–36.

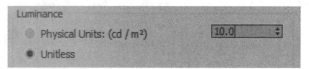

Figure 9–36

13. Render the **Camera01** viewport again The illumination is displayed around the globe as shown in Figure 9–37.

Figure 9–37

14. Save your work as **MymrIlluminatedMaterials.max**.

9.2 Exposure Control

Lighting, Materials, and Exposure Control are all used together to produce a real-world rendered image.

- **Exposure Control** parameters are a global adjustment used to modulate the output levels and color range of renderings and viewport display to expected values. Although the exposure control methods are optional when using scanline renderer, they are mandatory when working with mental ray.

- The Autodesk 3ds Max software has the ability to incorporate exposure control in the viewport but is dependant on the driver being used. To display exposure control in the viewport and modify it interactively use the Nitrous or Direct 3D display drivers.

- The Autodesk 3ds Max software calculates real-world illumination values through mental ray. Computer monitors (and printed media) are only able to show a tiny fraction of the total brightness range visible to your eyes.

- Exposure control enables you to adapt the often large dynamic range (the variation of lighting levels) calculated by mental ray into the relatively small dynamic range that can be displayed on a computer screen or printed on paper.

Exposure Control Methods

The various exposure control methods are available in the *Environment* tab in the Environment and Effects dialog box (**Rendering>Environment** or **Rendering>Exposure Control**). In the Exposure Control rollout, select an exposure control method in the drop-down list, as shown in Figure 9–38.

- Exposure Control is used when the **Active** option is enabled.

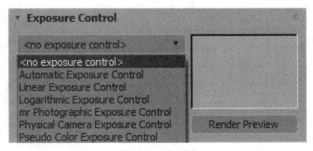

Figure 9–38

- **Automatic Exposure Control** attempts to automatically adjust the sample range of lighting levels. It is appropriate for still renderings with very large dynamic ranges. This method can cause flashing when animating, because different frames could be modulated differently.

- **Linear Exposure Control** interprets and adjusts the lighting levels linearly, which might provide better results when working with low dynamic ranges (small variations in lighting levels).

Only Logarithmic, mr Photographic, and Pseudo-Color exposure controls are supported by the mental ray renderer.

- **Logarithmic Exposure Control** interprets and adjusts the lighting levels with a logarithmic distribution, and provides additional controls that can be used effectively for animations.

- **mr Photographic Exposure Control** gives you the same type of control found in Logarithmic Exposure control, with values such as *Shutter Speed*, *Aperture* (fstops), and *Film speed*. In addition, there is a section that allows for *Shadow*, *Midtone*, and *Highlight* manipulation. Presets automatically adjust the settings, but if a rendering is overly bright or too dark, you can adjust the *Physical scale* setting to **Unitless**, and adjust its value.

- **Physical Camera Exposure Control** interprets and adjusts the exposure value and uses color-response curve to set exposure for physical cameras.

- **Pseudo Color Exposure Control** is used to generate a lighting analysis rendering colorized by luminance (light source brightness) or illuminance (the amount of illumination that arrives at a surface). The different colors in the render (shown in Figure 9–39) give a representation of lighting levels. The red areas depict overlit areas, blue are underlit, and the green areas are at a good lighting level.

Figure 9–39

Logarithmic Exposure Control Parameters

When **Logarithmic Exposure Control** is selected as the Exposure Control method, a corresponding rollout with parameters that are specific to this method is displayed, as shown in Figure 9–40.

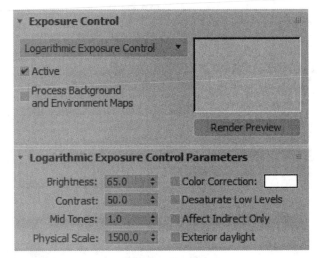

Figure 9–40

Brightness/ Contrast	Adjust the overall brightness and contrast of the rendered image. Brightness controls the perceived illumination of surfaces. Contrast can be used to adjust the difference between light and dark portions of the image. Images that appear washed out (with only a small difference in brightness levels) often benefit from increasing contrast.
Mid Tones	Enables you to shift the brightness levels of the middle portion of the color range. Increasing the midtones value brightens the middle tones of an image and lowering its value darkens them.
Physical Scale	Sets the real-world luminous intensity value of standard lights used with mental ray (multiplied by their multiplier parameter), measured in candelas. This value has no effect on scenes that have only Photometric or IES lights.
Color Correction	Enables you to adjust the color caste of an image so that the color in the swatch displays as white in the final rendering. This adjustment takes place automatically in human vision and is manually adjusted in some real-world cameras using balancing.
Desaturate Low Levels	Converts dark colors to shades of gray, simulating what happens to human vision under dim lighting.
Affect Indirect Only	Enables you to apply exposure control only to indirect lighting, not the direct lighting of your light objects. When working with standard lights this is a helpful option that enables you to manipulate the light object's direct illumination separate from the calculated ambient light.

Exterior daylight	Indicates that you are working with outdoor illumination values, which are much higher than is normally used indoors. When rendering with a camera outside in daylight this option is essential to avoid overexposure.

mr Photographic Exposure Control Parameters

When **mr Photographic Exposure Control** is selected as the Exposure Control method, a corresponding rollout containing parameters that are specific to this method is displayed, as shown in Figure 9–41. This method offers basic presets for daytime/nighttime lighting, and interior and exterior scenes.

- To control exposure, you can enter a single value or use any of the additional options available. These additional options are based on traditional camera and darkroom functionality.

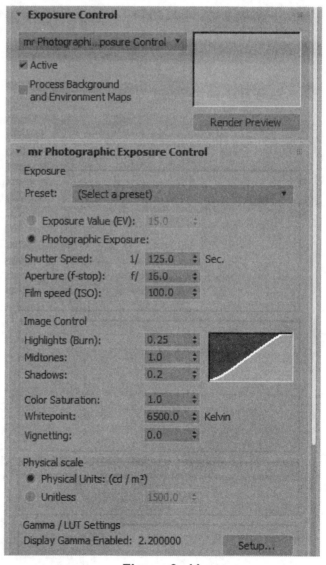

Figure 9–41

Preset	Provides you with predefined sets of values. Lets you select from Physically Based Lighting for Indoor or Outdoor for Daytime or Nighttime, or Non-Physically Based Lighting.
Exposure Value (EV)	Provides you with two options for defining exposure. Exposure Value (EV) is a single value to control the Exposure. Photographic Exposure provides a combination of 3 values to control the Exposure (Photographic Exposure).
Photographic Exposure	Provides three fields (*Shutter Speed*, *Aperture*, and *Film speed*) to control the exposure. The faster the shutter speed, the less light that is admitted into the camera. The lower the aperture (fstop) the wider the opening in the camera lens and thus the more light admitted. With film speed, the higher the number the faster the film, thus more light required.
Image Control	Provides controls similar to a darkroom technique in which you can burn and dodge to control shadows, highlights, and midtones independent of one another. Also provides tools for **Color Saturation** (use 0 for B&W renderings), **Whitepoint** to affect color tinting, and **Vignetting** to create a fuzzy elliptical gradation around the edges of the rendering.
Physical Scale	When this is set to Physical Units, the calculations occur based on the physical lighting and materials in the scene. When Unitless is set, you can enter a numeric adjustment to increase the energy in the scene. Use Unitless whenever the scene seems too dark or bright.
Gamma/ LUT Settings	Accesses the *Gamma and LUT* tab of the Customize> Preferences Viewports dialog box. Gamma is a method to adjust the rendering to suit a particular monitor or output device. Display Gamma, when enabled, controls what the monitor displays. Output gamma controls the brightness and contrast going to the output rendering. Warning: Changing gamma results in images that look one way in the Autodesk 3ds Max software, but look different in other programs such as Photoshop. For this reason be cautious when changing the Gamma.

Practice 9c

Working with Exposure Control

Practice Objective

- Assign NVIDIA mental ray renderer and work with mr Photographic Exposure Control parameters.

Estimated time for completion: 10 minutes

In this practice you will prepare an interior scene for global illumination with mental ray. You will assign NVIDIA mental ray renderer and then apply **mr Photographic Exposure Control** as the exposure control method. You will modify the parameters to adjust the lighting levels in the scene.

You must set the paths to locate the External files and Xrefs used in the practice. If you have not done this already, return to **Chapter 1: Introduction to Autodesk 3ds Max** and complete Task 1 to Task 3 in **Practice 1a: Organizing Folders and Working with the Interface**. You only have to set the user paths once.

Task 1 - Assign NVIDIA mental ray Renderer.

1. Open **mentalray_ExposureControl_start.max**.

*If a dialog box opens prompting you about a File Load: Mismatch, click **OK** to accept the default values.*

2. Verify that the **Camera - Lobby1** viewport is active. In the Main Toolbar, click  (Render Production). The scene is dark without any calculated ambient light or exposure control, as shown in Figure 9–42.

Figure 9–42

- The object named **Layer:VIZ-1-Ceiling Lights** consists of extruded circles representing the openings for the downlights. The openings display as lit in the renderings because a self-illuminated material has been assigned to them.

3. In the Rendered Frame Window, in the upper left area, click

    (Save Image) to save this rendering as a JPEG image file. In the Save Image dialog box, save the file in the *renderings* folder of your practice files folder with the name **1_No_Exposure_Control**. In the Save as type drop-down list, select **JPEG File (*.jpg,*.jpe,*.jpeg)**, as shown in Figure 9–43. Click **Save**.

File name: 1_No_Exposure_Control ▾ + Save

Save as type: JPEG File (*.jpg,*.jpe,*.jpeg) ▾ Cancel

Figure 9–43

4. In the JPEG Image Control dialog box, drag the slider to set *Quality* to **Best** (100) and click **OK**. Leave the Rendered Frame Window open for the rest of the practice.

You can also press <F10> to open the Render Setup dialog box.

5. In the Rendered Frame Window, click  (Render Setup).

   Alternatively, in the Main Toolbar, click 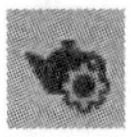 (Render Setup) or select **Rendering>Render Setup** to open the Render Setup dialog box.

6. In the upper area of the dialog box, in the Renderer drop-down list, select **NVIDIA mental ray** as shown in Figure 9–44. Verify that **NVIDIA mental ray** is displayed in the *Renderer* box.

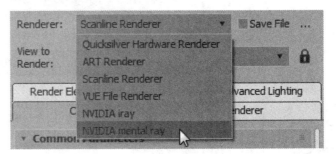

Figure 9–44

The additional panel only displays when NVIDIA mental ray is selected as the production renderer.

7. Note that an additional panel displays at the bottom of the Rendered Frame Window, as shown in Figure 9–45. This panel contains some of the settings for final gather, reflection, etc., which are available in the Render Setup dialog box. This enables you to change the settings easily.

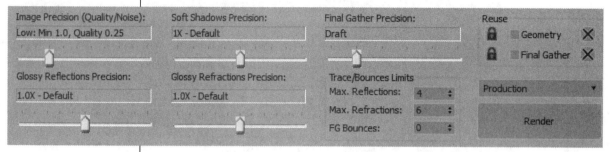

Figure 9–45

8. Click **Render** in the Rendered Frame Window. The rendering takes a little longer but it still looks dark.

9. In the Render Setup dialog box (Main Toolbar> 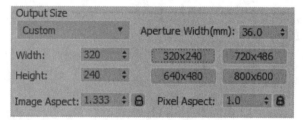 (Render Setup), verify that the *Common* tab is selected. In the Common Parameters rollout, in the *Output Size* area, click **320x240**, as shown in Figure 9–46.

Figure 9–46

10. Close the dialog box.

11. Render the scene and note that the rendered image is smaller and takes lesser time to render.

Task 2 - Work with Exposure Control.

Alternatively, select **Rendering> Exposure Control** *to open the Environment and Effects dialog box.*

1. In the Rendered Frame Window, click (Environment and Effects).

2. In the Environment and Effects dialog box, in the Exposure Control rollout, select **mr Photographic Exposure Control** in the drop-down list, as shown in Figure 9–47. Verify that **Active** is selected.

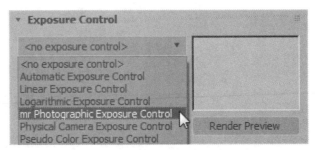

Figure 9–47

3. Click **Render Preview** and note that everything is black.

Use the spinner to reduce the Exposure Value EV and note the Render Preview. It updates interactively as you change this value.

4. In the mr Photographic Exposure Control rollout, in the *Exposure* area, select **Exposure Value (EV)** and using the spinner, reduce the Exposure value and note that the render preview becomes visible. Adjust the EV value until you have a good view of the tile floor in the preview window. You might try a value like EV = **6** or **7,** as shown in Figure 9–48.

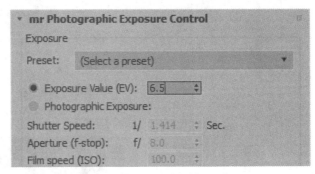

Figure 9–48

5. Click **Render** in the Rendered Frame Window. The scene displays brighter than before (as shown in Figure 9–49) under the same lighting conditions. Close the Environment and Effects dialog box.

Figure 9–49

6. In the **Camera - Lobby1** viewport, select any of the **Light–Downlight A-#** (note the name in the Command Panel). In the Command Panel, select the Modify panel (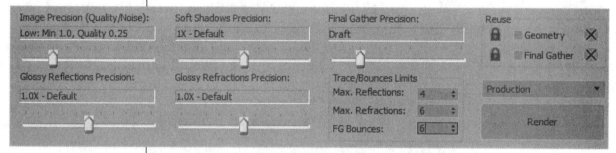). In the Intensity/Color/Attenuation rollout, in the *Color* area, select **HID Ceramic Metal Halide (Cool)**.

7. Render the scene again.

8. In the bottom panel of the Rendered Frame Window, in the *Final Gather Precision* area, verify that the slider is set to **Draft**. Set the *FG Bounces* to **6**, as shown in Figure 9–50.

Figure 9–50

9. Click **Render**. Note that there are subtle differences in the lighting in the back of the room, as shown in Figure 9–51.

Figure 9–51

10. In the Rendered Frame Window, click ![save] (Save Image) and save this rendering as **2_Exposure_Control.jpg** in the ...*renderings* folder.

11. Save your work as **mymentalray_ExposureControl_start.max**.

9.3 Daytime Lighting

Standard lights can be used to illuminate a nighttime interior scene or a scene that does not have openings to allow in daylight. Nighttime exterior scenes can be lit similarly, with outside light sources such as light fixtures and dim fill lights. Both interior and exterior scenes can be lit with specialized light objects during daytime.

Sunlight represents the direct illumination of the sun, as shown in Figure 9–52 (thick parallel arrows). The light that reflects off of the earth's surface and back down from the atmosphere (and the light that diffuses through the atmosphere on overcast days) is represented as skylight. Skylight illuminates a scene as if it were cast down from a hemispherical dome, as shown in Figure 9–52 (smaller, solid white arrows).

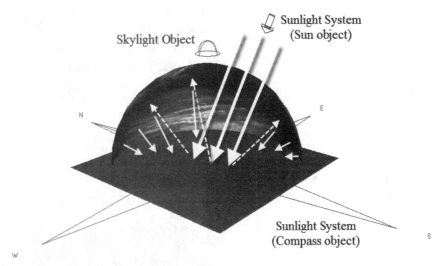

Figure 9–52

In Autodesk 3ds Max, you can create a **Daylight System** using either of the following methods:

*   Sunlight and Skylight systems

*   Sun Positioner and Physical Sky

Using the **NVIDIA** mental ray renderer, you can create a mental ray daylight system to render a physically based sun and sky lighting.

Sunlight and Skylight System

The Daylight system can be created by combining both Sunlight and Skylight systems.

Sunlight System

Sunlight can be modeled with a Sunlight system that includes a sun object (a direct light) and a compass object that is used to orient the sun in the scene. The angle of the sun's light can be controlled through the date, time, and location parameters. You can also animate the position of the sun over time for shadow studies.

Sunlight and **Daylight** objects are created as System objects, by selecting the Create panel (✛) and clicking ⚙ (Systems), as shown in Figure 9–53.

When creating a Sunlight system, locate the compass over the center of your site at an approximate ground elevation and control the sun's position using the Control Parameters, as shown in Figure 9–54. Once a sun object has been created, these Control Parameters become available in the Command Panel's Motion panel (⬤).

Figure 9–53

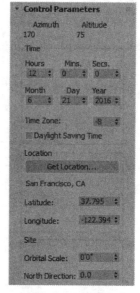

Figure 9–54

- Parameters in the *Time* and *Location* areas enable you to interactively position the sun in the correct location.

- The angle that indicates north in the current coordinate system can be entered in the *North Direction* field. This is used to orient the sunlight to your project geometry.

- The *Orbital Scale* value is the distance from the sun object to the compass (and the ground). The orbital scale should be large enough so that there are no objects behind the sun.

Sun objects are directional lights. Their Modify panel (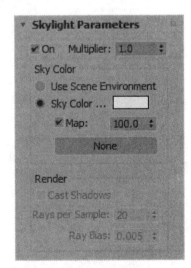) parameters are similar to those for directional lights. To generate shadows correctly, it is sometimes required to clear the **Overshoot** option in Directional Parameters rollout and increase the *Hotspot/Beam* value until it encompasses the entire site.

Skylight System

A Skylight object is not part of the Sunlight system, and is an entirely separate object. With a standard lighting approach, the illumination of a skylight object is not controlled by the date, time, or location settings of the sunlight system. The skylight's brightness (multiplier) parameter can be set manually and animated to change over time.

To create a **Skylight** object as a standard light object, in the Create panel (+), click (Lights), and then click **Standard**, as shown in Figure 9–55. Skylight objects have special controls available in the Skylight Parameters rollout, as shown in Figure 9–56.

Figure 9–55

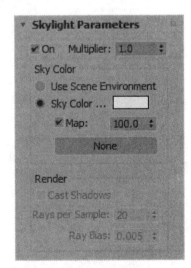

Figure 9–56

- The light cast from skylights can be colored based on the scene environment map. The **Use Scene Environment** option uses the environment that has been set up in the *Environment* tab in the Environment and Effects dialog box (**Rendering>Environment**).

- The **Sky Color** option enables you to use a single color or a map and it comes with the illumination capabilities in all renderers.

Skylight creates complex shadows that can be realistic and enhance scenes lit with natural lighting. The following settings help control the overall quality (and calculation time) of sky shadows:

Rays per Sample	The number of illuminated rays collected at each sampling point. Lower values result in faster renderings but grainier shadows. Set this value low for test renderings but increase it for the final product (use 15 for still images, but animations might need as much as 20 or 30 to avoid flickering).
Ray Bias	This is the minimum distance between two points for one to cast sky shadows on the other. Increasing this value in scenes with a lot of small detail might speed up rendering time without significantly lowering rendering quality.

Sun and Skylight Options

The following table displays the scene with different sun and skylight options:

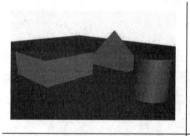	Scene with default lighting (no light objects or shadow casting).
	Scene with Sun (no skylight or ambient light). Note the pitch black shadows.
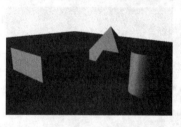	Scene with Sun and Skylight; no ambient fill lights or radiosity calculations have been added. Number of Rays = 4.

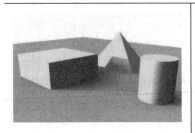	Scene with Sun and Skylight; no ambient fill lights or radiosity calculations have been added. Note that the shadows here are less grainy than the ones rendered above. Number of Rays = 10.
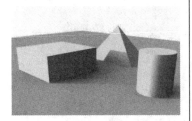	Scene with Sun and Skylight; no ambient fill lights or radiosity calculations have been added. Note that the shadows here are even less grainy than the ones rendered above. Number of Rays = 30. This result took 10x longer to render than the 4 Rays sample.

Sun Positioner Daylight System

New
in **2017**

A Sun Positioner enables you to create a light system that provides realistic sunlight with a full sky environment. This system uses a simple and intuitive workflow to create a geographically correct positioning and movement of the sun.

To create a **Sun Positioner** object:

1. In the Create panel ( ), click (Lights).
2. In the drop down list, ensure that **Photometric** is selected.
3. Click **Sun Positioner**, as shown in Figure 9–57.

• The Sun Positioner creates a Compass rose and a light source that mimics the sun. You can modify the settings of the sunlight system using the sun positioner parameters.

• The Display rollout (shown in Figure 9–58) enables you to control the display of the Compass Rose and set its radius. Using the **North Offset** option, you can set the cardinal direction that is used for placing the sun based on the date and time. In the *Sun* area, you can set the distance of the sun from the compass rose.

Figure 9–57

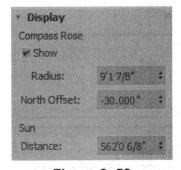

Figure 9–58

- The Sun Position rollout (shown in Figure 9–59) is used to set the position of the sun. The *Date & Time* area enables you to set the time, day, month, and year. You also have the option of using daylight savings time and setting the range of days to be used. In the *Location on Earth* area (shown in Figure 9–60), you can set the location using a database file, or set the Latitude and Longitude coordinates.

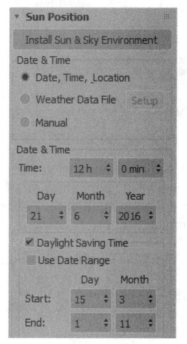

Figure 9–59

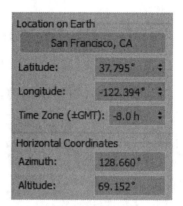

Figure 9–60

Image Based Lighting

Image Based Lighting (IBL) is a rendering technique that involves a scene representation of real-world light information as a photographic image. The image used is typically in a high dynamic range file format, such as, .HDR or .EXR. In the Autodesk 3ds Max software, this image is displayed as an environment map and used to simulate the lighting for the objects in the scene. This enables detailed real-world lighting to be used to light the scene.

Image Based Lighting is only available when **NVIDIA mental ray** is the active Production renderer. You can control the IBL settings in the *Global Illumination* tab>Skylights & Environment Lighting (IBL) rollout in the Render Setup dialog box, as shown in Figure 9–61. The **Skylight Illumination from IBL** is the default option used to provide the lighting information for the mental ray renderer. You can set the *Shadow Quality* by entering a value between **0.0** to **10.0**. You can select a *Shadow Mode* between **Transparent** (better quality and longer render time) and **Opaque**.

The higher value creates crisper shadows and longer render times.

Once the options have been set, you need to add a skylight ((Command Panel, click 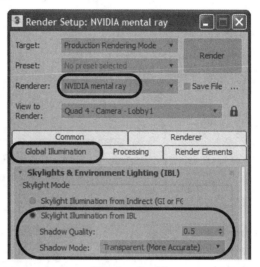 (Lights)>**Skylight**) to the scene and select **Use Scene Environment** (Skylights Parameters rollout) to use the lighting from the image.

Figure 9–61

Exterior Daylight with mental ray

Using the **NVIDIA** mental ray renderer, you can create a mental ray daylight system to render a physically based sun and sky lighting. The mental ray Daylight System includes a physical sun and sky. This can be seen in the Daylight Parameters in the Modify panel ( ). mental ray daylight calculates indirect illumination, so that you can illuminate an exterior scene with only a single light source. Early morning and late evening sunlight are tinged with color to create authentic looking renderings. Figure 9–62 shows a mental ray rendering using exterior daylight to illuminate the interior scene.

Figure 9–62

Practice 9d

Estimated time for completion: 15 minutes

*If a dialog box opens prompting you about a File Load: Mismatch, click **OK** to accept the default values.*

CountryRoad.hdr has been taken from the Environments folder in the Autodesk Showcase software.

Image Based Lighting

Practice Objective

- Light a scene using the light in an environment map image.

In this practice you will learn to light an exterior scene using an HDR image in the Image Based Lighting (IBL) technique for mental ray.

You must set the paths to locate the External files and Xrefs used in the practice. If you have not done this already, return to **Chapter 1: Introduction to Autodesk 3ds Max** and complete Task 1 to Task 3 in **Practice 1a: Organizing Folders and Working with the Interface**. You only have to set the user paths once.

1. Open **Retail Exterior.max**.

2. You need to have NVIDIA mental ray set as your Production Renderer to work with IBL. In the Main Toolbar, click

    (Render Setup) or select **Rendering>Render Setup**. In the upper area of the dialog box, in the Renderer drop-down list, select **NVIDIA mental ray.** Close the Render Setup dialog box.

3. Select **Rendering>Environment** or press <8> to open the Environment and Effects dialog box.

4. In the Common Parameters rollout, in the *Background* area, click **None** for Environment Map.

5. In the Material/Map Browser, expand the *Maps>General* categories and double-click on **Bitmap**.

6. In the Select Bitmap Image File dialog box, navigate to the ...\sceneassets\images folder and open **CountryRoad.hdr**. This image will provide the lights for the scene.

7. In the HDRI Load Settings dialog box, in the *Internal Storage* area, verify that **Real Pixels** and **Def. Exposure** are selected, as shown in Figure 9–63. Click **OK**.

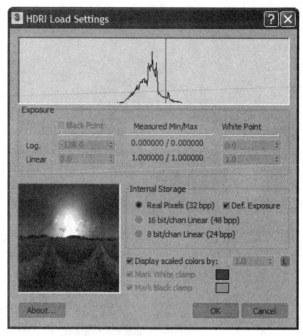

Figure 9–63

8. In the Environments and Effects dialog box, note that **None** has been replaced with **Map #9 (CountryRoad.hdr)**. Do not close the dialog box.

9. In the Main Toolbar, click ![icon] (Material Editor) to open the Slate Material Editor.

10. In the Environments and Effects dialog box, drag and drop **Map #9 (CountryRoad.hdr)** onto the *View1* sheet in the Slate Material Editor.

11. In the Instance (Copy) dialog box, verify that **Instance** is selected and click **OK**. The **Map # Bitmap** node is placed on the *View1* sheet.

12. In the *View1* sheet, double-click on the **Map # Bitmap** title bar to open its Parameter Editor.

13. In the Parameter Editor, in the Coordinates rollout, note that **Spherical Environment** is selected for *Mapping*, as shown in Figure 9–64. The light from the image will illuminate the scene from all directions.

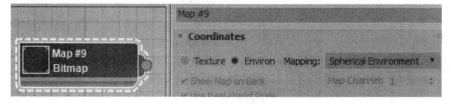

Figure 9–64

14. Close both the Slate Material Editor and Environment and Effects dialog boxes.

15. In the Command Panel>Create panel (✛), click

    💡 (Lights). In the drop-down list, select **Standard** and then select **Skylight**, as shown in Figure 9–65. In the Skylight Parameters rollout, in the *Sky Color* area, select **Use Scene Environment**, as shown in Figure 9–66.

Figure 9–65   **Figure 9–66**

It does not matter where you place the skylight because it is only a helper object.

16. In the **Camera - Southeast View** (the top left viewport), click in one of the parking lines to place the skylight as shown in Figure 9–67.

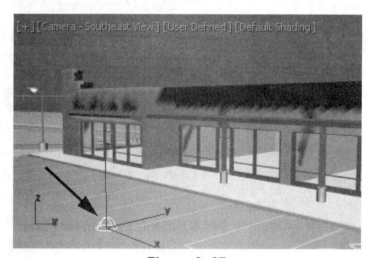

Figure 9–67

You do not require Final Gather if the scene is using the IBL image for lighting.

17. In the Main Toolbar, click 🐞 (Render Setup) to open the Render Setup dialog box. In the *Global Illumination* tab, in the Final Gathering (FG) rollout, clear **Enable Final Gather**. Close the dialog box.

18. Verify that Camera - Southeast View is active. Click

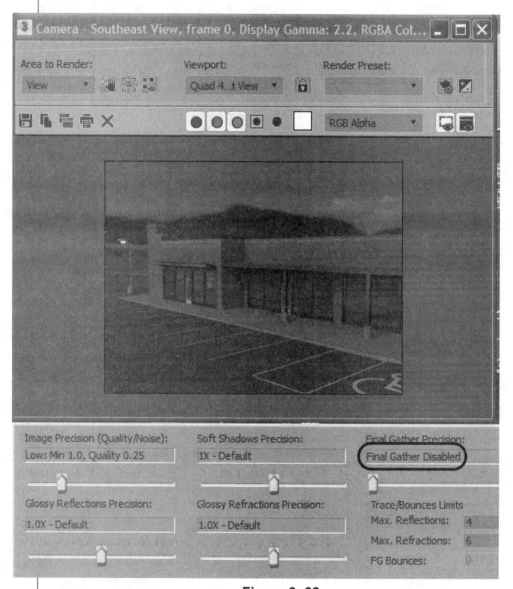

(Render Production) to render the scene, as shown in Figure 9–68. Note the environment background that was used and the lighting in the scene with the **Final Gather** disabled.

Figure 9–68

19. Close the Render Frame Window and save the file as **MyIBL.max**.

Practice 9e

Estimated time for completion: 15 minutes

*If a dialog box opens prompting you about a File Load: Mismatch, click **OK** to accept the default values.*

Lighting for an Exterior Scene with mental ray Daylight

Practice Objective

- Create a Daylight system with NVIDIA mental ray renderer.

In general, if you want a daylight system, it is recommended to use the mental ray daylight. In this practice you will create an NVIDIA mental ray daylight system and modify the parameter to get a realistic rendering of the scene.

You must set the paths to locate the External files and Xrefs used in the practice. If you have not done this already, return to **Chapter 1: Introduction to Autodesk 3ds Max** and complete Task 1 to Task 3 in **Practice 1a: Organizing Folders and Working with the Interface**. You only have to set the user paths once.

1. Open **Retail Exterior-Daylight.max**.

2. In the Main Toolbar, click ![Render Setup icon] (Render Setup) or select **Rendering>Render Setup**. In the Render Setup dialog box, in the Renderer drop-down list, select **NVIDIA mental ray** and close the dialog box.

3. Maximize the **Top** viewport and zoom to the extents.

4. In the Create panel (![plus icon]), click ![Systems icon] (Systems). In the Object Type rollout click **Daylight**, as shown in Figure 9–69.

Figure 9–69

The first click is the location of the compass rose. Keep holding the cursor and drag the mouse to resize the compass rose.

5. Near the approximate center of the **Top** viewport, click and drag out to create a compass rose similar to the size shown in Figure 9–70. The north and south points of the compass should approximately touch the top and bottom horizontal lines of the white layout area rectangle. Release the mouse button to complete the creation. You are still in the **Daylight** command.

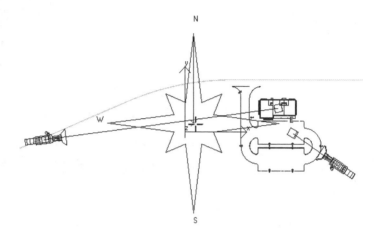

Figure 9–70

6. In the mental ray Sky dialog box, click **Yes**.

7. Note that the sun object is attached to the cursor as you are still in the **Daylight** command (Do not click). Press <L> to change to a **Left** view. Move the cursor up and down to graphically set the initial orbital scale of the sun object. Click when the sun is at a position as shown in Figure 9–71.

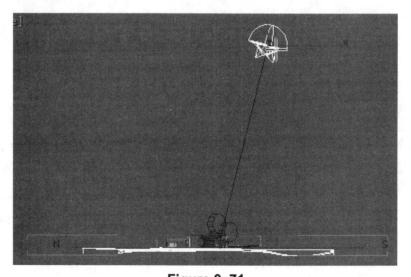

Figure 9–71

Once the Daylight System has been created, these parameters are located in the Motion panel

(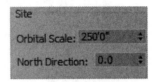) *in the Command Panel.*

8. Sun objects should be placed back from the scene for the shadows to be generated correctly. In the Control Parameters rollout, in the *Site* area, set *Orbital Scale* to **250'0"**, as shown in Figure 9–72.

Figure 9–72

9. In the Control Parameters rollout, in the *Location* area, click **Get Location...** and in the Geographic Location dialog box, select **Portland, ME**, and click **OK**.

10. In the Control Parameters rollout, in the *Time* area, set the following, as shown in Figure 9–73:

- *Hours:* **14**
- *Month*: **6**
- *Day*: **21**
- *Year*: **2016**

The location of the sun object changes based on the time and date. Press <Esc> to exit the **Daylight** creation command.

Figure 9–73

11. Maximize **Viewport** to show all four views and activate the **Camera - Southeast View** viewport. Click 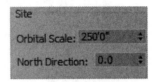 (Render Production) to render the view.

- Note that not much is displayed in the rendering and that the rendering is completely washed out.

mr Photographic Exposure Control is the recommended type for the mental ray renderer.

12. In the Rendered Frame Window, click 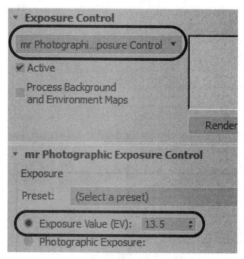 (Environment and Effects (Exposure Control)). Alternatively, select **Rendering>Exposure Control** to open the Environment and Effects dialog box. In the Environment and Effects dialog box, in the Exposure Control rollout, select **mr Photographic Exposure Control**. In the mr Photographic Exposure Control rollout, select **Exposure Value (EV)** and set it to **13.5** or **14**, (as shown in Figure 9–74) depending on the brightness of your display. Close the dialog box.

Figure 9–74

13. In the Rendered Frame Window, click **Render**. The rendering looks better.

14. In the bottom panel of the Rendered Window, in the *Trace/Bounces Limits* area, set *FG Bounces* to **2**, as shown in Figure 9–75.

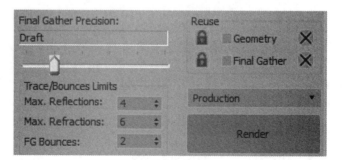

Figure 9–75

15. Click **Render**. Note a slightly brighter rendering, as shown in Figure 9–76.

16. Activate the **Perspective** view and use (Orbit) and pan to orbit to the north direction. Change the time of day to 7 am. In any viewport, select **Daylight001** (sun object) and in the

Command Panel, select the Motion panel ( ). In the Control Parameters rollout, in the *Time* area, set *Hours* to **7**. Activate the **Perspective** viewport and render the scene, as shown in Figure 9–77.

Figure 9–76

Figure 9–77

17. Save your work as **Mymr Daylight.max**.

Practice 9f

Viewport Lighting and Shadows

Practice Objective

- Set the different shading modes to display the shadows in the viewport.

Estimated time for completion: 5 minutes

In the Autodesk 3ds Max software you can view shadows directly in the viewport, without having to render them. In this practice you will learn how to enable Viewport Shading in your models.

You must set the paths to locate the External files and Xrefs used in the practice. If you have not done this already, return to **Chapter 1: Introduction to Autodesk 3ds Max** and complete Task 1 to Task 3 in **Practice 1a: Organizing Folders and Working with the Interface**. You only have to set the user paths once.

If a dialog box opens prompting you about a File Load: Mismatch, click OK to accept the default values.

1. Open **ViewportShadows_start.max**.
    - This file has a mental ray daylight system already added. The renderer used is also mental ray.

2. In the **Perspective** viewport, select the *Shading Viewport* (User Defined) and select **High Quality.** Note that the **Perspective** viewport display is washed out, although the shadows are displayed.

3. Select the *Shading Viewport* label again and select **Lighting and Shadows** to expand it. Note that **Illuminate with Scene Lights** is selected. This causes the washed out effect because the shadows are based on the scene lights.

For the shadows to be displayed in the viewport, your graphics card should support the Shader Model (2.0 or 3.0) and the display driver should be set to Nitrous Direct3D 11, Nitrous Direct3D 9, or Nitrous Software.

4. Select the *Shading Viewport* label again and select **Lighting and Shadows**. Clear the **Shadows** selection and note how the shadows disappear. Note also that the *Shading Viewport* label automatically changes to **User Defined** because the shadows are always displayed in the High Quality mode. Select **Shadows** to display the shadows in the viewport and change *Shading Viewport* label back to **High Quality.**

5. Select **Rendering>Exposure Control** or press <8> to open the Environment and Effects dialog box. Set the *Exposure Value (EV)* to a number between **13.5** and **15.0**, depending on the brightness of your display. This reduces the washed out effect, as shown in Figure 9–78. Close the dialog box.

Figure 9–78

6. In any viewport, select the **Daylight01** object, or alternatively, use the Scene Explorer to select the **Daylight01** light object.

In the Command Panel, select the Motion panel ( ). In the Control Parameters rollout, in the *Location* area, change the **North Direction** (using the spinner) and watch the shadows move in the **Perspective** viewport. In viewports, other than the **Perspective**, note that the **Daylight01** object also moves as you change the **North Direction**.

7. In the Control Parameters rollout, note that the month is set to **2** (Feb). Zoom in on the corner of the retail shop to get a closer look at the shadows. Note the long shadows, as shown in Figure 9–79.

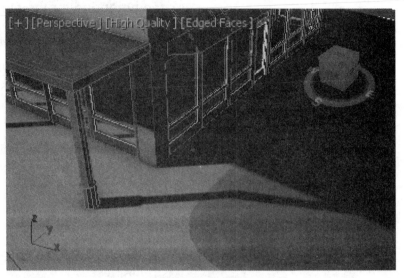

Figure 9–79

The shadows get longer in winter months and shorter in summer months.

8. Change the month to **7** (July) and review the shadows, as shown in Figure 9–80. The shadows get shorter.

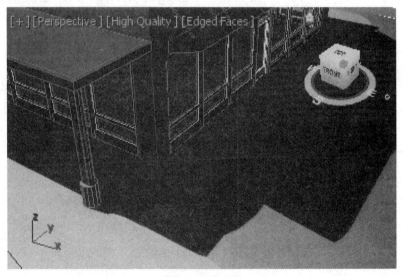

Figure 9–80

9. Select the **Visual Style** label and select **Lighting and Shadows**. Toggle **Ambient Occlusion** on and off (select and clear). Note the subtle change to the shadows in the viewport.

10. Save your work as **MyViewportShadows_start.max**.

Chapter Review Questions

1. With a Photometric light type, which type of Exposure Control is recommended for the Default Scanline Renderer?

   a. Automatic Exposure Control

   b. Linear Exposure Control

   c. Logarithmic Exposure Control

   d. Pseudo Color Exposure Control

2. Which photometric light distribution type only casts light in one hemisphere and mimics the way light emits from a surface?

   a. Uniform Spherical

   b. Uniform Diffuse

   c. Spotlight

   d. Photometric Web

3. Since photometric lights are based on real-world calculations of light energy, they are not scale-specific.

   a. True

   b. False

4. While using the **Logarithmic Exposure Control** as your exposure control method, which option converts dark colors to shades of gray, simulating what happens to human vision under dim lighting?

   a. Mid Tones

   b. Color Correction

   c. Desaturate Low levels

   d. Affect Indirect Only

5. Which of the following statements is correct?

   a. The angle of the sun's light cannot be controlled using date, time, and location parameters.

   b. The illumination of a skylight object is controlled by date, time, and location settings of the sunlight system.

   c. Skylight objects are directional lights and their modify parameters are similar to those for directional lights.

   d. Sunlight objects are directional lights and their modify parameters are similar to those for directional lights.

6. Which renderer should be the active Production renderer for the Image Based Lighting (IBL) rendering technique to become available?

   a. Scanline Renderer

   b. NVIDIA mental ray

   c. NVIDIA iray

   d. Quicksilver Hardware Renderer

   e. ART Renderer

Command Summary

Button	Command	Location
	Lights	• **Command Panel:** Create panel • **Create:** Lights
	Motion panel	• **Command Panel**
	Render Production	• **Main Toolbar** • **Rendering:** Render
	Render Setup	• **Main Toolbar** • **Rendering:** Render Setup
	Systems	• **Command Panel:** Create panel

mental ray Rendering

The NVIDIA® mental ray® renderer is one of the rendering engines available in the Autodesk® 3ds Max® software. This engine works well for visualization projects due to its global illumination system that enables the use of physically correct lighting and materials. Additionally, customization controls help you to further refine the results that are obtained using this rendering engine.

Learning Objectives in this Chapter

- Create realistic renderings using the NVIDIA mental ray renderer.
- Control the settings for photon mapping and final gather techniques to generate a smooth render.
- Enhance the quality of mental ray renderings using exposure controls and sampling quality.
- Create mental ray proxy objects.

10.1 Fundamentals of mental ray

The NVIDIA mental ray renderer, available with the Autodesk 3ds Max software, is a global illumination system that has been customized specifically for work with design visualization. It calculates physically based lighting using physically correct lights and physically based materials (such as the Autodesk materials or Arch & Design materials).

The mental ray renderer traces the paths of beams of light from their source (the CG light source) to the 3D surface and from the 3D surface onwards to the eye. It computes whether light reflects off the surface, passes through the surface, or is absorbed by the surface based on material definition.

To spread the light through the scene accurately, mental ray scatters points through the scene, which shoot out rays. Averaging occurs over these points with ray calculations to create the color for the pixels in the image. Figure 10–1 shows a mental ray rendering in process.

Figure 10–1

There are two basic methods for distributing light and color through the scene are available in mental ray. These are:

Photons are essential when caustic lighting effects are required.

- **Photon Mapping** is the method that calculates the pixels in a rendering and creates overlapping circular areas based on photon particles distributed by light energy through the scene. These circular areas blend together to create the lighting information in the scene. After calculation, the photon map file can be saved. Once calculated, it can be used in an animation using a moving camera. Photon mapping is useful when rendering interiors are lit by Photometric lights with intricate detail in low light areas.

- **Final Gather** is the method to be generally used for exterior renderings or interiors that are lit by exterior daylight coming through windows. It can be used with Photon Mapping.

mental ray Rendering

A mental ray rendering can approximate the real-world behavior of light. Using photometric lights and physically-based material parameters, mental ray can produce realistic ambient lighting. Some specifications of mental ray rendering are as follows:

- The mental ray renderer is intended to work with Photometric light objects: **Target Lights**, **Free Lights**, **mr Sun**, and **mrSkylight** objects. Standard lights can also be used if they are attenuated.

- The mental ray renderer can work with any material type. However, the Arch & Design materials have built-in mental ray adjustment controls, such as self-illuminance, reflectance, and transmission of light energy.

- mental ray calculates ambient light, thus reducing the time spent configuring ambient lights.

- **mr photographic Exposure Control** is required when lighting with mental ray.

- mental ray results can be stored as an .FGM (Final Gather Map) file and can reuse the calculations. Final Gather results are view-dependent. A mental ray solution can be rendered for multiple viewpoints, but each one must recalculate the Final Gather map for each frame where new geometry is revealed to the eye. When using an animated camera, you need to calculate the final gather map over the course of the animation (usually every 10 or 20 frames).

- The mental ray renderer can a lot of memory. It is recommended to find a balance between the least amount of memory usage and the most acceptable lighting results. Avoid using the **High** quality setting.

- The mental ray Light calculations can be used to create a lighting analysis for energy compliance.

The Autodesk® Revit® and AutoCAD® software use Autodesk materials and can share files with the Autodesk 3ds Max software.

Manually configured ambient light can be added as required, although it is an artistic fix and not a physically accurate solution.

> **Hint: Using .FGM Files**
>
> To speed up the process, calculate the .FGM (Final Gather Map) file using a smaller resolution. Once complete, use the .FGM file for the larger resolution rendering. You can also lower the *Sample per Pixel* **Minimum** and **Maximum** values to save time when calculating the .FGM file. These options are found in the Render Setup dialog box in the Sampling Quality rollout, in the *Renderer* tab.

10.2 mental ray Interior Rendering

Instead of using mental ray lighting when creating interiors without exterior lighting, you can use Photometric lights. When you create daylight and then render an interior scene (as shown in Figure 10–2), there is only direct light from the sun object. To realistically illuminate the interior scene and generate accurate lighting effects, you need to add indirect illumination using the mental ray renderer.

Figure 10–2

> **Hint: Autodesk Library Materials**
>
> It is recommended that you use Autodesk Library materials (which are based on Arch & Design materials) or Arch & Design materials with mental ray to generate the best quality surfaces.

To use mental ray, you should assign the NVIDIA mental ray as your renderer. In the Main Toolbar, click [icon] (Render Setup) or select **Rendering>Render Setup**. In the Render Setup dialog box, in the Renderer drop-down list, select **NVIDIA mental ray**, as shown in Figure 10–3. Close the dialog box.

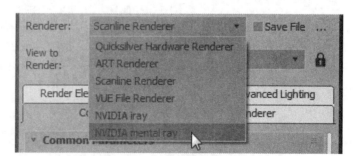

Figure 10–3

Global illumination is included in mental ray as part of generating indirect illumination in interior scenes. It can be obtained by either **photon tracing** or **final gathering**. Both methods use the photon mapping technique.

Photon Mapping

Photons are light particles that reflect, refract, and scatter across the diffuse surfaces based on materials applied to objects. Photons distribute energy quickly in the scene as they bounce from surface to surface.

> **Hint: Practice for Students**
>
> There is no practice using this Photon mapping. However, you can follow along with this lecture by opening **Mental_Interior_ Photons_Start1.max**.

*You should have assigned **NVIDIA mental ray** as your production renderer to display the Global Illumination options.*

Open the Render Setup dialog box, ( (Render Setup) or **Rendering>Render Setup**) and select the *Global Illumination* tab. In the Caustics & Photon Mapping rollout, in the *Photon Mapping* area, select **Enable**. By setting *Maximum Num. Photons per Sample* to a small number (1 or 2) and selecting **Maximum Sampling Radius** (as shown in Figure 10–4) you generate (click **Render** in the dialog box) swarms of small white circles that cover the surfaces, as shown in Figure 10–5.

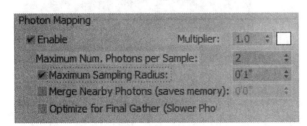

Figure 10–4

Figure 10–5

Slowly increase the **Maximum Sampling Radius** and the circles begin to join and overlap. In Figure 10–6, the *Maximum Num. Photons per Sample* and *Maximum Sampling Radius* are set to **1** and **0'2"** respectively, and in Figure 10–7, the values are set to **5** and **0'5"** respectively.

Figure 10–6

Figure 10–7

Increase the number of photons per sample by an order of magnitude. Continue increasing until you have a smooth photon-based solution. In Figure 10–8, the *Maximum Num. Photons per Sample* and *Maximum Sampling Radius* are set to **50** and **5'0"** respectively, and in Figure 10–9, the values are set to **500** and **5'0"**.

Figure 10–8

Figure 10–9

You might want to reduce the radius and increase the number of photons. The general rule is that when you decrease the radius by 2, you increase the maximum number of photons per sample times by **5.6 (4 x 1.4)**, and in the *Light Properties* area, increase the *Average GI Photons per Light* number by **1.4** photons.

To make the scene smoother, it is recommended that you add final gathering to it. Expand the Final Gathering (FG) rollout (*Global Illumination* tab), in the *Basic* area, toggle on **Enable Final Gather**, and set *Diffuse Bounces* to **2**, as shown in Figure 10–10.

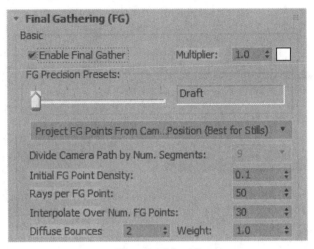

Figure 10–10

mr Photographic Exposure Control is the recommended exposure control method for the mental ray renderer.

After rendering, note that the brightness in the scene has improved, but is still a little dark because the exposure control options have not been set. In the Environment and Effects dialog box (**Rendering>Exposure Control** or, Rendered Frame Window> ⊞), in the Exposure Control rollout, select **mr Photographic Exposure Control** in the drop-down list, verify that **Active** is selected, and click **Render Preview**. The preview displays dark because no exposure value has been set. In the mr Photographic Exposure Control rollout, activate **Exposure Value (EV)** and using the spinner, set the EV value (**7.0 to 9.5**) until the lighting is improved in the Render Preview, as shown in Figure 10–11. Render the scene as shown in Figure 10–12.

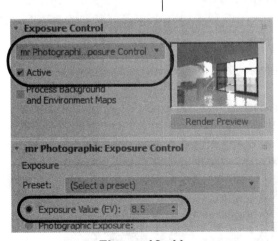

Figure 10–11

Figure 10–12

*If **Read/Write Photons to Photon Map Files** is already selected, click*

*...**to specify a folder and filename.*

When you get the required photon solution, you can save a photon map. This calculation is scene-based rather than specific to a viewport. To save a photon map:

1. In the Render Setup dialog box, in the *Global Illumination* tab, expand the Reuse (FG and Photons Disk Caching) rollout.
2. In the *Caustics and Photon Map* area, select **Read/Write Photons to Photon Map Files** in the drop-down list and specify a folder and filename in the Save As dialog box.
3. Click **Generate Photon Map File Now**, as shown in Figure 10–13. The file is saved as a binary .PMAP file (photon-map file).

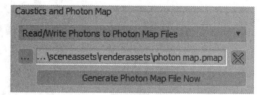

Figure 10–13

In many animations, especially with locked-down (non-moving) camera shots, a photon map saves you considerable rendering time. For interior renderings, photon mapping helps generate light in the scene and can smooth out flashing and shimmering problems in animations.

Photon Merging

Photon merging is similar to adaptive tessellation in radiosity. You can set a merge radius and the photons in that area are merged to conserve memory and calculation time.

For example, if you have two million photons in your scene, you might increase it to 10 million.

- Generally, the workflow for this is to set the merge radius less than 5% of the maximum sampling radius, and increase the number of photons drastically. You can save the photon map once your photon merging calculations are satisfactory and your image looks smooth.

- To enable Photon Merging, in the Caustics & Photon Mapping rollout, in the *Photon Mapping* area, toggle on **Merge Nearby Photons (saves memory)** and enter a radius, as shown in Figure 10–14.

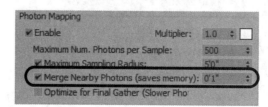

Figure 10–14

- For interior daylight scenes using mr Sky Portals (a photometric light type), you might be able to skip Photon Mapping entirely. However, for interior scenes with artificial illumination, use Photon Mapping to get the required results.

Final Gather

Final Gather is a viewport-based pixel computation that calculates indirect lighting by shooting rays throughout the scene. It creates final gather points that produce rays used to compute the brightness of the lighting.

- Bucket Rendering enables you to see different portions being rendered. If they are not rendered correctly, you can cancel the rendering, make the required modifications, and render again.

- In Render Setup dialog box, *Global Illumination* tab, in Final Gathering (FG) rollout, you can control the **Initial FG Point Density** and **Rays per FG Point** (as shown in Figure 10–15) to develop a smooth rendering. The Final Gather Presets set these numbers for you automatically.

- It is possible to display the final gather points in the renderings. In the Render Setup dialog box, in the *Processing* tab, expand the Diagnostics rollout. In the *Visual* area, select **Enable** and **Final Gather**, as shown in Figure 10–16.

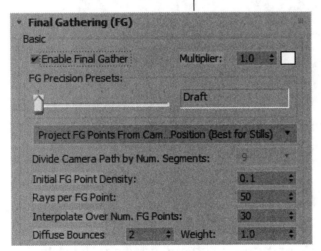

Figure 10–15

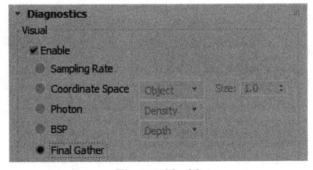

Figure 10–16

- When you render the scene, your rendering displays with green dots, as shown in Figure 10–17. Each dot represents a FG point.

Figure 10–17

Final Gather Parameters

The important **Final Gather** parameters are present in the *FG Precision Presets* area, as shown in Figure 10–18 (*Global Illumination* tab>Final Gathering (FG) rollout).

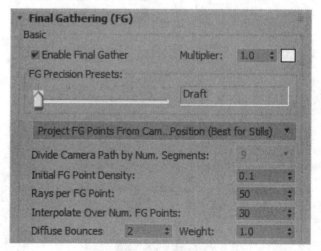

Figure 10–18

- **Initial FG Point Density:** Sets the grid spacing. Using too much density might introduce noise into the image. Remember that each point shoots rays in the scene.

- **Rays per FG Point:** Controls the number of rays shot into the scene from the FG point. If you set the **Interpolate Over Num. FG Points** to **1**, you have a one to one correspondence between Rays and Points. Increase the number of Rays and render to observe the effects. Increase the **Interpolate Over Num. FG Points** gradually to smooth the image. If your scene is evenly illuminated, you can use low values. The number of rays can be set from 50 to 500. If your scene contains a high contrast, you can use much higher values, in the 1000 to 10,000 range.

- **Interpolate Over Num. FG Points:** Determines the radius for smoothing, based on the number of points considered for the light calculation. The larger the number, the more points are considered in a single calculation. Setting this value to something high (between 100 and 250) should result in extremely realistic, artifact-free images. The workflow is to find the minimum radius that achieves realistic results, while maintaining detail in the scene.

- **Diffuse Bounces:** Defines the number of times the light bounces from surface to surface. Typical values range from 5 to 10, depending on the brightness required in the scene. Presets do not affect the *Diffuse Bounces* value.

*You can also use the Final Gather Precision slider directly in the bottom panel of the Rendered Frame Window to control **FG Precision Presets**.*

- **FG Precision Presets:** If you experience splotchiness on the wall, floor, or ceiling of an interior scene, you can increase the Final Gather Presets. Changing the *FG Precision Presets* from **Draft** to **Low** changes the values of **Initial FG Point Density** and **Rays per FG Point**, but all of the other settings remain the same. This eliminates some of the artifacts but increases rendering time. Changing to **Medium** should eliminate almost all artifacts, but can double rendering times. It is not recommended to use **High**, and **Very High** should only be considered when doing large-scale print work.

Hint: Additional Options in the Rendered Frame Window

A panel at the bottom of the Rendered Frame Window is available if the production renderer is set to **NVIDIA mental ray**. In addition to controlling the **Sampling Quality** and **Final Gather Precision**, sliders are available for *Precision of Glossy Reflections*, *Glossy Refractions*, and *Soft Shadows*. This is a global override to speed up rendering in the design stages.

Final Gather Map

Just like the Photon Map, you can write a Final Gather Map using the Render Setup dialog box.

- In the *Global Illumination* tab, expand the Reuse (FG and Photon Disk Caching) rollout. In the *Final Gather Map* area, select **Incrementally Add FG Points to FG Map Files** in the drop-down list and click ![...] to specify a path and filename. Then, click **Generate Final Gather Map File Now** as shown in Figure 10–19. Once the final gather map is generated, you can set the final gather map option to **Read FG Point Only from Existing FG Map Files**. This can be used to save time for long renderings by enabling you to reuse the final gather solution for future renderings without recalculation.

An additional panel displays at the bottom of the Rendered Frame Window when NVIDIA mental ray is selected as the active production renderer.

- You can also access this functionality directly from the Rendered Frame Window. In the bottom panel, select **Final Gather** in the *Reuse* area and click the Lock next to Final Gather, as shown in Figure 10–20.

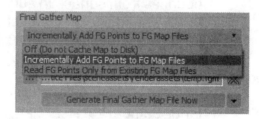

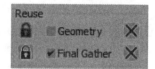

Figure 10–19   **Figure 10–20**

Exposure Control

Exposure Control (**Rendering>Exposure Control**, Exposure Control rollout) is recommended as part of the mental ray workflow. Select the **mr Photographic Exposure Control** (recommended exposure control method with mental ray), as shown in Figure 10–21. In the mr Photographic Exposure Control rollout, enable **Exposure Value (EV)** and click **Render Preview** to display an image in the thumbnail view. When the image is visible, make adjustments to the **Exposure Value (EV)** spinners and watch the image update interactively in the preview window. Selecting the spinner arrows adjusts the setting in increments of 10. You can also manually enter a numeric value. Controlling one number changes the entire range of values.

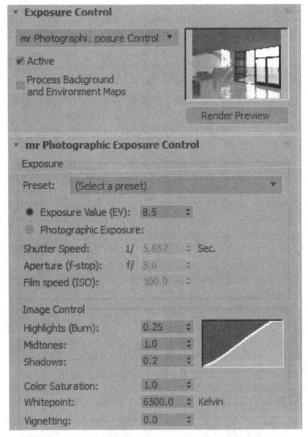

Figure 10–21

The changes can be applied to the whole scene to brighten the whole area, as shown in Figure 10–22. You can also apply Exposure control specifically to the midtone or shadow areas to brighten only those areas, as shown in Figure 10–23.

Figure 10–22

Figure 10–23

Hint: Photographic Exposure

If you are experienced with photography, you can consider using the **Photographic Exposure** option. This is the combination of *Shutter Speed*, *Aperture*, and *Film speed* values consistent with what is used in a traditional 35 mm camera, as shown in Figure 10–24.

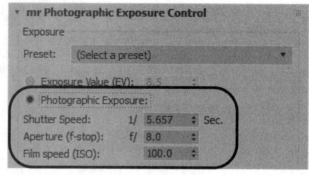

Figure 10–24

Sampling Quality

With mental ray renderer, you can use the Sampling Controls for antialiasing the rendered images. In the Render Setup dialog box, select the *Renderer* tab and expand the Sampling Quality rollout, as shown in Figure 10–25.

You can perform different kinds of sampling, by selecting the *Sampling Mode* in the drop-down list.

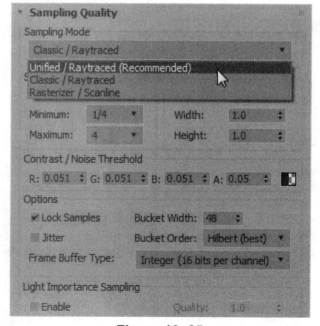

Figure 10–25

The **Unified/ Raytraced (Recommended)** method is used for quick rendering.

- Set the *Quality* of rendering to a range of **0.1 - 20.0** (the higher quality has lesser noise). The *Minimum* and *Maximum* values in the *Samples per Pixel* area (shown in Figure 10–26) provide controls similar to Supersampling in the scanline renderer. Increase the *Maximum* value to smooth out any jagged edges on diagonals. For this method, it is recommended that you adjust the *Quality* values rather than adjusting the *Minimum* and *Maximum* values. You can also access these settings in the bottom additional panel in the Rendered Frame Window and use the *Image Precision (Quality/Noise)* slider, which provides various presets for sample rate combinations, as shown in Figure 10–27.

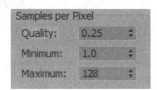

Figure 10–26

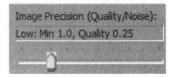

Figure 10–27

Do not assign the same value to Minimum and Maximum. The ratio of Minimum to Maximum is typically approximately 1:16.

The **Classic / Raytraced** method controls the antialiasing for the render. This method only uses the *Minimum* and *Maximum* sample rates, as shown in Figure 10–28.

- Consider using low values while determining the initial lighting. Increase these values when you are close to a more finished rendering. Use values, such as *Minimum* **4**, and *Maximum* **64** (or smaller) for a higher quality rendering and values of *Minimum* **1/16**, *Maximum* **1/4** for preview quality.

The **Rasterizer / Scanline** method uses *Shading* to assign a color to the micro-polygons and uses the *Visibility* samples to overset the image, as shown in Figure 10–29. This resolves the motion blur using many samples.

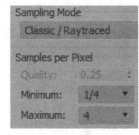

Figure 10–28

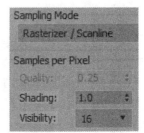

Figure 10–29

Ambient Occlusion (A0)

Ambient Occlusion is a type of light calculation that adds a detail enhancement effect by adding gradient shading to bring out subtle differences. It is a material effect that is part of the Arch & Design materials and some of Autodesk Material Library materials. This is enabled in the Special Effects rollout in the Parameter Editor of the material, in the Slate Material Editor, as shown in Figure 10–30.

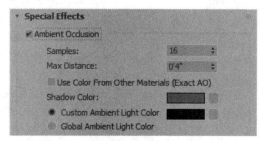

Figure 10–30

- Ambient Occlusion uses shaders to calculate the extent an area is inhibited by incoming light. It brings out detail in dark corners, along edges, and in bright places exposed to too much light.

- It has a *Max Distance* setting to speed up the rendering by limiting the radius considered. You can combine an extremely low final gather density (e.g., 0.1) with a small AO local radius (e.g., 4") to create quick renderings with good detail and smoothing.

In the film industry, it is common to create a separate Ambient Occlusion pass (called a dirt pass or beauty pass) on top of the rendering to enhance the details. You can create this kind of render pass using **Material Override**. You can enable Material Override in the Render Setup dialog box, in the *Processing* tab, in the Translator Options rollout. Placing an Arch & Design material in that slot temporarily overrides all materials in the scene. In Figure 10–31, the teapot has the Arch & Design material and in Figure 10–32, the teapot has an Override Material with an AO map.

Figure 10–31

Figure 10–32

Hint: Override Material

The **Override Material** can be used to remove the materials temporarily so that you can examine the lighting in your scene in isolation and make changes, as required.

Use **Final Gather** first and see how it looks. If the image has problems, generate a Photon solution to transport light energy into the scene. You can think of this as painting a broad light into the scene. Save a photon map. Use **Final Gather** again. It uses the Photon information and smooths it out into medium size details. Then, use **Ambient Occlusion** in the materials to bring out the small details. This can create quick, smooth, but detailed renderings.

Hint: Ambient Occlusion for Materials

You can apply Ambient Occlusion to the material. In the Slate Material Editor, open the material's Parameter Editor and in the Templates rollout, select **Enable Detail Enhancement**, as shown in Figure 10–33.

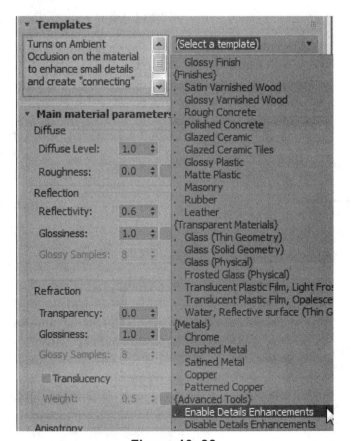

Figure 10–33

Practice 10a

Improving mental ray Speed, Quality, and using Material Overrides

Estimated time for completion: 35 minutes

Practice Objectives

- Setup Exposure Control options and Final Gather options.
- Improve the render quality and reuse the existing .FGM file.
- Apply **Material Override** to isolate the materials.

In this practice you will set Final Gather and exposure controls to get a decent interior render. You will save the Final Gather calculations, and reuse them in future renderings to save time during rendering. You will further enhance the renderings by modifying the Final Gather settings. You will also set the material overrides to temporarily remove materials examining the lighting in the scene.

You must set the paths to locate the External files and Xrefs used in the practice. If you have not done this already, return to **Chapter 1: Introduction to Autodesk 3ds Max** and complete Task 1 to Task 3 in **Practice 1a: Organizing Folders and Working with the Interface**. You only have to set the user paths once.

*If a dialog box opens prompting you about a File Load: Mismatch, click **OK** to accept the default values.*

Leave the Rendered Frame Window open for the rest of the practice (minimize/maximize as required).

While rendering, a Rendering window displays indicating the progress of the rendering. You can cancel the rendering anytime.

Task 1 - Working with Render Setup and Exposure Control.

1. Open **Final Gather Map Start.max**.

2. Verify that the **Camera - Lobby1** viewport is active. In the Main Toolbar, click ![teapot icon] (Render Production) to render the viewport. Note that the rendering is washed out and the ceiling is dark. In the Rendered Frame Window bottom panel, note that **Final Gather** is disabled and **Image Precision (Antialiasing)** is displayed indicating that the **Classic/Raytraced** *Sampling* option is used, as shown in Figure 10–34.

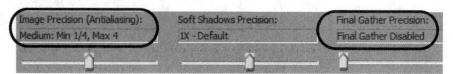

Figure 10–34

You can also press <F10> to open the Render Setup dialog box. Leave the Render Setup dialog box open for the rest of the practice.

3. In the Rendered Frame Window, click 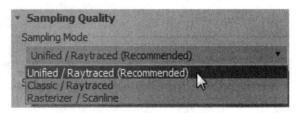 (Render Setup).

   Alternatively, in the Main Toolbar, click (Render Setup) or select **Rendering>Render Setup** to open the Render Setup dialog box.

4. Open the *Global Illumination* tab and expand the Final Gathering (FG) rollout. In the *Basic* area, select **Enable Final Gather**. Then, expand the Skylights & Environment Lighting (IBL) rollout and verify that **Skylight Illumination from (GI or FG)** is selected.

5. Select the *Renderer* tab, expand the Sampling Quality rollout, expand the Sampling Mode drop-down list and select **Unified /Raytraced (Recommended)**, as shown in Figure 10–35.

Figure 10–35

6. In the Render Setup dialog box or in the Rendered Frame Window, click **Render**.
   - It will take a few minutes to render because the Final Gather calculates the indirect lighting by shooting rays throughout the scene. Different portions are rendered as Final Gather uses Bucket Rendering.

Final Gather (mental ray) uses Bucket Rendering, whereas scanline rendering renders scanlines starting from the top of the image and going down.

   - In the bottom panel of the Rendered Frame Window, note that the **Final Gather** is activated and **Image Precision (Quality/Noise)** is displayed, indicating that the **Unified /Raytraced (Recommended)** *Sampling* option is used, as shown in Figure 10–36.

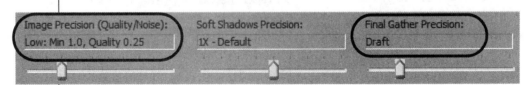

Figure 10–36

7. The rendering is too bright because the Exposure Controls have not been set. In the Rendered Frame Window, click

   (Environment and Effects (Exposure Control)). Alternatively, you can select **Rendering>Exposure Control** to open the Environment and Effects dialog box.

8. In the Environment and Effects dialog box, in the Exposure Control rollout, in the drop-down list, select **mr Photographic Exposure Control** and verify that **Active** is selected. Click **Render Preview**, which displays the washed out preview.

9. In the mr Photographic Exposure Control rollout, in the *Exposure* area, select **Exposure Value (EV)** and using the spinner increase the value till you get a better render preview (around **13**), as shown in Figure 10–37. Close the Environment and Effects dialog box.

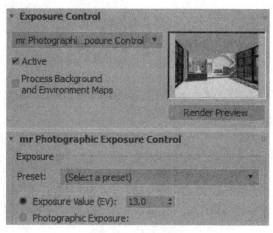

Figure 10–37

Task 2 - Improve rendering speed.

---

1. In the Render Setup dialog box, open the *Global Illumination* tab. Expand the Reuse (FG and Photons Disk Caching) rollout.

2. In the *Final Gather Map* area, click ![icon] as shown in Figure 10–38. In the Save As dialog box, enter **MyFinalGatherMap** as the name of the file. Note that *Save as type* displays **Final Gather Maps (*.fgm)**. Click **Save**. In the Render Setup dialog box, note that **Incrementally Add FG Points to Map Files** is automatically set and that the save location for the .FGM file is displayed, as shown in Figure 10–38.

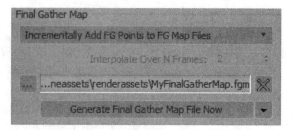

Figure 10–38

In the Rendered Frame Window, click

![icon] *(Render Setup). Alternatively, in the Main Toolbar, click*

![icon] *(Render Setup) or select **Rendering> Render Setup**.*

3. Select the *Common* tab. In the Common Parameters rollout, in the *Output Size* area, change the resolution by clicking **320x240**.

4. Return to the *Global Illumination* tab. In the Reuse (FG and Photons Disk Caching) rollout, in the *Mode* area, select **Calculate FG/Photons and Skip Final Rendering** and click **Generate Final Gather Map File Now**, as shown in Figure 10–39.

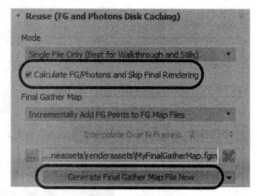

Figure 10–39

- Note that the completed rendering is smaller and does not look like a final rendered image because **Calculate FG/GI and Skip Final Rendering** is selected. It is used to save the Final Gather calculations, which are used in future renderings.

5. When the Final Gather Map calculation is finished, in the Render Setup dialog box, in the Reuse (FG and Photons Disk Caching) rollout, clear the **Calculate FG/GI and Skip Final Rendering** option.

6. In the Rendered Frame Window panel, in the *Reuse* area, verify that **Final Gather** is selected and click 🔒 next to it. This signals the renderer to skip the step of calculating the final gather map, and reuse the saved final gather map. Note that in the Render Setup dialog box, in the *Final Gather Map* area, the option has been automatically changed to **Read FG Points Only from Existing FG Map Files**, as shown in Figure 10–40.

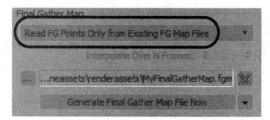

Figure 10–40

7. In the Render Setup dialog box, select the *Common* tab, and in the *Output Size* area, click **640x480** to change the resolution.

8. Click **Render** in the Rendered Frame Window or in the Render Setup dialog box. Note that a bucket rendering is not displayed while rendering because it skips the Final Gather Map calculation. The rendering is displayed as shown in Figure 10–41.

Figure 10–41

- The rendering is faster but the quality needs improvement. In the same camera view, you can keep reusing the final gather map.

Task 3 - Improve Rendering Quality.

If you change to a different view, you should create another .FGM file.

1. In the Render Setup dialog box, open the *Global Illumination* tab. In the Reuse (FG and Photons Disk Caching) rollout, in the *Final Gather Map* area, click [...] and save another FGM file as **MyFinalGatherMap2**.

*You can also change the **Final Gather Precision** in the bottom panel of the Rendered Frame Window.*

2. Expand the Final Gathering (FG) rollout. In the *Basic* area, slide the bar and set the *FG Precision Presets* value to **Medium**, as shown in Figure 10–42.

3. Select the *Common* tab and manually enter a custom output size with the following values, as shown in Figure 10–43:
   - *Width*: **160**
   - *Height*: **120**

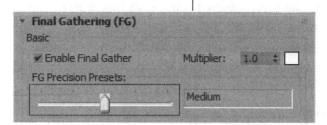

Figure 10–42

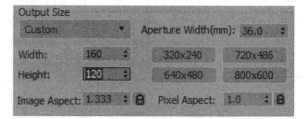

Figure 10–43

4. Return to the *Global Illumination* tab, in the Reuse (FG and Photons Disk Caching) rollout, click **Generate Final Gather Map File Now**. This could take some time to calculate (about 3-5 minutes) because the FG quality has been changed from *Draft* to **Medium**.

5. When the Final Gather Map calculation is finished, verify that in the Render Setup dialog box, in the *Final Gather Map* area, **Read FG Points Only from Existing FG Map Files** is set, as shown in Figure 10–44.

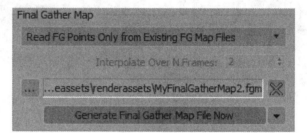

Figure 10–44

6. In the *Common* tab, click **640x480** and render. The rendering only takes little over a minute because it uses the Final Gather points from the saved file. Note that the splotchiness on the ceiling has decreased.

7. The image might still have jagged edges. In the bottom panel of the Rendered Frame Window, in *Image Precision (Quality/Noise)*, drag the slider to **Medium: Min 1.0, Quality 1.0**, as shown in Figure 10–45. Render again. The rendering is further improved.

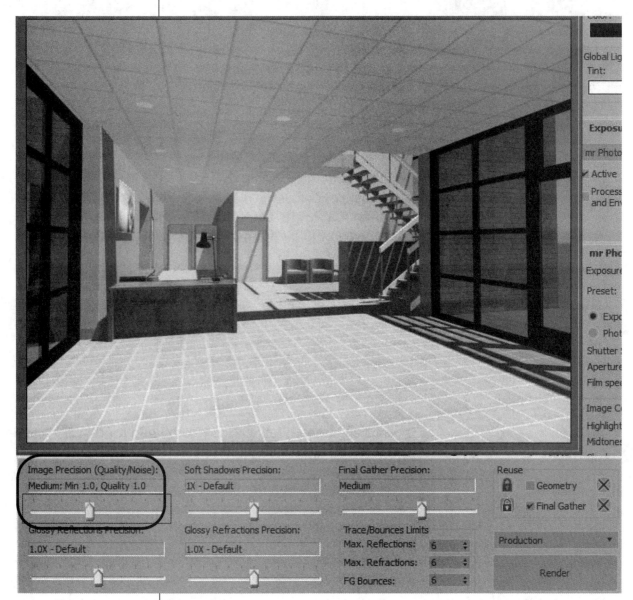

Figure 10–45

Task 4 - Set Material Override.

1. Open the Slate Material Editor.

2. In the Material/Map Browser, in the *Materials>mental ray* category, double-click on Arch & Design to add it as a node to the *View1* sheet and open its Parameter Editor.

3. Set the following, as shown in Figure 10–46:
   - Material name: **Override**
   - *Diffuse* area, *Color*: **white**
   - *Reflection* area, *Reflectivity*: **0**

Figure 10–46

4. Expand the Special Effects rollout and select **Ambient Occlusion**, as shown in Figure 10–47.

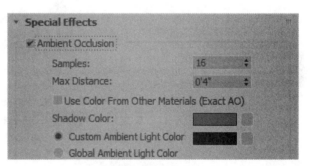

Figure 10–47

5. Move the Render Setup dialog box and place it next to the Slate Material Editor. Verify that the Override material node (*View1* sheet) is visible in the Slate Material Editor, as shown in Figure 10–48.

6. In the Render Setup dialog box, select the *Processing* tab. In the Translator Options rollout, in the *Material Override* area, select the **Enable** option.

The Render Setup dialog box, the Slate Material Editor, and the Rendered Frame Window are modeless dialog boxes and can remain open at the same time.

7. In the Slate Material Editor, in the *View 1* sheet, click and drag the **Override** material's output socket and drop it in the Render Setup dialog box, in the *Material Override* area, on *Material* **None**, as shown in Figure 10–48.

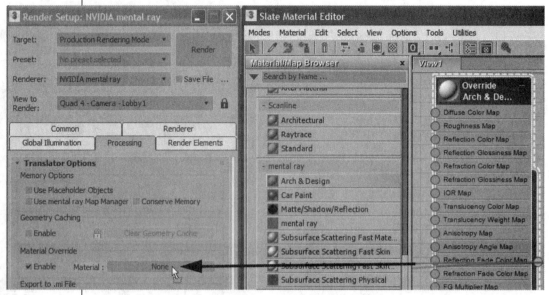

Figure 10–48

8. Verify that **Instance** is selected and click **OK**. Note that in the Render Setup dialog box, **None** is replaced by the material **Override** button, as shown in Figure 10–49.

Figure 10–49

9. Close the Slate Material Editor and the Render Setup dialog box. Minimize the Rendered Frame Window to display the viewports.

10. In the Scene Explorer ((Display None)> (Display Lights)), select **Light Downlight A00**. In the **Camera - Lobby1** viewport, right-click and select **Light On** in the quad menu, as shown in Figure 10–50. Note that in the viewport all of the downlights are displayed in (yellow) because the lights are instanced.

Figure 10–50

11. In the Command Panel, select the Modify panel (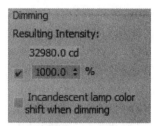). In the General Parameters rollout, in the *Light Distribution (Type)* drop-down list, select **Spotlight** as shown in Figure 10–51.

12. In the Intensity/Color/Attenuation rollout, in the *Dimming* area, enable **Resulting Intensity** by selecting the box before the % edit box and set the *% value* to **1000**, as shown in Figure 10–52.

Figure 10–51

Figure 10–52

13. Restore or maximize the Render Frame Window and click **Render** to render the scene. Note that the materials have been overridden in this scene and a single material is used throughout. This enables you to remove the materials temporarily to examine lighting in your scene. Your rendering might be slightly different than that shown in Figure 10–53.

Figure 10–53

14. Save your work as **MyFinal Gather Map Start.max**.

Practice 10b

Estimated time for completion: 20 minutes

*If a dialog box opens prompting you about a File Load: Mismatch, click **OK** to accept the default values.*

Adding a Sky Portal for Interior Lighting from Daylight

Practice Objective

- Add a Sky Portal to incorporate more light to the interior scene from the daylight system.

In this practice you will apply the Sky Portal object to the surface of the window frame using **AutoGrid**. You will also verify the direction in which the light should be pointing towards the inside of the scene.

The Sky Portal object is a photometric area light that magnifies the outdoor daylight and focuses it into the room. You must have a Skylight object (outdoor mr Sun and Sky Daylight system, Skylight, or IES Sky light) in the scene for Sky Portal to add light to the rendering. Sky Portal is dependent on the exterior lighting energy.

You must set the paths to locate the External files and Xrefs used in the practice. If you have not done this already, return to **Chapter 1: Introduction to Autodesk 3ds Max** and complete Task 1 to Task 3 in **Practice 1a: Organizing Folders and Working with the Interface**. You only have to set the user paths once.

1. Open **SkyPortal_Start.max**.

2. Activate the **Camera01** viewport and in the Main Toolbar, click ![icon] (Render Setup) or select **Rendering>Render Setup** to open the Render Setup dialog box. In the *Common* tab, in the Common Parameters rollout, in the *Output Size* area, click **320x240**. Then, click **Render**.
   - Note that Final Gather has been set for the render because the bucket rendering is being performed. The completed render displays light coming through the windows, as shown in Figure 10–54.

3. In the Rendered Frame Window, use the mouse wheel to zoom into the rendering for a closer look at the lamp, as shown in Figure 10–55. You can press, hold, and move the wheel to pan. The desk lamp is completely black (flat) without any lights being reflected. Close the Rendered Frame Window and the Render Setup dialog box.

Figure 10–54

Figure 10–55

4. Maximize the **Perspective** viewport and verify that the complete window is displayed in the viewport. Use **Zoom** and **Pan** to position the window, if required.

5. In the Command Panel>Create panel (⊞), click

 (Lights) and verify that **Photometric** is the default lighting type. In the Object Type rollout, click **mr Sky Portal** and select **AutoGrid**, as shown in Figure 10–56.

Figure 10–56

The rectangular window becomes the Sky Portal object.

6. Position (hover) the cursor over the bottom left corner of **FixedWindow04**. The Transform gizmo displays. Verify that the Y-axis (green) is displaying upward, and the Z axis (blue) is displaying outwards. (You might need to move the cursor slightly to point the gizmo in the right direction). Click at this point and drag the cursor to the upper right corner (as shown in Figure 10–57) to create a window. Release the cursor to display the white portal window. This creates a Sky Portal object that approximately matches the size of the frame.

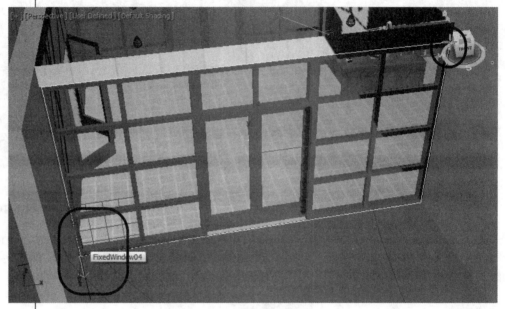

Figure 10–57

7. To verify that the light is pointing toward the correct direction (toward the inside of the room), with the skyportal still selected, click  (Select and Move) to display the move Transform gizmo at the center of the skyportal. Zoom into the Transform gizmo and note that a white arrow, overlapping the Y-axis of the gizmo, is pointing toward the building (i.e., through the window), as shown in Figure 10–58. This indicates the light direction is pointing correctly.

Figure 10–58

- If the light direction arrow is pointing towards the wrong direction, use the **Flip Light Flux Direction** option in the mr Skylight Portal Parameters rollout.

8. Zoom out and use the Y axis to move the sky portal slightly away from the **FixedWindow04** and towards you.

9. Using the viewport overlay, maximize the **Camera01** viewport.

In the Render Setup dialog box, you can click **640x480** *to set a higher resolution and display the effect of the sky portal clearly. This will increase the rendering substantially.*

10. Click  (Render Production). Zoom in on the lamp, as shown in Figure 10–59. Note the reflectivity and brightness on the lamp.

Figure 10–59

11. Save your work as **MySkyPortal_Start.max**.

- The **SkyPortal_Start.max** file contains the Architectural materials rather than Arch & Design materials. Therefore, the Sky Portal effect might not be drastically different.

There is a significant difference between Architectural materials and Arch & Design materials in responding to illumination.

- Figure 10–60 shows the materials converted to Arch & Design and the rendering has the *sky portal Multiplier* set to **30** to bring more light into the room.

Figure 10–60

10.3 mental ray Proxies

The mental ray proxy objects enable you to render large quantities of complex objects as instances so that they are only loaded into memory, as required, per bucket during the rendering process. Quick rendering is handy for objects that have a lot of detail and are repeated many times in the scene (such as vegetation and trees). These are proxy objects and can be rendered using **mental ray** in the Create panel

(+)> ● (Geometry), as shown in Figure 10–61.

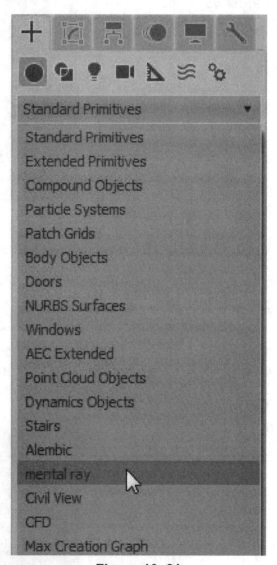

Figure 10–61

Practice 10c

mental ray Proxies

Practice Objective

- Create mental ray proxy objects.

Estimated time for completion: 10 minutes

You must set the paths to locate the External files and Xrefs used in the practice. If you have not done this already, return to **Chapter 1: Introduction to Autodesk 3ds Max** and complete Task 1 to Task 3 in **Practice 1a: Organizing Folders and Working with the Interface**. You only have to set the user paths once.

*If a dialog box opens prompting you about a File Load: Mismatch, click **OK** to accept the default values.*

1. Open **mentalray_proxies_start.max**. This is the far corner of the parking lot of the Retail Exterior file.

2. The scene is displayed in the **Perspective** view. Press <F3> to change to Wireframe mode.

3. In the Command Panel>Create panel (➕)>
   ⬤ (Geometry), select **mental ray** in the drop-down list.

4. In the Object Type rollout, click **mr Proxy**.

5. In the viewport, beside the plant, click and drag to create the mr proxy object (a bounding box will be created), as shown in Figure 10–62.

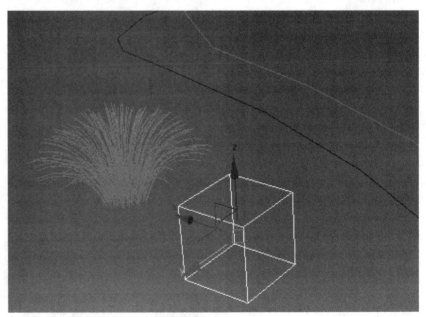

Figure 10–62

6. With this mr proxy object selected, in the Command Panel> Modify panel (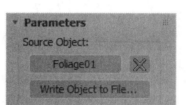), in the Parameters rollout, in the *Source Object* area, click **None**. In the viewport, select the **Foliage01** object (the plant). The name **Foliage01** displays on **None**, as shown in Figure 10–63.

7. Click **Write Object to File...**. In the Write mr Proxy file dialog box save the file as **RetailExteriorPlanting**. Note that this proxy object will be saved as an **mr Proxy Files (*.mib)** file.

8. In the mr Proxy Creation dialog box, accept the defaults and click **OK**. In the *Display* area of the Parameters rollout, note that a thumbnail and the vertices of the plant is displayed, as shown in Figure 10–64.

Figure 10–63 **Figure 10–64**

*You can open the Extras toolbar by right-clicking in an empty area in the Main Toolbar and selecting **Extras**.*

9. In the *Display* area, increase the *Viewport Verts* value to **1000** and press <Enter>.

10. Toggle to the four viewports views and in the Top viewport, use 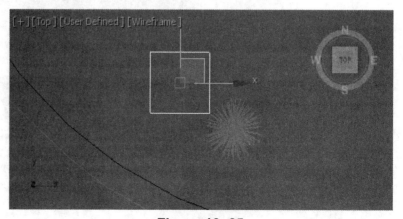 (Zoom Extents Selected). Zoom out slightly and move the proxy image to follow the curve of the path (green and black lines), as shown in Figure 10–65.

Figure 10–65

11. You can use the **Spacing** tool to plant a row of these proxies. Open the Extras toolbar, in the Array flyout, click

 (Spacing Tool), as shown in Figure 10–66.

Figure 10–66

12. In the Spacing Tool dialog box, click **Pick Path** and select the green line (Line01) drawn on the grassy area, as shown in Figure 10–67. Note that **Pick Path** is replaced by **Line01** in the dialog box. In the *Parameters* area, verify that **Count** is selected, increase the *Count* to **25** and press <Enter>. Click **Apply** and close the dialog box.

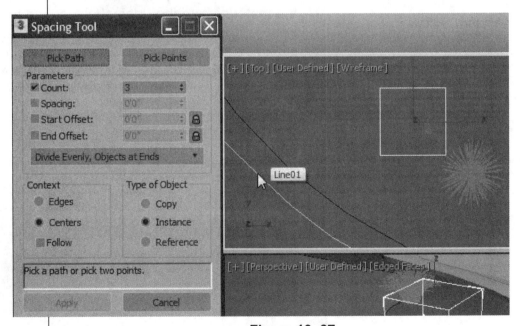

Figure 10–67

13. The plant proxies are placed along the Line01 path.

14. Activate the Perspective viewport and click  to render the scene, as shown in Figure 10–68.

Figure 10–68

15. Save your work as **Mymentalray_Proxies.max**.

Hint: Modify the Proxies to Add Variety

You can use the **Eyedropper** icon in the Material Editor to get the material from the original object and then apply it to the mr Proxies. You can make copies of this material, change it slightly, and then apply it to some of the proxies to break the monotony of the image, as shown in Figure 10–69. For variety, you can also scale and rotate the plants.

Figure 10–69

Chapter Review Questions

1. In mental ray, which option can be used to obtain global illumination?

   a. **Final Gather**

   b. **Exposure Control**

   c. **Sampling Controls**

   d. **Ambient Occlusion**

2. Which Sampling Mode uses *Quality*, *Maximum*, and *Minimum* values for adjusting antialiasing and motion blur?

   a. Unified / Raytraced (Recommended) mode

   b. Classic / Raytraced mode

   c. Rasterizer / Scanline mode

3. What does Ambient Occlusion use to calculate the extent of an area that is inhibited by the incoming light?

   a. Photons

   b. Glossiness

   c. Shaders

   d. Diffuse

4. What type of light object is required for the mr Sky Portal object to add and gather light in the scene?

   a. Omni light

   b. Spotlight

   c. Directional light

   d. Skylight

5. mental ray proxy objects enable you to render large quantities of only simple objects as instances?

   a. True

   b. False

Command Summary

Button	Command	Location
	Environment and Effects dialog box	• **Rendered Frame Window** • **Rendering:** Exposure Control
	Render Setup	• **Main Toolbar** • **Rendering:** Render Setup
	Spacing Tool	• **Extras Toolbar:** Array flyout

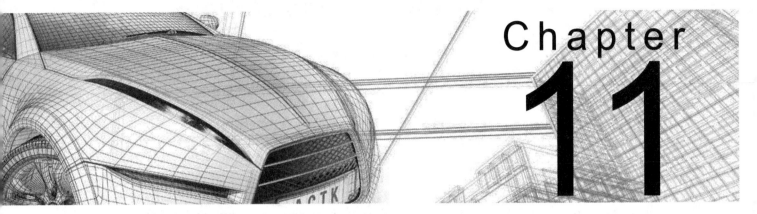

Rendering and Cameras

The Autodesk® 3ds Max® software is set so that the default rendering options provide excellent rendering results; however, understanding the different rendering options and presets that you can use to customize and save rendering settings will help you further control the results obtained in your renderings. Additionally, the use of cameras and background images can be included for further customization.

Learning Objectives in this Chapter

- Set the common options available in all of the renderers.
- Control specific options for NVIDIA® iray®, Scanline Renderer, and ART Renderer.
- Understand surface normals and their effects while rendering objects.
- Resolve face normal issues using various settings and rendering modes.
- Create scene states and render pass states using the State Sets feature.
- Create different types of cameras and control their parameters.
- Apply background images to viewports.
- Set the print resolution, paper size, and other options for a rendering.

11.1 Rendering Options

You can set, modify, and change the different options in the Render Setup dialog box, as shown in Figure 11–1. There are four ways to open the Render Setup dialog box:

- Select **Rendering> Render Setup**.

- Press <F10>.

- In the Main Toolbar, click 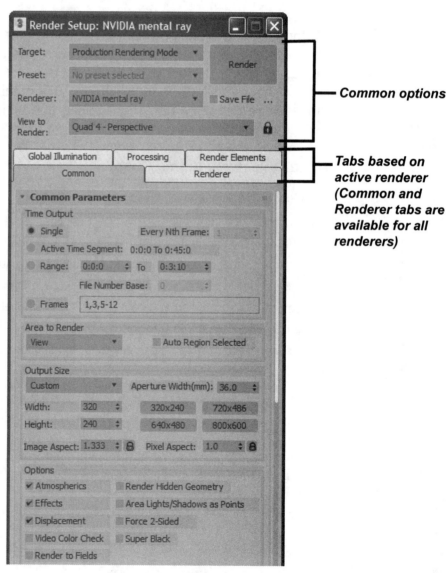 (Render Setup).

- In the Rendered Frame Window, click (Render Setup).

To quickly re-render the last rendered viewport (regardless of the active viewport) press <F9>. This eliminates the use of the Render Setup dialog box.

Figure 11–1

Common Options

Common options are available for all the renderers and are located at the top of the dialog box. These include:

- The **Target** drop-down list enables you to select the rendering options such as, Production, Iterative, A360 Cloud etc, as shown in Figure 11–2.

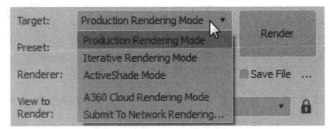

Figure 11–2

- The **Preset** drop-down list (as shown in Figure 11–3) enables you to swap between the available preset files or create, load, and save presets as RPS files using **Load Preset** and **Save Preset**. These presets are also accessed from the Render Shortcuts toolbar, as shown in Figure 11–4. When using the toolbar, you can save the current rendering settings as preset A, B, or C by selecting one of the corresponding buttons in the toolbar while holding <Shift>.

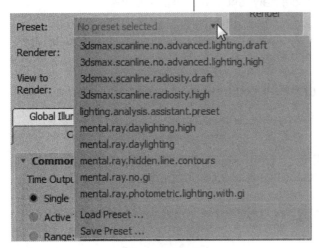

Figure 11–3

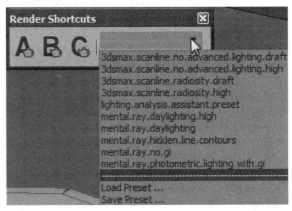

Figure 11–4

You can also select the rendering system in the Assign Renderer rollout in the Common tab of the dialog box.

- The **Renderer** drop-down list enables you to select the required rendering system, as shown in Figure 11–5.

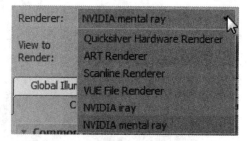

Figure 11–5

Quicksilver Hardware Renderer	Uses the system's graphics hardware (GPU) to quickly produce high-quality images. In order to use this renderer your graphics hardware must support Shader Model 3.0 (SM3.0) or a later version.
ART Renderer	A physically based renderer that uses the CPU only and renders the scene quickly.
Scanline Renderer	Intended to be used with both standard lighting (local illumination) and radiosity-based lighting.
VUE File Renderer	A legacy functionality that is not a graphical renderer. It uses ASCII text files to describe the position and transformation of objects, lighting, etc.
NVIDIA iray	Uses the NVIDIA iray rendering technology to accurately render racing light paths.
NVIDIA mental ray	A separate lighting and rendering system that determines illumination through the distribution of photons.

New
in **2017**

The tabs in the Render Setup dialog box change according to the active renderer.

Common Tab

The *Common* tab contains settings applicable to all rendering systems. Some of the options are described as follows:

Common Parameters rollout

- The *Time Output* area designates whether you are rendering a still frame (Single) or an animation. When rendering an animation you can specify to render the entire animation (Active Time Segment), a certain range (Range) or specify individual frames (Frames).

- The *Area to Render* area enables you to define what portion of the scene is rendered, such as View, Selected, Region, Crop, or Blowup.

- The *Output Size* area contains the render size options.

- The *Options* area enables you to select the objects and effects to render (**Atmospherics**, **Render Hidden Geometry**, etc.). You can also select the overrides (**Area Lights/Shadows as Points**, **Force 2-Sided**).

- The *Advanced Lighting* and *Bitmap Performance and Memory Options* areas provide additional options to further customize the rendering.

- The *Render Output* area enables you to specify a filename before rendering. Some of the commonly used file formats in which the rendering images are saved are as follows:

JPEG	The JPEG is a lossy format, which sacrifices quality in exchange for a smaller file size.
BMP	Windows Bitmap (24 bit, 16.7 Million Colors).
TGA	Targa (as 24 or 32 bit uncompressed).
PNG	Portable Network Graphics (as 24 or 48 bit color, no interlacing). This has the best file size to quality ratio as it offers the highest color depth with a smaller compression.
TIFF	Tagged Image File Format (24 bit color without compression).

Assign Renderer Rollout

In this rollout you can switch rendering systems and select the ActiveShade renderer that you want to use.

*Alternatively, they can be changed using the **Renderer** drop-down list in the Common area near the top of the Render Setup dialog box.*

Email Notifications Rollout

In this rollout you can set the option of having an email notification sent to you or another user whose email address has been specified. This is useful when the render is run without being monitored, in the case of lengthy renders.

Scripts Rollout

In this rollout you can enable the software to run a selected script before a rendering process has begun or after the process has been completed. The valid scripts that can be run are MAXScript file (.MS), macro script (.MCR), batch file (.BAT), and executable file (.EXE).

Renderer Tab

The *Renderer* tab displays renderer-specific options. It is provided for all of the renderers with render-specific options.

11.2 NVIDIA iray Renderer

The NVIDIA iray supports Sky Portal objects, translucency, and glossy refractions. The physically accurate renderer renders by tracing the light paths. Different from mental ray renderer that renders in buckets, iray renders by progressively refining the image until it has completed the render. Setup is minimal and simple, like a point and shoot camera.

- The iray renderer supports all of the mental ray materials, but only supports a subset of the Standard materials. Materials such as Arch & Design and Autodesk Library materials are available (with the exception of Autodesk Metallic Paint).

- The iray renderer supports Photometric lights (including mental ray daylight), mr Photographic Exposure Control, Batch rendering, Command Line rendering, and Backburner.

- When you select **NVIDIA iray** as the active renderer, the *Common* tab, *Renderer* tab, and *Render Elements* tab are available in the Render Setup dialog box.

Renderer Tab

The approach of the iray renderer is based on any of the three forms of time.

- In the iray rollout (shown in Figure 11–6) you can specify the length of time (in hours, minutes, and seconds), specify the number of iterations to complete, or you can run the rendering for an unlimited amount of time, enabling you to stop the rendering when you want.

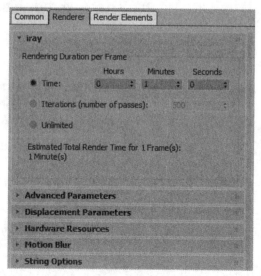

Figure 11–6

- In the Motion Blur rollout, you can enable the **Motion Blur** option to apply it to objects in a scene. You can specify the Shutter Duration that imitates the shutter speed of a camera. You can also set the number of segments for the blur and the number of iterations before the scene is updated to the next time sample.

- The Hardware Resources rollout displays information about your system's graphics support, as shown in Figure 11–7.

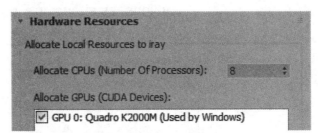

Figure 11–7

- A graphics card with CUDA enabled Graphics Processing Unit (GPU) can be used to speed up rendering.

- The String Options window in the String Options rollout enables you to specify various iray settings, which are saved with your current 3ds Max scene.

Render Elements Tab

In the *Render Elements* tab, you can render various elements. Up to 19 render elements can be rendered at a time including the alpha channel, irradiance data, normals etc.

The fact that you have a CUDA enabled GPU does not mean that it is used in your render calculations. As of the writing of this student guide, the complete Autodesk 3ds Max scene has to fit in the GPU memory for it to be used. A good measuring stick for the calculation's requirements is 1GB of video memory per 8 million triangles, and 3 bytes per pixel for any referenced bitmaps.

11.3 Scanline Renderer

The Scanline renderer generates a render by calculating a series of lines starting at the top and moving down. It is intended to be used with both standard lighting and radiosity based lighting.

Renderer Tab

The *Renderer* tab for the Scanline Renderer displays its specific options, as shown in Figure 11–8.

Figure 11–8

- The *Options* area enables you to globally enable or disable the use of all image maps (**Mapping**) or the calculation of all shadows (**Shadows**). The **Force Wireframe** option causes the scene geometry to render as wireframe objects with the **Wire Thickness** parameter listed below.

- The *Antialiasing* area contains options for antialiasing that smooths the jagged diagonal lines and curves in renderings but at a reduced quality, as shown on the left in Figure 11–9.

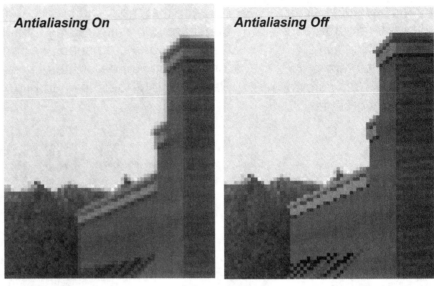

Figure 11–9

- SuperSampling (*Global SuperSampling* area) is an additional antialiasing pass applied to material textures. SuperSampling cuts down on noise, flickering, and moire patterns caused by dense material maps, as shown in Figure 11–10.

Supersampling Off

Supersampling On

Figure 11–10

Raytracer Tab

Raytracing is a rendering method used to calculate accurate reflections, refractions, and shadows. Raytracing is used for raytrace materials and some Architectural materials with shiny, transparent, or mirrored templates (e.g., glass, mirrors, etc.). Raytraced and area shadows cause raytracing to take place and for Scanline Renderer these are managed by the options in *Raytracer* tab, (as shown in Figure 11–11).

mental ray is recommended when a raytrace effect is required, rather than using the Scanline Raytrace features. mental ray has its own set of Raytracing controls.

Figure 11–11

- The **Maximum Depth** option is a measurement of how many reflections of reflections you want to permit. The default value of **9** might be excessive, while **3** might be as effective and requires much less rendering time.

- The **Cutoff Threshold** option is a percent value that causes the software to ignore rays that only contribute that percent or less of a pixel's color in the final rendering. Increasing this value reduces rendering time at a cost of lower accuracy.

- If you find that your raytraced reflections or shadows have jagged diagonal lines or curves, you can enable **Global Ray Antialiasing** to add smoothness.

- When cleared, the **Enable Raytracing** option disables all raytracing in the scene.

Several of these options relate to rendering performance. In many ways, these are black box parameters that need to be adjusted through trial and error for individual scenes.

Shadow types such as Advanced Raytraced also have antialiasing options.

New
in **2017**

11.4 ART Renderer

The Autodesk Ray Trace (ART) renderer is a path tracing renderer which generates fast and accurate renderings using few settings. ART is a physically based renderer and uses the computers CPU only. It supports photometric lights, the Sun Positioner, and physical material. ART is compatible with the Autodesk® Revit® software and is capable of creating highly accurate renderings of architectural scenes due to ART's support of the photometric and day lighting features in the Autodesk Revit software.

When you select **ART Renderer** as the active renderer, the *Common* tab, *ART Renderer* tab, and *Render Elements* tab are available in the Render Setup dialog box, as shown in Figure 11–12.

ART Renderer Tab

The *ART Renderer* tab displays the renderer-specific options, as shown in Figure 11–12.

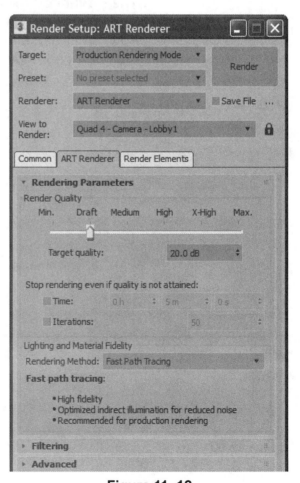

Figure 11–12

- The **Rendering Parameter** rollout enables you to set the *Target Quality,* which is measured in decibels (dB). A lower value is lower quality with more noise in the final image. A higher quality reduces the amount of noise in the final image, but the image takes longer to render.

- You can limit the time or number of iterations for a rendering in the *Stop rendering even if quality is not attained* area. This would prevent an image from taking too long to complete, but the resulting image might not have the desired quality.

- The *Lighting and Material Fidelity* area options are used to create image renderings. You can use the **Fast Path Tracing** method to render high fidelity, indirect illumination, or use the **Advanced Path Method** to generate final renders for true high fidelity images.

- The **Filtering** rollout enables you to activate **Noise Filtering** on final renderings. The **Anti-Aliasing** option sets the *Filter Diameter* in pixels and determines how the ART Renderer anti-aliases the edges in the image.

- The **Advanced** rollout has options to set the size of point lights in scene lighting using the **Point Light Diameter** value. You can also use the **Animate Noise Pattern** option to keep the noise pattern from being static in the final rendering.

Practice 11a

Working with Scanline Rendering Options

Practice Objective

- Set various rendering options to improve the rendering of the scene.

Estimated time for completion: 10 minutes

In this practice you will set some of the Rendering options. This practice uses the Default Scanline Renderer as the active renderer.

You must set the paths to locate the External files and Xrefs used in the practice. If you have not done this already, return to **Chapter 1: Introduction to Autodesk 3ds Max** and complete Task 1 to Task 3 in **Practice 1a: Organizing Folders and Working with the Interface**. You only have to set the user paths once.

*If a dialog box opens prompting you about a File Load: Mismatch, click **OK** to accept the default values.*

1. Open **Rendering Options.max**.

2. In the Main Toolbar, click (Render Setup) or select **Rendering>Render Setup** to open the Render Setup dialog box.

   - Near the top of the dialog box, in the common options, note that the *Renderer* is set as **Scanline Renderer**, as shown in Figure 11–13.

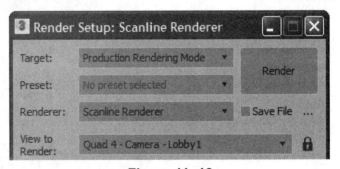

Figure 11–13

If this option is enabled, the software will recalculate radiosity for the material adjustments you make. They are very subtle, so you can ignore the recalculations for this practice.

3. In the *Common* tab, in the Common Parameters rollout, in the *Advanced Lighting* area, verify that **Use Advanced Lighting** is enabled, as shown in Figure 11–14. Clear **Compute Advanced Lighting when Required**, if required.

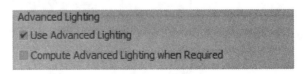

Figure 11–14

You can also click

(Render Production) in the Main Toolbar.

4. Ensure that the **Camera – Lobby1** viewport is active. In the Render Setup dialog box, in the *View to Render* edit box, ensure that **Quad 4 - Camera - Lobby1** is selected. Click **Render** in the Render Setup dialog box.

5. In the Rendered Frame Window, use the mouse wheel to zoom into the floor. Note that a moire pattern has formed on the tile floor, as shown in Figure 11–15.

Figure 11–15

6. In the *Renderer* tab, in the Scanline Renderer rollout, in the *Global SuperSampling* area, ensure that **Enable Global Supersampler** is cleared (as shown in Figure 11–16) to avoid calculating Supersampling for all materials.

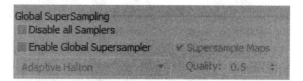

Figure 11–16

7. Open the Slate Material Editor. In the Material/Map Browser, expand Scene Materials and double-click on **Finishes. Flooring.Tile.Square.Terra Cotta** to display it in *View1* sheet, as shown in Figure 11–17.

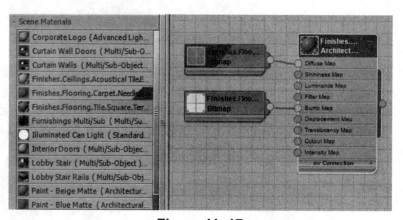

Figure 11–17

8. Double-click on the title bar of the material to open its Parameter Editor.

9. Expand the SuperSampling rollout and clear **Use Global Settings**, as shown in Figure 11–18. Use the default parameters including **Adaptive Halton** as the local supersampler.

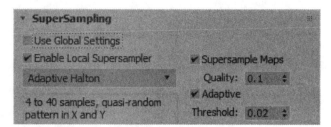

Figure 11–18

10. Render the **Camera – Lobby1** viewport and note that the moire pattern is somewhat reduced, but that the rendering time has increased. The visible edges of the sun's highlight area are also much better defined and antialiased. Some jaggedness displays along the rails in the curtain wall, as shown in Figure 11–19.

Figure 11–19

Clearing Raytraced self-reflections prevents the rails and mullions from reflecting in the glass.

11. Part of this jaggedness is caused by reflections of the shadows being cast near the glass. In the Render Setup dialog box, in the *Raytracer* tab, clear **Enable Self Reflect / Refract**, as shown in Figure 11–20.

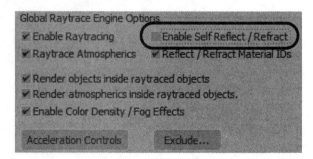

Figure 11–20

12. Render the scene. Note that the outside wall is jagged, and half of it is turned dark (as shown in Figure 11–23) as there is a significant refraction of the outside walls through the glass.

13. In the Slate Material Editor, in the Material/Map Browser, in the Scene Materials, double-click on Curtain Walls and Curtain Wall Doors to display in the *View1* sheet. Click

    (Lay Out All - Vertical) to arrange the materials vertically, as shown in Figure 11–21.

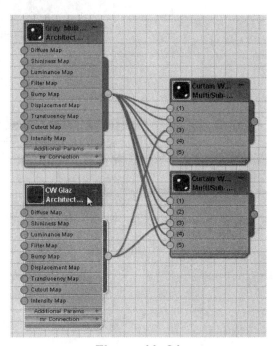

Figure 11–21

14. Double-click on the title **CW Glaz** (Architectural material) to open its Parameter Editor. In the Physical Qualities rollout, set the *Index of Refraction* to **1.0** (as shown in Figure 11–22) which results in no refraction.

With a Raytrace material you could disable refraction, whereas for an Architectural material reduce the Index of Refraction.

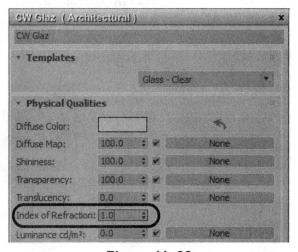

Figure 11–22

15. Render the scene again, as shown in Figure 11–24. The outside wall and rails are less jagged and the glass is less shiny than before.

Index of Refraction: 1.5

Figure 11–23

Index of Refraction: 1.0

Figure 11–24

16. Save your scene file as **MyRendering Options.max**.

11.5 Single vs. Double-Sided Rendering

Surface Faces and Rendering Modes

Autodesk 3ds Max 3D objects are treated as surface models rather than solids, to make calculations faster. 3D geometry is resolved into triangular faces when rendered.

Figure 11–25 displays two identical Box objects with the one on the right has all of its edges as triangular faces. To display triangular faces, right-click on the object, and select **Object Properties**. In the *General* tab, in the *Display Properties* area, clear **Edges Only**. If the viewport is set to Edged Face mode (<F4>), the triangular faces are displayed.

*In the Object Properties dialog box, in the Display Properties area, all of the options are grayed out if it is set to **By Layer** Change it to **By Object** for the options to be available.*

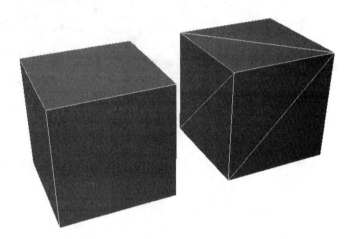

Figure 11–25

- In single-sided rendering mode, the faces are only displayed in the viewport and in renderings from the outside of the object. Therefore, no time is spent on calculating the inner faces of the object.

Working in single-sided mode is a more efficient way to render. It is recommended to use single-sided mode whenever possible.

- When using the scanline renderer, rendering in double-sided mode forces the Autodesk 3ds Max software to determine what the inside and the outside of each face looks like, adding significant rendering time.

Surface Normals

The Autodesk 3ds Max software determines which side of a face is visible in single-sided rendering mode using surface normals.

- Normals are imaginary vectors located perpendicular to one side of each face. The side that the normals project from is considered the front side or outside of the face.

- In single-sided mode, the Autodesk 3ds Max software renders faces whose vectors point towards the camera even if at very oblique angles, as shown in Figure 11–26.

- 3D objects such as primitives like these boxes automatically have their face normals pointing to the outside.

- Single-sided rendering mode can cause problems when object normals are inconsistent (inverted). In Figure 11–27, the box on the right has its top face normals pointing down instead of up. This can cause the box to have missing faces. (The back-facing edge lines are shown here for clarity but normally would not be visible.)

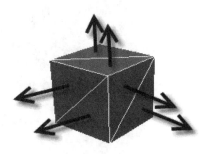 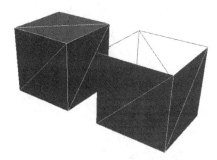

Figure 11–26   **Figure 11–27**

The viewport behavior might vary depending on your video driver.

- The faces with inverted face normals display in black in the viewport, but are invisible in the rendering To see through the faces that point away, right-click on the object, select **Object Properties** and in the *Display Properties* area, select the **Backface Cull** option.

Inconsistent face normals are a common result of importing 3D data from other applications.

- CAD software packages generally do not assign surface normals to 3D geometry. When you import this data into the Autodesk 3ds Max software, surface normals are automatically assigned to faces based on the order in which the vertices were created, which can result in inconsistent facings.

- When linking or importing 3D blocks and drawing from other software, there might still be inconsistent or inverted face normals, which need to be corrected.

Steps to Resolve Face-Normal Issues

If you experience missing faces due to inconsistent normals when working in a single-sided rendering mode, you can resolve them in several ways.

- If the data was imported or linked (.DWG or .DXF file), delete and re-import or reload the linked file and in the Import Options dialog box, select **Orient normals of adjacent faces consistently**, as shown in Figure 11–28. This option should be left off unless face-normal issues are present.

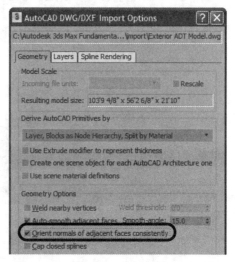

Figure 11–28

- If re-importing or reloading data is not feasible (or the data was not imported/linked) the Normal modifier can be used to unify faces. This object-space Modifier has the ability to flip all of the face normals when an object is completely inside out.

- If you have a small number of faces with normals pointing the wrong way (or a large number and some time to spend) you could manually flip and unify face normals. Using the **Edit Mesh** and **Edit Poly** modifiers, select the inverted polygon and then in the Surface Properties rollout use the **Flip** and **Unify** options, as shown in Figure 11–29.

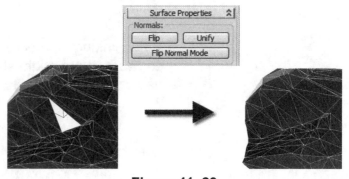

Figure 11–29

Enabling Double-Sided Mode

If you only have certain objects with face-normal issues that cannot be easily fixed, use **2-sided** materials. This renders the objects as double-sided that have double-sided materials, while rendering the rest of the scene geometry as single-sided. Different materials have the 2-sided options in different rollouts of the Parameter Editor.

- **Scanline>Standard** materials have the **2-Sided** option in the Shader Basic Parameters rollout, as shown in Figure 11–30.

- **Scanline>Architectural** materials have the **2-Sided** option in the Physical Qualities rollout, as shown in Figure 11–31.

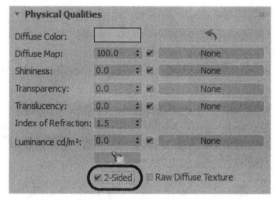

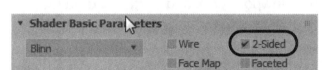

Figure 11–30

Figure 11–31

- **mental ray>Arch & Design** materials are two-sided by default. To have one-sided behavior, select **Back Face Culling** in the material's Advanced Rendering Options rollout, as shown in Figure 11–32. This can be handy in a viewport, but ensure the faces are the right direction if using mental ray.

You can enable double-sided mode globally to display the missing faces. Double-sided options are specific to each individual scene file.

- To render a scene double-sided, in the Render Setup dialog box, in the *Common* tab, in the *Options* area, enable **Force 2-Sided**, as shown in Figure 11–33. (When not selected, the Autodesk 3ds Max software renders in single-sided mode, regardless of any viewport settings.)

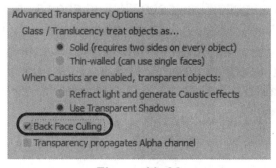

Figure 11–32

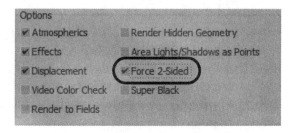

Figure 11–33

Practice 11b

Estimated time for completion: 5 minutes

At the university of Utah in 1975, Professor Martin Newell developed the teapot object. It was used for testing rendering algorithms. Today, the (Newell) teapot still exists in many 3D applications, including the Autodesk 3ds Max software.

Double-Sided Rendering Mode

Practice Objective

- Render an object as double-sided using a double-sided and single-sided material.

In this practice you will render an object as double-sided using a double-sided and single-sided material.

Task 1 - Assigning a double-sided material.

1. Reset the scene.

2. In the Command Panel>Create panel,(![plus]), click
   ![sphere] (Geometry), and in the Object Type rollout, click **Teapot**. In the **Perspective** viewport, click and drag to create the teapot object of any size.

3. With the teapot selected, select the Modify panel (![modify]) and in the *Teapot Parts* area of the Parameters rollout, clear **Lid**, as shown in Figure 11–34 to display the inside of the teapot, as shown in Figure 11–35. The faces on the inside of the teapot are visible because the **Backface Cull** option is not set by default.

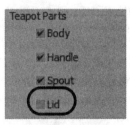

Figure 11–34

Figure 11–35

- The teapot selection has been cleared and its orientation has been changed to display the inside clearly.

4. Use ![orbit] (Orbit) to change the orientation of the teapot so that the inside is displayed. Select the teapot again if you had cleared its selection.

*In the Object Properties dialog box, in the Display Properties area, all of the options are grayed out if it is set to **By Layer**. Change it to **By Object** for the options to become available.*

5. Click 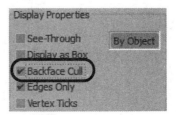 to open the Render Setup dialog box and ensure that the *Renderer* is set to **Scanline Renderer**.

6. Right-click on the selected teapot and select **Object Properties**. In the *General* tab, in the *Display Properties* area, click **By Layer** to change it to **By Object**, if required. Select **Backface Cull** (as shown in Figure 11–36) and click **OK**. The inside faces of the teapot become invisible.

Figure 11–36

7. Click  to render the scene. Note that the inside of the teapot is black, due to the black background, as shown in Figure 11–37. Leave the Rendered Frame Window open.

Figure 11–37

*You can also open the Environment and Effects dialog box by selecting **Rendering> Environment**.*

8. In the Rendered Frame Window, click ⊡ to open the Environment and Effects dialog box. In the Common Parameters rollout, in the *Background* area, click the **Color** swatch. In the Color Selector, change the color to white. Click **OK** and close the Environment and Effects dialog box.

9. Render the scene again. The faces inside the teapot are missing and display as white because of the background color.

10. Open the Slate Material Editor. In *Materials>General* categories, select the material **Double Sided**. Both the Facing and the Back materials are gray. Double-click on the **Facing** material node and assign a blue color to the **Diffuse** swatch. Similarly, double-click on the **Back** material node and assign a red color to the **Diffuse** channel. Drag and drop, or use 🗑 to assign the material to the teapot.

11. Render the scene. The inside faces are now visible in the rendering, as shown in Figure 11–38. The Object properties are overridden by the double-sided material.

Figure 11–38

Task 2 - Using the double-sided rendering option.

1. In the Slate Material Editor, select **Standard** in the *Materials>Scanline* list. The **Standard** material is not double-sided. Double-click to open the Parameter Editor and assign the color red to its **Diffuse** channel. Assign this material to the teapot. Close the Slate Material Editor.

2. Render the scene. The faces inside the teapot are missing and display as white because of the background color.

To open the Render Setup dialog box, click

*(Render Setup) in the Main Toolbar, or select **Rendering> Render Setup**.*

3. Open the Render Setup dialog box. In the *Common* tab, in the Common Parameters rollout, in the *Options* area, select **Force 2-Sided,** as shown in Figure 11–39.

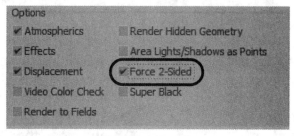

Figure 11–39

4. Render the scene. The teapot renders double-sided, as shown in Figure 11–40.

Figure 11–40

5. Save your work as **MyTeapot.max**.

11.6 State Sets

State Sets is a scene management/render pass manager in the Autodesk 3ds Max software. The State Sets dialog box enables you to record the changes made to the scene at different intervals and saves them in an hierarchical form. Select

Rendering>State Sets or click {image of icon} in the State Sets toolbar to open the State Sets dialog box, as shown in Figure 11–41. It opens in the tree view called *States* in which the states are recorded and managed.

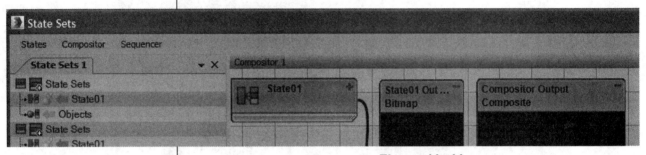

Figure 11–41

Some of the changes, such as using transforms, are not recordable by State Sets. See the Autodesk 3ds Max Help for a list of properties that can be used with the State Sets.

- The tree view opens with the master state at the top, which is displayed as {image}, and contains the **State01** state.

- You can add a new state by clicking {image} next to the master state or by selecting **States>Add State**. A new state with the name **State02** is added in the tree view, as shown in Figure 11–42.

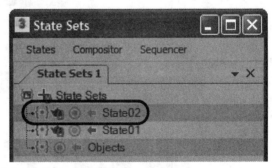

Figure 11–42

- To make a state current, click on the gray arrow. An active state is indicated by a green arrow.

- To record changes to a state, click (gray circle) next to the state. The (gray circle) changes to (black circle), indicating that the state is being recorded, and that you can start making changes to the scene. Once you have made your changes, click (black circle) to stop recording. The recorded changes are displayed as a children for this state, as shown in Figure 11–43.

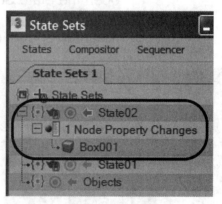

Figure 11–43

- You can add states and record changes in those states.

- To render all of the recorded states, in the State Sets menu bar, select **States>Render All States**, as shown in Figure 11–44. The states are rendered to files and saved in the path and filename specified in the Render Outputs panel.

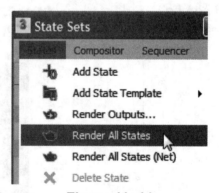

Figure 11–44

- To set a name and path for the output files, select **States>Render Outputs** to display the render outputs panel where you can browse and set the path for the files.

State Sets can bi-directionally interoperate with the Adobe After Effects CS4 (32-bit) and Adobe After Effects CS5/CS5.5 (64-bit). This requires that the files are copied from the Autodesk 3ds Max install folder into the After Effects install folder.

Compositer View

You can display the Compositor View by selecting **Compositor> Compositor View** in the dialog box menu bar with similar functionality to the View sheet in the Slate Material Editor.

Note that in the Compositor View, all of the wired states are displayed. You can modify the composition by modifying the nodes. You can select **Compositor>Compositor Link** to output the composition to the After Effects software or select **Compositor>Create PSD** to output the composition to an Adobe Photoshop .PSD file, as shown in Figure 11–45.

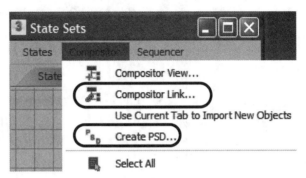

Figure 11–45

Camera Sequencer

You can use the Sequencer mode to set up an animation using multiple camera views. Select **Sequencer>Sequencer Mode** to activate a window along the bottom of the viewports with a track window indicating the cameras that are in use along with the range of frames for active cameras, as shown in Figure 11–46.

To add a camera, use ⊞ to add a state and then click on **None** and select camera from the menu. Click on the check box to enable the camera track.

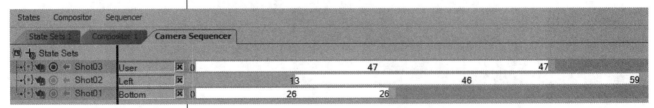

Figure 11–46

State Sets Toolbar

The State Sets toolbar (shown in Figure 11–47) enables you to quickly access the State Sets features.

Figure 11–47

- Click {icon} to open or close the State Sets dialog box. When you toggle it on and then select **Render All States** from the **States** menu in the State Sets dialog box, the state is rendered with the changed properties.

- Click {icon} to toggle the state render on or off. When you toggle it on and then select **Render All States** from the **States** menu in the State Sets dialog box, the state is rendered.

- Use the drop-down list to activate a state or access other controls.

- Click {icon} to open the Select Composite Link File dialog box where you can browse and use the selected .SOF (state output file).

11.7 Cameras

Cameras are created using ![camera icon] (Cameras), in the Command

Panel, in the Create panel (![plus icon]), as shown in Figure 11–48.

- Target cameras have a target object that can be selected and transformed separately from the camera itself.

- Free cameras do not have a target object.

- Physical cameras includes exposure control and other effects while framing the scene.

*Alternatively, you can create a camera by selecting **Create> Cameras**.*

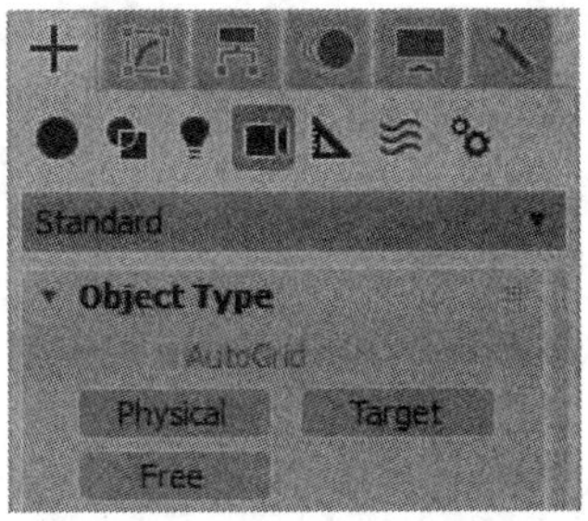

![Figure 11-48]

Figure 11–48

- Cameras can also be created on the fly to match a **Perspective** viewport using the **Views>Create Standard Camera From View**.or **Views>Create Physical Camera From View.**

Target and Free Camera Parameters

As with any other object, the **Camera** parameters are available

in the Command Panel, in the Modify panel (![modify icon]), as shown in Figure 11–49.

Figure 11–49

The **Camera** parameters found in the Parameters rollout for the Target and Free camera are:

- The focal length of real-world cameras is the distance between the focus point (the film or light-sensitive media) and the optical center of the lens. The **Lens** option available governs how much of the scene is visible to the camera. This corresponds to the focal length of real-world cameras.

- The camera focal lengths are directly related to that camera's field of view (FOV); an angular measurement of how much of the horizon can be seen by the camera. The field of view can be measured horizontally, vertically, or diagonally using the different field of view options, as shown in Figure 11–50.

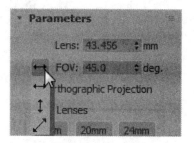

Figure 11–50

- Human vision is often approximated with a 45° field of view; it in fact varies from 60 degrees above to 75 degrees below the horizontal meridian. A focal length of 50mm is very commonly used in real-world cameras, which relates to about a 40° field of view in the Autodesk 3ds Max software.

- Other stock focal lengths are provided in the Autodesk 3ds Max software as button presets. Focal lengths below 50mm are considered short or wide-angle lenses, while those above 50mm are called telephoto lenses.

- The **Orthographic Projection** option (shown in Figure 11–51) causes a camera view to display as an orthographic or user view (axonometric rotated) rather than a three-point perspective.

- The camera's cone of vision is visible when the camera is selected, as shown in Figure 11–52. The **Show Cone** option causes it to remain visible after the camera is not selected.

- The **Show Horizon** option (shown in Figure 11–53) displays a dark gray line in the camera viewport representing the horizon in the camera view. It is helpful when aligning a camera to a background image.

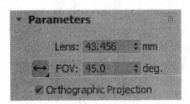

Figure 11–51

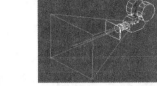

Figure 11–52

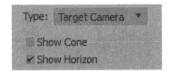

Figure 11–53

Hint: Two-Point Perspectives Through Cameras

By default, camera and perspective viewports show three-point perspective views. You can display a two-point perspective by adding a Camera Correction modifier to the camera object; select **Camera Correction** in **Modifiers>Cameras**, as shown in Figure 11–54. Two-point perspective causes vertical lines to remain vertical rather than converge over distance.

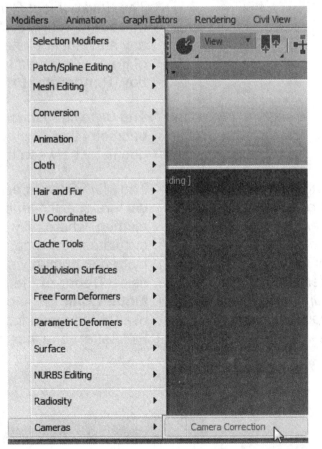

Figure 11–54

There are some additional **Camera** parameters, as shown in Figure 11–55.

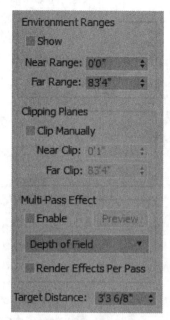

Figure 11–55

- The *Environment Ranges* area contains the distances measured from the camera between which you want to show any atmospheric effects assigned in the Atmosphere rollout of the *Environment* tab in the Environment and Effects dialog box (**Rendering>Environment**).

- The *Clipping Planes* area contains the cutoff distances for the geometry that displays in the camera. When enabled, only geometry between the clip distances is visible.

Depending on the selected effect, a Parameters rollout specific to that effect (Depth of Field Parameters or Motion Blur Parameters) opens below the Cameras Parameters rollout.

- The *Multi-Pass Effect* area (default is Depth of Field) is a camera-specific rendering effect that causes distance blurring, where only a certain point is in focus. This effect simulates how areas away from the focal point display blurred in human vision and photography. You can either select **Depth of Field (mental ray)**, **Depth of Field**, or **Motion Blur** (as shown in Figure 11–56) as an effect to be used in the rendering. You can also select the native Depth of Field effect of either mental ray, iray, or Quicksilver renderer.

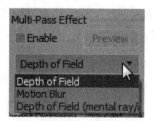

Figure 11–56

Physical Camera

The Physical Camera (as shown in Figure 11–57) is the best option for setting up photorealistic, physically based scenes. Physical Camera integrates framing the scene with per-camera exposure control, perspective control, distortion, depth of field, and motion blur. The options that can be incorporated while using the Physical camera is dependent on the active renderer.

The **Physical Camera** parameters (shown in Figure 11–58) are described as follows:

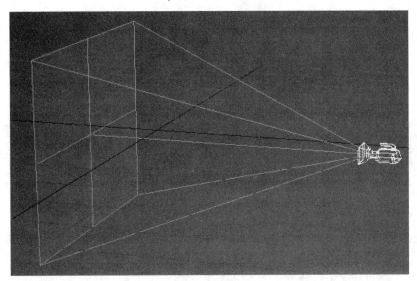

Figure 11–57

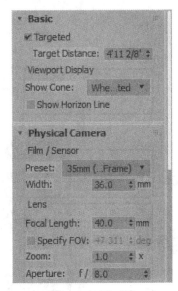

Figure 11–58

Basic rollout	When Targeted is selected, it defines properties for a target camera, and viewport display options.
Physical Camera rollout	Contains properties to define the scene view using real world camera values for accurate reproduction of a camera shot scene. Presets are available for common camera types which define Lens properties, focus, and shutter speed.
Exposure rollout	Defines exposure properties to be used with the physical camera. These properties do not affect the global exposure settings in the Environment settings.
Bokeh (Depth of Field) rollout	Properties to create a blurring effect in areas of the image that are out of focus. This effect is most apparent when the out-of-focus areas of the scene have small points of high contrast, typically from light sources or bright objects.
Perspective Control rollout	Properties to shift the perspective of the camera scene without changing the location or orientation of the camera.
Lens Distortion rollout	Settings to apply a camera distortion effect to the rendered image using cubic, or texture distortion.
Miscellaneous rollout	Enables clipping planes and modifies near and far environment ranges.

11.8 Background Images

The Autodesk 3ds Max software can use image files as viewport and rendering backgrounds. Background images are used to add detail to a scene or show a proposed construction project in its real-world context. You can load an image into the viewport background, independent of the rendering background (the environment map) or load it to both the viewport and rendering backgrounds.

How To: Enable a Background Image to Viewports

1. Select **Views>Viewport Configuration>***Background* **tab** (<Alt>+<B>) to open the Viewport Configuration dialog box in the *Background* tab, as shown in Figure 11–59.

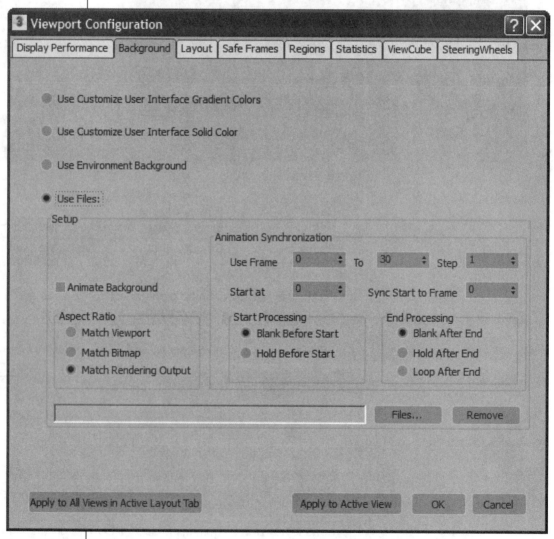

Figure 11–59

*If any option other than the **Use Files** option is selected, the Setup area is grayed out.*

2. Select **Use Files** to make the *Setup* area available for use.
3. In the *Aspect Ratio* area, select **Match Bitmap** to keep the aspect ratio of the image file constant.
4. Click **Files...** to browse for the image file and open it.
5. Click **Apply to Active View** or click **Apply to All Views in Active Layout Tab** to only display the image in the active viewport or to display it in all of the viewports.
6. Click **OK**.

How To: Assign an Environment Map to a Viewport

*Select **Rendering> Environment** to open the Environment and Effects dialog box.*

1. To enable an environment map to display in a viewport, you need to select the **Use Map** option and load a map using the *Environment Map* slot in the Environment and Effects dialog box, as shown in Figure 11–60. You can adjust the map parameters using an Instance of the map in Slate Material Editor, and opening its Parameter Editor.

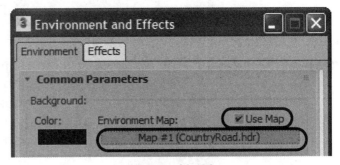

Figure 11–60

*Select **Views**>Viewport* **Configuration** *or press <Alt>+<B>.*

2. Select the viewport in which you want to display the map.
3. In the Viewport Configuration dialog box (*Background* tab), select **Use Environment Background** and click **OK**.

> **Hint: Updating a Background Image**
>
> Certain changes (e.g., change in resolution or aspect ratio) do not update the background image automatically. You should use <Alt>+<Shift>+<Ctrl>+<B> to update the background image in the active viewport. This command is not available if the active viewport does not display a background image.

Hint: Assign Background Image from Windows Explorer

You can also assign a background image directly from Windows Explorer by dragging and dropping the image file onto a viewport. A Bitmap Viewport Drop dialog box opens prompting you to select it as a viewport background or an environment map or both, as shown in Figure 11–61.

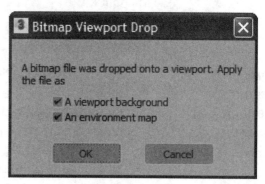

Figure 11–61

Aspect Ratio

The Autodesk 3ds Max software uses an aspect ratio to describe image proportions. It is the relationship between length and width of images, renderings, and viewports. For example, HDTV video can be created at a resolution of 1920 x 1080 pixels (1080p), which has an aspect ratio of 1.78 (1920 / 1080 = 1.78).

It is recommended to match the aspect ratio of a background image to the aspect ratio of a viewport and the rendered output. This enables you to see a more accurate representation of the final output in the viewports. The composition of a massing study displays different in the viewport (as shown in Figure 11–62) than it does in the rendered output (as shown in Figure 11–63) when their aspect ratios do not match.

Figure 11–62

Figure 11–63

You can maintain the aspect ratio of the viewport background using the options in the *Aspect Ratio* area in the Viewport Configuration dialog box, in the *Background* tab, as shown in Figure 11–64.

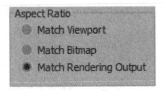

Figure 11–64

Match Viewport	Enables you to match the aspect ratio of the image to the aspect ratio of the viewport,
Match Bitmap	Enables you to lock the original aspect ratio of the image.
Match Rendering Output	Enables you to match the aspect ratio of the image to the active rendering output device.

Safe Frames

Safe Frames is a viewport display option that defines the portions of the viewport for rendered display. To enable this option, select the Viewport **+** label, and select **Configure Viewports** or select **Views>Viewport Configuration**. When the Viewport Configuration dialog box opens, select the *Safe Frames* tab, as shown in Figure 11–65.

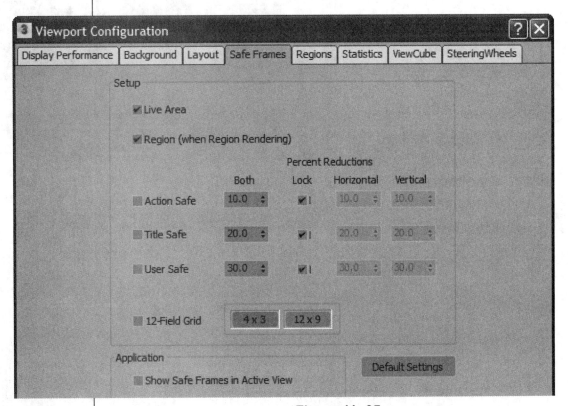

Figure 11–65

The *Safe Frames* tab provides setup options that relate to safe areas for animated action and titles when creating graphics for television. When set, these are displayed as rectangles in the active view, as shown in Figure 11–66:

- The outer rectangle is the *Live area*; the limits of what is rendered.

- The middle rectangle is the *Action safe area*, the recommended area for any animated action when creating graphics for television.

- The inner rectangle is the *Title safe area*, the recommended area for titles when creating graphics for television.

Figure 11–66

- The *User Safe* frame can be enabled, if required. It can be toggled on and customized to any proportion.

- The *12-Field Grid* frame displays a grid of cells (or fields) in the viewport. The 12-field grid yields either 12 (4x3) or 108 (12x9) cells and is used mainly by directors to reference specific areas of the screen.

Assigning Size and Aspect Ratio for Rendered Output

The rendering size (in pixels) and the aspect ratio of rendered output can be assigned in the *Output Size* area of the Render Setup dialog box, as shown in Figure 11–67 (**Rendering> Render Setup**>*Common* tab). There are several different presets available for output size.

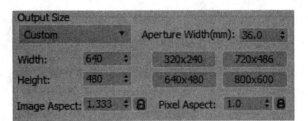

Figure 11–67

The pixel aspect ratio is determined by the image width and height.

Do not confuse the Image Aspect Ratio with the Pixel Aspect ratio. You can define the proportions of the pixel rectangle independent from the image. Consider the pixels to be individual tiles in a mosaic. The tiles can be narrow, long, or short and wide.

Hint: Use Standard Aspect Ratios

Be cautious about selecting random width and height values. Most output has a required width and height value for a particular media type. Problems occur because non-standard choices have been made for the rendering aspect ratio.

Practice 11c

Cameras and Background Images

Practice Objectives

- Apply a bitmap image as a background for the scene.
- Create a Physical Target Camera and modify the parameters.

Estimated time for completion: 20 minutes

In this practice you will apply a bitmap image as an Environment Map in a rendered scene, and as a Background Image in a viewport. You will then create a Physical Camera and modify its parameters to correctly display scene objects on top of the background image.

You must set the paths to locate the External files and Xrefs used in the practice. If you have not done this already, return to **Chapter 1: Introduction to Autodesk 3ds Max** and complete Task 1 to Task 3 in **Practice 1a: Organizing Folders and Working with the Interface**. You only have to set the user paths once.

Task 1 - Apply an Environment Map.

You will first configure an Environment Map to serve as a viewport and rendering background.

*If a dialog box opens prompting you about a File Load: Mismatch, click **OK** to accept the default values.*

1. Open **Rendering and Animation.max**.
   - This is the retail exterior scene with standard exterior lighting.

2. In the menu bar, select **Rendering>Environment**. The Environment and Effects dialog box opens.

3. In the *Environment* tab, in the Common Parameters rollout, in the *Background* area, click **None** for *Environment Map*.

4. In the Material/Map Browser, open the *Maps>General* categories and double-click on **Bitmap**.

5. In the Select Bitmap Image File dialog box, open **Background.jpg** (from the *...\Maps* folder).

- Note that **None** is replaced with **Map #9 (Background.jpg)** and **Use Map** is automatically enabled, as shown in Figure 11–68.

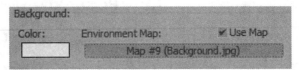

Figure 11–68

6. Close the Environment and Effects dialog box.

7. Activate the **Perspective** viewport and click  (Render Production). The tree line displays behind the model, as shown in Figure 11–69.

Figure 11–69

- Note that the image file is only displayed in the rendering as a background and not in the viewport.
- The position of the background image is not correct.

8. Close the Rendered Frame Window.

9. Ensure that the **Perspective** viewport is active, and then select the General viewport label (+)>**Configure Viewports** . In the Viewport Configuration dialog box, select the *Background* tab, if required.

You can also press <Alt>+<B> or select **Views>Viewport Configuration** *to open the Viewport Configuration dialog box.*

10. Select **Use Environment Background**, as shown in Figure 11–70. Click **OK**.

- Note that the image displays behind the scene in the **Perspective** viewport, but is not in the correct position.

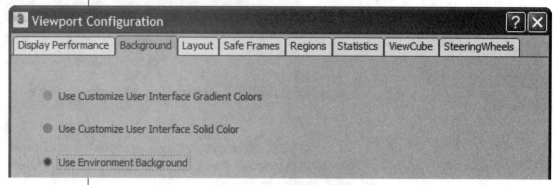

Figure 11–70

11. To modify the image, open the Slate Material Editor.

12. In the Material/Map Browser, in the *Scene Materials* category, double-click on **Map # (Background.jpg) [Environment]**, **to** place its node on the *View1* sheet, as shown in Figure 11–71.

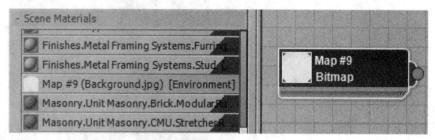

Figure 11–71

13. Double-click on the **Map # Bitmap** title bar to open its Parameter Editor.

14. In the Bitmap Parameters rollout, click **View Image**, as shown in Figure 11–72.

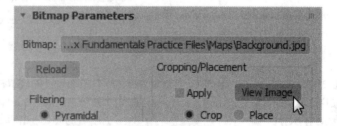

Figure 11–72

Programs such as Adobe Photoshop can be used to remove features that are not required in a background image.

- The Specify Cropping/Placement viewer displays a grassy field with the top of a trailer, as shown in Figure 11–73.

Figure 11–73

- In the Specify Cropping/Placement viewer, you can specify the image cropping (the limit of the area to be displayed) by re-sizing the red rectangle around the image. When required, cropping is enabled in the Bitmap Parameters rollout, in the *Cropping Placement* area, using the **Apply** option.

The Aspect value indicates if the image is being stretched or not.

15. Right-click and hold over the image to access the color and other image data information, as shown in Figure 11–74. The image is currently 1200 pixels wide by 750 pixels high. The Aspect value of 1.00 shows that this image is displaying normally. Close the Specify Cropping/Placement viewer.

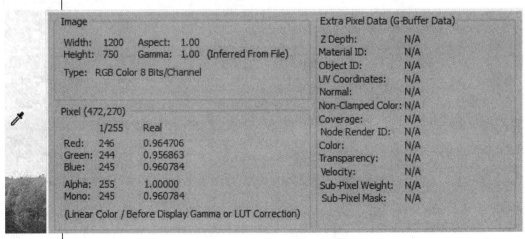

Figure 11–74

*The **Spherical Environment** is the default mapping option*

16. In the Map Parameter Editor (Slate Material Editor), in the Coordinates rollout, verify that **Environ** is selected. This indicates that the map is used as a 2D backdrop. In the Mapping drop-down list, select **Screen**, as shown in Figure 11–75. Close the Slate Material Editor.

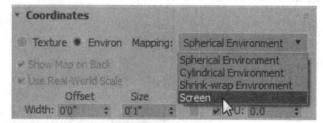

Figure 11–75

- In the **Perspective** viewport, note that the background image has updated and that a small portion of the tree line displays behind the right side of the building.

17. Render the **Perspective** viewport. The tree line in the image should display partially behind the model, as shown in Figure 11–76 (although the image is not yet in the correct position). Close the Rendered Frame Window.

Figure 11–76

Task 2 - Create a Camera.

The background photograph was taken from about the center of the westerly end of the proposed parking lot curb island location. The camera was approximately eleven feet above the proposed first floor elevation (on a ladder) and pointed horizontally towards a proposed interior wall corner and vertically to the level of the horizon. In this task you will create a camera approximately lined up with the background image. This type of approximation is required when exact measurements of camera position and other existing features are not available.

1. Activate the **Top** viewport and maximize it.

2. In the Command Panel>Create panel (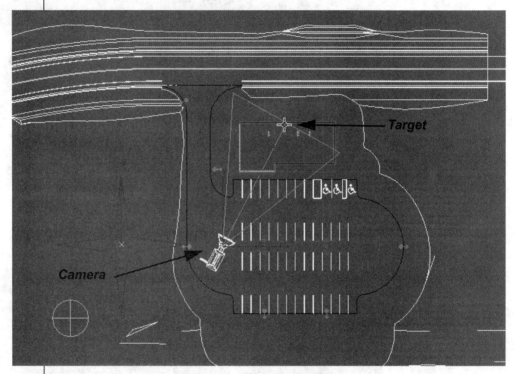), click

   (Cameras), and click **Physical**. Start with the approximate camera location (to the left of the middle double parking lot), click and drag to locate the target approximately over the model's back wall, and release to place the target, as shown in Figure 11–77.

Target

Camera

Figure 11–77

3. Maximize to the four viewports. Press <Esc> to exit the **Cameras** command and then activate the **Perspective** viewport.

4. Select the **Perspective** POV label and select **Cameras> PhysCamera001**. Note that the background image is visible in the viewport with the building being viewed at an angle from the bottom up, and that the top of the trailer might be visible in the front.

5. in the Scene Explorer, select the camera object by selecting

   PhysCamera001. In the Main Toolbar, click (Select and Move). In the Status Bar, note that Z elevation is **0.0**. Set Z to **11'0"**. Note that the tree lining is now visible behind the building along the left side and the trailer top is not visible.

6. You can now adjust the camera to display the image with respect to the building. In the **Top** Viewport, move the Camera object and keep looking in the **PhysCamera001** viewport until you get the scene similar to that shown in Figure 11–78.

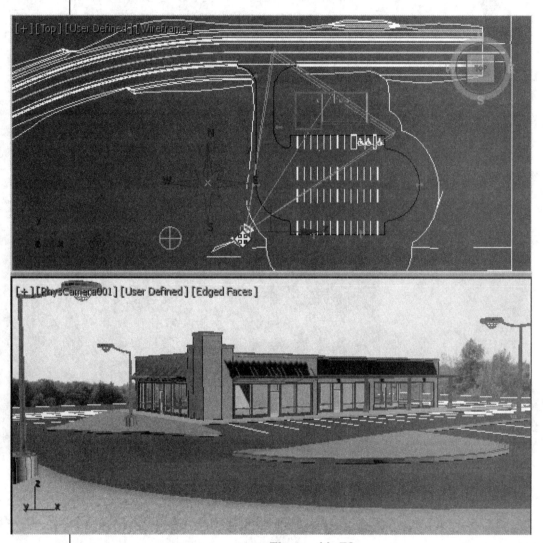

Figure 11–78

Task 3 - Approximately Match the Camera to the Background.

The background image has an aspect ratio of 1.6 (1200 pixels wide/750 pixels high). You will match the viewport and rendering to this aspect ratio.

1. In the Main Toolbar, click ![Render Setup icon] (Render Setup) or select **Rendering>Render Setup**.

2. In the Render Setup dialog box, in the Common Parameters rollout, in the *Output Size* area, set *Image Aspect* to **1.6.** Click 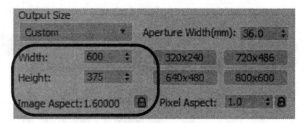 next to it to activate it. Then, set the *Width* to **600** pixels and press <Enter>, as shown in Figure 11–79. Note that the *Height* is automatically set to **375** because the *Image Aspect* is locked at **1.6.**

Figure 11–79

3. Close the dialog box. Activate the **PhysCamera001** viewport and render the scene to see the results.

4. Select the **PhysCamera001** POV label and select **Show Safe Frames**. Note the safe frames in the viewport, as shown in Figure 11–80.

Figure 11–80

Real-world 35mm cameras are named because of the diagonal measurement of their film, not their focal length.

5. Select the camera object in any viewport, if required, and in the Command Panel, select the Modify panel (⊡). In the Physical Camera rollout, note that in the Film/Sensor area, the Preset is set as **35mm** (Full Frame). This indicates that the photo was taken with a 35mm camera that had an adjustable lens.

6. In the Exposure rollout, click **Install Exposure Control.** In the Warning dialog box, click **OK** to replace the exposure control with the Physical camera exposure control.

7. Render the **PhysCamera001** viewport and note that the rendering is washed out.

8. In the Exposure rollout, change the Target EV value to around 8.5 - 9.5, as shown in Figure 11–81. Render the scene and note that the rendering is not washed out anymore.

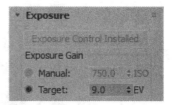

Figure 11–81

9. In the Basic rollout, in the *Viewport Display* area, select **Show Horizon Line**, as shown in Figure 11–82. In the **PhysCamera001** viewport, note that a black line displays across the middle of the viewport. It represents the horizon of the 3D model as seen by the camera.

10. You will adjust the position of the horizon. In the Perspective Control rollout, in the *Lens Shift* area, set the Vertical % value to **-10 %**, as shown in Figure 11–83. Note that the tree line is visible behind the building.

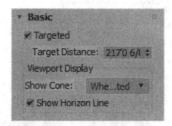

Figure 11–82

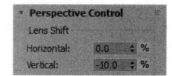

Figure 11–83

11. Verify that the **PhysCamera001** viewport is active and render the scene. Note that, with the help of some assumptions you have reasonably located the model over an existing photograph, as shown in Figure 11–84.

Figure 11–84

12. Save your work as **MyRenderingandAnimation.max**.

11.9 The Print Size Wizard

When you create renderings for print, the Print Size Wizard (shown in Figure 11–85) can help you select an appropriate rendering based on a required output resolution. To access the wizard, select **Rendering>Print Size Assistant**.

Figure 11–85

- A rendering's print resolution describes how many pixels show per printed inch, often referred to as pixels-per-inch on screen (ppi) or dots-per-inch on paper (DPI). Select the required dpi in the *Choose DPI Value* options.

Trial and error might be required to determine an appropriate resolution.

- Rendering time increases exponentially with size, so select the lowest resolution that provides an acceptable result.

- Many laser printers and plotters output between 300-600 DPI, however, when rendering values such as 72-150 DPI you can also get good results. High-end equipment plotting at 1200 DPI or better creates outstanding prints at 200-300 dpi and on high-quality paper.

- Higher quality paper can get better results than increasing resolution.

Practice 11d

Estimated time for completion: 5 minutes

If a dialog box opens prompting you about a File Load: Mismatch, click OK to accept the default values.

Using the Print Size Wizard

Practice Objective

- Set the print resolution, paper size, and other options for a rendering.

In this practice you will prepare a rendering for an A-size, 8.5"x11" print at 72 DPI. You want at least a 1/2" border around all sides and the aspect ratio of 1.6. Using the Print Size Wizard, you will set all the options to get the required print.

You must set the paths to locate the External files and Xrefs used in the practice. If you have not done this already, return to **Chapter 1: Introduction to Autodesk 3ds Max** and complete Task 1 to Task 3 in **Practice 1a: Organizing Folders and Working with the Interface**. You only have to set the user paths once.

1. Open **Print Wizard.max**.

2. Open the Print Size Wizard by selecting **Rendering>Print Size Assistant**. Verify that the printing units (*Choose Unit*) are set to **inches** and the orientation is set to **Landscape**.

3. In the Paper Size drop-down list, select **A – 11x8.5in**. Note in the viewport that this setting changes the aspect ratio (11"/8.5" = 1.29). Change the Paper Size back to **Custom**.

4. Set the *Paper Width* to **10** (11" minus a half-inch border on each side). When printing, the 1/2" border displays along both sides as long as you print this image centered on an 8.5" x 11" page at 72 DPI. On a hand-calculator work out the required rendered height 10"/1.6 = 6.25".

5. Set the *Paper Height* to **6.25** and select the *DPI* value of **72**, as shown in Figure 11–86. Press <Enter>. Note that the rendering size changes to 720 x 450 pixels.

Figure 11–86

6. Click **Render**.

   • Once rendered, you save the image and open it in an image editor or layout program to add your company logo, titles, labels, and other additional details.

   • You can also print directly to the current system printer by clicking 🖨 (Print Image) in the Rendered Frame Window.

7. Save the file as **MyPrint Wizard.max**.

Chapter Review Questions

1. Which renderer in the Autodesk 3ds Max software is not a graphical renderer and uses ASCII text files to describe the position and transformation of objects, lighting, etc.?

   a. Scanline Renderer

   b. VUE File Renderer

   c. Quicksilver Hardware Renderer

   d. NVIDIA mental ray renderer

2. When saving a rendering as an image file, which of the following format offers highest color depth with a smaller compression? In other words, this image file format is the best choice regarding file size to quality ratio.

   a. JPEG

   b. BMP (Bitmap)

   c. TGA (Targa)

   d. PNG (Portable Network Graphics)

   e. TIFF (Tagged Image File Format)

3. In rendering, which of the following is used to calculate accurate reflections, refractions, and shadows?

   a. Antialiasing

   b. SuperSampling

   c. Motion Blur

   d. Raytracing

4. In single-sided mode, the Autodesk 3ds Max software renders faces whose vectors point towards the camera.

   a. True

   b. False

5. What is the most commonly used focal length in real-world cameras?

   a. 30mm

   b. 50mm

   c. 70mm

   d. 90mm

6. For background images, which keys do you press to update the active viewport with the specific changes made to the image (the changes that do not update automatically)?

   a. \<Alt>+\<B>

   b. \<Alt>+\<Ctrl>+\<B>

   c. \<Alt>+\<Shift>+\<B>

   d. \<Alt>+\<Ctrl>+\<Shift>+\<B>

Command Summary

Button	Command	Location
	Cameras	• **Command Panel:** *Create* panel • **Create:** Cameras
	Effects and Environment dialog box	• **Rendered Frame Window** • **Rendering:** Environment
	Render Setup	• **Main Toolbar** • **Rendering:** Render Setup
	State Sets	• **State Sets Toolbar** • **Rendering:** State Sets
N/A	**Viewport Configuration dialog box>** *Background* **tab**	• **Views:** Viewport Background> Configure Viewport Background • **Keyboard:** <Alt>+<B>

Chapter

12

Animation

Animations created in the Autodesk® 3ds Max® software involve the use of Animation and Time Controls. These enable you to animate and keyframe a camera to create a walkthrough animation or to create single-frame images and then assemble them to create a movie.

Learning Objectives in this Chapter

- Work with Animation and Time Controls and set various options.
- Create animation output using the various approaches available.

12.1 Animation and Time Controls

Animations in the Autodesk 3ds Max software are created by playing back a number of still frames in rapid succession using desktop animation files such as .AVIs and .MOVs.

The Autodesk 3ds Max animation system offers powerful controls to create animations, ranging from simple camera movements to extremely complex sequences.

- Traditional movies play back a sequence of still images in rapid succession.

- Computer movie formats compile a sequence of still images into a compressed format, keeping track of the changes from frame to frame at the pixel level.

- Animations are based on Key Frames (or keys), which are time indexes at which objects change their position, rotation, scale, and/or a limited number of object parameters.

- The Autodesk 3ds Max software generates animations by interpolating between a small number of user-defined key frames – smoothly or otherwise.

- The animation controls enable you to create and play back a preview animation in one or more viewports.

Time Slider and Track Bar

The time slider and the track bar (shown in Figure 12–1) are found below the viewports and enable you to advance and reverse along an animation forward or backwards in time.

- The numbers below the time slider indicate the current time or frame number. Use the greater than (>) and lesser than (<) keys as shortcuts for moving the time slider a frame at a time.

- The shortcut menu in the Track bar contains the key properties and the controller properties. Selecting a key and then right-clicking displays all of the values for that key. Using the shortcut menu, you can also delete keys and use filter options for the display of the track bar.

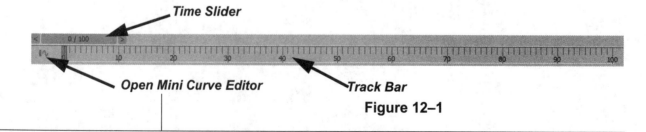

Figure 12–1

Enhanced
in 2017

- On the left side of the track bar, clicking 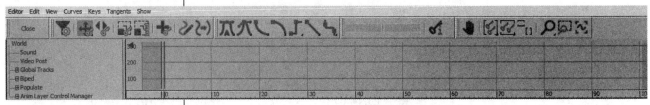 (Open Mini Curve Editor) opens the Mini Curve Editor (as shown in Figure 12–2), which replaces the track bar and the time slider. The Curve Editor contains a menu bar, toolbar, controller window, and the key window. You can collapse the Curve Editor by clicking **Close** at the left end of the Curve Editor toolbar.

Figure 12–2

Enhanced
in 2017

Hint: Track View: Using the Curve Editor and Dope Sheet

The Curve Editor and Dope Sheet are two animation data editors which graphically display and enable you to modify the animation controllers that are used to interpolate the objects in a scene.

- To open the Track View - Curve Editor, in the Main toolbar, click ![icon], or in the Menu Bar, select **Graph Editors>Track View- Curve Editor**.

- In the Curve Editor, the animation is displayed in the form of function curves, as shown in Figure 12–3. You can visualize and modify the motion by controlling the curves (i.e., tangent handles) at various keys.

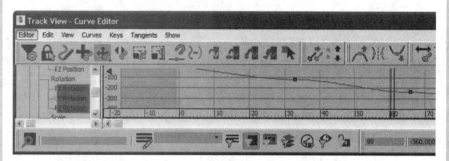

Figure 12–3

- To open the Track View - Dope Sheet, in the Menu Bar, select **Graph Editors>Track View- Dope Sheet**.

- In the Dope sheet, the animation is displayed in the form of a spread sheet displaying keys and ranges, as shown in Figure 12–4. You can visualize and modify the motion by controlling the keys directly.

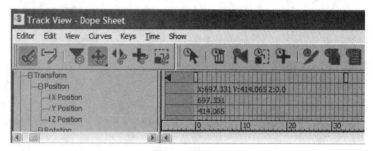

Figure 12–4

Animation and Time Controls

The Animation and Time Controls (shown in Figure 12–5) are found at the bottom right corner next to the Navigation Controls.

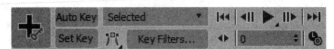

Figure 12–5

The various Animation and Time controls are described as follows:

<table>
<tr>
<td></td>
<td>Enables you to manually add an animation key at the time shown in the time slider.</td>
</tr>
<tr>
<td>Auto Key/ Set Key</td>
<td>Activates either Auto Key or Set Key Animation Modes.

• When Auto Key mode is active all movement, rotation, and scale changes are automatically stored as keys at the current frame. This method is more widely used by design visualizers. Press <N> as a shortcut to toggle on the mode.

• The Set Key mode enables you to create keys, set key information, and offers more control over the kinds of keys you create through filters by using [icon]. Its functionality was added primarily for character animators who used this methodology in other packages. Press <'> (single apostrophe) as a shortcut to toggle on the mode.</td>
</tr>
<tr>
<td>Previous/ Play/ Next</td>
<td>Enable you to play an animation in your viewport(s) and advance to the next or previous frame/key.

• When you click [icon] (Play Animation), the software plays the animation in the active viewport and replaces this icon with [icon] (Stop Animation).

• [icon] (Play Animation) is a flyout and contains [icon] (Play Selected), which only plays the selected objects in the active viewport.</td>
</tr>
</table>

*When either **Auto Key** mode or **Set Key** mode is active, their corresponding buttons display in red, indicating that you are in the animation mode.*

(Key Mode Toggle)	Enables you to move between frames or keys. • When you are in Key mode (active), the Previous and Next icons display as [icons] and enable you to jump to the previous or next keyframe. • Keyframes are set in the Time Configuration dialog box (Key Steps area). When Key mode is off, the Previous and Next icons are displayed as [icons] and you can jump to the previous and next frame.
(Go to Start)/ (Go to End)	Enable you to move directly to the beginning or end of an animation. The time slider jumps to the selected location.
86 (Current Frame)	Enables you to advance to a specific frame or time in the animation.
Key Filters...	Opens the Set Key Filters dialog box, which enables you to select the tracks on which the keys can be created. The track sets are created with the **Set Key** mode. The Selected drop-down list contains the created track sets and selection sets and enables you to select the required one quickly.
(Default In/Out Tangents for New Keys)	Contains a list of tangent types.
(Time Configuration)	Opens the Time Configuration dialog box.

Time Configuration

Clicking (Time Configuration) opens the Time Configuration dialog box (as shown in Figure 12–6) where you assign an animation, its length, playback rate, and other critical parameters. It is recommended to adjust these parameters before you start configuring an animation.

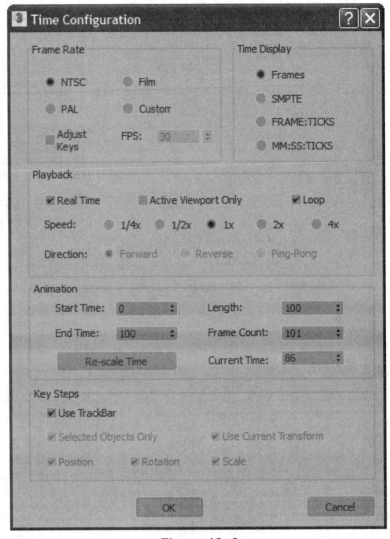

Figure 12–6

The *Frame Rate* area provides options to define how many still frames to show per second (FPS). When setting a frame rate, the goal is to create an animation that flows smoothly without rendering additional frames. The best choice for frame rate depends on the medium where you intend to play your animation.

NTSC	**National Television Standards Committee:** the standard television frame rate used across most of the Americas and Japan: 30 FPS.
PAL	**Phase Alternate Line:** the standard used across Europe: 25 FPS.
Film	Assigns the frame rate used in film production: 24 FPS.
Custom	Enables you to select a specific frame rate. Animations created for desktop and web-based presentations are often set 12-25 FPS.

The *Time Display* area provides options to select how you want to measure time during your animation.

Frames	Measures time in the number of frames that have elapsed since the beginning of the animation.
SMPTE	The time measurement standard used by the Society of Motion Picture Technical Engineers for video and television productions. This standard measures time in minutes, seconds, and frames separated by colons (such as 1:22:43).
FRAME:TICKS	Measures time in frames and ticks only. A tick is a unit of animated time that equals 1/4800 of a second.
MM:SS:TICKS	Measures time in minutes, seconds and ticks.

The *Playback* area provides options to control how the animation is played back in the viewports.

Real Time	Plays the animation at the real world playback rate, skipping frames, if required. Clearing this option displays all frames in sequence, even if it slows down the animation preview. This is used by most animators to inspect every frame for problems.
Speed	When **Real Time** is enabled, speed up or slow down the animation using this option or continually play using the **Loop** option.
Direction	When not using **Real Time** you can select to play the animation forwards, backwards, or ping-pong (forwards and backwards again) using the **Direction** option.
Active Viewport Only	Limits the animation preview to the active viewport, which might be required if system resources are taxed by the animation playback.

The options in the *Animation* area define the active time segment (the current animation length) between the starting and ending time.

Start Time	Can be equal to 0, a positive, or negative time value as required.
End Time	Can be equal to 0, a positive, or negative time value as required.
Length	The calculated time between the starting and ending points.
Frame Count	A value equal to the animation length + 1 frame, to account for the rendering of frame 0.

Current Time	Provides the frame you are on in the animation. Use this field to change to a different frame without exiting the dialog box.

When animation times are changed in this dialog box, the existing keys do not automatically scale to the new time. For example, if you lengthen an existing animation by increasing the end time, the current animation still stops at the old end time (unless you then manually adjust the keys).

To expand or contract an animation's overall length, click **Re-scale Time**, to open the Rescale Time dialog box, as shown in Figure 12–7. Changing the animation times spaces the existing keys along the new animation length.

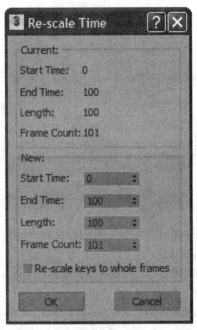

Figure 12–7

The *Key Steps* area provides options to limit how and which animation keys are created in Key mode. Leave the **Use TrackBar** option enabled to not limit key creation.

Progressive Display and Adaptive Degradation

The Progressive Display (only for Nitrous drivers) and Adaptive Degradation is a display option that can be very useful when playing animations in the viewport or when navigating large files

in the viewport. When enabled (in the Status Bar, click , or use <O> to toggle it on/off) it degrades an animation preview to a simpler display method to display the correct playback rate. It enables you to play a complex animation in a viewport at the correct speed, even if it means simplifying the display to a less detailed display mode, such as wireframe.

If you are using one of the legacy display drivers (Direct3D or Open GL), the Adaptive Degradation tab replaces the Display Performance tab in the Viewport Configuration dialog box.

In the Status Bar, right-click on 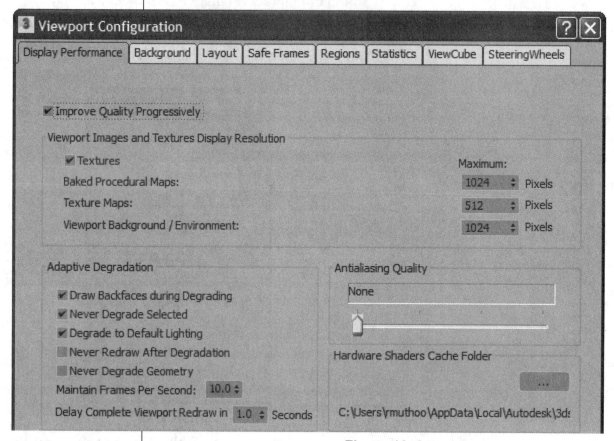 (Adaptive Degradation) to open the Viewport Configuration dialog box in the *Display Performance* tab, as shown in Figure 12–8. You can also open this dialog box by selecting **Views>Viewport Configuration** and then selecting the *Display Performance* tab. Alternatively, in the Viewport label, click [+] to display the label menu and select **Configure Viewports**. Using the menu bar or the Viewport label menu opens the dialog box in the *Visual Style & Appearance* tab. Select the *Display Performance* tab.

Figure 12–8

Improve Quality Progressively

This option (only available for Nitrous display drivers) enables you to improve the viewport quality through successive iterations. Once the iterations have been completed, a high quality rendered image is displayed in the viewport. You can also activate or clear this option in the menu bar (**Views> Progressive Display**).

Viewport Images and Textures Display Resolution

This area contains the following options:

Baked Procedural Maps	Enables you to set the resolution, in pixels, that is used to display the procedural maps in the viewports.
Texture Maps	Enables you to set the resolution in pixels, that is used to display the texture maps in the viewports.
Viewport Background / Environment	Enables you to set the resolution in pixels, that is used to display the environment and background maps.

Adaptive Degradation

The *Adaptive Degradation* area has the following options:

- When **Draw Backfaces during Degrade** is toggled on, the software draws the backface polygons while degrading the objects.

- When **Never Degrade Selected** is toggled on, the software does not degrade the selected objects.

- When **Degrade to Default Lighting** is toggled on, the software turns off all of the lights in the viewport with only the default lighting toggled on.

- When **Never Redraw after Degrade** is toggled on, the degraded objects display as is and do not redraw.

- When **Never Degrade Geometry** is toggled on, the geometry in the viewport is not degraded.

- The **Maintain Frames Per Second** option enables you to set the frame rate. The software maintains this frame rate through degradation.

- The **Delay Complete Viewport Redraw** option enables you to set a time in seconds, during which the viewports are not redrawn when degradation is complete.

> **Hint: Bitmap Proxy Images**
>
> Using Proxy images enables you to reduce the memory required for the 2D texture and increase the rendering speed. Expand Application Menu, select **References**, and select **Asset Tracking** to open the Asset Tracking dialog box. Use **Bitmap Performance and Memory>Global Settings** to set the proxy resolution.

Antialiasing Quality

Enables antialiasing in the viewport, which attempts to soften the rough edges in 3D Geometry. Note that higher quality settings can reduce system performance.

Hardware Shaders Cache Folder

The folder along with the complete path where the hardware shaders are saved is displayed. Click **...** to open the Configure System Paths dialog box and select a different location for saving your hardware shaders.

12.2 Walkthrough Animation

When animating cameras, it is often easier to have a camera follow a linear path than to configure the camera's position manually. For example, in Figure 12–9, you can animate a camera following a path going up a street to the house.

Figure 12–9

- To animate a target camera following a path, you create a helper object called a Dummy object, as shown in Figure 12–10. While a Dummy object is not required, it provides more control.

- The path can be a spline (shown in Figure 12–10) created in the Autodesk 3ds Max software or a linked/imported object. You then create a target camera and Dummy object and align them so they share a similar orientation. Multiple paths can be assigned and weighted during an animation.

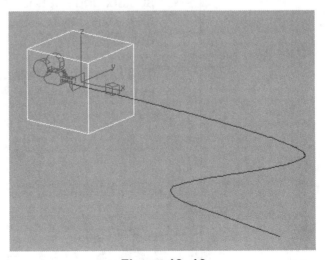

Figure 12–10

- To create a Dummy object, in the Command Panel>Create panel (➕), click ◢ (Helpers). In the Object Type rollout, click **Dummy**. A Dummy object is usually drawn in the **Top** viewport to ensure orientation with world space. Dummies have no parameters in the Modify panel and do not render in your final animation.

- In the Main Toolbar, use 🔗 (Select and Link) to link the Camera and Dummy.

- To animate the Dummy object and Camera, define a Path Constraint (**Animation>Constraints>Path Constraint**). A dotted line displays in the viewport, as shown in Figure 12–11. Select the spline to be used as the path. If you cannot see the path, you can press <H> to select the path by name from the Select From Scene dialog box.

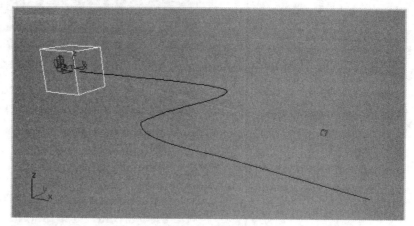

Figure 12–11

- Alternatively, the target object can be positioned over the subject and left unanimated. In this case, the target stays fixed over the building and the Dummy and Camera back animate along the path.

- The Dummy can follow the path using the **Follow** checkbox in the Motion panel.

Practice 12a

Creating a Turntable Animation

Practice Objective

Estimated time for completion: 20 minutes

- Animate a building by rotating a camera around it at keyframe intervals.

In this practice you will animate a camera rotating around the retail exterior building. You will add a dummy object on the building and set the key frames. Then apply rotation at the keyframes. You will then add interpolation to the keys using the dialog box and the Mini Curve Editor. This creates the illusion that the viewer is standing still and the building is revolving as if on a turntable.

You must set the paths to locate the External files and Xrefs used in the practice. If you have not done this already, return to **Chapter 1: Introduction to Autodesk 3ds Max** and complete Task 1 to Task 3 in **Practice 1a: Organizing Folders and Working with the Interface**. You only have to set the user paths once.

1. Open **Turntable_Animation_Start.max**.

2. Verify that the **Top** viewport is active and maximize it.

*If a dialog box opens prompting you about a File Load: Mismatch, click **OK** to accept the default values.*

3. Select the camera (**Turntable camera** is the only camera object) in the viewport. Click ![icon] (Zoom Extents All Selected) to display the camera, its target, and the entire building, as shown in Figure 12–12.

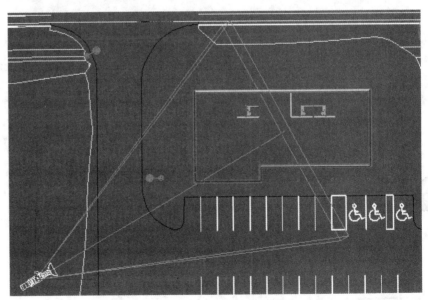

Figure 12–12

4. In the Command Panel>Create panel (![+]), click
   ![Helpers icon] (Helpers).

5. In the Object Type rollout, click **Dummy**. Starting from the camera target by clicking on the target (the small blue square in the center of the building), drag to create a dummy object (a square box) large enough to approximately extend beyond the two horizontal walls of the building, as shown in Figure 12–13.

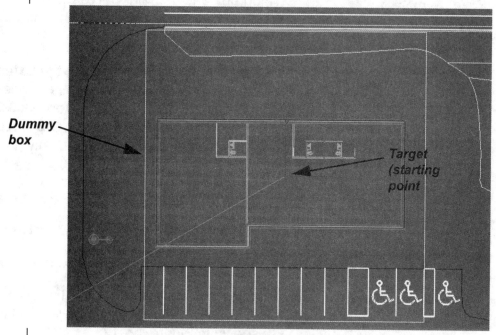

Figure 12–13

6. In the Main Toolbar, click ![link icon] (Select and Link). In the viewport, select **Turntable camera** (camera object). Note that the cursor displays as two linked squares when you hover it over the selected camera. Starting from the camera, click and drag the cursor to the Dummy object (box). A white dotted line displays between the camera and the dummy, as shown in Figure 12–14. Release the mouse to link the camera to the dummy.

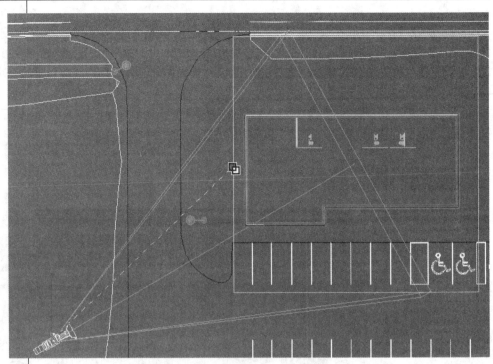

Figure 12–14

7. To test it, click ⊕ (Select and Move) and move the Dummy object. The camera should move with it. Undo the move after the test and click 🔲 (Select Object) to exit the **Move** command.

8. In the Animation playback controls, click 🕐 (Time Configuration) to open the dialog box. Set the following:

   • *Time Display*: **Frames**
   • *Animation* area - *End Time*: **99**

9. Click **OK**. Near the bottom of the viewport, note that the Time Slider displays as **0/99**.

10. Using the layout overlay, maximize the **Turntable camera** viewport.

11. In the Animation controls, click **Auto Key** (it displays in red) and drag the Time Slider to **frame 33**. The Track Bar displays a blue rectangle at frame 33, as shown in Figure 12–15.

Figure 12–15

*Click **Auto Key**. It displays in red, indicating that you are in the **Auto Key** animation mode. The slider bar area displays in red and a red border surrounds the current viewport.*

You can also use the Rotate gizmo to rotate the dummy object horizontally until the values on the screen display as [0.00, -0.00, -120.00].

12. In the Scene Explorer, using  (Display None) and (Display Helpers), select **Dummy001**. Verify that Dummy001 is displayed in the Name and Color rollout.

13. Click (Select and Rotate). In the Status Bar, in the *Z* field, enter **-120**, and press <Enter>, so that the building is rotated as shown in Figure 12–16.

Figure 12–16

14. Drag the Time Slider to frame **66** and rotate the dummy object another 120 degrees, by entering **-240** in the *Z* field of the Status Bar and press <Enter>, as shown in Figure 12–17.

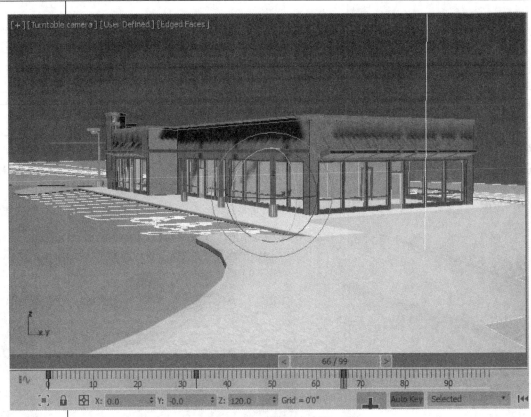

Figure 12–17

15. Drag the Time Slider to frame **99** and rotate the dummy object another 120 degrees, by entering **-360** in the *Z* field. Press <Enter>.

16. Play the animation by clicking ▶. Note that there is a pause with each revolution of the camera. Stop the animation by clicking ⏸.

17. If your animation has a lag, in the Status Bar, click ⬡ (Adaptive Degradation).

The working of the Adaptive degradation depends on your system configuration. You might not see the wireframe model while using Adaptive Degradation.

18. In the Animation controls, click ▶. Note that over time, the objects change into a wireframe model and animate smoothly. Stop the animation by clicking ⏸. Note that the model is redrawn as shaded almost immediately.

19. Right-click on ⬡ (Adaptive Degradation) to open the Viewport Configuration dialog box in the *Display Performance* tab. In the *Adaptive Degradation* area, set *Delay Complete Viewport Redraw in* to **5.0** seconds. Click **OK** to close the dialog box

If the animated object is not selected, the modified keys (green) is not displayed in the timeline.

20. Click 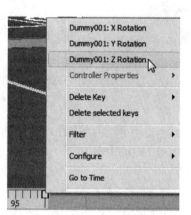. Let the animation play in the viewport until the complete model has been degraded to a wireframe model and then click ▣. Note that the model remains a wireframe for 5 seconds before it is redrawn as a shaded model.

21. Verify that the Dummy object is selected. To fix the pause at each revolution, right-click on the green key in the timeline at frame 99 and select **Dummy001: Z Rotation**, as shown in Figure 12–18. You can Pause the animation, if it is still running.

22. In the dialog box that opens, expand the *In* interpolation to display the interpolation tools flyout, as shown in

Figure 12–19. Click ⟋ (Linear interpolation).

Figure 12–18

Figure 12–19

23. Similarly, change the *Out* interpolation to ⟍ (Linear interpolation), as shown in Figure 12–20.
    - This sets the interpolation to Linear at frame 4 (99).

24. You will set the interpolation to Linear for the other three frames (0, 33, 66). In the upper left corner of the dialog box,

    click ◄ (left arrow) (as shown in Figure 12–20), to advance to key **1**, which is the key number. The *Time* displays as **1** and the *Value* displays as **0.0**, as shown in Figure 12–21. Set the *In* and *Out* Interpolation to **Linear** for key 1.

Figure 12–20

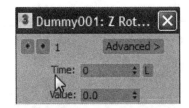

Figure 12–21

25. Repeat for the remaining keys **2** and **3** (frames 33 and 66),

    using ![icon] (right arrow) to move to the required key. Close the dialog box.

26. Click ![play icon] to play the animation. It should loop without any pause.

27. Click ![pause icon] to stop the animation.

28. In the Main toolbar, click ![Track View icon] (Track View) to open the Curve Editor. It displays the key window (right side) containing keys (small gray squares) and the linear slanting line (blue line) that displays the animation, as shown in Figure 12–22. You might have to zoom and pan inside the key window for the keys to display.

29. Hover the cursor over the Controller window (left side). It displays as a **Hand** icon. Hold and drag it up until the dummy object is listed with its applied Transforms, as shown in Figure 12–22.

30. In the Rotation node of the dummy object, select **X Rotation**, **Y Rotation**, and **Z Rotation**, if not already selected, as shown in Figure 12–22.

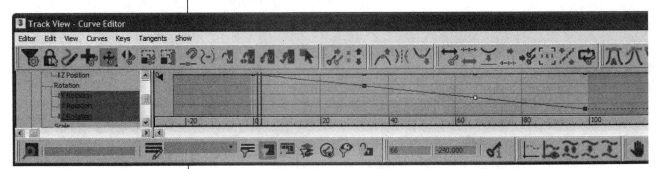

Figure 12–22

The selected key in the Curve Editor is represented as white in color.

31. In the Key window, on the blue line, select the key (small gray square) at frame 33. It displays in white indicating that it has been selected, as shown in Figure 12–23. In the Curve Editor toolbar, click (Set Tangents to Slow).
   - Note that a slight curve is added at this frame 33.

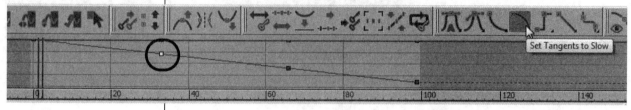

Figure 12–23

32. Click ▶ to play the animation and note that the animation slows down slightly when it reaches frame 33. Click ⏸ to stop the animation.

33. Add **Set Tangents to Slow** to the keys at frame 0, 66, and 99. Slight curves are added to these frames, as shown in Figure 12–24.

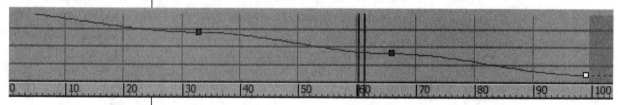

Figure 12–24

34. Click ▶ to play the animation and click ⏸ to stop.

35. Click **Close** at the left end of the Curve Editor toolbar to close the Curve Editor.

36. Save your work as **MyTurntable_Animation.max**.

Practice 12b

Keyframing a Camera Animation

Practice Objective

- Animate a camera to fly over the site.

In this practice you will add a camera to the scene and set the animation for the camera. You will then modify the animation by creating a new key and modifying the camera position at this key. This approach is similar to manually configuring a walkthrough or driveby animation.

You must set the paths to locate the External files and Xrefs used in the practice. If you have not done this already, return to **Chapter 1: Introduction to Autodesk 3ds Max** and complete Task 1 to Task 3 in **Practice 1a: Organizing Folders and Working with the Interface**. You only have to set the user paths once.

Task 1 - Save the Previous Render Options as a Preset.

1. Open **Presets.max**.

2. Before you configure the animation you should save all of the rendering settings for the still rendering. In the Render Shortcuts toolbar, in the Presets drop-down list, select **Save Preset**, as shown in Figure 12–25.

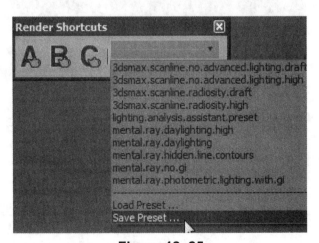

Figure 12–25

3. In the Render Presets Save dialog box, in the *File name* edit box, enter **Retail_Exterior_with_Background** to save your current render settings and click **Save**.

4. In the Select Preset Categories dialog box that opens, leave all of the preset categories as highlighted and click **Save**.

Task 2 - Configure the Camera Animation.

1. Maximize the **Top** viewport and zoom out till the building, parking lot, and the end of the road on the left side is displayed.

2. In the Command Panel>Create panel (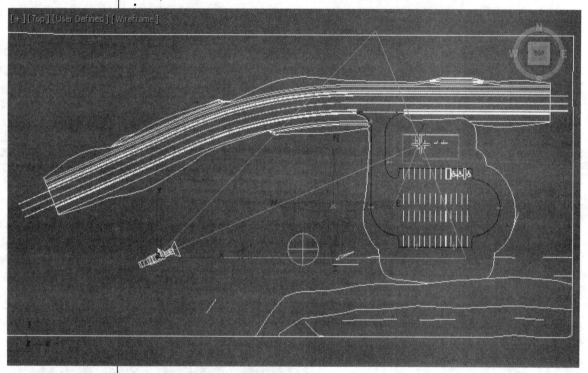), click

   (Cameras). In the Object Type rollout, click **Target**. Create a camera and the target in the approximate positions, as shown in Figure 12–26.

Figure 12–26

3. With the new camera selected, select the Modify panel

   ( ). Leave the camera with the default parameters but change its name to **Camera - Flyover**.

4. Maximize to display all four viewports. Right-click in the **Front** viewport to activate it. Change that view to show the **Camera - Flyover** view (as shown in Figure 12–27) by selecting the **Front** Point of View label and selecting **Cameras>Camera – Flyover**.

Figure 12–27

5. In the Animation controls, click 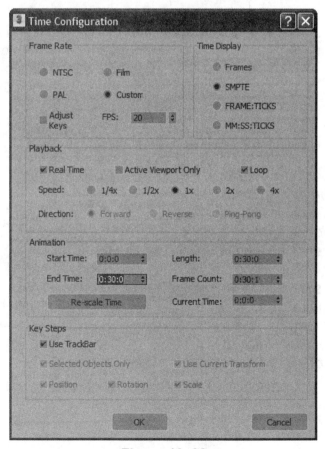 (Time Configuration). In the *Frame Rate* area, select **Custom**, set *FPS* to **20**, and in the *Animation* area, set *End Time* to **0:30:0**, as shown in Figure 12–28. Verify that all of the other values match the values in Figure 12–28. Your animation is 30 seconds long and intended for desktop playback at 20 FPS. Click **OK**.

Figure 12–28

6. Verify that the Time Slider is currently located at time **0:0:0**, as shown in Figure 12–29.

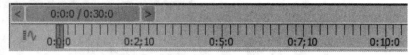

Figure 12–29

7. Click **Auto Key**. It displays in red. Note that the Time Slider and outline of **Camera - Flyover** viewport also display in red.

8. Drag the Time Slider all of the way to the *end time* of **0:30:0**, as shown in Figure 12–30. Note the blue marker on the scale.

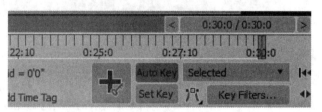

Figure 12–30

9. Verify that the **Camera - Flyover** object is selected (note the name in the Modifier Stack. Click 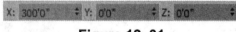 (Select and Move) and in the Status Bar, in the *Transform Type-In* area enter **X = 300'0"**, **Y = 0'0"**, and **Z = 0'0"**, as shown in Figure 12–31. The roundoff error might change your X-coordinate to a value just below 300' (this often happens, but does not significantly affect this animation).

Figure 12–31

*If you do not click **Auto Key** again to toggle the mode off, you create an unintended animation. The camera's animation keys are visible along the time slider as colored boxes (as long as the camera is selected). Right-click to modify or delete a key.*

10. Click **Auto Key** again to toggle off Auto Key mode.

11. Slide (scrub) the Time Slider left and right and watch the camera move. With the **Camera - Flyover** viewport active,

click ▶ to see a preview of the animation.

12. ▶ is changed while the animation is playing. Stop the

animation by clicking ▮▮. Move to the beginning by clicking

◄◄ .

Task 3 - Modify the Animation by Adding a New Key.

You are currently skimming at elevation 0 which makes you fly directly through some slopes of the terrain. To make the animation look more like a flyover you will add another key in the middle of the animation and raise the camera up in the Z-direction at that point.

1. Verify that the **Camera – Flyover** camera is selected.

2. Move the Time Slider to exactly **0:15:0** (the midpoint of the animation) and click ➕ (Set Keys). A new key is created at this point.

3. In the Time Slider, right-click on this new key and select **Camera – Flyover: Z Position**. Set the *Value* to **30'0"**, press <Enter> and close the dialog box.

4. Click ⏮ to return to the beginning and click ▶ to preview the animation. Note the vertical change has been adjusted but now at around the midpoint the camera is too close to the building. You will pull the camera back from the building at the midpoint. Stop the animation by clicking ⏸

5. Drag the Time Slider to exactly **0:15:0** and click **Auto Key**.

6. Right-click in the **Top** viewport and verify that the **Camera – Flyover** camera is still selected (if not, then select it). Click ✥ (Select and Move) and in the Status Bar, in the *Transform Type-In* area, set the following, as shown in Figure 12–32:
   - *X:* **15'0"**
   - *Y:* **-120'0"**
   - *Z:* **30'0"**

   This moves the **Camera – Flyover** camera away from the building. Since this is done in **AutoKey** mode the camera's existing key at 0:15:0 is updated with this new position.

Figure 12–32

If done without being in Auto Key mode you would move the camera at frame 0 and at all other keys.

7. Click **Auto Key** to toggle it off. Click ⏮ to return to the beginning and click ▶ to preview the animation. Stop the animation by clicking ⏸.

8. Click 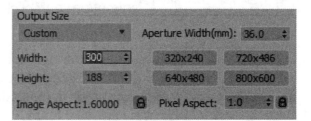 (Render Setup) to open the Render Setup dialog box. In the *Common* tab, in the Common Parameters rollout, *Output Size* area, set *Width* to **300** and press <Enter>, as shown in Figure 12–33. With the aspect ratio locked at 1.6 a rendering *Height* of **188** is automatically calculated.

Figure 12–33

9. In the *Time Output* area select **Active Time Segment** (entire animation). Normally you select a filename and location to render to.

10. Near the top of the dialog box, in the Preset drop-down menu, select **Save Preset** and save the rendering settings as **RetailExteriorAnimation.rps**. Save all preset categories.

11. Save the file as **MyCameraAnimationFlyover.max**.

Practice 12c

Creating a Walkthrough Animation

Estimated time for completion: 10 minutes

Practice Objective

- Animate a camera object along a path in a scene.

In this practice you will merge a .MAX file, which has a hemispherical dome with a simple sky texture and ground color applied to be used as a background for the current scene. You will also merge a file in which the path has been created.

You must set the paths to locate the External files and Xrefs used in the practice. If you have not done this already, return to **Chapter 1: Introduction to Autodesk 3ds Max** and complete Task 1 to Task 3 in **Practice 1a: Organizing Folders and Working with the Interface**. You only have to set the user paths once.

*If a dialog box opens prompting you about a File Load: Mismatch, click **OK** to accept the default values.*

1. Open **Camera Animations.max**.

2. In the **Application Menu>Import**, select **Merge**. In the dialog box, select **Sky and Ground Dome.max** from your practice files folder. Click **Open**.

3. In the Merge dialog box, select **Sky and Ground Dome** and click **OK**.
   - The Dome object has been turned inside-out by the normal modifier so that in single-sided rendering mode its surfaces can only be seen from the inside. This enables the dome to be seen in the renderings when a camera is inside the dome.

4. In the **Application Menu>Import>Merge**, select **Animation Path.max**. Click **Open**.

5. In the Merge dialog box, select **Animation Path 3D** and click **OK**. This 3D path is located along the proposed ground surface of the access road, as shown in Figure 12–34.

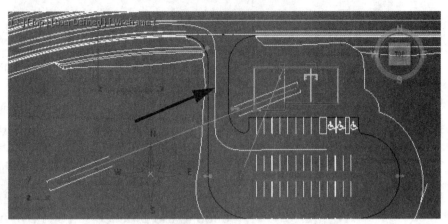

Figure 12–34

6. Maximize the **Top** viewport.

7. Using the Scene Explorer, select the object group **_Site Model** ((Display None) and (Display Groups)).

8. Right-click in the viewport and select **Freeze Selection** in the quad menu. The Site model geometry displays in a dull gray color and you can easily see the blue path that travels along the street. If required, use **Pan** to display the complete path in the viewport.

9. In the Command Panel>Create panel ( ), click

 (Cameras). In the Object Type rollout, click **Target**. Click near the left end of the path to place the camera, drag to the center of the building and release to set the target, as shown in Figure 12–35. In the Name and Color edit box, enter the name of the camera as **Walkthrough_Cam01**.

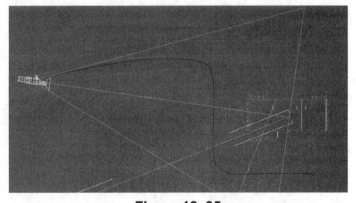

Figure 12–35

10. In the viewport, zoom into the Camera object. Click in the viewport to clear any selection.

11. In the Command Panel>Create panel (), click

    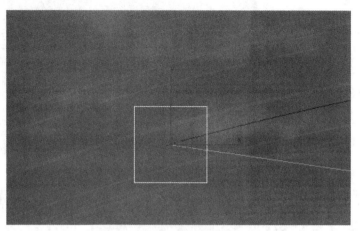 (Helpers). Click **Dummy**.

If you were flying a camera through the interior of a design you would align the camera to the dummy at this point. In this animation it is not required for this type of exterior flyby.

12. Click and drag to create the Dummy object around the Camera by starting at the beginning of the animation path spline, as shown in Figure 12–36.

Figure 12–36

13. In the Main Toolbar, click 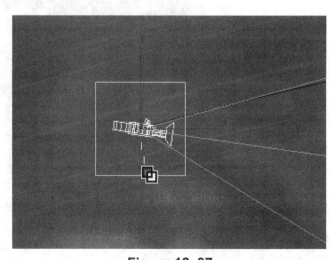 (Select and Link).

14. In the viewport, select and hold the newly created **Walkthrough_Cam01** object to define it as the child object. Drag the cursor to the outline of the **Dummy**. A dotted line displays between the cursor and the object, and the dummy object turns yellow, as shown in Figure 12–37. Release to link the camera to the **Dummy**.

Figure 12–37

When you hover the cursor over the path, it should turn yellow to show that it is going to be selected. Once it turns yellow, click to select it.

15. To check it, in the Main Toolbar, click 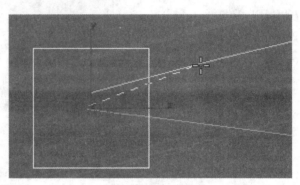 and move the Dummy. You should see the Camera move with it. This confirms that the linkage is correct. Undo the move.

16. Now you will constrain the dummy to the path. Select the Dummy object in the viewport and select **Animation> Constraints>Path Constraint**. The cursor is connected with a dotted line to the pivot point of the Dummy object. Click anywhere over the blue spline (Animation Path 3D) to select it as the animation path, as shown in Figure 12–38. The pivot point of the dummy automatically shifts to coincide with the start point of the path.

Figure 12–38

17. Zoom out till the entire blue path is displayed. Click 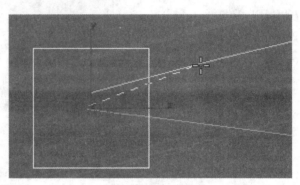 to play the animation. The Dummy and the camera animates along the path, as shown in Figure 12–39. Click 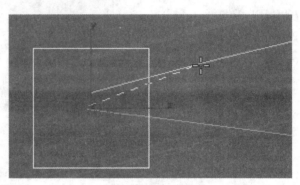 to stop the animation.

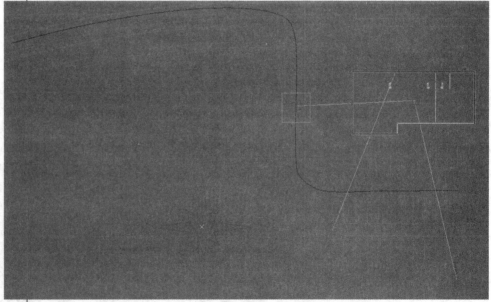

Figure 12–39

18. Maximize to display all four viewports. Activate the **Camera01** viewport and change it to the **Walkthrough_Cam01** viewport (select the **POV** label and select **Cameras>Walkthrough_Cam01**).

19. Click ► to play the animation. The animation might be improved if the camera was higher off the ground.

20. Click |◄◄ to go to the start of the animation, at frame zero.

Use the Scene Explorer, use ■ (Display Cameras) and select **Walkthrough_Cam01,** *child of* **Dummy001**.

21. Since the Camera is a child of the Dummy you can add transforms to the Camera without affecting the Dummy's animation. Select **Walkthrough_Cam01.Target** object and in the Modify panel rename it as **Camera_Flyby**.

22. With the **Camera_Flyby** object selected, in the Main Toolbar, right-click on ✛ (Select and Move) to open the Move Transform Type-In dialog box.

23. In the Absolute:World, change the Z-value to **6'0"**. Close the dialog box. Since **Auto Key** is off this lifts the Camera for the entire animation.

24. Play the animation in the **Camera_Flyby** viewport. Stop the animation.

25. Right-click on the viewport and select **Unfreeze All**. The Site model is displayed with full color. Play the animation again.

26. Save your work as **MyCameraAnimationFlyby.max**.

12.3 Animation Output

There are two strategies for creating animation output:

- Render directly to a single, composite animation file such as a .MOV or .AVI. This is generally recommended for previews.

- Render each still image (such as .PNG, .JPEG, .BMP, .TIFF, etc.) and later combine the stills into a composite animation using the Autodesk 3ds Max RAM Player, Video Post, or 3rd party post-production software.

You can select an animation output option in the Render Output File dialog box. To open this dialog box, open the Render Setup dialog box and expand the Common Parameters rollout in the *Common* tab. In the *Render Output* area, click **Files...**, as shown in Figure 12–40.

Figure 12–40

The Render Output File dialog box opens. In the Save as type drop-down list (shown in Figure 12–41), you can select to render to a single, compressed animation file (.MOV or .AVI) or to individual frames (such as .PNG, .JPEG, .BMP, .TIFF, etc.). If you select to render as individual frames, you need to provide the name once and the software automatically creates individual files for each frame, which are numbered sequentially.

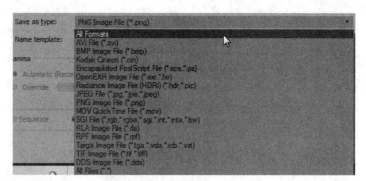

Figure 12–41

Assembling Animations

It is recommended to render files individually and then combine them into an animation. The Autodesk 3ds Max RAM player is a utility used for comparing two images side-by-side, or for previewing and compiling animations.

The RAM player (shown in Figure 12–42) can be opened in the menu bar by selecting **Rendering>Compare Media in RAM Player**.

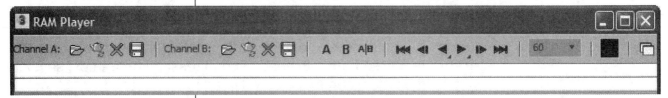

Figure 12–42

Click 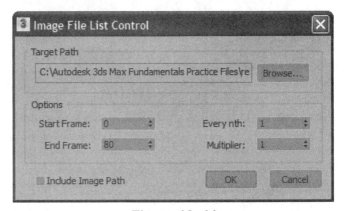 (Open Channel A) to open the Open File dialog box, shown in Figure 12–43. Enter the path and the first filename of the sequentially numbered image files. Selecting the **Sequence** option opens all of the files, which are named as specified in the *File name* field.

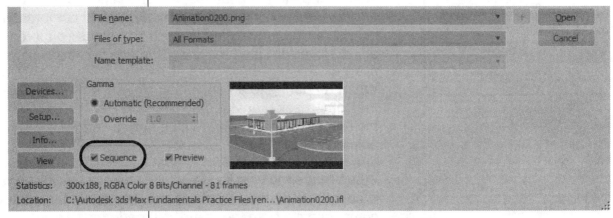

Figure 12–43

An image file list (.IFL) is an ASCII list of which files were used and in which order.

Once you open the specified image file, the Image File List Control dialog box opens (as shown in Figure 12–44), which displays the folder where the image file list (.IFL) is being created. The dialog box also provides you with options to limit the animation to certain frames.

Figure 12–44

Use the various playback options in the RAM Player to play the created animation.

Rendering files individually and then combining them into an animation later has various advantages, such as:

- A lot of time is spent calculating the information to create a rendered frame. Instead of compressing the frames, save them as a sequence of still images for access to all of the information later.

- When rendering individual frames, all of the previously saved frames remain available after a catastrophic error such as a system crash, disc error, power outage, etc. Therefore, you only need to re-render the missing frames required to complete your animation.

- When rendering animations, material, lighting or geometry, errors might occur in certain frames. Unlike compressed animation files, rendering to frames enables you to easily adjust, fix errors, and re-render the affected frames.

- When rendering to an animation file you need to first select the compression or video quality settings. If you do not like the results, select another value and re-render the entire animation.

- When rendering to stills, select a quality value after rendering is complete to try different settings and save out another composite file from the same still renderings.

- Rendering to a still image file format that supports an alpha channel (transparency) enables you to use a compositing package such as Combustion or Adobe After Effects for post-production processing and assembly.

Practice 12d

Creating Animation Output

Practice Objective

- Create an animation preview and create single-frame file images.

In this practice you create single-frame file images at 5 frame intervals and save them as .PNG file format. You will then assemble the individual frame images to create a movie using the RAM Player.

Estimated time for completion: 15 minutes

You must set the paths to locate the External files and Xrefs used in the practice. If you have not done this already, return to **Chapter 1: Introduction to Autodesk 3ds Max** and complete Task 1 to Task 3 in **Practice 1a: Organizing Folders and Working with the Interface**. You only have to set the user paths once.

Task 1 - Create Still Frames.

If a dialog box opens prompting you about a File Load: Mismatch, click OK to accept the default values.

1. Open **Camera_Animation_Start_Render.max**.

2. Make the **Camera - Flyover** viewport active.

3. Click ![icon] (Time Configuration) to open the Time Configuration dialog box. Change the *Time Display* to **Frames**.

4. In the *Animation* area, note that the *End Time* is set to **600** indicating that you have a 600 frame animation. Click **OK**.

5. Note that the *Time slider* should display as **0/600**, but it does not. Open the Time Configuration dialog box again (![icon]) and click **Re-scale Time** in the *Animation* area. The Re-scale Time dialog box opens. Click **OK** in both of the dialog boxes, and note that the *Time slider* is updated to display **0/600**.

*Rendering 600 frames might take a long time. You can select a shorter range and set the **Every Nth Frame** option to make it manageable.*

6. Click 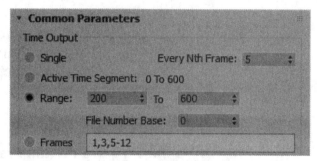 (Render Setup) to open the Render Setup dialog box. In the *Common* tab, verify that the Common Parameters rollout is expanded and do the following, as shown in Figure 12–45:

    *   In the *Time Output* area, select **Range**.
    *   Set a *Range* of **200** to **600**.
    *   Set *Every Nth Frame* to **5**.

    This renders every 5th frame between 200 and 600, which is a total of 81 frames of animation.

Figure 12–45

In the Render Output File dialog box, in the Save as type drop-down list, you can select to render to a single, compressed animation file (.MOV, .AVI), or to individual frames. If you select a single-frame file format (such as .PNG, .JPEG, .BMP, .TIFF, etc.), you will then automatically create individual files for each frame, numbered sequentially.

7. In the *Render Output* area, click **Files...**.

8. The Render Output File dialog box opens. Locate the *...\renderings* folder. Set the *Save as type* to **PNG Image File (*.png)**, and in the *File name* enter the name **Animation**. Click **Save**.

9. In the PNG Configuration dialog box, select **RGB 24 bit** and leave **Alpha channel** enabled. Click **OK**.

10. In the Render Setup dialog box, click **Render** to begin creating individual renderings for each frame.

11. The Rendered Frame Window opens with each frame being rendered and the Rendering dialog box opens (as shown in Figure 12–46), displaying information about the renderings, number of files to be rendered, estimate of the remaining rendering time, render settings, etc.

    *   It might take some time to complete the 81 frames of the animation, so you can stop the process with some frames completed or let it continue until all of the frames have completed.

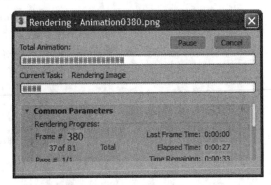

Figure 12–46

12. Close the Rendered Frame Window and Render Setup dialog box.

Task 2 - Assemble the Final Animation.

It is called a RAM player because it loads these images into RAM.

1. In the menu bar, select **Rendering>Compare Media in RAM Player** to open the RAM player. The RAM player is a utility used for comparing two images side-by-side or previewing and compiling animations.

2. In the *Channel A* area, click   (Open Channel A), as shown in Figure 12–47.

Figure 12–47

3. In the Open File, Channel A dialog box, browse to the ...*renderings* folder. Select **Animation0200.png** and verify that **Sequence** is enabled, as shown in Figure 12–48. Click **Open**.

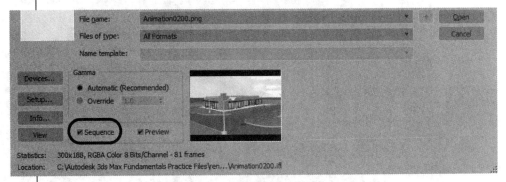

Figure 12–48

- The **Sequence** option enables the system to open all of the PNGs named **Animation*.png**.

4. The Image File List Control dialog box opens, as shown in Figure 12–49. It displays the folder where the image file list (.IFL) is being created. Click **OK**.

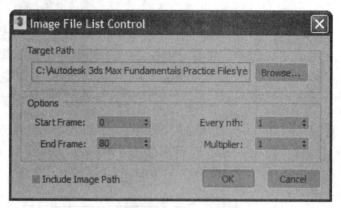

Figure 12–49

5. The RAM Player Configuration dialog box opens. It enables you to change the image size or aspect ratio on import, and to limit the number of frames to use and the maximum amount of RAM you want to dedicate to this process. Click **OK**.

6. After the animation has loaded into the RAM player you can play back the animation at different frame rates by selecting a number in the drop-down list, as shown in Figure 12–50.

   Click ▶ (Playback Forward) to play the animation. Select different frame rates and play the animation to see the effect.

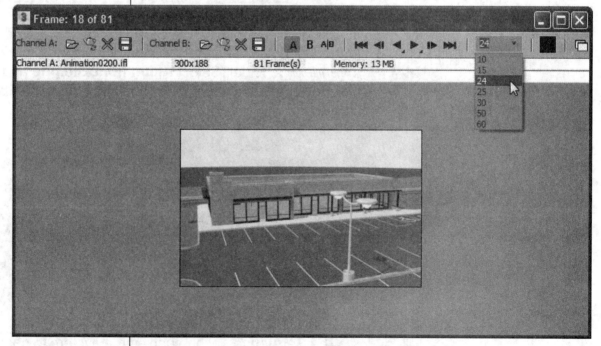

Figure 12–50

7. To save a desktop animation file, click ▣ (Save Channel A).

8. In the Save File, Channel A dialog box, browse to the ...*renderings* folder. Set *Save as type* to **AVI File (*.avi)**. Save the animation as **FlybyAnimation**.

9. In the AVI File Compression Setup dialog box, for the *Compressor*, select **MJPEG Compressor**, set the *Quality* to **60**, and click **OK**.

10. Save your work as **MyCameraAnimation.max**.

11. Navigate to your renderings folder and play **Flyby Animation.avi** file to watch the animation.

If the quality of the animation is not as required, you could try other methods or qualities until you have an acceptable result.

Chapter Review Questions

1. Activating (toggling on) which option in the Animation Controls changes **Previous**, **Play**, **Next Frame** (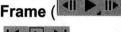) to **Previous**, **Play**, and **Next Keyframe** (⏮ ⏯ ⏭)?

   a. **Auto Key** animation mode

   b. **Set Key** animation mode

   c. ⬌ (Key Mode)

   d. ➕ (Set Keys)

2. A frame rate of 30 frames per second (FPS) is best suited for which medium?

   a. NTSC

   b. PAL

   c. Film

   d. Custom

3. When animation times are changed in the *Animation* area in the Time Configuration dialog box, the existing keys automatically scale to the new time.

   a. True

   b. False

4. Which category in the Create panel (➕) contains **Dummy** as its Object Type?

   a. ⬤ (Geometry)

   b. ⬛ (Shapes)

   c. ◼ (Cameras)

   d. ◣ (Helpers)

5. If you render each still image (such as .PNG, .JPEG, etc.), which utility can you use to combine the stills into a composite animation?

    a. Media Player

    b. RAM Player

    c. Batch Render

    d. Panorama Exporter

Command Summary

Button	Command	Location
Auto Key	Auto Key animation mode	• **Animation Controls Toolbar**
	Cameras	• **Command Panel:** *Create* panel • **Create:** Cameras
	Curve Editor	• **Main Toolbar** • **Graph Editors:** Track View - Curve Editor
	Default In/Out Tangents for New Keys	• **Animation Controls Toolbar**
N/A	Dope Sheet	• **Graph Editors:** Track View - Dope Sheet
	Go to End	• **Animation Controls Toolbar**
	Go to Start	• **Animation Controls Toolbar**
	Helpers	• **Command Panel:** *Create* panel
	Key Mode	• **Animation Controls Toolbar**
	Mini Curve Editor	• **Track bar**
	Previous, Play, Next Frame	• **Animation Controls Toolbar**
	Progressive Display	• **Status Bar**
	Render Setup	• **Main Toolbar** • **Rendering:** Render Setup
	Select and Link	• **Main Toolbar**
Set Key	Set Key animation mode	• **Animation Controls Toolbar**
	Set Keys	• **Animation Controls Toolbar**
	Time Configuration	• **Animation Controls Toolbar**

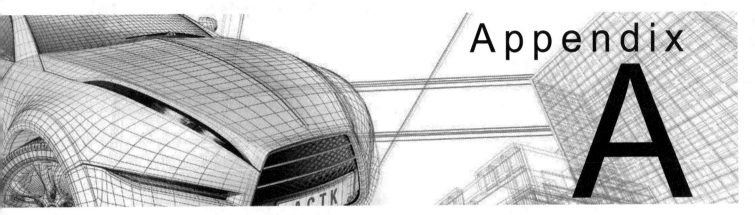

Optional Topics

There are some additional tools available in the Autodesk® 3ds Max® software that you can use when creating and rendering models. This appendix provides details about several additional tools and commands.

Learning Objectives in this Appendix

- Access Autodesk 3ds Max Help and use the various Help tools.
- Work with Architectural materials and the Compact Material Editor.
- Replace objects in a scene with AutoCAD® blocks or other Autodesk 3ds Max objects.
- Create a Lighting Analysis using the Lighting Analysis Assistant.
- Create hierarchies by collecting objects together with parent/child relationship.
- Customize the user interface elements.

A.1 Getting Help with Autodesk 3ds Max

The Help menu contains an extensive list of help options, which are organized as submenus so that finding information is easy. Some of the available help options are as follows:

*You can also press <F1> or select **Help>Autodesk 3ds Max Help**.*

1. The **Autodesk 3ds Max Help** is robust, well illustrated, and often the fastest way to find what an option or parameter controls and how to use it. This help is in the form of HTML files at autodesk.com website. There are a variety of ways to access this help. In the InfoCenter, click or expand ▾ and select **3ds Max Help**.

2. The **Autodesk 3ds Max Tutorials** (select **Help>Tutorials**) offer thorough and comprehensive learning materials to get you started with almost all of the features in the Autodesk 3ds Max software. The tutorials are in the HTML format at autodesk.com website. You can download the Tutorials and the files required for the tutorials from http://www.autodesk.com/3dsmax-tutorials-scene-files-2016. Install the files on your local hard drive for use as you are completing the tutorials.

3. **3ds Max Communities:** Select **Help>3ds Max Communities>AREA Product Community** and **AREA Discussion Forums** provides a single location for users to closely interact. In addition to the Autodesk 3ds Max forum, the AREA contains forums for other entertainment products, such as Mudbox, Motionbuilder, FBX, Maya.

4. **3ds Max Services and Support**: Select **Help>3ds Max Services and Support>SupportCenter** to connect to the support site. It has many frequently updated technical support articles available. There might also be documents describing how to fix commonly occurring problem. Autodesk Subscription customers also have access to email support directly from Autodesk. You can also connect with other Autodesk 3ds Max users and share information using the Autodesk 3ds Max Facebook page.

5. **3ds Max Resources and Tools:** Select **Help>3ds Max Resources and Tools**, as shown in Figure A–1 to access White Papers, the downloadable Vegetation Library, a Keyboard Shortcut Map, etc.

6. **Feedback:** The Autodesk 3ds Max software provides various **Speak Back** options, as shown in Figure A–2. Selecting an option connects you to web pages for reporting a bug in the software or making a request for small enhancements and new features. It also enables you to activate the Desktop Analytics Program.

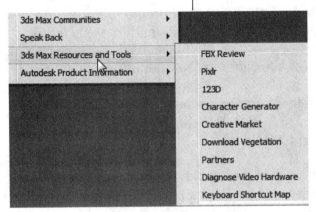

Figure A–1

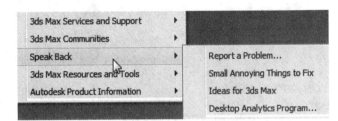

Figure A–2

7. **Other web communities:** There is a lot of information available on the Internet for the Autodesk 3ds Max software. Simple keyword searches can quickly find other sites that provide tutorials and helpful tips.

A.2 Compact Material Editor

- The Autodesk 3ds Max software contains two editors for working with materials:
  - Slate Material Editor: Used to design and build materials where the material components are displayed graphically.
  - Compact Material Editor: Used when the materials have already been created and you just need to apply them.

- The Compact Material Editor can be opened by clicking

  (Compact Material Editor) in the Main Toolbar (Material Editor flyout), or by selecting **Rendering>Material Editor> Compact Material Editor**.

- It is possible to have a material in the scene that has not been loaded into the editor. You can add a scene material to the editor by using (Get Material).

- **Options>Options…** in the Material Editor offers controls that can help speed up performance when several large or complex materials are present in the editor.

- A material shown in a sample slot is previewed as applied to a 3D object. A map previewed in a sample slot is shown as a flat 2D rectangle.

- Figure A–3 shows the various options available in the shortcut menu. The options enable you to copy the materials from one slot to another, rotating and resetting the rotation of the material sample, and set the number of slots.

You can also use

(Pick Material from Object) in the Material Editor and select the object in the viewport.

It is recommended that the sample material contain a scene material for the Select by Material option to be available. The Highlight Assets in ATS dialog is available if the material contains a map.

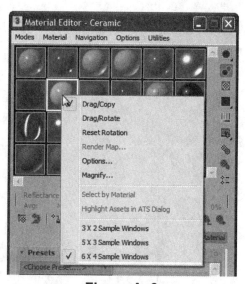

Figure A–3

- The Material Editor toolbars (shown in Figure A–4) work in the same way as the tools present in the Slate Material Editor.

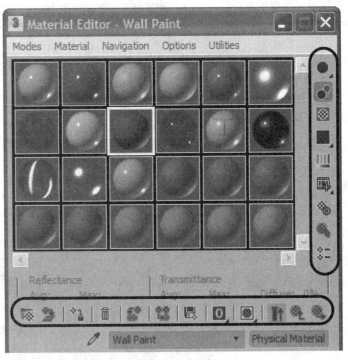

Figure A–4

The Material/Map Browser is embedded in the Slate Material Editor.

*You can also open the Material/Map Browser independently by selecting **Rendering> Material/Map Browser** in the menu bar.*

- The Material/Map Browser can be accessed by clicking

  (Get Material). Once you have located a required material in the browser, drag it from the browser to a scene object or to a sample slot in the Material Editor.

- Previews of the materials can be shown in a list, or as buttons. The display can be changed in the right-click menu, as shown in Figure A–5.

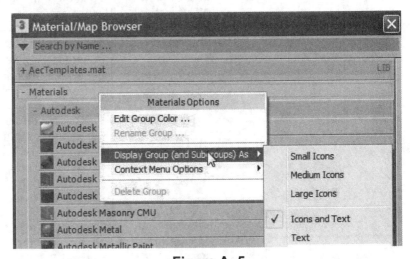

Figure A–5

A.3 Architectural Materials

Architectural materials offer a simplified interface over Standard materials because they have limited control (directly selecting a shader, some specular parameters, etc.). Architectural materials offer additional, built-in controls for translucency, refraction, and global illumination renderers.

Architectural Material Parameters

Architectural materials use Templates to assign shaders, which are predefined with many common material types (such as metals, paint, plastic, masonry, etc.). Selecting a template automatically populates other values in the Physical Qualities rollout, as shown in Figure A–6.

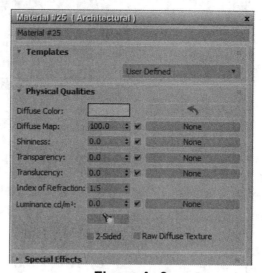

Figure A–6

Diffuse Color/ Diffuse Map	Located at the top of the Physical Qualities rollout, which are identical to those for Standard materials.
Shininess	Similar controls to the Specular Level of Standard materials. Architectural material highlights are generated through the **Shininess** and **Index of Refraction** parameters.
Transparency	The overall percentage that a material is transparent. For example, clear glass materials could be assigned transparencies between 90 and 100%.
Translucency	A measure of how much light is scattered as it passes through the object.
Index of Refraction (IOR)	Controls refraction and reflection. Typical values include 1.0 for air (effectively no refractive distortion), 1.33 for water, 1.5-1.7 for thick glass, and 2.5 for diamond.

Materials assigned in other software legacy translate into the Autodesk 3ds Max software as Architectural materials. All materials now import as Autodesk Materials.

Luminance	The amount of physically-based light the material emits. Unlike the Self-Illumination parameter of Standard materials, objects assigned Architectural materials can actually add light to scenes through this parameter as if they were light objects. (For example, illuminated materials are often used to represent neon tubes.)
Bump Maps	Can be assigned in the Special Effects rollout.

Architectural materials do not have Ambient Color controls because these materials are designed to work with radiosity, which directly calculates ambient illumination.

Architectural materials indicate when a reflectance value is out-of-range by colorizing the value in the Material Editor (based on the selected material template). Values that are too low are shown in blue and those that are too high are shown in red. Reflectance values that are out-of-range can be adjusted in a number of ways:

- When using a simple diffuse color (no diffuse image map), lower the overall value (V) of the color.

- The reflectance of Architectural materials can be reduced by entering a lower value for the *Reflectance Scale* in the Advanced Lighting Override rollout, as shown in Figure A–7.

- To lower reflectance when using a diffuse color map with Standard materials, assign the diffuse color to black and enter a value less than 100% for the diffuse color map. A value such as 95%, would reduce the brightness of the map by approximately 5%, as shown in Figure A–8.

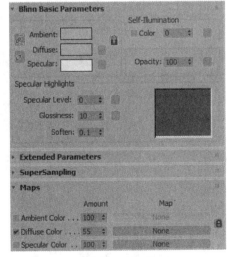

Figure A–7

Figure A–8

Hint: Converting Materials

You can manually convert the Architectural materials to Arch & Design materials by rebuilding them individually.

A.4 Object Substitution

Linked or imported AutoCAD Blocks can be automatically replaced with 3D objects using the **Substitute** modifier.

- The Objects to be replaced (such as linked AutoCAD blocks) should be located with the correct 3D coordinates (including elevation) and rotation for the replacing object.

- The substituting object needs to be one object. For example, the light pole could be used if it was collapsed to a single mesh object. (To do so, right-click on the base object in the Modifier Stack and select **Convert to Editable Poly or Mesh**. Then use the object's **Attach** in the Command Panel to join the other parts to the mesh. Materials and mapping can be preserved during this operation).

- The substitute object can be present in the same scene as the object to be replaced or it can be XRefed in from another scene.

- Although this is commonly used for AutoCAD blocks, other Autodesk 3ds Max objects can be substituted as well with this modifier.

Practice A1

Substituting the Parking Lot Light Poles

Practice Objective

- Replace 2D symbol based objects with 3D photorealistic object blocks.

In this practice you will substitute completed 3D light pole objects for 2D blocks in a scene using the **Substitute** modifier.

Estimated time for completion: 10 minutes

You must set the paths to locate the External files and Xrefs used in the practice. If you have not done this already, return to **Chapter 1: Introduction to Autodesk 3ds Max** and complete Task 1 to Task 3 in **Practice 1a: Organizing Folders and Working with the Interface**. You only have to set the user paths once.

*If a dialog box opens prompting you about a File Load: Mismatch, click **OK** to accept the default values.*

1. Open **Substitution_Start.max**.

2. Switch the viewport to **Wireframe shading** by pressing <F3>.

3. Zoom out on the area of the parking lot to display the flat, circular, and square symbols joined by a line (green), as shown in Figure A–9. These objects in the parking area are 2D light pole blocks. The parking lot surface has been hidden so that you can see the lamp symbols.

Figure A–9

4. In the Scene Explorer, use ■ (Display None)> 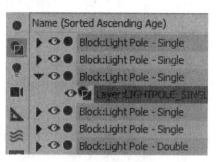 (Display Shapes) and expand any one of **Block:Light Pole - Single**. Select the **Layer:LIGHTPOLE_SINGLE**, as shown in Figure A–10.

Figure A–10

5. In the Command Panel, select the Modify panel (▨) and then select **Substitute** in the Modifier List. Only one 2D object is required to be selected because AutoCAD blocks link in as instances of each other, as indicated by the bold type in the Modifier Stack, as shown in Figure A–11.

6. Verify that the **Substitute** parameters match the parameters, as shown in Figure A–12 (default). Click **Select XRef Object...**.

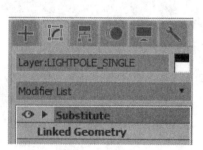

Figure A–11

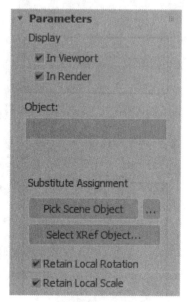

Figure A–12

7. In the Open File dialog box, open the source file, **Light Poles for Substitution.max** from your practice files folder.

8. In the XRef Merge dialog box, select the object named **LP_Single** and click **OK**.

9. In the Warning message dialog box, select **Apply to All Duplicates** to keep both materials, and click **Auto-Rename Merged Material**.

10. In the Substitution Question dialog box, click **Yes** to enable the substitute object's material to be used in this scene. Note that the 2D light pole blocks are replaced by the 3D single lightpole objects.

11. Repeat this process for one of the **Layer:LIGHTPOLE_ DOUBLE** objects (expand **Block:Light Pole - Double**), substituting **LP_Double** from **Light Poles for Substitution.max**.

12. In the viewport, change to **High Quality** in the *Shading Viewport* and **Default Shading** in the *Per-View Preference* label menu. Both the single light poles and double light poles are displayed, as shown in Figure A–13.

   • The **Substitute** modifier enables you to take a 2D symbol on an instanced object and replace it with a 3D photorealistic one several times in a scene, thus saving memory.

Figure A–13

13. Save your work as **MyCivilBaseSubstitution.max**.

A.5 Lighting Analysis

*The **NVIDIA mental ray** is required to be the active renderer for Lighting Analysis. It also requires mental ray materials with physically correct settings.*

The Autodesk 3ds Max software can create a lighting analysis rendering colorized by illumination or luminance values. The lighting analysis can be done using mental ray to physically correct lights and materials. Light meter objects can be placed in the scene to measure lighting. All of this is controlled using the Lighting Analysis Assistant dialog box, as shown in Figure A–14, (**Enhanced Menu Bar>Lighting Analysis>Lighting Analysis Assistant**).

In the Quick Access Toolbar, select Default with Enhanced Menus in the Workspaces drop-down list.

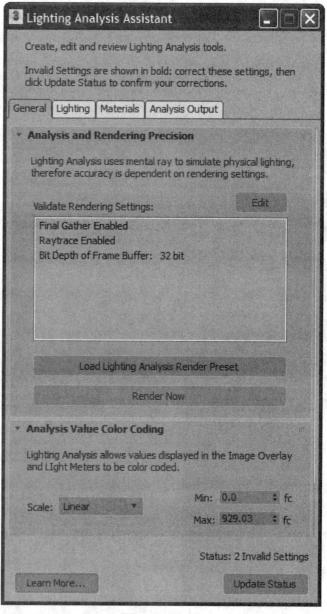

Figure A–14

There are four tabs in the Lighting Analysis Assistant dialog box: *General*, *Lighting*, *Materials*, and *Analysis Output*.

General Tab

The *General* tab validates that the rendering settings are correct. You must have Final Gather and Raytrace enabled and Bit Depth must be set to 32 bit. If any of these settings are incorrect, they are flagged in the Analysis and Rendering Precision rollout and must be corrected by recalculating the validation/ approval.

The Analysis Value Color Coding rollout enables you to adjust the color values displayed in the viewport, as shown in Figure A–15. By lowering the maximum value you can quickly find a pleasing range of colors for your output.

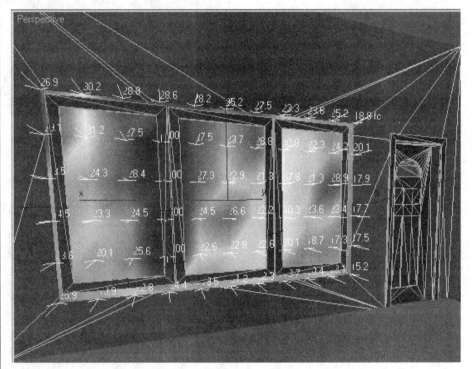

Figure A–15

Lighting Tab

In the *Lighting* tab (shown in Figure A–16), you can create mr Daylight System if one does not exist. You also have quick access to the settings for the sun/sky and daylight positions. If you are doing artificial light calculations (interiors) you can also create photometric lights from here. This dialog box checks for lights that have invalid settings and enables you to select and correct them.

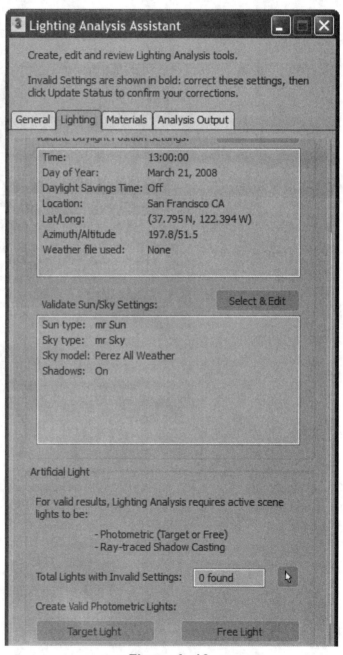

Figure A–16

Materials Tab

The *Materials* tab (shown in Figure A–17), validates the Materials in the scene.

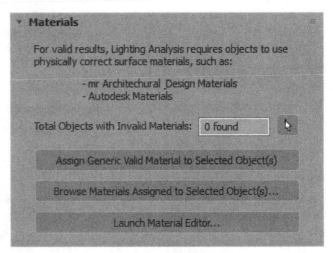

Figure A–17

The Lighting calculations require mr Arch & Design materials or Autodesk materials. If you have a scene that does not have the correct materials, they are flagged in the *Total Objects with Invalid Materials* field. Click the select arrow to select these objects in the viewport. You can then assign new materials to them yourself using the Material Editor or Material/Map Browser. If you do not care about the specific qualities of the material, you can use **Assign Generic Valid Material to Selected Object(s)**.

Hint: Adding Materials

Do not use **Assign Generic Valid Material to Selected Object(s)** on all of the selected objects in an interior. Doing so removes the glass from the windows and skylights. It is a better practice to add your own materials.

Analysis Output Tab

The *Analysis Output* tab (shown in Figure A–18) enables you create light meter objects.

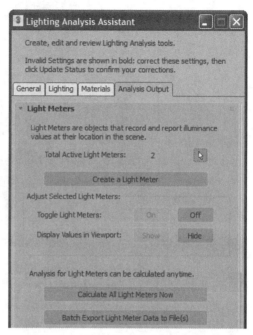

Figure A–18

To create a Light Meter object, click **Create a Light Meter** and drag a window around the objects in the viewport, as shown in

Figure A–19. You can create light meters using ◣ (Helpers) in the Command Panel's Create panel, which is a shortcut to the function. Alternatively, you can select **Lighting Analysis>Create>Light Meter**. You can use **AutoGrid** to create light meters over windows or other surfaces. Once the light meter is created, ensure that it is selected and go to the Modify panel and adjust the parameters to create the density of the value output.

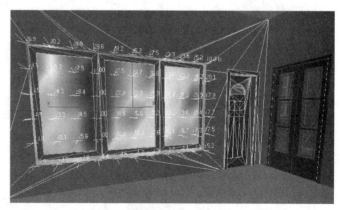

Figure A–19

You can calculate all of the Light Meters at once or batch export the light meter data to files. These files can be used for LEED 8.1 Certification for energy compliance of government standards.

You can see the values of the light meters in the viewport or you can add them to your rendering as an Image Overlay. In the Image Overlay rollout, click **Create Image Overlay Render Effect**, to create an Image Overlay. All of the Image Overlay settings and the output settings are listed.

The render effect that adds the printed values on top of the picture that you render displays as shown in Figure A–20.

Figure A–20

Practice A2

Estimated time for completion: 15 minutes

*If a dialog box opens prompting you about a File Load: Mismatch, click **OK** to accept the default values.*

*The **NVIDIA mental ray** must be the active renderer for Lighting Analysis. It also requires mental ray materials with physically correct settings.*

Conduct a Lighting Analysis

Practice Objective

- Create a Lighting Analysis for a scene by creating light meter objects.

In this practice you will create lighting Analysis for a scene by creating light meter objects. You will then overlay the values over the render.

You must set the paths to locate the External files and Xrefs used in the practice. If you have not done this already, return to **Chapter 1: Introduction to Autodesk 3ds Max** and complete Task 1 to Task 3 in **Practice 1a: Organizing Folders and Working with the Interface**. You only have to set the user paths once.

1. Open **Lighting_Analysis_mental_ray_start.max**.

2. In the Enhanced Menu bar, select **Lighting Analysis> Lighting Analysis Assistant**.

3. In the Lighting Analysis Assistant, verify that the *General* tab is selected. In the Analysis and Rendering Precision rollout, in the *Validate Rendering Settings* area, note the rendering settings, as shown in Figure A–21.

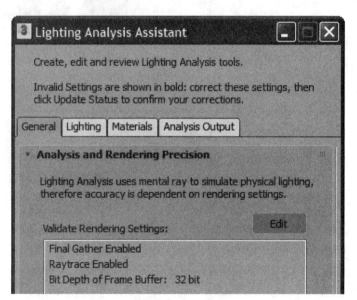

Figure A–21

4. In the Lighting Analysis Assistant, select the *Analysis Output* tab. In the Light Meters rollout, click **Create a Light Meter**. Leave the dialog box open, but move it over the doors area in the viewport so you can work in the window.

5. In the Command Panel, note that 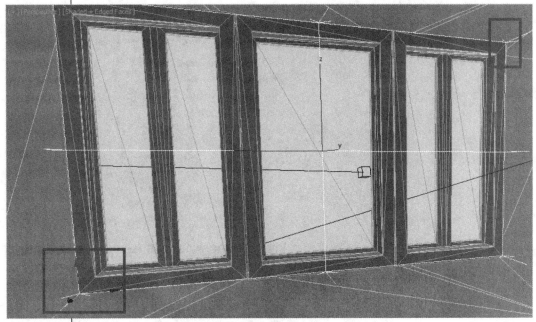 (Helpers) is automatically opened and **LightMeter** is selected. Toggle on **AutoGrid** at the top of the Object Type rollout.

6. In the viewport, note that the cursor displays a tripod. Hover the cursor over the lower left corner of the three large window objects and ensure that the Y-axis (green) is pointing up vertically and that the Z-axis (blue) is pointing outwards (towards you). Click and drag across to the diagonally opposite corner of all the three windows and release the mouse, creating a selection window., as shown in Figure A–22.

Figure A–22

7. With the selection window still selected, select the Modify

panel ( ). Note that the **LightMeter Helper** is displayed in
the Modifier Stack. In the Parameters rollout, set *Length
Segs:* to **7** and *Width Segs:* to **10** and press <Enter>, as
shown in Figure A–23. In the viewport, note that the
segments are added to the helper window object. This
increases the density of lighting analysis values. In the
Display rollout, verify that **Show Viewport Text** is selected.

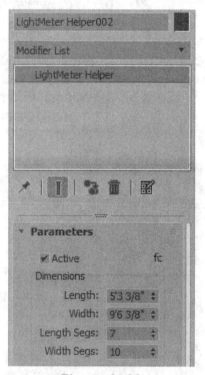

Figure A–23

8. In the Lighting Analysis Assistant, open the *Materials* tab and
verify that **0 found** is displayed as *Total Objects with Invalid
Materials*. This indicates that nothing needs to be corrected.

   • If you have any non-Physical materials assigned, an error
     displays. You can automatically assign a generic valid
     material to the selected objects in the scene.

   • If you click **Assign Generic Valid Material to Selected
     Object(s)** you lose transparency in the window glass.
     Reassign an Arch & Design thin glass to fix this problem.

9. Select the *Analysis Output* tab, in the Light Meters rollout,
click **Calculate All Light Meters Now**. A progress bar is
displayed in the Status Bar in the viewport. Once the
calculations are complete, the light meter values are
displayed in the viewport.

The full rollout might not be displayed. Use the

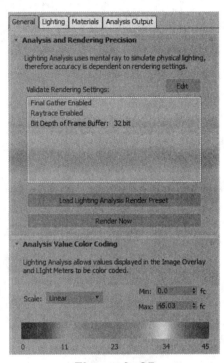 *(Hand) icon to drag it up.*

10. Select the *General* tab and expand the Analysis Value Color Coding rollout. Change the value for the *Max* spinner (as shown in Figure A–24) and you should see the colors change in the viewport on the light meter. Set a max value (approximately **45 fc**) where the maximum portion displays as green, similar to that shown in Figure A–25.

    • Green indicates a good lighting level.

    • Red indicates overlit areas.

    • Blue indicates underlit areas.

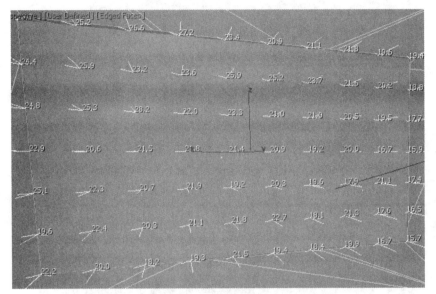

Figure A–24

Figure A–25

11. You can add these values to the renderer output as an overlay. Select the *Analysis Output* tab, in the Image Overlay rollout, next to *Validate Image Overlay Settings,* click **Edit**.

12. The Environment and Effects dialog box opens to the *Effects* tab.

13. In the Effects rollout, click **Add....** In the Add Effect dialog box, select **Lighting Analysis Image Overlay** to add the effect to the overlay and click **OK**.

14. In the *Parameters* area, note the Display Options settings. The first two options enable you to display the numbers over the whole image or only over the light meter object.

15. Set the options as shown in Figure A–26 (**Show Numbers On Entire Image (Screen Grid)** cleared and the remaining selected). Close the Environment and Effects dialog box.

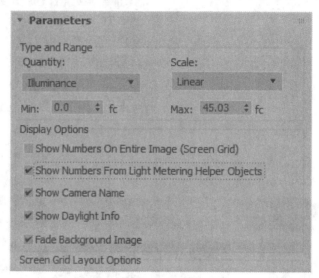

Figure A–26

16. Render the scene by clicking . It will take some time to complete the rendering process. In the Rendered Frame Window, the Image overlay is displayed when the rendering is complete, as shown in Figure A–27. A Lighting Analysis Data dialog box opens as well.

Figure A–27

17. Close the Lighting Analysis Data dialog box. In the Rendered Frame Window, save the rendered image as **LightingAnalysis.jpg**.

18. Save the scene file as **MyLightingAnalysis.max**.

A.6 Creating Hierarchies

Autodesk 3ds Max Hierarchies are collections of objects linked together with parent/child relationships. When used, transforms applied to a parent are automatically passed to its children. Connecting multiple objects in a hierarchical chain can enable sophisticated animations such as the motion of jointed robotic arms.

Most modifiers (such as Substitute) must be applied to the objects in the hierarchy rather than the parent.

In the case of the hierarchy file link options, incoming AutoCAD blocks are brought in as multiple objects so that they can maintain multiple material assignments from AutoCAD. They display together with a Block/Style Parent object, enabling you to transform the block as a unit by selecting the parent. The parent object itself does not have any geometry and does not render.

Practice A3	**Create Hierarchies**

Practice Objective

- Create hierarchical relationships between objects.

Estimated time for completion: 10 minutes

In many animations you will want to create hierarchical relationships so that objects move together when moved. Once you have linkages, you can animate them using forward kinematics in which you move the parent and rotate the children.

You must set the paths to locate the External files and Xrefs used in the practice. If you have not done this already, return to **Chapter 1: Introduction to Autodesk 3ds Max** and complete Task 1 to Task 3 in **Practice 1a: Organizing Folders and Working with the Interface**. You only have to set the user paths once.

*If a dialog box opens prompting you about a File Load: Mismatch, click **OK** to accept the default values.*

1. Open **Lamp Start Linking.max**. This is a model of a desk lamp, as shown in Figure A–28.

Figure A–28

2. In the Scene Explorer, use ■ (Display None) and ● (Display Geometry) and note the six geometry objects in the scene. The names are not indented, indicating that there are no linkages.

3. In the viewport, move the Base object that is at the bottom of the lamp. Note that it moves by itself and the other objects are unaffected. Undo the move and clear the selection.

4. In the Main Toolbar, click (Select and Link). Starting at the top, select and hold each object and drag a dotted line to its parent. You will repeat the process five times as follows:

- Select **Lampshade** and link it to **Upper Arm - Lamp**.
- Select **Upper Arm - Lamp** and link it to **Lower Arm**.
- Select **Lower Arm** and link it to **Lower Hub**.
- Select **Lower Hub** and link it to **Stand**.
- Select **Stand** and link it to **Base**.

5. In the Main Toolbar, click (Select Object) to end the linking process.

6. In the Scene Explorer, note that only **Base** is visible. Expand Base to display its dependent, **Stand**. Expand all of the children to display the dependencies, as shown in Figure A–29.

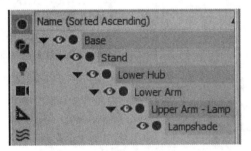

Figure A–29

7. Move the Base and note that the entire lamp moves with it. The base is the parent object and other objects are children and descendants. Undo the move.

8. Rotate the Lower Arm and note that the Upper Arm - Lamp and Lampshade, go along with the rotation. The Lower Hub, Stand, and Base are not part of the rotation. Undo the rotations.

9. Save your scene file as **MyLampStartLinking.max**.

Practice A4

Estimated time for completion: 10 minutes

*If a dialog box opens prompting you about a File Load: Mismatch, click **OK** to accept the default values.*

Create an Assembly Animation

Practice Objective

- Create animation assembly to bring the different parts of an object together.

It is common to create an animation of a design that builds up over time. In this practice you will create an animation of the assembly of a lamp.

You must set the paths to locate the External files and Xrefs used in the practice. If you have not done this already, return to **Chapter 1: Introduction to Autodesk 3ds Max** and complete Task 1 to Task 3 in **Practice 1a: Organizing Folders and Working with the Interface**. You only have to set the user paths once.

In this kind of animation, you will add keyframes to the end of the animation and then adjust the start and end ranges for each component.

1. Open **Lamp Start Linking Animation.max**.

2. In the Animation Controls, click 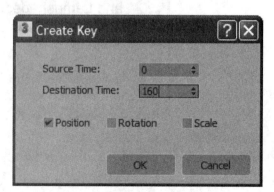 (Time Configuration). In the Time Configuration dialog box, in the *Animation* area, set the *End Time* to **200** and click **OK**.

3. Press <Ctrl>+<A> to select all objects in the viewport at once.

4. In the Time Slider, right-click on the **0/200** slider bar to open the Create Key dialog box. Clear **Rotation** and **Scale** leaving **Position** selected and set the *Destination Time* to **160**, as shown in Figure A–30. Click **OK**.

Figure A–30

- A Position key for all objects is placed at frame 160. Note that in the Track Bar, a red box is set at 160, as shown in Figure A–31.

Figure A–31

5. Click **Auto Key** to activate it (it will display in red).

6. Verify that your slider bar is located at **0** (0/200). Clear the object selection, and move each individual object randomly on the screen, similar to that shown in Figure A–32. (The placement of the objects can be different to that shown in the image.)

If all of the objects are selected, click in empty area in the viewport to clear the selection and then select each object separately.

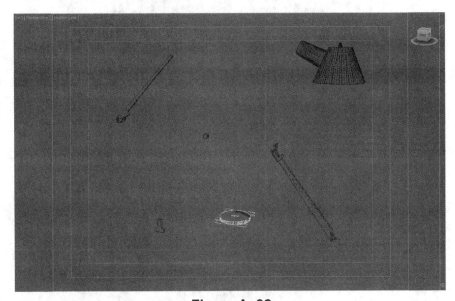

Figure A–32

7. Click (Play) and note that the components drift into their correct locations at frame 160. Stop the animation.

8. Save your scene file as **MyLampAnimation.max**.

Hint: Set the Selection Range

To have the components assemble one after another, using <Ctrl> select both keys in the Time Slider. Right-click and select **Configure>Show Selection Range**. A bar is added below the track bar indicating the duration of movement for the selected component. You can now move the ends of the range to control when the object starts to move and when it finishes. The shorter the line, the quicker the movement of the object.

A.7 Customizing the User Interface

The Autodesk 3ds Max software has a flexible and highly customizable user interface that can be modified using the Customize User Interface dialog box, as shown in Figure A–33. Select **Customize>Customize User Interface**.

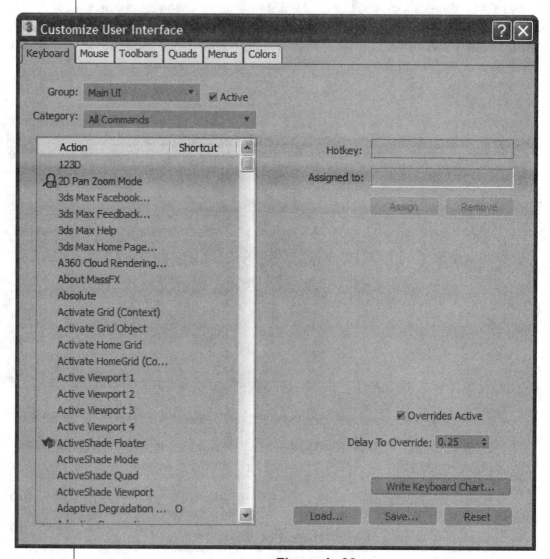

Figure A–33

- The settings located in each tab can be saved or swapped out independently with **Load...** and **Save...**.

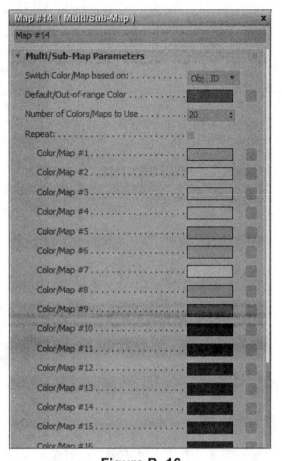

Figure B–16

6. Set *Number of Colors/Maps to Use* as **6**, as shown in Figure B–17. This identifies the first six materials as active for the shader when rendering.

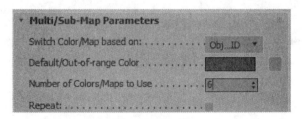

Figure B–17

Task 2 - Assign Maps to Materials.

In this task you will use another mental ray shader that has already been created and assigned. The steps in the previous task were included to describe how to create a new mental ray shader.

1. In the *View1* sheet, delete both the mental ray material and its Multi/Sub-Map node.

Each material has a unique channel assigned to it that corresponds with its position in the list. Each of these channels has a default color that can be modified. You can assign up to 100 materials using this shader.

2. In the Material/Map Browser, in the *Scene Materials* category, double-click **Chair Fabric**. In the *View1* sheet, note that this is a mental ray material and that its Multi/Sub-Map has already been created. The first six channels in the Multi/Sub-Map have been assigned to chairs 2 through 6. You will assign the material to chair 1.

3. In the **Camera01** viewport, set the *Shading Viewport* to **High Quality**.

4. In the **Camera01** viewport, select the seat back of the first chair on the left (Seat42), as shown in Figure B–18. The seat fabric and the frames are separate objects so only the seat part of the model is selected.

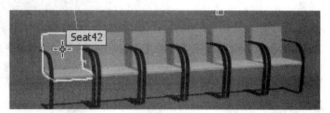

Figure B–18

5. In the Modify panel ( )>Modifier Stack, in the Editable Poly modifier of the seat, select **Polygon**. In the viewport, note that the complete seat is highlighted (red).

6. In the Polygon: Material IDs rollout, set *Set ID* as **1** and press <Enter>, as shown in Figure B–19.

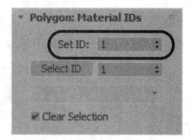

Figure B–19

7. In the *View1* sheet of Slate Material Editor, select the **Chair Fabric** mental ray node and click (Assign Material to Selection).

8. In the Command Panel>Modifier Stack, select **Editable Poly** to exit Sub-object mode.

9. For this scene, the remaining five channels were assigned separately to the remaining chairs and has already been completed. For example, seat 2 uses material channel 2 and seat 3 uses channel 3. To review the materials that are assigned to the six channels, in the *View1* sheet, double-click on the Fabric Multi/Sub-Map node title bar heading to open the Parameter Editor, as shown in Figure B–20. Note that the **Number of Colors to Use** is set to **6** and are colored in six different colors, ranging from green to brown.

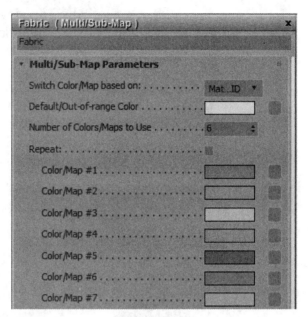

Figure B–20

10. In the viewport, select all six chair seat/backs and click

    (Assign material to Selection) to ensure that the materials are assigned.

11. Render the **Camera01** view. The six seats display with their different color materials.

Task 3 - Add Additional Seats to the Scene.

You will now populate the space with additional rows and columns of seats and adjust the **Multi/Sub-Map** parameters to make it more interesting.

1. Select **Frame42** to **Frame47** (all six frames) and **Seat42** to **Seat47** (all six seats) (Use Scene Explorer with ■ (Display None) and ● (Display Geometry)).

2. In the Status Bar, click  (Selection Lock) to lock this selection, as shown in Figure B–21.

Figure B–21

3. Activate the **Top** viewport. Click (Zoom Extents Selected) and pan the seats down.

4. Click (Select and Move). Hold <Shift> and drag the chairs towards the top of the screen (as shown in Figure B–22) to create a new (cloned) row of seats. Ensure that enough space is left between the two rows and release <Shift> and cursor.

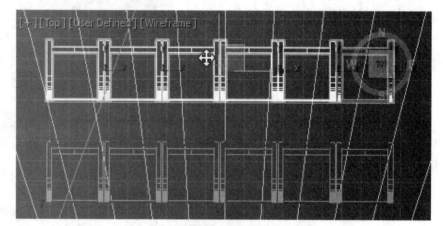

Figure B–22

5. In the Clone Options dialog box, select **Instance** and set the *Number of Copies* to **8**. Click **OK**.

6. Click (Select Object) to exit the Move transform. You now have a total of 54 chairs in one main grouping, as shown in the Camera01 viewport in Figure B–23.

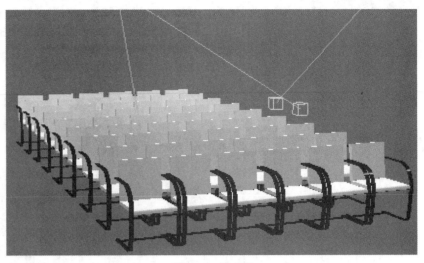

Figure B–23

7. Select all 54 chairs and their frames and lock the selection
( ). Zoom out in the **Top** viewport to see all of the chairs.

Using and <Shift>, drag all of the chairs to the left (on the X axis) to create a second group column of 54 chairs, as shown in Figure B–24. In the Clone Options dialog box, verify that **Instance** is selected and the *Number of Copies* are set to **1**. Click **OK**.

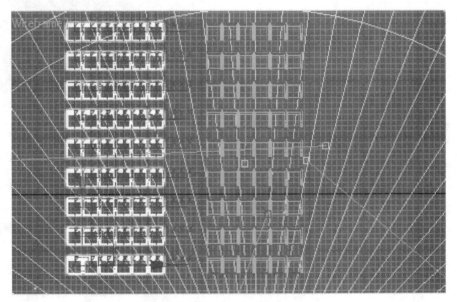

Figure B–24

8. As the group is still selected, press <Shift> and drag it to the right on the other side of the original group to create a third group column as **Instance** and set *Number of Copies* to **1**. You now have a total of 162 chairs.

9. Render the **Top** viewport, as shown in Figure B–25. Note that each group of six columns has the same regular color of chair from front to back

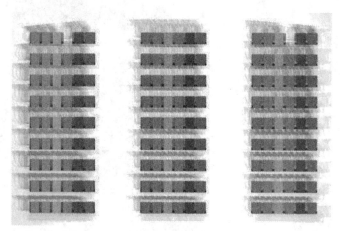

Figure B–25

You are not restricted to using solid colors with the Multi/Sub-Map shader and you can also apply maps to one or more materials. In such cases, the map replaces the color swatch.

10. In the Slate Material Editor, double-click on the Fabric Multi/Sub-Map title bar heading. In *Switch Color/Map based on* drop-down list, select **Random,** as shown in Figure B–26.

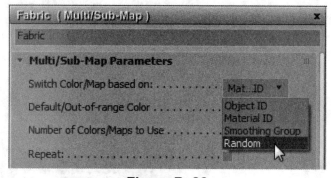

Figure B–26

11. Render the **Top** viewport, as shown in Figure B–27. Note that the uniform color by column has been replaced with a more random layout color pattern.

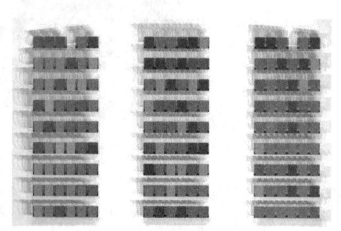

Figure B–27

Task 4 - Modify the Chair Frame Material.

The chair frames have a black glossy color applied to them but as the material is an Arch & Design type, you can change its look.

1. In the Slate Material Editor, in the Material/Map Browser, in the *Scene Materials* category, double-click on **Chair Chrome** material to add it to the *View1* sheet and open its Parameter Editor (Double-click the title bar heading).

2. In the Templates drop-down list, select **Copper**, as shown in Figure B–28.

The material has previously been assigned to the frame.

Figure B–28

3. Render the **Camera01** viewport, as shown in Figure B–29. It displays a view of your chairs with random mental ray Multi/Sub-Map material applied to the chairs.

Figure B–29

4. Save the file as **Mymentalchairs.max**.

Practice B4

Shadow Study Animation

Practice Objective

- Animate the Daylight System to create a shadow study.

Estimated time for completion: 15 minutes

In this practice you will animate the movement of the daylight throughout a day in the exterior scene to create an animated shadow study. This study will provide an accurate representation of how daylight will cast shadows in the scene.

1. Open **Shadow Study.max**.

2. Activate the **Camera01** viewport, if not already active. This is the non-animated camera view. Change the *Shading Viewport* to **High Quality**.

3. In the Animation controls, click 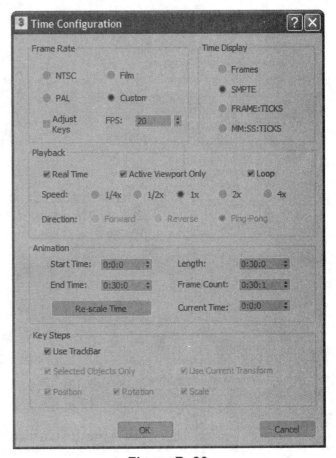 (Time Configuration). Verify that your default settings match the settings shown in Figure B–30. Click **OK**.

Figure B–30

4. In this shadow study you will animate the **Daylight001** object using keyframing. Select the **Daylight001** object in the **Compass001** helper object (Use the Scene Explorer,  (Display None) and (Display Groups)). Verify that the Time Slider is located at a time of **0:0:0** (frame 0), as shown in Figure B–31.

Figure B–31

5. In the Command Panel, select the Motion panel ( ). Start the shadow study animation at frame 0, representing **6:00 AM**. In the Control Parameters rollout, set the current time and date as shown in Figure B–32. Your *Azimuth* and *Altitude* values might be different.

Figure B–32

6. In the Animation Controls, click **Auto Key** (displays in red). While in **Auto Key** mode, drag the time slider to the end time of **0:30:0**, as shown in Figure B–33.

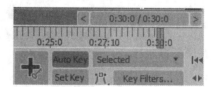

Figure B–33

7. At this time (**0:30:0**) change the sun's position to 7:00 PM by entering **19** in the *Hours* edit box in the Command Panel.

8. Click **Auto Key** again to end Auto Key mode.

9. Slide the Time Slider left and right (scrub) and in the viewports, watch the **Daylight001** object progress across the sky during the animation.

10. Open the Render Setup dialog box (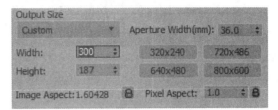 (Render Setup)). In the *Common* tab, in the *Output Size* area, set *Width* to **300**. With your aspect ratio locked at 1.6, it automatically calculates the *Height* of **187**, as shown in Figure B–34.

Figure B–34

11. In the *Time Output* area, set *Every Nth Frame* to **20** and verify that the **Active Time Segment** is selected, as shown in Figure B–35.

This enables you to always render **Camera01** *even if another viewport is active.*

12. In the *View to Render*, verify that the current viewport is set to **Quad 4 - Camera01** and click 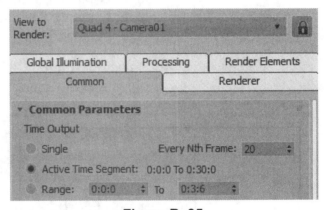, as shown in Figure B–35.

Figure B–35

13. In the *Render Output* area, click **Files....** Render the animation to still frames named **shadow study.jpg** in the ...*renderings* folder. If prompted to specify the JPEG quality, use the highest quality **JPEG** option.

14. Click **Render** to begin animating the individual frames of the animation through the course of a day from 6.00 a.m. to 7.00 p.m. Note the change in brightness of the daylight and the movement of the shadows from one frame to another.

15. When done, use the RAM Player (**Rendering>Compare Media in RAM Player**) to combine them into a compiled animation file called **Shadow Study.mov** or **Shadow Study.avi**.

16. Save the scene file as **My Shadow Study.max**.

Practice B5

Assigning the Renderable Spline Modifier

Practice Objective

Estimated time for completion: 10 minutes

- Make the 2D lines renderable so that they are visible in the renderings.

The Renderable Spline modifier enables you to make linework renderable. In this practice, you will assign a width to the pavement markings so that they will render appropriately.

1. Open **Renderable Spline.max**.

2. Render the viewport and note that the parking lot does not display the corridor markings, parking lines, and handicap symbols.

3. Open the Layer Explorer (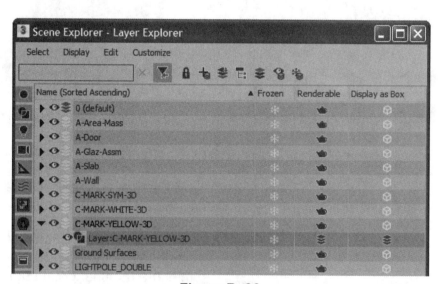 (Layer Explorer)). Expand the layer **C-MARK-YELLOW-3D**, as shown in Figure B–36. The layer contains a single object, the combined AutoCAD 3D lines that make up the yellow pavement markings.

4. Select the **Layer:C-MARK-YELLOW-3D** object to select the objects in the scene.

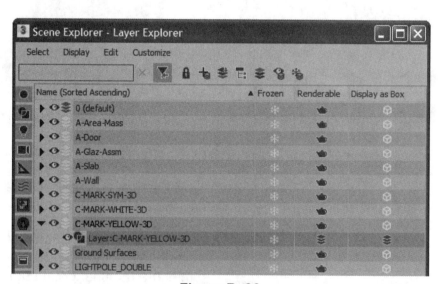

Figure B–36

5. In the Command Panel, select the *Modify* tab. In the Modifier List, select **Renderable Spline**. It is displayed in the Modifier Stack, as shown in Figure B–37.

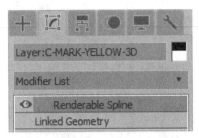

Figure B–37

6. In the Parameters rollout, select **Rectangular** and set the following, as shown in Figure B–38:

    *   *Width*: **0'3"**
    *   *Aspect*: **0.167**

    The *Length* automatically updates to **0'0 4/8"**. In your model, the *Length* translates into the vertical height of the pavement markings.

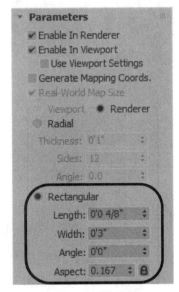

Figure B–38

7. In the Modifier Stack, right-click on **Renderable Spline** and select **Copy**.

8. In the Layer Explorer, expand **C-MARK-WHITE-3D** and select **Layer:C-MARK-WHITE-3D**. In the Modifier Stack, right-click on Linked Geometry and select **Paste** to add **Renderable Spline** with the same parameters. In the Parameters rollout, change the *Width* to **0'6"**.

9. Similar to Step 8, copy the **Renderable Spline** to **Layer:C-MARK-SYM-3D** in **C-MARK-SYM-3D**.

10. In the viewport, zoom into the parking lot area and note that the spline markings get some width, as shown in Figure B–39.

 • The markings might not display entirely above the pavement due to the approximate nature of the viewport display and your computer's display driver and settings.

Figure B–39

11. Assign each of these marking layers to not cast shadows. In the Layer Explorer, select and right-click on one of these layers (not the object inside the layer) and select **Properties**. In the Layer Properties dialog box, in the *Rendering Control* area, clear the **Cast Shadows** option and click **OK**. The setting is changed for other two layers automatically.

12. Render the viewport and note the parking lines and the handicap signs are all visible in the rendering.

13. Save your work as **MyRenderable Spline.max**.

Hint: When Not to Cast Shadows

Surfaces with abrupt elevation changes require shadows to look realistic, because the raised areas of a surface need to cast shadows on themselves or other objects to look believable. To speed up rendering time, do not cast shadows on flat ground surfaces that do not have much relief for shadows. The pavement markings are meant to be completely flush with the pavement, without any appreciable height to make shadows.

Practice B6

Using Script for Converting Materials

Practice Objective

- Convert the Architectural materials to Arch & Design materials.

Estimated time for completion: 15 minutes

The conversion script of mental images, developed by Zap Anderson (http://mentalraytips.blogspot.com),converts Architectural Materials to Arch & Design materials. In this practice you will work with this script to convert the Architectural Materials to Arch & Design. You will also adjust the settings for the Arch & Design materials to achieve a realistic rendering.

1. Exit the Autodesk 3ds Max software, if you have it open.

2. Using Windows Explorer, locate the script file **Macro_mrArchMtlTools.mcr** in the ...\Scripts folder (*C:\Autodesk 3ds Max Fundamentals Practice Files\scripts*). Copy **Macro_mrArchMtlTools.mcr** and paste it into the *scripts* folder in the Autodesk 3ds Max 2017 installation directory. (Normally found in *C:\Program Files\Autodesk\3ds Max 2017\scripts.*)

3. Launch the Autodesk 3ds Max software.

4. Open **Convert_Materials_start.max**.

5. Open the Slate Material Editor and in the Material/Map Browser, in the *Scene Materials* category, note that the three **Finishes** materials are Architectural materials, as shown in Figure B–40.

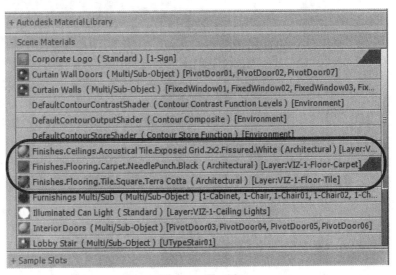

Figure B–40

6. In the Command Panel, click 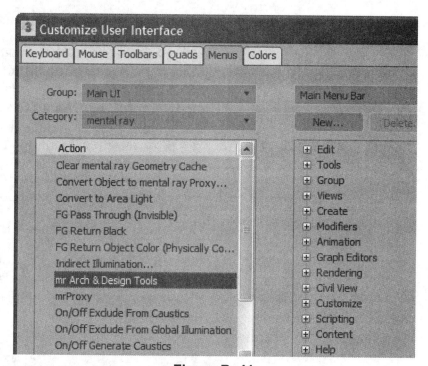 (Utilities) and click **MAXScript**.

*In the MAXScript rollout, use **Open Script** to open the script file.*

7. In the MAXScript rollout, click **Run Script** and select **Macro_mrArchMtlTools.mcr** in the Autodesk 3ds Max 2017 installation directory (Program Files). Click **Open**. By running it, you retrieve it into the Autodesk 3ds Max interface.

8. Select **Customize>Customize User Interface**.

9. In the Customize User Interface dialog box, select the *Menus* tab and in the Category drop-down list, select **mental ray**. In the Action list, select **mr Arch & Design Tools**, as shown in Figure B–41.

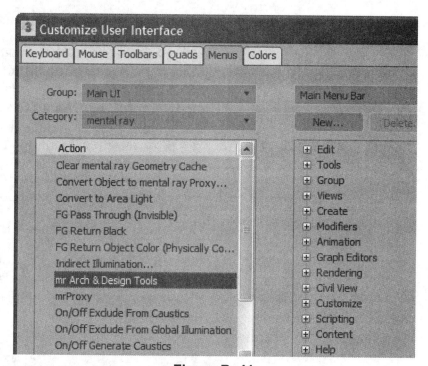

Figure B–41

10. On the right side of the dialog box, expand the **Scripting** menu. Drag the **mr Arch & Design Tools** action onto the **Scripting** menu, placing it after Run Script, as shown in Figure B–42. Close the dialog box.

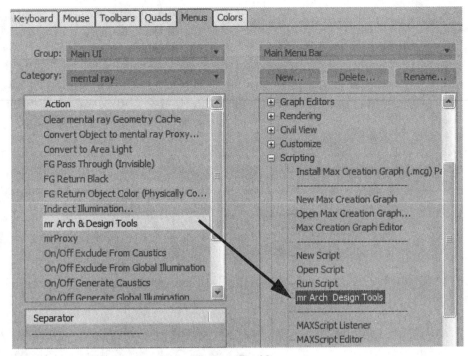

Figure B–42

11. The tool is now available from the **Scripting** menu. Select **Scripting>mr Arch Design Tools**, as shown in Figure B–43. The mrArch&Design Utilities dialog box opens, as shown in Figure B–44.

Figure B–43

Figure B–44

12. In the Affect Materials rollout, verify that **...in scene** is selected.

13. In the Ambient Occlusion rollout, click **Turn AO ON in all Arch & Design Materials** and **Force AO radius**. This adds detail enhancement to all of the materials.

14. In the Convert Materials rollout, click **Convert Materials to mr Arch & Design** and close the mr Arch&Design Utilities dialog box.

15. Open the Slate Material Editor, and in the Material/Map Browser, in the *Scene Materials* category, note that the Architectural materials (Finishes materials) are now Arch & Design materials, as shown in Figure B–45.

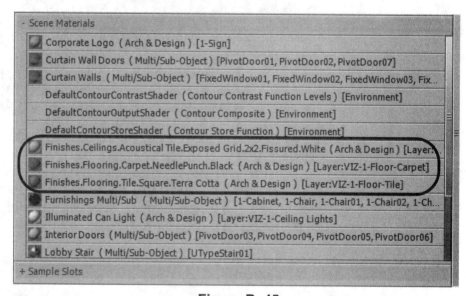

Figure B–45

Adjusting the materials is required after conversion.

16. Render the **Camera01** view, as shown in Figure B–46. Leave the Rendered Frame Window open. You will adjust the materials and lighting.

Figure B–46

Use Scene Explorer,

 *(Display None) and*

 *(Display Shapes).*

17. To toggle on the Self-Illumination for the materials of the overhead lights, select the **Layer:VIZ-1-Ceiling Lights** objects. In the Slate Material Editor, in the *Scene Materials*, double-click the **Illuminated Can Light** material to place it on the *View1* sheet.

18. Open its Parameter Editor (Double-click the title bar heading). In the Self-Illumination (Glow) rollout, select **Self Illumination (Glow)**.

19. Render the **Camera01** view again.

20. In the Slate Material Editor, verify that in the *Luminance* area **Unitless** is selected. Try increasing this value and rendering until the lights in the ceiling are brighter.

21. The desk lamp material is incorrect so you will need to create a new one. In the Slate Material Editor, in the Material/Map Browser, in the *Materials>mental ray* categories, double-click on **Arch & Design** to place it on the *View1* sheet.

22. Double-click on the title bar heading of the new material to open the Parameter Editor, and do the following, as shown in Figure B–47:

    • Rename the material **Desk Lamp**.

    • In the Templates drop-down list, select **Glossy Finish.**

    • Change *Diffuse* color to **Black**.

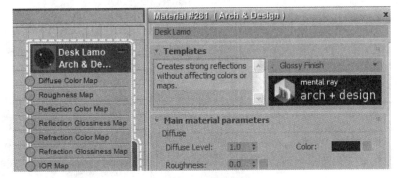

Figure B–47

23. In the viewport, select the desk lamp and in the Slate Material Editor, click (Assign Material to Selection).

24. Render the **Camera01** view again, as shown in Figure B–48.

Figure B–48

The Arch & Design materials and mrPhotographic exposure control are recommended for use with mental ray to achieve highly realistic results.

25. Open the Environment and Effects dialog box.

    (**Rendering>Environment** or  (Environment and Effects) in the Rendered Frame Window).

26. In the Exposure Control rollout, select **mr Photographic Exposure** control, and in the *Exposure* area, select **Exposure Value (EV)** and lower the *EV* value to **11.0**.

27. In the *Image Control* area, adjust the *Highlights (Burn)*, *Midtones*, and *Shadows* values. Increase the *Whitepoint* value to **10000**.

28. Render the **Camera01** view, as shown in Figure B–49. Note that the color is tinted and is a more yellow/sepia color, which looks warmer.

Figure B–49

29. Save your work as **MymrMaterials.max**.

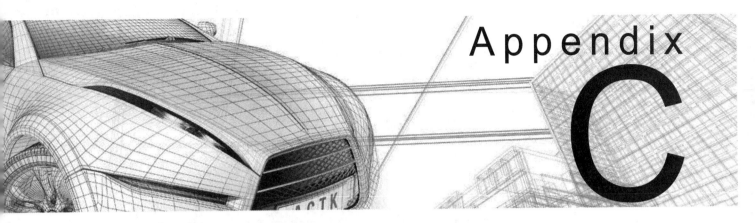

Autodesk 3ds Max Certification Exam Objectives

The following table will help you to locate the exam objectives within the chapters of the *Autodesk 3ds Max 2017: Fundamentals* student guide to help you prepare for the Autodesk 3ds Max Certified Professional exam.

Exam Topic	Exam Objective	Student Guide	Chapter & Section(s)
Animation	Create a path animation and evaluate an object along the path	• Autodesk 3ds Max Fundamentals	• 12.2
	Identify Controller types		
	Identify playback settings	• Autodesk 3ds Max Fundamentals	• 12.1
	Locate the value of keys in the Time Slider	• Autodesk 3ds Max Fundamentals	• 12.1
	Use a Dope Sheet		
Cameras	Differentiate camera types	• Autodesk 3ds Max Fundamentals	• 11.4
	Edit FOV (Field of View)	• Autodesk 3ds Max Fundamentals	• 11.4
Data Management/Interoperability	Differentiate common file formats and usages	• Autodesk 3ds Max Fundamentals	• 1.1 • 3.1 & 3.2
	Use the import feature to import model data	• Autodesk 3ds Max Fundamentals	• 3.1 & 3.2
Effects	Identify Space Warp types		
	Use atmosphere effects		
	Use particle systems		

Exam Topic	Exam Objective	Student Guide	Chapter & Section(s)
Lighting	Compare Attenuation and Decay	• Autodesk 3ds Max Fundamentals	• 8.2
	Identify parameters for modifying shadows	• Autodesk 3ds Max Fundamentals	• 8.4 • 9.1
	Add a volumetric effect		
Materials/ Shading	Identify Standard materials	• Autodesk 3ds Max Fundamentals	• 6.1, 6.3, & 6.4
	Use the Slate Material Editor	• Autodesk 3ds Max Fundamentals	• 6.2 & 6.5 • 7.2
Rigging	Use Character Studio for Rigging		
	Create simple Bipeds		
	Use the Skin modifier		
Modeling	Differentiate reference coordinate systems	• Autodesk 3ds Max Fundamentals	• 4.4
	Differentiate workflow	• Autodesk 3ds Max Fundamentals	• 1.2
	Identify Clone types	• Autodesk 3ds Max Fundamentals	• 4.5
	Differentiate standard versus extended primitives	• Autodesk 3ds Max Fundamentals	• 4.1
	Identify and use line tool creation methods	• Autodesk 3ds Max Fundamentals	• 5.1
	Identify Vertex types	• Autodesk 3ds Max Fundamentals	• 4.3 • 5.1
	Use object creation and modification workflows	• Autodesk 3ds Max Fundamentals	• 4.3, 4.6 • 5.2 to 5.5, 5.7
	Use polygon modeling tools	• Autodesk 3ds Max Fundamentals	• 4.6
	Use ProBoolean	• Autodesk 3ds Max Fundamentals	• 5.5
Rendering	Differentiate Renderers	• Autodesk 3ds Max Fundamentals	• 10.1 • 11.1
	Identify rendering parameters	• Autodesk 3ds Max Fundamentals	• 10.2 • 11.1 & 11.2
UI/Object Management	Describe and use object transformations	• Autodesk 3ds Max Fundamentals	• 4.2
	Identify Selection Regions and methods	• Autodesk 3ds Max Fundamentals	• 2.3
	Use Viewports	• Autodesk 3ds Max Fundamentals	• 1.8 • 2.1 & 2.2
	Set up and use Scenes	• Autodesk 3ds Max Fundamentals	• 1.8 • 2.4 • 11.3

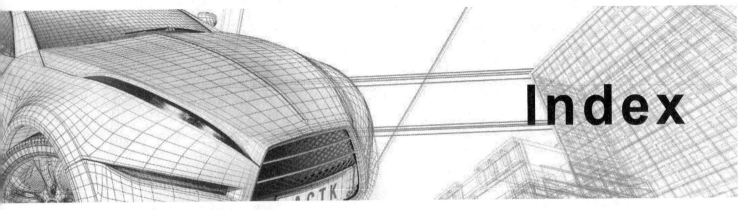

Index

About Us

SDC Publications specializes in creating exceptional books that are designed to seamlessly integrate into courses or help the self learner master new skills. Our commitment to meeting our customer's needs and keeping our books priced affordably are just some of the reasons our books are being used by nearly 1,200 colleges and universities across the United States and Canada.

SDC Publications is a family owned and operated company that has been creating quality books since 1985. All of our books are proudly printed in the United States.

Our technology books are updated for every new software release so you are always up to date with the newest technology. Many of our books come with video enhancements to aid students and instructor resources to aid instructors.

Take a look at all the books we have to offer you by visiting SDCpublications.com.

NEVER
STOP
LEARNING

Keep Going

Take the skills you learned in this book to the next level or learn something brand new. SDC Publications offers books covering a wide range of topics designed for users of all levels and experience. As you continue to improve your skills, SDC Publications will be there to provide you the tools you need to keep learning. Visit SDCpublications.com to see all our most current books.

Why SDC Publications?

- Regular and timely updates
- Priced affordably
- Designed for users of all levels
- Written by professionals and educators
- We offer a variety of learning approaches

TOPICS

3D Animation
BIM
CAD
CAM
Engineering
Engineering Graphics
FEA / CAE
Interior Design
Programming

SOFTWARE

Adams
ANSYS
AutoCAD
AutoCAD Architecture
AutoCAD Civil 3D
Autodesk 3ds Max
Autodesk Inventor
Autodesk Maya
Autodesk Revit
CATIA
Creo Parametric
Creo Simulate
Draftsight
LabVIEW
MATLAB
NX
OnShape
SketchUp
SOLIDWORKS
SOLIDWORKS Simulation